The Oxford Handbook of
Psychology and Spirituality

OXFORD LIBRARY OF PSYCHOLOGY

Editor in Chief PETER E. NATHAN

The Oxford Handbook of Psychology and Spirituality

Edited by

Lisa J. Miller

OXFORD
UNIVERSITY PRESS

OXFORD
UNIVERSITY PRESS

Oxford University Press is a department of the University of Oxford. It furthers the University's
objective of excellence in research, scholarship, and education by publishing worldwide.

Oxford New York
Auckland Cape Town Dar es Salaam Hong Kong Karachi
Kuala Lumpur Madrid Melbourne Mexico City Nairobi
New Delhi Shanghai Taipei Toronto

With offices in
Argentina Austria Brazil Chile Czech Republic France Greece
Guatemala Hungary Italy Japan Poland Portugal Singapore
South Korea Switzerland Thailand Turkey Ukraine Vietnam

Oxford is a registered trademark of Oxford University Press in the UK and certain other countries.

Published in the United States of America by
Oxford University Press
198 Madison Avenue, New York, NY 10016

© Oxford University Press 2012

First issued as an Oxford University Press paperback, 2014.

Library of Congress Cataloging-in-Publication Data
The Oxford handbook of psychology and spirituality / edited by Lisa Miller.
  p. cm.—(Oxford library of psychology)
  ISBN 978–0–19–972992–0 (hardcover); 978–0–19–935734–5 (paperback)
  1. Psychology, Religious. I. Miller, Lisa J. II. Title: Handbook of psychology and spirituality.
  BL53.O97 2012
  200.1'9—dc23
  2011042331

To Margo and Sid. Thank you for awe, wonder, and love.

SHORT CONTENTS

OXFORD LIBRARY OF PSYCHOLOGY

The *Oxford Library of Psychology,* a landmark series of handbooks, is published by Oxford University Press, one of the world's oldest and most highly respected publishers, with a tradition of publishing significant books in psychology. The ambitious goal of the *Oxford Library of Psychology* is nothing less than to span a vibrant, wide-ranging field and, in so doing, to fill a clear market need.

Encompassing a comprehensive set of handbooks, organized hierarchically, the *Library* incorporates volumes at different levels, each designed to meet a distinct need. At one level are a set of handbooks designed broadly to survey the major subfields of psychology; at another are numerous handbooks that cover important current focal research and scholarly areas of psychology in depth and detail. Planned as a reflection of the dynamism of psychology, the *Library* will grow and expand as psychology itself develops, thereby highlighting significant new research that will impact on the field. Adding to its accessibility and ease of use, the *Library* will be published in print and, later on, electronically.

The *Library* surveys psychology's principal subfields with a set of handbooks that capture the current status and future prospects of those major subdisciplines. This initial set includes handbooks of social and personality psychology, clinical psychology, counseling psychology, school psychology, educational psychology, industrial and organizational psychology, cognitive psychology, cognitive neuroscience, methods and measurements, history, neuropsychology, personality assessment, developmental psychology, and more. Each handbook undertakes to review one of psychology's major subdisciplines with breadth, comprehensiveness, and exemplary scholarship. In addition to these broadly conceived volumes, the *Library* also includes a large number of handbooks designed to explore in depth more specialized areas of scholarship and research, such as stress, health and coping, anxiety and related disorders, cognitive development, or child and adolescent assessment. In contrast to the broad coverage of the subfield handbooks, each of these latter volumes focuses on an especially productive, more highly focused line of scholarship and research. Whether at the broadest or most specific level, however, all of the *Library* handbooks offer synthetic coverage that reviews and evaluates the relevant past and present research and anticipates research in the future. Each handbook in the *Library* includes introductory and concluding chapters written by its editor to provide a road map to the handbook's table of contents and to offer informed anticipations of significant future developments in that field.

An undertaking of this scope calls for handbook editors and chapter authors who are established scholars in the areas about which they write. Many of the nation and world's most productive and best-respected psychologists have agreed to edit *Library* handbooks or write authoritative chapters in their areas of expertise.

For whom has the *Oxford Library of Psychology* been written? Because of its breadth, depth, and accessibility, the *Library* serves a diverse audience, including graduate students in psychology and their faculty mentors, scholars, researchers, and practitioners in psychology and related fields. Readers will find in the *Library* the information they seek on the subfield or focal area of psychology in which they work or are interested.

Befitting its commitment to accessibility, each handbook includes a comprehensive index, as well as extensive references to help guide research. And because the *Library* was designed from its inception as an online as well as a print resource, its structure and contents will be readily and rationally searchable online. Further, once the *Library* is released online, the handbooks will be regularly and thoroughly updated.

In summary, the *Oxford Library of Psychology* will grow organically to provide a thoroughly informed perspective on the field of psychology, one that reflects both psychology's dynamism and its increasing interdisciplinarity. Once published electronically, the *Library* is also destined to become a uniquely valuable interactive tool, with extended search and browsing capabilities. As you begin to consult this handbook, we sincerely hope you will share our enthusiasm for the more than 500-year tradition of Oxford University Press for excellence, innovation, and quality, as exemplified by the *Oxford Library of Psychology*.

Peter E. Nathan
Editor-in-Chief
Oxford Library of Psychology

ABOUT THE EDITOR

Lisa J. Miller

Dr. Lisa J. Miller is a foremost expert in spirituality and psychology having published over 70 related research articles and academic chapters. She has lectured nationally and internationally on spirituality in mental health, as well as to policy makers on Capitol Hill, community organizations, educators, and parents. Dr. Miller is a graduate of Yale University and the University of Pennsylvania, and currently serves as Director of Clinical Psychology and Associate Professor at Columbia University Teachers College. Dr. Miller currently is an Associate Editor for the Psychology of Religion and Spirituality, an APA research journal, and has served as President of the Society for the Psychology of Religion and Spirituality of the American Psychological Association.

ACKNOWLEDGMENTS

I am very honored and appreciative to be invited by Oxford University Press to edit this *Handbook of Psychology and Spirituality*. This life-changing experience has brought me into relationship with exceptionally deep-thinking and spiritually minded scientists and healers. This generous gift from Oxford has created the space to centralize the brilliant and revolutionary research within spiritual psychology that previously was dispersed across journals and scattered think tanks. This handbook provides a map marked where science walks the edge of a 21st Century spiritual psychology.

It has been a delight to work with the editorial team at Oxford University Press, foremost Chad Zimmerman, who generously has shared his wisdom on the big, specific, and in between of publishing. His wise sense of the word is most present throughout this handbook. My gratitude to Sarah Harrington for granting me the gift of editor, to Anne Dellinger for her thoughtful editing and artistic work, and to Megha Shiva Kumar from Newgen Knowledge Works for superb management of the production of this handbook.

I give my heartfelt thanks to each author in this handbook. Long overdue appreciation is due to the mentors who supported this work before it was popular: my beloved doctoral mentor, Martin Seligman; my postdoctoral mentors, Myrna Weissman and David Shaffer; Carole Dweck; William Beardslee; Teachers College Provost Tom James; my colleagues at Teachers College; and The William T. Grant Foundation for funding the first 5 years of my research. Additional appreciation goes to my forward-thinking, brilliant, and steadfast colleagues in Division 36 of the American Psychological Association, many of whom are in this volume.

During the time in which this handbook was developed, two of our outstanding scholars have died. Dr. Joseph Ciarrocchi and Dr. Peter Benson, were brave, dignified, and brilliant scholars. It is a true honor to have some of their final work in this handbook. We miss them.

CONTRIBUTORS

Samuel H. Barkin
Columbia University
New York, NY

Mario Beauregard
Departments of Psychology and Radiology
University of Montreal
Montreal, Quebec, Canada

William F. Bengston
Department of Sociology
St. Joseph's College
Patchogue, NY

Peter L. Benson
Search Institute
Minneapolis, MN

Jennifer F. Bernard
Department of Psychology
University of New Mexico
Albuquerque, NM

Chris J. Boyatzis
Department of Psychology
Bucknell University
Lewisburg, PA

Christopher T. Burris
Department of Psychology
St. Jerome's University
Waterloo, Ontario, Canada

Gail Christopher
W.K. Kellogg Foundation
Battle Creek, MI

Joseph W. Ciarrocchi
Department of Pastoral Counseling and
    Spiritual Care
Loyola University Maryland
Baltimore, MD

Lillian Comas-Díaz
Department of Psychiatry and Behavioral
    Sciences
George Washington University
Washington, D.C.

Jeanne Dalen
Oregon Research Institute
University of New Mexico
Albuquerque, NM

Larry Dossey
Medical City Dallas Hospital
Dallas, TX

Julie J. Exline
Department of Psychology
Case Western Reserve University
Cleveland, OH

Harris Friedman
Department of Psychology
University of Florida
Gainesville, FL

Matt Fritts
Samueli Institute
Alexandria, VA

Amit Goswami
Center for Quantum Activism
Eugene, OR

Bruce Greyson
Department of Psychiatry and
    Neurobehavioral Sciences
University of Virginia
Charlottesville, VA

Sean P. Hatt
Department of Counseling Psychology
Santa Clara University
Santa Clara, CA

Ralph W. Hood, Jr.
Department of Psychology
University of Tennessee at Chattanooga
Chattanooga, TN

Chad Johnson
Department of Human Relations
University of Oklahoma
Norman, OK

Maeba Jonas
Yale Divinity School
Yale University
New Haven, CT

Susan Jonas
Samueli Institute
Alexandria, VA

Wayne B. Jonas
Samueli Institute
Alexandria, VA

Brendan D. Kelly
Department of Adult Psychiatry
University College Dublin
Mater Misericordiae University Hospital
Dublin, Ireland

Stanley Krippner
College of Psychology and Humanistic
    Studies
Saybrook University
San Francisco, CA

Elizabeth J. Krumrei
Psychology Department
Pepperdine University
Malibu, CA

David Lukoff
Institute for Transpersonal Psychology
Palo Alto, CA

Annette Mahoney
Psychology Department
Bowling Green State University
Bowling Green, OH

Mark R. McMinn
Department of Clinical Psychology
George Fox University
Newberg, OR

Elizabeth Midlarsky
Teachers College
Columbia University
New York, NY

Lisa J. Miller
Teachers College
College of Physicians and Surgeons
Columbia University
New York, NY

Anthony S. J. Mullin
Teachers College
Columbia University
New York, NY

James M. Nelson
Chinese and Japanese Studies
Valparaiso University
Valparaiso, IN

Andrew B. Newberg
Department of Radiology
University of Pennsylvania School of
    Medicine
Philadelphia, PA

J. Alexis Ortiz
Department of Psychology
University of New Mexico
Albuquerque, NM

Justin J. Orton
Department of Psychology
George Fox University
Newberg, OR

Crystal L. Park
Department of Psychology
University of Connecticut
Storrs, CT

Kartikeya C. Patel
Institute for Transpersonal Psychology
Palo Alto, CA

Ralph L. Piedmont
Department of Pastoral Counseling and
    Spiritual Care
Loyola University Maryland
Baltimore, MD

Thomas G. Plante
Department of Psychology
Santa Clara University
Santa Clara, CA

Carole A. Rayburn
Clinical, Consulting, and Research
    Psychologist
Independent Practice
Silver Spring, MD

John K. Rempel
Department of Psychology
St. Jerome's University
Waterloo, Ontario, Canada

C. Edward Richards
Teachers College
Columbia University
New York, NY

P. Scott Richards
  Department of Counseling Psychology and
    Special Education
  Brigham Young University
  Provo, UT

Lee Joyce Richmond
  School of Education
  Loyola University Maryland
  Baltimore, MD

Linda Riebel
  College of Psychology and Humanistic
    Studies
  Saybrook University
  San Francisco, CA

Eugene C. Roehlkepartain
  Search Institute
  Minneapolis, MN

Eric D. Rose
  Department of Psychology
  Case Western Reserve University
  Cleveland, OH

Ruth Rosenbaum
  National Psychological Association for
    Psychoanalysis
  New York, NY

Peter C. Scales
  Search Institute
  Minneapolis, MN

Gary E. Schwartz
  Laboratory for Advances in Consciousness
  Department of Psychology
  The University of Arizona
  Tucson, AZ

Stephan Schwartz
  Samueli Institute
  Alexandria, VA

Randye J. Semple
  Keck School of Medicine
  Department of Psychiatry and the
    Behavioral Sciences
  University of Southern California
  Los Angeles, CA

Jeanne M. Slattery
  Department of Psychology
  Clarion University of Pennsylvania
  Clarion, PA

Brent D. Slife
  Department of Psychology
  Brigham Young University
  Provo, UT

Bruce W. Smith
  Department of Psychology
  University of New Mexico
  Albuquerque, NM

Kimberly N. Snow
  Graduate Department of Clinical
    Psychology
  George Fox University
  Newberg, OR

Len Sperry
  Medical College of Wisconsin
  Florida Atlantic University
  Boca Raton, FL

William A. Tiller
  Department of Materials Science and
    Engineering
  Stanford University
  Palo Alto, CA

Joseph P. Wagenseller
  C. G. Jung Institute of New York
  New York, NY

Fraser N. Watts
  Faculty of Divinity
  University of Cambridge
  Cambridge, UK

Kathryn T. Wiggins
  Department of Psychology
  University of New Mexico
  Albuquerque, NM

Everett L. Worthington, Jr.
  Department of Psychology
  Virginia Commonwealth University
  Richmond, VA

Carl E. Thoresen
  Department of Psychiatry and Behavioral
    Sciences
  Stanford University
  Stanford, CA

CONTENTS

Introduction

Lisa J. Miller

Psychology is a vital expeditionary among the disciplines of academia—eager to grow and attuned to the moment and culture in which we live. We are flexible, adaptable and alert. We reflect the partially veiled yet most compelling and necessary concerns of contemporary people. Our language is understood by a broad range of people, our innovations rapidly absorbed by surrounding culture, and thereby we co-create our contemporary zeitgeist.

Psychology consistently dialogs with the times: hysteria in the 1900s, IQ testing in the 1940s, groupthink in the 1950s, stereotyping in the 1960s and 1970s, depression in the 1980s and 1990s, and positive psychology in the 2000s. Psychology lives in this way along the edge of cultural history and is propelled by each new generation. Our research rapidly informs cultural advancement and methods of healing, together forging our contribution.

Science is particularly exciting on this temporal edge. To my graduate students, I liken psychological research to the journey in *Gulliver's Travels*—our inquiry reveals magnificent and varied sites, shocking and awe inspiring. Stepping back, we have actually stayed home, but we crafted a new lens through which to perceive humans and our place in the world. In our current era, we now rise as a culture in our awareness of spirituality. The language, operative concepts and assumptions of our culture increasingly hinge on spiritual ways of seeing, knowing, and living, such as: non-attachment, attunement, synchronicity, and handing-over to a Higher Power. Spiritual psychology as a scientific discipline, taken seriously, authentically, and with academic freedom, naturally brings forth a reexamination of psychology's core ontological assumptions—perhaps our greatest opportunity for contribution to the field.

This handbook highlights the cutting edge of an expanded psychology, encouraged by a subfield of psychology that directly addresses a broadened ontology. At the dynamic edge of the field of psychology and spirituality exists a body of work that works from a broadened set of ontological assumptions.

The authors of the forty chapters in this handbook see spirituality as being fundamental to the human constitution and foundational to the nature of our surrounding world. By deeply integrating spirituality into the existing landscape of psychology, they collectively reveal an entirely new formulation of psyche. In this handbook, spirituality is understood as ontologically real. Psyche connects us with the greater spirit, or consciousness, that is in us, through us and around us.

The research outlined in this volume picks up a lost thread to the social sciences—one extending from the ideals of the Socratic dialogs, suspended in psychology in the 20th century due to an exclusive vogue of secular materialism (except, of course, the unbridled and honest inquiry into spiritual psychology of William James). This formulation of psyche—in which the human mind is part and parcel of living spiritual reality—expands psychology by a Copernican magnitude. It demands that we move beyond the exclusive mechanistic and materialist view of the human mind as atomistic—authorized as the maker of meaning upon an inert world—to that of the human mind as dialectical. The dialectical human mind is in dialog with a conscious and sacred world and emanates from the same source as the world around us.

In this handbook, we define an emerging field within a spiritual psychological framework, that of postmaterialism, a science beyond the limitations of exclusive ontological materialism and mechanism. For some of the scholars herein, this radical shift is quite explicit; for others it is implicit or the ground on which they work, and yet others are silent on issues of ontology. In all cases, the science in this handbook forms a pastiche of different view of human psyche in the surrounding world than found in 20th Century psychology. Postmaterialist spiritual psychology includes the view that consciousness is the fundamental strata of all surrounding reality, of which our human mind is part and parcel. Consciousness as the fabric of the reality allows for a universe with guiding intention that is inherently teleological and in which all ground is sacred.

Postmaterialist spiritual psychology can live alongside and cross-fertilize work conducted from a materialist perspective; the two are not exclusive, and both are true. Materialist science merely needs to make its assumptions clearer as it sustains a vital place abreast work conducted from other ontological contexts. Materialism, however, in light of the past two decades of science, can no longer suffice as the exclusive rubric through which we view the human psyche. From a postmaterialist perspective, the conscious universe reifies sometimes as matter. Consciousness contributes towards the unfolding of material events. For instance, William Bengston in chapter 35 experimentally shows the effects of consciousness in the context of a rigorous controlled trial on the healing of cancerous tumors in mice. The consciousness of the lab technician and the preintervention "bondedness" of consciousness between mice in the treatment condition and control condition, yield in the control mice a response to the treatment they did not directly receive. Findings of a blind so-called placebo effect in mice, suggest that materialist experimental design might benefit from regard for postmaterial scientific consideration.

Scientists in this handbook view the brain in multiple new ways, including as an antenna, as a materialization or material representation of energy or consciousness, and as an expression of superposition of consciousness. Direct experience is understood as a way of knowing from the greater consciousness. The human brain is not exclusively a thought-making machine, but rather an innate channel for dialog with a conscious, surrounding reality. In other words, the brain is not more real than thoughts simply because it is tangible, and it is no longer endowed as the sole source of consciousness. This view of the human mind allows for the wisdom and information that surround us to touch our lives, inform our decisions, heal us, and guide our collective human activities. We are free from an egocentric prison of ontological centrality. From this perspective, it can be asked: is putting the human brain in the center of consciousness analogues to putting the earth at the center of the cosmos?

This postmaterialist ontology resonates as profoundly true for the rising generation of university students. This paradigm speaks to the lived reality of our current day students. On November 19, 2010, some of the contributors from this handbook traveled to Columbia University to share with our graduate students the ideas represented in this volume. These eminent researchers shared the new expanded psychological science, emphasizing the gains brought through postmaterialist understanding of spirituality, such as the oneness of consciousness, existence of a sacredness of source, and a teleology of development that inherently carries purpose.

As intellectual forerunners whose academic rigor is matched by their innovations, these senior scholars have persevered at points in their careers beyond material biases and professional obstacles, echoing those encountered by fellow revolutionaries in thought. It was therefore with great delight, and foremost surprise, that these eminent scholars entered the Columbia University Teachers College auditorium to discover hundreds of student interested in their work. These intellectual heroes were welcomed with tremendous enthusiasm into our largest auditorium—filled to capacity, standing room only, students leaning on the back walls, sitting on the banisters and lining the stairwells. The groundswell of students representing a historical cultural and intellectual transition away from 20th century strict materialism towards 21st century views that a greater consciousness, or spirit, exists throughout all reality.

Research studies presented in the conference and reported in this handbook validate a way of healing through use of our psyche to engage the greater consciousness that exists in us, through us and around us. Schwartz and Dossey (Chapter 34) solidly support the phenomena of spiritual healing, nonlocally and nonmechanistically, through assembling elegant scientific studies on spiritual healers such as that by landmark study Jeanne Achterberg and colleagues (2005). Achterberg put both patients and practiced indigenous healers in magnetic resonance imaging (MRI) machines. At specific and irregular time intervals, the experimenter asked the healer to work. As the healer started to use the customary method of intention, prayer or invoking the spiritual presence, the MRI showed distinct changes in brain function of the healer. Separated by distance and any sensory connection, the patient at these very same moments started to show the same changes in brain function as detected by MRI. This elegant experimental design shows that consciousness heals through nonlocal means, when an ultimate source of life or healing was invoked. This is a remarkable notion, but it is not entirely surprising- or really surprising at all- to many within the new generation of students. The 21st century students generally consider this study confirmatory of their sense or direct experience of the healing. As one student listener explained, "Everyone has their own healing story, and this is science confirming that it is true for everyone—this is reality."

Students, most in their twenties and thirties, responded to contributors of this handbook with verve saying, "This is the education that we want; the old scientific models feel dead to us. These ideas make sense to us." And "I need to know this way of working if I am to become a healer." Several students echoed, "I already assume a spiritual reality. Most of us do. So now what? We want to learn from this perspective."

My beloved mentor from my days as a doctoral student, Martin Seligman, founder of the positive psychology movement, always took an interest and was visibly curious about the ideas of students. At a dinner table full of accomplished scholars, Seligman almost always sat near a student, and would listen with intensity and an open mind to the ideas of students. Although students still need training in method and form, Seligman advocated that the new generation of scholars already knows something important, which is not immediately apparent looking only retrospectively. Who are this generation of students but the emerging guides for our evolving field?

This Oxford handbook answers the demands of the students by introducing an expanded psychology in which spirituality is taken as ontologically real. The authors apply postmaterialism to topics such as mental health and wellness, how to heal, and development. To a generation of students, many of whom meditate and speak overtly and casually of synchronicity and karma, postmaterialism is a natural understanding from which they search, but often cannot find, scholarship in the social and healing sciences. The students I have taught at Columbia for about a decade have been living implicitly or explicitly beyond this Copernican leap. This is why students listened in the hundreds with wide eyes to guest scholars for four hours on a Friday night, asking for a different education. This handbook provides some of the finest work that scientists and healers have discovered to respond to the forward-thinking, curious and hungry seeker.

The rigid traditional boundaries of academic departments may be a relic of strict materialism— whereas here we study humans, there we study animals, and there we study atoms or machines. This handbook starts with consciousness as the root of the human experience, and psychology as the human relationship to consciousness. The handbook constitutes a living think tank, diligently prepared over the past decade through rigorous research by leading academic researchers and healers, endemically crossing boundaries of so-called subfields. Into this exciting movement of intellectual history, I invite our reader to meet 63 leading intellectuals. As you pull up a seat at the round table, know that the opinions are as rigorous, forward thinking, and empirically supported as any in our era. Together, these scholars offer an augmented scientific language and a set of models and methods for inquiry toward a more knowing and more healing psychology.

I honor the distinct and lucid voices in this handbook so dearly that I will not paraphrase but rather introduce our shared endeavor. My contribution to the handbook has been that of editor, which I interpreted as a charge to hold an honest intellectual space free from the censor of intellectual vogue, and only to edit any given chapters in the direction of clarity and fullness (which rarely was needed).

At this juncture in history, there is radical climate change, multiple wars, epidemics of new diseases, and volatile economies across the world. Right now, the danger is immanent, and we must learn to live in dialog with the greater consciousness that is in us, through us, and around us. The dialog formed through the psychotherapeutic models in this handbook, such as awakening to the daily sacredness of living in spiritual awareness psychotherapy (American Psychological Association, 2004), are generalizable models for living with what Wayne Jonas and colleagues (Chapter 23) call our three pressing areas of need: recognition of the global village, awareness of the environment, and deep understanding of health. The innovation of science in the past 10 years pushes us, right on time, past the 20th-century models of mind, affording us a new opportunity to keep up with our surrounding reality.

We live in a postmaterialist era, through which at the moment perhaps we are being pushed, even led, by wisdom in our young students to build upon this cutting edge of the postmaterialist spiritual psychology (Miller, 2010). Psychology, in our century of history, has always evolved propelled by the wisdom of the people. I hope that through the science in this volume we collectively contribute toward an intellectual shift that can face up to the worldly dangers unexplained and unresolved by an exclusively 20th century materialist perspective. The scholars herein offer an updated intellectual and scientific frame through which to perceive a highly volatile and transitional world—to gird a bright new way of thinking and to sustain a new way of living. Evidence, language, and new models refine the inchoate awareness expressed by our young students. Taken to heart this awareness can spawn spiritual activism, as suggested in chapter 38 by quantum physicist Amit Goswami. Perhaps spiritual activism is a foundational intellectual quantum perspective to undergurd the world-wide movement for social and political change spearheaded by young adults.

The science in is Oxford University Press Handbook, entered fully and with an open mind, shows our universe to be alive, guiding and so very sacred. The scientific perspective that all consciousness is one and sacred may reawaken our appreciation of living beings around us, all life.

References

Achterberg, J., Cooke, K., Richards, T., Standish, L. J., Kozak, L, & Lake, J. (2005). Evidence for correlations between distant intention and brain function in recipients: A functional magnetic resonance imaging analysis. *Journal of Alternative and Complementary Medicine, 11,* 965–971.

American Psychological Association (Producer). (2004). *Spiritual awareness psychotherapy* [video/DVD] by Lisa Miller with Jon Carlson. Available from http://www. apa.org/videos/

Miller, L. (2010). Watching for light: Spiritual psychology beyond materialism. *Psychology of Religion and Spirituality, 2*(1), 35–36.

PART 1

Epistemological and Ontological Assumptions in History and Culture

The History and Current State of Research on Psychology of Religion

Ralph W. Hood, Jr.

Abstract

Religion and spirituality were major concerns of the early American psychologists. Largely influenced by the American Protestant experience of revivals, psychologists focused upon conversion using the biblical narrative of Paul as a prototype of sudden radical transformation. Many of the early psychologists sought to give reductionist explanations for both religion and spiritual phenomena as they sought to dissociate psychology from the popular cultural view of parapsychology and spiritualism. William James was the most notable exception, insisting on the possible ontological reality of the objects of both religious and psychic phenomena. Psychoanalysis influenced by the French medical tradition continued exploring religion, with Sigmund Freud offering an explanation of religion first simply as an illusion but finally as a mass delusion, thereby linking religion and madness. As American psychology sought to emulate the German tradition of experimental psychology within the limits of natural science, interest in religion waned. The reemergence of a psychology of religion came in the 1960s, partly influenced by interim concerns with authoritarianism and prejudice and cognitive dissonance theory, all of which had a marginal concern with religion. The cultural unrest of the 1960s sparked renewed interest in new religious movements and psychedelic states of consciousness, both of which fueled the psychology of religion. The field is now well established with a division in the American Psychological Association (APA) and an APA journal. Numerous other journals assure that the psychology of religion and now spirituality will continue to be identifiable areas of specialty within psychology.

Key Words: authoritarianism, cognitive dissonance, conversion, deconversion, entheogens, mysticism, ontological, parapsychological, religious orientation, spiritual transformation

Introduction

Concern with both histories of psychology and research on psychology is of recent origin. Division 36 of the APA had its origins in the American Catholic Psychological Association's concern for encouraging Catholics to pursue the science and profession of psychology. In 1971 this organization, which was disbanded in 1968, was reorganized as an ecumenical group, Psychologists Interested in Religious Issues (PIRI), and sought divisional status in what Benjamin (1977) has chronicled as APA's ever-increasing speciation expressed in its burgeoning divisional creations. After an initial failure in 1974, PIRI achieved division status in 1975 with Virginia Sexton as its first president (Hood, 1998). *Psychology of Religion*, the division's current name, emerged out of a struggle in which the outgoing executive committee under the presidency of Ralph Hood in 1992 voted to propose the name be *Psychology and Religion*, a decision never sent to membership for vote because it was immediately changed again to *Psychology of Religion* by the incoming executive committee under the presidency of Ray Paloutzian. This recommendation was sent to the membership and was accepted. The proposal to change the name to *Psychology of Religion and Spirituality* recently passed by a simple majority vote, but the newsletter editor of the division, W. Paul Williamson, noted that the bylaws required a two-thirds majority vote and hence the announcement of the name change was withdrawn (Hood, in press). A recent vote of members of Division 36 successfully changed the name to the Society for the Psychology of Religion and Spirituality.

This brief history of Division 36 illustrates the basic problem of writing any history but one exacerbated when the object of study is as emotionally volatile as religion. As Benjamin (2009) has noted, "History is not what happened in the past. It is what historians tell us happened in the past" (p. 1, emphasis in original). Until recently, histories of psychology have been Whig histories, written by insiders in the discipline rather than trained historians, and thus tend to support one view of psychology among many differing views as how to define the discipline (Butterfield, 1931/1965). Taylor has documented this with respect to Boring's (1929) almost iconic history of experimental psychology in which William James's own priority in establishing a laboratory of psychology at Harvard is minimally recognized in favor of Wundt's laboratory in Leipzig, Germany, in order to bolster Boring's vision of psychology as necessarily an experimental science in the tradition of the natural sciences. How one defines psychology is part of the means by which a given history is recognized. The history of psychology has its own divisional status (Division 26) that precedes that of Psychology of Religion in the APA, yet as a research specialty the history of psychology is little more than 40 years (Benjamin, 2009, p. 1). Thus, the issue of tracing the history of the psychology of religion depends on how each discipline is conceived. Rather than focusing upon a psychology *of* religion, an enterprise Belzen (2010) argues is fraught with conceptual pitfalls, our focus will be upon psychology *and* religion, that short-lived divisional name for what is likely in the future (whether *of* or *and*) the wedding of religion with spirituality (Paloutzian & Parks, 2005).

The First Period of Psychology and Religion

It is widely acknowledged that the early American psychologists concerned themselves with both religious and spiritual issues, including spiritualism (Coon, 1992). Part of this concern was the cultural fact of the American Protestant experience with its focus upon revivals and conversion experiences and

with what Taves (1999) has identified as the tension between psychologists and religionists on religious experience as opposed to experiencing religion. The fear for some and the hope for others was that religious experience could be adequately explained by psychological processes absent the need for any supernatural reference. With the exception of William James, almost to a person the earliest psychologists of religion believed in a psychology of religion, not a psychology and religion. In the early months of 1881, G. Stanley Hall delivered a series of public lectures at Harvard University. His topic was religious conversion, and much of the material he covered was later incorporated into his classic two-volume study of adolescence (Hall, 1904). Those committed to psychology as a natural science were courageous enough to tackle some of the most profound and meaningful religious phenomena of the time as lacking any supernatural necessity. However, the newly emerging psychology was linked in the popular mind with religious and parapsychological phenomena, including spiritualism (Coon, 1992). While many associated the new science of psychology with the documentation of spiritual phenomena, American psychologists divided along lines claiming to debunk or support such phenomena (Hood, in press). Hall eventually went on to write a two-volume treatise entitled *Jesus, the Christ, in Light of Psychology* (1917), foreshadowing psychohistorical works on religious figures most commonly associated with psychoanalysis, the psychology that emerged not out of German experimentalists but from French physicians and, of course, the influence of Sigmund Freud. However, when psychologists of the German experimental model studied religion, they focused upon Protestantism associated with American culture. Thus, not surprisingly, American psychology of religion emerged as a psychology of North American Protestant Christianity—a bias that still dominates the field to this day (Gorsuch, 1988). The two major topics of concern were religious experience and conversion.

Religious Experience and Conversion

Edwin Starbuck and James H. Leuba had been Hall's students at Clark University, arguably the only school of psychology of religion in the early period. Leuba (1896) published the first psychological journal article on conversion; this was rapidly followed by an article by Starbuck (1897) on conversion and by his first book-length treatment of the topic (Starbuck, 1899). Not surprisingly, Leuba's and Starbuck's research methods paralleled

Hall's, including the use of questionnaires and personal documents. Another early investigator, Coe (1916), added quasi-experimental techniques to the investigation of religious converts influenced by the American Protestant experience and revivals. These early investigators tended to focus upon dramatic cases of sudden conversion, using purely psychological principles that provided essentially reductionist interpretations. Pratt, one of James's students at Harvard, focused upon gradual converts, whose experiences were less dramatic, required intellectual seeking, and were hypothesized to be more genuinely characteristic of conversion within both Christianity and other religious traditions. However, as revival phenomena declined in American culture, so did psychologists' concern with conversion, so much so that as the 1960s approached, W. H. Clark (1958) bemoaned the fact that psychology had all but abandoned the study of conversion. He was to miss the anticipation of the renewed concern with religious conversion as the psychology of religion reemerged in what we identify as its second period, which will be discussed next.

The Exceptional Case of America's Exceptional Psychologist

If the early American psychologists sought to define psychology as natural science providing for a reductionist explanation of religious and spiritual phenomena, William James provided a nonreductionist basis for not a psychology of religion but for a complementary psychology and religion. His widely acknowledged first classic text, *Principles of Psychology* (1890/1981), limited psychology to a metaphysic associated with the German commitment to natural science metaphysics. However, he abandoned this commitment as only "provisional" in the abridgement of this text (James, 1892, p. 468), and in the second of his classic texts he produced what is less a psychology of religion than a text on psychology and religion (Hood, 2008).

James's (1902/1985) classic work *The Varieties of Religious Experience* has continued to influence psychologists since it was initially delivered as the Gifford Lectures at the beginning of the 20th century. James set the tone for contemporary empirical work in the psychology of religious *experience* that is nonreductive (Hood, 2000). He also anticipated the current concern with spirituality as opposed to religion, and in the words of Fuller (2001, p. 130) is the exemplar of what it means to be "spiritual but not religious." More than one psychologist has noted that if James were wiring today, his lectures would

undoubtedly be entitled *The Varieties of Spiritual Experience* (Gorsuch & Miller, 1999).

Like many American psychologists James's sought to illuminate conversion, relying heavily upon the research of his contemporaries, especially Edwin Starbuck and James H. Leuba. However, unlike many of the American psychologists of religion, James argued that religious thought was warranted by the fact that psychological reductive theories of religious experience were incomplete. A science of psychology must accept that ontological possibility of transcendence variously experienced. A reductive view of mysticism was insufficient on both methodological and conceptual grounds. The natural science limits provisionally acknowledged in the *Principles* were transcended in the *Varieties*. This is no more evident than in the contrasting evaluation of mysticism by James and the staunch defender of the naturalist Germanic experimental tradition, Leuba. Leuba (1925) argued that mysticism was at best an inferior or pathological state, whereas for James (1902/1985, p. 301) it was the "root and centre" of religion and an empirical indicator of a broader consciousness shared by both psychology and religion. Thus, even though the *Varieties* comes early in the first period of the psychology of religion, it foreshadowed the lack of concern with religious belief by psychologists, who all but adopted methodologies and frameworks such as behaviorism that left religion bereft of any serous ontological claims. Psychologists began to see psychology and religion as supporting incompatible ontological claims (Leuba, 1916, 1934). James's approach was rejected by American psychologists and became part of what Taylor (1999) has termed a "shadow culture." The exception was the French medical tradition, which birthed the science of psychoanalysis associated with another exceptional psychologist, Sigmund Freud. Its history is best documented by Ellenberger (1970), whose history of dynamic psychology is both authoritative and indicative of the close relationship between this species of psychology and religious and spiritual traditions.

Psychology of Religion: The Case of Freud and Psychoanalysis

While Ellenberger (1970) has made the case for the centrality of essentially religious concerns in the diversity of theories, he subsumes under the phrase "dynamic psychology" American psychology of religion focused in the early period upon Freudian theory and its claim to have found a natural scientific explanation for religion. While the concern with religion among the German tradition of a laboratory-based natural science waned, psychologists in the emerging psychoanalytic tradition took up the mantle of religion in training schools loosely affiliated with universities but heavily influential in programs concerned with clinical psychology. The early parallel is with James, whose treatment of psychology as if it were or could be a natural science was provisional and was countered by Freud's insistence that psychology as a natural science was finally achieved with the science of psychoanalysis (Grünbaum, 1984, 1987). Hence, Grünbaum rightly notes that like all natural science theories, psychoanalytic theories in general and Freud's theory of religion in particular are to be judged by empirical criteria. Here the issue is not to explore Freud's view of religion in depth but simply to note that this tradition of French medical concerns balanced the Germanic concern with laboratory science as the most influential effect on American culture and on popular ideas of psychology. No psychology has had as much influence on culture, arts, and literature as psychoanalysis. It also provided a powerful reductive explanation of religion that few contemporary psychologists of religion, even within the psychoanalytic tradition, support (Belzen, 2009). Critics of psychoanalysis note that it postulates its own myth of early childhood drama (the ontogenetic thesis) and of early humankind (the phylogenetic thesis) in what became the cornerstone of classical psychoanalysis. The Oedipal drama, especially for males, linked the desire for the mother with that of disposing the father in a dynamic seen as thinly masked in both Judaism (a religion of the father) and Christianity (a religion of the son). Ultimately, Freud saw religion as a falsification of reality. God was interpreted as a projected idealized father derived from the Oedipal drama. The decline of religion was predicated on Freud's assumption that it characterized the infantile stage of humankind. While American academic psychology largely ignored religion from 1930 through 1960, psychoanalysis in its classical Freudian variety produced literally thousands of articles and books, providing a huge cultural impact on how Europeans and Americans viewed themselves. Efforts to test psychoanalytic theories by naturalistic scientific methods have, not surprisingly, found psychoanalytic theories largely deficient, especially in their reductionist claims with respect to the objects of religious belief (Belzen, 2009; Meissner, 1984; Pruyser, 1968. Thus, psychoanalysis paralleled the early German-influenced experimentalists in exhausting within the first

generation of scholars what psychology as a natural science could say about religion. The instructive exemplar here is the only meeting between the two exceptional psychologists (James and Freud) who provide our integrating theme for the early period of the psychology of religion in America.

James and Freud

If James was self-consciously aware of the provisional nature and likely limits of natural science with respect to psychological questions that are accentuated in the psychology of religion, Freud was less open to the possibility of such limits (Meissner, 1984). In his analysis of the Freud/Pfizer correspondence, Meissner documents that Pfizer had raised the issue about Freud's rhetorical use of "science" as both an effort to establish the legitimacy of psychoanalysis and a rather naïve commitment to a particular metaphysic (Meissner, 1984, pp. 73–103). James did the same in his critique of Freud. Having only meeting him once (at Clark University), he is reported to have said by Ernst Jones, one of Freud's earliest biographers, "The future of psychology is yours" (Richardson, 2006, p. 514). However, this is less likely correct in light of Freud's letter to Ms. Calkins of September 19, 1909. There James noted a more cautious appreciation of Freud and psychoanalysis:

> I strongly suspect Freud, with his dream-theory, of being a regular *halluciné*. But I hope that he and his disciples will push it to its limits, as undoubtedly it covers some facts, and will add to our understanding of "functional" psychology, which is the real psychology.
> (*Perry*, 1935, p. 123)

Likewise, in the *Varieties* in a less thinly veiled reference to Freud, James echoed what has become a standard critique of classical Freudian theory: the refusal to abandon or limit the pansexual motivation *for* and explanation *of* the content of certain religious beliefs. James rejected the claim that religious belief was "perverted sexuality" (James, 1902/1985, p. 18).

> The plain truth is that to interpret religion one must in the end look at the immediate content of the religious consciousness. The moment one does this, one sees how wholly disconnected it is in the main from the content of sexual.
> (*James*, 1902/1985, p. 19)

With James championing the immediate content of religious consciousness, a descriptive psychology of religion merged with the narrative psychology that foreshadowed James as paving the way for the phenomenological psychology of religion that would find its place in the reemergence of an American psychology of religion in the 1960s, where mysticism would be the focus of systematic empirical study, with much of it from a Jamesean perspective (Hood, 1995, 2002, 2008a). However, in the eclipse of the psychology of religion after the first generation of American interest, two areas of research kept religion at least within the focus of those developing psychological theory within a natural science perspective. Those areas were authoritarianism and prejudice and cognitive dissonance and prophecy. Each in its own way would contribute to the emergence of the identification of two complementary paradigms for the psychology of religion in the only two *Annual Review of Psychology* pieces on psychology and religion in the reemergence of the study of religion by psychologists in the 1960s (Emmons & Paloutzian, 2003; Gorsuch, 1988).

Religion and Prejudice

Research on prejudice stimulated psychological interest in religion at least as an aside when religion per se was of little interest to American psychologists. It also laid the foundation for both of the paradigms that would characterize the reemergence of the psychology of religion, the measurement/correlational paradigm identified by Gorsuch (1988) and the interdisciplinary paradigm recommended by Emmons and Paloutzian (2003).

Research on authoritarianism and religion implicated at least some forms of religious commitment with prejudice. The first is arguably the longest research tradition in American social psychology published as *The Authoritarian Personality* (Adorno, Frenkel-Brunswik, Levinson, & Sanford, 1950). This research, which will be discussed more fully later, linked a concern with measurement and quantitative data with classical Freudian theory to produce a linkage that was largely unanticipated. While researchers had predicted a positive relationship between authoritarianism and prejudice, the linkage that there could be a religious form of the expression of authoritarianism was not. As we shall see later, many researchers consider the relationship between fundamentalist religion, authoritarianism, and prejudice to be as empirically established as any finding in the psychology of religion

Another concern with prejudice and religion came from Allport, who would initiate what would be the major focus of the reemergence of the psychology of religion, in America, the measurement of religious orientation and the various links between religious orientation and prejudice. Here we need but note that Allport's classic text on prejudice was published in 1954 in the eclipse of the psychology of religion, and his seminal paper on religious orientation and prejudice was published in the middle decade of the emergence of the psychology of religion (Allport & Ross, 1967). Thus, authoritarianism, prejudice, and religion were empirical themes in the period of the eclipse of the psychology of religion that made the reemergence of a psychology of religion possible as the discipline found a new footing in America in the 1960s. The current status of this research will be discussed later in this chapter.

Cognitive Dissonance and Failed Prophecy

Cognitive dissonance was first proposed by Festinger (1957) and was being further modified during his famous field study of a flying saucer group that prophetically predicted the end of the world. Yet the success of the theory was not in field research on apparently failed prophecy but in the laboratory and experimental tradition of the German psychological tradition, which was only provisionally endorsed by William James. The theory has been so successful in experimental social psychology that just 4 years before Festinger's death, Jones claimed, "Because the main propositions of dissonance theory have been confirmed with sufficient regularity, there is not a great deal to be gained from further research in this area" (1985, p. 57). Basic to Festinger's theory is that cognitions more or less map reality. Hence, there is pressure for individual beliefs to be congruent with reality—whether physical, psychological, or sociological (Festinger, 1957, pp. 10–11). This has led some researchers to puzzle over how it is that individuals can maintain membership in religious groups when they make predictions that are falsified. The classic study by Festinger, Riecken, and Schacter is entitled *When Prophecy Fails* (1953), framed within the natural science assumption that failed prophecy was an empirical fact. This participant observation study of a religious group that predicted the end of the world provided a fortuitous opportunity to test a belief Festinger and his colleagues were sure would be falsified. In light of the general focus on consistency in psychological social psychology, it was assumed that a clearly falsified prophecy would produce an objectively identified state of dissonance that would motivate the believers to both increase their commitment to their beliefs and also seek to increase proselytization. Hence, the interest in prophecy was simply a concern with disconfirmed belief in a real-life setting and not any genuine interest in the psychology of religion per se by dissonance theorists. Festinger also took a hand at some historical speculations on "unfulfilled prophecies and disappointed messiahs" (1957, pp. 3–32) in a time when American psychologists were largely ignoring religious issues. Part of the appeal of the theory of cognitive dissonance has always been its counterintuitive predictions. In an obituary for Festinger in the *American Psychologist*, the renowned social psychologist Zarjonc equated Festinger's standing in social psychology with that of Freud in clinical psychology (1990, p. 661). Two central counterintuitive hypotheses are as follows: Clearly falsified beliefs will be held even more intensely after falsification; and when prophecies fail, groups will increase active proselytization. As we shall see, the former hypothesis has been supported in the laboratory. Central to Festinger's theory is that cognitions can be dissonant. When cognitions are dissonant, they serve to motivate the believer to reduce this dissonance. The assumption of a real-world stance when prophecies are clearly confirmed or disconfirmed is a black-and-white realist stance that Festinger brought from the laboratory to his participant observation field study, an issue that we will address when we discuss dissonance theory and the reemergence of the psychology of religion. However, after affirming support for his theory in this field study, theorists largely abandoned the distinctive religious issue of failed prophecy for creative laboratory studies of cognitive dissonance. This indicated that the interest of social psychologists was not in researching religious issues but in simply noting how a theory partly derived from a study of failed prophecy could claim by creative laboratory studies to establish a counterintuitive psychological theory that could apparently be easily extrapolated to religious prophecies of little interest and unstudied by a psychology wedded to experimental methods and creative laboratory studies (Zarjonc, 1990, p. 661). However, theory lay waiting for psychologists of religion to test in the spirit of the call for a *multilevel interdisciplinary paradigm* (Emmons & Paloutzian, 2003, p. 395; emphasis in original) for the study of religion in the only one other than Gorsuch's (1988) *Annual Review of Psychology* to review of the psychology of religion entry to date.

The Reemergence of Psychology of Religion in America

Given that a serious history of psychology in its numerous speciations has yet to be written out, the view of the history of psychology of religion in America is a Whig history, self-conscious in its effort to present a view of psychology of religion compatible with several assumptions. With William James, we assume that psychology need not restrict itself to natural science assumptions and is unlikely to continue to do so if the call for the new paradigm is taken seriously—and we assume that it will be and applaud the possibility of a genuinely multilevel interdisciplinary paradigm that is nonreductive. It will likely have to be a psychology and religion, not simply a psychology of religion (Hood & Williamson, 2008). This paradigm echoes what actually fostered the reemergence of the psychology of religion, as mentioned earlier. To characterize this reemergence, we need to note the interdisciplinary matrix within which the psychologists interested in religion could maintain a sense of professional identity absent specific journals committed to the psychology of religion.

Interdisciplinary Associations and Journals

It is more than likely that many of these senior psychologists of religion today had their start as members of the Society for the Scientific Study of Religion, an interdisciplinary organization that began as the Committee for the Scientific Study of Religion in 1949 (Nelsen, 1998, p. 482). By the mid-1950s the name was changed to the Society for the Scientific Study of Religion, and by the mid-1960s the *Journal for the Scientific Study of Religion* was established, one goal of which was "to encourage the study of religion through the media of their respective sciences" (Nelsen, 1998, p. 482). Among the early members were eminent representatives of various disciplines, such as Gordon W. Allport in psychology, Talcott Parson and Pitrim Sorokin in sociology, and Paul Tillich in theology. The first of four psychologists to edit the journal was James Dittes (Hood, 2000). The society was dedicated to precisely the paradigm that Emmons and Paloutzian had called for, and it was this flagship journal that allowed an outlet for psychological studies of religion alongside those of other disciplines. Other journals had more explicit faith interests, such as the flagship journal for the Religious Research Association, *Review of Religious Research*. These two journals allowed for many involved in the reemergence of the psychology of religion to have publication possibilities. However, the net effect was that research on the psychology of religion area remained on the periphery of scientific respectability. Some psychologists of religion began to insist that more natural scientific studies linked to at least quasi-experimental paradigms were needed to bring the psychology of religion into mainstream psychology (Batson, 1977).

The shift encouraged new journals more directly identified with psychology to emerge. Some were not associated with faith commitment; others were more explicit in their faith orientation. The titles reveal their orientation: *Journal of Psychology and Theology*; *Journal of Psychology and Christianity*; *Journal of Religion*; *Journal of the Psychology of Judaism*; and *The International Journal for the Psychology of Religion*. Some new journals were more interdisciplinary in nature, such as *Mental Health, Religion and Culture* and most recently *Spirituality and Health International*. The *Archiv für Religionspsychologie* (*Archives for the Psychology of Religion*), the yearbook of the Internationale Gesellschaft für Religionspsychologie (International Association for the Psychology of Religion), founded in 1914, has been revived and now publishes three issues per year with more studies by American psychologists. Pertinent literature continues to grow at a rapid rate across the globe. Specialty journals such as the *Journal of Muslim Mental Health* address religious traditions other than Christianity, long dominant in the American psychology of religion. Other journals such as *Journal of Management, Spirituality and Religion* suggest that other specialty journals distinguishing spirituality from religion are likely. Finally, the Division of the Psychology of Religion of the APA now has its official journal, *Psychology of Religion and Spirituality*. Likewise, several general and specialty handbooks have been published and many more are in press. Thus, the psychology of religion has indeed reemerged. We shall mark its boundaries and concerns in light of the factors we think contributed to its reemergence.

Themes in the Reemergence of Psychology of Religion

Our survey of major themes in the reemergence of the psychology of religion is necessarily selective. We use as our guide the call for a new multilevel interdisciplinary paradigm that is nonreductive (Emmons & Paloutzian, 2003) and that therefore is as much prospective as it is retrospective. The themes we select are those that are likely to endure and continue to define psychology and religion for the foreseeable future.

The Bracketing of Ontological Claims

While early psychologists of religion addressed ontological claims relative to religion, a second generation of psychologists made progress by bracketing

ontological claims—essentially claiming that psychology cannot address ontological issues. The best exemplar of this is the recognition that Freud's theory of religion was not simply illusion (a product of wish fulfillment) but in fact delusion; a claim about a reality that does not exist could not sustain critical philosophical scrutiny (Grünbaum, 1984, 1987). The issue allowed a second generation of psychoanalytic theorists to focus upon object relations and the psychological process involved in experiences of God images (Meissner, 1984; Rizzuto, 1979). Many contemporary psychoanalysts avoid the controversy surrounding Freud's theory of religion by denying that psychoanalysis needs to address ontological issues (Belzen, 2009). The issue that psychology cannot directly address ontological issues also heavily influenced American clinical psychology, where the APA cautions that terms such as *hallucination* must be interpreted in terms of the believer's culture. The last several revisions of *The Diagnostic and Statistical Manual of Mental Disorders* (*DSM*) have included cautions about identifying hallucinations as pathological if there is normative support for these practices. This was made especially clear in *DSM-III-R*:

> When an experience is entirely normative for a particular culture—e.g., the experience of hallucinating the voice of a deceased in the first few weeks of bereavement in various North American Indian groups, or trance and possession states occurring in culturally approved ritual contexts in much of the non-Western world—it should not be regarded as pathological.
> (*American Psychiatric Association*, 1987, p. xxvi)

The effect of bracketing the psychologist's ability to assess ontological claims has the effect of freeing the contemporary psychology of religion to explore the psychological processes involved in religiously interpreted phenomena without regard to their correspondence to reality. Thus, both religious apologists and those in opposition to religion stand on equal footing. This has led contemporary researchers to explore issues of mental health and coping without regard to truth claims of the belief content of religious cognitions involved in such processes. While this is an advantageous move, it is limiting, and a dialog between psychology and religion remains crucial (Hampson & Boyd-MacMillan, 2008).

Religion, Mental Health, and Coping

Perhaps the major area of research with the reemergence of the psychology of religion has been the focus upon relationships between religion and mental health. Given the bracketing of ontological claims, religion and mental health may be orthogonal constructs. While psychologists are free to evaluate the psychological ramifications of particular religious beliefs and practices, the evaluation is on purely psychological criteria. Empirically identifying the correlates of mental health constructs with diverse forms of religious expression does not entail that even pathological processes might be positively framed within religious discourse (Hood & Byrom, 2010; Poloma & Hood, 2006). The empirical literature relating religion and mental health is complex and resists easy summary (Hood et al., 2009, ch. 11). However, the conceptual bracketing of ontological issues is widely accepted to mean psychologists cannot have either a purely psychological theory of religion insofar as it is a cultural phenomenon (Belzen, 2010).

A similar situation exists with respect to religious coping. With the reemergence of the psychology of religion, Pargament (1997) and his colleagues began an extensive series of empirical studies focusing upon how individuals use religion to cope. This research continues and as with religion and mental health, the complexity defies easy summary. However, the fact that believers do not simply believe but use their religion is well established.

Religious Orientation

Outside clinical concerns with religion, mental health, and coping, there is little doubt that the reemergence of psychology of religion was linked to Allport's concern and measures of religious orientation. A variety of measures of intrinsic, extrinsic, and later quest religion dominated the empirical literature through the 1980s. Much of the focus was on what religious orientations are linked to prejudice. Much of the debate reminds one of classical debates in learning theory, and the issues are as much conceptual as empirical. One camp has essentially seen intrinsic religious orientation as unrelated or negatively related to prejudice. Another camp gives that honor to the quest religious orientation and argues that intrinsic religious orientation only wishes to appear nonprejudicial. As with other areas, the empirical literature defies easy summary (Hood et al., ch. 12).

Authoritarianism and Fundamentalism

Closely related to the literature on religion and prejudice is the reemergence of a concern with personality and prejudice. Much of this research has been by Altemeyer and Hunsberger (2005), who

essentially argue that fundamentalism is a religious expression of right-wing authoritarianism and fosters prejudice, both general and that which is specifically religiously proscribed. The terrorist attacks on 9/11 in the United States have fueled added interest in religious fundamentalism, which is often conceptually linked to terrorism. However, caution is needed because we have little empirical data linking religious fundamentalism to terrorism, and most fundamentalists even when standing in opposition to the host culture do not employ violent tactics. The conditions under which any religious group employs violence is an empirical issue not yet adequately addressed. Hood, Hill, and Williamson (2005) have documented that many of the summary claims of psychologists with respect to religious fundamentalists lack empirical support and are suggestive of stereotyping by researchers whose own beliefs are distant from those they study.

Conversion and Deconversion

There is little doubt that the cultural fervor of America in the 1960s contributed to the reemergence of the psychology of religion. Just as the role of religious revivals and awakenings in American culture led the early psychologists to be concerned with conversion (Taves, 1999), the emergence of what became identified as new religion led psychologists to focus upon the process of conversion once more. Furthermore, setting the stage for the Emmons and Paloutzian's (2003) call for a new interdisciplinary paradigm, studies of conversion to new religious movements were dominated by sociologically trained social psychologists. One of the most widely adopted social psychology textbooks of the 1960s teamed a psychologist (Paul F. Secord) with a sociologist (Carl W. Backman), who tried to create an interdisciplinary social psychology, noting that "social psychology can no longer be adequately surveyed by a person trained in only one of its parent disciplines" (Secord & Backman, 1964, p. vii). The new studies of conversion radically altered classic views of religious conversion as a sudden process resulting in radical transformation of personality, heavily influenced by Paul in the Protestant tradition (Richardson, 1985). The new paradigm emphasized the active search for meaning in which converts explore the religious landscape by converting and deconverting from various religious groups; they do so in a continual process of actively searching for meaning and purpose, but their personalities are altered far less than their worldviews (Paloutzian, Richardson, & Rambo, 1999).

Associated with a return to interest in conversion and the new paradigm of active seeking was the process of deconverison, or the process by which one leaves a religious group either because he or she is exiting religion altogether or is seeking alternative religious groups. The complexity of deconversion is as empirically complex as that of conversion and in some ways represents a mirror image. However, it also reflects the religious climate of the host culture (Streib, Hood, Keller, Csöff, & Silver, 2008). Furthermore, transformations not specifically framed in religious contexts have led to studies of spiritual transformation, rather than to religious conversion, especially among those identified as spiritual but not religious (Hood, 2003b).

Cognitive Dissonance and the Call for a New Paradigm

Perhaps most indicative of the new paradigm mentioned earlier is the fact that psychologically oriented social psychologists who committed to laboratory studies of cognitive dissonance and socially oriented social psychologists who committed to field studies have reached almost opposite conclusions with respect to dissonance theory.

This is crucial because Festinger's theory requires that beliefs be proven false. In his own words, they must be "unequivocal and undeniable" (Festinger, 1957, p. 3). Such an objectivist stance is naïve with respect to how beliefs actually operate in real-life contexts and assumes that psychologists are authorities on ontological issues such as "falsification" of beliefs. As Carroll (1979, p. 184) noted when applying cognitive dissonance theory to biblical prophecy, there are no simple objective criteria by which one can identify failed prophecy because what outsiders (especially researchers) see as failed prophecy is seldom seen that way by insiders. Hence, psychologists tend to intrude an objectivist stance when they claim a given belief has been falsified. Tumminia (1998, p. 165) notes, "what appears to be seemingly irrefutable evidence of irreconcilable contradictions to outsiders, like Festinger, can instead be evidence of the truth of prophecy to insiders." Carroll (1979, p. 176) further notes that among believers there is a transcendental dimension to prophecy that secures it from what is only an apparent failure. Sociologically oriented social psychologists have noted this as well, recognizing that failed prophecy entails hermeneutical considerations that make claims to "unequivocal and undeniable" falsification perpetually problematic.

Sociologically oriented social psychologists have tended to take an insider's perspective and to focus upon interpersonal processes that maintain a socially constructed reality incapable of any simply falsification. "Failed prophecy" is thus a negotiated term and depends upon negotiated claims to reality for meaning (Carroll, 1979; Pollner, 1989). Furthermore, among prophetic groups, prophecy is less central than outsiders assume. The exclusive focus upon prophecy leads outsiders to assume that the major concern of the group is prophecy and ignores the complex cosmology that serves to integrate the group (Melton, 1985). Participant observation studies of prophetic groups have begun to show how rare increased proselytization is as a reaction to what is only apparently failed prophecy (Stone, 2000). Zygmunt (1972, p. 245) defines prophecy as a prediction that a "drastic transformation of the existing social order will occur in the proximate future through the intervention of some supernatural agency." The recognition of the transformation is socially constructed and hence not capable of unequivocal or undeniable failure. Thus, from the insider's perspective, prophecy cannot fail. The denial of failure of prophecy is the most common response from within prophetic groups as members struggle to stay within the group and to seek a proper interpretation of what must be only an apparent failure (Carroll, 1979; Dein, 1997, 2001; Melton, 1985; Tumminia, 1998). Increased proselytization is actually an uncommon response to failed prophecy (Stone, 2000). As Dein (2001) notes, dissonance theory too often is utilized to persuade others that those who stay within prophetic groups are irrational and driven by forces they do not understand. The task is to understand how believers confront a more spiritual understanding of prophecy than a simple literal understanding of its "failure" (Carroll, 1979; Dein, 200l).

Chemically Facilitated Mysticism

There were few texts that could be identified as psychology of religion in the eclipse of the field that followed the first generation of researchers. An exception was *The Psychology of Religion* by Clark (1958). Clark was one of the founding members of the Society for the Scientific Study of Religion and had a lifelong interest in mysticism. If we use the 1960s as our target decade for the reemergence of the psychology of religion in America, we be remiss not to identify dynamism fueled by hippie culture, the anti-Vietnam protest, and the use of psychedelic drugs as contributing to the intense interest in mysticism that has always occupied a significant role in the psychology of religion. Stevens has aptly documented this complex cultural dynamic in his book, which is aptly titled *Storming Heaven* (1987).

Clark's interest in psychedelics was in the possibility that they could facilitate mystical experience. Leary's career as a clinical psychologist blossomed into him becoming an iconic cult figure in the psychedelic movement. However, he also was the PhD director of what is arguably the single most cited quasi-experimental study in the psychology of religion, widely known as the "Good Friday" experiment (Pahnke, 1966). This flawed double-blind study attempted to demonstrate that a psychedelic drug administered in an appropriate setting could facilitate mystical experience. Doblin (1991) confirmed the positive results of the original Pahnke study in most of the original participants nearly a quarter of a century later. Most recently, Griffiths, Richards, Johnson, McCann, and Jesse (2008) have demonstrated in a rigorously designed double-blind study that psilocybin in an appropriate setting can facilitate mystical experiences. They were fortunate to be able to use as a guide one of the foremost authorities on psilocybin associated with the original Pahnke project (Richards, 2008). The relevance of drugs for facilitating mystical experiences has led psychologists of religion to champion the term *entheogen* for these chemicals and harkens back to debates between the earliest psychologists of religion such as Leuba and James over the meaning and value of mystical experience and of the various means used to facilitate it.

Non–Chemically Facilitated Mysticism

The value of both Pahnke's study and that of Griffiths and his colleagues is that they used questionnaires associated with Stace's (1960) common core theory of mysticism. A measure derived from Stace's criteria of mysticism is the Mysticism Scale first developed by Hood (1975). This widely used scale has allowed empirical assessment of mysticism and has been used in correlational and quasi-experimental studies to demonstrate that not only entheogens but many other conditions such as isolation tanks and nature experiences can facilitate mystical experiences. Furthermore, factor structure of the scale is consistent across diverse cultures, suggesting that there may be a common core to mystical experiences that various cultures and traditions interpret differently (see Hood et al., 2009, ch. 11). The importance of mysticism and its measurement has been and will continue to be of concern to those studying the psychology of religion. It is another

theme in the reemergence of the psychology of religion that illustrates an interdisciplinary focus, utilizing data derived from Stace's initial cross-cultural work to develop an empirical measure confirming Stace's basic phenomenologically derived common core, and allowing for empirical research that can distinguish mystical experience from its interpretation (Hood, 2003a).

Future Prospects for the Psychology of Religion

It is always risky to predict future prospects and expansion in the psychology of religion. However, given the opportunity to take this risk, we will outline five areas in which the psychology of religion might both expand and prosper—each of which, however, is assured to be contested by some. The areas to be briefly explored include a return to the ontological question; the limits of social constructionist or neo-Kantian views of psychology; the importance of parapsychology as the heir to spiritualism; the emergence of faith-specific psychologies; and the influence of funding agencies.

The Ontological Question Revisited

Psychologists are poorly trained in both the philosophical options for the discipline. Both Freud and James gained wide audience not simply for their psychologies but because they confronted ontological questions integral to religion.

Given his belief in the phylogenetic origin of religion, Freud denies the central historical truth claims of Christianity. He may be wrong (and most psychoanalysts think he is), but the point is that he could deny the ontological claims of one tradition given his belief in the ontological claims of his own findings. The widely acknowledged abandonment of the seduction theory has been shown to mask truth claims integral to feminist concerns with actual seduction and abuse (Hood, 1997). On the other hand, James was confident that the empirical facts of his study of varieties of religious experience warranted the ontological claim of an expanded consciousness integral to the great faith traditions (Hood, 2008). Thus, the psychology of religion cannot be satisfied with simply bracketing out ontological claims but must acknowledge how its findings and theories support certain ontological possibilities over others. It is not simply the search for the sacred that is important but also the response to it (Hampson & Boyd-MacMillan, 2008; Porpora, 2006). What is responded to is not to be ignored, even if the issue forces psychologists of religion to be more philosophically and theologically informed. The sociologist Pitrim Sorokin, a founding member of the Society for the Scientific Study of Religion, provided a model for the incorporation on the ontological claims of religion in his treatise on love, which was incorporated into part of the framing by Poloma and Hood (2006) of their study of an emerging Pentecostal church in which the claim that Godly love was a major motivating force was empirically explored in terms of Sorokin's model.

The Importance of Parapsychology

The ontological issue noted earlier interfaces with the well-established relationship between reports of religious and spiritual experiences and a variety of parapsychological phenomena (Hood, 1989, 2008a). The empirical associations are of less concern than the fact that the psychology of religion has a long history of linkage to psychic phenomena. James is again the exemplar, maintaining memberships in both the American Psychological Society and the American Society for Psychological Research. Many of the early founders of psychology of religion in America were members of both groups but dropped membership in the latter when it refused to deny the ontological reality of paranormal phenomena (Coon, 1992; Taylor, 1996). Yet it is clear that parapsychology is the legitimate heir of the spiritualism that occupied much of James's interest. Advances in scientific methods that allow for non local causation will be an integral part of the psychology of religion and spirituality in the future (Walach, Kohls, von Stillfried, Hinterberger, & Schmidt, 2009). It is worth noting here that both James and Freud were members of American and European societies devoted to the study of parapsychological phenomena.

The Emergence of Faith-Specific Therapies

One of the conundrums of psychology has been the problem often represented as a value issue with respect to therapies. Much of the current debate between religion and spirituality is empirically linked to the authority institutions have over individual views.

Religion is often seen as involving institutional rues, rituals, and regulations based upon beliefs defended as dogma. Those who accept this have a powerful vehicle with which to express their spirituality. However, an emerging minority in America and already a majority in some European countries see themselves as spiritual but not religious (Streib et al., 2008). The emergence of psychologists with warrants to treat psychoreligious and psychospiritual problems (Lukoff & Turner, 1992) and the massive involvement of spirituality in all aspects of health (Koenig, McCullough, & Larson, 2001) will likely lead to spiritually informed diagnostics and treatments. Given the considerable diversity of faith-based beliefs, both diagnostics and treatments will become more faith specific. This is already the case with respect to APA-approved schools with religious proscriptions opposed to homosexuality and will likely increase as psychologists who identify as spiritual but not religious confront others who are both religious and spiritual.

The Influence of Funding Agencies

Psychology of religion has always been influenced by wealthy individuals and foundations seeking to fund particular patterns of research. The first generation of psychologists of religion readily accepted funds to study psychic phenomena associated in popular American culture with "psychology." However, they took funds and used them to debunk psychic claims (Coon, 1992). James was the major exception, and this is why he was more rejected than accepted among the first generation of psychologists (Taylor, 1996, 1999).

While psychologists have a variety of funding agencies to which they can appeal for research grants, until recently all were committed to natural science assumptions and would be unlikely to fund any research that took the ontological issues in psychology of religion seriously. The emergence of Sir John Templeton and the Templeton Foundation has altered this dramatically for the psychology of religion and is likely to direct much of the research in the psychology of religion for the future. For the first time, massive grants are readily available, many in the millions, and most are perceived as seeking to explore positive aspects of religion consistent with the late Sir John's view. Some psychologists of religion have bemoaned this as essentially introducing a conservative Christian bias into prominence in the discipline (Wulff, 2006). However, psychologists of religion need not conform to any Templeton agenda. The issue is simply that entire areas emerge largely due to Templeton funding. The parallel is to pharmaceutical companies that direct the path of much of the research on drugs. What is at stake is whether psychologists of religion will continue to pursue research outside of the major funding agencies. It is largely such unfunded research that contributed to the reemergence of psychology of religion, and it need not succumb to the temptation to alter course based upon available funds. It is also worth emphasizing that Templeton-funded research is often published in high-quality, peer-reviewed journals, so it is not the quality but the direction of research that seems perplexing to some. This tension hopefully will be resolved as the endorsers of the call for a new paradigm take seriously the need for a multilevel interdisciplinary approach and realize that a nonreductive one will of necessity be a psychology and religion, not simply a psychology of religion.

References

Adorno, T. W., Frenkel-Brunswik, E., Levinson, D. J., & Sanford, R. N. (1950). *The authoritarian personality*. New York: Harper & Row.

Allport, G. W. (1954). *The nature of prejudice*. Cambridge, MA: Addison-Wesley.

Allport, G. W., & Ross, J. M. (1967). Personal religious orientation and prejudice. *Journal of Personality and Social Psychology, 5*, 432–443.

Altemeyer, B., & Hunsberger, B. (2005). Fundamentalism and authoritarianism. In R. F. Paloutzian & C. L. Parks (Eds.), *Handbook of the psychology of religion and spirituality* (pp. 378–383). New York: The Guilford Press.

American Psychiatric Association (1987). *Diagnostic and statistical manual of mental disorders* (3rd ed., rev.). Washington, DC: Author

Batson, C. D. (1977). Experimentation in psychology of religion: An impossible dream? *Journal for the Scientific Study of Religion, 16*, 413–418.

Belzen, J. (2010). *Towards cultural psychology holy of religion: Principles, approaches, and applications*. New York: Springer

Belzen, J. A. (2009). *Changing the scientific study of religion: After Freud*. New York: Springer.

Benjamin, L. T., Jr. (1977). The origin of psychological species: History of the beginnings of the American Psychological Association divisions. *American Psychologists, 52*, 725–732.

Benjamin, L. T., Jr. (Ed.) (2009). *A history of psychology: Original sources and contemporary research* (3rd. ed.). Malden, MA: Oxford University Press.

Boring, E. G. (1929). *History of experimental psychology*. New York: Century.

Butterfield, H. (1965). *The Whig interpretation of history*. New York: Norton. (Original work published 1931).

Carroll, R. P. (1979). *When prophecy failed: Cognitive dissonance in the prophetic traditions of the Old Testament*. New York: Seabury Press.

Clark, W. H. (1958). *The psychology of religion*. New York: Macmillan.

Coe, G. A. (1916). *The psychology of religion*. Chicago: University of Chicago Press.

Coon, D. J. (1992). Testing the limits of sense and science: American experimental psychologists combat spiritualism, 1880–1920. *American Psychologist, 47*, 143–151.

Dein, S. (1997). Lubavitch: A contemporary messianic movement. *Journal of Contemporary Religion, 12*, 191–204.

Dein, S. (2001). What really happens when prophecy fails: The case of Lubavitch. *Sociology of Religion, 62*, 383–401.

Doblin, R. (1991). Pahnke's "Good Friday" experiment: A long-term follow-up and methodological critique. *Journal of Transpersonal Psychology, 23*, 1–28.

Ellenberger, H. F. (1970). *The discovery of the unconscious: The history and evolution of dynamic psychology*. New York: Basic Books.

Emmons, R. A., & Paloutzian, R. (2003). Psychology of religion. *Annual Review of Psychology, 54*, 377

Festinger, L. (1957). *A theory of cognitive dissonance*. Evanston, IL: Row-Peterson.

Festinger, L., Riecken, H. W., & Schachter, S. (1953). *When prophecy fails*. Minneapolis: University of Minnesota Press.

Fuller, R. C. (2001). *Spiritual but not religious: Understanding unchruched America*. New York: Oxford University Press.

Gorsuch, R. L. (1988). Psychology of religion. *Annual Review of Psychology, 39*, 201–221.

Gorsuch, R. L., & Miller, W. R. (1999). Assessing spirituality. In W. R. Miller (Ed.), *Integrating spirituality into treatment* (pp. 47–64). Washington, DC: American Psychological Association.

Griffiths, R. R., Richards, W. A., Johnson, M. W., McCann, U. D., & Jesse, R. (2008). Mystical-type experiences occasioned by psilocybin mediate the attribution of personal meaning and spiritual significance 14 months later. *Journal of Psychopharmacology, 22*, 621–632.

Grünbaum, A. (1984). *The foundations of psychoanalysis: A philosophical critique*. Berkeley: University of California Press.

Grünbaum, A. (1987). Psychoanalysis and theism. *The Monist, 70*, 152–192.

Hall, G. S. (1904). *Adolescence: Its psychology and relations to physiology, anthropology, sociology, sex, crime, religion and education* (2 vols.). New York: Appleton.

Hall, G. S. (1917). *Jesus, the Christ, in light of psychology* (2 vols.). Garden City, NY: Doubleday.

Hampson, P. J., & Boyd-MacMillan, E. M. (2008). Turning the telescope around: Reciprocity in the psychology-theology dialogue. *Archive for the Psychology of Religion, 30*, 93–113.

Hood, R. W., Jr. (1975). The construction and preliminary validation of a measure of reported mystical experience. *Journal for the Scientific Study of Religion, 14*, 29–41.

Hood, R. W., Jr. (1989). Mysticism, the unity thesis, and the paranormal. In G. K. Zollschan, J. F. Schumaker, & G. F. Walsh (Eds.), *Exploring the paranormal* (pp. 117–130). New York: Avery

Hood R. W., Jr. (1997). Psychoanalysis and fundamentalism: Lessons from a feminist critique of Freud. In J. L. Jacobs & D. Capps (Eds.), *Religion, society, and psychoanalysis* (pp. 42–67). Boulder, CO: Westview Press.

Hood, R. W., Jr. (1995).The soulful self of William James. In D. Capps & J. L. Jacobs (Eds.), *The struggle for life: A companion to William James' The varieties of religious experience* (pp. 209–219). Newton, KS: Mennonite Press.

Hood, R. W., Jr. (1998). American Psychological Association (APA), section on psychology of religion (Division 36). In W. H. Swatos (Ed.), *Encyclopedia of religion and society* (p. 15). Walnut Creek, CA: Altamira.

Hood, R. W., Jr. (2000). American psychology of religion and the Journal for the Scientific Study of Religion. *Journal for the Scientific Study of Religion, 39*, 531–543.

Hood, R. W., Jr. (2002). The mystical self: Lost and found. *The International Journal for the Psychology of Religion, 12*, 1–20.

Hood, R. W., Jr. (2003a). Conceptual and empirical consequences of the unity thesis. In J. A. Belzen & A. Geels (Eds.), *Mysticism: A variety of psychological perspectives* (pp. 17–54). Amsterdam: Rodopi.

Hood, R. W., Jr. (2003b). Spirituality and religion. In A. L. Greil & D. Bromley (Eds.), *Religion and the social order: Vol. 10: Religion: Critical approaches to drawing boundaries between sacred and secular* (pp. 241–265). Amsterdam: Elsevier.

Hood, R. W., Jr. (2008a) *Mysticism and the paranormal*. In J. H. Ellens (Ed.), *The psychology of miracles*: God, science, and psychology in the paranormal,(Vol. 3, pp. 16–37). Westport, CT: Praeger.

Hood, R. W., Jr. (2008b). Theoretical fruits from the empirical study of mysticism: A Jamesian perspective. *Journal für Psychologie, 16,* Jfp–3.

Hood, R. W., Jr. (2010). Towards cultural psychology of religion: Principles, approaches, and applications: An appreciative response to Belzen's invitation. *Mental Health, Religion, and Culture, 13,* 397–406.

Hood, R. W., Jr. (in press). Psychology and religion. In V. S. Ramachdran (Ed.), *Encyclopaedia of human behavior*. New York: Academic Press.

Hood, R. W., Jr., & Byrom, G. (2010). Mysticism, madness, and mental health. In J. H. Elles (Ed.), *The healing power of religion: How faith helps humans thrive* (Vol. 3, pp. 171–191). Westport, CT: Praeger.

Hood, R. W., Jr., Hill, P. C., & Williamson, W. P. (2005). *The psychology of religious fundamentalism*. New York: The Guilford Press.

Hood, R. W., Jr. & Williamson, W. P. (2008). Contemporary Christian serpent handlers and the new paradigm for the psychology of religion. *Research in the Social Scientific Study of Religion, 19,* 59–89.

Hood, R. W., Jr., Hill, P. C., & Spilka, B. (2009). *The psychology of religion: An empirical approach* (4th ed.), New York: Guilford.

James, W. (1981). *The principles of psychology*. Cambridge, MA: Harvard University Press. (Original work published in 1890).

James, W. (1892). *Psychology: The briefer course*. New York: Henry Holt.

James, W. (1985). *The varieties of religious experience*: A study in human nature. Cambridge, MA: Harvard University Press. (Original work published 1902).

Jones, E. E. (1985). Major developments in social psychology during the past five decades. In G. Lindzey & E. Aronson (Eds.), *The handbook of social psychology*. (2nd. ed., Vol. 1, pp. 47–108). Reading, MA: Addison-Wesley.

Koenig, H. G., McCullough, M. E., & Larson, D. B. (2001). *Handbook of religion and health*. New York: Oxford University Press.

Leuba, J. H. (1896). A study in the psychology of religious phenomena. *American Journal of Psychology, 7,* 309–385.

Leuba, J. H. (1916*). Belief in god and immortality, anthropological and statistical study*. Boston: Sherman & French.

Leuba, J. H. (1925). *The psychology of religious mysticism*. New York: Harcourt Brace.

Leuba, J. H. (1934). Religious belief in American scientists. *Harper's, 169,* 292–300

Lukoff, D., Lu, F., & Turner, R. (1992). Toward a more culturally sensitive DSM-IV: Psychoreligious and psychospiritual problems. *Journal of Nervous and Mental Disease, 180,* 673–682.

Meissner, W. W. (1984). *Psychoanalysis and religious experience*. New Haven, CT: Yale University Press.

Melton, J. G. (1985). Spiritualization and reaffirmation: What really happens when prophecy fails. *American Studies, 26,* 17–29.

Nelsen, H. M. (1998). Society for the Scientific Study of Religion. In W. H. Swatos (Ed.), *Encyclopedia of religion and society* (p. 482). Walnut Creek, CA: Altamira.Pahnke, W. N. (1966). Drugs and mysticism. *International Journal of Parapsychology, 8,* 295–320.

Paloutzian, R. F., & Parks, C. L. (Eds.). (2005). *Handbook of the psychology of religion and spritiuality*. New York: The Guilford Press.

Paloutzian, R. F., Richardson, J. T., & Rambo, L. R. (1999). Religious conversion and personality change. *Journal of Personality, 67,* 1047–1079.

Pargament, K. I. (1997). *The psychology of religion and coping*. New York: The Guilford Press.

Perry, W. (1935). *The thought and character of William James* (Vol. 2). Westport, CT: Greenwood Press.

Pollner, M. (1989). *Mundane reason: Reality in everyday sociological discourse*. Cambridge, England: Cambridge University Press.

Poloma, M. M., & Hood, R. W., Jr. (2006). *Blood and fire: Godly love in a Pentecostal emerging church*. New York: New York University Press.

Porpora, D. V. (2006). Methodological atheism, methodological agnosticism and religious experience. *Journal for the Theory of Social Behavior, 36,* 57–75.

Pruyser, P. W. (1968). *A dynamic psychology of religion*. New York: Harper & Row.

Richards, W. A. (2008). The phenomenology and potential import of states of consciousness facilitated by psilocybin. *Archive for the Psychology of Religion, 30,* 189–199.

Richardson, J. T. (1985). The active vs. passive convert: Paradigm conflict in conversion/recruitment research. *Journal for the Scientific Study of Religion, 24,* 163–179.

Richardson, R. D. (2006). *William James: In the maelstrom of American modernism*. Boston: Houghton Mifflin

Rizzuto, A-M. (1979). *The birth of the living God: A psychoanalytic study*. Chicago: University of Chicago Press.

Secord, P. F., & Backman, C. W. (1964). *Social psychology*. New York: McGraw-Hill.

Stace, W. T. (1960). *Mysticism and philosophy*. Philadelphia: Lippincott.

Starbuck, E. D. (1897). A study of conversion. *American Journal of Psychology, 8,* 268–308.

Starbuck, E. D. (1899). *The psychology of religion*. New York: Scribner.

Stevens, J. (1987). *Storming heaven: LSD and the American dream*. New York: Harper & Row.

Stone, J. R. (2000). *Expecting Armageddon: Essential readings in failed prophecy*. New York: Routledge.

Streib, H., Hood, R. W., Jr., Keller, B., Csöff, R-M., & Silver, C. (2008). *Research in contemporary religion: Vol. 4: Deconversion: Qualitative and quantitative results from cross-cultural research in Germany and the United States*. Göttingham, Germany: Vandenhoeck & Ruprecht.

Taves, A. (1999). *Fits, trances, and visions: Experiencing religion and explaining experience from Wesley to James*. Princeton, NJ: Princeton University Press.

Taylor, E. (1996). William James on consciousness beyond the margin. Princeton, NJ: Princeton University Press.

Taylor, E. (1999). *Shadow culture: Psychology and spirituality in America*. Washington, DC: Counterpoint.

Tumminia, D. (1998). How prophecy never fails: Interpretative reason in a flying saucer group. *Sociology of Religion, 59,* 157–170.

Walach, H., Kohls, N., von Stillfried, N., Hinterberger, T., & Schmidt, S. (2009). Spirituality: The legacy of parapsychology. *Archive for the Psychology of Religion, 32,* 277–308.

Wulff, D. M. (2006) A field in crisis. Is it time to start over? In H. M. Poelofsma, J. S. M. Corveleyn, & J. W. van Sane (Eds.), *One hundred years of the psychology of religion* (pp. 11–32). Amsterdam: VU University Press.

Zarjonc, R. B. (1990). Leo Festonger (1919–1989). *American Psychologist, 45,* 661–662.

Zygmunt, J. F. (1972). When prophecy fails: A theoretical perspective on the comparative evidence. *American Behavioral Scientist, 16,* 245–268.

Theoretical and Epistemological Foundations

James M. Nelson *and* Brent D. Slife

Abstract

The psychology of religion and spirituality (PRS) involves applying the methods and procedures of psychological science to the study of religion and spirituality. Since PRS is a scientific endeavor, best practices in the field will always involve a thorough understanding of the scientific process, such as that provided by contemporary philosophers of science. One of the most important things to be learned from these writers is that all science—including inquiry in PRS—involves methodological, epistemological, ethical, and ontological assumptions that greatly affect the conduct of scientific work. A brief review of these assumptions in PRS suggests that current scientific practices in the field fall short in a number of ways, making it difficult for investigators to truly increase our understanding of the important psychological processes involved in religious activities and spiritual experience. We explore the nature of these assumptions and their problems, and offer a possible alternative framework that will help advance the science of PRS.

Key Words: philosophy of science, methodology, naturalism, positivism, hermeneutics

Introduction

The state of theory in the psychology of religion and spirituality (PRS) is a study in contrasts. William James, the founder of the field, was one of the greatest theoretical psychologists of all time. His writings not only provide a fine legacy of thinking about religious experience, but also include many profound works on the nature of knowledge and human inquiry. Given this history, one would expect the field of PRS to have a rich body of discussions about the theoretical foundations of the discipline.

Sadly, the current state of affairs does not match these expectations. Recent commentators (e.g., Hood, Hill, & Spilka, 2009) have noted the need for theory in PRS. Some have complained about the lack of an overarching theoretical model to help tie together results in the field (e.g., Kirkpatrick, 2005). It is also the case that PRS depends heavily on theory from other branches of psychology, such as psychodynamic thought, social psychology, evolutionary thought, and cognitive neuroscience, but it has contributed little unique theory of its own.

We believe that these theoretical problems are a symptom of deep philosophical difficulties in PRS. In particular, we believe that most PRS researchers operate using an antiquated and inadequate philosophy of science, and that this deficiency inhibits progress in our field. In this chapter, we attempt to outline and illustrate these problems, and we provide some ideas about possible solutions.

Definitions and Concepts

Many researchers view science as a hypothesis-testing enterprise. In this traditional view, investigators develop and test hypotheses based on *models* that specify structural relationships among constructs in a theory. These *hypotheses* are propositions about states of affairs—properties of things or relations between things (Armstrong, 1997, p. 1) that are proposed by a *theory*, a cluster of statements expected to provide an accurate *description* and *explanation* of phenomena, as well as guidance in the development of study methodology. Quantitative studies are often thought to be the best way of confirming (or disconfirming) these types of propositions (Carnap, 1974/1995, pp. 105–114).

However, this view of scientific research is only partly correct, as it leaves out a number of important parts of the picture. First, testing and verification is just half of the epistemological enterprise in science. The other part is *discovery*, the uncovering of new ideas that can form the basis for hypotheses to be tested. A vibrant, progressive scientific enterprise must eventually look outside the cycle of hypothesis and theory for new possibilities. The discovery of new ideas links up with the verification process to form the *scientific epistemological cycle* of exploration and testing. In general, PRS has been much weaker in the discovery end of this cycle.

Also often overlooked is the issue of *underdetermination*, the fact that any given set of data can be interpreted in several ways and may support other theories or hypotheses not being tested in a study (Bruner, 1991; Crowe, 2005). It is a logical error to assume that just because data fit a particular hypothesis, they *only* fit that hypothesis or explanation for the data. Data are, in principle, consistent with a limited number of other hypotheses and do not determine or prove any of them conclusively (Gahde & Stegmüller, 1986; cf. Quine, 1953, pp. 20–46). In this sense, they also do not "tell" us the "reality" of the phenomena under investigation. Scientific data are not a "map of" or "reflection of" reality; they are, in fact, not very meaningful until they are interpreted, and many interpretations are possible.

This interpretive element of science means that empirical findings are dependent upon more than just data (Lakatos, 1978; van Fraassen, 2002, p. 124). Scientists hold unproven assumptions that guide their interpretations of the data and the conduct of their investigations (cf. Barrow, 1998; Godfrey-Smith, 2003, pp. 149–155; Nagel & Newman, 2001, pp. 109–113). Unfortunately, the significance of these assumptions is often underestimated. Four types of presuppositions are of particular importance: methodological, epistemological, ethical, and ontological or metaphysical.

Methodological assumptions are beliefs about how scientific research should be conducted. They have been central to the identity of PRS. The modern definition of psychology—the scientific study of behavior—specifies a *method or logic of approach* as well as an object of study for the field.

Epistemological assumptions are beliefs about the nature of knowledge and provide an often unrecognized backing for methodological assumptions made by researchers. These assumptions limit the kinds of questions that can be asked in research studies (Rescher, 1982, p. 151) and the sorts of empirical data that are considered relevant.

Ethical assumptions in science revolve around the goals or values that stand behind the research program and standards for acceptable research practices. These presuppositions provide an often unacknowledged foundation for scientific methodology and epistemology. They include what are typically called *epistemic values*—the aspects of inquiry that are deemed important, such as coherence, simplicity of explanation, and strength of explanatory power. Typically a balance of these virtues is desirable. For example, a focus only on complexity produces models too difficult to test, whereas an exclusive emphasis on simplicity produces explanations that lack fit with reality or explanatory power (Lewis, 1973, pp. 73–74; Lewis, 1986, pp. 121–124; Lewis, 1999, pp. 231–236; Mittelstaedt & Weingartner, 2005, pp. 142–154; Popper, 1935/2002, pp. 110–115; Rescher, 1973; van Fraassen, 1989, pp. 47–50). Also at issue are *epistemic virtues*—qualities, skills, or capacities of the investigator that are desirable in the pursuit of knowledge, such as fairness, open-mindedness, or the ability to think holistically. These are similar in many ways to general virtues studied by ethicists (Garcia, 2003; Hookway, 2003; Zagzebski, 1996).

Ontological and metaphysical assumptions are fundamental to the other three categories. These presuppositions are ideas about what is in the world and how it works. Some of these are *entailed assumptions* that must be true in order for the research program to be valid (cf. Quine, 1953, pp. 1, 130), while others are *gratuitous assumptions* that may be dearly held but are not necessary for the program to produce valid scientific knowledge. Although scientists often believe that their work is free of metaphysics, in fact, all scientific progress is dependent on such assumptions. One cannot have a theory of knowledge without some ideas about the objects that the area of knowledge seeks to understand (Bhaskar, 1989, pp. 13–27; cf. Gasser & Stefan, 2007).

Assumptions in these four categories are essential to the collection and interpretation of scientific data. They provide a critical theoretical framework that helps us understand research in PRS.

Traditional Research Programs in Psychology of Religion and Spirituality

Most mainstream PRS researchers presume, knowingly or unknowingly, a particular system of these four categories of assumptions drawn from the philosophies of naturalism and positivism (Nelson, 2006, 2009, pp. 43–66; Slife, 2004b; Slife & Whoolery, 2006). While there is little consensus among theorists about the exact description of these philosophies (cf. Rea, 2002), *naturalism* is often thought to involve a quest for natural laws or law-like causal regularities in the universe. *Positivism* is a complex philosophical position developed in the early 19th century by Auguste Comte and modified by early 20th-century philosophers of the Vienna school, such as Ruolf Carnap and Herbert Feigl. We call the combination of these philosophies *positivistic naturalism* (PN).

In the sections that follow, we describe PN in detail, as well as its effects on the scientific practice of PRS. We illustrate our points using a number of high-quality studies as examples, although the themes we describe can be found in virtually any mainstream PRS investigation. Our intention here is not to criticize or even fully analyze these studies; rather, our aim is to use them to illustrate many of the strengths and weaknesses of PN. Since the strengths of this research tradition are well known, we describe these only briefly, putting an emphasis on delineating weaknesses that are less frequently acknowledged.

Methodological Assumptions

Although ontological and metaphysical assumptions are the most fundamental part of a research program, PN discussions of theory begin (and typically end) with methodology. This is because the key to obtaining knowledge in PN revolves around the methodological practice of *operationalization*, where the experimenter constructs a study to (a) measure publicly observable phenomena using (b) methods that maximize repeatability and reliability (law-like regularities), sometimes even at the expense of validity (Bridgman, 1927/1993; Feigl, 1949). In operationalization, validity can be assumed if the procedure seems reasonable; it is established later in other studies, thus giving it a subsidiary role to reliability. In PRS, it is typically further assumed that much of human behavior could be conceptualized as discrete variables that have direct and typically linear relationships with phenomena exhibiting a normally distributed frequency of occurrence. For instance, this kind of thinking can be seen in a thought-provoking study on spiritual transcendence and religious involvement (Piedmont, Ciarrochi, Dy-Liacco, & Williams, 2009), in which the authors state that in order to "disaggregate" religion and spirituality, they have developed measurement scales "to operationalize these two sets of constructs in a manner that solidly grounded them in both psychological theory and sound measurement practice" (p. 163). Many of these assumptions are rarely stated explicitly in PRS research, but they are tacitly assumed in the statistics employed during data analysis and interpretation.

Moreover, virtually all investigations in mainstream PRS use operationalizations of one sort or another. The researcher frequently has an interest in some "variable" that is not directly observable, and thus the researcher must change it to something else—operationalize it—in a way that is acceptable to PN methods. For example, spirituality and religiosity are themselves not directly observable, so these constructs are routinely operationalized as questionnaires and scales. No researcher assumes that the scores on these scales are identical with a person's spirituality or religiosity, yet the relationship between what is measured (performance on the questionnaire) and the unobserved topic being operationalized (e.g., spirituality) is rarely discussed.

These method assumptions obviously have many perceived advantages and benefits. For instance, many scholars consider these assumptions to lend an important specificity and clarity to what is studied. Also, the observability of operationalizations permits them to be easily replicated by other researchers, because other scholars can presumably observe the same phenomena, and thus come to the same findings, if they are valid and generalizable.

However, PN operationalization is also deeply problematic. First, the fact that many of the variables of interest in PRS (and psychology generally) are not directly publicly observable led natural scientists such as Percy Bridgman (who developed operationalization) to oppose its use in disciplines like psychology. Hugs and kisses are not love, and a score on a spiritual transcendence inventory is not spirituality. Because the relationship between the unobserved construct and the observable operationalization is not itself observable, it is in principle not knowable from an empirical perspective and is thus uncertain. It seems highly unlikely that any of the current operationalizations of important constructs such as "religion" or "spirituality" or their relationships with other variables completely represent all aspects of what they hope to measure. Certainly, current operationalizations have been criticized on a number of grounds (Slife, Wiggins, & Graham, 2005), such as the need for measures that take into account important aspects of cultural context (Kisala, 2003; Presser & Stinson, 1998; Sherkat & Ellison, 1999). Thus, PRS studies in the PN tradition do not yield a certain relation to their unobserved topic of interest, nor is there a way of completely correcting this problem using PN methods.

Second, repeatability and reliability require the further assumption that all people will respond to a particular measurement procedure in similar ways, an assumption that is questionable in many circumstances, particularly when using an instrument with people from very divergent cultural backgrounds (van de Vijver & Leung, 1997). Questionable measurement assumptions and procedures such as these make it difficult to interpret findings like the differential response of various cultural groups, for example, in studies looking at correlates of religiosity like well-being (e.g., Lavric & Flere, 2008).

Third, because scales are operationalizations designed to test the ideas of an experimenter, there is a danger of circularity—building into the scale the very thing the researcher hopes to find. For instance, the scale used to measure spiritual transcendence in Piedmont et al. (2009) is extolled as a good scale because of its strong reliability. However, the scale (1) has items that assume practices like prayer or worship have the same meaning regardless of culture or religious tradition and (2) explicitly reflects an understanding of spirituality that is "very distinct from theological understandings of the concept" (p. 5; cf. Piedmont, 2001; Piedmont & Leach, 2002). The data from the instrument are then used to support the claims that spirituality is (a) invariant across cultures and (b) different from religiousness—in other words, the very thing that was assumed in the construction of the scale. Needless to say, the justificatory power of such an argument seems questionable, yet this illustrates some of the typical problems of PN methodological assumptions. The addition of more methods or questionnaires (cf. Paloutzian & Park, 2005) does not solve this difficulty if these new methods are built on the same problematic assumptions.

Epistemological Assumptions

In PN, knowledge consists of abstract propositions that are "naturalistic" and describe law-like regularities. A law-like explanation is one that attempts to characterize a phenomenon in abstract terms and point to its regularity. It depicts relations between phenomena as necessary and causal, perhaps offering predictive power (Armstrong, 1983, pp. 96–99; cf. Bhaskar, 1974/2008, pp. 53–205; Harker, 2008; Hempel, 1968; Kistler, 2006, pp. 143–144; Mittelstaedt & Weingartner, 2005; Nagel, 1961, pp. 73–78; Rescher, 1970, p. 12; van Fraassen, 1989, pp. 26–38). In the PN view, the propositions are thought to be best if they are universal and independent of context.

PRS research often follows the assumption that looking for invariant, causal relationships should be the focus of investigation. Authors (e.g., Piedmont et al, 2009) attempt to identify "causal relationships" or "causal precedence" between variables (pp. 164–165). They argue that an invariant definition fills a "basic scientific need" (p. 175), and that if such a definition cannot be found, perhaps "the numinous should be eliminated from research altogether" (p. 175). True to the invariance valued by PN, only universals appear to matter, and if a particular aspect of religion or religious practice is not a universal phenomenon, it is not worthy of scientific study. This line of thinking rejects the suggestion of Hill and his colleagues (2000) that universal definitions for some terms (e.g., religion or spirituality) are inappropriate or impossible.

Many articles in the field also appear to assume the PN view that investigators are "passive sensors of given facts" (Bhaskar, 1989, p. 51), and that it is possible to examine the world as a completely neutral observer, having a "view from nowhere" (Nagel, 1986). Reviews that emphasize the empirical basis of PRS (e.g., Hood, Hill, & Spilka, 2009, pp. 21–53, 477–488) often seem to imply the achievability or at least desirability of scientific objectivity.

The philosophy of science literature has long recognized many problematic features about these PN epistemological assumptions:

1. Scholars who study scientific method and practice reject the idea that all relationships are causal (cf. e.g., Smith, 2007), which means that a primary, if not exclusive, focus on causality may lead authors to claim the existence of causal relationships that are not actually supported by their analyses. Authors in PRS frequently recognize this problem by acknowledging that their analytic procedures "cannot prove causality among a set of variables" but then often fail to follow through with this observation and argue that some variables have "a causal impact" on others (Piedmont et al., 2009, p. 170). These types of statements have a further problem in that they are descriptive rather

than explanatory, and so provide little information about why the relationship exists or how it works. Statements of mechanism rather than regularity may be more informative (cf. Rodgers, 2010; Wright & Bechtel, 2007).

2. It is widely acknowledged that even classical natural laws are not universal but are only valid at certain levels of explanation or under certain conditions and circumstances (Carrier, 1998; Chalmers, 2009; Fodor, 1991; Mittelstaedt & Weingartner, 2005, p. 176; van Fraassen, 1980, pp. 124–126;). For example, boulders don't have religion, but people do, and so regularities about it function only at the human level. Yet the contextual particularity of religious and spiritual regularities is rarely recognized in PRS programs of research. It goes without saying, perhaps, that every study or set of studies is relative to a particular population at a particular time and place, yet many researchers discuss their findings as if they are *automatically* generalizable to other populations, times, and places without providing justification for this assumption.

PRS researchers who recognize this problem have used a number of unsuccessful strategies to deal with it. Some investigators acknowledge problems of generalizability, but this is then forgotten as other PRS scholars make use of their work, assuming it applies to their subjects. In other words, they merely assume that most populations, times, and places are interchangeable parts, and thus the results produced by one set of "parts" are generalizable to other parts of the world. Other scholars try to avoid the problem by focusing on phenomena that they consider to be universal (e.g., Sinnott, 2001), but this closes the door to research on important topics that do not appear to meet this criteria. Some research (e.g., Piedmont & Leach, 2002) has attempted to correct the problem by including important contextual variables like culture, but while the intent of such work is admirable, it often suffers from methodological problems and fails to meet contemporary standards for cross-cultural research (cf. van de Vijver & Leung, 1997).

In fact, the need for universal definitions and findings is only important if one is bound within the confines of the PN research program. For instance, one could reject the PN universality assumption and consider the possibility that the relationship between religion and spirituality varies from group to group, perhaps individual to individual and era to era. We could ask, for example, whether individuals who are spiritual and religious might have different correlates of their spirituality than those reporting themselves to be spiritual but not religious.

3. Most philosophers of science would reject the idea that detached objectivity is possible. As we have seen, both the practice of science and the interpretation of its data are dependent upon the theoretical presuppositions of the investigator, who is thus inextricably part of the picture. Perhaps the term "fairness" would be a better statement of a realistic epistemic value.

Ethical Assumptions

PN generally takes an *instrumental* view of science, which means that the primary purpose of an inquiry is to increase human power and our ability to pursue desired goals (Nelson, 2009, p. 57). It is assumed in this view that the participants in the research need not directly benefit from their involvement (i.e., they are "instruments"), although they should not be directly harmed by it. The subjects of these studies are means to other ends, such as an increase in predictive power or some attractive outcome like practical clinical applications that might be achieved in the future.

However, PN claims of substantial benefits are often vague about the exact nature of these contributions or how they will come about. Past PRS studies in the PN tradition are said to be "amazingly vast, involving high-level research" that "spoke directly to human life" with "myriad sophisticated methods and data-analytic techniques," providing "the starting point from which the psychology of religion can step forward to make its most important contributions to the science of psychology and to human welfare" (Paloutzian & Park, 2005, p. 4). These are glowing assessments, but what are the actual concrete applications of these data, and how will these applications be made? What is the relationship between the often small amount of variance predicted and the practical significance of the study findings? These tantalizing hints of greater benefits for humanity remain unspecified. Moreover, many scholars have questioned the ethic of treating study "participants" as a means to some other end (Clegg & Slife, 2005). The notion that participants "gain research experience" is sometimes used to justify this form of research, although this hardly seems like an important contribution to human welfare. The point here is not that the PN tradition lacks ethics, but that its research does not appear to be making substantial progress toward the important values and goals that it hopes to achieve. Unfortunately, many psychologists may not even know of an alternative to an unrealized instrumentalism. We describe such as system in the section on "An Alternative Research Program in Psychology of Religion and Spirituality—Hermeneutics."

Ontological and Metaphysical Assumptions

PN has three primary ontological and metaphysical commitments: physicalist monism, individual essentialism, and the Law of Three Stages.

1. *Physicalist monism* is the view that (a) the only real things are material objects and the laws of physics that govern them (Armstrong, 1997, p. 6), and (b) this physical world is organized in a simple, unified, hierarchical fashion, with physical, chemical, and biological processes and structures at the foundation. In PRS, this implies that psychological, social, and spiritual processes ultimately and completely depend on these lower level processes, and thus it is possible to understand phenomena at higher levels on the basis of lower level processes: Psychology can be reduced to physics, and spirituality can be reduced to psychology or biology. Ironically, this also means that PN researchers begin (before conducting any research) by rejecting certain beliefs (e.g., the existence of a nonphysicalist God) that are fundamental for many of the religious traditions they are studying (cf. Slife & Reber, 2009).

This assumption seems to be common among contemporary researchers. Kirkpatrick (e.g., 2005, pp. 2–10), for example, has argued that evolutionary theory can provide a single monistic physicalist framework for PRS. Paloutzian and Park (2005) also argue that PRS can be integrated in a common framework with the life sciences, although they also assert that religion is a unique phenomenon, which seems to sit uneasily with their monistic views. Other scholars, however, note that good science may not form grand systems of explanation but rather many mini theories appropriate to a particular context (e.g., James, 1909/1996b; van Fraassen, 1980, p. 87; Wendt & Slife, 2009).

2. *Individual essentialism* is the PN position that in the human realm the primary reality is that of the individual. Relationships and group membership may be important but do not make up what is essential about the human person. Within PRS, this emphasis can be seen in the focus on individual religious behavior,

as opposed to the few studies that have been devoted to understanding the activity of religious communities (e.g., Pargament, Silverman, Johnson, Echemendia, & Snyder, 1983). Individualism is inherent in most PRS work but is more obvious in some lines of research, such as hedonic models of spirituality (cf. Cantor & Sanderson, 1999; Diener, Suh, Lucas, & Smith, 1999). A focus on "spirituality" (defined as an individual activity) as opposed to "religion" (in part a group phenomenon) fits well with this individualistic emphasis (cf. e.g., Sinnott, 2001).

3. The *Law of Three Stages* is the metaontological position that the best statements about reality are scientific ones, and that theological or philosophical statements involve more primitive stages of thinking that will eventually be replaced by scientific discourse (Comte, 1830–1842/1998). Logical positivists in the 20th century strengthened the Law of Three Stages and held that any type of metaphysical or ethical statement was nonsensical or merely an expression of emotion. Thus, discussions about ontological or metaphysical assumptions were thought to be unnecessary and empty of content (e.g., Carnap, 1950). This is sometimes referred to as a *deflationary* metaphysical stance.

The Law of Three Stages appears in PRS research in at least two ways. First, there is a general absence of any discussion about philosophical presuppositions. Even basic assumptions required by statistical procedures are rarely addressed, leaving the reader uncertain about the accuracy of the inferences made in the data analysis. Second, there is an apparent reluctance to deal with theological or religious concepts. Studies often attempt to separate themselves from metaphysical or theological concerns, and some journal editorial policies specifically exclude many studies that attempt to grapple with these issues (e.g., Piedmont, 2009).

These ontological assumptions are not problem free. In fact, a host of scholars have examined these presuppositions and identified a number of difficulties:

1. Physicalist monism appears to be inaccurate because complex dynamic systems—such as the human mind and social organizations—have emergent properties that are unique and are not entirely explainable from a knowledge of lower level laws (cf. Bhaskar, 1989, pp. 63, 77–80; Murphy, 1998). The partial independence of these levels suggests that the program of attempting to

unify science around a single theory and method is not realizable (Carrier, 2000; Dupre, 2004; Morrison, 2000; Wendt & Slife, 2009).

2. Individual essentialism is problematic, because the reduction of social constructs to personality variables limits our ability to understand the relational nature of religion and spirituality. Individual essentialism is also not consistent with what we know about the intensely relational nature of human person (Gergen, 2009; Slife, 2004a).

3. The Law of Three Stages causes numerous difficulties for scientific work by creating a problematic blindness toward assumptions and presuppositions (Nelson, 2009; Slife & Williams, 1995)—they are "philosophical" and so not part of "real science." For instance, all statistical procedures used in psychology make assumptions; normal distribution of variables, linearity of relationships, and independence of error terms are common presumptions. Complex procedures and phenomena may have additional or different assumptions, such as multivariate normality. Violation of these assumptions may lead to inaccurate interpretations of the data. Unfortunately, these issues are rarely discussed in PRS reports, and we certainly cannot take for granted that these assumptions have been met, particularly for complex spiritual and religious phenomena.

The avoidance of theological constructs appears to offer no benefits and significant disadvantages. If, in fact, spirituality is a universal phenomenon, it should appear in the world's theologies and religious traditions, and the wisdom of those traditions should be of essential relevance to any understanding of the topic. Practices we study (e.g., prayer) also have a religious or theological meaning that must be part of any full understanding of the behavior. Rejection of this "data" of wisdom seems counter to the empirical and scientific ideal of considering all the data and evidence relevant to answering a question.

Conclusions About Positivistic Naturalism

There is no question that the PN research program has brought with it some advantages and positive outcomes. First, PN contains within it an optimistic assessment of scientific progress that has motivated researchers to conduct many empirical investigations. This has led to a large body of work and taught us much about religion. Second, the dominance of PN as a general model in psychology as well as PRS has encouraged the application of traditional psychological theories to the study of religion, often with interesting results. These are tremendous achievements that must be appreciated.

Unfortunately, as we have seen, the PN program also has a number of serious weaknesses. Its allergy to philosophy and religious thought has hampered our ability to discuss important theoretical issues and presuppositions. This has led to meager development of theory (O'Connor, 1997), problematic study design or data interpretation, and other problems. These weaknesses in PN are seldom recognized in the PRS literature because alternative philosophies of science for investigating religion and spirituality are rarely acknowledged. In other words, PN has essentially been the "only game in town" for the PRS, so its comparative advantages and disadvantages have not been well understood (Slife, Reber, & Faulconer, in press). To correct this, we will later outline a hermeneutic alternative, which is admittedly too brief to serve as a "how to" but may help prevent the reification of PN as "the only real science" and aid in the understanding of its strengths and weaknesses.

Increasing Recognition of Positivistic Naturalism Difficulties

As it happens, some scholars and researchers have begun to see the weaknesses of PN and have articulated various concerns about that research program (e.g., Browning & Cooper, 2004; Jones & Butman, 1991; Nelson & Slife, 2006; Yarhouse, Butman, & McRay, 2005). Authors like Richard Gorsuch (2002a, 2002b) have suggested that the scientific study of religion, particularly if it is conceived from a PN point of view, has important limitations:

1. Science generally expects that information be objectively connected in a public manner so that other scientists may repeat and verify the findings. However, many of the things discussed by religious traditions are inherently nonrepeatable events (e.g., religious experiences) and so do not fit well within this methodology.

2. Philosophy (and sometimes theology) can and should have a role in helping psychologists to sort out theoretical issues, because it offers a "big picture" that empirical psychologists often lack.

3. There is a fundamental difference between the nomothetic, "that which can be generalized," and the idiographic, "that which is unique (and therefore not generalizable)" (2002a, p. 50).

Science is a process that assists us in identifying the nomothetic, but we live in an idiographic world that requires other approaches for its full understanding and appreciation, such as the arts. Spirituality also assumes that there are valid sources of knowledge beyond science, so that a rigid scientism is misplaced.

A critical discussion that is more sympathetic to the traditional PN framework is that of Hood, Hill, and Spilka (2009). They argue that the field's "status as a science is based largely on its methodology—that is, its use of scientific methods to study the phenomena of interest" (p. 21). Measurement is the crucial issue, how things are operationalized; they tell us "what a researcher means" by a particular term (p. 11). In line with an emphasis on law-like regularities, reliability is prioritized before validity (p. 28), and quality depends on how definitions and studies conform to "certain standards of good measurement" (p. 12). They assume that a "naturalistic perspective" underlies all scientific investigation, even though reductionism risks "sacrificing the richness and depth of the object of study" (p. 25). The metaphysical and epistemological assumptions inherent in this perspective are nowhere discussed.

On the other hand, Hood and his colleagues also see many of the limitations involved in PN. They acknowledge that theory is important to inquiry, and that PRS has largely been dependent on other areas of psychology for theoretical models (pp. 6, 482). They accept the nomothetic-idiographic distinction offered by Gorsuch (p. 26) and appear to argue that ideographic exploration using qualitative and other methods is an appropriate part of PRS, thus trying to avoid some of the reductionism found in PN accounts of religion. However, it is not clear how this embrace of ideographic investigation and methods is consistent with their commitment to naturalism, since the version of naturalism practiced in psychology (PN) involves a commitment to law-like explanation. The use of qualitative methods without challenging the PN framework does not necessarily produce advantages. Many qualitative methods are underlain explicitly with non-PN philosophies of science (Denzin & Lincoln, 2005; Slife & Gantt, 1999), so that conducting qualitative methods without their respective philosophies of science could undermine their unique benefits.

The critique of PN assumptions within traditional PRS has led to a couple of strategies designed to overcome the weaknesses of the PN program. First, investigators with religious orientations have developed research programs based on traditions such as theism or Buddhist thought (cf. Epstein, 1995; Murphy, 2007; Slife & Reber, 2009). These types of discussions have more recently tended to be constructive rather than critical, and to focus on personal and professional ways of integrating traditional psychology with religious ideas and practices (e.g., McMinn, Mood, & McCormick, 2009; Mikulas, 2007; Sandage & Shults, 2007). However, they largely neglect to build a philosophy of science that could offer a better alternative to the PN program. Second, other scientists have attempted to formulate a new and more adequate philosophy of science for PRS using hermeneutic theory. We now turn to this alternative.

An Alternative Research Program in Psychology of Religion and Spirituality—Hermeneutics

While the philosophical roots of hermeneutics stretch back into the classical period, modern theory is based on the work of a number of Continental philosophers, including Wilhelm Dilthey, H.-G. Gadamer, and Paul Ricoeur (1992). Some authors see a hermeneutic approach as standing in opposition to PN (cf. Luyten & Corveleyn, 2007), while others see it as complementary, focusing more on the discovery aspect of the scientific epistemological cycle in contrast to the PN focus on verification (cf. O'Connor, 1997). Many hermeneutic ideas resonate with the pragmatic psychology developed by William James (1902/1961, 1912/1996a, 1909/1996b), such as his emphasis on lived experience, as well as his concepts of radical empiricism and a pluralistic universe. Interestingly, pragmatic philosophy is becoming a significant contender outside of PRS as a basis for understanding scientific epistemology (e.g., Almeder, 2007). Hermeneutics also eschews the scientism inherent in the PN approach, which privileges psychology and scientific understanding over its object of study and the wisdom available in religious traditions. Hermeneutics works better with a conceptualization of PRS as a dialogical endeavor, as a dialogical model treats psychology and religion as equal partners that can learn from each other (Nelson, 2009).

In this section, we note the metaphysical, ethical, epistemological, and methodological conceptions that are assumed in hermeneutics, and we contrast these with assumptions made in PN. We then illustrate how these different assumptions can lead to very different kinds of research on the same topic. This is done by looking at two studies on the God concepts of individuals. We compare a God image and self-esteem (GISE) study by Benson and Spilka (1973) with a roughly contemporaneous work on God-image formation (GIF) by Ana-Maria Rizzuto (1974; cf. Rizzuto, 1979). The former study (GISE) is executed from within the PN tradition, while the latter (GIF) is psychodynamic and like many of its type of study fits more within the hermeneutic framework (Vergote, 1997). As a brief introduction, the GIF study describes "the unconscious process of forming, and relating to, the internalized image of God" (p. 88) through a detailed analysis of the case studies of two patients, while the GISE study uses correlational analysis of questionnaire-type data to show that self-esteem is "related positively to loving God-images and negatively to rejecting-impersonal-controlling definitions of God" (p. 306).

Ontological and Metaphysical Assumptions

Unlike the PN approach, hermeneutic theory begins with an examination of fundamental ontological and metaphysical assumptions before moving to a consideration of method.

1. *Rejection of physicalist monism.* Hermeneutic theorists believe that what is important in the human world is not just material objects or events but the *meaning* that these things have for the people who are involved (de Boer, 1997). Hermeneutic perspectives also typically reject a monistic stance that sees no essential difference between human and nonhuman aspects of the world. This ontological claim has epistemological implications, as it suggests that the methods of the natural sciences have inherent limitations in the study of the human person (Richardson, 2006). In this sense, PRS researchers cannot exclusively follow the methodology of the natural sciences (*Naturwissenschaften*) but should also look to the human sciences (*Geistewissenschaften*) for access to a broader set of information sources and theoretical constructs (Dilthey, 1989, pp. 56–72). Thus, the hermeneutic program generally rejects an exclusive focus on the reductionism and scientism of the PN program (Bhaskar, 1989, pp. 66–67; Schneider, 2000). The hermeneutic program is consistent with the position that procedures from outside science can give us knowledge (cf. Audi, 2003).

2. *Rejection of individual essentialism.* Generally, hermeneutic researchers have a more relational view of the human person than is found in PN. It focuses on people and the context within which they live and develop, and thus it is sensitive

to sociocultural factors (O'Connor, 1997; Slife, 2005).

3. *Rejection of metaphysical deflationism and scientism.* The Law of Three Stages calls for the elimination of theological or philosophical language and the substitution of scientific thought. The hermeneutics program calls for a different approach. First, ethical and metaphysical assumptions are considered an unavoidable and essential part of the investigator's preconceptions and must be understood if research is to be appropriately evaluated. Second, because of the affirmation of pluralism, science is good but scientism is ultimately false, because there are important aspects of the human world that are not reducible to scientific law.

The GIF study broadly reflects hermeneutic positions on these issues. It focuses on the meaning of the God image for each subject, while the GISE study is concerned instead with the relationships between values of operationalized psychological variables. The GIF study focuses on relational issues, attempting to categorize different types of God images "in the same way in which we describe and categorize different types of interpersonal relations" (p. 88). God can be influential in the lives of study participants. On the other hand, the GISE authors assert on the basis of their study that important attitudes toward religion by the subjects are not due to relational processes but can be reduced ultimately to "psychological processes of the individual" (p. 308). Also, differences can be seen in the amount of time devoted to discussion of theoretical presuppositions between the two papers. The PN study devoted 1/13.5 pages (about 7.5%), while the hermeneutic study had 6.5/16.5 pages (about 39.5%). There was no treatment of assumptions in the GISE study, for instance, there was no discussion of whether their data met the underlying requirements of the statistical procedures used in the data analysis.

Ethical Assumptions

Hermeneutics approaches the ethical foundations of research in several ways. First, issues of fact are not seen as strictly separate from issues of value, so that "facts" cannot be discussed without considering ethical issues. PN argues that these can and should be separate. Second, the purpose of hermeneutic inquiry is to increase understanding rather than the PN emphasis on instrumental power. Finally, hermeneutic research is very participant centered, with attention to the benefits of the participants along with gains for the investigator, whereas PN studies tend to be more focused on the goals and needs of the researcher.

The GIF and GISE studies follow these ethical patterns, with the GIF case study discussions touching on the ethical or value implications of the God image for the participants. The ethical implications of self-esteem in the GISE are not mentioned. The GIF study was conducted in the context of a helping therapeutic relationship, whereas no information is provided about how the GISE study is beneficial to participants.

Epistemological Assumptions

The hermeneutic research program is based upon a different understanding of the nature of knowledge and how it can be acquired.

1. *Rejection of knowledge as invariant propositions.* Hermeneutics generally holds that (a) some kinds of knowledge can only be represented in a narrative or story format (cf. Bruner, 1991; O'Connor, 1997), and (b) the truth or falsity of propositions about human action is highly dependent on their context, making universality something that is rare or nonexistent (cf. Packer, 1985, 1988). Epistemological strategies like PN that focus on universals may have difficulty understanding the inherent particularity of individual states of affairs and experiences (cf. Armstrong, 1997, pp. 95–112, 123–127; Lewis, 1999, pp. 325–331). The open, narrative product of hermeneutic inquiry—including its inherent critical perspective on assumptions—can be especially valuable because it may help psychologists formulate new questions and hypotheses of interest, strengthening the discovery end of the epistemological cycle, which historically has been weak in PRS. It is also particularly oriented to the investigation of certain topics like religious development and experience (Vergote, 1997).

This view is not incompatible with statements by philosophers of science. For instance, Roy Bhaskar argues that epistemologically, while natural science typically involves the study of closed systems with predictable regularities, social scientists investigate open probabilistic systems with multiple determinants, so that it is impossible to perform decisive tests about the nature of objects and their interrelationships. Unlike the situation in natural science, the objects of study in social sciences are constantly changing (Bhaskar, 1989, pp. 79–83, 185–187; cf. Vergote, 1997). The oxygen we study today is

likely to be the same as that discovered by Joseph Priestley in 1774, but the contemporary situation of religion and spirituality is certainly different today than it was in 18th-century England (Taylor, 2007). Furthermore, natural science is based on external observation of phenomena, whereas in the social sciences—including PRS—researchers draw upon the self-reports of intentional, self-conscious agents.

2. *Rejection of expert objectivity.* Hermeneutics generally holds that no knowledge is gained from a completely neutral point of view but depends upon a preunderstanding of ideas and values that offers a beginning point for interpretation (Gadamer, 1989). This is not greatly different than some contemporary points of view about the scientific enterprise (e.g., Ellis & Stoeger, 1996). A number of scholars argue that some kinds of assumptions about objectivity may actually be harmful to the study of the human person. For instance, van Fraassen argues that science as an objectifying enterprise treats the world as composed of objects that have no inherent value, raising the concern that "no objectifying inquiry can reveal what persons are or who persons are among things in the world" (2002, p. 191).

The GIF and GISE studies reflect these differences in epistemological assumptions about invariance and universality. The subjects in the GISE study were 128 male Catholic high school students who considered religion important. While the authors acknowledge that the findings of their study are "tentative," they do not indicate that this very specific sample offers any limitations on their findings. Demographic variables were included primarily as covariates in partial correlational analyses; that is, the analyses attempted to remove contextual variables as a factor in the model, thus—counter to hermeneutics—attempting to aspire to an acontextual view of the relationship between self-esteem and God image. Despite this aspiration, the authors of the GISE admit that they "do not provide many details about the relationship" between self-esteem and God image, particularly at the individual case level, and that "interpreting how individuals actually develop these God-images is difficult" (p. 307).

Assumptions of expert objectivity can also be seen in the GISE study, where the process starts with the investigator's point of view rather than the beliefs of the subjects. The authors indicate that they want to explain "theorized relationships between self-regarding attitudes and God-images" by using "cognitive consistency theory" from personality and social psychology (p. 297). On the basis of these theories, they hypothesized relationships between God images and two "self-regarding" attitudes: self-esteem and feelings of personal control (p. 298). While all analyses were correlational in nature, including partial correlations and comparing models, the authors felt justified in making quasi-causal statements, such as "self-esteem influences God-images," even though they recognize that "other explanations of the data need to be investigated, and refuted, in order to maximize the credibility of this position" (p. 306). On the other hand, the GIF study tries as much as possible to see the image of God from the point of view of the subjects, using their language and concepts. The investigator also has a point of view, but it is clearly stated and then remains more in the background.

Methodological Assumptions

Hermeneutic views of epistemology have methodological implications. As described earlier, PN research is built around the notion of operationalization, where measures are constructed that fit the epistemology of the methods and advance the agenda (and predictions) of the investigator. The investigator is viewed as an expert in the development of the measurement procedures, while the subjects being studied are thought to have simplistic views of phenomenon under investigation or to be ignorant of the true state of affairs (e.g., Leuba, 1912, pp. 249–256). Reliability and observability are thought to be the fundamental requirements of the measurement procedure, which tends to privilege quantitative approaches over qualitative ones. The result is a study that looks at a state of affairs from the presumably neutral or unbiased view of the researcher.

The hermeneutic approach reverses this picture in two ways. First, the subjects being studied are viewed as having irreplaceable knowledge of the phenomenon under investigation, so that any measurement procedure must make sense from the point of view of those being studied. In practice, this view results in a primary focus on the validity of measurement and tends to privilege qualitative procedures. The end result is an understanding that emphasizes the subject's point of view. Results are not thought to be neutral but to emerge from the prior points of view of the subject and investigator, leading to a new understanding. This process is sometimes referred to as the *hermeneutic circle* (cf. Ricoeur, 1981, p. 93). It provides the possibility

of new ideas, enhancing, once again, the discovery aspect of the scientific epistemological cycle.

Subjects in the GISE study were given a 23-item self-esteem scale and a 23-item locus of control scale, and asked single questions about age, grade, and their father's occupation, as well as three questions rating the amount of religious activity in the home. Semantic differential and Q-sort items were given to obtain measures of various aspects of God image, which the investigators appear to have operationalized as the subject's perceptions of God's qualities or dispositions (e.g., controlling, angry, loving, stern). Reliability statistics were reported for the God-image measures, but no validity information was reported. Variables were considered as single items, but no interaction effects were included in analyses. A key point here is that the subjects could only report aspects of the God image that they were asked about. In contrast, the GIF interviews asked general questions that allowed the subjects to tell their own story, which could include their own ideas and concepts in addition to those of the researcher.

Conclusions: The Need for Theory in Psychology of Religion and Spirituality

Good science is progressive, helping us to discover new points of view that remain fallible but have advantages over the previous viewpoints (Mittelstrass, 2000; Rescher, 1982, pp. 100, 172–174, 210–215, 246–247). However, it is impossible to fully evaluate the rationality and truth value of an individual viewpoint or body of research unless we also understand the underlying assumptions behind the research (cf. MacIntyre, 1977). We believe that the sophisticated tools provided by philosophers of science can help us to understand our tradition, identifying and potentially correcting its problems and limitations.

As a case in point, our conceptual analysis of the PN program in PRS indicates that its assumptions, though advantageous in some respects, nevertheless lead to a number of methodological and interpretive problems. Perhaps most prominently, PN provides no systematic facilitation of the discovery aspect of the scientific epistemological cycle, leading ultimately to little PRS progress. Many other serious limitations with the PN system are only readily apparent in the light of an alternative, such as hermeneutics. Hermeneutics has its own advantages and disadvantages (Slife, 2010), but the predominance of PN calls for at least a new awareness, if not an entirely different way of doing things. A reflection on the problems of PN and alternative possibilities, such as hermeneutics, suggests a number of needed changes:

• Removal of the PN "allergy" to philosophy so that PRS scholars can have open, constructive discussions about important theoretical issues that affect their work.

• Movement beyond the 19th-century suspicion of theological and religious ideas so that those in the field better appreciate their object of study and take advantage of the ideas it has to offer.

• Reevaluation of the suitability of an implicit naturalistic law framework for PRS, involving at least a movement away from trying to describe abstract natural laws toward a focus on contextual and particular mechanisms that can help us better understand the phenomena of interest.

• Recognition that a hermeneutic approach to PRS would overcome some of the problems inherent in the PN research program. Eventually, this would lead to more use of qualitative methods and a strengthened ability for the field to generate its own new ideas.

How might PRS come to grips with these attractive possibilities? While gazing into the future is always hazardous, several possible scenarios present themselves.

1. The field could undertake a deep self-examination, leading to a broad acceptance of many changes. This is the most desirable but least likely alternative. Psychology as a discipline has shown a remarkable ability to ignore or marginalize the discussion of theoretical and philosophical issues, suggesting that attempts for progress in PRS will not meet with eager acceptance.

2. PRS could totally reject any discussion of these issues and any of the proposed changes. This also seems unlikely, because many scholars recognize the need for new ideas in the discipline, and calls for broader use of qualitative methodologies are increasingly heard at professional meetings and on PRS electronic mailing lists. The increasing internationalization of PRS will also make resistance to change difficult as scholars from other cultures begin to question traditional Western Enlightenment values that underlie the PN research program.

3. A subgroup of scholars within PRS might recognize the need for reform and undertake changes in their own work, while the mainstream community continues in the old PN tradition.

This creation of a new academic subcommunity within PRS is similar to how the field has responded to past critiques, as in the creation of Christian professional societies, training programs, and journals in the latter part of the 20th century. This offers advantages but also can lead to fragmentation in the field and an inability of various subcommunities to learn about and utilize knowledge acquired by colleagues working in other groups.

4. A dialogical pluralism would recognize and support the existence of competing research programs, while at the same time providing means of mutual respect and dialog (Richardson, Fowers, & Guignon, 1999; Slife & Gantt, 1999). This seems the most likely desirable change outcome, but one that will not occur unless professional structures (e.g., journals, meetings) are created to support dialog and not systematically exclude scholarship from competing research programs. This must be a high priority of professional societies related to work in PRS.

In both the past and the present, PRS has a tradition of attracting many of the finest minds in psychology to its task. Our hope is that these scholars will recognize the exciting possibilities opened by new ways of doing things and embrace these as we move into a second century in the psychological study of religion and spirituality.

References

Almeder, R. (2007). Pragmatism and philosophy of science: A critical survey. *International Studies in the Philosophy of Science, 21*, 171–195.

Armstrong, D. (1983). *What is a law of nature?* Cambridge, England: Cambridge University Press.

Armstrong, D. (1997). *A world of states of affairs*. Cambridge, England: Cambridge University Press.

Audi, R. (2003). *Epistemology: A contemporary introduction to the theory of knowledge* (2nd ed.). New York: Routledge.

Barrow, J. (1998). *Impossibility: The limits of science and the science of limits*. Oxford, England: Oxford University Press.

Benson, P., & Spilka, B. (1973). God image as a function of self-esteem and locus of control. *Journal for the Scientific Study of Religion, 12*, 297–310.

Bhaskar, R. (1989). *Reclaiming reality: A critical introduction to contemporary philosophy*. London: Verso.

Bhaskar, R. (2008). *A realist theory of science*. London: Verso. (Original work published 1974).

Bridgman, P. (1993). *The logic of modern physics* (Reprint ed.). Salem, NH: Ayer. (Original work published 1927).

Browning, D. S., & Cooper, T. D. (2004). *Religious thought and the modern psychologies* (2nd ed.). Minneapolis, MN: Augsburg Fortress.

Bruner, J. (1991). The narrative construction of reality. *Critical Inquiry, 18*, 1–21.

Cantor, N., & Sanderson, C. A. (1999). Life task participation and well-being: The importance of taking part in daily life. In D. Kahneman, E. Diener, & N. Schwarz (Eds.), *Well-being: The foundations of hedonic psychology* (pp. 230–243). New York: Russell Sage Foundation.

Carnap, R. (1950). Empiricism, semantics and ontology. *Revue Internationale de Philosophie, 4,* 20–40.

Carnap, R. (1995). *An introduction to the philosophy of science* (M. Gardner, Ed.). New York: Dover. (Original work published 1974).

Carrier, M. (1998). In defense of psychological laws. *International Studies in the Philosophy of Science, 12,* 217–232.

Carrier, M. (2000). How to pile up fundamental truths incessantly: On the prospect of reconciling scientific realism with unending progress. In M. Carrier, G. Massey, & L. Ruetsche (Eds.), *Science at century's end: Philosophical questions on the progress and limits of science* (pp. 92–109). Pittsburgh, PA: University of Pittsburgh.

Chalmers, D. (2009). Ontological anti-realism. In D. Chalmers, D. Manley, & R. Wasserman (Eds.), *Metametaphysics: New essays on the foundations of ontology* (pp. 77–129). Oxford, England: Clarendon Press.

Clegg, J. & Slife, B. D. (2005). Epistemology and the hither side: A Levinasian account of relational knowing. *European Journal of Psychotherapy, Counseling and Health, 7,* 65–76.

Comte, A. (1998). Course on positive philosophy. In G. Lenzer (Ed.), *Auguste Comte and positivism: The essential writings* (pp. 71–306). New Brunswick, NJ: Transaction. (Original work published 1830–1842).

Crowe, B. (2005). Heidegger and the prospect of a phenomenology of prayer. In B. Benson & N. Wirzba (Eds.), *The phenomenology of prayer* (pp. 119–133). Bronx, NY: Fordham University.

de Boer, T. (1997). Inquiry into the foundations of a hermeneutical psychology: A critique of unpure reason. In J. Belzen (Ed.), *Hermeneutical approaches in psychology of religion* (pp. 35–49). Amsterdam: Rodopi.

Denzin, N. K., & Lincoln, Y. S. (Eds.). (2005). *The Sage handbook of qualitative research.* Thousand Oaks, CA: Sage.

Diener, E., Suh, E. M., Lucas, R. E., & Smith, H. L. (1999). Subjective well-being: Three decades of progress. *Psychological Bulletin, 125,* 276–302.

Dilthey, W. (1989). *Selected works: Volume 1: Introduction to the human sciences* (R. Makkreel & F. Rodi, Eds.). Princeton, NJ: Princeton University.

Dupre, J. (2004). The miracle of monism. In M. De Caro & D. Macarthur (Eds.), *Naturalism in question* (pp. 36–58). Cambridge, MA: Harvard University Press.

Ellis, G., & Stoeger, W. (1996). Introduction to general relativity and cosmology. In R. Russell, N. Murphy, & C. Isham (Eds.), *Quantum cosmology and the laws of nature* (2nd ed., pp. 35–50). Vatican City State: Vatican Observatory.

Epstein, M. (1995). *Thoughts without a thinker: Psychotherapy from a Buddhist perspective.* New York: Basic Books.

Feigl, H. (1949). Operationism and scientific method. In H. Feigl & W. Sellars (Eds.), *Readings in philosophical analysis* (pp. 498–509). New York: Appleton-Century-Crofts.

Fodor, J. (1991). You can fool some of the people all of the time, everything else being equal: Hedged laws. *Mind, 100,* 19–34.

Gadamer, H. G. (1989). *Truth and method* (2nd rev. ed., J. Weinsheimer & D. Marshall, Trans.). New York: Continuum.

Gahde, U., & Stegmuller, W. (1986). An argument in favor of the Duhem-Quine thesis: From the structuralist point of view. In L. Hahn & P. Schilpp (Eds.), *The philosophy of W. V. Quine* (pp. 117–136). La Salle, IL: Open Court.

Garcia, J. (2003). Practical reason and its virtues. In M. DePaul & L. Zagzebski (Eds.), *Intellectual virtue: Perspectives from ethics and epistemology* (pp. 81–107). Oxford, England: Clarendon Press.

Gasser, G., & Stefan, M. (2007). The heavy burden of proof for ontological naturalism. In G. Gasser (Ed.), *How successful is naturalism?* (pp. 159–181). Frankfurt, Germany: Ontos Verlag.

Gergen, K. (2009). *Relational being: Beyond self and community.* Oxford: Oxford University.

Godfrey-Smith, P. (2003). *Theory and reality: An introduction to the philosophy of science.* Chicago: University of Chicago.

Gorsuch, R. (2002a). *Integrating religion and spirituality?* Westport, CT: Praeger.

Gorsuch, R. (2002b). The pyramids of sciences and humanities: Implications for the search for religious "truth." *American Behavioral Scientist, 45,* 1822–1838.

Harker, D. (2008). On the predilections for prediction. *British Journal of the Philosophy of Science, 59,* 429–453.

Hempel, C. (1968). Maximal specificity and lawlikeness in probabilistic explanation. *Philosophy of Science, 35,* 116–133.

Hill, P., Pargament, K., Hood, R., McCullough, M., Swyers, J., Larson, D., & Zinnbauer, B. J. (2000). Conceptualizing religion and spirituality: Points of commonality, points of departure. *Journal for the Theory of Social Behavior, 30,* 51–77.

Hood, R., Jr., Hill, P., & Spilka, B. (2009). *The psychology of religion: An empirical approach* (4th ed.). New York: The Guilford Press.

Hookway, C. (2003). How to be a virtue epistemologist. In M. DePaul & L. Zagzebski (Eds.), *Intellectual virtue: Perspectives from ethics and epistemology* (pp. 183–202). Oxford, England: Clarendon Press.

James, W. (1961). *The varieties of religious experience.* New York: Collier. (Original work published 1902).

James. W. (1996a). *Essays in radical empiricism.* Lincoln: University of Nebraska Press. (Original work published 1912).

James, W. (1996b). *A pluralistic universe.* Lincoln: University of Nebraska Press. (Original work published 1909).

Jones, S., & Butman, R. (1991). *Modern psychotherapies: A comprehensive Christian appraisal.* Downers Grove, IL: InterVarsity.

Kirkpatrick, L. (2005). *Attachment, evolution, and the psychology of religion.* New York: The Guilford Press.

Kisala, R. (2003). Japanese religiosity and morals. In L. Halman & O. Riis (Eds.), *Religion in secularizing society: The Europeans' religion at the end of the 20th century* (pp. 205–222). Leiden, The Netherlands: Brill.

Kistler, M. (2006). *Causation and laws of nature.* London: Routledge.

Lakatos, I. (1978). *The methodology of scientific research programmes: Philosophical papers* (Vol. 1, J. Worrall & G. Currie, Eds.). Cambridge, England: Cambridge University Press.

Lavric, M., & Flere, S. (2008). The role of culture in the relationship between religiosity and psychological well-being. *Journal of Religion and Health, 47,* 164–175.

Leuba, J. (1912). *A psychological study of religion: Its origin, function and future.* New York: Macmillan.

Lewis, D. (1973). *Counterfactuals.* Cambridge, MA: Harvard University Press.

Lewis, D. (1986). *Philosophical papers* (Vol. 2). New York: Oxford University Press.

Lewis, D. (1999). *Papers in metaphysics and epistemology*. Cambridge, England: Cambridge University Press.

Luyten, P., & Corveleyn, J. (2007). Attachment and religion: The need to leave our secure base: A comment on the discussion between Granqvist, Rizzuto, and Wulff. *International Journal for the Psychology of Religion, 17*, 81–97.

MacIntyre, A. (1977). Epistemological crises, dramatic narrative and the philosophy of science. *Monist, 60*, 453–472.

McMinn, M., Mood, G., & McCormick, A. (2009). Integration in the classroom: Ten teaching strategies. *Journal of Psychology and Theology, 37*, 39–47.

Mikulas, W. (2007). Buddhism & Western psychology: Fundamentals of integration. *Journal of Consciousness Studies, 14*, 4–49.

Mittelstaedt, P., & Weingartner, P. (2005). *Laws of nature*. Berlin: Springer.

Mittelstrass, J. (2000). Nicholas Rescher on the limits of science. In M. Carrier, G. Massey, & L. Ruetsche (Eds.), *Science at century's end: Philosophical questions on the progress and limits of science* (pp. 76–83). Pittsburgh, PA: University of Pittsburgh.

Morrison, M. (2000). Unity and the limits of science. In M. Carrier, G. Massey, & L. Ruetsche (Eds.), *Science at century's end: Philosophical questions on the progress and limits of science* (pp. 217–233). Pittsburgh, PA: University of Pittsburgh

Murphy, N. (1998). Supervenience and nonreducibility of ethics to biology. In R. Russell, W. Stoeger, & F. Ayala (Eds.), *Evolutionary and molecular biology: Scientific perspectives on divine action* (pp. 463–490). Vatican City State: Vatican Observatory.

Murphy, N. (2007). Naturalism and theism as competing research traditions. In G. Gasser (Ed.), *How successful is naturalism?* (pp. 49–75). Frankfurt, Germany: Ontos Verlag.

Nagel, E. (1961). *The structure of science: Problems in the logic of scientific explanation*. New York: Harcourt, Brace & World.

Nagel, E., & Newman, J. (2001). *Godel's proof* (Rev. ed.). New York: New York University.

Nagel, T. (1986). *The view from nowhere*. New York: Oxford University Press.

Nelson, J. (2006). Missed opportunities in dialogue between psychology and religion. *Journal of Psychology and Theology, 34*, 205–216.

Nelson, J. (2009). *Psychology, religion, and spirituality*. New York: Springer.

Nelson, J. M., & Slife, B. D. (2006). Introduction to the special issue. *Journal of Psychology and Theology, 34*(3), 191–192.

O'Connor, K. (1997). Reconsidering the psychology of religion: Hermeneutical approaches in the contexts of research and debate. In J. Belzen (Ed.), *Hermeneutical approaches in psychology of religion* (pp. 85–108). Amsterdam: Rodopi.

Packer, M. (1985). Hermeneutic inquiry in the study of human conduct. *American Psychologist, 40*, 1081–1093.

Packer, M. (1988). Hermeneutic inquiry: A response to criticisms. *American Psychologist, 43*, 133–136.

Paloutzian, R., & Park, C. (2005). Integrative themes in the current science of the psychology of religion. In R. Paloutzian & C. Park (Eds.), *Handbook of the psychology of religion and spirituality* (pp. 3–20). New York: The Guilford Press.

Pargament, K., Silverman, W., Johnson, S., Echemendia, R., & Snyder, S. (1983). The psychosocial climate of religious congregations. *American Journal of Community Psychology, 11*, 351–381.

Piedmont, R. (2001). Spiritual transcendence and the scientific study of spirituality. *Journal of Rehabilitation, 67*, 4–14.

Piedmont, R. (2009). Editorial. *Psychology of Religion and Spirituality, 1*, 1–2.

Piedmont, R., Ciarrochi, J., Dy-Liacco, G., & Williams, J. (2009). The empirical and conceptual value of the spiritual transcendence and religious involvement scales for personality research. *Psychology of Religion and Spirituality, 1*, 162–179.

Piedmont, R., & Leach, M. (2002). Cross-cultural generalizability of the Spiritual Transcendence Scale in India: Spirituality as a universal aspect of human experience. *American Behavioral Scientist, 45*, 1888–1901.

Popper, K. (2002). *The logic of scientific discovery*. London: Routledge. (Original work published 1935).

Presser, S., & Stinson, L. (1998). Data collection mode and social desirability bias in self-reported religious attendance: Church attendance in the United States. *American Sociological Review, 63*, 137–145.

Quine, W. V. (1953). *From a logical point of view*. Cambridge, MA: Harvard University Press.

Rea, M. (2002). *World without design: The ontological consequences of naturalism*. Oxford, England: Clarendon Press.

Rescher, N. (1970). *Scientific explanation*. New York: Free Press.

Rescher, N. (1973). *The coherence theory of truth*. Oxford, England: Clarendon Press.

Rescher, N. (1982). *Empirical inquiry*. Totowa, NJ: Rowman and Littlefield.

Richardson, F. (2006). Psychology and religion: Hermeneutic reflections. *Journal of Psychology and Theology, 34*, 232–245.

Richardson, F. C., Fowers, B. J., & Guignon. C. B. (1999). *Re-envisioning psychology: Moral dimensions of theory and practice*. San Francisco: Jossey-Bass.

Ricoeur, P. (1981). *Hermeneutics and the human sciences: Essays on language, action, and interpretation* (J. Thompson, Ed. & Trans.). Cambridge, England: Cambridge University Press.

Ricoeur, P. (1992). *Oneself as another* (K. Blamey, Trans.). Chicago: University of Chicago.

Rizzuto, A-M. (1974). Object relations and the formation of the image of God. *British Journal of Medical Psychology, 47*, 83–99.

Rizzuto, A-M. (1979). *The birth of the living God: A psychoanalytic study*. Chicago: The University of Chicago Press.

Rodgers, J. (2010). The epistemology of mathematical and statistical modeling: A quiet methodological revolution. *American Psychologist, 65*, 1–12.

Sandage, S., & Shults, F. L. (2007). Relational spirituality and transformation: A relational integration model. *Journal of Psychology and Christianity, 26*, 261–269.

Schneider, H. (2000). Metaphors and theoretical terms: Problems in referring to the mental. In M. Carrier, G. Massey, & L. Ruetsche (Eds.), *Science at century's end: Philosophical questions on the progress and limits of science* (pp. 193–210). Pittsburgh, PA: University of Pittsburgh.

Sherkat, D. E., & Ellison, C. G. (1999). Recent developments and current controversies in the sociology of religion. *Annual Review of Sociology, 25*, 363–394.

Sinnott, J. (2001). Introduction: Special issue on spirituality and adult development, Part 1. *Journal of Adult Development, 8*, 199–200.

Slife, B. (2004a). Taking practice seriously: Toward a relational ontology. *Journal of Theoretical and Philosophical Psychology, 24*, 157–178.

Slife, B. D. (2004b). Theoretical challenges to therapy practice and research: The constraint of naturalism. In M. Lambert (Ed.), *Handbook of psychotherapy and behavior change* (pp. 44–83). New York: Wiley.

Slife, B. D. (2005). Testing the limits of Henriques' proposal: Wittgensteinian lessons and hermeneutic dialogue. *Journal of Clinical Psychology, 61*, 107–120.

Slife, B. D. (2010). *Method decisions: The advantages and disadvantages of quantitative and qualitative modes of inquiry.* Paper presented at the Chinese Psychology of Religion Conference, Pasdena, CA.

Slife, B. D., & Gantt, E. (1999). Methodological pluralism: A framework for psychotherapy research. *Journal of Clinical Psychology, 55*(12), 1–13.

Slife, B. D., & Reber, J. S. (2009). Is there a pervasive implicit bias against theism in psychology? *Journal of Theoretical and Philosophical Psychology, 29*(2), 63–79.

Slife, B. D., Reber, J., & Faulconer, J. (in press). Problems of ontological dualism in psychological science. In R. Proctor & J. Capaldi (Eds.), *Psychology of science: Implicit and explicit reasoning.* New York: Oxford University Press.

Slife, B. D., & Williams, R. N. (1995). *What's behind the research? Discovering hidden assumptions in the behavioral sciences.* Thousand Oaks, CA: Sage Publications.

Slife, B., & Whoolery, M. (2006). Are psychology's main methods biased against the worldview of many religious people? *Journal of Psychology and Theology, 34*, 217–231.

Slife, B., Wiggins, B., & Graham, J. (2005). Avoiding an EST monopoly: Toward a pluralism of methods and philosophies. *Journal of Contemporary Psychotherapy, 35*, 83–97.

Smith, S. (2007). Causation and its relation to "causal laws." *British Journal for the Philosophy of Science, 58*, 659–688.

Taylor, C. (2007). *A secular age.* Cambridge, MA: The Belknap Press of Harvard University.

van de Vijver, F., & Leung, K. (1997). *Methods and data analysis for cross-cultural research.* Thousand Oaks, CA: Sage

van Fraassen, B. (1980). *The scientific image.* Oxford, England: Clarendon Press.

van Fraassen, B. (1989). *Laws and symmetry.* Oxford, England: Clarendon Press.

van Fraassen, B. (2002). *The empirical stance.* New Haven, CT: Yale University.

Vergote, A. (1997). Cause and meaning: Explanation and interpretation in the psychology of religion. In J. Belzen (Ed.), *Hermeneutical approaches in psychology of religion* (pp. 11–34). Amsterdam: Rodopi.

Wendt, D., & Slife, B. D. (2009). Recent calls for Jamesian pluralism in the natural and social sciences: Will psychology heed the call? *Journal of Mind and Behavior, 30*(3), 185–204.

Wright, C., & Bechtel, W. (2007). Mechanisms and psychological explanation. In P. Thagard (Ed.), *Philosophy of psychology and cognitive science* (pp. 31–79). Amsterdam: Elsevier.

Yarhouse, M., Butman, R., & McRay, B. (2005). *Modern psychopathologies: A comprehensive Christian appraisal.* Downers Grove, IL: InterVarsity.

Zagzebski, L. (1996). Virtues of the mind: An inquiry into the nature of virtue and the ethical foundations of knowledge. Cambridge, England: Cambridge University Press.

Parameters and Limitations of Current Conceptualizations

Fraser N. Watts

Abstract

The current state of the psychology of religion is reviewed, and it is argued that there would be mutual benefit in it having closer links with general psychology. At present the psychology of religion is too selective in the range of phenomena it covers, and it should be broader geographically and in terms of faith traditions. In view of the diversity of religion, better ways of classifying religious phenomena are needed if research is to work with homogeneous categories. Though questionnaire methods have played an important role, the psychology of religion would benefit from making more use of both experimental methods and qualitative, first-person accounts. The "outsider's" perspective of the psychology of religion could usually be brought into dialog with the insider's perspective of theology. Finally, there is a case for developing an approach to the psychology of religion that tackles applied practical, applied issues while remaining research based.

Key Words: general psychology, consciousness, taxonomies, data, theology, applied

Introduction

There have been two main phases of activity in the psychology of religion. The first active period was from 1890 to 1930, in the early decades of psychology, and considerable advances were made. Then, after a lull in the middle of the 20th century, there was a second wave of increasingly vigorous activity in the latter decades of the 20th century (see Paloutzian, 1996). It is that second wave of activity that will be evaluated in this chapter. What are the strengths and weaknesses of what has been achieved? What are the challenges facing the field now, and how should it develop?

The uneven development of the psychology of religion (with a vigorous early phase, followed by a lull, and then a revival) calls for comment. The decline of the psychology of religion toward the middle of the 20th century was probably associated partly with the secularization (if not of society as a whole, at least of the community of academic

psychologists) and partly with the methodological turn toward behaviorism. The revival of the psychology of religion was in turn associated with the methodological emancipation of psychology that took place in the 1970s and a return to the admissibility of a broader range of data and theories. However, in this new phase, the psychology of religion was mainly the interest of a minority of religiously sympathetic psychologists, rather than of the discipline as a whole. In this it differed from the cognitive science of religion that has developed in the 21st century, which has been predominantly the interest of people unsympathetic to religion.

Links With General Psychology

The psychology of religion is probably much less central to the discipline now than it was early in the 20th century. It has become a specialist area that a relatively small proportion of psychologists know about. However, if it is not to be a completely isolated part of the discipline, it is important for it to maintain close links with the general body of psychological theory and research. It is an encouraging feature of contemporary psychology of religion that such links are now developing.

The majority of psychologists who do research on religion have other psychological research interests as well. That is partly a consequence of the fact that there are very few specialist posts in the psychology of religion. Most people who work in the field teach psychology more broadly, even if their research is largely focused on the psychology of religion. Some psychologists of religion have posts in religion or theology departments, rather than psychology departments; they risk becoming more isolated from mainstream psychology, but they are probably a minority. Most of those working on the psychology of religion have posts in social psychology in departments of psychology.

Another important issue in determining the relation of psychology of religion to the discipline as a whole is where research and theory on the psychology of religion is published. There is a growing range of specialist journals, including the *International Journal for the Psychology of Religion*, the *Archive for the Psychology of Religion*, and most recently the APA journal, *Psychology of Religion and Spirituality*. There are also confessional journals, such as the *Journal of Psychology and Theology* and the *Journal of Psychology and Christianity*. Specialist journals help the psychology of religion to develop identity and coherence, and papers published in such journals are likely to be read by a good proportion of people in the field. The downside is that they will probably only be read by psychologists who specialize in religion; that tends to keep the psychology of religion isolated from the rest of the discipline. From that point of view, it is helpful for at least some papers in the field to be published in mainstream psychology journals, and there is a growing trend in that direction.

I suggest that the psychology of religion benefits from having close links with other areas of general psychology, and that two-way links are desirable. Research in the psychology of religion can benefit from close connections with theories and methods in most areas of mainstream psychology. Equally, the psychology of religion provides an interesting and valuable field of applied psychology in which it would be beneficial to test a wide range of theories from mainstream psychology.

Strengthening links between general psychology and psychology of religion is more complex than it might first appear, partly because of the range and diversity of psychology itself. Psychology is partly a biological science, partly a social science, and the assumptions and methods of those two areas of psychology are very different from one another. There have been few attempts to integrate biological and social areas of psychology and, for the most part, they remain separate from one another. Biological psychologists know little about social psychology, and vice versa.

Despite that, I would argue that there is a strong case for psychologists trying to hold their discipline together (see Watts, 1992). Humans are both biological and social creatures, and any comprehensive understanding of human nature needs to take biological and social aspects into account. If disciplines such as psychology abandon the attempt to integrate their disparate wings, we would effectively be giving up on the attempt to develop a broad, comprehensive, systematic understanding of human nature. Religion is itself a phenomenon that needs to be understood from different perspectives, including the biological and the social. There is increasing interest in the suggestion that there is an evolutionary predisposition to religiousness (see Kirkpatrick, 2005) and the suggestion that the brain is hardwired for religion (see Newberg, Rause, & D'Aquili 2002). Yet it is also undeniable that religious activity takes culturally specific forms and is itself a social activity.

One of the conceptual issues this raises is whether any aspect of religion should be regarded as primary, from a causal point of view. There is always a tendency in biological psychology to assume that biological levels of explanation are foundational to everything else. However, even though biological life is obviously essential to human existence, that need not necessarily be accompanied by biological reductionism. It is a coherent alternative, for example, to espouse some kind of emergentism (Clayton & Davies, 2006) or nonreductive physicalism (Brown, Murphy, & Malony, 1998), in which nonbiological aspects of religious life are seen as emerging from the biological but are not reducible to it. Once nonbiological aspects of religious life have emerged, they take on their own forms. It is best to think about human nature in systemic terms, such that each aspect of human life is seen as being influenced by, and in turn influencing, all others.

There is a somewhat parallel issue about the relationship between individual and social aspects of religion and which should be regarded as "primary." In defining religious experience, William James

(1902/2002) focused on the experience of "individual men in their solitude" (p. 31); it is a long-standing criticism of William James that he ignored the social context out of which religious experience arose and assumed that the individual was primary (see Lash, 1990). Some of these criticisms seem overdone, and they may lead to the other extreme by assuming that society is primary and the individual secondary. Here, too, I would recommend a systemic approach in which the concept of "primacy" is discarded. It seems clear that the religiousness of an individual is influenced by society and also that the religious culture of a society is influenced by particular individuals within it. Influences in both directions should be recognized, and there is no reason to prioritize one over the other.

It is one of the attractive features of religion as a psychological topic that it integrates different features of general psychology. For example, religious development connects with general developmental and life span psychology; the psychology of religious organizations such as churches connects with general organizational psychology; the study of group processes in religion connects with the general study of group processes; and the study of cultural differences in psychological functioning connects with cultural psychology. The study of individual differences in religion connects with the broader study of personality in various ways: basic personality differences, such as the "Big Five" dimensions, affect how people are religious. The study of relationships with God connects with the general study of relationships, including attachment processes. The study of religious coping mechanisms connects with the general study of coping processes, while the study of emotions in religion (anger, for example) connects with the general study of emotion (Watts, 2007). The study of the evolution of religion connects with evolutionary psychology, and the study of brain processes in religious practices (such as meditation) connects with neuropsychology. And so on.

Considerable progress has been made in establishing these connections. However, it is also apparent that some connections are stronger than others, and that explicit connections with some particular areas of general psychology largely remain to be developed. At present, the psychology of religion has closest connections with personality and social psychology. The growing wave of activity in the psychology of religion since 1970 has coincided with the growth of cognitive psychology, which has increasingly become the dominant theoretical language of contemporary psychology. It is arguable that the psychology of religion would benefit from closer links with cognitive psychology.

The most conspicuous deficiency in contemporary psychology of religion is a body of good and fruitful theory. It is probably fair to say that a relatively small proportion of research in the psychology of religion is driven by theory, and there is a conspicuous dearth of broadly applicable theories in contemporary psychology of religion. I have argued elsewhere that dual-level theories of cognitive processes have broad application in the psychology of religion (Watts, 2002). However, more such examples are needed. There is probably no more pressing need in the psychology of religion than the need for better theory. Nothing would do more to strengthen the links between general psychology and the psychology of religion.

The Concept of "Religion"

The psychology of religion needs to broaden the range of cultural contexts in which it studies religion. Psychology has often been very restricted in its sources of data. The era of the "white rat" in psychology is largely over, but all too much psychology is still based on the study of American college students. There are some special populations, such as those receiving health care, who have been studied quite extensively. The psychology of religion is probably better from this point of view than many other areas of psychology because it has often studied people who are engaged in religion outside campus settings, but its scope is still not as broad as it should be.

One limitation is geographical, in that the vast majority of current data is from North America. There is a significant body of data from northern Europe but too little from the rest of the world. There are some areas of psychology, such a sensory psychology, where we can expect findings to be universal, and there it matters less if the source of data is restricted. However, that is not true of religion; we cannot extrapolate what we know about American religion to global religion.

Another limitation is that the vast majority of current psychology of religion is concerned with the Christian religion. There are exceptions: There is a certain amount of empirical psychology of Judaism (see Linke, 1999) and a journal devoted to the *Psychology of Judaism*. However, there is as yet very little comparable psychological study of Islam. There has been a good deal of research on certain Indian religious practices such as transcendental meditation, and states such as mindfulness, and there is also a coherent theoretical psychology emanating from Buddhism. However, the psychological study of Indian religion is so far very selective and limited, compared to the study of Christianity.

These two problems (geographical narrowness and selectiveness in the faith traditions studied) are, of course, interrelated. Most psychological research on religion is carried out in America, and non-Christian religions are generally not well represented there, though it is perhaps surprising that there has not been more psychological study of American Judaism. Yet it is not just that we cannot generalize from one faith tradition to another, without checking that the generalizations are justified. The more radical point is that one cannot justifiably assume that there is a general category of "religion" that encompasses such diverse examples as Christianity and Buddhism. There are good reasons for thinking that "religions" are far from comparable.

The concept of a "religion" is culturally specific and a product of the Enlightenment, and it can itself be subjected to deconstruction (see Lash, 1996). It is a concept that has gone through a radical transformation over the last 200 years or so, as parts of the world have become more secular. "Religion" is a very different phenomenon in a culture where almost everyone shares the same faith tradition from what it is in a culture that is multifaith and partly secular. Elective religions like Christianity and Western Buddhism are radically different from those such as Islam and Judaism that are inextricably intertwined with cultural identity. We have, as yet, only the most rudimentary understanding of the psychology of such nonelective religions.

Religion, any religion, is a multifaceted phenomenon and includes (at least) behavior, experience, and beliefs. It is important in any adequate psychology of religion to keep all these in focus and to be alert to the relationship between them. The dominance of behaviorism in the middle of the 20th century was perhaps one of the factors that created an unfavorable climate for the psychology of religion. More than most topics in psychology, religion cannot be studied adequately without taking account of beliefs and experience. It could well be that religion provides a particularly good opportunity for examining how behavior, beliefs, and experience interrelate in a systemic way.

There has recently been a movement to broaden the psychology of religion to include the psychology of spirituality as well. In one sense, that is a welcome development and reflects a growing concern with values and practices that are broadly "spiritual" but lie outside organized religion. It is sensible to broaden the psychology of religion to include the study of the kind of spiritual values and practices that are characteristic of religion, even when they are found outside an explicitly religious context. The problem, if there is one, is that it makes the boundaries of the "psychology of religion and spirituality" very blurred and could threaten the coherence of the discipline. There is a need for balance here, and we probably do not yet have clarity about where the boundaries of the psychology of spirituality should be drawn.

Religion and Consciousness

There are specific issues that arise at the intersection of the psychology of religion and the psychology of consciousness. It has been part of the agenda for the psychology of religion, at least since William James's classic, *The Varieties of Religious Experience* (1902/2002), which suggested that religious experience is "pure" and unmediated. It is common to find such claims in the mystical traditions of most religions, especially that religious practices such as meditation play an important role in inducing a pure form of consciousness. It is interesting to see William James present such claims as a scientific hypothesis, and similar claims can be found in the contemporary literature, for example, in the work of Robert Forman (1990).

Nevertheless, claims that religious practices induce a pure form of consciousness are controversial and have been strongly criticized on various grounds (see Katz, 1978; Proudfoot, 1985). To many, it seems completely implausible that there should be any human experience or consciousness at all that is not shaped and influenced by personal background and social context. Indeed, to some such as Katz, claims about "pure" religious consciousness may not reflect actual experience at all, just the repeating of claims that have been learned from religious teachers.

I am sympathetic to these criticisms, but much depends on whether claims about pure consciousness are made in absolute or relative terms. Though it may be implausible to suggest that religious practices can induce states of consciousness that are unaffected by any background factors whatsoever, it may well be the case that background factors play a stronger role in influencing some forms of consciousness than others, and that some religious practices play a role in reducing (if not eliminating) their impact. I suggest that there are no a priori reasons for dismissing out of hand that weaker form of the pure consciousness hypothesis, and that it merits empirical investigation.

There is a certain prima facie plausibility in a two-factor theory of religious consciousness, in which there is (1) a component of relatively "pure" experience in which background factors played a less significant role than in most states of consciousness and (2) a component in which background factors (including the religious tradition in which a person had been steeped) played a more significant role. That would be in some ways analogous to Schachter and Singer's theory of emotional experience (1962), which postulates (1) a physiological state that can be manipulated pharmacologically and (2) interpretations of that state that can be manipulated by what films people watch and so on. There seems likely to be an analogy between emotional and religious experience, and it would not be surprising if similar psychological theories emerged in both contexts.

There are both empirical and theoretical considerations that support a distinction between two components of mystical consciousness, one minimally interpretative, and one in which interpretative processes play a fuller and more normal role. Such a distinction emerges from factor analysis of Ralph Hood's mysticism scale (see Hood, Hill, & Spilka, 2009). The first factor reflects an experience of unity; the second factor incorporates religious claims. This two-factor questionnaire structure supports a two-factor theory of religious experience. Furthermore, a two-factor theory of mystical experience sits well with cognitive theories that postulate two levels of human cognition, such as interacting cognitive subsystems, which has been applied to religion by Watts (2002).

Religious practitioners are sometimes resistant to the idea that mystical consciousness is shaped by human processes. However, there seems no good theological reason to resist that idea; the belief that there is a transcendent God whose presence is experienced in mystical consciousness does not necessarily depend on the assumption that there is a direct relationship between supernatural mind and the human mind. In most faith traditions, it would be assumed that both the material created order (including the physical brain) and human society arise from a transcendent creator, and that experience of that creator is mediated through material and social aspects of the created order.

The Need for Taxonomies

The psychology of religion of the last few decades has been marked by a growing awareness of the complexity of the phenomena being investigated. In the first half of the 20th century there was still much interest in the most general question of all, "Why are people religious?" That question has largely been abandoned. (The main current exception is the neuropsychological hypothesis that people are religious because they are "hardwired" for religion, though that is an idea that makes little connection with the kind of empirical data that psychologists of religion are largely concerned with.) Broad, general questions have given way to a concern with taxonomies and moderator variables.

Not all religious people are the same; thus, one cannot generalize about them. In fact, they are so diverse that there is little chance of making headway with any questions in the psychology of religion unless we distinguish different kinds of religious people. An early and very influential distinction was drawn by Gordon Allport (1950) between intrinsic and extrinsic kinds of religious people (intrinsics are people for whom religion is the master motive in their lives; extrinsics are people for whom the attraction of religion lies more in its indirect consequences). The salutary discovery was these two kinds of religious people tended to differ from nonreligious people in opposite directions. Though the empirical literature is complex and untidy (see Batson & Ventis, 1982), the tendency is for intrinsic religious people to have unusually low levels of social prejudice and for extrinsic religious people to have unusually high levels. In parallel, intrinsic religious people tend to have unusually good mental health, whereas extrinsic people tend to have poor mental health. With such diversity among religious people, how can psychology possibly generalize about them?

So taxonomies are clearly essential in the psychology of religion, but we need to be discriminating about them. Good taxonomies are enormously helpful, but there is an infinite number of possible taxonomies, and not all are equally helpful. The field cannot cope with too great a multiplicity of taxonomies; we need to seek as much consensus as possible about a limited number of them.

I suggest that there are four main criteria for a good taxonomy in the psychology of religion. First, the way people are allocated must be reliable, whatever the methodology used. If it is a questionnaire, we need good test-retest reliability. If people are allocated on the basis of interviews, we need good inter-rater agreement. Second, the different categories should be as homogeneous as possible; there is little to be gained from subdividing people into types if some of the so-called types are really a ragbag of very different kinds. (That is a point on which the category of "intrinsic" religiousness has not fared too well.) Third, we need the different categories to be associated with differences on a reasonably broad range of measures. It is one of the good features of the intrinsic/extrinsic distinction that it does indeed map onto a broad range of differences. Fourth, we need substantial and significant differences between the categories; there is little to be gained from dividing people if the resulting subgroups are barely distinguishable from one another.

It is not only taxonomies of people that are needed; we also need taxonomies of phenomena. There are many religious phenomena that need to be subdivided before we can hope to get good answers to questions about who engages in them and what effects they have. For example, there is no point in asking what kinds of people are likely to have a conversion experience when different conversion types are so different from one another. The distinction between sudden and gradual conversion types is over a century old and still useful. Sudden and gradual conversion types differ in a broad range of ways such as age, religious outlook, social attitudes, and so on.

However, there are many other religious phenomena for which we do not have a good taxonomy. For example, there is an extensive body of research on glossolalia, such as what kinds of religious people are likely to engage in it (Malony & Lovekin, 1985). However, research has not made as much headway as it might and, on many measures, there may be nothing distinctive about glossolalics. Alternatively, it may be the case that there are different kinds of glossolalia, and that the people engaging in them are very different from one another. If so, we will not get clear results until we have a good taxonomy of different kinds of glossolalia. There are some promising distinctions in the literature, such as that between "serious" and "playful" glossolalia, but we do not yet know how best to subdivide people who engage in this particular religious activity. The same is true of many religious phenomena.

Data: Beyond the Questionnaire

In recent decades, the psychology of religion has made significant strides in broadening its range of data. However, there is more that needs to be done in this direction. Probably the most used methodological tool in the psychology of religion so far has been the questionnaire, and we have developed an impressive body of questionnaires measuring many different aspects of religion (Hill & Hood, 1999). Many have good psychometric properties, or at least good reliability.

However, there are significant limitations in questionnaire methodology, which suggest that the psychology of religion should not be too dependent on it. One key problem is validity. It is often hard to find good external criteria against which questionnaires can be validated. Despite the best efforts of careful researchers, we often do not know exactly what particular questionnaires are measuring (in the sense of knowing what determines variance in responses to the questionnaire). Too often, questionnaires are given labels that reflect what they were intended to measure, or what they appear at face value to be measuring, in the absence of data to demonstrate that that is what they do actually measure. Questionnaires are of limited value if, as is often the case, we do not know for sure exactly what they are measuring.

There are also pitfalls in summing responses to different questions to produce an overall score for a scale. It has the advantage of producing scores that are more stable and reliable than responses to individual questions, but there are also disadvantages in the summation method. It is usually the case that a relatively small amount of the variance in responses to each question is determined by variance that is common to all the questions in a scale. In addition, common variance may not be what is of most psychological interest; it may sometimes be responses to individual questions that are most illuminating. The reliability that results from summing responses to different questions to form an overall scale has disadvantages as well as advantages.

Questionnaires are usually affected by response sets, such as social desirability bias. If so, how people respond to a questionnaire will be affected by what responses they assume will present them in the best light. If religiousness is thought to be desirable, people will present themselves as more religious than they actually are. Furthermore, for some aspects of religiousness (such as concepts of God), there may be a discrepancy between consciously held concepts and more latent, implicit ones. What people think they believe about God (and say they believe) may be discrepant from more deeply held, implicit assumptions about God. A distinction between two such levels of cognition has been made in many contexts in recent psychology, and it also has been applied to the psychology of religion. It is a distinction that can be characterized in nontechnical language as one between "head" knowledge and "heart" knowledge. Questionnaires systematically tap into "head" knowledge and give little indication of what "heart"-level concepts people may have.

I do not intend to underestimate the huge contribution that questionnaires have made to the psychology of religion. Of course, their contribution has been massive. They are useful not only as measurement tools; the factorial structure of a questionnaire is often of considerable theoretical interest as well. For example, as already indicted, the factorial structure of items in Ralph Hood's mysticism questionnaire sheds light on the fundamental nature of mystical experience.

However, as valuable as questionnaires have been, I do want to suggest that the psychology of religion would benefit in the future from being less exclusively dependent on them. There are two directions in which it would be useful to broaden and, though they may seem to be pointing in opposite directions, I believe both could have a valuable contribution to make. On the one hand, there is a need for more objective, laboratory methods. On the other, there is a place for a broader range of qualitative and self-report measures.

The laboratory approach that is currently arousing most interest is the use of brain scanning while people are engaged in religious practices. However, there are many problems with it that should make us cautious. Because the research is so expensive, the sample of subjects is often very small. There are also often considerable individual differences from one subject to another. The range of religious practices that can be studied in this way is very limited, and the context is highly artificial, with the result that the data may be atypical. However, the main problem relates to the interpretation of the results. It is of little interest to know which area of the brain is associated with particular religious tasks unless we also know the function and significance of the part of the brain involved. Too often, in reports of scanning studies, claims are made about the significance of the brain area concerned that rely simply on the authority of the investigator and have no other scientific basis.

Recently, an attempt has been made to introduce into the psychology of religion the kind of experimental tasks that have been the mainstay of experimental cognitive psychology for several decades, where the standard way of investigating attention, memory, and so on has been to give people tasks from which inferences can be made. Use of such a methodology in the psychology of religion is still in its infancy. However, there are experimental tasks

that provide interesting measures of religiousness (see Barrett & Keil, 1996). What remains to be explored is whether they have any advantages. For example, the fact that they are less subject to social desirability effects might lead them to have better predictive power than self-report methods. All that remains to be investigated.

Qualitative Data, First-Person Accounts, and Constructionism

Psychology, generally, has had a difficult relationship with qualitative methods. Opinions have tended to polarize, with some people having a strong ideological commitment to them, and others disparaging them. I suggest that the psychology of religion should avoid both extremes, and simply make judicious use of qualitative methods alongside other methodologies. Polarized views about qualitative methods arise, in part, from exaggerating the difference between quantitative and qualitative methods. Summaries of qualitative data often involve statements to the effect that there is more of one thing than another. Wherever such comparisons are made, there is no reason in principle why they should not be made in numerical form.

There is now a range of qualitative methods available, many of which are regularly used in other areas of psychology such as clinical psychology (Good & Watts, 1996). These include discourse analysis, account analysis, case-study methodology, and so on. As with any other research method, it is always helpful to be clear about exactly what method is being used and why. The main thing that is needed, if qualitative research is to be fruitful, is a rigorous way of analyzing the data. The value of qualitative research has recently been enhanced by growing sophistication in qualitative methods of data analysis, which are now increasingly available in computerized form. Sadly, qualitative research in the psychology of religion is all too often undertaken with little idea of how the data will be analyzed or what conclusions it might lead to.

There has recently been an increasing enthusiasm for "grounded theory" methods among qualitative researchers. It is one of the distinctive features of the grounded theory approach that it avoids formulating hypotheses before analyzing the data. However, it is important to note that not all qualitative methods need to avoid hypotheses. Indeed, it is often difficult to reach significant generalizations on the basis of qualitative research without formulating hypotheses at some stage. There is much to be said for a two-stage methodology in which, in the first stage, data are analyzed without prior hypotheses. However, that analysis can be used to generate hypotheses that are then tested in a phase of hypothesis-driven research. It is obviously possible to have more confidence in conclusions that are confirmed in a hypothesis-testing stage than in conclusions reached, without prior hypotheses, from a single data set.

One important advantage of qualitative methods is perhaps that they allow a place for a first-person perspective. Psychology has mostly been heavily committed to a third-person, objectivizing perspective. However, it can be illuminating for that to be augmented by a first-person narrative about religious beliefs, experiences, and practices, focusing on the perspective of the person concerned. There are strands within social psychology that have been much influenced by postmodern philosophy and that have developed a critique of the objectifying style of psychology that often leaves no room for a first-person perspective. The postmodern claim is that people can only know something by engaging with it in a participatory way, and that they mislead themselves if they imagine that they can understand anything by being as detached from it as possible, or even if they imagine such detachment is actually possible. Here again, I would advise against extremism and suggest that first-person approaches can make a useful contribution to the psychology of religion, but so can more traditional, "objective" methodologies.

This leads to another debate that has often become overpolarized (like the debate between qualitative and quantitative methods). I suggest that there are strengths and weaknesses in both objective and personal-perspective methodologies. There is also nothing incompatible between them, and no reason why they should not be used in conjunction with one another. It would be too extreme to suggest that psychology should abandon objectifying methods in favor of first-person narratives, but to use them in conjunction with each other can be very illuminating.

A related critical perspective comes from social constructionism. Here it is important to distinguish a moderate form of social constructionism that recognizes people's concepts about religion (and everything else) are influenced by the social, cultural, and linguistic context in which they occur. That is a limited point but, as far as it goes, seems obviously correct. It is very different to maintain a strong, reductionist form of constructionism (sometimes called constructivism) that is inclined to suggest that people's concepts are simply social constructions and have no other reality.

Applying that distinction to religious beliefs, it is one thing to claim that people's concepts of God are influenced by their social and cultural context. That is hard to dispute. It is quite another matter to claim that people's concepts of God reflect nothing but prevailing social assumptions. That implies that the belief that there is a "real" God must be invalid. That is a kind of conclusion that I suggest neither psychology nor social theory is entitled to draw.

Links With Theology and Religious Studies

Though I have argued for close links between the psychology of religion and mainstream general psychology, I also want to urge that the psychology of religion should have close links with theology and other areas of religious studies. I see nothing incompatible in the psychology of religion facing both ways, toward both general psychology and religious studies. In a sense, the link with theology can be seen as a natural extension of concern for the first-person perspective. In studying any phenomenon, it makes sense to take some account of the perspective of those engaged in it. For example, in studying glossolalia, it makes sense to bring the beliefs and attitudes of those practicing it with the objectifying approaches and methodologies characteristics of the natural sciences.

Religious practitioners often make assumptions that go beyond the reach of the scientific study of religion. In particular, religious practitioners usually assume the activity and presence of God, and the psychology of religion cannot, in principle, confirm or disconfirm that assumption. It is a subtle matter whether and how empirical data relate to the assumptions of theism. I suggest that there is a helpful analogy between a scientific paradigm and theism (see Barbour, 1974). There are somewhat variable assumptions about the empirical status of paradigms. However, the most persuasive view is that (a) there is no direct way in which data can prove or disprove paradigmatic assumptions, but that (b) in the long run data can render paradigmatic assumptions more or less plausible. I suggest that the same is true of theism. In one sense, theism, like a scientific paradigm, is conjectural. However, it is a rationally motivated conjecture, and its possibility is affected by empirical considerations.

So I suggest that the psychology of religion has provided several lines of data that are consistent with the assumptions of theism and that render theism more plausible than it might otherwise be, even though they do not provide a logical argument in favor of theism. The frequency of powerful, spontaneous religious experience, the psychological benefits of prayer and religious coping mechanisms, and the propensity of young children to think in terms of supernatural agents, are all what you might expect on theistic assumptions. However, they do not prove those assumptions correct, and they can be explained without them. To put it another way, the psychology of religion provides a rich data set on which a "natural theology" can be built, provided it is recognized that the data are merely suggestive and not the basis of a conclusive argument.

At other points, the empirical data yielded by the psychology of religion suggest refinements to the assumptions of religious practitioners. For example, religious people who speak in tongues usually assume that it reflects the work of the Holy Spirit. Like general theistic assumptions, that is not proved or disproved by the scientific data. The empirical fact that speaking in tongues is associated with psychological benefits is at least consistent with it. However, in my view, scientific research on glossolalia certainly does challenge the assumption that people who speak in tongues are miraculously speaking a genuine language with which they have had no previous acquaintance. For example, it does not have the rhythmic structure of language (Samarin, 1972). Accepting that point does not justify the further conclusion that speaking in tongues is not, in some sense, inspired by the Holy Spirit and of spiritual benefit and significance. That may still be the case, but it means that speaking in tongues should be seen as some kind of general "ecstatic utterance" rather than a normal language. This illustrates how a constructive dialog between psychology and religion might lead to a refinement of the assumptions of religious practitioners.

Another very different point of intersection between the psychology of religion and theology arises from the fact that theological reflection can be treated as a data set that can be studied by psychological methods. There is now a substantial body of work studying scriptural texts from a psychological point of view (see Rollins & Kille, 2007) and similar methods can be extended to other historical theological texts. The evolution of theological ideas can also be treated as a form of cultural evolution and studied from the perspective of evolutionary psychology. Yet another methodology is to study analogies and correspondences between psychological theories and theological ideas. This has probably been used most extensively in Jungian psychology,

but it is not in principle confined to it. For example, the concept of individuation seems to have parallels in various theological ideas such as sanctification.

It is also potentially fruitful for the psychology of religion to have contact with other aspects of religious studies, especially the sociology of religion. The distinction between psychology and sociology is, to some extent, an artificial one. Religion cannot be studied satisfactorily, either from a purely individual perspective or from a purely social perspective. In fact, both disciplines concern themselves with the interaction between individual and society in religion. That is a feature of the social psychology of religion in the discipline of psychology and part of "social interactionism" within the discipline of sociology. One problem in developing a more fruitful interaction between the psychology and sociology of religion is that sociology is sometimes less empirical than psychology. It will be the more empirical aspects of the sociology of religion that will most fruitfully be brought into dialog with the psychology of religion.

The Case for an Applied Psychology of Religion

So far, the psychology of religion has been largely concerned with basic issues, such as trying to understand what sorts of people engage in particular forms of religion, what conditions particular forms of religion arise in, what effects they have, and so on. Those are the kind of basic questions that any area of psychology needs to address. However, there is potentially a wide range of practical applications of the psychology of religion that also merit attention. They have not yet been as fully developed as they might be, but it is likely that the 21st century will see a growing body of applied work on the psychology of religion.

So far, the main area of application has been on the borderline of clinical psychology and the psychology of religion. There has been growing interest in clinical psychology on issues dealing with faith and spirituality, and there has recently been a rich range of publications in this area. Steps have also been taken toward formulating the competence with faith and spirituality issues to which every clinical psychologist should aspire.

However, those clinical and pastoral applications of the psychology of religion are only a small proportion of what could potentially be developed. For example, a body of work could be developed on the interface of educational psychology and the psychology of religion, concerned with the educational work of the churches and faith communities. Additionally, a richer occupational psychology could be developed of ministers and other religious professionals, concerned with their selection, continuing professional development, personal problems, and so on. There could be a richer organizational psychology concerned with religious institutions and structures, and the particular ways in which they function. In each of these areas there is groundwork to build on, but much more could be developed.

In the applied psychology of religion there is an important distinction to be drawn between healthy and unhealthy forms of religion (see Watts, Nye, & Savage, 2002). One strand of the applied psychology of religion will be concerned with facilitating the work of healthy religious processes and institutions. Another strand will be concerned with addressing dysfunctionality within religious institutions and, at the extreme, helping to protect people from damaging and intrusive forms of religion. For example, religions are prone to give rise to intense forms of conflict, and that seems likely to reflect the fact that strongly felt issues of principle are involved. Psychology can contribute to conflict resolution within religious institutions (Boyd-MacMillan, Savage, & Liht, 2008). One dangerous form of religion about which there is particular concern at present is the radicalization of young Muslims. It seems likely that there are patterns of thinking that make people vulnerable to such radicalization, and it is possible to develop educational programs targeted at correcting that.

These are only examples of the broad range of applications of the psychology of religion that can potentially be developed. As the psychology of religion moves into a more practical, applied phase, it is important that there should continue to be close links with research. Indeed, in all areas of psychology, some of the most fruitful theoretical developments have arisen from tackling applied problems. So there is no reason why an applied psychology of religion should not make a substantial and important contribution to the research literature. The basic principles that should guide applied work, here as in other areas of psychology, are that all interventions should arise from a research-based theoretical understanding of the problem that is being addressed and should also be evaluated by research and refined in the light of rigorous evaluation.

Conclusion

The psychology of religion has made considerable strides since it regained momentum in the latter part of the 20th century. However, it faces a number of challenges. If it is to fulfill its potential, it is recommended that it should

- strengthen links with general psychology,
- broaden the range of phenomena it studied.
- find better ways of classifying them,
- expand the range of data it uses,
- enter into dialog with theology, and
- develop a stronger tradition of applied research.

References

Allport, G. W. (1950). *The individual and his religion, a psychological interpretation.* New York: Macmillan.

Barbour, I. G. (1974). *Myths, models and paradigms: The nature of scientific and religious language.* London: SCM.

Barrett, J. L., & Keil, F. C. (1996). Conceptualizing a nonnatural entity: Anthropomorphism in God Concepts. *Cognitive Psychology, 31,* 219–247.

Batson, C. D., & Ventis, W. L. (1982). *The religious experience: A social-psychological perspective.* New York: Oxford University Press.

Boyd-MacMillan, E. M., Savage, S. B., & Liht, J. (2008). *Transforming conflict: Conflict transformation amongst senior church leaders with different theological stances.* York: Foundation for Church Leadership.

Brown, W. S., Murphy, N. C., & Malony, H. N. (1998). *Whatever happened to the soul? Scientific and theological portraits of human nature.* Minneapolis, MN: Fortress Press.

Clayton, P., & Davies, P. C. W. (2006). *The re-emergence of emergence: The emergentist hypothesis from science to religion.* Oxford, England: Oxford University Press.

Forman, R. K. C. (1990). *The problem of pure consciousness: Mysticism and philosophy.* New York: Oxford University Press.

Good, D., & Watts, F. N. (1996). Qualitative research. In G. Parry & F. N. Watts (Eds.), *Behavioural and mental health research: A handbook of skills and methods* (2nd ed., pp. 253–276). Hove, England: Erlbaum (UK), Taylor and Francis

Hill, P. C., & Hood, R. W. (1999). *Measures of religiosity.* Birmingham, AL: Religious Education Press.

Hood, R. W., Hill, P. C., & Spilka, B. (2009). *The psychology of religion: An empirical approach* (4th ed.). New York: The Guilford Press.

James, W. (2002). *The varieties of religious experience: A study in human nature.* New York: Modern Library. (Original work published in 1902).

Katz, S. T. (1978). *Mysticism and philosophical analysis.* New York: Oxford University Press.

Kirkpatrick, L. A. (2005). *Attachment, evolution, and the psychology of religion.* New York: The Guilford Press.

Lash, N. (1990). *Easter in ordinary: Reflections on human experience and the knowledge of God.* Notre Dame, IN: University of Notre Dame Press.

Lash, N. (1996). *The beginning and the end of "religion."* Cambridge, England: Cambridge University Press.

Linke, S. B. (1999). *Psychological perspectives on traditional Jewish practices.* Northvale, NJ: Jason Aronson.

Malony, H. N., & Lovekin, A. A. (1985). *Glossolalia: Behavioral science perspectives on speaking in tongues.* New York: Oxford University Press.

Newberg, A. B., Rause, V., & D'Aquili, E. G. (2002). *Why God won't go away: Brain science and the biology of belief* (2nd ed.). New York: Ballantine Books.

Paloutzian, R. F. (1996). *Invitation to the psychology of religion* (2nd ed.). Boston: Allyn and Bacon.

Proudfoot, W. (1985). *Religious experience*. Berkeley: University of California Press.

Rollins, W. G., & Kille, D. A. (2007). *Psychological insight into the Bible: Texts and readings*. Grand Rapids, MI: William B. Eerdmans.

Samarin, W. J. (1972). *Tongues of men and angels: The religious language of Pentecostalism*. New York: Macmillan.

Schachter, S., & Singer, J. (1962). Cognitive, social and psychological determinants of emotional states. *Psychological Review, 69*, 379–399.

Watts, F. N. (1992). Is psychology falling apart? Presidential address to the British Psychological Society. *The Psychologist, 5*, 489–494.

Watts, F. N. (2002). *Theology and psychology*. Aldershot, England: Ashgate.

Watts, F. N. (2007). Emotion regulation and religion. In J. J. Gross (Ed.), *Handbook of emotion regulation* (pp. 504–520). New York: The Guilford Press.

Watts, F. N., Nye, R., & Savage, S. B. (2002). *Psychology for Christian ministry*. London: Routledge.

Progress in Physics and Psychological Science Affects the Psychology of Religion and Spirituality

Everett L. Worthington, Jr.

Abstract

In the present chapter, I argue that general culture is strongly influenced by three assumptions that have derived from modern science. These include the following: (1) Big numbers in time and space make anything thought to be statistically possible to eventually be thought of as likely. (2) We can be optimistic that this will eventuate in progress. (3) Life is all about relationships. The main implication of these assumptions is that the psychology of religion will soon become the psychology of religion and spirituality. Based on a review of quantum mechanics and cosmology, I suggested that there are four types of spirituality: (a) religious spirituality, (b) human spirituality, (c) nature or environment spirituality, and (d) cosmos spirituality (or transcendent spirituality). Each of these is defined in terms of close or intimate connection or relationship with a different object, and each has been formed primarily by the wonder, awe, and lack of determinancy found in different fields of study—theology, psychological science, biological science, and physics, respectively.

Key Words: religion, spirituality, physics, neuroscience, psychology, optimism, consciousness

Introduction

In this chapter, I will address these questions. What is spirituality? Why has it replaced (or supplemented) religion as being of interest to some people in many cultures—not the least of which is the subculture of scientists studying the psychology of religion and spirituality? And what is the future of the psychology of religion—does it include a psychology of spirituality?

My answers to those questions are obviously more complex than can be unambiguously addressed in a single chapter. My theme is this: The transformation of the psychology of religion into the psychology of religion and spirituality is directly traceable to the macro-lessons learned from physics and trickle-down effects into psychological science, religion, and culture. A parallel discourse could have dealt with biology in addition to physics, but I did not focus on it within the present chapter. There are three relevant macro-lessons

from physics: (1) Big numbers make uncertainties seem likely. (2) Optimism about scientific progress generalizes to optimism about life. (3) Physics is about relationships. Understanding those lessons can help us gain perspective on the future of the psychology of religion and spirituality and to see it within cultural context. Obviously, this present chapter does not focus on reviewing research on psychology, but it looks instead to physics (and mentions parallels in biology) to attempt to shed some light on the psychology of religion and spirituality.

If you are hesitating to continue reading because you are not a particle or cosmological physicist, I hope you will be assured that I will deal with the technicalities of physics only at a general conceptual (and not mathematical) level. Regardless of whether you have technical expertise as a physicist, you can still be informed (and I hope stimulated) by the present chapter.

Interesting Finding

We begin with an amazing finding. In the 2000 census in England, about 390,000 people identified their religion as Jedi [remember the movies in the two *Star Wars* trilogies]. In Australia, 79,000 wrote in Jedi as their religion. In New Zealand, 58,000 Jedis forced their way (sheepishly) into the census. In Canada, 20,000 Jedi knights unsheathed their light sabers on the census takers. How did this happen, and what does it represent?

In contemporary culture, science fiction seems to have become intermixed with religion. How? Let us reflect on *Star Wars* as an illustration of how this occurs.

In the first *Star Wars* trilogy, Luke Skywalker and Han Solo struggle to save the Federation from the Emperor and his henchman, Darth Vader. (Importantly, there is a cooperative federation of life from various sources within the multiverse.) In the climactic third movie, Jedi knight, Luke Skywalker battles the Emperor spiritually by engaging in a physical fight with Darth Vader. Vader was Luke's father and previously a Jedi knight, but he was corrupted by the dark side of the Force. Luke wins his father back to the Light Side of the Force through love. Destruction-oriented anger is Luke's enemy. When anger is exercised, the dark side gains ground. Importantly, while the spiritual battle is going on between Luke and the Emperor, Han Solo is fighting a battle of flesh and blood (aided by the unlikely personalized Ewoks) against the anonymous depersonalized storm troopers and machines on the nearby planet, Endor. Thus, the movie is a parable in which there are simultaneously parallel battles being waged in the realms of human flesh and transcendent spirit. Both battles must be won for the light side of the Force to prevail. Spiritual life and physical life are open systems, and the information in each feeds into the other.

Themes in Science Fiction

One unified message of science fiction is this: There is life out there, and it has evolved to parallel human life. If we can find the beneficial communities and learn from them and subdue the aggressiveness of the hostile communities, then life all over creation will be better off. Life, then, is seen as an open system in which the system can be enriched through flow from another system.

Second, science fiction experiences are often myths of human connection versus technological depersonalization, good versus evil, justice versus injustice, and human redemption versus human sinfulness. These myths are similar to the themes at the center of world religions. Science fiction, of course, is not science and not religion. It is a combination of popular science and cultural narrative that often deals with the same questions that religion deals with. As such, it provides an entranceway into the interaction of science with religion and spirituality—again, two systems that can and do interact. In the general population, which sets the stage for a science of religion and spirituality because these views are commonly held by research participants, there is a sense that, more and more frequently, an assumption deriving from science—which I will call *the optimistic "law" of big numbers*—provides a basis for many people's spirituality. Let's examine this assumption.

Science Fiction and the Optimistic "Law" of Big Numbers
An Assumed "Law" of Nature

Science fiction regularly assumes that existence derives from evolutionary theory. This assumption has become so widely accepted that it is not usually recognized as an assumption. It is taken as a law of nature. The "law" is this: *Life is all about big numbers and possibilities; if the numbers are big enough, possibilities can be probabilities; if the numbers are even bigger, possibilities can be likelihoods.*

Thus, the reasoning goes, if something has the remotest possibility of ever occurring, with enough trials, it will inevitably occur. Several corollaries follow this "law" of big numbers. The corollaries lead reasoning along a road that can suggest more emphasis on spirituality. This flow of logic is not inevitable, but, I submit, it has frequently been embraced, leading to an enhanced sense of spiritual existence. Let's examine these corollaries.

Corollary #1: The cosmos is so large and adaptation is such a ubiquitous principle that there is a likelihood of life on other planets.

Life requires chemicals, energy, and water. All that we know suggests that chemicals are widely scattered, although distributed in local "communities" instead of being evenly distributed. Energy is available from stars, black holes, and dark matter. It is also available from geothermal energy in the core of many planets, making an energy source not strictly dependent on a planet's surface interaction with its nearest star(s). (Some scientists now believe that life on Earth actually began deep in the ocean near geothermal vents and was not empowered by our sun within surface pools of water.) Water exists in various places even in our little solar system (e.g., at the polar caps on the moon, in the past on Mars [though surface water seems to have evaporated], in a large moon of Jupiter, and so on; so water likely exists in many places throughout the cosmos. Thus, with chemicals, energy, and water available at billions and billions (I couldn't resist making reference to Carl Sagan's tag line) of sites, then chances are high that life has formed or can form in other places than on Earth.

Corollary #2: There is a distinct possibility that such life will be intelligent. Steven J. Dick (1996) in *The Biological Universe* has suggested that planetary systems are common. Life originates where conditions are favorable. Evolution culminates in life, and life evolves toward its culmination in intelligence.

From our point of view as humans, intelligence appears to offer huge adaptive advantage. Life requires transmission of information (at a minimum, generational genetic information), and intelligence seems to be the most efficient way we can imagine of transmitting information. Hence, we assume life progresses toward intelligence as it unfolds. Thus, we conclude that more highly evolved life is likely to be more intelligent than is human life.

Corollary #3: Extraterrestrial life—at least in some localities, given big enough numbers—will both (a) attend to people and (b) care about people.

We may also assume that 100% aggressive and competitive life cannot thrive. According to the logic of evolution, some reconciliative mechanisms must evolve to balance the competitive pressures (Kirkpatrick, 2005; McCullough, 2008). If those affiliative mechanisms exist, the assumption goes, those affiliative mechanisms must result in some places that might be benevolent toward outgroup members. That is, there is a possibility that intelligent life can see benefits in befriending outgroup members. If there is a possibility, then with enough big numbers, such life must inevitably occur.

Corollary #4: Given large enough numbers, extraterrestrials somewhere must want to make contact with Earth, interact peacefully (like benevolent extraterrestrials in *Close Encounters of a Third Kind*, or *E. T.*, rather than hostile invading extraterrestrials in *War of the Worlds*), and if contact is made, people will survive, thrive, and be better. This is based on an assumption that benevolent extraterrestrials will want to extend friendship and benevolence to outgroups. The optimistic belief is that different cultures can enrich each other by sharing resources to deal with each other's deficiencies.

Analysis

These are *optimistic* assumptions at almost every point. I am frankly skeptical of the optimism. The assumptions represent modernity with its general assumption of progress and postmodernity with its belief in and value on relationship. The optimistic assumption of progress encourages many people to favor space exploration, hoping for optimistic outcomes. And the relational assumption, that reality is defined relationally, suggests that meetings with extraterrestrials would open new relational possibilities.

At first blush, the "law" that life is all about big numbers might suggest a sense of hope and connection. We might be tempted to conclude that we can find meaning and salvation from our humdrum existence through yielding to the authority of science and trusting to the "law" of big numbers and to the hoped-for benevolence of other cultures.

I am not suggesting that we should care that much about science fiction. (I happen to enjoy it in limited doses, but that is beside the point.) I am suggesting, rather, that the popularity of science fiction in common culture is an indication of the way many people in our culture think: Big numbers and optimism about spiritual encounters will lead to beneficial effects for humanity. (This optimism exists even as many people reject traditional religions and other people are caught up in fervent adherence to traditional religions.)

Let's analyze this mindset. James A. Herrick (2008), professor of communication at Hope College, a historically Christian university, has analyzed the mythologies represented by the Jedi findings in the census of 2000. Here is his analysis:

> For centuries, Christianity has provided the Western world with a coherent narrative…[F]or more than three centuries we have been in the process of slowly dismantling and discarding traditional religious narratives…In their place we have constructed a new set of myths transforming science into a spiritual project serving a vision of the future, suggesting that questionable benefits will arise from our involvement with unseen intelligences from other planets or dimensions or times, and even rendering the life of the individual person as inconsequential step along the way to something better.
> (p. 38)

Second, an optimistic outcome of the law of big numbers is not necessarily a foregone conclusion. In fact, in distinction to the reasoning that says, with big enough numbers, we can inevitably expect a benevolent connection with extraterrestrial life, we must face the consequence of being wrong. We might observe that pessimistic assumptions that favor isolationism and separatism are just as likely to be shown veridical, but they are not favored by modernity. Other assumptions—that even among other extraterrestrial cultures, those beings might not want to be in contact with us anyway—are also possible, but they are generally looked down on by postmodernity, which has a largely relational view of existence.

The chances of meeting a benevolent extraterrestrial culture are *at best* 50–50. If we assume that it is possible that hostile-competitive and benevolent extraterrestrial cultures exist in about equal numbers, the chances of meeting each type *first* is at best 50–50. It might be only the first contact that is determinative—especially if the culture is hostile-aggressive—like the *War of the Worlds* marauders. There are no big numbers at work here. Even if all of the assumptions of the "law" and the first three corollaries hold (and that is a BIG if), the first extraterrestrial culture we meet will be benevolent, hostile, or mixed. Our chances are at best 50–50. They are *far* less if we figure in the probabilities in supporting the law and all of the corollaries. They are even distantly less when we consider that evolutionary theory probably would predict that most outgroup relations will be more competitive than cooperative (with reconciliative mechanisms usually limited to ingroup relations). Thus, the beginning guess—that it might be a 50–50 probability between first contact of a benevolent compared to a hostile society, highly unlikely. I am tempted to observe that betting on a benevolent first contact seems to be a bad bet.

Where Did the "Law" of Big Numbers Come From?

Religion is vibrant worldwide, but in many scientific countries, it is being replaced by spirituality. Why? The answers are multifaceted, but I will suggest four below. First, the populations of the most developed countries are aging, resulting in more people who are approaching their end of life and looking for transcendent meaning. Second, in the minds of many, religion has fallen short of its promise of a meaningful narrative, within this modern culture. Third, science has provided a positive, optimistic narrative. Fourth, technological developments, especially in communication and transportation, have placed people in contact worldwide and provided a sense of interconnectivity, connection,

and intimacy—the essence of spirituality. Taken together, these four trends have stimulated many people to look beyond religion for a needed sense of connection to things transcendent.

Aging World Population

Aging elders and their aging caretakers confront the decay of body and mind. Overall, life can look grim as we approach death. However, the human spirit needs hope. To meet this existential need, humans search for meaning. There is a particular need for optimistic causes. People have found these in issues like enthusiasm over saving the planet, early post-election Obamamania, volunteerism, and the "can do" generation that led to much optimism in the face of a global financial crisis in 2009. (At present, now in 2012, as I revise these words written in 2009, some of the dew appears to have evaporated from the promising bloom of early 2009 as the economic crisis has spread throughout the world and the global economic outlook shows signs of very slow recovery.)

Disappointment in Religion

Religious conflicts undermine a sense that religion can lead to world peace. Rather, religion looks like a source of impassioned differences, and religious conflict can seem inevitable. Communication technology has made it possible for worldwide viewing of violence from interreligious conflict. This is particularly salient for people in the United States, England, and Spain after terrorist attacks within the last decade by religious radical fundamentalists. Prolific 24-hour-per-day news reporting and inherent bias in reporting negative events more than positive have made people worldwide more aware of such conflict than in the past (Mischel & Brooks, 2011). Furthermore, better global interconnectivity in travel and communication brings religions into contact with each other more than in prior centuries. That increases the probability of conflict (and also of beneficial interaction).

Even within religions certainty has been eroded. As religious information about one's own religion has become more accessible, divergent viewpoints and intrareligious theologies are encountered more frequently. These introduce more doubt about religion than in the times when people lived and worked in more culturally uniform settings.

Progress in Science

Sciences—in particular physics and biology—have provided poster children for people's sense of progress. The liberal sense of progress in the early

20th century was violently exploded in World Wars I and II. Nuclear bombs set off an age of anxiety. Yet nuclear physics and quantum mechanics—despite being tarred with fallout from the bomb—combined to uncover the Standard Model of Particle Physics, which is the new reductionist explanation of the physical world. A bit later, in the 1950s, the discovery of DNA and subsequent development of molecular biology, molecular genetics, and the mapping of the human genome have suggested an understanding of the biology that opens new vistas (unresolved ethics questions notwithstanding). Science has fed technology, placing cultures worldwide into contact through electronics, fiber optics, and airplane travel.

Progress in Technology

Technological connectedness (e.g., the Web, e-mail, blogs, Facebook, Blackberries, Twitter) makes people think in terms of connectedness. Connectedness is the essence of spirituality. Thus, technology has been increasingly directing people's attention toward the spiritual.

Resulting Spirituality

Based on these four factors, I suggest that people's need for spiritual connection, which historically had been met through religion and religious communities, is increasingly met through other means—which I describe as three secular spiritualities (in addition to religious spirituality). These secular spiritualities will be discussed in a later section of this chapter. Before looking at them, however, I will review more specifically how physics contributed to a more secularly spiritual worldview.

What Modern Physics Taught People
Science of Modern Physics

Thus far we have considered social trends and pressures that push and pull people toward spirituality and generally away from organized religion. We have considered the assumption flowing from science to general culture (as seen in science fiction entertainment) that life is about big numbers and thus given sufficient numbers of cases, anything that has a finite probability of occurring could become a definite possibility. We now look more closely at where that assumption arose: in quantum and relativistic physics. We see that physics has developed such that a sense of absolutism that has traditionally been the foundation of the various religions has been undermined. It has been replaced with probabilistic reasoning.

In 1900, William Thompson (who called himself Lord Kelvin) announced that science seemed to be approaching an authoritative account of nature. He suggested that only two small clouds remained that needed explanation—blackbody radiation and the inability to measure the speed of Earth in absolute space—then science would be virtually complete (except for the mopping up of some details). Resolving those two "little" problems, of course, transformed physics in the early part of the 20th century. They led to relativistic physics on one hand and quantum physics on the other.

Even prior to Einstein, the stage was set for the deluge descending from those clouds. While many precursors could be identified, we focus on one. In 1887, Albert Michelson and Edward Morley conducted a classic experiment that solved one of the troubling aspects of Newtonian physics. The idea was that some unmeasurable field, luminiferous ether (or just ether), flowed around us. Assume, then, that ether is flowing north and south. If a light wave moved north for distance d (aided by the flow of ether) and then south for distance d (fighting against ether), the light wave should be expected to take a different time to make that round trip than a different light wave moving at the same speed but cutting at 90 degrees to the flow of ether and going distance d east, then returning to the west. Thus, if a light beam were split at the source into two right-angle beams, they should be expected to arrive back at the source out of phase. (This is a consequence of Newtonian laws of motion.) Michelson and Morley experimentally showed that the light did not arrive out of phase but perfectly in phase. The speed of light in a vacuum was in fact invariant, regardless of its orientation within the field of ether. That assumption of an invariant speed of light formed an anchor for Einstein's (1905) theorizing about the relativity of time and space. If the speed of light did not change depending on frame of reference, then length and time had to change. Einstein's relativistic theories undermined a sense of absolutes in time and space, leaving only one measure—the speed of light in a vacuum—as being absolute. The fallout of relativity theory was a bolstering of the previously articulated worldviews that questioned absolutes—particularly Hegel's. Hegel reasoned, for example, that traditional rationality had depended on an understanding of thesis-antithesis. A statement and its opposite could not both be simultaneously true. Hegel, however, posited that it was process that was absolute—the dialectical process that theses and antitheses were always resolved into syntheses, which became new theses, which had antitheses, which were resolved in syntheses, and so on. Just as Einstein found that *c* was constant but space and time were interrelated, with the power and authority of science, he reinforced and empowered Hegel's notion that the dialectical process was absolute, and truths were interrelated. (Note that Darwin had followed a similar Hegelian logic in the theory of evolution by reproductive advantage.)

Einstein was not a friend of quantum mechanics. He never could resolve classical relativity theory with quantum mechanics. The Copenhagen interpretation of quantum mechanics suggested that particles could be represented by wave functions (and waves could be represented as particles). According to this interpretation, by measuring a system, the measurement causes the calculated set of probabilities of the system to "collapse" to the value measured. This aspect of the mathematics is called wave function collapse. Neils Bohr (1972–2006) and Werner Heisenberg (1958) put forth this theory. Erwin Schrödinger provided an elaboration of the theory. Schrödinger's (1935) hypothetical cat is a thought-experiment illustration, using reduction ad absurdum, to illustrate wave function collapse. Schrödinger suggested that we imagine a cat in a room; the cat is either dead or alive (we don't know which). Until a measurement is made, Schrödinger's cat is *both* dead and alive (or neither dead nor alive) to those outside the room. This gives rise to quantum "entanglement," in which two particles that have interacted (and are thus entangled) cannot be independently described without describing the other. Say that an electron and its antimatter counterpart, a positron, were created simultaneously in a linear accelerator. Certain properties, such as mass energy, electric charge, and spin angular momentum must be conserved in such accelerator interactions. If, according to the energy involved, we know that one particle is the electron and the other the positron, the entangled particles are not identified until one is measured. Once one is measured, the other particle is determined, even though it is not measured.

Bell's (1964) theorem suggested that when hidden (e.g., as yet unmeasured) particles are concerned, only a limited number of variables can produce the probabilistic predictions of quantum mechanics. Quantum entanglement, then, suggests, using Bell's theorem, that with two entangled particles, either we give up the idea that particles have definite properties, or else all particles must be connected by a web of instantaneous communication links. Such instantaneous communication links, of course, have provided more grist for the science fiction industry. Hugh Everett III (1957) argued that every possible outcome of every quantum event takes place in a limitless branching series of parallel universes—of which we can only see one; however, all are intertwined. (This is the premise of the time travel movies like Claude van Damme's *Time Cop* and the trilogy starring Michael J. Fox, *Back to the Future*.)

RETURNING TO LORD KELVIN

Now, we are about 100 hundred years post Lord Kelvin's somewhat optimistic assessment of science as complete—except for those two little clouds. What do we learn from a century of relativistic cosmology and quantum physics? Apparently not too much. Consider the book by John Horgan (1996), *The End of Science*. Horgan argues that we just about have answered all of the really meaningful questions in science. Except for mopping up a few pesky details, of course.

BIG-SCALE PHYSICS

Since 1998, we have accumulated evidence for "dark energy," which is supposed to arrive from some force that seems to be at work to accelerate the universe's expansion (Peebles & Ratra, 2003). This energy seems to have been manifest since the universe was estimated to be about 7 billion years old. Before that, it was probably masked by gravity. But, like dark matter, we do not really understand the nature of dark energy. Could it be possible that this could be similar to one of Lord Kelvin's (1900) little clouds? Explaining dark energy might require a fundamental change in the understanding of gravitational theory. There might be other clouds around. It seems that galactic clusters may have existed at about 3 billion years. But according to current theory, it should not have been possible for the cosmos to have that much structure. This suggests a second little cloud that might not be fully explained at present. Or perhaps there is a third cloud. We might not be reading the microwave background radiation correctly. That is the basis for much of our current understanding of the cosmos.

SMALL-SCALE PHYSICS

Perhaps the crowning glory of physics has been the development of the Standard Model of Particle Physics (Coughlan, Dodd, & Gripaios, 2006). The Standard Model unifies the electro-weak theory (which combines classical electromagnetism and the weak nuclear force) and a second strong nuclear force (which is explained by Quantum Chromodynamics, an analogy for the way colors combine). But the Standard Model has a couple of clouds on its horizon also. The rest mass of the neutrino has been theorized to be zero, yet now (one of those pesky problems) new evidence suggests that it might have rest mass. That suggests that changes might be needed in the Standard Model. In addition, the Standard Model is a renormalizable model, which means that the fundamental masses must be measured, not derived theoretically. This might suggest that some modifications might again be forthcoming, and there might even be fundamental particles more basic than the six quarks and six leptons (electrons, muons, tauons, and neutrinos flavored as each). Finally, the search for the Higgs boson, which physicists hope to detect with the operation of the European Organization for Nuclear Research (CERN), is still (in early 2012) in progress. The (shall we call it pesky and allusive) Higgs boson still has not been found. Even the development of string theory (and superstring theory) has not solved these problems. Particle physics assumes that the smallest fundamental units in physical existence are point particles. String theory (and superstring theory and M-theory; Greene, 1999) suggests that the most fundamental unit of physical existence is best represented as a loop, not a point.

Thus, as we look at both the very large and very small units of physics, we find enough annoying unexplained clouds to have true concern about rain. According to current physics models, the physical universe seems probabilistic at the core, but we have virtually no certainty that we possess the best understanding of the physical world. (Ironically, in late 2011—long after I wrote this chapter—the world has witnessed both evidence that flies in the face of relativity theory and also some indication of the limitations of the Heisenberg uncertainty principle. It is too early to tell the impact those discoveries might have on modern physics, but I think it is safe to say that the physics weather is distinctly cloudier now in 2012 than it was in 2010.)

Nevertheless, we usually can bet on our best current understanding of reality (relative to simply making up a story about what might occur in the future of physics). From both relativistic and quantum physics, we find the law of big numbers and a sense that, given enough time, probabilities will become possibilities, and possibilities will become likelihoods.

The Science of Biology (Briefer)

I have focused on modern physics. I easily could have made the same argument for modern biology.

SMALL-SCALE BIOLOGY

In biology, the operation of genetics and processes of intra- and intercellular signaling, regulatory, and monitoring networks that affect cellular metabolism seem much more complex than had been thought. These fundamental processes are ill understood. Furthermore, with genetics, we have come far beyond single-gene determinism. We now believe that all genes exist in all cells. But what is it that makes a cell take on a particular function? How do proteins turn on particular parts of DNA? The complexities are mind wrenching, so we fall back on an appeal to probability. Certainly, this does not deter molecular biologists from trying to uncover all of the biological mechanisms possible. But it erodes certainty that the human will ever be fully understood.

BIG-SCALE BIOLOGY

Although Darwin's (1859/2009) theory of evolution (with classical Mendelian genetics) predated modern physics (and both nodded intellectually to Hegel's earlier articulated dialectical idealism), the theory of evolution as a worldview is a relatively recent phenomenon. Evolutionary theory is the icon for probabilistic thinking. Adaptation is a guiding principle that selects which random events will have an impact on the population. Given enough time, material, and energy and an environmental system that makes something possible, evolutionary thinkers usually conclude that it is—at someplace in the vast multiverse—possible if not likely.

Mystery and Wonder at Root, Observables in Daily Life

Clearly, with physics and biology, there is a sense of mystery and wonder coming from the scientific disciplines. Much of the wonder comes about because the physical reality and biological reality seem to be probabilistic at core, and therefore, deep reality is unpredictable (and often awe inspiring; yet sometimes awful). Furthermore, because science is understood only by highly trained secular "priests" (i.e., scientists) who hold the keys to the kingdom, science speaks authoritatively—especially as far as the lay person is concerned. Of course, I am oversimplifying, but I am trying to make several arguments. (1) Physics and biology have shifted people's fundamental view of the nature of reality away from a sense of certainty to senses (a) of probability; (b) that given enough time and space, the law of big numbers will come about: namely, what is statistically possible will (with enough time) become probable, then likely, then inevitable; and (c) that individual entities are less important than the relationships between and among the entities. This is coupled with (d) the general sense of optimism from the adoption of a cultural narrative of change, problem solving, and progress, which I described in the previous section. These developments have provided a proscience backdrop that is optimistic at root.

Notice, importantly, that despite people's general beliefs that sciences have told us that life is indeterminant and uncontrollable, people nonetheless see the physical world. They experience the physical events in their own and others' lives. What is ephemeral (probabilistic, indeterminant, uncontrollable) at core must be seen and acted on in a concrete way in life. It is in this context of an indeterminant substrate of behavior and an observable life that we must understand psychological science.

Physics, Psychological Science, and the Invisible and Probabilistic Substrate of Consciousness

Many exciting advances in social science research are aimed at neuroscience, psychological science broadly conceived, and multiculturalism. This extends to positive psychology and, as we will see, to a psychology of religion and spirituality.

PHYSICISTS AND THE STUDY OF CONSCIOUSNESS

Probably the area of psychological science that is most highly and directly involved with modern physics is the study of consciousness. Consciousness is a puzzle that has entertained philosophers for centuries. It is apparently nonmaterial, yet it must have physical substrate. Furthermore, definitions are problematic. What is consciousness anyway? We all have it—even children—and yet we are not disturbed that we lose it each night.

So is consciousness material? That is, is consciousness a product of and reducible to brain states? Almost no one will argue that consciousness is *nothing but* the way our brain processes work—structure and function. Almost no one would argue that if we remember a dream or perceive a particular shade of red if the frequency of light is precisely specified, that we would activate precisely the same arrangements of neurons in the same areas of the

brain doing the same functions that would have produced the dream originally or the perception of red originally. That is, it is physically impossible that every unique mental event has a corresponding unique pattern of brain activity. As miraculous and complex as brains are, there simply are not enough neurons to support such a model. How, then, can limited brain apparatus produce the varieties of conscious experience? That is the puzzle.

But intrepid modern physicists have ventured into trying to deal with explaining consciousness. Let's reason with the physicist. Bohr's Copenhagen model of the atom has replaced the picture of a large nucleus with electrons revolving around it as if this were a miniature solar system. Instead, the Bohr atom views the atom's arrangement as completely probabilistic. Electrons have multiple probable states of energy and multiple probable positions. However, both energy and position are probabilistic according to the Heisenberg (1958) uncertainty principle. Experimental results actually describe a microcosm in which the particles occupy multiple states and multiple locations at the same time. The very act of measurement—if it occurs—collapses these to a single state.

Physicist Eugene Wigner (1960) speculated on a connection between quantum physics and consciousness. In trying to mediate between Heisenberg and Bohr (who saw reality in terms consistent with logical positivism) and Hugh Everett (with his multiple intertwined realities, 1957), Wigner suggested that the *consciousness* of the observer is what causes collapse of the wave function, not realist philosophy or splitting of observers. Wigner asserted that consciousness causes collapse. Thus, Wigner's interpretation of quantum mechanics suggests that observation *by a conscious observer* makes the wave function collapse to a single observable state. He claimed that the rules of quantum mechanics are correct; however, only the material world is subject to quantum mechanics. But external observers—who are not subject to quantum mechanics (namely human minds)—can make measurements on the brain, and when they do, the measurements cause wave function collapse.

Later, physicist David Bohm (2002) advanced Wigner's speculations. Bohm applied the theoretical and observational aspects of quantum physics directly to the functions of the brain and to the problem of consciousness. Bohm's student Yakir Aharonov (Aharonov & Bohm, 1959) showed that an electromagnetic field could have effects in otherwise fully shielded regions of space, which is the

Aharonov-Bohm effect. Bohm advanced the thesis that the brain at the quantum level is an informational system such that the mental and material merge. Matter and mind are inseparable aspects of a single whole.

The very achievements of modern physics have created a cultural mindset. That mindset is composed of several elements. First, certainty has been tossed from the window and replaced by relativity of time and space. Second, quantum physics showed us that we cannot trust commonsense conceptions. The measurement of entangled particles whose total spin, for example, must be conserved between the two, exists in an indeterminant state. But, if at some time, one is measured, then suddenly the other particle is also defined. Physicists also tell us of the pairing of matter and antimatter items whose states are simply indeterminable. Nor is it possible to say how such entanglement occurs. Is it a materialist process? Or is it a mental, consciousness-based process? Third, mostly, we believe what we observe. Fourth, so somehow we jump from an understanding of the physical universe (and conscious "universe") as probabilistic to what we observe, which we take to be the basis for making conscious decisions.

SPIRITUALITY BECOMES (OFTEN) A REPLACEMENT FOR RELIGION IN SCIENTIFIC-IMBUED SOCIETIES

Let us note the similarity to religion here. We live in a material world, yet most religions tell us there is an unseen world that is unpredictable, noumenal, and not controllable. What religions have traditionally done, science—since modern physics, modern molecular biology, and modern neuroscience—has done. The modern sciences have given people an alternative view of life, and the view is not religious. Similarly, it is not satisfactory to call it mere physics, mere biology, or mere neuroscience. People long for something that transcends mere materialism. So we capture the essence of this unpredictable, noumenal, uncontrollable world, which nevertheless yields some concrete observations, by calling it *spiritual*.

Psychological Science, and How the Invisible and Probabilistic Substrate of Consciousness Relates to "Observables" in Consciousness

Suppose it actually is the case that only by way of observation and measurement, by way of the introduction of some element or derived product of consciousness, that quantum uncertainties collapse into determinate states. (Note that the distance apart of the two entangled particles is irrelevant.) The influence that consciousness or its derivatives might have is not by way of contact but by way of that dimensionless entity, information. This could suggest such things as one consciousness, entangled with another, could influence it across space and perhaps time. This borders on mystical religious theory. Possibly. However, Bohm did not address the very nature of consciousness, the uniqueness of its possessor, the relationship of consciousness to more specific mental states and functions. There are more things not explained than things that are explained.

How can something so statistical *feel* so non-statistical? The nature of reality, remember, is seen by most people—not just scientists—as being statistical in essence. Yet our experience seems anything but statistical. It seems concrete. How can an essentially statistical model of reality produce sharp and concrete images in our minds (and brains)? Mental life is about reasoning logically or at least concretely. Quantum physics has overturned the classical world of absolute space, mass, time, and motion. However, the very essence of mental life for most of us, is the capacity to reason and arrive at an answer, not a statistical equation. A critic might argue that the correct model of brain function—if it is to be derived from quantum physics—must be thoroughly statistical and that goes against all of our experience.

A neuroscientist proposes a way that probabilistic brain states can create reproducible observables (mental images). However, let's look briefly into a theory of brain, mind, and consciousness proposed by thoroughgoing materialist Gerald M. Edelman (2004), winner of the Nobel Prize for his research on biology (namely the structure and diversity of antibodies). Edelman summarizes his almost militantly naturalistic and materialistic theory of consciousness in *Wider Than the Sky*.

Imagine an impressionist painting employing pointillism. In pointillism, thousands of dots of paint are arrayed such that when one stands at a distance from the painting, one sees an integrated picture. Our perception integrates the individual points into a Gestalt. Imagine, too, that the picture were one of the young woman–old woman perceptual Gestalt. When one concentrates, one can see a young woman, but when one focuses on a different context, the perception of the old woman emerges. One can shift attention back and forth between the two images.

Now note that if one-tenth of the points making up the picture were randomly turned off, the overall integrity of one's perception would not be affected. If those were turned back on and another one-tenth were activated, again the picture would not be compromised. This quality is known as "degeneracy" (p. 43). *Degeneracy* is the quality of being able to produce a particular mental representation by numerous combinations of underlying dots. The same picture could be presented even though an exact replication of exact same points might never be repeated.

The brain produces a flow of consciousness by a complex interaction of neurons stimulated by environment, associations (e.g., prefrontal association cortex), memories of the immediate past and present scenes (e.g., hippocampus), neurons in the inner-brain areas responsible for motion (e.g., basal ganglia, cerebellum, and thalamus), other brain areas, and body. The relationships among brain areas are crucial to thought and memory, not the firing of individual cells or even patterns of cells or the activation of discrete neural circuits. There is "degeneracy" in the circuits and neurons. Different neurons and circuits can produce the same concepts, mental images, or memories—just as different dots could produce the same perception of the impressionist painting—because the different neurons and circuits have the same relationships to each other.

It is similar relationships among neurons (not merely the firing of specific neurons) that form the same memory—or virtually the same. Perhaps different associations, thoughts, feelings, or situations shift the relationships, or perhaps attention directs input to different aspects of the impressionist pointillism picture. In these cases, the memory shifts and evolves.

In addition, different areas in the brain are integrated into a common integrated perception through "reentrant pathways" (p. 39). These are internal loops from cortex to inner brain to cortex and back again. Reentrant pathways are not like paths taken by NASCAR drivers looping in well-confined paths. Reentrant pathways are more like the paths of bumper-car drivers. Generally they may move counterclockwise, but their paths wind helter-skelter and rarely overlap from circuit to circuit.

Edelman has developed a theory of mind, brain, and consciousness. He calls it a "theory of neuronal group selection (TNGS)" (pp. 39–40) because its principles are based on Darwin's ideas that survival fitness drives system change. (Obviously, Darwin did not apply his theory of selection to describe the operation of neurons.) Edelman's theory describes how some relationships among neurons survive and others do not.

Edelman attempts to explain mind and consciousness depending solely on what is known about the structure and function of the brain and on what is being discovered by new tools of brain science. These new findings include microbiological findings about how neurons work, what neurotransmitters they emit and how those neurotransmitters operate, and how cell biology is influenced by DNA and the genetic code. They also include findings that measure the functioning of areas of the brain.

Different "core states" (p. 45) do not represent an image or concept in a one-to-one correspondence. Many different core states can produce a given image or concept. Let's look at an experiment summarized by Edelman that shows that (a) different neural firing can produce the same conscious experience, (b) the brain integrates information (represented by related activity in widely separate brain areas), and (c) human conscious experience seems to be unique.

Edelman's experiment uses (pp. 108–112) binocular rivalry. Our eyes see slightly different images continually. Our brain tries to reconcile the two images into one perceived visual image. The study enhanced the rivalry between the different images cast on left and right retina by having a person stare at a pattern of right-angle crossed lines. The vertical lines were red; the horizontal ones, blue. The participant wore glasses with one red lens (allowing the retina to see only the blue lines, which were horizontal and seem purple) and one blue lens (allowing that retina to see only the red lines, which were vertical and seem purple). The brain, of course, continually tried to put the images together. Because the rivalry between the retinal images was so keen, the brain could not blend the images. People perceived the vertical lines. Then perhaps a few seconds later they perceived the horizontal lines. Back and forth, irregularly. In the study, participants indicated perceiving the vertical lines by pressing a switch with one hand. When they perceived the horizontal lines, they pressed a switch with the other hand. (They never pressed both switches at the same time.)

I have used the word "perceive" to mean that the participant is aware of or conscious of seeing. Actually, the light was being seen, or sensed, continually by both eyes. Thus, by this method, what one was conscious of seeing could be separated from what one actually saw. Magnetoencephalography (MEG) was used to measure brain activity. Mathematical methods integrating MEG data revealed the portions of the brain operating when the participant reported perceiving horizontal or vertical lines and the portions of the brain operating when the person did not report seeing one (or the other) lines. Other mathematical methods can detect when brain areas far away from perception or visual sensation sites were activated in coordination with seeing or perceiving.

The results were remarkable. First, when the vertical lines were *reported* to have been perceived (for example), different pathways and areas were stimulated each time perception shifted from vertical (to horizontal and back again) to vertical. Thus, each instance of perceiving exactly the same vertical lines was produced by completely different underlying neural events. It is the *relationships among the neurons*—like randomly selected points in an impressionist painting—rather than specific neurons or pathways that give rise to perception. Second, different areas in the brain—even at considerable distances apart—were highly correlated with the perception of vertical lines. For instance, some areas of the brain perceive vertical edges. Others perceive horizontal edges. Some perceive brightness. Some, color. Some, thickness of lines. In short, the brain is marvelously integrated, and it integrates information from all over the cortex. Also, as with the reports of vertical lines, the relationships among the neurons—not the specific neurons themselves—were important. Third, not only were pathways within a single participant unique, but no two participants showed the same brain *activity* patterns when perceiving vertical lines.

RELATIONSHIPS

Edelman's work on consciousness suggests one additional lesson: Relationships are important. It is not the specific neurons or brain areas that are important. It is their relationships to each other that are important.

Physicists have shown how entangled particles interact, even if separated at great distance, because of their previously established relationship with each other. From a social science point of view, we can now see that relationships are of fundamental importance within the brain. If we can be as bold as some of the theologian physicists, we might suggest the same analogy. Nature is relational at its core.

In this section on consciousness, we have shown, using Edelman's research and theorizing, how a probabilistic model of brain activity can produce conscious experiences that consist of mental images and processes that are repeatable and seem "real." In the chapter thus far, I have argued that physics,

biology, and now psychological science (looking only to neuroscience as a representative of psychological science) have converged in laying the groundwork for how a scientifically impregnated society can gestate and then give birth to a replacement of religion: secular spirituality. Secular spirituality is about relationships. (We saw how important that was in Edelman's theorizing.) It also provides an explanatory scheme, or sense of meaning, that is rooted in the unpredictable, greater-than-thou, ephemeral, and uncontrollable idea of something unseen. Yet it provides a connection with things that are very visible, tangible, and realistic. These serve as the elements of spirituality in modern secular society.

The Transformation of Psychology of Religion Into the Psychology of Religion and Spirituality
Definitions of Spirituality

Spirituality is hard to define (Zinnbauer et al., 1997). It seems to involve personal experience, but what kinds of personal experience? Spirituality is a closeness or connection with some object. What kind of object? One reason spirituality might be hard to define is that the object of closeness and connection is not carefully specified. I have identified four objects and thus four types of spirituality. (There might be others, which would give rise to other types of spirituality.) God (as different religions conceive of God) is the object of closeness and connection in religious spirituality. Each of the three secular spiritualities has an object that its corresponding science says, at its core, is indeterminant, uncontrollable, and awe inspiring and yet yields clear observables.

- Humanistic spirituality
- Environmental or nature spirituality
- Cosmos spirituality (because people might even think beyond the "cosmos" I also call this transcendent spirituality)

These are the objects to which people seek closeness, connection, and relationship: God, humankind, nature or environment, and the cosmos. These four spiritualities correspond to four causal and cultural phenomena—religion and three sciences: (a) psychological science, (b) subatomic physics and biology, and (c) cosmological physics, respectively.

Our field was originally conceived as the psychology of religion (Starbuck, 1899). Scientists studied the way individuals and religious groups related to the Divine and to each other. However, in recent years, our field has become the psychology of religion *and spirituality*. Witness the American Psychological Association Division 36 journal, the *Psychology of Religion and Spirituality*.

The shift in worldview that came about due to the discoveries in relativistic and quantum physics, biology, and neuroscience has led to a shift. No longer is it merely that one's relationship with the Divine is filled with awe, wonder, and uncertainty. Now, the cosmos is full of wonder and awe (i.e., cosmos spirituality). Nature at the level of particle physics or string theory and both molecular biology and evolution provides a similar sense of wonder, awe, and fundamental indeterminacy (i.e., nature spirituality). Psychological science has developed to the extent that people do not merely equate psychology with psychotherapy or psychoanalysis. Instead, now psychological science often is associated with brain images, neuroscience, biological roots of behavior, behavioral genetics, and even cognitive neuroscience. Psychology as psychotherapy has been replaced by a psychological science full of awe, wonder, and indeterminacy (i.e., humanistic spirituality).

Because of the development and discoveries in the various sciences, spirituality is defined differently. It has gained popular acceptance because it "makes sense" given the multiple ways the modern physics, modern biology, and modern psychological science.

Why Are We So Optimistic?

We appear to be increasingly evolving into a spiritual culture. This is not merely because we have had a twentieth century of scientific progress. Rather, some scientific developments—notably, the nuclear bomb and biological warfare—have ushered in an age of anxiety around the 1950s. But in recent decades, we seem to have ignored the age of anxiety and have once again taken up a narrative of progress.

There is so much evidence of evil in the world that this seems startling. Baumeister, Bratslavsky, Finkenauer, and Vohs (2001) summarized a principle in life: The bad is stronger than the good. People appear to be hardwired by evolution to give special attention to any negative event in life. If we do not attend to a positive event, we merely miss out on a reward, but if we do not attend to a negative event, it very well could kill us. Thus, attending to present events that could be negative or threatening provides an evolutionary selective advantage. In the present, perceiving the negative is rewarded. To overcome one bad event requires five or more good events (Baumeister et al., 2001).

But, then, how can people today be so optimistic about the future? Why do people hope for a breakthrough to a more positive humanity? Why do we believe—against a realistic probability—the likelihood of finding a beneficent E. T.? Why do we count on the likelihood of progress?

The answer is that just as survival rewards attending to the bad events that occur in the present, it also rewards hope in the future. Without hope, little progress can happen. Without hope, we do not look for progress, so we often cannot take advantage of it when it occurs. This leads us (presumably due to its selective advantage) to look for positive in the future. We ignore the instances of lack of progress or even of moral regress, and we focus on the evidence for hope. That focus keeps us moving forward rather than resting on our laurels and not pursuing new horizons.

This suggests that spirituality will be pursued vigorously. Religion, which is more conservative than spirituality, will be maintained by societies and people within the societies who are concerned with risk and lack of stability. Spirituality is defined by Koenig, McCullough, and Larson (2001) as "unmoored." Spirituality is more about change than stability—going with the flow rather than being tied to the dock—and more about the future than the past. Spirituality is pursued by the adventuresome. Religious spirituality is an adventurous mindset within the boundaries of religion. But the more speculative secular spiritualities come from the secular and scientific roots of culture: psychological science and multiculturalism, which fuel humanistic spirituality; biology, which fuels environmental and nature spirituality; and relativistic physics, which fuels cosmos spirituality. Popular science and science fiction in the entertainment media fuel the transmission of the secular scientific spiritualities.

Conclusion

Let me speculate about the shape of the future of the psychology of religion and spirituality on the basis of the line of reasoning I have developed in this chapter. Importantly, I believe that there is a future. Religion and spirituality are not going to be reduced to physics, biology, neuroscience, or psychological science. With that in mind, let's tackle three points in conclusion.

The Future for New Researchers in the Field of the Psychology of Religion and Spirituality

We are in a time of transition. We are not in a full-fledged scientific revolution, but we might learn from examining such revolutions. Philosopher of science Thomas Kuhn (1970) examined past scientific revolutions and showed that established scientists usually did not participate with gusto in a scientific revolution. Established scientists usually (though not always) continued with their established programs of research. As philosopher of science Imre Lakatos (1978) noted, these programs tended to be either degenerating or vibrant. Degenerating programs were those that were finding their peripheral propositions shown untrue, their midlevel propositions attacked, and their core propositions besieged. Scientists in degenerating programs of research were revising their theories. However, other programs of research were more vibrant. In those, although peripheral propositions might be under attack, the core was secure; normal science could revise the periphery and continue to map out questions. I believe that the psychology of religion is a vibrant program of research, not a degenerating one. However, no field can remain stagnant. The attention to spirituality will inevitably necessitate the increased study by established researchers of religious spirituality.

Kuhn showed that new researchers who recently enter a field under siege or who are in training to enter that field tend to embrace the new. New researchers have little to risk. They can afford to take chances on research and still—if things do not work out—reshape and redeem their careers. I believe, then, that lots of new researchers will invest heavily in the psychology of spirituality—especially involving human spirituality, nature spirituality, and cosmos spirituality.

However, personal beliefs and values also direct people toward research and scientific careers on certain topics. Many religious people are drawn to science (though they seem, by surveys, to be a minority relative to nonreligious people). Still, religious values will continue to push people to study psychology of religion and religious spirituality, just as others are pushed by their more spiritual and secular values to study psychology of spirituality.

The Future of the Psychology of Religion Will Be Increasingly Relational

Besides focusing more attention on the study of the psychology of religious spirituality, I believe that the psychology of religion will also be more relational. The interconnectivity of particles in multiple simultaneous states suggests that life is relational. That is clearly true in studying the life of humans in relationship with the Sacred. More relational models will be articulated in a similar mode as Shults

and Sandage's (2006) relational spirituality and as our model of relational spirituality and forgiveness (Davis, Hook, & Worthington, 2008).

In addition, the relationships between and among religions will become increasingly important. There are many social, political, and technological reasons for this, but many of these reasons exist today because of scientific and technological advances and because of implications from relativistic and quantum mechanical principles that relativized time and space, energy and mass, and created a picture of reality that has undermined concrete metaphors replacing them with probabilistic ones. Like quantum particles, multiple religions coexist in multiple geographical regions, political entities, and socioeconomic strata. When we attend to the conflicts—such as when news reports that a riot has broken out between Shiite and Sunni people in Iraq—the measurement (i.e., observation) of the event collapses our attention on the conflict and in essence gives it substance—a sense of reality that we were unaware of previously. Furthermore, when the conflict erupts in Iraq, like subatomic particles connected because of entanglement, conflicts can erupt in other geographical areas (within and outside the country), political entities (e.g., other countries), and socioeconomic strata.

We are interconnected more each day around the world. *The World Is Flat*, claimed columnist Thomas L. Friedman (2005). It has been leveled by technology in the form of communication and information technology, transportation, and economic system. Individualism and collectivism (Oyserman, Coon, & Kemmelmeir, 2002) affect religious and spiritual experiences, and they are being brought together with increasing frequency in the flat world. The impact of each and on the permeability of the systems of religion as individualistic and collectivistic cultures interact will provide many challenges for psychologists of religion in future generations.

Development of psychological measurement is always crucial to the transformation of science (Galison, 2003). Brain-scanning equipment has allowed a study of the coordination of brain states with subjective experiences. Neuroscientists have located centers of the brain that are activated when religious or spiritual experiencing, meditation, prayer, or worship occurs. Of course, few people hold to a reductionist view that religious experiences are at one with brain states (Jeeves & Brown, 2009), but these brain functions and structures are correlated with spiritual experiences. Development of new technologies for measurement might open even more revelatory findings.

The existence of multiple simultaneous states suggests that theology and psychological scientists might be describing the same phenomena on occasion, but by discussing the phenomenon in one language—that of theology or of psychological science—the issues become crystallized around that discipline. The psychology of religion needs to develop a methodology for discussing topics of mutual interest in ways that allow the mutual flow of information across boundaries—from theology to psychology and vice versa.

Mystery and awe drive the field. Sometimes today, the sense I have picked up, especially from some recent graduates, is that the territory of the psychology or religion has been mapped (except for those few troublesome clouds) and that the only exploration left is in the psychology of spirituality. Yet if we have learned anything from the study of physics, we have learned that there is always a transformative discovery just around the corner. Recall Lord Kelvin. Let us not lose the awe and mystery of what we have discovered, and let us heed the lessons of physics in maintaining a focus on discovery in the psychology of religion and religious spirituality.

Future of the Psychology of Religion and Spirituality

In speculating about the future of research in the psychology of spirituality, we must remain cognizant of Berger et al.'s finding that most people are more involved in religion than in spirituality (see Berger et al., 1999). Namely, religion is alive and well worldwide and permeates countries, socioeconomic groups, and political systems. He describes interest in spirituality, however, as being largely localized to the academy, intellectual, and professional classes, and geographically concentrated in Western Europe and places influenced by Western European intellectual tradition—such as liberalism in the United States. Berger et al. argue that writers, artists, researchers, and university professors often believe that religion has heard its own death knell because those intellectuals travel to other countries and interact with people largely in the same profession as they—professors with professors, business people with business people. When interest in spirituality is localized by social class or profession, such international exposure provides an incorrect assessment of how widespread an interest in "unmoored" spirituality is—that is, spirituality with connections cut off from traditional religion. In England in 2001, according to Wikipedia, the population at the time of the 2001 census was 49,138,831 (http://en.wikipedia.org/wiki/Demographics_of_England; accessed June 16, 2009). We find that about 42 million claim Christianity; 9 million, none; 1.5 million, Muslim; 0.5 million, Hindu; 0.39 million, Jedi Knight; 0.33 million, Sikh; 0.26 million, Jewish; 0.15 million, Buddhist; and 0.3 million, Spiritualist (http://www.vexen.co.uk/UK/religion.html). Clearly, even in England, in which few people actively participate in their religion, the major religions do not seem to be replaced by spiritualist religions. However, the numbers of spiritual-but-not-religious people are growing and are currently not insubstantial.

Because we live in a technologically, interpersonally, and culturally interrelated flat world, it is likely that religionists, secularists, and spiritualists will interact and will influence each other across all boundaries. The influence of spirituality on traditional religions will likely grow. But we also note that the influence of traditional religion on spirituality may also grow. We know from our experience in the world—from cosmological and quantum physics, from microbiological, genetic, and evolutionary science, and from psychological science—we do not live in a closed system. Boundaries will be mutually penetrated. Ideologies will spread out. It is likely that humanistic, naturalistic, and cosmological (or transcendental) spiritualities will be increasingly embraced, but religious spirituality will also thrive as the systems interpenetrate. For the foreseeable future, we will be a psychology of both religion and spirituality. The psychology of religion and spirituality will continue to increase the study of different nonreligious spirituality even as it must continue to study religions.

Final Point

We need a psychology of religion and spirituality, not just a psychology of religion or a psychology of spirituality or a secular psychology that is gutted of religious and spiritual attention. Readers of this chapter are in the academy, which Berger et al. (1999) name as one of those bastions of secularism and of spirituality. We should not delude ourselves into believing that religion is passé. Instead, we should turn our attention to it with renewed vigor, even as we turn our attention to the four different types of spirituality with enthusiasm.

Overview

In the present chapter, I argued that general culture—witness the science fiction entertainment industry and results of the 2000 census for examples—is strongly influenced by the assumptions that have derived from modern science. Subatomic and relativistic physics and psychological science and neuroscience have fueled these three general cultural beliefs: (1) big numbers in time and space make anything probabilistic become likely; (2) we can be optimistic that this will eventuate in progress; (3) and life is all about relationships.

Concerning (1) and (2), I questioned the inherent optimism on the basis of realism. Big numbers do not always lead to positive outcomes, and we could imagine negative outcomes just as easily as positive outcomes and assume they would be inevitable. However, on the side of optimism, I noted that evolution selects for hope, which motivates inquiry and intentional adaptation. We do live in an open system, and by exploring and seeking to optimize communication across system boundaries, we provide more discovery opportunities.

The third proposition, that life is all about relationships, not only accords with postmodern philosophy (and thus finds resonance with many in our world that straddles modernity and postmodern living) but also the relationality of life might yield solutions to traditional puzzles like the nature of consciousness. Furthermore, and of focal interest to the present essay and Handbook, relationality provides the key to developing new studies into spirituality. We must not only attend to religious spirituality but also to forms of spirituality that have derived (I argue) from the modern sciences. Based on the three types of science I reviewed, I suggested that four types of spirituality will be the focus of attention. These are (a) religious spirituality (from traditional religion and based on closeness and connection to God), (b) human spirituality (rooted in psychological science), (c) nature or environment spirituality (rooted in physics and biology), and (d) cosmos or transcendental spirituality (rooted in cosmological physics). Each of these is defined in terms of close or intimate connection or relationship with a different object, and each has been formed primarily by the wonder, awe, and lack of determinacy found in different fields of study—theology, psychological science, biological science, and physics, respectively. Thus, the future of our field, which has been traditionally the psychology of religion, has made its shift. The field will soon become, if it has not already, the psychology of religion and spirituality.

References

Aharonov, Y., & Bohm, D. (1959). Significance of electromagnetic potentials in the quantum theory. *Physical Review, 115*(3), 485–491.

Baumeister, R. F., Bratslavsky, E., Finkenauer, C., & Vohs, K. D. (2001). Bad is stronger than good. *Review of General Psychology, 5*, 323–370.

Berger, P. L., Sacks, J., Martin, D., Weiming, T., Weigel, G., Davie, G., & An-Naim, A. A. (Eds.). (1999). *The deseculariztion of the world: Resurgent religion and world politics.* Washington, DC: Ethics and Public Policy Center.

Bell, J. S. (1964). On the Einstein Podolsky Rosen paradox. *Physics, 1*, 195–200.

Bohm, D. (2002). *The essential David Bohm* (Lee Nichol, Ed.). London: Routledge.

Bohr, N. (1972/2006). *Collected works, Vol. 1–12.* Amsterdam: Elsevier.

Coughlan, G. D., Dodd, J. E., & Gripaios, B. M. (2006). *The ideas of particle physics: An introduction for scientists* (3rd ed.). Cambridge, England: Cambridge University Press.

Darwin, C. (2009). *The origin of species: By means of natural selection, or the Preservation of favoured races in the struggle for life.* London: John Murray. (Original work published 1859).

Davis, D. E., Hook, J. N., & Worthington, E. L., Jr. (2008). Relational spirituality and forgiveness: The roles of attachment to God, religious coping, and viewing the transgression as a desecration. *Journal of Psychology and Christianity, 27*, 293–301.

Dick, S. J. (1996). *The biological universe: The twentieth century extraterrestrial life debate and the limits of science.* Cambridge, England: Cambridge University Press.

Edelman, G. (2004). *Wider than the sky: The phenomenal gift of consciousness.* New Haven, CT: Yale University Press.

Einstein, A. (1905). Zur Elektrodynamik bewegter Körper [On the electrodynamics of moving bodies]. *Annalen der Physik, 17*, 891.

Everett, H., III. (1957). "Relative state" formulation of quantum mechanics. *Review of Modern Physics, 29*, 454–462.

Friedman, T. L. (2005). *The world is flat: A brief history of the twenty-first century.* New York: Farrar, Strauss and Giroux.

Galison, P. (2003). *Einstein's clocks, Poincaré's maps: Empires of time.* New York: W. W. Norton.

Greene, B. (1999). *The elegant universe: Superstrings, hidden dimensions, and the quest for the ultimate theory.* New York: W. W. Norton.

Heisenberg, W. (1958). *Physics and philosophy: The revolution in modern science.* London: Goerge Allen & Unwin.

Herrick, J. A. (2008). *Scientific mythologies: How science and science fiction forge new religious beliefs.* Downers Grove, IL: InterVarsity Press.

Horgan, J. (1996). *The end of science: Facing the limits of knowledge in the twilight of the scientific age.* Boston: Addison Wesley (Helix Books).

Jeeves, M., & Brown, W. (2009). *Neuroscience, psychology and religion: Illusions, delusions, and realities about human nature.* Philadelphia: Templeton Foundation Press.

Kirkpatrick, L. A. (2005). *Attachment, evolution, and the psychology of religion.* New York: Guilford Press.

Koenig, H. G., McCullough, M. E., & Larson, D. (2001). *Handbook of religion and health.* London: Oxford University Press.

Kuhn, T. S. (1970). *The structure of scientific revolutions* (2nd ed). Chicago: University of Chicago Press.

Lakatos, I. (1978). *The methodology of scientific research programmes: Philosophical papers, Volume 1.* Cambridge, England: Cambridge University Press.

McCullough, M. E. (2008). *Beyond revenge: The evolution of the forgiveness instinct.* San Francisco: Jossey-Bass.

Michelson, A. A., & Morley, E. W. (1887). On the relative motion of the Earth and the luminiferous ether. *American Journal of Science, 34,* 333–345.

Mischel, W., & Brooks, D. (2011). The news from psychological science: A conversation between David Brooks and Walter Mischel. *Perspectives on Psychological Science, 6*(6), 515–520.

Oyserman, D., Coon, H. M., & Kemmelmeier, M. (2002). Rethinking individualism and collectivism: Evaluation of theoretical assumptions and meta-analyses. *Psychological Bulletin, 128,* 3–72.

Peebles, P. J. E., & Ratra, B. (2003). The cosmological constant and dark energy. *Reviews of Modern Physics, 75,* 559–606.

Schrödinger, E. (1935, November). Die gegenwärtige Situation in der Quantenmechanik [The present situation in quantum mechanics]. *Naturwissenschaften, 23,* 807–812; 823–828; 844–849.

Shults, F. L., & Sandage, S. J. (2006). *Transforming spirituality: Integrating theology and psychology.* Grand Rapids, MI: Baker Academic.

Starbuck, E. D. (1899). *The psychology of religion.* New York: Charles Scribner's Sons.

Thompson, W. (Lord Kelvin). (1900, April). *Nineteenth century clouds over the dynamical theory of heat and light.* Royal Institution lecture, London, April 27, 1900.

Wigner, E. (1960). The unreasonable effectiveness of mathematics in the natural sciences. *Communications on Pure and Applied Mathematics, 13*(1), 1–14.

Zinnbauer, B. J., Pargament, K. I., Cole, B., Rye, M. S., Butter, E. M., Belavich, T. G., et al., (1997). Religion and spirituality: Unfuzzying the fuzzy. *Journal for the Scientific Study of Religion, 36,* 549–564.

CHAPTER 5

Complementarities in Physics and Psychology

C. Edward Richards

Abstract

This article explores one of the profound complementarities in quantum physics and psychology: the reflexive nature of observation both on the objective (physics) and the subjective (psychological) side. It seeks to provide a logical chain of evidence from quantum mechanics to quantum effects in biological systems, to quantum effects in neurological systems. It then discusses the implications for psychology and pedagogy. Should quantum theory become the dominant paradigm for explaining consciousness, the implications for psychology are profound indeed. However, neuroplasticity, whether explained by classical or quantum effects, has already launched a revolution in our understanding of how changing one's intentions and thoughts affects both behavior and the brain.

Key Words: quantum physics, psychology, pedagogy, consciousness, neuroplasticity

Introduction

This chapter explores one of the profound complementarities in quantum physics and psychology—the reflexive nature of observation both on the objective (physics) and the subjective (psychological) side. It reviews a few of the more interesting features of quantum mechanics, recent research on quantum effects in biological systems, and finally proposes some implications for both psychology and pedagogy. At least two kinds of arguments support a comparison between quantum physics and psychology. The first, and weaker of the two, argues that physics is the one discipline to which all others owe primacy. Quantum physics is well established and highly predictive, and much of our modern technology depends upon it. All other disciplines from biology to psychology would benefit from working theoretically by analogy. The second and more powerful argument is that quantum physics describes reality as it is—all other levels of reality, including chemistry, biology, and psychology, are necessarily quantum. Thus,

other disciplines are merely perspectives on the one reality. It follows that, to the extent we really want to understand life and consciousness, we need to use a theoretical model that actually explains aspects of life and consciousness that the classical model cannot explain.

Our discussion in this chapter first explores a few ways in which thoughtful quantum physicists first saw and discussed the reason for an analogy between quantum mechanics and consciousness and then turns to research that actually might support a focus on the latter argument. Finally, we discuss the implications for psychology and pedagogy.

Niels Bohr, commenting on provocative similarities between reflective thinking and quantum physics, once mused:

> The apparent contrast between the continuous onward flow of associative thinking and the preservation of the unity of the personality exhibits a suggestive analogy with the relation between the wave description of motions of material particles,

governed by the superposition principle, and their indestructible individuality.

(*cited in Rosenblum & Kuttner*, 2006, p. 193)

If one observes the content of a thought (its position), this act of observation will have an immediate effect upon the speed of its movement in the mind, holding it as it were, before the mind's gaze and sharpening its focus; conversely, watching a thought arise and pass away from consciousness (its motion) has a constraining effect on one's ability to focus sharply upon it. By analogy, the uncertainty principal in quantum physics confirms this relationship between method, observer, and outcome: by observing the position of a subatomic particle, you cannot accurately describe its motion. Conversely, observing the motion of the particle restricts one's ability to identify its position. The choice of devices we use to record these two features of consciousness and quantum behavior have an immediate impact on what we pay attention to—and what we find (Stapp, 2007).

Additionally, investigating the materialist underpinnings of naïve realism in both physics and psychology exposes the persistent enigma of communication. If a mind does exist separate from a brain, how do they then communicate with each other? Furthermore, how can a "nonmaterial" mind influence a material brain? Bell's theorem, which was articulated to establish the minimum conditions for Einstein's realist position that things really exist and they are separable has been thoroughly experimentally tested and falsified, much to Bell's dismay. Einstein once sarcastically quipped, "When I look up at the moon, I'd like to believe it is really there." A number of experimental tests of Bell's theorem support the finding that quantum particles are neither real nor separate. Given the fact of entanglement, how then does one entangled particle communicate its simultaneous change in spin to its twin—even when that twin is a billion light years away? The hidden variable theory proposed by Einstein, Podolsky, and Rosen (EPR) implies some as yet unknown variable that causes the entanglement. Numerous experiments have shown that this solution would require the unknown variable to exert its influence faster than the speed of light. Thus far, based on available research evidence, physicists prefer to accept nonlocality over the hidden variable theory.

Similarly problematic, a photon in the double-slit experiment generates a wave interference pattern that is essentially a probability distribution. In classical physics, the immediate question arises: "a probability distribution of what?" However, in the quantum world there is no "what." The probability distribution of the photon and the description of where one can locate "it" are identical. On the hard anvil of this conundrum, conventional metaphors completely break down. When we think of a wave—for example, ripples in a lake—the substratum is the water. Nobel Prize laureate John Wheeler's famous quip "A bit is it" turns out to be wrong.[1] The quantum world has no substratum, no object, no bit—only a probability distribution of where it might be found—*if you looked*. Isn't it relatively fascinating that while thought has correlates in the brain, thought itself has no color, shape, mass, energy, or location? Paradoxically, creative thought acts in the world: it produced quantum theory, Mona Lisa's smile, and the San Francisco Bridge.

Most physicists now agree that no sharp boundary exists between the quantum and the classical world. To make this point crystal clear, physicist Anton Zeilinger (2008), writing in the science journal *Nature*, observed:

> For example (as is well known from early quantum mechanics and is now supported by experiment), there is no fixed boundary between the classical and the quantum world. The same object can behave as a quantum system in one situation, for example when it is isolated from the environment, or as a classical system in another. Fullerenes and even biological macromolecule are typical examples, showing quantum interference in two-slit experiments whereas they can be seen in a tunneling electron microscope, for instance, at classically well defined locations. (p. 3)

As Zeilinger confirms, the experimental conditions and the observer determine whether an object is classical or quantum. The limit on the size of object is an experimental limit, *not a theoretical limit*. Furthermore, quantum activity is ongoing beneath the apparent solidity and separable appearance of large objects.

Our final example from the quantum mechanics literature concerns the notion of quantum tunneling. Lenard Susskind, Nobel laureate and professor of physics at Stanford University, describes tunneling in an intuitively easy way to understand. Imagine a series of uniform hills—if drawn on paper, they would look like a wave pattern. Now imagine a small marble at the top of one of the hills being given a slight push; it rolls down one side and back up the other, back down and up, and so on until the marble comes to rest at its lowest point. In classical physics the marble is constrained by its original speed, mass, and gravity. It eventually comes to rest at the bottom of the valley between the hills. In quantum mechanics it is possible—although counterintuitive—to "tunnel" through the hill and have the marble appear in the next valley over, without having to climb back up the surface. In other words, quantum tunneling occurs when an object passes through a barrier, even though it doesn't have enough energy to do so according to classical physics. Another, related quantum phenomena is that an elementary particle, under specific conditions, can be observed to make a ghost of itself in another location that has the same electromagnetic signature as the original: one particle is a virtual particle and the other is the original particle. Yet the ghost-twin virtual particle behaves in exactly the same way as the original. Collectively, physicists describe the preceding examples as "quantum weirdness." As Niels Bohr suggested, several such analogies between consciousness and quantum mechanics lead us to consider whether advances in one field might provoke an advance in the other. Rosenblum and Kuttner (2006) concur, arguing these analogies are now providing testable experiments between the subjective realm of consciousness in psychology and the objective realm of consciousness in quantum physics (p. 194).

We began this inquiry with a review of quantum mechanics and will now follow with parallel developments in biological systems, including recent developments in neurobiology. The final section proposes a theory of learning in psychology using self-awareness training as a reflexive example and a line of inquiry for potential testable hypotheses consistent with the previous review of research.

Quantum Physics and the Enigma of Consciousness

This section[2] begins with a necessary distinction between what we might call subjective consciousness (psychology) and objective consciousness (the facts of quantum physics).

If we posit the existence of an objective consciousness that moves faster than the speed of light, it violates Planck's constant and is unobservable according to the mathematics of quantum physics. Yet what is unobservable may indeed be inferred to exist despite the fact that experiments to detect faster-than-light particles have not been successful so far (e.g., zero energy tachyons). While "beforeness" might not be an appropriate category to describe

reality prior to the big bang, current explanations that describe the entire universe appearing out of emptiness are evocative of the problem of consciousness in the brain. For example, Filk and von Muller (2009) use the term *status nascendi* (state of birth) to describe a kind of "coming into existence" without observable antecedents. In this case, it seems the coming into existence of our universe (of high-energy particles) and the coming into existence of consciousness (human thought) also have interesting parallels that they explore at length in their provocative essay.

The big bang theory of the universe is also known as the Singularity. Another way of understanding it is that at the very first moment of the universe, Einstein's famous equation of general relativity ($E = mc^2$) fails as mass becomes zero and energy becomes infinite (Steinhardt & Turok, 2007, p. 37). One explanation proposed for the emergence of time is the Hartle-Hawking argument: the big bang was not the abrupt switching on of time at some singular first moment, but the emergence of time from space in an ultrarapid but nevertheless continuous manner. From a human perspective, the big bang was very much a sudden, explosive origin of space, time, and matter. But Hartle-Hawkings posit, if we look very, very closely at that first tiny fraction of a second of existence, we find no precise on-off switch for the beginning of time but rather a Zeno-like paradoxical quality of always-halving-but-never-arriving. Thus, the Hartle-Hawking theory of the origin of the universe seems to say two contradictory things: first, time did not always exist; and second, there was no first moment of time. To paraphrase a sly observation by Roger Penrose, quantum mechanics makes absolutely no sense. (Penrose, 1994)

Perhaps quantum mechanics' weirdness in the spooky-action-at-a-distance, quantum tunneling, and entanglement problem may be a window into those aspects or interpretations of indeterminacy that function outside of space/time/gravity constraints. Certainly, the trends in physics toward understanding the universe in terms of "information" rather than materiality are drawing closer to a view that sees consciousness or awareness as a fundamental unifying state. Information does not deny materialism. Rather, matter might be construed as an emergent property of information—and life, an emergent property of the interaction of complexity, information, space-time, and matter.

One major problem in this conversation is the urge of those who believe in deities of one kind or another, to conflate information with an

Informer—the old deus ex machina (God from the machine) problem rearing its unhappy head once again. It might be surprising to find that a substantial majority of highly regarded physicists subscribe to an anthropic principle—not in the traditional theistic sense, but in the sense that the universe is self-aware. However, for most of these physicists, nothing extra is implied.

The Anthropic Principle

We have choices to make about how we go about investigating the world around us. Today, a number of highly intelligent and thoughtful scientists follow some version of the *anthropic principle* as a starting point in their work. The anthropic principle essentially argues that the universe we experience is the way it is because we are here to observe it—or conversely, if the universe weren't compatible with life, we wouldn't be here to observe it. To oversimplify, the entire universe exists to produce intelligent life forms that can study it. It is a fascinating proposition: the universe is intrinsically designed to evolve life forms capable of an ever-widening arc of self-knowledge and self-awareness. If this is true, then deepening our self-understanding and our understanding of the universe mirrors the intentionality of the universe. Again, it may be the case that mirror neurons reflect this higher order anthropic principle.[3] Physicist Amit Goswamit, among others, a proponent of the strong version of the anthropic principle, argues that the universe is a self-aware entity.[4]

The anthropic principle is not merely wishful thinking: in fact, it is a bit of an embarrassment for scientists. Our universe has evolved, according to the best astrophysicists, in dependence upon unbelievably precise and sensitive initial conditions. About 15 numbers called *physical constants* summarize these initial conditions. For example, Newton's law of gravity depends upon a gravitational constant that explains the strength of the attractive power of gravity. Three other very precise numbers explain the strong and weak nuclear forces. The speed of light is another well-known constant. Planck's constant fixes the smallest possible size of atoms and how far back into the history of the universe we can see. Together, these constants determine the shapes, sizes, and relationships of super nova and atoms, mosquitoes and sharks, water lilies and redwoods. The anthropic principle argues that an image of a universe as a chance event that is so exquisitely constrained by the mathematical constants of scientific discovery, constants not only true for all times and places in the universe but also required at very

precise levels of accuracy in order for the universe to have come into existence in the first place, violates the principle of Occam's razor—everything else equal "the simplest explanation is best." As noted physicist Freeman Dyson has dryly written, "...the universe in some sense must have known we were coming" (Dyson, 1979, p. 250).

Alan Guth of MIT has estimated that the occurrence of a big bang some 14 billion years ago would have required matter possess the very specific density of 1 part in about 10^{55}! For example, one exponent either way, say 10^{54} or 10^{56}, is sufficient to produce conditions that would have put an end to the universe before Earth or humanity could have evolved. Second, the big bang theory has a problem known as the horizon problem. No matter where one looks in the universe the big bang seems to have produced uniform background radiation. The big bang seems to have exploded all at once and in perfect symmetry. That fact implies 10^{83} detonators would have had to explode at precisely the same moment to produce the universe we now observe.

However, the sharpest challenge for physicists is known as *the singularity problem*. What precipitated the big bang in the first place? What was the first cause? Planck's constant prohibits us from having any knowledge of what occurred from Alpha time to $10-^{43}$ or what physicists call Planck's time. In plain English, during the first few microseconds of the universe, neither space nor time existed; therefore, these microseconds are essentially preexistent and unknowable. Even more problematic, how can one have a concept called *microseconds*, when neither space nor time yet existed? Even language fails us. Finally, we have a number of observational problems, including a huge amount of missing matter and energy, now called dark matter and dark energy.[5]

Regarding the existence of dark energy and matter, data from NASA's WMAP satellite support a two-decades-old theory (inflation) that the universe expanded rapidly from the size of a marble to billions of light years across in a trillionth of a second following its cataclysmic birth. Apparently, neither the speed of light, nor anything else for that matter, was yet a constant. According to the most recent WMAP data, normal matter, the stuff of people, planets, and pulsars, is only 4% of the combined matter and energy of the universe. Dark matter and dark energy comprise the remaining 96%. The WMAP data imply that the universe is vastly larger than the roughly 14 billion light year radius we can view from Earth; in fact, so much larger that we cannot even assume that the part we can see is representative of the composition of the rest of it. According to Stanford University physicist Leonard Susskind, "We and all that we can see, are no more than a tiny dot in an unimaginably large sea of space and time" (Vergano, 2006). Assuming these results hold, then the 14 billion light year radius of the singularity may not be singular at all and Planck's constant becomes a local horizon.[6] What we know about cosmology might be a mere hiccup in a vast cosmological sea of existence.

One universal feature of existence seems to be that whatever exists includes information as its fundamental characteristic—even thoughts qualify in this regard. Thus, thought can be considered as a subclass of information along with feelings, sensations and intuitions, entanglement, indeterminacy, and superposition. All subatomic particles, dark energy, and vacuums contain information. However, for information to come into existence, it too must be perpetually *status nascendi*. I leave it open to the reader to decide whether information exists absent an observer.

If self-awareness is an intrinsic quality of the universe, then our reflections are merely an expression of that generic quality—all human thought is the universe seeking to understand itself using human evolution to increase its capacity for self-reflection. From this radical view of reality, physics and psychology are merely the subjective and objective complements of self-discovery and the argument for a common theoretical approach is compelling.

Many physicists have explored and proposed ideas like those outlined earlier. Actually, a long tradition exists in which consciousness is considered a necessary condition for existence of the quantum world—at least since the Copenhagen interpretation.[7] Certainly one of the earliest, most extensive, and interesting exchanges between a psychologist and a physicist occurred in the letters between Wolfgang Pauli and Carl Jung (see Miller, 2009).

As another example, David Bohm (1980) introduced the parallel concepts of an *implicate* and *explicate* order. When physicists deal with the microscopic world of quantum mechanics, it is the implicate order that rules, and when they deal with the classical physics of the macroscopic, the explicate order prevails. As Vannini concludes, "according to Bohm, consciousness coincides with the implicate order" (2008, p. 169).

Physicists working at CERN with the Large Hadron Collider are seeking to push back their investigations into the formation of the universe to one-thirtieth of a billionth of a second before the big bang, when some infinitesimally small, undefined, ephemeral X exploded into what we now know as the universe. In the world of physics, emptiness is what is before time, space, and causality. There seems to be no connection to psychology whatsoever. Yet in the emerging field of psychology, which seeks to integrate experiences of *presence* into the life experience of clients as a state of awareness that is neither preoccupied with the past, nor absorbed in fantasies about the future, but is grounded in the body and the breath with an acute sense of immediacy. Hence, we may be able to close some ground between the psychological experience of presence defined as the timeless now, and emptiness defined as that condition existing prior to space, time, and causality. Recent experiments with the Zeno effect suggest that it is possible to postpone quantum randomness indefinitely with sustained attention to the initial condition. Analogously, this "backward" influence of attention on brain function puts to rest the old classical dualism between thought and brain: thought changes the mind of the thinker (Schwartz & Begley, 2002; Stapp, 2007).

In an effort to explain the problem of what happened before time, space, and causality, physicist Paul Davies quotes St. Augustine in stating that the world was made "not in time, but simultaneously with time." As Davies goes on to explain, the origin of the universe—what we now call the big bang—was not simply the sudden appearance of matter in an eternally preexisting void, but the coming into being of space-time itself. Space-time comes into being simultaneously with the cosmic origin. There was no "before," no endless ocean of time for a god, or a physical process, to wear itself out in infinite preparation.[8]

The systems perspective emphasizes the processes and relationships among the components of complex adaptive organisms—whether in physics, chemistry, biology, or psychology—and uses a common language to describe the behavior of the system. For example, in evolutionary biology one speaks of fitness landscapes and adaptation. At the same time, much of evolutionary theory uses the metaphorical language of effort, competition, and struggle, straitjacketing the theory itself with the causal determinism of classical physics. However, when one adds a feedback loop and describes the relationships between species and landscapes as mutually influenced, as, for example, in developmental biology, the language from the mathematics of complexity theory that speaks of attractors, basins of attraction, repellers, and trajectories has superior explanatory power. Thus, a new language is emerging that has been accelerated by the study of complex adaptive systems and developmental biology (Goodwin, 1994, chapter 6; Minelli, 2009). A parallel process is developing in the language of quantum mechanics and quantum explanations for biological and chemical processes. We now increasingly find the language of quantum effects—entanglement, decoherence, quantum tunneling, and the Zeno effect—sprinkled throughout the biological and psychological literature. While this transfer of quantum metaphor to psychology can admittedly range from the ridiculous to the sublime, it does speak to the compelling power of quantum theory that so many researchers use quantum mechanics in their own areas of research. It seems that the language of science has now superseded the language of religion and mythology—even as religion fights a rearguard action by explaining mysticism in the language of quantum mechanics.

We think we understand the world before us, and we function in it more or less reasonably well using antique Newtonian notions of causality—and for the most part it works. Paradoxically perhaps, the deepening appreciation for complex adaptive models and the subtle and profound hierarchy of emergent properties of reality are leading the most curious and speculative of researchers to align themselves with models that are more holistic and mirror the complexity they are finding in their area of expertise. Despite our fascination with quantum mechanics, one may still imagine that the Newtonian world is the "real deal" and that this quantum stuff is the esoteric realm of the fantastic and very, very small. Yet according to a growing number of physicists, including Nobel laureate Robert Laughlin, it is the other way around. Newtonian regularities emerge only because of underlying quantum structures that are themselves emergent properties of, as yet not understood, even more fundamental, and unifying structures, if string theory proves true (Laughlin, 2005).

Laughlin writes, "Since principles of organization—or more precisely, their consequences—can be laws, these can themselves organize into new laws, and so on. The laws of electron motion beget the laws of thermodynamics and chemistry, which beget the laws of crystallization, which beget the laws of engineering. The natural world [Newtonian world] is thus [embedded within] an interdependent hierarchy of descent" (Laughlin, 2005, p. 7). At this point in our understanding of physics, we do not know if it is "evolution all the way down"—and

all the way up—nor whether even the laws of quantum mechanics are local or apply to a multiverse (a reality comprised of infinite universes and perhaps many kinds of physics).

Laughlin goes on to say that a signature of emergent organizational phenomenon is a sharp phase transition. He cautions that the important thing to focus on is not the transition itself, but *the emergent exactness* that necessitates it (Laughlin, 2005, p. 40). A common example of phase transition is that of water as it goes from liquid to solid in the form of ice. Scientists are now making a major shift in research, moving from studying ever-smaller parts of the universe to understanding how nature organizes itself. Even fundamental things, in other words, are not necessarily absolutely fundamental. Laughlin argues that:

> From the reductionist standpoint, physical law is the motivating impulse of the universe. It does not come from anywhere and implies everything. From the emergentist perspective, physical law is a rule of collective behavior, it is a consequence of more primitive rules of behavior underneath (although it need not have been), and it gives one predictive power over a limited range of circumstances. Outside this range, it becomes irrelevant, supplanted by other rules that are either its children or its parents in a hierarchy of descent.
> (2005, p. 80)

Laughlin describes the classical and the quantum as emergent properties of nested levels of reality. But, he argues, even deeper, and as yet undiscovered levels may offer more fundamental explanations.

Perhaps no more radical findings in recent astrophysics have upended conventional thinking about the divide between the classical (macro) and the quantum (micro) worlds more than resolution of the debate about black holes and whether information escapes from them. The tale of the battle for the hearts and minds of the physics community is admirably recounted by Stanford University physicist Leonard Susskind (2008) in his eminently readable *The Black Hole Wars*, where he recounts his battle with Stephen Hawkings and explains how he discovered (with Dutch physicist Gerard 't Hooft) that the universe is a hologram and that quantum mechanical uncertainties function on the massive scales of black holes. If anything put the last nail in the coffin of size and decoherence constraining quantum effects in large bodies, Suskind's and 't Hooft's theoretical accomplishments have done so. Susskind concludes,

As weird as the Holographic Principle is—and it is very weird—it has become part of the mainstream of theoretical physics. It is no longer just a speculation about quantum gravity; it has become an everyday working tool, answering questions not only about quantum gravity but also about such prosaic things as the nuclei of atoms...I don't know anything less intuitive about the world than this. Getting our collective heads around the Holographic Principle is probably the biggest challenge that we physicists have had since the discovery of Quantum Mechanics. (pp. 301–305)

If we live in such a world as Laughlin and Susskind describe, then we need to become much more highly self-aware that our understanding of existence, and our own part in it, is highly provisional, depending on the level of analysis, and equally relational, depending on the subset of the universe we are examining. While Laughlin and Susskind are concerned with the black holes and the structure of the universe, it suggests that we also live in a world where a hierarchy of descent or ascent is but one dimension. Since we are, ourselves, an emergent property of life—and it is not at all certain that we are anywhere near the end of that process either—the possibilities for coevolution are increasingly real. Indeed, there is much more evidence that we are a transitory evolutionary species than a completed one—which implies an entirely new line of psychological inquiry where intention and consciousness can change the very nature of our being. And our being is itself redefined by a web of environments and relationships. Psychology, to the extent it deepens its response to the call of the quantum world, will become less tightly focused on ego and identity and more focused on the processes of formation, reformation, and polymorphism.

Quantum theory is absolutely the single best experimentally verified theory we have currently. Its predictive power is breathtakingly accurate—but the gaps are there and increasing. Many physicists have also believed it is an incomplete theory as did Schrodinger himself. What happens when our stories about ourselves no longer satisfy or work? Changing our creation stories—whether at the level of individuals or universes—expands our openness to other viewpoints, and our senses to other sources of input hitherto neglected (Morowitz, 2002).

Postmodernism has launched a powerful critique of the privileged position of the observer and, by doing so, has forced the observer back into the world as a participant. It is now widely accepted in science and social science that the mere presence of an observer influences what is observed. Now that we have established in principle no real size limits on quantum effects in large bodies are theoretically valid, it raises the question of whether any inroads have been made experimentally to demonstrate quantum effects in biological or "wet" systems.

Quantum Effects in Biological Systems

This section reviews some very recent research that has experimentally demonstrated plausible quantum effects in biological systems. We begin with research in plants, birds, reptiles, amphibians, and mammals and then turn to neurological arguments for quantum effects in the human brain. This digression seems to be an important part of the chain of evidence necessary to understand how it is plausible for quantum effects to occur in the mind-brain complex.

Darwin's theory of evolution is rooted in a methodological and philosophical paradigm of science that is founded upon classical Newtonian physics. This historical bias is well described by Robert Nadeau and Manas Kafatos in their book *The Nonlocal Universe* (1999):

> In Darwin's view, the struggle for existence occurs "between" an atomized individual organism and other atomized individual organisms in the same species, "between" an atomized individual organism of one species with that of a different species, or "between" and atomized individual organism and the physical conditions of life. (p. 108)

Thus, Darwins' biological evolutionary machine resembles the classical atomic theory of the interactions of discrete objects. The universal "struggle for life" is analogous to the universal presence of gravity. Although Darwin included the notion of randomness in his theory of mutation of species, his model remained essentially mechanistic.

The emergentist perspective now gaining a foothold in physics is also becoming more established in the biological sciences.[9] For example, from the study of microorganisms, we now know that they are so universal and ubiquitous at all levels of life, both on and within the very organisms of living systems, the distinction between "whole and parts" completely breaks down and must be replaced with the perspective that the whole and parts are within each other—all organisms are emergent aspects of the self-generative activity of life. The more sophisticated way to study organisms is "in their embedded relations to the whole" (Nadeau & Kafatos, 1999, p. 109). As one illustrative example close to home, the average human frame has approximately 100 trillion cells, yet only 10 trillion are human cells! The remaining cells are largely bacteria with a few random parasites and fungi added (Buckman, 2003). But the important point here is that only a tenth of the cells contained within our frame are actually our own. Some of these are parasitical and some have powerful symbiotic relationships with our human DNA-based cells, such that we could not live without them. Stuart Kauffman (1995), writing in *At Home in the Universe* concludes, "All evolution is co-evolution." We may now also have to conclude that all development is codevelopment. If evolution is really coevolution, this means that the unit of analysis is not species but ecosystems. Similarly, if development is really codevelopment, then the unit of analysis is not individuals but ecosystems and the mutually interdependent niches within them.

Basic to life on Earth, as we well know, is the amazing process of photosynthesis, which converts sunlight into energy that can be used by plant life to produce chlorophyll. If we could establish that quantum processes explained the nearly perfect levels of energy conversion in photosynthesis, then the case for a generalized quantum mechanics would be much stronger. In fact, this has been established only very recently. An article in *Discovery* magazine describes the results:

> Inside the black box, optics manufactured to billionths-of-a-meter precision detect something extraordinary: Within the bacterial proteins, dancing electrons make seemingly impossible leaps and appear to inhabit multiple places at once. Peering deep into these proteins, Fleming and his colleagues at the University of California at Berkeley and at Washington University in St. Louis have discovered the driving engine of a key step in photosynthesis, the process by which plants and some microorganisms convert water, carbon dioxide, and sunlight into oxygen and carbohydrates. More efficient by far in its ability to convert energy than any operation devised by man, this cascade helps drive almost all life on earth. Remarkably, photosynthesis appears to derive its ferocious efficiency not from the familiar physical laws that govern the visible world but from the seemingly exotic rules of quantum mechanics, the physics of the subatomic world.
>
> (*Anderson,* 2009)

Another very interesting bit of research on quantum effects in biology demonstrates results consistent with a quantum effect at the level of DNA. P. P. Gariaev and his colleague Vladimir Poponin (1992, 1995) have demonstrated in their work with the DNA phantom effect that every molecule of DNA exerts a nonlocal field effect on the material locale surrounding it, in some cases up to 30 days after the DNA source molecule has been removed. Gariaev and Poponin's work—because DNA is as fundamental to the reproduction of life as is the production of chlorophyll by plants—may support a more general conclusion that among living organisms, that nonlocality operates simultaneously with chemosynaptic neuronal processes at all scales and in all living things (Gariaev 1991).[10] DARPA, the Pentagon's research think tank, also seems to believe that sufficient evidence of quantum effects exists at the biological level that it has launched a research initiative to investigate quantum mechanical effects in biological systems. Citing the previous research on photosynthesis, DARPA says there are other biological examples of quantum effects—including an explanation, perhaps, for how birds are able to navigate along the Earth's magnetic fields (Shachtman, 2008).

Our mental models of center and periphery (the classical solar model of Copernicus) are highly redundant in the sciences: the atomic structure in molecules, the nucleus in the cell, and the neuron in the brain. These models are variously under attack by quantum theory in physics, recent research on cellular epigenetics, and the case for the intelligence of the cell being located at the cell's boundary rather than its center. For example, biologist Bruce Lipton (2008) refers to the cellular nucleus as the "gonads" of the cell, and the work of Andrew Koob (2009) emphasizes the importance of the glia in the brain, comprising 90% of the brain's volume and responsible for wavelike communication in the brain with neurons. According to Koob, the neurons are analogous to highways and glia to cities: the real intelligence in the brain lies in the glia. A parallel shift is also occurring in research focus, largely as the result of quantum effects in physics, seeking and finding wavelike patterns of influence in biological systems rather than the simple on-off switching of classical models of DNA.

The emerging field of ecological-developmental biology is one illustration of the need for the kind of sensitivity to levels required by an emergentist perspective. While taxonomies are useful and perhaps even necessary heuristics, they can also reinforce linear and hierarchical mental models and can encourage systemic blinders. In biology, as one illustration, genes do not explain organs or bilateral symmetry (Minelli, 2009). This potential for systemic blindness is less true for those researchers who are sensitive to the levels of reality and the corresponding shifts in rules that accompany the levels. The emerging field of ecological-developmental biology is one illustration of the shift in awareness among researchers to a systemic perspective, where the focus widens to include environmental interdependency and polymorphism.

Are there useful analogies to biology? Biological phenotypes respond to environmental cues like temperature, predators, and species density both incrementally and probabilistically. How we appear is not solely determined by DNA. The presence of melanin produces the dark hair on otherwise white mammals at the tips of the ears, nose, tail, and feet—in this example, of Siamese cats and Himalayan rabbits. Researchers have discovered this effect is due to lower body temperature at the extremities. In the case of Himalayan rabbits, it has been demonstrated that if one shaves the hair off the back of the rabbit and repeatedly applies ice packs, the white hair will turn dark. In another example, the sex of some turtles and reptiles is determined by specific temperature variations during fetal development. These two sets of examples support the arguments for polymorphism.

What evolutionary developmental biology teaches us is that psychology might benefit from more attention to boundary-spanning disciplinary exploration—for example, fusing insights from biological developmental theory, neuroplasticity, and clinical intervention. One promising line of inquiry is to investigate the role that epigenetics plays in gene expression, trait formation, and stress markers and behavioral interventions that can establish alternative neural pathways—which, in turn, can establish phenotype plasticity, lower stress levels, and disease formation and ultimately polymorphism at the level of human traits (Gilbert & Epel, 2009).

Psychology and Consciousness

Psychology, for its part, presumes consciousness except for the most radical theories of behaviorism. At the same time, the emergence of the study of neuroplasticity and psychological states is demonstrating a powerful backward causality of conscious behavior on brain physiology. The verification and power of will and intention (applied consciousness) on brain structure has created a revolution in neurology that is still largely pending in psychology

but holds promise for a complete change in theory, research, and practice.

Experimentally, the feedback loop between intentional control of mind states and significant changes in brain structure are now well established. It seems crystal clear that the causal direction is no longer unidirectional from brain to mind, but rather characterized by complex cyclical feedback loops, including epigenetic, developmental, and environmental contingencies and, potentially, the intentional cultivation of mind states and experiences. As one example, long-time practitioners of meditation possess very different brain structures from those who do not practice.[11] The intentional alteration of the brain via behavioral practices like meditation has forever altered conventional wisdom about the mind-body problem. Furthermore, the emerging evidence supporting the existence of quantum effects within the brain and the possibility that the brain relies foundationally upon quantum effects for significant core-level functions may one day result in shifting the border between the classical (macro) and quantum (micro) decidedly toward the macro and perhaps destroys the distinction altogether. As discussed previously, physics experiments have now entangled clusters of molecules rather than subatomic particles, and biological systems like photosynthesis are now showing evidence of quantum effects, so the boundary is fast eroding on that side as well.

Roger Penrose has proposed one model of how this happens in the brain. Gödel's theorem (Kurt Gödel, 1906–1978) plays a role in Penrose's theory of quantum effects in the brain. This theorem demonstrates that no system of axioms is sufficiently powerful to generate all mathematical truths. Penrose, following Gödel, claims that the human mind must have nonalgorithmic capabilities that go beyond axioms and rules. And, indeed, the human mind can recognize those parts of arithmetic that transcend the systems of axiom—which, of course, Gödel's mind demonstrated by showing the limits of mathematics as a symbol system. Not all theorists concur with this interpretation.[12] Nevertheless, Penrose suggests that this nonalgorithmic aspect of consciousness comes from its connections with quantum physics (Hameroff 1996).

A thoughtful and ambitious study by Schwartz, Stapp, and Beauregard (2008) takes on the relationship between quantum physics in neuroscience and psychology. It simultaneously seeks to demonstrate that quantum physical theory does a better job of explaining certain fundamental characteristics in the brain than does classical physics and at the same time explains how volition and attention alter the brain itself in a form of intentional neuroplasticity.

The fatal flaw in the classical model, according to Schwartz, Stapp, and Beauregard, which is generally a robust approximation for quantum theory, is that it eliminates the causal efficacy of conscious effort in experiments that require quantum dynamics be used in principle. If we succumb to the enticement of FAPP (for all practical purposes) and the classical model when it leaves unexplained critical features of neural processing and especially the role of choice and consciousness in human agency, then we miss important opportunities to improve therapeutic choice of treatment, patient recovery from trauma and suffering, and the design of clinically relevant research. As Schwartz, Stapp, and Beauregard state,

> . . . once the transition to a quantum description is made, the principles of quantum theory must, in order to maintain rationale consistency and coherency, be used to link the quantum physical description of the subject's brain to his stream of conscious experiences. The conscious choices of human agents thereby become injected nontrivially into the causal interpretation of neuroscience and neuropsychology experiments. This caveat particularly applies to those experimental paradigms in which human subjects are required to perform decision-making or attention-focusing tasks that require conscious effort.
>
> (2008, p. 7)

We already have an emerging body of evidence that the client's commitment to think and act in ways that alter the habituated feedback loops reinforcing phobias and traumatic experiences can alter brain chemistry and brain function. As Kurt Lewin so famously quipped, "Nothing is so practical as a good theory" (1945, p. 129).[13]

Neuroplasticity itself seems to be intimately related to astrocyte growth, the most prominent form of glia in the brain. If so, then astrocyte cells respond to intention and attention. According to Koob (2009), "in the 1990s, Fred Gage and colleagues at the Salk institute confirmed that [brain] cell division occurs in the human hippocampus; other labs have shown that the [brain] cells dividing in humans are astrocytes" (p. 85). One study in particular is noteworthy. In 2006, researchers from Sweden in collaboration with researchers from the United States and Australia studied the brains of cadavers who had lived during the mid-1950s when massive amounts of heavy carbon were released into

the atmosphere as a result of aerial nuclear testing. Since cortical gliogenesis in adult humans was already established, they could document the presence of the radioactive carbon in post-1950s brain cells. None of the new growth radioactive cells were found to be neurons. They were all glia (Koob, 2009, p. 95).

Ultimately, neuroplasticity may be a misnomer. It seems as likely that glia are responsible for brain plasticity and plasticity in the brain may be a general feature of bioplasticity from which the brain is not excluded. Furthermore, within the brain the causal direction may well be from astrocyte to neuronal development insofar as neuroplasticity is concerned.

Perhaps somewhat ironically, the burgeoning use of positron emission tomography (PET) scanning and functional magnetic resonance imaging (fMRI) to map the correlates of mental states with brain activity are predicated upon advances in quantum mechanics. At the same time, many researchers in neurobiology are very resistant to quantum models of neurology. One cannot help but wonder whether the presence of quantum technology is producing outcomes consistent with a quantum perspective a la the paradox of Schrodinger's cats, where the choice of methods cannot be separated from the nature of the outcome. Indeed, quantum mechanics requires that the choice of experiment will determine whether classical or quantum effects are observed.

One conclusion that emerges from this abbreviated exploration of recent developments in physics and psychology is that a certain metacognitive pattern can be observed between the evolution of physics, developmental biology, and neuroplasticity—with significant implications for psychology and the use of mind training as a therapeutic intervention. Before we can really explore this further, it is necessary to establish some agreed-upon terminology for our discussion of a psychology and pedagogy of self-awareness.

Self-Awareness and Pedagogy

William James, in his classic text *The Principles of Psychology*, makes the case that intention, will, and mental effort can affect the choices we make and have real consequences in our lives. His theory of psychology was overrun by the advent of behaviorism and the research of B. F. Skinner, which denied the existence of consciousness. The rise of behaviorism in the 1950s and the corresponding decline in the role of consciousness in human behavior is just another example of how classical physics and the mechanical materialism of the era profoundly truncated our worldview (James, 1983). However, given the recent research findings on neuroplasticity and the role of astrocytes in brain growth, James's arguments for the power of directed intention to influence one's neural development have enjoyed a resurgence and figure prominently in recent work (Schwartz & Begley, 2002; Schwartz, Stapp, & Beauregard, 2008).

Given the dynamical and recursive nature of self-observation, we need, as a minimum, a typology of learning into which we can structure our categories of thought so that we do not become lost. Gregory Bateson (1904–1980), an eminent biologist and systems theorist, influenced diverse fields, including cybernetics, family therapy, and communications studies (Hawkins, 2004, p. 410).[14] He developed a useful heuristic and one I've used for more than 25 years in my own thinking about pedagogy. According to Tosey (2006), Bateson posits five types of thought, although he said little about the highest type. These are described in Table 5.1. One should read from the bottom of Table 5.1 to the top, although the types should not be viewed as a hierarchy or pyramid.

Several important points need to be considered in understanding Bateson's approach. First and foremost, for Bateson, the brain and mind were not contiguous: the mind existed in a much wider social and environmental space—for Bateson, thinking was inherently social and environmental (Blakeslee, 2007). This view is consistent with the evolutionary developmental biological perspective, which now challenges an overemphasis on the individual as a unit of analysis. Some distinctive features of Bateson's *levels of learning* bear special attention:

• Higher orders of recursion allow certain problems to be solved more easily but create new challenges of integration and human development. In this sense, Bateson's recursive model of learning is generative but not hierarchically progressive. Learning to learn does not solve one's difficulties with learning—it does offer new challenges and opportunities for growth and understanding. At the same time, it does qualitatively alter one's perspectives and opportunities for insight.

• The feedback loops in Bateson's *levels-of-learning* are not closed loops. They function simultaneously and are mutually influential as one would expect in a dynamical open systems model. Feedback loops are also sensitive to variations in the presence of supports and challenges in the environment. Thus, as one example, learning involves processing information that may be self-contradictory. This is another example of an emergentist perspective, which requires us to remain sensitive to relative truths and levels of meaning and not apply taxonomies outside of their domain of relevance.

• Higher orders of recursion produce the conditions for "metacommunication" about the way communication is to be understood. A reciprocal influence between these levels affects both the original communication and the insights about communication more generally. As an illustration, imagine a Buddhist saying to you, "Buddhism is not what you think." If you do not understand the joke, you will experience the statement as a declaration that you do not understand Buddhism, even if you think you do. However, if you understand the context, you will realize the statement could also mean *thinking is not adequate to understanding Buddhism*. By this the Buddhist might be implying the heart of

Table 5.1 Bateson's Levels of Learning

Learning IV	"…would be *change in Learning III*, but probably does not occur in any adult living organism on this earth."
Learning III	…is *change in the process of Learning II*, e.g., a corrective change in the system of *sets* of alternatives from which choice is made.
Learning II	…is *change in the process of Learning I*, e.g., a corrective change in the set of alternatives from which choice is made, or it is a change in how the sequence of experience is punctuated.
Learning I	…is *change in specificity of response* by correction of errors of choice within a set of alternatives.
Learning 0	…is characterized by *specificity of response*, which—right or wrong—is not subject to correction.

Source: From Tosey (2006).

Buddhism can be found in the meditative practice that transcends thought altogether and abides in a ground of self-awareness that is simultaneously bright, clear, and compassionate in its profound wisdom. Now, realizing the double meaning of the statement, *Buddhism is not what you think*, you may laugh, and that laughter is a signal to the one who made the statement that you understand. A metacommunication has occurred. Similar statements are frequently made by physicists and misunderstood by their students—for example, when the mathematical physicist Roger Penrose said, "Quantum mechanics makes absolutely no sense."

• Mismatches between levels have real communicational and psychological effects. Russell and Whitehead's approach to this problem in their theory of logical types was to ban all such sentences by cleanly separating statements at different logical levels. Bateson has wisely pointed out that good logic may be bad natural science. As the preceding example suggests, some of the most interesting forms of communication and a great deal of humor depend upon the tension created by this mismatch in levels of communication. Poetry, theater, and jazz thrive on it, and in the Zen tradition, the use of koans and the conversation between teacher and student depend upon this tension.

As we will see shortly, Bateson provides us with a robust conceptual map for meditation and a metacognitive map for understanding the subtle variations on the levels of practice, with sufficient training, one can accomplish.

With deference to Bateson's formative work, and as Lutz, Dunne, and Davidson (2007) recount at length, a considerable amount of confusion exists about the terms used to describe and explain various practices and internal states in meditation even within the Buddhist tradition, never mind including in our purview Christian, Vedic, or Shamanic traditions. In fact, *meditation* is such an inclusive word that this author prefers to use a more elaborate description: *the pedagogy, practice, and consequences of self-awareness*.[15] The reason for this preference is that it helps us to untangle what we are speaking about and what consequences we expect as a result of our efforts.

The language and terminology that one finds most prevalent in the Western traditions are meditation, mindfulness, peaceful abiding, focused awareness, focused attention, open presence without an object, bare attention, or the ground of awareness. As you can see, this encourages a conflation of practices,

approaches, techniques (pedagogy), and expected outcomes (Germer 2005, Grossman et al., 2004).

Since the kinds of practices are wide ranging, the cultures of the practices are very old—certainly many are prior to the common era—and even highly trained practitioners disagree on how to translate from Sanskrit, Pali, Tibetan, or even Chinese or Japanese in the Zen traditions, it seems helpful to clarify what the terms mean in the context of this chapter. The following terms are not only an explanation of meaning but also an outline of the basic concepts required for an intellectual understanding of the practice of self-awareness.[16]

1. Ground of awareness: This is the fundamental nature of human beings and presumably all forms of life. It is a self-organizing feature of nature. Even an amoeba has a preference for a sugar solution over a salt solution and will seek one and avoid the other. In practical terms self-awareness training is about seeking to rediscover our own basic nature. This very ground from which all of our seeking and searching takes place is already here: our fundamental challenge is to recognize our own nature.

2. Attention: Attention has two aspects important to our pedagogy of self-awareness: (1) focused attention, which is the application of awareness by using our will or intention to direct attention upon some object, process, or condition; and (2) metacognitive attention—or attention to attention. This is an autopoietic[17] feature of awareness. (William James famously said, "Thought is the thinker.") Awareness is reflexive: it is capable of attending to itself. This fact is critical for a pedagogy of self-observation because it makes possible the act of noticing when our attention has wandered away from the object of our focus (e.g., the breath) and it makes possible the return of awareness to the object of focus. Thus, the practitioner is both attending to the breath and noticing when the awareness of breath is lost and exercising the intention to return to breath awareness. Absent the reflexivity of self-awareness, we would be condemned to study ourselves only in others. Introspection would be fruitless.

3. Subject/object: The subject in this case is our own identity as an observing self. The object is something other than the observing self and can be a thing (a stone), a process (I'm having difficulty breathing), a condition (I am experiencing suffering), or a thought (I don't like suffering).

The subject/object dichotomy is better understood in this context as two ends of a pole that can be lengthened or shortened depending upon one's goals. To illustrate, assume you are a surgeon and an operation is upcoming. As you plan the surgery, you might be very objective, emotionally cool, and quite analytical about the risks and rewards of alternative procedures. However, when you speak to the patient, you might draw very close to him or her and be quite empathic and reassuring while discussing the options. Later, when you enter into surgery, you are again cool, rational, and objective. Thus, we can understand the subject/object distinction as a flexible continuum of experience and perspective. The nature of the continuity of opposites becomes increasingly transparent as one observes one's own thought. In this case an insight experientially occurs that the subject and object are distinctions held in the same field of awareness and analyzed by it: Thought is the thinker.

4. Intention: The pedagogy of self-knowledge requires that we mobilize our energy and focus that energy on a specific goal and set of practices to realize that goal. Without a clear intention and a commitment to sustain that intention and a mobilization of the commitment in the form of practice, we are unlikely to realize the goal.

5. Practice: Commitment and intention are necessary but not sufficient. We must mobilize the resources and actually practice because it is a skill set that requires practice and effort to improve. It also generally requires an instructor who has at least some familiarity with the issues discussed here but, more important, generates the result spontaneously in his or her own presence. In this sense meditation is not an activity of thought but of awareness. One who is deeply entrained in that particular state of consciousness provides a resonating influence on the minds of those around him or her that facilitates a similar state. Typically, students cannot maintain the state on their own until they have worked closely and deeply with the teacher for many years.

6. Reflection: In addition to mobilizing our intention, we need to reflect upon our understanding of the practice and our experience with the practice. The former is conceptual knowledge and the latter experiential knowledge. It is quite necessary to cycle around these two repeatedly as we proceed with our self-inquiry. In fact, intention can be focused and strengthened by understanding the importance of the goal, examining how the goal will improve our lives or the lives of others, and by considering the consequences of not pursuing the goal. This kind of intellectual reflection is an important component of self-awareness training.

7. Insight: Insight follows reflection. It is an emergent property of practice and reflection and is not something we can predict or even expect, but we know that practice and reflection are a necessary but insufficient condition for insight to develop. It is very much like the analogy used by a Zen master I read many years ago explaining the experience of *Kensho* or what might be called momentary enlightenment in the Japanese Zen tradition. He said that one could do nothing to produce *Kensho* any more than one could make lightning strike. However, he laughed and said, "If you run around in an open field with a long copper rod held overhead during a thunderstorm, you can surely increase the odds." This "activity" was his metaphor for intensive study, practice, and reflection.[18]

One might argue that psychology is the art and science of self-awareness. As John Dewey, the famous philosopher and educator, once wrote, "Education is not *for* life: it *is* life." And, Bateson would agree, as life is not only intrinsically educational, it is also intrinsically social.

When a psychologist establishes the conditions for self-awareness, the client begins to see how the strategies and defense mechanisms she once used to manage her self-concept and her relationships with others are dysfunctional to her emerging sense of self (Bateson's Level I learning). At a deeper level the psychologist and client may also begin to understand that they are not outside the client's experience, that the therapist and the client interact and have mutual influences upon each other (transference and countertransference). This would be Bateson's Level II learning. The therapeutic directionality in classical psychology has now shifted from linear and away from the therapist and toward the client into a feedback loop (Hofstadter, 2007). At some point in the relationship the therapist begins to discover that his or her intentionality for the client contains an espoused theory that influences the field of development of the client—a theory in action. Gendlin, in a major review of what predicts success in therapy, found that those who could feel and describe a "felt sense" in their bodies were significantly more likely to benefit from therapy than those who could not, independent of the type of therapy. He also developed techniques to help individuals acquire the skills to feel, recognize, and describe this felt sense in their own therapeutic settings. This finding lends more support to the notion that one can be trained to improve one's self-awareness, and that training has real implications for our mental health and well-being (Ferrari & Sternberg, 1998). At Bateson's Level III learning, one is able to alter the sets of assumptions and consider options among the systems of interaction and sets of intentions, for example, moving from a classical to a quantum model of neuroplasticity, which simultaneously alters theory, practice, and the definition of the possible.

The preceding review of terminology and basic concepts also has embedded within it a path of practice that follows progressive stages of development from novice to journeyman to master practitioner. Table 5.2, presented by Lutz, Dunne, and Davidson (2007, p. 513), provides an elegant and simple outline that I have adapted slightly to our purposes.

The first stage of practice at Level 0 (Table 5.2) is primarily concerned with developing the basic condition of stability of focused attention. From the view of an accomplished practitioner of self-awareness, the human condition is characterized very broadly by attention-deficit disorder. Most of us cannot focus on anything for more than a few moments at a time, and we make matters worse by seeking to multitask everywhere we go. The emphasis at stage one is primarily focusing on the object of our attention, whether the breath, sensations, a sound, a mantra, or an object of observation like an icon, an image, or even a small stone. One possible line of reflection is focused on the aversion-attraction polarity that leads the mind around in circles.[19] While focusing on our object of attention, we soon see that the mind is restless and quickly abandons the object for more interesting terrain. Over time we may begin to see a pattern in our aversion to holding the object steady before our mind, and the mind's eagerness to attend to something else—anything else (Richards, 2009).

One insight that really shifts our understanding of the attraction-aversion distraction cycle is that this is simply a habit of the mind, that it is completely mechanical and impersonal. If we sustain our reflective activity with sufficient effort, the pattern emerges as an insight into the impersonal nature of mental activity. Furthermore, conversation with others will bring the further insight that this pattern can be generalized to mental functioning among many practitioners. This insight should make us more compassionate toward others.

The second stage shifts emphasis just slightly to developing the witness capacity in the awareness (Langer 1997, Moore & Malinowski, 2009). This is developed by reserving a small part of our awareness for the simple task of noticing when our attention wanders from our focus. At this point our awareness is split between the object and the subject (our own awareness of our practice). The intention is to keep the witness active and present throughout the practice and focused on the object. Evidence of progress is determined by how quickly the witness notices when the mind has wandered. (Please remember that "witness" and "object" are really two aspects of the same mind.) The strength of the intention to practice can be monitored by how quickly the mind releases its noticing of wandering and returns its attention and focus to the object. Ideally, this is done without self-recrimination or other forms of storytelling, whose only purpose is to distract the mind from keeping its intention. Reflection is focused on these elements of practice and maintaining clarity about the state of the practice, then considering antidotes to the distresses that arise in practice from too much tension or too much dullness while focusing on the object.

The third stage is a much more advanced practice only possible when the attention focused on the object and the object become "fused" as it were. At this stage attention is effortless, stable, and vivid. The experiencer and the experienced are

Table 5.2 Path of Practice

Stage	Object	Subject	Metacognition	Intention	Reflection	Insight
0	+	−	−	Object	Aversion-attraction loop	The habitual nature of mind
1	−	+	+	Subject	Tension-laxity loop	Tuning the practice
2	−	−	+	Metacognition	Subject-object loop	It's not what you think!
3	□	□	++	Ground awareness	No mind	Nothing's changed

"−" = deemphasize; "+" = emphasize; "□" = absent.

indistinguishable, and the subject/object distinction collapses. Now the intention shifts from the original object to this state of fusion itself. It is an extremely subtle practice, where attention shifts from foreground to background, from the subject-object distinction, to the field. The field is observed by competence in maintaining stability and focus over some period of time, although it can also be experienced as spontaneous and unexpected. One focus for reflection is the lesson that one cannot use the mind to produce this effect. It arises as an emergent property of the practice itself in the same way art emerges from competence and sustained practice with the medium. One possible insight for the practitioner is that awareness is preexistent—before sensations, feelings, or thoughts (Damasio 1999, 2010, McCrae 2009, Pert 2000). Hence, the Zen koan: "What was your original face—before your mother was born?"

The fourth and final stage occurs when the practitioner and the practice collapse back into the ground of awareness. At this stage the practitioner's identity is synonymous with the ground of awareness. Reflection has stopped and the profound insight that "nothing has changed" is understood. This is an extremely difficult level to explain because it is beyond concepts, language, time, space, and causality. It is very similar to the moment before Planck's constant in physics—we can point, but we cannot really explain without digging ourselves a deeper hole. (The first step when you find yourself digging yourself into a deeper and deeper hole is to stop digging!) Imagine that there was in fact a single theory of everything and one night, while experiencing a particularly vivid dream, you realized it. You woke up the next morning and you knew it and you understood it. Now, how would you explain it?

What is very interesting about these steps and levels of practice is that they correspond so well to both levels in psychology and levels in physics. In Table 5.3, we see that a rough correspondence can be found between an evolving theory of quantum physics, psychology, and pedagogy. One can also find a correspondence with an emergentist perspective, which catalyzes the insights from one level to the next, and a pedagogy of self-awareness training. It is in the absence of an explicit model of how to proceed that some teachers of meditation have disserved their students by misunderstanding their developmental levels and the challenges and supports required to meet their needs (Drago-Severson, 2009, Kegan 1982). This model is also a useful heuristic for research on the backward influences of intention and attention on neuroplasticity. The results will surely be affected by the level of learning practiced, by the level of awareness of the practitioner, and by methods and levels of understanding of the researchers. For example, the concept

Table 5.3 Physics, Psychology, and Pedagogy

Stage	Object	Subject	Metacognition	Intention	Reflection	Insight	Level in Psychology	Level in Physics
0	+	+	Identification	Reaction	None	I am my experience	Behavioral	Prerational
1	+	−	−	Object	Aversion-attraction loop	The impersonal nature of mind	Client-centered therapy	Classical Newtonian physics
2	−	+	+	Subject	Tension-laxity loop	Tuning the practice	Interactionist therapy	Ecological theory
3	−	−	+	Metacognition	Subject-object loop	It's not what you think!	Therapeutic field/positive psychology	Copenhagen interpretation in quantum physics
4	□	□	++	Ground awareness	No mind-no loop	Nothing's changed	Transcendental-ism/self-actualization	Bohm's implicate order

Stages are analogous to Bateson's levels.
"−" = deemphasize; "+" = emphasize; "□" = absent.

of *emptiness* in psychology has traditionally been equated with feelings of meaningless, *anomie*, and alienation. When a client presents these feelings, the traditional psychological approach has viewed them as a problem to be solved or made to go away rather than an opening into a higher stage of human development. Most psychologists will seek to have the patient replace these feelings with a progressively healthier sense of self or ego according to the therapist's own developmental level. Yet a therapist and client both at Level III (or higher) will view descriptions of emptiness very differently. Thus, the correlates of neural activity or its absence will require competence with higher orders of learning; such investigations are necessarily complicated and contingent—and made more so when therapist and client are either unaware of their own developmental level, at widely differing levels of development, or the client is actually acting from a higher level than the therapist.

In the highest form of psychology—a psychology that is still emerging from the ferment of the 20th century—a possibility exists that psychologists will see their work as enabling the self-actualization of developing human beings and themselves (Bar-On, 2001). The *psyche* in psychologist will again come alive. If this does not occur, then the codevelopment of physics and psychology risks becoming a technocratic enterprise, where instruments are used to classify neurosis based on brain waves and brain formation and psychology will become a corporatized method of sorting people into occupations and/or institutions.

Given our current addiction to power over others, this dark side of the relationship between physics and psychology needs to be acknowledged and brought into the light. But it would be inopportune to end on a dark note given that so much possibility lies ahead for progress. The language of quantum mechanics has been evolving for at least 100 years, yet in a world of billions, a few thousand might really understand it. (In this, I must confess my double ignorance of both the highest levels of physics and psychology.) Yet, as an avid student of both, I have found abundant clues to follow—dropped by the best teachers in both traditions—hinting that consciousness may be the common denominator in the complex and contradictory equations of the subjective and the objective domains of reality (Wallace 2006, 2007).

At the same time one cannot be sanguine about the possibility that the control of quantum materials

via nanotechnology may lead to molecular-sized pharmaceuticals, computer implants, and other medical devices that will rapidly blur the distinction between man and machine. As Sarewitz and Woodhouse (2003) have written in a thoughtful and provocative essay in *Nanotechnology* magazine about technological innovation and its impact on society:

> If innovations as apparently modest as the metal stirrup and the cotton gin can transform society to its roots in a period of decades or less, what of technologies now on the horizon that aim to revolutionize the very processes by which new materials are designed and produced, that are blurring the boundary between the inanimate and the living, that may combine the powers of machine intelligence and human consciousness?
> (p. 64)

Given our obsession with control over nature and the difficulty society has with globally raising its learning level to what Bateson would identify as Level II or Level III, we may not be able to solve our next confrontation with technology and social change with the kind of wisdom and foresight required to avoid its worst scenarios. Certainly psychologists could play a role in this, but the profession has increasingly been dominated by pharmaceuticals and short-term clinical interventions intended to adjust clients to their circumstances rather than challenge the circumstances themselves.

Should quantum theory become the dominant paradigm for explaining consciousness, the implications for psychology are profound indeed. However, neuroplasticity, whether explained by classical or quantum effects, has already launched a revolution in our understanding of how changing one's intentions and thought affects both behavior and the brain itself (Doidge 2007, Goleman 1995, 2006, Siegel 2001, Ramachandran 2011). Still to be explored are biofeedback devices using audio and visual response to brain-wave patterns to acquire training effects with much more efficiency and depth. If it takes 20 or more years to attain the effects recently demonstrated by highly advanced practitioners of meditation, that effort-to-outcome ratio is likely to discourage all but the most able and dedicated from acquiring the skill levels needed to produce the demonstrated effects. My own explorations in the area of biofeedback indicate that it might be highly effective at lowering the height of this barrier and producing desirable behavioral and physiological effects in far less time, cost, and effort. This has implications for the introduction of creative modalities in psychological practice and in teaching and learning.[20]

Conclusion

This chapter has sought to provide a logical chain of evidence from quantum mechanics to quantum effects in biological systems, to quantum effects in neurological systems. Quantum mechanics is well established, but the research in biological systems is barely underway, and it is certainly highly speculative whether quantum effects will replace classical physical explanations in the future. However, quantum mechanics is beginning to capture serious attention and research dollars. As the technology improves based on quantum mechanics, it follows that the experiments will also improve in rigor and definitiveness, although it is likely to take another decade or more to provoke a shift in the theoretical models of biological systems from classical to quantum. Our understanding of the universe has moved from a closed to an open and perhaps infinite system.

A revolution in biology is replacing hierarchy, taxonomy, and fixed systems with open, adaptive, and process-focused models that are taking advantage of the mathematics of chaos and complexity theory, as well as applying swarming models and complex adaptive systems theory (Cohen & Stewart 1994, Gell-Mann 1994, Holland 1995, Johnson 2001). Finally, our understanding of the human brain/mind complex as highly plastic throughout the life span and influenced by thought is also encouraging theoretical interest in models of complex adaptive behavior. How are we to understand macro-trends in modeling the universe and our roles in it?

The word "universe" is very interesting—*uni verse*—"one song" or "one story." Native peoples, such as the Navajo (Dine), often sing their stories of creation. Singing and storytelling are synergistic; the singing not only recounts the story, it empowers it. The song of creation holds all that exists together. Similarly, every person has a fundamental story to they tell about himself or herself and that story is the story of his or her Self. We are literally held together, or torn apart, by the power of our story, just as in physics our universe is held together or torn apart by the power of the story we tell about it. Whether created by the gods while churning an ocean of milk, or by the big bang, or destroyed by a great flood, or a collapsing sun, or in the vast cycles of sleep and awaking caused by Brahma, or the random collisions of the multiverse, our creation and destruction stories shape our worldview just as our personal creation and destruction stories shape our understanding of our life and our death in the larger mythology of our worldview.[21] Could it be that we are backing our way into a unified theory of everything?

Notes

1. For a detailed explanation of why, see Susskind (2008).

2. The title of this section is adapted from Rosenblum and Kuttner's provocative book, *Quantum enigma: Physics encounters consciousness* (2006). I highly recommend this book to readers interested in a deeper understanding of the implications of the ubiquitous presence of consciousness in all versions of quantum mechanics.

3. Mirror neurons are neurons that fire both when a person acts and when a person observes another person perform the same action.

4. See, for example, Goswami (1993).

5. Stanford physicist Lenard Susskind is not worried about dark matter because he believes that it can be explained by as-yet-undiscovered subatomic particles. However, he says that dark energy is very problematic because there is just far too much of it for the standard model to account for.

6. These findings seem to support the "many universes" version of astrophysics.

7. For an interesting summary of the history of the main proponents and variations in this approach, see Vanninni (2008).

8. A competing perspective argues that our universe is but one of an infinite cycle of collisions between our universe and a parallel world. The big bang was not the beginning of time but the bridge to a past filled with infinitely repeating cycles of evolution. See Steinhardt and Turok (2007), *Endless universe: Beyond the big bang—Rewriting cosmic history.*

9. For example, the recent journal *NeuroQuantology*, founded in 2002, has numerous articles devoted to the subject of quantum theory and research in biological systems.

10. For a thoughtful and cautious commentary on quantum effects in physiology, see P. Wolynes (2009).

11. See, for example, Davidson et al. (2003); Lazer et al. (2005); Lutz et al. (2004); and Pagnoni and Cekic (2007).

12. For a review of criticisms of the Penrose-Hameroff theory and Hameroff's response, see Hameroff (2007).

13. Some examples of the research of the effects on cerebral functioning by redirecting emotional response using cognitive reframing and mindfulness practices include Beauregard et al. (2001); Levesque et al. (2003); Ochsner et al. (2002); Paquette et al. (2003); and Schwartz et al. (1996).

14. I am particularly indebted to Paul Tosey (Centre for Management Learning & Development School of Management) and his paper *Bateson's Levels of Learning: A Framework for Transformative Learning?* Available at http//:www.NLPresearch.org

15. See, for example, Richards (2009).

16. The author's bias is to separate the religious history of the techniques of self-awareness training from the pedagogy, practice

techniques, and outcomes, using a scientific approach to their investigation.

17. The term was originally introduced by Chilean biologists Humberto Maturana and Francisco Varela in 1972:

> An autopoietic machine is a machine organized (defined as a unity) as a network of processes of production (transformation and destruction) of components which: (i) through their interactions and transformations continuously regenerate and realize the network of processes (relations) that produced them; and (ii) constitute it (the machine) as a concrete unity in space in which they (the components) exist by specifying the topological domain of its realization as such a network. See: Capra, Fritjof (1997). *The Web of Life* for a general introduction to the ideas behind autopoiesis.

18. For an interesting study by a Zen practitioner experiencing *Kensho* while conducting an fMRI of his brain blood flow patterns, see Austin (1998).

19. Reflections and insights can be several; Table 5.2 only provides one example of each.

20. It would require another chapter to cover this material. Some promising lines of inquiry include use of emotionally responsive computer simulations with children, the use of brain-wave technology to support communication and mobility with severely handicapped children and adults, and the use of bio-feedback technology to intentionally create specific brain-wave states. See, for example, Fehmi and Robbins's (2007) work with biofeedback.

According to the June 29, 2009 issue of *Science Daily*, Japan's BSI-TOYOTA Collaboration Center has successfully developed a system that controls a wheelchair using brain waves in as little as 125 milliseconds. With over 2.5 million people in wheelchairs, this technology will have a very high potential to influence both the education and the mobility of handicapped persons. It will also have many other applications where remote operation of robots and other forms of technology are faster and more efficient by using brain waves.

21. For two utterly fascinating books on worldview in mythology, see Jaynes (1976) and de Santillana (1977).

References

Anderson, M. (2009, February). Is quantum mechanics controlling your thoughts? *Discover Magazine*. Retrieved December 2011, from http://discovermagazine.com/2009/feb/13-is-quantum-mechanics-controlling-your-thoughts

Austin, J. H. (1998) Zen and the brain: Toward and understanding of meditation and consciousness. (2nd ed.) Cambridge, MA: MIT Press.

Bar-On, R. (2001). EI and self actualization. In J. Ciarrochi, J. Forgas, & J. Mayer (Eds.), *Emotional intelligence in everyday life* (pp. 82–97). New York: Psychology Press.

Beauregard, M., Levesque, J., & Bourgouin, P. (2001). Neural correlates of conscious self-regulation of emotion. *Journal of Neuroscience*, 21, RC165

Blakeslee, S., & Blakeslee, M. (2007). *The body has a mind of its own*. New York: Random House.

Bohm, D. (1980). *Wholeness and the implicate order*. Oxford, England: Routledge.

Buckman, R. (2003) *Human wildlife*. Baltimore: John Hopkins University Press.

Cohen, J., & Stewart, I. (1994). *The collapse of chaos: Discovering simplicity in a complex world*. New York: Penguin Group.

Damasio, A. (1999). *The feeling of what happens: Body and emotion in the making of consciousness*. New York: Harcourt.

Damasio, A. (2010). *Self comes to mind: Constructing the conscious brain*. New York: Pantheon.

Davidson, R. J., Kabat-Zinn, J., Schumacher, J., Rozenkranz, M., Muller, D., Santorelli, S. K., ... et al., (2003). Alterations in brain and immune function produced by mindfulness meditation. *Psychosomatic Medicine*, 65, 564–570.

de Santillana, G. (1977). *Hamlet's mill: An essay investigating the origins of human knowledge and its transmission through myth*. Jaffery, NH: David R. Godine.

Doidge, N. (2007). *The brain that changes itself*. New York: Penguin Press.

Drago-Severson, E. (2009). *Leading adult learning*. Thousand Oaks, CA: Corwin Press.

Dyson, F. (1979). *Disturbing the universe*. New York: Harper & Row.

Fehmi, L., & Robbins, J. (2007). *The open-focus brain: Harnessing the power of attention to heal mind and body*. Boston: Trumpeter Press.

Ferrari, M., & Sternberg, R. J. (1998). *Self-awareness: Its nature and development*. New York: The Guildford Press.

Filk, T., & von Muller, A., (2009) Quantum physics and consciousness: The quest for a common conceptual foundation. *Mind and Matter*, 7(1), 59–79.

Gariaev, P. P., Chudin, V. I., Komissarov, G. G., Berezin, A. A., & Vasiliev, A. A. (1991). Holographic associative memory of biological systems. *Optical Memory and Neural Networks*, 1621, 280–291.

Gariaev, P. P., Grigor'ev, K. V., Vasil'ev, A. A., Poponin, V. P., & Shcheglov, V. A. (1992). Investigation of the fluctuation dynamics of DNA solutions by laser correlation spectroscopy. *Bulletin of the Lebedev Physics Institute*, 11–12, 23–30.

Gariaev, P. P., & Poponin, V. P. (1995). Vacuum DNA phantom effect in vitro and its possible rational explanation. *Nanobiology*.

Gell-Mann, M. (1994). *The quark and the jaguar: Adventures in the simple and complex*. New York: W.H. Freeman & Co.

Germer, C. K., Siegel, R. D., & Fulton, P. R. (2005). *Mindfulness and psychotherapy*. New York: The Guilford Press.

Gilbert, S. F., & Epel, D. (2009). *Ecological developmental biology: Integrating epigenetics, medicine and evolution*. Sunderland, MA: Sinauer Associates.

Goleman, D. (1995). *Emotional intelligence: Why it can matter more than IQ*. New York: Bantam.

Goleman, D. (2006). *Social intelligence: The new science of human relationships*. New York: Bantam.

Goodwin, B. (1994). *How the leopard changed its spots: The evolution of complexity*. New York: Charles Scribner's Sons.

Goswami, A. (1993). *The self-aware universe: How consciousness creates the material world*. New York: Jeremy P.Tarcher/Putnam.

Grossman, P., Niemman, L., Schmidt, S., & Walsch. H. (2004). Mindfulness-based stress reduction and health benefits: A meta-analysis. *Journal of Psychosomatic Research*, 57, 35–43.

Hameroff, S. (1996). Orchestrated reduction of quantum coherence in brain microtubules: A model for consciousness.

Mathematics and Computers in Simulation, 40(3–4), 453–480.

Hameroff, S. (2007). The brain is both neurocomputer and quantum computer. *Cognitive Science: A Multidisciplinary Journal,* 31(6), 10–35

Hawkins, P. (2004). Gregory Bateson: His contribution to action research and organization development. *The Journal of Action Research,* 2(4), 409–423.

Hofstadter, D. (2007). *I am a strange loop.* New York: Basic Books.

Holland, J. (1995). *Hidden order: How adaptation builds complexity.* New York: Helix Books.

Jaynes, J. (1976). *The origins of consciousness in the breakdown of the bicameral mind.* New York: Houghton Mifflin.

James, W. (1983). *The principles of psychology.* Cambridge, MA: Harvard University Press. (Original work published 1890).

Johnson, S. (2001). *Emergence: The connected lives of ants, brains, cities, and software.* New York: Scribner.

Kauffman, K. (1995). *At home in the universe: The search for the laws of self-organization and complexity.* New York: Oxford University Press.

Kegan, R. (1982). *The evolving self: Problem and process in human development.* Boston: Harvard University Press.

Koob, A. (2009). *The root of thought.* Upper Saddle River, NJ: Pearson Education.

Langer, E. J. (1997). *The power of mindful learning.* Boston: Persus Publishing.

Laughlin, R. B. (2005). *A different universe: Reinventing physics from the bottom down.* New York: Basic Books

Lazar, S. W., Kerr, C. E., Wassermand, R.H., Gray, J.R., Greve, D. N., Treadway, M. T.,... Fischl, B. (2005). Meditation experience is associated with increased cortical thickness. *Neuroreport,* 16(17), 1893–1897.

Levesque, J. et al. (2003). Neural circuitry underlying voluntary suppression of sadness. *Biol. Psychiatry,* 53, 502–51

Lewin, K. (1945). The research center for group dynamics at Massachusetts Institute of Technology. *Sociometry,* 8, 126–35.

Lewin, R. (1992). *Complexity: Life at the edge of chaos.* New York: Macmillan.

Lipton, B. (2008). *The biology of belief: Unleashing the power of consciousness, matter and miracles.* Hay House Inc.

Lutz A, Dunne JD, Davidson RJ (2007) in Cambridge Handbook of Consciousness, Meditation and the neuroscience of consciousness: an introduction, eds Zelazo P, Moscovitch M, Thompson E (Cambridge, MA: Cambridge University Press), pp 499–554.

Lutz, A., Greischar, L. L., Rawlings, N. B., Ricard, M., & Davidson, R. J. (2004). Long-term meditators self-induce high amplitude gamma synchrony during mental practice. *Proceedings of the National Academy of Sciences USA,* 101(46), 16369–16373.

Maturana, H., & Varela, F. (1980). *Autopoiesis and cognition: The realization of the living.* Holland: D. Reidel Publishing Company. Originally published as *De Maquinas y Seres Vivos.* (1972). Chile: Editorial Universitaria S.A.

McCrae, R. R. (2009). The physics and chemistry of personality. *Theory and Psychology,* 19(5), 670–687.

Miller, A. I. (2009). *Deciphering the cosmic number: The strange friendship of Wolfgang Pauli and Carl Jung.* New York: WW Norton.

Minelli, A. (2009) *Forms of becoming: The evolutionary biology of development.* Princeton, NJ: Princeton University Press.

Moore, A., & Malinowski, P. (2009). Meditation, mindfulness and cognitive flexibility. *Consciousness and Cognition,* 18,176–189.

Morowitz, H. I. (2002). *The emergence of everything: How the world became complex.* New York: Oxford University Press.

Nadeau, R., & Kafatos, M. (1999). *The non-local universe: The new physics and matters of the Mind.* New York: Oxford University Press.

Ochsner, K. N., et al. (2002). Rethinking feelings: an FMRI study of the cognitive regulation of emotion. *J. Cogn. Neurosci.,* 14, pp. 1215–1229.

Pagnoni, G., & Cekic, M. (2007). Age effects on gray matter volume and attentional performance in Zen meditation. *Neurobiology of Aging,* 28(10), 1623–1627.

Paquette V, Levesque J, Mensour B, Leroux JM, Beaudoin G, Bourgouin P, Beauregard M (2003): Change the mind and you change the brain: Effects of cognitive-behavioral therapy on the neural correlates of spider phobia. *Neuroimage,* 18, 401– 409.

Penrose, R. (1994). *Shadows of the mind: A search for the missing science of consciousness.* New York: Oxford University Press.

Pert, C. (2000). *Your body is your subconscious mind.* Coulder, CO: Sounds True.

Ramachandran, V.S. (2011). *The tell-tale brain: A neuroscientist's quest for what makes us human.* New York: W. W. Norton & Company.

Richards, C. E. (2009). Toward a pedagogy of self, *Teachers College Record,* 111(12), 2372–2379.

Rosenblum, B., & Kuttner, F. (2006). *The quantum enigma: Physics encounters conscious.* New York: Oxford University Press.

Sarewitz, D., & Woodhouse, E. (2003). Small is powerful. *Nanotechnology,* pp. 63–83.

Schwartz, J.M., Stoessel, P.W., Baxter, L.R., Martin, K.M., Phelps, M.E. (1996). Systematic changes in cerebral glucose metabolic rate after successful behavior modification treatment of obsessive-compulsive disorders. *Arch Gen Psychiatry,* 53, 109–11.

Schwartz, J. M., & Begley, S. (2002). *The mind and the brain.* New York: Harper Collins.

Schwartz, J., Stapp, H., & Beauregard, M. (2008). *Quantum physics in neuroscience and psychology: A neurophysical model of mind/brain interaction.* Retrieved December 2011, from http://www-physics.lbl.gov/~stapp/PTB6.pdf

Shactman, N. (2008, September 3). Pentagon explores quantum biology. *Wired.* Retrieved December 2011, from http://www.wired.com/dangerroom/2008/09/pentagon-explor/

Siegel, D. (2001). *The developing mind: How relationships and the brain interact to shape who we are.* New York: The Guilford Press.

Stapp, H. (2007). *Mindful universe.* Berlin: Springer Verlagen.

Steinhardt, P. J., & Turok, N. (2007). *Endless universe: Beyond the big bang—rewriting cosmic history.* New York: Broadway Books.

Susskind, L. (2008). *The black hole wars.* New York: Little, Brown & Co.

Tosey, P. (2006). Bateson's levels of learning: A framework for transformational learning?. University of Tilburg, UK: Universities' Forum for Human Research Development Conference. Retrieved from http://epubs.surrey.ac.uk/1198/

Vannini, A. (2008). Quantum models of consciousness. *Quantum Biosystems, 1(2)*, 165–184.

Vergano, D. (2006, March 17). Big bang unfolded in the blink of an eye. *USA Today*, p. 2A.

Wallace, A. B. (2006). *The attention revolution: Unlocking the power of the focused mind.* Boston: Wisdom Publications.

Wallace, A. B. (2007). *Hidden dimensions: The unification of physics and consciousness.* New York: Columbia University Press.

Wolynes, P. (2009) Some quantum weirdness in physiology. *Proceedings of the National Academy of Sciences USA, 106*(41), 17247–17449.

Zeilinger, A. (2008, January). Split world. Book review of "Decoherence and the Quantum-to- Classical Transition" by Maximilian Schlosshauer. *Nature*. Retrieved December 2011, from http://www.nature.com/nature/journal/v451/n7174/full/451018a.html

PART 2

Personality and Social Psychology: Universalism, Absolutism, and Relativism

Personality, Spirituality, and Religion

Eric D. Rose *and* Julie J. Exline

Abstract

The current review explores advances made over the last 10 years (1999–2009) in research linking personality with spirituality and religion. Contributions from the fields of behavior genetics, attachment, the trait approach, and the study of values are analyzed to address four major topics. First, the roots of religious and spiritual life as well as pathways that lead both toward and away from spirituality and religiousness are described. Second, recent contributions to the controversial discussion of religious and spiritual prosociality are presented. Third, evidence for a connection between religiousness and spirituality with self-control and morality is explored. And finally, recent advances in the study of prejudicial attitudes and behavior on the part of religious and spiritual individuals are reviewed. The chapter concludes with a brief critique of the current state of empirical research linking personality with spirituality and religion, along with ideas for enhancing future research.

Key Words: personality, religion, spirituality, traits, values, behavior genetics, attachment, prosociality, self-control, prejudice

Introduction

Ten years have passed since the *Journal of Personality* published a special issue on religion in the psychology of personality. The editor of the issue, Robert Emmons, bemoaned the lack of attention to religious and spiritual topics among personality psychologists (Emmons, 1999). Since that time, the psychology of religion has embraced the paradigms of mainstream personality psychology (e.g., attachment theory, behavior genetics, and the trait approach), and this cross-pollination has been very fruitful.

The current review explores advances made in four major areas of the empirical study of personality and religion/spirituality over the last 10 years. First, we address roots and pathways in the development of the adult religious/spiritual personality. Second, we explore the link between religiousness, spirituality, and prosociality. Third, we look

at the relationship between religion, self-control, and morality. And last, we explore advances in the study of religion and prejudice. While the study of religious and spiritual personality has certainly advanced in other domains, these four areas were considered primary in terms of the attention granted them in the literature.

With rare exceptions, this review limits itself to articles published in the year 1999 or later. The key criteria for a study to be reviewed were that it addressed one of the four issues mentioned earlier and that it advanced knowledge of what it means to be a religious or spiritual person. Thus, articles with a particular focus on topics such as prayer (which nonreligious people do) and images of God (which nonreligious people have) are not represented here. Studies of childhood personality and articles of a sociological nature were also excluded. The scope of this chapter was further limited by excluding studies that addressed the relationship between religion and mental health. Though they fall well within the rubric of religion and personality, studies of religious coping and defense were also excluded, as space would not permit their review.

A Brief Introduction to Models Referenced in This Review

In the remainder of this review frequent references are made to religious orientation (Allport & Ross, 1967) as well as to the Five Factor Model of personality (McCrae & John, 1992) and The Schwartz Value Survey (Schwartz, 1992). For readers unfamiliar with these models, brief introductions are provided. A general overview of the relationship between traits, values, and religiousness is also presented.

RELIGIOUS ORIENTATION: INTRINSIC, EXTRINSIC, AND QUEST

Despite the proliferation of measures of religion and spirituality, religious orientation remains one of the most widely used measures of religiousness (Allport & Ross, 1967). An *intrinsic* religious orientation is one in which religion is embraced as an end unto itself, rather than as a means to achieve other goals. In contrast, an *extrinsic* religious orientation is one in which the individual uses religion as a means of fulfilling other needs or desires. Batson (1976) suggested a third category of motivation—religion as a *quest*. This third category is meant to reflect a style of religious questioning generated by confrontation with the challenges and tragedies of life.

TRAITS AND VALUES

Over the last 10 years, the trait approach to measuring the religious personality has relied largely on the Big Five and Five Factor Models of personality. The Big Five is a lexically based model of personality (Goldberg, 1981), while the Five Factor Model was developed through questionnaire research (McCrae & John, 1992). These two models are highly similar, with a nearly identical factor structure. Each consists of bipolar conscientiousness, extraversion, agreeableness, and neuroticism factors. However, while the Five Factor Model contains a fifth factor labeled as openness, the Big Five labels its fifth factor as intellect or imagination. Each factor is thought to be further divisible into various primary traits or facets.

In truth, the Five Factor Model only seems to account for a modest amount of variance in religiousness (see Piedmont, 1999b). Furthermore, facet-level analyses add little or nothing to the explanation of variance in religiousness and spirituality beyond what can be predicted by the general factors alone (see Saroglou & Fiasse, 2003; Saroglou & Munoz-Garcia, 2008). Nevertheless, consistent patterns of findings have emerged modestly relating religiousness to agreeableness, conscientiousness, and openness, and these findings will be highlighted in the remainder of this review.

More impressive than the relationship between religiousness and traits has been the ability of values to predict religiousness. While traits describe a person as she is, values are motivational and aspirational descriptors of the individual as she wishes to be (see Saroglou & Munoz-Garcia, 2008). Over the last 10 years The Schwartz Value Survey (Schwartz, 1992) has achieved recognition as a comprehensive, cross-culturally valid, and predictive measure of values (Saroglou, Delpierre, & Dernelle, 2004). The Schwartz Value Survey includes 10 values of importance that are often conceptualized as existing along three axes (Fontaine, Duriez, Luyten, Corveleyn, & Hutsebaut, 2005). On one axis are values relating to self-transcendence (e.g., benevolence, universalism) versus values of self-enhancement (e.g., power, achievement). A second axis holds values relating to openness to change (e.g., self-direction, stimulation) versus conservation (e.g., security, tradition). A third axis emphasizes hedonism versus acceptance of external limits (e.g., conformity, tradition).

In two studies, both using international samples, participants were administered measures of religiousness, the Five Factor Model and The Schwartz Value Survey (Roccas, Sagiv, Schwartz, & Knafo, 2002; Saroglou & Munoz-Garcia, 2008). In both studies values accounted for a sizable portion of variance in religiousness, whereas traits added little or nothing to the prediction of religiousness. When the order of regression was reversed, traits accounted for a modest portion of variance in religiousness, whereas the addition of values significantly and sizably increased prediction. Saroglou and Munoz-Garcia (2008) also extended this finding to the prediction of spirituality, where findings were identical.

Roots and Pathways

Over the past 10 years research has illuminated the often surprising paths that lead individuals toward or away from religious and spiritual life. We will see that there are many different paths from youth to adult religiousness (or irreligiousness). Along the way, genetics, early relationships with caregivers, and personality traits each exert unique influence in shaping adult religiousness and spirituality.

Behavior Genetics

Briefly, behavior genetics is a methodology that allows researchers to quantify the extent to which individual differences in a given variable are attributable to either inherited genetic factors, shared environmental factors, or nonshared environmental factors. Shared environmental factors exert a similar influence on all members of a group (e.g., the impact of divorce in a family). In contrast, nonshared environmental factors uniquely impact individuals within a group (e.g., how a loss uniquely impacts a particular family member). Because variance attributed to nonshared factors includes measurement error, this factor can be inflated by the use of measures with poor reliability; this is a particular problem in studies of religiousness.[1]

INCREASING GENETIC CONTRIBUTIONS FROM EXTERNAL TO INTERNAL RELIGIOUSNESS

One major theme to emerge from the study of behavior genetics and religion is that personal and internal aspects of religious life (e.g., belief) are more influenced by genetics and less influenced by shared environment than are external and impersonal aspects of religious life (e.g., religious affiliation; Bradshaw & Ellison, 2008). It has been suggested that genetics exert greater influence on internal aspects of religious life because religious beliefs express internally motivated wants, needs, and wishes. In contrast, external aspects of religious life are prone to social pressures and thus are more influenced by shared environments (Bradshaw & Ellison, 2008).

Based on a review of prior research as well as findings from their own study of nearly 15,000 twins and family members, D'Onofrio, Eaves, Murrelle, Maes, and Spilka (1999) concluded that religious affiliation is primarily determined by shared environmental factors. Genetic contributions to religious affiliation appear to be limited to a small contribution among women. Genetic contributions to religious behaviors such as church attendance are more substantial, and recent estimates suggest genetic contributions of roughly 18% to 19% (D'Onofrio et al., 1999) versus 32% (Bradshaw & Ellison, 2008). Shared environmental factors seem to contribute somewhere between 16% and 21% to church attendance (Bradshaw & Ellison, 2008; D'Onofrio et al., 1999).

Heredity makes its greatest impact on internal belief aspects of religious life. Bouchard, McGue, Lykken, and Tellegen (1999) uncovered that 43% of the variance in intrinsic religiousness was attributable to genetics, compared to 39% for extrinsic religiousness. Bradshaw and Ellison found that genetics accounted for 27% of religious belief salience and 29% of spirituality, respectively. Genetics also appears to contribute significantly to whether one espouses religion in a conservative way. Bradshaw and Ellison (2008) reported genetic influences of 41% to 44% for biblical literalism and exclusivist beliefs (see also D'Onofrio et al., 1999).

INCREASING GENETIC CONTRIBUTIONS WITH AGE

Retrospective reports suggest that with age the influence of genetics on religiousness grows, whereas the influence of shared environments dwindles. Genetics accounts for only a small portion of the variance in retrospective ratings of childhood religiousness (12%, Koenig, McGue, Krueger, & Bouchard Jr., 2005; 19%, Bradshaw & Ellison, 2008), whereas shared environment accounts for roughly 53% to 56% (Bradshaw & Ellison, 2008; Koenig et al., 2005). In contrast, one study showed that genes account for 44% of current variance in religiousness, while shared environment drops to an 18% portion (Koenig et al., 2005). It has been argued that these changes reflect the increased autonomy and decreased family influence that accompanies late adolescence (Koenig et al., 2005).

The finding that genetic influences on religiousness increase with age may be moderated by external versus internal aspects of religion. Retrospective reports suggest that during childhood internal aspects of religion (e.g., belief) are more genetically determined than aspects of external religiousness (e.g., church attendance). As one ages, the influence of heredity on internal aspects of religious life remains fairly stable (Koenig et al., 2005). What seems to undergo a significant increase is the influence of heredity on *external* aspects of religiousness. This may reflect how external aspects of religious life become more subject to personal choice with age (see Koenig et al., 2005).

MEDIATING FACTORS

One important task for future research will be to identify the means through which genes influence religiousness. Research by D'Onofrio and colleagues (1999) found that the same genes that influenced church attendance in their sample also influenced social attitudes (e.g., attitudes toward sexuality). The same was not true of personality traits, which were uncorrelated with church attendance in this study. These findings suggest that genes may influence religiousness not via personality traits, but rather through social attitudes.

SUMMARY

Behavior genetics research has forced reevaluation of the prevalent assumption that people become religious solely through environmental influence (D'Onofrio et al., 1999). Nevertheless, the current literature suffers from numerous shortcomings. Bradshaw and Ellison (2008) lament a general lack of replications and inattention to measurement of many important aspects of religious life.[2] Research is also overly reliant on potentially biased retrospective reports, and measures with poor reliability inflate variance associated with nonshared genetic factors.

Attachment and Religiousness

For the last 20 years researchers have explored the possibility that differences in religiousness are attributable to variance in attachment styles. Attachment is the evolution-based drive to remain close to caregivers (Bowlby, 1969). Early attachment relationships are considered vital for the development of healthy models of self and other and for the internalization of a capacity for emotion regulation (e.g., Gable & Isabella, 1992). In a secure attachment relationship a child learns that he is worthwhile, that his caretaker is dependable, and that emotion is tolerable. In an insecure attachment relationship a child comes to think of herself as unlovable, others as nondependable, or emotion as intolerable.

Research on *concurrent* relationships between attachment and religiousness has yielded inconclusive findings. Knowing whether a person is currently securely or insecurely attached offers little help in consistently predicting religiosity. A majority of studies have found that securely attached adults are more religious or have a stronger relationship with God than insecurely attached adults (e.g., Granqvist & Hagekull, 2000; Kirkpatrick, 1998; Kirkpatrick & Shaver, 1992). However, significant effect sizes reported in these studies tended to be weak. Also, some studies failed to find any significant relationship between adult attachment and current religiousness (Granqvist & Hagekull, 2000, 2001), while other studies found that some forms of insecure attachment were actually associated with greater current religiousness (see Byrd & Boe,

2002; Granqvist & Hagekull, 2000; Kirkpatrick & Shaver, 1992).

In contrast, research that accounts for differences across time has yielded more consistent findings. Retrospective and longitudinal research shows that knowing about attachment style is actually quite helpful in predicting future religiousness. Two major temporal pathways to later religiousness have emerged, one beginning with secure attachment and the other beginning with insecure attachment.

FROM SECURE ATTACHMENT TO LATER RELIGIOUSNESS

Findings suggest that securely attached children have an increased likelihood of becoming religious adults with personal/positive relationships with God, but only when they view the parents they grew up with as being religious (Granqvist, 1998; Kirkpatrick & Shaver, 1990). To explain these findings, Granqvist and Hagekull (1999) proposed that the securely attached children of religious parents become more religious over time through the internalization of parental values. Granqvist and Hagekull (1999) developed the PBRS, a measure of "parental-based socialization of religiosity," and found that it was positively correlated with secure attachment among a university sample but notably without any moderating effects of parental religiousness.

Granqvist and Hagekull (1999) found that religious change in the lives of individuals with secure childhood attachment involves a unique cluster of attributes: For these individuals gradual, nonintense religious change tends to begin at a young age and involves internalization of parental standards. In support of this model, Granqvist and Kirkpatrick (2004) found that compared to sudden converts, gradual converts scored modestly but significantly higher on the PBRS, and they evidenced a trend toward greater retrospective maternal attachment security.

Dickie, Ajega, Kobylak, and Nixon (2006) proposed an alternative model to explain why the securely attached children of religious parents grow to become religious adults. Through path analyses they uncovered that self-concept mediates the path from nurturing contemporary relationships with parents to contemporary religiousness and closeness to God. For young adult men, having a nurturing mother led to increases in self-esteem, which, in turn predicted greater religiousness and closeness to God. Among young adult women, seeing either parent as nurturing positively influenced a daughter's sense of self as powerful and or nurturing, which in turn led to increased notions of God as powerful and nurturing.

FROM INSECURE ATTACHMENT TO LATER RELIGIOUSNESS

A second pathway to later religiousness begins with insecure attachment. A significant portion of insecurely attached children find their way to religion and a positive relationship with God, but only when they are the children of irreligious parents (Granqvist, 1998; Kirkpatrick & Shaver, 1990). A fascinating aspect of this phenomenon is that the participants in question (who were insecurely attached) reported more religiousness and a closer relationship with God than more securely attached participants (see Granqvist, 1998; Kirkpatrick & Shaver, 1990).

Interestingly, research also shows that insecure attachment during adulthood is predictive of religious changes down the road, and this seemingly regardless of parental religiousness. In 6-month and 4-year longitudinal studies, Kirkpatrick (1997, 1998) found that after controlling for baseline levels of religiousness, students with various forms of insecure attachment were most likely to undergo the most significant religious change. In the 4-year study (Kirkpatrick, 1997) this included a greater likelihood of finding a new relationship with God and undergoing a conversion experience.

The discovery that insecurely attached individuals are more likely than their secure counterparts to undergo sudden and dramatic religious change experiences is perhaps the strongest and best replicated finding in the attachment and religion literature. This finding was confirmed at a modest effect size in a recent meta-analysis that included an overall sub-sample of nearly 100 sudden converts (Granqvist & Kirkpatrick, 2004). While the vast majority of the studies in this meta-analysis used Christian samples, Pirutinsky (2009) found that converts to and from Orthodox Judaism also showed greater attachment insecurity than Jews who had not undergone conversions.

The sudden conversions of insecurely attached individuals involve a cluster of experiences that tend to occur later in life and are uniquely tied to problems in relationships and the regulation of painful emotion (see Granqvist, 1998; Granqvist & Hagekull, 1999, Granqvist & Kirkpatrick, 2004; Kirkpatrick & Shaver, 1990). The *emotional compensation hypothesis* suggests that insecurely attached individuals turn to religion to compensate for deficits in emotional regulation. An emotion-based religiosity scale (EBRS) developed by Granqvist and Hagekull (1999) was found to be negatively correlated with a scale measuring religion based on socialization, suggesting that these really are two different sides of religiousness.

Thus far only one study has shown the soothing effect that religious change can have on the emotional distress of the insecurely attached individual. Brown et al. (2004) found that regardless of attachment style, all of the widows in his longitudinal study showed greater temporary increases in religiousness compared to controls. However, an increase in the importance of religious beliefs led to a reduction in grief feelings only for insecurely attached widows (but not for securely attached widows). Note, however, that this study was limited through use of a two-item measure of attachment insecurity, one that (at face level) may actually tap into loneliness more than insecurity.

FROM INSECURE ATTACHMENT TO RELIGIOUS DRIFTING

Though it has received less empirical attention, a third pathway seems to run from insecure attachment to religious parents to later adult irreligiousness. Kirkpatrick and Shaver (1990) found that among those with avoidant attachment styles, having a perceived-as-religious mother during childhood predicted present negative feelings about God and religion. Bierman (2005) found that within an adult sample, retrospective reports of paternal abuse negatively predicted religious involvement and religious self-concept. While this latter study did not account for parental religiousness, it does offer validation of a pathway from insecure attachment to later irreligiousness.

ATTACHMENT AND SPIRITUALITY

The one study that addresses the relationship between attachment and spirituality suggests the presence of a pathway from insecure attachment to higher levels of later spirituality. Granqvist and Hagekull (2001) found that insecure childhood (but not adult) attachment was more prevalent among a sample of self-identified "new age" religionists as compared to a Lutheran sample. Furthermore, among all participants a continuous measure of "new-agedness" was positively correlated with insecure childhood (but not adult) attachment.

No evidence emerged to suggest that the spiritual change that occurred in the lives of new age individuals was either gradual or sudden. However, spiritual change within the new age sample was positively correlated with insecure attachment. Furthermore, themes of religion compensating for emotional distress were positively correlated with insecure maternal attachment among the new age sample. New age affiliation among a subsample of Lutherans was also positively correlated with a scale measuring the use of religion as a means of compensating for emotional distress. These findings are complemented by Bierman's (2005) finding that the presence of physical abuse by a nonparent was a positive predictor of spiritual self-concept later in life.

MODERATING EFFECTS OF GENDER AND VARIETIES OF INSECURITY

Many attempts have been made to uncover any moderating effects of gender on the aforementioned relationships. In the meta-analysis described earlier, Granqvist and Kirkpatrick (2004) found that sex differences were negligible both in terms of participant gender and with regard to paternal versus maternal attachment. It is similarly unclear that varieties of insecure attachment (i.e., anxious versus avoidant) moderate the aforementioned findings in any patterned and consistent way.

SUMMARY

By elaborating on religious pathways, studies of attachment have contributed significantly to our understanding of the religious personality. Limits of the literature include heavy reliance on self-report of attachment styles[3] as well as the use of potentially biased retrospective self-reports of childhood attachment. Finally, it is worth considering issues of generalizability because much of the research described was done among Swedes, a relatively secular group (see Granqvist & Hagekull, 2001).

Personality Trait Pathways

A growing body of literature highlights the pathways from personality traits to later religiousness and spirituality. The most replicated finding thus far is that conscientiousness during adolescence is predictive of later life religiousness (Heaven & Ciarrochi, 2007; McCullough, Tsang, & Brion, 2003), and one study replicated this finding while controlling for teenage religiousness (Wink, Ciciolla, Dillon, & Tracy, 2007). Wink and colleagues (2007) note that while these findings might mean that conscientious teens become more religious adults, it is equally plausible that conscientious teens are less likely than nonconscientious peers to become irreligious over time. Heaven and Ciarrochi (2007) also found evidence for moderating effects of gender and personality

change on the relationship between conscientiousness and later religiousness. In their study increases in conscientiousness between the first and second years of high school predicted greater religiosity during the third year of high school, but only for girls.

Findings regarding pathways from agreeableness to religiousness are more equivocal and appear to be moderated by gender. McCullough, Tsang, and Brion (2003) found that teenage agreeableness failed to predict later life religiosity. Wink and colleagues (2007) accounted for teenage religiousness and found strong effects for females only. Not only was teenage agreeableness predictive of later religiosity, but teenage religiosity was also predictive of later life increases in agreeableness.

Finally, it seems that teenagers who are open to new experiences have a greater likelihood of becoming spiritual older adults. Wink and colleagues (2007) found that teenage openness was predictive of greater spirituality in late adulthood, even after controlling for teenage religiousness. Unfortunately, this study was limited by not being able to control for teenage spirituality.

Agreeableness, Prosociality, and Religion

Many teachings of the world's major religions emphasize kindness, generosity, and peacefulness. Over the last 10 years, research has tackled the question of whether these religious ideals are internalized by religious adherents. In other words: Are religious people kind people?

SELF-REPORTED TRAITS

The Big Five factor of agreeableness is largely a measure of interpersonal style, assessing a range of interaction extending between poles of antisocial and prosocial tendencies (see Costa, McCrae, & Dye, 1991; Wilkowski, Robinson, & Meier, 2006). The results of two recent meta-analyses suggest that religiousness and self-reported agreeableness are positively correlated at a modest effect size, one that ranges between 0.13 and 0.20, depending on how one categorizes measures of religion (Lodi-Smith & Roberts, 2007; Saroglou, 2002). Findings from recent facet-level analyses remarkably suggest that religiousness is modestly positively associated with nearly every facet of self-reported agreeableness (Saroglou & Fiasse, 2003; Saroglou & Munoz-Garcia, 2008). These facets include Altruism, Compliance, Straightforwardness, Trust, Modesty, and Tender-Mindedness (Costa et al., 1991).

Nevertheless, the effect sizes noted earlier are not robust, and one does not have to look hard to find studies that fail to find an association between agreeableness and various forms of religiousness (e.g., Duriez & Soenens, 2006; Leak & Fish, 1999). These nonassociations beg the question of whether there are factors that moderate the relationship between religiousness and agreeableness.

Some forms of religiousness may be more strongly associated with self-reported agreeableness than others. In their recent meta-analysis, Lodi-Smith and Roberts (2007) found that self-reported agreeableness tends to have a significant effect size of 0.21 with measures of commitment to religion and internalization of religious values but a nonsignificant effect size of 0.04 with measures of religious affiliation or behavior. Duriez (2004) found that among the religious portion of a Belgian undergraduate sample, self-reported trait empathy was significantly correlated with having a "symbolic" interpretation of religion, as opposed to a more literal interpretation of religion. While this latter finding hints that prosociality may be more prominent among religious liberals, Streyffeler and McNally (1998) found no difference in the agreeableness scores of liberal and fundamentalist churchgoers.

Another potential moderator is the measure of agreeableness used. Saucier and Skrzypinska (2006) found that the while a Big Five measure of agreeableness did not correlate with religiousness, a positive correlation emerged between religiousness and a Five Factor Model measure of agreeableness. The authors suggest that the former measure loads heavily on gentle nonhostility, whereas the latter loads more on compliance.

SELF-REPORTED VALUES

In a recent meta-analysis using 21 independent samples, general religiousness was found to have a modest positive effect size with the prosocial value of benevolence ($d = 0.14$; Saroglou et al., 2004). Religiousness was also modestly negatively correlated with valuing power ($d = -0.09$), and the rank order of these values did not differ significantly across religions. There are two potential moderators at work in these value relationships. First, using some indicators of socioeconomic development, it was found that the more robust a country's economic development, the more positive the correlation between religiousness and benevolence and the more negative the correlation between religiousness and power (Saroglou et al., 2004). Another potential moderator is symbolic versus literal religiousness. Fontaine, Luyten, and Corveleyn (2000) found that religious literalism was not significantly correlated with valuing benevolence or devaluing power. In contrast, those who espoused a more symbolic religiosity placed a high value on benevolence and also exhibited a nonegocentric devaluing of hedonism and achievement. Similar findings were reported by Fontaine and colleagues (2005).

Should We Believe the Self-Reports?

In their influential review, Batson, Schoenrade, and Ventis (1993) concluded that the consistent positive associations between intrinsic religiousness and self-reports of compassion and tolerance are mediated by socially desirable responding. They argued that intrinsic religiousness is positively associated not so much with being helpful and tolerant, but rather the desire to appear that way. In the wake of Batson and colleagues' conclusion, many researchers have designed studies of religious prosociality using various non-self-report methodologies. Following the model outlined by Saroglou, Pichon, Trompette, Verschuren, and Dernelle (2005), we report findings from observer reports, studies of unconscious processes, and experimental procedures.

OBSERVER REPORTS OF RELIGIOUS PROSOCIALITY

Observers consistently seem to recognize religious people as being kind or altruistic. Saroglou and Fiasse (2003) found that participants' self-reported religiousness was modestly positively correlated with maternal ratings of participant agreeableness. In a later study, Saroglou and colleagues (2005, study 3) found that religious teens and young adults were rated by peers as being altruistic and were rated by siblings as being both altruistic and empathic. In a separate study (Saroglou et al., 2005, study 4), religious teens and young adults were rated by colleagues, though not siblings, as being altruistic and empathic.

Similar findings have emerged based on the reports of observers and interviewers with no intimate knowledge of or relationship with participants. For example, Wink and colleagues (2007) found that among a White middle-class sample, religiousness in older adulthood was positively correlated with an independent rater's Q-sort measure of agreeableness. Also, a longitudinal study by Dillon, Wink, and Fay (2003) revealed that being religious at any point during one's adulthood was predictive of an observer recognizing traits of generativity (i.e., concern for future generations) later in life.

TAPPING THE UNCONSCIOUS: PRIMING STUDIES AND PROJECTIVE METHODS

Priming methods have become popular means to examine the relationship between religiousness and prosociality. Pichon, Boccato, and Saroglou (2007) found that undergraduate participants primed with positively valenced religious words had increased prosocial/charitable behavior and faster recognition of "prosocial" words than nonprimed controls. In two studies, Shariff and Norenzayan (2007) gave participants $10 and instructions that any money not taken for oneself would be given to an anonymous second participant. In both studies participants primed with words relating to the "divine" left more money for the other player and also were more likely to take and leave an equal amount (i.e., $5) as compared to those who received a control prime.

It is unclear whether these priming effects are moderated by participants' religiousness. In the only research to look for these moderating effects, results were mixed (Shariff & Norenzayan, 2007). In one study, the "divine" prime was effective regardless of participant level of religiousness, while in a second study the prime only worked for participants who reported belief in God. Perhaps most interesting is that in both studies belief in God by itself was *not* a significant predictor of giving, and it only significantly predicted giving in conjunction with the prime in the second study.

Lastly, Saroglou and colleagues (2005, study 1) asked undergraduates to look at cards depicting frustrating interpersonal situations and to imagine what the protagonist in the card would say. General religiousness was negatively correlated with having projections rated as aggressive by experimenters. Religious fundamentalism was unrelated to experimenter ratings.

EXPERIMENTAL EVIDENCE

Ahmed (2009) compared the behavior of a group of religious students studying to be imams (i.e., Muslim clergy) against a group of secular students. In two games players were left with the choice of whether to selfishly keep money granted to them by the experimenter or to share with other players. Across both studies religious students contributed more than the nonreligious students. Interestingly, this difference was accounted for by the fact that in both games a significantly lower percentage of religious people gave zero money. Among those who gave, however, there was no difference between the religious and secular students.

The Limits of Religious Prosociality

The aforementioned research suggests that religious prosociality is a real phenomenon. As described next, however, this effect seems to be moderated by at least two major factors. First, while religious individuals may be kind in a proactive sense, their prosociality may not extend into situations that tend to prompt vengeful or retaliatory behavior. Second, a variety of studies suggest that some forms of religious compassion may not extend to members of outgroups or to individuals who violate religious values.

VENGEFULNESS AND RETALIATORY AGGRESSION

While religious individuals tend to report being nonvengeful, findings suggest that these reports should be viewed with some skepticism. In one study religious conservatism was negatively correlated with self-reported trait vengefulness but uncorrelated with participant ratings of how vengeful they would be in various scenarios that were hypothetically vengeance inducing (Cota-McKinley, Woody, & Bell, 2001).

Greer, Berman, Varan, Bobrycki, and Watson (2005) found that undergraduate participants who scored higher on intrinsic religiousness and church activity tended to report lower trait vengefulness scores, and these findings were not mediated by socially desirable responding.[4] However, also included in this study were two tasks in which participants were given the opportunity to retaliate after being the target of a confederate's aggression. Despite self-reports of reduced aggression among frequent churchgoers and those with high intrinsic religiosity, only participants who scored high on the Quest scale *acted* with less vengeance. Leach, Berman, and Eubanks (2008) similarly found that intrinsic religiousness was negatively correlated with self-reported trait aggression but not correlated with a behavioral measure of retaliatory aggression.

Further skepticism about the relationship between general religiousness and nonvengeance comes from a variety of priming studies. Using a behavioral paradigm similar to Greer and colleagues (2005), Leach, Berman, and Eubanks (2008) found no differences in retaliatory aggression between students primed to read a popular magazine and those primed to memorize a Bible passage or to connect with their higher power. Finally, some evidence suggests that exposure to text that describe acts of religiously sanctioned vengeance may actually increase aggressive behavior, even among irreligious participants (Bushman, Ridge, Das, Key, & Busath, 2007). Bushman and colleagues exposed participants to a passage describing an act of cruelty and later measured participants' aggressiveness in a competitive task. The most aggressive reactions belonged to participants who were led to believe that the passage was of biblical origin and who were additionally exposed to a passage in which God sanctioned a vengeful response.

IN-GROUP VERSUS OUT-GROUP COMPASSION

In the same meta-analysis that found that benevolence was modestly valued by religious individuals, universalism was modestly devalued ($d = -0.09$; Saroglou et al., 2004).[5] Saroglou and colleagues (2004) interpret this finding by suggesting that religious benevolence may be limited to those in one's ingroup. Support for this interpretation emerged in a study where undergraduate participants were presented with scenarios in which either a known party or a stranger was in need (Saroglou et al., 2005, study 4). Religiousness was positively correlated with helping known parties but not with helping strangers. Spirituality, in contrast, was positively associated with helping all targets without discrimination.

A series of studies by Batson and colleagues (1999) suggested that some forms of religiousness may be negatively associated with a specific form of compassion and kindness, one that centers on those who violate religious values. In an experimental setting, Batson and colleagues (1999) instructed a sample of Christian undergraduates to divide their time between two tasks. Participants were told that working longer on one task would increase the odds of a stranger winning a raffle, while greater effort on the second task would offer the same benefit to one of three supposed "disclosers." In one condition, the discloser was a homosexual who planned to use any money won to attend a gay-pride rally. In a second condition, the discloser was a homosexual who planned to use any money won to visit grandparents. In the final condition, the discloser did not mention sexual orientation and noted a plan to use the money to visit grandparents.

Participants who scored high on the intrinsic religiosity scale were less willing to help any gay discloser, regardless of what the person planned to do with the money. Batson and colleagues interpreted this finding to mean that intrinsically religious individuals were less willing to help an individual who violates religious values. Also, the finding that highly intrinsic participants did not help a gay

person visit his or her grandparents (as opposed to helping him or her attend a gay-pride rally) also suggests that intrinsically religious people may find it difficult to "love the sinner while hating the sin" (Batson et al., 1999).

Just as Saroglou and colleagues (2005) found that highly spiritual individuals were capable of universal compassion, Batson and colleagues found a similar phenomenon with individuals high in Quest. Those who scored high on the Quest scale did not discriminate against gay disclosers who planned to visit grandparents. Those who scored high in Quest were, however, less willing to help a gay discloser who planned to attend a gay-pride rally. Batson and colleagues interpret this latter finding as a legitimate expression of loving the sinner while hating the sin (since offering to help someone attend a gay-pride rally would have constituted promotion of sin). Later research showed that the universal compassion of high Quest scorers (and their ability to love the sinner and hate the sin) even extended to two groups who specifically violated Quest values of tolerance and open-mindedness: antigay individuals (Batson, Eidelman, Higley, & Russell, 2001) and religious fundamentalists (Batson, Denton, & Vollmecke, 2008).

SPIRITUALITY

Saroglou and Munoz-Garcia (2008) found that spiritual individuals valued benevolence and devalued power and achievement. In contrast to the values of religious individuals, spiritual types did not devalue universalism (Saroglou & Munoz-Garcia, 2008). From a trait perspective, studies have revealed positive associations between spirituality and self-reported agreeableness, empathy, and altruism (see Henningsgaard & Arnau, 2008; MacDonald, 2000; Saroglou et al., 2005). One facet-level study suggests that spirituality is positively correlated with all aspects of self-reported agreeableness (Saroglou & Munoz-Garcia, 2008), while in another study spirituality was only positively correlated with self-reports of tender-mindedness (Saroglou & Fiasse, 2003).

There is, however, some controversy as to whether spirituality is truly positively correlated with agreeableness, or whether spirituality only appears to be associated with agreeableness due to a mutual positive correlation with religiousness. McCullough and Willoughby (2009) found that within their undergraduate sample, a positive correlation between spirituality and agreeableness did not survive when controlling for religiousness. Similarly, spirituality was not correlated with agreeableness in a study that purposely isolated distinct factors of religiousness and spirituality (Saucier & Skrzypinska, 2006).

Nevertheless, observers tend to see spiritual people in a prosocial light. Across two studies, Saroglou and colleagues (2005) found that targets that self-identified as spiritual were seen as altruistic and empathic by peers and colleagues. In one (but not both) of these studies siblings also saw spiritual targets as altruistic and honest. Findings also suggest that spirituality is associated with prosocial behavior in experimental settings. Research shows that spirituality is uncorrelated with retaliatory aggressive behavior (Leach et al., 2008) and positively associated with indiscriminant helping behavior (Saroglou et al., 2004).

Based on these findings, one might assume the falsity of the common criticism of spirituality as a self-centered practice (e.g., Bellah, Madsen, Sullivan, Swidler, & Tipton, 1985). However, consider findings from a longitudinal study of a sample born in the 1920s: Dillon and colleagues (2003) found that spirituality in early adulthood was a *negative* predictor of observer reports of generosity in late adulthood. In middle adulthood spirituality became more important to a larger portion of the sample, and the spirituality of middle-aged and older adults positively predicted self and observer reports of generative concern for others in old age. These results raise fascinating questions, particularly as none of the other findings reviewed here suggest that young adult spirituality is tied to selfishness (not contemporaneously, at least).

SUMMARY

We echo the conclusions reached by Saroglou and colleagues (2005), who describe the relationship between religiousness and prosociality as a "limited reality." They further note that "...religious people are not delusional or dishonest when they report agreeableness, helping and other prosocial dispositions: others perceive them as altruists and they really tend to act in a prosocial way to some extent, with some people, and under some conditions" (2005, pp. 344–345). Future research will hopefully extend current findings by clarifying the factors that underlie the connection between religion and prosociality.[6]

Self-Control, Conscientiousness, and Morality

Baumeister and Exline (1999) noted the centrality of self-control in religious morality. They suggested that the greatest sins reflect lapses of self-control, whereas the most praiseworthy virtues require disciplined self-regulation. Self-control is inarguably central in religious philosophy, but to what extent is self-control reflected in the personality of religious and spiritual individuals? Moreover, if self-control really is a core aspect of the religious personality, does this make religious people more moral than others?

SELF-REPORTED TRAITS

In a recent narrative review McCullough and Willoughby (2009) reviewed 12 studies from the past 20 years (13 including their own study), each measuring the relationship between religion and primarily self-report measures of self-control. Positive correlations ranging from 0.21 to 0.38 were reported for all but one study, and correlations were impressively consistent across religion, region, and age. McCullough and Willoughby (2009) also concluded that existing evidence supports the notion that the connection between religiousness and various positive social outcomes (e.g., lower drug use; Walker, Ainette, Wills, & Mendoza, 2007) is at least partly explicable through religion's association with heightened self-control and delay of gratification.

The Big Five trait of conscientiousness is relevant to a discussion of religion and self-control.[7] Conscientiousness is often conceptualized as being comprised of the two lower order traits of *proactive* striving for achievement or competence, and *inhibitive* dependability or impulse control (e.g., Hough, 1992; Mount & Barrick, 1995). In a recent study, Saroglou and Munoz-Garcia (2008) found that measures of religiousness were positively correlated with both inhibitive and proactive aspects of conscientiousness.

More generally, however, evidence for the presence of a consistent positive association between religiousness and conscientiousness is underwhelming. Saroglou's 13-study meta-analysis (2002) demonstrated that self-reported conscientiousness was positively but modestly correlated with general/intrinsic religiousness and open/mature/spiritual religiousness. In their more recent meta-analysis of 36 studies, Lodi-Smith and Roberts (2007) found that general religiousness was not significantly correlated with self-reported conscientiousness.

One explanation for these inconsistent findings is that the positive correlation between conscientiousness and religion is moderated by style of religiousness. In the latter meta-analysis described earlier, conscientiousness had a significant albeit modest effect size ($d = 0.12$) with measures of commitment to religion and internalization of religious values; however, it had a nearly nonexistent effect size with measures of religious affiliation or behavior. This moderating effect is well illustrated by the findings of a recent study of sexual restraint (Rowatt & Schmitt, 2003). Among undergraduates, higher intrinsic religiousness scores were positively correlated with sexual restraint, relationship exclusivity, and seeking out a long-term mate. Findings were reversed for participants with an extrinsic religious style, and extrinsic religiousness was positively correlated with use of short-term sexual strategies, attempts at mate poaching, and the belief that sex without love is acceptable.

Finally, skepticism as to an association between conscientiousness and religiousness should be somewhat tempered by recent observer reports that confirm that others see religious people as more conscientious. Saroglou and Fiasse (2003) found that participant religiousness was positively predicted by the extent to which participants' mothers rated participants as conscientious. Also, Wink and colleagues (2007) found that among a sample of mainly White, middle-class Protestants, religiousness in older adulthood was positively correlated with independent rater's Q-sort measurements of conscientiousness.

VALUES

In the meta-analytic review of religiosity and values described earlier (Saroglou et al., 2004), religiousness showed its two highest positive associations with valuing tradition ($d = 0.45$) and conformity ($d = 0.23$). Religiousness was most strongly associated with devaluing hedonism, stimulation, and self-direction (effect sizes of -0.30, -0.26, and -0.24, respectively). The rank order of these values did not significantly differ across religions (i.e., Jews, Muslims, and Catholics). Findings were, however, moderated by economic factors: Greater socioeconomic development in participants' countries meant that religiousness was associated with somewhat less valuing of traditionalism as well as less devaluing of self-direction. These findings suggest that being more religious is associated with valuing existing social institutions and devaluing personal/egoistic strivings, particularly in wealthier nations.

EVIDENCE FOR A CONNECTION BETWEEN RELIGIOUSNESS AND MORALITY

The scholarly skepticism regarding the positive correlation between religiousness and self-reported prosociality and altruism also extends to self-report of religious morality. The *social desirability hypothesis* would be that religiousness is not associated with advanced morality so much as a desire to be *seen* as highly moral (see Burris & Navara, 2002). We think that this skepticism can be maintained in a more nuanced way that addresses different aspects of morality, including moral identity, moral reasoning, and moral behavior.

Religious teachings surely emphasize morality, but it is important to wonder at what level moral teachings are incorporated into individual religious identity. Aquino and Reed (2002) recently developed a two-factor measure of moral identity. An internalization factor measured the centrality of moral values to the self-concept, whereas a symbolization factor tapped a desire to project a moral self-image into the social world through external behavior and appearance. Religiousness was positively correlated with symbolization and with a total moral identity score but was not significantly correlated with internalization. These findings support the social desirability hypothesis and suggest that, for some religious samples, moral identity is not internalized.

In contrast to moral identity, moral reasoning refers to a learned capacity to reason about moral issues. Concerns over social desirability should reasonably be decreased with regard to moral reasoning, as observer-rated capacities are difficult to fake. Two recent studies suggest a positive relationship between religiousness and moral reasoning. Maclean, Walker, and Matsuba (2004) found a positive correlation between intrinsic religiousness and interviewer-rated level of moral reasoning among a relatively irreligious undergraduate sample.[8] In a more recent study, postconventional moral reasoning (the highest of Kohlberg's levels of moral reasoning) was positively predicted by Quest religiousness, but only among participants who also achieved high scores on a measure of commonsense judgment and practical reasoning skills (Cottone, Drucker, & Javier, 2007). These findings suggest that some forms of religiousness may be positively associated with moral reasoning and hint at the importance of moderating effects.

Most concretely, researchers are curious about whether religious people will behave morally in various experimental situations. Findings suggest that priming participants with religious concepts tends to lead to moral behavior, but it remains unclear whether one must be religious for these priming effects to emerge.

Across two studies Randolph-Seng and Nielsen (2007) asked participants to perform a simple circling task on which high performance would be rewarded. Participants were instructed to record the number of items correctly circled and report this to the experimenter. Secretly, the experimenter also counted the number of correct responses. In both studies, none of the participants who received a supraliminal religious prime cheated by overreporting correct responses. In contrast, participants who received neutral primes overreported success with significantly more frequency. The second study accounted for participant religiousness and found that intrinsic religiousness was not predictive of cheating behavior, either by itself or in interaction with the religious prime.

In contrast, Carpenter and Marshall (2009) found that both participant religiousness and religious priming are integral to moral behavior. Undergraduate participants were left alone under observation by hidden camera and given a coin to use to help decide whether they themselves or an anonymous coparticipant should be entered in a cash raffle. Moral hypocrites told experimenters that the moral thing to do was either flip a coin or simply give the raffle ticket to the other participants, but they were caught on camera acting against their stated morals. By themselves neither intrinsic religiousness nor an overt religious prime significantly predicted moral hypocrisy. However, a significant interaction emerged such that there was significantly more moral congruence among highly intrinsic participants who received a religious prime.

SPIRITUALITY AND CONSCIENTIOUSNESS, SELF-CONTROL, MORALITY

Studies of the relationship between spirituality, self-control, and morality are more sparse than studies involving measures of religiousness. From a values perspective, spiritual individuals, unlike religious individuals, do not seem to value tradition and conformity, nor do they devalue hedonism or self-direction (Saroglou & Munoz-Garcia, 2008). From a trait perspective, research on the relationship between spirituality and conscientiousness currently offers conflicting findings. In one study spirituality was positively correlated with conscientiousness and both its proactive and inhibitive aspects (Saroglou & Munoz-Garcia, 2008). More recently, McCullough and Willoughby (2009) found that *negative* correlations of spirituality with both conscientiousness and self-control were suppressed due to the presence of variance associated with religiousness. Future

research on the connection between spirituality and self-control should account for the potential confounds with religiousness and the potential moderating effects of different measures of spirituality.

Religion, Openness, and Prejudice

Gordon Allport (1954) is credited with recognizing the contradiction that religion seems simultaneously tied to prosociality and prejudice.[9] Since his time researchers have struggled to reconcile these seemingly opposing realities.[10] Prior reviews have dealt with the topic extensively and thoughtfully (e.g., Batson & Burris, 1994; Hood, Spilka, Hunbserger, & Gorsuch, 1996). The last 10 years have seen progress in identifying patterns of moderation and mediation in the relationship between religiousness and both racial prejudice and prejudice against homosexuals. We begin our review by highlighting how religiousness is connected with traits and values associated with tolerance.

TRAITS

The Five Factor Model contains no particular focus on tolerant or prejudicial traits, and perhaps the closest analog is the openness factor. Recently, growing attention has been focused on the positive relationship between openness and spirituality (e.g., Saucier & Skrzypinska, 2006). This positive correlation survives controlling for religiousness and gender (Wink et al., 2007) and is supported not only by self-ratings but also by openness ratings made by participants' mothers (Saroglou & Fiasse, 2003) and experts using a Q-sort (Wink et al., 2007). Spirituality is positively correlated with nearly all facets of openness, including openness to aesthetics/feelings, values, and fantasy (see Saroglou & Fiasse, 2003). And yet spirituality is not associated with openness to *everything*; a recent study found a negative correlation between spirituality and openness to actions (Saroglou & Munoz-Garcia, 2008).

In contrast, negative correlations have emerged between openness and traditional religiousness among an adult community sample (Saucier & Skrzypinska, 2006) and with the major long-term life goal of participating in religious activities among undergraduates (Roberts & Robins, 2000). It seems that the negative correlation between religiousness and openness may at times be suppressed by the inclusion of variance associated with spirituality. Once variance associated with spirituality is removed, the nonassociation between religiousness and openness is unmasked and a negative correlation emerges (e.g., McCullough & Willoughby, 2009).

Facet-level analyses suggest a more nuanced relationship between religiousness and openness, one that may be moderated by self-reports versus observer reports. Analysis of participant self-ratings in one facet-level analysis showed that religiousness was associated with being less open to values. But according to these same participants' mothers, religiousness was positively correlated with being open to ideas (Saroglou & Fiasse, 2003). Another potential moderator of the relationship between religiousness and openness is emotional versus classical religiousness. Saroglou and Munoz-Garcia (2008) found that classical religiousness was negatively correlated with openness to actions and to ideas. Emotional religiousness (i.e., experiencing religion in an emotional way; not to be confused with the use of religion as a form of emotional compensation, described earlier) was also negatively correlated with openness to actions but was positively correlated with openness to aesthetics/feelings.

RELIGIOUS FUNDAMENTALISM
AND PREJUDICE: CORRELATIONS
AND EXPLANATIONS

Religious fundamentalism (RF) involves avoidance of questioning one's religious beliefs and rare consideration of alternate points of view. Recent meta-analytic [11] and narrative reviews make it clear that RF is consistently positively associated with self-reported homosexual prejudice (Hunsberger & Jackson, 2005; Whitley Jr., 2009). Meta-analytic results also show that RF is positively associated with self-reported racist attitudes. However, the effect size for this association is roughly two-and-a-half times smaller than the effect size for antihomosexual attitudes (Whitley Jr., 2009). In their narrative review, Hunsberger and Jackson (2005) reported that nearly half of the studies reviewed found no association between RF and racial prejudice.

Over the past 10 years researchers have made progress in understanding the connection between RF and prejudice. Laythe, Finkel, and Kirkpatrick (2001) suggested that RF is actually a composite of two competing tendencies: belief style and belief content. The style of the RF is closed-minded, insular authoritarianism, and Laythe and colleagues suggested that it was this style that positively links RF with prejudice. The second proposed component of RF was fidelity to traditional Christian beliefs. The authors proposed that this Christian Orthodoxy would negatively predict racial biases and have a sample-dependent impact on antigay biases. Later analyses supported a two-component

model by confirming that authoritarian attitudes and Christian Orthodoxy accounted for a sizable 60% of the variance in RF (Laythe, Finkel, Bringle, & Kirkpatrick, 2002).

The model suggested by Laythe and colleagues (2001, 2002) was confirmed with regard to racist attitudes. Racist attitudes were positively predicted by authoritarianism and negatively predicted by Christian Orthodoxy (Laythe et al., 2002). The removal from religious fundamentalism of variance associated with one component led to the strong emergence of the effect of the other factor (e.g., when authoritarianism was held constant, RF became a negative predictor of racial prejudice). When both aspects were held steady, RF added nothing to the prediction of racism (Laythe et al., 2002). This pattern of findings was later replicated using an implicit measure of racist attitudes (see Rowatt & Franklin, 2004).

The model was only partially supported with regard to antihomosexual biases. In simultaneous regressions homosexual prejudice was negatively predicted by Christian Orthodoxy but positively predicted by both RF and authoritarianism. These findings suggest that among some samples Christian Orthodoxy will predict lower self-reported gay prejudice (see also Jonathan, 2008). It also suggests that something beyond an authoritarian style of belief links RF with antihomosexual prejudice.

Altemeyer (2003) suggested an alternative explanation for the prejudice of RFs. He proposed that RF prejudice represents the continuation of early training in ingroup preferences. Using a sample of college students and their parents, Altemeyer found strong positive correlations of RF with racist/antigay attitudes and found an even stronger positive correlation between RF and religious ethnocentrism, or a preference for one's religious ingroup over religious outgroups. Altemeyer suggested that the relative strength of this distaste for religious outgroups stems from early life emphasis on training in us-versus-them religious distinctions more so than training in other distinctions such as race and gender. RF undergraduates confirmed that identification with family religion was stressed in their families, while gender and race were relatively unstressed.[12] Unfortunately, this study was limited by its use of retrospective reports and the lack of a measure of social desirability bias.

QUEST RELIGIOUSNESS AND
THE ABSENCE OF PREJUDICE

When it comes to issues of prejudice, the open-mindedness of those with a Quest orientation seems to work in the opposite fashion of religious funda-mentalism. In Whitley Jr.'s (2009) meta-analytic review, Quest was significantly associated with lower racial prejudice, and it was the only religious factor related to positive attitudes toward homosexuals (see similar conclusions in Hunsberger & Jackson, 2005). Quest has also been shown to be tied with positive implicit attitudes toward homosexuals (Tsang & Rowatt, 2007). One interesting and as yet unex-plained finding is that Quest is nearly twice as strongly (negatively) associated with homosexual prejudice as with racial prejudice (see Whitley Jr., 2009).

INTRINSIC RELIGIOUSNESS AND HOMOSEXUAL (BUT NOT RACIAL) PREJUDICE

Another finding is in need of explanation: Intrinsic religiousness shows consistent positive correlations with antigay attitudes but negative correlations with racial prejudice. This conclusion has emerged in recent narrative and meta-analytic reviews (Hunsberger & Jackson, 2005; Whitley Jr., 2009). Researchers have taken one of two approaches in addressing this finding.

The first approach has been to address reasons why religion might treat gays and those of other races differently. Batson and Burris (1994) sug-gested that religious communities typically censure racial prejudice, but they simultaneously tolerate or even promote antigay prejudice. Horvath and Ryan (2003) suggested that religious intolerance toward gays stems from the belief that being gay is controllable, whereas controllability is an obvious nonfactor for race. In a study of discriminatory hir-ing practices, path analyses showed that religiosity was directly positively linked with antigay attitudes and with beliefs that homosexuality is controllable. Furthermore, the relationship between religiosity and antigay attitudes was partially mediated by the belief that homosexuality is controllable (Horvath & Ryan, 2003; see also Haslam & Levy, 2006).

A second approach takes the stance that intrinsic religiousness is not tied with prejudice against gay individuals so much as with intolerance of homosex-ual sexuality and general extramarital promiscuity. Veenlivet (2008) found that compared with the rest of their undergraduate sample, highly intrinsic par-ticipants exhibited negative attitudes toward homo-sexual sexual behavior. At the same time, highly intrinsic participants with greater prior exposure to the message that one is meant to "love the sinner, hate the sin" were no different from the rest of the sample in terms of beliefs about how homosexu-als should be treated in society. In contrast, highly intrinsic participants not exposed to the "love the sinner" message exhibited more negative attitudes toward gays in society.

A similar suggestion was made by Mak and Tsang (2008), who proposed that intrinsically religious people may not be prejudiced against homosexu-als so much as intolerant of any form of extramari-tal promiscuity. They used the same methodology employed in the Batson studies (described earlier), and each undergraduate participant received a note from one of four disclosers: a gay promiscuous dis-closer; a gay celibate discloser; a not-gay promiscu-ous discloser, and a not-gay celibate discloser. High intrinsic religiousness was associated with giving less help to all promiscuous disclosers, but intrinsic reli-giousness was not associated with any sort of bias against gay disclosers.

The notion that intrinsic religiousness is not associated with prejudice toward gay individuals is countered by findings from at least two studies. First, recall the findings from Batson and colleagues (1999), described earlier. Second, Wilkinson (2004) administered a multidimensional measure of homophobia to an undergraduate sample. Intrinsic religiousness and Christian Orthodoxy were both modestly to moderately positively correlated with each of the scales, including fear of contact with gays, immorality beliefs, intolerance of gays having rights, and stereotypes about gays.

EXTRINSIC RELIGIOUSNESS AND RACIAL (BUT NOT HOMOSEXUAL) PREJUDICE

Meta-analytic findings and narrative review sug-gest that extrinsic religiousness is not significantly or consistently associated with homosexual prejudice (Hunsberger & Jackson, 2005; Whitley Jr., 2009). In contrast, extrinsic religiousness showed a positive effect size with regard to racial prejudice (Whitley Jr., 2009) and is most often positively correlated with racial prejudice (Hunsberger & Jackson, 2005). This finding remains largely unexplained.

CURRENT AND FUTURE TRENDS IN RESEARCH ON RELIGION AND PREJUDICE

Drawing on coping theory, Pargament, Trevino, Mahoney, and Silberman (2007) suggest that the prejudices of religious individuals may be a form of negative coping with perceived threats to one's ingroup. Prejudice protects the ingroup by maintain-ing vigilance and distance from a value-threatening outgroup. This model differs from prevalent trait approaches to prejudice in that it appreciates situ-ational variables. Increased prejudice is posited in the presence of threat or negative coping, whereas decreased prejudice is predicted in low-threat situations or when more positive coping is used.

Support for this model emerged in a recent study by Pargament and colleagues (2007) where between 7% and 17% of an undergraduate sample agreed that Jews desecrated Christianity (i.e., were a threat to Christian values) in either the past or the present. The perception of Jews as *current* (as opposed to historic) desecrators of Christianity significantly predicted perceived conflict with Jews and anti-Semitism over and above various demographic and trait factors that typically predict prejudice (e.g., authoritarianism). The use of negative strategies to cope with the perception that Jews are a threat (e.g., by viewing Jews as demonic) was also positively correlated with anti-Semitism and perceived conflict with Jews. In contrast, more positive coping strategies were negatively associated with anti-Semitism/conflict.

The work of Pargament and colleagues (2007) also exemplifies another current trend in the literature: the study of connections between religion and prejudice against groups other than gays and racial minorities. Harper (2007) suggested that in certain settings nonreligious people can be a minority group targeted for prejudice by a religious majority. The author found evidence that religious undergraduates' descriptions of nonreligious people had an overall negative valence. Attitudes toward Muslims have also been the focus of recent study. Rowatt, Franklin, and Cotton (2005) found that Christian undergraduate participants showed evidence of both explicit and implicit bias against Muslims relative to Christians and that various measures of religiousness (i.e., RF, intrinsic, quest) showed unique patterns of correlation with these biases.

Finally, many recent studies have taken advantage of the Implicit Attitude Test (IAT) as a means of studying unconscious attitudes regarding prejudice. On the IAT, participants are asked to sort words into categories while the researcher measures sorting speed. The notion behind the IAT is that participants sort faster when two concepts are positively associated in their minds but sort slower when the connection is weak or negative. For example, a prejudiced individual would sort words in the gay-pleasant category more slowly than words in the straight-pleasant category.

One consistent finding from these studies is that implicit antihomosexuality has unique correlates and mediators with religious factors that differentiate it from more explicit antihomosexual prejudice (e.g., Rowatt et al., 2005, 2006). For example,

Tsang and Rowatt (2007) found that a positive correlation between intrinsic religiousness and explicit antihomosexuality was mediated by authoritarian attitudes, while a (marginally significant) positive correlation between intrinsic religiousness and implicit antihomosexuality was not.

Beyond this, however, clear patterns have yet to emerge to explain what predicts implicit antihomosexual attitudes. Two recent studies performed simultaneous regressions to predict antihomosexual attitudes using RF, Christian Orthodoxy, and authoritarianism. In one study, RF emerged as the only significant predictor of implicit antihomosexual attitudes (Rowatt et al., 2006) while in another study, authoritarianism was the only predictor of implicit antihomosexuality, and then only among non-Christians (Jonathan, 2008).

Conclusions and Future Directions

The last 10 years have seen significant progress in the study of the religious and spiritual personality. In one sense, this progress is due to the accumulation of research findings to the point where meta-analytic techniques can now be employed to address long-standing questions and debates. This is clearly an advantage in the study of religion and prejudice, where meta-analysis has revealed fascinating and nuanced patterns of correlation (see Whitley Jr., 2009). Meta-analytic data have also been invaluable in helping to elaborate the relationship of religiousness with traits and values.

But perhaps more important, recent progress is also attributable to researchers in the psychology of religion and spirituality embracing theoretical paradigms and research methods employed in the mainstream personality literature. During the last decade this sampling has been evident in numerous ways. Research exploring connections of religion with behavior genetics, attachment, and the Five Factor Model have increased our understanding of the roots and pathways of religious life. The use of priming studies has offered new insights into the long-standing debate over the validity of self-reported prosociality among the religious. And path analyses are helping us to understand how it is that being religious leads to greater self-control, which in turn leads to positive outcomes for society.

Despite these advances, there are a number of areas where research into the religious and spirituality personality can still grow. One clear disadvantage of the current literature is the relative lack of empirical research on religious affect and motivation.[13] In our review of the literature, studies on affect and motivation were clearly in the minority. The study of affect is integral to an understanding of religiousness, as should be evident from findings reviewed earlier regarding the relationship between affect, attachment, and religiousness. Research on religious affect and motivation may increase as researchers draw their attention away from trait approaches and toward the study of values (which are inherently motivational units) and situational pressures (e.g., Pargament et al., 2007).

The study of personality in the psychology of religion would also benefit from continued exploration of aspects of personality that are uniquely relevant to religious and spiritual individuals (for a similar critique, see McCrae, 1999). Some research has already begun to address these unique areas. For example, Piedmont (1999a) identified a trait of "spiritual transcendence," which was not only independent of the Five Factor Model but predicted important outcomes over and above the FFM. Recent studies of sanctification, or the process of making something sacred or holy, also represent an advance in the study of areas unique to religion and spirituality. Research suggests that sanctification is a meaningful construct with significant predictive value (e.g., Murray-Swank, Pargament, & Mahoney, 2005).

Finally, the study of the religious and spiritual personality would benefit from addressing the lack of measurement sophistication in self-report measures of religiousness. There are two major costs associated with this problem. First, poor reliability and careless self-reporting can lead to the loss of much of the nuance and subtlety extant in religious life. Second, researchers waste valuable resources by constantly reinventing redundant measures. We offer two potential solutions to this problem. First, increased use of expert ratings would allow researchers to be uncompromising in the study of more nuanced aspects of religious life.[14] Second, efforts should be made to design a measure of religion and spirituality akin in validity, reliability, and comprehensiveness to the Five Factor Model and the Schwartz Value Survey. Such a measure would create a shared language among researchers and would dramatically reduce measurement overlap.

Notes

1. Bradshaw and Ellison (2008) provide an excellent summary of behavior genetics methodology. D'Onofrio and colleagues (1999) discuss assortative mating and the challenges it presents to the behavior genetic study of religion.

2. In their own research Bradshaw and Ellison (2008) found that genetics accounted for an impressive 65% of variance in being "born again."

3. In one study of attachment and religion, Ross (2007) found that self-reported attachment style agreed with expert ratings only with regard to secure features of attachment. Otherwise self-reports were more generous than expert ratings by painting respondents as more stable in relationships, less dependent, more autonomous, and more caring.

4. Quest was uncorrelated with trait vengeance in this study. Interestingly, greater donation of church money was not only positively correlated with self-reported trait vengeance (as was extrinsic religiousness), but it was also the only variable associated with greater retaliatory aggression (Greer et al., 2005).

5 Universalism was particularly devalued by religious participants in Mediterranean countries and by religious individuals from economically underdeveloped countries (Saroglou et al., 2004).

6. Saroglou and colleagues (2005) offer evidence that the relationship between religion and prosociality is not mediated by attachment style, empathy, or honesty. Excellent discussions on other potential mediators are offered by Shariff and Norenzayan (2007) and Ahmed (2009).

7. While this section on self-control highlights findings regarding conscientiousness, it is noteworthy that both agreeableness and conscientiousness have been suggested as deriving from a common developmental process of heightened self-control (see Ahadi & Rothbart, 1994).

8. Findings from this study are limited by use of a religious orientation scale with a relatively irreligious population.

9. Hunsberger and Jackson (2005) argue persuasively for extending definitions of religious prejudice to include not only instances of straightforward negativity but also instances of stifling positive treatment (e.g., paternalism).

10. Readers are encouraged to review Hunsberger and Jackson (2005) for thoughtful commentary on how religious people can be simultaneously prosocial and intolerant.

11. Meta-analytic techniques are limited by their inability to perform regression analyses. This is unfortunate, because many measures of religiousness clearly overlap, and it would be helpful to determine which measures account for the lion's share of prejudicial attitudes.

12. Fifty-seven percent of high fundamentalists in this study noted that their parents never emphasized racial distinctions when participants were young.

13. A comparable critique was made 10 years ago by Hill and Hood, Jr. (1999).

14. Westen (1996) discussed similar costs of using self-report over expert ratings in reference to the trait approach.

References

Ahadi, S. A., & Rothbart, M. K. (1994). Temperament, development, and the Big Five. In C. F. Halverson, Jr., G. A. Kohnstamm, & R. P. Martin (Eds.), *The developing structure of temperament and personality from infancy to adulthood* (pp. 189–207). Hillsdale, NJ: Erlbaum.

Ahmed, A. M. (2009). Are religious people more prosocial? A quasi-experimental study with Madrasah pupils in a rural community in India. *Journal for the Scientific Study of Religion, 48*(2), 368–374.

Allport, G. W. (1954). *The nature of prejudice.* Cambridge, MA: Addison-Wesley.

Allport, G. W., & Ross, J. M. (1967). Personal religious orientation and prejudice. *Journal of Personality and Social Psychology, 5,* 432–443.

Altemeyer, B. (2003). Why do religious fundamentalists tend to be prejudiced? *The International Journal for the Psychology of Religion, 13*(1), 17–28.

Aquino, K., & Reed, A., II. (2002). The self-importance of moral identity. *Journal of Personality and Social Psychology, 83*(6), 1423–1440.

Batson, C. D. (1976). Religion as prosocial: Agent or double agent? *Journal for the Scientific Study of Religion, 15*(1), 29–45.

Batson, C. D., & Burris, C. T. (1994). Personal religion: Depressant or stimulant of prejudice and discrimination? In M. P. Zanna & J. M. Olson (Eds.), *The psychology of prejudice: The Ontario symposium* (Vol. 7, pp. 149–169). Hillsdale, NJ: Erlbaum.

Batson, D. C., Denton, D. M., & Vollmecke, J.T. (2008). Quest religion, anti-fundamentalism, and limited versus universal compassion. *Journal for the Scientific Study of Religion, 47*(1), 135–145.

Batson, C. D., Eidelman, S. H., Higley, S. L., & Russell, S. A. (2001). "And who is my neighbor?" II: Quest religion as a source of universal compassion. *Journal for the Scientific Study of Religion, 40*, 39–50.

Batson, C. D., Floyd, R. B., Meyer, J. M., & Winner, A. L. (1999). "And who is my neighbor?": Intrinsic religion as a source of universal compassion. *Journal for the Scientific Study of Religion, 38*, 445–457.

Batson, C. D., Schoenrade, P., & and Ventis, W. L. (1993). *Religion and the individual: A social-psychological perspective.* New York: Oxford University Press.

Baumeister, R. F., & Exline, J. J. (1999). Virtue, personality, and social relations: Self-control as the moral muscle. *Journal of Personality, 67*(6), 1165–1194.

Bellah, R. N., Madsen, R., Sullivan, W., Swidler, A., & Tipton, S. M. (1985). *Habits of the heart: Individualism and commitment in American life.* Berkeley: University of California Press.

Bierman, A. (2005). The effects of childhood maltreatment on adult religiosity and spirituality: Rejecting God the father because of abusive fathers? *Journal for the Scientific Study of Religion, 44*(3), 349–359.

Bouchard, T. J., McGue, M., Lykken, D., & Tellegen, A. (1999). Intrinsic and extrinsic religiousness: Genetic and environmental influences and personality correlates. *Twin Research, 2*, 88–98.

Bowlby, J. (1969). *Attachment and loss: Vol. 1. Attachment.* New York: Basic Books.

Bradshaw, M., & Ellison, C. G. (2008). Do genetic factors influence religious life? Findings from a behavior genetic analysis of twin siblings. *Journal for the Scientific Study of Religion, 47*(4), 529–544.

Brown, S. L., Nesse, R. M., House, J., & Utz, R. L. (2004). Religion and emotional compensation: Results from a prospective study of widowhood. *Personality and Social Psychology Bulletin, 30*, 1165–1174.

Burris, C. T., & Navara, G. S. (2002). Morality play or playing morality? Intrinsic religious orientation and socially desirable responding. *Self and Identity, 1*(1), 67–76.

Bushman, B. J., Ridge, R. D., Das, E., Key, C. W., & Busath, G. L. (2007). When god sanctions killing: Effects of scriptural violence on aggression. *Psychological Science, 18*(3), 204–207.

Byrd, K. R., & Boe, A. (2002). The correspondence between attachment dimensions and prayer in college students. *The International Journal for the Psychology of Religion, 11*(1), 9–24.

Carpenter, T. P., & Marshall, M. A. (2009). An examination of religious priming and intrinsic religious motivation in the moral hypocrisy paradigm. *Journal for the Scientific Study of Religion, 48*(2), 386–393.

Costa, P. T., Jr., McCrae, R. R., & Dye, D. A. (1991). Facet scales for agreeableness and conscientiousness: A revision of the NEO Personality Inventory. *Personality and Individual Differences, 12*(9), 887–898.

Cota-McKinley, A. L., Woody, W. D., & Bell, P. A. (2001). Vengeance: Effects of gender, age, and religious background. *Aggressive Behavior, 27*, 343–350.

Cottone, J., Drucker, P., & Javier, R. A. (2007). Predictors of moral reasoning: Components of executive functioning and aspects of religiosity. *Journal for the Scientific Study of Religion, 46*(1), 37–53.

Dickie, J. R., Ajega, L. V., Kobylak, J. R., & Nixon, K. M. (2006). Mother, father, and self: Sources of young adults' God concepts. *Journal for the Scientific Study of Religion, 45*(1), 57–71.

Dillon, M., Wink, P., & Fay, K. (2003). Is spirituality detrimental to generativity? *Journal for the Scientific Study of Religion, 42*(3), 427–442.

D'Onofrio, B. M., Eaves, L. J., Murrelle, L., Maes, H. H., & Spilka, B. (1999). Understanding biological and social influences on religious affiliation, attitudes, and behaviors: A behavior genetic perspective. *Journal of Personality, 67*(6), 953–984.

Duriez, B. (2004). Taking a closer look at the religion-empathy relationship: Are religious people nicer people? *Mental Health, Religion and Culture, 7*, 249–254.

Duriez, B., & Soenens, B. (2006). Personality, identity styles, and religiosity: An integrative study among late and middle adolescents. *Journal of Adolescence, 29*, 119–135.

Emmons, R.A. (1999). Religion in the psychology of personality: An introduction. *Journal of Personality, 67*(6), 873–888.

Fontaine, J. R. J., Duriez, B., Luyten, P., Corveleyn, J., & Hutsebaut, D. (2005). Consequences of a multidimensional approach to religion for the relationship between religiosity and value priorities. *The International Journal for the Psychology of Religion, 15*(2), 123–143.

Fontaine, J. R. J., Luyten, P., & Corveleyn, J. (2000). Tell me what you believe and I'll tell you what you want: Empirical evidence for discriminating value patterns of five types of religiosity. *The International Journal for the Psychology of Religion, 10*(2), 65–84.

Gable, S., & Isabella, R. A. (1992). Maternal contributions to infant regulation of arousal. *Infant Behavior and Development, 15*, 95–107.

Goldberg, L. R. (1981). Language and individual differences: The search for universals in personality lexicons. In L. Wheeler (Ed.), *Review of personality and social psychology* (Vol. 2, pp. 141–165). Beverly Hills, CA: Sage.

Granqvist, P. (1998). Religiousness and perceived childhood attachment: On the question of compensation or correspondence. *Journal for the Scientific Study of Religion, 37*(2), 350–367.

Granqvist, P., & Hagekull, B. (1999). Religiousness and perceived childhood attachment: Profiling socialized correspondence and emotional compensation. *Journal for the Scientific Study of Religion, 38*, 254–273.

Granqvist, P., & Hagekull, B. (2000). Religiosity, adult attachment, and why 'singles' are more religious. *The International Journal for the Psychology of Religion, 10*(2), 111–123.

Granqvist, P., & Hagekull, B. (2001). Seeking security in the new age: On attachment and emotional compensation. *Journal for the Scientific Study of Religion, 40*(3), 527–545.

Granqvist, P., & Kirkpatrick, L. A. (2004). Religious conversation and perceived childhood attachment: A meta-analysis. *The International Journal for the Psychology of Religion, 14*(4), 223–250.

Greer, T., Berman, M., Varan, V., Bobrycki, L., & Watson, S. (2005). We are a religious people; we are a vengeful people. *Journal for the Scientific Study of Religion, 44*(1), 45–57.

Harper, M. (2007). The stereotyping of nonreligious people by religious students: Contents and subtypes. *Journal for the Scientific Study of Religion, 46*(4), 539–552.

Haslam, N., & Levy, S. R. (2006). Essentialist beliefs about homosexuality: Structure and implications for prejudice. *Personality and Social Psychology Bulletin, 32*(4), 471–485.

Heaven, P. C. L., & Ciarrochi, J. (2007). Personality and religious values among adolescents: A three-wave longitudinal analysis. *British Journal of Psychology, 98*, 681–694.

Henningsgaard, J. M., & Arnau, R. C. (2008). Relationships between religiosity, spirituality, and personality: A multivariate analysis. *Personality and Individual Differences, 45*, 703–708.

Hill, P. C., & Hood, R. W., Jr. (1999). Affect, religion and unconscious processes. *Journal of Personality, 67*(6), 1015–1046.

Hood, R. W., Jr., Spilka, B., Hunberger, B., & Gorsuch, R. L. (1996). *The psychology of religion: An empirical approach* (2nd ed.). New York: The Guilford Press.

Horvath, M., & Ryan, A. M. (2003). Antecedents and potential moderators of the relationship between attitudes and hiring discrimination on the basis of sexual orientation. *Sex Roles, 48*(3/4), 115–130.

Hough, L. M. (1992). The "Big Five" personality variables-construct confusion: Description versus prediction. *Human Performance, 5*, 139–155.

Hunsberger, B., & Jackson, L. M. (2005). Religion, meaning and prejudice. *Journal of Social Issues, 61*, 807–826.

Jonathan, E. (2008). The influence of religious fundamentalism, right-wing authoritarianism, and Christian orthodoxy on explicit and implicit measures of attitudes toward homosexuals. *The International Journal for the Psychology of Religion, 18*, 316–329.

Kirkpatrick, L. A. (1997). A longitudinal study of changes in religious belief and behavior as a function of individual differences in adult attachment style. *Journal for the Scientific Study of Religion, 36*(2), 207–217.

Kirkpatrick, L. A. (1998). God as a substitute attachment figure: A longitudinal study of adult attachment style and religious change in college students. *Personality and Social Psychology Bulletin, 24*(9), 961.973.

Kirkpatrick, L. A., & Shaver, P. R. (1990). Attachment theory and religion: Childhood attachments, religious beliefs and conversion. *Journal for the Scientific Study of Religion, 29*(3), 315–334.

Kirkpatrick, L. A., & Shaver, P. R. (1992). An attachment-theoretical approach to romantic love and religious belief. *Personality and Social Psychology Bulletin, 18*(3), 266–275.

Koenig, L. B., McGue, M., Krueger, R. F., & Bouchard, T. J., Jr. (2005). Genetic and environmental influences on religiousness: Findings from retrospective and current religiousness ratings. *Journal of Personality, 73*, 471–488.

Laythe, B., Finkel, D. G., Bringle, R. G., & Kirkpatrick, L. A. (2002). Religious fundamentalism as a predictor of prejudice: A two-component model. *Journal for the Scientific Study of Religion, 41*(4), 623–635.

Laythe, B., Finkel, D., & Kirkpatrick, L. A. (2001). Predicting prejudice from religious fundamentalism and right-wind authoritarianism: A multiple regression approach. *Journal for the Scientific Study of Religion, 40*, 1–10.

Leach, M. M., Berman, M. E., & Eubanks, L. (2008). Religious activities, religious orientation, and aggressive behavior. *Journal for the Scientific Study of Religion, 47*(2), 311–319.

Leak, G. K., & Fish, S. B. (1999). Development and initial validation of a measure of religious maturity. *The International Journal for the Psychology of Religion, 9*(2), 83–103.

Lodi-Smith, J., & Roberts, B. W. (2007). Social investment and personality: A meta-analysis of the relationship of personality traits to investment in work, family, religion, and volunteerism. *Personality and Social Psychology Review, 11*(1), 1–19.

MacDonald, D.A. (2000). Spirituality: Description, measurement, and relation to the five factor model of personality. *Journal of Personality, 68*(1), 153–197.

Maclean, A. M., Walker, L. J., & Matsuba, M. K. (2004). Transcendence and the moral self: Identity integration, religion and moral life. *Journal for the Scientific Study of Religion, 43*(3), 429–437.

Mak, H. K., & Tsang, J-A.(2008). Separating the 'sinner' from the 'sin': Religious orientation and prejudiced behavior toward sexual orientation and promiscuous sex. *Journal for the Scientific Study of Religion, 47*(3), 379–392.

McCullough, M. E., Tsang, J., & Brion, S. (2003). Personality traits in early adolescence as predictors of religiousness in early adulthood: Findings from the Terman longitudinal study. *Personality and Social Psychology Bulletin, 29*(8), 980–991.

McCullough, M. E., & Willoughby, B. L. B. (2009). Religion, self-regulation, and self-control: Associations, explanations, and implications. *Psychological Bulletin, 135*(1), 69–93.

McCrae, R. R., & John, O. P. (1992). The Five-Factor Model: Issues and applications. *Journal of Personality, 60*(2), 175–215.

McCrae, R. R. (1999). Mainstream personality psychology and the study of religion. *Journal of Personality, 67*(6), 1209–1218.

Mount, M. K., & Barrick, M. R. (1995). The Big Five personality dimensions: Implications for research and practice in human resources management. *Research in Personnel and Human Resources Management, 13*, 153–200.

Murray-Swank, N. A., Pargament, K. I., & Mahoney, A. (2005). At the crossroads of sexuality and spirituality: The sanctification of sex by college students. *The International Journal for the Psychology of Religion, 15*(3), 199–219.

Pargament, K. I., Trevino, K., Mahoney, A., & Silberman, I. (2007). They killed our Lord: The perception of Jews as desecrators of Christianity as a predictor of anti-Semitism. *Journal for the Scientific Study of Religion, 46*(2), 143–158.

Pichon, I., Boccato, G., & Saroglou, V. (2007). Nonconscious influences of religion on prosociality: A priming study. *European Journal of Social Psychology, 37*, 1032–1045.

Piedmont, R. L. (1999a). Does spirituality represent the sixth factor of personality? Spiritual transcendence and the five-factor model. *Journal of Personality, 67*(6), 985–1013.

Piedmont, R. L. (1999b). Strategies for using the five-factor model of personality in religious research. *Journal of Psychology and Theology, 27*(4), 338–350.

Pirutinsky, S. (2009). Conversion and attachment insecurity among Orthodox Jews. *The International Journal for the Psychology of Religion, 19*, 200–206.

Randolph-Seng, B., & Nielsen, M. E. (2007). Honesty: One effect of primed religious representations. *The International Journal for the Psychology of Religion, 17*(4), 303–315.

Roberts, B. W., & Robins, R. W. (2000). Broad dispositions, broad aspirations: The intersection of personality traits and major life goals. *Personality and Social Psychology Bulletin, 26*(10), 1284–1296.

Roccas, S., Sagiv, L., Schwartz, S. H., & Knafo, A. (2002). The big five personality factors and personal values. *Personality and Social Psychology Bulletin, 28*(6), 789–801.

Ross, T. (2007). Attachment and religious beliefs: Attachment styles in Evangelical Christians. *Journal of Religion and Health, 46*(1), 75–84.

Rowatt, W. C., & Franklin, L. M. (2004). Christian orthodoxy, religious fundamentalism, and right-wing authoritarianism as predictors of implicit racial prejudice. *The International Journal for the Psychology of Religion, 14*(2), 125–138.

Rowatt, W. C., Franklin, L. M., & Cotton, M. (2005). Patterns and personality correlates of implicit and explicit attitudes towards Christians and Muslims. *Journal for the Scientific Study of Religion, 44*(1), 29–43.

Rowatt, W. C., & Schmitt, D. P. (2003). Associations between religious orientation and varieties of sexual experience. *Journal for the Scientific Study of Religion, 42*(3), 455–465.

Rowatt, W. C., Tsang, J., Kelly, J., LaMartina, B., McCullers, M., & McKinley, A. (2006). Association between religious personality dimensions and implicit homosexual prejudice. *Journal for the Scientific Study of Religion, 45*(3), 397–406.

Saroglou, V. (2002). Religion and the five factors of personality: A meta-analytic review. *Personality and Individual Differences, 32*, 15–25.

Saroglou, V., Delpierre, V., & Dernelle, R. (2004). Values and religiosity: A meta-analysis of studies using Schwartz's model. *Personality and Individual Differences, 37*, 721–734.

Saroglou, V., & Fiasse, L. (2003). Birth order, personality, and religion: A study among young adults from a three-sibling family. *Personality and Individual Differences, 35*, 19–29.

Saroglou, V., & Munoz-Garcia, A. (2008). Individual differences in religion and spirituality: An issue of personality traits and/or values. *Journal for the Scientific Study of Religion, 47*(1), 83–101.

Saroglou, V., Pichon, I., Trompette, L., Verschuren, M., & Dernelle, R. (2005). Prosocial behavior and religion: New evidence based on projective measures and peer ratings. *Journal for the Scientific Study of Religion, 44*(3), 323–348.

Saucier, G., & Skrzypinska, K. (2006). Spiritual but not religious? Evidence for two independent dispositions. *Journal of Personality, 74*(5), 1257–1292.

Schwartz, S. H. (1992). Universals in the content and structure of values: Theoretical advances and empirical tests in 20 countries. In M. P. Zanna (Ed.), *Advances in experimental social psychology* (Vol. 25, pp. 1–65). San Diego, CA: Academic Press.

Shariff, A. F., & Norenzayan, A. (2007). God is watching you: Priming God concepts increases prosocial behavior in an anonymous economic game. *Psychological Science, 18*(9), 803–809.

Streyffeler, L. L., & McNally, R. J. (1998). Fundamentalists and liberals: personality characteristics of Protestant Christians. *Personality and Individual Differences, 24*(4), 579–580.

Tsang, J., & Rowatt, W. C. (2007). The relationship between religious orientation, right-wing authoritarianism, and implicit sexual prejudice. *The International Journal for the Psychology of Religion, 17*(2), 99–120.

Veenlivet, S. G. (2008). Intrinsic religious orientation and religious teaching: Differential judgments towards same-gender sexual behavior and gay men and lesbians. *The International Journal for the Psychology of Religion, 18*, 53–65.

Walker, C., Ainette, M. G., Wills, T. A., & Mendoza, D. (2007). Religiosity and substance use: Test of an indirect-effect model in early and middle adolescence. *Psychology of Addictive Behaviors, 21*, 84–96.

Westen, D. (1996). A model and a method for uncovering the nomothetic from the idiographic: An alternative to the Five-Factor Model? *Journal of Research in Personality, 30*, 400–413.

Whitley, B. E., Jr. (2009). Religiosity and attitudes towards lesbian and gay men: A meta-analysis. *The International Journal for the Psychology of Religion, 19*, 21–38.

Wilkinson, W. W. (2004). Religiosity, authoritarianism, and homophobia: A multidimensional approach. *The International Journal for the Psychology of Religion, 14*(1), 55–67.

Wilkowski, B. M., Robinson, M. D., & Meier, B. P. (2006). Agreeableness and the prolonged spatial processing of antisocial and prosocial information. *Journal of Research in Personality, 40*, 1152–1168.

Wink, P. L., Ciciolla, L., Dillon, M., & Tracy, A. (2007). Religiousness, spiritual seeking, and personality: Findings from a longitudinal study. *Journal of Personality, 75*(5), 1051–1064.

Overview and Development of a Trait-Based Measure of Numinous Constructs: The Assessment of Spirituality and Religious Sentiments (ASPIRES) Scale

Ralph L. Piedmont

Abstract

Interest in spiritual and religious (numinous) constructs has grown rapidly in the past decade. Corresponding to this interest, numerous scales have been developed to capture these qualities. The presence of so many different measures has generated some difficulties for the field, including the lack of a developed database that supports the psychological validity of many of these instruments. The Assessment of Spirituality and Religious Sentiments (ASPIRES)[1] scale addresses these concerns by clearly operationalizing spirituality and religiousness as psychological constructs that have universal relevance. This chapter provides an overview on the development and psychometric integrity of the scale. It also provides an overview of research that has examined the incremental, cross-cultural, and clinical validity of the instrument. It is concluded that the ASPIRES scale provides empirically sustainable definitions of spirituality and religiousness that reinforce their nonredundancy with established personality constructs and their relevance in predicting a wide array of psychosocially significant outcomes.

Key Words: ASPIRES, spirituality, religiousness, validity, assessment

Introduction

Research activity in the areas of religion and spirituality has grown tremendously over the past decade (Emmons & Paloutzian, 2003). Interest in how individuals make meaning for their lives in terms of a relationship to some ultimate being has become quite developed. Research across the medical, psychological, and anthropological fields has consistently shown the positive psychological and physical value of such beliefs and practices.

As a result of this interest, a number of scales have been developed and applied. However, the presence of so many different measures has generated some difficulties for the field. First, many of these scales reflect a very specific, theological perspective and are thus unsuitable for use with individuals from diverse faith traditions. Second, the theological models from which these scales were developed frequently do not readily generalize to many therapeutic contexts. Finally, there exists little developed psychometric evidence for many scales, leaving little developed validity information available for understanding their utility (see Hill & Hood, 1999).

The Assessment of Spirituality and Religious Sentiments (ASPIRES) scale was developed to address these concerns. The ASPIRES scale is a nondenominational measure that is relevant for working with individuals across a wide range of faith traditions as well as appropriate for use with nonreligious or agnostic persons. It conceptualizes numinous variables as psychological constructs that have universal relevance. The ASPIRES scale also has a validated observer rating form for use with couples or in contexts where a self-report may be unfeasible (e.g., for use with terminally ill or forensic samples). Also available are short-form versions when brief assessments are required.

The ASPIRES scale measures two major dimensions of numinous functioning: Religious Sentiments (RS) and Spiritual Transcendence (ST). The RS component is composed of two domains. The first, *Religious Involvement*, reflects how actively involved a person is in performing various religious rituals and activities (e.g., frequency of attending religious services). Also contained in this domain is the level of importance these activities represent to the person. The second domain, *Religious Crisis*, examines whether a person may be experiencing problems, difficulties, or conflicts with the God of his or her understanding and/or faith community. Both domains examine the value an individual attaches to his or her involvement in specific, ritual-oriented, religious activities.

The second dimension measured by the ASPIRES scale is Spiritual Transcendence (ST). ST represents a motivational construct that reflects an individual's efforts to create a broad sense of personal meaning for his or her life. Those high on transcendence are able to find a larger sense of meaning and purpose to life that goes beyond their immediate sense of time and place. Transcendent individuals have a developed sense of transpersonalism and feel an attachment to nature and communities. Those low on transcendence have a more materialistic orientation to life that stresses more of the "here and now" of life.

There are three correlated facet scales to ST: *Prayer Fulfillment*, the ability to create a personal space that enables one to feel a positive connection to some larger reality; *Universality*, the belief in a larger meaning and purpose to life; and *Connectedness*, feelings of belonging and responsibility to a larger human reality that cuts across generations and groups. These dimensions have been shown to represent aspects of the individual independent of the personality dimensions of the Five-Factor Model (FFM). Furthermore, scores on these scales evidenced predictive validity over and above the FFM in explaining interpersonal style, coping ability, sexual attitudes, psychological maturity, and well-being (Piedmont, 2009). Thus, anyone interested in obtaining a comprehensive description of a person ought to include these dimensions. By conceptualizing spirituality as a trait-based construct, ST fits well with established psychological paradigms and its nondenominational nature makes it an appropriate assessment for all individuals, regardless of religious faith tradition or cultural background. From a clinical perspective, information from the ASPIRES scale can be useful for understanding a client's personal sense of meaning—his or her ultimate sense of purpose and life direction.

The purpose of this chapter is threefold. First, to outline the conceptual foundation to the constructs contained by the ASPIRES scale, including how the variables are defined, their psychological nature, and anticipated relations to larger personality dimensions. It is important to note that the constructs presented here are assumed to be *psychological* as opposed to *theological* realities. As such, the model underlying the ASPIRES scale seeks to provide a platform for deriving empirically testable hypotheses. Second, to outline the methods employed for developing the ASPIRES scale and to overview the reliability and validity of the inventory and its different forms. Most important, the issue is to demonstrate that the dimensions of the ASPIRES scale represent aspects of human functioning *not contained* by traditional measures of personality. Finally, to summarize some of the clinical and cross-cultural research using the ASPIRES scale. One central assumption of spirituality is that it represents a universal human quality. Thus, for any psychological model to be comprehensive in terms of description and explanation, it will need to include the numinous constructs. It is hoped that readers will come away from this chapter viewing the ASPIRES scale as an essential assessment tool and appreciating the empirical significance of spiritual and religious constructs when they are operationalized by an instrument that is firmly grounded in psychological methods and theories.

History and Development of the ASPIRES Scale

The original work with the ASPIRES scale began with the development of the Spiritual Transcendence Scale (STS; Piedmont, 1999, 2001). The goal of this effort was to create an empirically sound measure that would capture the fundamental aspects of spirituality; those numinous qualities (e.g., awe, wonder, an appreciation of, and search for, the sacred) that underlie and are common to all religious faiths. To demonstrate that these spiritual qualities represented something distinct from already existing personality dimensions, three empirical criteria were to be met: (1) the new spiritual constructs would need to be shown to be independent of existing personality dimensions as represented by the FFM; (2) the spiritual dimension would need to be at a comparable level of generality as the domains of the FFM, in that it would have to subsume several, smaller "facets"; and, (3) spirituality would have to be recoverable over multiple sources of information (e.g., across ratings sources and measures; McCrae & Costa, 1996).

It was hypothesized that spirituality is a motivational drive that propels us to create a broad sense of personal meaning within an eschatological context. In other words, knowing that we are going to die, each of us needs to construct some sense of purpose and meaning for the life being led. Why am I here? What purpose does my life serve? Why should I do the things I do? These are important questions that each of us needs to answer and our responses to them set the tempo, tone, and direction of our lives. Managing our sense of mortality is an innate task for our species (e.g., Greenberg, Solomon, & Pyszczynski, 1997), and ideally, these answers help to pull together the many disparate threads of existence into a more meaningful coherence that gives us the will to live productively. However, there are many different types of answers to these existential questions, with some responses providing more emotional support and psychological resilience than others.

One way of categorizing responses to these existential questions is along the time frame people use to understand their lives. For example, some individuals may perceive their lives within the immediate context they inhabit, responding to the specific needs and demands of the here and now (a relatively short event horizon). Others may view their lives as part of a specific generation or cohort, and personal meaning develops in relation to how these people view their commitments to others in their generation and those that follow them (a more moderate event horizon). Finally, still others may view their lives as part of some eternal ontological pathway that involves responsibilities toward others in both the here and now and in the next life (a long event horizon). The broader the event horizon one uses to create meaning, the more stability, resilience, and personal satisfaction one can experience. Spiritual Transcendence is the psychological force that motivates us to create broad event horizons for viewing our lives (Piedmont, 2004a, provides a model for describing this meaning-making process).

Spiritual Transcendence represents a universal human capacity to stand outside of one's own immediate existence and to view life from a broader, more integrated whole. To varying degrees, we increasingly realize that there is a larger meaning and purpose to our lives. We are single threads in a larger tapestry of existence; although small and limited, each thread makes a unique contribution to the overall texture and imprint of the woven piece.

In developing the Spiritual Transcendence Scale (STS), a consortium of theological experts from diverse faith traditions, including Buddhism, Hinduism, Quakerism, Lutheranism, Catholicism, and Judaism, was assembled. This focus group was used to identify qualities of spirituality that were common to all of these faiths. A number of dimensions were identified (e.g., existentiality, tolerance of paradoxes, nonjudgmentality, gratefulness), and these individuals then wrote items that they believed reflected these various qualities. Those items, along with others developed by the author, were then analyzed within the context of the FFM and it was determined that spirituality represented a unique, distinct individual-differences construct (see Piedmont, 1999). As noted earlier, succeeding research studies supported the universal nature of the construct and its predictive utility (e.g., Piedmont, 2006; Piedmont, Ciarrocchi, Dy-Liacco, & Williams, 2009). Piedmont (2004a) provides a larger conceptual model for understanding Spiritual Transcendence within various types of meaning and their corresponding strengths and weaknesses.

Over the course of several years, three limitations to the STS became apparent. First, the language used for the items was, in places, very sophisticated. Several rather esoteric and arcane phrases were employed (e.g., "peak experience," "levels of consciousness") that may not have been understood by younger or less educated respondents. To compensate for these, the original scale included a short *Glossary of Terms* to help define these words. This made the scale cumbersome for use in some domestic samples and in many cross-cultural contexts. A second limitation was the Connectedness facet scale, which consistently generated very low alphas. Although a strong predictor of various outcomes, it was hoped that a more internally consistent scale would improve the applicability of the construct. Finally, there was no short form. Although only 24 items long, in some applications the STS was deemed burdensome (e.g., with use by elderly). It was thought that having a smaller scale that captured the broad construct might be useful.

As a result of these concerns, a new list of 38 items was created and given along with the STS to a sample of 466 undergraduate students. Using correlational and factor analytic analyses, a new set of STS items were identified, and these items constitute the Spiritual Transcendence Scale now contained in the ASPIRES scale. The revised STS consisted of 23 items (10 original items and 13 new items). The alpha reliabilities for the scales were as follows: 0.95 for Prayer Fulfillment, 0.82 for Universality, 0.68 for Connectedness, and 0.89 for the Total Score. The new STS facet scales evidenced good convergent and discriminant validity as well as demonstrating incremental validity in predicting psychosocial criteria over and above personality. The original and revised STS correlated substantially (r's = .83, .89, .55, and .87 for Prayer Fulfillment, Universality, Connectedness, and total score, respectively), indicating that the two instruments share much in common. Interestingly, the Connectedness scales are not as overlapping as the others, given that only one of the original items was retained on the new facet scale.

The items for the new STS scale are all quite readable and no glossary of terms is necessary. The alpha for the Connectedness form was slightly higher than originally found, but not much more. It may be that Connectedness represents a more complex construct than the other two facet scales. Also created were short-form versions for both self-ratings and observer ratings. These instruments are discussed in more detail later.

Thus, individuals who have used the earlier versions of the STS should find a significant amount of continuity with the ASPIRES version. One can have confidence that the validity data accrued on the original STS will be applicable to the current version.

Religious Sentiments Scale

The first six items on the Religious Sentiments Scale have been a part of the ongoing research process using the STS from the beginning. These items have always been used as convergent validity criteria for the STS. However, more recent research examining the empirical utility of religious versus spiritual constructs (Piedmont, Ciarrocchi, Dy-Liacco, & Williams, 2009) has shown the predictive and incremental validity of religious constructs in their own right. As such, it was deemed appropriate to include these items along with the STS.

Added to these were six additional items. Two of them (items 7 and 8) reflect one's commitment to his or her beliefs and the status of those commitments, respectively. The former is hypothesized to be a potential moderator of religiosity's relationship to external criteria. The latter was included as a way to identify those individuals whose faith may have suddenly increased (e.g., had a religious transformation) or decreased (e.g., had a religiously disappointing

experience). In both instances, such individuals may provide important insights into how religion and spirituality impact psychosocial functioning. By including this item, users have a mechanism for identifying individuals in spiritual transformation. Studying such individuals has important implications for research on personality stability and change (see Miller & C'deBoci, 1994).

The final four items were included to address issues of religious crisis. A factor analysis of the items from the Multidimensional Measurement of Religiosity/Spirituality (MMRS; Fetzer/National Institute on Aging Working Group, 1999) showed similar items to form a factor independent of religiosity, spirituality, and personality (Piedmont et al., 2006). What is of interest about these items is that they appear to address the negative side of religiosity (i.e., when faith and belief become sources of personal and social distress). This represents a whole new area of investigation and may provide new insights into how individuals develop a personal sense of equilibrium. Empirically, the items emerged as their own factor, and it is up to future research to outline the larger value of these items. It is hoped that the incorporation of these items into the ASPIRES scale will stimulate just such activity.

SENTIMENTS VERSUS MOTIVES

It needs to be pointed out that these items capture religious involvements and experiences, as well as the importance attributed to those beliefs. As such, they represent an aspect of functioning very different from the qualities assessed by the Spiritual Transcendence Scale (STS). While the STS is believed to represent an intrinsic, inherited quality of the individual, these items reflect instead personal *sentiments*. The term "sentiments" is an old term in psychology, and it reflects emotional tendencies that develop out of social traditions and educational experiences (Ruckmick, 1920; Woodworth, 1940). Sentiments can be very powerful motivators for individuals and have very direct effects on behavior. However, sentiments, like love, gratitude, and patriotism, do not represent innate, genotypic qualities like spirituality. That is why the expression of sentiments can and does vary across cultures and time periods. Sentiments may also be more amenable to change and modification.

Spiritual Transcendence, on the other hand, is hypothesized to represent a fundamental, inherent quality of the individual. Such a construct is referred to as a *motive*. Motives are nonspecific affect forces that drive, direct, and select behavior.

As an intrinsic source of motivation, motives influence the basic adaptive orientation of individuals to their environments. Motives represent universal aspects of human behavior and are found in all human cultures. As a basic building block to personality, motives are the source for many acquired sentiments. Spiritual Transcendence represents a basic motivation for people to create a durable sense of personal meaning, to find a broader social and teleological context for understanding the goal and purpose of life.

Thus, the ASPIRES scale makes an important distinction between spirituality and religious involvements (i.e., religiosity). Using structural equation modeling (SEM), Piedmont, Ciarrocchi et al. (2009) have empirically demonstrated the two constructs, although very much related to one another (latent, disattenuated correlation was Lambda = 0.71), reflected different psychological sets of variables. The best-fitting SEM models indicated that one's religious sentiments were shown to develop out of one's spiritual motivations. As such, spiritually motivated individuals may, or may not, choose to develop religious sentiments. In fact, spirituality may underlie a number of different types of sentiments, (e.g., patriotism, love, social activism). Conversely, an individual low on spirituality but reared in an environment that is heavily religiously committed may develop a strong sense of religious sentimentality. However, he or she will lack a transcendent orientation (e.g., a belief in the unitive nature of life). Hence, the two constructs are related but should not be considered isomorphic. Piedmont et al. (2009) demonstrated that the two sets of variables predict different sets of psychosocial outcomes, underscoring the need for both sets of constructs to explain one's numinous orientation.

This underlying theoretical model to the ASPIRES scale is certainly in need of additional testing and no doubt refinement. However, it does provide a conceptual starting point for understanding the nature of these two sets of constructs as *psychological constructs*, and the ASPIRES scale provides an empirical point of departure for such tests.

Applications for the ASPIRES Scale

The ASPIRES scale incorporates a wide range of numinous constructs under a single umbrella. All the items contained in this scale have a demonstrated empirical utility in predicting psychosocial outcomes and/or have a tremendous amount of potential conceptual value for those who are interested in spiritual and religious phenomena.

There are numerous applications for the ASPIRES scale. It can be used for conducting pastoral or religious assessments of clients in health care settings. It can quickly identify needs to be addressed by pastoral staff. The scale is also useful for conducting medical outcome research; for charting the role of spiritual and religious constructs on the emotional well-being, survival rates, and treatment responsiveness of patients. It is a very useful instrument for studying end-of-life issues with terminally ill or elderly samples. In some circumstances, the Short Form may be very appropriate when time or attention issues are salient. The empirical robustness and pedigree of the ASPIRES scale makes it a useful component of any assessment battery for those undertaking research studies in clinical, I/O, personality, or social psychological contexts. What is particularly beneficial in these contexts is the availability of a validated rater version, which allows for the collection of an independent source of data that can verify self-reported information. Finally, the growing movement in positive psychology makes the ASPIRES scale an increasingly relevant instrument for understanding a uniquely human quality: the creation of a life-directing sense of personal meaning.

The following section will provide some basic psychometric information about the underlying structure of the ASPIRES scales and their incremental validity in predicting a wide array of psychosocial outcomes.

Psychometric Information

The information presented in this section was obtained from a sample of 424 individuals (120 men and 291 women, 13 indicated no gender). Participants were obtained from four different locations: Massachusetts, Illinois, Mississippi, and Maryland. Most were undergraduate students but also included were graduate students in pastoral counseling and general adults. Participants ranged from 17 to 62 years of age (mean age = 21 years), with most being Caucasian (84%) (6% were African American, 3% each were Asian and Hispanic, and the remaining 4% were Arabic or did not indicate a racial preference). There were a variety of religious faith traditions, with most being Christian (82%). Another 9% represented Jewish, Hindu, Muslim, and Buddhist faith traditions and 6% indicated as being atheist or agnostic (3% did not indicate a religious preference).

These individuals were also asked to find two people who knew them for at least 3 months to rate them on both the ASPIRES scale and other measures. However, 364 participants obtained two ratings, while 34 obtained only 1. Concerning the observers, most knew their targets fairly well and for a relatively long period of time (mean = 8.33 years).

Normative Data

SPIRITUAL TRANSCENDENCE SCALE

The Spiritual Transcendence Scale (STS) measures three correlated facets: Prayer Fulfillment, Universality, and Connectedness. Items comprising these subscales are listed in Tables 7.2 and 7.3. Items are rated from 1 "*strongly disagree*" to 5 "*strongly agree.*" Items are counterbalanced to control for the effects of acquiescence.

One working hypothesis regarding ST is that it develops as one ages. Because spirituality refers to the personal meaning one creates for the life being led, as one ages mortality becomes more salient and concerns develop about bringing a sense of personal closure. For this reason, it is believed that older people are more concerned with spiritual issues than younger ones. One consequence of this is that older people are expected to have higher scores on ST than younger ones. Another working hypothesis is that given the relational nature of spirituality (i.e., making and maintaining caring relationships with others), women are expected to have higher scores than men.

A 2 (gender) by 3 (age group) Multivariate Analysis of Variance was conducted using the three ST facet scales as the dependent variables. A significant age effect (Wilks' Lambda = 0.863; multivariate $F (6,806) = 10.29$; $p < .001$) was obtained. Univariate analyses showed significant age effects for all three facet scales, and post-hoc tests noted that each age group had significantly different scores from every other age group across the three facet scales. For the Prayer Fulfillment and Universality scales, increasing age was associated with increasing mean levels. However, for the Connectedness scale, just the opposite pattern was found: Increasing age was associated with *lower* mean scores. This suggests that the items relating to the need for approval from others, both living and dead, is a more relevant aspect of spirituality for younger rather than older individuals. Thus, the ASPIRES scale captures aspects of spirituality relevant for both adolescents and adults.

A significant gender effect was also observed (Wilks' Lambda = 0.97; multivariate $F (3,403) = 4.48$; $p < .004$). As expected, women scored significantly higher than men on all facets. Similar findings were obtained with total ST scores. When scoring the ST scales, it is necessary to control scores for gender and age. It is recommended that the normative data presented in the Technical Manual (Piedmont, 2005) be used to calculate T-scores. Such a transformation can help one to determine how similar obtained scores are to those in this normative data set. T-scores carry a mean of 50 and a standard deviation of 10. Values between 45 and 55 are considered average. T-scores above 55 are *high* and those below 45 are *low*.

It should be pointed out that the ASPIRES scale is the *only* measure of numinous constructs that has an observer rating form. This is based on the working assumption that spiritual and religious (i.e., numinous) constructs represent broad-based aspects of personality that find clear expression in daily behavior. These constructs are sufficiently distinct and salient that observers can readily identify them. Research has strongly supported this contention by demonstrating significant correlations between self-rated ST scores and scores obtained from observers. The magnitude of such convergence is similar to that found with the major personality dimensions of the FFM.

As such, observer ratings can provide useful information about the spiritual and religious sentiments of individuals. Observer ratings can be utilized when working with couples, either for premarital evaluations or for marital therapy. Ratings would also be useful in medical contexts where individuals may not be able to provide their own assessments either due to age or physical debilitation.

The Technical Manual also provides normative information based on responses obtained from the raters. As with self-reports, scores obtained from the rater version should, ideally, be compared to values presented here, with respect to age and gender *of the person being rated*. Note that the normative values for the observer ratings are different from those obtained with self-reports. Different types of raters will generate different types of score distributions. One should not use self-rated normative data for evaluating observer ratings.

RELIGIOUS SENTIMENTS SCALES

There are 12 items that comprise the Religious Sentiments (RS) section. These items were selected because of their demonstrated value in the research literature. Although these items constitute two larger scales (Religious Involvement and Religious Crisis), the items themselves have considerable practical value in their own right. Individuals interested in pastoral assessments can readily determine how salient religion is to a person by examining responses to each item.

Four of the items in this section were included because they address spiritual crisis. There are times when individuals do find themselves in conflict, either with the tenets of their faith or directly with the God of their understanding. In each circumstance, a person may find herself in a state of stress, emotional conflict, and personal apprehension. Such individuals may also find themselves isolated from their faith group or even from other loved ones in their lives. Traditional psychological assessments do not consider spiritual causes for symptoms of emotional distress (although *DSM-IV* does have codes for describing these types of issues). As a result, appropriate interventions may be overlooked.

In examining the items for this section, another 2 (gender) by 3 (age group) MANOVA was conducted using the 12 RS items as the dependent variable. A significant age effect was obtained (Wilks' Lambda = 0.782; multivariate $F (24,770) = 4.23$; $p < .001$). Univariate analyses showed significant effects for all but two items ("God is punishing me" and "I feel isolated from my faith group"). Interestingly, no significant gender effect was found. Thus, men and women did not score differently on these items. As such, scores on the two religiosity scales need to be adjusted for age. This is accomplished by using the normative data available in the technical manual to create T-scores.

It is clear that men and women as well as individuals of different ages have different normative response patterns on the ASPIRES scales. As such, it is important that raw scores not be used in analyzing ASPIRES data, but rather normative adjusted scores that will automatically adjust for these differences. An additional value of having normative data on these scales is that it enables researchers to determine the representativeness of their samples.

Factor Structure

Self-reported scores from the 23 items comprising the ST scale were subjected to a principal components analysis. Three factors were expected to emerge from the data and the Scree Test indicated that three factors were appropriate. Three factors were extracted and obliquely rotated and the results are presented in Table 7.1. As can be seen, all but one item loaded on its intended dimension. Only the item "Death does stop one's feelings of

Table 7.1 Pattern Loadings From a Principal Components Analysis of the Self-Reported Spiritual Transcendence Scale Items

Spiritual Transcendence Item	Component		
	1	2	3
PF1	**.70**	.03	−.13
PF2	**.65**	.21	−.03
PF3	**.75**	−.02	.00
PF4	**.85**	−.07	.05
PF5	**.74**	.17	−.05
PF6	**.90**	−.06	−.03
PF7	**.86**	−.02	.06
PF8	**.86**	.01	.01
PF9	**.87**	−.06	.11
PF10	**.79**	.01	.03
UN1	**.33**	**.59**	.00
UN2	.07	**.78**	.01
UN3	.23	**.64**	−.16
UN4	−.07	**.41**	.26
UN5	.27	**.39**	.04
UN6	.21	**.47**	.29
UN7	.21	**.62**	.21
CN1	.07	−.17	.06
CN2	.09	−.27	**.75**
CN3	.06	−.20	**.83**
CN4	−.03	.05	**.65**
CN5	.07	.20	**.32**
CN6	−.10	.16	**.35**

Notes: Loadings ≥ .30 are in boldface type.
CN, Connectedness; PF, Prayer Fulfillment; UN, Universality.
Source: Reprinted with permission of author from Piedmont (2005).

emotional closeness to another" did not load significantly on any factor.

Although the facts are expected to be significantly correlated, the component correlation matrix showed the three factors to be relatively independent (Factor 1 correlated $r = .25$ with Factor 2 and $r = .18$ with Factor 3; Factor 2 correlated $r = .14$ with Factor 3). Thus, the ST items evidenced the expected putative structure.

Table 7.2 Pattern Loadings From a Principal Components Analysis of the Self-Reported Religiosity Items

Religiosity Item	Component 1	Component 2
1. Frequency read Bible/Torah	**.84**	.01
2. Frequency read religious literature	**.84**	−.03
3. How often pray	**.81**	.13
4. Frequency attend religious services	**.80**	.04
5. Have a personal, close relationship with God	**.80**	−.05
6. Experience a union with God	**.79**	.00
7. How important are your religious beliefs (higher score = greater importance)	**.73**	.04
8. Over past 12 months, have religious involvements changed (higher score = increase)	**.47**	−.17
9. Feel that God is punishing	−.05	**.86**
10. Feel abandoned by God	.05	**.85**
11. Feel isolated from faith group	.04	**.75**
12. Unable/unwilling to involve God in personal decisions	**−.41**	**.43**

Notes: N = 411. Loadings ≥ .30 are in boldface type.
Source: This table is reprinted with permission of author from Piedmont (2005).

The 12 RS items were also subjected to a principal components analysis. Items 7 ("How important to you are your religious beliefs") and 8 ("Over the past 12 months, have your religious interests and involvements...") were scored so that higher scores indicated more positive sentiments. The Scree Test for these data suggested that two factors be extracted. Items were again obliquely rotated and the results are presented in Table 7.2. The first eight items constitute a dimension named *religiosity*. It reflects the degree of involvement an individual has in performing various religious activities as well as the importance of the values that underlie those activities. It is interesting to note that items 5 and 6, which concern the quality of relationship one has to the God of one's understanding, also load on this dimension. Thus, involvement in ritual behaviors and experiences of connection to a higher being are very much related to one another.

The second factor was termed *Religious Crisis* and contained the last four items of the section. These items all reflect some level of conflict and isolation from both one's religious faith group and from the God of one's understanding. These two factors were significantly correlated ($r = −.35$), indicating that those in spiritual crisis tended to be less involved in religious ritual and to have a more distant relationship with the God of one's understanding.

Scales were created to represent these two factors. For the Spiritual Crisis scale, scores on the four items were simply summed. Because the items on the Religiosity scale contained different response categories, scores on each of these items were first standardized and then aggregated to form a total score. This was done to insure that each item made an equal contribution to the total score. Simply summing raw scores would give an unfair advantage to those items with larger variances (i.e., those items with more response options), allowing them to have more influence on the total score. This was not done with the religious crisis items because they all have the same 5-point response scale.

Internal Consistency

Alpha reliability coefficients were calculated for scores obtained across the six scales for both the self-report and observer versions. These results are presented in Table 7.3. As can be seen, the ST overall and facet scales of Prayer Fulfillment and Universality evidenced adequate levels of reliability, in both the self and observer forms. The Connectedness scale showed a lower level of consistency. Some of this can be attributed to Item 7 ("Death does stop one's feelings of closeness to another"). Deleting this item raised the alpha to 0.58 in the self-report scores and to 0.67 in the

Table 7.3 Alpha Reliabilities and Cross-Observer Convergence for the Self and Observer Versions of the Spiritual Transcendence and Religiosity Scales

Scale	Self-Report (α)	Observer Report (α)	Self-Observer (r)
Spiritual Transcendence Scales			
Prayer Fulfillment	.94[a]	.93[c]	.69***[e]
Universality	.78	.76	.43***
Connectedness	.49	.55	.28***
Total Scale Score	.89	.90	.63***
Religious Sentiments Scales			
Religious Involvement	.89[b]	.92[d]	.84***[f]
Religious Crisis	.75	.82	.41***

Notes: *** $p < .001$, two-tailed.
[a]$N = 419$.
[b]$N = 411$.
[c]$N = 399$.
[d]$N = 396$.
[e]$N = 396$.
[f]$N = 396$.
Source: This table is reprinted with permission of author from Piedmont (2005).

observer scores. Historically, this scale has generated lower alpha reliabilities, although it would evidence higher retest coefficients. It may be that this dimension of spirituality is, by nature, relatively complex. Measures of internal consistency may underestimate its true reliability. Consistent with this view has been the findings that correlations with external criteria have always shown the dimension to be useful. It is up to future research with this scale to determine the utility of this dimension. Reliability estimates for scores on the two Religious Sentiment scales show them to be quite adequate in both the self and observer samples.

Validity Information

CONVERGENT VALIDITY

One manner of documenting the validity of a scale is to demonstrate cross-observer convergence. This approach answers the question, "Does what individuals say about themselves agree with what knowledgeable observers say about them?" Finding such consensus supports the value of a test score as representing an objective quality of the individual that finds clear expression in overt behavior. Cross-observer convergence is a powerful way to demonstrate validity for any measure of psychological traits because it avoids spurious associations due to common method. In short,

two self-report measures will always correlate with each other because the same person is taking both instruments. Whatever psychological mechanisms underlie a person's performance on one test will also contribute to performance on the other. This will make the two scales correlate. However, because raters do not share the same motivations for responding as the person himself/herself, correlations between a self-report and observer rating will not be contaminated by this "correlated error." Thus, cross-observer convergence provides a more accurate estimate of association.

Table 7.3 provides convergence values for the six ASPIRES scales. As can be seen, each scale correlates significantly across the two information sources. Thus, the information contained in the self-report scores agrees substantially with what knowledgeable informants report. There are two important conclusions to be drawn from these data. First, the level of convergence is as high as, and in some cases higher than, what is found with the major personality dimensions of the FFM. Thus, spiritual and religious constructs can be measured with a comparable level of accuracy as other personality traits. Second, religious and spiritual qualities do not represent solipsistic aspects of the individual. Rather, these traits find clear expression in overt behavior

Table 7.4 Correlations Between the Spiritual Transcendence and the Religious Sentiments Scales for Both the Self-Report and Observer-Ratings Forms

Spiritual Transcendence Scale	Religious Sentiment Scale	
	Religious Involvement	Religious Crisis
Self-Report Data (N = 420)		
Prayer Fulfillment	.81***	−.46***
Universality	.44***	−.31***
Connectedness	.08	−.09
Total Score	.74***	−.45***
Observer Rating Data (N = 399)		
Prayer Fulfillment	.85***	−.38***
Universality	.60***	−.38***
Connectedness	.21***	−.17**
Total Score	.80***	−.40***

Notes: ** $p < .01$; *** $p < .001$; two-tailed.
Source: This table is reprinted with permission of author from Piedmont (2005).

and are sufficiently salient that they can be accurately identified by others.

Table 7.4 provides the intercorrelations between the ST and RS scales in both the self and observer samples. As can be seen in both samples, Religiosity is positively correlated with Spiritual Transcendence, and Religious Crisis is negatively associated. This is not unexpected, whereas research has shown that Spirituality and Religiosity represent two highly correlated dimensions. However, such overlap does not indicate that the two should be collapsed into a single dimension (Piedmont et al., 2009).

DISCRIMINANT VALIDITY

Spiritual and religious phenomena are considered to represent aspects of the individual not contained in traditional personality constructs. Working from the perspective of the FFM (an empirically derived, comprehensive taxonomy of traditionally defined personality constructs), it has been argued that spirituality represents the sixth major dimension of personality (Piedmont, 1999). A developing body of research is supporting this position. For the purposes of this report, self-report scores from the ASPIRES scale were jointly factor analyzed with self-reported scores on the FFM dimensions. The Scree Test indicated two possible factors, which were extracted and obliquely rotated. The results of this analysis are presented in Table 7.5.

As can be seen, the five ASPIRES scales all loaded significantly (i.e., > 0.30) on the first factor. All the scales, with the exception of Religious Crisis loaded positively on this dimension, indicating a positive convergence among these scales. Religious

Table 7.5 Pattern Loadings for the Joint Factor Analysis of ASPIRES Scales and the Personality Dimensions of the Five-Factor Model

Scale	Component	
	1	2
Prayer Fulfillment	.90	−.01
Universality	.67	−.08
Connectedness	.36	.12
Religious Involvement	.85	−.06
Religious Crisis	−.56	.32
Neuroticism	−.04	.71
Extraversion	−.04	−.67
Openness	−.16	−.39
Agreeableness	.15	−.59
Conscientiousness	.18	−.63

Source: This table is reprinted with permission of author from Piedmont (2005).

Table 7.6 List of Psychological Measures Completed by the Normative Sample

Measure	Constructs	Authors
Hope Scale	Belief that things will turn out fine	Snyder, Sympson, Ybasco, Border, Babyak, & Higgins (1996)
Satisfaction with Life Scale*	General life contentment	Diener, Emmons, Larsen, & Griffin (1985)
Affect Balance Scale*	Positive and negative affect	Bradburn (1969)
Delighted-Terrible Scale*	Overall rating, high score = delighted	Andrews & Withey (1976)
Attitudes Toward Abortion Scale*	Pro-choice vs. pro-life	Single item scale developed by author
Self-Actualization Scale*	Psychological maturity	Jones & Crandall (1986)
Self-Esteem	Feelings of esteem and self-worth	Rosenberg (1979)
Prosocial Behavior Scale*	Prosocial behavior	Rushton, Chrisjohn, & Fekken (1981)
Purpose in Life Test	Personal meaning for life	Crumbaugh (1968)
Individualism Scale*	Individualism vs. collectivism	Dion & Dion (1991)
Social Support Scale	Belonging to a faith group	Fetzer Institute & National Institute on Aging
Sexual Attitudes	Erotophilia vs. erotophobia	Fisher, Byrne, White, & Kelly (1988)

Note: *Observer ratings obtained on these scales.
Source: This table is reprinted with permission of author from Piedmont (2005).

Crisis, which loaded negatively, reflects a moving away from a transcendent meaning orientation. The FFM domains evidenced negligible loadings on this factor (all loadings below 0.20). Factor 2 evidenced significant loadings for all the personality dimensions. The pattern of these loadings indicated a personality profile for this sample that was high on Neuroticism and low on the remaining factors. Only the Religious Crisis scale loaded significantly positively on this domain and explains the FFM configuration: Those high on Religious Crisis evidence emotional dysphoria and an interpersonally detached style. The correlation between the two factors was $r = .14$. Thus, the religious and spiritual scales of the ASPIRES scale appear to capture aspects of the individual that are relatively independent of those qualities defined by the FFM.

CONSTRUCT VALIDITY: PREDICTING OTHER CRITERIA

Allport (1950) asserted that religious sentiments are a central, organizing aspect of an individual's psychological world. This interest in numinous constructs centers on the conviction that spirituality represents the core of a person. It reflects the fundamental manner in which a

person positions himself/herself adaptively to the world at large. As such, spiritual and religious constructs should be related to a wide range of psychosocially salient constructs, including well-being, psychological growth and maturity, and interpersonal style.

To this end, participants in this normative study completed an array of psychological scales, which are listed in Table 7.6. The constructs measured included feelings of life satisfaction and well-being, psychological maturity, interpersonal style, and attitudes toward sexuality. Ratings were also obtained on a subset of these scales. Table 7.7 provides the correlations between self-rated scores on the ASPIRES scales and self and observer ratings on these constructs.

As can be seen, the ASPIRES scales correlate significantly with these psychosocial criteria. The pattern of correlations is similar for both the self- and observer-rated outcomes. These results indicate that the numinous constructs contained on the ASPIRES maintain substantive overlap with a wide range of psychosocial outcomes. To obtain an index of overall overlap (i.e., effect size), a series of multiple regression analyses were conducted where each of the psychosocial variables served as

Table 7.7 Correlations Between Self-Reported ASPIRES Scales and Self-Ratings and Observer Ratings on the Psychosocial Variables

Psychosocial Outcome	ASPIRES Scale						R^2
	Relig	Rel Crisis	PF	UN	CN	Total STS	
Hope	.22***	−.35***	.21***	.21***	.06	.24***	.14***
Satisfaction with Life	.25***	−.45***	.28***	.26***	.09	.31***	.22***
Positive Affect (ABS)	.18***	−.22***	.21***	.18***	.15**	.25***	.08***
Negative Affect (ABS)	−.25***	.30***	−.19***	−.21***	.09	−.19***	.14***
Delighted-Terrible Scale	.28***	−.41***	.24***	.25***	.05	.27***	.20***
Attitude Toward Abortion	.33***	−.15**	.23***	.11*	.01	.20***	.11***
Self-Actualization	.21***	−.31***	.18***	.30***	−.11*	.20***	.18***
Self-Esteem	.21***	−.38***	.22***	.19***	.02	.22***	.15***
Prosocial Behavior	.17***.	−.07	.13**	.10*	.08	.14**	.03*
Purpose in Life	.35***	−.49***	.38***	.37***	.06	.41***	.30***
Individualism	−.13**	.22***	−.16**	−.28***	−.21***	−.26***	.13***
Social Support	.18***	−.19***	.21***	.06	.21***	.21***	.09***
Sexual Attitudes Scale (high score-erotophilia)	−.34***	.18***	−.27***	−.07	−.14**	−.25***	.14***
Observer Ratings							
Delighted-Terrible	.23***	−.30***	.21***	.18***	.10*	.23***	.10***
Attitude Toward Abortion	.42***	−.21***	.36***	.19***	.05	.33***	.18***
Positive Affect (ABS)	.11*	−.17***	.10	.08	.03	.10*	.03*
Negative Affect (ABS)	−.26***	.28***	−.21***	−.15**	.03	−.19***	.11***
Satisfaction With Life	.18***	−.30***	.18***	.12*	.12*	.19***	.10***
Self-Actualization	.15**	−.16***	.10*	.19***	.00	.14**	.06***
Individualism	−.14**	.18***	−.14**	−.14**	−.12*	−.17***	.05***
Prosocial Behavior	.24***	−.05	.18***	.17***	.03	.19***	.07***

Notes: * p < .05; ** p < .01; *** p < .001; two-tailed.
CN, Connectedness Scale; PF, Prayer Fulfillment; Relig, Religiosity Scale; Rel Crisis, Religious Crisis Scale; UN, Universality.
Source: This table is reprinted with permission of author from Piedmont (2005).

the dependent variable. The five ASPIRES scales (not including the Total STS score) were then simultaneously entered as predictors. The resulting multiple R^2's are presented in the last column of Table 7.7.

As can be seen, the ASPIRES scales predict from 3% (Prosocial Behavior Scale) to 30% (Purpose in Life Scale), with a median explained variance of 11%. Although the ASPIRES scales do not explain the majority of variance in these scales, they do account for a substantial amount of variance that is certainly practically significant.

INCREMENTAL VALIDITY

Perhaps the most important question to ask about numinous constructs is whether they can explain variance in outcomes *over and above* what can already be explained by using established measures of personality. Finding variables that correlate with other variables is not a difficult task. However, finding variables that *add* significantly to our predictive power is more challenging.

The ultimate goal of assessment is to identify those constructs that maximally explain a given outcome. Ideally, these predictors should have minimal

Table 7.8 Incremental Validity of the ASPIRES Scales Over Demographic Variables and the Five-Factor Model Domains in Predicting Psychosocial Outcomes

Psychosocial Outcome	Demographics R^2	FFM δR^2	ASPIRES δR^2	ASPIRES Predictors
Self-Outcomes				
Hope	.05***	.29***	.04***	RC
Satisfaction Life Scale	.02*	.31**	.10***	RC, UN
Positive Affect	.01	.15***	.04***	CN, PF
Negative Affect	.08***	.23***	.02***	RC
Delighted	.01	.29***	.08***	RC, UN
Attitude Abortion	.01	.06***	.09***	R
Self-Actualization	.11***	.25***	.05***	RC, CN, UN, PF
Self-Esteem	.04***	.35***	.05***	RC
Prosocial Behavior	.02*	.07***	.02**	R
Purpose in Life	.05***	.42***	.08***	RC, UN
Individualism	.03**	.20***	.05***	UN, CN
Social Support	.01	.05***	.04***	PF, CN
Sexual Attitudes	.10***	.06***	.09***	R
Observer Outcomes				
Delighted	.00	.20***	.04***	RC, R
Attitudes-Abortion	.02*	.11***	.12***	R
Positive Affect	.03**	.10***	.01*	RC
Negative Affect	.10**	.13***	.02***	RC
Satisfaction Life Scale	.01	.20***	.03***	RC
Self-Actualization	.06***	.11***	.00	—
Individualism	.02*	.15***	.00	—
Prosocial Behavior	.03**	.03	.05***	R, RC

Notes: $^*p < .05$; $^{**}p < .01$; $^{***}p < .001$; two-tailed.
C, Connectedness; PF, Prayer Fulfillment; RC, Religious Crisis; R, Religiosity; UN, Universality.
Source: This table is reprinted with permission of author from Piedmont (2005).

overlap among themselves and maximum overlap with the criterion. To develop such a multidimensional model requires an understanding of what qualities underlie the universe of individual differences. In short, what is needed is a good taxonomy.

The FFM represents one such taxonomy. The FFM is an empirically derived framework of individual difference constructs. Developed over many decades, this model postulates five broad dimensions to personality: Neuroticism (the tendency to experience negative affect); Extraversion (the extent to which one enjoys social activities); Openness (the proactive seeking of new experiences); Agreeableness (a compassionate vs. antagonistic orientation toward others); and Conscientiousness (ability to pursue long-range goals and personal organization). These five dimensions have been found to explain the majority of reliable variance among scales that measure traditional personality constructs. The FFM has been shown to be quite robust and together can be useful in predicting a wide range of outcomes.

For a new scale to be useful, it would need to demonstrate that it does significantly increase one's predictive ability over the FFM constructs. This is the ultimate test of any new construct. As was shown earlier, the dimensions of the ASPIRES scale are mostly independent of the FFM. However, it needs to be demonstrated that the ASPIRES dimensions can provide significant, unique explanatory power over the FFM domains.

To accomplish this, a series of hierarchical multiple regression analyses were conducted. The psychosocial variables in Table 7.6, both the self and observer ratings, served as the dependent variables. On step 1 of the analysis, the demographic variables of age and gender were entered. On step 2, self-rated markers of the FFM domains were entered. On step 3, using forward entry, the five ASPIRES scales were entered. A partial F-test determined whether the ASPIRES scales provided any significant increment in the explained variance. The results are presented in Table 7.8.

As can be seen, the FFM dimensions explained significant amounts of variance in all but one of the outcome variables. The ASPIRES scales made significant *additional* increases in the explained variance over and above the FFM ($\Delta\Delta R^2$ column). On average, the ASPIRES scales added 5% additional variance. The most relevant question to ask at this point is, "Does a 5% gain in explained variance represent a practically significant effect?" The answer is "Yes." It should be kept in mind that the R^2s are partial coefficients; they represent what each construct has to offer once the predictive effects of *both* personality *and* the other covariates have been removed. Thus, these values are low because there is little reliable variance left to explain in the criteria. Nunnally and Bernstein (1994) have observed that increases in R^2 are generally very small by the time a third substantive predictor is added to a regression equation. As more predictors are added, their incremental contributions will be increasingly smaller. Hunsley and Meyer (2003) suggested that an R^2 increase of between 0.02 and 0.04 would indicate a reasonable contribution for a variable entered on the third step. Given that the numinous variables in the present study are being added into the regression equations on the *seventh step*, the 5% additional variance appears to represent a quite robust contribution.

Another way to evaluate the practical contribution of the ASPIRES scales is to compare directly their explanatory power to that of the FFM. This can be done by comparing the R^2 values in Table 7.7 with the corresponding FFM R^2 values in Table 7.8. The result provides a more direct test of the zero-order predictiveness of this numinous domain relative to the empirically powerful FFM. Making this comparison shows the ASPIRES scales to be relatively robust predictors. In some instances, the predictive power of the religious and spiritual constructs was as great as the contribution made by personality. For example, the FFM predicts 20% of the overall variance in the Individualism scale, while the ASPIRES scales together explain 13% of the overall variance. Similarly, the FFM explains 7% of the variance in Prosocial Behavior, while the religious constructs explain 3%. In other instances, where the FFM may explain the lion's share of the variance (e.g., 42% of the variance in the Purpose in Life test), the numinous constructs also explained healthy amounts of the variance (e.g., 30% of the total variance in the Purpose in Life Test). What is perhaps of greater interest is that there are aspects of the individual better predicted by the numinous variables. Those scales relevant to sexual attitudes (e.g., Attitude Rating Toward Abortion and the Sexual Orientation Scale) were much more related to religiosity and spirituality (R^2s of 0.11 and 0.14, respectively) than they were to the dimensions of the FFM (R^2s of 0.06 and 0.06, respectively).

These data clearly indicate that these two measures of religiosity and spirituality are variables with predictive depth and potential conceptual power. As a single block, they compared favorably to the predictive power of the major personality dimensions represented by the FFM. Their ultimate value, however, may lie in their ability to explain some aspects of human activity (e.g., sexuality) better than the more traditional personality variables.

Short-Form Psychometric Properties

Although the ASPIRES scale is a relatively brief instrument, there may be situations where its length may be onerous. For example, for use with elderly or terminally ill individuals, the item load may be too much for such individuals to focus and concentrate on. Or, in circumstances where ratings are required from busy professionals, a brief form may be seen as more "doable" than a longer one. In response to these considerations, a short-form version has been developed, including both the self and observer rating versions.

For the Religious Sentiments section, only the first four items have been included (those dealing with the frequency of engaging in various religious practices). For the Spiritual Transcendence Scale, nine items were selected, three from each of the facet scales. The chosen items from each facet scale were those that evidenced the highest item-total correlations for their facet.

Using information from the normative sample, basic psychometric information about the short forms can be derived. Table 7.9 presents the alpha reliabilities and correlations with the long form. As can be seen, the brief versions of the scales evidence adequate levels of internal consistency. Correlations with the long forms indicate that the smaller scales capture much of the same information contained by their longer versions.

French and Piedmont (2004) examined the self-report version of the Short Form in a sample of 207 adults (French & Piedmont, 2004). Alpha reliabilities were comparable to those presented here. The Spiritual Transcendence facet scales correlated with a number of psychosocial outcomes (e.g., self-actualization, self-esteem, well-being, and prosocial behavior), even after the predictive effects of the FFM personality domains were controlled. Piedmont, Kennedy, M. Sherman, N. Sherman, and Williams (2008) examined the self and observer versions of the Short Form in both a student and community sample. Factor analyses evidenced a four-factor solution in the self-report data (the three STS scales plus the Religious Involvement scale), while only a three-factor solution was obtained in the observer-ratings data (the Religious Involvement items also loaded on the Prayer Fulfillment dimension). Significant cross-observer convergence was found (convergent correlations ranged from 0.27 for Universality to 0.77 for Religious Involvement). Both versions evidenced significant incremental validity over

personality in predicting an array of psychosocial outcomes.

Piedmont, Werdel, and Fernando (2009) examined the Short Form in a multifaith sample of Sri Lankans. Scores on the scales produced levels of internal consistency comparable to value obtained with the American normative sample. A factor analysis of the Spiritual Transcendence items revealed the underlying three correlated factor structure. Finally, mean score differences between the Christian and Buddhist groups also provided some validity for the scales. Thus, the Short Form scales can provide an empirically robust assessment of these numinous constructs, both across cultures and faith groups. However, the Short Form does not contain the Religious Crisis items.

Overview of Research Using the ASPIRES Scale
Cross-Cultural and Cross-Faith Findings

One of the major assumptions behind the ASPIRES scales is that they capture a universal aspect of human psychological functioning. Spirituality and religiosity are uniquely human qualities that find expression in all human cultures across every era. As such, the dimensions contained in the ASPIRES scale should be found reliable and valid across faith traditions and cultures. The accruing evidence supports this position.

Goodman (2002) gave the ST scales to a sample of conservative, reformed, and orthodox Jews. She found the ST scales to be reliable in all three samples and to significantly predict outcomes. Piedmont and Leach (2002) gave the ST scales and elements of the Religiosity scale (in English) to an Indian sample of Hindus, Muslims, and Christians.

Table 7.9 Alpha Reliabilities for the Self and Observer Versions of the ASPIRES Short Form and Correlations With the Long Form

ASPIRES Scale	Self-Report (α)	Observer (α)	Correlation With Long Form-Self	Correlation With Long Form-Observer
Prayer Fulfillment	.89	.89	.94***	.90***
Universality	.59	.82	.89***	.88***
Connectedness	.68	.71	.81***	.84***
Total Score	.76	.81	.90***	.92***
Religious Involvement	.80	.88	.94***	.96***

Notes: N for self-reports = 420; N for observer ratings = 399.
*** p < .001, two-tailed.
Source: This table is reprinted with permission of author from Piedmont (2005).

The ST scales evidenced alpha reliabilities comparable to those found in the United States. However, the Connectedness scale was found to be quite low. Furthermore, the ST scales were found to evidence significant incremental validity over the FFM personality domains in predicting emotional well-being and psychological maturity.

Cho (2004) translated the ST items into Korean and distributed the form to middle-aged married couples. The sample was comprised of evangelical Christians. The ST scales were found to significantly predict fear of intimacy. Bourdeau, Hinojosa, Perez, and Chu (2004) translated the ST scales into Spanish for use with gay Latino men. Alpha reliabilities were lower than those found in American samples, especially for Connectedness. However, the scales were found to capture native Meso-American religious themes that are not found with the more Christian-based spirituality measures.

Wilson (2004) gave the ST scales in English to a sample of aboriginal Canadians who were receiving inpatient treatment for alcoholism. The ST scales were found to be quite reliable (overall alpha for total ST scale was 0.90) and the overall score correlated significantly with other measures of spirituality and ethnic identity.

Piedmont (2007) translated the ST scales into Tagalog, a native language of the Philippines. This translation was given to a large adult sample across several different island locations. This sample was overwhelmingly Catholic. Alpha reliabilities were comparable with American samples, save Connectedness, which was much lower in both the self- and observer-rating versions. However, test-retest reliabilities were found to be very high for all scales (the 7-day-retest coefficient for Connectedness was 0.77). Thus, the lower alpha reliabilities for scores on the Connectedness scale appear to reflect the scale to be rather complex rather than unreliable. Piedmont found the expected three correlated factor structure in both the self and observer versions. Also, he found significant self-other convergence. The ST scales were also found to evidence significant incremental validity over the FFM personality domains. Perhaps most interesting, a comparison of the English and Tagalog versions of the scales showed the translation to be metrically equivalent to the original English version. Thus, the concepts of spirituality inherent in the English language can be found in a language that does not share a common lexical or cultural heritage with English. This finding is evidence that ST represents a universal quality of humans.

Finally, Rican and Janosova (2010) employed a Czech translation of the ASPIRES scale in assessing a sample of undergraduate Czech students. What is noteworthy about this study is the strong cultural atheistic orientation of the culture. Nonetheless, the Spiritual Transcendence scales evidenced independence from the domains of the FFM and correlated significantly with other measures of spirituality that were developed in this culture. Taken as a whole, the research data provide clear support for considering ST as a broad-based motivational construct. It is relevant for understanding behavior across diverse faith traditions and cultural backgrounds.

Clinical Applications

Spirituality constructs are finding wide application in mental and physical health centers. Spirituality is considered to be an important element of coping and healing. Several studies have used the ST scales as a predictor of such outcomes. Furthermore, low levels of spirituality (or conflicted spirituality) are seen as a risk factor for negative mental health outcomes.

Golden, Piedmont, Ciarrocchi, and Rodgerson (2004) showed that the ST scales evidenced significant incremental validity over the FFM personality domains and work environment in predicting burnout among Methodist clergy. The PF scale was the best predictor, in that those clergy who were not satisfied in their personal connection with the Transcendent experienced higher levels of burnout.

Bartlett, Piedmont, Bilderback, Matsumoto, and Bathon (2003) employed the ST scales with chronic arthritis sufferers. They found that the total ST score was a significant predictor of positive affect and general health (as measured by the SF-36), even after controlling for age, disease activity, physical function, and depressive symptoms.

Piedmont (2004b) used the ST scales with a sample of outpatient substance abuse treatment clients. The ST was given both before and after treatment. Alphas were consistent with those found in nonclinical samples. All scales evidenced significant retest reliabilities over the 8-week treatment period. Most important, Time 1 ST scores were found to significantly predict Time 2 self-report measures of coping ability, stress experience, and well-being. These relationships held even when controlling for personality, gender, and marital status. Controlling for these demographic variables, it was also found that Time 1 ST scores predicted Time 2 counselor ratings of treatment efficacy. The dimensions of Connectedness and Universality were the most salient predictors in these analyses, indicating that one's sense of attachment to and responsibility for larger social realities plays an important role in substance abuse recovery.

Wilson (2004) also found that ST scores were significantly related to self-ratings of abstinence self-efficacy among an inpatient sample of aboriginal Canadians. Universality was identified as the significant predictor of abstinence, even after the effects of gender and length of time in the AA program were controlled.

Finally, Piedmont, Hassinger, M. Sherman, N. Sherman, and Williams (2007) examined the relations between the ASPIRES scales and Axis II functioning in two college student samples. Using two different measures of Axis II functioning, it was found that the Religious Crisis scale evidenced consistent, significant associations with characterological impairment across both samples and measures. The spirituality scales were found to be independent of the pathognomic process once personality and Religious Crisis were controlled. Using SEM analyses, the model that hypothesized that Religious Crisis was a causal predictor of dysfunctionality evidenced best fit to the data (as opposed to the pathology being the cause of the religious distress).

The developing literature on the ASPIRES scales shows them to be useful predictive constructs in a number of clinical environments. The value of the instrument is twofold: (1) It is a psychometrically robust instrument across diverse populations; and (2) it is a robust predictor of psychosocial outcomes related to psychological growth, well-being, coping ability, psychopathology, and responsiveness to treatment.

The Value of the ASPIRES Scale for Research and Practice

The field is literally awash with measures of spirituality and religiousness, with new instruments appearing regularly in the journal literature. Absent any consensual definitions of spirituality and religiousness or any framework (empirical or conceptual) to organize this information, others have already pointed out the serious scientific difficulties such an overwhelming tide of scales poses for the field (Gorsuch, 1990; Hill et al., 2000; Piedmont et al., 2009). Koenig (2008) has flatly stated that if the field cannot organize and define its constructs, then the numinous should be eliminated from research altogether. The ASPIRES scale was developed explicitly to address these issues of meaning

and measurement so that a scientifically credible database could begin to be assembled.

In their review of the relations between personality, spirituality, and religiousness, Rose and Exline (this volume) outline several specific measurement areas in need of development in the field. For example, Rose and Exline (Chapter 6, this volume) noted the need for "continued exploration of aspects of personality that are uniquely relevant to religious and spiritual individuals." Such work would help to identify those specific qualities that define spiritual experiences. Although the ASPIRES was rationally developed to capture universal aspects of numinous functioning, by employing an empirical methodology that stressed the discriminant and incremental validity of the numinous scales over the domains of the FFM, the ASPIRES scale provides empirically sustainable operationalizations of spirituality and religiousness that reinforce their nonredundancy with these established personality constructs. This results in two significant benefits to the field.

First, the ASPIRES scale provides very clear definitions for spirituality and religiousness that have been found stable across samples, cultures, religions, and information sources. In a field that cannot find rational consensus on defining these two basis constructs, the scales of the ASPIRES provide a refreshing point of empirical consistency that has the potential for organizing the many different, and redundant, measures in the field. The ASPIRES scales can serve as the basis for a shared language for the development of a comprehensive model of numinous constructs. Second, because there is a conceptual model underlying the ASPIRES scales that articulates the psychological mechanisms by which spirituality and religiousness operate, the ASPIRES scales can be useful in the development and testing of causal models that address the underlying psychological processes that impact, and are impacted by, numinous constructs. For example, my colleagues and I (Piedmont et al., 2007, 2009) have employed the ASPIRES scales in a variety of studies evaluating the causal role of spirituality on a variety of psychosocial outcomes. Using SEM, we examined the extent to which spirituality was either a product of, or an input to, various psychological constructs. The ASPIRES scales have been shown to evidence causal priority in predicting such outcomes as affective well-being, psychological maturity, and characterological dysfunctionality.

Rose and Exline also noted that the field needs to design and build better measures of spirituality, with better psychometrics and less reliance on self-reports being two key issues. The ASPIRES scale does represent one of the better validated instruments in the field today, with a large and growing research database that demonstrates its relevance for assessing numinous qualities across faith groups and cultures. The findings from these studies clearly support the value of the ASPIRES scales as universal aspects of human functioning (e.g., Rican & Janosova, 2010).

Aside from its psychometric strengths, the ASPIRES scale has a number of important features that commend its use. First, it is written in simple, easy-to-understand language that requires only a seventh grade reading level. This makes the scale available for use with both younger samples and with more diverse community groups. Second, items are differentially reflected in order to control for acquiescence effects in responding, a salient source of error present in many newer spirituality scales. Third, the ASPIRES scale is the *only* instrument in the field to have a validated rater form. Ratings provide an important counter point to self-reports. Observer ratings provide significant, valid information about a target that cannot be obtained from a self-report, and they do not suffer from the same sources of response error. Therefore, convergence between self and observer ratings provides strong evidence that numinous constructs do not represent solipsistic aspects of the individual, but rather aspects of functioning that are observable in behavior and are consensually defined. Fourth, the ASPIRES scale also has self and observer short-form versions to provide greater flexibility to researchers and clinicians to assess numinous constructs in a wide range of contexts. Finally, the ASPIRES scale now has a computer-based interpretive program that allows users to input scores directly into a program and receive a four-page report that includes T-scores based on age and gender along with explanations of what those scores represent about the individual. It should be a useful tool in both clinical and pastoral care contexts.

Taken as a whole, the ASPIRES scale represents one of the more conceptually sophisticated, psychometrically robust, and technologically advanced instruments in the field of the Psychology of Religion today. It addresses many of the conceptual and technical problems identified by researchers in the field (e.g., Buss, 2002; Gorsuch, 1990; Sloan & Bagiella, 2002) and provides amenities few other instruments possess (e.g., a comprehensive technical manual, computer-based interpretive program, long and short forms, self and observer versions). It is hoped that this chapter will stimulate interest in the ASPIRES scale and in its ability to advance both research and clinical

practice in the field. The methodology by which the ASPIRES scale was developed can serve as a model for both the development of new instruments in this area and as a standard for evaluating existing instruments. A greater reliance on empirically sound models, methods, and measures will help to crystallize the scientific significance of numinous constructs for the social and physical sciences.

Note

The ASPIRES scale is a copyright protected instrument. Forms, manual, and scoring program can be obtained by contacting the author. Specimen sets are available upon request.

References

Allport, G. W. (1950). *The individual and his religion.* New York: Macmillan Company.

Andrews, F. M., & Withey, S. B. (1976). *Social indicators of well-being: American's perceptions of life quality.* New York: Plenum.

Bartlett, S. J., Piedmont, R. L., Bilderback, A., Matsumoto, A. K., & Bathon, J. M. (2003). Spirituality, well-being and quality of life in persons with rheumatoid arthritis. *Arthritis Care and Research, 49,* 778–783.

Bourdeau, B., Hinojosa, O., Perez, E., & Chu, K-L. (2004). *Understanding the spirituality of gay Latino men: A cross-cultural validity study.* Paper presented at the 2nd Annual Mid-Winter Research Conference on Religion and Spirituality, Columbia, MD.

Bradburn, N. M. (1969). *The structure of psychological well-being.* Chicago: Aldine.

Buss, D. M. (2002). Sex, marriage, and religion: What adaptive problems do religious phenomena solve? *Psychological Inquiry, 13,* 201–203

Cho, I. (2004). *An effect of spiritual transcendence of fear of intimacy.* Unpublished Master's thesis, Torch Trinity Graduate School of Theology, Seoul, Korea.

Crumbaugh, J. (1968). Purpose-In-Life Test. *Journal of Individual Psychology, 24,* 74–81.

Diener, E., Emmons, R. A., Larsen, R. J., & Griffin, S. (1985). The satisfaction with life scale. *Journal of Personality Assessment, 49,* 71–75

Dion, K. K., & Dion, K. L. (1991). Psychological individualism and romantic love. *Journal of Social Behavior and Personality, 6,* 17–33.

Emmons, R. A., & Paloutzian, R. F. (2003). The psychology of religion. *Annual Review of Psychology, 54,* 377–402.

Fetzer/National Institute on Aging Working Group. (1999, October). *Multidimensional measurement of religiousness/spirituality for use in health research: A report of the Fetzer/National Institute on Aging Working Group.* Kalamazoo, MI: Fetzer Institute.

Fisher, W. A., Byrne, D., White, L. A., & Kelly, K. (1988). Erotophobia-erotophilia as a dimension of personality. *Journal of Sex Research, 25,* 123–151.

French, A., & Piedmont, R. L. (2004). *An evaluation of the reliability and validity of the Revised Spiritual Transcendence Scale Short Form.* Paper presented at the Annual Mid-Winter Conference on Religion and Spirituality, Columbia, MD.

Golden, J., Piedmont, R. L., Ciarrocchi, J. W., & Rodgerson, T. (2004). Spirituality and burnout: An incremental validity study. *Journal of Psychology and Theology, 32,* 115–125.

Goodman, J. M. (2002). *Psychological well-being in the Jewish community: The impact of social identity and spirituality.* Unpublished Ph.D. dissertation, Kent State University, Kent, OH.

Gorsuch, R. L. (1990). Measurement in psychology of religion revisited. *Journal of Psychology and Christianity, 9,* 82–92.

Greenberg, J., Solomon, S., & Pyszczynski, T. (1997). Terror management theory of self-esteem and cultural world views: Empirical assessments and conceptual refinements. In M. P. Zanna (Ed.), *Advances in experimental social psychology* (pp. 61–139). San Diego, CA: Academic Press.

Hill, P. C., & Hood, R. W., Jr. (1999). *Measures of religiosity.* Birmingham, AL: Religious Education Press.

Hill, P. C., Pargament, K. I., Hood, R. W., McCullough, M. E., Swyers, J. P., Larson, D. B., & Zinnbauer, B. J. (2000). Conceptualizing religion and spirituality: Points of commonality, points of departure. *Journal for the Theory of Social Behavior, 30,* 51–77.

Hunsley, J., & Meyer, G. J. (2003). The incremental validity of psychological testing and assessment: Conceptual, methodological, and statistical issues. *Psychological Assessment, 15,* 446–455.

Jones, A., & Crandall, R. (1986). Validation of a short index of self-actualization. *Personality and Social Psychology Bulletin, 12,* 63–73.

Koenig, H. G. (2008). Concerns about measuring "spirituality" in research. *Journal of nervous and Mental Disease, 196,* 349–355.

McCrae, R. R., & Costa, P. T., Jr. (1996). Towards a new generation of personality theories: Theoretical contexts for the five-factor model. In J. S. Wiggins (Ed.), *The Five-Factor Model of personality: Theoretical perspectives.* New York, NY: Guilford Press.

Miller, W. R., & C'deBoci, J. (1994). Quantum change: Toward a psychology of transformation. In T. F. Heatherton & J. L. Weinberger (Eds.), *Can personality change?* (pp. 253–280). Washington, DC: American Psychological Association.

Nunnally, J. C., & Bernstein, I. H. (1994). *Psychometric theory* (3rd ed.). New York: McGraw-Hill.

Piedmont, R. L. (1999). Does spirituality represent the sixth factor of personality? Spiritual transcendence and the five-factor model. *Journal of Personality, 67,* 985–1013.

Piedmont, R. L. (2001). Spiritual transcendence and the scientific study of spirituality. *Journal of Rehabilitation, 67,* 4–14.

Piedmont, R. L. (2004a). The Logoplex as a paradigm for understanding spiritual transcendence. *Research in the Social Scientific Study of Religion, 15,* 263–284.

Piedmont, R. L. (2004b). Spiritual transcendence as a predictor of psychosocial outcome from an outpatient substance abuse program. *Psychology of Addictive Behaviors, 18,* 213–222.

Piedmont, R. L. (2005). *Assessment of Spirituality and Religious Sentiments Scale, technical manual.* Baltimore: Author.

Piedmont, R. L. (2006). Spirituality as a robust empirical predictor of psychosocial outcomes: A cross-cultural analysis. In R. Estes (Ed.), *Advancing quality of life in a turbulent world* (pp. 117–134). New York: Springer.

Piedmont, R. L. (2007). Cross-cultural generalizability of the Spiritual Transcendence Scale to the Philippines: Spirituality as a human universal. *Mental Health, Religion, and Culture, 10,* 89–107.

Piedmont, R. L. (2009). The contribution of religiousness and spirituality to subjective well-being and satisfaction with life.

In L. J. Francis (Ed.), *International handbook of education for spirituality, care and well-being* (pp. 89–105). New York: Springer.

Piedmont, R. L., Ciarrocchi, J. W., Dy-Liacco, G. S., & Williams, J. E. G. (2009). The empirical and conceptual value of the Spiritual Transcendence and Religious Involvement Scales for personality research. *Psychology of Religion and Spirituality, 3,* 162–179.

Piedmont, R. L., Hassinger, C. J., Sherman, M. F., Sherman, N. C., & Williams, J. E. G. (2007). The relations among spirituality and religiosity and Axis II functioning in two college samples. *Research in the Social Scientific Study of Religion, 18,* 53–74.

Piedmont, R. L., Kennedy, M. C., Sherman, M. F., Sherman, N. C., & Williams, J. E. G. (2008). A psychometric evaluation of the Assessment of Spirituality and Religious Sentiments (ASPIRES) scale short form. *Research in the Social Scientific Study of Religion, 19,* 163-181.

Piedmont, R. L., & Leach, M. M. (2002). Cross-cultural generalizability of the Spiritual Transcendence Scale in India. *American Behavioral Scientist, 45,* 1886–1899.

Piedmont, R. L., Mapa, A. T., & Williams, J. E. G. (2006). A factor analysis of the Fetzer/NIA Brief Multidimensional Measure of Religiousness/Spirituality (MMRS). *Research in the Social Scientific Study of Religion, 17,* 177–196.

Piedmont, R. L., Sherman, M. F., Sherman, N.C., & Williams, J. E. G. (2008). A psychometric evaluation of the Assessment of Spirituality and Religious Sentiments (ASPIRES) Scale: Short Form. *Research in the Social Scientific Study of Religion, 19,* 163–181.

Piedmont, R. L., Werdel, M. B., & Fernando, M. (2009). The utility of the Assessment of Spirituality and Religious Sentiments (ASPIRES) Scale with Christians and Buddhists in Sri Lanka. *Research in the Social Scientific Study of Religion, 20,* 131–146.

Rican, P., & Janosova, P. (2010). Spirituality as a basic aspect of personality: A cross-cultural verification of Piedmont's model. *The International Journal for the Psychology of Religion, 20,* 2–13.

Rose, E. D., & Exline, J. J. (2012). Personality, spirituality and religion. In L. Miller (Ed.), *Oxford handbook of psychology of spirituality and consciousness* (pp. 85–103). New York: Oxford University Press.

Rosenberg, M. (1979). *Conceiving the self.* New York: Basic Books.

Ruckmick, C. A. (1920). *The brevity book on psychology.* Chicago: Brevity Publishers.

Rushton, J. P., Chrisjohn, R. D., & Fekken, G. C. (1981). The altruistic personality and the self-report altruism scale. *Personality and Individual Differences, 2,* 293–302.

Sloan, R. P., & Bagiella, R. (2002). Claims about religious involvement and health outcomes. *Annals of Behavioral Medicine, 24,* 14–21.

Snyder, C. R., Sympson, S. C., Ybasco, F. C., Borders, T. F., Babyak, M. A., & Higgins, R. L. (1996). Development and validation of the state Hope Scale. *Journal of Personality and Social Psychology, 70,* 321–335.

Wilson, T. (2004). *Ethnic identity and spirituality in the recovery from alcoholism among aboriginal Canadians.* Unpublished Master's thesis, University of Windsor, Windsor, ON, Canada.

Woodworth, R. S. (1940). *Psychology* (4th ed.). New York: Henry Holt & Co.

Good and Evil in Religion:
The Interpersonal Context

Christopher T. Burris *and* John K. Rempel

Abstract

Based on an integrative review of cross-cultural literature concerning virtues, moral foundations, and values, we suggest that traditional religions' common understanding of "the good" centers on self-transcendence, manifest intrapersonally as an emphasis on self-control, and interpersonally as love, or motivation to preserve and promote others' well-being. Complementarily, we suggest that "evil" centers on self-enhancement, manifest interpersonally as moral compartmentalization, and interpersonally as hate, or the desire to diminish others' well-being. Not all love is "good," and not all hate is "evil" within faith traditions, however, and we consider examples of each of these subversions. We also consider the functional role of love and hate within religion, and we suggest that the emotions that accompany love-related episodes may sometimes serve as experiential validation of a faith tradition's claims, and that intentional evocation of strong negative emotions in quasi-religious contexts may buttress an unstable self-image. Finally, we offer broad suggestions for future research.

Key Words: good, evil, love, hate, morality, religion

Introduction

When used in isolation, the connotations of "good" and "evil" can be as tame as generic approval (good) or chided impishness (evil) but, especially when used in tandem, their import can be considerably more grave and expansive: "Good and evil" involve the cosmic, the mythic, the supernatural. Not surprisingly, then, good and evil are central matters of concern for religion. Indeed, across traditional religions at least, followers are exhorted to seek out and strive for that which is good, whereas evil is deemed "necessary" at best or, more often, as a "problem" or an "adversary." Commonly, good and evil are seen as being in conflict, often personified as gods, avatars, and saviors clashing with devils, demons, and minions. In the midst of it all are human beings, whose interconnected lives are tapestries of suffering and triumph as they attempt to confront both evil and good within the context of their traditions, personal beliefs, and relationships.

Notwithstanding the recurrent use of "good" and "evil" or their linguistic equivalents within faith traditions, an important question is whether there is a superordinate understanding of both good and evil that is evident across faith traditions. Thus, our goal in the present chapter is to identify the respective conceptual cores of understandings of good and evil within the context of religion, and subsequently to reflect on the individual and relational implications of these emergent understandings. To do so effectively, it seems prudent first to set forth a defensible conceptual definition of religion.

What Is Religion?

Positing an overarching conceptual definition of religion is a daunting task, and the results are often so vulnerable to deconstruction that the authors of a major recent overview of the empirical psychology of religion literature (Hood, Hill, & Spilka, 2009) consciously opted to focus instead on operational definitions. From our perspective, however, a conceptual definition of religion seems useful for delineating our domain of discourse, especially to the extent that key definitional components of religion figure prominently in religious conceptualizations of good and evil. Thus, we begin with our own *psychological, individual-level* definition of religion that is situated amid the human needs for meaning, control, and relationship identified by Hood et al. (2009) as central to comprehending how religion functions in human life. Specifically, we define religion as *ascribing importance to an entity in the absence of "objectively justifiable" criteria (meaning), and subsequently attempting to appropriate it (control) and/or relate to it (relationship).*

The components of this definition deserve some commentary. First, we use the intentionally broad term "entity," thereby allowing a religion's Entity to be impersonal (such as a force or a principle) as well as personal (such as a deity or revered ancestor). We would therefore have no problem with the characterization of communism as religion (McFarland, 1998), for example. Second, inherent in our definition is the idea that it is the elevation of the Entity to a position of prominence (cf. Tillich's, 1959, concept of "ultimate concern"; see also Emmons, 1999) that gives religion its motive power, its often striking capacity to reorder a person's life around a central theme (cf. Allport's, 1950, concept of "sentiment"). Third, the elevation of the Entity occurs "in the absence of 'objectively justifiable' criteria": This qualification is necessary to underscore the fact that the elevated status of a religion's Entity at the individual level is fundamentally private and subjective—that is, it is not based either on *direct observation* or *social consensus*, in contrast to most other "knowing." That is, religion—at least among the devout—*feels* true, and it is therefore not easily dislodged: Here we are reminded of research by Hunsberger and Altemeyer (2006), who reported that 100% of religious fundamentalists—as well as 50% of self-identified atheists—stated that the hypothetical discovery of "hard" scientific-historical evidence that definitively disconfirmed their beliefs concerning whether God exists would *not* lead them to change their beliefs. Collectively, we suggest that these three components of our definition map onto humans' need for meaning.

The motivational implications of a religion's elevation of an entity, in turn, map onto humans' need for control and/or relationship, depending on the nature of the Entity itself. Obviously, if an entity is assumed to be impersonal, control is relevant but relationship is not: Luke Skywalker was admonished to "*use* the Force," not to befriend or placate it. This conceptualization is a magical one, giving rise to religious systems in which control themes are evident in the use of ritual or visualization to effect changes in the external world (both seen and unseen), for example. In contrast, when religion's Entity is assumed to be personal, both control and relationship themes can be addressed within the religious system: At times, devotional acts may be intended to effect change, as in petitional prayer or offerings, whereas at other times the attention directed toward the Entity may resemble simulated conversation.

With our individual-level definition of religion, there is the risk that any analysis of good and evil can become tautological. Presumably, any entity that has been elevated to the level of ultimate importance would be good by definition. This tells us nothing new about religious conceptions of "good," however. Moreover, if a religious system is solipsistic or wholly impersonal, "evil" may be irrelevant. Consequently, we will examine the concepts of "good" and "evil" as they manifest their religious significance in the human arena; that is, we suggest that good and evil are *inescapably interpersonal*. In particular, as we will argue, relational and power/control themes figure prominently in religious conceptions of good and evil. Consider the Hebrew story of Job, wherein Satan bet Yahweh that Job would lose faith when stripped of his family, possessions, and health. To use our terminology, Satan—an exemplar of evil entities—asserted that Job would no longer consider elevation of Yahweh as meaningful when his (Job's) need for relationship and control was thwarted.

What Is "Good"?

Psychology has a long history of avoiding—or at least avoiding the appearance of—prescriptivism. Of course, even at the descriptive level there has always been the tacit recognition that, at the psychological level, the human organism experiences some things as desirable or beneficial and other things as harmful or aversive. Within the growing field of positive psychology (e.g., Seligman & Csikszentmihalyi, 2000), this implicit understanding has become more explicit, fueling a deliberate search for the principles of, and tools for fostering, the "good life."

Of particular relevance to the current discussion, Dahlsgaard, Peterson, and Seligman (2005) sought to identify a set of ubiquitous virtues (i.e., the psychological strengths of character that contribute to a well-lived life) by reviewing Confucianism, Taoism, Buddhism, Hinduism, Athenian philosophy, Judaism, Christianity, and Hinduism. Their six *core virtues* appear in Table 8.1.

Not surprisingly, *transcendence* as Dahlsgaard et al. (2005) defined it is emphasized within the overtly religious traditions. These authors also claimed that, of the six core virtues, only *justice* and *humanity* are prominently featured across all of the traditions examined, however.

Haidt and colleagues (Haidt & Graham, 2007; Haidt & Joseph, 2004) have recently taken a very different approach toward cataloguing and understanding human virtues. Rather than focusing on established traditions, they developed their Moral Foundations Theory by examining established anthropological and evolutionary ideas of morality. Their goal was to pinpoint the "interlocking sets of values, practices, institutions, and evolved psychological mechanisms that suppress or regulate selfishness and make social life possible" (Haidt, 2008, p. 70) by identifying the widely held virtues for which there is published evolutionary support. The five moral foundations identified by them appear in Table 8.2.

There is a straightforward correspondence between the moral foundations of harm/care and fairness/reciprocity, described by Haidt and colleagues as *individualizing foundations*, and the virtues of humanity and justice identified by Dahlsgaard et al. (2005). The remaining three—ingroup/loyalty,

authority/respect, and purity/sanctity, which are collectively labeled *binding foundations*—are focused on forming and maintaining coalitions and marking group boundaries, establishing social structure and order, and suppressing the carnal, "animal" nature. There is much overlap of content between these three foundations and Dahlsgaard et al.'s core virtues of courage, wisdom, temperance, and transcendence, although the two schemes differ with respect to how the content is grouped.

Both Dahlsgaard et al. (2005) and Haidt (2008) took a "top-down" approach toward discovering the structure and content of what humans consider "good" by identifying the common themes evident in existing literature. Complementing this is the "bottom-up" approach that Schwartz (1992) and colleagues used to identify the common content and structure of values across cultures. For Schwartz, values are the beliefs and associated emotions that represent desirable global goals or the behaviors that promote the realization of those goals. Thus, values have a motivational foundation and act as guiding life principles and standards for selecting and evaluating behavior, people, and events.

In a set of studies with over 25,000 participants from 44 countries, Schwartz (1992) found evidence to support his hypothesized structure of 10 categories of values: power, achievement, hedonism, stimulation, self-direction, universalism, benevolence, tradition, conformity, and security. These values form a circumplex in which adjacent values share congruent goals and opposing values are linked to incongruent goals: Table 8.3 shows the values in consecutive order around the circumplex.

Table 8.1 The Six "Core Virtues" Identified by Dahlsgaard and Colleagues

Humanity	Interpersonal strengths that involve befriending and caring for others; examples include love and kindness
Justice	Civic strengths that underlie healthy community life; examples include fairness, leadership, and citizenship or teamwork
Courage	Emotional strengths that involve the exercise of will to accomplish goals in the face of opposition, external or internal; examples include bravery, perseverance, and authenticity (honesty)
Temperance	Strengths that protect against excess; examples include forgiveness, humility, prudence, and self-control
Wisdom	Cognitive strengths that entail the acquisition and use of knowledge; examples include creativity, curiosity, judgment, and perspective (providing counsel to others)
Transcendence	Strengths that forge connections to the larger universe and thereby provide meaning; examples include gratitude, hope, and spirituality

Table 8.2 Five "Moral Foundations" Identified by Haidt and Colleagues

Harm/care	Basic concerns for the suffering of others, including virtues of caring and compassion
Fairness/reciprocity	Concerns about unfair treatment, inequality, and more abstract notions of justice
Ingroup/loyalty	Concerns related to obligations of group membership, such as loyalty, self-sacrifice, and vigilance against betrayal
Authority/respect	Concerns related to social order and the obligations of hierarchical relationships, such as obedience, respect, and proper role fulfillment
Purity/sanctity	Concerns about physical and spiritual contagion, including virtues of chastity, wholesomeness, and control of desires

Furthermore, Schwartz and Boehnke (2004) have also secured empirical support for the suggestion that the values circumplex is organized around two superordinate, bipolar dimensions in which *self-transcendence* values (benevolence and universalism) oppose *self-enhancement* (power and achievement) values, and *openness to change* values (self-direction, stimulation, and hedonism) oppose *conservation* values (tradition, conformity, and security). Although these two orthogonal dimensions are interpretive additions to the empirically based circumplex structure of values ratings—and

alternate dimensions can and have been proposed (e.g., Schwartz, 2006)—we would suggest that the self-transcendence/self-enhancement dimension captures core motivational processes of direct relevance to the analysis of good and evil.

More specifically, the contents of the six virtues identified by Dahlsgaard et al. (2005) and the five moral foundations identified by Haidt (2008) are located on the self-transcendence side of Schwartz's (1992) values circumplex. That is, *all* of the virtues and moral foundations map onto values that reflect the goal of benefitting targets beyond the individual

Table 8.3 Schwartz's Ten Value Categories With Descriptions and Specific Values

Power	Social status and prestige, control or dominance over people and resources (social power, authority, wealth, preserving my public image, social recognition)
Achievement	Personal success through demonstrating competence according to social standards (successful, capable, ambitious, influential, intelligent)
Hedonism	Pleasure and sensuous gratification for oneself (pleasure, enjoying life, self-indulgence, sexuality)
Stimulation	Excitement, novelty, and challenge in life (daring, a varied life, an exciting life)
Self-direction	Independent thought and action choosing, creating, exploring (freedom, independent, choosing own goals, creativity, curious, self-respect)
Universalism	Understanding, appreciation, tolerance, and protection for the welfare of all people and for nature (broad-minded, social justice, equality, a world at peace, a world of beauty, unity with nature, protecting the environment, wisdom)
Benevolence	Preservation and enhancement of the welfare of people with whom one is in frequent personal contact (helpful, honest, forgiving, loyal, responsible, true friendship, mature love)
Tradition	Respect, commitment, and acceptance of the customs and ideas traditional culture or religion provide (humble, devout, respect for tradition, moderate, detachment, accepting my portion in life)
Conformity	Restraint of actions, inclinations, and impulses likely to upset or harm others and violate social expectations or norms (obedient, politeness, honoring parents and elders, self-discipline)
Security	Safety, harmony, and stability of society, of relationships, and of the self (national security, social order, sense of belonging, family security, clean, reciprocation of favors, healthy)

self. This is largely consistent with Schwartz (2007), who found that more than 80% of a sample of 100 Israeli adults surveyed labeled all of the benevolence values on the Schwartz Value Survey as moral, and that at least 70% labeled all or most of the universalism, conformity, tradition, and security values as moral.

Note that there is a lack of correspondence in one respect: Schwartz's Israeli respondents considered security values to be moral and self-direction values as amoral even though self-direction is more closely aligned with the self-transcendence dimension than is security. However, both security and self-direction are at the periphery of the self-transcendence dimension, and so their moral nature may be more open to cultural interpretation. That is, given the Israeli context, security is likely to be an especially salient and moral concern at the group level. In the same way, self-direction values such as creativity, independence, and freedom may be ascribed higher moral ratings in more individualistic cultures where group threat is less salient. Overall, however, the self-transcendence/self-enhancement dimension seems to reflect a morality dimension in which "goodness" is embodied in the virtues and moral frameworks identified by Dahlsgaard et al. (2005) and Haidt (2008) that go beyond self-interest and span Schwartz's (1992) openness to change/conservation dimension.

Religion, Politics, and "the Good"

The openness to change/conservation dimension, which is orthogonal to the self-transcendence/self-enhancement dimension, appears to underlie liberal/conservative ideological differences in both political and religious domains. In the political domain, for example, research by Haidt and others (e.g., Graham, Haidt, & Nosek, 2009; Haidt & Graham, 2007; McAdams, Albaugh, Farber, Daniels, Logan, & Olson, 2008) has repeatedly found that people who self-identify as politically conservative tend to endorse conservation values, whereas political liberals consistently endorse openness to change values—although, for both groups, the endorsed values may fall on either side of the self-transcendence/self-enhancement continuum. Graham et al. (2009) have also shown that political conservatives in general are more likely to endorse the individualizing and binding moral foundations equally, whereas political liberals show a strong preference for the individualizing moral foundations. Moreover, van Leeuwen and Park (2009) recently demonstrated that sensitivity to threat—specifically,

the belief that the world is a dangerous place—predicted more conservative political beliefs, and that this was mediated by greater endorsement of binding moral foundations. The key point here is that, to the extent that self-transcendence defines that which is "good," political ideology is arrayed along a dimension that is essentially orthogonal to "goodness."

In the religious domain the picture is somewhat more complex. In a meta-analysis of studies that have examined the relationship between values and traditional religiosity, Saraglou, Delpierre, and Dernelle (2004) found that greater religiosity was most strongly (and logically) linked to tradition-related values, with more modest but still positive associations with values related to conformity, security, and benevolence. In contrast, traditional religiosity tended to be inversely associated with endorsement of values that reflected hedonism, stimulation, self-direction, achievement, power, and universalism. Thus, in general, traditional religiosity appears to be associated primarily with values representing both conservation and self-transcendence. When spirituality rather than religiosity is the predictor, however (see Hood et al., 2009, for an extensive discussion of the conceptual distinction), the positive associations with benevolence and the negative associations with power and achievement remain, but associations with the remaining values are essentially zero (Saroglou & Munoz-Garcia, 2008). Thus, like political ideology, religiosity and spirituality shows conservative/liberal variation yet, despite these variations, conceptualizations of "good" remain squarely within the self-transcendence domain.

This pattern is further clarified when we look at the correlations between more liberal religiosity and moral foundations. In an analysis of ongoing online data collection of moral foundations and political orientation, Haidt, Graham, and Joseph (2009) identified four clusters. In addition to the liberal (high on individualizing and low on binding moral foundations) and conservative (moderately and equally high on individualizing and binding moral foundations) groups described earlier, they found two others. The first was high on individualizing and also relatively high on binding moral foundations. Labeled the "Religious Left" by Haidt et al., this group expressed concern for all types of moral behavior—and thus, by extension, appeared to endorse self-transcendent values at both ends of the conservation/openness to change continuum. Haidt et al. cited Jim Wallis, the founder of Sojourners—a

Christian-based social justice organization—as an exemplar of this group.

The other group was low across the board—as low as the conservatives on individualizing and as low as the liberals on binding moral foundations. Haidt et al. (2009) labeled this group "Libertarians," in reference to the philosophical position that regards personal liberty as the only significant value, and cited the radical individualism of novelist/philosopher Ayn Rand as an exemplar. The desire for unfettered personal freedom is most certainly consistent with motivation to enhance the self. In and of itself, this is not necessarily problematic. The issue, however, as implied by Schwartz's (1992) circumplex, is that prioritization of self-enhancement can have a zero-sum quality: The pursuit of power, stimulation, hedonism, and achievement sets the stage for anarchy, selfishness, and the sacrifice of others' well-being for personal gain.

Overall, the foregoing analysis shows a remarkable convergence in what people across time, place, and tradition consider as "good": The virtues and moral foundations identified are consonant with valuing the well-being of people, places, and objects that transcend the self. Indeed, Balliet, Joireman, Daniels, and George-Falvy (2008) found that trait empathy—the dispositional capacity to take the perspective of others—was positively correlated with self-transcendent values and negatively correlated with self-enhancement values. Moreover, as we will now articulate, the motivation to transcend one's own interests in the service of others' well-being is manifest, at the interpersonal level, as love. Hence, it is not surprising that "love" is a recurrent emphasis across many faith traditions.

What Is "Love"?

After a survey of the dominant conceptualizations of love and their associated shortcomings in the psychological literature, Rempel and Burris (2005) postulated that love is best understood as a *motive associated with the goal of preserving or promoting the well-being of the other*. This motivational conceptualization of love allows for the postulation of distinct love types based on whether the ultimate goal of the love motive is benefiting the other (as in *altruistic* love), or whether benefiting the other is instead a means to some self-focused end, for example, prolonging pleasurable contact with the other in the case of erotic love.

This idea that different types of love are associated with different types of ultimate goals proves critical when attempting to understand how religions deal with love: Altruistic love (e.g., Post, 2002) is especially valorized, as evidenced by the near-ubiquitous enshrinement of the principle referred to as "The Golden Rule" in the Christian tradition, that is, non-contingent efforts to treat others as one wishes to be treated (Ontario Consultants on Religious Tolerance, 2010). In its most dramatic form, altruistic love implies self-sacrifice: "Greater love hath no man than this, that a man lay down his life for his friends" (John 15:13). At the same time, self-sacrifice often finds its way into religion in a multitude of milder forms, given traditional religion's recurrent advocacy of self-control (McCullough & Willoughby, 2009).

In contrast, instrumental or nonaltruistic forms of love are less revered, viewed with suspicion, or even condemned as an outright mockery of true love. For example, in a number of traditions, erotic love is seen as problematic because it fosters particularistic attachments and/or self-gratification, and because this distracts from pursuit of the Entity, celibacy may be prescribed. In other contexts, however, erotic love may instead be co-opted in the service of spiritual development, as in the case of Hindu Tantra (Urban, 2003). A strikingly innovative example of this is the "Loving Jesus Revelation" articulated by The Family International (2004)—a Christian-based new religious movement—wherein adult followers are encouraged, among other things, to express receptive devotion to Christ through the use of sexually explicit language and visualizations during periods of private prayer.

Thus, religion's adoption of self-transcendence as a guiding principle leads to religion's corresponding prescription, at the interpersonal level, to adopt the goal of preserving and promoting others' well-being for its own sake. That is, in terms of the core definitional elements of religion discussed earlier, personal power is subordinated to relational connection. If benefiting the other is not the demonstrable ultimate goal, then religions are much more circumspect, however. Indeed, explicitly self-serving motivation for prosocial behavior may be viewed with derision: "Therefore when thou doest thine alms, do not sound a trumpet before thee, as the hypocrites do in the synagogues and in the streets, that they may have glory of men. Verily I say unto you, they have their reward" (Matthew 6:2). If, however, the ultimate goal is framed as a spiritual one, nonaltruistic forms of love are viewed more permissively.

Good: A Summary

In sum, we suggest that the concept of *good* is based on self-transcendent values: Being mindful of others, individuals are admonished to temper their own appetites as well as actively contribute to others' well-being. Thus, the "good"—in its most rarefied interpersonal form—is altruistic love. If our conceptual analysis is correct thus far, then it also seems reasonable to expect that what is labeled "evil" will embody one or more variants of self-enhancement in interpersonal contexts.

What Is "Evil"?

Although we are not aware of a text-based summary of "core vices" analogoud to the core virtues identified by Dahlsgaard et al. (2005), Cenkner's (1997a) edited volume assembled representative interpretations of evil across the major faith traditions. We therefore rely primarily on that volume for our survey of religious conceptualizations of evil, with the caveat that contributors seldom defined evil outright, and so we inferred their working definitions of evil based on how they used the term.

Judaism

In the Judaic tradition, the Torah links evil to chaos, a breakdown of order, and a human tendency toward violence, according to James (1997). Isenberg (1997) echoed the latter theme in his comments concerning the rabbinic view of humanity's split nature, which includes *yetzer*, or an inborn tendency toward evil. He also contrasted evil with "justified suffering" (p. 20) and explicated the Kabbalistic understanding that evil stems from "broken connections" or relationships: Adam's "original sin" was to see himself as separate, and hatred and destruction is the result (p. 27).

Christianity

From a Christian perspective, although Zwerner (1997) ultimately interpreted the crucifixion of Jesus as a redemptive, transformative event, it nevertheless also exemplifies evil, understood as "unmerited suffering" (p. 50). More formally, she defined evil as "any actions or states of affairs which intend and/or realize destructive effects for human persons, their relationships, or the natural environment" (p. 44). Stenger (1997) likewise noted the intimate link between Christ's crucifixion and evil in antidotal uses of the sign of the cross "to ward off evil powers" at various points in Christian history (p. 60).

Islam

According to Al-Ghazali's (1997) interpretation of the Islamic worldview, evil is to be understood within the framework of *adl* ("placing something in its proper stead") versus *zulm* ("placing something in an improper or wrong place where it does not belong," p. 74). Humans must therefore prioritize spiritual strivings and physical/material concerns properly; failure to do so results in an "unbalanced and exclusive pursuit of selfish purpose" (p. 74). The identified interpersonal consequences are considerable: "[A]ll evil known in human history has arisen from humankind's malice and ill will against and among each other" (p. 76).

Buddhism

From a (Theravedan) Buddhist standpoint, Vajiragnana (1997) identified evil as "that which is opposed to the attainment of enlightenment" (p. 99). Evil, then, is ultimately that which corrupts or defiles the mind, thereby constraining one's ability to perceive reality in its truest sense. The three essential "defilements or passions are greed, hatred and delusion" (p. 101).

Hinduism

From a broader, cosmological perspective in classic Hindu thought, evil is assumed not to exist. It is, however, acknowledged as a phenomenological reality akin to pain and suffering (Kaplan, 1997). D'Sa (1997) asserted that evil manifests "wherever wholeness is rejected or neglected and partiality is the norm" (p. 148): Evil is fragmentation stemming from misguided perception. Cenkner (1997b), in his consideration of Hindu philosopher Tagore's work, characterized evil as "alienation, isolation, and unrelatedness" (p. 136)

Satanism

Complementing these treatments of evil in mainstream religious traditions is a satanic perspective, at least as articulated in *The Satanic Bible* (LaVey, 1969). Therein, the label "evil" is generally viewed with disdain, portrayed as being used pejoratively by self-proclaimed "good" individuals to refer to those who, mindfully or not, live according to satanic principles such as "indulgence instead of abstinence" and "vengeance instead of turning the other cheek" (p. 25). Speaking on behalf of Satanists, LaVey ultimately—albeit begrudgingly—embraced the "evil" label, however: "So, if 'evil' they have named us, evil we are—and so what! The Satanic Age is upon us! Why not take advantage of it and LIVE!" (p. 45).

Emergent Themes

At the broadest, most inclusive level of analysis, we would suggest that the representation of "evil" across these various traditions can be understood as a specific articulation of self in relation to the social world that has both "omission" and "commission" facets (cf. self-control versus active promotion of the other's well-being in "good" discussed earlier). From an omission standpoint, evil can be understood as the *refusal to engage in self-transcendence* or "laziness taken to its ultimate, extraordinary extreme" (Peck, 1978, p. 278). From a commission standpoint, evil can be understood as *overt self-enhancement at the expense of others' well-being.* Thus, evil is the conceptual inverse of good as we characterized it earlier: Reflecting back on the core elements of religion, it is the prioritization of personal power and control over relational connections. The consequences of this prioritization, we suggest, are *suffering* and *fragmentation*, which can manifest both intrapersonally and interpersonally.

Psychological Perspectives on Evil as Suffering

Social-psychological analyses of "evil" to date have focused primarily on the suffering outcome. As we will soon illustrate, however, fragmentation as a subtext or context is not infrequent. Within such analyses, "evil" is used as an a priori label to refer to a discrete category of large-scale destructive behaviors such as genocide: Darley (1992), Miller (2004), Staub (2003), and Waller (2002) exemplify this approach.

Complementing such efforts to treat evil "objectively" are conceptual frameworks that acknowledge the *subjectivity* of the label itself, that is, that "evil" is a matter of perception and interpretation (Baumeister, 1997), with corresponding attention to when and with what effects the label is applied. Exemplifying the latter approach, Burris and Rempel (2008a, 2011) proposed that—at least in interpersonal contexts—the label "evil" is especially likely to be applied to behavioral instances of *intentional, unjustifiable harm.* Viewed in this way, the behavioral prototype of evil is the mirror image of the prototype of good, that is, intentional, unmitigated attempts to benefit the other, of which altruistic love is the purest exemplar.

Indeed, just as love is the interpersonal embodiment of "good," we suggest that the interpersonal embodiment of "evil" is *hate*, understood as a motive associated with the goal of diminishing or destroying the well-being of the other (Rempel & Burris, 2005). Moreover, just as a motivational conceptualization of love allows us to postulate the existence of love types based on whether ultimate goal of the

love motive is benefiting the other or is instead a means to some form of self-benefit, so it is possible to postulate the existence of hate types wherein making the other suffer can be intended either for its own sake or as a means to some other end. Thus, in the case of nihilistic hate, destruction of the other is the ultimate goal, whereas, for example, diminishing the other's well-being can also be a means to the end of restoring a sense of justice and order, as in the case of redress.

Importantly, just as altruistic love is held as the ultimate standard for interpersonal goodness across many faith traditions and instrumental forms of love are regarded as less noble, so hate is most likely to be regarded as the embodiment of interpersonal evil and thus subject to condemnation by religion *when its ultimate goal is perceived to be unjustified.* Thus, when hate is seen as justifiable, it does not match the behavioral prototype of evil, that is, intentional, unjustifiable harm. For example, the Hebrew Bible states: "The fear of the LORD is to hate evil" (Proverbs 15:13), so when evil itself is the target, hate is not condemned but extolled as a manifestation of being in proper relationship with the Entity.

In fact, when the focus is on what is perceived to be a justifiable end (e.g., executing justice or restoring order), people actually may tend not to regard the intent to harm as "hate." A striking example of this sort of subversion appears in the Hebrew story of Abraham, who, although ultimately stayed by God, was willing to kill his own son as a sacrificial tribute. Thus, if "love" of God is the ultimate goal, then the instrumental harm may not be seen as issuing from hateful intentions or judged to be evil. Indeed, as a patriarchal figure who is revered across the three most influential Western (or *Abrahamic*) religions, it is clear that Abraham's reputation was not irreparably marred by his homicidal intentions toward his son that—by contemporary standards—would be regarded as traumatizing and abusive. Others, such as political enemies flagrantly portrayed as "enemies of God" (Keen, 1986), are not so lucky, however: Their acts of intended harm are seen as unjustifiable and, therefore, as "evil." Engaging in "evil" behaviors, in turn, is seen as sufficient cause to brand the actors as "evil" individuals, a process that Ellard, Miller, Baumle, and Olson (2002) referred to as "demonizing."

At the extreme, such "evil" individuals are perceived to embody what Baumeister (1997) referred to as the "myth of pure evil." According to the myth, evildoers intentionally perpetrate harm, destruction, and chaos on innocent victims merely for the pleasure of doing so. In addition to this sadistic core, evildoers are also egotistical, greedy, savage, and filled with a rage that they have difficulty controlling. Finally, such individuals are seen as *irredeemably* evil. This is a damning indictment, facilitating the justification of harsh treatment of evildoers, for as Baumeister (1997, p. 69) put it, "... there is no point in being patient, tolerant, and understanding when one is dealing with evil" (see also Peck, 1983). Indeed, Rempel and Burris (2010) found that greater endorsement of the myth of pure evil predicted increased endorsement of a cluster of exceedingly harsh punishments directed toward a repeat sex offender, including a life sentence with solitary confinement and surgical castration. Moreover, Burris and Rempel (2011) found that branding a target as "evil" predicted interpreting his ambiguous behaviors as exemplifying prototypic "evil" behavior, which in turn predicted harshly punitive responses toward him.

Here we see an exacerbating symbiosis between "evil" and suffering: The intentional infliction of suffering is seen as "evil" when perceived to be unjustified. This can lead to labeling the perpetrator as irreparably "evil," in which case even his or her ambiguous behavior is suspect and he or she becomes a target for the infliction of severe harm or even annihilation. Concurrently, few individuals, religious or not (excepting perhaps some bemused Satanists), are likely to view their own desires to inflict suffering on others as "evil" because they see their intentions as justified, so evil can become self-perpetuating.

Religious and Psychological Perspectives on Evil as Fragmentation

In addition to evil's recurrent link to human suffering across a variety of religious perspectives is its recognition as a fragmenting force, that is, as something that creates and/or accentuates separations and divisions. Such fragmentation can be intrapersonal, as noted earlier in Hindu commentaries that articulated evil in terms of isolation and resistance to wholeness; it can also be interpersonal. For example, "he that soweth discord among the brethren" is on the list of those things that the Hebrew God "hates" (Proverbs 6:19).

A striking articulation of the fragmentation theme appears in Roman Catholic priest Malachi Martin's (1992) commentary concerning five alleged cases of demonic possession, wherein he opined that the raison d'être for demonic entities is their hatred

for (God and) humanity, manifest as a "need to disrupt, to soil, to destroy, to make ugly, to deform" (p. 417). This theme was echoed by *The Exorcist*'s Father Merrin, who, when asked why the possession of young Regan occurred, stated: "I think the point is to make us despair...To see ourselves as...animal and ugly...To reject the possibility that God could love us" (Blatty, Marshall, & Friedkin, 1973). Thus, as the preternatural embodiment of evil, demons are portrayed as being motivated by hate to inflict harm by defacing and (ultimately) isolating their human targets (see also Peck, 1983).

The fragmentation tactic is graphically portrayed when, in reference to Slayer's album *God Hates Us All*, lead vocalist Tom Araya remarked in the film documentary *Metal: A Headbanger's Journey* that "God doesn't hate...[but] it's a great fucking title...I think it'll fucking piss a lot of people off" (McFayden, Dunn, & Wise, 2005). The tactic is two-pronged: (1) The deity, often portrayed in Christian-influenced contexts as loving humanity, is instead depicted as (universally) hateful, which in effect magnifies the gap between God and humanity; (2) promulgation of the depiction of God as hate-filled is itself expected to provoke opposition.

Fragmentation has appeared as a theme in a number of psychological treatises on evil as well. Peck (1983), for example, suggested that the paramount motivation of "evil" individuals is to avoid taking responsibility for their misdeeds, fueled by an absolute intolerance of the associated guilt and shame. The two primary deflection mechanisms are hypothesized to be scapegoating (i.e., letting others—often dependents—bear the burden), and excessive attention directed to maintaining a respectable or virtuous public image (which is presumed to be severely at odds with their private motives). Under severe press, however, these deflection mechanisms may fail, leading to a disorganization of thought that resembles a "mild schizophrenic-like disturbance" (p. 129).

Darley (1996), drawing on Lifton's (1986) analysis of doctors in Nazi death camps, likewise posited that one means by which individuals can become complicit with an evil-producing organization is by a nonconscious "doubling" process whereby a "personality is formed that is designed to cope with the exigencies of the killing situation, but one which can and does access the skills and knowledge of the prior personality." Moreover, paralleling Peck (1983), this internal fragmentation "promotes the avoidance of guilt" (Darley, 1996, p. 206). In addition, Darley (1992) pointed to "diffusion and fragmentation of responsibility" as contributors to the perpetration of evildoing at the organizational level. The vector is similar to the one identified by Peck: "Higher-ups have a good deal of room to maneuver to keep cover-ups on track without leaving evidence of their complicity. Thus they can participate in evil without leaving a trail and generally escape the sanctions that, at least occasionally, are visited on some middle-level personnel" (Darley, 1992, p. 32).

Baumeister (1997) cited organizational factors similar to those identified by Darley (1992, 1996). Moreover, at the individual level, he underscored the functionality of *low-level thinking*, an often meticulous focus on procedures and details that can effectively mask the larger implications of one's actions, for "[w]rongness is largely a high-level judgment that requires evaluating the higher meaning of actions according to broad, meaningful principles. If one can avoid thinking at that level, the wrongness does not appear" (p. 340).

Evil: A Summary

The religious and psychological voices sampled here are in harmony with respect to conceptualizing evil as rooted in the willful promotion of—or refusal to extend—the self that manifests as harm/suffering and both individual and interpersonal fragmentation. We have suggested that, just as love is the sine qua non of good, so hate (the intent to diminish or destroy another's well-being) and evil (the conceptual inverse of good) are often closely connected: Hate is often judged to be "evil," but *only when seen as unjustified*. So, for example, "killing for God" is not likely to be judged as "evil" by the perpetrator because the act may be framed as a means of expressing one's devotion to that deity. This underscores the subjectivity associated with application of the "evil" label.

Once applied, the consequences of the "evil" label are often considerable, however, in that branding a person as irredeemably evil is perhaps the ultimate justification for harming, isolating, or even destroying that person. Thus, the profound irony is that evil is often judged by the suffering and chaos it creates, yet evildoers themselves seldom embrace the "evil" label as applicable to themselves or their behavior—preferring instead to obfuscate the moral implications of their behavior by compartmentalizing their thinking or to justify their own behavior by displacing blame onto others, especially those whom they have labeled "evil." In so doing, it would seem that evil feeds its own destructive fire.

Good and Evil, Love and Hate, Means and Ends

Across mainstream religious contexts, we have argued that the conception of what is "good" centers on themes of self-transcendence, of which love—especially altruistic love—is the interpersonal manifestation. This is perhaps not surprising within a tradition such as (orthodox) Christianity, wherein an inherently relational Trinitarian God provided a model of self-sacrifice in the crucifixion and death of Christ: "For God so loved the world, that he gave his only begotten son…" (John 3:16). Similar themes are also evident in Kabbalistic Judaism, wherein sex with one's partner on the Sabbath is seen as healing the rift in God, who "is a number of relationships: husband/wife; father/mother; brother/sister; king/queen, etc." (Isenberg, 1997, p. 29). More striking, however, is Buddhism's prescription (in absence of a relational deity) of four modes of living—loving-kindness, compassion, altruistic joy, and equanimity—as steps on the path toward enlightenment, which is conceptualized as a release from suffering into "*nibbana*… [the] ultimate reality, the highest state which lies beyond both good and evil" (Vajiragnana, 1997, p. 99). Indeed, within Buddhism are bodhisattvas who forgo, at least temporarily, their own pursuit of this nonattached, enlightened state in order to teach others.

The key question here is *why* do religions advocate love, particularly altruistic love? Certainly, the experience of love and its associated emotions is generally positive, and the motivational orientation of love, by definition, is toward benefiting the other (see Rempel & Burris, 2005). We also know, for example, that religious involvement can enhance personal well-being (e.g., Smith, McCullough, & Poll, 2003) as well as foster cooperation and group solidarity (e.g., Norenzayan & Shariff, 2008). Thus, to the extent that religious and philosophical traditions involve striving for "the good life," it seems reasonable to wonder whether the experience of love is itself a contributor to positive outcomes such as these.

In addition to these possible links, we suggest that the experience of love itself may, in fact, reinforce a spiritual worldview. That is, we submit that the experience of love for others, as well as witnessing prosocial episodes that are potentially motivated by love, can include a temporary suspension of the default sense of separation between self and other that is facilitated by a shift in one's perceptual field. The resulting sense of unity—which is the core of mystical experience (see Hood et al., 2009)—and the attendant emotions can bolster an individual's confidence in the validity of his/her personal convictions concerning the nature of the unseen. As Hood et al. put it: "[M]ysticism is an experience that provides sufficient warrant for belief in God or ultimate reality" for some—that is, "mystical experience has evidential force" (p. 332).

The most direct support for this proposition in reference to one's own experience comes from our own unpublished data in which participants read one of two tragic newspaper stories (concerning a woman grieving the drive-by shooting death of her infant grandson or an elderly disabled man who crawled for help as his dying wife lay pinned beneath a tractor). They subsequently completed a self-report measure of emotional empathy (an emotion that has been linked to altruistic motivation/love—see Batson, 1991), as well as a subset of items from Hood's (1975) Mysticism scale either before or after reading the stimulus story. Among women, a sense of oneness, absorption into something larger, space-time distortion, and a sense of the sacred as assessed by the Mysticism scale items that were completed after reading the story were all linked to greater self-reported empathy. Although men's responses to the Mysticism items following the story showed that they were just as likely as women to experience a shift away from the default sense of the self as separate, they—if anything—tended to report correspondingly *less* empathy, suggesting that they may have found the experience threatening (cf. Batson et al., 1996). At the same time, a prior history of mystical experiences (as indicated by responses to the Mysticism items *before* reading the stimulus story) was associated with greater reported empathy among men.

Provocatively consistent with the capacity of vicarious or observed love to foster self-transcendence is Haidt's (2003) analysis of *elevation*, conceptualized as the emotional inverse of disgust that is "triggered by people behaving in a virtuous, pure, or superhuman way" (p. 281). Importantly, most of the exemplars of "elevation triggers" reported by Haidt refer to witnessing prosocial acts that are potentially compatible with altruistic love, and the consequences of witnessing such actions include feeling not only warm and aspiring (i.e., to be a better person oneself) but also prosocial and affiliative.

In the language drawn from a spiritual autobiography cited by Haidt, when one feels empathy for another, the sense is that "love pours out," whereas when one experiences elevation, "love pours in" (p. 287). In either case, this language suggests that the

usual boundary that separates self from the rest of the world, including other people (see Burris & Rempel, 2008b), has been temporarily suspended, and as Hood et al. (2009) suggested, "awareness of limits makes the experience of [mystical] transcendence possible" (p. 366). Thus, notwithstanding the stereotypes of sannyasis, anchorites, and other mystical seekers as willfully solitary, the triggers of mystical experience are often emotive and interpersonal—such as "sex, childbirth, [and] watching children" (Wulff, 2000, p. 410).

In contrast to love, which appears capable of suspending the usual boundaries between self and the rest of the world, hate seems to widen the gap between self and other. LaVey's (1969, p. 29) satanic diatribe made this abundantly clear: "Hate your enemies with a whole heart, and if a man smite you on one cheek, SMASH him on the other!; smite him hip and thigh, for self-preservation is the highest law!" Here hate is the prescribed motive force behind harming the other in excess of what justice would require: The response is thus consistent with nihilistic hate, and so the appeal to "self-preservation" or physical survival seems unconvincing.

The rationale for this satanic edict seems much more comprehensible, however, if the "self" to be preserved is a psychological one. Baumeister (1997) presented a convincing case that "unstable egotism" or "insecure grandiosity" is a motive force behind a sizable portion of interpersonal hostility. To understand the dynamics, consider a chemically dependent individual who seeks out ever-increasing doses of his or her drug of choice to achieve a high and/or stave off the excruciating experience of withdrawal. In pursuit of this, he or she may be willing to discard the respect, trust, and well-being of previously valued others. Now replace "drug of choice" with "positive self-evaluation." An inordinately high opinion of oneself is extremely difficult to maintain, yet affected individuals are often strongly motivated to do so in order to avert the potentially overwhelming feelings of shame associated with deflation of the self-image.

Hate—which, at its core, involves subordinating others' well-being to one's own purposes—can thus be understood, at least in part, as a preemptive strike directed toward anticipated threats to one's grandiose self-image. Very simply, whereas we have argued that the experience of love may have evidential force with respect to validating (traditional forms of) faith, hate can function to validate the self—specifically, an inflated, unstable self-image. Suggestively consistent with this analysis is the welcome page of the official Church of Satan Web site (http://www.churchofsatan.com), which presents a number of towering, somber, costumed characters—one of whom is brandishing a sword toward the viewer—accompanied by the caption: "We're looking for a few outstanding individuals." LaVeyian Satanism thus pairs brazen elitism with the enshrining of hatred—a combination that may appeal especially to individuals with an inflated, unstable sense of self. Indeed, just as acts associated with empathy or elevation arguably facilitate self-transcendence, so may rage-filled, disgust-evoking acts of desecration serve to elevate the self of the practitioner. For example, LaVey (1972) outlined one "Black Mass" ritual in which participants drink urine expelled by a satanic nun and the celebrant inserts a stolen consecrated host (deemed the body of Christ in Roman Catholic teachings) into the vagina of the female "altar" body before throwing the host on the floor and stamping on it.

Conclusion and Future Directions

Notwithstanding the expanse of our subject matter, we have tried to extract what we believe are a number of structural and thematic commonalities with respect to how good and evil are construed across faith traditions (for a summary, see Table 8.4). Where possible, we have also attempted to review relevant empirical findings, although the research literature on good and evil *as constructs* (rather than labels applied to a phenomenon of which the researcher approves or disapproves) is rather limited. The "up" side of this is that the connections that we have tried to make in this chapter point to a breadth of possible lines of research that have scarcely been developed. We will highlight just a few.

First, the link between interpersonal experiences and religious experience deserves further articulation and testing. For example, we have pointed to evidence that emotional empathy may serve as a mystical trigger by temporarily altering how people experience the boundary between themselves and the rest of the world, and we have also speculated that intentionally evoked negative emotions within quasi-religious contexts may be especially appealing to individuals with an inflated, unstable sense of self because such emotions may serve to buttress that sense of self. The impact of other emotions and relationship-related variables should also be explored. For example, Burris and Rempel (2008b) found that chronic sensitivity to physical threat predicted a greater desire to avoid evil among single, uninvolved people and people in relationship who were primed to think of themselves as "me" rather than "us," but that this link disappeared among people in relationships (who by default think in terms of "us"). It seems entirely plausible that (lack of) involvement in an intimate relationship may shift how people articulate and connect to "the good" as well.

Table 8.4 A Summary of Structural and Thematic Construals of Good and Evil in Religion

A. Principles	Good	Evil
B. Personal ideals	Values	
	Self-transcendence: well-being of others; self-control	Self-enhancement: suffering of others; fragmentation (interpersonal, intrapersonal)
C. Interpersonal context	Motives	
	Love: sacrifice self for other; idealized, unless it obstructs spiritual growth	Hate: sacrifice other for self; condemned, unless target is "evil"
D. Subversions	Benefit other for self → [self-enhancement]	[hate in service of "love"] → sacrifice other for Entity
E. Sample means and ends	Empathy, elevation: validating faith	Disgust, rage, desecration: validating (inflated, unstable) self

Second, the implications of religious variations in conceptions of morality deserve additional consideration. We have argued here that there is considerable convergence of opinion across faith traditions concerning the "goodness" of self-transcendence values, yet there also appears to be some divergence along the conservation/openness to change dimension between conservatives and liberals or "religious" versus "spiritual" individuals. We therefore wonder, for example, whether extreme adherents on either end of the latter values dimension are prone to viewing those at the other end as "moral outgroups" by construing the others' prosocial behaviors as not simply evidence of having different priorities but as a commitment to self-enhancement rather than self-transcendence.

Third, we have only begun to explore the ramifications of the "evil" label. We already have evidence that labeling someone as "evil" allows for the disinhibition of hostile intentions directed toward him or her, and that exposure to "evil" symbols (e.g., a swastika or an inverted pentagram) is sufficient to make the "myth of pure evil" more accessible. At the same time, we have also shown that symbolic evil cues tend to polarize people's judgments of a target, leading those who perceive evil as a destructive force to be more punitive and those with a less virulent concept of evil to be more lenient (see Burris & Rempel, 2011). It is an open question as to whether the variations in conceptualizations of evil across faith traditions—a greater emphasis on suffering or fragmentation, for example—likewise has different implications. Moreover, we are not aware of any research that has examined the implications of being labeled "evil" or the lengths to which some individuals may go to avoid (or possibly embrace) this label.

Finally, the manifestation of evil that we have labeled "fragmentation" merits empirical investigation, particularly when juxtaposed against the human motivation to establish and maintain a sense of continuity—that is, a sense that the self endures over time (Sani, 2008). Particularly among those faith traditions for which continuity is especially important (as evidenced by an interest in genealogy, promotion of offspring, or preservation of sacred texts and artifacts, for example), one can easily see how the threat of interpersonal fragmentation would be especially powerful. Also interesting, however, is the phenomenon of intrapersonal fragmentation, particularly in light of Peck's (1983) claim that evil individuals will sometimes be attracted to positions of religious prominence because this assists in diverting attention (their own, as well as others') away from the moral implications of their evil deeds. Without question, intrapersonal fragmentation remains a troubling, poorly understood phenomenon.

These are but a few examples of the wide-ranging research directions available when we consider the interpersonal dimensions of topics as vast and consequential as good and evil. Yet as we deliberated on the concepts of good and evil in a religious context from a psychological perspective and considered the core message of this analysis, we were reminded of a story attributed to Jesus concerning the last judgment (Matthew 25: 31–46) in which humanity is divided into "sheep" (i.e., those who will enter paradise) and "goats" (i.e., those who will be rejected). The backdrop is cosmically significant: Evil shall be banished forever and only good shall remain. Nevertheless, the good and the evil do not appear here as heroes and villains engaged in a supernatural clash. Instead, humanity is divided based on whether they fed the hungry, gave the thirsty a drink, offered shelter to a stranger, clothed the naked, and visited the sick and imprisoned. That is, humanity was separated into "good" and "evil" based on their willingness to transcend their own personal interests and perform simple, intimate acts on behalf of another.

References

Al-Ghazali, M. (1997). The problem of evil: An Islamic approach. In W. Cenkner (Ed.), *Evil and the response of world religion* (pp. 70–79). St. Paul, MN: Paragon House.

Allport, G. W. (1950). *The individual and his religion.* New York: Macmillan.

Balliet, D., Joireman, J., Daniels, D., & George-Falvy, J. (2008). Empathy and the Schwartz value system: A test of an integrated hypothesis. *Individual Differences Research, 6,* 269–279.

Batson, C. D. (1991). *The altruism question: Toward a social-psychological answer.* Hillsdale, NJ: Erlbaum.

Batson, C. D., Sympson, S. C., Hindman, J. L., Decruz, P., Todd, R. M., Weeks, J. L., ... Burris, C. T. (1996). "I've been there, too": Effect on empathy of prior experience with a need. *Personality and Social Psychology Bulletin, 22,* 474–482.

Baumeister, R. F. (1997). *Inside human violence and cruelty.* New York: W. H. Freeman.

Blatty, W. P., Marshall, N. (Producers), & Friedkin, W. (Director). (1973). *The exorcist* [Motion picture]. United States: Warner Brothers.

Burris, C. T., & Rempel, J. K. (2008a). The devil you think you know: A psychology of evil. In N. Billias (Ed.), *Territories of evil* (pp. 13–28). Amsterdam: Rodopi.

Burris, C. T., & Rempel, J. K. (2008b). Me, myself, and us: Salient self-threats and relational connections. *Journal of Personality and Social Psychology, 94,* 944–961.

Burris, C. T., & Rempel, J. K. (2011). "Just look at him": Punitive responses cued by "evil" symbols. *Basic and Applied Social Psychology, 33*, 69–80.

Cenkner, W. (1997a). *Evil and the response of world religion.* St. Paul, MN: Paragon House.

Cenkner, W. (1997b). Hindu understandings of evil: From tradition to modern thought. In W. Cenkner (Ed.), *Evil and the response of world religion* (pp. 130–141). St. Paul, MN: Paragon House.

Dahlsgaard, K., Peterson, C., & Seligman, M. E. P. (2005). Shared virtue: The convergence of valued human strengths across culture and history. *Review of General Psychology, 9*, 203–213.

Darley, J. (1996). How organizations socialize individuals into evildoing. In D. Messick & A. Tenbrunsel (Eds.), *Codes of conduct: Behavioral research into business ethics* (pp. 13–43). New York: Russell Sage Foundation.

Darley, J. M. (1992). Social organization for the production of evil. *Psychological Inquiry, 3*, 199–218.

D'Sa, F. X. (1997). A new understanding of the Bhagavad-Gita: Trinitarian evil. In W. Cenkner (Ed.), *Evil and the response of world religion* (pp. 142–156). St. Paul, MN: Paragon House.

Ellard, J. H., Miller, C. D., Baumle, T. L., & Olson, J. M. (2002). Just world processes in demonizing. In M. Ross & D. T. Miller (Eds.), *The justice motive in everyday life: Essays in honor of Melvin Lerner* (pp. 350–362). Cambridge, England: Cambridge University Press.

Emmons, R. A. (1999). *The psychology of ultimate concerns.* New York: The Guilford Press.

The Family International. (2004). *The "Loving Jesus" revelation.* Retrieved February 2010, from http://www.thefamily.org/dossier/statements/lj.htm

Graham, J., Haidt, J., & Nosek, B. A. (2009). Liberals and conservatives rely on different sets of moral foundations. *Journal of Personality and Social Psychology, 96*, 1029–1046.

Haidt, J. (2003). Elevation and the positive psychology of morality. In C. L. M. Keyes & J. Haidt (Eds.), *Flourishing: Positive psychology and the life well-lived* (pp. 275–289). Washington, DC: American Psychological Association.

Haidt, J. (2008). Morality. *Perspectives on Psychological Science, 3*, 65–72.

Haidt, J., & Graham, J. (2007). When morality opposes justice: Conservatives have moral intuitions that liberals may not recognize. *Social Justice Research, 20*, 98–116.

Haidt, J., Graham, J., & Joseph, C. (2009). Above and below left–right: Ideological narratives and moral foundations. *Psychological Inquiry, 20*, 110–119.

Haidt, J., & Joseph, C. (2004). Intuitive ethics: How innately prepared intuitions generate culturally variable virtues. *Deadalus, Fall*, 55–66.

Hood, R. W., Jr. (1975). The construction and preliminary validation of a measure of reported mystical experience. *Journal for the Scientific Study of Religion, 14*, 29–41.

Hood, R. W., Jr., Hill, P. C., & Spilka, B. (2009). *The psychology of religion: An empirical approach* (4th ed.). New York: The Guilford Press.

Hunsberger, B. E., & Altemeyer, B. (2006). *Atheists: A groundbreaking study of America's nonbelievers.* Amherst, NY: Prometheus.

Isenberg, S. R. (1997). From myth to psyche to mystic psychology: The evolution of the problem of evil in Judaism. In W. Cenkner (Ed.), *Evil and the response of world religion* (pp. 16–31). St. Paul, MN: Paragon House.

James, G. G. (1997). The priestly conceptions of evil in the Torah. In W. Cenkner (Ed.), *Evil and the response of world religion* (pp. 3–15). St. Paul, MN: Paragon House.

Kaplan, S. (1997). Three levels of evil in Advaita Vedanta and a holographic analogy. In W. Cenkner (Ed.), *Evil and the response of world religion* (pp. 116–129). St. Paul, MN: Paragon House.

Keen, S. (1986). *Faces of the enemy: Reflections of the hostile imagination.* San Francisco: Harper & Row.

LaVey, A. (1969). *The satanic bible.* New York: Avon Books.

LaVey, A. (1972). *The satanic rituals.* New York: Avon Books.

Lifton, R. J. (1986). *The Nazi doctors: Medical killing and the psychology of genocide.* New York: Basic Books.

Martin, M. (1992). *Hostage to the devil: The possession and exorcism of five contemporary Americans.* San Francisco: Harper San Francisco.

McAdams, D. P., Albaugh, M., Farber, E., Daniels, J., Logan, R. L., & Olson, B. (2008). Family metaphors and moral intuitions: How conservatives and liberals narrate their lives. *Journal of Personality and Social Psychology, 95*, 978–990.

McCullough, M. E., & Willoughby, B. L. B. (2009). Religion, self-regulation, and self-control: Associations, explanations, and implications. *Psychological Bulletin, 135*, 69–93.

McFarland, S. G. (1998). Communism as religion. *The International Journal for the Psychology of Religion, 8*, 33–48.

McFayden, S., & Dunn, S. (Producers), Dunn, S., McFayden, S., & Wise, J. J. (Directors). (2005). *Metal: A headbanger's journey* [Motion picture]. Canada: Seville Pictures.

Miller, A. G. (2004). *The social psychology of good and evil.* New York: The Guilford Press.

Norenzayan, A., & Shariff, A. F. (2008). The origin and evolution of religious prosociality. *Science, 322*, 58–62.

Ontario Consultants on Religious Tolerance. (2010). *Shared belief in the "golden rule" (a/k.a. ethics of reciprocity).* Retrieved February 2010, from http://www.religioustolerance.org/reciproc.htm

Peck, M. S. (1978). *The road less traveled: A new psychology of love, traditional values and spiritual growth.* New York: Simon & Schuster.

Peck, M. S. (1983). *People of the lie: The hope for healing human evil.* New York: Simon & Schuster.

Post, S. G. (2002). The tradition of agape. In S. G. Post & L. G. Underwood (Eds.), *Altruism and altruistic love: Science, philosophy, and religion in dialogue* (pp. 51–64). London: Oxford University Press.

Rempel, J. K., & Burris, C. T. (2005). Let me count the ways: An integrative theory of love and hate. *Personal Relationships, 12*, 297–313.

Rempel, J. K., & Burris, C. T. (2010, January). *Belief in the "myth of pure evil" and sentencing recommendations for child sex offenders.* Poster presented at the Annual Meeting of the Society for Personality and Social Psychology, Las Vegas, NV.

Sani, F. (2008). *Self-continuity: Individual and collective perspectives.* New York: Psychology Press.

Saroglou, V., Delpierre, V., & Dernelle, R. (2004). Values and religiosity: A meta-analysis of studies using Schwartz's model. *Personality and Individual Differences, 37*, 721–734.

Saraglou, V., & Munoz-Garcia, A. (2008). Individual differences in religion and spirituality: An issue of personality traits and/or values. *Journal for the Scientific Study of Religion, 47*, 83–101.

Schwartz, S. H. (1992). Universals in the content and structure of values: Theoretical advances and empirical tests in 20 countries. In M. P. Zanna (Ed.), *Advances in experimental social psychology* (Vol. 25, pp. 1–65). New York: Academic Press.

Schwartz, S. H. (2006). A theory of cultural value orientations: Explication and applications. *Comparative Sociology, 5,* 137–182.

Schwartz, S. H. (2007). Universalism values and the inclusiveness of our moral universe. *Journal of Cross-Cultural Psychology, 38,* 711–728.

Schwartz, S. H., & Boehnke, K. (2004). Evaluating the structure of human values with confirmatory factor analysis. *Journal of Research in Personality, 38,* 230–255.

Seligman, M. E. P., & Csikszentmihalyi, M. (Eds.). (2000). Positive psychology: An introduction. *American Psychologist, 55*(1), 5–14.

Smith, T. B., McCullough, M. E., & Poll, J. (2003). Religiousness and depression: Evidence for a main effect and the moderating influence of stressful life events. *Psychological Bulletin, 129,* 614–636.

Staub, E. (2003). *The psychology of good and evil: Why children, adults, and groups help and harm others.* New York: Cambridge University Press.

Stenger, M. A. (1997). The ambiguity of the symbol of the cross: Legitimating and overcoming evil. In W. Cenkner (Ed.), *Evil and the response of world religion* (pp. 56–69). St. Paul, MN: Paragon House.

Tillich, P. (1959). *Theology of culture* (R. C. Kimball, Ed.). New York: Oxford University Press.

Urban, H. B. (2003). *Tantra: Sex, secrecy, politics, and power in the study of religions.* Berkeley: University of California Press.

Vajiragnana, M. (1997). A theoretical explanation of evil in Theraveda Buddhism. In W. Cenkner (Ed.), *Evil and the response of world religion* (pp. 99–108). St. Paul, MN: Paragon House.

van Leeuwen, F., & Park, J. H. (2009). Perceptions of social dangers, moral foundations, and political orientation. *Personality and Individual Differences, 47,* 169–173.

Waller, J. (2002). *Becoming evil: How ordinary people commit genocide and mass killing.* New York: Oxford University Press.

Wulff, D. (2000). Mystical experience. In E. Cardeña, S. J. Lynn, & S. Krippner (Eds.), *Varieties of anomalous experience: Examining the scientific evidence* (pp. 397–440). Washington, DC: American Psychological Association.

Zwerner, J. M. (1997). The discovery of Christian meaning in suffering: Transformation and solidarity. In W. Cenkner (Ed.), *Evil and the response of world religion* (pp. 43–55). St. Paul, MN: Paragon House.

Religion, Altruism, and Prosocial Behavior: Conceptual and Empirical Approaches

Elizabeth Midlarsky, Anthony S. J. Mullin, *and* Samuel H. Barkin

Abstract

This chapter examines two important aspects of human functioning: altruism and religion. Beginning with older, more philosophical and rhetorically based discourse on the link between the two phenomena, definitions of altruism and religion are discussed and reviews of the empirical research conducted separately on each are presented. We then address the question: What empirical evidence exists about the manifestations of these phenomena and the extent to which they are related to one another? The complex, multifaceted nature of both altruism and religion are acknowledged, and we argue that cross-disciplinary approaches are needed for progress to be made. At the same time, we note that both altruism and religion are powerful enough to have both salutary and toxic effects that make it critical that they be the focus of research efforts. Suggestions for future research are then offered.

Key Words: altruism, religion, religiosity, prosocial behavior, sociobiology

Introduction

In some respects, the concepts of altruism and religion are intertwined. Altruism—motivated by the desire to do good deeds or help others, without expectation of reward, reciprocation, or recognition—is significant for essentially all of the world religions (Neusner & Chilton, 2005). In Judaism, Rabbi Akiva, the Talmudic sage and scholar, asserted that "love thy neighbor" (Leviticus 19:18) is a fundamental value. Rabbi Abraham Isaac Kook taught that altruism toward humanity leads to altruism expressed to the force behind all giving—the Creator—and is thus the ultimate goal of creation (Bokser, 1978). In Christianity, altruism is central to the teachings of Jesus, especially in the Sermon on the Mount and the Sermon on the Plain. Indeed, the day before his assassination, speaking in support of a strike by sanitation workers, Martin Luther King Jr. enjoined his audience to follow Jesus's lesson of the Good Samaritan. He

said, "The question is not, 'If I stop to help this man in need, what will happen to me?' If I do not stop to help the sanitation workers, what will happen to them?" (Yarbrough & Eidenmuller, 2010).

In Sufism one must engage in *I'thar* (altruism) by forgetting one's own concerns and devoting oneself to the other (Gulen, 2004); in Islam, *I'thar* is the highest form of nobility (Singer, 2008). Altruism, in the form of love (increasing joy in others) and compassion (relieving suffering in others) is the key factor in all forms of Buddhism, and one's own happiness is the natural consequence of altruism (Harvey, 2000).

In all of these religions, altruism is an important and even central goal. The expectation is that religion should help each sincerely religious individual to achieve altruism. The difficulty lies in the rather nonhumanistic concept of original sin, particularly as found in Judaism and Christianity (and echoed in Sigmund Freud's concept of the "id"), which must be overcome by the intrinsically egoistic individual.

The term "altruism" itself was coined in the French (*altruisme*) by Auguste Comte (1852/1966), champion of a positivistic, science-based social system. In contrast to the religious view that human beings are innately selfish (tainted by original sin), Comte's "scientific" view was that people are innately altruistic. There must, Comte believed, be a new, scientific religion—the "Religion of Humanity"—whose goal would be to subsume oneself to "the Great Being" in which the goal was to live for others (*vivre pour altrui*).

The emphasis on subsuming individuality to the group in order to achieve the greatest common good has been a theme among the Hutterites, a group of German Christian Anabaptists. This group has been a cooperative and even altruistic one in which members avoid personal gain and work to achieve goals for the collectivity (Bower, 1995). The Israeli kibbutz, designed as an experiment in which all were viewed as equal participants in achieving the common good, worked efficiently as long as its highly idealistic members were motivated by an essentially altruistic ideology. Beginning in about the mid-1980s, as this orientation began to wane, the kibbutz movement went into decline (Don, 1996). Altruria, a short-lived Utopian community in Sonoma, California, was formed on the basis of altruistic and Christian religious ideals in 1894. The experiment was abandoned within the year because of unbridgeable financial problems (Budd, 1956).

Nevertheless, the idea that religion facilitates altruism has been widely promulgated (Norenzavan & Shariff, 2008). The existence of many dramatic examples of altruism by religious leaders has helped to promote this idea. During the Holocaust, for example, religious figures included Catholic priests (Oliner & Oliner, 1988), several prominent religious figures in the Bulgarian Orthodox Church (Todorov, 1999), and the Protestant minister who inspired and organized the entire population of Le Chambon, a Protestant town in France, to save thousands of Jewish lives (Hallie, 1979; Midlarsky, Jones, & Corley, 2005). These anecdotal accounts notwithstanding, research on the relationship between altruism and religion has been limited and largely inconclusive. This is not surprising, as both religion and altruism are multidimensional concepts, best understood through a multidisciplinary lens. In psychology alone, a comprehensive understanding requires investigation of the personality, social, developmental, health, mental health, and neuropsychological aspects of altruism.

As many researchers have noted (e.g., Smith, 2003; Spilka, Hood, Hunsberger, & Gorsuch, 2003),

while often interesting and thought provoking, we cannot rely exclusively on philosophical or theological explanations of the relationship between altruism and religion. Rather, we must adopt an empirical approach to assess the extent to which these two constructs are linked and *how*. This chapter, then, is a literature review that aims to explore the relationship between religion and altruism. The intention is to provide insight into some of the complexities of the subject and to highlight some areas in need of additional academic attention and expansion. We begin with separate treatments of the definitions and empirical perspectives on religion and altruism. We then consider the relationship between religion and altruism, and we end with suggestions for future work in this domain.

Religion
Definitions and Theoretical Perspectives

It is difficult to write about a construct whose definition is elusive. However, while Spilka and his colleagues assert that "more books have been written on this topic than any other in the history of humanity," they claim that this effort has resulted in neither cohesion, agreement, nor clarity (Spilka, Hood, Hunsberger, & Gorsuch, 2003, p. 9). In a similar vein, Asad (1993) posited that there can be no universal definition of religion. This is partly due to Asad's belief that such a definition is embedded in historical discourses on the subject and therefore is difficult to unravel.

From an etymological perspective, "religion" is derived from *religio*, a Latin word that is typically defined as "obligation." The *Oxford English Dictionary* (2008) defines religion as an "action or conduct indicating a belief in, reverence for, and desire to please a divine ruling power; the exercise or practice of rites or observances implying this." Religion is a construct that differs from religiousness or religiosity, a personality trait that, in turn, varies both between and within individuals (Darley & Batson, 1973), and which is often treated as a synonym for religion. Religion also differs from spirituality, which is often secular and, as such, is separate from formal religion. People involved with religion tend to accept traditional forms of religious authority and inhabit a space purposefully created for religious worship. People embracing secular spirituality appreciate individual autonomy as an alternative to an external religious authority and create their own spiritual space and experience (Wuthnow, 1998). Spirituality entails recognition by the individual of one's ultimate connection to a reality outside oneself, with humanity, and with a presence outside the natural world. Those who espouse full commitment to a faith have claimed that true spirituality cannot be experienced by the secular. However, Stetzer and colleagues assert that spirituality exists outside of religion whenever human emotions of awe, wonder, and reverence are experienced when observing or studying nature or the universe (Stetzer, Stanley, & Hayes, 2009).

In contrast to the autonomy inherent in spirituality, religion may begin in one person, but it becomes a "communication of a world view, or a created reality, that people develop as a group" (Dow, 2004, p. 2). The universality of religion among human societies appears to be linked to the fact that human beings have the capacity to recognize that personal existence has a discrete beginning, a finite duration, and ultimately an end. As a result, each human being is faced with questions concerning the meaning and value of life, the relationship of the individual to all of humanity, to creation, and to the Creator. Religion prescribes rituals based on what Stark and Bainbridge (1987) labeled the supernatural premise, or supernatural assumptions. In this chapter, the focus will be on formal religion and its individual manifestation—religiosity (or religiousness)—in relationship to altruism. According to Emmons and Paloutzian (2003), the distinction made between religion and spirituality is artificial, and there are as many shared qualities between them as there are qualities that distinguish them. Spirituality simply represents an expansion of religion, rather than necessarily supplanting it (Hill et al., 2000). Nevertheless, this chapter will focus on altruism and religion, as religion is experienced within an organized community that teaches, preaches, and engages in rituals.

Empirical Perspectives

Operational definitions, mainly in the form of psychological measures administered to individuals, have varied, taking either single or multiple aspects of religious phenomena into consideration. As these definitions are based on human responses, it is appropriate to note that they are actually definitions of religiosity or religiousness. Among the many examples are the approach taken by Hoge (1972), who validated a scale of intrinsic religious motivation as his operational definition of religion. Both Altemayer and Hunsberger (1992), and Fulton, Gorsuch, and Maynard (1999) focused on fundamentalism as their measure and operational definition of religion. Other researchers employed dyadic concepts,

such as Allport and Ross (1967), who distinguished between intrinsic and extrinsic religion, and Allen and Spilka (1967), who described committed versus consensual religion. Likewise, Smith (2003) advocated a multidimensional approach. One example of a multidimensional conception is a six-dimension scale, subsumed under three components—cognitional, emotional, and behavioral aspects of religiosity (Cornwall, Albrecht, Cunningham, & Pitcher, 1986). A second example resulted from factor analyses of religiousness in the Black community, which yielded such components as the private, subjective, nonorganizational, and organizational aspects of religiosity, as well as the intensity of denominational identity (Taylor, Chatters, & Levin, 2004). A third example is the result of work by Lam and Rotolo (2000), who identified four dimensions of religiosity: participatory, private, affiliative, and theological. Batson (1976), as well as Batson and his collaborators (Batson, Eidelman, Higley, & Russell, 2001), distinguish three types of religiosity, based on their antecedents: egoistic (religiousness based on self-interest), intrinsic (based on faith, belief), and quest (the search for meaning by an individual who can tolerate doubt and ambiguity).

The "quest" type of religiosity bears some resemblance to the sixth stage of faith development posited by James W. Fowler (1981, 1991). The sixth stage, usually occurring in midlife, is a "conjunctive" faith that acknowledges paradox. In this stage of development, the individual continues the quest for meaning and for the full comprehension that marks the seventh stage, termed "enlightenment," which only so few people can attain. Unfortunately, there has been little success in creating and validating an operational definition of Fowler's complex theory (Barnes & Doyles, 1989; Leak, Loucks, & Bowlin, 1999), which limits its utility as a means for studying religion.

Altruism
Definitions and Theoretical Perspectives

The word "altruism" is often used interchangeably with a host of others, including "aiding," "helping," "volunteering," and "prosocial behavior" (Dovidio, Piliavin, Schroeder, & Penner, 2006; Midlarsky, 1991; Midlarsky & Kahana, 2007). Nevertheless, altruism is a distinct construct, which can be viewed as a subcategory of prosocial behavior. In prosocial behavior, there is an intention to help the other. In altruism, a relatively rare form of behavior, the intention to help is other-oriented rather than egoistic. Also, the anticipated cost of the behavior to the altruist (up to and including death) far outweighs any expected extrinsic gain (Midlarsky, 1968; Piliavin & Charng, 1990). By this definition, the Christian woman who sheltered a Jewish family during the Holocaust because she was enjoined to do so by a minister whom she feared was acting prosocially but not altruistically. However, the non-Jewish rescuers who helped Jews during the Holocaust despite the fact that they anticipated no gain for themselves, and were risking their lives by helping, were behaving altruistically. Research has indicated that these heroic individuals were high in altruistic moral judgment and in empathic concern (Fagin Jones & Midlarsky, 2007; Midlarsky, Fagin Jones, & Corley, 2005).

The use of the term "prosocial behavior" as a default in place of "altruism" appears to be based on a concern that many of the helping behaviors under investigation are not *really* altruistic. For well over a century, we have lived in a milieu strongly influenced by several lines of thought—reward-based American behaviorism, Hedonism within philosophy, Freud's antihumanistic view of the basic (*id*) nature of humanity, and certain interpretations of Darwin. While none of these theories was fully accepted in itself, their confluence has been very influential (Midlarsky, 1968). Thus, the general view has been that to be certain that an act is altruistic, one must somehow prove that it is not actually egoistic (e.g., Batson et al., 1988). Or, as was so famously said by Little Buttercup,

> Things are seldom what they seem
> Skim milk masquerades as cream…
> (Gilbert & Sullivan, in *HMS Pinafore*)

What is so interesting in all of this is that when psychologists study more negative phenomena, such as greed, selfishness, or violence, there seems to be less of a need to discover whether those phenomena are "really" what they seem to be, or instead are obscuring the "truth" of the situation. What we emphasize here is that there should be no need to insist that all prosocial acts are altruistic or that all altruists behave prosocially (Midlarsky & Midlarsky, 2003). Altruism is not the same as "agreeableness"(Wiggins, 1996), which includes compliance, a characteristic that may be lacking in at least some of the most courageous altruists (Midlarsky, Fagin Jones, & Corley, 2005). Furthermore, it is unnecessary and even inappropriate to assume that "everyday" altruism occurs to the same degree as it does in the case of the Holocaust heroes, even in people who are genuinely altruistic. Like so many other motives and personality traits, individual differences in altruism should be understood to range along a continuum from low to high, rather than being expressed uniformly across individuals and situations.

Also, as Batson and Shaw (1991) have suggested, we should think in terms of a *pluralism* of prosocial motives—that we can have altruistic and egoistic motives simultaneously.

Several bodies of theory have been brought to bear in the attempt to comprehend altruism, of which two are the evolutionary and the psychological. For the sake of completeness, we note that the field of evolutionary psychology remains controversial and has not yet undergone sufficient empirical development to permit evaluation at this time (Segerstrate, 2000).

The evolutionary and psychological approaches both address the altruistic paradox, first identified in 1883 by Lester Ward (1883), the first president of the American Sociological Association. The altruistic paradox raises the question of why a behavior would be performed when it puts an individual at risk, and when neither the acquisition nor expression of altruism is associated with reward for the individual. Theorists within psychology have addressed this paradox in several ways. For example, evolutionary theory has largely interpreted Darwin's (1871, 1981) "survival of the fittest" as referring to survival of the fittest *individual* (but see De Waal, 2008; Kropotkin, 1902/1972), so that the evolutionary biologist Richard Dawkins (1976) could write that in regard to individual generosity, biological human nature had nothing to offer. To insure altruism, we would have to *teach* altruism to inherently selfish organisms, according to Dawkins. The frustration with this interpretation of Darwin led others, such as Wilson (1975), to interpret and expand Darwin's concept to encompass both *individual* fitness and *inclusive* fitness. Inclusive fitness indicates that survival may be best insured when individuals have viable offspring (as in individual fitness) and when survival is insured of those closest to the individual through shared genes, as in kin selection.

Wilson (1975), who has been credited with the development of sociobiology, may have done so largely because of the need to explain altruism. In his seminal volume, Wilson provides numerous examples of what appears to be altruism throughout the animal kingdom. As Stephen Jay Gould (1980, p. 261) wrote:

> Why should our nastiness be the baggage of an apish past and our kindness uniquely human? Why should we not seek continuity with other animals for our "noble" traits as well?

What we ask, as well, is why it seems so difficult to acknowledge that human beings can be altruistic that it has become normative to use the term "prosocial" in its place. We seem to have no problem with characterizing acts as violent or passive, for example, without worrying about whether our use of these words somehow obscures their "true nature." Perhaps this tendency to doubt the possibility of the existence of altruism is based on the continued influence of the evolutionary, philosophical (Hedonistic), and psychoanalytic viewpoints enumerated earlier, along with others that have so long shaped the zeitgeist. Perhaps in view of the evidence of violence, of even genocidal proportions (Midlarsky, 2005), it has seemed particularly difficult to believe that altruism is a "natural" aspect of human nature. The virtual lack of research on altruism may also be based on what has seemed to be the more urgent desire to learn to prevent negative behaviors, rather than to emphasize the positive aspects of human functioning.

In arguing against biological explanations of altruism, Campbell (1975) notes that, indeed, forms of caring, such as rudimentary forms of mother–child attachment, may be subject to biological explanation. However, the more complex forms observed in human beings may be best explained by the mechanisms of social, rather than biological, evolution. For example, individualistic societies, such as that found preeminently in the United States, value altruism quite differently than do collective societies, like the Hindu (Diener & Suh, 2003; Kitayama, Markus, Matsumoto, & Norasakkunkit, 1997). Illustrations abound of the numerous types of social adaptation that have occurred throughout human societies and cultures, as reflected in doggerel by A. F. J. (1939) in the *Journal of Abnormal and Social Psychology*.(cited in S. B. Sells, 1963).

The Arapesh eat a little flesh.
They live secure but futile.
They're not competitive or harsh,
As are the Kwakiutl.

Bachiga think that food and drink
Should come from lone endeavor.
The Zuni, herding sheep in peace,
Cooperate forever.

Samoans feel the great ideal
Is helping one another
Ojibwas try to stand alone
And no one loves his brother.

The Maori loaned whate'er they owned
From Kingdom Come til now;
But interest rates are very high
Among the Ifugao.

Empirical Perspectives

According to evolutionary theory, people are inherently selfish. When prosocial action is observed, it is based on the biological need to insure one's own survival or the survival of those who have the closest genetic link to the recipient. In a series of studies, Japanese and American participants responded to scenarios depicting a "life-threatening" situation or a "trivial" situation, in both of which helping was needed. In both the American and Japanese samples, helping increased as a monotonic function of genetic overlap with the sibling (0.50 overlap) receiving more help than nieces and nephews (0.25 overlap), and then first cousins (0.125). The strength of the relationship was greater in response to the "life-and-death" scenario. The amount of helping in that situation also decreased as the age of the recipient increased, presumably because of the lesser "fitness" of the older recipients. Interestingly, though, "trivial" helping was directed more at older recipients than to those described as middle aged.

In regard to psychological research on altruism, a great deal of research attention was paid to this phenomenon in the late 1960s through the mid-1980s, especially by social and developmental psychologists. Psychology was beginning to expand beyond the almost unilateral emphasis on violence (including genocidal violence), abuse, and psychopathology to more positive domains, such as altruism, responsibility, morality, and gratitude. In these early attempts to move toward a positive—and thus a more "balanced"—set of perspectives within psychology, altruism has become a popular domain of inquiry.

Enthusiasm for the study of altruism quickly abated, however, when the largely laboratory-based, experimental researchers were confronted with "problems" concerning the motives for the observed prosocial behavior and their measurement. It is relatively simple to come up with examples of prosocial *activity*—whether helping, donation behavior, emergency intervention, rescue, trivial, or "normative" behaviors such as holding an elevator door or picking up dropped pencils. In the early studies these were typically treated as behavioral manifestations of *altruism*, in the absence of any evidence or even curiosity about the motives of the helper. In asking the question *"why"* about these behaviors, a series of well-done studies were conducted on child socialization and on factors such as gender, perceived need, locus of control, similarity to the recipient, and dependency, to name only a few. In this context, it is not surprising that the use of the term "altruism" became a troublesome distraction from the "real" work of making the world a more peaceful place. The spotlight was therefore turned on "prosocial" behavior, in order to avoid the need to confront troubling questions about motivation.

In the research that *was* concerned with altruism, two possible motives were consistently studied. These were empathy (Davis, 1994; Hoffman, 2001) and moral judgment (Eisenberg, 2009). The basic premise has been that when a helpful act is performed by a person high in empathy, moral judgment, or both, then that behavior can be considered to be altruistic. Particularly in the case of what Midlarsky has termed "altruistic moral judgment" (Midlarsky, Kahana, Corley, Schonbar, & Nemeroff, 1999) to distinguish it from Kohlberg's approach (Kohlberg, Levine, & Hewer, 1983), the good of the recipient is placed above all other considerations; this conception is very close to the cognitive facet of altruism. Similarly, among operational definitions of empathy, the one that has important links to altruism is the Interpersonal Reactivity Index (IRI; Davis, 1994). This measure offers four components: personal distress, fantasy empathy, perspective taking, and empathic concern. Of the four, empathic concern, the centerpiece is altruistic concern for the other. In all of the other components, the potential benefactor's own discomfort (personal distress), ability to comprehend the other's situation (perspective taking), or the proclivity to share and even experience the emotions of characters in books or movies (fantasy empathy), egoism is a more central element.

Social psychologist Daniel Batson has wrestled with the question of whether empathic concern, which is an important explanatory mechanism for altruism, can provide a link with explanations from evolutionary biology. In evolutionary biology, as noted earlier, helpfulness is motivated by inclusive fitness, in order to insure survival of at least a portion of one's genes; thus, helping of strangers is likely to be a rare event. This reasoning finds its counterpart in research by social psychologists, whose experiments have explored the role of similarity to the recipient as a predictor of helping (Krebs, 1987).

If, indeed, there is an evolutionary basis for altruism, then it should be found in the "maternal instinct," as expressed in parental nurturance. If empathically motivated altruism is genetically based, then more help should be given to those most similar to the helper. In a study conducted by Batson, Lishner, Cook, and Sawyer (2005), college women read a story in which a volunteer helped someone named Kayla, who was a female college junior, an adult dog, a puppy, or a 3-year-old child. The women saw themselves as most similar to the college junior, but despite the perceived similarity, empathic concern for Kayla the student was lower than for the other three, all of whom were child-like figures.

Other studies also support a genetic link between empathic concern and altruism. For example, research has been conducted using the methodology of twin studies, which compare the degree of similarity of identical twins who share most of their genes, to fraternal twins, who share a lesser proportion. Results of these studies have indicated that between 50% (Rushton, Fulkes, Neale, Nias, & Eysenck, 1986) and 71% (Matthews, Batson, Horn, & Rosenman, 1981) of the variation in empathy is heritable. More recent research indicates that the when the dimensions of empathy (empathic concern, personal distress, perspective taking, and fantasy empathy) are analyzed separately, empathy seems somewhat heritable, but less so than previously found in the studies by Matthews and collaborators, and by Rushton and his collaborators (Davis, Luce, & Kraus, 1994). Furthermore, work on the development of empathy indicates that socialization can override any genetic influences at as early as 20 months of age (Zahn-Waxler, Schiro, Robinson, Emde, & Schmitz, 2001).

In research on the relationship between moral judgment and altruism, researchers have sought to discover whether higher stages of moral cognition predict higher rates of help that is given on the basis of altruistic principles. According to Bar-Tal and Raviv (1982), the stages of cognitive development reflect increasing increments in unselfish motives as the person develops. In the lower stages, helping is prompted by the anticipation of specific rewards and punishments. With growing maturity, higher stages are reached wherein the cognitions promoting helping are first markedly egoistic (to meet norm-based expectations), then they are hedonistic (because helping makes one feel better), and next because reciprocation is expected. If the highest altruistic stage is attained, then the moral motive is the intention to help the recipient. In this work, as in research on prosocial moral reasoning by Eisenberg (1982), the question was not whether people at higher stages of moral development help more, but rather the extent to which their helping is altruistic rather than egoistic. In work on what has been termed altruistic moral judgment (Midlarsky et al., 1999), the highest form of moral reasoning was found to distinguish Holocaust rescuers from bystanders (Midlarsky, Fagin Jones, & Corley, 2005). What is important is that although altruism may be based to some extent on genetic predispositions, psychosocial and environmental factors are critical in shaping behavior as complex as altruistic behavior. The two intrinsic factors that have been cited as predictors of altruism, and which are close to our conceptions of the meaning and nature of altruism, are moral judgment and empathy, both of which can develop through the seasons of life (Midlarsky & Kahana, 1994). In the following we consider the possibility that religion, which, like altruism, can transcend the self in its higher stages of development, is related to altruism in important ways.

Religion, Prosocial Behavior, and Altruism

Is there evidence that religion and altruism are associated with one another? There is frequently an assumption that religion is necessary if altruism is to occur. Most if not all of the world religions teach—through exhortations, religious writings, and religious exemplars such as the saints—the importance of doing good deeds for altruistic reasons (Beit-Hallami & Argyle, 1997; McFadden, 1999). And, indeed, Smith (2003) found that church attendance and self-definition as a "strong" member of one's faith predicted what he termed "altruism."

There is research evidence both linking religion to prosocial behavior and disputing the strength, or even the existence, of such a link. To begin with, Hood, Hill, and Spilka (2009) have written that although prosocial behavior may be associated with religion, it is not the exclusive province of those committed to faith. As they point out, current society offers many opportunities to help in secular as well as in religious settings. Many people, including those who are nonreligious or antireligious, assist others. Thus, even when religion predicts prosocial behavior, as in cases where people make donations during participation in religious services, nonreligious, religiously unaffiliated people may help as much but in other contexts (Spilka et al., 2003).

Batson and his colleagues have argued that being more religious cannot be equated with being more helpful. Furthermore, their review of the empirical literature up to 1993 concluded that religious people show no more active concern for those in need than do people who are less religious; they only present

themselves as more concerned (Batson, Schoenrode, & Ventis, 1993). More recently, Saroglou and his associates discussed existing discrepancies between results of research employing self-report and research using experimental and quasi-experimental methodologies. In some research, religiousness does predict prosocial behavior. People who report that they view religion as important, and place a high value on it, report that they work more hours and are generally more committed to volunteer activity than are people who do not place a high value on religion (Kupper & Bierhoff, 1999; Penner, 2002). There is a general assumption within social psychology that experimentation is a methodology that is far more rigorous and more likely to lead to valid results than is self-report methodology. Self-report data may be biased by the desire to respond in socially desirable ways. Left out of this, though, is acknowledgment of the biases in experimentation—ranging from the typical use of artificial laboratory settings, and to operational definitions that consist of short-term responses that are usually neither costly nor time consuming, and demand characteristics, such as desire to appease the experimenter (Midlarsky, 1968; Midlarsky & Bryan, 1967). In situations of the kind studied in experiments, the effect of religiosity often has only modest effects. As noted earlier, although volunteering and other forms of prosocial action may be prompted by egoistic and/or altruistic motives, people who report that they see religion as important, and place a high value on it, work more hours and are generally more committed as volunteers than are people do not place a high value on religion (Kupper & Bierhoff, 1999; Penner, 2002).

There are indeed instances in which religious people *report* altruistic tendencies but do not necessarily *behave* prosocially. However, results of four recent studies have indicated that there is indeed an impact of religiousness on actual helping behavior, albeit a modest one. The primary findings suggested that religious young adults tended not to be aggressive when dealing with hypothetical daily hassles, and that although female students' religiosity was associated with willingness to help people described as "close" in hypothetical situations, this helping tendency was not extended to those unknown to them. On the other hand, religious people not only reported high altruistic behavior and empathy but were also perceived as high in altruism and empathy by peers (friends, siblings, or colleagues). Results also indicated that helping by religious people is not an artifact of gender, social desirability bias, security in attachment, empathy, or honesty (Saroglou, Pichon, Trompette, Vershueren, & Dernelle, 2005).

Although the results of studies on religion and altruism have generally not been strong, much of the work has focused on relatively low-cost short-term helping—and it is in those situations in which religiosity has had no effect or modest effects. When we examine research on volunteering and other behaviors that occur over a longer time period, college students who are committed to their religion emerge as more involved, and give more time—as relief workers, tutors, and social justice activists, to name just three—than do college students who are not religiously committed (Benson et al., 1980; Hansen, Vandenberg, & Patterson, 1995). George Gallup (1984) conducted a survey in which he found that among the 12% of Americans who were "highly spiritually committed," 46% voluntarily helped infirm and poor people, in contrast to the 22% who were rated as "highly uncommitted." Results of his 1987 survey indicated that people who attended religious services on a weekly basis gave two and a half times more money to charity than did those who never attended religious services. This pattern was confirmed in surveys conducted in 1990 and 1992 (Gallup and Lindsay, 1999).

The relationship between religious participation and donations has also been echoed in the relationship between religion and volunteer behavior. Results of the Westat (2001) Poll, in which telephone surveys were conducted with 4,216 adults aged 21 and above, religious participation was a predictor of volunteering. That is, 54% of those who attended religious services volunteered, in contrast to 32% of nonattenders. These respondents also donated more time to volunteer activities. Also, when Americans giving time and/or money to religious groups were compared with those involved solely in secular charitable activities, even after controlling for economic resources, they were also more generous in giving to secular charitable appeals and volunteer efforts.

Research has indicated that older adults are very generous, over long periods of time, particularly when they are high in religiosity (Midlarsky & Kahana, 1994). Among the non-Jewish altruistic rescuers of Jews during the Holocaust, there were higher degrees of religiousness than among the bystanders (Oliner & Oliner, 1988).

Religion, Prosocial Behavior, and Altruism

Is there evidence, then, that religion and altruism are related? There is frequently an assumption that religion is necessary if altruism is to occur. Most if not all of the world religions teach—through exhortations, religious writings, and religious exemplars, such as the saints—the importance of doing good deeds and becoming truly altruistic (Beit-Hallami & Argyle, 1997; McFadden, 1999).

In other treatments, intense religious experience of a higher presence or power—first studied by William James (1902)—has been found to deepen commitment to religion. Of those reporting religious experiences, Hays (1990) found that 56% attended church. People reporting religious experiences tend to have more positive feelings toward others and express the desire to help them. In addition to wishing to help others, religious people may engage in altruistic behavior. Among what is admittedly a minuscule number of believers, altruism has led to saintly behavior. Among the courageous, altruistic gentile rescuers of Jews during the Holocaust, who risked their lives in order to save the lives of others, many said that religious faith guided their behavior; there were, however, a similar number who helped for secular reasons (Oliner & Oliner, 1988). In our own research on these Holocaust heroes, several spoke of being prompted to do so for religious reasons, in contrast to none of the bystanders. Nevertheless, despite this qualitative finding, religion was not among the variables discriminating Holocaust rescuers from bystanders (Midlarsky, Fagin Jones, & Corley, 2005).

Although some of the research evidence points to religion as a cause of altruism (though some does not), religion can also have adverse effects. When the highest stage of faith is reached, the individual may be able to transcend his or her own concerns and experience the connection to the Creator and to all of humanity (Fowler, 1991). However, when people accept religious authority in a concrete way and become religious extremists, then adverse effects may occur. Under certain circumstances, those who adhere to a religion that demands courses of action that can lead to great rewards (and when not performed, lead to terrifying punishments) may become prejudiced, and even violent terrorists (Juergensmeyer, 2000). Religion may block empathy for others who are believed to violate one's religious values (Jackson & Esses, 1997). Research of this kind argues for the need for a universally compassionate religious style, in which people in need are helped regardless of their belief system (Batson et al., 2001).

Conclusions and Future Directions

Research on both altruism and religion has become increasingly well developed. Nevertheless, a great deal remains to be done. Both altruism and religion are multidimensional phenomena, both of which require multidisciplinary study if they are to be full understood. Despite attention paid to religion, no widely accepted definition has emerged. *Altruism* is a word that has been supplanted in the psychology literature by the term *prosocial*, largely because of concern about whether prosocial behavior is "truly" altruistic or, instead, is egoistic. However, just as people who attend religious services may be doing so for multiple reasons—including the need for affiliation, support, and the need to do the "right thing"—generosity may be attributable to both egoistic and/or altruistic reasons, varying with the potential recipient and the situation. The person whose religiosity is based on having attained the highest stage of faith in the Creator may well be as rare as the person whose helping is based solely on altruistic motives.

Thus, we argue that few helpers have only a single motive, and it may be appropriate to recognize that among those who respond to the needs of others with prosocial behavior, few do so out of altruistic motives alone. Even if there is an "altruistic gene," in addition to or in place of a "selfish gene," it is likely that the complex sequences involved in human behavior require extensive psychosocial development as well.

It is also important that in contrast to the view that both altruism and religion are "good," both can have adverse outcomes. Religion can prompt violence, prejudice, and terrorism, although it can also lead to lower rates of drug and alcohol addiction and sexual acting out. Generosity, even when motivated by altruistic reasons, can lead to dependency of the recipient. Self-sacrifice on behalf of a victim on the basis of altruistic moral principles or empathic concern can lead to neglect (e.g., of one's own family) or even destruction of others (as in the case of Himmler; Midlarsky, 2005; Midlarsky & Midlarsky, 2003).

Concerning the relationship between altruism and religion, a great deal of research is needed, if it is to be better understood. Some suggestions for future work in this domain are as follows:

1. Sociobiologists argue that there may be a biological substratum for complex behaviors, including human altruism. Additional research is needed to more firmly establish conceptual and causal links between the biological and the social/behavioral sciences in this domain,

2. More research is needed to develop measures and other operational definitions of both religion and altruism.

3. Spontaneous, low-cost helping and long-term care for others that is costly for the benefactor may have different preconditions, including different religious antecedents. This possibility needs to be investigated.

4. Religious faith and principled altruism may be experienced and expressed more fully as predisposed individuals move through the life course. More work is needed on the dimensions of altruism and religion, and the links between them at developmental stages from childhood through late life.

Finally, this chapter was designed to separately review theoretical and empirical dimensions of altruism and religion, and the fledgling research on the relationship between them. Both phenomena are critical in human behavior and interaction. Further research is warranted, and it may well result in an enhanced ability to contribute to the well-being of individuals and of groups.

References

Allen, R., & Spilka, B. (1967). Committed and consensual religion. *Journal for the Scientific Study of Religion*, 6, 191–206.

Allport, G. W., & Ross, J. M. (1967). Personal religious orientation and prejudice. *Journal of Personality and Social Psychology*, 5, 432–443.

Altemayer, B., & Hunsberger, B. (1992). Authoritarianism, religious fundamentalism, quest, and prejudice. *International Journal for the Psychology of Religion*, 2, 113–133.

Asad. T. (1993). *Genealogies of religion*. Baltimore: Johns Hopkins University.

Barnes, M., & Doyles, D. (1989). The formation of a Fowler scale. *Review of Religious Research*, 30, 412–420.

Bar-Tal, D., & Raviv, A. (1982). A cognitive-learning model of helping behavior development. In N. Eisenberg (Ed.), *The development of prosocial behavior* (pp. 199–218). New York: Academic.

Batson, C. D. (1976). Religion as prosocial. *Journal for the Scientific Study of Religion*, 15, 29–45.

Batson, C. D., & Shaw, L. L. (1991). Evidence for altruism: Toward a pluralism of prosocial motives. *Psychological Inquiry*, 2(2), 107–122.

Batson, C. D., Dyck, J., Brandt, J. Batson, J., Powell, A., McMaster, M., & Griffitt, C. (1988). Five studies testing two new egoistic alternatives to the empathy-altruism hypothesis. *Journal of Personality and Social Psychology*, 55, 52–77.

Batson, C. D., Eidelman, S., Higley, S., & Russell S. (2001). "And who is my neighbor?" II. Quest religion as a source of universal compassion. *Journal for the Scientific Study of Religion*, 40, 39–50.

Batson, C.D., Lishner, D., Cook, J., & Sawyer, S. (2005). Similarity ad nurturance: Two possible sources of empathy for strangers. *Basic and Applied Psychology*, 7, 15–25.

Batson, C. D., Schoenrode, P., & Ventis, W. (1993). *Religion and the individual*. New York: Oxford.

Beit-Hallami, B., & Argyle, M. (1997). *Religious behavior, courage, belief, and experience*. New York: Routledge.

Benson, P., Dehority, J., Garman, L., Hanson, E., Hochschwender, M., Lebold, C.,...Sullivan, J. (1980). Intrapersonal correlates of nonspontaneous helping behavior. *Journal of Social Psychology, 110,* 87–95.

Bokser, B. Z. (Ed.). (1978). *Abraham Isaac Kook.* Mahwah, NJ: Paulist Press.

Bower, B. (1995). Return of the group. *Science News, 48,* 330.

Budd, L. J. (1956). Altruism arrives in America. *American Quarterly, 8,* 40–52.

Campbell, D. T. (1975). On the conflicts between biological and social evaluation and between psychology and moral tradition. *American Psychologist, 30,* 1103–26.

Comte, A. (1966). *Catechism positivistic.* Paris: Flammarion. (Original work published 1852).

Cornwall, M., Albrecht, S. L., Cunningham, P. D., & Pitcher, B. L. (1986). The dimensions of religiosity. *Review of Religious Research, 27,* 226–244.

Darley, J. M., & Batson, C. D. (1973). "From Jerusalem to Jericho": A study of situational and dispositional variables in helping behavior. *Journal of Personality and Social Psychology, 27*(1), 100–108.

Darwin, C. (1981). *The descent of man, and selection in relation to sex.* Princeton, NJ: Princeton University Press. (Original work published 1871).

Dawkins, R. (1976). *The selfish gene.* New York: Oxford University Press.

De Waal, F. B. M. (2008). Putting the altruism back into altruism. *Annual Review of Psychology, 59,* 279–300.

Diener, E., & Suh, E. (Eds.). (2003). *Subjective well-being across cultures.* Cambridge, MA: MIT Press.

Don, Y. (1996). The importance of behaving altruistically: Altruism as an efficiency boosting factor in the kibbutz. *Journal of Rural Cooperation, 24,* 17–26.

Dovidio, J. F., Piliavin, J. A. Schroeder, D. A., & Penner, L. A. (2006). *The social psychology of prosocial behavior.* Mahwah, NJ: Erlbaum.

Dow, J. W. (April 15–18, 2004). *Religions and evolutionary theory.* Paper presented at the Central States Anthropological Society meetings, Milwaukee, WI.

Emmons, R., & Paloutzian R. (2003). The psychology of religion. *Annual Review of Psychology, 54*(1), 377–402.

Fagin Jones, S., & Midlarsky, E. (2007). Courageous rescue during the Holocaust. *Journal of Positive Psychology, 2*(2), 136–147.

Fowler, J. W. (1981). *Stages of faith.* San Francisco: Harper & Row.

Fowler, J. W. (1991). Stages in faith consciousness. In F. K. Oser & W. G. Scarlett (Eds.), *Religious development in childhood and adolescence* (pp. 27–45). San Francisco: Jossey-Bass.

Fulton, A. S., Gorsuch, R. L., & Maynard, E. A. (1999). Religious orientation, antihomosexual sentiment, and fundamentalism among Christians. *Journal for the Scientific Study of Religion, 38,* 14–22.

Gallup, G., Jr. (1984, March). Religion in America. *The Gallup report.* Report No. 222. Princeton, NJ: Princeton Religion Research Center.

Gallup, G., Jr., & Lindsay, D. (1999). *Surveying the religious landscape.* Harrisburg, PA: Morehouse.

Gould, S. J. (1980). *The evolution of gryphaea.* New York: Arno.

Hansen, D., Vandenberg, B., & Patterson, M. (1995). The effects of religious orientation on spontaneous and nonspontaneous helping behavior. *Personality and Individual Differences, 19,* 101–104.

Hays, D. (1990). *Religious experience today.* London: Maubrey.

Hoffman, M. L. (2001). *Empathy and moral development.* New York: Cambridge University Press.

Gulen, M. F. (2004). *Key concepts in the practice of Sufism.* Rutherford, NJ: Fountain.

Hallie, P. (1979). *Lest innocent blood be shed: The story of the village of Le Chambon and how goodness happened there.* New York: Harper & Row.

Harvey, P. (2000). *An introduction to Buddhist ethics.* New York: Cambridge University Press.

Hill, P. C., Pargament, K. L., Hood, R. W., McCullough, M. E., Swyers, J. P., Larson, D. B., & Zinnbauer, B. J. (2000). Conceptualizing points of departure. *Journal for the Theory of Social Behavior, 30,* 51–77.

Hoge, D. (1972). A validated intrinsic religious motivation scale. *Journal for the Scientific Study of Religion, 11*(4), 369–372.

Hood, R. W., Hill, P. C., & Spilka, B. (2009) *The psychology of religion: An empirical approach.* (4th Ed.). New York: Guilford.

Jackson, L., & Esses, V. (1997). Of scripture and ascription. *Personality and Social Psychology Bulletin, 23,* 893–906.

James, W. (1902). *The varieties of religious experience* (2nd ed.). New York: Longmans.

Juergensmeyer, M. (2000). *Terror in the name of G-d.* Berkeley: University of California.

Kitayama, S., Markus, H., Matsumoto, H., & Norasakkunkit, V. (1997). Individual and collective processes in the construction of the self. *Journal of Personality and Social Psychology, 72,* 1245–1266.

Kohlberg L., Levine, C., & Hewer, A. (1983). *Moral stages.* New York: Harper.

Krebs, D. (1987). The challenge of altruism in biology and psychology. In C. Crawford, M. Smith, & D. Krebs (Eds.), *Sociology and psychology* (pp. 81–118). Hillsdale, NJ: Erlbaum.

Kropotkin, P. (1902/1972). *Mutual aid: A factor of evolution.* New York: New York University.

Kupper, B., & Bierhoff, H. (1999). Love your neighbour, do good to him: The helping behaviour of volunteers in relation to motives and religiosity. *Zeigschrift fur Differentielle und Diagnostische Psychologie, 20,* 217–230.

Lam, P-Y., & Rotolo, T. (2000). Examining the relationship between religiosity and life satisfaction. *Research in the Scientific Study of Religion, 11,* 133–153.

Leak, G., Loucks, A., & Bowlin, P. (1999). Development and initial validation of an objective measure of faith development. *International Journal for the Scientific Study of Religion, 9,* 105–124.

Matthews, K., Batson, C. C., Horn, J., & Rosenman, R. (1981). "Principles in his nature which interest him in the fortune of others...": The heritability of empathic concern for others. *Journal of Personality, 49,* 237–247.

McFadden, S. (1999). Religion, personality, and aging. *Journal of Personality, 67,* 1081–1104.

Midlarsky, E. (1968). Aiding responses: An analysis and review. *Merrill Palmer Quarterly, 14,* 229–260.

Midlarsky, E. (1991). Helping as coping. In M. S. Clark (Ed.), *Review of personality and social psychology: Prosocial behavior* (Vol. 12, pp. 238–264). Newbury Park, CA: Sage.

Midlarsky, E., & Bryan, J. H. (1967). Training charity in children. *Journal of Personality and Social Psychology, 5,* 409–415.

Midlarsky, E., Fagin Jones, S., & Corley, R. (2005). Personality correlates of heroic rescue during the Holocaust. *Journal of Personality, 73,* 907–934.

Midlarsky, E., & Kahana, E. (1994). *Altruism in later life.* Newbury Park, CA: Sage.

Midlarsky, E., & Kahana, E. (2007). Life course perspectives on altruism, health, and mental health. In S. G. Post (Ed.), *Altruism and health outcomes* (pp. 56–60). New York: Oxford University.

Midlarsky, E., Kahana, E., Corley, R. Schonbar, R., & Nemeroff, R. (1999). Altruistic moral judgment among older adults. *International Journal of Aging and Human Development, 49,* 39–53.

Midlarsky, M. (2005). *The killing trap.* New York: Cambridge University Press.

Midlarsky, M., & Midlarsky, E. (2003, June). *Understanding Himmler: Altruistic punishment and genocide.* Paper presented at the International Association of Genocide Scholars meetings, Galway, Ireland.

Neusner, J., & Chilton, B. (Eds.). (2005). *Altruism in world religions.* Washington, DC: Georgetown University.

Norenzavan, A., & Shariff, A. F. (2008). The origin and evolution of religious prosociality. *Science, 322*(5898), 58–62.

Oliner, S., & Oliner, P. (1988). *The altruistic personality.* New York: Free Press.

Oxford University Press. (2008). *Concise Oxford English dictionary* (11th ed., rev.). Oxford, England: Author.

Penner, L. (2002). Dispositional and organizational influences on sustained volunteering. *Journal of Social Issues, 58,* 447–467.

Piliavin, J., & Charng, H. (1990). Altruism. *Annual Review of Sociology, 16,* 27–65.

Rushton, J. P., Fulker, D. W., Neale, M. C., Nias, D., & Eysenck, H. J. (1986). Altruism and aggression: The heritability of individual differences. *Journal of Personality and Social Psychology, 50,* 1192–1198.

Sagerstrate, U. (2000). *Defenders of the truth: The battle for science in the sociobiology debate, and beyond.* Oxford, England: Oxford University Press.

Sells, S. B. (1963). An interactionist looks at the environment. *American Psychologist, 118*(11), 696–702.

Seraglou, V., Pichon, I. Trompette, L., Verschueren, M., & Dernelle, R. (2005). Prosocial behavior and religion. *Journal for the Scientific Study of Religion, 44,* 323–348.

Singer, A. (2008). *Charity in Islamic society.* New York: Cambridge University Press.

Smith, T. W. (2003, June), *Empathy, altruism, and religion.* Paper presented at the meeting of the National Opinion Research Center, University of Chicago, Chicago, IL.

Spilka, B., Hood, R. W., Hunsberger, B., & Gorsuch, R. (2003). *The psychology of religion: An empirical approach* (3rd ed.). New York: The Guilford Press.

Stark, R., & Bainbridge, W. S. (1987). *A theory of religion.* New York: Peter Lang.

Stetzer. E., Stanley, R., & Hayes, J. (2009). *Lost and found: The younger unchurched and the churches that reach them.* Nashville, TN: B & H Publishing Group.

Taylor, R., Chatters, L., & Levin, J. (2004). *Religion in the lives of African Americans.* Thousand Oaks, CA: Sage.

Todorov, T. (1999). *The fragility of goodness. Why Bulgaria's Jews survived the Holocaust.* Princeton, NJ: Princeton University Press.

Ward, L. F. (1883). *Dynamic sociology.* New York: Appleton.

Westat, Inc. (2001). *Giving and volunteering in the United States.* Washington, DC: Independent Sector.

Wiggens, J. S. (Ed.) (1996). *The five-factor model of personality: Theoretical perspectives.* New York: Guilford.

Wilson, E. O (1975). *Sociobiology: The new synthesis.* Cambridge, MA: Harvard University Press.

Wuthnow, R. (1998). *After heaven: Spirituality in America since the 1950s.* Berkeley: University of California Press.

Yarbrough, J. M., & Eidenmuller, M. E. (July 8, 2010). *I've been to the mountaintop.* Retrieved from http://www.americanrhetoric.com/speeches/mlkivebeentothemountaintop.htm

Zahn-Waxler, C., Schiro, K., Robinson, J., Emde, R., & Schmitz, S. (2001). Empathy and prosocial development in young MZ and DZ twins. In R. Emde & J. Hewitt (Eds.), *Infancy to early childhood* (pp. 141–162). London: Oxford University Press.

PART 3

Spiritual Development, Family, and Culture

Spiritual Development During Childhood and Adolescence

Chris J. Boyatzis

Abstract

Social-scientific research on spiritual and religious development is burgeoning. Amid this growth, there is progress but lack of consensus in defining spiritual development. A social-ecology model of spiritual development is offered, with a focus on the family context as well as other social contexts. Studies that have examined the interaction effects of multiple dimensions of religiosity and spirituality on children's outcomes are highlighted. Adolescent well-being has received extensive attention, with ample evidence of the positive role of religion and spirituality in youth development but uncertainty on the causal mechanisms. Many future directions are offered, including a call for refined methodology with longitudinal design and in-depth qualitative methods as well as greater incorporation of perspectives outside of psychology: cultural anthropology, comparative religion, and religious education/children's theology.

Key Words: child, adolescent, spirituality, religion, family, social ecology, definition, well-being, methodology

Introduction

Not long ago, religious and spiritual development were rather neglected domains of development, comprising a conspicuously tiny fraction of research on child and adolescent development (Benson, Roehlkepartain, & Rude, 2003; Boyatzis, 2003a). Fortunately, spiritual development is now a significant domain in its own right. For example, dissertations on children and spirituality have surged; most of the dissertations ever done on this topic have appeared since 2000. Many volumes on religious and spiritual development have appeared recently, including the landmark volume, *The Handbook of Spiritual Development in Childhood and Adolescence* (Roehlkepartain, King, Wagener, & Benson, 2006); other edited books (e.g., Allen, 2008; Dowling & Scarlett, 2006) the new periodical, *International Journal on Children's Spirituality*; and a spate of special journal issues on the

topic: *Review of Religious Research* (Boyatzis, 2003b), *Applied Developmental Science* (King & Boyatzis, 2004), *The International Journal for the Psychology of Religion* (Boyatzis, 2006), *New Directions for Youth Development* (Benson, Roehlkepartain, & Hong, 2008), and *Research in the Social Scientific Study of Religion* (Boyatzis & Hambrick-Dixon, 2008). In addition, the most recent edition of the prestigious *Handbook of Child Psychology* had for the first time a chapter on religious and spiritual development (Oser, Scarlett, & Bucher, 2006). The field of spiritual development is working toward the mainstream like never before.

It is a challenge, then, to review this burgeoning literature. To do justice to the many topics in religious/spiritual development would strain this chapter's limits. Due to space limitations here and the availability elsewhere of many sources, I will delimit my review. For example, I forego review of attachment theory to explain children's or adolescents' relationships with God, an approach that examines the "high degree of structural and functional similarity between child-parent and believer-God relationships" (Granqvist & Dickie, 2006, pp. 197–198). Nor do I discuss the major area of children's religious cognition—concepts of God, prayer, the afterlife, and so on (for reviews as well as critiques of cognitive stage theory, see Boyatzis, 2005, 2009; Johnson & Boyatzis, 2006; Scarlett, 2006). I have also chosen to focus on normal populations, although recent work (see Kim, McCullough, & Cicchetti, 2009; Miller & Kelley, 2005) explores studies on psychiatric or atypical populations. (Dew et al. [2009] describes an exemplary prospective, short-term longitudinal approach of adolescent psychiatric patients, showing that a loss of faith over time predicted less improvement in their depression.) Finally, I have chosen not to explore the "dark side" of religion and spirituality for children and youth, though others have (e.g., Mahoney & Tarakeshwar, 2005; Wagener & Maloney, 2006).

What I do review are recent attempts to define spiritual development and then research on religion and spirituality within the family. While conventional wisdom is that the family is the crucial locus of religious and spiritual development, it is surely not the only one. Hence, a section of this chapter is devoted to the broader social ecology that includes but goes beyond the family. I review cutting-edge research that demonstrates the value of measuring multiple religious constructs and analyzing their interaction. In addition, the role of spirituality and religion in adolescent well-being and thriving will be discussed, with attempts to describe mechanisms that may explain why religion is related in healthy ways to adolescent well-being. Because several other handbooks have been published recently, I feel obligated to discuss literature in this chapter that is *very recent*. Toward that end, fully 91% of the sources cited here were published in 2000 or later, with 42% from 2006 on. Another focus is to examine religion and spirituality in children's and teens' lives. Although there is growing literature on religion in parents' lives (e.g., Mahoney & Tarakeshwar, 2005), my interest is restricted to how religion might relate to parenting *behaviors* that may directly or indirectly affect children's religious and spiritual development. Finally, I suggest important new directions for the field, especially in methods and design and engagement with other disciplines.

Challenges and Progress in Defining Spiritual Development

Most attempts to define spiritual development have concluded that there is no consensus on how to define spirituality (Zinnbauer & Pargament, 2005), in part because spirituality seems to parallel notions of psychological well-being in general and because of its overlap with religion. In this chapter, I will often use the terms "spiritual" and "religious" interchangeably. In the research literature they still overlap each other so much that to restrict the discussion to only spirituality research would be to systematically ignore a wealth of relevant information.

If it seems difficult to define "spirituality," it is even more difficult to define "spiritual development." Some scholars suggest there has been more effort to define spirituality than spiritual development and conclude, "There is no consensus about what 'this domain' (of children's spirituality) really is" (Roehlkepartain, Benson, King, & Wagener, 2006, p. 4). If children develop spiritually, *what* develops? A metatheoretical constraint operating here, suggests Jacquie Mattis, is the Western assumption that spiritual maturity requires passage of time (Mattis, Ahluwalia, Cowie, & Kirkland-Harris, 2006). In contrast, many communities, whether indigenous peoples or some Eastern religions, attribute spiritual capacities to children even before birth. To understand spiritual development, then, entails resolving a prior question: "When does selfhood/beingness, and therefore spiritual life, begin?" (Mattis et al., p. 283). In my opinion, secular social science has not wrestled enough with this key question, though scholars in comparative religion and children's theology have (e.g., Bunge, 2001, 2008). Despite more work needed in that domain, there has been progress from a Western social-scientific worldview toward definitions.

Scholars at The Center for Spiritual Development recently offered this definition of spiritual development: Growth in "the intrinsic capacity for self-transcendence, in which the self is embedded in something greater than the self, including the sacred...shaped both within and outside of religious traditions, beliefs, and practices" (Benson et al., 2003, pp. 205–206). Here is a similar definition: "Spirituality is the intrinsic human capacity for self-transcendence in which the individual participates in the sacred—something greater than the self. It propels the search for connectedness, meaning, purpose, and ethical responsibility. It is experienced, formed, shaped, and expressed through a wide range of religious narratives, beliefs, and practices, and is shaped by many influences in family, community, society, culture, and nature" (Yust, Johnson, Sasso, & Roehlkepartain, 2006, p. 8).

These definitions are valuable because they characterize spirituality as (a) a natural human propensity (consistent with the "biological argument" for innate spirituality; Hay, Reich, & Utsch, 2006); (b) socialized and shaped by multiple experiences, sometimes within organized religion but also outside of it; and (c) characterized by a sense of connectedness and relationality to what is beyond the self, what has been termed "relational consciousness" (Hay & Nye, 1998). Spirituality, then, is not restricted to a particular religious doctrine or sacred entity; God or some theistic version thereof is not a priori the only transcendent entity with which a child could experience a relationship. In addition, these definitions suggest that during ontogenesis, children's relational consciousness emerges *prior* to religious socialization: Children are spiritual beings first and then are acculturated (or not) in a religious tradition that channels intuitive spirituality into particular expressions (rituals, creeds, etc.) that have been passed through the faith tradition. These definitions also make clear that children's spirituality is subject to many influences, from family to culture. It behooves us, then, to use a social ecology model to understand children's spirituality within a complex web of social influences and institutions, and later in this chapter I take such an approach. However, a problem arises from the prior definitions' use of "sacred." Namely, what does "sacred" mean to a child, and how could we find out? Answering these questions remains a serious task for our field. One possible approach could be with the construct of sanctification (Pargament & Mahoney, 2005), though it isn't clear how this construct would apply, theoretically or methodologically, to children.

Recently, Johnson and Boyatzis (2006) proposed that spiritual development proceeds from intuitive understanding to increasingly reflective thought. Young children possess powerful inference mechanisms for intuitively sorting out reality and the supernatural. Such intuition is integrated with increasing reflection and scaffolded by cultural practices that orient the child to cultural modes of spiritual knowing and being. Thus, spiritual development arises not from mere acquisition of knowledge about the transcendent but from increasingly meaningful and organized experiential connections of the self to, in William James's words, the "something more."

One statistical step that could help the field is the use of factor analysis to identify major constructs (spirituality, religiosity) comprised of specific behavioral, cognitive, or emotional variables. Dowling et al. (2004) factor-analyzed data from 1,000 adolescents, and distinct latent constructs of spirituality and religiosity emerged. In their analysis, religiosity consisted of four variables: beliefs about the impact of religion on one's behavior, one's religious views (e.g., about God), feelings about God's restrictions and rules for people, and being involved in a faith institution. The spirituality factor consisted of helpfulness toward others and lower preoccupation with the self. Other such studies on diverse samples and various measures may yield comparable or different constructs.

The Value of Assessing Multiple Contexts: A Social-Ecology Approach

A social-ecology model (Bronfenbrenner, 1979) posits multiple contexts of influence on children's development. These contexts range from the most proximal "microsystems," such as family, school, the peer group, or the religious community, to more distal ones, such as macrosystem dominant cultural values and ideologies. This model helps us examine the role of different contexts on religious and spiritual development. Another value is its description of "mesosystems" or linkages between microsystems (e.g., the home-church connection, the parent–peer group connection). Though most work (and hence this chapter) will focus on the family, I will also describe studies that illustrate these mesosystems at work.

One helpful framework is a sociocultural model that emphasizes the influence of knowledgeable adults who use guided participation in culturally meaningful practices to help the child move to higher competence (Vygotsky, 1978). Hence, parents, relatives, clergy, religious educators, youth ministers, and other adults can act as mentors who guide apprentices—children and teens—to more advanced levels of understanding and engagement in practices, creeds, and modes of expression. A second framework is a transactional model that posits that children and parents influence each other in recurrent exchanges (Kuczynski, 2003). This characterization of bidirectional interaction contrasts sharply with traditional views that presume parents (and other adults) influence children in a unilateral P→C fashion; this "transmission" model dominated socialization research for decades, but scholars now endorse a more dynamic conceptualization of adult–child interactions as having bidirectional and often multidirectional flows of influence.

The Family as a Context of Spiritual and Religious Development

Children grow in a complex interlocking web of social contexts. Although social-ecology models posit that it takes a village to raise a child, we might say that the family is "the first village" of religious and spiritual development (Boyatzis, Dollahite, & Marks, 2006). As Lisa Miller (2008) stated in a recent presidential address to Division 36 of the American Psychological Association, parents are children's "spiritual ambassadors," who can support "children's inchoate spirituality with ongoing spiritual dialog."

In the family, whatever input children receive from their parents not only must be processed through the child's inherent cognitive structures but may also be mediated through external factors such as sibling relationships. In this view, children's beliefs may undergo initial revision due to parent testimony (Harris & Koenig, 2006) but also may show ongoing revisions due to "secondary adjustments" through "third-party discussions" (Kuczynski, 2003, p. 10) that could include siblings, for example, and recursive discussions between multiple family members; these dynamics are common in family life. Our field knows little about these complex multidirectional dynamics in which parents and children influence *each other's* spiritual growth. I would expect that some families reveal a distinct "parent-as-mentor, child-as-apprentice" role structure; in other families, there may be more fluidity between these roles (see Boyatzis, 2004). In some families the child may be viewed as something of a "spiritual savant." Some parents—especially African American, Caribbean, and African—speak of their young children as "old souls" or as having "come here to teach me something" (Mattis et al., 2006). Many cultural and ethnic groups view children as spiritual beings at birth, as "spiritual emissaries" from the "other side" of an ancestral spirit realm (e.g., Gottlieb, 2006). Some families may use only one of these modes consistently, whereas other families may display more flexibility and different configurations at different times due to changes in a child's and parents' spiritual maturation. The culturally influenced discourse styles and parental attributions of children as spiritual beings should be studied as antecedents, correlates, and sequelae of children's spiritual development.

Within these dynamics, it is likely that parents influence their children as in other realms, through induction of beliefs (from subtle persuasion to dogmatic insistence), disciplinary tactics, rewards and punishments, and behavioral modeling. For example, work from England has underscored the power of parental modeling as a key influence on the prayer behavior of children (Francis & Brown, 1990; also see Silberman, 2003). While progress has been made to understand such processes, there is much more to learn. Researchers need to study how religion operates in immediate ways within family interaction and activity.

Parent–Child Conversation About Religion and Spirituality

Ongoing conversation about religion may be an important mechanism through which parents and children co-construct religious and spiritual meaning (Boyatzis, 2004). Recent studies have examined parent–child communication in the home. One study of Christian families (Boyatzis & Janicki, 2003) with children ages 3 to 12 asked parents to complete a religious conversation diary for 2 weeks as well as complete survey measures on the topics, frequency, setting, and processes in such conversations. Diary entries were recorded close to three times per week on average, a frequency corroborated by survey data from parents. Content analyses of diaries revealed that children were active participants in conversations about religion and spirituality—they initiated and terminated about half of conversations, spoke as much as parents did, and frequently asked questions and offered their own views. These data support the view that in family communication about religion, children are active participants rather than passive recipients of ideas "transmitted" by parents, and that in many families a "bidirectional reciprocal" style is more prominent than a unilateral parent-to-child dynamic.

In another study, Flor and Knapp (2001) assessed two-parent Christian families in the rural South through computerized questionnaires done at families' homes. Regressions revealed that frequent bidirectional communication about religion predicted children's importance of religion. What the authors labeled as children's religious behavior (worship attendance and, perhaps oddly, belief in God) was predicted by higher bidirectional faith discussion with parents. Bidirectional faith discussion predicted modest but unique variance in children's religiosity. These patterns were especially apparent in same-sex dyads (mother-daughter, father-son).

A third recent study assessed more qualitative aspects of family communication about religion. Dollahite and Thatcher (2008) surveyed and interviewed parents and adolescents in highly religious Jewish, Christian, and Muslim families, who described various techniques through which parents tried to shape youths' religiosity (e.g., family devotions, church attendance, praying with children). However, in interviews, parents and adolescents both cited conversations more frequently (more than 75% of each group) than any other method; the adolescents rated conversations as the most important means through which parents shared their faith. Dollahite and Thatcher identified two kinds of discourse styles in their families, "youth-centered" conversations that focus on the adolescents' spiritual needs and issues and "parent-centered" conversations that emphasize parents talking rather than listening to children and not taking the adolescents' views or concerns as priorities. Youth-centered talks were more common than "parent-centered" conversations, which were described in only 12% of interviews. The youth-centered model is akin to the bidirectional parent ←→ child dynamic described earlier (Boyatzis & Janicki, 2003; Flor & Knapp, 2001). Youth-centered conversations were described by not only adolescents but also parents as more positive experiences. These findings provide a potential explanation for why Flor and Knapp (2001) found that higher parent–child communication predicted higher religiosity in youth: Such conversations are positive experiences for youth who are then more likely to internalize parents' religious values. A Presbyterian father described this youth-centered style by saying, "I take the approach of coming alongside rather than trying to parent down to them" (p. 630). This style may help youth adopt parents' religious values as well as strengthen the parent–child relationship more broadly.

Taken together, these studies—two employing both quantitative and qualitative methods—offer ample evidence that many families use an open, bidirectional communication style. Subsequent research might emulate their use of diverse methods that yield different insights. These studies also provide data that such conversations have positive impact on youths' religiosity, although more work will be needed to confirm such a result. The extant research relies on self-report, which could be tainted by social desirability effects or memory and reporting problems. In addition, the research takes a snapshot of family life; longitudinal data will give stronger evidence that parent–child faith discussion

at Time 1 is causally related to youth religiosity at Time 2. In any event, designs need to account for the impact that youth may have on their parents' spirituality. Too little published work recognizes this possibility.

Many questions remain for future research on parent–child communication, such as, do families of different religious affiliations differ in religious communication style? How do parent and child personality variables affect faith-communication styles? Does spiritual disclosure in families reflect, or cause, healthy parent–child intimacy in general? Does religious communication uniquely contribute to children's well-being, beyond other parenting variables? Answers to these would be interpreted more clearly if data were collected on discussion about various topics (school, romance, etc.) to determine whether religion is discussed more, less, or similarly to other, more secular domains in the child's life, and whether it matters more or less to children's and adolescents' spirituality and well-being in general.

The Value of Measuring Multiple Variables and Their Interactions

Many researchers have used limited assessments of religiosity, as one review found that more than 80% of studies on religion and family measured religiosity with only one or two items (Mahoney, Pargament, Swank, & Tarakeshwar, 2001). Given the multifaceted nature of religiosity and, of course, the complexity of parenting, we can assume that when researchers measure different religiosity variables they will better capture the role of religion in parenting and family life. Here I describe a few studies that confirm the power of examining the interactions between multiple dimensions of religiosity in the family.

One of the most pressing challenges for parents is disciplining their children. This process is related to parents' religious makeup. While it is known that parents with conservative Christian affiliations approve of spanking and use it more often with their children than do nonconservative Christian parents, a stronger predictor of spanking than religious affiliation is the parents' theological conservatism, that is, biblical literalism and inerrancy, thinking that children possess original sin, and belief in expiatory punishment (Gershoff, Miller, & Holden, 1999). This link between religiosity and spanking has been further elucidated by a superb recent study.

Murray-Swank, Mahoney, and Pargament (2006) measured several indices of religious belief in mothers, including their theological conservatism and sanctification of their roles as parents, or how much the mothers imbued their role with sacred and holy qualities and saw themselves as doing "God's work." Neither conservatism nor sanctification was related independently to the mothers' use of spanking. However, in regressions, mothers' use of spanking was predicted by the interaction between mothers' conservatism and sanctification scores. Specifically, mothers who were theologically conservative were more likely than other conservative mothers to spank their children if they also viewed their parent role as sacred and holy; in contrast, mothers who were theologically liberal were less likely than other liberal mothers to spank their children if they also viewed their role as sacred and holy. Thus, "the link between sanctifying one's role as a parent and using corporal punishment…was moderated by how conservative or liberal a mother was in her interpretation of the Bible" (p. 283).

Another study examined sanctification of the parental role in relation to children's moral conduct. Volling, Mahoney, and Rauer (2009) examined parental disciplinary strategies and beliefs about the sanctification of parenting (i.e., endowing it with sacred and divine significance). These parenting measures were examined in relation to the development of young children's conscience. Maternal and paternal sanctification of parenting was positively related to their use of positive socialization techniques (e.g., approving good behavior, recognition when child was nice) and the use of induction (e.g., focusing on consequences of the children's wrongdoing). For our purposes, the key finding was that parents' use of positive socialization techniques combined with their sanctification of parenting to predict children's conscience development. Children's moral conduct was most mature when fathers were high in induction and high in sanctification of their parent role. A similar interaction obtained for children's affective discomfort; that is, after acting badly, children's guilt, apologizing, and concern for others was highest when fathers and mothers used positive socialization techniques *and* were high in sanctification of parenting.

A third study (Dumas & Nissley-Tsiopinis, 2006) analyzed a diverse sample of families with preschoolers. Parents reported on their sanctification of the parenting role and on their style of religious coping in response to children's oppositional behavior. Sanctification did not predict children's behavior. Interestingly, children's oppositional behavior increased when parents' overall religiousness was low and when mothers engaged in frequent negative religious coping (expressing anger at God, feeling God has abandoned them). This problematic behavior in children was most apparent only at the intersection of different expressions of religiosity.

A fourth study (Abar, Carter, & Winsler, 2009) examined the effects of African American parents' religiosity and parenting style on their late adolescents and college students, whose religiosity was measured on the Valuegenesis Youth Survey with items such as "I like to worship and pray with others" and "I feel God's presence in my relationships." Although there was no main effect of authoritative parenting or parent religiosity on youths' own religiosity, a significant interaction emerged, as higher authoritative parenting combined with higher parental religiosity to predict modest but unique variance in youths' own religiosity.

Collectively, these recent, high-quality studies demonstrate the power of measuring multiple variables of interest and then analyzing interactions between them to more clearly understand how religion is associated with children's development.

Interaction of Family and Peer Influences

Although the family matters for children's spirituality, a social-ecology model considers the interplay between different social contexts. One fine example comes from Schwartz (2006), who measured adolescent spirituality in relation to parent and peer religiosity. Data were collected at a large international Christian youth conference in Canada on the youths' religious belief and commitment and "perceived faith support" from parents and friends. Support was assessed with items such as "my parents (friends) and I talk about how we are doing as Christians" and "my parents (friends) show me what it means to be an authentic Christian."

Teenagers' own religiosity was predicted by their parents' and friends' religiosity; teens with stronger faith had parents and peers with stronger faith. But most interesting was that parents' influence was mediated by friends' religiosity: After controlling for friends' faith support, parents' faith support predicted teens' religiosity less strongly. Thus, our understanding of adolescent spirituality is enriched by measuring the interplay of different contexts in which youth develop, an approach consistent with theoretical models of faith development (Fowler, 1981).

A similar result emerged from a national study of US youth by Gunnoe and Moore (2002) on childhood and adolescent predictors of religiosity in early adulthood. Mothers' religiosity and religious training in childhood were significant predictors of young adult religiosity, but one of the most potent predictors was the frequency of worship attendance by one's peers during adolescence. In a similar study, Regnerus, Smith, and Smith (2004) analyzed data from the National Longitudinal Study of Adolescent Health, a database of youth from grades 7 to 12. The surveys included two religiosity outcomes for youth: worship attendance and importance of religion. Relative influences were computed for the religiosity of parents, peers, the youths' schools, and local county norms (of worship attendance). Teens' worship attendance was related most strongly to their parents' attendance, but peers' religiosity and local county worship norms were also strong predictors of youth attendance. The importance of religion in the youths' schools turned out to be the strongest predictor of the importance that the adolescent subjects themselves placed on religion. Together, these studies confirm the value of a social-ecology approach that analyzes links between multiple influences.

Peers and Siblings

Peer relations constitute a major arena of human growth, and they may be central in spiritual development. The equality and symmetry in peer relationships provide opportunities for children to learn and exercise empathy, care, and compassion. A peer's trust must be earned, and won; this is in contrast to parents, who, to paraphrase Robert Frost, have to take you in when you go home. It is plausible that the exercise of interpersonal concern in this "horizontal" peer context could be positively associated with greater spirituality and enhanced personal connectedness to a transcendent "vertical" entity. Contemporary childhood in the West is jammed with organized activities. Are these beneficial, or not, for spiritual growth? Does the soccer player's connection to the team enhance her sense of connectedness to other forces beyond the self? Is the solitary adolescent diarist and poet more directly in tune with his innermost self? Do children with intimate friendships have greater spiritual depth and sense of the sacred? Are youth avidly listening to the cacophony of the peer group (or media) less sensitive to the "small, quiet voice" inside that seems essential to the spiritual? Unfortunately, the literature is silent on these matters, which, to me, outline an important research agenda. In short, friendship could be a crucial locus for spiritual growth, for good and bad.

Because children play a lot with peers, some activity may have a spiritual and religious nature—if only we could study this topic to find out. A colorful anecdote from a colleague is illustrative. As a Roman Catholic child, she would cut out small pieces of white Wonder bread and compress them into flat disks to "play communion" with her younger sisters. She gave these "communion wafers" to her siblings along with grape juice as the Eucharistic blood of Christ (served in gaudy wine glasses to help demarcate the specialness of the ritual). Decades later, this woman recalls that her parents commended such religious play, saying it proved the girl was "taking religion seriously." This kind of ritualistic play with siblings or peers may occur more often than social scientists realize (in part because such play could transpire in private, children-only settings), but we should find ways to explore it, at least through interviews with children or parents or retrospective reports.

The Context of Culture

Beyond the peer group, culture is a vital context in a social-ecology model, and it is high time that we widen our aperture beyond American borders. In one study (De Roos, Iedema, & Miedema, 2003), Dutch children's God concepts were assessed in structured interviews. The children's mothers had a variety of religious affiliations and their children were enrolled in schools that varied in emphasis on religion. Findings showed that mothers' affiliation and the schools' religious orientation had independent effects on children's God concepts. Another study assessed children's God concepts in relation to mothers' and teachers' God concepts (De Roos, Iedema, & Miedema, 2001). Mothers' and teachers' God concepts predicted children's God concepts, but in different ways. Parents' beliefs were most associated with rational aspects of children's concepts, but teachers' beliefs were more predictive of biblical features in children's God concepts. Furthermore, even after controlling for parents' religious affiliation, there was an independent effect of school on children's concepts.

Tirri, Tallent-Runnels, and Nokelainen (2005) interviewed fifth- and sixth-grade children in Finland, the United States, Hong Kong, and Bahrain, and found that the types of moral, religious, and spiritual questions asked by these children reflected their dominant cultural religions. Across these nations, girls asked more spiritual and religious questions than boys did. Another study in the Netherlands assessed identification with one's religious group and views of other religious groups in Christian, Muslim, and nonreligious early adolescents (Verkuyten & Thijs, 2010). The findings revealed that a third of the Christian and nonreligious participants expressed negative feelings toward Muslims, and Muslim youth expressed negative feelings toward Christians, nonbelievers, and Jews. Furthermore, the Muslim youth had high religious ingroup identification, which was associated with more negative feelings toward nonbelievers and Jews. This study did yield a finding with educational policy implications: Increased opportunities for contact in school between youth from different groups were related to more positive interactions between the groups. There are other insightful treatments of culture, ethnicity, and spirituality, one of the most enlightening by Mattis et al. (2006).

Religion and Spirituality and Adolescent Well-Being

On national surveys, religion matters to American children and adolescents. In one national study (Smith, 2005), 51% of adolescents said that religion was "very" or "extremely" important in their daily lives, and in another (Smith, Faris, Denton, & Regnerus, 2003) nearly one-third of youth said religion was "very" or "pretty" important. According to Smith et al. (2003, p. 130), the "vast majority of American youth pray regularly." Such data give us one level of insight, but circling numbers on surveys or answering an interviewer's questions is one thing and living a life that embodies faith is quite another. As Regnerus (2003, p. 395) quipped, "Many teenagers are themselves religious—or at least their parents take them to church." In his interview study of more than 200 American teenagers, Christian Smith made this critique of adolescent spirituality: "The overwhelming number of U.S. teens engage and value religion, not for the sake of God, or the common good of a just society... but for the instrumental good it does them" (2005, p. 150). If this is true, it's necessary to analyze more deeply religious and spiritual *meaning* in youths' lives rather than simply behaviors or beliefs. In the meantime, let us consider some recent studies on youths' well-being and their spirituality and religion.

It is now clear that religion and spirituality are assets in adolescents' lives. Many reviews have found that higher religiosity and spirituality are associated with better mental health (Miller & Kelley, 2005; Regnerus, 2003; Wong, Rew, & Slaikeu, 2006). For example, higher intrinsic religiosity is related to lower anxiety in at-risk high-school students (Davis, Kerr, & Robinson-Kurpius, 2003) and with better psychological adjustment in a mixed-ethnicity

sample of young adolescents (Milevsky & Levitt, 2004). One study of teenage mothers found that greater involvement with church and reliance on church members and officials were related to better academic outcomes, self-esteem, and lower depression in these adolescent mothers (Carothers, Borkowski, Lefever, & Whitman, 2005). Caputo (2004) analyzed a national sample of adolescents and found that youth of parents who had stronger feelings about their religion and more frequent religious practices had better health and lower substance abuse.

Milot and Ludden (2009) found that rural adolescents' religious importance predicted lower substance use even after accounting for parental support. Religious importance predicted lower school misbehavior and higher academic motivation, and worship attendance predicted higher grades.

Davis and Epkins (2009) tested whether 11- to 12-year-olds' private religious practices (e.g., prayer, scripture reading, listening to religious programs) would buffer them against the impact of family conflict. The children's religious practices showed no direct association with their depressive and anxiety symptoms, but they did moderate relations between family conflict and youths' anxiety and depression. Specifically, family conflict was more strongly related to youths' depression and anxiety when they were low, but not high, in private religious practices. These findings were akin to those from a study showing that children who prayed frequently were significantly higher in protective resources such as social connectedness and sense of humor (Rew, Wong, & Sternglanz, 2004). In another study, Catholic and Protestant 12- to 15-year-olds in the United Kingdom had stronger sense of purpose in life the more frequently they prayed (Robbins & Francis, 2005).

While suggestive of positive benefits of religious or spiritual practices, these studies do not confirm any specific mechanisms. It seems plausible that prayer and other private practices may calm young adolescents' emotions (and sympathetic nervous systems) and provide a sense of healthy respite or distance from conflict, as well as help the youth generate helpful perspectives or solutions to problems. Future research should assess more deeply what prayer "does" for children and adolescents. In any event, correlational studies cannot demonstrate causal effects. One reason is that some studies do not tease apart the youths' private practices from family practices. For example, in the Davis and Epkins study it is impossible to tell whether listening to religious programs—a behavior they measured—was a solitary or family event, or if youth chose such events on their own volition or due to parents' insistence. We need more refined measures and to supplement surveys with qualitative approaches; as Davis and Epkins suggest, researchers could simply "ask preadolescents to describe the meaning behind their religious behaviors" (2009, p. 712). Isn't it time that we do this?

In a study that illustrates the value of studying multiple social contexts in teenagers' lives, Regnerus and Elder (2003) found that, after controlling for other relevant factors, youth who live in high-poverty areas were more likely to stay on track academically if they were also high in church attendance. In contrast, youth in the same high-poverty areas but who were low in church attendance were more likely to fall behind academically. Thus, religious involvement can ameliorate broader risk factors such as community poverty presumably through giving the youth exposure to positive models and norms in the faith community that would reinforce values and behaviors that would promote academic success. The authors claimed that worship attendance could be important for academics because the faith community serves as a sanctuary for those youth living amid neighborhood risk and dysfunction.

Although there is a paucity of studies with longitudinal designs, such an approach was used by Kerestes, Youniss, and Metz (2004), who followed a sample of American youth from 10th to 12th grades (roughly 15–16 and 17–18 years of age). A specific interest of theirs was how the trajectory in youth religiosity across that interval was linked to changes in risk behaviors (e.g., drug use) and civic involvement (e.g., desire to perform volunteer service). The most positive behavioral profile (high civic involvement, low drug use) appeared in the youth who were highly religious at both grade levels. The more interesting finding was that youth who went from being initially high in religiosity to low in religiosity 2 years later also sharply increased their use of marijuana and alcohol; in contrast, youth going from initially low to high in religiosity 2 years later showed increased desire for civic involvement.

While the aforementioned studies demonstrate that religion is linked to adolescent well-being, some studies are getting closer to the reason. In a national survey of 20,000 American adolescents, Wagener, Furrow, King, Leffert, and Benson (2003) found that the positive impact of teenagers' religious involvement on their well-being was mediated through the mechanism of exposure to social capital and developmental assets within the religious community. Social engagement in religious communities reduced risk behaviors and increased youths' psychosocial thriving and well-being. In another study, Furrow, King, and White (2004) assessed identity, meaning, and prosocial concerns in a diverse sample of 800 American public high school students. Structural equation analyses supported a model in which religious identity was significantly linked to stronger and more positive "personal meaning" and "prosocial concerns." In the model, religious identity was a latent variable comprised of youths' responses to items that tapped how active they were in their church and how "traditional" and "committed-ethical" they saw themselves. The prosocial concerns score, derived from a standardized measure, predicted higher scores on personal responsibility, empathy, and helpfulness toward others. In a related study, Dowling et al. (2004) used structured equation modeling (SEM) to test the contributions of spirituality and religiosity to adolescent well-being (e.g., a hopeful future, search for a positive identity). Religiosity was comprised of traditional topics (such as views of God, engagement with a faith community, impact of religious beliefs on one's behavior), and spirituality entailed an orientation to do good work for others along with lower self-involvement. The structural models revealed that adolescent thriving was related to spirituality directly, religiosity directly, and spirituality through religiosity. Together, the findings show that exemplary youth development has spirituality as a crucial component, which is "not fully commensurate with other key dimensions of an adolescent's inner life, such as religiosity" (Dowling et al., 2004, p. 11).

Taken together, the aforementioned studies highlight some important conclusions. First, these different studies illuminate definitional challenges. For example, a cluster of positive and good behaviors regarding concern for others was labeled as "prosocial concerns" in one study (Furrow et al., 2004), yet in another study a cluster of very similar behaviors was labeled as "spirituality" (Dowling et al., 2004). This difference of semantic opinion seems problematic. Some scholars (notably Zinnbauer & Pargament, 2005) have emphasized that the core of "spirituality" is a relationship to what one considers "the sacred." Is serving others always a "sacred" or spiritual act? Is the perfunctory high school service project always a genuine manifestation of spirituality or something else? More definitional debate and clarity is needed, and at this point a valid conclusion may indeed be that it is "premature—and potentially dangerous" to settle on one definition (Roehlkepartain et al., 2006, p. 6).

A second conclusion from these studies is that religion matters for adolescent well-being. Specifically, religion provides a personal and social forum for enhanced meaning and concern about others and desire to do good in the community. While this is a reasonable "religion is good for youth" picture to paint, it is important to note that in the aforementioned studies there is ample variance *unexplained* by religion in the models, indicating that more samples and models should measure other variables. In the meantime, there surely is evidence amassing that religion and spirituality are assets in youths' well-being, promoting better functioning and enhancing one's sense of purpose and meaning in life. Youth who are engaged in a value-laden and moral context that religion can provide seem to emerge with an enhanced spiritual sensibility that promotes attitudes and actions to contribute to the greater good (Lerner, Dowling, & Anderson, 2003).

Another study that explored adolescent well-being by Desrosiers and Miller (2008) tested a large mixed-ethnicity sample with a wide age range across adolescence. The purpose of their study was to tease apart the effects associated with congregational religious factors from more personal spiritual ones, these constructs coming from separate subscales of the Brief Multidimensional Measure of Religiousness/Spirituality. Youths' lower alcohol use was predicted by higher scores on subscales the authors referred to as "personal spirituality" variables: forgiveness, daily spiritual experience, and positive religious coping. Lower alcohol use was also predicted by higher scores on public religion variables, such as perceived support from one's congregation. In contrast, when youth perceived more problems in their congregation (measured on items such as "how often are the people in your congregation critical of you and the things you do?"), they scored higher in anxiety. Desrosiers and Miller suggested that a more personal spirituality—an "internalized, dyadic relationship" with God—protects against an intrapersonal spiritual void that alcohol may be used to fill (p. 248). The religious community also provides protective functions that reduce anxiety in adolescents, perhaps due to the social support given in a congregation perceived by the youth to be helpful and concerned toward the adolescent. However, when adolescents feel that their congregation is critical and unsupportive, they lose any sense of support and hence suffer more anxiety. The causal arrows between these variables are

uncertain, as the authors recognize, but their study is helpful: It utilized multiple measures of religiosity/spirituality, which allows one to identify which dimensions are related differentially to specific psychological outcomes; it intentionally tested an a priori distinction between "religion" and "spirituality" (the latter being defined in part by a personal relationship with God); and it attempted to identify mechanisms through which spirituality and religiosity may benefit or harm adolescents' well-being.

When Parents and Adolescents Differ

What happens in families where children and parents have different religious commitments? In many families, parents do not share the same religious faith—what has been termed "religious heterogamy." Using data from the National Survey of Families and Households, Petts and Knoester (2007) found that parents' religious heterogamy was associated with their children's use of illegal substances but had no association with children's self-esteem, satisfaction with life, or school performance. Stokes and Regnerus (2009) used the Add Health database to examine families in which the adolescent and parent did not share the same religious practices or beliefs (what they termed "religious discord"). When parents valued religion more than their adolescents did, the adolescents described having poorer relations with their parents. However, there was no evident link to the parent–child relationship when the adolescent valued religion more than the parent did. Some denominational effects emerged, as religious discord was associated with poorer parent–child relationships especially in evangelical Protestant families. Data from the National Longitudinal Study of Adolescent Health show that the more religious mothers and their adolescent children are, the less often the children are delinquent; however, the effect of one's religiosity depends on the other. Pearce and Haynie (2004) found that children's delinquency was higher when a mother or child was very religious and the other was not. While such findings are intriguing, causality remains unclear. Difference of belief may nudge a child toward trouble, or religious heterogamy may be just one dimension of a problematic relationship that itself would increase the odds for trouble.

Conclusion and Future Directions

On whether religion is linked to better outcomes, the jury is in. On whether religion *causes* well-being, the jury is still out. The vast majority of studies are correlational, with obvious limitations. Most measures are self-reports with their inherent constraints. While recent publications have used multiple regressions and structural equation modeling for more powerful analyses, there are many extraneous variables still unaccounted for, and these may explain or mediate links between religiosity and well-being. It is possible that religiosity is yoked to other qualities—personality traits, environmental factors, hormonal and genetic profiles—that could help explain the healthy role of religion. Consider studies that find that higher religiosity predicts better diet, exercise, and sleep. Before we conclude that religion is in some way responsible for such healthy behavior, it would be wise to measure potential third variables. In this case, the personality trait of conscientiousness could be relevant. Conscientiousness is positively related to religiosity (Piedmont, 2005) and surely the aforementioned health behaviors. In sum, our current approaches leave us vulnerable to many "spurious" relationships if we fail to test third-variable candidates, and not just additional indices of religiosity.

Even if we make strides toward stronger models, a genuine understanding of how religion works will require longitudinal designs that assess people in childhood and follow them over time. Such designs will answer many questions: How do childhood forms of religiosity relate to and predict adult religiosity? Are there childhood temperamental traits or psychological profiles that start a trajectory to particular religious outcomes? Is childhood openness or impulsiveness predictive of adult religious orientations, such as existential curiosity and quest rather than defensiveness and dogmatic closure? Contrary to presumptions that parenting or environmental variables shape children's spirituality, longitudinal designs will help us identify forms of childhood spirituality that may emerge early and then evoke subsequent socialization efforts.

Our field has been dominated by large- and sometimes small-sample studies using self-reports, usually on paper-and-pencil surveys that yield quantitative data. While such approaches help us chart structural relations between variables, especially when tested in SEM approaches, they are limited in showing how and why variables may be linked, and they surely do not address the meaning of religious behaviors or beliefs to those who perform or hold them. The reigning quantitative approach, then, must be complemented by a more meaning-centered, qualitative analysis. The limits of quantitative approaches were captured eloquently by the comparative-religion scholar Wilfred Cantwell Smith (1991, p. 7): "Such scholars might uncharitably be compared to flies crawling on the outside of a goldfish bowl, making accurate and complete observations on the fish inside, measuring their scales meticulously, and indeed contributing much to a knowledge of the subject, but never asking themselves, and never finding out, how it feels to be a goldfish."

To learn what it feels like to be a goldfish, so to speak, requires a qualitative methodology (Boyatzis & Newman, 2004). In-depth qualitative studies could emulate the approaches used in, for example, Hay and Nye (1998) and Robert Coles's (1990) magnificent book, *The Spiritual Life of Children*. A perusal of the conversations in these books will confirm that a genuine understanding of spirituality in children's lives requires sensitive adults who are willing to go to "the deep water" (pardon the pun), listening in extended conversations to children to learn about their spiritual lives.

Other innovative qualitative methods use expressive writing. For example, Van Dyke and Elias (2008) coded for religious themes in essays written by public-school children on values that were important to the children. Another study asked adolescent girls to examine their own diaries and poetry for expression of spirituality and learned that the most common themes were creating solitude, preserving sensitivity, and connecting beyond the self (Sinats et al., 2005).

Our neglect of the personal meaning of children's spirituality comes partly from the hegemony of cognitive developmentalism. These models, presupposing an invariant march toward rational logic away from other modes, have perpetuated the Western post-Enlightenment emphasis on cognition. This brought a concomitant dismissive attitude toward other forms of knowing. In counterpoint is theologian and religious educator John Westerhoff (2000), who asserts that consciousness entails two modes of consciousness, one intellectual and one intuitional and experiential, the latter characterized by nonverbal, nonlinear processes. I concur that "the development and integration of both modes of consciousness is essential to the spiritual life" (Westerhoff, 2000, p. 70). That our field has not begun to understand spiritual *experience* is an understatement and to remedy this will require us to go deeper, beyond the mapping of variables in sophisticated analyses and into the heart of children's spiritual experience.

In addition to expanding our methodologies, we should broaden our perception of different scholarly disciplines that may enhance our understanding of spiritual and religious development. Let me nominate two disciplines that, typically neglected, could be most helpful: cultural anthropology and children's theology/religious education. Cultural anthropology will help us understand that our social-science paradigm is steeped in implicit culture-bound ideologies. The study of children's religiosity and spirituality in diverse cultures will illuminate our biases and enrich our knowledge of religious and spiritual development (see Mattis et al., 2006). Finally, religious education and children's theology is a vibrant field, with major edited volumes (Bunge, 2008; Yust et al., 2006), journals, and conferences, yet none of these endeavors show up on the social-science radar. A closer examination of work in religious education and children's theology would help social scientists understand how religions may affect children. To focus on one aspect of faith traditions, many religions have rituals and sacraments that are essential mechanisms to provide children with a sense of connectedness to the tradition's sacred transcendent entity as well as connectedness to the faith community around the child. Milestone sacraments for children in different traditions include baptism, confirmation, confession, bar or bat mitzvah, and so on. Psychologists might want to learn more about how children understand and experience such events. Organized religions prioritize these events, but do *children* feel transformed by them? Qualitative and ethnographic work is needed; a fine example is Bales's (2005) ethnographic account of Roman Catholic children's First Communion.

In sum, children's religious and spiritual development is receiving scholarly attention like never before, and in this chapter I have tried to describe our accomplishments in mapping out children's religious and spiritual development. At the same time, I have tried to convey that we still have much to learn about the deep territory of spirituality so central to child development and our humanity.

Author's Note

This chapter is dedicated to the memory of Dr. Kelly Murray, formerly of Loyola University Maryland, whose beautiful life ended tragically early. Kelly was a talented professor and clinical psychologist, an advocate for girls' well-being, a dedicated wife, and a loving mother to six daughters.

References

Abar, B., Carter, K. L., & Winsler, A. (2009). The effects of maternal parenting style and religious commitment on self-regulation, academic achievement, and risk behavior among African-American parochial college students. *Journal of Adolescence, 32,* 259–273.

Allen, H. C. (Ed.). (2008). *Nurturing children's spirituality: Christian perspectives and best practices.* Eugene, OR: Cascade.

Bales, S. R. (2005). *When I was a child: Children's interpretation of First Communion.* Chapel Hill: University of North Carolina Press.

Benson, P. L., Roehlkepartain, E., & Hong, K. (Eds.). (2008). Spiritual development [Special issue]. *New Directions for Youth Development, 118.*

Benson, P. L., Roehlkepartain, E. C., & Rude, S. P. (2003). Spiritual development in childhood and adolescence: Toward a field of inquiry. *Applied Developmental Science, 7,* 204–212.

Boyatzis, C. J. (2003a). Religious and spiritual development: An introduction. *Review of Religious Research, 44,* 213–219.

Boyatzis, C. J. (Ed.). (2003b). Religious and spiritual development [Special issue]. *Review of Religious Research, 44*(3).

Boyatzis, C. J. (2004). The co-construction of spiritual meaning in parent-child communication. In D. Ratcliff (Ed.), *Children's spirituality: Christian perspectives, research, and applications* (pp. 182–200). Eugene, OR: Wipf & Stock.

Boyatzis, C. J. (2005). Children's religious and spiritual development. In R. F. Paloutzian & C. L. Park (Eds.), *Handbook of the psychology of religion and spirituality* (pp. 123–143). New York: The Guilford Press.

Boyatzis, C. J. (Ed.). (2006). Unraveling the dynamics of religion in the family and parent-child relationships [Special issue]. *The International Journal for the Psychology of Religion, 16*(4).

Boyatzis, C. J. (2009). Examining religious and spiritual development during childhood and adolescence. In L. Francis (Ed.), *The international handbook of education for spirituality, care, and well-being* (pp. 51–68). New York: Springer.

Boyatzis, C. J., Dollahite, D. C., & Marks, L. D. (2006). The family as a context for religious and spiritual development in children and youth. In E. C. Roehlkepartain, P. E. King, L. Wagener, & P. L. Benson (Eds.), *The handbook of spiritual development in childhood and adolescence* (pp. 297–309). Thousand Oaks, CA: Sage.

Boyatzis, C. J., & Hambrick-Dixon, P. (Eds.). (2008). Adolescent spirituality [Special section]. *Research in the Social Scientific Study of Religion, 19.*

Boyatzis, C. J., & Janicki, D. (2003). Parent-child communication about religion: Survey and diary data on unilateral transmission and bi-directional reciprocity styles. *Review of Religious Research, 44,* 252–270.

Boyatzis, C. J., & Newman, B. (2004). How shall we study children's spirituality? In D. Ratcliff (Ed.), *Children's spirituality: Christian perspectives, research, and application* (pp. 166–181). Eugene, OR: Wipf & Stock.

Bronfenbrenner, U. (1979). *The ecology of human development.* Cambridge, MA: Harvard University Press.

Bunge, M. (Ed.) (2001). *The child in Christian thought.* Grand Rapids, MI: Eerdmans.

Bunge, M. (Ed.) (2008). *The child in the Bible.* Grand Rapids, MI: Eerdmans.

Caputo, R. K. (2004). Parent religiosity, family process, and adolescent outcomes. *Families in Society, 85,* 495–510.

Carothers, S. S., Borkowski, J. G., Lefever, J. B., & Whitman, T. L. (2005). Religiosity and the socioemotional adjustment of adolescent mothers and their children. *Journal of Family Psychology, 19*, 263–275.

Coles, R. (1990). *The spiritual life of children*. Boston: Houghton Mifflin.

Davis, K. A., & Epkins, C. C. (2009). Do private religious practices moderate the relation between family conflict and pre-adolescents' depression and anxiety symptoms? *The Journal of Early Adolescence, 29*, 693–717.

Davis, T. L., Kerr, D. B., & Robinson-Kurpius, S. E. (2003). Meaning, purpose, and religiosity in at-risk youth: The relationship between anxiety and spirituality. *Journal of Psychology and Theology, 31*, 356–365.

De Roos, S. A., Iedema, J., & Miedema, S. (2001). Young children's descriptions of God: Influences of parents' and teachers' God concepts and religious denomination of schools. *Journal of Beliefs and Values, 22*, 19–30.

De Roos, S. A., Iedema, J., & Miedema, S. (2003). Effects of mothers' and schools' religious denomination on preschool children's God concepts. *Journal of Beliefs and Values, 24*, 165–181.

Desrosiers, A., & Miller, L. (2008). Substance use versus anxiety in adolescents: Are some disorders more spiritual than others? *Research in the Social Scientific Study of Religion, 19*, 237–254.

Dew, R., Daniel, S., Goldston, D., McCall, W., Kuchibhatla, M., Schleifer, C., Triplett, M., & Koenig, H. (2009). A prospective study of religion/spirituality and depressive symptoms among adolescent psychiatric patients. *Journal of Affective Disorders, 120*, 149–157.

Dollahite, D. C., & Thatcher, J. Y. (2008). Talking about religion: How religious youth and parents discuss their faith. *Journal of Adolescent Research, 23*, 611–641.

Dowling, E., & Scarlett, W. G. (Eds.). (2006). *Encyclopedia of spiritual development in childhood and adolescence*. Thousand Oaks, CA: Sage.

Dowling, E. M., Gestsdottir, S., Anderson, P. M., von Eye, A., Almerigi, J., & Lerner, R. M. (2004). Structural relations among spirituality, religiosity, and thriving in adolescence. *Applied Developmental Science, 8*, 7–16.

Dumas, J. E., & Nissley-Tsiopinis, J. (2006). Parental global religiousness, sanctification of parenting, and positive and negative religious coping as predictors of parental and child functioning. *The International Journal for the Psychology of Religion, 16*, 289–310.

Flor, D. L., & Knapp, N. F. (2001). Transmission and transaction: Predicting adolescents' internalization of parental religious values. *Journal of Family Psychology, 15*, 627–645.

Fowler, J. (1981). *Stages of faith*. San Francisco: Jossey-Bass.

Francis, L. J., & Brown, L. B. (1990). The predisposition to pray: A study of the social influence on the predisposition to pray among eleven-year-old children in England. *Journal of Empirical Theology, 3*, 23–34.

Furrow, J. L., King, P. E., & White, K. (2004). Religion and positive youth development: Identity, meaning, and prosocial concerns. *Applied Developmental Science, 8*, 17–26.

Gershoff, E. T., Miller, P. C., & Holden, G. W. (1999). Parenting influences from the pulpit: Religious affiliation as a determinant of corporal punishment. *Journal of Family Psychology, 13*, 307–320.

Gottlieb, A. (2006). Non-Western approaches to spiritual development among infants and young children: A case study from West Africa. In E. C. Roehlkepartain, P. E. King, L. Wagener, & P. L. Benson (Eds.), *The handbook of spiritual development in childhood and adolescence* (pp. 150–162). Thousand Oaks, CA: Sage.

Granqvist, P., & Dickie, J. (2006). Attachment and spiritual development in childhood and adolescence. In E. C. Roehlkepartain, P. E. King, L. Wagener, & P. L. Benson (Eds.), *The handbook of spiritual development in childhood and adolescence* (pp. 197–210). Thousand Oaks, CA: Sage.

Gunnoe, M. L., & Moore, K. A. (2002). Predictors of religiosity among youth aged 17–22: A longitudinal study of the National Survey of Children. *Journal for the Scientific Study of Religion, 41*, 613–622.

Harris, P. L., & Koenig, M. A. (2006). Truth in testimony: How children learn about science and religion. *Child Development, 77*, 505–524.

Hay, D., & Nye, R. (1998). *The spirit in the child*. London: Fount.

Hay, D., Reich, K. H., & Utsch, M. (2006). Spiritual development: Intersections and divergence with religious development. In E. C. Roehlkepartain, P. E. King, L. Wagener, & P. L. Benson (Eds.), *The handbook of spiritual development in childhood and adolescence* (pp. 46–59). Thousand Oaks, CA: Sage.

Johnson, C. N., & Boyatzis, C. J. (2006). Cognitive-cultural foundations of spiritual development. In E. C. Roehlkepartain, P. E. King, L. Wagener, & P. L. Benson (Eds.), *The handbook of spiritual development in childhood and adolescence* (pp. 211–223). Thousand Oaks, CA: Sage.

Kerestes, M., Youniss, J., & Metz, E. (2004). Longitudinal patterns of religious perspectives and civic integration. *Applied Developmental Science, 8*, 39–46.

Kim, J., McCullough, M. E., & Cicchetti, D. (2009). Parents' and children's religiosity and child behavioral adjustment among maltreated and non-maltreated children. *Journal of Child and Family Studies, 18*, 594–605.

King, P. E., & Boyatzis, C. J. (2004). Exploring adolescent religious and spiritual development: Current and future theoretical and empirical perspectives. *Applied Developmental Science, 8*, 2–6.

Kuczynski, L. (2003). Beyond bidirectionality: Bilateral conceptual frameworks for understanding dynamics in parent-child relations. In L. Kuczynski (Ed.), *Handbook of dynamics in parent-child relations* (pp. 3–24). Thousand Oaks, CA: Sage.

Lerner, R. M., Dowling, E. M., & Anderson, P. M. (2003). Positive youth development: Thriving as a basis of personhood and civil society. *Applied Developmental Science, 7*, 172–180.

Mahoney, A., Pargament, K. I., Swank, A., & Tarakeshwar, N. (2001). Religion in the home in the 1980s and 90s: A meta-analytic review and conceptual analysis of religion. *Journal of Family Psychology, 15*, 559–596.

Mahoney, A., & Tarakeshwar, N. (2005). Religion's role in marriage and parenting in daily life and during family crises. In R. F. Paloutzian & C. L. Park (Eds.), *Handbook of the psychology of religion and spirituality* (pp. 177–198). New York: The Guilford Press.

Mattis, J. S., Ahluwalia, M. K., Cowie, S-A. E., & Kirkland-Harris, A. M. (2006). Ethnicity, culture, and spiritual development. In E. C. Roehlkepartain, P. E. King, L. Wagener, & P. L. Benson (Eds.), *The handbook of spiritual development in childhood and adolescence* (pp. 283–296). Thousand Oaks, CA: Sage.

Milevsky, A., & Levitt, M. J. (2004). Intrinsic and extrinsic religiosity in preadolescence and adolescence: Effect on psychological adjustment. *Mental Health, Religion, and Culture, 7*, 307–321.

Miller, L. (2008, August). *Pedagogical approach to spiritual awareness*. Presidential address to Division 36 (Psychology of

Religion). Presented at the annual meeting of the American Psychological Association, Boston, MA.

Miller, L., & Kelley, B. S. (2005). Relationships of religiosity and spirituality with mental health and psychopathology. In R. Paloutzian & C. L. Park (Eds.), *Handbook of psychology and religion* (pp. 460–478). New York: The Guilford Press.

Milot, A. S., & Ludden, A. B. (2009). The effects of religion and gender on well-being, substance use, and academic engagement among rural adolescents. *Youth and Society, 40*, 403–425.

Murray-Swank, A., Mahoney, A., & Pargament, K. I. (2006). Sanctification of parenting: Links to corporal punishment and parental warmth among Biblically conservative and liberal mothers. *The International Journal for the Psychology of Religion, 16*, 271–288.

Oser, F., Scarlett, G. W., & Bucher, A. (2006). Religious and spiritual development throughout the life span. In W. Damon & R. M. Lerner (Eds.), *Handbook of child psychology: Vol. 1: Theoretical models of development* (6th ed., pp. 942–997). New York: Wiley.

Pargament, K. I., & Mahoney, A. (Eds.). (2005). Sanctification: Seeing life through a sacred lens [Special issue]. *The International Journal for the Psychology of Religion, 15*(3).

Pearce, L. D., & Haynie, D. L. (2004). Intergenerational religious dynamics and adolescent delinquency. *Social Forces, 82*, 1553–1572.

Petts, R. J., & Knoester, C. (2007). Parents' religious heterogamy and children's well-being. *Journal for the Scientific Study of Religion, 46*, 373–389

Piedmont, R. L. (2005). The role of personality in understanding religious and spiritual constructs. In R. Paloutzian & C. L. Park (Eds.), *Handbook of the psychology of religion and spirituality* (pp. 253–273). New York: The Guilford Press.

Regnerus, M. D. (2003). Religion and positive adolescent outcomes: A review of research and theory. *Review of Religious Research, 44*, 394–413.

Regnerus, M. D., & Elder, G. H., Jr. (2003). Staying on track in school: Religious influences in high- and low-risk settings. *Journal for the Scientific Study of Religion, 42*, 633–649.

Regnerus, M. D., Smith, C., & Smith, B. (2004). Social context in the development of adolescent religiosity. *Applied Developmental Science, 8*, 27–38.

Rew, L., Wong, Y. J., & Sternglanz, R. W. (2004). The relationship between prayer, health behaviors, and protective resources in school-age children. *Issues in Comprehensive Pediatric Nursing, 27*, 245–255.

Robbins, M., & Francis, L. J. (2005). Purpose in life and prayer among Catholic and Protestant adolescents in Northern Ireland. *Journal of Research on Christian Education, 14*, 73–93.

Roehlkepartain, E. C., Benson, P. L., King, P. E., & Wagener, L. (2006). Spiritual development in childhood and adolescence: Moving to the scientific mainstream. In E. C. Roehlkepartain, P. E. King, L. Wagener, & P. L. Benson (Eds.), *The handbook of spiritual development in childhood and adolescence* (pp. 1–15). Thousand Oaks, CA: Sage.

Roehlkepartain, E. C., King, P. E., Wagener, L., & Benson, P. L. (Eds.). (2006). *The handbook of spiritual development in childhood and adolescence*. Thousand Oaks, CA: Sage.

Scarlett, G. (2006). Toward a developmental analysis of religious and spiritual development. In E. C. Roehlkepartain, P. E. King, L. Wagener, & P. L. Benson (Eds.), *The handbook of spiritual development in childhood and adolescence* (pp. 21–33). Thousand Oaks, CA: Sage.

Schwartz, K. D. (2006). Transformation in parent and friend faith support predicting adolescents' religious faith. *The International Journal for the Psychology of Religion, 16*, 311–326.

Silberman, I. (2003). Spiritual role modeling: The teaching of meaning systems. *The International Journal for the Psychology of Religion, 13*, 175–195.

Sinats, P., Scott, D. G., McFerran, S., Hittos, M., Cragg, C., Leblanc, T., & Brooks, D. (2005). Writing ourselves into being: Writing as spiritual self-care for adolescent girls. Part one. *International Journal of Children's Spirituality, 10*, 17–29.

Smith, C. (2005). *Soul searching: The religious and spiritual lives of American teenagers*. New York: Oxford University Press.

Smith, C., Faris, R., Denton, M. L., & Regnerus, M. (2003). Mapping American adolescent subjective religiosity and attitudes of alienation toward religion: A research report. *Sociology of Religion, 64*, 111–133.

Smith, W. C. (1991). *The meaning and end of religion*. Minneapolis, MN: Fortress Press.

Stokes, C. E., & Regnerus, M. D. (2009). When faith divides family: Religious discord and adolescent reports of parent–child relations. *Social Science Research, 38*, 155–167.

Tirri, K., Tallent-Runnels, M. K., & Nokelainen, P. (2005). A cross-cultural study of pre-adolescents' moral, religious and spiritual questions. *British Journal of Religious Education, 27*, 207–214.

Van Dyke, C. J., & Elias, M. J. (2008). How expressions of forgiveness, purpose, and religiosity relate to emotional intelligence and self-concept in urban fifth-grade students. *American Journal of Orthopsychiatry, 78*, 481–393.

Verkuyten, M., & Thijs, J. (2010). Religious group relations among Christian, Muslim and nonreligious early adolescents in the Netherlands. *The Journal of Early Adolescence, 30*, 27–49

Volling, B. L., Mahoney, A., & Rauer, A. J. (2009). Sanctification of parenting, moral socialization, and young children's conscience development. *Psychology of Religion and Spirituality, 1*, 53–68.

Vygotsky, L. S. (1978). *Mind in society*. Cambridge, MA: Harvard University Press.

Wagener, L. M., Furrow, J. L., King, P. E., Leffert, N., & Benson, P. (2003). Religion and developmental resources. *Review of Religious Research, 44*, 271–284.

Wagener, L. M., & Maloney, H. N. (2006). Spiritual and religious pathology in childhood and adolescence. In E. Roehlkepartain, P. E. King, L. Wagener, & P. L. Benson (Eds.), *The handbook of spiritual development in childhood and adolescence* (pp. 137–149). Thousand Oaks, CA: Sage.

Westerhoff, J. W., III. (2000). *Will our children have faith?* (Rev. ed.). Toronto: Anglican Book Centre.

Wong, Y. J., Rew, L., & Slaikeu, K. D. (2006). A systematic review of recent research on adolescent religiosity/spirituality and mental health. *Issues in Mental Health Nursing, 27*, 161–183.

Yust, K-M., Johnson, A. N., Sasso, S. E., & Roehlkepartain, E. C. (Eds.). (2006). *Nurturing child and adolescent spirituality*. New York: Rowman & Littlefield.

Zinnbauer, B., & Pargament, K. I. (2005). Religiousness and spirituality. In R. F. Paloutzian & C. L. Park (Eds.), *The handbook of the psychology of religion* (pp. 21–42). New York: The Guilford Press.

Questions Left Unaddressed by Religious Familism: Is Spirituality Relevant to Nontraditional Families?

Annette Mahoney *and* Elizabeth J. Krumrei

Abstract

Given the growing pluralism in family structures, this chapter highlights the role of religion and spirituality in the formation and maintenance of diverse types of families. We outline commonalities and differences that exist among major world religions about forming and maintaining family relationships. Consistent with the predominant conceptual model called *religious familism*, most research on faith and family life focuses on traditional families (i.e., married heterosexual couples with biological children). We summarize findings on these families that largely assess spirituality indirectly via markers of religious participation (e.g., religious affiliation, attendance, salience). We then review in more detail research on spirituality within nontraditional families, focusing on families comprised of cohabiting couples, same-sex couples, and single parenthood because these nontraditional families have received the most, albeit limited, empirical attention. Given evidence of the interdependence of religion and traditional family forms, research is needed to determine the relevance of spirituality for nontraditional families.

Key Words: cohabitation, couples, homosexuality, family, marriage, parenting, religion, same-sex couples, spirituality

Introduction

The idealized vision of *family* in mid-20th century America consisted of an employed father married to a stay-at-home mother caring for the couple's biological children (described by Smith, 1993, as the standard North American family). Demographically, the prevalence of this *traditional* family formation peaked in the United States in the 1950s at 43% of all households (Edgell, 2006), since which time there has been growing pluralism in family structures. For example, whereas the 1960s saw 91% of American minors living with married, biological parents, this rate dropped to 60% of minors by 2009, with 26% of minors living with single parents, 6% with married stepparents, and 8% with cohabiting couples or nonparental caregivers (US Census Bureau, 2009). Furthermore, 62% of US women in the late 1990s reported they had cohabited with a partner prior to

marriage (Kennedy & Bumpass, 2008), and up to 65% of children are expected to spend part of their childhood living with an unmarried couple due to nonmarital births among cohabiting couples or nonmarital unions following divorce (Bumpass & Lu, 2000). Obviously, a traditional family life cycle of heterosexuals getting married prior to cohabitation and first-time pregnancy, with the union ending by death, is declining in the United States.

The traditional family formation emerged in America partly under the influence of Christianity (Edgell, 2006; Ruether, 2000). Sociological discussion about religion and family often focuses on ways these two institutions have been interdependent. The term *religious familism* refers to the ideology that the family is the central unit of social order and should be governed by certain religious imperatives (Edgell, 2006; Edgell & Docka, 2007; Wilcox,

2004). Religious familism in the United States has valued certain forms of the family above others, emphasizing stable heterosexual marriages that produce children and exclude nonmarital sex (Edgell & Docka, 2007). Perhaps as a result, little research has examined the role of religion and spirituality within nontraditional families, leaving many unanswered questions about what influence, if any, spirituality plays within the growing number of these families.

In this chapter, we spotlight a central paradox regarding spirituality and family life. Namely, considerable theological dissension exists within and across religious subcultures about moral norms regarding family structure, whereas consensus tends to exist across religions about how family members should act to maintain family relationships after they are formed. In exploring this distinction between family structure and family process when it comes to commonalities and differences in major world religions, we draw on the conceptual framework of *relational spirituality* (Mahoney, 2010). The vast majority of empirical research on religion and family has focused on traditional families, and we briefly summarize relevant findings. In addition, we highlight the largely unstudied possibility that people in nontraditional families may also find spirituality relevant to their home life. For example, one qualitative study with same-sex couples from the southern United States found that nearly all viewed their union as having spiritual significance and meaning (Rostosky, Riggle, Brodnicki, & Olson, 2008), a finding consistent with the high religious attendance and prayer rates of US sexual minorities (Sherkat, 2002). To facilitate more research on diverse families, we showcase findings and unaddressed questions about spirituality in the formation and maintenance of relationships among three types of nontraditional families that have received the most, albeit limited, empirical attention: cohabitating heterosexual couples, same-sex couples, and single parents.

Conceptual Issues in the Scientific Study of the Interface of Family and Religion-Spirituality
Conceptualizing Family
The traditional family model in Western societies has been facilitated through a wide range of institutional, legal, and economic arrangements, not the least of which has been its legitimization by religious authority (Edgell & Docka, 2007). Nevertheless, diversity in family forms has existed historically and globally (Stacey, 1997). As Abma and Martinez

(2006) pointed out, until recently those who lived outside of the normative rules to create family systems did so because of external circumstances, such as a ban on marriage for those without property. However, in many modern industrialized societies, it is increasingly unclear what is the exception and what is the rule regarding the boundaries that define a family. The normative parameters have become complex as individuals functionally take on marital or parental roles for brief or indefinite periods in absence of legal or biological ties. One could ask whether family includes only biological or legally related people, or extends to cohabiting (same or opposite gendered) partners, their (biological or otherwise) children, additional caretakers of the children, and so forth.

Martin (1998) posed several premises for expanding the standard family model, including that family not be defined on the basis of the biological relationship between members, the number of households, the number of parents, the gender of the parents, or the sexual orientation of the parents and children. Rather, she proposed an alternative model where family be defined based of the functionality and psychology of the family unit. As an example, parents in this model are defined as those who are committed to raising a child, regardless of their biological relationship to the child, their legal rights and responsibilities, the number of parents present, and whether the parents have sexual relationships with one another. In this chapter we examine how religion and spirituality relate to some diverse family structures that fall within such an expanded model of family.

Conceptualizing Religion and Spirituality
Ambiguity surrounding the demarcation of *family* is akin to the tensions surrounding the boundaries of *religion* versus *spirituality*. These two domains are increasingly polarized in popular culture and social science literature (Zinnbauer & Pargament, 1999). Being religious tends to be portrayed as membership in an organized religious group; adherence to institutional doctrine, worship, or rituals; and external social control by religious authority. Being spiritual is often depicted as involving a personal connection to the sacred; a private search for enlightenment, purpose, meaning, or virtues; and internal spiritual motivation. Yet 65% of Americans describe themselves as "spiritual and religious," with another 15% to 20% claiming to be "spiritual but not religious," and 5% to 10% saying they are "religious but not spiritual" (Marler & Hadaway, 2002).

Thus, in studying the role of spirituality in family functioning, researchers are challenged to develop conceptual models that recognize the growing destitutionalization of spirituality while recognizing that participation in organized religion is a major pathway most people use to foster their spirituality.

Pragmatically, when it comes to empirical findings on the intersection of faith and family, abstract theoretical debates over the definitions of religion versus spirituality are essentially moot because researchers have relied so heavily on single items to tap these overlapping domains. About 75% to 85% of peer-reviewed, published studies conducted in the past 30 years assess whether a given family member endorses affiliates with a particular religious tradition, attends religious services, or says that religion or spirituality is personally important (Mahoney, 2010; Mahoney, Pargament, Swank, & Tarakeshwar, 2001). In short, most controlled research assesses a given family member's overall engagement in public (e.g., affiliation, attendance rates) or private (e.g., frequency of prayer) forms of religiousness. Because of the global nature of these items, it is difficult, if not impossible, to identify unique spiritual beliefs or practices found within or outside of organized religion that could impact family relationships.

Relational Spirituality as a Conceptual Lens: Focus on Formation and Maintenance of Diverse Family Relationships

Mahoney (2010;in press) recently developed a conceptual framework called *relational spirituality* to delineate the multifaceted and complex interface of spirituality and family life, and to highlight unique and specific psychospiritual processes that could facilitate or undermine relationship functioning in both traditional and nontraditional families (Mahoney, 2010; in press). In this framework, "spirituality" is defined as the "search for the sacred" (Pargament & Mahoney, 2002), a definition that encompasses the formation, maintenance, and transformation of one's connection to the sacred. The sacred includes concepts of God, the divine, and the transcendent and extends to virtually any aspect of life that can become part of the sacred via its association with, or representation of, divinity (Mahoney, Pargament, & Hernandez, 2010). Spirituality includes unconventional pathways people take outside of institutional religion in their search for the sacred and well-worn pathways pursued within institutional religious contexts. Parallel

to the search for the sacred, individuals also search for family relationships in three interactive stages over time: (a) formation, which refers to creating and structuring a familial bond; (b) maintenance, which refers to sustaining the quality and stability of chosen relationships; and (c) transformation, which refers to coping with family or life stressors that call for fundamental changes in the structure or processes of family relationships. The integration of the searches for the sacred and relationships constitutes *relational spirituality*.

This chapter elaborates the portion of Mahoney's relational spirituality framework that addresses the role of spirituality in structuring and maintaining diverse types of family forms. Readers are referred elsewhere for an elaboration of numerous in-depth psychospiritual processes that may operate within families (Mahoney, in press). In particular, we focus here on the fact that widespread controversies in public discourse about family structures seem to reflect underlying theological disputes over what type of family is spiritually legitimate and optimal (e.g., heterosexual marriage with biological children versus same-sex marriages and parenthood with nonmarital births). However, diverse faith communities tend to promote similar virtues for how family members should act to sustain healthy family relationships as signs of relationship success (e.g., commitment, sacrifice, love). Before proceeding to review empirical findings, we offer illustrations of the divergent and overlapping theological positions on the formation and maintenance, respectively, of traditional and nontraditional families.

Theological Perspectives on the Formation and Maintenance of Family Relationships

It is beyond the scope of this chapter to delineate all of the many beliefs and practices pertaining to family life within major world religions (see Browning & Clairmont, 2007; Onedera, 2008). Furthermore, doctrinal and ritual variations exist within each religion that stem from differences in regional and sectarian religious traditions, sociocultural influences, interpretation of sacred texts, and personal preferences. Thus, we have chosen to highlight general traditional and progressive theological stances advocated within various world religions about (1) what kinds of family relationships should be formed and (2) how family members should treat each other to maintain their relationships. Perhaps increased attention to theological orientations about these two distinctive normative questions will spark more scientific research on diverse types of families.

Formation of Family Relationships

PREDOMINANT THEOLOGICAL VIEW INFLUENCING SOCIAL SCIENCE RESEARCH

Most empirical research on faith and family has overwhelmingly involved national or community samples from the United States (Mahoney, 2010; Mahoney et al., 2001) and thus participants who are predominately affiliated with a Christian denomination. For example, 70% to 75% of parents of US adolescents describe themselves as Catholic or Protestant, with 10% or 15% endorsing "none" for affiliation (Smith, 2005). It is understandable therefore that much of the interpretation about empirical links between global markers of religious involvement and family functioning within social science literature relies on religious familism as a conceptual framework since mainline Protestantism has been a dominating historical influence on discourse about family life in American culture (Ruether, 2000). To reiterate, religious familism refers to the ideology that the family should be governed by certain religious positions on family life emphasized by mainline religions, particularly by conservative branches of American Protestantism (Edgell, 2003, 2006; Wilcox, 2004). For example, in conservative Christianity, marriage is considered to be an explicit expression for the commitment of a man and woman to one another that provides the necessary structure for sexual intimacy and childbearing, resulting in nonmarital sex, same-sex marriage, cohabitation, single parenthood, and stepfamilies being morally undesirable (Zink, 2008). In sum, religious familism reflects doctrines rooted in traditional Christianity that idealize and reinforce mid-20th-century, middle-class views of "the good family," consisting of married heterosexuals with biological children (Edgell, 2003, 2006; Edgell & Docka, 2007).

The conceptual lens of religious familism is consistent with predominant theological positions in Islam and Judaism that uphold and defend the biological nuclear family as the spiritual ideal for a family structure. For example, within conservative and orthodox Judiasm, marriage followed by procreation mirrors the very nature of God (Onedera, 2008; Wertheimer, 2007). In Islam, marriage is also considered to be inherently religious (Al-Jibaly, 2000) and a religious obligation to complete one's faith (Altareb, 2008). Because marriage is considered the only legitimate way for men and women to be alone together, alternative family formations, such as cohabitation and same-sex unions, are ruled out as viable options within Islam (Altareb, 2008). Thus, most monotheistic traditions argue that a family headed by a married heterosexual pair is the ideal context to bear and raise human beings (Dorff, 2008).

ALTERNATIVE THEOLOGICAL VIEWS

There are other common theological models that have had less influence on social science research. In Confucianism, for example, family is defined not as a nuclear unit but as an extended unit that often involves four generations living together (Meyer, 2007). Similarly, a traditional Hindu family consists of multiple generations living in the same household with a common kitchen and jointly owning property (Meyer, 2007; Williams, 2007). Both Hinduism and Confucianism value family identity above self-identity and individual needs (Meyer, 2007; Williams, 2007). In fact, the Hindu concepts of self and family are integral rather than separate concepts. Williams (2007) has pointed out that immigrants with other religions have begun to raise anew the question of defining the family in American society.

Parallel to the increased acceptance of diverse family structures during the 20th century in American society generally (Jensen, 2006; Stacey, 1997), theological justifications emerged within progressive segments of Christianity that rejected "natural law" rooted in biological ties as the guiding principle to demarcate the boundaries of family and instead defended nontraditional family forms, such as same-sex marriages, childless marriages, and single or adoptive parenthood (Ruether, 2000). For example, many liberal Protestants affirm same-sex relationships and honor same-sex covenants as vehicles of God's creation and grace in a similar fashion as opposite-sex marriage (Cook, 2008). Ruether (2000) provides an insightful description of recent shifts in ideologies about the family in progressive segments of the Christian community set within her highly recommended analysis of the ever-changing history of diverse Christian perspectives on family life since 1st-century Christianity.

Similar shifts can be observed in some Jewish groups within the United States. For example, changing social patterns within the Jewish community in America have prompted a reconsideration of fundamental assumptions concerning the composition of the Jewish family with marriage as the ideal (Wertheimer, 2007). The Jewish community currently includes many singles, single parents, blended families, and homosexual families resulting in contemporary Jews stretching Jewish norms to apply to these new circumstances (Dorff, 2008). This is made clear in the Central Conference of American Rabbis' statement on human sexuality (1998):

> In our age, the traditional notion of family as being two parents and children (and perhaps older generations) living in the same household is in the process of being redefined. Men and women of various ages living together, singles, gay and lesbian couples, single-parent households, etc., may be understood as families in the wider, if not traditional sense. "Family" also has multiple meanings in an age of increasingly complex biotechnology and choice.

This reveals a shift in some theologians' views of the preference for biological parameters to define the structure of family, but not necessarily the value of family systems. The statement emphasizes that "[t]he importance of family, whether biologically or relationally based, remains the foundation of meaningful human existence." Reform Judaism continues to emphasize the family as the primary unit of intimacy grounded in relational processes of respect, trust, and love.

In sum, the conceptual lens of religious familism implies that religion's primary, perhaps exclusive, function for family life is to shore up the formation of traditional nuclear family structures. Here the word *religion* implicitly refers to traditional monotheistic religions. Yet reliance on this theological lens to guide scientific research ignores many questions about faith for diverse families. Does religion impact the formation of families for those involved in religious groups or individuals who theologically affirm nontraditional family structures? What, if any, spiritual beliefs or practices impact choices to form nontraditional families, particularly given that poor or working-class Caucasians disproportionally belong to these families and are most likely to feel excluded or judged by ethnically similar religious congregations (Edgell, 2006)? Will religion become increasing irrelevant to modern families as biologically intact, nuclear families increasingly decrease in number? With these questions in mind, we turn to theological rationales regarding the maintenance of the family relationships.

Maintenance of Family Relationships

In contrast to the marked differences within and across religious traditions on the formation of family relationships, we have been struck by the degree of consensus regarding theological views on what people should do to sustain the family relationships that they do form. Because of this, we focus our discussion in this section on broad theological consensuses on ideal ways to sustain couple and parent–child relationships.

MARRIAGE-COUPLES' RELATIONSHIPS

Religious wedding ceremonies not only signify the formation of couples' relationships but also offer windows into the virtues that couples promise to live out to fulfill the sacred nature of their bond. Thematically, the following virtues are widely heralded on religious grounds as means that couples should use to sustain their relationships across the conservative to progressive spectrum within Christianity, Judaism, Islam, Hinduism, and Confucianism traditions: compassionate love, self-sacrifice, commitment, respect, honesty, forgiveness, gratitude, and accountability (Onedera, 2008). It is important to note that although a minority of highly fundamentalist religious subgroups may imply that husbands have religious rights to physically or sexually dominate their wives, the majority of theological voices across major world religions do not endorse domestic violence or sexual aggression within marriage (Onedera, 2008). On the other hand, theological consensus places a high premium on sexual monogamy within marriage as well as same-sex relationships. Readers are referred elsewhere for a discussion on variations in theological opinions on the gendered roles that men and women should fulfill as spouses or parents (Gallagher, 2003; Hernandez & Mahoney, in press; Mahoney, 2010).

PARENT–CHILD RELATIONSHIPS

Many world religions have religious rituals and prayers to signify the importance of bringing children into the world. These religious practices signal the significance of childrearing in the family and community, and highlight the responsibilities of parents to place their highest priority on facilitating their children's spiritual, moral, psychological, and physical development. Thematically, the following virtues are emphasized for parents across the conservative to progressive spectrum within Christianity, Judaism, Islam, Hinduism, and Confucianism to sustain parent–child relationships: model and dispense love, self-sacrifice, commitment, protectiveness, and an investment of resources to ensure the child's well-being (Onedera, 2008). It is important to realize that although some religious subgroups, such as conservative Christians, emphasize that parents should instill a sense of obedience in children and condone the spanking as a discipline method, leaders of major world religions within Western, industrialized countries do not advocate child physical abuse (Browning & Clairmont, 2007). Furthermore, Christian subcultures that support spanking also emphasize that parents balance this strategy with high levels of involvement, affection, positive parenting techniques, and other effective disciplinary strategies (Bartkowski & Xu, 2000).

Religion and Functioning of Families of Heterosexual Couples: Major Empirical Findings

Forming a Marital Relationship

People across the globe rank religious similarity as an important factor when searching for a spouse, and little has changed in the past 50 years in how much Americans desire a mate with a similar religious affiliation (see Mahoney, 2010 for review). Couples also decide early in their courtship whether (non)religious compatibility matters. That is, the percentage of couples who have the same religious affiliation does not change across the stages of dating, being sexually intimate, cohabiting, or marrying (Blackwell & Lichter, 2004). Conservative Protestants (CP), along with Catholics, Latter Day Saints (LDS), and Jews, are the most likely to marry people with the same affiliation, with 50% to 65% of these believers entering same-faith unions (Sherkat, 2004).

After adults establish an intimate relationship, they make choices about its structure. Religious involvement promotes getting married. Members of CP or LDS families (particularly women) and anyone who views religion as highly important more frequently enter marriage by age 23 (see Mahoney, 2010 for review). Effects of religious affiliation on earlier marriage timing also hold for Catholics and moderate Protestants, whereas Jews, liberal Protestants, and the unaffiliated tend to delay marriage. Religious attendance also encourages marriage following a nonmarital birth (e.g., Wilcox & Wolfinger, 2007) and making the transition from cohabitation into marriage (e.g., Duvander, 1999).

Forming a Parent–Child Relationship

For centuries, religions have encouraged married couples to procreate. Although recent overall female and male fertility rates in the United States have not varied due to affiliation with a predominant religious group or attendance, the personal importance of religion continues to be tied to higher birth rates by women (Mahoney, 2010). Consistent with religious traditions that teach that motherhood should be reserved for marriage, this link is especially strong for women over age 24, who are more likely to be married, and disappears in subsamples of younger women. Furthermore, women who say religion is unimportant are more likely to have unplanned births, especially during adolescence (Hayford & Morgan, 2008), or to remain childless into middle age (Abma & Martinez, 2006). Women's plans to have children are also tied to greater importance of religion in their lives, regardless of how often they attend services of their particular faith tradition. This link holds for women who do or do not hold socially conservative attitudes toward feminism or family life emphasized by some religious groups (Hayford & Morgan, 2008). Overall, women who value their faith are more likely to have children and want to be mothers.

Virtually no peer-reviewed research is available on religion and men's desire to be fathers or their rates of parentage. Researchers, however, have sought to examine whether fathers involved in conservative Protestant churches spend more time than other fathers with their children after they are born, rather than being distant or absent; numerous studies have not found this to be the case for contemporary married men (see Mahoney, 2010 for more details). On the other hand, across religious denominations, married fathers who attend religious services more often are more likely to spend time playing with their biological children (Mahoney, 2010). These findings imply that men who are more intensively involved in the faith tradition of their choice may be more motivated to invest time in creating a father–child bond.

Maintenance of Family Relationships by Married Couples

MAINTAINING THE QUALITY OF MARITAL RELATIONSHIPS

Over the past three decades, multiple studies have found that higher levels of general religiousness of one or both spouses has been related to greater marital satisfaction (e.g., Clements, Stanley, & Markman, 2004; Wilcox & Wolfinger, 2008; Wolfinger & Wilcox, 2008), less marital conflict (e.g., Curtis & Ellison, 2002) and physical aggression (e.g., Ellison & Anderson, 2001), and lower risk of divorce (e.g., Brown, Orbuch, & Bauermeister, 2008). See Mahoney et al. (2001) and Mahoney (2010) for further elaboration of this growing body of work.

MAINTAINING THE QUALITY OF PARENT–CHILD RELATIONSHIPS

With regard to parent–child relationships, higher levels of religious activity by parents and adolescents predicts better parent–youth relationship quality (e.g., Bartkowski & Xu, 2000), greater parental affection (e.g., Wilcox, 1998), more positive discipline practices (e.g., Volling, Mahoney, & Rauer, 2009), and lower prevalence of child physical abuse (e.g., Brown, Cohen, Johnson, & Salzinger, 1998). See Mahoney et al. (2001) and Mahoney (2010) for an exhaustive review of these and related findings.

NUANCES REGARDING FINDING ABOUT FAMILY AND FAITH

As the representative findings cited earlier indicate, higher general religiousness tends to predict better quality in family relationships. Yet the findings are not as simple as they may seem. It is important to consider several nuances. One issue to consider is not merely individual family members' religiousness but also similarities between family members when it comes to religion. For example, spousal similarity in attendance tends to be more strongly linked to marital satisfaction and stability in national surveys than just one spouse's attendance (Myers, 2006). Furthermore, marked discrepancies among couples regarding religious issues are rare, but they are linked more to arguing about money and the division of household labor (Curtis & Ellison, 2002) and to higher divorce rates (Vaaler, Ellison, & Powers, 2009). The parallel has also been found among parent–child relationships. For example, religious dissimilarity between parents and adolescents is associated with more relational discord and distance (Stokes & Regnerus, 2009).

An even more important issue involves uncovering conceptually what it is about religion that makes a difference in family life. Constructs that focus on spiritual cognitions or behaviors specifically about family relationships yield greater insight than nonspecific items about a given family member's religiousness (e.g., affiliation, attendance, general salience of religion). For instance, studies show that couples who view their marriage as sacred and connected to God report greater marital quality and commitment (e.g., Ellison, Henderson, Glenn, & Harkrider, 2011; Mahoney et al., 1999) and less risk of infidelity (Fincham, Lambert, & Beach, 2010). Furthermore, studies such as these, which directly assess the perceived spiritual nature of marriage (i.e., sanctification) yield more robust and consistent linkages than general markers of personal religiousness. Religious traditions also offer families unique ways to interact behaviorally as dyads or family units that may facilitate relationship quality (Mahoney, 2010, in press). For example, deep spiritual dialogs

between college students and their mothers predict greater collaboration in dealing with disagreements, even after controlling for discussion of other sensitive topics (Brelsford & Mahoney, 2008). The meaning attributed to shared spiritual activities also appears to matter. For example, marital satisfaction is tied more closely to couple's perceived meaning of shared spiritual rituals than their mere frequency (Fiese & Tomcho, 2001; Marks, 2004).

Another issue to recognize is that while some beliefs and behaviors rooted in religion may help family relationships, other manifestations of religion may be harmful. For example, whereas religious service attendance has generally been tied to lower self-reported extramarital sex in national surveys (e.g., Burdette, Ellison, Sherkat, & Gore 2007), the odds of an affair paradoxically increase for high attenders who do not feel close to God and for low attenders who do feel close to God (Atkins & Kessel, 2008). Thus, religion may pose a risk factor if dissonance exists between public and private forms of spirituality. In addition, family members can turn to religion in ways that escalate rather than reduce their conflicts. For example, parents and college students who triangulate God into the middle of their conflicts in destructive ways seem to be worse off than those who leave God out of the dispute entirely (Brelsford & Mahoney, 2009). Similarly, although family prayer is tied to better child adjustment, open marital conflict about religious issues is related to poorer child adjustment (Bartkowski, Xu, & Levin, 2008). Overall, religion offers protective or risk factors for families of married couples with children, depending on the nature of the religious beliefs or behavior under investigation; for greater elaboration, see Mahoney (2010) and Mahoney, in press

Religion and the Functioning of Nontraditional Families

Little research has addressed the role of religion and spirituality for nontraditional families (Mahoney, 2010; in press). Nearly all studies either exclude diverse family structures or occasionally combine them with traditional families within their samples (e.g., studies that combine married and cohabiting couples). Thus, research is only just emerging on whether religion and spirituality shape the formation or maintenance of nontraditional adult unions and parent–children relationships. We now examine peer-reviewed findings published in journals on the role of religion in family functioning among diverse family structures and highlight questions that await exploration.

Same-Sex Unions: Forming and Maintaining

FORMING

In the 1991–2000 General Social Surveys, 4.3% of men and 3.1% of women reported that they had had same-sex sexual partners during the preceding 5 years, percentages larger than those identifying as "other" races, Episcopalians, or Jews (Sherkat, 2002). National surveys also highlight the relatively high levels of public and private religiousness by sexual minorities (Sherkat, 2002). For example, although gays, lesbians, and bisexual individuals tend to hold less orthodox views of the Bible and are more likely to be apostates than heterosexuals, gay men report similar rates of religious attendance and prayer as heterosexual men (Sherkat, 2002). Furthermore, although male bisexuals engage in the lowest levels of public religious activity compared to other gender/sexuality combinations, over 60% believe the Bible is divinely inspired. Despite the relevance of religion and spirituality generally to the lives of homosexuals, however, we know little about whether religion or spirituality influences the formation of same-sex unions. In terms of mate selection, one study based on a recent Internet survey (N = 218,195) found that homosexual participants assigned less importance to religious similarity when seeking a partner than heterosexual participants (Lippa, 2007).

Given that legal marriage has only very recently become an option for same-sex couples in a few American states, research on links between religion or spirituality and the transition from cohabitation to marriage is, not surprisingly, unavailable. One study suggests that higher levels of spirituality may motivate same-sex couples to engage in symbolic and legal actions to form a partnership that would be more difficult to dissolve. Namely, Oswald, Goldberg, Kuvalanka, and Clausell (2008) examined 150 lesbians and gay men in same-sex relationships and found that the importance of religion in their daily life predicted whether they had engaged in a formal commitment ceremony with their partner. Every unit increase in the importance of religious beliefs increased the odds of having had a commitment ceremony 1.6 times, even after controlling gender and relationship duration. Individuals were also more likely to have established legal ties with their partner, such as owning joint property, establishing a will or power of attorney, registering as domestic partners, or entering into civil marriage, if they were involved in a supportive spiritual community.

Various case studies and qualitative interviews also suggest that same-sex couples draw on religious beliefs in their conceptualization of what it means to marry or be partners (McQueeney, 2003), rely on religion to find meaning in their relationship commitment (Lewin, 1998), and use religion to sanctify and attribute spiritual significance to their relationships (Rostosky, Riggle, et al., 2008; Suter, Bergen, Daas, & Durham, 2006). These initial studies raise the fascinating, but unresearched, possibility that a major reason why some same-sex couples fight for the right to get formally married is because they want their union to be recognized by themselves and society as having the same degree of spiritual legitimacy and symbolic meaning as heterosexual unions consecrated via weddings. Notably, alternative options to marriage are multiplying in modern societies to structure adult partnerships. Thus, the implicit and explicit spiritual meaning that wedding rituals bestow upon a union, usually witnessed by friends and family with similar spiritual values (liberal or conservative), may become the most distinctive factor that discriminates "marriage" from adult partnerships that are privately cemented between the pair via legal or economic contracts. Perhaps future research will help determine whether forming a union within a spiritual context helps sustain the relationship beyond the impact of other factors.

MAINTAINING

Descriptively speaking, about half of same-sex partners are religiously similar to each other, and one study by Rostosky, Otis, Riggle, Kelly, and Brodnicki (2008) examined whether this factor is tied to relationship quality. These researchers administered various single-item measures regarding religious affiliation and frequency of public and private religious activities and an index of intrinsic religiosity to a community sample of 90 same-sex couples. They found that 53% of the couples were similar in their religious affiliation (or nonaffiliation); 65% in frequency of religious attendance (whether this was low, moderate, or high); 54% in frequency of private religious activities; and 47% in intrinsic religiosity index score. Yet, unlike findings with heterosexual married couples, similarity in religious attendance or activities was not linked to the same-sex couples' relationship satisfaction. On the other hand, being more similar in intrinsic religiosity (i.e., depth and salience of internal religiousness) was correlated with greater relationship satisfaction. Thus, sharing personal religious and spiritual values covaries with same-sex couples' relationship satisfaction.

Rostosky, Otis et al. (2008) also conducted interviews with 40 of the 90 couples. Although the conversational prompts did not specifically ask about religion, 45% of the couples spontaneously brought up religion as pertaining to their relationships. Relevant themes included how religion had functioned as either a challenge or source of support in their relationship, how they negotiated retaining versus abandoning public religious involvement, and how they crafted meaningful personal and private religiousness. Rostosky, Riggle et al. (2008) also conducted qualitative interviews with 14 same-sex couples that revealed that the couples used religious and spiritual values to understand and undergird their relationships. Overall, Rostosky and colleagues' ground-breaking studies suggests that spirituality is an important resource for many same-sex couples who often engaged in spiritual activities together and tried to negotiate intracouple differences in religious expression in ways that met the needs of both partners.

One other study we located conducted among adolescents suggests that religion can be a protective factor against partner physical aggression among same-sex couples (Halpern, Young, Waller, Martin, & Kupper, 2004). Specifically, according to US national survey data, among 117 males and females aged 12–21 years who reported exclusively same-sex romantic or sexual relationships in the previous 18 months, participants who said that religion was important to them were at lower risk for violence in the relationship than those who did not view religion as important. Of course, as is the case with heterosexual couples, religious differences among homosexual couples could potentially also add conflict in the relationship. Kaufman and Raphael (1996) offer illustrative depictions of ways that individuals within a same-sex union are likely to differ with regard to their needs to express the spiritual dimension of life; for example, they may come from different religious traditions and have different levels of religious observance and depth of faith. Kaufman and Raphael (1996) also usefully describe how some same-sex partners may respond to religious differences by imposing their views on their partner or by disparaging the partner's preferences, which, in turn, can intensify conflict.

Overall, as is empirically true for married heterosexuals, initial scholarship suggests that religion can be a potential source of strength and strain for same-couples. We were unable to locate studies on the role that religion plays in decisions same-sex couples make to become biological parents or the quality of their parent–child and coparenting relationships. Thus, much room remains for research on religion and the creation and maintenance of family units headed by same-sex couples.

Cohabiting Heterosexual Unions: Forming and Maintaining

FORMING A COHABITING UNION

Increasingly married couples are cohabiting before they enter marriage. Among recent marriage cohorts (married 1997–2001), 62% of women had cohabited prior to marriage (Kennedy & Bumpass, 2008). Thus, cohabitation is becoming a normative route to marriage. Very recent national data also indicate that women who cohabited with one or more partners prior to marriage are no more likely to divorce than those who did not cohabit (Goodwin, Mosher, & Chandra, 2010). Moreover, couples with formal plans to marry prior to residing together are no more likely to divorce than those who did not cohabit (Goodwin et al., 2010). Thus, research has begun to burgeon on what shapes the decision to form a cohabiting relationship.

We located no peer-reviewed studies that address whether spiritual factors shape men or women's selection of cohabiting partners or tangible commitments to marry prior to cohabiting (e.g., engagement ring, wedding date set). For example, some individuals may reserve cohabitation for partners they view as a "soul mate" or believe God intends for them to marry, or for relationships they perceive as being part of a larger spiritual plan. Research conducted in the 1980s and 1990s documented that global markers of religiousness lowered the likelihood of the practice of cohabitation in that era (e.g., Lehrer, 2004). A recent stellar study indicated that the importance of religion in daily life and attendance, not denomination, are key factors that discourage or delay cohabitation for contemporary young adults. Specifically, in a longitudinal study of American youth, Eggebeen and Dew (2009) found that conservative Protestants cohabited less often as teens than nonaffiliated youth, but after the former group entered adulthood, their cohabitation rates were equal to mainline Protestants or non-Catholic groups, and greater than Catholics. Yet within *all* religious groups, adolescents who were high in attendance and importance of religion cohabited less in the future than those who were low in both factors. Nevertheless, one-third of highly devout youth did chose to cohabit, with mainline and conservative Protestants most likely to marry their partners, whereas Catholics converted their unions into marriage no more often than nonaffiliated youth.

Reciprocally, other research indicates that the decision to cohabit tends to undermine young adults' participation in organized religion over time, especially for those who had been most devout. For example, Stolzenberg, Blair-Loy, and Waite (1995) followed a large sample of men and women from the ages of 22 to 32, and cohabitation reduced church membership much more than marriage increased it. Similarly, national surveys over time with 15,197 adolescents indicated that those who cohabited were most likely as adults to disaffiliate from their religious denomination (Uecker, Regnerus, & Vaaler, 2007). Cohabitors also reported marked decreases over time in service attendance and religious salience, which dropped 44%, compared to each other family formation assessed, including being single, married, or having child(ren) in the household (Uecker et al., 2007). Thornton, Axinn, and Hill (1992) also observed that individuals who cohabited between the ages of 18 and 23 had significantly lower rates of religious participation than those who had not cohabited, even when controlling for initial levels of religious participation at age 18. This study reported that the decision to cohabit led to a greater reduction in religious participation among those belonging to religious groups that are most opposed to sex outside of marriage. Specifically, cohabitation reduced religious participation more for Catholics and fundamental Protestants than for nonfundamentalist Protestants. Thus, the negative effect of cohabitation on religious engagement seems greatest among young adults who originally took religion and spirituality the most seriously.

One possible explanation for such findings is that the cognitive dissonance resulting from inconsistencies between personal choices and traditional religious teachings may tend to push individuals away from organized religion. For instance, those who cohabit may question traditional religious rationales regarding intimate relationships, which may accompany skepticism of religious authority in other areas (Thornton et al., 1992). It is noteworthy that the links between cohabitation and decline in religious attendance in Uecker et al.'s (2007) study remained powerful even after controlling for sexual activity. Thus, a theoretical explanation should also account for the public nature of cohabitation that is unique from the potentially private nature of other religiously nonsanctioned sexual relationships that could equally cause cognitive dissonance. Additional theoretical explanations for the links between cohabitation and decline in religious attendance may include that participation in many religious communities may be less rewarding for cohabiting couples whose family structure falls outside of traditional norms. As a result, cohabiting individuals may experience direct and indirect criticism from fellow believers (Thornton et al., 1992; Uecker et al., 2007). Overt, inferred, and even anticipated disapproval from a religious community may account for the decrease in religious attendance and the increased religious disaffiliation among those who cohabit (Stolzenberg et al., 1995). Overall, people who cohabit, especially if they do not transition into marriage, are mostly likely to withdraw from religious participation; this seems especially likely for people who were most religious to begin with and in religious subcultures most opposed to nonmarital sex. This raises challenges for religious institutions given the growing ubiquity of nonmarital cohabitation across the life span.

MAINTAINING COHABITING UNIONS

Three studies offer initial evidence that spiritual or religious factors could facilitate the quality of nonmarital cohabitation unions. First, Wolfinger and Wilcox (2008) found that among unmarried couples from low-income, urban centers who recently had a baby, higher rates of religious attendance by a father was tied to his higher relationship satisfaction and greater emotional support from the mother. These findings duplicated results with married fathers in this sample. In contrast, mothers' individual religious attendance was not linked to relationship quality for either married or unmarried women. In another study of this same sample of predominantly ethnic minorities (a.k.a. "fragile" families), however, higher religious attendance by *both* partners was tied to both parents reporting higher relationship satisfaction and emotional support toward each other and less conflict over his sexual fidelity (Wilcox & Wolfinger, 2008). Third, Henderson and Ellison (2010) examined several religious factors in a national sample of adults in a cohabiting or steady dating relationship (oversampled of African American and Latinos). They found that individuals who said they (1) shared core religious and spiritual values with their partners and (2) believed God was at the center of their bond were more satisfied with their relationship. The former factor also predicted expectations to marry. Furthermore, these links persisted after controlling for acts of kindness, consideration, and criticism between partners and demographic characteristics.

In contrast, attending services together did not predict satisfaction net of controls.

Taken together, these initial studies suggest that religion and spirituality may offer unmarried heterosexuals resources to sustain positive relationship dynamics, even though the structure of their union falls outside of marriage, the context that religious traditions advocate as optimal for an intimate, sexual relationship. More research is needed to identify specific psychospiritual mechanisms that may account for these findings. Hypothetically, for example, individuals who are able to draw on a felt relationship with God to be appropriately assertive and forgiving in a cohabiting relationship may be better equipped to navigate conflicts and sustain mutual love and good communication. Alternatively, feelings of spiritual ambivalence and guilt in the eyes of God and conflicts with a spiritual community about cohabitation could increase the risk that individuals become excessively dependent on their partners for emotional or financial support, and thus are less able to set limits or exit the relationship if it becomes dysfunctional. These, and other fascinating questions, await investigation (Mahoney, in press).

Single Parenthood: Forming and Maintaining

FORMING

We were interested in locating research for this chapter on the role of single women or men who formed a parent–child relationship through non-marital birth or adoption. Only one study appears to exist on the role of religion in facilitating adoption, but this study was restricted to married women (Hollingsworth, 2000). No research appears to exist on the role of religion in decisions by unmarried or married individuals to use assisted reproductive technology to become pregnant. Finally, despite decades of intense public debate and research about the intersection of religion and societal *attitudes* about abortion, only three studies could be found that focus directly on the role of religion in unmarried, pregnant women's actual decision to obtain an abortion versus to sustain a pregnancy after they conceived (Adamczyk, 2008, 2009; Adamczyk & Felson, 2008), which are based on national survey data with unmarried adolescents. Pregnant teens who are more religious are more likely to marry prior to giving birth and thereby avoid abortion, based on a general index that combines private (i.e., prayer and personal importance of religion) or public (i.e., attendance and youth group activities) markers

(Adamczyk & Felson, 2008). Among pregnant teens who *remain* unmarried, neither public nor private religiousness influences abortion decisions, net of demographic controls (Adamczyk, 2009; Adamczyk & Felson, 2008). However, unmarried teens who report a conservative Protestant affiliation are more likely to give birth rather than terminate their pregnancy than Catholics, mainline Protestants, and Jews, but they are no more likely to make this choice than religiously unaffiliated teens (Adamczyk, 2008; Adamczyk & Felson, 2008). Finally, having attended a high school with a high proportion of conservative Protestants appears to discourage abortion behavior when women get pregnant in their twenties, but not as teens (Adamczyk, 2009). Adamczyk (2008) also found no evidence living in counties heavily populated by conservative Protestants influences teens' abortion decisions. Overall, these findings suggest that adopting conservative Protestant identity and close ties in this religious network translates into being more willing to become a mother out of wedlock, perhaps because these conservative Protestant subcultures value motherhood and pro-life choices above career or educational alternatives. Clearly more research is merited on the intersection of religion and spirituality, and becoming a single parent by choice.

MAINTAINING

Several studies on low-income and disproportionally minority mothers suggest that religion may facilitate good parenting practices in the absence of a biological father and under adverse economic and social conditions. Among single mothers, greater religious attendance and personal salience of God or spirituality has been tied to more maternal satisfaction, efficacy, authoritativeness, and consistency as well as less parental distress and risk of child abuse (Cain, 2007; Carothers, Borkowski, Lefever, & Whtiman, 2005; Hill, Burdette, Regnerus, & Angel, 2008; Sparks, Peterson, & Tangenberg, 2005). For instance, Carothers et al. (2005) gauged adolescent mothers' involvement with religious communities prenatally and when their children were 3, 5, and 8 years old. Although only half of these mothers participated in a religious community, higher embeddedness was tied to lower subsequent maternal depression and risk of child abuse, and to better child adjustment. In another 2-year, longitudinal study, Hill et al. (2008) found that mothers living in low-income urban environments who frequently attended religious services later reported greater satisfaction with parenting and viewed the role as less stressful or irritating than women who attended less frequently, even after controlling for social support, self-esteem, and depression. These findings imply that religion may offer valuable coping resources to sustain healthy, positive parenting practices for single parents in adverse conditions.

Yet the global or trait measures of general religiousness used in the aforementioned research obscures the fact that certain specific manifestations of religion may exacerbate poor functioning in stressful circumstances. Extensive research on religious coping methods to deal with nonfamilial stressors (e.g., natural disasters, illness) shows that while maladaptive religious coping is less common than adaptive religious coping, it consistently predicts undesirable psychosocial and health outcomes (Pargament, 1997, 2007). Consistent with this, in the sole study that assessed specific religious struggles in parenting among mothers found that this was associated with lower investment and satisfaction in parenting (Dumas & Nissley-Tsiopinis, 2006). Clearly, more research is needed on the ways spirituality can be a source of solace and support or added source of strain in single parents' efforts to maintain positive relationships with their children.

Comments on Other Family Structures

In this chapter, we have highlighted research on religion and spirituality within families based on heterosexual marriage, same-sex unions, cohabitation, and single parenthood. Clearly, other nontraditional types of families could be studied because little is known about how faith operates within families headed by grandparents, foster parents, stepparents, multiple partners (as is the case with polygamy and polyamory), and people who have divorced, chosen to be childless, or encountered fertility difficulties. Interestingly, adults without children are less religiously active than those with children and are more likely to drop out of organized religion (Edgell, 2006). Divorced adults and their children also tend to decrease their attendance at religious services and switch or disaffiliate from a given denomination, although adult children of divorce report feeling as close to and supported by God as those from nondivorced families (e.g., Zhai, Ellison, Glenn, & Marquardt, 2007). Voluntarily childless women also report lower levels of religious attendance and affiliation compared to the overall population or childless women who plan to have children in the future (Abma & Martinez, 2006). The tendency for individuals in nontraditional families to distance themselves from religious groups

suggests that reciprocal influences exist between involvement in organized religion and decisions regarding family structure. These bidirectional linkages challenge religious communities to help never-married or divorced parents, or couples who are intentionally childless or infertile feel welcome in religious social networks that are disproportionally comprised of biologically nuclear families. Edgell and Docka (2007) note that the standard North American family model has shown remarkable persistence as a spiritual ideal despite the fact it has never been the encompassing reality for most Americans. We hope the persistence of this ideal does not hinder social scientists from further investigating the impact of religion and spirituality, for better or worse, on families in their many forms.

Conclusions

There is growing pluralism in contemporary family structures. Individuals establish familial ties with others and make decisions about the structure and roles within these relationships. Adults seek out partners with whom to live, with marriage often pursued as a goal. People create parent–child relationships, via conception and birth, adoption, or informal caretaking relationships. These bonds persist for time periods and in different combinations to create family units. Diversity exists in religious values about various family structures as does theological controversy about the spiritual and moral legitimacy of various family forms. When it comes to morality, people's values will differ (see also the discussion in Yarhouse & Burkett, 2002). However, social scientific methods are powerless to speak to matters of ultimate truth and morality. People must decide how to combine information gathered from scientific and religious ways of knowing to inform their choices. Empirical research is confined to examining the correlates and outcomes of beliefs and behaviors. Although social scientists can offer information about the manifestations of religion that are generally associated with psychological and interpersonal processes and outcomes, they cannot resolve theological debates as to whether normative values about family structure should be based on biological and legal ties or on the quality of relational processes. Furthermore, an inherent and often lengthy lag in time is inevitable between the rapid changes occurring in modern family life and scientific findings that speak to these transformations. For instance, it will be some time before same-sex couples in stable, long-term unions raise enough children to compare rigorously these children's adjustment to those raised by married heterosexuals who do not divorce. A scientific comparison of these two types of intact, dual-parent families would help untangle whether the biological composition or the quality of family relationships (or both) shapes relational and individual outcomes. Yet individual differences within each type of family will most likely far outweigh the impact, on average, of group membership. Issues related to diverse family structures and transitions can pose confusion for individuals who face them. Both individuals and religious communities face difficult normative decisions about whether to embrace or reject the growing pluralism in family structures (Edgell, 2006; Ruether, 2000). An intriguing empirical question is what kinds of religious or spiritual beliefs or practices seem to contribute to individual, familial, and societal well-being or discord in navigating the complex search for family bonds.

This chapter highlights that certain aspects of religion are associated with maintaining stable and well-functioning family relationships. Many religions promote virtues that facilitate positive family processes and offer resources that decrease the risk of family dysfunction (Mahoney, 2010; Mahoney, in press). Religious resources may be particularly helpful to families with diverse structures who may be exposed to a greater amount of stress and discrimination and may lack some traditional sources of community and familial support. On the other hand, it is also possible that certain religious beliefs, practices, or interactions can heighten family distress.

Access to religious participation and fit with religious communities for those with diverse family structures will depend in part on the approaches of religious communities. Edgell (2003, 2006) observes that the major religious institutions in the United States developed a template for ministry during the 1950s based on a traditional family formation that declined soon thereafter. Despite major changes in the makeup of American families, many religious groups organize ministry around the cultural ideal (Edgell, 2006) or operate with a "stretched" version of the standard family ideal, for example, by accommodating changes in gender roles and sexual orientation expectations (Edgell & Docka, 2007, p. 30). A minority of churches have focused on institutionally adjusting to nontraditional models of the family, for example, by embracing congregants as single individuals, elevating the status of the extended family, or relinquishing biological relatedness as a spiritually optimal characteristic of parent–child relationships.

Directions for Research on Spirituality and the Family

Our review highlights the need for further research to evaluate how spirituality operates in varying family formations with diverse religious backgrounds. An enormous amount of work remains to identify maladaptive and adaptive influences of spirituality for diverse families. Attention to both positive and negative manifestations of religion and spirituality can aid in decreasing simplistic stereotypes and can facilitate dialog among groups of diverse persuasions. Additional in-depth findings about nontraditional families could also inform religious leaders who face challenges reconciling the growing gap between religious and societal norms about acceptable family structures. Future research may discover, for instance, that many individuals avoid participating in organized religion because traditional theological stances about nontraditional families foster a sense of being marginalized by religious communities, create internal dissonance, and seem irrelevant to the realities of contemporary family relationships.

To achieve the goal of gathering information about the multifaceted roles of religion for family relationships, greater depth is needed with regard to conceptual models. Many of the studies on religion and family functioning fail to articulate clearly what it is about religion that matters. More fine-grained models of the role of religious beliefs and behaviors in family life are required to explore how religion influences family outcomes in ways that are unique from other psychological or social processes. For example, in research on religious participation and cohabitation and same-sex unions, religious participation is often interpreted as a proxy for psychosocial constructs that are not specific to religion. The argument that religious constructs may be important in their own right, and not merely endogenous to couple relationships, will be more persuasive when studies address specific psychospiritual mechanisms (Mahoney, in press).

Along similar lines, reviews of the literature on the role of religion in family life in general, and for diverse family structures in particular, revealed that most researchers have made use of limited and superficial measures of religion (Mahoney, 2010; Mahoney et al., 2001). Many studies have relied on single or few items consisting of presence or type of religious affiliation, religious service attendance, overall importance of religion, or similarity within couples on these variables. Fewer studies used in-depth measures of an individual family member's faith. It is even rarer for studies to delve into how family members incorporate faith within their relationships. Inquiry into the influence of religion should encompass not only individual but also relational functioning. An emerging exception is a growing body of research on the sanctification of marriage, sexuality, and intimate relationships (Mahoney et al., 2010). Similarly, relational spiritual functioning can be tapped by examining the prevalence, nature, and influence of family members engaging in spiritually dialogs (e.g., Brelsford & Mahoney, 2008) or activities focused on a relationship, such as praying for or with a partner (e.g., Fincham et al., 2010). Other forms of relational spirituality involve people relying on a felt connection to the divine to guide family life. For example, in coping with marital conflict, Butler and Harper (1994) articulated helpful and harmful ways that a spouse may privately turn to God to navigate marital conflict. From a family system's perspective, connections to the divine can operate alongside other family relationships, with or without the awareness of other family members. Other research questions involve whether violating certain religious values about family structure pose relational risks to individuals within diverse family structures. Future studies may reveal painful, irreconcilable divisions about the family forms that people within and across subcultures affirm as sacred.

Greater richness in the conceptualizing and measurement of religion and spirituality in family life will facilitate research findings that are more persuasive to theorists, practitioners, or policy makers regarding unique benefits or risks that religion offers for family relationships. This could help policy makers communicate clearly in the public square, family practitioners relate effectively to clients, and religious organizations clarify messages about the family. When data are available about specific religiously based beliefs or behaviors that increase favorable family outcomes such as stability, communication, and relationship satisfaction, and decrease unfavorable family outcomes such as divorce, distress, and violence, these can be used to educate people about the more malleable religious factors tied to family success. Finally, findings about traditional and nontraditional families that offer more nuance could facilitate constructive dialogs about the role of religion and spirituality within and across families and communities of believers and nonbelievers alike. Ultimately, as scientific evidence about the risks and rewards of intertwining the domains of faith and family becomes more visible, this will enhance compassion and communication between families of all kinds.

References

Abma, J. C., & Martinez, G. M. (2006). Childlessness among older women in the United States: Trends and profiles. *Journal of Marriage and Family, 68*, 1045–1056.

Adamczyk, A. (2008). The effects of religious contextual norms, structural constraints, and personal religiosity on abortion decisions. *Social Science Research, 37*, 657–672.

Adamczyk, A. (2009). Understanding the effects of personal and school religiosity on the decision to abort a premarital pregnancy. *Journal of Health and Social Behavior, 50*, 180–195.

Adamczyk, A., & Felson, J. (2008). Fetal positions: Unraveling the influence of religion on premarital pregnancy resolution. *Social Science Quarterly, 89*, 17–38.

Al-Jibaly, M. (2000). *The Muslim family: Vol. 1. The quest for love and mercy: Regulation for marriage and wedding in Islam.* Arlington, TX: Al-Kitab & As-Sunnah Publishing.

Altareb, B. (2008). The practice of marriage and family counseling and Islam. In J. D. Onedera (Ed.). *The role of religion in marriage and family counseling* (pp. 89–104). New York: Routledge.

Atkins, D. C., & Kessel, D. E (2008). Religiousness and infidelity: Attendance, but not faith and prayer, predict marital fidelity. *Journal of Marriage and Family, 70*, 407–418.

Bartkowski, J. P., & Xu, X. (2000). Distant patriarchs or expressive dads? The discourse and practice of fathering in conservative Protestant families. *The Sociological Quarterly, 41*, 465–485.

Bartkowski, J. P., Xu, X. H., & Levin, M. L. (2008). Religion and child development: Evidence from the early childhood longitudinal study. *Social Science Research, 37*, 18–36.

Blackwell, D. L., & Lichter, D. T. (2004). Homogamy among dating, cohabiting, and married couples. *Sociological Quarterly, 45*, 719–737.

Brelsford, G. M., & Mahoney, A. (2008). Spiritual disclosure between older adolescents and their mothers. *Journal of Family Psychology, 22*, 62–70.

Brelsford, G. M., & Mahoney, A. (2009). Relying on God to resolve conflict: Theistic mediation and triangulation in relationships between college students and mothers. *Journal of Psychology and Christianity, 28*, 291–301.

Brown, J., Cohen, P., Johnson, J. G., & Salzinger, S. (1998). A longitudinal analysis of risk factors for child maltreatment: Findings of a 17-year prospective study of officially recorded and self-reported child abuse and neglect. *Child Abuse and Neglect, 22*, 1065–1078.

Brown, E., Orbuch, T. L., & Bauermeister, J. A. (2008). Religiosity and marital stability among Black American and White American couples. *Family Relations, 57*, 186–197.

Browning, D. S., & Clairmont, D. A. (2007). *American religions and the family: How faith traditions cope with modernization and democracy.* New York: Columbia University Press.

Bumpass, L., & Lu, H. H. (2000). Trends in cohabitation and implications for children's family contexts in the United States. *Population Studies, 54*, 29–41.

Burdette, A. M., Ellison, C.G., Sherkat, D. E., & Gore, K. A. (2007). Are there religious variations in marital infidelity? *Journal of Family Issues, 28*, 1553–1581.

Butler, M. H., & Harper, J. M. (1994). The divine triangle: God in the marital system of religious couples. *Family Process, 33*, 277–286.

Cain, D. S. (2007). The effects of religiousness on parenting stress and practices in the African American family. *Families in Society-the Journal of Contemporary Social Services, 88*, 263–272.

Carothers, S. S., Borkowski, J. G., Lefever, J. B., & Whitman, T. L. (2005). Religiosity and the socioemotional adjustment of adolescent mothers and their children. *Journal of Family Psychology, 19*, 263–275.

CCAR Ad Hoc Committee on Human Sexuality Report (1998). *Kulanu: All of us – A program and resource guide for gay, lesbian, bisexual, and transgender inclusion.* Central Conference of American Rabbis (CCAR), 259–264. Retrieved February 2012, from http://www.bjpa.org/Publications/details.cfm?PublicationID=7816

Clements, M. L., Stanley, S. M., & Markman, H. J. (2004). Before they said "I do": Discriminating among marital outcomes over 13 years. *Journal of Marriage and Family, 66*, 613–626.

Cook, C. J. (2008). The practice of marriage and family counseling and liberal Protestant Christianity. In J. D. Onedera (Ed.), *The role of religion in marriage and family counseling* (pp. 73–87). New York: Routledge.

Curtis, K. T., & Ellison, C. G. (2002). Religious heterogamy and marital conflict—Findings from the national survey of families and households. *Journal of Family Issues, 23*, 551–576.

Dorff, E. N. (2008). The practice of marriage and family counseling and Judaism. In J. D. Onedera (Ed.), *The role of religion in marriage and family counseling* (pp. 135–151). New York: Routledge.

Dumas, J. E., & Nissley-Tsiopinis, J. (2006). Parental global religiousness, sanctification of parenting, and positive and negative religious coping as predictors of parental and child functioning. *The International Journal for the Psychology of Religion, 16*, 289–310.

Duvander, A. Z. E. (1999). The transition from cohabitation to marriage. *Journal of Family Issues, 20*, 698–717.

Edgell, P. (2003). In rhetoric and practice: Defining 'The good family' in local congregations. In M. Dillon (Ed.), *Handbook of the sociology of religion* (pp. 164–179). New York: Cambridge University Press.

Edgell, P. (2006). *Religion and family in a changing society.* Princeton, NJ: Princeton University Press.

Edgell, P., & Docka, D. (2007). Beyond the nuclear family? Familism and gender ideology in diverse religious communities. *Sociological Forum, 22*, 25–50.

Eggebeen, D., & Dew, J. (2009). The role of religion in adolescence for family formation in young adulthood. *Journal of Marriage and Family, 71*, 108–121.

Ellison, C. G., & Anderson, K. L. (2001). Religious involvement and domestic violence among US couples. *Journal for the Scientific Study of Religion, 40*, 269–286.

Ellison, C. G., Henderson, A. K., Glenn, N. D., & Harkrider, K. E. (2011). Sanctification, stress, and marital quality. *Family Relations, 60*, 404–420.Fiese, B. H., & Tomcho, T. J. (2001). Finding meaning in religious practices: The relation between religious holiday rituals and marital satisfaction. *Journal of Family Psychology, 15*, 597–609.

Fincham, F. D., Lambert, N. M., & Beach, S. R. H. (2010). Faith and unfaithfulness: Can praying for your partner reduce infidelity? *Journal of Personality and Social Psychology, 99*, 649–659.

Gallagher, S. K. (2003). *Evangelical identity and gendered family life.* New Brunswick, NJ: Rutgers University Press.

Goodwin, P. Y., Mosher, W. D., & Chandra, A. (2010). Marriage and cohabitation in the United States: A statistical portrait based on Cycle 6 (2002) of the National Survey of Family Growth. *National Center for Health Statistics.* Retrieved December 2011, from http://www.cdc.gov/nchs/data/series/sr_23/sr23_028.pdf

Halpern, C. T., Young, M. L., Waller, M. W., Martin, S. L., & Kupper, L. L. (2004). Prevalence of partner violence in same-sex romantic and sexual relationships in a national sample of adolescents. *Journal of Adolescent Health, 35*, 124–131.

Henderson, A. K., & Ellison, C. G. (2012) *Religion and relationship quality among cohabiting and dating couples.* Manuscript submitted for publication.

Hayford, S. R., & Morgan S. P. (2008). Religiosity and fertility in the United States: The role of fertility intentions. *Social Forces, 86*, 1163–1188.

Hernandez, K., I., & Mahoney, A. (in press). *Balancing sacred callings in career and family life.* P. Hill & B. Dik (Eds.), *Advances in workplace spirituality: theory, research and application.* Information Age Publishing.

Hill, T. D., Burdette, A. M., Regnerus, M., & Angel, R. J. (2008). Religious involvement and attitudes toward parenting among low-income urban women. *Journal of Family Issues, 29*, 882–900.

Hollingsworth, L. D. (2000). Who seeks to adopt a child? Findings from the national survey of family growth. *Adoption Quarterly, 3*, 1–24.

Jensen, L. A. (2006). Liberal and conservative conceptions of family: A cultural-developmental study. *International Journal for the Psychology of Religion, 16*, 253–269.

Kaufman, G., & Raphael, L. (1996). *Coming out of shame: Transforming gay and lesbian lives.* New York: Doubleday.

Kennedy, S., & Bumpass, L. (2008). Cohabitation and children's living arrangements: New estimates from the United States. *Demographic Research, 19*, 1663–1692.

Lehrer, E. L. (2004). The role of religion in union formation: An economic perspective. *Population Research and Policy Review, 23*, 161–185.

Lewin, E. (1998). *Recognizing ourselves: Ceremonies of lesbian and gay commitment.* New York: Columbia University Press.

Lippa, R.A. (2007). The preferred traits of mates in a cross-national study of heterosexual and homosexual men and women: An examination of biological and cultural influences. *Archives of Sexual Behavior, 36*, 193–208.

Mahoney, A. (2010). Religion in the home from 1999–2010: A decade review from a relational spirituality framework. *Journal of Marriage and Family, 72*, 805–827.

Mahoney, A. (in press). The spirituality of us: Relational spirituality in the context of family relationships. In K. I., Pargament, J. J. Exline, & J. W. Jones (Eds.) *APA handbook of psychology, religion, and spirituality: Vol I.* American Psychological Association.

Mahoney, A., Pargament, K. I., & Hernandez, K. I. (in press). Heaven on earth: Beneficial effects of sanctification for individual and interpersonal well-being. In J. Henry (Ed.), *Oxford book of happiness.* Oxford, UK: Oxford University Press.

Mahoney, A., Pargament, K. I., Jewell, T., Swank, A. B., Scott, E., Emery, E., & Rye, M. (1999). Marriage and the spiritual realm: The role of proximal and distal religious constructs in marital functioning. *Journal of Family Psychology, 13*, 321–338.

Mahoney, A., Pargament, K. I., Swank, A., & Tarakeshwar, N. (2001). Religion in the home in the 1980s and 90s: A meta-analytic review and conceptual analysis of religion, marriage, and parenting. *Journal of Family Psychology, 15*, 559–596.

Marks, L. (2004). Sacred practices in highly religious families: Christian, Jewish, Mormon, and Muslim perspectives. *Family Process, 43*, 217–231.

Marler, P. L., & Hadaway, C. K. (2002). "Being religious" or "being spiritual" in America: A zero-sum proposition? *Journal for the Scientific Study of Religion, 41,* 289–300.

Martin, A. (1998). Clinical issues in psychotherapy with lesbian-, gay-, and bisexual- parented families. In C. J. Patterson & A. R. D'Augelli (Eds.), *Lesbian, gay, and bisexual identities in families: Psychological perspectives* (pp. 270–291). New York: Oxford University Press.

McQueeney, K. (2003). The new religious rite: A symbolic interactionist case study of lesbian commitment rituals. *Journal of Lesbian Studies, 7,* 49–70.

Meyer, J. F. (2007). Confucian "familism" in America. In D. S. Browning & D. A. Clairmont (Eds.), *American religions and the family: How faith traditions cope with modernization and democracy* (pp. 168–184). New York: Columbia University Press.

Myers, S. M. (2006). Religious homogamy and marital quality: Historical and generational patterns, 1980–1997. *Journal of Marriage and Family, 68,* 292–304.

Onedera, J. D. (2008). *The role of religion in marriage and family counseling.* New York: Routledge.

Oswald, R. F., Goldberg, A., Kuvalanka, K., & Clausell, E. (2008). Structural and moral commitment among same-sex couples: Relationship duration, religiosity, and parental status. *Journal of Family Psychology, 22,* 411–419.

Pargament, K. I. (1997). *The psychology of religion and coping: Theory, research, practice.* New York: The Guilford Press.

Pargament, K. I. (2007). *Spiritually integrated psychotherapy: Understanding and addressing the sacred.* New York: The Guilford Press.

Pargament, K. I., & Mahoney, A. (2002). Spirituality: Discovering and conserving the sacred. In C. R. Snyder (Ed.), *Handbook of positive psychology* (pp. 646–675). Washington, DC: American Psychological Association.

Prebish, C. S. (2007). Family life and spiritual kinship in American Buddhist communities. In D. S. Browning & D. A. Clairmont (Eds.), *American religions and the family: How faith traditions cope with modernization and democracy* (pp. 185–196). New York: Columbia University Press.

Rostosky, S. S., Otis, M. D., Riggle, E. D. B., Kelly, S., & Brodnicki, C. (2008). An exploratory study of religiosity and same-sex couple relationships. *Journal of GLBT Family Studies, 4,* 17–36.

Rostosky, S. S., Riggle, E. B., Brodnicki, C., & Olson A. (2008). An exploration of lived religion in same-sex couples from Judeo-Christian traditions. *Family Process, 47,* 389–403.

Ruether, R. R. (2000). *Christianity and the making of the modern family.* Boston: Beacon Press.

Sherkat, D. E. (2002). Sexuality and religious commitment in the United States: An empirical examination. *Journal for the Scientific Study of Religion, 41,* 313–323.

Sherkat, D. E. (2004). Religious intermarriage in the United States: Trends, patterns, and predictors. *Social Science Research, 33,* 606–625

Smith, C. (with M.L. Denton). (2005). *Soul searching: The religious and spiritual lives of American teenagers.* New York: Oxford University Press.

Smith, D. E. (1993). The Standard North-American Family— SNAF as an ideological code. *Journal of Family Issues, 14,* 50–65.

Sparks, A., Peterson, N. A., & Tangenberg, K. (2005). Belief in personal control among low-income African American,

Puerto Rican, and European American single mothers. *Journal of Women and Social Work, 20,* 401–415.

Stacey, J. (1997). *In the name of the family: Rethinking family values in the postmodern age.* Boston: Beacon Press.

Stokes, C. E., & Regnerus, M. D. (2009). When faith divides family: Religious discord and adolescent reports of parent and child relations. *Social Science Research, 38,* 155–167.

Stolzenberg, R. M., Blair-Loy, M., & Waite, L. J. (1995). Religious participation in early adulthood: Age and family life cycle effects on church membership. *American Sociological Review, 60,* 84–103.

Suter, E., Bergen, K., Daas, K., & Durham, W. (2006). Lesbian couples' management of public–private dialectical contradictions. *Journal of Social and Personal Relationships, 23,* 349–365.

Thornton, A., Axinn, W. G., & Hill, D. H. (1992). Reciprocal effects of religiosity, cohabitation, and marriage. *American Journal of Sociology, 98,* 628–651.

Uecker, J. E., Regnerus, M. D., & Vaaler, M. L. (2007). Losing my religion: The social sources of religious decline in early adulthood. *Social Forces, 85,* 1667–1692.

U.S. Census Bureau, Housing and Household Economic Statistics Division, Fertility & Family Statistics Branch. (2010). *Current population survey, 2009 annual social and economic supplement.* Retrieved January 25, 2010, from http://www.census.gov/population/socdemo/hh-fam/cps2009/tabC9-all.xls

Vaaler, M. L., Ellison, C. G., & Powers, D. A. (2009). Religious influences on the risk of marital dissolution. *Journal of Marriage and Family, 71,* 917–934.

Volling, B. L., Mahoney, A., & Rauer, A. J. (2009). Sanctification of parenting, moral socialization, and young children's conscience development. *Journal of the Psychology of Religion, 1,* 53–68.

Wertheimer, J. (2007). What is a Jewish family? The radicalization of Rabbinic discourse. In D. S. Browning & D. A. Clairmont (Eds.), *American religions and the family: How faith traditions cope with modernization and democracy* (pp. 151–167). New York: Columbia University Press.

Wilcox, W. B. (1998). Conservative Protestant childrearing: Authoritarian or authoritative? *American Sociological Review, 63,* 796–809.

Wilcox, W. B. (2004). *Soft patriarchs, new men: How Christianity shapes fathers and husbands.* Chicago: University of Chicago Press.

Wilcox, W. B., & Wolfinger, N. H. (2007). Then comes marriage? Religion, race, and marriage in urban America. *Social Science Research, 36,* 569–589.

Wilcox, W. B., & Wolfinger, N. H. (2008). Living and loving "decent": Religion and relationship quality among urban parents. *Social Science Research, 37,* 828–848.

Williams, R. B. (2007). Hindu family in America. In D. S. Browning & D. A. Clairmont (Eds.), *American religions and the family: How faith traditions cope with modernization and democracy* (pp. 197–210). New York: Columbia University Press.

Wolfinger, N. H., &Wilcox, W. B. (2008). Happily ever after? Religion, marital status, gender and relationship quality in urban families. *Social Forces, 86,* 1311–1337.

Yarhouse, M. A., & Burkett, L. A. (2002). An inclusive response to LGB and conservative religious persons: The case of same-sex attraction and behavior. *Professional Psychology: Research and Practice, 33,* 235–241.

Zhai, J. E., Ellison, C. G., Glenn, N. D., & Marquardt, E. (2007). Parental divorce and religious involvement among young Adults. *Sociology of Religion, 68*, 125–144.

Zink, D. W. (2008). The practice of marriage and family counseling and conservative Christianity. In J. D. Onedera (Ed.), *The role of religion in marriage and family counseling* (pp. 55–71). New York: Routledge.

Zinnbauer, B., & Pargament, K. (1999). The emerging meanings of religiousness and spirituality: Problems and prospects. *Journal of Personality, 67*, 889–919.

Motherhood and Female Faith Development: Feminine Tapestry of Religion, Spirituality, Creativity, and Intuition

Carole A. Rayburn

Abstract

The influence of mothers, motherhood, and the concept of Mother of God and Mother God on female faith development are examined in light of religion, spirituality, creativity, and intuition. It is held that it is necessary for the female child to learn of egalitarian relationships in creation so that she may assume her balanced and equal place in the world as a creation of nature and a Higher Power. These lessons she most often learns at the knee of a loving, protective, wise, and caring mother. The importance for girls and women to consider gender issues along with development of faith, religion, spirituality, and theology cannot be overemphasized.

Key Words: creativity, faith development, faith of our mothers, female faith, intuition, maternal faith nurturance, maternal spirituality, matriarchal psyche-spirit, motherhood and faith, religious/spiritual tapestry

Introduction

In a world still largely patriarchal, how do girls and women find a theology, religion, and spirituality with which they can identify? How do they develop a faith born out of gender-affirmative, female-enhancing, and egalitarian realizations that satisfy their search for truth and knowledge, soothe their minds, bodies, and souls, and increase their joy of living? How do they develop a faith that enables them to reach out to a transcendent Higher Power and to see themselves in the big tapestry of universal creation? Is it possible for girls and women to truly see themselves as equal participants in a religious and/or spiritual realm if only male leaders dominate the sacred and the secular worlds? If the "Other" is always male, and the model of holiness is always a male God, a male Savior, and a male Holy Spirit, exactly where do female persons envision themselves in the panorama of creation, believing, salvation, dedication, and reverence to the holy or transcendent? We will examine faith, faith development, religion and religiousness,

spirituality, creativity, and intuition in attempting to answer these questions.

Faith

Faith has been defined as a "firm belief in something for which there is no proof; complete trust; something that is believed, particularly with strong conviction; especially a system of religious beliefs" (Merriam Webster, 1993, p. 418). In whom is such complete trust usually placed by very young children?

In most cases, it is the mother who has the major role in childrearing and instruction of values, traditions, morals, and other educational matters from the earliest stages of the child's growth and development. The mother–child bonding is particularly strong between a mother and her daughter, the two females being able to identify with each other through the similarities of their bodies, emotions, and gender roles (both stereotypical and more acceptable, chosen ones). While the female child may admire the gender differences between her and her father and any male siblings, her comfort level at comparing herself to another female—her mother and any female siblings—is usually considerable and greater. The young female child more easily models herself in her mother's image. If from a very early age she receives from her mother physical and emotional tender loving care, protection, instruction in how to manipulate the environment and cope with the world, teaching of important values and lessons of good and bad, she understandably views her mother as a special conveyor of religiousness, spirituality, faith development, and morality in her life.

Because of these vital experiences, it is no surprise that later on, when she is taught that she was created by a divine being, a Higher Power, God, who is described as a Creator, Protector, Savior, and possessor of goodness and truth, and loving kindness, that she can readily identify these with her mother. Indeed, she has probably figured out that it was her mother who was more visibly and intimately connected with her own conception and birth, and who played the more major role in her upbringing. While she may see her father as strong, loving, and caring, and as a provider for his family, she may more often turn to her mother in times of trauma. The mother would be seen as the parent who has experienced more similar events to her daughter and thus might be more insightful and understanding about whatever troubles her daughter.

Faith Development

Faith development involves the process by which faith engenders spirituality. Relatedly, spirituality (a search for purpose and meaning through an internal drive for a relationship with God or a supreme being) development has been viewed as a process of faith development (Thomas & Hewitt, 2009).

Fowler (1981) proposed a six-stage model of faith development that, while not universally applicable to all cultures (Vygotsky, 1978), nonetheless served as a paradigm of the faith process. In the Intuitive-Projective Faith stage, children become aware of the acceptable and unacceptable actions and beliefs of parenting persons and what these mean in broad terms. Wanting to please the parent, especially the caretaker mother, they quickly associate those issues on which the mother places positive values with the good and acceptable and those on which she places negative values as bad things to be avoided.

Trusting in one's mother and her perceptions of life, ethics, and morality is very important for children, especially in early childhood. In older children,

religious symbols and myths within the faith tradition are more the area of concern. What and who is God, who made the world and its inhabitants, and where does the child see herself fitting in the universe of creation? What or who will keep her safe as she recites, "Now I lay me down to sleep, I pray the good Lord my soul to keep" or its equivalent and ponders what it really means to "be kept safe" and what potential harms and injuries may assail her. The mother's role in guiding particularly her female children and adolescents is vastly important here.

Mothers walk a tightrope in conveying the subtleties of gender differentiation in the faith realm while avoiding the symbols, images, and stereotypical taboos that would later lead to discrimination and disenfranchisement of females. From the point of view of religion, the patriarchy often defined femalekind as inferior and "less pure" in terms of godliness; this theme of supposed inferiority would later fly in the face of females identifying with religious feminism.

The second stage of Literal Faith would envision mothers as faithful promoters of particular beliefs, values, and attributes. Such maternal messages might be passed on with strong convictions and received by their children unquestioningly. Teachings about a loving Creator, punishments for bad behavior, and the necessity for being loving and kind to others may be passed on to daughters and their brothers by their mothers at this time.

In the third stage, Synthetic Conventional Faith, through a noncritical evaluation of faith, adolescents identify with a specific faith perspective and rituals. Those outside this understanding are viewed as "others." The idea that only those who believe in a certain theology, religion, spirituality, or who hold a particular denominational faith and practice specific rituals are good, acceptable persons may gain relevance here. Here mothers can be instrumental in inculcating views and rituals that encourage an affirmative empowering womanhood within the faith beliefs. As in the Quaker tradition, female children can be raised in egalitarian ways that promote the realization of their maximum potentials as persons of God, faith, religiousness, and/or spirituality (Raum, 2004; Rayburn, 2007a).

In Individuative-Reflective Faith, Fowler's fourth stage, older adolescents and adults are challenged to analytically pull apart the rituals and myths of their religion and to evaluate their spiritual paths with a critical eye (Datan, 1982; Gavin, 1982; Meadow, 1982; Propst, 1982; Rayburn, 1993). In comparing their views with the views of others, they refine their faith development and spiritual identity in ways that map out personal and distinct paths. Here the mother may foster within her daughter, through her earlier instruction and example, the freedom and encouragement to delve more deeply into her beliefs in ways that engender more valid and satisfying reflections about her faith. Here the daughter may feel more comfortable in examining concepts of theology, religion, and spirituality, such as the existence of God or a Higher Power, the fatherhood and/or the motherhood of God, and where she fits into the spiritual community and/or the kingdom of God. Though more orthodox patriarchal teachings may insist that girls and women are fully satisfied with their identities as religious or spiritual beings through their association and identity with the men—fathers, brothers, and husbands—in their lives, only through the egalitarian religious/spiritual upbringing, especially by her mother, are daughters truly able to fully identify with the godly, the holy, the realm of the godly and the sacred (Bradford, 1982; Gavin, 1982; Johnson, 1981; Rayburn, 1981, 1982, 1989, 2001, 2002a,b, 2008a,b,c; Rayburn, Natale, & Linzer, 1982).

Conjunctive Faith, the fifth stage in Fowler's theory of faith development, involves adults' ability to attain an appreciation of faith systems while at the same time not being restricted by these systems. For instance, in more patriarchal faith traditions, girls and women may be able to differentiate the overall pleasing teachings of their denominations while not accepting any validity of female inferiority at any level of religious/spiritual practice (Rayburn, 1981, 2002a,b, 2008a,b,c). Much of this insightfulness and analytical differentiation depends on the modeled strength of the mother and the philosophical, spiritual egalitarianism that gets passed onto daughters. To have a strong faith development in the absence of an equally strong sense of self as a child of God—or at least of the universe in the spiritual realm—might be possible but most assuredly would not be a healthy freeing of girls and women in the sense of their highest spiritual actualization.

Girls and women may look closely at the roles of women in Scripture (Eve, Miriam, Ruth, Naomi, Esther, Deborah, Bathsheba, Delilah, Virgin Mary, Mary Magdalene, Mary and Martha, Lydia, Phoebe, and Juno—a disciple of Christ), in religious movements and inspirations (Joan of Arc, Juliana of Norwich, Catherine of Siena, Teresa of Avila, Hildegard of Bingen, Rose of Lima, Machig Lapdron, Achi Chokyi Droma, Dorothy Day, Mother Teresa of Calcutta, Mother Mary Elizabeth Seton, Ellen Gould White, and Mary Baker Eddy), and spiritual movements and inspirations (Kandro Rinpoche, Sojourner Truth, Mary Daly, Rosemary Radford Ruether, and Lynn Gottlieb). Examining the language of theology and religion—and how such noninclusive language may threaten to exclude them from the total picture of religiousness and spirituality—becomes more important. Such inspection of language may have been influenced by her mother's earlier teachings about the religious, spiritual, and gender issues in faith development (Espin, 2008; Prestbo & Staats-Westover, 2008; Rayburn, 1984, 2008a, 2008b, 2008c).

Searching for female role models in their quest for universal meaning, girls and women want to discern the leadership roles in the secular and sacred worlds that they can take on as their own. They may enter into a prolonged struggle with the patriarchy in defining, refining, and reshaping their images of the Higher Power, the ultimate in life, and their leadership roles in ecclesia as well as in the world in general (Durka, 1982; Natale, 1982; Rayburn, 1979, 1989; Rayburn & Richmond, 2002b; Rayburn, Richmond, & Rogers, 1982, 1983, 1986, 1994; Richmond, Rayburn, & Rogers, 1985). In an enchanting book written especially for her daughter to explain the role of the rabbi who is also a mother and wife, Mindy Portnoy (1986) describes in *Ima on the Bima* the simultaneous roles of the religious professional and mother. The wonderment and awe of girls seeing their mothers performing this ecclesial role has far-reaching effects. Such a child would adapt a broad worldview that would not limit such religious and spiritual involvement to men. Any restrictions on women's participation even at the highest levels of ecclesia would cause a psychological clash and cause her distress and strain should she encounter discrimination in religious leadership roles.

Universalizing Faith, Fowler's final stage, deals with transcendent, moral, and religious actions. Does the woman recognize and even invite the transcendent and mystical Higher Power—God, spiritual teacher, guru, or even Mother Nature herself—as a vital influence in and on her life? Does she have deep respect and gratitude for life itself and for the giver or creator of life? Does she understand and reverently value her independence on the transcendent forces in her existence? Besides having fear and anxiety about death and dying, does she appreciate the tremendous gift of life and the balance of death in the overall panorama of creation? Does she have some theological, philosophical, spiritual concept of a redeemer, redemptive powers, or salvific influences on her vulnerability in attempting to cope with life and its myriad mysteries? Do ideas of right and wrong, and good and evil penetrate her sense of perceiving, feeling, and interacting with others? Are her religious/spiritual actions moderated by moral considerations? Are even her ethics influenced by such thoughts of right and wrong as she attempts to incorporate the sacred with the secular in her life and in her transactions with others?

No matter what side of these issues her mother has taken and whether the woman decides to agree with her mother or mother surrogate or to go counter to the script, the maternal messages will nonetheless be of decided importance. Through a mother's bent toward creative themes and intuitive openness, daughters are encouraged and more enabled to open themselves to the transcendent and to allow that which is unseen, immaterial, and intangible to come through and enrich, enliven, and bless their lives.

As a child, the daughter may have been exposed to creation in ongoing life, as with the pregnancy of cats and dogs and the birth of fascinating new lives of romping kittens and puppies. She may well have witnessed her own mother's pregnancy and been told of the coming birth of a sibling. Creation stories and events center on the mothers and grandmothers who pass on to female children the creation themes, the beginnings and giving of life, and the interdependence of all who live on all others who share living. Mothers can encourage and provide opportunities for their daughters to learn about, appreciate, and care for the environment and the plants and animals of the earth (McElroy, 1998; Prestbo & Staats-Westover, 2008; Randour, 2000a, 2000b; Rayburn, 2008a, 2008b, 2008c; Rayburn & Richmond, 1998, 2000, 2002a,; Reedy, 2008; Weahkee, 2008). In the National and International Religion Report (1990), a most extensive faith development study of Americans, respondents were asked "who" or "what" had had the most positive influence on their religious faith; the significant response, across age, gender, and denomination, was "my mother."

Religion and Religiousness

Girls and women are more apt to identify themselves with being spiritual than with being religious, though one proclivity does not necessarily entirely exclude the other (Rayburn, 2001; Rayburn & Richmond, 2002a,b). Furthermore, while religiousness and religion ideally have spirituality at their core,

they are not the same (Nicolas, DeSilva, Coutinho, & Prater, 2008; Rayburn, 1996, 2007a,b; Rayburn & Richmond, 2002b).

Definitions and Concepts of Religion and Religiousness

Religion has been defined as "the service, worship of God or the supernatural"; devotion or commitment to religious observance or faith; a personal set of doctrines or "institutionalized system of religious attitudes, beliefs, and practices" (Merriam-Webster, 1993, p. 988).

Religion has been defined as "the rites, texts, rituals, and formalized structures for persons practicing a doctrine" (Gregerson, 2008, p. 196). Simon (2008) defines *religion* as a religious, organized community. In their studies of religiousness and creating the Inventory on Religiousness (Rayburn & Richmond, 1997), religiousness was operationally defined as having three main factors: Belief and Spiritual Growth; Transcendence (awareness and appreciation of one's life being influenced and guided by a Higher Power or a supernatural force); and Caring for Others. Furthermore, in this study, a significant ($p = .001$) relationship was found between Physical and Psychological Well-Being (Inventory on Well-Being; Rayburn & Richmond, 2002a,b, 2006) and the Inventory on Spirituality's Seeking Goodness and Truth; greater significance was found between well-being and spirituality than between well-being and religiousness. To the extent that mothers pass on positive messages from religion and religious doctrine and tenets, as well as from any rituals, practices, and theopsychosocial beliefs and attitudes about girls and women, those female persons will probably associate religion and religiousness with their development of higher self-esteem and positive identity/image. Where female persons from sacred writings and holy events have been denigrated or even seen as sources of evil (e.g., Augustine's statement that women were the gateway to hell, temptresses, etc.) would not engender healthy connections of girls and women with religion and religiousness.

Motherhood of God

Julian of Norwich (Beers, 1992,1999; Long, 1995; Marcell,2008), 1342–1412, anchoress and avowed solitary who devoted her life to prayer and meditation, anticipated by six centuries the most creative and highly regarded thoughts on feminist Christian theology. In her *Revelation of Love*, she writes of God's love shown by joy and deepest compassion, rather than with regard to law and duty. In her visions of 16 different revelations, she named both God and Christ as "mother" and she put forth a fully developed spirituality of the Motherhood of God. In wisdom, she did this within the parameters of an orthodox understanding of the Christian faith.

Pope John Paul I also spoke to the Motherhood of God issue: "God is not only our Father but even more so our Mother, who wants only to be good to us, wants only to love us, especially if we are bad" (Cuthell, 2009). The current Pope, Benedict XVI, sees God's forgiveness of sins for those who are repentent as more a female than a male side of God, and theologian Hans Kung views the acknowledgment by the Vatican that God transcends the sexes as long overdue (Owen, 1999). In early church history, those who held to God the Mother concepts included Clement of Alexandria, Gregory Nazianzus, Origen, Irenacus, John Chrysostom, Jerome, Ambrose, Augustine, Anselm, Aquinas, Thomas A'Kempis, Bernard of Clairvaux, Julian of Norwich, Martin Luther, Teresa of Avila, and Gertrude of Helfta. Clement spoke of Christ as spiritual milk drawn from "the Father's breast of love," and of Jesus being both father and mother. Anselm asked of Jesus: "Are you not also a mother? . . . If you had not been in labor, you could not have borne death, and if you had not died, you could not have brought forth." Teresa of Avila spoke of sustaining and comforting streams of milk that flowed from Jesus's breasts. Other images of the motherhood of God include biblical references from Ruth 2:12, God as a mother bird; and Matthew 23:37, Jesus lamenting that he would have drawn the people of Jerusalem under his wings as a mother hen does her chicks.

Mary Baker Eddy (Start, 1979), founder of the Christian Scientist Church, added a spiritual interpretation to the Lord's Prayer: After "our Father," Eddy added "Father-Mother God." More than 100 years prior to the feminist movement, Eddy rejected an exclusively male image and an exclusively Father image in her theology. (On a personal note, when the present writer was in a very male-dominated seminary with 350 male and only five female seminarians, she and at least one of the other three women prayed to "Mother-Father God.")

J. Philip Wogaman (1998), a Methodist minister, saw God as neither male nor female but believed that God has both father-like and mother-like attributes. Lester Start (1979), a Baptist minister, in his concepts about the Motherhood of God, cited the feminine traits of God in Christianity, in Buddhism, and in Hinduism. Start related that the Holy Bible pronouncement that God's eternal love and mercy is like a mother's love for her infant (Isaiah 42:14; 45:10; 49:15; 66:13), God is like an eagle watching over her nest (Deuteronomy), Jesus is in the bosom of God (John 1: 18), and the motherly description of God in Hosea 11 ("When Israel was a boy, I loved him: I called my son out of Egypt. It was I who taught Ephaim how to walk, I who had taken them in my arms, but they did not know that I harnassed them in leading strings and led them with bonds of love—that I had lifted them like a little child to my cheek, that I had bent down to feed them"). In speaking about Buddhism, Start sees the feminine traits of God in Kwan Yiu, goddess of mercy, who was the Chinese Madonna. In Hinduism, there are a myriad of female deities who are associated with gods. To Start, attributing exclusively masculine traits to God would be quite strange, since both female and male principles are needed. For him, viewing God as creative love without the image of mother-love as well a father-love would be difficult, because creative love and the creative spirit of God require both maternal and paternal qualities and images.

Wewerka (2008), speaking of her Buddhist beliefs, drew strength from the extremely careful reasoning in Buddhism's analysis of life and its focus on monitoring, awareness, and observing the mind aimed at ending suffering. It was a goddess who related Buddha's teaching that gender limitations are not placed on males and females but rather that the absolute mind is not subject to any duality. Tara, a female bodhisattva of compassion, had been a king's daughter named Wisdom Moon. Refusing to change her form to that of a man, she is considered the "perfection of knowledge" and "the mother of all Buddhas" from whom everything originated. In the beginning stages of Buddhism, not the Buddha but the female principle, *prajnapamita*, was the representation. The childhood faith of Wewerka was not Buddhism, and she did not learn this belief system from her mother or family but rather as an adult and feminist woman—from other women in her adult environment.

Lone Jensen Broussard (2012), a Unitarian Universalist minister, writing a sermon on "The Motherhood of God," stated, "Ideal motherhood is God as we would like to imagine her, feeding us, keeping us safe, holding us tight, loving us, guiding us, and embracing us." Though she does not believe God to be male or female, she calls the life force that sustains the fabric of life "the ever birthing and destroying, creative life force of swirling galaxies and tiny insects…Goddess or Mother" (p. 3). She calls for women to reclaim the power of nurturing, and she declares that her denomination has recognized from early on the feminine divine spirit and the idea of God as mother. Since 1863, Unitarian Universalists have had women ministers (pp. 3–4).

Read (1979) commented that it is vital to have both motherhood and fatherhood images of God if we are to see God as truly God. The symbolism of creativity is essential to the concept of the motherhood of God.

Weiner (2008) considered Kabbalah, the mystical Jewish writings, with the Shekinah, as the Heavenly Mother and the "good-breast mother" being received as the sustenance of the hungry and even ravenous seeker of wisdom, truth, and knowledge. Furthermore, Job and Proverbs described Wisdom as the female principal partner of God.

Embodied and Engendered Considerations in Godhood

Added to the second-rate value assessment of women in holy writings are the ways in which females and their biological, psychological, and sociological attributes are linked by males to theology and power structure to determine their limitations. Parts of the female body and female bodily functions may be held against women in their interactions with others. Taboos against the issuance of menstrual blood and the menses itself were common: Biblical patriarchal authorities saw the menses as a negative condition that rendered women unclean, impure, and in need of separation for a period of time from the society of men for a ritual or other cleansing. Yet no such purification procedures appear to have been required for the discharge of semen, even in the case of nocturnal emissions.

Indeed, the embodied, engendered God—most always seen in traditional patriarchal theology—is a male and in the Trinity eliminates any true identity of females with the Godhead (Rayburn, 1995). Menstrual blood exists primarily when women are either not pregnant or have had a disruption of their pregnancy. Did the patriarchs intend for women to be ever-pregnant to be considered "pure"? Furthermore, female virginity but much less male virginity is stressed in most traditional religions. Even words and concepts pertaining to religion and the religious are painted in masculine strokes: *Testimony, testament, seminary,* and *seminal*

all derive from the testicles and semen or the seed bed (Rayburn, 2002).

Fertility Goddesses

From earliest times, in most cultures, goddess images reflected the fertility of women, their power, strength, nurturing, devotion, and wisdom (Daly, 1968,1973; Eppig, 2008; Prestbo & Staats-Westover, 2008; Tummala-Narra, 2008). These goddesses had exaggerated breasts, vaginas, hips, and abdomens, drawing attention to their powers of creation, nurturance, and even ability to deny such attendance to the life-giving force. Stedman (1996) pointed out that the earth as mother, the Great Mother Goddess, gave birth from her womb to all living things, who returned to her womb after birth. This powerful embodiment of the female principle as life force, ruled over sky, earth, and the underworld. With the ever-present renewed productivity of the earth and constant recurrences of the rhythms of the moon, this image was reinforced. Furthermore, women, who had menstrual cycles coinciding with lunar cycles and had the power of procreation and nurturing, served as the earthly shadow of this powerful goddess image.

Goddesses were revered by special rituals and ceremonies, such as "Cakes for the Queen of Heaven" (Prestbo & Staats-Westover, 2008), to praise their vital contribution to life. These goddesses included Astarte, the star goddess; Nut, the night sky; Oya, the Yoruban goddess of the whirlwind; Demeter, the Great Mother; Kali, the Hindu goddess of destruction; the Queen of Heaven; and "Earth Mother" (Prestbo & Staats-Westover, 2008). The Earth Mother was the creator of all things, which began with her and returned to her at their death; she was responsible for creation, generation, regeneration, nurturing, and growth of all life.

The 1970s goddess movement encouraged and enlivened creative feminism, with the proclamation that God was (and still is) a woman, or at the very least, a feminine personage of the Godhead. Since women were traditionally treated as inferior to men and felt powerless and in need of a solidly unifying feminine force, they sought strong feminine images of madonnas and goddesses. A goddess movement, resulting in the Daughters of Gaia, and based on the spiritual lessons of several female spiritual leaders, practices female-affirming rituals (such as the coming of age at various special times of females' lives: birth, pregnancy, wisdom of the hag, etc.; Prestbo & Staats-Westover, 2008).

The Hebrews of Old Testament times strongly rejected the female principle associated with pagan fertility religions related to Baal in Canaan and the focus of these goddesses on generation and agriculture. Eppig (2008) noted that a third of local deities were female, such as "Earth Mother." Stedman (1996) commented that legends abounded in ancient times of an earlier matriarchal period and a violent rebellion by men in which they seized female authority (and, we might add, female self-esteem and individualism).

The Hebrews of those ancient times seemed to feel the fervent need—at times—to corrupt and pervert the image of women, seeing them as sorceresses, temptresses, and as evil beings. Interestingly, since these ancient times never lacked in male pagan gods (and the ancient statues did not lack in male fertility gods with pronounced phalluses), the Hebrews did not rule out the male principle in their newly created religion. In fact, in many respects, they seemed to worship the masculine principle at the decided cost of the female principle. Furthermore, if the argument is taken from the need to denounce many pagan deities (both female goddesses *and* male gods) and to then proclaim the divine and righteous worship of one God (even later as the trinitarian three-in-one Godhead was expanded in Christianity), the question is why the male principle becomes the center of the new religion. Were not male as well as female pagan deities thought equally culpable and without value as true deities worthy of worship, and were not both male gods as well as female goddesses present in considerable number at the time of the changing of the God belief system? It is no wonder that something resonated in modern-day women when they read Mary Daly's *The Church and the Second Sex* (1968) and *Beyond God the Father* (1973).

Kristeva (1982) spoke of the maternal core that exists within the image of God, but it has been transformed into the paternal symbolism in Christianity. The masculine imagery of God and its accompanying exclusion of women from power structures in ecclesia has led to extreme difficulty in the development of women's identity within religion and spirituality.

Spirituality
Definitions of Spirit and Spirituality
Merriam-Webster (1993, p. 1134) defines *spirit* as an animating or vital principle held to give life to physical organisms; supernatural being or essence. *Spirituality* is defined as "of, or relating to, consisting of, or affecting the spirit; of, or relating to sacred matters; ecclesiastical rather than lay or temporal; concerned with religious values; of, or relating to supernatural beings or phenomena."

Eppig (2008) sees spirituality as the deepest longing to transcend concerns about personal security, self-esteem, and control so as to integrate work and relationships around the desire to build a better world. To Simon (2008), spirituality is an individual, idiosyncratic matter (as contrasted with religion, a religious organized community matter). Clamar (2008) views spirituality as a very individual and personal experience that mediates between body, soul, and self, animating and giving a fervent and affiliative life force.

Gregerson (2008), referring to God with feminine identity, viewed spirituality as the inner experience of the sacred, with God lifting people to Her bidding, transcending mundane consciousness, bringing together diverse spiritual traditions, and humanistic and scientific knowledge of gender and psychology.

Schneiders (1986) saw spirituality as the experience of striving to integrate one's self-transcendent life toward the perceived ultimate value. Siderits (2008) held that spirituality is that which integrates science and meaning, with the universe having a force that unites life and gives it meaning (she was influenced by free-thinking women, such as Elizabeth Cady Stanton and Ursala Goodenough). Richmond (2008) defines *spirituality* as that which has "spiritus," or animation or enlivenment, that comes from within; awareness of the connection between the best and most dearly held values within the self to that believed to be the greatest in the universe; personal experience associated with reverence and awe; and awareness of the connection between the self and all that animates, enlivens, and gives meaning.

Nicolas, DeSilva, Coutinho, and Prater (2008) view spirituality as a connection that may or may not be experienced with religion; feeling, belief, or connection in that which is higher than the individual; individual and personal experience or feeling involving a sense of love, connection, and happiness with self and God. To them, a strong sense of spirituality is best developed when women continually explore and share their spirituality with other women.

Spirituality may also be seen as the essence of one's being and the fervent heartfelt and soulful caring for others, reaching beyond oneself to a transcendent Higher Power (God, Holy Spirit, supernatural being or divine guide, guru, eternal teacher, etc.). It has a mystical, healing power in bringing about change in persons and situations for the better; its quality of selflessness displays the best in others as it flows from them, focusing on the transcendent, and calls these individuals to the aid of others. Spirituality brings out the best in humankind, encouraging individuals to identify with other parts of life because they want not only the best for themselves but others as well. With spirituality, the concept of sisterhood and also brotherhood takes on a genuine dimension of love and caring, expressed joyfully and abundantly. Extending beyond our humanness, guided by transcendent influences, it goes beyond members of one's own group identity, often to others very unlike ourselves.

Rayburn and Richmond (1996), in developing the Inventory on Spirituality, operationally defined *spirituality* as having three main factors: Transcendence (horizontal)—Seeking Goodness and Truth, and valuing peacefulness, cooperation, and forgiveness; Transcendence (vertical)—Spiritual Growth, with realizing and attending to external influences on our lives (God, Higher Power, nature, trusted guide or teacher, etc.); and Caring for Others (people, animals, plants, all of the universe). Being spiritual was regarded as requiring no adherence to any religious belief. A spiritual person might be religious or might be churched, unchurched, agnostic, or atheistic. Whereas religiousness was regarded as doctrinal, holding to specific tenets of a faith system, and possibly involving an organized community of believers, spirituality more concerned a fervent caring for others, searching for the good and true, and recognizing the guidance of forces outside oneself that influenced one's life paths.

Rayburn and Comas-Diaz (2008) wrote of WomanSoul, women's spirituality, as affirming, nurturing, creative, and compassionate. They also saw spirituality as compassionate illuminate, the fervent caring for the best for others and radiating with spiritual enlightenment (Rayburn, 2008a).

Comas-Diaz (2008) proposed "spirita," a way of being, a spirituality of resistance, protest, evolution, revolution, and promoting of global social justice. Spirita is the dark-skinned feminism of color.

The Holy Spirit

Duckworth (2006) wrote of Mary, the mother of Jesus, as the Mother of God, the *Theotokas* or *God-bearer*. This title was bestowed on the Virgin Mary at the third Ecumenical Council in the 5th century. Duckworth then examined the role of the Holy Spirit, the third divinity of the Christian trinity, called the Comforter and the Advocate. In Hebrew, *ruach* (feminine noun—Hebrew has no neuter nouns) is "the spirit of God" and in Greek *pneuma* (neuter noun) is "breath" or "wind" or that which dwells within us, around us, between us, leading us into wisdom, understanding, and inspired action. The feminine + the neuter nouns describing the Holy Spirit strongly suggest that the Holy Spirit may be regarded as the feminine being of the trinitarian Godhead. Prestbo and Staats-Westover (2008) reminded us that Sophia or Wisdom was once the honored name of the Holy Spirit, reflecting the feminine aspect of the female principle in the trinity.

Biblical Scripture has described the Holy Spirit as the Teacher; Comforter; Inspirer; Peacemaker; Intercessor; Purifier; Sanctifier; Producer of the fruit of all goodness, righteousness, truth, love, joy, peace, gentleness, and faith; Bestower of wisdom, knowledge, and healing; Worker of miracles and prophesy, grace, communion, and life. The Holy Spirit has been represented as a dove, fire, wind, and other nonhuman forms. All of these seem to concern more feminine attributes than masculine ones. Traditionally, Christians attribute their spirituality as coming from the Holy Spirit.

Images of God

In a study by Kanis (2003), graduate students in a religious philosophy course at a Roman Catholic college saw the Holy Spirit as a somewhat neurotic woodland sprite a bit akin to Peter Pan's Tinkerbell. In light of Jesus saying that he was leaving the Holy Spirit with humankind to instruct and guide them in the last days of the earth, this perception of the third personage of the Trinity was most disturbing. Before the students rated the Holy Spirit on the Big Five Personality Factors (Costa & McCrae, 1992), they were provided printed descriptive terms for the Holy Spirit from Scripture: "The Holy Spirit (Old Testament RUACH, New Testament PNEUMA) is a neuter noun. Scripture has described the Holy Spirit as a Teacher, Comforter . . . and prophesy, grace, communion, and life." God has been a voice calling out to Adam and Eve and a burning bush, and Christ has appeared to humans in human form. The Holy Spirit, however, represented in nonhuman forms such as a dove, fire, and wind, may have been ranked by humans as of less significance and credibility in comparison to God and Christ. Furthermore, though we are instructed to pray in the name of all three personages of the Trinity, many of us pray to God only and in the name of Christ, again leaving out or even forgetting the existence of the Holy Spirit. More familiarity with images of God and Jesus may increase our comfort level with these personages, leaving us with a spiritual imbalance. Since Christians are taught that their spirituality comes from the Holy Spirit, frequent or even occasional neglect of the Holy Spirit would do harm to not only their spirituality but also to the potential of their spiritual nature. From the Hebrew and Greek neuter nouns for the Spirit, some theologians have perceived the Holy Spirit as the female principle of the Godhead. If at least subconsciously the Holy Spirit is perceived as feminine, would the Holy Spirit become more neglected, discounted, trivialized as a wood nymph or woodland sprite; would girls and women identify with the Holy Spirit; would the gender identity bring more balance to the spiritual and religious psyche of girls and women; and would this create a much-needed corrective balance to the male psyche and the unrealistic idea of a totally all-male Godhead?

In a follow-up study, "The Images of God: Have We Forgotten the Holy Spirit?" (Rayburn, 2003), respondents chose adjectives in the Life Choices Inventory (LCI) (Rayburn, Hansen, Siderits, Burson, & Richmond, 1999, 2004) to describe God, Christ, and the Holy Spirit, along agentic (power- or career-mindedness, or traditionally more male-oriented values or lifestyles) or communal (family- or community-mindedness or more traditionally female-oriented values or lifestyles) life choices. They also rated these three personages of the Godhead on the Big Five personality traits/NEO-R (Costa & McCrae, 1992), as well as on the Inventory on the Supreme and Work (ISAW) (Rayburn & Richmond, 1999) Concept of the Supreme. In addition, the respondents rated themselves on the LCI, the Inventory on Religiousness (IR) (Rayburn & Richmond, 1997), and the Inventory on Spirituality (IS) (Rayburn & Richmond, 1996). On all of these measures, the Holy Spirit was given the lowest rating. On the NEO-R Neuroticism, in which a high score is interpreted as being sensitive, nervous, moody, easily experiencing unpleasant emotion (anger, anxiety, vulnerability to stress, depression), the Holy Spirit had the lowest mean score (40.50), coming after self (45.93), Jesus (41.44), and God (40.98). This suggested that the Holy Spirit was seen as more emotionally stable, secure, and confident than the others rated.

The Bipolar Adjectives Rating Scale, BARS (Piedmont, 1995), an adaptation of the NEO-R (Costa & McCrae, 1992), was used for studying the images of the Holy Spirit, God, and Jesus.

On the NEO-R Extraversion (outgoing, energetic, action-oriented, enthusiastic, talkative, assertive) and Agreeableness (friendly, compassionate, cooperative, concerned with social harmony, generous, helpful, willing to compromise, having an optimistic view of others and believing others to be trustworthy, good, and honest—all the attributes usually given to the Holy Spirit in Scripture), the Holy Spirit came out only third in line (Extraversion for Jesus, 54.63; God, 50.67; Holy Spirit, 49.84; and self, 48.32; Agreeableness for Jesus, 57.02; God, 52.18; Holy Spirit, 51.57; and self, 51.02). Thus, unlike the description of the Holy Spirit in Scripture, the emergent picture here is of a more shy and withdrawn, less assertive, enthusiastic, and energetic personage, more outspoken, less compassionate, cooperative, generous, caring, and helpful than Jesus and God.

For Openness to Experience (creative, imaginative, sensitive to beauty, inventive and open to new ideas, curious) and for Conscientiousness (organized, efficient, self-disciplined, acting dutifully, aiming for and needing achievement), the Holy Spirit ranked at the very bottom of the four rankings, with mean scores for Openness for Jesus, 58.42; God, 57.41; self, 55.20; and Holy Spirit, 54.13, and for Conscientiousness for Jesus, 58.42; self, 54.04; God, 52.83; and Holy Spirit, 49.51.

On the LCI Agentic and Communal factors, for Total LCI (with its Agentic + Communal, alpha = 0.8831), respondents' self mean score was 164.25; score for Jesus was 155.56; for God, 153.69; and for the Holy Spirit, 138.84. For the Agentic factor (alpha = 0.8429), the respondents' self mean score was 79.78; for Jesus, 72.19; for God, 71.88; and for the Holy Spirit, 64.00. For the Communal factor (alpha = 0.8374) mean score, the self was 84.47; for Jesus, 83.38; for God, 81.81; and for the Holy Spirit, 74.84. Again, the Holy Spirit had the lowest rating on both the power- and career-minded traditionally male pursuits and interests and the family- and community-mindedness traditionally female pursuits and interests. Interestingly, respondents rated themselves at the highest level of the ratings on all three measures. There were high correlations between God Agentic and Holy Spirit Agentic ($r = .718^{**}$, $p = .000$) and God Communal and Holy Spirit Agentic ($r = .634^{**}$, $p .000$), as well as Jesus Agentic and Holy Spirit Agentic ($r = .558^{**}$, $p = .000$) but not Jesus Communal and Holy Spirit Agentic ($r = .253$, $p = .169$). Holy Spirit Agentic and Self Agentic had an $r = .377^{*}$, $p = .036$. For God Communal and Holy Spirit Communal, $r = .700^{**}$, $p = .000$ (not significant with Jesus Communal, $r = .353$, $p = .051$), and with self Communal, $r = .518**$, $p = .003$.

In the ISAW Concept of the Supreme (alpha = 0.9772 for the 15 items), respondents' perception of God's response was a mean score of 129.78; for self, 120.69; for Jesus, 120.34; and for the Holy Spirit, 114.32. On the ISAW Concept of the Supreme, respondents are asked to rate how they think that each personage of the Godhead would rate "the Supreme" (defined in the instructions as "God," "Supreme Being," "Higher Power," "Divine Being," "Divine Spirit," "nature," "divinely inspired teacher," or whomever or whatever they regarded as "the Supreme") and also answer these perceptions about how they perceive the Supreme. Some of the items on which "the Supreme" was rated are Creator/Creation; Judge/Judgment; Peacemaker/Peace; Nurturer/Nurture; Love; and Center of one's being. On other studies (Rayburn, 2001; Rayburn & Richmond, 2002) women scored higher means for spirituality than for religiousness, though they showed interest in both, whereas men often had higher scores on religiousness but not at all on spirituality. Furthermore, while men were significantly more likely to see themselves as agentic but infrequently communal, women identified with both agentic and communal, though more communal at times.

There is a consistent pattern in these mean score rankings. The Holy Spirit was rated at the bottom of Neuroticism, Openness, Conscientiousness, Agentic + Communal, Agentic or power-traditional male mindedness, and also Communal or family-/community- mindedness/traditional female-oriented, and in perception/concept of "the Supreme." For Extraversion and Agreeableness, the Holy Spirit was rated next to the bottom, above only respondents' self-ratings on this factor. Thus, although seen as more emotionally stable than self, Jesus, and God, the Holy Spirit did not seem to have too much to commend her or him. This is quite contrary to the glowing description of the Holy Spirit in Scripture. Are God and Jesus so often written about in holy writings that humans sense a lot of distance and lack of awareness, appreciation, and understanding of the Holy Spirit's being and vital role? What does this indicate for the Christian believer who sometimes attributes spirituality as emanating from the Holy Spirit? What does such neglect portend theologically as well as spiritually?

Madonnas and Saints

Icons of the Virgin Mary, such as the Black Madonna, have abounded throughout the world and have given new hope to women and ethnic minorities (Comas-Diaz, 2008; Eppig, 2008). Comas-Diaz (2008) wrote about the many icons of the Black Virgin Mary or *Vierges Noires*, associated with Astarte, Isis, Demeter, Black Artemis, Cibele, Kali, Tara, Inana, and Lilith. It was easy for Comas-Diaz to identify with Our Lady of Monserrat or *la Moreneta* (the dark-skinned one), highly esteemed in Puerto Rico. This and similar black madonnas satisfied the longing of particularly ethnic minority women for more identity and inclusion in the spiritual world.

Austria (2008), writing about spirituality in the resilient Filipinos, a multicultural people who have survived many political upheavals, related that they draw much strength from the Virgin Mary and from women saints, each having a special month dedicated to her, such as *Nuestra Senora Guia*, Our Lady of the Way *Nuestra Senora de Paz Buen Viaje*, *La Naval de Manila*, Our Lady of Perpetual Help, *Virgen de los Desamparados*, and Our Lady of Immaculate Conception.

Espin (2008) related that her childhood was so influenced by the lives of saints and their sacrifices that she dreamt of imitating them and even becoming a saint herself. While she questioned the Spanish language and its attribution of engendered nouns, adjectives, and verbs to males even in cases in which this was illogical, she drew upon the possibilities presented by female saints for an expanded role for girls and women. Wanting to share such broader roles with other women, she decided to remain in the faith tradition of her youth, despite her awareness of its patriarchal oppression of women and ethnic minorities. Sensing a need to renew and revitalize her religious tradition, she fought for liberation from within. Saints (such as Rose of Lima, Mariana Parades of Quito, Teresa of Avila, Teresa of Los Andes, and Edith Stein) helped her to hold onto her cultural identity even while fighting political struggles, social tensions, and injustices.

Wewerka (2008) has been influenced by great female teachers and practitioners of Buddhism: Machig Lapdron, Yeshe Tsogyel, Achi Chokyi Drolma, and Gochen Tulku Rinpoche. It is a Buddhist belief that differences between women and men are not put forth by the teachings themselves but by the cultures in which the teachings are given.

Creativity and Intuition

Creativity is essential to all of life and to women's interactions: giving birth to something new—children, ideas, the life force and peace, and harmony, and beauty. Furthermore, women's spirituality or WomanSoul is sharing, caring, affirming, nurturing, creative, and compassionate. Compassionate Illuminate is compassionate caring for others, wisdom, and searching for goodness and truth: caring for the best for others and radiating with spiritual enlightenment (Rayburn, 2008a, 2008c; Rayburn & Comas-Diaz, 2008).

In developing the Creative Personality Inventory (Rayburn, 2005a), creativity was operationally defined as that which brings into existence something new through imaginative skill or design rather than imitating previous product, thoughts, or ideas. The creative personality would be flexible, original, imaginative, and unique in thinking. Factors involved in the CPI were Newness and Creativity, Enthusiasm, Joy in Creating, Joy of Challenge, and Uniqueness (Rayburn, 2005a, 2006, 2008b). The CPI has an overall alpha reliability of 0.891 for the 29 items.

Intuition as operationally defined in the development of the Intuition Inventory (II) (Rayburn 2005b, 2006, 2008b) was seen as involving direct knowledge or conviction gained by contemplating through immediate apprehension or cognition; the power or faculty of receiving direct, immediate knowledge or cognition without evident rational inference or thought. There is an interrelatedness surrounding intuition, transcendence, seeking goodness and truth, openness and flexibility in obtaining knowledge and what is good and true, and caring for others. The overall alpha reliability for the 21 Intuition Inventory items is 0.892. The three main factors are Confidence in Making Conclusions, Intuitive Thinking, and Sensitivity, Compassion. In a comparison between Criterion group versus Matched group, all of the CPI and II factors except the CPI Joy of Challenge were highly significantly correlated. Intuition operates in a mysterious fashion, entering our sense of awareness like a breath of air suddenly appearing as from out of nowhere and having a sense of urgency and accuracy transcending the individual's efforts to consciously bring about such an understanding.

In *WomanSoul*, a book on women's spiritual inner life (Rayburn & Comas-Diaz, 2008), 23 professional women of various backgrounds, including psychology, biological science, social work, ministry, and teaching, considered spirituality as the most important factor in inspiring them and as being highly related to creativity and intuition. The enlivening and creative force of "Spirit" has been viewed especially by women as freeing and affirmative and allowing them to optimally appreciate and use their intuition and creativity toward maximum productivity and self-actualization in relating to the full world of people, animals, plants, that is, to all of life and to the life force (Rayburn & Richmond, 2002).

Highly correlated to the CPI and II factors are the Inventory on Spirituality (Rayburn & Richmond, 1996) factors of Caring for Others (all of life, with an awareness and appreciation of true interdependency on others for protection and survival; expansion of kindness and social responsibility toward all, incorporating protection of the environment, awareness of and sensitivity to the beauty, awesomeness, and wonderment of the world and of life), Transcendence (knowledge of some strong external life force or influence pulling the self toward caring for other and seeking the good and true; the often mystical persuasive force is unwavering and connects with the ordinary world of experience and ultimate reality, taking us into a realm of otherworldly thoughts and feelings, into the unique and highly unusual; intuition plays a large part in this aspect of transcendence), and Seeking of Goodness and Truth (the analytical aspect of authenticity seeking within the fiery fervor of spirituality; the urgent seeking for a sense of meaning, purpose, mission, and challenge; creativity plays a significant part in the search for goodness and truth).

Rayburn and Richmond (Rayburn, 2006, 2008b) held that from spirituality comes the development of creativity and the openness from which intuition is born, fostered, nourished, and celebrated. Moved by the Spirit, we get the impetus to bring forth new, often mystical ideas and connections. Often women appear to be more trusting of intuition and fear less to express themselves through such insightful knowledge and information. *Intuition* has been defined as "quick and ready insight" and "the power or faculty of attaining direct knowledge or cognition without evident rational thought and inference" (Merriam-Webster, p. 615). *Creativity* has been defined as being creative—having the quality of being created rather than imitated (Merriam-Webster, p. 272). Richmond found that graduate counseling students in a Catholic college, discussing themes important to their lives and identities, in which men wrote about warlike and aggressive themes (such as "Onward Christian soldier, marching as to war..."), while even nuns—who had never been married nor had any children—related to themes of creation, childbirth, delivery, and nurturing (Richmond, 1995).

Applications of Motherhood and Female Faith Development to Psychotherapy

Incorporating Hindu Indian spirituality into her psychotherapeutic work, Tummala-Narra (2008) related that the "soul" had often been linked to the feminine and "mind" to the masculine, but Hindu goddess images speak to women's ideals of power, strength, nurturance, devotion, influence, and intelligence. She emphasized that women, particularly mothers, play a critical role in handing down spiritual traditions and practices to children and youth. Questioning religious practices and rituals that exclude women from power or link them with evil and destructive aspects of power, such as uncleanliness and impurity during their menstrual cycle, she applauded Hindu imagery with its fluidity of masculine and feminine images and of human and animal forms.

Pfunder (2008), working psychotherapeutically with her ill mother, discovered a Sufi road to ecstasy, longing, and surrender that was vital to her personal and psycho-spiritual survival in an almost overwhelming relationship with her mother. Sufi chanting, drumming, dancing, whirling, and meditative movement brought her into ecstatic states of being, sacredness, and spirituality, adding to her optimal professional and personal actualization.

Richmond (2008) has experienced many religious and spiritual orientations and integrated them to benefit herself and her clients. Through such personal and professional networking, she has enriched her work as an academic, counselor, and consultant.

Greene (2008) related that her grandmother and mother were instrumental in spiritually inspiring her and teaching her both the positive and the oppressive sides of religion and spirituality. She was grateful for the Christian denominations to which most African American women belong and find organized leadership opportunities. She has used this knowledge and awareness in her work with others.

Clamar (2008), with her eclectic, diverse experiences, worked with older women in therapy and counseling. She saw spirituality as giving them more opportunities for communal as well as agentic solutions to problems, plus flexibility and openness. Simon (2008) was inspired by spiritual but not religious parents—good and caring people, who pointed to religion as engendering war and conflict but to spirituality with love at the cornerstone of connectedness. She approached God from the natural order, with the creative process and its unfolding pattern of change. Nicolas, DeSilva, Coutinho, and Prater (2008) do spiritually inspired psychotherapeutic work with their students.

Miller (2008) shared her uplifting, soulful, healing work with children and their families, working from the vantage point of being a superb mother/therapist role model, passing on vital messages of spirituality and other meaningful lessons for life. She has developed her own Spiritual Awareness Psychotherapy, a transformative and spiritually interactive role that children have with the universe and its lessons. As the therapist, she brings out the child's ability and role as spiritual guide to her or his family and the community at large.

Conclusion

Motherhood is intimately linked to female faith development, and concepts of "Mother of God," Motherhood of God," female goddesses, madonnas and saints, and the Holy Spirit have played a vital and viable role in the formation of female faith development. Lessons that mothers have taught by example and more formal instruction have formed the basis of female religiousness and spirituality. The tapestry of motherhood in weaving female faith development involves teachings about religiousness and spirituality, and it is intimately related to creativity and intuition.

References

Austria, A. M. (2008). Spirituality and resilience of Filipinos. In C. A. Rayburn & L. Comas-Diaz (Eds.), *Woman Soul: The inner life of women's spirituality* (pp. 119–126). Westport, CT: Praeger.

Beer, F. (1992). *Women and mystical experience in the Middle Ages.* Rochester, NY: Boydell Press.

Beer, F. (1999). *Julian of Norwich: Revelations of divine love and the motherhood of God.* NY: D. S. Brewer.

Bradford, M. L. (1982). Committed Mormon women and how they cope: A personal approach. *Journal of Pastoral Counseling, 17*(1), 23–28.

Broussard, L. J. (2012). "The Motherhood of God" Sermon of May 10, 2009, Retrieved January 2010, from http://myblockseo.com/lone-jensen-broussard/mother-of-god-sermon-lone-jensen-broussard.pdf and http://myblockseo.com/lone-jensen-broussard/mother-of-god-sermon-lone-jensen-broussard.htm

Clamar, A. (2008). Spirituality: An eclectic force in life. In C. A. Rayburn & L. Comas-Diaz (Eds.), *WomanSoul: The inner life of women's spirituality* (pp. 139–142). Westport, CT: Praeger.

Comas-Diaz, L. (2008). Illuminating the Black Madonna: A healing journey. In C. A. Rayburn and L. Comas-Diaz (Eds.), *WomanSoul: The inner life of women's spirituality* (pp. 85–91). Westport, CT: Praeger.

Costa, P. T., Jr., & McCrae, R. R. (1992). *Revised NEO Personality/Inventory (NEO-PI-R) and NEO Five-Factor*

Inventory (NEO-FFD manual). Odessa, FL: Psychological Assessment Resources.

Daly, M. (1968). *The church and the second sex*. Boston: Beacon Press.

Daly, M. (1973). *Beyond God the father*. Boston: Beacon Press.

Datan, N. (1982). Toward a taxonomy of patriarchy: Survival imperatives, ritual, and reform in Jewish tradition. *Journal of Pastoral Counseling, 17*(10), 5–8.

Duckworth, P. (2006, May 14). *Easter V. Year B*. Sermon delivered at St. Ambrose, Foster City, CA. Retrieved January 2010, from http://www.stambrosefostercity.org/sermon.05.14.06.doc

Durka, G. (1982). Women and power: Leadership in religious organizations. *Journal of Pastoral Counseling, 17*(1), 69–74.

Eppig, E. (2008). Worldviews and women's spirituality. In C. A. Rayburn & L. Comas-Diaz (Eds.), *WomanSoul: The inner life of women's spirituality* (pp. 3–18). Westport, CT: Preager.

Espin, O. M. (2008). My "friendship" with women saints as a source of spirituality. In C. A. Rayburn & L. Comas-Diaz (Eds.), *WomanSoul: The inner life of women's spirituality* (pp. 71–84). Westport, CT: Praeger.

Fowler, J. W. (1981). *Stages of faith*. NY: Harper & Row.

Gavin, E. (1982). Stress and conflict of Catholic women in relation to feminism. *Journal of Pastoral Counseling, 17*(1), 9–13.

Greene, B. (2008). African American women, religion, and oppression: The use and abuse of spiritual beliefs. In C. A. Rayburn & L. Comas-Diaz (Eds.), *WomanSoul: The inner life of women's spirituality* (pp. 153–166). Westport, CT: Preager.

Gregerson, M. B. (2008). A quiet soul listens to her: Women, spirituality, and psychology. In C. A. Rayburn & L. Comas-Diaz (Eds.), *WomanSoul: The inner life of women's spirituality* (pp. 193–206). Westport, CT: Praeger.

Johnson, S. (1981). *From housewife to heretic: One woman's struggle for equal rights and her excommunication from the Mormon church*. Garden City, NY: Doubleday.

Kanis, S. (2003, March). *Women's spirituality*. Paper presented at the Spirituality and Religion Conference, APA Division 36, Psychology of Religion, Loyola College, Baltimore, MD.

Kristeva, J. (1982). *Powers of horror: An essay on abjection*. New York, NY: Columbia University Press.

Long, T. L. (1995). Julian of Norwich's "Christ as Mother" and medieval constructions of gender. Presented at the Madison Conerence on English Sufies, James Madison University, March 18,1995. Retrieved January, 2012, from http://community.tncc.edu/faculty/longt/papaers/Julian_Xt_as_Mother.html

Marcell, R. (2008, December). *Julian of Norwich and the "Motherhood of God."* http://robert-marcell.suite101.com/julian-of-norwich-a85969. Retrieved 1/22/2012.

McElroy, S. C. (1998). *Animals as teachers and healers*. New York: Ballentine.

Meadow, M. J. (1982). Religious unchurched women: Yearnings, frustrations, and solutions. *Journal of Pastoral Counseling, 17*(1), 29–32.

Merriam-Webster's Collegiate Dictionary. (1993). Springfield, MA: Merriam-Webster.

Miller, L. (2008). Spiritual awareness in life and psychotherapy. In C. A. Rayburn & L. Comas-Diaz (Eds.), *WomanSoul: The inner life of women's spirituality* (pp. 221–236). Westport, CT: Praeger.

Natale, S. M. (1982). Dynamics in religious organizations which induce stress. *Journal of Pastoral Counseling, 17*(1), 57–60.

National and International Religion Report. (1990). 4, March 12, 1990.

Nicolas, G., DeSilva, A. M., Coutinho, M., & Prater, K. (2008). Voicing my own gospel: Stories of spirituality from young women. In C. A. Rayburn & L. Comas-Diaz (Eds.), *WomanSoul: The inner life of women's spirituality* (pp. 247–258). Westport, CT: Praeger.

Owen, R. (1999) Pope praises "God the Mother" to pilgrims. *The London Times*, September 10, 1999. Retrieved Januray, 2012, from http://www.truthbeknown.com/mother.htm

Pfunder, J. (2008). Colors of the invisible Sufi healing. In C. A. Rayburn & L. Comas-Diaz (Eds.), *WomanSoul: The inner life of women's spirituality* (pp. 167–178). Westport, CT: Praeger.

Piedmont, R. (1995). Big-Five adjective marker scales for uses with college students, *Psychological Reports, 77*, 160–162.

Portnoy, M. A. (1986). *Ima on the Bima: My mommy is a rabbi*. Minneapolis, MN: Lerner Publishing.

Prestbo, D., & Staats-Westover, H. (2008). The goddess has returned! In C. A. Rayburn & L. Comas-Diaz (Eds.), *WomanSoul: The inner life of women's spirituality* (pp. 19–38). Westport, CT: Praeger.

Propst, R. (1982). Servanthood defined: Coping mechanisms for women within Protestant Christianity. *Journal of Pastoral Counseling, 17*(10), 14–18.

Randour, M. J. (2000a). *Animal grace: Entering a spiritual relationship with our fellow creatures*. Novato, CA: New World Library.

Randour, M. J. (2000b, August). *Changing of the Gods: Emergence of the women's spirituality movement*. Paper presented at the Third Millennium Women and Spirituality Symposium—Addressing the Wounds of Traditionalism at the American Psychological Association Annual Conference, Washington, DC.

Raum, E. (2004). *American lives: Alice Paul*. Chicago: Heinemann Library.

Rayburn, C. A. (1979, April 4). Wilson, Bradford discuss women's status in Adventist Church. *Student Movement* (Andrews University), p. 9.

Rayburn, C. A. (1981). Some reflections of a female seminarian: Woman, whither goest thou? *Journal of Pastoral Counseling, 16*(2), 61–65.

Rayburn, C. A. (1982). Seventh-day Adventist women: Values, conflicts, and resolutions, *Journal of Pastoral Counseling, 17*(1), 19–22.

Rayburn, C. A. (1984). Impact of nonsexist language and guidelines for women in religion. *Journal of Pastoral Counseling, 19*(1), 5–8.

Rayburn, C. A. (1989). Power struggles, equality quests, and women in ecclesia. *Journal of Pastoral Counseling, 24*, 145–150.

Rayburn, C. A. (1993). Ritual as acceptance/empowerment and rejection/disenfranchisement. In L. A. Northup (Ed.), *Women and religious ritual* (pp. 87–101). Washington, DC: Pastoral Press.

Rayburn, C. A. (1995). The body in religious experience. In R. W. Hood, Jr. (Ed.), *Handbook of religious experience* (pp. 476–494). Birmingham, AL: Religious Education Press.

Rayburn, C. A. (1996, August 12). *Religion and spirituality: Can one exist independently of the other?* Paper presented at the American Psychological Association Annual Conference, Toronto, Canada.

Rayburn, C. A. (2001). Theobiology, spirituality, religiousness, and the Wizard of Oz. William C. Bier Award Address. *Psychology of Religion Newsletter, 26*(1), 1–11.

Rayburn, C. A. (2003, March 28). *Images of God: Have we forgotten the holy spirit?* Paper presented at the Mid-Winter Research Conference on Religion and Spirituality, Loyola College in Maryland, Timonium, MD.

Rayburn, C. A. (2005a). *Creative Personality Inventory (CPI).* Washington, DC: US Copyright Office.

Rayburn, C. A. (2005b). *Intuition Inventory (II).* Washington, DC: US Copyright Office.

Rayburn, C. A. (2006). Development of the Creative Personality Inventory and the Intuition Inventory. In S. M. Natale (Ed.), *Conflict and the "sleep of reason"* (pp. 105–112). New York: Global Scholarly Publications and Oxford University Centre for the Study of Values in Education and Business.

Rayburn, C. A. (2007a). Alice Paul: Constitutional amendment mover and ERA author. In E. A. Gavin, A. Clamar, & M. A. Siderits (Eds.), *Women of vision: Their psychology, circumstances and successes* (pp. 61–78). New York: Springer Publishing.

Rayburn, C. A. (2007b, March 2). *Health, religiousness, spirituality: Aging wine/newer wineskins?* Paper presented at the American Psychological Association Division 36 Mid-Winter Conference on Research on Religion and Spirituality, Loyola University, Columbia, MD.

Rayburn, C. A. (2008a). Compassionate illuminate: Spirituality's caring for others, seeking goodness and truth, peacefulness, and that "T" word—transcendence. *Child and Family Behavior Therapy, 30*(2), 195–198.

Rayburn, C. A. (2008b). Implications of creativity and intuition springing forth from spirituality. In S. M. Natale (Ed.), *Beatitude past utterance: Balancing life, career, values, ethnics* (pp. 143–152). New York: Global Scholarly Publication and Oxford University Centre for the Study of Values in Education and Business.

Rayburn, C. A. (2008c). The saving grace of spirituality: Restoring hope, vitality, and creative joy. In C. A. Rayburn & L. Comas-Diaz (Eds.), *WomanSoul: The inner life of women's spirituality* (pp. 39–56). Westport, CT: Praeger.

Rayburn, C. A., & Comas-Diaz, L. (Eds.). (2008). *WomanSoul: The inner life of women's spirituality.* Westport, CT: Praeger.

Rayburn, C. A., Hansen, L. S., Siderits, M. A., Burson, J., & Richmond, L. J. (1999, 2004). *Life Choices Inventory (LCI).* Washington, DC: US Copyright Office.

Rayburn, C. A., Natale, S. M., & Linzer, J. (1982). Feminism and religion: What price holding membership in both camps? *Counseling and Values, 26*(8). 154–164.

Rayburn, C. A., & Richmond, L. J. (1996). *Inventory on Spirituality (IS).* Washington, DC: US Copyright Office.

Rayburn, C. A., & Richmond, L. J. (1997). *Inventory on Religiousness (IR).* Washington, DC: US Copyright Office.

Rayburn, C. A., & Richmond, L. J. (1998). Theobiology: Attempting to understand God and ourselves. *Journal of Religion and Health, 37*(4), 345–356.

Rayburn, C. A., & Richmond, L. J. (1999). *Inventory on the Supreme and Work (ISAW).* Washington, DC: US Copyright Office.

Rayburn, C. A., & Richmond, L. J. (2000). Theobiology: Its relevance to deeper understanding, In S. M. Natale, A. F. Libertella, & G. Hayward (Eds.), *On the threshold of the millenium: Business, education, and training, a values-laden process* (pp. 281–288). Lanham, MD: University Press.

Rayburn, C. A., & Richmond, L. J. (Eds.). (2002a). Theobiology: Interfacing theology and science. (Devoted issue). *American Behavioral Scientist, 45*(12), 1793–1811.

Rayburn, C. A., & Richmond, L. J. (2002b). Women, whither goest thou? To Chart a new course in religiousness and spirituality and to define ourseves! In L. H. Collins, M. R. Dunlap, & J. C. Chrisler (Eds.), *Charting a new course for feminist psychology* (pp. 167–189). Westport, CT: Praeger.

Rayburn, C. A., & Richmond, L. J. (2004). *Inventory on religiousness.* Washington, DC:US Copyright Office.

Rayburn, C. A., Richmond, L. J., & Rogers, L. (1982). Women, men, and religion: Stress within sanctuary walls. *Journal of Pastoral Counseling, 17*(1), 75–83.

Rayburn, C. A., Richmond, L. J., & Rogers, L. (1983). Stress in religious leaders. *Thought: Fordham University Quarterly Review, 58*(230), 329–344.

Rayburn, C. A., Richmond, L. J., & Rogers, L. (1986). Men, women, and religion: Stress in leadership roles. *Journal of Clinical Psychology, 42*(3), 540–546.

Rayburn, C. A., Richmond, L. J., & Rogers, L. (1994). Women religious professionals and stress. In L. B. Brown & H. N. Malony (Eds.), *Religion, personality, and mental health* (pp. 167–173). New York: Springer-Verlag.

Read, D. H. C. (1979). Fourth Sunday in Lent (Mothering Sunday) The motherhood of God. *The Expository Times, 5,* 145–146.

Reedy, R. (2008). Women, science, and spirituality. In C. A. Rayburn & L. Comas-Diaz (Eds.), *WomanSoul: The inner life of women's spirituality* (pp. 57–67). Westport, CT: Praeger.

Richmond, L. J. (1995, August). *Career development: Sermons of female pastoral counseling students.* Paper presented at the American Psychological Association Annual conference, New York, NY.

Richmond, L. J. (2008). Strange attractors or hand of God: A spiritual journey. In C. A. Rayburn & L. Comas-Diaz (Eds.), *WomanSoul: The inner life of women's spirituality* (pp. 237–246). Westport, CT: Praeger.

Richmond, L. J., Rayburn, C. A., & Rogers, L. (1985). Female rabbis: A "species" at risk? *Journal of Pastoral Counseling, 23*(1), 11–15.

Schneiders, S. M. (1986). Feminist spirituality. In J. M. Conn (Ed.), *Women's spirituality: Resources for human development* (pp. 30–67). New York: Paulist Press.

Siderits, M. A. (2008). Journeying in twilight: Agnosticism and spirituality. In C. A. Rayburn & L. Comas-Diaz (Eds.), *WomanSoul: The inner life of women's spirituality* (pp. 179–192). Westport, CT: Praeger.

Simon, J. (2008). Stepping stones in a full life. In C. A. Rayburn & L. Comas-Diaz (Eds.), *WomanSoul: The inner life of women's spirituality* (pp. 129–138). Westport, CT: Praeger.

Start, L. (1979, December 9). *"The motherhood of God."* Retrieved January 2012, from http://hdl.handle.net/10920/9018

Stedman, E. (1996). *A woman's worth.* Palo Alto, CA: Discovery Publishing.

Thomas, A. J., & Hewitt, A. A. (2009). Promoting resilience of African-American children through spirituality and religion. *Children, Youth, and Family News, Summer,* 7–9.

Tummala-Narra, P. (2008). Hindu Indian spirituality, female identity, and psychoanalytic psychotherapy. In C. A. Rayburn & L. Comas-Diaz (Eds.), *WomanSoul: The inner life of women's spirituality* (pp. 209–220). Westport, CT: Praeger.

Vygotsky, L. S. (1978). *Mind in society: The development of higher psychological processes.* Cambridge, MA: Harvard University Press.

Weahkee, R. L. (2008). American Indian women and spirituality. In C. A. Rayburn & L. Comas-Diaz (Eds.), *WomanSoul: The inner life of women's spirituality* (pp. 107–118). Westport, CT: Praeger.

Weiner, M. B. (2008). Living Kabbalah. In C. A. Rayburn & L. Comas-Diaz (Eds.), *Woman soul: The inner life of women's spirituality* (pp. 143–152). Westport, CT: Praeger.

Wewerka, R. (2008).View of women, spirituality, and Tibetan Buddhism. In C. A. Rayburn & L. Comas-Diaz (Eds.), *Woman soul: The inner life of women's spirituality* (pp. 97–105). Westport, CT: Praeger.

Wogaman, J. P. (1998*). Speaking the truth in love: Prophetic preaching to a broken world*. Louisville, KY: Westminster John Knox Press.

Colored Spirituality: The Centrality of Spirit Among Ethnic Minorities

Lillian Comas-Díaz

Abstract

Spirituality is a way of life and a coping strategy for many people of color. Most ethnic minorities share a collective unconsciousness—a culturally relevant spirituality that helps them to struggle against oppression. Consequently, a colored spirituality is a culturally relevant syncretistic practice that focuses on cultural resilience, consciousness, and liberation. In this chapter, I present people of color's spirituality. I conclude by discussing what a colored spirituality offers to mainstream healing.

Key Words: people of color, spirituality, resilience, cultural consciousness, liberation

Introduction

Since the dawn of time, people have explored the mystery of life and death through spirituality. Like most individuals, people of color endorse a variety of religious and spiritual beliefs. Although religion plays a major role in the lives of many people of color, spirituality offers them cultural relevance. This means that most people of color find solace and support, and make meaning out of adversity through their spirituality (Cervantes & Parham, 2005). Indeed, spirituality validates ethnic minorities' experience as a source of healing and power.

People of color in the United States embrace a variety of spiritual beliefs. Moreover, their spiritual development is encased in specific cultural contexts (see Abalos, 1998; Allen, 1992; Hamilton & Jackson, 1998; Wade-Gayles, 1995). For instance, due to their history of slavery, many African Americans celebrate the Spirit as a coping mechanism against oppression. About 85% of African Americans describe themselves as "fairly religious or very religious" and cite prayer as a most common coping strategy (Satcher, 2001). As a result, most African Americans have a legacy of interacting with spiritual forces via visions, dreams, trance,

and worship. Likewise, additional spiritual activities such as speaking in tongues, dancing in the spirit, prophecies, spirit possession, and others originate in African mysticism (Baker, 2007). Certainly, African Americans tend to practice an action-oriented spirituality, where music, movement, and faith are major elements (Wimberly, 1991).

On the other hand, the diversity among American Indian nations makes difficult the identification of common spiritual values. Nonetheless, spirituality is a way of life among Native Americans, who believe in the interconnection of spirit, mind, and body. This shared Native American spiritual perspective includes interconnectedness, the sacred responsibility to teach and guide, and the acknowledgment that it is human to make mistakes (Trujillo, 2000). Moreover, American Indian spirituality teaches the value of sharing, cooperation, and noninterference (Sue & Sue, 2008).

Like other people of color, Asian Americans have diverse religious and spiritual orientations. However, Asian American spirituality is influenced by Eastern philosophies and traditions. Such Eastern orientations emphasize the achievement of enlightenment through the development of diverse levels of consciousness (Wilber, 2000). Indeed, many Asian Americans engage in a bicultural orientation; that is, they exhibit a Western cultural practice in the workplace and engage in traditional Eastern approaches at home (Tan & Dong, 2000). What is more, Asian American traditional spirituality tends to be holistic and to focus on liberation. Within this context, liberation is defined as the freedom from negative elements that cause imbalance. Consequently, attaining liberation leads to being in harmony with the cosmos.

Although most of the Latinos are nominally Catholic, there is ample religious diversity among this population. While a significant number of Latinos are leaving the Catholic Church, many are converting to Protestantism, and some Latinas are choosing Islam (Martin, 2006). In the face of adversity, oppression, immigration, and dislocation, many Latinos reconnect with their indigenous spiritual beliefs through syncretism. Syncretistic religions such as *Candomblé* (Zea, Mason, & Murguia, 2000), *Santería* (Gonzalez-Wippler, 1989), *curanderismo* (Kiev, 1968), *espiritismo* (Comas-Díaz, 1981), and others combine traditional ethnic beliefs such as African religions, North and South American animism, and shamanism with mainstream Western religions. These syncretistic forms of spirituality emerged out of psychosocial turmoil to empower individuals through the reconnection with their ancestry and history. Such affiliation strengthens cultural identity, rescues cultural values, and offers historical continuity.

Translocation and cultural adjustment are important developmental milestones for many immigrants of color. More succinctly, these experiences tend to profoundly influence their spiritual practices. In other words, many immigrants of color use their spirituality as a way of coping with cultural shock, economic distress, and cultural adjustment. Regardless of immigration status, a colored spirituality offers a sense of belonging to a community, as well as a relief from emotional distress caused by acculturation pressure and racism.

Despite people of color's cultural diversity, a historical bond connects many ethnic minorities. A colored spirituality is a form of collective unconsciousness that unites most ethnic minorities through a common history of oppression. Numerous people of color adhere to a colored spirituality in order to cope with a legacy of cultural trauma. Historical cultural trauma entails the succession of traumatic events and oppression that members of a cultural group endure from one generation to the next (Evans-Campbell, 2008). When ethnic minorities become conscious of their sociopolitical and historical circumstances, they embrace a colored spirituality that encourages the use of cultural beliefs, symbols, and traditions for healing and liberation. A colored spirituality affirms the centrality of Spirit among ethnic minorities through an amalgamation of indigenous traditions with dominant religious beliefs. As a lived spirituality (Castillo, 1994), this syncretistic approach addresses the psycho-spiritual needs of many people of color.

Soul Wounds

Ethnic minorities' history of cultural oppression nurtured the practice of a colored spirituality. Many people of color are bonded through a shared history of ethnocultural and racial trauma. Such a formative legacy creates deep attachments, distinguishing people of color who have endured cultural oppression from those whom have not. Moreover, this traumatic legacy fosters identification, affiliation, and group membership related to racial and cultural oppression (Comas-Díaz, 2007).

A history of cultural oppression is a common denominator for individuals who endorse a colored spirituality. Certainly, being the *other* is a mark of cultural oppression. Color, the manifestation of historical and cultural trauma in the United States, bonds many ethnic minorities. Such legacy of racial subjugation subordinates gender, sexual orientation, and class identities to the condition of being oppressed (Almquist, 1989). Indeed, cultural-racial trauma is a formative experience for many visible people of color. Moreover, people of color have been subjected to cultural imperialism—the attempts to intellectually and culturally dominate the oppressed. The effects of cultural imperialism are nefarious to its victims because cultural imperialism universalizes and establishes as a norm the dominant group's experience and culture (Young, 1990). Consequently, dominant group members define the individuals in the oppressed group and designate them as deviant and inferior (Young, 1990). As a result, victims of cultural imperialism become the *other* and thus seriously compromise their cultural values (Said, 1994).

When people of color become disconnected from their indigenous roots, they develop a fractured identity. Along these lines, losing one's identity causes imbalance, distress, and illness. Additionally, cultural imperialism robs the oppressed of their agency, mastery, and ability for critical analysis. Beth Roy (2007) argued that individual psychodynamics represent internalized oppression. Within this framework, cultural imperialism acts as a contemporary manifestation of colonization through the repression of people of color's ethnic beliefs. Indeed, the American Psychological Association's first president of color, Kenneth B. Clark (1989), identified the condition of Americans of color as colonization.

Cultural oppression inflicts soul wounds to its victims. Soul wounds result from a legacy of cultural trauma, ungrieved losses, internalized oppression, and learned helplessness (Duran, 2006). Soul wounds are the offspring of ethnic minorities' history of slavery, colonization, genocide, US annexation wars, and survivor syndrome, among other oppressive experiences inflicted upon people of color. Soul wounds are a response to cultural and spiritual hegemony. They lead to a negation of the self. As cultural oppression elicits a psychological adaptation to the realities of domination, victims internalize powerlessness and develop identity conflicts (Freire, 1973). Indeed, numerous people of color suffer from an oppressed (or colonized) mentality consisting of emotional alienation, self-denial, assimilation, and strong ambivalence (Memmi, 1965). Likewise, chronic alienation results in a psycho-spiritual anomie, a condition that aggravates people of color's soul wounds.

Most people of color encounter contemporary oppression. Many contend with social defeat, or the condition arising when an individual is forced into a menial position as an outsider, unable to attain the social rewards of a dominant group member (Cantor-Graae & Selten, 2005).

Being the *other* exposes visible people of color to racial microaggressions. The assaults that people of color receive on a regular basis solely because of their race and/or ethnicity, racial microaggressions include being the target of racial profiling, being harassed in public spaces, ignored by clerks who favor White customers, being confused with the help, and other degrading experiences (Pierce, 1995).

To heal their soul wounds and achieve liberation, victims of cultural oppression need to find their own voice to name and describe their condition (Fanon, 1967). Many ethnic minorities commit to a colored spirituality in order to repair an oppressed mentality and reformulate a fractured identity. As a result, a colored spirituality attempts to heal soul wounds through the rescue and affirmation of individuals' ethnocultural and indigenous roots. Moreover, a colored spirituality offers people of color opportunities for hope and redemption. As ethnic minorities incorporate their indigenous beliefs into dominant religions, they affirm a colored spirituality, rescue their ancestry, and ground their identity into a collective self.

An Invisible Altar: Culturally Relevant Spirituality

Most Western religions have engaged in cultural imperialism through their repression of people's indigenous spiritual beliefs. Unfortunately, many of the dominant religions have historically functioned as instruments of colonization. Consequently, Western religions have had a devastating effect on the collective identity of indigenous groups, particularly on American Indians (Trujillo, 2000). In contrast, a colored spirituality emerged out of such repression to offer solace, support, and hope to people of color. Similar to the invisible church where African slaves used to worship to conceal their indigenous beliefs from their masters (Cook & Wiley, 2000), many people of color place their spirituality in an invisible altar. Such an altar enthrones a culturally relevant spirituality. In other words, a colored spirituality surfaced out of cultural oppression to affirm, sustain, and redeem ethnic minorities' indigenous beliefs.

Indeed, a colored spirituality addresses the psycho-spiritual needs of many ethnic minorities in a culturally relevant manner. Moreover, a culturally relevant spirituality promotes emotional and spiritual salvation (Early, 1996). Grounded in a collectivistic worldview, a colored spirituality helps people of color to deepen their existential sense of meaning and purpose in life. Consequently, the spirit world is omnipresent among most people of color.

Regardless of their religiosity, numerous people of color, including African Americans (Boyd-Franklin, 2003), Asian Americans (Sue & Sue, 2008), American Indians/Native Americans (Allen, 1992), and Latinos (Comas-Díaz, 2006), have an awareness of their spiritual ancestry. For example, traditional Latino culture emphasizes animism—the belief that everything in life, whether human, animal, material, and or ecological, has a spirit (De La Cancela- & Zavala, 1983). Moreover, the Pew Hispanic Center and Pew Forum on Religion and Public Life (2007) found that while remaining committed to traditional church teachings, many Latino Catholics reported familiarity with supernatural experiences, such as divine healings and speaking in tongues—experiences that are more typical of Protestant revival movements than traditional Catholic Church.

Relatedly, many Native Americans believe in a sacred interconnection of everything in the cosmos (Garret & Garret, 1994). Likewise, traditional Asian Americans accept the existence of the supernatural and thus honor the spirit of their ancestors through specific practices (Tan & Dong, 2000). Indeed, the wisdom of ancient Eastern practices has enriched the spiritual lives of many Asian Americans. Moreover, traditional African culture assigns spirituality a central role in life (Mbiti, 1969). Furthermore, many African Americans have been praying for generations (Cook & Wiley, 2000) and thus have a long history of spiritual communion.

In the following section I examine a colored spirituality's culturally responsiveness to collectivistic ethnic minorities. Specifically, I illustrate this process through a discussion of transpersonality and cultural consciousness.

Transpersonality

Most people of color acknowledge the metaphysical dimension of existence (Sue & Sue, 2008). In other words, they recognize the interpenetration of the material and the nonmaterial worlds. Such orientation embraces transpersonality—a manifestation of the metaphysical aspect in life. Transpersonality entails the development of identity beyond personal and individual contexts (Scotton, 1996). A sociocentric way of relating, transpersonality involves the ability to transcend the individual self into a self-other-cosmic identity. Transpersonality fosters the interpenetration of cosmic influences in people's lives (Comas-Díaz, 2011). An illustration of transpersonality is the permeability of boundaries between the living and deceased individuals. Since many people of color believe that the contact between significant others does not end with death, they continue their relationship with the dead through dreams, visions, and other supernatural avenues (Council of National Psychological Associations, 2003).

Along these lines, numerous people of color endorse a transpersonal agency—a spiritual principle that recognizes the role of supernatural factors in people's lives (Keller, 2002). This concept relates to the belief in the co-creation of reality (Comas-Díaz, 2006). Transpersonal agency refers to the sharing of a personal sense of mastery with an external power. Simply put, many people of color share their agency with transpersonal entities—spiritual, natural, supernatural, and or cosmic influences (destiny, karma, fortune).

Another expression of transpersonality is the belief in a cosmic locus of control. Indeed, due to their cultural oppression, many people of color adhere to a combined internal and external locus of control, where the context determines which locus of control will prevail. For example, the Serenity prayer is an illustration of a cosmic locus of control: "God, give me the grace to accept with serenity the things that cannot be changed, courage to change the things which should be changed, and the wisdom to distinguish one from the other."

People who adhere to a colored spirituality recognize the pervasive influence of context in their life. Thus, their spirituality is anchored in cultural, family, group, environmental, sociopolitical, and historical contexts (Ho, 1987). Consequently, belief in transpersonality is expressed through cultural forms. For example, many Latinos believe in magical realism—an interpenetration of reality with fantasy (Maduro & Martinez, 1974). Magical realism infuses fantasy and mystery into Latino life (Comas-Díaz, 2006). Interestingly, magical realism has been successfully used as a psychotherapeutic approach for Latinos (De Rios, 1997).

When ethnic minorities are grounded in a colored spirituality, they reconnect with their indigenous legacies, enhance their coping strategies, and become empowered. Therefore, a colored spirituality is culturally relevant because it fosters cultural resilience, encourages cultural consciousness, and promotes liberation. In the following section I discuss these elements.

Cultural Consciousness

Spirituality and resilience have a reciprocal relationship; they promote each other. For example, milestones and crises provide individuals with opportunities to reconnect with spirituality. Interestingly, an ideological ethnicity denotes the tendency to find meaning in life challenges by revisiting cultural and spiritual beliefs (Harwood, 1981). Consequently, a colored spirituality affirms ideological ethnicity as it fosters spiritual development by helping individuals to make meaning out of adversity. Such a perspective offers resilience, hope, and redemption to oppressed individuals. Similarly, a colored spirituality reframes the meaning of illness as a spiritual crisis (Grof & Grof, 1989), as well as an opportunity for self-improvement (Muñoz & Mendelson, 2005).

Additionally, minorities endorse a colored spirituality to cope with historical and contemporary cultural trauma. Resilience is a major component of people of color's cultural consciousness. Such coping style has been termed "cultural resilience." A host of values and practices that promote coping mechanisms and adaptive reactions to trauma and oppression within an indigenous and ethnic context, cultural resilience (Elsass, 1992) is a survivalist and resourceful response to oppression and adversity.

Cultural resilience can be expressed as revision, adaptation, and subversion. It empowers individuals to resist and revise the dominant discourse. For example, Black Christian theologians reinterpreted Jesus as a person of color and a racial liberator (West & Glaude, 2004). Many African American theologians modified Christian traditions, beliefs, and scriptures in order to deconstruct culturally oppressive narratives and thus help people of color to recover their voices (Brown, 1989; Thomas, 1998). Hence, a spirituality-based cultural resilience helps people of color to revise the meaning of being the *other*. For example, as several African American women walked the wounded healer path, they became "chosen vessels" in order to impart wisdom and courage to their communities (Osaigbovo, 2002).

To resist oppression, cultural resilience encourages adaptation. For example, culturally resilient individuals adapt by endorsing a syncretistic consciousness. The capacity to simultaneously hold multiple beliefs, shift from one perspective to another, and integrate several cultural orientations, a syncretistic consciousness helps to create a new reality out of divergent positions (Sandoval, 1998). Likewise, a syncretistic consciousness allows individuals to enact different identities according to the specific context. Also known as a multicultural brain, a syncretistic consciousness enhances people of color's coping with power dynamics, emphasizes diverse aspects of their identity according to context, and promotes transformation (Comas-Díaz, 2008). A syncretistic consciousness is a survivalist mechanism (Moya, 2001) associated with cultural adaptation and biculturalism. Empirical research found that bilingual bicultural individuals incorporate two cultures, have distinct sets of culture-specific concepts, and develop mental frameworks that activate different aspects of their identities (Luna, Ringberg, & Peracchio, 2008). The survivalist aspect of a syncretistic consciousness is related to what W. E. B. Du Bois (1903) called African Americans' double consciousness, where individuals cope with the dominant White society while being situated in an ethnic minority context. A syncretistic consciousness enhances coping, survival, and creativity.

Yet another function of a spiritual cultural resilience is subversion. Insurgence aims to change an oppressive status quo. As many White Americans used their Christian religion to sustain slavery, African Americans used their colored spirituality as a liberation force (Cook & Wiley, 2000). To illustrate, numerous people of color questioned beliefs, traditions, practices, and structures of dominant religions in order to foment social changes. Consequently, they revised the dominant dogma, subverted the established canon, and chose divine figures with dark skin (Kidd, 2002). For example, Black Madonna worship is prevalent among some people of color because it promotes resilience against oppression, sexism, and racism (Kidd, 2005). Black Madonnas are syncretistic dark ancient goddess who became Christian liberation fighters (Begg, 1985; Galland, 1990).). Our Lady of Guadalupe, the syncretism of a Catholic Virgin with the Mexican goddess Tonantzin, helped Mexicans to obtain their independence and encouraged Mexican Americans to fight racism in the Untied States (Castillo, 1994). Notwithstanding a colored spirituality goal of subversion, the first step in liberation is the development of cultural consciousness.

A colored spirituality helps ethnic minorities to reconnect with their psycho-spiritual roots. As a result, it fosters cultural consciousness—the affirmation, identification, and celebration of people's ancestry, history, and culture. Cultural consciousness encourages ethnic minorities to recognize, reclaim, and recover their indigenous values and strengths. When cultural consciousness helps ethnic minorities to reacquaint with their history and culture, it promotes their psycho-spiritual redemption. Moreover, this type of consciousness helps people of color to recuperate from cultural amnesia. Furthermore, cultural consciousness promotes color consciousness—ethnic minorities' identification, affirmation, and acceptance of their "darkness" or non-White physical characteristics. For these reasons, healing the soul wounds begins with the awakening of cultural and racial consciousness.

African American spirituality is an excellent example of such racial and cultural awakening. Black churches have used African motifs such as clothing, adornments, African music, instruments, and dance, in addition to libations, and calling upon ancestors to promote an African American cultural consciousness. Moreover, adherents to a colored spirituality tend to define their identity in a relational context. That is, they incorporate family, group ancestry, ethnic community, and spirituality into their sense of self and cultural identity. Similarly, the process of rescuing psycho-spiritual strengths enhances cultural and racial identity. Such a process helps ethnic minorities to combat racism—at the individual, institutional, and societal levels. More important, cultural consciousness helps people of color to challenge their internalized racism and oppression.

Cultural consciousness promotes divergent thinking—the creative act of producing as many ideas as possible. A divergent thinking is associated with creativity. Indeed, many of the cultural resilient responses are creative expressions (Comas-Díaz, 2008). Thus, it is not surprising that research has documented that multicultural experiences enhance creativity (Leung, Maddux, Galinsky, & Chiu, 2008). Moreover, when ethnic minorities reconnect with their cultural roots, they become spiritually awakened and thus empowered (Tisdell, 2006). Succinctly put, cultural consciousness helps people of color to transcend a survivalist mentality and to work toward liberation. Certainly, cultural consciousness offers people of color redemption, transformation, and liberation in a culturally relevant manner.

Liberation

> The greatest weapon in the hands of the
> oppressor is the mind of the oppressed.
> —Stephen Bantu Biko (1971)

Reconnecting with our cultural and spiritual roots paves the road to empowerment. Certainly, the ultimate goal of colored spirituality is liberation. Due to their history of soul wounds, many ethnic minorities are in need of liberation approaches. Within this perspective, a colored spirituality promotes insurgence, activism, and social justice. Indeed, adherents to a colored spirituality populate the annals of the US civil rights movements.

African American spirituality offers credence to this assertion. A central tenet in African Christian churches is the promotion of racial liberation (Cook & Wiley 2000). Thus, a colored spirituality acts as a social witness for reform (Townes, 1995). To illustrate, African American clergy has a long history of preaching liberating messages and establishing Afrocentric Christian schools. Indeed, the African American spiritual consciousness emerged to promote agency, empowerment, and emancipation. Even African American churches that are not Afrocentric tend to promote liberation while providing opportunities for African Americans to attain community participation, leadership skills, and

management positions that are not available in the dominant society (Boyd-Franklin, 1989; Cook & Wiley, 2000). Moreover, the Black theology movement as well as Elijah Muhammad's Nation of Islam called for African American self-sufficiency and self-empowerment (Cook & Wiley, 2000).

Similarly, Latinos have a legacy of engaging in spiritual liberation practices. The Spanish (Latin) word *misericordia* (mercy) translates into English as "miserable heart" and means "having pain in your heart for the pains of another and taking pains to do something about the pain" (Ploplis, 2010). In other words, *misericordia* calls for the liberation of the oppressed. Consequently, Liberation theology was born in Latin America. To foment social justice and combat poverty and inequality among Latino(a)s, Liberation theologians side with the poor and oppressed (Gutierrez, 1971). Influenced by Liberation theology, Paulo Freire (1973), a Brazilian educator, developed *conscientizacion* as a teaching method. A critical consciousness process, *conscientizacion* teaches individuals to engage in a dialectical dialog with their world, become aware of their circumstances, and initiate transformative actions. Moreover, a critical consciousness encourages oppressed individuals to ask: What? Why? How? For whom? Against whom? By whom? In favor of whom? In favor of what? To what end? (Freire & Macedo, 2000). As people of color answer these questions, they explore the existential meaning of their life.

Infused with liberation theology principles, Latino spirituality tends to be communal, in addition to culturally and linguistically responsive. Similarly, the Black liberation theologies emphasize the needs of the marginalized and view salvation as liberation from White oppression (West & Glaude, 2004). As previously indicated, many Black theologians and clergy added their voice to the cries of freedom that mobilized civil rights movements. Simply put, a colored spirituality aims at social justice. It promotes liberation and encourages solidarity among oppressed individuals. Definitely, the dictum "liberate yourself by liberating others" is a colored spirituality principle.

Along these lines, a colored spirituality opens spaces for individuals who are oppressed at multiple levels. For example, African American women's feminism—womanism—affirms female strengths, fights oppression, and promotes collective social justice (Walker, 1983). Womanists resist, rebel, and empower themselves and their ethnic communities by preserving and *integrating* their female colored spirituality into mainstream religion (Comas-Díaz, 2008). Likewise, *mujerismo* (from the Spanish word *mujer*—meaning woman) blends Latina feminism, cultural studies, and folk spirituality. Similar to their womanist sisters, *mujeristas* fight against sexism, racism, neocolonialism, and other types of oppression (Isasi-Díaz, 1994). Both womanist and *mujerista* movements are embedded in liberation theology and advance social justice.

A New-Ancient Narrative: Colored Spirituality and Healing

Spiritually and healing are intimately connected for many people of color. Traditional African and Latino spirituality have a strong healing legacy (Mbiti, 1969; Ruiz, 1997). To illustrate, many ethnic minority spiritual organizations offer culturally appropriate healing and counseling services, 12-step programs, support services, and community resources (Wimberly, 1991). Likewise, healing is a spiritual activity for many American Indians, since intention, words, and feelings have a powerful role in native medicine (Ruiz, 1997). Moreover, everything in life, including events, interactions, memories, and positive experiences and places, has a healing potential in the American Indian worldview (Sue & Sue, 2008).

Due to their legacy of cultural trauma, numerous ethnic minority group members expect healing to bear a spiritual component (Coelho, 2003; Maduro & Martinez, 1974); thus, they seek the help of spiritual healers. Most traditional healers such as *curanderos*, *espiritistas*, shamans, *yerberos* (*hierberos*), medicine wo/man, and or *sobadores* examine health and well-being through a holistic prism. That is, they believe that illness results from a disharmony between the mind, body, sprit, and cosmos. Additionally, folk healers hold a relational mirror to reflect individuals' health. In other words, they believe that a disruption in relationships with significant others is the root of distress. Therefore, spiritual healers define healing as a holistic practice that involves ancestral and sacred affiliations (Morones, & Mikawa, 1992). Such relational healing helps to ground sufferers to a cultural context. Indeed, proponents of a colored spirituality assert that healing occurs when we reconnect with who we are (Ruiz, 1997). Consequently, the purpose of spiritual healing is to be awakened, conscientized, and liberated.

Interestingly, the healing properties of non-Western spiritual and philosophical traditions are permeating the general public. As a result, Americans of all colors are using healing traditions based on ancient colored spirituality. When illness threatens individuals' sense of intactness and connection to the world, non-Western healing traditions provide them with a participatory experience of empowerment, authenticity, and an enlarged self-identity (Kaptchuk & Eisenberg, 1998). Moreover, empirical research found "new" practices such as yoga, acupuncture, Ayurveda, meditation, mindfulness, herbs, and many others to be the most widely used healing approaches among Americans (Walsh & Shapiro, 2006). According to the National Center for Complementary and Alternative Medicine, 38% of adults and about 12% of children in the United States use complementary and alternative medicine (Barnes, Bloom, & Nahin, 2008). The majority of people using these healing approaches stated that they find them to be more congruent with their own values, beliefs, and orientation toward health and life.

Currently, healers from diverse spiritual paths and professional backgrounds are examining the curative attributes of colored spirituality traditions such as *curanderismo* (Kiev, 1968), *espiritismo* (Comas-Díaz, 1981), *Santería* (Gonzalez-Wippler, 1989), shamanism (Villoldo, 2000), *Candomblé*, and *Umbanda* (Zea et al., 2000). In many instances, a *syncretism of syncretism*, such as a blending of *espiritismo* with Buddhism, is promoting holistic healing to the next developmental stage. Such movement contributes to the evolution of a new-ancient healing narrative. This development infuses syncretism and holism into the dominant healing. It attempts to heal the individual, group, world, and cosmos. In sum, a colored spirituality restores individuals' sense of belonging, promotes self-healing, and commits to social justice.

Conclusion

Painted with vivid hues, the altar of a colored spirituality is visible to those who seek to see. The ongoing evolution of a colored spirituality is aided by a fundamental set of qualities. Some of these qualities include being resilient, syncretistic, communal, relational, holistic, metaphysical, committed, and emancipatory. Table 13.1 summarizes the characteristics of a colored spirituality.

In summary *a colored spirituality* mobilizes ethnic minorities to achieve a critical knowledge of themselves, helps to overcome their oppressed mentality, and facilitates taking control of their lives. A colored spirituality fosters consciousness by asking individuals to liberate themselves by liberating others. Such

Table 13.1 Colored Spirituality's Main Characteristics

- Resilient (emphasis on cultural strengths)
- Survivalist (emphasis on collective survival)
- Culturally responsive
- Contextual (connected to cultural, historical, sociopolitical, and ecological contexts)
- Syncretistic
- Oral (transmitted orally)
- Physical (expressed through singing, dancing, somatic rituals)
- Communal (honors the fellowship of people of color)
- Relational (heart to heart)
- Holistic (interconnection of mind, body, and spirit)
- Emancipatory (collective liberation)
- Cohesive (it promotes collective solidarity)
- Metaphysical
- Active (action oriented)
- Committed (social justice and racial equality)

a relational liberation facilitates the development of solidarity among oppressed individuals and guarantees the enduring evolution of a colored spirituality. A colored spirituality has relevance for everyone because its syncretistic flexibility addresses human needs by culturally adapting to individuals' unique contexts.

Future Directions

Theologians, academicians, practitioners, and others can benefit from examining colored spirituality. Specifically, they can explore the following questions:

How can a colored spirituality improve the development of health services?

How can a colored spirituality contribute to the establishment of life-enhancing programs?

What can a spiritual syncretism contribute to individual and collective well-being?

What can we learn from a colored spirituality's commitment to social justice and global welfare?

References

Abalos, D. (1998). *La comunidad Latina in the United States*. Westport, CT: Praeger.

Allen, P. G. (1992). *The sacred hoop*. Boston: Beacon Press.

Almquist, E. (1989). The experience of minority women in the United States. In J. Freeman (Ed.) *Women: A feminist perspective* (4th ed., pp. 414–445) Mountain View, CA: Mayfield.

Baker, P. (2007). *African American spirituality, thought and culture* (2nd ed.). Lincoln, NE: I Universe.

Barnes, P. M., Bloom, B., & Nahin, R. (2008, December). *CDC National Health Statistics Report #12. Complementary and Alternative Medicine Use Among Adults and Children: United States, 2007*. National Healh Statistics Reports. Hyattsville, MD: National Center for Health Statistics.

Begg, E. (1985). *The cult of the black virgin*. London: Arkana/ Penguin Books.

Biko, S. B. (1971). *Speech in Cape Town*. Retrieved January 2010, from http://africanhistory.about.com/od/bikosteve/p/qts_biko.htm

Boyd-Franklin, N. (2003). *Black families in therapy: Understanding the African American experience* (2nd ed.). New York: The Guilford Press.

Brown, E. B. (1989). Womanist consciousness: Maggie Lena Walker and the Independent Order of Saint Luke. *Sign, 14*, 610–633.

Cantor-Graae, E., & Selten, J-P. (2005). Schizophrenia and migration: A meta-analysis and review. *American Journal of Psychiatry, 162*, 12–24.

Castillo, A. (1994). *Massacre of the dreamers: Essays on Xicanisma*. New York: Penguin.

Cervantes, J. M., & Parham, T. A. (2005). Towards a meaningful spirituality for people of color: Lessons for the counseling practitioner. *Cultural Diversity and Ethnic Minority Psychology, 11*(1), 69–81.

Clark, K. B. (1989). *Dark ghetto: Dilemmas in social power* (2nd ed.). Middletown, CT: Wesleyan University Publishers.

Coelho, P. (2003). *El peregrino* [The pilgrim]. Mexico City: Grijalbo.

Comas-Díaz, L. (1981). Puerto Rican *espiritismo* and psychotherapy. *American Journal of Orthopsychiatry, 51*(4), 636–645.

Comas-Díaz, L. (2006). Latino healing: The integration of ethnic psychology into psychotherapy. *Psychotherapy, Theory, Research, Practice and Training, 43*(4), 436–453.

Comas-Díaz, L. (2007). Ethnopolitical psychology: Healing and transformation. In E. Aldarondo (Ed.), *Promoting social justice in mental health practice* (pp. 91–118). Mahwah, NJ: Erlbaum.

Comas-Díaz, L. (2008). *Spirita*: Reclaiming womanist sacredness in feminism. *Psychology of Women Quarterly, 32*, 13–21.

Comas-Díaz, L. (2011). Interventions with culturally diverse populations. In D. Barlow (Ed.), *Oxford handbook of clinical psychology* (pp. 868–887). New York: Oxford University Press.

Cook, D. A., & Wiley, C. Y. (2000). Psychotherapy with members of African American churches and spiritual traditions. In P. S. Richards & A. E. Bergin (Eds.), *Handbook of psychotherapy and religious diversity* (pp. 369–420). Washington, DC: American Psychological Association.

Council of National Psychological Associations. (2003). *Psychological treatment of ethnic minority populations*. Washington, DC: The Association of Black Psychologists.

De La Cancela, V., & Zavala Martinez, I. (1983). An analysis of culturalism in Latino mental health: Folk medicine as a case in point. *Hispanic Journal of Behavioral Sciences, 5*(3), 251–274.

De Rios, M. D. (1997). Magical realism: A cultural intervention for traumatized Hispanic children. *Cultural Diversity and Mental Health, 3*(3), 159–170.

Du Bois, W. E. B. (1903). *The souls of black folk*. Chicago: McClurg.

Duran, E. (2006). *Healing the soul wound: Counseling with American Indians and other native people*. New York: Teachers College Press.

Early, G. (1996). Understanding Afrocentrism: Why Blacks dream of a world without Whites. In G. C. Ward & R.

Atwan (Eds.), *The best American essays 1996* (pp. 115–135). New York: Houghton Mifflin Company.

Elsass, P. (1992). *Strategies for survival: The psychology of cultural resilience in ethnic minorities.* New York: New York University Press.

Evans-Campbell, T. (2008). Historical trauma in American Indian/Native Alaska communities. *Journal of Interpersonal Violence, 23*(3), 316–338.

Fanon, F. (1967). *Black skin, White masks.* New York: Grove Press.

Freire, P. (1973*). Education for critical consciousness.* New York: Seabury.

Freire, P., & Macedo, D. (2000). *The Paulo Freire reader.* New York: Continuum.

Galland, C. (1990). *Longing for darkness: Tara and the Black Madonna.* New York: Compas/Penguin Press.

Gonzalez-Wippler, M. (1989). *Santería: The religion: faith, rites, magic.* New York: Harmony.

Garret, J.T. & Garret, M.W. (1994). The path of good medicine: Understanding and counseling Native American Indians. *Journal of Multicultural Counseling and Development, 22,* 139–144.

Gutierrez, G. (1971). *A theology of liberation.* Maryknoll, NY: Orbis Books.

Grof, S., & Grof, C. (Eds.). (1989). *Spiritual emergency: When personal transformation becomes a crisis.* New York: Jeremy P. Tarcher/Putnam.

Hamilton, D. M., & Jackson, M. H. (1998) Spiritual development: Paths and processes. *Journal of Instructional Psychology, 25*(4), 262–270.

Harwood, A. (1981). *Ethnicity and medical care.* Cambridge, MA: Harvard University Press.

Ho, M. H. (1987). *Family therapy with ethnic minorities.* Newbury Park, CA: Sage.

Isasi-Díaz, A. M. (1994). *Mujeristas*: A name of our own. Sisters Struggling in the Spirit. In N. B. Lewis (Ed.), *A women of color theological anthology* (pp. 126–38) Louisville, KY: Women's Ministries Program, Presbyterian Church (USA).

Kaptchuk, T. J., & Eisenberg, D. M. (1998). The persuasive appeal of alternative medicine. *Annals of International Medicine, 129,* 1061–1065.

Keller, H. (2002). Culture and development: Developmental pathways to individualism and interrelatedness. In W. J. Lonner, D. L. Dinnel, S. A. Hayes, & D. N. Sattler (Eds.), *Online readings in psychology and culture* (Unit 11, Chapter 1) Bellingham: Center for Cross-Cultural Research, Western Washington University.

Kiev, A. (1968). *Curanderismo: Mexican American folk psychiatry.* New York: Free Press.

Kidd, S. M. (2002). *The secret life of bees.* New York: Penguin Putnam.

Kidd, S. M. (2005, April 13). *The illuminating Black Madonna.* Lecture presented at the Washington National Cathedral, Washington, DC.

Leung, A. K-Y., Maddux, W., Galinsky, A., & Chiu, C-Y. (2008). Multicultural experience enhances creativity: The when and how. *American Psychologist, 63*(3), 169–181.

Luna, D., Ringberg, T., & Peracchio, L. A. (2008). One individual, two identities: Frame-switching among biculturals. *Journal of Consumer Research, 35*(2), 279–293.

Maduro, R. J., & Martinez, C. F. (1974, October). Latino dream analysis: Opportunity for confrontation. *Social Casework, 55,* 461–469.

Martin, R. (2006). Latinas choosing Islam over Catholicism. *NPR.* Retrieved January 2010, from http://www.npr.org/templates/story/story.php?storyId=6133579

Mbiti, J. S. (1969). *African religions and philosophy.* London: Heinemann Educational Publishers.

Memmi, A. (1965). *The colonizer and the colonized.* Boston: Beacon Press.

Morones, P. A., & Mikawa, J. K. (1992). The traditional Mestizo View: Implications for modern psychotherapeutic interventions. *Psychotherapy, 29*(3), 458–466.

Moya, P. M. L. (2001). Chicana feminism and postmodernist theory. *Signs: Journal of Women in Culture and Society, 26,* 441–483.

Muñoz, R. F., & Mendelson, T. (2005). Toward evidence-based interventions for diverse populations: The San Francisco General Hospital Prevention and Treatment Manuals. *Journal of Clinical and Consulting Psychology, 73*(5), 790–799.

Osaigbovo, R. F. (2002). *Chosen vessels: Women of color, keys to change.* Downers Grove, IL: InterVarsity Press.

Pew Hispanic Center and Pew Forum on Religion & Public Life. (2007, April 27). Latinos and the transformation of American religion. Retrieved on July 20, 2009, form http://www.pewhispanic.org/2007/04/25/changing-faiths-latinos-and-the-transformation-of-american-religion/

Pierce, C. M. (1995). Stress analogs of racism and sexism: Terrorism, torture and disaster. In C. V. Willie, P. P. Reiker, & B. S. Brown (Eds.), *Mental health, racism and sexism* (pp. 277–293). Pittsburgh, PA: University of Pittsburgh Press.

Ploplis, T. (2010). Divine mercy Sunday. *Mother Cabrini Messenger, 72*(1), 1–2.

Roy, B. (2007). Radical psychiatry: An approach to personal and political change. In E. Aldarondo (Ed.), *Promoting social justice in mental health practice* (pp. 65–90). Mahwah, NJ: Erlbaum.

Ruiz, M. (1997). *The four agreements: A Toltec wisdom book.* San Rafael, CA: Amber-Allen Publishing.

Said, E. W. (1994). *Culture and imperialism.* New York: Vintage Books.

Sandoval, C. (1998). Mestizaje as method: Feminists-of-color challenge the canon. In C. Trujillo (Ed.), *Living Chicana theory* (pp. 352–370). Berkeley, CA: Third Woman Press.

Satcher, D. (2001). Mental health: Culture, race, and ethnicity. *US Department of Health and Human Services.* Retrieved on January 2010, from http://www.surgeongeneral.gov/library/mentalhealth/cre/execsummary-1.html

Scotton, B. W. (1996). Introduction and definition of transpersonal psychiatry. In B. W. Scotton, A. B. Chinen, & J. R. Battista (Eds.), *Textbook of transpersonal psychiatry and psychology* (pp. 3–8) New York: Basic Books.

Sue, D. W., & Sue, D. (2008). *Counseling the culturally diverse: Theory and practice* (5th ed.). New York: Wiley.

Tan, S-Y., & Dong, N. J. (2000). Psychotherapy with members of Asian American churches and spiritual traditions. In P. S. Richards & A. E. Bergin (Eds.), *Handbook of psychotherapy and religious diversity* (pp. 421–444). Washington, DC: American Psychological Association.

Thomas, L. E. (1998, Summer). Womanist theology, epistemology, and a new anthropological paradigm. *Cross Currents.* Retrieved December 2011, from http://www.crosscurrents.org/thomas.htm

Tisdell, E. J. (2006). Spirituality, cultural identity, and epistemology in culturally responsive teaching in higher education. *Multicultural Perspectives, 8*(3), 19–25.

Townes, E. M. (1995). *In a blaze of glory: Womanist spirituality as social witness*. Nashville, TN: Abingdon Press.

Trujillo, A. (2000). Psychotherapy with Native Americans: A view into the role of religion and spirituality. In P. S. Richards & A. E. Bergin (Eds.), *Handbook of psychotherapy and religious diversity* (pp. 445–466). Washington, DC: American Psychological Association.

Villoldo, A. (2000). *Shaman, healer, sage: How to heal yourself and others with the energy medicine of the Americas*. New York: Harmony Books.

Wade-Gayles, G. (Ed.). (1995). *My soul is my witness: African-American women's spirituality*. Boston: Beacon Press.

Walker, A. (1983). *In search of our mothers' gardens: Womanist prose*. New York: Harcourt Brace Jovanovich.

Walsh, R., & Shapiro, S. (2006). The meeting of meditative disciplines and Western psychology: A mutually enriching dialogue. *American Psychologist, 61*(3), 227–239.

West, C., & Glaude, E., Jr. (Eds.). (2004). *African American religious thought: An anthology*. Louisville, KY: Westminster John Knox Publishers.

Wilber, K. (2000). *Integral psychology: Consciousness, spirit, psychology, therapy*. Boston: Shambhala.

Wimberly, E. P. (1991). *African American pastoral care*. Nashville, TN: Abingdon Press.

Young, M. I. (1990). *Justice and the politics of difference*. Princeton, NJ: Princeton University Press.

Zea, M. C., Mason, M., & Murguia, A. (2000). Psychotherapy with members of Latino/Latina religions and spiritual traditions. In P. S. Richards & A. E. Bergin (Eds.), *Handbook of psychotherapy and religious diversity* (pp. 397–419). Washington, DC: American Psychological Association.

Models of Spiritual Development

Harris Friedman, Stanley Krippner, Linda Riebel, *and* Chad Johnson

Abstract

This chapter focuses on exploring various models of spiritual development. It first addresses philosophical dilemmas underpinning the concept of spiritual development by questioning whether these can be addressed without metaphysical assumptions embedded in religious worldviews and thus understood in any consensual way across different historical and cultural contexts. Traditional models of spiritual development are then reviewed, drawing from indigenous, Eastern, and Western cultures. Integrative-philosophical and scientific models, including those from the psychology of religion, transpersonal psychology, and neurobiology, are then presented. The chapter concludes by noting the complexities involved in understanding spiritual development accompanied by suggestions on future directions for these models by highlighting their commonalities and differences and by providing some evaluative perspectives for thinking critically about them.

Key Words: spiritual, transpersonal, developmental, cultural, metaphysical

Introduction

In the Biblical book of Genesis, Jacob, one of the patriarchs of Judaism, dreamed that he saw a ladder that reached from earth to heaven, on which angels were ascending and descending. Such vertical models, which imply ascending to a higher or descending to a lower realm, have been frequently used to describe spiritual development. Implicit in all vertical models is a hierarchical belief that some stages of development, or rungs on the ladder, are higher or lower than others. Other models of spiritual development avoid value-laden imagery. For example, spiritual development can be seen as going in many directions, which makes comparing and ranking various states unnecessary (Ferrer, 2009). Spiritual development can also be seen as expanding in a horizontal, rather than vertical, direction, such that there is no higher or lower, but only different patterns of expansiveness (Friedman, 1983). In this chapter, we attempt to describe these and several other models of spiritual development.

It is beyond the scope of a chapter to set forth and compare all of the many approaches to spiritual development stemming from the myriad of religious traditions, each of which may contain more than one model of spiritual development. Instead, we sample a few models we consider representative from indigenous, Eastern, and Western cultures. Then, we discuss philosophical models of spiritual development and end with scientific approaches. We hope to provoke thought about these models by highlighting their commonalities and differences, as well as by providing some evaluative perspectives for thinking critically about them. In light of the many variant uses of the three key terms in our title, *spirituality*, *model*, and *development* are defined in some detail below.

Spirituality

As a concept, spirituality has been increasingly differentiated from religiosity (Bartoli, 2007). Religiosity is now frequently seen as pertaining to an organized system of beliefs about the sacred, along with rituals, rules, and other requirements of a belief system endorsed by a group (Fuller, 2001; Pargament, 1997). Such connotations have implicit social and cultural meanings, referring to something external to the individual (although these may be internalized).

Religious institutions, while supporting positive values such as community and life-structuring rituals, tend to be flawed in one major way: Certainty about the truths of one's own religion sometimes leads people to become intolerant. Taken to extremes, this leads to dire consequences, such as genocides (Harris, 2004). Superstition, sexism, dogmatism, and fanaticism appear in many religions, including indigenous, Eastern, and Western, and crusades, genocides, jihads, and holy wars have led many in the West to reject formal religion, propelling books voicing antireligious sentiments to bestseller status (e.g., Dawkins, 2006; Dennett, 2006).

By contrast, spirituality is increasingly seen as an inner process of connectedness with the sacred, a psychological process internal to the individual (Gallup & Jones, 2000; Sperry & Shafranske, 2005). Of course, there is significant overlap between the two terms, as spirituality historically has been experienced through religion. But a person engaged in a religious group may or may not have had spiritual experiences per se, and a person who has had spiritual experiences may or may not be part of a religious group (Friedman & Pappas, 2007). This distinction between spirituality and religiosity apparently is growing more salient in modern industrial cultures (Miller & Thoresen, 2003).

Spirituality, even when distinguished from religiosity, has been variously defined: that which "infuses human beings with inspiration (from in-"spirit"), creativity, and connection with others" (Fukuyama & Sevig, 1999, p. 4); involves a "presence or absence of an individual's focus on higher, broader, and deeper life meanings that transcend ordinary existence" (Krippner & Welch, 1992, p. 122); and the "human quest for personal meaning and mutually fulfilling relationships among people, the nonhuman environment, and for some, God" (Canda, 1998, p. 243), to name just a few. Spirituality has been viewed as cognitive or affective, related to transcendence or to everyday life, to enhanced ego development or regression to infantile states, and to devotion to diverse transformational paths (Porter, 1995).

Clearly, spirituality is a diffuse and multifaceted construct. MacDonald (2000) analyzed a number of spirituality measures based on varying underlying concepts of spirituality and found five factors: cognitive, experiential/phenomenological, existential well-being, paranormal beliefs, and religiousness. MacDonald also identified several outlying factors that did not fit well with his five-factor model (e.g., self-expansiveness; Friedman, 1983).

Lately, spirituality has been somewhat commodified based on its presumed tangible benefits, such as higher levels of mental and physical health (Elmer, MacDonald, & Friedman, 2003; Gartner, 1996). However, spirituality can also be related to harmful occurrences, such as psychopathology (Johnson & Friedman, 2008), poor health (Magyar-Russell & Pargament, 2006), vulnerability to the seduction of cults, neglect of practical concerns, and exploitation of followers (Kornfield, 1993). Climbing Jacob's ladder of spiritual development can lead to many outcomes, both ascending and descending—and some may not be pleasant destinations.

One example of difficulties associated with spiritual development is conversion, the adoption of new religious beliefs that differ significantly from previous beliefs, which plays a crucial role in some people's spiritual development. This poses a real conundrum regarding spiritual development. An adherent of the new faith may view converts as advancing in development by discovering the "true" faith, while a member of the previous faith may see them as guilty of one of the worst sins, apostasy. A convert takes on not only a new religious identity but also a new set of values and behaviors. Insofar as conversion is often part of spiritual development, it illustrates the relativism that seems inherent in any model of spiritual development.

The difficulties in assessing spiritual development are illustrated by the case of Mother Mary Theresa of Calcutta, who, in 1946, claimed that Jesus Christ had spoken to her on a train trip to Darjeeling, urging her to leave her teaching position in order to work with the disadvantaged. How do we reconcile this with the discovery that she later lived for decades feeling abandoned by her God? Less than 3 months before receiving the Nobel Prize, she had written to a spiritual confidant, "The . . . emptiness is so great—that I look and do not see—listen and do not hear" (van Biema, 2007, p. 35). Her published letters revealed that, except for one brief interlude, she had not felt the presence of God for the last five decades of her life (Kolodiejchuk, 2001). This loss of contact apparently started when she began tending the poor in Calcutta and eventually became so severe that she began to doubt the existence of heaven and even of God. This loss of contact was, to her, a painful and unwanted descent for which she never found an explanation, yet she continued her service and never publicly disavowed her faith. How would we evaluate these contradictory accounts? Did her loss of faith represent a descent (with many years of tireless devotion to the poor simply a compensation) or an ascent (demonstrated by her capacity to persevere in many good works even in the absence of inspiration)?

Model

We look at the various conjectures about spirituality as *models*, which we define as follows: "a model matches the reality that it describes in some important ways" and "a model is simpler than that reality" (Rodgers, 2010, p. 5). There are many ways to examine models of spiritual development. For example, one could compare models from different cultural vantages, such as breaking them down into broad categories such as indigenous, Eastern, or Western (although cultural diffusion has cross-fertilized these in numerous ways so they are not "pure" categories). Or one could compare the basis on which truth claims are made: faith-based (religious), logical or other systematic approaches to inquiry not based on empiricism (philosophical), and empirical approaches (scientific).

In addition, spiritual development models vary considerably in form. Some are described verbally as in myths or theories, mathematically as in numerological or modern dynamic systems approaches, graphically as in maps or cartographies, or in other ways. Representations may be relatively straightforward and logical (in the sense of following defined rules for relating symbols) or appear quite alogical or even paradoxical (apparently not following any form of logic or even intending to defy logical grasp, as in Zen Buddhist koans and the parables of Jesus that attempt to point beyond the limitations of logic). Some models rely heavily on metaphor and we note that metaphors hold value not only in the study of spiritual matters (Metzner, 1998) but also have been widely used in science throughout its history (Leary, 1990). In this chapter, we are guided by the metaphor of Jacob's ladder.

Some approaches to spiritual development do more than merely describe: they attempt to explain how spirituality might evolve. They may employ conventional mechanisms (such as biological, social, psychological, and cultural factors) or supernatural mechanisms (such as *karma* and *grace*). Those that link variables together in an attempt to explain how

a process unfolds over time can be properly referred to as "theories." Those theories amenable to empirical scrutiny (e.g., falsification) may be seen as scientific, while those that adhere to criteria of logic (e.g., being internally consistent) without demanding empirical support might be deemed philosophical.

We do not claim that any model (or type of model) is necessarily better for understanding or facilitating spiritual development. As Western psychologists operating within the scientific tradition, we acknowledge that some readers might find our approach to spiritual development woefully lacking in light of their own traditions, but we hope we are not disrespectful in our attempt to understand and classify them.

Development

Development usually implies a process of growth across time. It is often assumed that such growth is desirable (as in the idea of maturation), and a failure to develop at a proper rate or to an expected destination (as in developmental delay) is undesirable. As we shall see, even a process that is generally deemed favorable may include real or apparent reverses. Discontinuity between stages of development is often assumed, but some thinkers advocate viewing spiritual development more as a continual process (Hood, Spilka, Hunsberger, & Gorsuch, 1996), rather than a process of moving from one discrete stage to another.

Spiritual development, in some models, allows for influences that transcend the physical, such as contact with a divine entity or a sense of profound interconnectedness with the universe. Until recently, Western psychology has generally adhered to the prevailing materialistic paradigm of most sciences, but this situation may be changing (Brydon-Miller & Tolman, 1997; Polkinghorne, 1983).

Spiritual development can be seen primarily as intrapersonal (as changes residing within the individual) or interpersonal (residing among individuals in relationship to community). For example, one divide among Buddhists is between the Theravadan and Mahayanan lineages, the former focusing more on the enlightenment of individuals, while the latter emphasizes collective enlightenment more. Development can also be transpersonal, in the sense of pointing to something beyond the individual as an isolated being and that interconnects the individual to the sacred or cosmos in which, inextricably, one is always embedded (Friedman, 1983).

Some traditions posit a teleology or defined end purpose, such as ending *dukkha* (suffering, or attachment to the impermanent, within Buddhism) or attaining salvation (the attainment of blessed eternal life, within Christianity). In other models, there is no defined terminus and one's spiritual development may be seen as continually unfolding, becoming richer and more profound until death, and, according to some traditions, even continuing after death across multiple lifetimes.

In some models, spiritual development may be seen as unexpectedly sudden, as in a rapid conversion (e.g., that of the Christian apostle, Paul) or enlightenment (the immediacy of some Zen Buddhist attainments of *samadhi*). Bucke (1901/1969) asserted that cosmic consciousness comes suddenly and unbidden. In other systems, change is seen as gradual, requiring painstaking effort (years of deprivation and suffering), whereas in others it may be seen as unattainable by any effort (contingent on passively receiving *grace* or subject to *karma* from previous incarnations). In some models, spiritual development is seen as unidirectionally progressive (always upward toward a defined goal), whereas in others it is seen as consisting of both ascents and descents, intermixed in various ways. Spiritual development has also been viewed as both widely variant across individuals and invariant in which everyone progresses through the same stages at roughly the same rate. The very notion of spiritual development over time is not universal. At least one thinker (Tolle, 1999) disputed the importance of time itself, stating that dwelling on it is actually a spiritual obstacle.

There have been many attempts to organize spiritual beliefs. One typology was proposed by Rawlinson (1997), who characterized them on two dimensions: hot versus cool and structured versus unstructured. Hot traditions emphasize relationship to a personal spiritual being, while cool traditions emphasize inner growth. Structured traditions emphasize the need to follow specific methods, while unstructured traditions emphasize no specific path. Given the sheer number of approaches and their possible permutations for understanding spiritual development, any summary, including ours, is necessarily limited.

Philosophical Questions

These numerous models of spiritual development vary in basic philosophical ways, which require examination. For example, does spiritual development necessarily imply some underlying reality apart from the material plane or are people's beliefs (not withstanding whether they relate to anything substantial in any veridical manner) worthy of study in and of themselves? As psychologists, we write from the latter perspective without taking a position on the metaphysical assumption in the former. Spiritual development may be conceptualized as aimed toward a hypothetical end point (or range of end points) seen as more "real" than the ordinary world. Those traditions that see ordinary reality as illusory (e.g., as a veil of illusion or *maya*) may be quite different from those that would use empirical tests (e.g., the scientific tradition) to understand spiritual development. For instance, many forms of meditative practice, which generally involve the self-regulation of attention and concentration, use a model of development to describe the process of deepening the meditative experience itself, rather than necessarily conceptualizing it as a pathway to any sort of spiritual terminus. In these models, such end points may be welcome as a positive side effect of meditation but may not necessarily be fundamental to the regimen itself. In other models, a metaphysical terminus, such as eternal salvation or enlightenment, may be the only desired end point and all salutary benefits at the more mundane level on the way to achieving this spiritual outcome are seen as secondary or even superfluous.

Regardless, any model of spiritual development implies that change can be recognized. Some traditions use specific tests, such as "passing" Zen koans by receiving a teacher's approval of one's answer, to demonstrate progressive spiritual attainment, whereas others are less clear in defining progress. These considerations illustrate some of the perplexing epistemological questions involved in this inquiry.

Traditional Models of Spiritual Development

There are many traditional models of spiritual development. We, of course, do not attempt to provide an overview of all but, instead, provide a few representative examples. We use the broad categories of indigenous, Eastern, and Western to organize this presentation, noting that the order of their presentation is unrelated to any belief in the primacy or superiority of any of the traditions discussed.

Indigenous Models of Spiritual Development

There are many indigenous models of spiritual development. Eliade (1951/2004) subsumed many of these under the term *shamanism,* which he believed typically focused on reinstating a sacred balance that had been disrupted. He proposed that experiences of death and resurrection (which occur during rituals such as fasting, torture, or use of psychedelic substances) form a universal core element of spiritual development in the shaman (a development not shared by members of his or her community). The spiritual development of the shaman requires repeated visits to the spirit worlds (often requiring multiple deaths and rebirths) and reaps progressively increasing powers; the shaman can eventually at will ascend to higher realms or descend to lower realms, often described metaphorically as through climbing a tree (a metaphor comparable to Jacob's ladder).

Aspirants for the title of *sangoma*, a spiritual practitioner and healer among the Zulu tribe in southern Africa, for example, undergo trials congruent with this model (Watson, 1982). Other shamanic traditions around the world have well-developed sequences of tasks or skills that aspirants must successfully complete or acquire. Typically, they involve services to their community and clients, such as guarding against sorcery, treating pain and disease, interpreting dreams, resolving family and clan disputes, finding lost objects, locating game during hunting seasons, and arranging ceremonies for such transitions as childbirth, adolescence, marriage, menopause, and death (Krippner, 2002; Walsh, 2007).

Thus, the shamanic path to spiritual development is not primarily one of individual self-improvement or enlightenment, but rather a path of community service. As the shaman's skills and knowledge increase, his or her success in helping the community is the gauge of his or her spiritual development.

Western Models of Spiritual Development

Spirituality in Western culture has been dominated by the Abrahamic (Judeo-Christian-Islamic) tradition for over two millennia. However, it should be noted that many other rich traditions were suppressed or totally eliminated, such as the mystery schools of the ancient Mediterranean (Burkert, 1987) and the Celtic priesthood (Anderson, 1998), and there are residual traces even today of these formerly vibrant traditions.

Within Judaism, spiritual development has long been judged through being well versed in the Bible and its associated books, as depth of knowledge in these sacred texts was the mark of understanding the will of God. Learning was not restricted to simple ritualistic recitation of the laws but to the capacity to apply them in daily life and live according to God's plan. Spiritually developed individuals

demonstrate wisdom and compassion through righteously applying the law, as well as balancing justice and forgiveness within their communities. Esoteric mystical traditions within Judaism included the act of blessings with the literal process of the breath (as in the Jewish patriarchs breathing upon their successors in bestowing their blessings).

In Hassidism, one variant of mystical Judaism, the very person of a righteous one is seen as the embodiment of wisdom and compassion, while in Kabalistic Judaism, spiritual development grows in levels from focus on the individual to focus on others, and eventually to focus on God (Berke & Schneider, 2006). According to these authors, the first level focuses on obeying rituals, such as the dietary laws, without a deeper appreciation of their meaning; this stage is seen as that of the animal soul. The next level involves emergence of complex interpersonal understandings, dealing with concepts such as justice; this is seen as the wind soul. The subsequent level develops into a relationship with God, which involves the further actualization of righteousness (putting the will of God into practice); this is seen as the breath soul. The next levels involve experiencing spirituality as disconnected from the body and, eventually, a unitive experience may be attained.

Mystical schools within the Muslim tradition also focus on realizing their relationship to Allah, using methods such as contemplation, movements, and storytelling. Whirling dervishes, members of one Muslim Sufi order, twirl in circles to alter consciousness in order to grow closer to Allah. Members of another Muslim sect, the Druze, hold that spiritual development occurs over several lifetimes; this concept of reincarnation, which is otherwise little known in contemporary Western traditions but was part of early Christianity, is also found in some strands of mystical Judaism, as well as in Hindu, Buddhist, and many Eastern traditions (Chari, 1967). According to Rafea, Rafea, and Rafea (2005), Islamic spiritual development is judged through matching worldly affairs with the will of Allah, aligning the secular with the sacred in accord with Allah's laws. This is broken into steps: conviction (through a combination of faith and will) that Allah alone is supreme; submission to Allah; ability to distinguish between what Allah does and does not will; and finally, completely identifying with Allah's will, harmonizing not just with the sacred but with the entire world.

In the Christian tradition, the Biblical New Testament (John 2:12–14) provides a dichotomous model of spiritual development by emphasizing three stages of growth paralleling physical maturation: childhood, young adulthood, and mature adulthood, each with its spiritual characteristics. There is also a long tradition of celebrated Christian saints, such as Thomas Aquinas and Saint John of the Cross, who were recognized for their profound spiritual development based on their attainments. Aquinas proposed stages of spirituality, such as dividing charity into three parts, starting with "beginners," who need encouragement; the "proficient," who need to strengthen their capacity to love; and the "perfect," who are at union with God (Torrell, 2003). Saint John of the Cross (2003) described the soul's 10-step journey climbing a ladder of love (like Jacob's ladder), progressing from body concerns to union with God and, most famously, passing through the "dark night of the soul." The rungs (stages) are as follows: languishing with love for God and the loss of desire for all things other than God; ceaseless preoccupation with finding God; perseverance in the face of obstacles, accompanied by a sense of worthlessness in comparison to magnitude of the task; gratitude for all that God has already granted and acceptance that no more can be asked; impatience and longing to unite with God; increased charity and purity, as well as repeated contact with God; vehemence in asking for God's love; holding tightly onto God; perfection sensed as sweetness; and finally, being totally merged with God. Noteworthy, this tenth stage was not expected to be achieved within a human's lifetime.

Some modern Protestant communities, while not offering an explicit developmental path, honor certain signs of spiritual development. For example, in some Pentecostal churches, handling venomous snakes with impunity and engaging in glossolalia (speaking in tongues) are seen as evidence of high spiritual development. Another widespread and influential spiritual movement in the contemporary United States, which is anchored in Christianity, is the 12-step approach in which spiritual goals and practices are promoted as tools for mastering behavioral and substance addictions (Krippner, 2005). Twelve-step programs are emphatically stage based, and skipping a stage is seen as possibly leading to relapse (Alcoholics Anonymous, 2001).

Eastern Religious Models of Spiritual Development

There are many Eastern religious models of spiritual development, including those of Hinduism (Vedanta), Taoism, Buddhism, Confucianism, Jainism, Sikhism, and Shintoism. If any generalizations can be made validly across their great diversity, they seem, in contrast to the Western traditions, to more explicitly contain self-experiments and encourage critical and reflective thinking on the part of the seeker to appraise his or her spiritual development. These include millennia-old systematic change processes that require cognitive control, disciplined effort, and self-reflective awareness that could take decades to master, such as formal meditation practices.

In the West, religion has been viewed as primarily theocentric, emphasizing a relationship to a personal divine figure; by contrast the Eastern traditions, for example, Buddhism and Taoism, often emphasize nonduality and an impersonal divine (Cortright, 1997). However, some Eastern traditions are theocentric, including Shintoism, which boasts a pantheon of divinities. Eastern religions have been sometimes presumed to be "more spiritual" than those religions from the West by Westerners under the sway of romanticism (Friedman, 2005), but Eastern traditions also have their outer trappings and inner constraints. For example, although Buddhism is often characterized as not being a religion (and sometimes is characterized as a philosophy or even a psychology), Buddhist beliefs include faith assumptions, such as Buddha's alleged "enlightenment" in which supposedly he became free of karma, a concept inextricably linked to a doctrine of reincarnation. Furthermore, the basic appeal of this religion is on the faith that, since Buddha obtained liberation from karma, others who might follow in His path can also obtain the same result. This and many other tenets of Buddhism (and most religions) are empirically untestable and thus nonscientific, although many attempt to misclassify Buddhism as a psychological science (Friedman, 2009).

One sophisticated Eastern model for spiritual development is the *Yogasutras*, attributed to the scholar Patanjali in the 2nd century BCE; its eight "limbs" or steps laid the basis for Ashtong Yoga, one of many disciplines purported to "quiet the mind," transcend one's usual identity, and "know God" (Yati, 2009). This yoga system proposes many tools for spiritual development: meditation and mindfulness; postures and breathing practices; moderation in lifestyle; and positive virtues such as honesty and not injuring others. Spiritual development is seen as related to attainment of these qualities. The outer forms of yoga (physical strength and flexibility in *hatha* yoga) are easier to evaluate than the more subtle aspects of this path.

The Buddha's "eightfold path" includes aspiring toward right (or complete) perspective, right intention, right speech, right action, right livelihood, right effort, right awareness, and right concentration. The first two are said to produce wisdom, the next four to change conduct, and the final two to improve meditation. These eight aspects of the path are not necessarily sequential, like the rungs of Jacob's ladder, but are to be developed simultaneously, each supporting the others (Sangharakshita, 2007; Snelling, 1991).

One symbolic representation of spiritual development from the Zen Buddhist tradition is the Ten Ox-Herding Pictures (Suzuki, 1960), which depict stages in finding and taming a lost bull, an allegory for the search for enlightenment. It starts with searching for the lost bull (realizing there is something more to life), followed by discovery of its footprints (recognizing a spiritual path). Then, the bull is glimpsed (the goal of enlightenment is perceived), followed by catching it in a struggle (disciplined effort). The bull is finally tamed (practice becomes more natural) and is ridden home, accompanied by joy. Then, the bull is forgotten (transcended); finally, self and bull are both forgotten (all is experienced as emptiness). The source of oneness is reached and the seeker returns to the community to share the fruits of spiritual development with others. One's place on this allegory indicates one's level of spiritual maturity, according to this Buddhist model.

Another approach within Hindu and Buddhist traditions is based on *chakras*, Sanskrit for "turning wheels," purported focal points in one's "etheric body" (or "subtle energy body"). Although some traditions speak of five, six, eight, or even twelve chakras, the best-known versions define seven: the root, sacral, solar plexus, heart, throat, brow, and crown chakras. The chakra levels where one's supposed energy mostly resides, as well as the relative balance among chakra energy, can be used to assess spiritual development (e.g., one whose energy is primarily in the base chakra, related to survival, would be seen as less developed than one whose heart chakra predominates). In this sense, the human body and its supposed energy systems are like Jacob's ladder, with each chakra being like a rung. The level of one's overall chakra energy indicates one's spiritual development.

In some yogic traditions, as seekers develop spiritually a type of energy (*kundalini*) is said to rise upward like a serpent from the root to the crown, terminating if discipline has been sufficiently rigorous in a unitive experience (Avalon, 1919; Goswami,

1980). This developmental sequence may take years of meditative work and is not without risk. One well-known seeker, Krishna (1971), awakened his kundalini "serpent" without supervision, resulting in disequilibrium that took years to resolve.

Spiritual development through activation of the chakras has taken somewhat different forms in Tantra, Shakta, Tibetan Buddhism, Vajrayana Buddhism, and Himalayan Bonpo, among others, and in the more recent writings of Aurobindo (1962) and Bhatnagar (Bhatnagar & Lassey, 2009). The latter adept has incorporated Western psychological principles into his developmental model and has prescribed detailed exercises, such as the visualization of various chakras to facilitate spiritual growth.

Taoist paths to spiritual development also emphasize working with one's *subtle body* (the sheath that allegedly envelops the physical body and extends beyond it), often through internal alchemy, visualization exercises, or ritualized movement such as *qigong*, thought to promote mental and physical health (Chia, 1993). These practices interact with traditional Chinese medicine and the purported circulation of *qi* energy through its alleged network of some 265 acupuncture points and the dozen or so meridians that are thought to connect them. Healthy regimens are prescribed to balance one's *yin* and *yang* propensities (i.e., one's receptive and expressive propensities). Here, spiritual development takes an embodied approach. However, *qi* is not seen as merely physical, although there are alleged practical benefits for the practitioner's physical, mental, emotional, and sexual health by unblocking energy channels and increasing energy balance (Mayer, 2003; Meech, 2007).

Integrative-Philosophical Models of Spiritual Development

Underhill (1911/1961) was one of the first scholars to look across various traditions and provide an organizing scheme of spiritual development. She proposed that five stages lead toward the ultimate goal of mystical spirituality, the merging of the individual soul with God or the Absolute. The first is "awakening," in which one becomes conscious of the divinity, followed by the second, "purgation," in which one struggles to eliminate personal imperfections. The third stage of "illumination" is often mistaken as the last stage, as it is accompanied by a glimpse of "transcendence." Extraordinary mystics, however, go through a fourth stage, which St. John of the Cross called "the dark night of the soul," a profound sense of abandonment by God. Then, if surrender to God's will occurs, there is a final stage with complete loss of the individual self and a permanent union with the absolute. By organizing descriptions of people's experiences, Underhill used a philosophical, rather than faith-based, approach and her integration resembles Jacob's ladder in terms of a vertical hierarchy of spiritual states with development consisting of passing from each state to the next "higher" one.

More recently, Wilber (1980, 1997, 2000, 2004) organized a massive amount of material into a coherent framework of spiritual development. Taking a cultural-historical approach, Wilber (1980) described four fundamental phases in the evolution of human consciousness. In Wilber's earliest era, the sense of self was wholly identified with physical being and the primordial forces of nature. Consciousness later became separated from the physiological life of the body, but it had not advanced beyond a childlike sense of magically mingling in this world. In this second era, the myths structuring this reality were still bound to the body, but an external world was recognized and responsibility for events was magically assigned to it. In the third era, with the advent of more complex forms of language some 12,000 years ago, the verbal mind climbed out of the body and into a world of extended time. The physical world could now be represented, manipulated, and narrated through mental symbols, making it possible to use complex shared symbols to understand and control one's impulses and world. However, the cognitive abilities necessary for self-reflection were not yet well developed and so the individual's emerging sense of self drew from images of the culture's mythology. As the capacities for self-reflection evolved and the individual's assumptions could be tested through deductive reasoning, emerging perhaps some 3,000 years ago in different parts of the world, a self-observing aspect of the psyche came into being. This marked the beginning of Wilber's fourth era, characterized by the differentiation of the separate personal ego, the capacity to step back and observe oneself. The current era, Wilber's fourth, is dominated by the rational, self-reflecting, individual ego. In primordial times meaning was lodged in the group; today it is primarily centered in the individual.

Wilber (2000) also created a model of spiritual development based on his examination of Western and Eastern reports of mystical development. One can, Wilber asserted, progress from "gross-level mysticism" to the "causal," "subtle," and "integral"

stages. The last of these represents the resolution of one's conflicts and imbalances in favor of a unity of thought, feeling, and action. Wilber contended that children do not have ready access to the higher spiritual realms. He did not dispute the claim that children were capable of having some sort of spiritual experiences, only that they cannot skip developmental stages. He argued that children's absence of strong ego boundaries means they cannot differentiate between themselves and the environment, a capacity that characterizes higher level mystical experiences. According to Wilber (1980, 2000), pre-egoic spirituality differs from "trans-egoic" spirituality and to equate them is to commit a "pre/trans fallacy." Wilber's model is probably the most impressive modern example of a vertical model similar to Jacob's ladder.

However, Wilber's model has been questioned by many, including Washburn (2003) and Taylor (2009). Washburn's model is less hierarchical, allowing for alternating ascents and descents. Taylor conceptualized spiritual experiences as occurring at many different levels of intensity, and reports of the spirituality of children meet his criteria for being authentic spiritual experiences, albeit at lower intensity levels. Taylor's model describes five levels that may occur developmentally or may be encompassed within a single experience.

1. A heightening of physical perception; the world seems brighter, more colorful, and more intricate.

2. A sense of the "aliveness" of ordinarily inanimate phenomena; the world comes alive.

3. A sense of meaning, harmony, and benevolence pervading one's surroundings or the world as a whole.

4. A sense of inner well-being, peace, bliss, or joy.

5. An awareness of spirit in the world—what Christian mystics call deification, what some Buddhist traditions refer to as *nirvikalpa samadhi*.

These experiences can occur in a solitary context or in a communal context, such as group sporting activities, lovemaking, or in a group artistic performance (including among members of the audience at such a performance). Taylor (2009) found support for his position from Loevinger's (1976) speculation that a child's openness to experience is reduced during maturation but might be regained at higher levels of ego development. Taylor concluded that spiritual experiences are accessible to individuals at both Wilber's pre-egoic and trans-egoic levels, but that certain aspects of "transegoic" spiritual experiences are not a part of the preegoic experiences, for example, the realization that one's "ego self" is not one's "true self." This debate about childhood spirituality is also reflected in Hay and Nye's (1998) notion of "relational consciousness," which is proposed as a noncognitive spiritual construct that presumably bypasses linear cognitive development constraints and allows for the equal validity of childhood and adult spiritual experiences.

Philosophical models of spiritual development use various classification schemes, but in general they use concepts not easily amenable to empirical testing or they have not subjected their speculations to empirical tests, although they may have integrated empirical data into a theoretical edifice. What separates them from scientific approaches is this lack of being open to empirical examination, although the boundaries between philosophy and science are not always clearly delineated.

Psychological Models of Spiritual Development

Many psychologists have proposed stage theories of spiritual development within the scientific tradition, which calls for some form of empiricism, using sensory perception to gain information to support or disconfirm a theory. For example, Roehlkepartain, Benson, and King (2005) presented an overview of various theories of spiritual development in childhood and adolescence. In the quantitative traditions of research, measurement is essential and there is a robust literature using measures relevant to this topic. There is also an abundance of tools designed to assess spirituality, including over 100 identified constructs related to spirituality and the transpersonal (MacDonald, Friedman, & Kuentzel, 1999; MacDonald, Kuentzel, & Friedman, 1999; MacDonald, LeClair Holland, Alter, & Friedman, 1995). Many additional measures have been developed since these review papers, evidencing a growing research tradition (MacDonald & Friedman, 2002). There is also a strong qualitative research tradition in studying spiritual development, as well as a variety of emerging mixed-method approaches (Robbins & Friedman, 2009).

Psychology of Religion

One of the earliest psychologists of religion, Allport (1969) distinguished between immature and mature religious sentiments. Immature religion uses less developed thought processes, which are concrete and magical (as in accepting sacred scriptures literally), while mature religion uses more developed thought processes (as in seeing sacred scriptures metaphorically). His ideas developed into related concepts of intrinsic and extrinsic religion, which can be seen as a stage delineation, albeit with only two stages. Allport's work generated a tremendous amount of empirical research (see Hood et al., 1996), placing it in the realm of science. However, even a scientific approach must face the conceptual conundra we have pointed out. For instance, some religious traditions hold that accepting scripture literally demonstrates a higher level of spiritual development, whereas other traditions may see uncritical literalism as a relatively undeveloped stage of spirituality.

Morality is the focus of another widely used psychological approach to spiritual development. Kohlberg (1971) was influenced by the well-known Piagetian stages of cognitive development, as he created a model of moral reasoning consisting of six stages. Individuals at presumed different stages of moral development provide different justifications or condemnations of actors in given vignettes. Kohlberg postulated three main stages: a "preconventional" approach based on self-interest without concern for another, a "conventional" approach based on prevailing moral values, and a "postconventional" approach that sometimes contradicted prevailing moral values in service of a higher good. He saw his stages as universal, but progression through the stages occurring at different rates in different cultures. Of particular interest to our discussion is Kohlberg's belief that some people regressed into earlier stages, depending on life circumstances (just as the angels both ascended and descended Jacob's ladder). Kohlberg also sometimes speculated about a seventh stage of cosmic and transcendental morality.

If moral decision making represents an aspect of spirituality, one's primary form of moral reasoning can be seen as an indicator of spiritual development. Interestingly, some spiritual traditions explicitly defy notions of morality and encourage adherents to break extant taboos. For example, Jesus admonished his followers to shirk the day-to-day responsibilities of family and other conventional ties in order to follow Him, such as to ignore Sabbath rules in order to help others, while some Hindu tantric practices encourage violating social norms, such as codes of sexual conduct, in order to gain liberation. Thus, moral criteria cannot form a uniform approach to understanding spiritual development, since morality itself is so variable. In addition, as religions ossify, the fundamental moral messages of their founders, which often were quite radical, frequently become distorted into instruments of social control benefiting the status quo.

The Freudian approach attempted to build a scientific theory of development devoid of reliance on any vestiges of religion and spirituality (i.e., considering religion and spirituality as prima facie signs of failure to mature). However, several followers of this approach created revisions and extensions of Freudian theory that did encompass spiritual development. Erikson (1980) extended Freud's theories across the entire life span into an eight-stage model of development. Although each stage can be linked to spiritual development, perhaps most salient to this discussion is Erikson's last stage, integrity versus despair. Erikson argued that, at the end of life, the developmental crisis needing resolution is finding meaning with life itself, including its inevitable end in death. To the extent that this successful resolution requires facing at least existential, if not spiritual, concerns, achieving it can be a mark of spiritual development.

Gilligan (1982) took exception to Kohlberg and Erikson, pointing out that their models were male centered and hierarchical. Her interviews with women indicated that, when faced with moral decisions, they thought more about caring and connection than about abstract rules. Gilligan interpreted the fact that females tended to score lower on Kohlberg's measures of moral development as an artifact of the model, rather than a demonstration that the moral development of women is in some way inferior to that of men. Her critique exemplifies the dilemma of imposing any uniformly vertical model of spiritual development, as these may not only be culturally and historically limited but also gender biased.

Perhaps the best-known stage theory of spiritual development is based on both cognitive (Piagetian) and affective (Freudian and Eriksonian) precursors. Fowler (1981) envisioned spiritual development as a sequence of seven universal stages: "Primal or Undifferentiated" faith during the first two years (focused on security issues and not on faith per se), "Intuitive-Projective" faith in preschoolers (focused on unconscious material and magical beliefs), "Mythic-Literal" faith in grade-school preadolescents (focused on following rules, such as in adhering to conventional justice), "Synthetic-Conventional" faith in adolescence (focused on conformity), "Individuative-Reflective" faith in early adulthood (focused on struggles to find personal meaning), "Conjunctive" faith in middle adulthood (focused

on achieving reconciliation of paradoxes), and last a "Universalizing" faith, similar to other models of transcendence. As a scientific theory, this developed into a robust research tradition (Leak, 2008).

The psychology of religion, as an empirical scientific tradition, has provided many avenues to understanding spiritual development, typically involving the use of measures and surveys. However, much of this research has been based on a Judeo-Christian approach to spirituality and, as mentioned, may not be very universally applicable.

Transpersonal Psychology

The word "transpersonal" was first introduced into psychology by William James in a 1905 lecture and used in 1942 by Carl Jung as the German term *uberpersonlich*, which his English translators rendered as "transpersonal" (Vich, 1988). A few years later, this term was also used by Murphy (1949) and then in the 1960s others picked up the term (Sutich, 1969) as a type of unifying framework. Friedman (1983) applied the term "transpersonal self-expansiveness" to experiences in which one's sense of identity extends beyond its ordinary limits to encompass wider, broader, and deeper aspects of the cosmos. Friedman (2002) later argued that the transpersonal perspective allows a scientific approach to understanding such phenomena that can benefit from the wisdom of religious traditions and spiritual experiences without being bound by their underlying assumptions, a point to which we will return in our conclusion.

In contrast to the psychological study of religion from a more or less "objective" position (such as exploring demographic patterns related to phenomena), transpersonal psychology also embraces the "subjective" study of the experiential aspects of spirituality. Today the distinction between transpersonal psychology and the psychology of religion is fading, as there is a call to broaden the psychology of religion by renaming it the "psychology of religion and spirituality" (Emmons & Paloutzian, 2003). Some scientific research has come out of the transpersonal psychology tradition (e.g., Tart, 2009), but most of the work has been experiential. One example of a transpersonal scientific research tradition stems from the Self-Expansiveness Level Form (SELF), a self-report test measuring transpersonal self-expansiveness, defined as "the amount of True Self which is contained within the boundary demarcating self from not-self through the process of self-conception" (Friedman, 1983, p. 38). The SELF measures three levels of self-expansiveness derived through using a spatial-temporal cartography in which there is a personal level of the here and now, a transpersonal level in which identity expands beyond present place and time such that self dissolves as a separate entity, and a middle level between the personal and transpersonal. In this regard, the SELF was specifically designed not to measure a vertically hierarchical level of spiritual development, but rather a horizontal expansion of the self-concept across space and time. This approach has also resulted in an empirical research tradition, placing it within the realm of science (Pappas & Friedman, 2007).

Neurobiological Models of Spiritual Development

The neurobiological approach to spiritual development, now in its infancy, uses emerging technologies (fMRI, QEEG, etc.) that can measure the physical expressions or concomitants of spiritual variables. For instance, activation of certain brain states (theta and perhaps gamma brain waves) or the development of certain brain areas (following years of meditation) lends itself to neurobiological study. Spiritual traditions have long discussed physical factors, such as breath and alleged "subtle energies" (*qi* or *prana*), in relationship to spiritual development. A convergence of interest in traditional spiritual issues and these new scientific methods has begun to occur, such as by Krishna (1971), who held several seminars with scientists, attempting to elicit their cooperation in verifying the existence of "kundalini energy," which he felt held the key not only to spiritual development but also to human genius and creativity. Motoyama (1971, 2009) claimed to have invented a technology for measuring acupuncture points, meridians, and chakras, asserting that his data validate the existence of these ancient constructs, and called for independent replication of his studies. Alper (2001) and McNamara (2009) have linked the neurobiology of spirituality to human evolution, and the latter author has proposed that religion was a primary force in the evolution of self-awareness.

The neurobiology of spirituality is therefore emerging as a distinct discipline, with studies of meditation, near-death experiences, dissolving of ego boundaries, and other phenomena taking place with rigorous methodologies. In this regard, accounts of extraordinary experiences studied through the tools of neuroscience are attracting the attention of scholars (Cardeña, Lynn, & Krippner, 2000; Krippner & Friedman, 2010). It is even conceivable that one day spiritual development might be assessed by neurobiological indicators (e.g., the overall ratio of theta to beta brain waves produced during meditation, the activation of certain areas in the left temporal lobe of the brain, etc.). This would not necessarily be an exercise in reductionism but rather an acknowledgment of neurobiological concomitants to spiritual life.

Conclusion

This chapter began with the metaphor of Jacob's ladder as a starting point for discussing models of spiritual development, but there is another lesson to be learned from this biblical account. Once Jacob reached the top of the ladder, Jehovah gave Jacob and his descendants dominion over all the land that they could see. This promise could represent the rewards of spiritual development (Maslow, 1968). But when it is interpreted literally, as by some of Jacob's descendants who base their claims to political and economic control of Judea and Samaria on this story, it causes no end of turmoil, bloodshed, and warfare. This illustrates some of the very real challenges for understanding spiritual development, for taking a sacred text literally can have high costs to humanity and the earth. We believe that understanding more deeply and being able to facilitate spiritual development could benefit people in important ways. The models we have described serve as one set of tools to explore this possibility.

Another approach is to recognize barriers to spiritual development. These can be microsocial (as in conformity pressures from other individuals), macrosocial (as in pressures from collective structures such as laws), or individual, as in character flaws. For instance, Trungpa (1973) defined "spiritual materialism" as a pursuit of enlightenment driven by egoistic needs. Clearly, this whole area is one of great challenges and potential rewards, as well as one where the costs can be high if no integration is found.

Ferrer (2009) has argued for a participatory approach to spirituality and its development. He proposed abandoning any predetermined ultimate criteria for evaluating spiritual development, as they can soon collapse into dogmatic formulations. He argued that this does not mean abandoning discernment, but that we simply recognize that spiritual truth claims cannot be argued in terms of ontology, because their multiplicity is both a natural and essential expression of a mystery to be celebrated. He maintained that this is not an abdication of the obligation to evaluate the differential worth of various paths, but that we need other grounds to evaluate competing truth claims. He was especially averse to the use of any predetermined doctrines (spiritual hierarchies) and instead suggested the consequences of different paths be used to evaluate them. Specifically, he proposed two guidelines: an assessment of how a path might liberate practitioners from self-centeredness, and another assessment of how a path might lead to a person's fulfillment. These proposals recall the pragmatic solution proposed by James (1890) for resolving conflicts between positions (such as belief in free will versus determinism) by looking at their fruits. In this way, different paths to spiritual development may not be universally inferior or superior, just different—and spiritual development may not be subsumable within any one system of understanding or measured in any unidimensional way.

Future Directions

We have attempted to capture some of the many complexities involved in understanding models of spiritual development and hope we have supplied readers with some useful concepts to aid their study of this important and provocative avenue of human inquiry. Whether readers see Jacob's ladder of spiritual development as vertical, horizontal, circular, or something else, we wish them well in their quest. Finally, we hope that the panoply of models of spiritual development does not obscure the goal of so many individuals and traditions to further spiritual development, whether it is seen as salvation, enlightenment, or plain healthy living in a fully embodied state of the here and now.

Questions Presenting Future Directions for the Field, Difficult Problems To Be Solved, or Topics That Remain To Be Addressed

How might spiritual development be significantly influenced by historical and cultural context?

Can spiritual development ever be understood in a universal way across all cultures and all times?

Can there be models of spiritual development that do not rely on untestable metaphysical assumptions?

Can a unifying scientific model of spiritual development be constructed that appropriately addresses the complexity and multidimensionality of this area?

What empirical research methods (or mixed methods) might best address the complexity of spiritual development?

What innovative or new methods might be created or utilized to study spiritual development?

What are possible genetic components of spiritual development?

How might spiritual development models better integrate the body, embodiment, and/or somatic phenomenology?

How might neuroscience inform, modify, or guide spiritual development models?

How might current research with psychedelics and/or pharmaceuticals enhance our understanding of spiritual development?

References

Alcoholics Anonymous. (2001). *The story of how many thousands of men and women have recovered from alcoholism.* (4th ed.) New York: Alcoholics Anonymous.

Allport, G. (1969). *The individual and his religion* (9th ed.). New York: Macmillan. (Original work published 1950).

Alper, M. (2001). *The "God" part of the brain* (5th ed.). Brooklyn, NY: Rogue Press.

Anderson, R. (1998). *Celtic oracles: A new system for spiritual growth and divination.* New York: Random House.

Aurobindo, S. (1962). *The future evolution of man.* Twin Lakes, WI: Lotus Press.

Avalon, A. (1919). *The serpent power.* London: Dover.

Bartoli, E. (2007). Religious and spiritual issues in psychotherapy practice: Training the trainer. *Psychotherapy: Theory, Research, Practice, 44,* 54–65.

Berke, J., & Schneider, S. (2006). The self and the soul. *Mental Health, Religion and Culture, 9,* 333–354.

Bhatnagar, S., & Lassey, D. (2009). *Microchakras: Inner tuning for psychological wellbeing.* Rochester, NY: Inner Traditions.

Brydon-Miller, M., & Tolman, D. L. (1997). Transforming psychology: Interpretive and participatory research methods [Special Issue]. *Journal of Social Issues, 53*(4), 597–603.

Bucke, R. M. (1969). *Cosmic consciousness.* New York: E. P. Dutton. (Original work published 1901).

Burkert, W. (1987). *Ancient mystery cults.* Cambridge, MA: Harvard University Press.

Canda, E. (1998). Therapeutic transformation in ritual, therapy, and human development. *Journal of Religion and Health, 27,* 205–220.

Cardeña, E., Lynn, S. J., & Krippner, S. (Eds.). (2000). *Varieties of anomalous experience: Examining the scientific evidence.* Washington, DC: American Psychological Association.

Chari, C. T. K. (1967). Reincarnation: New light on an old doctrine. *International Journal of Parapsychology, 9,* 217–222.

Chia, M. (1993). *Awaken healing light.* Los Angeles: Healing Tao Books.

Cortright, B. (1997). *Psychotherapy and spirit: Theory and practice in transpersonal psychotherapy.* Albany, NY: SUNY Press.

Dawkins, R. (2006). *The God delusion.* New York: Houghton Mifflin Harcourt.

Dennett, D. (2006). *Breaking the spell: Religion as natural phenomenon.* New York: Viking Adult.

Eliade, M. (2004). *Shamanism: Archaic techniques of ecstasy.* Princeton, NJ: Princeton University Press. (Original work published 1951).

Elmer, L., MacDonald, D., & Friedman, H. (2003). Transpersonal psychology, physical health, and mental health: Theory, research, and practice. *The Humanistic Psychologist, 31,* 159–181.

Emmons, R. A., & Paloutzian, R. F. (2003). The psychology of religion. *Annual Review of Psychology, 54,* 377–402.

Erikson, E. H. (1980). *Identity and the life cycle.* New York: W. W. Norton.

Ferrer, J. N. (2009). The plurality of religions and the spirit of pluralism: A participatory vision of the future of religion. *International Journal of Transpersonal Psychology, 28,* 139–151.

Fowler, J. W. (1981). *Stages of faith.* New York: Harper & Row.

Friedman, H. (1983). The Self-Expansiveness Level Form: A conceptualization and measurement of a transpersonal construct. *The Journal of Transpersonal Psychology, 15,* 37–50.

Friedman, H. (2002). Transpersonal psychology as a scientific field. *International Journal of Transpersonal Studies, 21,* 175–187.

Friedman, H. (2005). Problems of romanticism in transpersonal psychology: A case study of Aikido. *The Humanistic Psychologist, 33,* 3–24.

Friedman, H. (2009). Xenophilia as a cultural trap: Bridging the gap between transpersonal psychology and religious/spiritual traditions. *International Journal of Transpersonal Studies, 28,* 107–111.

Friedman, H., & Pappas, J. (2007). Towards a conceptual clarification of the terms religious, spiritual, and transpersonal as psychological constructs. In A.Baydala, J. Pappas, & W. Smythe (Eds.), *Cultural healing and belief systems* (pp. 22–54). Calgary, AB: Temeron Books.

Fukuyama, M., & Sevig, T. (1999). *Integrating spirituality into multicultural counseling: Multicultural aspects of counseling and psychotherapy.* Thousand Oaks, CA: Sage Publications.

Fuller, R. C. (2001). *Spiritual, but not religious: Understanding unchurched America.* New York: Oxford University Press.

Gallup, G., Jr., & Jones, T. (2000). *The next American spirituality: Finding God in the twenty-first century.* Colorado Springs, CO: Cook Communications.

Gartner, J. (1996). Religious commitment, mental health, and prosocial behavior: A review of the empirical literature. In E. P. Shafranske (Ed.), *Religion and the clinical practice of psychology* (pp. 187–214). Washington, DC: American Psychological Association.

Gilligan, C. (1982). *In a different voice.* Cambridge, MA: Harvard University Press.

Goswami, S. S. (1980). *Layayoga: The definitive guide to the chakras.* London: Routledge & Kegan Paul.

Harris, S. (2004). *End of faith: Religion, terror, and the future of reason.* New York: W. W. Norton.

Hay, D., & Nye, R. (1998). *The spirit of the child.* London: Fount.

Hood, R. W., Jr., Spilka, B., Hunsberger, B., & Gorsuch, R. (1996). *The psychology of religion: An empirical approach.* New York: The Guilford Press.

James, W. (1890). *The principles of psychology* (Vol. 2). New York: Henry Holt.

Johnson, C., & Friedman, H. (2008). Enlightened or delusional? Differentiating religious, spiritual, and transpersonal experience from psychopathology. *Journal of Humanistic Psychology, 48*(4), 505–527.

Kohlberg, L. (1971). The claim to moral adequacy of a highest stage of moral development. *Journal of Philosophy, 70,* 636–646.

Kolodiejchuk, B. (2001). *Mother Teresa: Come be my light.* New York: Doubleday.

Kornfield, J. (1993). *A path with heart.* New York: Bantam.

Krippner, S. (2002). Conflicting perspectives on shamans and shamanism: Point and counterpoints. *American Psychologist, 57,* 962–977.

Krippner, S. (2005). Spirituality across cultures, religions, and ethnicities. In R. H. Cox, B. Ervin-Cox, & L. Hoffman (Eds.), *Spirituality and psychological health* (pp. 204–240). Colorado Springs: Colorado School of Professional Psychology.

Krippner, S., & Friedman, H. L. (Eds.). (2010). *Mysterious minds: The neurobiology of psychics, mediums, and other extraordinary people.* Santa Barbara, CA: Praeger/ABC-CLIO.

Krippner, S., & Welch, P. (1992). *Spiritual dimensions of healing.* New York: Irvington.

Krishna, G. (1971). *Kundalini: The evolutionary energy in man.* Boston: Shambhala.

Leak, G. (2008). Factorial validity of the Faith Development Scale. *International Journal for the Psychology of Religion, 18*(2), 123–131.

Leary, D. E. (Ed.). (1990). *Metaphors in the history of psychology.* New York: Cambridge University Press.

Loevinger, J. (1976). *Ego development.* San Francisco: Jossey-Bass.

MacDonald, D., & Friedman, H. (2002). Assessment of humanistic, transpersonal and spiritual constructs: State of the science. *Journal of Humanistic Psychology, 42,* 102–125.

MacDonald, D., Friedman, H., & Kuentzel, J. (1999). A survey of measures of spiritual and transpersonal constructs: Part one: Research update. *Journal of Transpersonal Psychology, 31,* 137–154.

MacDonald, D., Kuentzel, J., & Friedman, H. (1999). A survey of measures of spiritual and transpersonal constructs: Part two-additional instruments. *Journal of Transpersonal Psychology, 31,* 155–177.

MacDonald, D., LeClair, L., Holland, C., Alter, A., & Friedman, H. (1995). A survey of measures of transpersonal constructs. *Journal of Transpersonal Psychology, 27,* 1–66.

MacDonald, D. A. (2000). Spirituality: Description, measurement, and relation to the five factor model of personality. *Journal of Personality, 68,* 157–197.

Magyar-Russell, G., & Pargament, K. (2006). The darker side of religion: Risk factors for poorer health and well-being. In J. H. Ellens (Ed.), *Where God and science meet: How brain and evolutionary studies alter our understanding of religion: Vol. 3. The psychology of religious experience* (pp. 105–131). Westport, CT: Praeger/Greenwood.

Maslow, A. (1968). *Toward a psychology of being.* New York: Van Nostrand.

Mayer, M. (2003). Qigong clinical studies. In W.B. Jonas (Ed.), *Healing, intention, and energy medicine* (pp. 121–137). London: Churchill Livingston.

McNamara, P. (2009). *The neuroscience of religious experience.* New York: Cambridge University Press.

Meech, P. (2007). *Mysteries of the life force: My apprenticeship with a chi kung master.* Boulder, CO: Sentient Publications.

Metzner, R. (1998). *The unfolding self: Varieties of transformative experience.* Novato, CA: Origin Press.

Miller, W. R., & Thoresen, C. E. (2003). Spirituality, religion, and health. *American Psychologist, 58,* 24–35.

Motoyama, H. (1971). *Hypnosis and religious superconsciousness.* Tokyo: Institute for Religious Psychology.

Motoyama, H. (2009). *Being and the logic of interactive function.* Tokyo: Human Science Press.

Murphy, G. (1949). Psychical research and personality. *Proceedings of the Society for Psychical Research, 49,* 1–15.

Pappas, J., & Friedman, H. (2007). The construct of self-expansiveness and the validity of the Transpersonal Scale of the Self-Expansiveness Level Form. *The Humanistic Psychologist, 35*(4), 323–347.

Pargament, K. (1997). *The psychology of religion and coping: Theory, research, practice.* New York: The Guilford Press.

Polkinghorne, D. E. (1983). *Methodology for the human sciences: Systems of inquiry.* Albany, NY: SUNY Press.

Porter, G. (1995). Exploring the meaning of spirituality and its implications for counselors. *Counseling and Values, 40,* 69–79.

Rafea, A., Rafea, A., & Rafea, A. (2005). *The book of essential Islam: Spiritual training system of Islam.* Dorset, England: Book Foundation.

Rawlinson, A. (1997). *The book of enlightened masters: Western teachers in Eastern traditions.* Chicago: Open Court.

Robbins, B., & Friedman, H. (Eds.). (2009). Special issue on methodological pluralism. *The Humanistic Psychologist, 37.*

Roehlkepartain, E., Benson, P., & King, P. (2005). Spiritual development in childhood and adolescence: Moving to the scientific mainstream. In E. Roehlkepartain, P. King, L. Wagener, & P. Benson (Eds.), *The handbook of spiritual development in childhood and adolescence* (pp. 1–16). Thousand Oaks, CA: Sage.

Rodgers, J. (2010). The epistemology of mathematical and statistical modeling: A quiet methodological revolution. *American Psychologist, 65,* 1–12.

Sangharakshita, U. (2007). *The Buddha's noble eightfold path.* London: Windhorse.

Snelling, J. (1991). *The Buddhist handbook: A complete guide to Buddhist schools of teaching, practice, and history.* Rochester, NY: Inner Traditions.

Sperry, L., & Shafranske, E. (2005). *Spiritually oriented psychotherapy.* Washington, DC: American Psychological Association.

St. John of the Cross. (2003). *Dark night of the soul.* Mineola, NY: Dover.

Sutich, A. (1969). Some considerations regarding transpersonal psychology. *Journal of Transpersonal Psychology, 1,* 11–20.

Suzuki, D. T. (1960). *Manual of Zen Buddhism.* New York: Grove Press.

Tart, C. T. (2009). *The end of materialism: How evidence of the paranormal is bringing science and spirit together.* Oakland, CA: New Harbinger/Noetic Books.

Taylor, S. (2009). Beyond the pre/trans fallacy: The validity of pre-egoic spiritual experience. *Journal of Transpersonal Psychology, 41,* 22–43.

Tolle, E. (1999). *The power of now.* Novato, CA: New World.

Torrell, J. (2003). *Saint Thomas Aquinas: Spiritual master.* Washington, DC: Catholic University of America Press.

Trungpa, C. (1973). *Cutting through spiritual materialism.* Boston: Shambhala.

Underhill, E. (1961). *Mysticism.* New York: E. P. Dutton. (Original work published 1911).

Van Biema, D. (2007, September 3). Her agony. *Time,* pp. 35–43.

Vich, M. (1988). Some historical sources of the term "transpersonal." *Journal of Transpersonal Psychology, 20,* 107–110.

Walsh, R. (2007). *The world of shamanism: New views of an ancient tradition.* Woodbury, MN: Llewellyn.

Washburn, M. (2003). *Embodied spirituality in a sacred world.* Albany, NY: SUNY Press.

Watson, L. (1982). *Lightning bird.* New York: Dutton.

Wilber, K. (1980). *The Atman project.* Wheaton, IL: Quest Books.

Wilber, K. (1997). An integral theory of consciousness. *Journal of Consciousness Studies, 4,* 71–92.

Wilber, K. (2000). *Integral psychology.* Boston: Shambhala.

Wilber, K. (2004). *Integral spirituality: A startling new role for religion in the modern and postmodern world.* Boston: Shambhala.

Yati, N. C. (2009). *Principles and practices of Patanjali's Yoga Sutras.* New Delhi, India: D. K. Printworld.

PART 4

Prayer, Intention and Sacred Dialogue in Treatment: Western Traditions

15A

Spiritually Sensitive Psychotherapy: An Impending Paradigm Shift in Theory and Practice

Len Sperry

Abstract

This chapter reports on a current paradigm shift that appears to be under way in how spiritually sensitive psychotherapy is conceptualized and practiced. I describe and discuss six indications of this shift and its implications.

Key Words: paradigm shift, postmaterialist perspective, consciousness, well-being therapy, positive psychology, positive psychotherapy, spiritual development

Introduction

Today, clients increasingly expect that spiritual issues will be incorporated in psychotherapy (Lesser, 1999). Through their ethics codes and diversity policies, the mental health professions also expect that therapists will be sensitive to spiritual issues. Such expectations require many therapists who were indifferent or less sensitive to spirituality to become more sensitive to it. While a small number of therapists endeavored to deal with such issues over the past several decades, it has only been recently that formal approaches to spiritually oriented therapy have emerged (Sperry & Shafranske, 2005). Many of these approaches are simply modifications of existing therapeutic systems such as psychoanalysis (Rizzuto, 2005), Jungian psychotherapy (Corbett & Stein, 2005), cognitive-behavioral therapy (Tan & Johnson, 2005), interpersonal psychotherapy (Miller, 2005), and the humanist psychotherapies (Elkins, 2005). Unfortunately, such approaches can have inherent limitations relative to their theoretical and scientific bases that can limit their clinical value, utility, and efficacy.

Fortunately, this is a particularly propitious moment for spiritually sensitive psychologists and other psychotherapists to be alive and professionally engaged as a paradigm shift in the theory and practice of spiritually sensitive psychotherapy appears to be under way. In my opinion, this impending paradigm shift promises to radically alter the way in such therapies are conceptualized and practiced, and presumably the way in which trainees are educated. Table 15.1 lists six indicators of this impending shift. This chapter describes and discusses these indicators. This discussion can provide a broad context in which to read and reflect upon the approaches described in subsequent chapters of this section of the Handbook.

The Impending Paradigm Shift in Psychotherapy

Paradigm shift refers to a revolution or significant change in the basic assumptions and practices in a science. Paradigm shift contrasts with "normal science" in which common assumptions remain unchanged and any "developments" in the field are simply evolutions or modifications of existing practices (Kuhn, 1962). While originally directed to the physical sciences, the paradigm shift perspective is also useful in understanding developments in the social sciences. For example, the "cognitive revolution" is considered in to be a paradigm shift in the

Table 15.1 Indicators of an Impending Paradigm Shift in Psychotherapy

1. Shift from a materialist to postmaterialist psychology and psychotherapy
2. Shift from a psychologization of spirituality to an integrative, holistic spirituality
3. Shift from a psychopathology focus to a consciousness and spiritual growth focus
4. Recovery of virtue and the influence of positive psychology on psychotherapy
5. Development of new therapies based on positive psychology and well-being models
6. Development of competencies in psychotherapy practice and training

science of psychology. It is argued that the cognitive revolution shifted the central focus away from a purely behavioral approach to human behavior and toward the acceptance of cognition as necessary for an integrative and fuller understanding of psychological factors influencing human behavior. That shift occurred from the late 1960s through the 1970s and resulted in cognitive-behavioral therapy, which is now the most commonly practiced psychotherapy in the world. However, since the original version of Beck's cognitive therapy (1976) was based on essentially the same materialist and reductionist assumptions as Wolpe's behavior therapy (1969), it is questionable whether paradigm shift technically occurred, at least in the early days. More recently, however, basic assumptions compatible with a postmaterialist perspective are evident in the so-called third wave of cognitive and behavioral therapies (Hayes, Follette, & Linehan, 2004).

Today, it appears that a concomitant paradigm shift is under way in the overall theory and practice of psychotherapy (Sperry, 2011). It appears that this concomitant shift has and will continue to impact spiritually sensitive psychotherapy. In addition, other change factors will be noted that have been and are operative in the paradigm shift occurring in spiritually sensitive psychotherapy. Six indications of this impending change are described here.

Shift From a Materialist to Postmaterialist Psychology and Psychotherapy

From the earliest times psychology was understood as "the study of the soul." Since the late 19th century in its quest to become a science, that is, scientific psychology, psychology sought to free itself from its roots in "value-based" philosophy and become "value-free" like physics and the biological sciences. Psychology also adopted a perspective and a method, that is, the scientific method, which were decidedly materialist. This materialist perspective includes the following premises: Phenomena that exist are measurable. Human life is a material phenomenon, wherein the mind is an expression of matter. Furthermore, God, afterlife, free choice, and other spiritual phenomena are essentially false projections of the mind.

Reductionism and dualism are two philosophical constructs that underlie this materialist perspective. Reductionism is a way of understanding the complex nature of a phenomenon by reducing it to the interactions of its parts, or to simpler or more fundamental phenomena. Reducing grief or spiritual striving to a neuroscience construct such as neurotransmitter activity is an example of reductionism. Like reductionism, dualism is a central tenet of the perspective that posits the dual nature of reality. While Descartes championed the mind-body split, many in psychology separate the mind from the brain (Sperry, 2010).

Although reductionism is an essential construct in the materialist perspective, dualism is not. This is evident in the new unified theory of psychology (Henriques, 2004a). This theory advocates that for psychology to become truly scientific, it must relinquish its adherence to mind-brain dualism and embrace the nondualist theory called scientific naturalism, which posits that all mental process are basically biologically determined and measurable (Rand & Hardi, 2005). Adopting such a theory and its underlying philosophical premises promises that the psychological sciences will experience dramatic scientific developments as well as increased respect within the scientific community (Henriques, 2004b). Although it allows for the scientific study of religion and spirituality, the proposed unified theory is problematic since values considered central to spirituality, such as love and serving others, are incompatible with scientific naturalism. Besides being materialist, the proposed unified theory is reductionist in that it "reduces" phenomena such as spiritual transcendence to neurobiology and biochemistry. More accurately, the unified model represents a biologization of spirituality. Not surprisingly, some have expressed considerable concern about such a unified theory and have called for alternatives (Slife, 2005).

In the materialist reductionism perspective, the universe is considered a mechanical system like a clock (Newton, 1713), the body and brain are localized bits of matter, and every action in this classical view of physics is determined by mechanical forces, that is, localized causality. Subjective experiences such as human consciousness, intuition, thoughts, and feelings are simply passive bystanders of such a mechanical system and its processes. Furthermore, reductionism and dualism characterize this perspective. By contrast, postmaterialist perspectives are more holistic instead of reductionist, less characterized by nonlocal causality, and more consistent with quantum physics (Bohm & Hiley, 1993). Accordingly, human consciousness, intuition, thoughts, and feelings are under the control of an individual with free will.

The alternative to reductionism is nonreductionism or holism (Sperry & Mansager, 2004), while an alternative to scientific naturalism is quantum field theory, which is nondualist. Interestingly, the need for a holistic psychotherapy approach that is sensitive to spiritual issues, particularly spiritual growth and development, is becoming a felt need among an increasing number of therapists today.

Shift From a Psychologization of Spirituality to an Integrative, Holistic Spirituality

A current and troubling concern is the "psychologization" of spirituality (Cortright, 1997). Psychologization refers to the therapeutic influence that modern psychology exerts on understanding the spiritual life. In a psychologized spirituality, spirituality is "reduced" to psychological constructs. Such psychological reductionism involves an overreliance and uncritical adoption of such constructs as "self-fulfillment" and "self-realization." This is problematic because true spiritual growth involves transformation of self, that is, self- emptying, rather than self-absorption, which fosters narcissism (Sperry, 2002b). A more recent form of reductionism is the "biologization" of spirituality in which spirituality is reduced to neurology and biochemical processes such as the so-called God gene (Hamer, 2004).

Some therapeutic approaches unwittingly foster such psychologization of spirituality, and understanding the underlying relationship of spirituality to psychology is useful in choosing such an approach. While there is yet to be a consensus definition of spirituality (McSherry & Cash, 2004; Sperry, 2005), it is possible to describe the various ways the relationship of spirituality and psychology has been described or implied in psychological and spiritual theories. If one articulates the relationship between the domains of spirituality and psychology in terms of two sets of factors—whether the domains are the same or different, and which domain has primacy over the other—it is possible to derive five different relationships. These five relationships represent a taxonomy (Sperry & Mansager, 2007), which is briefly described as follows:

1. Psychology and spirituality are viewed as essentially the same with psychology having primacy. There is little or no need for spiritual interventions or disciplines necessary to effect development. This is the epitome of psychological reductionism, and it is exemplified by the classical psychoanalytic approach (Freud, 1927/1995).

2. Psychology and spirituality are essentially the same, with spirituality having primacy. This view is represented by classical Jungian psychotherapy (Jung, 1963) and a few traditional approaches to spiritual direction and pastoral counseling (May, 1992). This is the epitome of spiritual reductionism.

3. Psychology and spirituality are essentially different, with psychology having primacy. This view is representative of some spiritually oriented psychoanalytic approaches (Shafranske, 2005), as well as some existential-humanist approaches (Elkins, 2005).

4. Psychology and spirituality are essentially different, with spirituality having primacy. In this view, growth in one domain such as the psychological can be reflected in the other but is not inevitable. Thus, one can be saintly but neurotic. This view is representative of a number of the transpersonal approaches to psychotherapy (Cortright, 1997), spiritually oriented interpersonal psychotherapy (Miller, 2005), as well as spiritually oriented cognitive-behavioral therapy (Tan & Johnson, 2005).

5. Psychology and spirituality are essentially different, with neither having primacy nor being reducible to the other. When client concerns involve symptom or problem resolution, psychotherapeutically oriented strategies are indicated, whereas when concerns involve ultimate questions and answers, spiritually oriented strategies are indicated. This view is representative of the holistic orientation (Sperry & Mansager, 2004).

This taxonomy identifies the first four orientations as being reductionist with the fifth as holistic, that is, nonreductionist. Reductionist approaches are less likely to be developmentally oriented. On the other hand, holistic approaches are postmaterialist in perspective and more likely to be strengths based and growth oriented.

Growth-oriented, spiritually sensitive psychotherapies tend to emphasize constructing meaning and the transcendent over decreasing symptoms and impairment, that is, an emphasis on meanings more than on observation of facts. Such therapy requires a focused listening to the client's experience to understand his or her meaning. In short, "(s)piritually sensitive psychotherapists offer a particular kind of listening, a listening that is receptive to the meanings of psychological difficulties within a broad and transcendent context" (Shafranske & Sperry, 2005, p. 25). Not surprisingly, such approaches are based on a postmaterialist perspective.

Shift From a Psychopathology Focus to a Spiritual Growth and Consciousness Focus

Basically, conventional psychotherapy practice is psychopathologically focused (Sperry, 2002a). This means that therapeutic interventions are directed at reducing symptoms and improving functioning. Such a pathological focus is not uncommon in spiritually sensitive psychotherapy, at least for two of the three usual indications for it, that is, coping with a serious stressor, or a crisis of faith or meaning, whereas the third, spiritual growth, is not (Shafranske & Sperry, 2005; Sperry, 2010). While a focus on spiritual growth may seem more consistent with traditional spiritual direction, today individuals are increasing seeking out psychotherapists rather than ministers to foster their spiritual as well as psychological development. Others are turning to mindfulness practices and spiritual coaching (Belf, 2003). This is not to suggest that spiritual growth has no place in the first two indications of spiritually sensitive psychotherapy. Instead, it is proposed that spiritual growth should be an expected outcome for all three indications, albeit a secondary outcome for the first two and the primary outcome for the third. This section begins with a description of the three common indications for psychotherapy that is sensitive to spiritual and religious issues and concerns. Then, it discusses consciousness and levels of consciousness as indicators of spiritual development.

There is increasing recognition that spiritual and religious issues are common in and outside of therapy. *DSM* has responded to this recognition with the V-Code "Religious or Spiritual Problems" (V62.89). It is a diagnostic category for religious or spiritual problems that includes distressing experiencing involving the loss or questioning of one's faith, problems associated with conversion to a new faith, or of questioning one's spiritual values (American Psychiatric Association, 2000). This designation primarily reflects the second of the three indications for spiritually integrated psychotherapy.

COPING WITH A SERIOUS STRESSOR

Perhaps the most common of the three clinical indications of spiritually integrated psychotherapy involves the use of spiritual resources in coping with serious stressors and tragedies. The range of stressors is quite broad and includes serious health problems, significant personal losses or professional losses, as well as difficult interpersonal and family conflicts. Common religious and spiritual resources for coping with such stressors include prayer, attendance at religious services, emotional support of a faith community, and so on (Pargament, 1997). Spiritually sensitive therapists can assist such distressed clients in identifying and utilizing such spiritual resources to cope more effectively.

Case Example

Patricia is a 34-year-old, single, African American female who sought therapy following the death of her mother. During the brief spiritual assessment of the initial evaluation, Patricia revealed that while she considered herself a deeply spiritual person, she had stopped attending church as an adolescent against her mother's wishes. Because of a recent job transfer out of town, she had no support from either a faith community or from her extended family. In the weeks following her mother's death, she had become increasingly depressed, anxious, tearful, and guilt ridden. Her constant thought was that her deeply religious mother 'begged me not to take that job transfer and look what happened. I should have listened to her." At some level she knows this thought is "ridiculous but my guilt is crushing me and maybe God is punishing me for leaving my mother." Her expectation is that therapy will help her cope better, reduce symptoms, and clarify her issues. While spiritually sensitive psychotherapy can help her meet these expectations, it could also foster her personal and spiritual growth.

CRISES OF FAITH AND MEANING

Any number of tragedies and stressors can provoke a crisis of faith or meaning. These can include betrayals, the death of a child, or other losses resulting in a crisis of faith or meaning in life. Such crises are also called spiritual struggles. "Spiritual struggles are signs of spiritual disorientation, tension, and strains. Old roads to the sacred and old understandings of the scared itself are no longer compelling. In their place, people struggle to reorient themselves and find a new way to the sacred or a new understanding of the sacred" (Pargament, 2007, p. 112). Pargament (2007) identifies three types of spiritual struggles: interpersonal, intrapersonal, and divine. Interpersonal struggles involve family, friends, or congregations about matters such as gossiping, cliquishness, hypocrisy, or disagreement with doctrine. Intrapersonal struggles typically involve uncertainty or doubt about spiritual matters or serious doubts about one's religious tradition. A third form of struggle involves tensions between an individual and the divine often in the face of critical life events when an individual comes to question or doubt God's existence or the belief that God is caring and benevolent in the face of adversity. Such questioning and doubts are referred to as crises of faith. These struggles can be temporary expressions of spiritual pain that quickly resolve, or they may be protracted experiences that result in anxiety or depressive conditions with lowered physical and relational functioning and quality of life (Exline & Rose, 2005).

Case Example

Leila is a 47-year-old, married female who complains of worsening anger, confusion, insomnia, and "down moods" of 4 months duration. It appears that her symptoms began soon after a priest in her parish was indicted for sexual misconduct with an adolescent. It appears that while Leila had no such history, her younger brother had been abused by a priest from age 13 to 15. After the indictment Leila reports that she stopped all church involvement and began questioning her faith in "a God that would let such terrible things happen to kids." While spiritually sensitive psychotherapy can be directed at resolving this spiritual crisis, presumably it could also foster her personal and spiritual growth.

SPIRITUAL GROWTH

Spiritual growth refers to the development and formation of the whole person by an intentional focus on increasing the person's self-aware consciousness, self-transcendence, and transformation (Sperry, 2002b). It involves developing the person's spiritual and interior life with spiritual practices and disciplines such as prayer, fasting, simplicity, solitude, and worship (Walsh, 1999). Such spiritual formation can also include the more intimate and in-depth process of spiritual direction (May, 1992; Sperry, 2002b).

Case Example

Martin, a 43-year-old, married executive, had just made an appointment with a psychologist who practiced spiritually integrated psychotherapy. He had been referred by a friend who was involved in "growth counseling" with the psychologist. Martin sought help in "toning down my obsession with work" and "getting more balance in my professional, family, personal, and spiritual life." While Martin regularly worked 60 hours a week, the same or less than his fellow executives, he did not find his work satisfying or as meaningful as it had been in the past. He attributed this to a mid-life crisis in which he felt increasingly disconnected from his family and friends and "spiritually impoverished." Spiritually sensitive psychotherapy that is informed by spiritual direction can presumably help Martin achieve this outcome.

LEVELS OF CONSCIOUSNESS

Consciousness is commonly understood as the awareness of one's existence, sensations, thoughts, and feelings. Self-aware consciousness is the uniquely human capacity to remember and reexperience the past in the immediacy of one's own intuitions. Individuals differ in their capacity for self-conscious awareness depending on their degree of adaptability and their "level of awareness of the context in which … (they) live" (Cloninger, 2004, p. xvi). Four differing levels of self-conscious awareness can be identified. They are as follows: little or no conscious awareness; minimal awareness; moderate awareness; and maximal awareness. These levels of awareness reflect levels of spiritual development that have long been described in early Judeo-Christian literature, beginning with the Bible. Initially, three "ages" of spiritual growth and development—beginner, proficient, and perfect—were described. While favored by Origen and Augustine, these "ages" were replaced by the "ways" of purgative, illuminative, and unitive during the Middle Ages. More recently, efforts to combine the "ages" and "ways" have resulted in three "stages" of the spiritual life (Garrigou-Lagrange, 1938). These stages or levels appear to be comparable to the levels of conscious awareness.

Clinically speaking, these levels of self-aware consciousness can be approximated in terms of functionality and impairment on the Global Assessment of Functioning scale (GAF), which is Axis V of *DSM-IV-TR* (American Psychiatric Association, 2000). Furthermore, level of self-aware consciousness can also be approximated from the duration of the individual's response to distress and upset.

Specifically, individuals with very high levels of self-awareness have a very short-lived response to even moderate to severe distress, while individuals with very low levels seem to experience distress for several hours or even days. These four levels of self-aware consciousness with their clinical correlates can be described as follows (Sperry, 2010).

Level 0

Individuals here tend to experience very little or no awareness and instead engage in emotional thinking, act in an egocentric fashion, seek immediate gratification, and display impulsivity and emotional instability. They often carry diagnoses of severe personality disorders, substance dependence, or psychoses. Furthermore, their experience of distress typically lasts for several hours or even a few days at a time until a sense of calm is reestablished. Their GAF scores tend to be lower than 60.

Level 1

Individuals here tend to experience a minimal level of awareness. Accordingly, their actions are purposeful and although still somewhat egocentric, they have some impulse control and can delay gratification. Generally, they can function relatively well in nonstressful situations, but they fare poorly when under moderate stress during which they can exhibit a range of negative affects. The duration of their experience distress and upset usually lasts for hours. Their GAF scores tend to be in the range of 60 to 74.

Level 2

Individuals here tend to experience a moderate level of awareness. They are mature and are aware of others' needs as well as their own subconscious thinking. Their demeanor is characterized by calmness and patience. They typically experience positive emotions and are able to observe themselves and others with little need to judge or blame. As a result, they deal reasonably well with conflicts and relationships. The duration of their experience distress and upset usually lasts for minutes to an hour or so. Their GAF scores tend to be in the range of 75 to 90.

Level 3

Individuals here tend to experience a maximal level of awareness. This translates to effortless calm, impartial awareness, creativity, and loving behavior. They are in touch with previously unconscious thoughts and motivations, possess a balanced outlook on life, and no longer struggle with wishful thinking and conflicts. Consequently, their experience of distress and upset is very short lived and momentary. Their GAF scores tend to be at the highest levels, that is, in the 90s. Cloninger (2004) has described a similar but different view of consciousness levels.

Recovery of Virtue and the Influence of Positive Psychology on Psychotherapy

Although Maslow used the term "positive psychology" in 1954 and subsequent psychologists emphasized the promotion of mental health over the treatment of mental illness, Martin Seligman is considered the father of the modern positive psychology movement (Seligman & Csikszentmihalyi, 2000). Positive psychology's roots are in humanist psychology with its focus on happiness and fulfillment. Earlier influences on positive psychology came primarily from philosophical and religious sources that predated the development of scientific psychology. Chief among these was Aristotle's belief that happiness is constituted by rational activity in accordance with "virtue." Christianity further developed virtue with its emphasis on the four cardinal virtues (prudence, temperance, justice, fortitude) and the three theological virtues (faith, hope, charity), which served as a counterpoint to the seven deadly sins or vices, which centered on self-indulgence and narcissism.

Until the advent of scientific psychology in 1879 when Wundt established the first laboratory in experimental psychology, virtue was central to psychology. Virtue is traditionally defined as the disposition that moves one to accomplish moral good, or more contemporaneously, as a value in action (Peterson & Seligman, 2004). Essentially, virtue was "lost" for more than a century as scientific psychology developed, until its recent "recovery" as the positive psychology movement emerged. The publication of *Character Strengths and Virtues: A Handbook and Classification* by Peterson and Seligman (2004) represents a landmark research effort in identifying and classifying the positive psychological traits of persons. It identifies six classes of virtue consisting of 24 measurable character strengths. These include the following: (1) Wisdom and Knowledge: characterized by creativity, curiosity, open-mindedness, love of learning, perspective, and innovation; (2) Courage: characterized by bravery, persistence, integrity, and vitality; (3) Humanity: characterized by love, kindness, and social intelligence; (4) Justice: characterized by citizenship, fairness, and leadership; (5) Temperance: characterized by forgiveness and mercy, humility, prudence, and self-control; and (6) Transcendence: characterized by appreciation of beauty and excellence, gratitude, hope, humor, and spirituality (Peterson & Seligman, 2004).

The recovery of the virtue tradition by positive psychology has influenced the practice of psychotherapy. The next section describes two such approaches.

Development of New Therapies Based on Positive Psychology and Well-Being Models

As suggested earlier, spiritually sensitive psychotherapy approaches based on materialist and reductionist premises are out of step with the impending paradigm shift, in contrast with approaches that are more holistic and based on virtues, strengths, and consciousness. In terms of levels of consciousness, cognitive-behavioral therapy and many conventional psychotherapy approaches appear to be primarily focused on Level 0 and Level 1 of consciousness and related clinical considerations. That is problematic for two reasons: First, treatment end points are limited to symptom reduction and at most to relapse prevention. These end points are particularly problematic in long term, chronic conditions such as in recurrent depression wherein residual symptoms persist in the majority of patients upon successful treatment of their illness (Fava, Rafnelli, Cazzaro, Conti, & Grandi, 1998). Second, when the goal of therapy is reduction of symptoms and impairment, but not increased personal effectiveness and well-being, relapse is likely and perhaps even inevitable. Based on a 6-year follow-up study of a novel treatment prevention strategy, it was speculated that merely being in remission of symptoms was insufficient to prevent relapse and that the absence of well-being actually creates conditions of vulnerability for relapse (Fava et al., 2004).

What is needed is another type of treatment, a more holistic therapy that can move clients beyond reduction of symptoms and impairment to complete symptom remission and higher levels of consciousness. In short, a therapy approach is needed that can promote growth to Level 2 functioning and higher. Whereas conventional approaches seem to focus largely on the assessment of symptom and deficits and specify a diagnosis, a holistic, growth-oriented approach should focus more on the assessment of consciousness, strengths, and positive experiences and actions. General treatment goals would likewise differ. Where conventional approaches would emphasize reducing symptoms

and impairment (Levels 0 and 1), Level 2 goals would emphasize increasing self-awareness and spiritual development.

POSITIVE PSYCHOTHERAPY

Seligman and colleagues at the University of Pennsylvania have developed a way to treat conditions like depression by focusing on virtues, building positive emotions, and increasing the client's sense of meaning, instead of simply reducing symptoms such as sadness (Seligman, Rashid, & Parks, 2006). This approach utilizes a combination of 12 exercises that can be practiced individually or in groups. The technique, "using your signature strengths or virtues," is a primary intervention in positive psychotherapy. When tested in a randomized controlled trial, it was found that this technique did lead to positive treatment outcomes (Seligman, Rashid, & Parks, 2006). Seligman's positive psychotherapy approach is one of a number of emerging forms of psychotherapy influenced by positive psychology. Another promising approach is well-being therapy.

WELL-BEING THERAPY

Well-being therapy is a theoretically and empirically derived treatment approach with promising treatment outcomes data (Fava et al., 2004). Well-being therapy was developed by Fava (2003) specifically as a relapse preventive strategy in the residual phase of affective disorders, and for nonresponders to standard treatment for affective disorders. Subsequently, it was expanded as a treatment intervention for anxiety disorders, including obsessive-compulsive disorder (Fava & Ruini, 2003). More recently, it has been utilized as a strengths-based strategy in school counseling and in life coaching (Ruini, Belaise, Brombin, Caffo, & Fava, 2006). Several studies show its superiority when compared to cognitive-behavioral therapy alone, including a 6-year follow-up of nonmedication treatment for preventing recurrence in depression, which showed that when well-being therapy strategies were included in treatment, results were only 40% relapse rate compared to 90% rate with clinical management (Fava et al., 2004). Based on Ryff's (1989) model of well-being, well-being therapy is structured, directive, and problem oriented, yet it is client centered in that the client's positive appraisals of well-being lead the course of treatment. This contrasts with most other therapy approaches in which the therapist takes considerable responsibility in specifying destination and goals of treatment and leading the process. Well-being therapy is an eight-session therapeutic intervention that emphasizes both self-observation, as well as interactions with the therapist. Interestingly, the therapist's role in well-being therapy is more that of a coach, with the client being largely responsible for leading the change process.

The overall goal of well-being therapy is to enhance the client's sense of well-being. This is accomplished by a threefold strategy: First, enhance the client's awareness of positive moments. Second, discuss and change negative thoughts that disrupt episodes of well-being. Third, improve the clients' impairments in six well-being dimensions. The therapeutic process in well-being therapy is rather straightforward. It begins with teaching the client to record (in a structured diary) current episodes of well-being and thoughts that sidetrack those experiences. It then involves reinterpreting those thoughts viewed from an observer's standpoint. Then, it utilizes reinterpretations to increase a sense of well-being in any of the six well-being dimensions that are impaired. A variety of therapeutic interventions are utilized in well-being therapy. These include cognitive restructuring, distancing, fostering positive thinking, homework, happiness interventions, and spiritual practices. Well-being therapy can be provided individually or in small groups. It has been used with adults, older adults, children, and adolescents in clinical and in nonclinical settings (Fava & Ruini, 2003). Well-being therapy is a directive and structured treatment approach in which the focus of treatment can be specified. As it is currently formulated, in the initial sessions, the focus is on identifying periods of well-being through a structured diary. Clients are taught to rank episodes of well-being on a scale from 0 to 100, where 0 represents the absence of well-being and 100 represents the most intense well-being that could be experienced. The focus on intermediate sessions is on discovering how thoughts and behaviors characteristically prevent well-being, once this pattern is recognized. These sessions emphasize self-monitoring moments and feelings of well-being. During these sessions the therapist encourages the client to engage in pleasurable activities each day, and specific strategies for enhancing well-being are discussed. The final sessions focus more directly on impaired dimensions of well-being. The therapist guides the client in recognizing errors in thinking and in generating alternate interpretations (Fava & Ruini, 2003).

Development of Competencies in Psychotherapy Practice and Training

Competency is the current zeitgeist in psychotherapy practice and training. Not simply another approach or training method, competency represents a veritable paradigm shift in psychotherapy training and practice. As such, it is challenging much of what is familiar and comfortable. Thus, requirement standards are beginning to be replaced with competency standards, core competencies are replacing core curriculums, and competency-based licensure is on the horizon. This trend is already evident in medical training, where competency standards have replaced requirement standards and competency-based examinations are a requirement for medical licensure.

The shift to psychotherapy competency is also an accreditation standard in psychiatry training programs, which now require that trainees demonstrate competency in at least three psychotherapy approaches. Training programs in clinical psychology programs have solidly embraced competencies, and marital and family therapy and professional counseling programs are poised to follow suit. Because competencies involve knowledge, skill, and attitudinal components, competency-based education is very different in how psychotherapy is taught, learned, and evaluated. Not surprisingly, models of instruction and supervision must necessarily change. The emergence of competencies on the center stage of training and practice reflects several societal trends, among them the demand for professional accountability and evidence-based practice. Fortunately, the expectation that therapists demonstrate the effectiveness of their therapeutic work parallels the recent upsurge in treatment outcomes research.

Six core psychotherapy competencies have been described. They are as follows: (1) articulate a conceptual framework for psychotherapy practice; (2) develop and maintain an effective therapeutic alliance; (3) develop an integrative case conceptualization and treatment plan based on an integrative assessment; (4) implement interventions; (5) monitor treatment progress and outcomes and plan for termination process; and (6) practice in a culturally sensitive and ethically sensitive manner (Sperry, 2010, 2011).

Currently, there is no consensus on competencies involving spiritually sensitive psychotherapy. Nevertheless, some have also endeavored to establish competencies and ethical guidelines for spiritually sensitive practice (Gonsiorek, Richards, Pargament, & McMinn, 2009; Richards, 2009). While the current lack of consensus on competencies leaves a void for psychologists and psychotherapists practicing in this area, it provides both a challenge and an opportunity for this specialty field to develop and mature.

There are, however, two notable developments to aid professional counselors and psychologists. The Association for Spiritual, Ethical, and Religious Values in Counseling (ASERVIC), a division of the American Counseling Association (ACA), has published a list of competencies: "Competencies for Addressing Spiritual and Religious Issues in Counseling" (ASERVIC, 2009; Cashwell & Young, 2005). It is noteworthy that these competencies have been recently revised and extended (ASERVIC, 2009). This revised document includes 14 competencies of which the first six are cognitive competencies, for example, "can describe the similarities and differences between spirituality and religion," while the last five are clinical competencies. These involve assessment, diagnosis, goals setting, and the utilization of spiritually sensitive treatment interventions.

The American Psychological Association's (APA) Division 36 (Psychology and Religion) has developed some preliminary guidelines ("Preliminary Practice Guidelines for Working with Religious and Spiritual Issues") that focus on assessment, therapy, and diversity considerations in the practice of spiritually oriented psychotherapy (cf. Appendix 2.1, Hathaway & Ripley, 2009). While these guidelines have not been formally adopted by the APA, they "represent the sorts of common best practice recommendations from exemplar clinicians who specialize in addressing religious and spiritual issues in practice" (Hathaway & Ripley, 2009, p. 33).

A tentative list of competencies for spiritually sensitive psychotherapy that "map" to the list of core psychotherapy competencies (Sperry, 2010; 2011; 2012) is included in Table 15.2. These were derived, in part, from Sperry (2012) and Aten and Leach (2009).

Concluding Comments

Six different indicators have been described to support the contention that a paradigm shift is occurring in the theory and practice of spiritually oriented psychotherapy. This paradigm shift is likely to be more far reaching and substantive than the "cognitive revolution" that shifted the focus from a behavioral to a cognitive-behavioral perspective. The shift from a materialist and reductionist perspective to a postmaterialist and holistic perspective with an emphasis on self-aware consciousness constitutes a radical and revolutionary change with many implications. For example, a number of the historical and contemporary psychotherapy approaches identified as being sensitive to spiritual issues appear to be

Table 15.2 Core Competencies of Spiritually Sensitive Psychotherapy

1. Articulate an integrative and holistic conceptual framework for psychotherapy that is spiritually sensitive

2. Develop and maintain an effective therapeutic alliance sensitive to the spiritual dimension that adequately deals with spiritual transference, countertransference, and resistance

3. Include spirituality in the case conceptualization and treatment plan based on an integrative assessment and diagnosis that includes the spiritual dimension

4. Implement spiritual and psychological interventions, including referral to spiritual resources if indicated

5. Monitor and evaluate overall treatment progress and outcomes as well as incorporate spiritual dimension in the termination process

6. Practice in a culturally sensitive and ethically sensitive manner, acknowledging cultural and religious factors

more consistent with a materialist perspective than with a postmaterialist perspective. An indicator of this is their reductionist view of spirituality and psychology. Thus, it should not be too surprising then that these approaches may only be able to offer limited help to individuals seeking spiritual growth and development.

The model of consciousness and spiritual development levels described here articulates four different levels of goals that can serve as a taxonomy for choosing psychotherapeutic approaches and interventions. Unfortunately, most existing therapeutic approaches, including the majority of spiritually sensitive approaches, are well suited for Level 0 and 1, while approaches like positive psychotherapy and well-being therapy are sensitive to Level 2 spiritual issues and goals. The time has come for the development of other spiritually sensitive psychotherapy approaches that target the various levels of consciousness. In tandem with the paradigm shift that is occurring in psychotherapy competencies, it may well be that the shift under way in spiritually sensitive psychotherapy may be propelled forward synergistically with increasing interest in consciousness phenomena. For example, research on the clinical applications of mindfulness has greatly increased in the past few years at the same time more clinicians are utilizing mindfulness methods with clients, and even practicing mindfulness themselves.

References

American Psychiatric Association. (2000). *Diagnostic and statistical manual of mental disorders* (4th ed., Text rev.). Washington, DC: Author.

Association for Spiritual, Ethical and Religious Values in Counseling (ASERVIC). (2009). Competencies for Addressing Spiritual and Religious Issues in Counseling. *Interaction, 10*(10), 3, (Fall).

Aten, J., & Leach, M. (Eds.). (2009). *Spirituality and the therapeutic process: A comprehensive resource from intake to termination.* Washington, DC: American Psychological Association.

Beck, A. (1976). *Cognitive therapy and the emotional disorders.* New York: International Universities Press.

Belf, T. (2003). *Coaching with spirit.* San Francisco: Pfeiffer/Jossey-Bass.

Bohm, D., & Hiley, B. (1993). *The undivided universe: An ontological interpretation of quantum theory.* London: Routledge.

Cashwell, C., & Young, S. (2005). *Integrating spiritual and religion into counseling: A guide to competent practice.* Alexandria, VA: American Counseling Association.

Cloninger, C. R. (2004). *Feeling good: The science of well-being.* New York: Oxford University Press.

Corbett, L., & Stein, M. (2005). Contemporary Jungian approaches to spiritually oriented psychotherapy. In L. Sperry & E. Shafranske (Eds.), *Spiritually oriented psychotherapy* (pp. 51–73). Washington, DC: American Psychological Association.

Cortright, B. (1997). *Psychotherapy and spirit. Theory and practice in transpersonal psychotherapy.* Albany, NY: SUNY Press.

Elkins, D. (2005) A humanistic approach to spiritually oriented psychotherapy. In L. Sperry & E. Shafranske (Eds.), *Spiritually oriented psychotherapy* (pp. 131–152). Washington, DC: American Psychological Association.

Exline, J., & Rose, E. (2005). Religious and spiritual struggles. In R. Paloutzian & C. Parks (Eds.), *Handbook of the psychology of religions and spirituality* (pp. 315–330). New York: The Guilford Press.

Fava, G. (2003). Well-being therapy: Conceptual and technical issues. *Psychotherapy and Psychosomatics, 68,* 171–179.

Fava, G., Rafnelli, C., Cazzaro, M., Conti, S., & Grandi, S. (1998). Well-being therapy: A novel psychotherapeutic approach for residual symptoms of affective disorders. *Psychological Medicine, 28,* 475–480.

Fava, G., & Ruini, C. (2003). Development and characteristics of a well-being enhancing psychotherapeutic strategy: Well-being therapy. *Journal of Behavioral Therapy and Experimental Psychiatry, 34,* 45–63.

Fava, G., Runi, C., Rafnelli, C., Finos, L., Conti, S., & Grandi, S. (2004). Six year outcome of cognitive behavior therapy for prevention of recurrent depression. *American Journal of Psychiatry, 161,* 1872–1876.

Freud, S. (1927/1995). *The future of an illusion.* New York, NY: Norton.

Garrigou-Lagrange, R. (1938). The three ways of the spiritual life. London: Burns & Oates.

Gonsiorek, J. C., Richards, P. S., Pargament, K. I., & McMinn, M. R. (2009). Ethical challenges and opportunities at the edge: Incorporating spiritual and religion into psychotherapy. *Professional Psychology: Research, and Practice, 40,* 385–395.

Hamer, D. (2004). *The God-gene: How faith is hardwired into our genes.* New York: Doubleday.

Hathaway, W., & Ripley, J. (2009). Ethical concerns around spiritual and religion in clinical practice. In J. Aten & M. Leach (Eds.), *Spirituality and the therapeutic process: A comprehensive resource from intake to termination* (pp. 25–52). Washington, DC: American Psychological Association Hathaway & Ripley.

Hayes, S., Follette, V., & Linehan, M. (Eds.). (2004). *Mindfulness and acceptance: Expanding the cognitive-behavioral traditions.* New York: The Guilford Press.

Henriques, G. (2004a). The development of the unified theory and the future of psychotherapy. *Psychotherapy Bulletin, 39,* 4, 16–21.

Henriques, G. (2004b). Psychology defined. *Journal of Clinical Psychology, 60,* 12, 1207–1221.

Jung, C. (1963). *Memories, dreams, reflections.* New York: Vintage Books.

Kuhn, T. (1962). *The structure of scientific revolutions.* Chicago: University of Chicago Press.

Lesser, E. (1999). *The new American spirituality: A seeker's guide.* New York: Random House.

May, G. (1992). *Care of mind, care of soul.* San Francisco: Harper/Collins.

McSherry, W., & Cash, K. (2004). The language of spirituality: An emerging taxonomy. *International Journal of Nursing Studies, 41,* 151–161.

Miller, L. (2005). Interpersonal psychotherapy from a spiritual perspective. In L. Sperry & E. Shafranske (Eds.), *Spiritually oriented psychotherapy* (pp. 177–206). Washington, DC: American Psychological Association.

Newton, I. (1713). *Principia mathematica.* London: Mothe-Cajori.

Pargament, L. (1997). *The psychology of religion and coping: Theory, research, practice.* New York: The Guilford Press.

Pargament, L. (2007). *Spiritually-integrated psychotherapy: Understanding and addressing the sacred.* New York: The Guilford Press.

Peterson, C., & Seligman, M. (2004). *Character strengths and virtues: A handbook and classification.* Oxford, England: Oxford University Press.

Rand, K., & Hardi, S. (2005). Toward a consilient science of psychology. *Journal of Clinical Psychology, 61*(1), 7–20.

Richards, P. S. (2009). Toward religious and spiritual competence for psychologists: Some reflections and recommendations. *Professional Psychology: Research, and Practice, 40,* 389–391.

Rizzuto, A. (2005). Psychoanalytic considerations about spiritually oriented psychotherapy. In L. Sperry & E. Shafranske (Eds.), *Spiritually oriented psychotherapy* (pp. 31–50). Washington, DC: American Psychological Association.

Ruini, C., Belaise, C., Brombin, C., Caffo, E., & Fava, G. (2006). Well-being therapy in school settings: A pilot study. *Psychotherapy and Psychosomatics, 75,* 331–336.

Ryff, C. (1989). Happiness is everything, or is it? Explorations on the meaning of psychological well-being. *Journal of Personality and Social Psychology, 6,* 1069–1081.

Seligman, M., & Csikszentmihalyi, M. (2000). Positive psychology: An introduction. *American Psychologist, 55,* 5–14.

Seligman, M., Rashid, T., & Parks, A. (2006). Positive psychotherapy, *American Psychologist, 61,* 774–788.

Shafranske, E. (2005). A psychoanalytic approach to spiritually oriented psychotherapy. In L. Sperry & E. Shafranske (Eds.), *Spiritually oriented psychotherapy* (pp. 105–130). Washington, DC: American Psychological Association.

Shafranske, E., & Sperry, L. (2005). Addressing the spiritual dimension in psychotherapy: Introduction and overview. In L.

Sperry & E. Shafranske (Eds.), *Spiritually oriented psychother-apy* (pp. 11–29). Washington, DC: American Psychological Association.

Slife, B. (2005). Testing the limits of Henriques' proposal: Wittgensteinian lessons and hermeneutic dialogue. *Journal of Clinical Psychology, 61*(1), 107–120.

Sperry, L. (2002a). From psychopathology to transformation: Retrieving the developmental focus in psychotherapy. *Journal of Individual Psychology, 58*, 398–421.

Sperry, L. (2002b). *Transforming self and community: Revisioning pastoral counseling and spiritual direction*. Collegeville, MN: Liturgical Press.

Sperry, L. (2005). Is a consensus definition of spirituality possible? Theory construction in spiritually-oriented psychotherapy. *Research in the Social Scientific Study of Religion, 16*, 207–219.

Sperry, L. (2010). Psychotherapy sensitive to spiritual issues: A post-materialist psychology perspective and developmental approach. *Psychology of Religion and Spirituality, 2*, 46–56.

Sperry, L. (2011). *Core competencies in counseling and psychother-apy: Becoming a highly competent and effective therapist*. New York: Routledge.

Sperry, L. (2012). *Spirituality in clinical practice: Theory and practice of spiritually oriented psychotherapy, Second edition*. New York, NY: Routledge.

Sperry, L., & Shafranske, E. (Eds.). (2005). *Spiritually oriented psychotherapy*. Washington, DC: American Psychological Association.

Sperry, L., & Mansager, E. (2004). Holism in psychotherapy and spiritual direction: A course correction. *Counseling and Values, 48*(7), 149–160.

Sperry, L., & Mansager, E. (2007). The relationship of psychol-ogy and spirituality: An initial taxonomy for spiritually-oriented counseling and psychotherapy. *Journal of Individual Psychology, 63*, 359–370.

Tan, S., & Johnson, W. (2005). Spiritually-oriented cogni-tive behavior therapy. In L. Sperry & E. Shafranske (Eds.), *Spiritually oriented psychotherapy* (pp. 77–103). Washington, DC: American Psychological Association.

Walsh, R. (1999). *Essential spirituality: The seven central practices to awaken heart and mind*. New York: Wiley.

Wolpe, J. (1969). *The practice of behavior therapy*. New York: Pergamon.

15B

Journey From a Materialist to a Postmaterialist Perspective— A Portrait

Len Sperry

Abstract

It is not uncommon for the course of one's professional and personal life to evolve. Often this evolution involves significant changes in assumptions and premises about science and human nature. The career trajectory of a professional clinician and researcher is described in terms of three distinct phases: materialistic, dualistic, and postmaterialistic.

Key Words: Materialism; postmaterialism; dualism; philosophy of science

Presumably, individuals can and do evolve or shift from a materialist to a postmaterialist perspective. How this evolution occurs is not particularly clear, nor have there been many illustrations of this process in print, particularly of clinician-researchers. Here is one such example. The portrait is about Dr. E. and describes three distinct periods or phases of the evolution in his professional and personal life. For convenience, they are labeled: materialist, dualist, and postmaterialist phases. Some aspects of this portrait are disguised.

Background

Dr. E. is a 55-year-old, married, Caucasian male who had completed a MD and a residency in psychiatry as well as a PhD in biochemistry. Dr. E. teaches, researches, and practices psychiatric medicine in an academic medical center. He is a tenured full professor with appointments in the medical school in psychiatry and in the graduate school in biochemistry.

Dr. E. has remained at the same institution in which he received his graduate school and medical training.

Materialist Phase

The materialist perspective is sometimes referred to as scientific naturalism in philosophical and scientific circles. A hallmark of this perspective is that all reality is a function of matter. Human life is likewise a material phenomenon and mind is considered the expression of matter. Constructs like God and the afterlife are considered to be false projections of the mind. Human nature is viewed as neutral and human persons are considered to be the products of evolution. Freedom and free choice are also false projections of the mind, and individualism is emphasized over the communal. Generally speaking, human life has no transcendent purpose. Instead, the only reasonable purpose in life is to maximize pleasure and minimize pain. Reductionism is a central value and constructs in this perspective. For psychology and psychiatry, this means that behavior and personality are reduced to biological mechanism and explanations. Similarly, higher order constructs such as love and spirituality are also reduced to biological explanations, for example, the God gene. For better or worse, this materialist perspective underlies most undergraduate and graduate education in the Western world, particularly in the sciences. For example, I recall the fervor of a graduate school professor proclaiming that the indisputable marker of whether a phenomenon or construct truly exists is if it could be measured!

Dr. E. was probably subtly imbued with the materialist perspective during his medical training. For a long time, the culture of medical science has favored this perspective. Dr. E. reflected that modern psychology and psychiatry have almost no awareness of the limitations of materialism. He recalls hearing and reading critiques of this perspective in undergraduate courses. Since the critiques were so dissonant with his graduate school and medical training, he did not attempt to reconcile these critiques with his own beliefs, until later in his professional life. He recalls being convinced at the beginning of his clinical research career that personality could be explained satisfactorily with genetic coding and other psychobiological mechanisms. This view persisted until he began researching the influence of memory on personality development. But he was shocked to found that an individual's autobiographical memories were social constructions as perceived in the present, rather than actual memories of past events. Because the materialist perspective could not provide a convincing explanation for this phenomenon, he became increasingly disenchanted and began to question this perspective.

Dualist Phase

While there are various forms of dualism, some commonalities can be noted. The basic premise is that persons are both material and immaterial. While the brain is considered material, mind and spirit are nonmaterial substances that involve consciousness and self-awareness. This duality is expressed in the "mind-body problem" in which the challenge is to describe the relationship between mental and physical processes (e.g., interactionism or parallelism). In psychology and medicine, the basic concern is determining which sphere (mind or brain) is primarily responsible for illness and how each sphere affects the other. Human nature is largely considered bad or tainted by most religions. For example, Calvinists (and cultural Calvinists) view human nature as depraved, and individuals are divided between the good or the elect and the bad. Human behavior and feelings are the results of upbringing and impulses as well as unconscious processes or maladaptive thinking. Individualism is typically emphasized over the communal. Human life may or may not have a transcendent purpose, but through insight and effort it is possible to achieve personal adjustment or even fulfillment in life.

By his 41st birthday, Dr. E. was enjoying the perks of an academic career. He had been a tenured full professor with appointments in two departments for 2 years. He had received and continued to receive federal research funds, and he had a modest publication record. But he also experienced some confusion and discontent as his "world just didn't compute like it used to." He now attended to the physical and mental health of his patients, recognizing that each played a role in the pathogenesis of his or her illness. He recalls becoming more connected with patients in his clinical work. In the past, he had seen patients for medication management but now was spending more time with them and integrating psychotherapy. In fact, he found that patients did better with this combined therapy and he enjoyed this form of clinical work. Before, he was convinced that medical interventions, like psychotropic medications, were all that patients needed to stabilize and possibly improve. But reflection on his practice style showed that most patients were not doing well with this treatment regimen.

Then there was the matter of his daughter, Amy. He had agreed with his wife, who was a devout Episcopalian, that Amy would be raised in the faith. This meant Dr. E. started attending church services, something he had not done since high school, and becoming involved in a range of activities at the parochial school his daughter was now attending. Now, matters like sin and salvation were on his radar. His own religious upbringing was in the Presbyterian Church, and as he started to read about religion, particularly about Calvinism, he began to question his life. He also began to pray again. One of his friends in whom he had confided his confusion and discontent, said it sounded like the male midlife crisis. He wasn't sure about that but he did recognize that his life over the past 20 or so years had been largely "unexamined," and he tentatively concluded that there was more to life than competing for grants on narrower and narrower topics. His current research had also moved beyond the physiological markers to include the psychological substrates of personality development.

Postmaterialist Phase

The basic assumption is that all that exists is indivisibly related through a common universal source. Human persons are considered to be embodied spirits, and human nature is viewed as basically good. A quantum view of life is embraced, and while reductionism and dualist thinking are viewed as limiting, as is Newtonian physics, they are not fully dismissed. Human persons are considered to be influenced by past positive and negative experiences, yet they have free will and the capacity to develop beyond trauma or handicaps, particularly through self-aware consciousness. Because of the belief that all things and human persons are connected, a realistic balance between communal and individual needs and aspirations is valued. Generally speaking, life is understood as having a transcendent purpose involving increased levels of consciousness and the universal unity of being.

Dr. E.'s life continued to evolve. He was now in his mid-50s and his daughter was now in college. He was now practicing a more integrative form of treatment. He mused that when he began practice his treatment philosophy was to treat diseases with empirically based treatments. Now, his philosophy was to foster optimal health and well-being in his patients while treating their symptoms. He had been appointed medical director of the medical school's psychiatry clinic, which meant that he had increased responsibility for supervising psychiatry residents and clinical psychology interns. He took this responsibility seriously and endeavored to role model competent and compassionate patient care. His research focus had broadened and reflected his fascination with the quantum perspective. Funding was now becoming available for "integrative" research and he was successful in securing it. About 5 years ago he was doing research on memory and personality development and was surprised to find that research subjects' autobiographical memory did not always coincide with their semantic memory of early life recollections. He tried to make sense of his finding: Autobiographical memory appeared to be a social construction reflecting the subject's current perceptions rather than objective past reality.

Certainly, this was inconsistent with the scientific naturalism perspective in which he had been trained. It resulted in a careful examination of his basic assumptions about science and life. As a result, his research on personality began to extend to the development of self-aware consciousness in adults.

For 4 years he had been practicing mindfulness meditation and was experiencing a sense of centeredness and increased connectedness with people and nature. He noticed that relationships with colleagues and friends had also changed, as he was more drawn to those who were also interested in a broader view of life. He reports that his life is full and meaningful and his relationships, particularly with his wife and now married daughter, are life giving and enjoyable. He believes he has achieved a balance in his life that had been a constant struggle for him, particularly during the first 30 years of his career.

Concluding Note

This portrait is not meant to suggest that the phases described are, in any way, normative. Rather, the three labels, materialist, dualist, and postmaterialist, seem to reasonably characterize the life experience of Dr. E. It is conceivable that others' journey to a postmaterialist perspective might not involve a dualist phase. However, it seems that individuals who have a religious upbringing, wherein goodness and badness, sin and grace, and so on are central to that worldview, may begin at a dualist phase. Or, like Dr. E., wherein medical and graduate school training was so formative, individuals might "regress" to a materialist perspective.

Honoring Religious Diversity and Universal Spirituality in Psychotherapy

P. Scott Richards

Abstract

Spirituality is a universal human concern and capacity, but there is great diversity in the world concerning how spirituality is understood and practiced. Within this context of diversity, it is a challenging task for psychotherapists to learn how to ethically and effectively work with spiritual issues during treatment in order to facilitate their clients' journeys of healing and growth. This chapter describes some principles and practices that may assist psychotherapists in their efforts to succeed at this important challenge, including seeking understanding and competency in religious and spiritual aspects of diversity, selecting a spiritually oriented treatment framework and approach, finding common spiritual ground with clients, and creating a spiritual space that helps clients access the resources of their faith and spirituality during their healing journeys. The chapter concludes with a brief discussion of future directions and needs in this domain.

Key Words: psychotherapy, spirituality, religious diversity, counseling, theism, training, research

Introduction

The teachings of the major world religions and the writings of many philosophers, theologians, and social scientists converge in agreement that spirituality is a universal human concern and capacity—a basic condition of human existence (Emmons, 1999; Finnegan, 2008; Holmes, 2007; Tacey, 2004). As expressed by Sue, Bingham, Porche-Burke, and Vasquez (1999):

> Understanding that people are cultural and spiritual beings is a necessary condition for a psychology of human existence . . . in addition to rationality, life consists of emotions, intuitions, and spirituality . . . A psychology that fails to recognize this aspect of human existence is a spiritually and emotionally bankrupt discipline . . . Moreover, a psychology based solely on the separation of science and spirituality and that uses primarily the segmented and reductionistic tenets of the natural sciences is

one that may not be shared by three quarters of the world nor by the emerging culturally diverse groups in the United States.
> (p. 1065)

Although there is widespread agreement that spirituality is a universal human characteristic and capacity, there is great diversity in how it is understood and expressed (Holmes, 2007; Tacey, 2004; Zinnbauer, Pargament, & Scott, 1999). Perhaps the most common and diverse way that spirituality is understood and expressed is through religious beliefs and practices. There is an enormous amount of religious diversity in the world, including five major Western or theistic religions (i.e., Judaism, Christianity, Islam, Zoroastrianism, and Sikhism) and six major Eastern world religions (i.e., Hinduism, Buddhism, Jainism, Shintoism, Confucianism, and Taoism) (Smart, 1993, 1994). Within each of these world religions numerous subdivisions or subtraditions can be found, reflecting even greater diversity in belief and practice (Richards & Bergin, 2000; Smart, 1993, 1994).

In addition to those who understand and express their spirituality through a religious tradition, growing numbers of people find meaning and give expression to their spirituality outside of one of the major world religions (Finnegan, 2008; Tacey, 2004). For example, many people find understandings about spirituality within transpersonal, humanistic, and existential philosophical traditions (e.g., Elkins, 2005; Lukoff & Lu, 2005). Many others understand and express spirituality in a private, individualist manner devoid of ties to institutions or formal theological and philosophical frameworks (Finnegan, 2008; Sperry & Shafranske, 2005; Tacey, 2004). Finally, approximately 16% of the world's population consider themselves atheistic or nonreligious (e.g., nonbelievers, agnostics, free thinkers, secularists) (Barrett & Johnson, 2002). Atheists and nonreligious persons also grapple with spiritual concerns as they face universal human questions about the origin of life, meaning and purpose, morality, love, suffering, evil, and death. Atheistic and naturalistic worldviews, much like the world's religious traditions, attempt to provide conceptual frameworks and social support for understanding and expressing universal spiritual questions and needs (Richards & Bergin, 2005).

Within this context how can psychotherapists learn to ethically and effectively use language and interventions that respect and honor religious and spiritual diversity? Furthermore, how can they access that which is universal in human spirituality in order to facilitate their clients' journeys of healing and growth? Although these are challenging tasks, they are achievable. The purpose of this chapter is to describe some principles and practices that may assist psychotherapists in their efforts to succeed at this important challenge.

The chapter begins with a description of why it is important for psychotherapists to grow in their understanding and respect of various religious and spiritual beliefs, practices, and traditions and how they can do so. Next, psychotherapists are encouraged to select a spiritually oriented treatment framework and approach that fits their personal worldview and theoretical orientation. The need for psychotherapists to understand clients' spiritual language and views and to find common spiritual ground with them is discussed and suggestions are offered about how they can do this. Recommendations are also made concerning how psychotherapists can create a spiritual space that allows clients to access the resources of their faith and spirituality during their healing journeys. The chapter concludes with a brief discussion of future directions and needs in this domain, including developing a research evidence base for spiritually oriented treatment approaches and training the next generation of helping professionals.

Develop Competency in Religious and Spiritual Aspects of Diversity

For psychotherapists to work effectively and ethically with spiritual clients and issues, it is essential for them to develop competency in religious and spiritual aspects of diversity. This is important for several reasons (Richards & Bergin, 2000). First, psychotherapists are ethically obligated to seek an understanding of religious aspects of diversity so that they can "ensure the competence of their services" with religious clients (APA, 2002a, p. 1064). Shafranske and Malony (1996) argued that "it is incumbent that clinicians develop at least a rudimentary understanding of religion in its institutional expressions" (p. 566). They pointed out that religious affiliation "may be a far more potent social glue than the color of one's skin, cultural heritage, or gender...Religious identification for some may be the thread that unites individuals into a social unit...religion must be taken account of as a factor in any appreciation of individual difference and cultural diversity" (p. 564).

Although multicultural specialists have helped mental health professionals become more aware of differences due to race, ethnicity, gender, sexual orientation, and so on, they have given relatively little attention to religious and spiritual aspects of diversity (Smith & Richards, 2005). Because of this neglect, many professionals are not adequately prepared to work sensitively and effectively with religious clients. Ethical violations may occur if psychotherapists disregard the importance of their clients' religious beliefs and values (Bergin, 1980; Worthington, 1986, 1988).

Second, psychotherapists will enjoy more credibility with religious clients and leaders if they obtain training in religious and spiritual diversity. Many religious people have an unfavorable view of the mainstream mental health professions and a distrust of psychotherapy (Richards & Bergin, 2000; Worthington, 1986). Several studies have found that devoutly religious persons are often reluctant to seek psychotherapy because they fear that secular therapists may misunderstand, pathologize, and seek to undermine their religious beliefs

(Richards & Bergin, 2000; Weaver, Koenig, & Larson, 1997; Worthington, Kurusu, McCullough, & Sanders, 1996). Religious clients want to receive services from psychotherapists who are willing and capable of working with them in a religiously sensitive and competent manner (Worthington, 1988). Developing competency in religious aspects of diversity and building trust with people from diverse religious backgrounds could lead to increased referrals from religious leaders and communities and increase the likelihood that religious people will receive mental health services when needed.

Third, competency in religious diversity may help psychotherapists understand how to more fully access the healing resources in religious communities to assist their clients. There is a growing body of evidence that religious and spiritual beliefs, practices, and influences can both prevent problems and help promote coping and healing where problems have occurred (Benson, 1996; Koenig, McCullough, & Larson, 2001; Pargament, 1997). Spiritual views of psychotherapy, along with spiritual assessment and intervention techniques, have been proposed to help therapists more fully understand how they can draw upon the religious and spiritual resources in their clients' lives to assist them in coping and healing. However, an understanding of clients' religious beliefs and backgrounds is an essential foundation or prerequisite for using such resources and interventions. When therapists have specific knowledge about the religious background and beliefs of their clients, they often enjoy greater credibility and it is easier for them to understand how their clients' religious beliefs and culture may be intertwined with the presenting problems and symptoms. It also is easier for them to select spiritual and secular interventions that are in harmony with their clients' spiritual worldview and values.

The foundational skills of religiously and spiritually sensitive psychotherapists are similar to those required of effective multicultural counselors, including awareness of one's own cultural and racial heritage and values; respect for and comfort with cultures, races, and values that are different from one's own; understanding of how a client's cultural and racial heritage could affect his or her worldview and sense of identity; awareness of how one's helping style could affect clients from different cultural and racial backgrounds; and sensitivity to situations where it may be appropriate to refer a client to someone of her or his own culture or race (Sue & Sue, 1990; Sue et al., 1982). Spiritually sensitive psychotherapists also acquire specialized knowledge and training about religion and spirituality. This enables them to generalize their multicultural attitudes and skills to religious and spiritual clients and issues (Richards & Bergin, 2000). Several recommendations have been made about how psychotherapists can increase their competency to work with clients from diverse religious and spiritual backgrounds, including gaining a general understanding about the world religions; seeking in-depth knowledge about religious traditions frequently encountered in psychotherapy; gaining expertise in the psychology and sociology of religion; reading books or taking workshops or classes about working with spiritual issues in psychotherapy; staying current with scholarly literature about religion and spirituality in mental health and psychotherapy; seeking supervision or consultation from colleagues who have expertise in religious and spiritual aspects of diversity and treatment; and engaging in personal spiritual exploration and growth practices (Brawer, Handal, Fabricatore, Roberts, & Wajda-Johnston, 2002; Miller, 2011; Richards & Bergin, 2000, 2005; Shafranske & Malony, 1996; Young, Cashwell, Wiggins-Frame, & Belaire, 2002).

Select a Spiritually Oriented Treatment Approach

A large number of spiritually oriented treatment approaches have been developed during the past couple of decades that affirm the universality and importance of human spirituality in therapeutic change. Buddhist, Hindu, Christian, Jewish, Muslim, and ecumenical theistic approaches have been proposed (e.g., Collins, 1988; Epstein, 1995; Hedayat-Diba, 2000; McMinn, 1996; Pargament, 2007; Rabinowitz, 1999; Richards & Bergin, 2000; Rubin, 1996; Spero, 1985). Some scholars have also incorporated spiritual perspectives and interventions into cognitive, interpersonal, humanistic, Jungian, multicultural, psychodynamic, and transpersonal psychologies (e.g., Fukuyama & Sevig, 1999; Griffith & Griffith, 2002; Helminiak, 1996; Kelly, 1995; Lovinger, 1984; Nielsen, Johnson, & Ellis, 2001; Richards & Bergin, 2004; Sperry, 2001; Sperry & Shafranske, 2005; Swinton, 2001; West, 2000). Compared to 15 years ago when very little had been published about integrating spirituality into treatment, psychotherapists now have a wide variety of spiritually oriented approaches to choose from.

It is essential for psychotherapists to select a spiritually oriented treatment approach that is consistent with their personal worldviews if they wish to work sensitively and effectively with religious and spiritual issues during treatment. Fear and Woolfe (1999) suggested that "Therapists need to operate within a theoretical orientation which encompasses the same underlying metatheoretical assumptions as their personal philosophy" (p. 253). They reasoned that congruence between therapists' personal philosophical values and theoretical orientation is necessary to promote professional development and therapeutic efficacy, and to prevent burnout.

Consistency between a therapist's personal worldview and theoretical orientation is also necessary for ethical practice. There is much agreement that ethical practice requires therapists to be clear about their own worldview and values (e.g., Arthur, 2001; Halbur & Halbur, 2006; Ibrahim, 1985; Neiymeyer, Prichard, Lyddon, & Sherrard, 1993; Richards & Bergin, 2005; Tjeltveit, 1999). Therapists who are clear and congruent in regard to their personal and professional beliefs and values are more capable of handling values issues that arise in therapy in an ethical manner (Richards, Rector, & Tjeltveit, 1999).

Picking an approach that is consistent with their life philosophy can be challenging for psychotherapists, especially if their worldview seems to differ significantly from that endorsed by the larger therapeutic community (O'Grady, Bartz, Boardman, & Richards, 2006). All mainstream secular psychotherapy traditions are grounded in the theology of the naturalistic-atheistic worldview, which denies the importance and reality of spiritual influences in human health and healing (Bergin, 1980; Dixon, 2002; Slife, 2004). Because the naturalistic-atheistic theology or worldview assumes that spiritual realities *do not* exist, psychotherapists may feel pressured to abandon their spiritual worldview in their professional practice. This seems counterintuitive and counterproductive given that the majority of people in the world, including psychotherapy clients, believe in spiritual realities. Psychotherapists will be more effective if they adopt a therapeutic orientation that is in harmony with their own spiritual beliefs and then learn to use it in an effective and ethical manner.

An important first step when deciding upon a spiritually oriented approach is for psychotherapists to carefully examine, explore, and articulate their own personal spiritual worldview or theology. This could require considerable personal spiritual exploration and searching, depending on where the psychotherapist is at in his or her own spiritual journey (Miller, 2011). Once they have done this, they can learn about the various spiritually oriented psychotherapy approaches that have been developed and select one that is most consistent with their own spiritual beliefs. Psychotherapists need to ensure that their spiritual approach is not only consistent with their own beliefs, but that it is internally consistent in its theology, philosophy, personality theory, and therapeutic practices and techniques (O'Grady et al., 2006). A number of activities can be helpful in selecting and integrating a therapeutic framework and orientation into one's sense of personal and professional identity, including personal introspection, meditation, prayer, and/or contemplation; reading books and sacred writings about spirituality and spiritual exploration; participating in group or class discussions about spirituality; writing a personal counseling philosophy paper; engaging in videotaped session review with peers and/or supervisors; and consulting with spiritually minded colleagues (Halbur & Halbur, 2006; Miller, 2011; O'Grady et al., 2006).

I now briefly describe my own spiritually oriented therapeutic orientation—a strategy called theistic integrative psychotherapy (Richards, 2005a, 2005b; Richards & Bergin, 2005). I do this for two reasons. First, I share my approach as one example of how a spiritually oriented framework can serve as a conceptual framework for applied practice. Second, I share my approach so that readers can better understand the basis for my recommendations in the remainder of the chapter about how to explore and affirm spirituality during treatment in order to facilitate clients' journeys of healing and growth. In describing my theistic spiritual strategy, I am not trying to advocate that all psychotherapists adopt it as their framework for treatment. As previously stated, it is important that psychotherapists select a conceptual framework and therapeutic approach that is consistent with their own spiritual beliefs.

Theistic Integrative Psychotherapy

During the past few decades, many researchers and practitioners throughout the world have contributed to the development of theistic spiritual perspectives and approaches in mainstream psychology and psychotherapy. Surveys have shown that approximately 30%–50% of psychotherapists are members of one of the theistic world religions, believe in God, and use spiritual interventions in their professional practices (e.g., Bergin & Jensen, 1990; Shafranske, 2000; Shafranske & Malony, 1990). In my own practice, I integrate theistic perspectives and interventions with several of the mainstream secular psychotherapy traditions (Richards, 2005a). A variety of other theistically informed psychotherapy approaches have been described in the literature, including psychodynamic, interpersonal, humanistic, and cognitive ones (e.g., Richards & Bergin, 2004; Sperry & Shafranske, 2005).

Figure 16.1 illustrates that the conceptual framework for my theistic integrative approach includes theological premises that are grounded in the theistic worldview, philosophical assumptions that are consistent with the theistic worldview, a theistic personality theory, and a theistic view of psychotherapy. The theological foundations of my approach are based in the worldview of the theistic world religions. There is great diversity between and within the theistic world religions, but they also share important theological beliefs, including the ideas that God exists, human beings are the creations of God, there is a divine purpose to life, human beings can communicate with God through prayer and other spiritual practices, God has revealed moral truths to guide human behavior, and the human spirit or soul continues to exist after mortal death (Richards & Bergin, 1997).

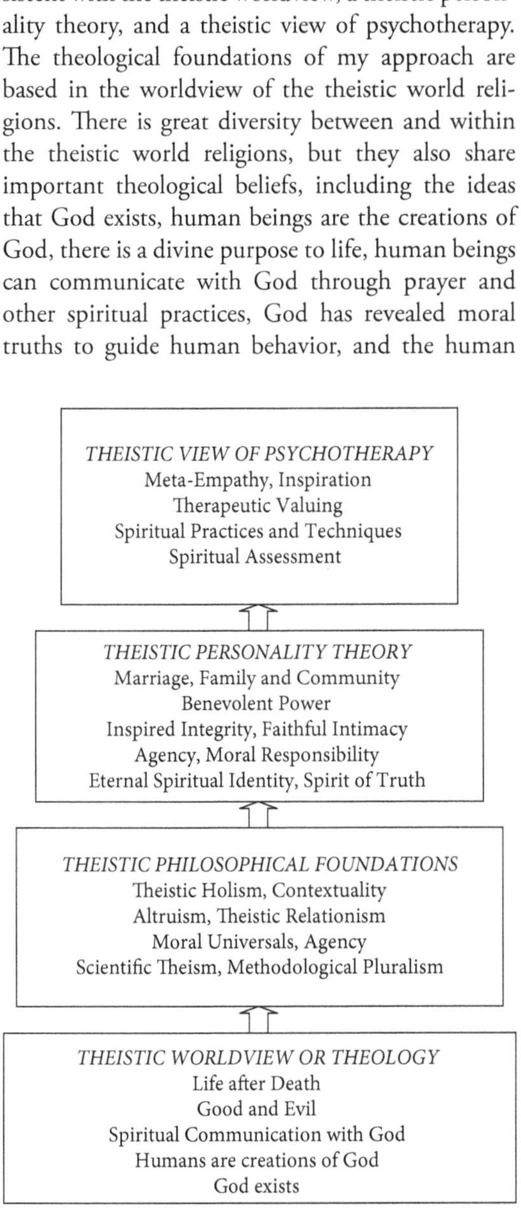

My theistic integrative psychotherapy approach is grounded in a number of philosophical assumptions that are consistent with theism, including scientific theism, theistic holism, human agency, theistic morality, theistic relationism, altruism, and contexuality. Although it is beyond the scope of this chapter to discuss all of these philosophical perspectives, this has been done elsewhere (e.g., Griffin, 2000; Richards & Bergin, 2005; Slife, 2004; Slife, Hope, & Nebeker, 1999). Here I briefly discuss only three of these assumptions to illustrate how my theological beliefs influence my philosophical assumptions. As mentioned earlier, the theistic worldview is founded on the belief that human beings are creations of God, that they must learn to choose between good and evil, and that they have a responsibility to love and assist others. The philosophy of *human agency* assumes that humans have the ability to willfully choose their behavior. *Theistic morality* assumes that good and evil exist within the context of a situation and that humans are morally responsible to choose good over evil. *Altruism* assumes that humans can act altruistically for the sake of others without the incentive of personal benefits. I accept these philosophical assumptions because they are more consistent with my theological views than are the naturalistic assumptions of *determinism, ethical relativism*, and *hedonism*, which assume that human behavior is determined by external forces, morality is relativistic, and humans can only act in their own self-interest (Slife, Mitchell, & Whoolery, 2004; Slife & Williams, 1995; Williams, 1992).

The theistic worldview also has many potential implications for personality theory, which can only be briefly mentioned here, but that have been described in more detail elsewhere (Miller & Delaney, 2005; Pargament, 2007; Richards & Bergin, 2005; Sperry & Shafranske, 2005). According to the theistic perspective, the core essence of identity and personality is spiritual. Human beings are composed of both a mortal body and an eternal spirit or soul that continues to exist beyond the death of the mortal body. People who believe in and live congruently with their eternal spiritual identity are more likely to develop in a healthy manner socially and psychologically (Richards & Bergin, 1997). People who neglect their spiritual growth and well-being are more likely to suffer poor mental health and unfulfilling relationships. Therapeutic change is facilitated when clients access the resources of their faith and spirituality (Richards & Bergin, 2005).

THEISTIC VIEW OF PSYCHOTHERAPY
Meta-Empathy, Inspiration
Therapeutic Valuing
Spiritual Practices and Techniques
Spiritual Assessment

THEISTIC PERSONALITY THEORY
Marriage, Family and Community
Benevolent Power
Inspired Integrity, Faithful Intimacy
Agency, Moral Responsibility
Eternal Spiritual Identity, Spirit of Truth

THEISTIC PHILOSOPHICAL FOUNDATIONS
Theistic Holism, Contextuality
Altruism, Theistic Relationism
Moral Universals, Agency
Scientific Theism, Methodological Pluralism

THEISTIC WORLDVIEW OR THEOLOGY
Life after Death
Good and Evil
Spiritual Communication with God
Humans are creations of God
God exists

Figure 16.1 Theological, philosophical, theoretical, and applied foundations of theistic integrative psychotherapy. Adapted from Richards, P. S., & Bergin, A. E. (2005). *A spiritual strategy for counseling and psychotherapy* (2nd ed.). Washington, DC: American Psychological Association. Used with permission.

Table 16.1 summarizes some of the key characteristics of the theistic integrative psychotherapy approach. One important implication of the theistic conceptual framework for the practice of psychotherapy is that psychotherapists may wish to encourage their clients to explore how their personal spirituality may assist them during treatment and recovery. Clients who have faith in God's healing power and draw upon the spiritual resources in their lives during psychological treatment may receive added strength and power to heal and change (Richards & Bergin, 2005). Another implication of the theistic framework for practice is that there are values and principles that influence healthy human functioning, such as integrity, honesty, forgiveness, repentance, humility, love, spirituality, marital commitment, sexual fidelity, family loyalty and kinship, benevolent use of power, and respect of human agency (Bergin, 1980, 1985, 1991; Miller, 2005). Such values can provide psychotherapists with a way of assessing whether their clients' lifestyles are healthy, as well as some basis for evaluating what therapeutic goals to endorse (Jensen & Bergin, 1988).

Another implication for practice is that both psychotherapists and clients may on occasion obtain spiritual enlightenment to assist in treatment and recovery (O'Grady & Richards, 2010; Richards & Bergin, 2005; West, 2000). By providing space for meditative or prayerful moments, psychotherapists and clients may experience inspired insights. Finally, another implication is that psychotherapists can use a variety of spiritual practices and interventions to assist clients in their spiritual journeys and growth, including spiritual imagery, mindfulness and contemplative meditation, sacred writings, spiritual discussions, and referral for spiritual direction. More information about these topics is provided later in this chapter.

Affirming Universal Spirituality and Using It as a Resource in Treatment

Psychotherapists can affirm that which is universal in spirituality by seeking to understand clients' views of spirituality and to find common spiritual ground with them. When seeking to understand and affirm spirituality with clients from diverse religious and spiritual traditions, it can be helpful for psychotherapists to have some understanding about the diverse ways that spirituality may be understood in the world. Beginning with a broad perspective about spirituality can help psychotherapists give clients room to explore and clarify their beliefs about what spirituality means to them.

The world religions differ somewhat in their teachings about spirituality and how it is developed. Nevertheless, as can be seen in Table 16.2, there are some general similarities among them. For example, the theistic world religions teach that humans are spiritual beings created in the image of God. These religions also emphasize the importance of human beings' relationships with God and living in harmony with God's moral laws. The Eastern religious traditions also emphasize the importance of correct living and spiritual enlightenment, but they do not view spiritual progression as dependent on one's relationship with or obedience to a Supreme Being. There is agreement between all of the world religions that humans are spiritual beings and that spiritual enlightenment and growth is a universal human potentiality. More detailed information about the spiritual understandings and perspectives of the religious traditions of the world can be found in books, videos, DVDs, and on the World Wide Web.

Another source of insight about the nature of spirituality can be found in social science literature. Table 16.3 provides a sampling of the numerous definitions of spirituality that have been offered by social scientists. As can be seen, although there is considerable variability in the definitions, commonalities can be found, including the notions that spirituality (1) is a universal human characteristic and need; (2) involves a search for the sacred or transcendent in life; (3) contributes to people's sense of meaning, purpose, and values; (4) involves living congruently with one's beliefs and values; (5) contributes to a universal love of humanity; and (6) is not the same as religion, though it is often associated with religious beliefs and experiences. Spirituality may include experiences such as feeling compassion, loving, being loved, feeling hope, receiving inspiration, being honest and congruent, feeling a sense of life meaning and purpose, enjoying relationships with family and friends, feeling a connection or relationship with a higher power or God, meditating, contemplating, and enjoying nature.

I now offer some therapeutic perspectives and recommendations that my colleagues and I have found helpful in our efforts to affirm and access the healing influence of spirituality in our work with clients with diverse spiritual beliefs. These perspectives and recommendations are grounded in the theistic framework for psychotherapy described earlier in this chapter and not all of them may fit

Table 16.1 Distinguishing Characteristics of Theistic Integrative Psychotherapy

Goals of Therapy	Therapist's Role in Therapy	Role of Spiritual Techniques	Client's Role in Therapy	Nature of Relationship
Spiritual view is part of an eclectic, multisystemic view of humans and so therapy goals depend on the client's issues. Goals directly relevant to the spiritual dimension include the following: (a) help clients affirm their eternal spiritual identity and live in harmony with the Spirit of Truth; (b) assess what impact religious and spiritual beliefs have in clients' lives and whether they have unmet spiritual needs; (c) help clients use religious and spiritual resources to help them in their efforts to cope, change, and grow; (d) help clients resolve spiritual concerns and doubts and make choices about role of spirituality in their lives; and (e) help clients examine their spirituality and continue their quest for spiritual growth.	Adopt an ecumenical therapeutic stance and, when appropriate, a denominational stance. Establish a warm, supportive environment in which the client knows it is safe and acceptable to explore his or her religious and spiritual beliefs, doubts, and concerns. Assess whether clients' religious and spiritual beliefs and activities are affecting their mental health and interpersonal relationships. Implement religious and spiritual interventions to help clients more effectively use their religious and spiritual resources in their coping and growth process. Model and endorse healthy values. Seek spiritual guidance and enlightenment on how best to help clients.	Interventions are viewed as very important for helping clients understand and work through religious and spiritual issues and concerns, and for helping clients draw on religious and spiritual resources in their lives to assist them in better coping, growing, and changing. Examples of major interventions include cognitive restructuring of irrational religious beliefs, transitional figure technique, forgiveness, meditation and prayer, Scripture study, blessings, participating in religious services, spiritual imagery, journaling about spiritual feelings, repentance, and using the client's religious support system.	Examine how their religious and spiritual beliefs and activities affect their behavior, emotions, and relationships. Make choices about what role religion and spirituality will play in their lives. Set goals and carry out spiritual interventions designed to facilitate their spiritual and emotional growth. Seek to use the religious and spiritual resources in their lives to assist them in their efforts to heal and change. Seek God's guidance and enlightenment about how to better cope, heal, and change.	Unconditional positive regard, warmth, genuineness, and empathy are regarded as an essential foundation for therapy. Therapists also seek to have charity or brotherly and sisterly love for clients and to affirm their eternal spiritual identity and worth. Clients are expected to form a working alliance and share in the work of change. Clients must trust the therapist and believe that it is safe to share their religious and spiritual beliefs and heritage with the therapist. Clients must know that the therapist highly values and respects their autonomy and freedom of choice and that it is safe for them to differ from the therapist in their beliefs and values, even though the therapist may at times disagree with their values and confront them about unhealthy values and lifestyle choices.

Source: Reprinted from Richards, P. S., & Bergin, A. E. (2005). *A spiritual strategy for counseling and psychotherapy* (2nd ed.). Washington, DC: American Psychological Association. Used with permission of the authors and publisher.

Table 16.2 View of Spirituality of the Major World Religious Traditions

	View of Spirituality
Western Religious Traditions	
Judaism	Obedience to God's laws and worshiping Him leads to character development (acquisition of qualities such as goodness, humility, and holiness). Humans can communicate with God through prayer and worship. God responds to people reaching out to Him.
Christianity	Accepting Jesus Christ as Savior will lead one to good works, a moral life, and devotion and worship. This will allow one to receive the influence of the Holy Spirit and partake of other fruits of the spirit (e.g., love). Through prayer and the influence of the Holy Spirit, human beings can communicate with God and receive God's help, influence, and grace.
Islam	Obeying God's law as revealed in the Qur'an and "giving up" worldly things allows people to grow spiritually. The path of spiritual growth involves overcoming vices such as arrogance, greed, and dishonesty. This leads to higher levels of religious experience and union with God. Humans can communicate with God through prayer, meditation, and repetition of set phrases or the name of God.
Zoroastrianism	Choosing good over evil, prayer, and meditation will help people on the pathway to spiritual growth. Human beings can communicate with God through prayer.
Sikhism	Through dependence on God, human beings can overcome their ego and pride and achieve spiritual liberation and growth and a mystical union with God. Spiritual growth leads one to the qualities of love, faith, mercy, and humility. Humans can communicate with and worship God, particularly through prayer and singing.
Eastern Religious Traditions	
Hinduism	Spirituality is achieved through good works, knowledge, and worship and devotion (one of the three paths to salvation). Ultimately, spiritual growth leads to a realization of the oneness of all things (Brahman-Atman) and to a release from the rounds of rebirth. People can communicate with the deities and receive assistance from them.
Buddhism	In Theravada Buddhism spiritual enlightenment and eventual nirvana come from renouncing the world, believing in the Four Noble Truths, and following the Eightfold Middle Path. In Mahayana Buddhism loving service, faith, and compassion (not celibacy or asceticism) are seen as the keys to spiritual growth and enlightenment. Mahayana Buddhists may worship helping beings.
Jainism	Spiritual enlightenment is viewed as pure omniscient consciousness or infinite knowledge. Release from karma-matter and spiritual enlightenment is gained through overcoming attachment to worldly things (asceticism), faith in the Jain saints, right knowledge, right conduct (e.g., *ahisma* or nonviolence), and meditation.
Shinto	Spirituality is perhaps best thought of as feelings of appreciation and closeness to nature and enjoyment of life. Human beings can worship the *kamis* (deities) in order to "secure their continued favor" (Palmer & Keller, 1989, p. 87).
Confucianism	There are no teachings about spiritual communication with deity or about transcendent spiritual enlightenment. Confucius did describe what he believed are the characteristics of a "superior man" or "true gentleman." These qualities included "li (the code of moral, social conduct), jen (virtue, compassion, love), yi (righteousness), and te (virtue)" (Nigosian, 1994, p. 200).
Taoism	Living in harmony with the Tao is the pathway to inner harmony and peace. An important principle of the Tao is *we-wei*, that is, the principle of nonaction. *We-wei* is "a call to passive action…One should not resist, confront, or defy. One should not lay down…rules, or requirements…Only sincere humility, minimal desires, and pure spontaneity can enable one to find the Way" (Palmer & Keller, 1989, p. 70).

Source: Adapted from Richards, P. S., & Bergin, A. E. (1997). *A spiritual strategy for counseling and psychotherapy.* Washington, DC: American Psychological Association. Used with permission of the publisher and authors.

Table 16.3 Examples of Social Scientists' Conceptions of Spirituality

Source	Definition/Description
ASERVIC (1996, paragraphs 3–4)	"Spirit may be defined as the animating life force, represented by such images as breath, wind, vigor, and courage. Spirituality is the drawing out and infusion of spirit in one's life. It is experienced as an active and passive process. Spirituality is also defined as a capacity and tendency that is innate and unique to all persons. This spiritual tendency moves the individual toward knowledge, love, meaning, peace, hope, transcendence, connectedness, compassion, wellness, and wholeness. Spirituality includes one's capacity for creativity, growth, and the development of a value system. Spirituality encompasses a variety of phenomena, including experiences, beliefs, and practices. Spirituality is approached from a variety of perspectives, including psychospiritual, religious, and transpersonal. While spirituality is usually expressed through culture, it both precedes and transcends culture."
Burke and Miranti (2001, p. 602)	"Spirituality refers to a way of being in the world that acknowledges the existence of, and the desire to be in relationship with, a transcendent dimension or higher power. This spiritual tendency is believed to move the individual toward knowledge, hope, love, transcendence, connectedness, and compassion."
Elkins et al. (1988, p. 10)	"Spirituality which comes from the Latin spiritus, meaning 'breath of life' is a way of being and experiencing that comes through awareness of a transcendental dimension and that is characterized by certain identifiable values in regard to self, others, nature, life and whatever one considers to be the Ultimate."
Elkins (1998, pp. 32–33)	"Spirituality is universal. It is available to every human being…It is a human phenomenon. This does not mean that it has no divine component, but it does mean that spirituality is an inborn, natural potential of the human being…The common core of spirituality is found at the inner phenomenological level. Spirituality manifests in countless outer forms…underneath these outward forms, there is a common longing for the sacred, a universal desire to touch and celebrate the mystery of life. It is in the depths of the soul that one discovers the essential and universal dimensions of spirituality…Spirituality has to do with our capacity to respond to the numinous. The essential character of spirituality is mystical…There is a certain mysterious energy associated with spirituality. Every culture has recognized a life force that moves through all creation. The soul comes alive when it is nurtured by this sacred energy, and one's existence becomes infused with passion, power, and depth…The aim of spirituality is compassion."
Finnegan (2008, p. 12–13)	"Spirituality is the place where we meet primordial reality and wrestle with the forces of primordial experience that date back to the very origins of our human lives. It is a space for self-knowledge and self-transcendence and the processes they set in train. It is the space where we encounter the forces of shadow and repression and interpret or misinterpret them, contain them safely as we respond to the upward call of the divine and the awe-inspiring wonder of God, or give way to the darker powers of disorder and destruction. Spirituality is a space where lovers meet and in the meeting God is found. It is holy ground and sacred space, a place where pilgrims meet as journeys pause, a space where rituals flourish and worship prospers. It is a space for prayer, meditation and the wise contemplative gaze. It is the meeting place of harmony, community, integrity, generosity, love, faith and hope, motivation and intentionality, and the turning of the mind away from sole concern with the self…Spirituality is a journey, a quest, a path, a way. It is a journey of discovery, a quest for meaning, a path to a fuller life, a way of love and embraced destiny; dancing with the Holy One, new songs of devotion and awe rising from the depths of soul."

(continued)

Table 16.3 (continued)

Source	Definition/Description
Helminiak (1996, p. 32)	Spirituality is (1) "the human spiritual nature as such: the spiritual component in the human being; that which makes humans spiritual;" (2) "concern for transcendence: the sense that something in life goes beyond the here and now and the commitment to that something;" (3) "a lived reality: (a) in the general sense: all those aspects of human living that help enhance and unfold the human spiritual capacity, (b) in the social or cultural sense: particular ways of advancing spiritual growth as advocated by different traditions or school, e.g., Hindu spirituality, Methodist spirituality, (c) in the individual sense: the beliefs and practices that a particular person follows in order to nourish his or her spiritual sensitivities and growth."
James (1902, pp. 31–32)	Spirituality [James used the term "personal religion"] is "the feelings, acts, and experiences of individual men in their solitude, so far as they apprehend themselves to stand in relation to whatever they may consider the divine."
Kelly (1995, pp. 4–5)	Spirituality is "grounded in a dimension of reality beyond the boundaries of the strictly empirically perceived, material world…is a deep sense of belonging, of wholeness, of connectedness, and of openness to the infinite."
Martin and Carlson (1988, p. 59)	"Spirituality is a process by which individuals recognize the importance of orienting their lives to something nonmaterial that is beyond or larger than themselves…so that there is an acknowledgment of and at least some dependence upon a higher power, or Spirit."
Maugans (1996, p. 11)	"Spirituality can be defined as a belief system focusing on intangible elements that impart vitality and meaning to life's events."
Miller and Thoresen (2003, p. 27)	Spirituality includes "the notion of being concerned with life's most animating and vital principle or quality, often described as giving life or energy to the material human elements of the person." Spirituality "includes a broad focus on the immaterial features of life, regarded as not commonly perceptible by the physical senses (e.g., sight, hearing) that are used to understand the material world."
Pargament (2007, p. 32–33)	Spirituality is "a search for the sacred." "At the heart of the sacred lies God, divine being, or a transcendent reality."
Piedmont et al. (2007, p. 55)	"Spirituality represents our efforts to create meaning and purpose for our lives. This need for meaning is seen as an intrinsic universal human capacity."
Richards and Bergin (2005, p. 22)	Spirituality is "a state of being attuned with God or the Divine Intelligence that governs or harmonizes the universe." It involves a "search for and harmony with God and the sacred." Characterized by "thoughts and feelings of enlightenment, vision, harmony with truth, transcendence, and oneness with God."
Sperry and Shafranske (2005, p. 17)	"For many people spirituality is anchored in a quest for a direct, unmediated experience of the transcendent realities in which they once more confidently believed."
Vaughan (1996, p. 336)	"Spirituality presupposes certain qualities of mind, including compassion, gratitude, awareness of a transcendent dimension, and an appreciation for life which brings meaning and purpose to existence."
Wuthnow (1998, p. vii)	"At its core, spirituality consists of all the beliefs and activities by which individuals attempt to relate their lives to God or to a divine being or some other conception of a transcendent reality."
Zinnbauer, Pargament, and Scott (1999, p. 909)	"Spirituality is the search for the sacred" and "has to do with the paths people take in their efforts to find, conserve, and transform the sacred in their lives."

other spiritually oriented therapeutic approaches. I encourage psychotherapists to modify my perspectives and recommendations, where needed, in order to ensure that they practice in a consistent way with their own spiritual framework and approach.

Prepare Spiritually for Psychotherapy Sessions

Being an effective psychotherapist requires a great deal of professional and personal preparation. In addition to professional education and training, and emotional insight and well-being, psychotherapists who wish to incorporate spirituality into treatment may find they are more effective if they engage in personal spiritual preparation. Several research studies provide evidence that many psychotherapists prepare spiritually for psychotherapy sessions by praying, meditating, contemplating, or by engaging in other spiritual practices that help them to be spiritually attuned (e.g., Chamberlain, Richards, & Scharman, 1996; O'Grady & Richards, 2010; West, 2000).

O'Grady and Richards (2010) interviewed over 300 helping professionals from a diversity of spiritual traditions and professional specialties and found that most of them reported that they seek to be open to spiritual influences in their work. They offered a number of suggestions about how helping professionals can become more spiritually attuned in their work, including (a) being open to inspiration and spiritual influences, (b) actively seeking spiritual guidance, (c) nurturing a relationship with God, (d) living a virtuous life, and (e) being present in relationship with clients. Collectively, this diverse group of helping professionals strongly affirmed the belief that spiritual preparation can open the door to inspiration and other spiritual influences and experiences during treatment. As expressed by one counseling psychologist:

> Begin each session with the intention and attitude to seek the highest good of your client and be a channel, "instrument" of God's presence. Cultivate an attitude of humility and authentic presence in therapy. As therapists, we are often changed by the encounter as much as the client. When we relate deeply to another, God may be present.
> (*O'Grady & Richards*, 2010, p. 64)

Create a Safe and Spiritually Open Therapeutic Relationship

It is important to establish a spiritually safe and open therapeutic relationship with clients. Religion and spirituality are considered private topics, even sacred, by many clients. Many religious people have fears that mental health professionals will not respect and may even seek to undermine their religious beliefs and values (Richards & Bergin, 2000; Worthington, 1986). In addition, some clients believe that religion and spirituality are taboo topics in psychotherapy, perhaps believing that the separation between church and state in government extends to the mental health professions, or perhaps being aware that many psychotherapists are unwilling or unprepared to address these topics (Henning & Tirrell, 1982; Richards & Bergin, 2005). Whatever the reason may be, clients who do not feel a great deal of trust for their psychotherapists are unlikely to freely discuss their spiritual beliefs and values.

Psychotherapists can help clients feel safe to discuss religious and spiritual issues in treatment by explicitly informing them that it is permissible and appropriate for them to do so if they desire. Psychotherapists can do this verbally and in a written informed consent document given to clients at the beginning of treatment. Psychotherapists can also let clients know that they view spiritual beliefs as a potential resource for treatment. Questions about clients' religious and spiritual backgrounds on intake questionnaires can also help open the door to spiritual discussions. Communicating a willingness to explore spiritual issues without prematurely disclosing specific details about their own religious beliefs can help psychotherapists establish trust with a wide range of clients (Richards & Bergin, 2005).

It is also important for psychotherapists to communicate interest and respect when clients self-disclose information about their spiritual beliefs. Psychotherapists can let clients know that they respect them for having the courage to discuss their religious and spiritual beliefs. If religious differences and value conflicts with clients arise during treatment, they must be dealt with in a respectful and tolerant manner. When value conflicts occur, psychotherapists should openly acknowledge their values and explicitly affirm that their client has the right to differ from them without having their intelligence or morality questioned. Sometimes it is necessary to consider whether the value conflict is so threatening that referral would be in the best interest of the client (Richards et al., 1999).

Conduct a Religious and Spiritual Assessment

It is important for psychotherapists to conduct a religious-spiritual assessment of their clients as part of a multidimensional assessment strategy (Richards & Bergin, 2005). Many helpful publications about religious and spiritual assessment are now available (e.g., Chirban, 2001; Gorsuch & Miller, 1999; Hill & Hood, 1999; Hill & Pargament, 2003; Pargament, 2007; Richards & Bergin, 2005).

In the initial session or two, psychotherapists should do a history of the religious and spiritual background of every client, including the positive and negative experiences in their religious backgrounds and their current religious affiliation or spiritual framework. It can be helpful to explore what is meaningful to clients in regard to spiritual matters and what is not, and to find out how much time they devote to various religious practices, such as scripture study, prayer, church attendance, meditation, private religious experiences, and service.

Psychotherapists should seek understanding about how clients' religious beliefs and background may contribute to their conflicts, impasses, and difficulties. An effective clinical interviewing process invites clients to share in a safe environment their true thoughts, feelings, and beliefs about spirituality and the role of it in their lives (Berrett, Hardman, & Richards, 2010). By asking clients questions about their religious background and current spirituality, inviting them to elaborate when needed, psychotherapists can gain much insight into how clients' spirituality may be intertwined with emotional, psychological, and relationship issues.

When conducting a spiritual assessment, it is also important to clarify clients' religious and spiritual strengths and resources. It is also helpful to understand the positive, the uplifting, and the strengthening aspects of clients' spirituality and religious community and how this may assist them in treatment. Gathering information and seeking clarifications about clients' spirituality may be needed throughout the course of treatment.

Learn the Language of Clients' Spirituality

As psychotherapists conduct a religious and spiritual assessment, they have the opportunity to begin to understand their clients' language of spirituality. There are a number of spiritual themes that seem to be universal in the human family that can help psychotherapists and clients find common ground for understanding each other's spiritual language. These themes include experiences such as love, faith, suffering, meaning and purpose, responsibility, repentance, forgiveness, gratitude, belonging, congruence, honesty, family, community, enlightenment, transcendence, and the quest for a relationship with a

higher power or Creator. These can be talked about with clients and doing so can help expand psychotherapists' understanding of their clients' spirituality as well as clients' understanding of their own spirituality.

In seeking to learn the language of their clients' spirituality, psychotherapists can ask clients to help them understand their views and language of spirituality. In developing this relationship of sharing and understanding, psychotherapists create a spiritual space and safe environment in which clients can do their work. As clients share and use their language of spirituality, this often strengthens their deeply held beliefs, which can be an anchor in difficult times. Explorations about spiritual beliefs and understandings can edify and build clients up toward understanding who they really are and who they can become.

As psychotherapists grow in understanding of clients' spiritual language, they will be more capable of joining, respecting, supporting, challenging, and nurturing clients in their spiritual beliefs in a way that facilitates recovery (Berrett et al., 2010). As clients develop and understand their own spiritual language, it can help strengthen their sense of spiritual identity and feelings of worth and goodness.

Create a Space for Spiritual Awareness and Experiences

In addition to providing a spiritually safe and open therapeutic relationship for clients, it is important for psychotherapists to make efforts to create *spiritual space* for their clients or, in other words, to create an environment that gives clients the opportunity to recognize and affirm spiritual insights, impressions, and experiences (Miller, 2005; Richards & Bergin, 2005; West, 2000). Psychotherapists can help clients recognize and explore spiritual feelings and experiences that occur both within and outside of the therapy hour.

West (2000) suggested several things that can help create a space for the recognition of spiritual influences and experiences in psychotherapy, including (a) accepting that therapy can be a spiritual space; (b) tolerating silence so that the spiritual space can unfold; (c) listening in a deep and holistic manner to words, feelings, and spiritual impressions; (d) speaking authentically by appropriately sharing feelings of the heart; and (e) accepting the spiritual experiences that occur. Griffith and Griffith (2002) also discussed attitudes and skills that are helpful for creating a spiritual space, including (a) fostering curiosity, wonder, and openness to the being of the other; (b) attenuating cynicism and certainty; (c) promoting openness and respect by democratizing the structure of therapy; (d) communicating respect for clients' personhood; (e) paying attention to feelings and bodily sensations that permit spiritual experiences to be recognized, understood, and expressed; and (f) listening carefully to what clients spontaneously speak about when they feel safe and respected.

When psychotherapists are successful at creating a spiritual space for their clients, spiritual experiences, insights, and influences that seem to go beyond ordinary therapeutic processes may occur. For example, some psychotherapists have reported experiencing deep spiritual connection or communion with their clients (Chamberlain et al., 1996; O'Grady & Richards, 2010; West, 2000; White, 2002). Reminiscent of Buber's (1996) *I—Thou* relationship, this spiritual connection enhances psychotherapists' empathy and compassion for their clients and promotes healing and growth. Psychotherapists have described this experience in different ways, including (a) feeling part of something bigger than themselves or their clients, (b) feeling that grace is present, (c) feeling that God is present, (d) feeling the presence of healing energies or spiritual beings, and (e) feeling that something special has happened between the psychotherapist, client, and God (Chamberlain et al., 1996; O'Grady & Richards, 2010; West, 2000; White, 2002).

Within such a spiritual therapeutic space, some psychotherapists have also reported experiencing inspiration, enlightenment, and/or a heightening of their attributes and abilities that enabled them to (a) more clearly assess and understand their clients' problems, and (b) select and implement effective interventions (Chamberlain et al., 1996; O'Grady & Richards, 2010; West, 2000; White, 2002). These feelings of inspiration are sometimes described as promptings, intuitive hunches, and gut feelings. Psychotherapists often perceive that such spiritual impressions lead to more accurate understandings and assessments of their clients. Some psychotherapists have also reported that spiritual insights have enhanced their ability to appropriately select and effectively implement standard secular interventions, as well as commonly used spiritual interventions. At other times, spiritual impressions lead psychotherapists to say or do something in therapy that was not planned and that is not typically used but that clearly had positive therapeutic effects.

Help Clients Listen to the Spiritual Impressions of Their Hearts

Psychotherapists can help clients learn to listen to and follow the spiritual impressions and insights of their hearts. Listening to and following spiritual impressions of the heart is an important pathway toward recovery and healing (Richards, Hardman, & Berrett, 2007). People from diverse cultures and religions have for thousands of years considered the heart as a source of emotion, courage, wisdom, and spirituality (Childre & McCraty, 2001). According to McCraty, Bradley, and Tomasino (2004–2005), there is a large amount of contemporary scientific evidence supporting the idea that:

> the heart is a sensory organ and a sophisticated center for receiving and processing information. The nervous system within the heart (or "heart brain") enables it to learn, remember, and make functional decisions independent of the brain's cerebral cortex. Moreover, numerous experiments have demonstrated that the signals the heart continuously sends to the brain influence the function of higher brain centers involved in perception, cognition, and emotional processing. In addition to the extensive neural communication network linking the heart with the brain and body, the heart also communicates information to the brain and throughout the body via electromagnetic field interactions.
> (p. 15)

There is also growing evidence that the heart plays an important role in spiritual experiences, intuitive ways of knowing, and in healthy physical and emotional functioning (e.g., Childre & McCraty, 2001; McCraty, Atkinson, & Bradley, 2004a, 2004b; McCraty, Atkinson, & Tomasino, 2001).

According to my theistic view of psychotherapy, the heart is a metaphor for clients' eternal spiritual identity and a receptor for spiritual impressions and influences that come from the Creator (Richards & Bergin, 2005; Richards et al., 2007). Helping clients get in touch with and affirm their spirituality through the metaphor of the heart is typically nonthreatening and well accepted and can assist them in discovering or rediscovering their sense of identity as spiritual beings (Richards et al., 2007). Psychotherapy clients often acknowledge a lost or a broken heart. As clients become more aware of their spirituality and better at sensing those things that speak to their heart, they begin to challenge their negative self-perceptions.

Clients' hearts are the inner core of their being. The heart is more than feelings and it is more than thoughts. It receives spiritual impressions and conveys a sense of knowing and understanding (Richards et al., 2007). When clients become aware of their hearts as a source of information and a resource for self-direction, this can facilitate a growing sense of spiritual integrity and well-being.

Listening to the heart involves living in the present with optimism and spiritual awareness, rather than focusing on conflicts, confusion, and negative self-talk. The heart can help clients connect to their priorities, values, dreams, and deepest desires, which can help them in understanding and pursuing the most important path of their lives.

Listening to the heart also involves clarifying which principles are critical to live by, and then striving to live a life congruent with those self-chosen principles. It also involves recognizing truth in the moment. When truth is listened to and followed, change occurs. Once clients recognize what their heart is saying to them, they can make promises and commitments to themselves, God, and others and begin to act upon their heartfelt understandings and values with spiritual integrity. Spiritual integrity comes from a consistent pattern of living true to self-chosen beliefs and values (Miller, 2005; Richards & Bergin, 2005).

Clients will grow in self-respect as they find the courage to follow their hearts and to act on these internal prompts even in times when they feel overwhelmed, undeserving, or fearful. Learning to trust and follow the spiritual impressions of the heart is not a quick fix, but rather, an ongoing development of inner understanding and sense of purpose and direction (Richards et al., 2007).

Help Clients Affirm Their Spiritual Identity and Goodness

When psychotherapists understand clients' spiritual beliefs and values, they can watch for occasions when clients demonstrate faithfulness, hard work, endurance, humility, congruence, and other signs of character and strength. When this occurs, they can point it out in an affirming way to their clients. Many clients have a hard time seeing the good in themselves and so affirming their goodness and spirituality by giving feedback about specific occasions when they have behaved congruently, courageously, and honorably can have a positive impact. In doing so, psychotherapists are holding up a *therapeutic mirror* to the positive that clients often have a hard time seeing in themselves. Holding up the therapeutic mirror can help clients see their inherent spiritual worth and goodness (Berrett et al., 2010).

Shame, self-judgment, and self-contempt create a false negative identity. But as psychotherapists hold up a mirror for clients and help them see love in themselves and in their lives, then healing can take place. Clients gain confidence that if they listen to their hearts, they can give and receive love even while they are not completely recovered because love is part of who they are. It is part of their identity.

Receiving the reflected witness of their goodness through feedback, compliments, kindness, and love from others helps clients' sense of spiritual identity and integrity grow in positive ways. When clients see who they really are, they see that they are separate from their problems and mistakes. When clients live in harmony with their hearts, their spiritual identity is manifest in their countenance and in the way they live moment by moment. They feel at peace and lose the need for dysfunctional and self-defeating behaviors.

To reconnect with their hearts, clients need to once again let love in and let love out. Psychotherapists can explore how clients refuse love and what they can do to begin to open up their hearts and to receive love from other people. Psychotherapists can also help clients examine how they can show their love for others through word and action. This process involves labeling love as an expression of the heart and accepting love from others as a gift from their heart. By doing so, clients can begin to increase awareness of how much love there is around them and how much love they have to share with others. Love is a gift, whether it comes from God, oneself, or from significant others. Love can help heal the lonely, the empty, and the shameful sense of self.

Invite Clients to Engage in Spiritual Interventions and Practices

Psychotherapists can help clients access the resources of their spirituality by inviting them to engage in spiritual interventions and practices that are consistent with their spiritual beliefs. Religious and spiritual practices such as praying, meditating, contemplating, mindfulness, engaging in spiritual imagery, reading sacred writings, engaging in acts of worship and ritual, and seeking spiritual counsel and direction from spiritual leaders have been practiced for millennia by religious believers (Smart, 1993, 1994). There is growing empirical evidence that there is healing potential in such practices (e.g., Benson, 1996). Growing numbers of psychotherapists report encouraging clients to engage in these practices as adjunctive interventions during or outside of therapy sessions (Plante, 2009; Richards

& Bergin, 2005). Religiously devout and spiritually minded clients typically welcome the inclusion of spiritual perspective and interventions in treatment.

Spiritual practices and interventions are useful for helping clients challenge and modify unhealthy and inaccurate perceptions of God and self, overcome feelings of shame and unworthiness, gain a clearer sense of life's purpose and meaning, set self-chosen spiritual goals, learn to again listen to the spiritual impressions of their hearts, reaffirm their sense of spiritual identity and worth, and reconnect with God and significant others (Richards et al., 2007). There are many other potential benefits of such practices and interventions when they are used appropriately (Miller, 1999; Plante, 2009; Richards & Bergin, 2004, 2005; Richards et al., 2007). There is growing empirical evidence that spiritual adaptations to psychotherapy that incorporate such interventions with psychological treatment approaches are effective (Richards & Worthington, 2010; Smith, Bartz, & Richards, 2007).

Future Directions

Much scholarly work has been done during the past two decades in the psychology of religion field (Emmons & Paloutzian, 2003) that has great relevance to spiritually oriented treatment approaches because it helps provide a theoretical and empirical foundation for applied practice. Continued research in the psychology of religion is needed on topics such as, but not limited to, the nature of spirit, spirituality, and spiritual well-being; the nature of religious and spiritual development across the life span; the spiritual needs and issues of human beings; the relationship between religion and spirituality and various psychological disorders and human strengths; the prevalence and role of spiritual influences in therapeutic change and healing; and the development and application of research methodologies, procedures, and designs that allow researchers to validly study spiritual phenomena (Richards & Bergin, 2005).

There is also a pressing need for more research on spiritually oriented treatment approaches and on specific spiritual interventions (Richards & Worthington, 2010). Although there is a growing body of studies that provide general support for the efficacy of spiritually oriented treatment approaches, the database is still relatively small and has methodological limitations. Religiously accommodative cognitive treatment approaches for religious clients with depression and anxiety meet evidence-based standards of efficacy, but other spiritually oriented approaches need additional investigation. Methodologically pluralistic research strategies are needed, including quantitative and qualitative designs that do not reduce spiritual phenomena into a naturalistic framework (Richards & Worthington, 2010). More research on spiritually oriented psychotherapy with religiously and culturally diverse groups is also needed because to date most theory and research in this domain has focused on the Christian religious tradition and on Western (Euro-American) cultures.

Progress has also been made in conceptualizing and measuring religion and spirituality, including the publication of a handbook of religious and spiritual measures (Hill & Hood, 1999). Nevertheless, there is still a great need for the development of reliable, valid, and clinically useful assessment and outcome measures of religious and spiritual functioning that are applicable with clients from diverse religious and cultural backgrounds. Such work would allow psychotherapists and researchers to use them with confidence in treatment settings (Richards & Worthington, 2010). Historically clients' religious and spiritual functioning has rarely been assessed in psychotherapy outcome research. In recent years this has begun to change, but much more work is needed before the religious and spiritual outcomes of various psychotherapies will be adequately understood (Richards & Worthington, 2010).

Much progress has also been made in recent years in regard to training and education concerning spiritual issues in psychotherapy. For example, religion is now recognized as one type of diversity in the American Psychological Association's ethical guidelines (APA, 2002a) and in APA's *Guidelines on Multicultural Education, Training, Practice, and Organizational Change for Psychologists* (APA, 2002b). Growing numbers of multicultural books and journal articles give at least some attention to religious and spiritual aspects of diversity. Furthermore, many prominent multicultural scholars, and a majority of mental health professionals, now acknowledge that religion and spirituality are important aspects of multicultural diversity (Crook-Lyon, O'Grady, Smith, Golightly, & Jensen, 2005; Sue et al., 1999).

Despite the growing recognition that religion and spirituality are multicultural issues, surveys suggest that most graduate training programs in the mental health professions still do not systematically address these topics (Bergin, 1983; Bishop, Avila-Juarbe, & Thumme, 2003; Richards & Bergin, 2000;

Schulte, Skinner, & Claiborn, 2002; Shafranske, 2000). Thus, there remains a gap between professional beliefs and practice in regard to the inclusion of religion and spirituality in multicultural training. Efforts are needed to further close this gap until accrediting organizations, including the American Psychological Association, require all graduate training programs in the mental health professions to provide a substantial training component in religious and spiritual aspects of diversity and practice.

Conclusion

The movement to integrate spiritual perspectives and interventions into mainstream psychology and psychotherapy has matured during the past decade and continues to gain momentum. Spiritual worldviews contribute important insights into previously neglected aspects of human nature, personality, therapeutic change, and the practice of psychotherapy (Bergin, 1980; Jones, 1994). I hope that psychotherapists from diverse spiritual traditions will contribute to the effort to affirm that which is good in religious traditions and in personal spirituality so that these can serve more fully as healing and unifying influences in the lives of our clients and in all of the human family.

References

American Psychological Association. (2002a). *Ethical principles of psychologists and code of conduct.* Retrieved December 2011, from http://www. apa.org/ethics

American Psychological Association. (2002b). *Guidelines on multicultural education, training, practice, and organizational change for psychologists.* Retrieved December 2011, from http://www.apa.org/pi/oema/resources/policy/multicultural-guidelines.aspx

Arthur, A. R. (2001). Personality, epistemology and psychotherapists' choice of theoretical model: A review and analysis. *European Journal of Psychotherapy, Counseling and Health, 4,* 45–64.

Association for Spiritual, Ethical, and Religious Values in Counseling (ASERVIC). (1996). *Summit on spirituality white paper.* Alexandria, VA: Author.

Barrett, D. B., & Johnson, T. M. (2002). Religion. In *Britannica Book of the Year* (p. 303). Chicago: Encyclopedia Britannica.

Benson, H. (1996). *Timeless healing: The power and biology of belief.* New York: Scribner.

Bergin, A. E. (1980). Psychotherapy and religious values. *Journal of Consulting and Clinical Psychology, 48,* 75–105.

Bergin, A. E. (1985). Proposed values for guiding and evaluating counseling and psychotherapy. *Counseling and Values, 29,* 99–116.

Bergin, A. E. (1991). Values and religious issues in psychotherapy and mental health. *American Psychologist, 46,* 394–403.

Bergin, A. E., & Jensen, J. P. (1990). Religiosity of psychotherapists: A national survey. *Psychotherapy, 27,* 3–7.

Berrett, M. E., Hardman, R. K., & Richards, P. S. (2010). The role of spirituality in eating disorder treatment and recovery. In Maine, M., Bunnell, D., McGilley, B. (Eds.). *Special issues in the treatment of eating disorders: Bridging the gaps* (pp. 367–385). Maryland Heights, MO: Elsevier.

Bishop, D. R., Avila-Juarbe, E., & Thumme, B. (2003). Recognizing spirituality as an important factor in counselor supervision. *Counseling and Values, 48,* 34–46.

Brawer, P. A., Handal, P. J., Fabricatore, A. N., Roberts, R., & Wajda-Johnston, V. A. (2002). Training and education in religious/spirituality within APA-accredited clinical psychology programs. *Professional Psychology: Research and Practice, 33,* 203–206.

Buber, M. (1996). *I and thou* (W. Kaufmann, Trans.). New York: Simon & Schuster. (Original work published 1923).

Burke, M. T., & Miranti, J. (2001). The spiritual and religious dimensions of counseling. In D. C. Locke, J. E. Myers, & E. L. Herr (Eds.), *Handbook of counseling* (pp. 601–612). Thousand Oaks, CA: Sage.

Chamberlain, R. B., Richards, P. S., & Scharman, J. S. (1996). Spiritual perspectives and interventions in psychotherapy: A qualitative study of experienced AMCAP therapists. *AMCAP Journal, 22,* 29–74.

Childre, D., & McCraty, R. (2001). Psychophysiological correlates of spiritual experience. *Biofeedback, 29*(4), 13–17.

Chirban, J. T. (2001). Assessing religious and spiritual concerns in psychotherapy. In T. G. Plante & A. C. Sherman (Eds.), *Faith and health: Psychological perspectives* (pp. 265—290). New York: Guilford Press.

Collins, G. R. (1988). *Christian counseling: A comprehensive guide* (Rev. ed.). Dallas, TX: Word Publishing.

Crook-Lyon, R. E., O'Grady, K. A., Smith T. B., Golightly, T., & Jensen, D. R. (2005, August 20). *Should spiritual and religious issues be taught in graduate curricula?* Paper presented at the 113th Annual Convention of the American Psychological Association, Washington, DC.

Dixon, T. (2002). Scientific atheism as a faith tradition. *Studies in History, Philosophy, Biology, and Biomedical Science, 33,* 337–359.

Elkins, D. N. (1998). *Beyond religion: A personal program for building a spiritual life outside the walls of traditional religion.* Wheaton, IL: Quest Books.

Elkins, D. N. (2005). A humanistic approach to spiritually oriented psychotherapy. In E. P. Shafranske (Ed.), *Spiritually oriented psychotherapy* (pp. 131–151). Washington, DC: American Psychological Association.

Emmons, R. A. (1999). *The psychology of ultimate concerns: Motivation and spirituality in personality.* New York: The Guilford Press.

Emmons, R. A., & Paloutzian, R. F. (2003). The psychology of religion. *Annual Review of Psychology, 54,* 377–402.

Epstein, M. (1995). *Thoughts without a thinker: Psychotherapy from a Buddhist perspective.* New York: Basic Books.

Fear, R., & Woolfe, R. (1999). The personal and professional development of the counselor: The relationship between personal philosophy and theoretical orientation. *Counseling Psychology Quarterly, 12,* 253–262.

Finnegan, J. (2008). *The audacity of spirit: The meaning and shaping of spirituality today.* Dublin, Ireland: Veritas Publications.

Fukuyama, M., & Sevig, T. (1999). *Integrating spirituality into multicultural counseling.* Thousand Oaks, CA: Sage.

Griffin, D. R. (2000). *Religion and naturalism: Overcoming the conflicts.* Albany, NY: SUNY Press.

Griffith, J. L., & Griffith, M. E. (2002). *Encountering the sacred in psychotherapy: How to talk with people about their spiritual lives.* New York: The Guilford Press.

Halbur, D. A, & Halbur, K.V. (2006). *Developing your own theoretical orientation in counseling and psychotherapy*. New York: Pearson.

Hedayat-Diba, Z. (2000). Psychotherapy with Muslims. In P. S. Richards & A. E. Bergin (Eds.), *Handbook of psychotherapy and religious diversity* (pp. 289–314). Washington, DC: American Psychological Association.

Helminiak, D. A. (1996). *The human core of spirituality: Mind as psyche and spirit*. Albany, NY: SUNY Press.

Henning, L. H., & Tirrell, F. J. (1982). Counselor resistance to spiritual exploration. *Personnel and Guidance Journal, 61*, 92–95.

Hill, P. C., & Hood, R. W. (1999). *Measures of religiosity*. Birmingham, AL: Religious Education Press.

Hill, P. C., & Pargament, K. I. (2003). Advances in the conceptualization and measurement of religion and spirituality. *American Psychologist, 58,* 64–74.

Holmes, P. R. (2007). Spirituality: Some disciplinary perspectives. In K. Flanagan & P. C. Jupp (Eds.), *A sociology of spirituality* (pp. 23–42). Burlington, VT: Ashgate.

Ibrahim, F. A. (1985). Contribution of cultural worldview to generic counseling and development. *Counseling Psychologist, 13*, 13–19.

James, W. (1902). *The varieties of religious experience*. New York: Modern Library.

Jensen, J. P., & Bergin, A. E. (1988). Mental health values of professional therapists: A national interdisciplinary survey. *Professional Psychology: Research and Practice, 19*, 290–297.

Jones, S. L. (1994). A constructive relationship for religion with the science and profession of psychology: Perhaps the boldest model yet. *American Psychologist, 49*, 184–199.

Kelly, E. W. (1995). *Religion and spirituality in counseling and psychotherapy*. Alexandria, VA: American Counseling Association.

Koenig, H. G., McCullough, M. E., & Larson, D. B. (2001). *Handbook of religion and health*. New York: Oxford University Press.

Lovinger, R. J. (1984). *Working with religious issues in therapy*. Northvale, NJ: Jason Aronson.

Lukoff, D., & Lu, F. (2005). A transpersonal-integrative approach to spiritually-oriented psychotherapy. In E. P. Shafranske (Ed.), *Spiritually oriented psychotherapy* (pp. 177–233). Washington, DC: American Psychological Association.

Martin, J. E., & Carlson, C. R. (1988). Spiritual dimensions of health psychology. In W. R. Miller & J. E. Martin (Eds.), *Behavior therapy and religion* (pp. 57–110). Newbury Park, CA: Sage.

Maugans, T. A. (1996). The SPIRITual history. *Archives of Family Medicine, 5*(1), 11–16.

McCraty, R., Atkinson, M., & Bradley, R. T. (2004a). Electrophysiological evidence of intuition: Part 1. The surprising role of the heart. *Journal of Alternative and Complementary Medicine, 10*(1), 133–143.

McCraty, R., Atkinson, M., & Bradley, R. T. (2004b). Electrophysiological evidence of intuition: Part 2. A system-wide process. *Journal of Alternative and Complementary Medicine, 10*(2), 325–336.

McCraty, R., Atkinson, M., & Tomasino, D. (2001). *Science of the heart: Exploring the role of the heart in human performance*. HeartMath Research Center Publication No. 01–001. Boulder Creek, CA: Institute of HeartMath.

McCraty, R., Bradley, R. T., & Tomasino, D. (2004–2005). The resonant heart. *Shift: At the Frontiers of Consciousness, 5*, 15–19.

McMinn, M. R. (1996). *Psychology, theology, and spirituality in Christian counseling*. Wheaton, IL: Tyndale House Publishers.

Miller, L. (2005). Interpersonal psychotherapy from a spiritual perspective. In E. P. Shafranske (Ed.), *Spiritually oriented psychotherapy* (pp. 153–175). Washington, DC: American Psychological Association.

Miller, L. (2011). An experiential approach for exploring spirituality. In J. D. Aten, M. R. McMinn, & E. L. Worthington, Jr. (Eds.), *Spiritually oriented interventions for counseling and psychotherapy* (pp. 325–343. Washington, DC: American Psychological Association.

Miller, W. R. (1999). *Integrating spirituality into treatment: Resources for practitioners*. Washington, DC: American Psychological Association.

Miller, W. R., & Delaney, H. D. (Eds.) (2005). *Judeo-Christian perspectives on psychology: Human nature, motivation, and change*. Washington, DC: American Psychological Association.

Miller, W. R., & Thoresen, C. E. (2003). Spirituality, religion, and health: An emerging research field. *American Psychologist, 58*(1), 24–35.

Neiymeyer, G. J., Prichard, S., Lyddon, W. J., & Sherrard, P. A. D. (1993). The role of epistemic style in counseling preference and orientation. *Journal of Counseling and Development, 71*, 515–523.

Nielsen, S. L., Johnson, W. B., & Ellis, A. (2001). *Counseling and psychotherapy with religious persons: A rational emotive behavior therapy approach*. Mahwah, NJ: Erlbaum.

Nigosian, S. A. (1994). *World faiths* (2nd ed.). New York: St. Martin's Press.

O'Grady, K. A., Bartz, J., Boardman, R. D., & Richards, P. S. (2006, April 22). *Integrating secular psychotherapy orientations with a theistic worldview*. Paper presented at the 76th Annual Meeting of the Rocky Mountain Psychological Association, Park City, UT.

O'Grady, K. A., & Richards, P. S. (2010). The role of inspiration in the helping professions. *Psychology of Religion and Spirituality, 2*, 57–66.

Palmer, S. J., & Keller, R. R. (1989). *Religions of the world: A Latter-Day Saint view*. Provo, UT: Brigham Young University Press.

Pargament, K. I. (1997). *The psychology of religion and coping: Theory, research, practice*. New York: The Guilford Press.

Pargament, K. I. (2007). *Spiritually integrated psychotherapy: Understanding and addressing the sacred*. New York: The Guilford Press.

Piedmont, R. L., Hassinger, C. J., Rhorer, J., Sherman, M. F., Sherman, N. C., & Williams, J. E. G. (2007). The relations among spirituality and religiosity and axis II functioning in two college samples. *Research in the Social Scientific Study of Religion, 18*, 53–73.

Plante, T. G. (2009). *Spiritual practices in psychotherapy*. Washington, DC: American Psychological Association.

Rabinowitz, A. (1999). *Judaism and psychology: Meeting points*. Northvale, NJ: Jason Aronson.

Richards, P. S. (2005a). Theistic integrative psychotherapy. In E. P. Shafranske (Ed.), *Spiritually oriented psychotherapy* (pp. 259–285). Washington, DC: American Psychological Association.

Richards, P. S. (2005b). Theistic integrative psychology. *Psychotherapy Videotape Series VI (Spirituality)*. Washington, DC: American Psychological Association.

Richards, P. S., & Bergin, A. E. (1997). *A spiritual strategy for counseling and psychotherapy*. Washington, DC: American Psychological Association.

Richards, P. S., & Bergin, A. E. (Eds.). (2000). *Handbook of psychotherapy and religious diversity*. Washington, DC: American Psychological Association.

Richards, P. S., & Bergin, A. E. (2004). *Casebook for a spiritual strategy in counseling and psychotherapy*. Washington, D.C.: American Psychological Association.

Richards, P. S., & Bergin, A. E. (2005). *A spiritual strategy for counseling and psychotherapy* (2nd ed.). Washington, DC: American Psychological Association.

Richards, P. S., Hardman, R. K., & Berrett, M. E. (2007). *Spiritual approaches in the treatment of women with eating disorders*. Washington, DC: American Psychological Association.

Richards, P. S., Rector, J. R., & Tjeltveit, A. C. (1999). Values, spirituality, and psychotherapy. In W. R. Miller (Ed.), *Integrating spirituality in treatment: Resources for practitioners* (pp. 133–160). Washington, DC: American Psychological Association.

Richards, P. S., & Worthington, E. L., Jr. (2010). The need for evidence-based spiritually-oriented psychotherapies. *Professional Psychology: Research and Practice, 41*, 363–370.

Rubin, J. B. (1996). *Psychotherapy and Buddhism: Toward an integration*. New York: Plenum Press.

Schulte, D. L., Skinner, T. A., & Claiborn, C. D. (2002). Religious and spiritual issues in counseling psychology training. *Counseling Psychologist, 30*, 118–134.

Shafranske, E. P. (2000). Religious involvement and professional practices of psychiatrists and other mental health professionals. *Psychiatric Annals, 30*, 525–532.

Shafranske, E. P., & Malony, H. N. (1990). Clinical psychologists' religious and spiritual orientations and their practice of psychotherapy. *Psychotherapy, 27*, 72–78.

Shafranske, E. P., & Malony, H. N. (1996). Religion and the clinical practice of psychology: A case for inclusion. In E. P. Shafranske (Ed.), *Religion and the clinical practice of psychology* (pp. 561–586). Washington, DC: American Psychological Association.

Slife, B. D. (2004). Theoretical challenges to therapy practice and research: The constraint of naturalism. In M. J. Lambert (Ed.), *Bergin and Garfield's handbook of psychotherapy and behavior change* (5th ed., pp. 44–83). New York: Wiley.

Slife, B. D., Hope, C., & Nebeker, R. S. (1999). Examining the relationship between religious spirituality and psychological science. *Journal of Humanistic Psychology, 39*, 51–85.

Slife, B. D., Mitchell, L. J., & Whoolery, M. (2004). A theistic approach to therapeutic community: Non-naturalism and the Alldredge Academy. In P. S. Richards & A. E. Bergin (Eds.), *Casebook for a spiritual strategy in counseling and psychotherapy* (pp. 35–54). Washington, DC: American Psychological Association.

Slife, B. D., & Williams, R. N. (1995). *What's behind the research? Discovering hidden assumptions in the behavioral sciences*. Thousand Oaks, CA: Sage.

Smart, N. (1993). *Religions of Asia*. Englewood Cliffs, NJ: Prentice Hall.

Smart, N. (1994). *Religions of the West*. Englewood Cliffs, NJ: Prentice Hall.

Smith, T. B., Bartz, J. D., & Richards, P. S. (2007). Outcomes of religious and spiritual adaptations to psychotherapy: A meta-analytic review. *Psychotherapy Research, 17*, 643–655.

Smith, T. B., & Richards, P. S. (2005). The integration of spiritual and religious issues in racial-cultural psychology and counseling. In R. T. Carter (Ed.), *Handbook of racial-cultural psychology and counseling: Theory and research* (Vol. 1, pp. 132–160). New York: Wiley.

Spero, M. H. (Ed.). (1985). *Psychotherapy of the religious patient*. Springfield, IL: Charles C. Thomas.

Sperry, L. (2001). *Spirituality in clinical practice: Incorporating the spiritual dimension in psychotherapy and counseling*. New York: Brunner/Routledge.

Sperry, L., & Shafranske, E. P. (Eds.) (2005). *Spiritually oriented psychotherapy*. Washington, DC: American Psychological Association.

Swinton, J. (2001). *Spirituality and mental health care: Rediscovering a forgotten dimension*. London and Philadelphia: Jessica Kingsley Publishers.

Sue, D. W., Bergnier, J. E., Duran, A., Feinberg, L., Pedersen, P., Smith, E., & Vasquez-Nuttall, E. (1982). Position paper: Cross-cultural counseling competencies. *The Counseling Psychologist, 10*, 45–52.

Sue, D. W., Bingham, R., Porche-Burke, L., & Vasquez, M. (1999). The diversification of psychology: A multicultural revolution. *American Psychologist, 54*, 1061–1069.

Sue, D. W., & Sue, D. (1990). *Counseling the culturally different: Theory and practice* (2nd ed.). New York: Wiley.

Tacey, D. (2004). *The spirituality revolution: The emergence of contemporary spirituality*. New York: Brunner-Routledge.

Tjeltveit, A. C. (1999). *Ethics and values in psychotherapy*. New York: Routledge.

Vaughan, F. (1996). Spiritual issues in psychotherapy. In G. Jennings (Ed.), *Passages beyond the gate: A Jungian approach to understanding the nature of American psychology at the dawn of the new millennium* (pp. 336–345). Needham Heights, MA: Simon & Schuster Custom Publishing.

Weaver, A. J., Koenig, H. G., & Larson, D. B. (1997). Marriage and family therapists and the clergy: A need for clinical collaboration, training, and research. *Journal of Marriage and Family Therapy, 23*, 13–25.

West, W. (2000). *Psychotherapy and spirituality: Crossing the line between therapy and religion*. Thousand Oaks: Sage.

White, F. E. (2002). The lived-experience of psychospiritual integration: A qualitative study with licensed psychotherapists who actively integrate spirituality into their practice of psychotherapy (Doctoral dissertation, Institute for Transpersonal Psychology, 2002). *Dissertation Abstracts International: Section B: The Sciences and Engineering, 63*, 2613.

Williams, R. N. (1992). The human context of agency. *American Psychologist, 47*, 752–760.

Worthington, E. L., Jr. (1986). Religious counseling: A review of published empirical research. *Journal of Counseling and Development, 64*, 421–431.

Worthington, E. L., Jr. (1988). Understanding the values of religious clients: A model and its application to counseling. *Journal of Counseling Psychology, 35*, 166–174.

Worthington, E. L., Jr., Kurusu, T. A., McCullough, M. E., & Sanders, S. J. (1996). Empirical research on religion and psychotherapeutic processes and outcomes: A ten-year review and research prospectus. *Psychological Bulletin, 119*, 448–487.

Wuthnow, R. (1998). *After heaven: Spirituality in America since the 1950s*. Berkeley: University of California Press.

Young, J. S., Cashwell, C., Wiggins-Frame, M., & Belaire, C. (2002). Spiritual and religious competencies: A national survey of CACREP-accredited programs. *Counseling and Values, 47*, 22–33.

Zinnbauer, B. J., Pargament, K. I., & Scott, A. B. (1999). The emerging meanings of religiousness and spirituality: Problems and prospects. *Journal of Personality, 67*(6), 889–919.

Counseling and Psychotherapy Within and Across Faith Traditions

Mark R. McMinn, Kimberly N. Snow, *and* Justin J. Orton

Abstract

This chapter begins with general considerations for religiously and spiritually oriented psychotherapy, including the importance of seeing religion and spirituality as dimensions of cultural diversity, considering clients' welfare and autonomy, and maintaining competence. Three types of religious and spiritual intervention approaches are then discussed: assimilative, accommodative, and collaborative. Assimilative approaches introduce spiritual interventions or considerations into a standard psychotherapy approach. Accommodative approaches involve adapting a standard psychotherapy regimen to include religious or spiritual matters. Collaborative approaches entail a mental health professional and religious leader working in tandem for the sake of clients' welfare. Next, specific issues related to counseling within (when the client and counselor share the same beliefs) and across (when the client and counselor hold differing beliefs) faith traditions are offered. The chapter concludes with some thoughts regarding future directions of religious and spiritual interventions in counseling and psychotherapy.

Key Words: religion, spirituality, religious counseling, spiritual issues in psychotherapy, religious diversity, religiously accommodative psychotherapy, psychology-clergy collaboration

Introduction

With five minutes remaining in our final session, a psychotherapy client asked me (Snow), "So what do you think about me and God?" The majority of our sessions had been spent discussing specific sources of anxiety, concerns about the future, and ways of coping with these fears. My mind traveled back to conversations early on in therapy regarding my client's religious struggles, including some feelings of frustration and disappointment with God. Now in the waning moments of our sessions together he chose to broach the topic once more. It struck me that perhaps there was a well of unprocessed material waiting to be tapped, beliefs and values waiting to be uncovered—a vast driving force in my client's life. But then again, maybe my client's question reflected his comfort with me, as he chose to ponder issues of ultimate meaning even during the final

moments of our therapeutic work together. Perhaps his question was a measure of some success, suggesting that in treating his anxiety I had also helped him feel comfortable pondering profound questions about faith and his experience with the Divine.

As with the client described in this anecdote, most people who seek the services of counselors and psychotherapists have spiritual experiences and beliefs (Gallup Polls, 2009), they look to religion as they cope with life challenges (Pargament, 1997, 2007), and they face ultimate concerns that involve religion and spirituality (Emmons, 1999). Even with religion becoming less important to US residents over the past 15 years, 80% still report religion to be very important or fairly important to them, down from 87% in 1992. In 2008, 61% still belonged to a church or synagogue and 38% had attended services in the past 7 days (Gallup Polls, 2009). An additional portion of people—perhaps as many as one-third of all US residents—describe themselves as spiritual but not religious (Gallup, 2003).

Given the prominence of religion and spirituality in society, it is wise for mental health professionals to understand something about their clients' religious and spiritual beliefs and behaviors in order to provide effective assessment and treatment. But this is not to suggest that counselors and psychotherapists should be religious advisors, pastoral counselors, or spiritual directors. Although some overlap exists, the goals and methods of mental health counseling and psychotherapy are distinct from the goals and methods of spiritual interventions, and these distinctions ought to be respected and maintained (Gonsiorek, Richards, Pargament, & McMinn, 2009). Herein lies a major challenge facing contemporary mental health professionals, and a substantial challenge facing us as authors of this chapter: How do we embrace the importance of understanding spiritual and religious issues while still affirming the distinct contribution of mental health training and practice?

In this chapter, we first suggest several general considerations, including culture, client welfare, client autonomy, and therapist competence. Next, we look at existing interventions and describe three possible approaches: assimilative, accommodative, and collaborative. Then we turn our attention to counseling when the counselor and client share the same faith. Finally, we consider counseling when the counselor and client have different faiths.

General Considerations for Counseling Within and Across Faith Traditions
Religion and Spirituality as a Cultural Issue

Over the past several decades counselors and psychotherapists have become increasingly aware of the importance of understanding the cultural diversity among their clients (Sue & Sue, 2007). Every client, and every therapist, is shaped by the mores, assumptions, and values emerging from her or his ethnic and cultural communities. I (McMinn) recall working with a client many years ago who reported feeling like an incomplete woman because of her hysterectomy. After several weeks of using standard cognitive therapy strategies to help her see her situation differently, my supervisor pointed out that her beliefs about womanhood may actually be closely tied to the cultural community that helped define

her throughout the 167 hours each week that were not spent in my office. One hour per week in my office could not compete with powerful cultural messages that helped define her, nor was it fitting for me to try to compete with the community that helped her find hope and meaning and sustained her through challenging life situations. It was only when I recognized my cultural insensitivity (with the help of my supervisor), apologized to my client, and began helping her evaluate her beliefs in a more culturally inclusive manner that she made progress in therapy.

In the same way, religious and spiritual issues are often powerful influences for counseling and psychotherapy clients. If overlooked, the results of our interventions may be compromised, or even damaging to clients. Consider something as basic as the definition of health. An agnostic cognitive-behavioral therapist may see health as the capacity to reinterpret difficult life situations without letting the situations become too upsetting. In contrast, a devout Buddhist or Hindu client may desire to accept suffering as an inevitable part of living, and ultimately to transcend suffering through spiritual practices and the wisdom gained from spiritual mentors. A devout Jewish, Christian, or Muslim client may see health as the ability to maintain faith and find meaning in the midst of suffering.

Just as it is important for mental health professionals to know basic information about different cultures and ethnicities, so also it is important to have basic knowledge of different religious systems, spiritual beliefs, and practices. This basic knowledge can be obtained through taking a world religions course or reading a world religions text, by having open conversations with friends and acquaintances about their spiritual beliefs and practices, by attending workshops and seminars on religious and spiritual issues in psychotherapy, or by getting supervised training on the topic.

One challenge in learning about culture in psychotherapy is not to overgeneralize. For example, a therapist learning about Asian American culture may start assuming that all Asian American clients have communitarian values, emphasize achievement and diligence, avoid bringing shame to their families, and so on. But, of course, there are many cultures in Asia, various levels of acculturation to consider, and individual differences from one client to another. It would be a mistake to assume too much based on general knowledge of cultural categories. In the same way, knowing about religious systems can easily lead to overgeneralizations and faulty conclusions. It is important to recognize vast diversity within every major faith tradition, and to realize there is a good deal of individual variation in how people experience and express their faith-related beliefs.

Ms. Davison comes for psychotherapy because of a persistent generalized anxiety disorder that contributes to insomnia, inhibits her relationships, and leads to feelings of dread and apprehension about the future. She and her psychotherapist set goals for the first session—to learn ways to manage and reduce her feelings of anxiety, to establish closer relationships with family members and colleagues at work, to reduce her tendency toward perfectionism, and to sleep better as she learns to manage her anxiety. In the middle of the first session, Ms. Davison mentions that she is an elder at the Presbyterian church she attends, and that she would like a therapy approach that is respectful of her faith.

As the psychotherapist ponders the best treatment for Ms. Davison, it will be important to consider something about her religious faith, both in terms of understanding the basic themes of the Christian faith, and also in terms of the individual nuances of her particular faith experience. Christians generally believe in an afterlife, and they seek to live in a way that reflects the example of Jesus Christ. Perhaps Ms. Davison puts a good deal of pressure on herself to be perfect, and then feels defeated and anxious when she falls short of these lofty standards. But then again, Presbyterian theology emphasizes that good works can never earn approval with God—that is only accomplished by God's undeserved favor. So perhaps Ms. Davison's faith is actually a protective factor that keeps her from even greater levels of perfectionism and anxiety. And it will be important to consider that she is an elder in the church. What does her leadership role in a faith community say about the levels of stress she experiences, about the respect she garners in relationships, about how much weakness and struggle she can reveal to others in her faith community, and about her capacity to manage stress? What sort of gender issues might arise with being a woman leader in a religion that generally has male leaders? All these matters, and more, are worth exploring in the context of counseling.

Client Welfare

One of the most fundamental principles of professional psychologists and other health professionals is that we promote the welfare of our clients. This is foremost in the mental health practitioner's mind, just as it is foremost in our ethical standards. The

beginning words of ethics Principle A for psychologists read, "Psychologists strive to benefit those with whom they work and take care to do no harm. In their professional actions, psychologists seek to safeguard the welfare and rights of those with whom they interact professionally and other affected persons…" (American Psychological Association [APA], 2002, p. 1062).

Client welfare is important to consider when counseling within and across faith traditions. On one hand, because faith-related beliefs and practices are held as important to many clients, and because these beliefs and practices often enhance a person's well-being, it is important for mental health professionals to be respectful rather than dismissive when religious and spiritual issues come up in therapy. On the other hand, some religious and spiritual beliefs can be damaging to self and others, so at times it is important for mental health professionals to help clients think incisively about their various beliefs and practices. Both the positive and negative dimensions of religion and spirituality must be considered.

POSITIVE DIMENSIONS OF RELIGION AND SPIRITUALITY

For many years, it was common to hear or read psychologists' disparaging comments about religion (e.g., Ellis, 1962, 1971, 1983). But the tide has shifted. Many respected professionals, both religious and nonreligious, have made the study of religion and spirituality and health an established field within social science (see Miller & Thoresen, 2003; Powell, Shahabi, & Thoresen, 2003; Seeman, Dubin, & Seeman, 2003). Going along with this trend, the fields of counseling and professional psychology have become more open to religion and spirituality, both as an important diversity issue, and further, as a potential benefit to client health (Aten & Leach, 2009; Miller & Delaney, 2005; Pargament, 2007; Richards & Bergin, 2005; Shafranske, 1996; Sperry & Shafranske, 2005). We approach this topic with the assumption that religion may bring potential benefits to client health and wholeness.

This assumption has been supported by recent research suggesting that the relationship between religion and health is strikingly positive in terms of its average effects at the population level (see Koenig, McCullough, & Larson, 2001; Priester, Khalili, & Luvathingal, 2009). Epidemiological studies on the effects of religion on health and morbidity have explored both preventive and curative effects of religion and spirituality (for reviews of these findings and related measurement issues, see Hill & Pargament, 2003; Koenig et al., 2001; Miller & Thoresen, 2003). Religion's benefits extend to both physical and mental dimensions of health and well-being. While a majority of this research has focused on Christianity, the benefits of other religious faiths and nonreligious forms of spirituality have been supported as well.

There are several dimensions of religious life that may affect a person's understanding of health—either implicitly or explicitly—and engagement in healthful activities. First, religious and spiritual systems often help people make meaning of life, including the difficult aspects of life (Slattery & Park, 2011). Religious meaning is often promoted by associations with particular faith-based institutions, clergy, and by the sacred texts and traditions associated with the faith. For example, members of various religious institutions are taught to seek maturity in living through dedication to a purposeful life; among the various behaviors that may be emphasized are social action, altruistic behavior, peace seeking, forgiveness, community involvement, abstinent lifestyle, and relationship fidelity. Altruistic and prosocial behaviors have positive effects on mental health (Post, 2005; Schwartz, Meisenhelder, Ma, & Reed, 2002) while also serving the well-being of society as a whole. Other religious and spiritual traditions may emphasize seeking transcendence, and cultivation of an interior relationship with the divine. For those who are intrinsically religious, relationship with God is a powerful motivating force behind outward behavior. This meaning-making dimension of faith is often important to consider in working with religious and spiritual clients,

Second, being a member of a religious or spiritual community provides a social support network for adherents that should not be underestimated. Religious social support can offer clients valuable relationships; a socially transmitted understanding of their faith beliefs; shared experience of rituals related to coming of age, partnering, and death; and access to communal spiritual activities such as collective prayer and worship. In times of stress, religious activities can be positive forms of coping, whether practiced individually or with a group, offering people meaning and hope when facing either life trauma or everyday stressors (see Pargament, 1997, for an extensive review of religious coping).

Third, religious resources may be sources of help in the midst of life troubles. Many clergy spend a substantial amount of time counseling parishioners (Weaver, 1995), and many are open to collaborating with mental health workers (Benes, Walsh, McMinn, Dominguez, & Aikins, 2000; Edwards, Lim, McMinn, & Dominguez, 1999; Lish, McMinn, Fitzsimmons, & Root, 2003; McMinn, Aikins, & Lish, 2003; McMinn, Chaddock, Edwards, Lim, & Campbell, 1998). There is also a substantial amount of religious and spiritual self-help material available in bookstores, some of which has been written by counseling and psychology professionals and may prove very useful for bibliotherapy. And sacred texts can also be useful for self-help and bibliotherapy purposes. Paradoxically, one of the most vocal opponents of religion in professional psychology—Albert Ellis—conceded that "the Judeo-Christian Bible is a self-help book that has probably enabled more people to make more extensive and intensive personality and behavioral changes than all professional therapists combined" (Ellis, 1993, p. 336). Interestingly, Ellis even went on to coauthor a book addressing how to effectively use rational emotive behavior therapy with religious clients, respecting their beliefs and even incorporating scripture in the counseling process (Nielsen, Johnson, & Ellis, 2001). A number of accommodating approaches to therapy such as this one have been developed. Research has generally supported these approaches as similarly effective as nonaccommodating approaches, with the potential benefit of increasing client cooperation (McCullough, 1999).

The literature at this time clearly supports a positive link between religion and spirituality and health. Some researchers have suggested that the relationship is mediated by various factors; still, other researchers suggest that the benefits of religion and spirituality may extend beyond any mediating factors, being intrinsically tied to the very nature of religion and spirituality (see Hill & Pargament, 2003). It is possible that perceived closeness with God, as viewed from an attachment perspective, may be its own predictor of health (see Hill & Pargament, 2003). It is important to remember that degree of religiosity or spirituality will differ from client to client and, therefore, potential benefits of incorporating faith into the therapy process will have to be assessed on an individual basis.

As practitioners, then, it behooves us to understand how our clients benefit from their religious and spiritual practices. It is possible that the faith of our clients can contribute to positive therapeutic outcomes in a variety of ways—by fueling a desire and motivation for well-being, and by offering many potential resources that can be both psychologically and spiritually nurturing.

NEGATIVE DIMENSIONS OF RELIGION AND SPIRITUALITY

Although the historical tendency of the psychological community to declare spiritual beliefs and practices as harmful is reversing, religion and spirituality continue to be marginal concepts in academic and clinical settings (Young, Cashwell, Wiggins-Frame, & Belaire, 2002). Even among mental health professionals who accept the potential positive impact of spiritual and religious beliefs on the well-being of clients, there often remains reservation concerning some mainstream religious beliefs (O'Connor & Vandenberg, 2005). Though Ellis (2000) acknowledged the potential positive influence of spirituality and religion late in his career, and even coauthored a book on the topic (Nielsen et al., 2001), he continued to warn against a number of potential drawbacks. He wrote that those who accept spiritual and religious systems are at risk for prejudice and dubious mental-emotional health (Ellis, 1999, 2000; Ellis & Harper, 1997), ego inflation and conditional self-acceptance (Ellis, 2000), as well as extreme obsession that leads to poor self-care (Ellis, 2000; Ellis & Harper 1997; Ellis & MacLaren, 1998). Ellis's warnings against the potential negative consequences of holding religious and spiritual beliefs are neither unique (e.g., Greene, 2008) nor unsupported. Hood, Spilka, Hunsberger, and Gorsuch (1996) demonstrate that religiosity in the United States is indeed linked to rigid thinking, prejudice, and narrow-mindedness. Pargament, Kennell, Hathaway, and Grevengoed (1988) reported a pattern of passive religious coping that is linked to lower self-esteem, lower personal control, poorer problem-solving skills, and a greater intolerance for differences between people, and subsequent studies have found similar results (Hathaway & Pargament, 1990; McIntosh & Spilka, 1990; Schaefer & Gorsuch, 1991).

Moreover, highly religious individuals and those in spiritual distress may have negative anticipations of counseling in general and especially with non-religious counselors (Keating & Fretz, 1990). And although those with intrinsic faith commitments tend to be less prone to depression and hostility than others, those with extrinsic and prosocial approaches to faith have increased risk of physical complaints and psychological distress (Hackney & Sanders, 2003; Salsman & Carlson, 2005).

One of us (Orton) once saw a client whom we will call Joe. He was a model Marine sergeant—muscular, dedicated, and seemingly fearless. Joe's troops saw him as unshakable. Unbeknownst to his subordinates, Joe cried himself to sleep nearly every night, terrified that he was going to hell. No matter how much Joe tried to live up to his lofty spiritual standards, at the end of each day he knew he had failed. Failure, Joe's religious convictions taught, was inevitability met by terrible wrath. The man, who was so confident before others, was reduced to a weeping hulk when faced with the belief that God was against him. Joe's struggle highlights the reality that not all religious and spiritual experiences promote client welfare. Joe's pervasive experience of spiritual failure is not uncommon, as spiritual and religious distress often includes struggles with religious and moral guilt (Kennedy, 1999; Lukoff, Lu, & Turner, 1998), as well as anger toward God (Fitchett, Rybarczyk, DeMarco, & Nichols, 1999).

For clinicians committed to their client's welfare, these findings about negative religious experiences are concerning, especially because they are associated with poor health outcomes (Fitchett et al., 1999; McCullough, Hoyt, Larson, Koenig, & Thorsesen, 2000; Pargament, Koenig, Tarakeshwar, & Hahn, 2001). Johnson and Hayes (2003, p. 417) reported that clients with religious or spiritual concerns are "25% more likely than other clients to experience distress related to sexual concerns, 22%–29% more likely to experience distress related to relationships with peers, 34%–37% more likely to be concerned about thought of being punished for ones sins, and nearly twice as likely as other clients to be confused about their beliefs and values." Some conservative religious beliefs also contribute to internalized homophobia, which can be damaging to gay, lesbian, and bisexual clients (Bartoli & Gillem, 2008; Beckstead, 2001).

When considering client welfare, it is important to recognize both the positive and negative dimensions of religion and spirituality. Religious and spiritual beliefs can sustain and enhance mental health in difficult times, and they can also lead to distress and despair (Plante, 2011). Discerning the difference is one of the challenges of effective clinical work.

Client Autonomy

Psychotherapists have an ethical obligation to respect the autonomy and dignity of counseling and psychotherapy clients. The APA (2002) ethics code states:

> Psychologists respect the dignity and worth of all people, and the rights of individuals to privacy, confidentiality, and self-determination... Psychologists are aware of and respect cultural, individual, and role

differences, including those based on age, gender, gender identity, race, ethnicity, culture, national origin, religion, sexual orientation, disability, language, and socioeconomic status and consider these factors when working with members of such groups. Psychologists try to eliminate the effect on their work of biases based on those factors, and they do not knowingly participate in or condone activities of others based upon such prejudices.

(p. 1063)

This ethics principle serves as a reminder that religious persuasion is typically not the goal of mental health interventions. When religious values are discussed, it is within a context of affirming the client's right to self-determination. Consider the following case example:

Melissa is a 17-year-old high school student seeking help for depression. She discloses to her therapist that she is pregnant and trying to decide how to tell her parents. The following session, Melissa reports that she mustered the courage to tell her parents, who responded lovingly and supportively. They are suggesting that Melissa terminate the pregnancy. This seems like a good idea to Melissa also, but she wonders if she might regret the decision later. The father of the child wants nothing to do with Melissa or the decision about whether to abort the fetus. The counselor schedules a family session with Melissa and her parents to discuss the situation, and in the process he asks about religious values regarding abortion. Melissa does not identify with any religion. Her parents report being Catholic, but they state that they have lapsed from their faith and that this is not an important consideration. Melissa and her parents leave the session in agreement that abortion is the best option. This creates inner turmoil for the counselor, who is a committed Roman Catholic and opposed to abortion.

As difficult as this situation may be for the counselor, the client's autonomy remains a guiding principle for ethical counseling and a distinguishing feature between mental health counseling and religious guidance. The counselor is correct to assess religious values during the family session, and the counselor is also correct to grant Melissa—in consultation with her family—self-determination in the choice she faces. Likewise, if the roles were reversed—with a counselor who believed abortion to be the best option and a teenager who chose to give birth because of moral objections to abortion—then the counselor would likewise be obligated to be respectful of the client's values and autonomy.

Client autonomy should not be confused with unrealistic efforts to remove all persuasive influence from counseling and psychotherapy. Virtually all counseling and psychotherapy involves exerting influence. For example, a couples therapist may help a person become more communicative and assertive in a relationship, even if the person initially does not see any reason to change. An individual psychotherapist may empower a depressed client to exercise more frequently or use stress-provoking exposure techniques to treat a client with an anxiety disorder. An addictions counselor might help a client acknowledge a problem with alcohol abuse. Exerting influence is a common part of counseling and psychotherapy, but within the context of informed consent and in a way that is respectful of the client's self-determination and autonomy. Efforts to persuade a client to change religious viewpoints are generally discouraged in counseling and psychotherapy, and they may only be appropriate in certain situations. For example, if a psychotherapist is convinced that a client's religious views are causing damage to the client or others, then some level of persuasion might be fitting, but only if the psychotherapist's intent is described in the treatment consent form, if the religious change is clearly associated with a mental health outcome, and if the religious issues are discussed in a relational context where the client feels fully respected and accepted regardless of the outcome of the conversation.

Therapist Competence

The final general consideration discussed here pertains to therapist competence. As is true with any area of specialty or multicultural practice, competence in handling religious and spiritual issues requires adequate training, experience, and sensitivity. Consider the following situation:

You are working as a psychologist at a university teaching hospital. Much of your work involves consulting with physicians on medical/surgical floors and in outpatient clinics. Today you are called to an inpatient neonatal unit to visit with Ms. Ayer, a 26-year-old, first-generation Sikh immigrant from Punjab who recently gave birth to her first child, a 3-pound baby girl. Ms. Ayer has been commuting to the hospital each day to be with her child. The neonatal pediatrician who talks with Ms. Ayer frequently is concerned that she may be experiencing postpartum depression. The purpose of your consultation is to help the pediatrician determine whether Ms. Ayer is depressed and, if so, to recommend an appropriate treatment.

It is unlikely that the hospital in this situation employs a Sikh psychologist, so matching the religious values of client and therapist will not be possible. Still, the psychologist bears responsibility to be informed and respectful regarding the client's religious and spiritual values.

Hathaway and Ripley (2009) have provided a thoughtful list of "preliminary practice guidelines when working with religious and spiritual issues" (p. 46). They divide these guidelines into three areas: assessment guidelines, intervention guidelines, and multicultural/diversity guidelines. Notice that all three of these areas are relevant in the previous example of working with a Sikh immigrant who may be experiencing symptoms of postpartum depression.

Among the assessment suggestions, Hathaway and Ripley (2009) emphasize attentiveness to spiritual and religious concerns, including screening questions for all clients as well as more extensive assessment when spiritual and religious issues are particularly salient (see also Richards & Bergin, 2005). They also emphasize the importance of learning what is normative for a particular religious group so that a client's particular beliefs and behaviors can be interpreted in light of normative faith practices. In assessing Ms. Ayer, it will be important to know how closely she identifies with the Sikh faith, what immigrating to another country means about her connection to family and faith community, whether the father of the child is still part of her life, and, if so, the nature of that relationship. It will also be helpful to know the meaning of her giving birth to a girl, and how depression is viewed within her Punjabi culture and among others of similar faith.

Regarding intervention, it is important to seek client consent before using spiritually oriented interventions while also recognizing that established evidence-based interventions should be preferred over untested spiritually oriented interventions and that religious and spiritual treatment goals should always be relevant to the primary mental health treatment goals. With devout clients, competent therapists should understand and attempt to accommodate the client's spiritual and religious beliefs while not compromising the integrity of the treatment being offered. Also, it is important to recognize that religious and spiritual interventions may be harmful in some situations, such as working with a psychotic client who is having religious delusions (Hathaway & Ripley, 2009). If a psychologist were to offer treatment to the client in the previous case example, it would be important that the

primary goals of treatment be focused on mental health (e.g., treatment of postpartum depression) rather than on religious education or spiritual transformation. Religious and spiritual beliefs may be a frequent topic of conversation throughout the intervention, and perhaps some spiritually oriented techniques would be used, but the primary goals and methods of treatment would remain focused on mental health issues.

Finally, Hathaway and Ripley's (2009) multicultural/diversity suggestions emphasize that psychologists learn about clients' religious and spiritual values, that psychologists gain self-awareness of their own beliefs and values and do not coerce or impose their values on clients, and that psychologists be wise about whether to disclose their religious and spiritual views to clients. Hathaway and Ripley also state the importance of obtaining continuing education, supervision, and consultation, and encourage psychologists to recognize the complexity of religious and spiritual variables in relation to other areas of diversity such as sexual orientation, age, gender, and so on. In the previous example, it will be important for the psychologist to consider how giving birth to a female child may affect Ms. Ayer's perceptions of parenting, her relationship with the child's father, and others in her family and social support network.

We have offered four general considerations here—religion and spirituality as a cultural issue, welfare of the client, client autonomy, and therapist competence. These set a context for considering particular intervention approaches when counseling within and across faith traditions.

Intervention Approaches

Religion and spirituality may be integrated into counseling and psychotherapy in a variety of ways, making any taxonomy likely to minimize the creative and artistic aspects of mental health professionals' work. Still, taxonomies can be useful in order to consider the range of possible interventions and the place that each gives to religion and spirituality. We suggest three general types of approaches: assimilative, accommodative, and collaborative.

Assimilative Approaches

Therapists may choose to assimilate spiritual interventions in the context of a standard psychotherapy intervention. For example, a counselor may encourage an anxious client to engage in spiritual journaling (Frame, 2003; Wiggins, 2011) though the majority of each session is devoted to standard therapeutic activities such as cognitive restructuring, exposure treatments, considering developmental issues, exploring emotions, discussing past and current relationships, and so on. The spiritual intervention—journaling, in this case—is not the main focus of treatment, but it allows a client to consider how religious and spiritual matters may relate to symptom patterns and the other material being explored in the context of counseling. Schlosser and Safran (2009) provide a list of many spiritual interventions that can be employed in mental health treatment, including forgiveness, prayer, spiritual history, spiritual genograms, spiritual relaxation, and so on; and Aten, McMinn, and Worthington (2011) provide a more intensive exploration of several spiritual interventions. Some of these treatment methods can be assimilated into standard treatment, while others require that the treatment itself be altered to make intentional use of religious and spiritual interventions. Altering a treatment because of religious and spiritual considerations is considered an accommodative approach.

Accommodative Approaches

Whereas an assimilative approach may draw upon spiritual interventions from time to time, accommodative approaches are those that have been transformed by the integration of religious and spiritual principles and methods. Schlosser and Safran (2009) distinguish between spiritually accommodative approaches and spiritually oriented approaches, both of which would fall under our domain of accommodative approaches.

Spiritually accommodative approaches tend to be standard treatment protocols—often manualized treatments—that have been altered to incorporate a particular religious or spiritual approach. The most common example of this is cognitive-behavioral therapy that has been adapted for Christian clients, though cognitive-behavioral therapy has also been adapted for Muslim clients (Hook et al., 2010; Schlosser & Safran, 2009). For example, religious imagery may be used instead of standard imagery, and sacred writings may be used to help identify and correct dysfunctional thought patterns.

Schlosser and Safran (2009) describe spiritually oriented approaches as "less standardized and more inclusive" than spiritually accommodative approaches (p. 200). For example, a spiritually oriented approach can be seen in Benner's (2005) provocative model for integrating insight-oriented psychotherapy with spiritual direction, in Sperry's (2005) Integrative Spiritually Oriented

Psychotherapy, and in Richards and Bergin's (2005) Theistic-Integrative Psychotherapy. None of these approaches use treatment manuals, but rather they discuss how religious and spiritual worldviews and methods can be incorporated into the overall approach that a mental health professional employs.

Collaborative Approaches

A third category involves the collaboration of mental health professionals and religious leaders (Benes et al., 2000; Edwards et al., 1999; McMinn et al., 2003). Rather than assuming that a mental health professional can address the various spiritual and religious needs of their clients, the collaborative approach assumes that a religious leader or spiritual expert—typically someone who is already part of the client's life—can provide important guidance and support in the process of treatment. For example:

> A nonreligious counselor sees a married couple to help improve their relationship. Both husband and wife are Muslim. In the first session, it becomes clear to the counselor that certain religious issues are likely to affect the process and outcome of treatment. For example, the counselor does not feel adequately prepared to fully understand the couple's view of gender roles and sexuality. The counselor asks the husband and wife for written authorization to discuss basic treatment progress and questions about faith with the imam at the mosque where they attend. Both partners sign the authorization and express appreciation that their faith will be respected in the process of treatment.

As this example illustrates, when a counselor or psychotherapist lacks expertise in particular religious or spiritual beliefs, it is often wise to consult with a religious leader who is part of the client's social support system. At other times a client may be referred directly to a religious or spiritual leader to address a value or belief that is unfamiliar to the mental health professional.

Collaborative approaches can also be used outside of traditional psychotherapy interventions in order to enhance the mental health of larger groups of people. For example, Budd (1999) collaborated with chaplains in the US Air Force to develop an effective suicide prevention effort for Air Force personnel (see also Budd & Newton, 2005).

Determining Which Approach to Use

When should assimilative, accommodative, and collaborative approaches be used? We have no firm answers to this question because the creative dimensions of therapy and the diversity of client characteristics, interests, and needs demand flexibility in how spirituality and religion are addressed. We suggest three factors for mental health professionals to consider when determining which approach to use.

First, it is important to consider client beliefs and desires. Some clients are highly interested in incorporating religion and spirituality in treatment, and others are not. It is useful to assess this early in the treatment relationship. Richards and Bergin (2005) advocate a two-level approach to assessing religious and spiritual beliefs. The first level is to discern a global sense of the role of religion and spirituality in a client's life. This is typically done with a simple probe on the intake form or in the first interview. For example, "Tell me some about your religious and spiritual beliefs and how important they are to you." For clients who identify closely with religious and spiritual values, a more detailed level of assessment can be pursued. Here the clinician attempts to understand the client's experience of the Divine, the orthodoxy of the client's religious beliefs, how religion may be used for coping, a sense of the client's spiritual well-being, and so on. Assimilative approaches to treatment can be used in a wide variety of contexts, though they assume at least a modest level of interest in religion or spirituality on the client's part. Accommodative approaches are typically used with clients who have a high degree of commitment to a religious or spiritual worldview and would like their beliefs to play an important role in treatment. Collaborative approaches are likely to be used for clients who are part of a faith community and are interested in having a religious or spiritual leader involved with their treatment.

Second, it is important to consider issues of competence. Though a client may desire an accommodative approach, a counselor who has no training or experience with spiritually oriented interventions should not attempt to provide this treatment. Referring the client to another mental professional would be appropriate in this case. Similarly, assimilative approaches require some expertise in one or more spiritually oriented intervention and should not be attempted without some background or training on the part of the mental health professional. Collaborative approaches are generally accessible to all mental health professionals, assuming they have basic respect for religious leaders and can communicate effectively with them (McMinn et al., 2003).

Third, the research base for spiritual and religious interventions should be considered when selecting an intervention approach. We turn to this topic next.

Outcome Data on Religious and Spiritual Intervention Approaches

A recent and extensive review of religious and spiritual interventions revealed a total of 24 outcome studies on the topic (Hook et al., 2010). The interventions were used to treat a variety of problems, including anxiety, depression, and even schizophrenia. Almost all of the existing research is limited to what we have called accommodative approaches, and most of this focuses on what Schlosser and Safran (2009) call "spiritually accommodative approaches." That is, current research tends to focus on relatively standardized forms of treatment that have been adapted to include religious and spiritual variables. Most of the published studies have been with Christian interventions, though some have considered other faiths, including Islam, Buddhism, Taoism, and nonspecific spirituality (Hook et al., 2010). In general, research evidence suggests that some accommodative approaches are as effective as standard approaches, but most are not more effective than standard treatment. Of the 24 studies reviewed, Hook et al. (2010) deemed two therapies efficacious. Two additional therapies were deemed efficacious when combined with medication, two more when combined with existing inpatient treatments, and six treatments were considered possibly efficacious. Three treatments were not considered efficacious. Treatments in each category are listed in Table 17.1.

Most of these studies have methodological limitations, many use analog clients, and the standardization of treatment approaches leaves much to be desired. More and better research is needed to understand the effectiveness of religious and spiritual approaches to counseling and psychotherapy (McMinn, Worthington, & Aten, 2011).

In summary, we have described three types of intervention approaches that consider religious and spiritual issues. Assimilative approaches add religiously or spiritually oriented interventions or homework to a standard treatment approach. Accommodative approaches are treatments that have been modified from their standard form in order to introduce religious and spiritual issues. Collaborative approaches involve communicating with religious or spiritual leaders throughout the treatment process. The client's beliefs and desires, the psychotherapist's competence, and empirical support for various treatment options should be

Table 17.1 Religious and Spiritual Treatments With Empirical Support

Efficacious treatments

Christian accommodative cognitive therapy for depression

Twelve-step facilitation for alcoholism

Efficacious treatments when combined with medication

Muslim accommodative psychotherapy for depression

Muslim accommodative psychotherapy for anxiety

Efficacious treatments when combined with existing inpatient treatment

Spiritual group therapy for eating disorders

Buddhist accommodative cognitive therapy for anger

Possibly efficacious treatments

Christian devotional meditation for anxiety

Taoist cognitive therapy for anxiety

Christian accommodative group treatment for unforgiveness

Spiritual group treatment for unforgiveness

Christian accommodative group cognitive-behavioral therapy for marital discord

Christian lay counseling for general psychological problems

No evidence for efficacy

Spiritual group cognitive-behavioral therapy for anxiety

Muslim accommodative cognitive-behavioral therapy for schizophrenia

Christian accommodative cognitive-behavioral therapy for eating disorders

Source: Hook et al., 2010.

considered when determining which approach to use with a particular client.

Special Issues When Counseling Within Faith Traditions

Engaging in counseling with a client who shares a common faith system with the counselor provides both opportunity and possible barriers to success in promoting mental health. Indeed, being intimately familiar with core values and beliefs that a client holds can be of immediate benefit in the process of developing a helpful conceptualization of the client's strengths, needs, struggles, and desires. Though insider experience can be a rich resource to draw upon when conceptualizing clients, clinicians should be wary of relying on generalizations with clients who claim to share their religious and spiritual beliefs. When counseling within religious traditions, skilled psychotherapists will realize there are nuances within every belief system, and they will carefully assess for this rather than make assumptions.

Potential Benefits

Life for most is complex, and struggle is a common human condition. Regardless of the specific treatment goals, the process of therapy can be enriched for clients who feel confident that their therapist is a fellow companion traveling a similar faith journey. Common among many faith traditions is the teaching that fellow believers are spiritual brothers and sisters. Safety, understanding, loyalty, acceptance, and love between spiritual siblings are powerful ideas often wrapped within this common faith belief. Knowing that one's therapist is a spiritual sister or brother has power in establishing immediate alliance within the therapeutic relationship. Many therapists have experienced similar reactions from clients when a shared faith commitment is made known: "Thank goodness; I am so happy to hear that, I was really hoping you would share the same faith as me; I was worried you wouldn't be a believer; Good, now I know you are safe." In choosing a provider, clients may view the religious beliefs of a therapist as a deciding factor, potentially more important than the provider's education, experience, and training.

Cultural differences may serve as an obstacle to forming a therapeutic alliance, but when the psychotherapist and client share the same religious or spiritual faith, it often serves as a powerful point of connection even when other cultural characteristics are not shared. An example of this is seen in McMinn's (2006) work with a stressed and anxious client. McMinn, a European American man, and his client, an African American woman, created a therapeutic bond based on shared faith experience despite their other differences. Sisemore (2006) observes, "As this White male works with an African American woman, we assume cultural distance. Yet, they share a vital 'culture' in common, the Christian faith."

Beyond establishing rapport, seeking a counselor or psychotherapist with similar faith beliefs may help clients overcome the stigma that is commonly attached to seeking mental health treatment within some prominent religious groups. This barrier is most easily overcome if the counselor discloses information about similar faith beliefs to the client early in the treatment relationship. Thus, working within faith traditions can provide the safety and security that many clients need in order to enter into and benefit from professional counseling.

Potential Concerns

The psychotherapist working within faith traditions ought to take heed, however, for while doing so may promote an immediate connection with the client and facilitate openness to psychotherapy, it can later present a formidable barrier to the therapeutic process. Clients who knowingly share a religious tradition with their therapist may feel less comfortable discussing personal thoughts and behaviors that do not conform to what is generally considered acceptable within the system. Indeed, sharing common beliefs regarding what is morally acceptable may lead to feelings of shame within the client–therapist relationship when the client's behaviors conflict with religious norms and values. The power of unconditional positive regard experienced from therapist to client has been thoroughly researched, and this essential common factor in most therapeutic interventions can be sabotaged by the faith-sharing client's internal sense of shame.

Being an insider within a client's faith-influenced worldview can potentially limit a therapist's ability to assist a client in modifying thought processes or schemas. Perhaps the religious beliefs contribute in some way to the client's inability to identify and restructure thinking patterns that are maladaptive, such as when someone with a rigid belief system is forced to grapple with life circumstances that are fraught with complexity and ambiguity. Indeed, when faced with tragedy, it is not uncommon for people to struggle with their faith, even to the point of abandoning their beliefs altogether (Exline & Rose, 2005). For clients dissatisfied with a faith system that encourages reliance on long-established tenets to explain suffering and hardship, a therapist who shares the same faith might be tempted to focus on resolving the clients' questions rather than allowing the client to accept the ambiguity and uncertainty of life. Training and supervision can help a therapist working with clients who share his or her faith tradition to maintain a broad perspective when considering treatment options.

The possibility of detrimental internal reactions when working within faith traditions is not limited to clients. Therapists are prone to experiencing varying levels of personal distress as well, such as when working with clients who are struggling with faith beliefs, disillusioned with their faith, in the process of leaving their faith, or understand their faith in ways contrary to the therapist's interpretation. It is important in these instances for the clinician to avoid exerting undue power or influence over clients to bend their thought processes back into what the therapist deems religiously or theologically appropriate. Doing so would be overstepping the role of a psychotherapist. In this instance the psychotherapist would be attempting to assume the role of a religious leader. Whereas debating theology or spiritual issues may be appropriate for a rabbi, pastor, priest, or monk, doing so does not fall within the bounds of most professional psychotherapist–client relationships. For those therapists who believe such discussion might be helpful to a client, referral to religious and spiritual professionals within the clients' faith community is often the best solution.

Therapists working within faith traditions, particularly when clients come from the same religious community, should carefully consider the presence and effect of multiple role relationships. Working within one's own spiritual community highly increases the risk of clinicians forming multiple relationships with clients. Indeed, because of this Richards and Bergin (2005) discourage clinicians from working within their local congregations. They support this stance with a number of arguments. First, the client and therapist are more likely to make outside social contacts, as they frequent the same religious services. These contacts increase the risk of developing therapist-personal friend, therapist-lover, or therapist-business partner dual relationships. Second, clients who have shared intimate life details with a therapist who attends the same religious gatherings may feel embarrassed, awkward, and uncomfortable. Such clients may go on to discontinue attending religious services in order to avoid encountering their therapist. Third, therapists are more at risk of violating their clients' confidentiality. Therapists may inadvertently disclose information discussed in a therapy session, mistakenly believing it was learned outside of treatment.

Richards and Bergin (2005) recommend the following dos and don'ts for therapists practicing within their own faith communities (p. 187–188):

1. Therapists should avoid therapist–religious leader and therapist–religious associate dual relationships.

2. After carefully considering the circumstances, if a therapist believes that a dual relationship may be in a person's best interest, the therapist should, before entering into such a relationship, consult with his or her supervisor and professional colleagues to see whether they agree.

3. If the therapist and professional colleagues agree that the risk of a professional–religious dual relationship is warranted, the therapist should carefully define and limit the extent of the dual relationship and explain the risks and boundaries to the client.

4. The therapist should consult frequently with professional colleagues about the case as the dual relationship proceeds. If at any time the client, the therapist, or the therapist's professional colleagues believe the client is being harmed by the dual relationship, the therapist should terminate the relationship and refer the client to another therapist.

5. The therapist should continue to consult with and inform professional colleagues about the case until the dual relationship has ended and the case has been carefully documented.

Special Issues When Counseling Across Faith Traditions

Counseling across faith traditions brings potential challenges. Although these challenges can be bridged, it takes understanding and effort on the part of the therapist. For starters, most faith traditions inherently bring with them specific definitions of health and healing. While we would love to say that therapy is a purely objective enterprise, experience tells us that subjectivity always plays a role in the process of therapy. Just as counseling across cultures requires keen self-awareness on the part of the counselor, so also it is imperative that therapists explore their own religious and spiritual beliefs, and potential biases and limitations, when it comes to working across faith traditions. Training and supervision should be sought out where appropriate in order to maintain cultural sensitivity and to counter the potential pitfalls of issues such as countertransference, misguided interventions, and misdiagnoses stemming from cultural biases.

It is also useful to consider the disclosure of one's faith values. Therapists may choose to advertise their faith tradition, to join with religious leaders as sources of networking and referral for religious clients, or to disclose their faith within informed consent, either verbally or written. While this may appeal to some clinicians, others prefer to keep their personal lives more private. Still, there is always the possibility that clients may inquire about their psychotherapist's faith background. Answering such questions may encourage the establishment of rapport. Self-disclosure in this instance may be a culturally sensitive strength, as therapists can join their client around notions of ultimate meaning and spiritual quest, without having to share the same religious worldview. Exploring the client's reasons for asking such questions may lead to important insights that can add to the richness of therapy for the client.

A client may have fears about working with a therapist who does not share her or his worldview; these fears can be discussed openly, much as fears about ethnic and cultural differences might be discussed. Therapists may wish to share their theoretical orientation and typical way of conducting therapy; then, clients can choose whether to pursue psychotherapy. Most important may be the client's desire to see how the therapist responds to faith beliefs in general. Is the therapist respectful versus shaming, and open-minded versus stereotyping?

Some clients may be relieved to have a therapist who does not share their faith tradition but is rather a neutral party. For example, this might be the case when a client is struggling with faith beliefs, wrestling with issues that are not well received by the person's faith community, or struggling against religious power systems or unjust treatment by members of a religious community. In these cases, the therapist would do well to align with his or her client's experiences, while simultaneously avoiding criticism of the client's beliefs.

In addition to issues of disclosure, counselors and psychotherapists ought to consider basic knowledge of religious systems. Mental health professionals should have at least a basic understanding of world religions. This is a vital aspect of cross-cultural competency, which has been recognized by APA (2002) and continues to be a growing topic in the field. If their education has not included such a course, therapists can educate themselves about religious systems in advance.

When counseling across faith traditions, the knowledge that a psychotherapist brings into the consulting office should always be accompanied by a posture of learning and exploring with the client what faith has meant to him or her as an individual. As unique participants in their faith traditions, clients will present with highly varied experiences. Even within the majority of world religions, there are diverse streams and innumerable subtleties that go beyond the terms "Muslim" and "Christian," for example. Questions such as the following may be helpful:

What about your faith is most significant to you personally?

What does your faith look like in your daily life?

How do you view yourself, others, and the world in light of your faith?

Priester, Khalili, and Luvathingal (2009) suggest the following potential questions (pp. 107–108):

What was your experience of religion as a child?

What aspects of your parents' religion did you like and/or dislike?

Did you go through any major religious changes in your life? Any conversion experiences? Any changes in denomination?

What religious beliefs bring you the most comfort?

What religious practices bring you the most comfort or feelings of support?

At what point in your life did you feel closest to your God(s)?

At what point in your life did you feel most distant from God?

Finally, when providing mental health services across faith traditions, it is important to consider collaborative models of intervention, as described earlier in this chapter. If a patient's presenting problem is faith based in nature, or the person requests spiritually oriented interventions, it may be helpful to consult with a clergy member from the patient's religious faith tradition. Most religious clergy will be happy to consult, and doing so may again help to build rapport with the client. In some cases, a psychotherapist may wish to refer a client to a clergy member or layperson who shares the client's faith tradition, as an additional source of support. When considering referring a client to a clergy member for care, and also discontinuing treatment, it is important to consider why the client originally came to seek help from a psychotherapist, as well as the severity of the psychological symptoms being treated.

Conclusion

In this chapter we have discussed general considerations for religiously and spiritually oriented psychotherapy and counseling. These include viewing religion and spirituality as cultural diversity issues, considering the welfare of the client, respecting the client's autonomy, and maintaining competence. We then considered different intervention approaches, including assimilative, accommodative, and collaborative approaches. Finally, we addressed specific issues related to counseling when the client and counselor share the same beliefs, and when the client and counselor hold differing beliefs. In the process we have cited the sparse outcome literature that is available and suggested that a great deal more research is needed.

Most world religions teach something akin to the Golden Rule—that we should treat others the way we would like to be treated ourselves. Perhaps this is the most fitting and useful summary statement than can be offered when considering religious and spiritual issues—an area that has received relatively less attention than other forms of human diversity in counseling and psychotherapy. Until we have clearer research findings and clinical practice guidelines, it may be most useful to use the Golden Rule as a standard of care. Do we offer our clients the same sort of respect and autonomy that we ourselves wish to have with our spiritual and religious values? Do we have the basic knowledge to engage in informed conversation and understand the nuances of our clients' beliefs? Are we willing to keep mental health goals the first priority, recognizing the need to protect our clients by practicing within the scope afforded us by our training and professional credentials? Do we stay current with the literature so that we can offer clients the best care available, in a way that is sensitive to human diversity?

Future Directions

We suggest two primary areas for future development: research and training. Regarding research, there is currently a paucity of research on religious and spiritual approaches to psychotherapy, and what little has been reported has focused entirely on accommodative approaches. Most of these studies have focused on religion rather than spirituality that is not linked to religious belief. Questions for the future include the following:

1. What effects on outcome and therapeutic alliance result when a counselor or psychotherapist introduces a spiritually oriented intervention in an otherwise standard approach to treatment (assimilative approach)?

2. To what extent do the therapist and client need to share a similar faith perspective when an accommodative intervention is used?

3. We need to move beyond global questions of whether religiously based approaches are effective. A more refined question for the future is, Which therapies are useful for which individuals holding which religious and spiritual beliefs?

4. What interventions work best with those who identify themselves as spiritual but not religious?

As with research, training in religious and spiritual issues is still in its infancy. Practice standards are being discussed (Hathaway & Ripley, 2009), but they have not yet been developed and formalized, which means that no standardized training models or criteria are available. Moreover, there seems to be some ongoing resistance to training in religious and spiritual interventions, with a majority of APA internship training directors reporting that they do not foresee training students in religious or spiritual issues (Russell & Yarhouse, 2006) and only a small minority of APA accredited doctoral programs providing systematic education regarding religious and spiritual issues (Brawer, Handal, Fabricatore, Roberts, & Wajda-Johnston, 2002). Thus, we offer the following training-related questions:

1. What minimal standards in religious and spiritual issues should be expected of all professional psychology and counselor education training programs?

2. Much as cultural diversity training begins with self-awareness, how can self-awareness be enhanced regarding religious and spiritual worldview issues?

3. What sort of practicum and internship training opportunities might be available if we considered collaborative training opportunities within religious communities?

4. What ethical issues need to be considered and reconsidered in light of current practices for counseling within and across faith traditions?

Counselors and psychotherapists are routinely invited into the most intimate places of clients' lives. Some would call them sacred places. Learning to enter quietly, respectfully, and appreciatively is a worthy endeavor.

Further Reading

Aten, J. D., & Leach, M. M. (Eds.). (2009). Spirituality and the therapeutic process: A comprehensive resource from intake through termination. Washington, DC: American Psychological Association Books.

Aten, J. D., McMinn, M. R., & E. L. Worthington, Jr. (Eds.). (2011). Spirituality oriented interventions for counseling and psychotherapy. Washington, DC: American Psychological Association.

Pargament, K. I. (2007). Spiritually integrated psychotherapy: Understanding and addressing the sacred. New York: The Guilford Press.

Richards, P. S., & Bergin, A. E. (2005). A spiritual strategy for counseling and psychotherapy (2nd ed.). Washington, DC: American Psychological Association.

Sperry, L., & Shafranske, E. P. (Eds.). (2005). Spiritually oriented psychotherapy. Washington, DC: American Psychological Association.

References

American Psychological Association. (2002). Ethical principles of psychologists and code of conduct. American Psychologist, 57, 1060–1073.

Aten, J. D., & Leach, M. M. (Eds.). (2009). Spirituality and the therapeutic process: A comprehensive resource from intake through termination. Washington, DC: American Psychological Association.

Aten, J. D., McMinn, M. R., & Worthington, E. L., Jr. (Eds.). (2011). Spirituality oriented interventions for counseling and psychotherapy. Washington, DC: American Psychological Association.

Bartoli, E., & Gillem, A. (2008). Continuing to depolarize the debate on sexual orientation and religion: Identity and the therapeutic process. Professional Psychology - Research and Practice, 39, 202–209.

Beckstead, A. L. (2001). Cures versus choices: Agendas in sexual reorientation therapy. Journal of Gay and Lesbian Psychotherapy, 5, 87–115.

Benes, K. M., Walsh, J. M., McMinn, M. R., Dominguez, A. W., & Aikins, D. C. (2000). Psychology and the church: An exemplar of psychology-clergy collaboration. Professional Psychology: Research and Practice, 31, 515–520.

Benner, D. G. (2005). Intensive soul care: Integrating psychotherapy and spiritual direction. In L. Sperry & E. P. Shafranske (Eds.), Spiritually oriented psychotherapy (pp. 287–306). Washington, DC: American Psychological Association.

Brawer, P. A., Handal, P. J., Fabricatore, A. N., Roberts, R., & Wajda-Johnston, V. A. (2002). Training and education in religion/spirituality within APA-accredited clinical psychology programs. Professional Psychology: Research and Practice, 33, 203–206.

Budd, F., & Newton, M. (2005). Healing the brokenhearted: Cross and couch together. In M. R. McMinn & A. D. Dominguez (Eds.), Psychology and the church (pp. 89–93). Hauppauge, NY: Nova Science Publishers.

Budd, F. C. (1999). An Air Force model of psychologist-chaplain collaboration. Professional Psychology: Research and Practice, 30, 552–556.

Edwards, L. C., Lim, R. K. B., McMinn, M. R., & Dominguez, A. W. (1999). Examples of collaboration between psychologists and clergy. Professional Psychology: Research and Practice, 30, 547–551.

Ellis, A. (1962). Reason and emotion in psychotherapy. Secaucus, NJ: Lyle Stuart.

Ellis, A. (1971). The case against religion: A psychotherapist's view. New York: Institute for Rational Living.

Ellis, A. (1983). The case against religiosity. New York: Institute for Rational-Emotive Therapy.

Ellis, A. (1993). The advantages and disadvantages of self-help therapy materials. Professional Psychology: Research and Practice, 24, 335–339.

Ellis, A. (1999). How to make yourself happy and remarkably less disturbed. San Luis Obispo, CA: Impact Publishers.

Ellis, A. (2000). Spiritual goals and spirited values in psychotherapy. Journal of Individual Psychology, 56, 277–284.

Ellis, A., & Harper, R. A. (1997). A guide to rational living (3rd ed.). North Hollywood, CA: Melving Powers.

Ellis, A., & MacLaren, C. (1998). Rational emotive behavior therapy: A therapist's guide. San Luis Obispo, CA: Impact Publishers.

Emmons, R. A. (1999). The psychology of ultimate concerns: Motivation and spirituality in personality. New York: The Guilford Press.

Exline, J. J., & Rose, E. (2005). Religious and spiritual struggles. In R. F. Paloutzian & C. L. Park (Eds.), Handbook of the psychology of religion and spirituality (pp. 315–330). New York: The Guilford Press.

Fitchett, G., Rybarczyk, B. D., DeMarco, G. A., & Nichols, J. J. (1999). The role of religion in medical rehabilitation outcomes: A longitudinal study. Rehabitation Psychology, 44, 1–22.

Frame, M. W. (2003). Integrating religion and spirituality into counseling: A comprehensive approach. Belmont, CA: Brooks/Cole.

Gallup, G. H. (2003, February 11). Americans' spiritual searches turn inward. Retrieved July 2009, from http://www.gallup.com/poll/7759/Americans-Spiritual-Searches-Turn-Inward.aspx

Gallup Polls, Inc. (2009). Religion. Retrieved June 2009, from http://www.gallup.com/poll/1690/religion.aspx

Gonsiorek, J. C., Richards, P. S., Pargament, K. I., & McMinn, M. R. (2009). Ethical challenges and opportunities at the edge: Incorporating spirituality and religion into psychotherapy. Professional Psychology: Research and Practice, 40, 385–395.

Greene, B. (2008). African American women, religion, and oppression: The use and abuse of spiritual beliefs. In C. A. Rayburn & L. Comas-Diaz (Eds.), WomanSoul: The inner life of women's spirituality (pp. 153–166). Westport, CT: Praeger Publishers/Greenwood Publishing Group.

Hackney, C. H., & Sanders, G. S. (2003). Religiosity and mental health: A meta-analysis of recent studies. Journal for the Scientific Study of Religion, 42, 43–55.

Hathaway, W. L., & Pargament, K. (1990). Intrinsic religiousness, religious coping, and psychosocial competence: A covariance structure analysis. Journal for the Scientific Study of Religion, 29(4), 423–441.

Hathaway, W. L., & Ripley, J. S. (2009). Ethical concerns around spirituality and religion in clinical practice. In J. D. Aten & M. M. Leach (Eds.), Spirituality and the therapeutic process: A comprehensive resource from intake through termination (pp. 25–52). Washington, DC: American Psychological Association Books.

Hill, P. C., & Pargament, K. I. (2003). Advances in the conceptualization and measurement of religion and spirituality: Implications for physical and mental health research. American Psychologist, 58, 64–74.

Hood, R., Spilka, B., Hunsberger, B., & Gorsuch, R. (1996). The psychology of religion: An empirical approach (2nd ed.). New York: The Guildford Press.

Hook, J. N., Worthington, E. L., Jr., Davis, D. E., Jennings, D. J., II, Gartner, A. L., & Hook, J. P. (2010). Empirically supported religious and spiritual therapies. Journal of Clinical Psychology, 66, 46–72.

Johnson, C., & Hayes, J. (2003). Troubled spirits: Prevalence and predictors of religious and spiritual concerns among university students and counseling center clients. Journal of Counseling Psychology, 50(4), 409–419.

Keating, A. M., & Fretz, B. R. (1990). Christians' anticipations about counselors in response to counselor descriptions. Journal of Counseling Psychology, 37, 293–296.

Kennedy, S. M. (1999). Religious perfectionism: A first step toward conceptualization and assessment (Ph.D. dissertation, Pennsylvania State University, 1999). Dissertation Abstracts International, 59, 4531.

Koenig, H. G., McCullough, M. E., & Larson, D. B. (2001). Handbook of religion and health. Oxford, England: Oxford University Press.

Lukoff, D., Lu, F., & Turner, R. (1998). From spiritual emergency to spiritual problem: The transpersonal roots of the new DSM-IV category. Journal of Humanistic Psychology, 38, 21–50.

Lish, R. A., McMinn, M. R., Fitzsimmons, C. R., & Root, A. M. (2003). Clergy interest in innovative collaboration with psychologists. Journal of Psychology and Christianity, 22, 294–298.

McCullough, M. E. (1999). Research on religion-accommodative counseling: Review and meta-analysis. Journal of Counseling Psychology, 46, 92–98.

McCullough, M. E., Hoyt, W. T., Larson, D. B., Koenig, H. G., & Thoresen, C. (2000). Religious involvement and mortality: A meta-analytic review. Health Psychology, 19, 211–222.

McIntosh, D., & Spilka, B. (1990). Religion and physical health: The role of personal faith and control beliefs. Research in the Social Scientific Study of Religion, 2, 167–194.

McMinn, M. R. (2006). Christian counseling [DVD in APA Psychotherapy Video Series]. Washington, DC: American Psychological Association.

McMinn, M. R., Aikins, D. C., & Lish, R. A. (2003). Basic and advanced competence in collaborating with clergy. Professional Psychology: Research and Practice, 34, 197–202.

McMinn, M. R., Chaddock, T. P., Edwards, L. C., Lim, R. K. B., & Campbell, C. D. (1998). Psychologists collaborating with clergy: Survey findings and implications. Professional Psychology: Research and Practice, 29, 564–570.

McMinn, M. R., Worthington, E. L., Jr., & Aten, J. D. (2011). Spiritually oriented interventions: Future directions in training and research. In J. D. Aten, M. R. McMinn, & E. L. Worthington, Jr. (Eds.), Spiritually oriented interventions in counseling and psychotherapy (pp. 345–351). Washington, DC: American Psychological Association.

Miller, W. R., & Delaney, H. D. (Eds.) (2005). Judeo-Christian perspectives on psychology: Human nature, motivation, and change. Washington, DC: American Psychological Association.

Miller, W. R., & Thoresen, C. E. (2003). Spirituality, religion, and health: An emerging research field. American Psychologist, 58, 24–35.

Nielsen, S. L., Johnson, W. B., & Ellis, A. (2001). Counseling and psychotherapy with religious persons: A Rational Emotive Behavior Therapy approach. Mahwah, NJ: Erlbaum.

O'Connor, S., & Vandenberg, B. (2005). Psychosis or faith? Clinicians' assessment of religious beliefs. Journal of Consulting and Clinical Psychology, 73, 610–616.

Pargament, K. I. (1997). The psychology of religion and coping: Theory, research, practice. New York: The Guilford Press.

Pargament, K. I. (2007). Spiritually integrated psychotherapy: Understanding and addressing the sacred. New York: The Guilford Press.

Pargament, K. I., Kennell, J., Hathaway, W., & Grevengoed, N. (1988). Religion and the problem-solving process: Three styles of coping. *Journal for the Scientific Study of Religion, 27*, 1, 90–104.

Pargament, K. I., Koenig, H. G., Tarakeshwar, N., & Hahn, J. (2001). Religious struggle as a predictor of mortality among medically ill elderly patients: A 2-year longitudinal study. *Archives of Internal Medicine, 161,* 1881–1885.

Plante, T. G. (2011). Addressing problematic spirituality in therapy. In J. D. Aten, M. R. McMinn, & E. L. Worthington, Jr. (Eds.), Spiritually oriented interventions in counseling and psychotherapy (pp. 83–106). Washington, DC: American Psychological Association.

Post, S. G. (2005). Altruism, happiness, and health: It's good to be good. *International Journal of Behavioral Medicine, 12*(2), 66–77.

Powell, L. H., Shahabi, L., & Thoresen, C. E. (2003). Religion and spirituality: Linkages to physical health. *American Psychologist, 58,* 36–52.

Priester, P. E., Khalili, S., & Luvathingal, J. E. (2009). Placing the soul back into psychology: Religion in the psychotherapy process. In S. Eshun & R. A. R. Gurung (Eds.), *Culture and mental health: Sociocultural influences, theory, and practice* (pp. 91–114). Oxford, England: Blackwell Publishing.

Richards, P. S., & Bergin, A. E. (2005). A spiritual strategy for counseling and psychotherapy (2nd ed.). Washington, DC: American Psychological Association.

Russell, S. R., & Yarhouse, M. A. (2006). Religion/spirituality within APA-accredited psychology predoctoral internships. *Professional Psychology: Research and Practice, 37,* 430–436.

Salsman, J. M., & Carlson, C. R. (2005). Religious orientation, mature faith, and psychological distress: Elements of positive and negative associations. *Journal for the Scientific Study of Religion, 44,* 201–209.

Schaefer, C., & Gorsuch, R. (1991). Psychological adjustment and religiousness: The multivariate belief-motivation theory of religiousness. *Journal for the Scientific Study of Religion, 30*(4), 448–461.

Schlosser, L. Z., & Safran, D. A. (2009). Implementing treatments that incorporate clients' spirituality. In J. D. Aten & M. M. Leach (Eds.), Spirituality and the therapeutic process: A comprehensive resource from intake through termination (pp. 193–216). Washington, DC: American Psychological Association Books.

Schwartz, C., Meisenhelder, J. B., Ma, Y., & Reed, G. (2002). Altruistic social interest behaviors are associated with better mental health. *Psychosomatic Medicine, 65,* 778–785.

Seeman, T. E., Dubin, L. F., & Seeman, M. (2003). Religiosity/spirituality and health: A critical review of the evidence for biological pathways. *American Psychologist, 58,* 53–63.

Shafranske, E. P. (1996). Religious beliefs, affiliations, and practices of clinical psychologists. In E. P. Shafranske (Ed.), Religion and the clinical practice of psychology (pp. 149–162). Washington, DC: American Psychological Association.

Sisemore, T. A. (2006, December 27). Christian counseling: An area of cultural diversity? *PsycCritiques, 51*(52).

Slattery, J. M., & Park, C. L. (2011). Meaning-making and spiritually oriented interventions. In J. D. Aten, M. R. McMinn, & E. L. Worthington, Jr. (Eds.), Spirituality oriented interventions for counseling and psychotherapy (pp. 15–40). Washington, DC: American Psychological Association.

Sperry, L. (2005). Integrative spiritually oriented psychotherapy. In L. Sperry & E. P. Shafranske (Eds.), Spiritually oriented psychotherapy (pp. 307–329). Washington, DC: American Psychological Association.

Sperry, L., & Shafranske, E. P. (Eds.) (2005). Spiritually oriented psychotherapy. Washington, DC: American Psychological Association.

Sue, D. W., & Sue, D. (2007). Counseling the culturally diverse (5th ed.). New York: Wiley.

Weaver, A. J. (1995). Has there been a failure to support parish-based clergy in their role as frontline community mental health workers? A review. *The Journal of Pastoral Care, 49*(2), 129–149.

Wiggins, M. I. (2011). Spiritual journaling. In J. D. Aten, M. R. McMinn, & E. L. Worthington, Jr. (Eds.), Spirituality oriented interventions for counseling and psychotherapy (pp. 303–321). Washington, DC: American Psychological Association.

Young, J. S., Cashwell, C., Wiggins-Frame, M., & Belaire, C. (2002). Spiritual and religious competencies: A national survey of CACREP-accredited programs. *Counseling and Values, 47,* 22–33.

Psychoanalysis, Psi Phenomena, and Spiritual Space: Common Ground

Ruth Rosenbaum

Abstract

Psychoanalysis, psi phenomena (telepathy, clairvoyance, and psychokinesis), and spirituality might appear to be strange bedfellows. However, with the evolution of psychoanalytic theories of intersubjectivity and scientific studies of psi phenomena, a portrait has emerged of the kind of space within which the self exists. It is a space characterized by indistinct boundaries between self and other, a shared space, and it appears to be crucial for psychological growth and transformation. This concept of the self connecting with an "other" beyond its own localized boundaries is also the basis of spiritual experience and spiritually inspired forms of transformation, such as miracles and mystical states. In exploring the common ground shared by these overlapping territories of the self's expansive reach, we may discover the conditions that enhance the possibilities for change and growth in psychoanalysis and, in the process, approach a more comprehensive understanding of the nature of consciousness itself.

Key Words: psi phenomena, consciousness, conscious, unconscious, intersubjective field, attunement, resonance, spiritual space

Introduction

One does not need an elaborate study to conclude that nearly every human being, at some point in life, has wished or prayed for a miracle—for an event or outcome so unlikely that it would seem to be an impossibility. Whether it be recovery from a terminal illness, a much-needed windfall, a romantic connection, or an available parking spot, the appeal of a miracle is not only that it solves an immediate problem, but that it engenders a direct feeling of connection with something or someone beyond the self, whether defined as God, the universe, luck, or an infinite, ineffable "source." The experience of a miracle immediately lifts the self out of a space of isolation, and out of the predictability of the mundane, into an awareness of a larger, transcendent scope of reality within which all things are possible. This direct experience of the astonishing magnitude of reality has the potential to transform

our experience of being in the world and of being in ourselves.

What characterizes miracles, whether in casual form (any highly unlikely but beneficial event) or in Biblical form (e.g., the parting of the Red Sea, Christ's walking on water), is that they are "in some remarkable sense 'contrary to the normal course of nature'" (Flew, 1967, p. 347). In psychoanalysis, patient and therapist seek to transform what would ordinarily be "the normal course of nature," the "normal course" being the universal human tendency to engage repeatedly in life from the same set of perspectives, perspectives shaped by a complex tangle of nature, nurture, and culture, which often lead to various forms of suffering and lack of fulfillment. It truly seems like a miracle when a person who has experienced extreme trauma in childhood can emerge from a pattern of chronic self-destructive behavior to lead a constructive, enjoyable life, or when an "untreatable" schizophrenic, through a healing relationship with a therapist, can enjoy a productive, satisfying life, sometimes without medication (Dorman, 2004; Greenberg, 1964; Steinman, 2009). Even on a less dramatic scale, small changes in our habitual perspectives can have a profound effect on our capacity to experience joy and fulfillment in life.

To illuminate the kind of space in which the miracle of psychological transformation is most likely to take place, this chapter will focus on areas of convergence of psychoanalysis, spiritual space, and psi phenomena. Each of these three seemingly disparate realms facilitates experience outside the generally expected or "normal" course of events and, like the proverbial blind men trying to describe an elephant, each reveals a different aspect of the way the self participates in what psychologist and philosopher William James (1902/1985) called the "reality of the unseen" (p. 53). It appears, as will be discussed, that the process of psychological change and growth is reliant on permeable boundaries between self and other, and on modes of relating that are beyond logical, explicit description. These same features characterize spiritual experience and psi phenomena such as telepathy, clairvoyance, and psychokinesis.

What You Don't See Is What You Get: Our Implicit, Unseen Reality

Psychoanalytic theory rests on an unseen, elusive foundation: the unconscious. Supporting Freud's contention that unconscious mental processes dominate our behavior, motivation, and experience far more than do conscious processes, recent research in cognitive science indicates that the role of the unconscious in guiding our behavior is even greater than previously understood (Gilhooley, 2008). On the level of visual perception alone, scientists estimate that our eyes receive *and process* 10 million bits of information per second, of which only 16 can be engaged with consciously (Norretranders, 1998, p. 93), pointing to a truly "unseen" reality that is constantly affecting us yet far surpasses that which can be detected and processed by conscious awareness. The difference in proportion—10,000,000: 16—conveys some idea of the supremacy of unconscious mental activity over conscious, and that represents only one of our perceptual systems.

The existence of an unseen reality that permeates and enriches our "normal course" of quotidian activities and strivings is also the cornerstone of spirituality. In fact, spirituality involves a search for a deeper meaning or truth beyond what is evident on the surface of life. The mystic's exhilarating experience of oneness with everything and everyone points to a substrate of interconnectedness that eludes explicit observation. Spiritual space, the immeasurable space that surrounds and pervades our measured existence, is filled with infinite potential in which the self can participate and, in the process, shift from its "local" address in classical time and space to one which can be defined only by the absence of finite boundaries and measurements. The self in meditation, the self in prayer, the self in creative reverie, the self experiencing telepathy, the self in mystical union with nature or with another self in passionate lovemaking, and the self engaged with the "other" in the unique intimacy of the psychoanalytic relationship are all examples of the self's participation beyond its finite "seen" space.

What's Psi Got To Do With It?

Psi, a general term referring to types of communication or information transfer that defy common understanding of how such communication normally takes place, includes telepathy (communication between minds), clairvoyance (communication from environment to mind) and psychokinesis (the capacity to move objects or influence a physical system without any discernable physical means of doing so).[1] These phenomena indicate that the self participates in an as yet indefinable and unseen aspect of reality that defies our customary assumptions of the separation between our minds and our separation in time and space.

For example, remote viewing experiments, conducted at the Stanford Research Institute, and funded by the CIA, the Defense Intelligence Agency, the Army, the Navy, and NASA, demonstrated that subjects were able to draw or describe an undisclosed, randomly chosen target site that was visited and observed by an agent. The accuracy rate of these "remote viewings" produced against-chance odds of 10^{20} or a billion billion to one (Radin, 1997, p. 101). In other studies, the subject's accurate remote perceptions of the undisclosed site took place *before* the agent arrived at the site, and in some cases even before the site was selected. In these precognitive remote viewing experiments, conducted by the Princeton Engineering Anomalies Research Lab, accurate viewings produced odds against chance of a hundred billion to one (Radin, 1997, p. 105). Other studies of psi phenomena will be described later in this chapter, as they illuminate aspects of the intersubjective space shared by patient and therapist and of potential spiritual space.

Terms and Distinctions

Since the following terms can be used in different ways in different contexts, clarification as to their meaning in this discussion is important.

"Consciousness" refers to the process by which we engage in the perception, reception, creation, or contemplation of aspects of reality, either seen or unseen. It encompasses both conscious and unconscious mental processes.

The "unconscious" refers to that part of consciousness that is outside of awareness. It shares certain features with spiritual space, in that it is a nonlocal phenomenon (not confined by classical spatial parameters) and also transcends time (Freud, 1915/1957).

"Conscious" mental processes involve those aspects of consciousness of which we are aware. Conscious and unconscious mental processes are dynamic and fluid, in that something that was outside of awareness at one moment may enter conscious awareness at another, and vice versa.

One does not have to be conscious for consciousness to be engaged. For example, several studies (Kelly et al., 2007; Kihlstrom et al. 1990) demonstrate that patients who had been under deep general anesthesia, as well as patients in full cardiac arrest, have subsequently been able to cite details of conversation or behavior on the part of members of the surgical team, indicating that their consciousness had engaged with the environment even when conscious mental processes, by all known scientific measurements, were offline.

The Elephant in the Room: A Brief History of a Psychoanalytic Taboo

What an irony! Psychoanalysts invited the unconscious not only into the treatment room but also into popular culture. (Who has not heard of a "Freudian slip," defense mechanisms, or the id, ego, and superego?) Yet within the field of psychoanalysis, the concept of the unconscious has been carefully pruned so that experiences that appear to derive from similar soil, such as psi phenomena and spiritual experience, have, for the most part, been cordoned off from professional viewing. Psi phenomena, in particular, acquired such taboo status that analysts dared not make public their interest or possible belief in such phenomena for fear of damaging their reputations (Farrell, 1983; Mayer, 1996a, 2001, 2007).

For many decades, psychoanalysts had been practicing in the shadow of Freud's rejection of religion and spirituality. Writing of religion, he said:

> The whole thing is so patently infantile, so foreign to reality, that to anyone with a friendly attitude to humanity it is painful to think that the great majority of mortals will never be able to rise above this view of life.
> (*Freud,* 1930/1961b, p. 74)

Freud's major thesis was that religion was "the universal obsessional neurosis of humanity; like the obsessional neurosis of children, it arose out of the Oedipus complex, out of the relation to the father" (1927/1961a, p. 43).

As for spiritual experience, Freud (1930/1961b) made his view clear in his response to his friend Romain Rolland's description of a feeling he experienced often: "a sensation of 'eternity,' a feeling as of something limitless, unbounded—as it were, 'oceanic'" (p. 11). Freud stated that he could not discover this oceanic feeling in himself and, furthermore, that:

> the idea of men's receiving an intimation of their connection with the world around them through an immediate feeling…sounds so strange and fits in so badly with the fabric of our psychology that one is justified in attempting to discover a psychoanalytic—that is, genetic—derivation of such a feeling.
> (p. 12)

Though in recent years, many psychoanalysts (Bion, 1970/1995; Eigen 1998, 2001; Gargiulo, 2006/2007; Gottesfeld, 1985; Grotstein, 1998; Loewald, 1978; Matte-Blanco, 1975; Meissner, 1984) have recognized the legitimate place of a patient's religion and spirituality in analytic discourse, Roland (2011) points out that the field in general is still uncomfortable with elements of spiritual experience that lie outside the Judeo-Christian tradition. Also, few who write about spirituality and psychoanalysis consider the contribution that studies of psi phenomena can make to understanding the interconnectedness of self and other that is fundamental to both topics. Schermer (2003), for example, in an extensive exploration of psychology, psychoanalysis, and spirituality, pointedly excludes the subject of paranormal or psi phenomena (p. 26).

Interestingly, Freud (1922/1973a, 1925/1973b, 1933/1965, 1933/1973c, 1941d/1973) was more open to serious consideration of psi phenomena, particularly telepathy, than he was to religion or spirituality. Though he engaged in a complex dance of approach-avoidance regarding the subject, he was clearly fascinated by it and thought that psychoanalysis and telepathy were vitally related. "I should like to point out," he stated:

> that by inserting the unconscious between the physical and what has hitherto been regarded as mental, psychoanalysis has prepared the way for the acceptance of such processes as telepathy. If one gets used to the idea of telepathy one can account for a great deal by means of it.…
> (*Freud*, 1933/1973c, p. 108)

Freud was a member of both the British and the American Society for Psychical Research, and, in 1921, wrote to an acquaintance: "If I had my life to live over again I should devote myself to psychical research rather than to psychoanalysis" (Jones, 1957, p. 392). He proposed that telepathy was an activity of the unconscious mind, and that similar to the way in which one could learn about repressed unconscious wishes through dreams, one could also find "messages" from the unconscious in telepathically received material (Freud, 1922/1973a). He analyzed the readings of several fortunetellers, including one he called "a genuine 'medium'" (Freud, 1941/1973d, p. 62), and suggested that an unconscious wish could be transmitted from one person to another along with thoughts and factual material related to the wish. In fact, some of the apparently erroneous facts produced by the fortunetellers turned out to be accurate when viewed from the perspective of the clients' inner (unseen) reality—their unconscious wishes and fantasies, as opposed to their observable (seen) reality.

Yet, because it was Freud's priority to protect psychoanalysis from contamination from the occultists and table-tappers of the time and to assure its place in history as a scientifically based endeavor, he ultimately distanced himself from an area of exploration that may have allowed him to learn more about his overriding passion—the exploration of the unconscious. Though early on, a handful of analysts (Balint, 1955; Burlingham, 1935; Ehrenwald, 1948; Eisenbud, 1946, 1947; Servadio, 1935/1973) explored the subject of telepathy, particularly as it occurred in the analytic session, for the most part the subject remained associated with infantile or magical, delusional thinking.

As Eisenbud (1946), commented:

> one of the most remarkable facts in the history of the psychoanalytic movement is the indifference with which Freud's publications on the subject of telepathy have been received… In the more than twenty years that have elapsed since Freud's first publication on the subject in 1922, scarcely more than a half dozen psychoanalytic authors have made clinical contributions to the field, and most of these have published single communications followed by strange and enduring silences.
> (p. 32)

With a few exceptions, this silence endured for the next several decades.

In recent years, some analysts, among them Bass (2001), Eshel (2006), and Suchet (2004), have written about their patients' telepathic dreams and the uncanny "knowing" and unconscious communication that can take place in the analytic session. However, they describe these occurrences as special instances of patient–analyst interconnectedness, resisting acknowledgment of the larger para-psychoanalytic implications of such experiences. Eshel (2006), for example, after an in-depth exploration of a patient's telepathic dreams, concludes:

> I find that this account did not take me into the domain of occultism, but rather into *the occult of psychoanalysis and the psychoanalytic process*… particularly of patient–analyst unconscious interconnectedness in the psychoanalytic situation and its "impossible" extremes, defying space, time and personal boundaries.
> (p. 1622)

There are, however, some analytic writers—Farrell (1983), Lazar (2001), Mayer (1996a, 1996b, 2001, 2007), and Tennes (2007)—who have not conveniently subsumed anomalous occurrences in psychoanalysis under proprietary psychoanalytic terms like "unconscious communication." Instead, they have urged consideration of these occurrences as instances of a much deeper realm of experience of which psychoanalysis is a part, and they have challenged the field's sequestering of the Freudian unconscious from other manifestations of unconscious activity.

Zero Degrees of Separation?

One of the most important factors responsible for the softening of the taboo against open discussion of psi phenomena by psychoanalysts has been the acceptance of intersubjective and relational theories of psychoanalysis. These approaches overturned the classical analytic notion of the self as an encapsulated entity, separate from other selves. They represented a radical departure from the Freudian one-person psychology, in which the analyst was a "blank screen" onto which the patient projected his dysfunctional patterns, which were then to be observed, examined, and treated with specific techniques in order to bring about a cure, much as a medical doctor examines a physical body and then applies a treatment. Intersubjective theory ushered in a reformulation of how selves interact in space together, and proposed that the individual unconscious does not reside strictly within the individual (Loewald, 1988).

The intersubjective field is co-constructed by the subjectivities of patient and analyst (Atwood & Stolorow, 1984) and, as in Ogden's (1994) related concept of the "analytic third" (p. 4), it is an essence of the relationship between patient and analyst that transcends a linear summation of their explicit communication. This field, unique to each patient–therapist dyad, becomes an active part of the analysis, resulting in a continuous unfolding of moments of possibility created by patient, therapist, and the field itself as it arises and evolves out of their mutual interactions, both conscious and unconscious.

Winnicott (1975) foreshadowed intersubjective theory with his description of transitional objects and phenomena, characterized by a lack of clear boundaries between inner and outer, subject and object, self and other. He spoke of an "intermediate area of experience" that is essential to the infant's development, and that "throughout life is retained in the intense experiencing that belongs to the arts and to religion and to imaginative thinking, and to creative scientific work" (p. 242). Ferenczi (Ferenczi & Rank, 1924/1986) was also an early proponent of what, in the 1980s, came to be known as the "two-person psychology" (Modell, 1984) underlying analytic treatment. In both intersubjective and relational thinking (Kohut, 1984; Mitchell, 1988; Stolorow, 1991; Stolorow, Brandchaft, & Atwood, 1987), the analyst–patient relationship emerged as a poetic parallel to the observer–observed relationship in quantum physics, in that the observer (analyst) has a mutative effect on the observed (patient) simply by virtue of the act of observing. The patient is no longer exactly who he was once he steps into the office of a particular therapist with particular theories, experiences, and personality traits—thus, the oft-cited observation that Freudian patients have Freudian dreams, Jungian patients have Jungian dreams, and so forth (Hufford, 2003). In intersubjective theory, the patient is also an observer, thus changing and affecting the analyst, so that each member of the dyad is both observer and observed,

creating an ongoing Mobius strip of interactive, creative transformations of self and other.

Kulka (1997) and Gargiulo (2010) elaborate on a quantum context for psychoanalysis, and for the growth of the self, underscoring the parallel between quantum wave-particle phenomena, and the creation, out of a field of wave-like possibilities in the analytic session, of in-the-moment particle-like interpretations and meaning. Though a quantum context is not identical to a spiritual context (and some physicists would bristle at any analogy between the two), the qualities of spiritual space and quantum space are alike in that both are implied spaces of boundless potential, not defined by measurable physical dimensions. We do not see quantum or spiritual space, but we assume their presence because particles, events, information, and life seem to emerge from them.

The Nature of Intersubjective Space

The intersubjective nature of the growth of the self acquired even more substantiation from research on nonverbal communication between mother and infant (Beebe & Lachmann, 2002). Fascinating frame-by-frame analysis of videotaped interaction between mothers and babies as young as 4 months old reveals split-second shifts in their mutually shaping responses to each other. These studies vividly illustrate how the psychological growth of the infant occurs within a relational context, each member of the dyad affecting and regulating the other's responses, primarily on an implicit, unconscious level. As adults, we continue to grow "in relation" to others. Paradoxically, the discovery of our individual "separate" selves is dependent upon the fact that we are never wholly separate from others. (In spiritual experience a related paradox exists: Discovery of the self often occurs through self-lessness, through a merging of the self with the divine or with God. Thus, the self is simultaneously lost and found through surrender to a relationship with the "Other.")

Unmediated Resonance

Our consciousness engages in Winnicott's "intermediate area" (1975) to such an extent that it is reasonable to postulate that all experience emerges from an intermediate, intersubjective space. What is this space like? A clue to the nature of intersubjective space can be found in the activity of mirror neurons, a type of premotor neuron first discovered in the mid-1990s in the prefrontal cortex in monkeys (Gallese, Fadiga, Fogassi, & Rizzolatti, 1996), and then in human brains as well. It was found that the same mirror neurons were activated not only when the monkeys executed certain actions but also when they observed the same action being performed by others. In humans, for example, if a person raises his hand, the same neurons fire in the brain of someone watching him as fire in the hand-raiser's brain. These neurons play a role in our immediate experience of what another experiences, as well as in understanding, without words, the intention of others (Iacoboni et al., 2005). They may be the neural basis for empathy, for our attunement to each other's inner states (Iacoboni, 2008). Mirror neurons, however, initiate a different kind of empathy than the classical "putting oneself in another's shoes." In the "embodied simulation" that is associated with mirror neuron activity, we are automatically, and without conscious effort, in each other's shoes. According to Gallese (2003), one of the discoverers of mirror neurons, we all participate in a prereflexive "shared intersubjective space" (p. 160). The kind of empathy facilitated by mirror neurons suggests a possible "unmediated resonance" (Goldman & Sripada, 2005, p. 207) between human beings.

Up until now, mirror neuron activation has been found to occur only when there is direct sensory observation of another's action or expression, so that other instances of "unmediated resonance," such as the mystic's merging with the infinite, or telepathy, or some of the mysterious forms of intersubjective experience that occur in psychoanalysis, require further explanation. Gallese, Eagle, and Migone (2007), for example, state that mirror neurons cannot account for projective identification, in which the analyst is said to have reactions and feelings that have been projected into his psyche by the patient's unconscious or split-off emotions. Some writers, they comment, have suggested telepathy as an explanation (p. 150). Note that projection is not a one-way street: The analyst's unconscious projections can penetrate the patient's psyche as well. In fact, therapeutic action in work with psychotic patients often involves the patient's introjecting and assimilating parts of the analyst's healthier, stronger ego (Searles, 1976, pp. 158–159).

Perhaps mirror neurons will eventually be discovered that do not require direct observation through the five senses, so that "observation" may ultimately extend to the entire spectrum of what can be perceived and responded to by the unconscious. Though neuroscience may never fully explain all intersubjective phenomena, it does seem as though our neurobiological structure primes us for experiences in which the self is not separate from the other, and in which shared intersubjective space is the rule, not the exception. At a conference on Neurobiology and Attachment Theory in Psychotherapy (June 2006), Allan Schore spoke of the "immediate connection" triggered by right hemisphere to right hemisphere attunement between patient and therapist. (The right hemisphere of the brain is thought to be the site of most unconscious communication and information processing.) This unmediated brain-to-brain resonance, Schore said, is more fundamental to positive change in the patient than any particular technique or verbal intervention.

Fields Without Borders

Though contemporary psychoanalysis has, for the most part, embraced the concept of an interactive, intersubjective field, and of a "two-person" psychology, it has stopped short of exploring the space in which the dyadic intersubjective field exists, as if there is a fence around the field within which baby and mother, or patient and analyst, interact with one another. Intersubjective theorists Atwood and Stolorow (1984) state that "patient and analyst together form an indissoluble psychological system" (p. 64); however, they do not address the space within which this psychological system exists. From a more comprehensive perspective, one can view the analytic experience as created and affected not only by what occurs within the dyad but also by the field that permeates it. Just as there are no fixed boundaries between patient and therapist, there are no fixed boundaries between the dyadic intersubjective field and the space or field that surrounds and suffuses it.

Green (2000) commented that "…our thinking about the 'inter' in psychoanalysis cannot be confined only to that which takes place between the two members of a couple; it also refers to another order of determination that eludes the observation of their relations" (p. 21). Similarly, Tennes (2007) suggests that:

> from a two-person model, we must move to one that is triadic, but one in which "the third" is not simply a product of the psyches of patient and analyst but is, rather, a superordinate field that, however inadequate our capacity to explain it, informs and contains the analytic encounter.
> (pp. 510–511)

Following is a case example of the possible interpenetration of the patient–therapist field with a superordinate field. As suggested by this case, the patient–therapist intersubjective field appears to establish a relational dynamic interaction with the intangible space that lies beyond it. There is a parallel between the interactive patient–therapist relationship and the interactive relationship between the patient–therapist field and the field of a larger reality or potential spiritual space.

Interpenetrating Fields—A Case Example

(Note: The patient's name and certain details have been changed in order to disguise his identity.)

Sam first came to see me because of a debilitating depression following a significant job disappointment. He was 42, very handsome, had made a fair amount of money in his architecture business, was a "golden boy" in many respects, and yet he had never maintained a relationship with a woman for more than 2 months. Sam's women had to be much younger, perfect looking, and under the Sam microscope, no one came close. He had a few friends, but even they found some of his rigid views on certain issues hard to bear. Sadly for Sam, he applied the same contemptuous lens toward himself, and, at 42, his life was worth little to him because he had not fulfilled the grand vision he had for himself—not enough money, not enough status, and no perfect wife and kids.

One day, I was running a few minutes late for his session, and when he came into the office and sat down, he had a quizzical smile on his face.

"I'd like to know what you think of this. I don't think this is really worth talking about, but listen to what happened. I was waiting for you and I had this bag of M&Ms, and to pass the time, I tried to guess what color the next M&M would be before I took it from the bag. And, you know, I got all but one right! I mean, I don't think it's more than coincidence; I hate all that New Age-y stuff, but, it's kind of interesting."

With any other patient, I might simply have nodded and listened for what would follow. But with Sam, I recognized that this event, so outside his usual set of expectations as to how the world worked, had caught his attention. I tried not to let it wander.

"What do you find interesting about it?" I asked.

"Oh, nothing really," he backed off smugly. "I thought you might find it interesting; I think women like these kinds of things."

"Well, then, that was very nice of you to tell me about it. But, you know, if it were truly insignificant to you, if you were absolutely certain it was *mere* coincidence, I don't think you would have mentioned it," I challenged.

"I guess I was wondering if there might be something to it, I mean, do you think I might have some kind of talent?"

I knew I had to tread cautiously. To play into a belief that Sam had special powers would simply fuel the old template and reinforce his absolute belief that he was worthless unless he could occupy a greater-than-mortal position. I felt that a healthy dose of uncertainty was called for.

So I said, "I don't know about that, but I do think it means that there is something outside your usual way of seeing things that in some way intrigues you. Maybe it's liberating to think that there's something you haven't yet categorized. You know, maybe there are more things in heaven and earth than are dreamt of in your philosophy."

"That's from *Hamlet*, isn't it?" Sam asked.

I nodded.

"Well," said Sam, "I don't think that supports anything. I don't want a quote from literature. I hated all those humanities majors in college! I want a scientific explanation."

For the moment, I dropped my end of the rope in this tug of war, and Sam went on to talk about other things. But in the next several weeks, a series of unusual coincidences, or synchronicities, occurred in Sam's life. Each incident was unusual in itself, but the growing frequency with which they occurred was truly astonishing. The correct guessing of the M&M colors, and Sam's allowing me to linger on the subject, seemed to have attuned Sam's attention to notice other odd coincidences. He became like an excited schoolboy bringing in material for show and tell. And then, there occurred the mother of all synchronicities.

First, some background: When Sam was depressed, he would read about the lives of famous and powerful men, hoping to find some identification with them that might kindle a spark of his own sense of worth. At one point he came across a little-known book containing George Washington's personal diary. In it was a series of prayers Washington had written for himself to provide solace and inspiration.

Sam told me about his favorite of the prayers, albeit a bit sheepishly, since, as he said, it was a little "corny" and far too religious. But if it was good enough for George Washington, it was good enough for him. He proceeded to recite the first part of Washington's "Monday Morning" prayer for me:

> O eternal and everlasting God, I presume to present myself this morning before thy Divine majesty,

beseeching thee to accept of my humble and hearty thanks, that it hath pleased thy great goodness to keep and preserve me the night past from all the dangers poor mortals are subject to, and has given me sweet and pleasant sleep, whereby I find my body refreshed and comforted for performing the duties of this day, in which I beseech thee to defend me from all perils of body and soul...

(*Johnson*, 1919, pp. 26–27)

About the time of his discovery of the prayer, Sam, always in pursuit of hyper-macho endeavors, signed on to become a crew member of a ship on a perilous expedition near the Arctic Circle. He was gone for over 4 weeks. Upon his return, he came in for his first session, smiling somewhat cryptically.

"OK," he announced, "I have to acknowledge that there are some things that can't be explained by logic or science."

I was certainly intrigued.

Sam explained: Before his return to the United States, he took a side trip to Norway. On his second night in a village north of Oslo, he was having dinner at a restaurant, when a pretty young Norwegian woman drew his attention. He invited her to join him at his table. She was a college history major, and during their conversation, she happened to mention that her class was currently studying American history. One of her course requirements was that each student choose a prominent figure in American history and present a report to the class. She told Sam that she had chosen George Washington. What a coincidence, said Sam, and told her he'd recently read a book about Washington. Then, mainly to score points as a sensitive man, Sam told her of his discovery of Washington's prayers for guidance. As Sam began to recite the "Monday Morning" prayer—"O eternal and everlasting God, I presume to present myself this morning..." the young woman interrupted him and took up where he'd left off. In halting English, she recited the entire first part of the prayer, the same part Sam had recited to me.

After recounting these events, Sam just looked at me. We were both speechless. Then, Sam proceeded to get out pen and paper and insisted, just to make sure we weren't getting too carried away, that we try to calculate the odds against this happening by chance. And so, we went down Sam's list of questions and tried, together, to estimate the following: What percentage of Americans knows from memory this "Monday Morning" prayer by George Washington? Of those Americans, what percentage might have traveled to a village north of Oslo recently? Of that infinitesimally small group, what percentage would have dined in the same restaurant and at the same time as the young history student who dined there that evening? Then, we had to factor in: What percentage of Norwegians even knows of George Washington's "Monday Morning" prayer? And of those, what percentage could actually recite a substantial portion of the prayer?

Needless to say, the odds we came up with were, conservatively speaking, a gazillion to one against this happening strictly by chance. And then, events of an even more improbable, one could say miraculous, nature unfolded over the next several months. Without any obvious precipitating event, Sam began to question many of his fixed ideas about people and about himself. He started doing volunteer work at a hospital, and befriended an elderly man who lived near his home. He also fell in love with a woman unlike any he'd dated before (without the various "pedigrees" he'd always insisted upon) and has since married and had two children with her.

Although I can't be certain of this, it seemed that our mutual focus on the coincidence of Sam's guessing the M&M colors, an anomalous experience for him, and our shared interactive exploration and enjoyment of the synchronicities he subsequently reported, might have set up a resonance with a larger field of unseen reality that interacted with Sam's and my relationship. Then, in some inexplicable way, this interaction may have opened our field to the manifestation of a series of increasingly improbable coincidences, which, in turn, affected our work together.

Like Beebe's (Beebe & Lachmann, 2002) videotaped mother-infant pairs' subtle shaping of each other, Sam and I engaged in a delicate choreography around the subject of synchronicities, with each one of us accommodating both consciously and unconsciously to the other's very different starting positions, and ending up equally stunned by his experience in Norway. We both felt that our relationship had been touched by a relationship with something beyond our comprehension. The effect this had on Sam was transformative, as he was deeply affected by what he experienced as an engagement with the vastness of a reality well beyond the narrow psychic space within which he had originally existed. It also brought us closer and facilitated deeper work that resulted in very practical changes in his life and in his capacity for tolerance, love, and compassion for himself and others.

Psi Research—Illuminating the Superordinate Field

It is beyond the scope of this chapter to undertake a comprehensive review of recent scientific studies of psi phenomena. I have selected two types of psi research that touch on the concept of the space within which the self resides and that have implications for psychoanalytic work and for the nature of intersubjective fields in general. In addition, results from psi experiments point to the possible existence of an infinite spiritual space or "source" and to ways in which the unconscious may interact with that space.

One of the most highly regarded series of psi experiments was conducted over a period of 25 years, beginning in 1979, at the Princeton Engineering Anomalies Research (PEAR) Laboratory (cited earlier regarding remote viewing experiments). The PEAR Lab was established in 1979 by Robert Jahn, Dean Emeritus of the Princeton Engineering School and professor of Aerospace Sciences, and cofounder Brenda Dunne to explore the effect of human consciousness on physical systems.

A typical PEAR Lab experiment was designed to determine if human intention could have an effect on a random event generator's output which, according to chance, would normally be 50% 1's and 50% 0's. In these experiments, a human subject, or operator, would usually sit in front of the box-like generator as it produced and recorded thousands of rapidly streaming 1's and 0's, and would set an intention to try to shift the percentage of 1's or 0's higher or lower than the expected 50%. Some PEAR experiments, as well as those from other laboratories, showed that distance--even up to thousands of miles--between operator and machine did not diminish the subjects' ability to alter the chance statistics of the machine. A meta-analysis of 832 experimental random event generator studies, including the PEAR Lab studies, found that the impact of human intention on the machines' output yielded overall odds against chance of over a trillion to one (Radin, 1997, p. 140).[2]

In an interview with PEAR Lab cofounder Brenda Dunne (personal communication, February 11, 2004), she explained that most of the more successful operators tried to feel a kind of merging with the machine, to create, in her words, a kind of "third space" or "blurring of identities between human and machine." That approach, similar perhaps to a meditative state that softens the sensation of boundaries of the self, seemed to result in larger effects on the machine than when subjects focused more directly, and with more conscious effort, on willing the machine to change its statistically predictable output. This blurring of identities and creation of a "third space" is strikingly similar to the descriptions of what occurs between patient and analyst in the intersubjective field. Stern (2004) and the Boston Change Process Study Group (Stern et al., 1998) have proposed that change occurs in therapy precisely when therapists are willing to abandon their familiar framework and wade in more deeply to meet the patient in intersubjective waters or, one could say, to "blur" their habitual sense of themselves, their roles, and their linear assessment of the patient.

In the PEAR experiments, it appeared as though the against-chance effects took place outside of conscious control: After an initial conscious intention was selected (to either raise or lower the otherwise statistically predictable production of 1's and 0's), the unconscious aspect of consciousness seemed to take over and "deliver" the anomalous results. Here, too, there is a parallel to descriptions of the primacy of the role of the unconscious in therapeutic efficacy, that is, in altering the probable, "statistically likely" repetitive patterns in a person's inner and outer life. As Schore (June 2006), stated, in emphasizing the essential role of unconscious attunement between patient and therapist in positive treatment outcome: "The unconscious does better when left to do its own thing without the conscious mind on its shoulder." In psychoanalysis, it seems that interpretations, affective expression, and explicit communication are the visible, conscious scaffolding upon which implicit meaning, unconscious resonance, and transformational processes can perform their alchemy.

Unconscious Forays Into Quantum, Superordinate, and Spiritual Space

In a conceptual model of the relationship between the human mind and its material environment, based on the findings of the PEAR Lab and other psi studies, Jahn and Dunne (2001) propose that there is an interface between the conscious and the tangible (observable) physical world and an interface between the unconscious and the intangible (quantum-ruled) physical world. We are used to the former interface, as it obeys classical rules of time and space, cause and effect; what we see *is* what we get. The unconscious and the quantum intangible realms, however, both speak a counterintuitive logic-defying language—time does not exist as we normally conceive of it, nor does space. In both the unconscious and the intangible physical realms, events that we normally think of as impossible occur routinely: Think of the wildly improbable scenarios that emerge from our unconscious in dreams, and also of what Einstein called "spooky action at a distance" (Lindley, 1996)—the behavior of two paired particles, separated at a source, that seem to "know" and respond instantaneously to each other's spin and charge, even at great distances from each other.[3]

Jahn and Dunne (2001) speculate that at times the unconscious is able to carry information from the intangible physical realm with which it has undetectable but intimate contact, into conscious awareness, resulting in psi or anomalous phenomena such as remote viewing, human-machine effects, and telepathy.[4] They then suggest that perhaps this entire range of experience—from the world of conscious awareness and perceivable phenomena to the unseen unconscious and intangible physical realms—emanates from, or participates in, an even less comprehensible yet all-encompassing space they term the "Source." They describe the "Source" as an ineffable, infinite space that is inherently spiritual in that it gives rise to everything yet has no identifiable physical dimensions or properties of its own. This concept is similar to the Buddhist concept of emptiness—emptiness itself has no form and no substance, but is that from which all form and substance emerge.

Uncanny Intersubjective Influence

The extensive reach of the intersubjective field has been highlighted by another category of psi studies, primarily by Braud and Schlitz (1991), in which they explored the capacity of the average person to influence, from a distance, the biological systems of other people. In these studies, the distant subjects were monitored for changes in levels of physiological relaxation or arousal. As many as seven different physiological indices were used, including electrodermal response, heart rate, and muscle tension. The influencer was given computer-generated random instructions as to when to focus on either arousing or calming the distant subject, and when to direct attention away from the subject entirely, thus producing "no-mental-influence" control periods. Subjects were not informed of either the timing or direction of the influencers' intentions. Furthermore, influencers and subjects were separated not only by distance, but also, in some cases, by special soundproof and electromagnetically proofed rooms. The combined results of 37 such experiments showed a highly significant degree

of correlation between changes in the subjects' physiological levels of arousal or relaxation and the influencers' specific intentions. These studies yielded odds against chance of more than a hundred trillion to one (Radin, 1997, p. 153).

By whatever yet undiscovered means these phenomenal effects occurred, the nature of the intersubjective space involved appears to be similar to that involved in studies demonstrating the positive impact of prayer (including prayer from a distance) on the healing of physical conditions, often without the knowledge of those being prayed for (Byrd, 1988; Dossey, 1993; Harris, 1999; Springer & Eicher, 1999). If we can influence each other's physiology, even at a distance, and even without the recipient's knowledge of the intended influence, we have to radically shift our thinking about the effect intention has on the emotions of others as well (since physiology and emotion are themselves mutually interactive).

Future Directions: Implications and Possibilities for Psychoanalysis
Resolving an Identity Crisis

Psychoanalysis has been under pressure, particularly in the last two decades, to justify its existence and efficacy in a world of health insurance–mandated short-term fixes and drug treatments for psychological problems. Evidence-based research geared toward finding objective scientific support for psychoanalytic techniques such as analyzing the transference have become popular, as has the search for support from recent discoveries in neuroscience. However, in emphasizing this approach to prove its worth, the field has turned its attention away from its essential foundation in a nonobjective realm of experience: unconscious processes and the therapeutic relationship. Since it has become increasingly accepted that therapeutic change emerges primarily from a space characterized by unseen, unspoken interactions, rather than from identifiable techniques and theories, psychoanalysis may have to question its attachment to finding objective, empirical macro-world scientific validation. The strength of psychoanalysis lies in its clinical "facts" (the idiosyncratic moment-to-moment experience of each unique patient–therapist pair) and in its embrace of a quest for depth, self-awareness, growth, and transformation, more akin to some spiritual traditions than to the hard sciences. In fact, as noted earlier in the discussion of mirror neurons, even neuroscience may only be able to take us part of the way toward a full explanation of how psychoanalysis works.

While consciousness and the unconscious may be processed in the brain, they may not reside exclusively and locally within the brain, as suggested by the studies of patients' experiences under deep anesthesia or in cardiac arrest (referred to earlier in this chapter).

Since psychoanalysts take seriously the unseen, mutual influencing that occurs between patient and therapist, and since they acknowledge that unconscious mutual influencing is a major factor in early psychological development, then they should also take seriously the studies in psi phenomena that have as their central feature unseen, mutual influencing and communication.

A possible step toward raising awareness and stimulating discussion of the relevance of the psi unconscious to the Freudian unconscious would be to offer a course at psychoanalytic institutes that would present the growing body of rigorously conducted scientific investigations of psi phenomena. If the remnants of the irrational, long-standing taboo regarding psi phenomena could be shaken off, psychoanalysts would find that they are in a prime position both to learn from and contribute to the exploration of psi, given their daily focus on unconscious processes in their practices.

Intention and Influence

The psi phenomena described in this chapter suggest that an initial conscious intention, whether in the form of a thought, a feeling, or a prayer, may trigger inexplicable, unconscious activity or transfer of information that results in a measurable influence on either a human or nonhuman environment well beyond what would be expected by chance. With this perspective in mind, one can view the concept of intention as it occurs in the ongoing field of mutual influence between patient and therapist in ways that have not yet been considered. Though psychoanalysis has moved away from the idea that the analyst should be a "neutral" blank screen, perhaps it has not moved far enough.

COUNTERTRANSFERENCE AND NON-NEUTRALITY IN A NEW LIGHT

Though Freud considered countertransference (the range of feelings and reactions the analyst has to the patient) a problem to be overcome so that it did not interfere with the patient's treatment, contemporary relational and intersubjective theories regard countertransference feelings to be important clues to the patient's projections and unconscious patterns as they are enacted in therapy. In light of the results of psi studies, it seems that consideration should be given to a more active engagement of a specific kind of countertransference. For example, since conscious intention seems to be a catalyst for unconscious influence, should analysts be more conscious of their intentions toward and for their patient? Might it be therapeutic to consciously create certain kinds of intention? This latter suggestion would violate most current training protocols, which maintain certain aspects of classical analysis: One is not supposed to impose one's own wishes or suggestions or have an agenda for the patient. Certainly, a therapist should not have a vested interest in a patient's attending medical school rather than art school, for example, but it may be appropriate for a therapist to consciously intend that the patient achieve a sense of well-being, or overcome fears, or be liberated from the constraining armor of the past. Holding such a conscious intention may subtly shape a therapist's words, facial expressions, and affect in ways that could enhance the bond with the patient, but beyond that, it may unleash, beyond conscious awareness, unconscious anomalous influence in the direction of psychological healing.

Typically, analysts are encouraged to become aware of negative countertransferential feelings toward the patient, such as anger, irritation, boredom, frustration, and envy. While it is vitally important for these feelings to be acknowledged and explored in the interest of understanding the analyst, the patient, and the analyst-patient intersubjective field, perhaps a further step could be taken. Analysts could be trained to find or create a mental space (through simple meditation techniques, for example) within which they could hold positive intention, compassion, even love for the patient at the same time that negative feelings are acknowledged and analyzed. It is possible that, in creating this more expansive consciousness or mental space of positive intention, the analyst might attune the intersubjective patient–therapist field to greater interaction with the superordinate field that both permeates and lies beyond the two-person psychoanalytic endeavor. At the very least, psychoanalysts should consider thinking beyond both classical and contemporary meanings of transference and countertransference so as to integrate the scientific discoveries of the startling extent to which we transfer to, extract from, and influence one another, often beyond conscious awareness.

Resonance and Attunement

An unexpected finding emerged from the PEAR random event generator studies described earlier: It was found that when two people worked together to try to influence the output of the machine, they produced a larger effect than did a single person working alone, and couples with a strong emotional bond "achieved an effect size nearly seven times larger than that produced by those same people as individual operators" (Dunne & Jahn, 2005, p. 709). One can speculate that anomalous events are more likely to occur in a closely bonded relationship, and that a powerful attunement or resonance between people may heighten the likelihood of exceeding chance expectations, whether it be in the case of a random event generator's output, or in the case of a patient trying to change repetitive, predictable, limiting patterns in his life. In fact, several studies (Henry, 1998; Klein et al., 2003; Luborsky et al., 1985; Norcross, Beutler, & Levant, 2005; Wallerstein, 1995) have concluded that the quality of the bond, or working alliance, between patient and therapist plays a greater role in bringing about positive outcome in psychotherapy than does any specific theory or technique.

The Importance of the Personality of the Analyst

Ironically, what has turned out to be one of the most important factors contributing to healing in various kinds of psychotherapy, including psychoanalysis, was, in classical Freudian practice, to be avoided at all cost: the manifestation of the personality of the therapist. As indicated earlier in this chapter, analysts were expected to maintain "neutrality" and to appear as a "blank screen" to the patient. Indicative of the sea change that has occurred, in 2006 the APA Presidential Task Force on Evidence-Based Practice noted that: "Because of the importance of therapeutic alliance to outcome, an understanding of the personal attributes and interventions of therapists that strengthen the alliance is essential for maximizing the quality of patient care" (p. 278).

A question that needs to be further explored is what those personal attributes are and how people can learn to develop them. Siegel (2010) has elaborated on methods of cultivating aspects of the therapist's "presence" that contribute to attunement and resonance with the patient and has described the neurobiological basis for some of these aspects. Schore (June 2006), also speaking from a neurobiological perspective, cited the following traits as most important in establishing the crucial right hemisphere to right hemisphere resonance between patient and analyst: the analyst's sensitivity, or

"capacity to register and respond to very slight differences or changes in emotion," the expression of affect, and a deep sense of devotion and commitment to the patient's well-being.

"All technique," he said, "sits atop the therapist's ability to access the implicit realm," the implicit realm of unconscious resonance and other forms of nonverbal communication.

To explore the personality traits that might foster access to the implicit realm, it may be useful to investigate the states of mind of the more successful subjects in the studies of psi phenomena. It appears as though they were able, through some combination of conscious intention and unconscious attunement, to connect with or access an implicit realm in order to bring about the unexpected, improbable, miraculous-seeming results in the experiments. Jahn and Dunne (2004) have postulated certain features that seemed to facilitate the subjects' access to the implicit realm, among them a tolerance for uncertainty and an openness to alternative views of reality. I suggest that collaboration between psi researchers, psychologists, and psychoanalysts could lead to useful studies that would reveal more about the personality traits that are effective in both psi experiencing and in psychoanalysis.

Time and Psychoanalysis

Classical psychoanalytic treatment has focused primarily on remembering and analyzing the past so that distorted perceptions shaped in earlier periods of life will not continue to govern present experience. Whether emphasis was on the Oedipal or pre-Oedipal phases, psychological problems and their solutions were seen within a linear, chronological framework. Many contemporary writers, including Beebe and Lachmann (2002), Gargiulo (2010), Kulka (1997), Orange, Atwood, and Stolorow (1997), and Stern (1989), have emphasized the nonlinear, nontechnical element in psychoanalytic process, and the accelerations of growth and healing that can emerge from in-the-moment unfolding of unexpected possibilities that transcend both the patient's linear history and the linear narrative of the analysis. Since psi phenomena and spiritual experience (such as miracles, personal awakenings, and mystical revelations) also defy linear, probabilistic progressions, psychoanalysts may benefit from including these areas of human experience in their thinking about the scope of change that can be hoped for regarding each of their patients' lives. Furthermore, there may be ways, yet to be explored, of priming analysts' sensitivity to the opening of "windows" of emergent, nonlinear opportunities for transformation, without forfeiting investigation and understanding of the influence of past experience.

Conclusion

When a person seeks psychoanalysis, he or she is hoping for a way to expand possibilities in his or her life and to find release from constraining patterns and self-limiting thoughts and behavior that might otherwise seem impossible to change. More than technique or theory, the bond that forms in the intersubjective space that patient and therapist create and engage in together is the key to the emergence of new perspectives and transformation.

Intersubjective space is also the medium of psi phenomena and of spiritual experience. Experiments in psi phenomena home in on this shared space and provide a glimpse into what is normally an unseen substrate of our interconnectedness with each other and with our environment, both spiritual and material. Psi studies, historically shunned by the scientific and psychoanalytic communities, ironically provide measurable, quantifiable evidence of manifestations of our shared space (even though the fundamental mechanism of the effects remain, and may always remain, a mystery.)

While most people cannot experience the fullness of interconnectedness that is a mystic's raison d'être, we are all products of mystical space in that our very development from infancy on depends on implicit, unconscious, intersubjective modes of relating with others. The common ground of psi phenomena, spiritual space, and the psychoanalytic process points to the active role that this unseen space plays in every instant of our lives, mostly outside of our awareness. The field of psychoanalysis, clearly a denizen of unseen reality, could benefit, perhaps even renew itself, by embracing an exploration of the territories with which it shares space: psi phenomena and spirituality.

Notes

1. Recently the term "consciousness-related anomalies" has been used interchangeably with the term "psi phenomena," since it captures the main essence of the various manifestations of psi—that is, the role of consciousness in imparting or extracting information from an otherwise random system. For instance, telepathy involves extracting information from another mind, clairvoyance from a random source in the environment, and psychokinesis points to the role of consciousness in transferring information into a physical process or other aspect of the physical world with which it is engaged.

2. For questions about the scientific soundness of these studies, please refer to *Foundations of Physics*, "Evidence for Consciousness-Related Anomalies in Random Physical Systems" (Radin &

Nelson, 1989). The authors address "virtually all methodological criticisms raised to date" (p. 1504) and they demonstrate that the experimental effects produced have a "replication rate...as good as that found in exemplary experiments in psychology and physics" (p. 1510). See also Dean Radin's book, *Entangled Minds* (2006), for an extensive review of investigations confirming the validity of the results of the PEAR Lab program, and additional rebuttals to commonly raised methodological criticisms.

3. This phenomenon, described by Bell's theorem, of two initially paired particles separated by great distances, yet simultaneously correlating their behavior, was recently verified (Bouwmeester et al., 1997).

4. Jung (1952/1973) envisioned absolute knowledge existing "in a space-time continuum in which space is no longer space, nor time time" (p. 65). He theorized that the unconscious could engage with that continuum and carry knowledge from it into consciousness, similar to what Jahn and Dunne speculate.

References

APA Presidential Task Force on Evidence-Based Practice. (2006). Evidence-based practice in psychology. *American Psychologist*, *61*(4), 271–285.

Atwood, G. E., & Stolorow, R. D. (1984). *Structures of subjectivity: Explorations in psychoanalytic phenomenology*. Hillsdale, NJ: The Analytic Press.

Balint, M. (1955). Notes on parapsychology and parapsychological healing. *International Journal of Psychoanalysis, 36*, 31–35.

Bass, A. (2001). It takes one to know one: Or, whose unconscious is it anyway? *Psychoanalytic Dialogues, 11*, 683–702.

Beebe, B., & Lachmann, F. M. (2002). *Infant research and adult treatment: Co-constructing interactions*. Hillsdale, NJ: The Analytic Press.

Bion, W. R. (1995). *Attention and interpretation*. Northvale, NJ: Jason Aronson. (Original work published 1970).

Bouwmeester, D., Pan, J., Mattle, K., Eidl, M., Weinfurter, H., & Zeilinger, A. (1997). Experimental quantum teleportation. *Nature, 390*, 575–579.

Braud, W. G., & Schlitz, M. J. (1991). Consciousness interactions with remote biological systems: Anomalous intentionality effects. *Subtle Energies: An Interdisciplinary Journal of Energetic and Informational Interactions, 2*(I), 1–46.

Burlingham, D. T. (1935). Child analysis and the mother. *Psychoanalytic Quarterly, 4*, 69–92.

Byrd, R. C. (1988). Positive therapeutic effects of intercessory prayer in a cardiac care unit population. *Southern Medical Journal, 81*(7), 826–829.

Dorman, D. (2004). *Dante's cure: A journey out of madness*. New York: Other Press.

Dossey, L. (1993). *Healing words: The power of prayer and the practice of medicine*. San Francisco: Harper San Fransisco.

Dunne, B., & Jahn, R. G. (2005). Consciousness, information, and living systems. *Cellular and Molecular Biology, 51*, 703–714.

Ehrenwald, J. (1948). *Telepathy and medical psychology*. New York: W. W. Norton & Co.

Eigen, M. (1998). *The psychoanalytic mystic*. New York: Free Association Books.

Eigen, M. (2001). Mysticism and psychoanalysis. *Psychoanalytic Review, 88*, 455–481.

Eisenbud, J. (1946). Telepathy and problems of psychoanalysis. *The Psychoanalytic Quarterly, 15*, 32–87.

Eisenbud, J. (1947). The dreams of two patients in analysis interpreted as a telepathic rêve à deux. *The Psychoanalytic Quarterly, 16*, 39–60.

Eshel, O. (2006). Where are you, my beloved? *International Journal of Psychoanalysis, 87,* 1603–1627.

Farrell, D. (1983). Freud's 'thought-transference,' repression, and the future of psychoanalysis. *International Journal of Psychoanalysis, 64,* 71–81.

Ferenczi, S., & Rank, O. (1986). *The development of psychoanalysis.* Madison, CT: International Universities Press. (Original work published in 1924).

Flew, A. (1967). Miracles. In P. Edwards (Ed.), *Encyclopedia of philosophy* (pp. 346–353). New York: Macmillan and Free Press.

Freud, S. (1957). The unconscious. In J. Strachey (Ed. & Trans.), *Standard edition of the complete psychological works of Sigmund Freud* (Vol. 14, pp. 159–215). London: Hogarth Press. (Original work published 1915).

Freud, S. (1961a). The future of an illusion: Civilization and its discontents and other works. In J. Strachey (Ed. & Trans.), *Standard edition* (Vol. 21, pp. 5–56). London: The Hogarth Press. (Original work published in 1927).

Freud, S. (1961b). *Civilization and its discontents* (J. Strachey, Ed. & Trans.). New York: W. W. Norton & Co. (Original work published in 1930).

Freud, S. (1965). Dreams and occultism. In J. Strachey (Ed. & Trans.), *New introductory lectures on psycho-analysis* (pp. 38–70). New York: W. W. Norton & Co. (Original work published 1933).

Freud, S. (1973a). Dreams and telepathy. In G. Devereaux (Ed.), *Psychoanalysis and the occult* (pp. 69–86). New York: International Universities Press. (Original work published 1922).

Freud, S. (1973b). The occult significance of dreams. In G. Devereaux (Ed.), *Psychoanalysis and the occult* (pp. 87–90). New York: International Universities Press. (Original work published in 1925).

Freud, S. (1973c). Dreams and the occult. In G. Devereaux (Ed.), *Psychoanalysis and the occult* (pp. 91–109). New York: International Universities Press. (Original work published 1933).

Freud, S. (1973d). Psychoanalysis and telepathy. In G. Devereaux (Ed.), *Psychoanalysis and the occult* (pp. 56–68). New York: International Universities Press. (Original work published 1941).

Gallese, V. (2003). The manifold nature of interpersonal relations: The quest for a common mechanism. In C. D. Frith & D. M. Wolpert (Eds.), *The neuroscience of social interaction* (pp. 159–182). New York: Oxford University Press.

Gallese, V., Eagle, M. N., & Migone, P. (2007). Intentional attunement: Mirror neurons and the neural underpinnings of interpersonal relations. *Journal of the American Psychoanalytic Association, 55*(1), 131–176.

Gallese, V., Fadiga, L., Fogassi, L., & Rizzolatti, G. (1996). Action recognition in the premotor cortex. *Brain, 119,* 593–609.

Gargiulo, G. J. (2006/2007). Transcending religion: Reflections on spirituality and psychoanalysis. *The Annual of Psychoanalysis and Spirituality and Religion: Psychoanalytic Perspectives.* Catskill, NY: Mental Health Resources Publishers.

Gargiulo, G. J. (2010). Mind, meaning, and quantum physics: Models for understanding the dynamic unconscious. *Psychoanalytic Review, 97*(1), 91–106.

Gilhooley, D. (2008). Psychoanalysis and the "cognitive unconscious:" Implications for clriinical technique. *Modern Psychoanalysis, 33*(1), 91–127.

Goldman, A., & Sripada, C. S. (2005) Simulationist models of face-based emotion recognition. *Cognition, 94,* 193–213.

Gottesfeld, M. L. (1985). Mystical aspects of psychotherapeutic efficacy. *Psychoanalytic Review, 72,* 589–597.

Green, A. (2000). The intrapsychic and intersubjective in psychoanalysis. *Psychoanalytic Quarterly, 69,* 1–40.

Greenberg, J. (1964). *I never promised you a rose garden.* New York: Penguin Books.

Grotstein, J. S. (1998). The numinous and immanent nature of the psychoanalytic subject. *Journal of Analytic Psychology, 43,* 41–68.

Harris, W. (1999). A randomized, controlled trail of the effects of remote intercessory prayer on outcomes in patients admitted to the coronary care unit. *Archives of International Medicine, 159*(19), 2273–2278.

Henry, W. P. (1998). Science, politics, and the politics of science: The use and misuse of empirically validated treatment research. *Psychotherapy Research, 8*(2), 126–140.

Hufford, D. J. (2003). Response. *Journal of Folklore Research, 40*(1), 99–109.

Iacoboni, M. (2008). *Mirroring people.* New York: Farrar, Straus, and Giroux.

Iacoboni, M., Molner-Szakacs, I., Gallese, V., Buccino, G., Mazziotta, J. C., & Rizzolatti, G. (2005). Grasping the intentions of others with one's own mirror neuron system. *PLoS Biology, 3*(3), e79.

Jahn, R. G., & Dunne, B. (2001). A modular model of mind/matter manifestation (M5). *Journal of Scientific Exploration, 15*(3), 29–329.

Jahn, R. G., & Dunne, B. (2004). Sensors, filters and the source of reality. *Journal of Scientific Explorations, 18*(4), 547–570.

James, W. (1985). *The varieties of religious experience.* New York: Penguin Books. (Original work published 1902).

Jones (1957). *The life and work of Sigmund Freud: Volume 3. The last phase, 1919–1939.* New York: Basic Books, Inc.

Johnson, W. J. (1919). *George Washington, the Christian.* New York: The Abingdon Press.

Jung , C. G., & Pauli, W. (1973). *Synchronicity: An acausal connecting principle* (R. F. C. Hull, Trans.). Princeton, NJ: Princeton University Press. (Original work published 1952).

Kelly, E. F., Kelly, E. W., Crabtree, A., Gauld, A., Grosso, M., & Greyson, B. (2007). *Irreducible mind: Toward a psychology for the 21st century.* Lanham, MD: Rowman and Littlefield.

Kihlstrom, J., Schacter, D., Cork, R., Hurt, C., & Behr, S. (1990). Implicit and explicit memory following surgical anesthesia. *Psychological Science, 1,* 303–306.

Klein, D. N., Schwartz, J. E., Santiago, N. J., Vivian, D., Vocisano, C, Castonguay, L. G.…Keller, M. B. (2003). Therapeutic alliance in depression treatment: Controlling for prior change and patient characteristics. *Journal of Consulting and Clinical Psychology, 71*(6), 997–1006.

Kohut, H. (1984). *How does analysis cure?* Chicago: University Chicago Press.

Kulka, R. (1997). Quantum selfhood: Commentary on paper by Beebe, Lachmann, and Jaffe. *Psychoanalytic Dialogues, 7,* 183–187.

Lazar, S. (2001). Knowing, influencing, and healing: Paranormal phenomena and implications for psychoanalysis and psychotherapy. *Psychoanalytic Inquiry, 21,*113–131.

Lindley, D. (1996). *Where does the weirdness go? Why quantum mechanics is strange, but not as strange as you think.* New York: Basic Books.

Loewald, H. W. (1978). *Psychoanalysis and the history of the individual*. New Haven, CT: Yale University Press.

Loewald, H. W. (1988). Psychoanalysis in search of nature: Thoughts on metapsychology, "metaphysics," projection. *Annual of Psychoanalysis, 16*, 49–54.

Luborsky, L., McLellan, A. T., Woody, G. E., O'Brien, C. P., & Auerbach, A. (1985). Therapist success and its determinants. *Archives of General Psychiatry, 42*(6), 602–611.

Matte-Blanco, I. (1975). *The unconscious as infinite sets: An essay in bi-logic*. London: Duckworth.

Mayer, E. L. (1996a). Changes in science and changing ideas about knowledge and authority in psychoanalysis. *Psychoanalytic Quarterly, LXV*, 158–200.

Mayer, E. L. (1996b). Subjectivity and intersubjectivity of clinical facts. *International Journal of Psychoanalysis, 77*, 709–737.

Mayer, E. L. (2001). On "Telepathic dreams?" An unpublished paper by Robert J. Stoller. *Journal of the American Psychoanalytic Association, 49*(2), 629–657.

Mayer, E. L. (2007). *Extraordinary knowing*. New York: Bantam Books.

Meissner, W. W. (1984). *Psychoanalysis and religious experience*. New Haven, CT and London: Yale University Press.

Mitchell, S. (1988). *Relational concepts in psychoanalysis*. Cambridge, MA: Harvard University Press.

Modell A. H. (1984). *Psychoanalysis in a new context*. Madison, CT: International Universities Press.

Norcross, J., Beutler, L., & Levant, R. (2005). *Evidence-based practices in mental health: Debate and dialogue on the fundamental questions*. Oxford, England: Oxford University Press.

Norretranders, T. (1998). *The user illusion: Cutting consciousness down to size*. New York: Viking.

Ogden, T. H. (1994). The analytic third: Working with intersubjective clinical facts. *International Journal of Psychoanalysis, 75*(1), 3–19.

Orange, D. M., Atwood, G. E., & Stolorow, R. D. (1997). *Working intersubjectively: Contextualism in psychoanalytic practice* (Vol. 17). London: The Analytic Press.

Radin, D. (1997). *The conscious universe: The scientific truth of psychic phenomena*. San Francisco: Harper San Francisco.

Radin, D. (2006). *Entangled minds*. New York: Pocket Books.

Radin, D. I., & Nelson, R. D. (1989). Evidence for consciousness-related anomalies in random physical systems. *Foundations of Physics, 19*, 1499–1514.

Roland, A. (2011) *Journeys to foreign selves: Asians and Asian Americans in a global era*. Oxford, England: Oxford University Press.

Schermer, V. L. (2003). *Spirit and psyche: A new paradigm for psychology, psychoanalysis, and psychotherapy*. New York: Jessica Kingsley Publishers.

Schore, A. N. (2006, June). *Neurobiology and attachment theory in psychotherapy*. Workshop conducted at Mount Sinai Medical Center, New York.

Searles, H. F. (1976). Transitional phenomena and therapeutic symbiosis. *International Journal of Psychoanalytic Psychotherapy, 5*, 145–204.

Servadio, E. (1973). Psychoanalysis and telepathy. In G. Devereaux (Ed.), *Psychoanalysis and the occult* (pp. 210–220). (Original work published 1935).

Siegel, D. J. (2010). *The mindful therapist: A clinician's guide to mindsight and neural integration*. New York: W. W. Norton & Co.

Springer, S., & Eicher, D. (1999). Effects of a prayer circle on a moribund premature infant. *Alternative Therapies, 5*, 115–118.

Steinman, I. (2009). *Treating the untreatable: Healing the realms of madness*. New York: London Karnac Books.

Stern, D. B. (1989). The analyst's unformulated experience of the patient. *Contemporary Psychoanalysis, 25*, 1–33.

Stern, D. B. (2004). *The present moment in psychotherapy and everyday life*. New York: Norton.

Stern, D. N., Sander, L., Nathan, J., Harrison, A., Bruschweiler-Stern, N., & Tronick, E. (1998). Non-interpretative mechanisms in psychoanalytic therapy. *International Journal of Psychoanalysis, 79*, 903–921.

Stolorow, R. D. (1991). The intersubjective context of intrapsychic experience: A decade of psychoanalytic inquiry. *Psychoanalytic Inquiry, 11*, 171–184.

Stolorow, R. D., Brandchaft, B., & Atwood, G. (1987). *Psychoanalytic treatment: An intersubjective approach*. Hillsdale, NJ: The Analytic Press.

Suchet, M. (2004). Whose mind is it anyway? *Studies in Gender and Sexuality, 5*(3), 259–287.

Tennes, M. (2007). Beyond intersubjectivity: The transpersonal dimension of the psychoanalytic encounter. *Contemporary Psychoanalysis, 43*(4), 505–525.

Wallerstein, R. S. (1995). The effectiveness of psychotherapy and psychoanalysis: Conceptual issue and empirical work. In T. Shapiro & R. N. Emde (Eds.), *Research in psychoanalysis: Process, developmental, outcome* (pp. 299–312). New Haven, CT: International Universities Press.

Winnicott, D. W. (1975). *Through pediatrics to psycho-analysis*. New York: Basic Books.

Spiritual Aspects of Jungian Analytical Psychology: Individuation, Jung's Psychological Equivalent of a Spiritual Journey

Joseph P. Wagenseller

Abstract

This chapter includes a brief description of the life and work of Carl Gustav Jung, MD, with particular attention to his personal experience of the objective psyche and its articulation into a theoretical framework. Special emphasis is placed upon the transpersonal/spiritual dimension of the psyche and the applicability of Jung's theory and practice to achieve a dynamic relationship with the self. The individual's experience with the transpersonal aspect of the psyche is illustrated with examples from symptoms, dreams, and the phenomenon of synchronicity. Jung's psychological equivalent of a spiritual journey, known as the individuation process, is described and illustrated as an option for those for whom other, perhaps more traditional religious faiths and practices are no longer meaningfully effective. In conclusion, recommendations are made for future study and research.

Key Words: active imagination, analysis, archetype, individuation, individuation process, numinous, objective psyche, Self, synchronicity, transcendent function

Introduction

Following a brief biographical sketch of the life and early work of C. G. Jung, this chapter places his contribution in the context of the scientific and cultural era in which the psychoanalytic movement began, early 20th-century Europe.

Jung's work represents a combination of the influences of Schopenhauer, Carus, Nietzsche, Kant, and Freud, among others; his response to the psychiatric community of his time; and his own personal experiences of the depth of the psyche, which he called "a confrontation with the unconscious," along with his professional practice.

Jung's experiential understanding of the psyche in both the personal and transpersonal dimensions is described. Transpersonal aspects, such as dreams, symptoms, and the phenomenon of synchronicity are described and illustrated to delineate the spiritual, purposeful, or prospective thrust of the self, Jung's term for the superordinating phenomenon

that organizes and orchestrates the multidimensionality of the psyche as it guides the individual through the individuation process, Jung's term for the psychological equivalent of a spiritual journey.

Jung's Life and Early Work

To appreciate Jung's contribution, it is helpful to place him and his work in its historical and cultural setting, together with a little biographical information about the man, as his understanding of the psyche and his theoretical development grew out of experiences of the psyche, both his and those of others.

At the turn of the last century, when the psychoanalytic movement began in Europe, members of the psychiatric community had been trying to gain respectability for their specialty with their medical colleagues. Mental illness was still looked upon with abhorrence, fear, and judgment. Mental hospitals were still called insane asylums, and patients were treated cruelly and punitively. The psychiatric profession was emphasizing diseases of the brain and diagnostic skills; psychiatrists were concerned with making the profession of psychiatry scientifically respectable.

Culturally, turn-of-the-century Vienna was quite Victorian. Sexual repression was typical, as seen in the fact that Freud's early cases were with patients diagnosed as hysterical. They were understood to be suffering from sexual repression. With the emphasis of psychoanalysis upon the unconscious, the non-rational, instinctive aspect of the personality and infantile sexuality, it is no surprise that the professional community and the culture at large found this very threatening and responded with resistance and hostility.

Carl Gustav Jung (July 26, 1875– June 6, 1961)

Jung was born in the rural, farming community of Kesswil, Switzerland, where his father was a reformed Protestant minister. When Carl was 6 months of age, his family moved to Laufen, near the Rhine Falls. At an early age, he was intently occupied with trying to understand the larger questions of life, such as Truth, Eternity, and God. Carl's early mind was shaped by these preoccupations. Although he listened attentively to his father's religious teachings, he was confused by various ideas about Jesus, in particular. He prayed to God and experienced God as trustworthy and without contradictions. Thus, his concern with spirituality was a lifelong preoccupation, with a very early beginning.

As he grew older, he questioned his father about certain theological teachings he found difficult to accept. It was a great disappointment to him that his father seemed attached to a traditional, orthodox understanding and was reluctant to think for himself. Jung was always questioning. He felt that his father was trapped in having to represent the conventional beliefs and that he was discouraged and despondent.

Jung describes his mother as highly intuitive, mystical, and practically clairvoyant. As a boy, he often felt that she seemed to know what he was thinking and feeling before he even expressed it. As he mentions in *Memories, Dreams, Reflections*, this often left him with a spooky feeling. She spent several summers in a mental hospital, which was very difficult for Carl, as he found her intermittent unavailability, both physically and psychologically, to be distressing. She had lost two sons in infancy, prior to Carl's birth.

These traits of his parents would characterize his subsequent concern with religious matters. He had little interest in or patience with what he called "secondhand religion," a phrase he took from William James. He did not want to be told to believe someone else's experience. To him, direct experience was what he valued. His father represented secondhand religion, whereas his mother's experience was direct and mystical, more like his own.

A sister, Trudi, was born 9 years after Carl. They did not share much of a life together.

There was a persistent family legend that Jung's grandfather, C. G. Jung, had been the natural son of Goethe. Irrespective of whether the story was literally true, it was meaningful to Jung, as he felt attuned to much of what Goethe had written. Goethe's work on Faust especially fascinated Jung, as he realized the archetypal dimension of the drama. In a similar manner, Jung was focused upon one main idea or goal, namely, "the secret of the personality."

His companions were largely farm children whose interests and activities were very different from his emerging intelligence and inner experience. Thus, there was a natural setting in which he was quite unique among his peers. His memoirs tell us that he learned the early facts of sexuality from these children.

Jung's childhood experiences were such that he could not forget or ignore them. The fact that they seemed not to be understood or appreciated by others only made him more lonely and isolated. This combination of factors contributed to a deep interiority. His early childhood was characterized by solitary play and a vivid imagination. His deep absorption in play was such that he was quite upset if interrupted.

As a child, Jung had many psychological experiences that left a lasting impression upon him. At the age of 5, he had a dream that made such an impact on him that he puzzled over it for the rest of his life. Only much later, did he grow to understand it. In the dream, he was in a meadow, where he discovered a stone-lined hole in the ground. Inside was a stone staircase. Descending to the bottom, he found a curtain, behind which was a room about 30 feet long. On a red carpet stood a platform on which was a golden throne.

> Something was standing on it which I thought at first was a tree trunk twelve to fifteen feet high and about one and a half to two feet thick. It was a huge thing reaching almost to the ceiling. But it was of a curious composition: it was made of skin and naked flesh,

and on top there was something like a rounded head with no face and no hair. On the very top of the head was a single eye, gazing motionlessly upward.

It was fairly light in the room, although there were no apparent windows and no apparent source of light. Above the head, however, was an aura of brightness. The thing did not move, yet I had the feeling that it might at any moment crawl off the throne like a worm and creep toward me. I was paralyzed with terror. At that moment I heard from outside and above me my mother's voice. She called out, "Yes, just look at him. That is the man-eater!"
(*Jung & Jaffe*, 1963, pp. 11–12)

Many years later he realized that this was a phallus. Later still, he understood this to be a ritual phallus, which he took to be an underground nameless god related to initiation in the "secrets of the earth."

Other psychological phenomena from around this time included the carving of a small manikin, which he enclosed in a pencil case and hid in the attic. This secret gave him a sense of security, supporting his sense of identity and well-being at times when he felt the need of reassurance. He began to realize that he had two different personalities, one his conventional self-presentation, what he would later call the "persona," an extroverted aspect; and another, much deeper and wiser sense of self, which he would also later associate with the archetypal dimension of the psyche, an introverted experience of himself. This number two personality seemed to be of medieval times. In other words, from an early age, he had a sense of both the personal and transpersonal dimensions of his identity and the beginnings of the understanding and theory of the personality that would follow.

At the age of 9, he often liked to sit upon a particular stone and play an imaginary game, questioning his relationship to the stone, exploring what the stone meant to him and vice versa. His inner imaginative life often seemed more real to him than the outer life. He sensed that his experiences of the psyche were meaningful and to be honored. Jung held this regard for inner experience throughout his life. He valued it in every person he met and supported people to be true to their experience, not surrendering it to the collective beliefs of others. His lifelong motto was the importance of experiencing for oneself. This became the thread of his understanding of the spiritual dimension of the psyche and of the individuation process, the psychological equivalent of a spiritual journey. (For a full understanding of the relationship of Jung's life and work, the reader may wish to consult *Memories, Dreams, Reflections.*)

At the age of 12, Jung had a dream of God depositing a turd upon the dome of the Cathedral in Basel. He took this as a direct experience of God, who was above manmade religion. He felt a direct relationship with God. This became another secret that he thought others might have trouble accepting. He held these and other inner experiences as the beginnings of an inner life and personality formation that both gave him a sense of individuality and also contributed to isolating him from others. Also at the age of 12, he was pushed one day by another boy, resulting in him falling and hitting his head. For 6 months after the incident, Jung had fainting spells. These interfered with his school attendance and caused great distress to his father.

Following private school education in Basel, Jung decided to attend medical school, where, after much consideration, he chose psychiatry as his specialty because it combined his interests in the scientific world around him and the inner world of the psyche, including his wide-ranging study of world religions and philosophy.

Jung's doctoral thesis was entitled *On the Psychology and Pathology of So-Called Occult Phenomena*, reflecting his early interest in altered states of consciousness and the spirit realm of the psyche. His work with Theodore Flournoy on the productions of the trance state of mediums contributed to his understanding of creative, nonpathological aspects of the *psyche* as did his study of William James's *Varieties of Religious Experience.*

Around 1900, during his early years in the psychiatric profession, Jung worked at the Burgholtzli Clinic in Zurich with Eugen Bleuler, MD, studying patients diagnosed with dementia praecox (schizophrenia). He developed the Word Association Test, originally discovered by Wilhelm Wundt, and applied it to both psychotic and normal individuals

Following Jung's reading of Sigmund Freud's *The Interpretation of Dreams*, they corresponded for a year before Jung visited Freud in Vienna on February 27, 1907. That historic meeting and conversation lasted 13 hours. Both men were exploring the unconscious through the study of dreams. Jung had a particular interest in linking the thought formations of schizophrenia with dream formations. Freud had developed the method of free association. Jung had developed the Word Association Experiment. These two methods led them both to an understanding of "the complex," a largely unconscious psychodynamic, with a theme, or archetypal core, such as the Oedipus complex, a power complex, inferiority complex, or hero or victim complex. Jung called his early theory Complex Psychology, seeing the psyche as being comprised of many complexes, with the ego, the complex of identity, as the central one.

The two men became colleagues with great mutual respect. Jung tended to defer to Freud due to his age and greater experience. However, from the beginning there were important differences. Jung's early writing on Freud, from 1906 to 1916, defends Freud's theories on the sexual etiology of neurosis, theory of dreams, both manifest and latent content, wish fulfillment, condensation, and dream censor. However, as early as 1907, Jung expressed doubt about Freud's sexual theory, seeing it as only one of many components of the personality. Jung felt that Freud was dogmatic about the sexual theory and substituted sexuality for religion. Jung also commented upon the Oedipus complex, seeing it as only one of many complexes and not the sole root of all neurosis. While agreeing that the personal unconscious contained unacceptable aspects of the personality, he felt that it had a positive, creative, spiritual dimension as well. In *Memories, Dreams, Reflections*, Jung makes the point that he places great importance upon sexuality. However, he saw it as the expression of the chthonic spirit, which he called "the other face of God" (Jung & Jaffe, 1963, p. 168). He was concerned with not only the personal meaning and biological function of sexuality but also its spiritual aspect and numinous meaning.

Following their early mutual enthusiasm, Freud considered Jung to be his "heir apparent" to lead the psychoanalytic movement. As Freud and most of his followers in the early phase were Jewish, he was concerned that psychoanalysis not become identified with Judaism and welcomed Jung as a Protestant Christian, believing that Jung's affiliation would be beneficial to the cause.

As Freud's and Jung's relationship evolved, Jung found Freud unyielding in his attitude toward the psychoanalytic movement. Freud was so dogmatic about his theories that it seemed impossible to discuss them. On one occasion, they both heard a loud noise. Jung predicted it would happen again, which it did. It was caused by a splitting of a table, an instance of synchronicity, or meaningful coincidence. Jung suggested it might herald a split between them, but Freud dismissed the idea.

In 1909, Freud, Jung, and Ferenzi traveled together to Clark University in Worcester, Massachusetts, at the invitation of A. A. Brill and Stanley Hall. There they lectured for 7 weeks. American audiences were very interested in these early lectures about psychoanalysis, complexes, Freud's conflict theory, libido, repression, and others. During this time, Freud and Jung analyzed each other's dreams.

On one occasion, Freud was unwilling to offer any personal associations to his dream or to share the content of his personal life as it related to the dream, saying that it might undermine his authority within the psychoanalytic profession to do so. Jung was troubled at the thought that Freud's authority was more important to him than the meaning of the dream. Jung's idealization of Freud began to decline, as Freud seemed too one-sided and dogmatic. A dream of Jung's that contained two skulls was interpreted by Freud to suggest that Jung had a death wish toward him.

There was a growing tension between the two men over their differences about libido and sexual theory. In 1916, Jung published *The Psychology of the Unconscious*, what is now called *Symbols of Transformation*. In this work, he offered an interpretation of a case presented by Theodore Flournoy. In so doing, Jung illustrated his archetypal perspective, his theory of libido transformation, and his symbolic understanding of incest, portraying it as having a spiritual meaning or rebirth. Jung introduced his understanding of the purposeful thrust of archetypal dynamics, pointing to the potentiality for personality development lying within the symptoms of the individual. While working on the theory, Jung entitled a chapter "The Sacrifice." He knew that this chapter would cost him his friendship with Freud because of the archetypal perspective he included. Jung later realized that this was his own sacrifice. This was too much for Freud and amounted to the beginning of an irreparable break between them. Their friendship lasted from 1907 until 1913.

From 1913 to 1917, Jung was engaged in the preparatory work for *Psychological Types*. He explains in *Memories, Dreams, Reflections* that this work initially came from his need to define how his outlook differed from Freud's and Adler's. Also, however, in response to the setting, Jung felt that the psychiatric profession of his day took too negative and pejorative a view of those seeking treatment. He thought that the prevailing attitude toward psychopathology tended to label patients with diagnostic terms that demeaned them. In contradistinction to the then current practice of diagnosis, he developed his theory of psychological types, in which he described a full spectrum of psychological qualities and attributes, without judgment. In developing this perspective, he offered an entirely new and nonjudgmental attitude toward the human psyche. This was his effort to deal with the relationship of the individual to the world of people, places, and things.

Jung suggested that all individuals have access to the full range of these functions, extraversion/introversion, thinking, feeling, sensation, and intuition. Each, however, has his or her unique combination, usually accenting certain qualities, while others are less accessible. For example, we all have a tendency to relate to the world around us, of people, places, and things. This is our extroverted side. We are also related to our "inner world" of sensations, feelings, imagination, and so on. This is our introverted side. Most of us tend to be more naturally at home in one or the other of these tendencies.

We also use four other functions; thinking, feeling, sensation, and intuition. Again, most of us tend to be stronger in certain of these functions and weaker in others. Each of these typologies, taken to an extreme, may very well appear as pathological. These tendencies can be worked with to arrive at a better balanced personality. One's typology is determined by a mixture of hereditary qualities and life experiences. Over the course of a lifetime, often more recessive functions become more available, especially at midlife and thereafter.

In addition to offering a positive perspective for individuals to understand themselves, Jung's theory of psychological types is now widely used to assist in career counseling and guidance, such as through the well-known Myers-Briggs survey. It is also used in helping couples and families understand and appreciate their differences, rather than judging their differences as superior or inferior.

To relate typology to spirituality, Jung would understand that one's inferior function connects to the transpersonal, or archetypal, dimension of the psyche, causing the individual to experience it as numinous, mystical, or awesome.

Jung's Midlife Experience: "Confrontation With the Unconscious" and Midlife Theory (1914–1918)

Following Jung's separation from Freud, he encountered what he called a "confrontation with the unconscious" (1914–1918). During this time, he experienced powerful unconscious dynamics, constant inner pressure, uncertainty, and disorientation. He had archetypal dreams and experienced extrasensory phenomena, such as poltergeist, clairvoyance, and others, which he later addressed in his theory of synchronicity. In 1913, he had a vision of a "monstrous flood covering the land between the North Sea and the Alps. As it approached Switzerland, the mountains grew higher and protected the country. The sea turned into blood" (Jung & Jaffe, 1963, p. 175). Jung thought this indicated a coming psychosis.

During this turbulent time, Jung carefully observed these phenomena and pondered their meaning. He describes all of this in *Memories, Dreams, Reflections*. As he was undergoing this experience, he felt that there was purposefulness to this chaos, as if his psyche was being reorganized. Coming out of this experience—which might be called a psychotic process or a creative reorganization of the psyche, depending on your point of view—he began to formulate his understanding of the dynamics of the psyche. (A thorough overview of Jung's theory of the structure and dynamics of the psyche may be found in the References.)

As Jung was writing *Symbols of Transformation*, he became increasingly impressed with the mythological dimension of the psyche and pondered the notion of the "personal myth," considering the possibility that everyone has one. He began to wonder what his myth was.

Toward the end of 1913, Jung had a dream in which the figure of Siegfried was killed. Jung saw this as a representation of his unconscious identification with the hero myth or archetype. Seeing Siegfried as a Teutonic culture hero, representing the tendency to impose one's will upon others, he realized it was time to relinquish this attitude.

In abandoning the heroic attitude, which he equated with consciousness, Jung let himself experience the depths of the psyche. He returned to the imaginative play of his childhood experience, discovering the phenomenon of "active imagination" and the autonomy of the unconscious, the phenomenon that the unconscious has energy, initiative, and a life of its own.

In the experience of active imagination, he discovered that through an inner dialog with figures such as Philemon, an ancient wise man figure, who appeared to him in a dream, new and unexpected psychic phenomena occurred, introducing him to the discovery that the unconscious, both personal and transpersonal, is autonomous and expresses its own point of view. The archetypal realm of the unconscious he initially called the collective unconscious, and later the objective psyche.

Jung was convinced that man can tolerate a great deal of suffering, but he cannot stand a meaningless life. He was impressed with his observations that individuals and groups who hold beliefs which connect them with transpersonal meaning suffer less neurosis. In this context, he believed that practicing Roman Catholics, who experience their lives as meaningfully embraced by the sacraments of the church, are a good example. To live a sacramental life, in which daily life is understood symbolically and sanctified through a meaningful relationship with God, is to live a meaningful life. In his visit with the Pueblo Indians of New Mexico, Jung was likewise impressed that the members of this tribe understood themselves to be the children of Father Sun. They believed it was their responsibility to accompany Father Sun in his journey across the sky each day, through their devotional practices (Jung, 1976, p. 274).

In examples such as these, Jung was convinced of the need for a symbolic life, which connects us with the transpersonal. The phenomena of the personal myth and the destiny motif (discussed later in this chapter) are integral to this experience.

"Of all those who ever consulted me who were in the second half of life, no one was ever cured who did not achieve a spiritual outlook on life" (Jung, 1958, p. 334).

Jung's theory is often referred to as a therapy for the second half of life. It grew out of his experience. As previously mentioned, he felt that the theories of Freud and Adler, dealing with the development of personality, identity, career, relationships, and the resolution of sexual and power drives were good for the first half of life. In his *Collected Works*, Jung also described how all psychological theories tend to reflect the typologies of their originators. He compared the theories of Freud, introverted thinking; Adler, extroverted feeling; and himself, introverted intuition, in this regard.

Initially, he saw the individuation process as an experience of the second half of life. Later he revised this, recognizing that this process is lifelong. What has popularly became known as the "midlife crisis" has worked its way into common parlance. Today, everyone has some idea of this phenomenon. For some people it is a gradual process, not necessarily a crisis at all but simply a coming to terms, more realistically, with one's mortality and limited time and the importance of a larger perspective for one's life, such as has traditionally been offered by the religions of the world. Somewhere between the ages of 35 and 50 some people begin to feel a sense of restlessness, wanderlust, a quest for adventure, release from responsibility, redemption of lost childhood, or a desire for leisure and creativity.

For others, there may be more of an upheaval. This is especially true of individuals whose personalities have become more one sided. It might be said that the second half of life offers us the opportunity to rediscover those aspects of ourselves that have been lost. Where did we lose the path? Where did we diverge from being true to ourselves? Often these experiences take the form of a call or vocation to fulfill oneself through some new emphasis or value in one's life. See Paradigm of religious leaders in my article on "Spiritual Renewal at Midlife" (1998 pp. 269–270)

One woman dreamed that she discovered in her attic a chest containing the dreams and poems of her youth; for her this represents lost or abandoned idealism and creativity.

Another man, at retirement age, had a series of dreams in which he was taken back to his senior year in college, as if that point in time were a crossroads, there for him to consider a different path.

INDIVIDUATION PROCESS

Jung called his concept of the individuation process a "psychological equivalent of a spiritual journey." It includes several components such as his understanding of the personal myth, the hero's journey, the archetype of vocation, and the destiny motif. Each of these accents different qualities of the ego's experience of the self.

Jungian thought has always taken seriously the spiritual dimension of the psyche and the importance of spirituality in the lives of human beings. This was one of the major differences between Freud and Jung. Jung was interested in the belief systems of men and women, of whatever faith, as they enriched their lives with meaning and purpose and connected individuals with a Higher Power.

Spirituality, in broad terms, is meant as the inner life as it relates to what has been called the life of the soul—thoughts, feelings, imagination, images, insights, perceptions that pertain to and connect us with the transcendent. The more general term of "spiritual," rather than "religious," is being used in order to be inclusive and not limit our consideration to the major bodies of faith or great world religions. Nevertheless, many of these experiences may fit very well within one's particular experience of a traditional religion. Others of these experiences may not seem to do so, but they definitely get one's attention as coming from another realm of being, not under the control of the individual.

As Jung studied the many faiths of the world, he became convinced that there is a dimension of the psyche beyond the ego, or the conscious personality, which is universal and the source of spiritual experiences. He called this the self, that superordinating center of the personality which includes the entire psyche, conscious and unconscious. The self makes itself known to individuals in a variety of ways, which can be experienced directly. Some of these are dreams; symptoms, both physical and psychological; and experiences of synchronicity, or meaningful coincidences.

Jung discovered that the self has a larger perspective than the ego and often brings to our attention a different point of view for consideration. He recognized a purposeful orientation, or what philosophers would call a teleological function of the self. In other words, there is an inner force guiding us. Experiences such as dreams, symptoms, and synchronicities call this to our attention and reorient us, if we can discern their meaning

Many people consulted Jung because they had lost their faith; or the way in which they had understood it was no longer meaningful. Jung encouraged them to return to the religion of their earlier life, if they could, to deepen it or re-relate to it. For those who are not able, or do not wish to find such a perspective through religion, they may do so through what Jung called a psychological equivalent, the individuation process, which relates us to transpersonal phenomena and values.

Some individuals discover this inner orientation for themselves during their life experience. Many recognize this experience when they encounter Jung's articulation of it and feel affirmed. Others find their way to Jungian analysis, drawn by a search for greater transpersonal meaning and purpose and access to more of their potential.

Through the lifelong process by which we become the unique individuals we were created to be, we actualize our potentiality. It is a process through which, by integrating increasingly the unconscious aspects of the personality, the conscious personality gains more and more access to the self. The center of the personality shifts from ego to midpoint between the ego and the self.

Jung spoke of a spiritual dimension of the psyche from which people have powerful, transformative experiences that they formulate into various belief systems. He said that there are several elements to this dimension. The spiritual element, he suggested, is an organic aspect of the psyche that is expressed in symbols, which reveal a path of psychological development that points in a direction toward a goal. The goal is expressed in images of completion in a whole, which Jung called the self. The self is unique for each individual. It is found through the integration of the ego and the unconscious characterized by qualities of awe and wonder, which might be called numinous—qualities of unconditional authority, power, and value. These qualities also belong to the various images of God that have been enshrined in the great world religions of different cultures.

All spiritual experience is initially an individual's experience. Thus, Jung made the point that all such experience is also psychological experience, as it is the individual's psyche that has the experience. He coined the term "God-Image" to describe that aspect of the psyche that receives the experience of God. His study of William James's *The Varieties of Religious Experience* and Rudolph Otto's *The Idea of the Holy* helped him with the articulation of these life-changing experiences.

In saying that the subjective experience of the self and that of God are so similar that they cannot be distinguished, Jung aroused considerable controversy. This remark led to misunderstanding. He did not mean that the experience of God is only a psychological phenomenon, but that it is always through the psyche that we experience everything, including the Divine. He introduced the concept of the God image to discuss this, suggesting that the God image evolves in human consciousness.

The term "individuation" is used in a particular way by Jung and Jungians. Among some psychological orientations, individuation refers to the process of an infant and young child's separation from the mother, which takes place during the early period of a child's life. For Jung, however, the individuation process refers to the lifelong journey that each of us takes, during which we seek to fulfill, as much as possible, our potential. Just as the potential oak tree lies within each acorn, so the unique potential of each of us lies within the newborn infant.

Aristotle's concept of entelechy was influential in Jung's understanding that there is a unique pattern within the seed of each living being. Each of us is a unique incarnation of what it is to be a human being. Each individual has the opportunity to discover the particular man or woman he or she will be. Jung thought of this as a manner of understanding the "Imago Dei," the manner in which humankind is created in the image of God. He offered a corresponding way of considering the "imitation of Christ," namely to seek to be as true to one's own unique incarnation of the spirit as Christ was to his (Jung, 1958, p. 340).

Over the course of a lifetime, through an intricate combination of the unfolding of our genetic makeup, our life experience, including the formative experiences of our families of origin and other significant relationships and experiences and what we make of them, we individuate. For Jungians, then, unlike some schools of thought, we are all capable of significant growth and change all of our lives.

Jung's New Myth of Man

As it gradually dawns on people, one by one, that the idea of the evolution of the God image is not just an interesting idea but a living reality, it may become a new myth. Whoever recognizes this myth as his or her own personal reality will put his or her life in the service of this process. He or she will reflect upon his or her own unique incarnation of deity, experiencing life as meaningful and an example of Jung's understanding of the indwelling of the Holy Spirit and of St. Paul's "Christification of the many" (Edinger, 1984, p. 113).

As mentioned, some elements of the individuation process include the phenomenon of the personal myth, the hero's journey, the archetype of vocation, and the destiny motif. These are all variations on the ego's experience of the self. Brief descriptions follow.

The Personal Myth

The personal myth was first discussed by Jung, who suggested that everyone has a personal myth, irrespective of whether one is aware of it. By this he meant that there is at least one archetypal dynamic that is a dominant dynamic of each individual's psychology.

(Theoretically, there could be more than one dominant archetype directing an individual's life.) This dynamic will be expressed symbolically in dreams or other forms as a mythological motif, such as the hero, the victim, religious leader or healer, to name a few.

To the extent that the individual is unaware of this mythic dynamic affecting his or her life, he or she will be in its grips. Anything that we are identified with has power over us. If one is identified with an archetypal motif, one is being lived by it. Identification with the archetype will inflate the individual, causing him or her to appear grandiose, although often charismatic and attracting followers.

The idea of the personal myth was one that Jung first began to discover in some of his patients. He wondered why a particular individual would be connected with a particular mythological motif. They occurred, he discovered, because they are pertinent to the individual's psychology at a particular moment in his or her life. They represent something with which the individual needs to come to terms. Frequently, when an individual is challenged with an unfamiliar situation, he will discover within himself an effective response (Jung, 1988, p. 22). Later he may wonder where that ability came from. Jung would suggest that the archetype was constellated to support him at that moment; as if to say, "this is how humankind has dealt with this matter universally, from all times." Jung began to wonder what his personal myth was.

Jung, himself, had a dream in which Siegfried was killed. In contemplating that dream, he realized that Siegfried is a culture hero. He is one of the culture heroes of the culture in which Jung grew up—the culture of Germanic mythology. What Jung began to consider was that he had been unconsciously identified with the heroic attitude. The heroic attitude is one typically found in hero myths, in which the individual is growing in strength and mastery. It is an ego-centered style of life, appropriate to the first half of life.

He realized that it was time for him to relinquish this attitude.

Jung recognized, from his experience of the Siegfried dream, and others, that often people are identified with the myth, unconsciously fused with a certain dynamic of the unconscious and in its control. In the following, I will briefly illustrate the phenomenon of identification.

It is not uncommon, for example, for someone to say, "I don't want to be anything like my father or my mother" yet discover that one is nevertheless unconsciously just the same in some way. One man changed his name. He was originally named A.B., the same as his father. Wanting to be nothing like his father, he changed his name to B. A. What a surprise it was when he dreamed that "Not until you claim your given name will you resolve your father complex." Again, in many cases, young persons live out the unconscious of their parents.

Francis Wickes, an early Jungian analyst in New York City, was one of the first to write about this phenomenon. She started out as an elementary school teacher and became a Jungian analyst, working with children and their parents. She discovered that troubled children were frequently living out the unresolved conflicts of their parents. Children are very susceptible to the unconscious and absorb the emotions and traumas of others. Often they suffer from what the parents are not dealing with. Frequently they suffer from things that the parents need to become more responsible for, so that they are not unwittingly inflicted on the child. In her work with families, Mrs. Wickes began to delineate these dynamics and help parents take back their issues for themselves. Then, their children could then be relieved of that unnecessary suffering.

Hans Dieckman, from Berlin, had a similar but slightly different approach. He wrote about what he called *The Favorite Fairytale of Childhood* (Dieckmann, 1971). He discovered that, particularly in Europe where fairy tales are much more a part of children's experience, many people have a favorite fairy tale. What he learned was that the dynamics of that fairy tale, if you look at it and analyze it as if it were a dream, mirrors the psychology of the individual. If the individual's psychology has as one of its core challenges, the very motif of that fairy tale, then that becomes a central issue of that individual's individuation process.

This idea of the favorite fairy tale of childhood has within it the destiny motif. In symbolic, mythological language, as early as childhood one is called by what is part of one's life task. It is not uncommon to recognize that at an early age, a young person has an intuitive notion of something that he or she is going to deal with later in life. Or, if they don't recognize it, in retrospect, it begins to become clearer.

That is just another way in which someone recognized, clarified, and wrote about the theme of the personal myth. Fairy tales are very similar to myths. They are made up of the same symbolic, archetypal motifs.

Joseph Campbell also became very interested in the idea of the personal myth. He encountered it originally from Jung. Part of Campbell's idea was that if one is growing up in a particular culture, as long as that culture's belief system is meaningful, the individual can just grow up in it and find support for life, being embraced by the mythology.

You can use it, believe it, have initiations in it, and it will help move you along through life. But if it is no longer meaningful or viable for you, and if you are not at home with it, then you have to find your own individual belief system. This is true both for the personal myth and for one's personal spirituality.

The Destiny Motif

Closely related to, and integral to the ego-self dialog of the individuation process, over a lifetime, is the destiny motif, which occurs frequently in mythology, especially in the mythology of the hero. The myth of the hero has been called the mythological and cultural equivalent of the development of the ego. (See Campbell's *Hero With a Thousand Faces* and Otto Rank's *The Myth of the Birth of the Hero.*)

The destiny motif also occurs frequently in the stories of the great world religions and their leaders. Running through the destiny theme is the experience of synchronicity. Biblical examples include Moses, with the experience of the "Burning Bush," the Ten Commandments, and the Exodus; experiences of the prophets and their "Calls"; and the baptism of Christ and his experience in the wilderness (Wagenseller, 1995, pp. 167–172).

Both synchronicity and the destiny motif are very much part of the experience of modern-day men and women. The metaphor of the religious leader can also be seen as describing a particular process of midlife transformation for contemporary individuals, as described in my previously mentioned article.

Powerful, life-changing experiences, which are often encountered by individuals during midlife transformation, include a new vocation (Jung, 1954, pp. 175–186). The archetype of the call or vocation is an example of the phenomenology of the self that is experienced by the individual, moving him or her to redirect or rededicate his or her life purpose. An example of this is the experience of my classmate, Tom, mentioned later in the section on synchronicity, who left his work on creating bombs to become a cardiologist and establish cardiology centers in third-world countries.

Three frequently experienced phenomena of the individuation process that result from the activity of the self are symptoms, dreams, and synchronicity. Symptoms, dreams, and synchronistic experiences may or may not be believed to be spiritual, but they do emanate from what we call a transpersonal dimension of one's being or psyche. They are beyond the will or control of the ego and often at odds with it, as if they came from another consciousness and have a purpose within the personality.

Symptoms

Once the personality is fairly well established, there begins to be, either forcefully or more gradually, a reorganization of the personality. Elements that have not been included begin to surface and make a bid for integration. What has been repressed begins to surface; feelings, unmet needs, and distressing symptoms intrude upon one's awareness. Sometimes the need for change is more conscious.

An individual may experience a general dissatisfaction with oneself or one's life. For others, more acute symptoms may occur: Anxiety; depression; unwanted, intrusive, obsessional thoughts, including suicidal thoughts; compulsions and addictions; eating disorders; alcoholism; and so on will present themselves for consideration. Somewhere between the ages of 35 and 50 these changes begin to make themselves known.

In keeping with Jung's interest in taking a non-pejorative view of all psychological productions of the psyche, he studied symbol systems such as mythology and world religions, looking for patterns that were expressed similarly in them. Taking a symbolic view of the symptoms of his patients, he suggested that the symptom has within it the seeds of the cure. "A psychoneurosis, he suggested, must be understood, ultimately, as the suffering of a soul which has not discovered its meaning" (Jung, 1958, pp. 330–331). On another occasion, he suggested that the gods and goddesses of the Pantheon have become the diseases of modern-day men and women. He saw these gods and goddesses as symbolic projections of subpersonalities. By no longer honoring the transpersonal dynamisms of Aphrodite (love), Ares (aggression), Dionysos (ecstasy), and Hera (domesticity), individuals were either possessed by identification with these complexes or dissociated from them (Bolen, 1984, 1989).

Jung claimed that of all those who ever consulted him in the second half of life, no one was ever cured who did not achieve a spiritual outlook on life (Jung, 1958, p. 334). By this he meant not necessarily an orthodox religious point of view, although that may be the case for some, but its psychological equivalent, that which has been provided by the great world religions of various cultures—a depth or a height dimension that gives perspective to an individual's life, giving it meaning by placing it in a larger perspective.

By listening to the unpleasant symptoms of midlife challenge, taking a symbolic approach to them, and finding a more receptive attitude toward the rejected values within them, these neglected or rejected aspects of the personality become integrated. Through the application of the "redemptive attitude," sometimes referred to as "befriending the shadow," devalued elements of the personality, such as aggression, sexuality, spirituality, neediness, vocational issues, and others are met and included. As a result of this process, new life flowers; needs are met, vocational issues clarify, and spirituality blossoms.

Jung's approach toward the symbolic understanding of the meaning of symptoms is consistent with his view of the purposefulness of the self. The self manifests a wisdom beyond that of the ego and seems to know better what is needed. In other words, the meaning of the symptom discloses that a basic human need is being related to maladaptively, resulting in unnecessary suffering. This understanding goes right to the heart of all psychosomatic medicine, the mind/body connection, and often what it is that needs to be related to differently.

For example, when the founders of Alcoholics Anonymous were starting the organization, they consulted Jung. Essentially, his idea was that people who are caught in a compulsion for spirits need to find a different relation to the spiritual dimension of life. This is the principal of homeopathic medicine, "Like cures like." It was out of this advice and guidance that the founders of Alcoholics Anonymous included the spiritual dimension of the recovery process, referred to as the need for a "Higher Power." This has also been included in other 12-step, self-help programs such as Overeaters Anonymous.

Similar changes of attitude are helpful with other compulsions. As Jung has pointed out, compulsions are what once were known as "possessions." These are agonizing experiences in which one is controlled by the unconscious dynamic of a complex. Frequently it is such experiences that bring people into therapy. Usually what is needed is a different relationship to the particular dynamic by which the individual is gripped, whether it is one's sexuality, one's dependency needs, one's creativity, or one's power complex. Whatever the compulsion is, the individual needs a more accepting attitude toward the value and power embedded in the symptom. Usually the problem lies in the fact that the individual unconsciously judges the quality and devalues it.

In sexual addictions, he saw the need for a more conscious acceptance and integration of one's sexuality. In gambling and kleptomania, he might have suggested a more conscious acceptance of one's ambition and desire for material substance, as well as a willingness to work for it.

In short, when there is some aspect of our human nature that we do not accept and come to terms with in our personality, we are usually troubled by it eventually: frequently by being caught in the grips of unconscious dynamics such as obsessions and compulsions. Jungians view such troubling sufferings as eating disorders, sexual addictions and deviations, and other addictions as symbolic/

symptomatic manifestations of undervalued, natural human attributes.

All of the old seven deadly sins, for example, can be seen as natural, healthy components of the personality, when they are valued and integrated. They become problematic only to the extent that they are denied or repressed and gain an unconscious grasp on the individual. Two examples will help to illustrate this process.

A woman was attacked by a man in a park and fought him off with a violence she had never experienced before. She was so frightened of her power that she never wanted to feel it again. When it was pointed out to her that this power had effectively saved her from an unwanted experience, she began to see it as the antidote to her general dissatisfaction with her "lukewarm" life. The analyst used the myth of Heracles's Twelve Labors to illustrate the transformation of energy from murderous rage to the civilizing experiences resulting from the refinement of libido. The integration of her aggression was exactly what she needed to energize her life into one of greater fulfillment.

In another situation, a man who was in recovery from alcohol and drug addiction began to experience feelings of what he called "lust." By taking the "redemptive attitude" toward his sexuality, it became the antidote to his isolation and loneliness, leading to marriage and a family.

> Behind the neurotic perversion is concealed his vocation, his destiny; the growth of personality, the full realization of the life-will that is born with the individual. It is the man without *amor fati* who is the neurotic.
> (*Jung*, 1954 p. 185)

Illness as Vocation

Most illnesses bring with them emotional responses such as discouragement or depression. By applying Jung's prospective method to the experience, we can ask, "What is being asked of me in this suffering?" Depression, for example, can be understood as a call to go more deeply into ourselves in order to find another level of meaning from which to be living our lives (Harding 1970).

If each of us, in our own individual way, is trying to become the best he or she can be and to put together the best life that he or she can, then our sufferings and illnesses might be considered in the context of our best efforts. Illness may then be a compromise or a less than successful adaptation to some challenge of life, inviting us to consider a different view.

In other words, if all forms of illness, psychological and physical, are considered as maladaptive responses to some aspect of life, then we can see how these various instances of suffering participate in our experience of destiny and individuation. In this context, it will be important to reflect upon just what it might mean that one became ill with a particular form of suffering at a particular time in life. How is it that this is the best response I could make to the challenges of my life at this time? Illness can be seen then as a call, or vocation, to a change of life. For more on the "archetype of vocation," see a list of my work in the References.

Often religious and charismatic leaders experience a serious, life-threatening illness as an aspect of a conversion. St. Paul is an excellent example of this, being struck blind at the time of his conversion. Shamans typically undergo such physical and/ or psychological, spiritual ordeals as an aspect of their calling. Many men and women today undergo such upheavals during the midlife years, as did Jung. One individual, for example, during the early period of his analysis, was experiencing difficulties with vision, hearing, and balance. These symptoms disappeared miraculously, he felt, as he realized the maladaptiveness of the attitudes that brought him to analysis.

Dreams

When Sigmund Freud discovered what he called "The Royal Road to the Unconscious," his theory of dream analysis, many colleagues gathered around him to form the beginnings of the psychoanalytic movement. One of these was Carl Jung, who brought new dimensions to the understanding of dreams.

From early in their relationship, Jung differed from Freud with regard to their understanding of the unconscious and dreams. For Jung, in addition to dreams expressing repressed aspects of the personal unconscious, they also conveyed creative potential within the dreamer and offered a purposeful thrust connecting him and moving him toward the fulfillment of that potential.

This view became fully articulated in his commentary of a case of Theodore Flournoy's, referred to as Miss Miller, published in *Symbols of Transformation*. Jung was struck by the mythological character of many of these fantasies. While working on this case, he had several dreams of his own, suggesting that a break with Freud was emerging. (For a thorough coverage of Jungian dream theory and practice, consult the References.)

Some people begin to be attentive to their dreams in childhood and intuitively grasp that they have meaning. Some never remember their dreams. Others are engaged by them at a particular time in their lives. Following are examples of each.

There is a remarkable account, in *Man and His Symbols* (Jung, 1964 pp. 50–60), of a 10-year-old girl who wrote down a series of dreams that so captured her attention that she drew pictures of them and presented them to her father for Christmas. The father brought them to Jung, who had the sad task of telling him that they heralded his daughter's death. She died shortly thereafter. It has been observed and documented that when an individual's life is pressured by impending death, the preparation process may be telescoped, as is seen in this case.

Personally, although I have been aware of dreams throughout my lifetime, it was a series of three dreams within a week, when I was 25 years old, that made it clear to me that there were inner matters of a spiritual nature that needed attention before proceeding to my ordination to the priesthood. They engaged me and sent me off to do more inner work before returning to be ordained.

A man of 64 years of age was about to retire from a company he had worked for all of his adult life. He had been a hard-working, conscientious person, loyal to his employer and family. Just as he was about to retire, his company was taken over by another and he was left with much more reduced benefits than he had anticipated. His wife left him, and one of his sons deeply disappointed him. His distress was such that he had nothing to look forward to; he could see no reason to live. However, he began to remember vivid and powerful dreams for the first time in his life. Working with those dreams led him to a dramatic change of outlook and a remarkable new life, which included meeting, quite by chance, it seemed, a much younger woman from another part of the world and very different culture, and marrying her. This was an event he would never have expected. He also made his peace with those whom, he felt, had done him wrong, and he entered into a postretirement career full of traveling and writing, which he fully enjoyed.

As we begin to observe and attend to our dreams more closely and carefully, we may become deeply impressed by the intricacy of them. We begin to wonder, "Where do these dreams come from? Who is the author of my dreams? I could not have thought up this dream with my waking mind; I would never have imagined it." We develop a profound respect for this dimension, the transpersonal, or the source that is beyond our individual personal experiences

Gradually, it dawns upon us that the author of our dreams is remarkably creative. We realize that the author knows things that we do not know. There are perceptions of ourselves and others that are astoundingly insightful. A dream may offer an observation, from its perspective, on a situation that we had not considered. Some people are led through dreams back into their ancestry to discover meaningful information. In two instances known to me, individuals discovered their biological fathers as a result of their dreams.

We recognize that these dreams come from another dimension. They have a mind of their own—meaning that they are evidence of the autonomy of the unconscious. Often people have dreams they would prefer not to have. Sometimes people even dread sleep, anticipating disturbing dreams. Sometimes one may be awakened by a dream that is so upsetting that he or she is reluctant to return to sleep, out of concern that the dream may be continued; often it is.

Throughout this chapter, I will illustrate with dreams from already published books, and some from former analysands, who gave me permission to use them. All of what follows will illustrate the purposeful thrust of the self as it orchestrates the unconscious through dreams to awaken the dreamer to a new understanding and change of life.

In the Jungian approach to dream analysis, the dreamer is first asked his or her associations to the various elements of the dream, such as the setting, the people, action, and so forth. The dream can be understood both on what is called the objective, or outer level, or on the subjective level, in which all of the elements of the dream are understood as aspects of the dreamer's inner life. In addition to the dreamer's personal associations, Jungians are also attuned to what are known as archetypal motifs in a dream, such as the hero motif, or an initiation motif, or the theme of transformation, or creation.

For Jungian analysts, dreams can do a number of things: A dream can be therapeutically beneficial, even if it is not understood. The more a dream can be understood, however, the better. As new awareness brought by the dream becomes integrated into consciousness, the dynamic relationship between the dreamer and the unconscious changes. There is an ongoing dialog between the waking personality and the unconscious. The self is the author of our dreams and of our life's destiny.

Secondly, a dream can be diagnostically informative. Frequently a dream, told at the beginning of a therapeutic course of treatment, picturing the dynamic of the unconscious, helps inform the diagnostician. Often in the initial interview, a dream is reported that offers very helpful diagnostic and prognostic information. Here are two examples.

A young man in his early 30s, who had earned two masters degrees, but felt stuck and unable to engage with his life in any sort of effective way, had this dream: "I am presented with a butterfly and told I have to choose between the wings and the body."

It was clear to him in the dream that whichever he chose would result in killing the butterfly. Interestingly, the Greek work for butterfly is *psyche*. It is not uncommon for dreams to offer etymological information. The dream pointed up in a succinct, metaphorical image his body-spirit conflict.

In another instance, a dreamer presented this dream: "I am walking on the moon with a race of giants. The moon explodes and burns out my eyes." Within a week, the dreamer was hospitalized with a psychosis.

Thirdly, a dream can indicate the prognosis of the therapy. It can indicate the transferential disposition of the individual through the characterization of the therapist or therapy, such as portraying them as educational or legalistic, or similar to someone known from the past. Or it may suggest resistance through the unavailability of either the therapist or applicant. Dreams can alert the dreamer to physical illness as well as provide precognitive information.

There are also various types of dreams. Childhood dreams make a lasting impression; some of these are analogous to the favorite fairy tale of childhood and have embedded within them the life task of the individual.

Nightmares threaten the dreamer both during the dream and upon awakening because they threaten the individual's sense of identity and security. Here is an example. A huge gorilla is breaking down the door of the dreamer's bedroom. He had been so depressed he had been unable to get out of bed. The dream alerted him to the need to integrate his aggression.

Recurrent dreams: Some dreams recur until the dreamer gets the message. One woman who repeatedly dreamed of herself as a prostitute finally realized that she had been devaluing herself as a woman, continually deferring to the masculine.

Dream series: I will illustrate a dream series of my own.

Perhaps the main issue early in analysis was to sort out the impact of his relationship with his father and his sudden and traumatic death. Early dreams told that he was not dead, but still alive and at someone else's house. The dreamer was to go and bring him home. Once there, happy to have learned that his father was still alive, he found him grotesquely deformed as he had been for the day he lived after his stroke. Versions of this dream were repeated several times, until, in one of these dreams, the father sat up and said, "This means that the father in you is paralyzed." Just in case the dreamer did not understand.

Then, there was a series of dreams in which the dreamer's father would come to visit to see how the dreamer was getting along in his life. In one dream, the father was interested in the analysis. Interestingly to the dreamer, Jung describes in *Memories, Dreams, Reflections* that his father visited him after his death. In the last of this series, the father was the dreamer's age and size, although he had been considerably smaller. He visited the dreamer's family to meet them and embraced the dreamer.

A subset of these father dreams involved the dreamer's voice.

In the first, he was told that singing would help to resolve father issues by finding his own voice. Although understanding that this was not to be taken literally, he took voice lessons for 10 years with a teacher who taught from a psychological perspective. For many years, the dreamer's voice was one of the metaphors of his unconscious process until finally there was a dream in which he was singing in a choir of peoples of all nations in the ruins of the Temple of Jerusalem. The dreamer could hear the voices singing in their own languages and could hear his own in harmony with them.

The reader may be interested to know that, during the writing of this chapter, I had another dream that, after many years, again involved my voice and seemed to suggest the integration of various time periods in my life, singing the tune of a song learned in childhood ("The Ash Grove") but with words that wove together my boyhood and made reference to my early ministry and analytic training. It seemed as if the work on this section stirred me to present another singing dream that partnered feeling with understanding.

The series illustrates the progressive movement of the unconscious, as it symbolically represents the healing and integration process. In closing this section, I will recommend to the reader a section of Edward F. Edinger's book, *Ego and Archetype: Individuation and the Religious Function of the*

Psyche, in which he presents dreams of a metaphysical nature, preparing the dreamers for their deaths (1973, pp. 197 & ff).

Synchronicity as Grace

"To this day, God is the name by which I designate all things which cross my willful path violently and recklessly, all things which upset my subjective views, plans and intentions and change the course of my life, for better or worse" (author's correspondence with a man in Cambridge, England).

Synchronicity

Our attention may be drawn to the activity of the self in a number of ways. Two of these have already been mentioned, namely symptoms and dreams. A third is synchronicity, or other versions of what are often called paranormal or parapsychological experiences. All of these have the capacity to disrupt our lives, as Jung said in the earlier quote. They can change our intentions and plans completely.

Jung's theory of synchronicity was his effort to provide a theoretical overview for those experiences that connect an individual's psyche with unusual psychic events, such as clairvoyance, extrasensory perception, and others, such as numinous spiritual experiences, which seem to relate him or her to the cosmos and the transcendent.

By synchronicity, Jung meant the meaningful intersection or connection between two or more events, one inner and the other(s) outer, which cannot be proven to be causally connected, but which are meaningfully related. Usually there is a meaningful connection between one's subjective psychological experience, such as one's inner preoccupation, and the experiences that one encounters in life—meaningful coincidences.

A common example might be to think of someone one has not seen for some time. Suddenly the phone rings and that person has called. Or two people are recalling a third person whom neither has heard from in a long time, when suddenly that third person is in contact. Such an event catches our attention. Some people have these experiences frequently, others less so, but they make an impression.

I recently had such an experience, when approaching my fiftieth high school reunion; I pondered the fact that I had heard nothing of one of my classmates since graduation day. This friend, named Tom, had been a classmate since first grade. Many other classmates had been seen or heard of, but Tom was conspicuously missing.

Within a day of wondering what had become of Tom, he called me. No one else from the class called, but Tom did. It turned out that he had been a scientist making bombs, when he decided one evening to change and become a physician. He had become a cardiologist and had been establishing cardiology centers in third-world countries.

Synchronicity is the meaningful intersection between our own psychological condition and our experiences in life. Why is it that at a particular moment in my life I happen to have a certain experience that turns me in a certain direction, which makes a great difference in my life, which might have gone very differently? If I hadn't been open to or responded to the moment with a certain attitude, which might have been uncharacteristic of me, the whole experience would not have happened. This is the kind of experience that many people call "grace."

You begin to attend to what gets your attention. It begins to make sense. Something clicks and, like the subtle shift of a kaleidoscope, you shift into a different frame of mind and state of being. In Jungian terms, a different rapport is established between the ego and the self. Something is offered; you respond and cooperate. As a result, you and your life are changed.

For some people, these experiences of synchronicity occur at transition points in their lives. Often, when this is the case, they carry something of the destiny motif or archetype. People who are attuned to synchronicity in their lives tend to be more open to life's meaningful interruptions. They recognize the relationship between their psyches and the way in which their lives are encountered—the way in which they are able to respond to them, engage with them, and work out some degree of partnership with their destiny.

By way of illustration, I will share several such experiences. I went off to college, thinking I would become a clergyman. Part way through college, I was not so sure. The month before my senior year, my father died suddenly of a stroke.

Two days later I was walking along the river thinking about what I was going to do. I decided that I would "walk in my father's footsteps" in the hope that they would lead me to a deeper relationship with my heavenly Father, in relation to Whom I would discover more clearly who I was and what was to be my purpose and path in life. At that time, I knew nothing of Jung's work, but intuitively, I sensed the connection between the personal and archetypal father and its meaning for my destiny.

(Later, during my analysis, I came to understand the extent to which I had been identified with my father. I was not sure whether my vocation was really mine or a continuation of his.)

This was a kind of poetic, intuitive way of forming a plan or direction. After my graduation from college, I went on to the same seminary he had attended. Upon graduation, I went to my first parish in Richmond, Virginia, where I agreed, as a part of my work, to minister to a small group of deaf persons, who met there for worship. I went to Gallaudet College, in Washington, and learned sign language sufficiently to conduct services and engage in a pastoral ministry with them. By the end of my first year, the small group of about a dozen had grown to sixty families.

Around the end of my first year there, I was to be ordained as a priest, having been a deacon for a year. The Feast of Pentecost was approaching, and I was preparing a sermon on it, trying to think about how to make sense of phrases like "a rushing mighty wind" and "tongues of flame" to a group of people who might have some difficulty understanding them. Had I been preaching to the "hearing congregation" upstairs, I would have thought I knew just what I was talking about.

However, I was led back to explore just what was Pentecost in the first century. Clearly it was a pre-Christian celebration. I was reminded that Pentecost was a harvest festival, 50 days after the giving of the Law to Moses. I began to speculate that the Disciples, who were still hiding in the Upper Room, in fear, were celebrating this Jewish festival probably in connection with a commemoration of the Lord's Supper, as he had taught them, when they were transformed. What was described in these powerfully symbolic images gave them the conviction and the courage to overcome their fear and be empowered.

My thoughts further developed to the point that I felt they were no longer "orthodox," leaving me conflicted. These feelings and thoughts were powerfully underscored by a series of three dreams I had within one week. I had not paid a great deal of attention to my dreams before, but I knew intuitively that they meant that I was not ready to be ordained. I postponed my ordination indefinitely and took a leave of absence to go off and contemplate.

My first stop was to attend a weekend conference in Triangle, Virginia, entitled "The Apple and the Silver Cord," which was a series of dialogs between an Episcopal clergyman and the president of the C. G. Jung Foundation of New York City.

These dialogs helped me gain a freer and more symbolic understanding of what I had felt I needed to espouse too concretely. People I met at the conference invited me to visit with them on Bailey Island, Maine, where I met and had my first analytic sessions with Dr. Esther Harding.

In discussing some of my dreams with her, she was able to shed light on my conflicts and help me to see a way through them. In one dream, I wanted to make love with a woman with whom I had had a relationship. She said, "Not until you have resolved your vocational problem." In response to this dream, Dr. Harding pointed out succinctly, "You cannot have your soul (*anima*) until you resolve your vocational dilemma." This happened remarkably to me in two sessions.

Dr. Harding referred me to a Jungian analyst named Elined Kotchnig, who lived and practiced in Chevy Chase, Maryland. I saw her on my day off, a trip of approximately 120 miles each way. By the way, Mrs. Kotchnig was a Quaker, very active in Quaker retreats and studies at Pendle Hill, near Haverford, Pennsylvania, where my father had been so moved by Quaker mysticism. My analytic work enabled me to resolve my theological conflicts and return to my position in Richmond and be ordained.

The next wummer, I attended a week-long conference sponsored by the Jung Foundation and the Educational Center of St. Louis, intended for those in religious education. There I met people from all over the country and Canada. With many of them, I stayed in touch for many years. The conference included presentations such as Dr. Edinger's "Christ as Paradigm of the Individuating Ego" (the first time he presented it; it is now found in Ego and Archetype 1973); Esther Harding's "The Psychological Meaning of the Crucifixion"; Edward Whitmont's "The Redemption of Satan"; Ross Hainline's "The Unconscious Experienced as Fate"; and others. This was a very powerful week and it stirred my dream life deeply. It was clear to me that Dr. Edinger was the person with whom I wanted to work analytically. I spoke to him about it and he told me to contact him when I moved to New York City.

Within a few months, I was offered a position in Connecticut, which enabled me to move and begin my analysis, and later my training, at the Jung Institute. Around this time, I met the young woman who became my wife. We married, she completed her nursing training, I completed my analytic training, and we decided to begin a family.

However, 8 years later, we had still been unable to conceive. Then, one day in the spring of 1978, someone asked me if I would be the speaker on Mothers' Day at a Mothers and Daughters Communion Breakfast at a church in another community. In accepting the invitation, I was intrigued by the fact (coincidence, maybe to become a "meaningful coincidence?") that in 1978 Pentecost and Mothers' Day were being celebrated on the same day. I thought about that and spoke about how sometimes with our preconceived notions about such things as beliefs and theology, we miss what is before us.

I spoke about how the biblical tradition of the Old and New Testament and the Judeo-Christian tradition tended to think of God in masculine terms—a patriarchal god of Father, Son, and Holy Spirit. I reminded us of how earlier cultures had valued female goddesses. For example, the religion of Demeter and Persephone had been a very powerful one in Greek culture for centuries. I spoke about the uniqueness of the mother–daughter relationship. And I spoke about Sophia, who was described in the wisdom literature of the late Old Testament era, as a feminine counterpart of God, a feminine version of the Holy Spirit. I spoke of Jung's emphasis upon the missing feminine in the Godhead of Western religions. I spoke of being receptive and open to the unexpected encounters with the divine, not only in the Burning Bush and the Manger, but in other unexpected places. That afternoon, our daughter was conceived—a little feminine form of the spirit.

That was in May of 1978. On August 23 of that year, I was driving around Westport, Connecticut, when I passed a building I had passed many times before but to which I had never paid much attention. I thought to myself, "Someday I might like to start a center, where I could do my work of psychotherapy and Jungian analysis, share it with a group of colleagues, and invite others to teach and present their work. Maybe a building like that would lend itself to the purpose."

I was anticipating becoming a father and contemplating what sort of a father I wanted to be. I thought of my own father, as it was the anniversary of his death. I thought about what I had loved and admired about him and what I would want to develop differently in myself. One thing I knew was that I would like to become a better provider, in material terms, since, with his sudden death, our family lost our home and had only enough money to pay for his funeral.

I decided to stop in at a real estate office to speak with a broker I knew, just to speak about the idea and ask about its feasibility. I was thinking about a project, perhaps 10 years in the future. The woman I was looking for was not there, but her partner was. We met easily and I shared with him my thoughts. He asked me if I had a few minutes, which I did. He drove me to the very building in town that had caught my attention. He told me that this building was not yet on the market, but that it would be coming on the market soon. He said that he thought it would suit my purposes very well. I told him that I wasn't prepared to buy anything just yet; I was thinking of some years ahead. He told me that, if I could come up with the down payment, he was confident that he could fill the building with tenants within a month.

Within an hour, the challenge had been resolved. A second mortgage on our home provided the down payment and, true to his word, the broker filled the building with tenants, sufficiently to carry the cost.

In recent years, I have become more attuned to these experiences of synchronicity. On one occasion, I had three experiences within a 24-hour period that caught my attention.

I came out of a CVS pharmacy and paused on the sidewalk, when a woman drove up in a car, got out, and came directly up to me, holding out a magazine and asked me, "Are you interested in physical therapy?" I said, "Yes, but I don't think I need it just now." She said, "Alright," then got back in her car and drove away, not speaking to anyone else. That seemed odd to me. That was in Westport, Connecticut.

The next morning, walking to my office in Manhattan, a woman came up to me on the sidewalk, held out a magazine and said, "Do you want to be saved?" I said, "Yes, I think so, but not just at this moment."

Within 5 minutes, I walked into my office to find my phone ringing. It was the director of the Jung Foundation, who said, "We are planning the Summer Studies Program at the Foundation on the theme of 'Staying Sane in an Insane World.' We would like you to be the speaker on the last day on the subject of 'Keeping the Faith.'" I paused for a moment and said, "Let me think about it."

As I reflected upon the invitation and these incidents, it felt as if something was beckoning me. I wasn't sure what to make of this but felt that somehow life was addressing me and inviting me to respond in some way. I didn't want to speak on "Keeping the Faith" as such but offered a modified version, "Keeping Our Equilibrium During

Turbulent Times." It afforded me an opportunity to reflect upon just where I was then.

As I was thinking about what I wanted to speak about, more experiences occurred.

I received a phone call from another high school classmate, George Krevsky, whom I hadn't seen in 40 years. He told me how his life had evolved and of the chance meeting with Esther Smith. He spoke of how his conversation with this artist had resulted in his leaving his work as the director of Jewish Community Centers and establishing an art gallery in San Francisco.

The next week, Clyde Smith, another friend since age 5, called to tell me his mother had died. His mother was Esther Smith, the very woman about whom George had spoken the week before. A few years earlier Clyde had attended my mother's funeral; this had meant a lot to me. I told him to let me know when and where the memorial service would be and that I would be there. He expressed surprise and pleasure and asked if I would perform the service. I said, "Of course I would." We agreed to speak further in a few days. When we spoke, it turned out that his sister felt that her mother's memorial service should not be a Christian one, since she was Jewish and probably not even a religious service, since she was really more of a humanitarian. Clyde asked if I would still conduct the service. I said that I would, although we would need to reconsider it.

As I thought about Esther, I realized that her religion was her art and the appreciation and expression of beauty. I was reminded of John Keats's poem "Ode to a Grecian Urn." "Beauty is truth and truth beauty. That's all we know on earth and all we need to know." That became the theme of the service. People attending stood up one at a time and told stories of how she had touched their lives, caringly and courageously. In one story, Esther had been attending a concert to which some soldiers stationed nearby had been given tickets. They began to heckle one of the performers. Esther, five feet tall, stood up, stopped the concert, with about 500 people present, spoke about respect for difference, and sat down as the concert continued with no further heckling.

As we have heard, Jung discovered the meaningful and purposeful thrust of the disconcerting and disruptive events of his life His conviction that he was being engaged by a call he did not yet understand helped him to persevere through chaos to a new order. He experienced the reordering phenomenon of the self. Out of this reorganization of his personality, he discovered the individuation process, his own psychological equivalent of a spiritual journey, available to everyone in search of his or her path. The best way to lose oneself is by following someone else's path.

Conclusion

Tracing the spiritual dimension of life and the psyche throughout Jung's life and work, this chapter has illustrated his passion for the direct experience of God. Beginning with his exceptional childhood experiences of the depth of the psyche, his personal experiences were discovered to be individual versions of universal phenomena, which he later termed "archetypal."

For Jung, the real question is, "Is man related to anything greater than himself?"

His understanding of the "secret of the personality" evolved through his lifetime as his "main business," a term he took from Goethe. This refers to the relationship between the individual's experience of the transpersonal and those of others at all times and places, that which connects us with others and the universe. The discovery of the individuation process became the opportunity for the individual to find an attunement with the self and a dynamic spiritual journey unfolding from within. As the individuation process awakens through symptoms, dreams, and synchronicity, the individual discovers a relationship with the spiritual aspect of the personality.

Future Directions

Through Jung's experience of the "confrontation with the unconscious" and the creative reorganization of his psyche, he discovered the universal relevance and applicability of that phenomenon in his psychotherapeutic work with others.

Because of the very nature and emphasis of Jung's work on the sanctity of individual experience, it does not lend itself easily to research, which, by its very nature is concerned with the collective, numbers, statistics, percentages, and nonindividual data.

Future study might address a statistical analysis.

References

Dieckmann, H. (1971). The favorite fairytale of childhood as a therapeutic factor in analysis. In J. Wheelwright (Ed.), *The analytic process* (pp. 77–84). New York: Putnam.

Edinger, E. (1973). *Ego and archetype; Individuation and the religious function of the psyche*. Baltimore: Penguin Books.

Edinger, E. (1984). *The creation of consciousness*. Toronto: Inner City Books.

Harding, E. (1970). The meaning and value of depression. *Bulletin for the Analytical Psychology Club of New York*, 1–15.

Jung, C. G. (1954). The development of personality. In *Collected works* (Vol. 17, pp. 175–186). New York: Pantheon.

Jung, C.G. (1958). Psychology and religion: West and east. In M. Fordham (Ed.), *Collected works* (Vol. 11, Ch. V. p. 334). New York: Pantheon.

Jung, C. G. (1976). The symbolic life. In M. Fordham (Ed.), *Collected works* (Vol. 18, Ch. III, pp. 267–281). New York: Princeton University Press.

Jung, C. G., & Jaffe, A. (Eds.). (1963). *Memories, dreams, reflections*. (R. C. Winston, Trans.). New York: Pantheon.

Jung, C. G. (1988). In J. L. Jarrett (Ed.), *Nietzche's Zarathrustra*. Princeton University Press.

Jung, C. G. (1964). Approaching the Unconscious. In C. Jung & M. Von Franz (Eds.), *Man and his symbols* (pp. 58–60) New York: Doubleday.

Wagenseller, J. P. (1995). The archetype of vocation. In *Protestantism and Jungian psychology* (pp. 167–172. Tempe, AZ: New Falcon Publications.

Wagenseller, J. P. (1998). Spiritual renewal at midlife. *Journal of Religion and Health*, *37*(3), 265–272.

Further reading

Bolen, J. S. (1984). Goddesses in every woman. New York: Harper & Row.

Bolen, J. S. (1989). Gods in everyman. New York: Harper & Row.

Campbell, J. (1949). *The hero with a thousand faces*. Princeton, NJ: Princeton University Press.

Edinger, E. (1996). *The new God-image*. Wilmette, IL: Chiron.

PART 5

Mind, Awareness and Consciousness in Treatment: Eastern Traditions

Contemplative Traditions and Meditation

Brendan D. Kelly

Abstract

Most of the world's major religious and spiritual traditions incorporate elements of contemplative prayer or meditation, although the nature, prominence, and precise features of such practices vary between traditions. Neuroscientific findings indicate that meditation is associated with significant, enduring alterations in patterns of activity in specific brain areas (e.g., anterior cingulate cortex, dorsolateral prefrontal areas). These, in turn, are linked with the increased attention and alterations in experience of self associated with contemplative practice. Neuroscientific findings are complemented by clinical evidence of relationships between contemplative practice and positive psychological change, leading, for example, to the use of "mindfulness-based cognitive therapy" for depression (combining mindfulness-based techniques from Buddhist tradition with Western cognitive therapeutic approaches). There remains substantial potential for further research and ongoing dialog aimed at developing deeper, more integrated understandings of the spiritual, psychological, and biological effects of contemplative practice.

Key Words: meditation, spirituality, religion, Buddhism, Christianity, cross-cultural comparison, neurosciences, psychology, psychotherapy, mental disorders

Introduction

The word *meditate* is derived from the Latin word *meditari* (contemplate) and means to exercise the mind in contemplation, especially religious contemplation (Pearsall & Trumble, 1996, p. 898). Most of the world's major religious and spiritual traditions include elements of contemplative prayer or meditation as part of their practices, although the nature, prominence, and precise features of such contemplative practices vary significantly between traditions.

In the early 21st century, the practice of meditation is most immediately associated with Buddhist tradition in many parts of the world, although there are also substantial, often neglected elements of contemplation and meditation within Christianity, Islam, Hinduism, Judaism, and Taoism. There are also many nonspiritual, nonreligious traditions involving practices of contemplation and meditation, most of which resemble spiritual or religious contemplative practices in certain procedural respects but do not have explicitly religious or spiritual frameworks surrounding their practices.

This chapter aims to explore meditative practices within a range of contemplative religious or spiritual traditions, with particular focuses on Buddhism and Christianity.

Meditative Practices in the Buddhist Tradition
The Foundations of Buddhist Meditation

Buddhism is a spiritual, psychological, philosophical, and cultural tradition that has its roots in the story of Buddha or "awakened one" (Gethin, 1998; Harvey, 1990). The historical Buddha, Siddhārtha

Gautama, was born in India around 566 BC, the protected son of a chieftan. Siddhārtha, however, became dissatisfied with his life of privilege and left home to become a wandering ascetic. After years of self-mortification and meditation, Siddhārtha sat in prolonged meditation beneath a sacred Bodhi tree, and, after resisting many forms of temptation and attack, he achieved enlightenment, whereby he finally beheld the exact condition of all living beings and saw the cause and solution to suffering.

Many of the central principles of the Buddha's subsequent teachings are reflected in the Buddha's "four truths" and "eightfold path," both of which are central to the development of Buddhist psychology and, in turn, Buddhist contemplative practice. The four truths are concerned with human suffering (*duhkha*) and the way to overcome suffering:

(a) *Duhkha* refers to the unsatisfactoriness of human experience and behavior, highlighting a need to identify the root cause of *duhkha* and overcome it.

(b) *The roots of duhkha* lie in attachment (also translated as craving and "grasping" or "attachment"), hatred, and delusion, all three of which are implicit in human responses to sensory phenomena; this truth provides many of the underpinnings for Buddhism's focus on cognitive training, contemplative practice, and meditation.

(c) *The cessation of suffering* can be attained by conquering attachment, aversion, and delusion; this is known as *nirvāna* or *nibbāna*.

(d) *How to overcome duhkha:* The way to overcome *dukkha* is through Buddhism's eightfold path, based on the principles of wisdom, moral virtue, and meditation.

The eightfold path is chiefly concerned with achieving the cessation of suffering and is centred on the concepts of wisdom, moral virtue, and meditation.

WISDOM

(a) *Right view* refers to understanding things as they really are, based on the four truths; right view fundamentally informs all other elements of the eightfold path.

(b) *Right intention* refers to the volitional dimensions of wisdom; that is, a commitment to renunciation, goodwill, and development of compassion.

MORAL VIRTUE

(c) *Right speech* refers to abstaining from false or slanderous speech, harsh words, and idle,

purposeless chatter; that is, engaging in friendly, gentle, true speech.

(d) *Right action* refers to abstaining from actions that are harmful, deceitful, or dishonest, including harmful or dishonest sexual behavior; that is, engaging in kind, honest, and compassionate actions at all times.

(e) *Right livelihood* refers to earning one's living in a fashion consistent with the eightfold path; that is, avoiding, in particular, butchery, dealing in living creatures, and selling weapons or intoxicants.

MEDITATION

(f) *Right effort* refers to focusing one's mental efforts on achieving the goals set out in the eightfold path, promoting "wholesome" states and avoiding "unwholesome" ones.

(g) *Right mindfulness* refers to controlling cognition so as to see things as they really are; that is, clear-sighted and concentrated contemplation of body, feelings, state of mind, and phenomena.

(h) *Right concentration* refers to the development of mental "one-pointedness" or "wholesome concentration"; in Buddhist tradition, the key element in achieving this is the practice of meditation.

These eight elements are not sequential steps but interdependent principles, which, when taken together and skilfully applied within one's life, will lead one toward the end of suffering (*dukkha*) and the attainment of *nirvāna*, which is the ultimate and logical culmination of Buddhist practice (Das, 1997; Gethin, 1998).

Buddhist Meditation

The practice of meditation is a key component of the Buddhist eightfold path and, for many people, meditation forms the central and defining element of Buddhist spirituality and psychology. Consistent with this, Buddhist spiritually and psychology are deeply enmeshed with each other in both theory and practice, as reflected in the unsurpassed spiritual significance that Buddhism accords to the practice of meditation and the elaborate psychological framework that surrounds both the theory and practice of Buddhist meditation (Bodhi, 1999).

In psychological terms, the most detailed enunciation of the framework of Buddhist psychology is to be found in the *Abhidharma*, or "higher teaching," and described in detail in the seven books of *Abhidharma*, which the Buddha conceived 21 days after his awakening (Gethin, 1998). The indicative contents of the seven books of the Theravada *Abhidharma* (the oldest Buddhist tradition, which emerged from India) provide a clear demonstration of Buddhism's emphasis on a range of specific psychological concepts, including the definition and attainment of various states of consciousness, the significance of a range of specific cognitive practices, and the centrality of meditation to Buddhist spirituality *and* psychology:

(a) *Dhammasangani*: This book provides an overview or framework for the entire Abhidharma, outlining the overall categorization of states of consciousness and material phenomena, as well as explanations of important *Abhidharma* terminology.

(b) *Vibhanga*: This book provides detailed analyses of a range of important Buddhist concepts such as sense bases, dependent arising, mindfulness, the eightfold path, types of knowledge, and *dhammahadaya* (the essence of the doctrine).

(c) *Dhātukathā*: This book provides an analysis of all phenomena in relation to the essential Buddhist concepts of sense bases, aggregates, and elements.

(d) *Puggalapannatti*: This book examines different kinds of individuals and different levels of spiritual development, using an approach more similar to that of the *Suttas* (or more general teachings) than that of the traditional *Abhidharma*.

(e) *Kathāvatthu*: This book comprises a manual of debatable or undecided points in *Abhidharma* teachings and is generally ascribed to the Elder Moggaliputta Tissa.

(f) *Yamaka*: This book is concerned with the use of *Abhidharma* terminology and the resolution of ambiguities in relation to a range of areas, including sense bases, latent dispositions, and consciousness.

(g) *Patthāna*: This lengthy book, also known as the "Great Treatise," provides an analysis of the interrelations between different teachings within the *Abhidharma*, according to 24 varieties of conditional relations. The *Patthāna* presents an enormously detailed, systematic overview of much of Buddhist psychology and, in many ways, forms the heart of the teachings of the *Abhidharma* (Bodhi, 1999).

Consistent with this elaborate, detailed engagement with psychological processes and cognitive states, Buddhist tradition accords unsurpassed importance to the practice of meditation, including meditation for the attainment of calm (*samatha*) and meditation for the development of insight (*vipassanā*). Buddhist thought holds that the human mind is fundamentally pure but has become defiled; the purpose of meditation is to remove these defilements and see things as they really are. The five hindrances that most immediately require removal to this end are sense-desire, anger, torpor, restlessness, and doubt.

In practical terms, meditation for the attainment of calm (*samatha*) is generally commenced before development of insight (*vipassanā*), often by focusing meditative concentration on a single phenomenon (e.g., one's own breath). There are many accounts of the states of consciousness into which the meditative mind can then enter, and these are commonly described as the five *dhyānas*:

(a) *Vitarka*: The application of thought
(b) *Vicara*: Examining
(c) *Prīti*: Joy
(d) *Sukha*: Happiness
(e) *Cittaikagrata*: One-pointedness of mind (Gethin, 1998)

At the point of attaining the fourth *dhyana* (*Sukha* or happiness), the meditator can start to focus on the development of insight (*vipassanā*). The initial stages of this process can be conceptualized using the paradigm of the seven purifications:

(a) Purification of conduct
(b) Purification of consciousness
(c) Purification of view
(d) Purification by overcoming doubt
(e) Purification by knowledge and vision of what is path and not-path
(f) Purification by knowledge and vision of the way
(g) Purification by knowledge and vision

At this point, there are numerous other ways in which further meditative progress can be conceptualized, but all, if skilfully pursued, lead to the point of becoming an *arhat*, an individual who sees things as they really are and has attained *nirvāna* or *nibbāna*. Some of these accounts of various stages, paths, and purifications can appear complex and convoluted to some readers and practitioners. Many of these schemes, however, evolved into their present forms over centuries of Buddhist practice and may now serve multiple purposes. Not least among these purposes is their usefulness in affording milestones of progress for the meditator: Following the Buddhist path can involve lengthy meditative commitment, which may seem time consuming and repetitive; detectable milestones along the way can act as invaluable sources of encouragement for the weary or for those losing hope along the way.

A more detailed account of, and introduction to, broader themes in Buddhist psychology is provided by De Silva (2005), and a more focused account of Buddhist psychology in relation to Western psychology and psychiatry is provided by Kelly (2008).

One of the key concepts in much Buddhist psychology and spirituality, and, especially, Buddhist meditation, is "mindfulness," which refers to a careful awareness of one's own thoughts and feelings. In Buddhist psychology this concept is also known as *sati* and forms an important element of much meditative practice (Brazier, 2003). The aim of mindfulness practice is to promote awareness of, and connection with, cognitive and bodily states and processes. The emphasis remains on observation and labelling, rather than judging, changing, or acting. There are numerous ways to cultivate mindfulness in everyday life. One way is to provide a verbal label for certain predetermined phenomena throughout the day; for example, mentally labelling the position of one's body each time it changes (i.e., standing, sitting, walking, etc.). Similar approaches can be applied to emotional and cognitive phenomena, labelling each as it is observed. In Buddhist meditation, mindfulness of the body and breath are often used to cultivate contemplative states of mind.

Effects of Buddhist Meditation on the Brain

Buddhist meditation has significant effects on the human brain. Recent years have seen a substantial increase in research interest in this area, with a succession of studies confirming that the effects of Buddhist meditation on the physical brain are detectable, substantial, and enduring.

Brown, Forte, and Dysart (1984a), for example, studied visual sensitivity in individuals practicing Buddhist mindfulness meditation before and after a 3-month retreat, which involved 16 hours of mindfulness meditation each day. Following the retreat, practitioners were capable of detecting shorter single-light flashes and required shorter intervals to distinguish between consecutive flashes, compared to before the mindfulness retreat. This is consistent with previous studies (Brown, Forte, & Dysart, 1984b), as well as original Buddhist texts, which suggest that mindfulness meditation is associated with significant changes in human perception.

Benson, Malhotra, Goldman, Jacobs, and Hopkins (1990), in an especially detailed study of brain function in three Tibetan Buddhist monks,

also concluded that meditation was associated with significant changes in resting brain metabolism, as well as significant changes in electroencephalogram (EEG) readings or, more specifically, increased beta activity and asymmetry in alpha and beta activity between the hemispheres, indicating significant changes in patterns of brain electrical activity as a result of meditation.

In a similarly focused study, Newberg et al. (2001) studied the effects of meditation in eight experienced Buddhist meditators using advanced brain imaging technologies (single photon emission tomography) and reported significant changes in brain blood flow associated with meditation; more specifically, researchers reported increased regional cerebral blood flow in the cingulate gyrus, thalamus, inferior and orbital frontal cortex, and dorsolateral prefrontal cortex in the brains of meditators. Taken in conjunction with earlier, comparable neuroimaging studies (Newberg & Iversen, 2003), these findings confirm the substantial effects of contemplative practice on the physical brains of meditators.

These findings are also consistent with the work of Lutz, Greischar, Rawlings, Ricard, and Davidson (2004), who examined eight experienced Buddhist practitioners and ten student volunteers and reported that the Buddhist practitioners had significant changes in brain electrical activity during meditation; more specifically, researchers reported that meditation induced sustained EEG high-amplitude gamma-band oscillations and phase synchrony. In addition, however, the Buddhist meditators had certain changes in brain electrical activity (higher ratios of gamma-band activity to slow oscillatory activity over the medial frontoparietal electrodes) not only during meditation but also *after* meditation, suggesting that the changes in brain function induced by meditation last significantly longer than the meditation sessions themselves.

Overall, these findings, along with various other related studies (Hanson, 2009; Kelly, 2008), provide substantial scientific support for significant and enduring alterations in brain biology associated with meditation. In terms of specific alterations, there are signs of an emerging confluence among neuroscientific studies, suggesting that meditation is linked with detectable alterations in activity in specific brain areas, including the anterior cingulate cortex and dorsolateral prefrontal areas (Cahn & Polich, 2006). At a subjective level, these kinds of biological brain changes appear linked with both the increased attention and alterations in experience of self associated with meditation.

These findings are complemented by an emerging literature supporting a similarly robust relationship between contemplative practice and positive psychological change; that is, recent years have not only seen multiple studies demonstrating that meditation produces biological changes in brain function (as measured through patterns of electrical activity and blood flow) but also studies suggesting that contemplative practice can be associated with positive psychological change, as reflected in the alleviation of psychological symptoms or treatment of mental illness through the judicious use of selected contemplative practices and meditative techniques.

More specifically, various forms of Buddhist contemplative practices have been described as producing benefit for certain individuals with depression (Segal, Williams, & Teasdale, 2001), anxiety disorders (Emmanuel, 2001; Tapanya, Nicki, & Jarusawad, 1997), obsessive-compulsive disorder (Olson, 2003), substance misuse disorders (Barrett, 1997; Marlatt, 2002), disordered eating patterns (Albers, 2006), and disorders involving anger (DiGiuseppe, 1999; Leifer, 1999). Similar benefits have been described in relation to certain aspects of physical illnesses, including psychological care during cancer treatment (Lundberg & Trichorb, 2001), promotion of holistic health in HIV/AIDS (Logsdon-Conradsen, 2002), adjunctive care in chronic medical illness (Bonadonna, 2003), and terminal care (Barham, 2003; McGrath, 1998).

Of these diverse psychological and physical disorders, depression is the condition for which the role of Buddhist contemplative techniques has been explored in greatest depth. Williams, Teasdale, Segal, and Kabat-Zinn (2007) describe a treatment paradigm called "mindfulness-based cognitive therapy" for depression, which combines mindfulness-based techniques from Buddhist tradition with Western cognitive therapeutic approaches to depression. This therapeutic paradigm involves a combination of meditation, education, and cognitive therapy in order to reduce symptoms of depression and promote sustainable, balanced recovery. Similar approaches are increasingly being applied to a range of other issues within clinical psychology and psychiatry, including anxiety disorders, emotional dysregulation syndromes, anger problems, binge eating, suicidal behavior, and the psychological effects of trauma (Mace, 2008).

Mindfulness is proving to be an especially valuable psychological technique in the context of many existing forms of psychotherapy (Germer, Siegel, & Fulton, 2005; Segal et al., 2001), including cognitive-behavioral therapy (Kumar, 2002), dialectical behavioral therapy (Palmer, 2002; Robins, 2002), and acceptance and commitment therapy (Hayes, 2002). There is also a long-standing relationship between psychoanalysis and Buddhist practice, especially meditation (Fromm, Suzuki, & Demartino, 1960). More recently, there have been especially interesting considerations of the role of meditative practice in the context of depression in conjunction with other approaches, such as the use of psychotropic medication and various forms of psychotherapy (e.g., Epstein, 2007).

Buddhist Meditation: The Future

Recent years have seen substantially increased interest in the relationship between specific Buddhist techniques, especially mindfulness-based meditation, and positive psychological change or the alleviation of symptoms of psychological distress and mental illness (Brazier, 1995; Kelly, 2008). These meditative concepts and techniques are increasingly recognized as being potentially valuable not only for many individuals who experience psychological distress but also for many of those who seek to help others, such as therapists (Simpkins & Simpkins, 2009). These positive therapeutic developments are strongly underpinned by emerging knowledge of the substantial biological effects of Buddhist contemplative practice on the human brain (Hanson, 2009).

The subjective effects of integrating this evolving "brain science" of meditation with the psychological effects of Buddhist practice have been explored in depth by Austin (1999, 2006), who provides a particularly detailed summary of existing neuroscientific research into Zen meditation and consciousness, combined with a substantial knowledge of Buddhism from an experiential perspective. This is an especially valuable area of work because it links "objective" scientific data with "subjective" experience, and it opens up an important dialog between two spheres that are often regarded as separate, to the detriment of both.

Future years are likely to see continued increase in the use of Buddhist mindfulness and meditative techniques as components in psychotherapeutic approaches to a range of states of psychological distress and mental illness. This trend is both evidenced and advanced through the establishment of a Centre for Mindfulness Research and Practice at the University of Wales at Bangor in the United Kingdom (http://www.bangor.ac.uk/mindfulness). Future years are also likely to see increased research into, and practice-based interest in, contemplative traditions other than Buddhism including, most notably, meditative and contemplative practices within Christian traditions (Lopez, 2008).

Meditative Practices in the Christian Tradition
The Foundations of Christian Meditation

Meditative and contemplative practices form an important part of many traditions within Christianity. Christianity is a monotheistic religion that has been historically divided into three main branches (MacCulloch, 2009):

(a) *Roman Catholicism*, within which there are various churches, led by bishops, with the Pope, or Bishop of Rome, as highest authority on matters of faith

(b) *The Orthodox Church*, whose constituent churches are in communion with the Patriarchal Sees of the East, and which is the second largest constituent church within Christianity

(c) *Protestantism*, which includes a relatively broad variety of churches, all of which draw at least some of their beliefs and practices from John Calvin (1509–1564), Martin Luther (1484–1546), and/or Huldrych Zwingli (1484–1531)

All three branches of Christianity regard the Bible as the word of God, presented as two canonical collections of books: the Old Testament and New Testament (Armstrong, 2007). Various churches differ in the extent to which the words of the Bible are to be taken literally or interpreted as metaphor, especially in relation to the earlier books of the Old Testament. Notwithstanding these interpretative divergences, the key features of Christianity in most churches include the belief that Jesus Christ was the Messiah prophesized in the Old Testament and that He was persecuted, crucified, and buried. He was then resurrected from the dead and, after appearing to some people, ascended into heaven. It is also believed that Jesus will return from the dead to judge all human beings, living and dead. Those who are virtuous and those who truly have repented their sins will enjoy eternal life. In Christian scripture, Jesus is seen as teaching about God, being the son of God, and forming part of the "Holy Trinity," which comprises Jesus, God the Father, and the Holy Spirit.

The practice of Christianity varies between churches and traditions but generally involves group worship on Sunday, the day of the resurrection. Worship involves prayers, thanksgiving, sermonizing,

and celebrating the Eucharist, which is a form of liturgical worship involving a consecrated meal, generally of bread and wine, which Christians believe is transformed into the Body and Blood of Christ during the Eucharist (transubstantiation). Other Christian rites include the sacraments, which are specific rites initiated by Jesus to convey grace in various particular contexts:

(a) *The sacrament of baptism*, which is a Christian initiation rite soon after birth

(b) *The sacrament of confirmation*, which is Christian initiation as a young adult, strengthening Baptismal grace

(c) *The sacrament of the Eucharist*, which is a partaking of Jesus's sacrifice, often at Sunday worship

(d) *The sacrament of penance and reconciliation*, which involves confession of, and forgiveness for, sins

(e) *The sacrament of anointing of the sick*, which is a sacrament of healing, conveying grace to those in immediate danger of death

(f) *The sacrament of holy orders*, in which an individual devotes oneself to the work of God by, for example, becoming a priest or nun

(g) *The sacrament of matrimony*, which establishes between a couple a lasting and exclusive bond, sealed by God

In addition to Sunday Eucharist, the sacraments, and various other public activities linked with Christianity (e.g., pilgrimages), there are also many individual and group activities linked with Christian observance, including prayer, good works, and contemplative practices. Prayer can be practiced either individually or in groups, and it can include forms of ritual devotion such as "the rosary," which involves saying short prayers up to 50 times each (Storey, 2004). Good works can include charitable involvement, helping the sick or elderly, assisting the poor, or attempting to influence social and government policy in directions indicated by Christian teachings (Massaro & Shannon, 2002).

Christian Contemplative Practices

Contemplative practices form a significant element within many Christian traditions, but they are generally not accorded the same primacy that meditation is accorded in Buddhist traditions (Talbot, 2002). Within Buddhism, meditation is a necessary element on the path to enlightenment, whereas within Christianity, contemplative practices *can* represent an important element in one's spiritual life, but they do not have the same centrality that they possess in Buddhism. As a result, contemplative practices in Christian traditions have tended to be associated with particular historical individuals and particular groups of monks, nuns, and laypersons.

The individuals most strongly associated with contemplative traditions in the history of Christianity include the following:

• *Saint Augustine of Hippo* (354–430), a bishop, philosopher and theologian, was an immensely influential figure in the development of Western Christianity, and patron of the Augustinian religious order. Saint Augustine wrote extensively on matters of theology and, in Saint Augustine's view, contemplation was an extremely important method for reaching the truth about God. The production of specific psychological states while contemplating (e.g., joy at contemplative discovery) was epiphenomenal: The purpose of contemplation was to understand the truth about God and encounter that truth immediately and directly (Kenney, 2005).

• *Saint Thomas Aquinas* (1225–1274), an Italian priest in the Dominican Order, was another philosopher and theologian who placed considerable emphasis on "natural theology" and "natural law" (Maritain, 2008). Saint Thomas also emphasized Christian contemplative practice, arguing that Christian communities needed contemplative individuals within them in order to strengthen and deepen their faith.

• *Saint Ignatius of Loyola* (1491–1556) was a hermit and priest, who founded the Society of Jesus and encouraged followers to visualize and meditate on scenes from the life of Jesus Christ; this model of contemplative Christianity involved both intellectual and affective (emotional) components, centered on love (Caraman, 1990).

• *Saint Theresa of Ávila* (1515–1582), a Carmelite nun and mystic, described four stages of the "ascent of the soul," including (a) "mental prayer" or contemplation; (b) "prayer of quiet," a supernatural state in which the individual's soul is merged with God; (c) "devotion of union," a supernatural *and* ecstatic state that also involves an absorption of reason in God; and (d) "devotion of ecstasy or rapture," a state in which the individual's consciousness of being in one's body has disappeared and one enters the ultimate, mystical trance (Cohen, 1957; Hamilton, 1982).

• *Saint John of the Cross* (1542–1591), a Carmelite friar and priest, wrote extensively in the fields of poetry and Catholic mysticism

(De Nicolás, 1996; Kavanagh, 2000) and went on, with Saint Theresa of Ávila, to found the Disclaced Carmelites, a mendicant Catholic order with strong emphasis on silent prayer, enclosed living, and contemplative practice (Hamilton, 1982).

• *Thomas Merton* (1915–1968), a Trappist monk from the United States, had a strong interest in Buddhist contemplative practice and initiated dialog with Buddhist leaders and teachers, including the Dalai Lama and Thich Nhat Hanh, a celebrated Vietnamese Buddhist monk (Cunningham, 1999).

• *John Main* (1926–1982), a Benedictine monk, practiced and promoted Christian meditation throughout the 20th century (Harris, 2001). More specifically, Main developed a practice that involved sitting quietly for 20–30 minutes, letting one's thoughts pass without engaging with them, and constantly returning to a chosen "prayer-phrase" (similar to a mantra); one was simply being *with* God instead of trying to talk *to* God (Main, 2006). Main's work led to the emergence of the World Community for Christian Meditation in 1991.

Christianity, especially early Christianity, also had a notably strong monastic component, which often involved lengthy, solitary, and/or silent contemplation (Belisle, 2003). This tradition persists, in various forms, among diverse Christian orders and groupings today, including the following:

• *The Religious Society of Friends* (Quakers), which began in England in the mid-17th century, as a breakaway from English Puritanism, and now encompasses a range of different churches around the world, many of which are known for their social activism (including early opposition to the transatlantic slave trade). While the Religious Society of Friends engages in many different forms of prayer and devotion, one of the chief forms of worship is communal meditation, a form of silent prayer focusing on Jesus Christ (Dandelion, 2007). This is known as "unprogrammed worship" and lasts approximately 1 hour, during which time certain friends, if so moved, may rise and speak when they feel they are led by a spirit.

• *The Order of Cistercians* is a Catholic order of enclosed monks, whose first abbey was founded in 1098 by Robert of Molesme (1028–1111). The Order is characterized by literal observance of the rules of Saint Benedict, a commitment to manual labor and an atmosphere of silence (Tobin, 1996). One branch of the Cistercians, the Order of Cistercians of the Strict Observance (Trappists), places an especially strong emphasis on silence in order to permit greater focus on gaining a deeper understanding and love of God.

• *The Carthusian Order*, or Order of Saint Bruno, is a Catholic Order of enclosed monks and nuns, founded by Saint Bruno in 1084. The life of the Carthusian monk or nun is characterized by solitude, meditation, prayer, and manual work, with a strong emphasis on silent, solitary contemplative practice (Lockhart, 1999).

• *The World Community for Christian Meditation* was founded in 1991, based on the contemplative work of John Main, a Benedictine monk who practiced and promoted Christian meditation (Harris, 2001; Main, 2006). The World Community for Christian Meditation has its international center in London but has branches in many other countries, and it sees itself as a monastery without walls, devoted to Christian contemplative practice.

Various other Christian religious orders and groups include other, different kinds of meditative and contemplative practices within their traditions, sometimes in the broader context of an enclosed way of life (e.g., Camaldolese, Order of Saint Clare). One of the key differences between Christian and Buddhist meditation, however, is the role of God in Christian contemplative practice. While Buddhist meditation centers on cognitive training and concentration in order to see things as they really are and thus bring an end to suffering, Christian meditation focuses on coming into closer communion with God (e.g., the silent, "unprogrammed worship" of the Society of Friends). This difference is emphasized most clearly in the work of Saint Augustine, who regarded the production of specific psychological states while contemplating as incidental to the central purpose of contemplation, which is to encounter the truth about God, immediately and directly (Kenney, 2005).

The 20th century, however, saw the emergence of significant dialog between contemplative traditions and, in particular, renewed exploration of commonalities between Buddhist and Christian meditative traditions. Thomas Merton, for example, had a lengthy dialog with D. T. Suzuki (1970–1966), a celebrated Buddhist teacher, looking at the relationship between Christian and Buddhist contemplative traditions, and this was later published in Merton's *Zen and the Birds of Appetite* (Merton, 1968). More recently, Wallace (2007) has drawn attention to areas of convergence between Western and Eastern meditative traditions, noting that many Christian mystics (including Saint Augustine of Hippo) reported that some of the results of contemplative practice stemmed from clearer perceptions of God's true nature, the human soul, and laws of nature. At least some of these observations have significant echoes of Buddhist writings on the purpose and consequences of meditation, which include the removal of defilements and enhancement of perception of reality.

Effects of Christian Meditation on the Brain

Another source of evidence of potential convergence between Buddhist and Western contemplative traditions has emerged from neuroscientific study of the biological correlates of contemplative practices. While most neuroscientific research on meditation to date has focused on practitioners of Buddhist contemplative practice, there is a growing, although still limited, body of evidence regarding non-Buddhist forms of meditation.

Azari et al. (2001), for example, used functional neuroimaging to study brain activation in Christian and nonreligious individuals during recitation of psalms (scripture from the Hebrew Bible), a nursery rhyme, and parts of a telephone directory. During recitation of religious scripture, Christian subjects showed increased activation of a frontal-parietal circuit in the brain, involving the dorsolateral prefrontal, dorsomedial frontal, and medial parietal cortex. These areas play a significant role in sustaining reflexive evaluation of thought, and these results suggest that subjective religious experience may be, in significant part, a cognitive process. This is consistent with the strong emphasis placed on cognition in Buddhist psychological and contemplative tradition (Bodhi, 1999; Gethin, 1998; Kelly, 2008).

Newberg et al. (2003) studied changes in patterns of blood flow in the brains of Christian (Franciscan) nuns during verbal-based meditative practice. They found significant alterations in brain blood-flow patterns associated with meditation, including increased flow in the prefrontal cortex, inferior parietal lobes, and inferior frontal lobes, indicating increased brain activity in these areas. There was also an inverse correlation between blood-flow changes in the prefrontal cortex and superior parietal lobe on the same side. These findings suggest that meditative experiences may be mediated, at least in part, through differentiation of the superior parietal lobe, which is involved in the generation of normal sense of spatial awareness, among other tasks (D'Aquili & Newberg, 2000).

These findings are generally consistent with findings in the brains of Buddhist and other meditators, supporting a possible confluence of research findings, focusing on altered activity in specific brain areas (e.g., anterior cingulate cortex, dorsolateral prefrontal areas) and linking these with the increased attention and alterations in experience of self associated with contemplative practice (Cahn & Polich, 2006; Hanson, 2009; Kelly, 2008; Newberg et al., 2001; Newberg & Iversen, 2003). Taken together, these findings provide significant support for the idea that different forms of meditation, within differing spiritual traditions, may produce similar biological alterations in the brain. This area requires further study, however, as neuroscientific research to date has focused significantly on Buddhist meditation as opposed to other forms of contemplative practice, such as Christian meditation (Lopez, 2008). There may also be value in exploring differences between individual spiritual "cognitive styles": Tapanya, Nicki, and Jarusawad (1997), for example, studied levels of worry among Buddhist (Thai) and Christian (Canadian) elderly persons and reported that an extrinsic religious orientation among Buddhists, but not Christians, was linked to greater worry.

There is also a need for further research comparing the psychological and biological effects of religious and nonreligious contemplative practice. Wachholtz and Pargament (2005), for example, have found that spiritual and secular forms of meditation are associated with differing effects on anxiety, mood, spiritual health, and spiritual experiences. In terms of neurobiology, Azari et al. (2001), in their functional neuroimaging study, reported different patterns of brain activation in nonreligious individuals reciting a nursery rhyme compared to religious individuals reciting religious psalms, with the former showing significant activation of the left amygdala, which correlated significantly with their affective state. This area both merits and requires greater study.

Christian Meditation: The Future

Christianity has a long tradition of contemplative practice, dating from early monastic settlements, through the lives and works of many of the greatest leaders of Christian thought, including Saint Augustine of Hippo, Saint Thomas Aquinas, Saint Ignatius of Loyola, Saint Theresa of Ávila, and Saint John of the Cross. In the 20th century, spiritual leaders of Christian contemplative practice showed evidence of broader engagement with other contemplative traditions (e.g., Thomas Merton and Buddhism) and a desire to promote and renew Christian meditation on a broader, more inclusive basis (e.g., John Main and the World Community for Christian Meditation).

As a result of this strong tradition, the early 21st century sees the continuation of the contemplative practice of, among others, the Religious Society of Friends (Quakers), Order of Cistercians, Carthusian Order, Camaldolese, and Order of Saint Clare. The foundation of the World Community for Christian Meditation in 1991 has been accompanied by other evidence of renewed and broadening interest in Christian meditation: In 2005, the Carthusian Order was the subject of a widely distributed, award-winning documentary film, *Into Great Silence*, directed by Philip Gröning (Zeitgeist Films).

Notwithstanding evidence of increased dialog between Christian and Buddhist meditative traditions (e.g., Merton, 1968), there remain important differences between traditions, including, most notably, the role of God in Christian contemplative practice. Nonetheless, Christian sources still describe the results of contemplative practice as including clearer perceptions of God's true nature, the human soul, and laws of nature (Wallace, 2007), at least some of which have significant echoes of Buddhist writings on the purpose and consequences of meditation (Kelly, 2008).

In addition, neuroscientific studies of meditators of both Buddhist and Christian traditions also point to areas of commonality, focusing especially on altered activity in specific brain areas (e.g., anterior cingulate cortex, dorsolateral prefrontal areas) that are linked with the increased attention and alterations in experience of self commonly associated with contemplative practice in all traditions (Cahn & Polich, 2006; Hanson, 2009; Newberg et al., 2001; Newberg & Iversen, 2003). Future years are likely to see this area of research increase its focus on Christian and other non-Buddhist forms of meditation, the role of individual spiritual "cognitive styles" in relation to meditation, and further comparisons of the psychobiological effects of religious and nonreligious contemplative practice.

Meditative Practices in Other Spiritual and Religious Traditions
Islam

Islam is a religion based on the *Qur'an*, a book that is considered to be the word of God, and the example of Muhammad, the Islamic prophet (Armstrong, 2000). The five "pillars" of Islam provide the foundations of Muslim life:

(a) Faith in the Oneness of God and finality of the prophethood of Muhammad
(b) The establishment of the daily prayers
(c) Almsgiving and concern for the needy
(d) Purification of the self through fasting
(e) Pilgrimage to Makkah for all who are capable

There are many different branches within Islam, each with certain distinctive features; the main branches include Sunni, Shi'a, Sufism, and Kharijite. Islam has a strong tradition of frequent prayer involving meditation on God by reciting the Qur'an; this is known as *Ṣalāt* and produces spiritual peace and strength to help individuals in the tasks of their lives (Aslan, 2005). While the intensity of *Ṣalāt* results in it bearing many similarities with various forms of meditation from other spiritual traditions, Islam also has various other additional contemplative traditions, including, most notably, *tafakkur* and Sufism.

Tafakkur means "reflecting on the universe" in order to gain food for thought. *Tafakkur* is seen as a form of intellectual development that emanates from a higher level, from God. Receiving divine inspiration in this fashion permits personality growth and development, which, in turn, helps the individual to live life on a more spiritual level.

Sufism is a mystical form of Islam that has an especially strong focus on the spiritual and mystical aspects of the religion. Sufi meditation, also called *Muruqaba*, involves developing progressively deeper awareness of the self, ascending into an awareness of the universe and God. In some respects, the process of Sufi meditation is similar to that of Buddhism (developing particular forms of concentration), but the two traditions differ in terms of the role of God: In Sufi meditation, the final aim is for the individual to become extinguished within God, before returning with new knowledge of God and one's place in the universe.

Sufi meditation is often presented as possessing healing qualities, especially in relation to the healing spiritual journey from the realm of delusions into the realm of realities (As-Sayyid, 2005). Like Buddhism, this paradigm sees the self as originally pure but now defiled, and the process of meditation can return the self to its original state of purity. Sufi meditation is, however, considered controversial among certain scholars of Islam, albeit quite widely practiced and discussed among certain other groups (Frager & Fadiman, 1997; Karamustafa, 2007).

While here have been some comparative considerations of Sufism and Western psychological traditions, such as psychoanalysis (Nurbakhsh, 1978a, 1978b), and some considerations of the biological correlates of Sufi practice (e.g., Ernst, 1998), the neuroscientific literature in this area has not grown in recent years to the same extent as it has in relation to Buddhist practice. There is, nonetheless, substantial potential for much fruitful interaction between Sufi and Western psychological and neuroscientific traditions: Deikman (1977), in particular, felt that Western psychiatry could benefit significantly by engaging with Sufism's devotion to the development of higher intuitive and perceptual capacities, as well as Sufi conceptions of the conscious evolution of man and the ultimate realization of man's full capacities, for the benefit of all.

Hinduism

Hinduism is a religion that is rooted in the Indian subcontinent and is also known as *Sanātana Dharma* (eternal law). Hinduism is sometimes regarded as the world's oldest religion and appears to have myriad origins and contributing influences, resulting in an enormous diversity of practices and beliefs within Hinduism (monotheism, polytheism, etc.). Many branches of Hinduism are characterized by belief in reincarnation and *karma* (laws of cause and effect) (Flood, 1996).

While it is difficult to subdivide Hinduism into different schools, McDaniel (2007) describes six general types of Hinduism:

(a) *Folk Hinduism*, rooted in local cults and traditions relating to deities at communal level
(b) *Vedic Hinduism*, which is practiced by *brahmins* (educators, lawmakers, and preachers in Hindu tradition)
(c) *Vedantic Hinduism*, as based on the teachings or philosophies of the *Upanishads*, which are core Hindu scriptures (Mascaro, 2005)
(d) *Yogic Hinduism*, which emphasizes particular physical and mental disciplines and practices, as outlined in, for example, the *Yoga-sūtra of Patañjali* (Feuerstein, 1992)
(e) *Dharmic Hinduism*, based on the idea of *karma* and various traditional Hindu societal practices
(f) *Bhakti*, which places particular emphasis on the involvement of the individual in devotion and divine worship

Yogic Hinduism places a special emphasis on the practice of yoga, a collection of physical and mental disciplines that assist the individual in attaining states of physical and mental balance and unity. The roots of these practices are found in a wide variety of Hindu traditions and texts, including, for example, the *Yoga-sūtra of Patañjali* (Feuerstein, 1992). Yoga is both a form of meditation and a preparation for deeper contemplative practices (Brown & Gerbarg, 2009).

The practice of yoga can involve a range of observances, including abstaining from certain types of actions (e.g., violence, lying), observing certain qualities (e.g., purity, austerity), sitting in certain postures, specific patterns of breathing, specific patterns of focusing the senses and attention, contemplation, and the merging of consciousness with meditative objects (Feuerstein, 1992). Overall, there is much overlap between certain contemplative yoga practices and Buddhist meditation, reflecting the partially shared origins and courses of both traditions.

The practice of yoga has significant physiological and psychological effects. The physiological effects of yoga appear to stem from alterations in the parasympathetic drive, stress-response patterns, neuroendocrine system, and/or thalamic generators (Brown & Gerbarg, 2005a). There is also evidence that some of its physiological effects may be mediated by increased endogenous secretion of melatonin triggered by yogic practices (Harinath et al., 2004). In parallel with these neurophysiological findings, there have been suggestions that yoga may prove a useful complementary element in the management of various physical disorders, such as epilepsy (McElroy-Cox, 2009) and asthma (Pretorius, 2009), as well as having a potentially beneficial effect on longevity (Brown & Gerbarg, 2009; Bushell, 2009). More study is needed in all of these areas before systematic recommendations can be made.

Yogic practices also have significant psychological effects (Dalai, 1991), including increases in mindfulness (Shelov, Suchday, & Friedberg, 2009). Consistent with this, there is growing evidence to support the usefulness of yoga as an adjunctive treatment for stress, depression, anxiety, posttraumatic stress disorder, and substance abuse (Brown & Gerbarg, 2005b, 2009). In terms of depression, there is evidence that, at least in certain individuals, yoga may be superior to no treatment (Khumar, Kaur, & Kaur, 1993); comparable with electroconvulsive therapy and imipramine (an antidepressant medication) in terms of remission rates (Janakiramaiah et al., 2000); and have an adjunctive role for those who have benefitted from antidepressant medication but experience residual symptoms (Shapiro et al., 2007). While further evidence is needed before treatment guidelines can be made for specific disorders, including depression and anxiety (Krisanaprakornkit, Krisanaprakornkit, Piyavhatkul, & Laopaiboon, 2006), these remain very promising areas for further research.

Future years are likely to see continued increases in public interest in yoga in both Eastern and Western countries. In 1998, it was estimated that some 15 million American adults had already practiced yoga at some point in their lifetime, including 7.4 million during the previous year (Saper, Eisenberg, Davis, Culpepper, & Phillips, 2004). This pattern of use is likely to continue and increase in the coming years, both in America and elsewhere (Corliss, 2001).

There is also likely to be continued interest in the integration of existing scientific knowledge of the physiology and psychology of yoga, linking psychological, neurological, and immunological research findings into coherent, unified models (Kulkarni & Bera, 2009). In the broader context, there is likely to be increased interest in the articulation of models of yoga and meditative practice that integrate neuroscientific findings with subjective experiences of yoga and meditation (Austin, 1999, 2006; Deshmukh, 2006), contributing to the emergence of a more unified, integrated understanding of the subjective effects and objective biological correlates of yogic and contemplative practices.

Judaism

The practices and beliefs of Judaism originate in the Hebrew Bible and were further shaped by texts such as the *Talmud*. Judaism is one of the world's oldest monotheistic religions and is seen as an expression of the relationship between God and the Children of Israel. The practices and observances of Judaism include prayer several times daily, particular forms of dress, *Shabbat* (weekly day of rest), pilgrimage festivals, various dietary laws, and reading of scripture (Robinson, 2000).

There is a strong tradition of meditation and contemplative practice within Judaism (Davis, 2000). According to Judaism, creation is God made manifest, and the purpose of life is to know God and transform the world through compassion and justice. Jewish scriptures provide myriad examples of meditative behavior, demonstrating that contemplative practice has constituted an important element within the broader practice of Judaism for many centuries (Shapiro, 2000).

More specifically, the Jewish mystical, meditative tradition, *Kabbalah*, is fundamentally based on esoteric teachings relating the finite world of humans with the infinite world of the Creator (Matt, 1996). Many of the practices associated with *Kabbalah* are centered on contemplation, including visualization of the soul's journey, in order to come closer to, and develop a deeper understanding of, the Divine. Contemporary Judaism also incorporates a number of different, related meditative practices (Davis, 2000), including *Hisbonenus* (understanding through analytic and reflective study, generally of the *Torah*) and *Hisbodedus* (unstructured, individualized meditation with the aim of creating an individualized relationship with God and clarifying one's own motives).

There is significant overlap between some of the aims of meditation in the traditions of Judaism and Buddhism. In the context of Judaism, for example, Shapiro (2000) writes that the purpose of meditation is to free the meditator from the idea of permanence and the illusion of separation, thus producing a state of calm that permits the meditator to respond constructively to the challenges and opportunities of life. One of the key differences between these traditions, however, relates to the centrality of God in Judaism, in significant contrast to Buddhism.

In comparative terms, there have been myriad explorations of the relationships between psychoanalysis and mysticism (e.g., Leavy, 2009), including *Kabbalah* (Berke, 1996). Using a more cognitive framework, Birnbaum (2005) examined the issue of adolescent aggression in Jewish-Israeli society and proposed guided mindfulness meditation as a useful approach for facilitating growth toward autonomy, self-awareness, and healing. Consistent with this, Ben-Arye and colleagues (2009) examined the use of complementary and alternative therapies (yoga, meditation, guided imagery) in Israel and reported that women used such therapies more frequently than men, and that Jewish women used such therapies more frequently than Arab women.

From a more neuroscientific perspective, Drubach and Claassen (2008) considered the apparent conflict raised by the Jewish and Christian belief that God is ever-present and the fact that the brain is not constantly aware of such a presence. The authors used neuroscientific theories of perception to propose an approach to this dilemma based on the idea of neuronal habituation, producing an apparent "unawareness" of God, even though He is ever-present. As in other spiritual traditions, future years are likely to see continued research and neuroscientific model-building focusing on the biological correlates not only of specific beliefs and belief systems but also

various spiritual practices within Judaism, including meditation and other forms of contemplative prayer.

Taoism

The word Tao (*Dao*) means "way" or "path." Taoism (*Daoism*) refers to a group of spiritual and psychological traditions in East Asia, all of which place emphasis on nature, compassion, moderation, and humility (Oldstone-Moore, 2003). The key principles of Taoism include the Tao (*Dao*) itself; De (*Te*), which is active cultivation of the "Way" of virtue and integrity; Wu Wei, which means "doing without action"; and P'u, which means a state of receptiveness and readiness for Tao. Taoist philosophy has multiple spheres of influence, including health and medicine, as well as architecture, politics, and martial arts.

The most influential text in Taoism is the Tao Te Ching (*Daodejing*), which was written by Lao Tzu in the 3rd or 4th century BC (Tzu & Mitchell, 1999). The Tao Te Ching is centered on the nature of Tao, which, according to Taoism, transcends traditional concepts of form and categorization. As a consequence, the Tao Te Ching presents a series of thematically linked texts, with the overall aim of conveying the essential principles of Tao and guiding readers toward understanding the "way."

Taoist traditions include a range of meditative and contemplative practices (Cleary, 2000). Many of these techniques are centered on the breath because, in Taoism, breath is associated with Qi, which is the life force within each living being (Simpkins & Simpkins, 2009). Taoist practice aims to use breathing as a way to help internal energy flow better through the body, thus producing healing. The emphasis on breath as an element in meditation is similar to that in various Buddhist contemplative techniques, including Zazen.

Taoism sees emotions as a constantly changing flow, producing a dynamic balance between various emotions (e.g., happiness and sadness) (Simpkins & Simpkins, 2009). This conceptual approach provides a reason to experience the full range of emotions but also a reason not to become excessively involved in one emotion or another: The flow of various emotions is constant. In some ways, this approach is analogous to the cultivation of mindfulness of emotions in Buddhist tradition; that is, noting the presence of emotions and possibly labeling them but not engaging excessively with them as they pass and change (Brazier, 2003).

The principles and practices of Taoism have had significant influences on contemplative practices in other traditions, such as Buddhism, and many of the neuroscientific findings in relation to Buddhist meditation are likely to apply to analogous forms of Taoist practice (Lopez, 2008; Wallace, 2007). Taoism's particular emphasis on breathing is also the subject of neuroscientific attention (Squire, Berg, Bloom, Du Lac, & Ghosh, 2008) and is likely to form the focus of further, future research.

In terms of therapeutic applications, there is growing evidence of the use of Taoist practices, such as breathing techniques and meditative practices, in psychotherapeutic settings, especially in relation to stress reduction (Simpkins & Simpkins, 2009). More specifically, there is emerging evidence that the practice of Qigong, which uses controlled breathing and graceful movements to promote the circulation of Qi, may be associated with significant benefits in terms of positive mood, reduced anxiety, and enhanced pleasure, at least in certain individuals (Johansson & Hassmén, 2008). In addition, Qigong meditators show lower levels of neuroticism than nonmeditators, after controlling for gender, age, and education (Leung & Singhal, 2004).

Conclusions

Most of the world's major religious and spiritual traditions incorporate elements of contemplative prayer or meditation, although the nature, prominence, and precise features of such practices vary between traditions. Overall, interest in contemplative practice and meditation is continuing to grow significantly in the Western world, both in the general population and among researchers interested in the neuroscientific and clinical effects of contemplative practice.

Recent years have seen an especially notable increase in research interest in the neuroscience of contemplative practices, especially Buddhist meditation. Findings to date provide substantial scientific support for significant and enduring alterations in brain biology associated with meditation, with strong evidence of detectable alterations in brain activity in the anterior cingulate cortex and dorsolateral prefrontal areas associated with meditation (Cahn & Polich, 2006). These biological changes appear linked with both the increased attention and alterations in experience of self associated with meditation.

These findings are complemented by emerging evidence of relationships between contemplative practice and positive psychological change, with studies suggesting that specific contemplative practices may benefit some individuals with depression, anxiety disorders, obsessive compulsive disorder, substance misuse disorders, disordered eating patterns, disorders involving anger, emotional dysregulation syndromes, binge eating, suicidal behavior, and posttraumatic disorders. There has been particular clinical interest in the use of "mindfulness-based cognitive therapy" for depression, combining mindfulness-based techniques from Buddhist tradition with Western cognitive therapeutic approaches (Williams et al., 2007). Similar techniques may offer further benefits in relation to certain aspects of physical illnesses, including psychological care during cancer treatment, promotion of holistic health in HIV/AIDS, adjunctive care in chronic medical illness, and terminal health care.

While much of this research has focused on Buddhist traditions, there is increasing neuroscientific and clinical interest in contemplative practices from other spiritual traditions, including Christianity, Islam, Hinduism, Judaism, and Taoism. There is also growing evidence of increased dialog between meditative traditions and while there remain important differences between traditions (e.g., the role of God in Christian and Jewish contemplative practice, but not Buddhism), there are also significant areas of commonality; for example, Christian sources describe the results of contemplative practice as including clearer perceptions of God's true nature, the human soul, and laws of nature, and at least some of these descriptions have significant echoes of Buddhist writings on meditation.

The dialog between Buddhist tradition and "Western" neuroscience has been especially interesting in recent years (Lopez, 2008; Wallace, 2007) and led to the emergence of the Mind and Life Institute, dedicated to the establishment of a working partnership and research collaboration between modern science and Buddhism (http://www.mindandlife.org). An analogous dialog between Buddhist tradition and "Western" psychotherapeutic techniques has produced a long-standing relationship between Buddhism and psychoanalysis, and, more recently, integration of mindfulness techniques with existing forms of psychotherapy, including cognitive-behavioral therapy, dialectical behavioural therapy, and acceptance and commitment therapy.

Future Directions

Future years are likely to see a continued increase in public interest in meditation, monasticism

(Draper, 2009), and yoga (Corliss, 2001) in both Eastern and Western countries. There is also likely to be increased interest in other contemplative traditions that were not considered in this chapter, including those with lengthy histories (e.g., Jainism) and more recent schools (e.g. New Age meditative practices). These trends are likely to continue in parallel with deepening interest in the ways in which various aspects of psychology interact with contemplative traditions, especially as contemplative practices (such as meditation and yoga) continue to grow in popularity. Conceptually, these developments can be considered in three broad, thematic categories: neuropsychology and contemplative traditions; clinical psychology and contemplative traditions; and new concepts, questions, and queries.

Neuropsychology and Contemplative Traditions

In light of the enormous growth in neuroscientific interest in contemplative practice and brain function over past decades, it is likely that much future research in this area will remain focused on the detectable biological effects of meditation on the brain. Given that studies to date have focused largely (although not exclusively) on Buddhist practice, there is a need for further study of meditative practices from other contemplative traditions (such as Christianity), in order to compare results across practices and traditions.

From a neuropsychological perspective, there is a strong need for greater integration of neuroscientific findings about meditation with subjective experiences of contemplative practices (Austin, 1999, 2006; Deshmukh, 2006). The blending of objective with subjective sources will contribute to the development of a more unified, integrated understanding of the psychological effects and biological correlates of meditation. This process may be hampered by Western science's traditional difficulty with the integration of "subjective" experience with "objective" measurement and scientific techniques. Overcoming these methodological tensions may represent one of the key contributions that neuropsychological research into contemplative practice will bring to Western neuropsychological research.

There is also likely to be significant value in exploring differences between individual spiritual "cognitive styles" and identifying ways in which different individuals respond to contemplative practices, and their related psychological consequences. The consequences of these differing cognitive styles are also likely to vary across spiritual traditions (Tapanya et al., 1997), pointing to a possible need for multilevel conceptual models that take account of cognitive style, contemplative practice, spiritual tradition, *and* personal factors related to psychological and spiritual activities. The development and interpretation of such models will present a unique and valuable challenge to Western psychology.

Future research work in this area could also usefully consider the role of culture in mediating or modulating expressions of psychological states related to, or induced by, contemplative practice (Castillo, 2003). At present, there is a notable paucity of systematic considerations of cultural factors in relation to contemplative practices, despite a relatively substantial literature relating to other aspects of cross-cultural psychology (Berry, Poortinga, Segall, & Dasen, 2002). Previous work in cross-cultural psychology has much to offer in this context, not least through its considerations of methodological issues such as the selection of valid control groups and study samples, attaining an optimal balance between "etic" approaches (from outside the system) and "emic" approaches (from within the system), and engaging in meaningful considerations of cultural "equivalence" (Berry et al., 2002; Kelly & Feeney, 2007).

Clinical Psychology and Contemplative Traditions

From the perspective of clinical psychology, therapeutic interest is likely to continue to focus on mindfulness in the context of existing forms of psychotherapy, including cognitive-behavioral therapy, dialectical behavioral therapy, and acceptance and commitment therapy (Boseley, 2010). With psychotherapeutic and psychiatric practice increasingly emphasizing evidence-based paradigms of care, there is a need for further randomized controlled clinical trials to quantify the effects of mindfulness and meditation-based techniques for specific psychological disorders and mental illnesses.

The evidence-base to date is strongest for mindfulness-based cognitive therapy for depression (combining mindfulness-based techniques from Buddhist tradition with Western cognitive therapeutic approaches) (Williams et al., 2007). Similar approaches are now being applied in the contexts of anxiety disorders, emotional dysregulation syndromes, anger problems, binge eating, suicidal behavior, and the psychological effects of trauma (Mace, 2008). Further work is needed to clarify and consolidate the evidence bases for these interventions as forms of psychological therapy.

In terms of future research on mindfulness, Garland and Gaylord (2009) suggest four areas that they believe should be featured on the research agenda: (a) performance-based measures of mindfulness; (b) scientific evaluation of Buddhist claims made about mindfulness; (c) the neurophenomenology of mindfulness; and (d) measuring changes in mindfulness-induced gene expression. Further work in these areas would build on much existing research on correlates of mindfulness (Greeson, 2009) and help integrate robust considerations of mindfulness with existing neuroscientific findings.

These considerations of the role of mindfulness within Western psychotherapeutic and neuroscientific paradigms are useful, important, and to be welcomed. An exclusive focus on mindfulness to the exclusion of all else would, however, serve to obscure other aspects of contemplative practice that form key elements of most meditative traditions: Buddhist tradition, after all, accords substantial importance to the practice of meditation for *both* attainment of calm (*samatha*) *and* development of insight (*vipassanā*). While the existing scientific and psychological literature shows considerable evidence of benefits from attention, concentration, relaxation, and stress reduction, the issue of insight has been generally ignored in the integration of contemplative traditions into psychological therapies.

This relative neglect of the issue of insight in psychological considerations of contemplative practice stems chiefly from the West's strong tendency to separate psychological from spiritual practice. Many Eastern traditions (e.g., Buddhism) do not observe a robust division between psychological and spiritual matters. This makes a great deal of sense when one considers that an individual's psychological and spiritual beliefs and practices reside within the same brain, at the same time, and in the same sociocultural context as each other.

On this basis, the West's division between psychological and spiritual matters is, largely, a line which was drawn in the sand and which, as a result, can be altered or removed as circumstances require. In this context, the unfolding encounter between Eastern contemplative traditions and Western psychology offers an important opportunity to reexamine the relationship between spirituality and psychology in the West and refocus attention on the point of ultimate convergence for both spirituality and psychology: the individual human mind.

New Concepts, Questions, and Queries

The meeting of any two substantial traditions, or families of traditions, is a complicated, challenging, and exciting process. The emerging relationship between the family of (chiefly) "non-Western" contemplative traditions and the family of (chiefly) "Western" psychological traditions fits this paradigm perfectly, in all of its complexity, confusion, and excitement.

This meeting of traditions presents specific opportunities for established subdisciplines within "Western" psychological thought and practice, such as neuropsychology and clinical psychology (see earlier discussion). The overarching merit of such meetings of traditions, however, lies in the issues and challenges raised by one tradition for which the other tradition *has no category or language*. This element of the encounter between "Western" psychological traditions and "non-Western" contemplative traditions will probably produce the most exciting immediate challenges and the most lasting intellectual and cultural legacies to result from this encounter.

The tension between private and public paths to truth provides the clearest example of this to date. In Buddhist tradition, the path to truth lies in subjective or *private* exploration, through individual contemplative practice; even though practice may commonly occur in group settings, it is the *individual* who must meditate, contemplate, and achieve his or her own spiritual progress. In "Western" tradition, by contrast, the search for truth is conceived as a very public affair, involving open access to step-by-step methodologies, transparent scientific experimentation, and public articulation of results (in journals, newspapers, other media)—results upon which others may build. This is in stark contrast with Buddhism's requirement that each individual travels the journey for himself or herself. What does this contrast mean for the current meeting of Western and Eastern traditions, and what does psychology have to offer in this arena?

Psychological research has, traditionally, aimed to document, codify, and analyze individual psychological behavior in a scientific fashion and has not endorsed individual psychological practice as the path to truth to anything like the extent that Buddhism does. Consistent with this "Western" psychological approach, Christian contemplative traditions retain a focus on a predetermined outcome to individual contemplative practice (deeper realization of God) and, when compared to Buddhist tradition, place much less emphasis on the insight-revealing merits of the individual contemplative path.

Despite these differences in approach, or possibly *because* of them, psychology offers the most appropriate and adaptable arena in which contemplative practices can integrate and interact with Western psychological and spiritual traditions. Some methodological adaption may, however, be required. It is, for example, immediately apparent that Western psychology's division into subdisciplines (neuropsychology, cognitive psychology, clinical psychology, cross-cultural psychology, etc.), while offering a reassuring framework for the overwhelmed, does not lend itself readily to the holistic consideration of the possibilities opened up by contemplative traditions: Most contemplative traditions conceptualize the brain as a single, unified entity, integrating not only various psychological subdisciplines but also spirituality, into a single, holistic model of mind.

These tensions between approaches are to be welcomed. Dividing psychology into subdisciplines may serve specific purposes for researchers and teachers, but it may also distract from the ontological unity of the individual, living brain, which, after all, constitutes the ultimate root of *all* psychology. Committed, integrated psychological considerations of contemplative traditions can help restore a sense of balance by refocusing attention on the holistic experience of the individual mind and placing this in the broader context of its spiritual, cultural, *and* scientific settings.

Cross-cultural psychology, as conceptualized in Western traditions, also has much to offer to various schools of contemplative practice as part of these integrative, interpretative, and adaptive processes. The introduction of Buddhism to the United States, for example, has (arguably) resulted in the emergence of a distinct "Western" school of contemplative Buddhism. This adaptation of Buddhism to a new geographical context has political, cultural, spiritual, and even economic dimensions. But the most compelling way in which to approach this matter, at least initially, is through the prism of cross-cultural psychology (Berry et al., 2002), starting with an examination of the extent to which existing concepts and tools within cross-cultural psychology are appropriate to the systematic exploration of complex spiritual and cultural phenomena such as the integration of meditation into a new cultural and political context. At present, this area of research is a largely untilled field; the opportunities are at once substantial, challenging, and exciting.

There is, however, a need for caution. Given recent enthusiasm in relation to the neuroscience of meditation, and ongoing research into its clinical effects, it is useful for researchers to reflect upon the purpose of such cross-sectoral research, which is, surely, neither to "prove" that any given spiritual practice is "scientifically valid" nor to provide "spiritual justification" for specific forms of neuroscientific or clinical activity. The purpose of these cross-sectoral dialogs is, rather, to enrich endeavors in both fields and, hopefully, move toward a meaningful integration of objective and subjective forms of knowledge in relation to meditation. While there may be certain limits to which these goals can be achieved (Ernst, 1998), there clearly remains substantial potential for further research and ongoing dialog aimed at developing a deeper, more integrated understanding of the spiritual, psychological, and biological effects of contemplative practice, for the benefit of all.

Further Reading

Aslan, R. (2005). *No God but God: The origins, evolution and future of Islam.* New York: Random House.

Cahn, B. R., & Polich, J. (2006). Meditation states and traits: EEG, ERP, and neuroimaging studies. *Psychological Bulletin, 132,* 180–211.

Cleary, T. (2000). *Taoist meditation: Methods for cultivating a healthy mind and body.* Boston, MA: Shambala.

Cunningham, L. S. (1999). *Thomas Merton: The monastic vision.* Grand Rapids, MI: Wm. B. Eerdmans.

Dalai, A. S. (1991). *Psychology, mental health and yoga.* Twin Lakes, WI: Lotus Press.

Davis, A. (Ed.). (2000). *Meditation from the heart of Judaism.* Woodstock, VT: Jewish Lights Publishing/LongHill Partners.

De Silva, P. (2005). *An introduction to Buddhist psychology* (4th ed.). London: Palgrave Macmillan.

Flood, G. (1996). *An introduction to Hinduism.* Cambridge, England: Cambridge University Press.

Frager, R., & Fadiman, J. (Eds.). (1997). *Essential Sufism.* San Francisco: Harper San Francisco

Williams, M., Teasdale, J., Segal, Z., & Kabat-Zinn, J. (2007). *The mindful way through depression: Freeing yourself from chronic unhappiness.* New York and London: The Guilford Press.

References

Albers, S. (2006). *Mindful eating 101: A guide to healthy eating in college and beyond.* New York: Routledge.

Armstrong, K. (2000). *Islam: A short history.* London: Weidenfeld & Nicolson.

Armstrong, K. (2007). *The Bible: The biography.* London: Atlantic Books/Grove Atlantic Ltd.

As-Sayyid, N. M. (2005). *The healing power of Sufi meditation.* Washington, DC: Islamic Supreme Council of America.

Aslan, R. (2005). *No God but God: The origins, evolution and future of Islam.* New York: Random House.

Austin, J. H. (1999). *Zen and the brain.* Cambridge, MA and London: MIT Press.

Austin, J. H. (2006). *Zen-brain reflections.* Cambridge, MA: MIT Press.

Azari, N. P., Nickel, J., Wunderlich, G., Niedeggen, M., Hefter, H., Tellmann, L.,... Seitz, R. J. (2001). Neural correlates of religious experience. *European Journal of Neuroscience, 13,* 1649–1652.

Barham, D. (2003). The last 48 hours of life: A case study of symptom control for a patient taking a Buddhist approach to dying. *International Journal of Palliative Nursing, 9,* 245–251.

Barrett, M. E. (1997). Wat Thamkrabok: A Buddhist drug rehabilitation program in Thailand. *Substance Use and Misuse, 32*, 435–459.

Belisle, P-D. (2003). *The language of silence: The changing face of monastic solitude*. London: Darton, Longman and Todd.

Ben-Arye, E., Karkabi, S., Shapira, C., Schiff, E., Lavie, O., & Keshet, Y. (2009). Complementary medicine in the primary care setting: Results of a survey of gender and cultural patterns in Israel. *Gender Medicine, 6*, 384–397.

Benson, H., Malhotra, M. S., Goldman, R. F., Jacobs, G. D., & Hopkins, P. J. (1990). Three case reports of the metabolic and electroencephalographic changes during advanced Buddhist meditation techniques. *Behavioral Medicine, 16*, 90–95.

Berke, J. H. (1996). Psychoanalysis and Kabbalah. *Psychoanalytic Review, 83*, 849–863.

Berry, J. W., Poortinga, Y. H., Segall, M. H., & Dasen, P. R. (2002). *Cross-cultural psychology: Research and applications* (2nd ed.). Cambridge, England: Cambridge University Press.

Birnbaum, L. (2005). Adolescent aggression and differentiation of self: Guided mindfulness meditation in the service of individuation. *Scientific World Journal, 5*, 478–489.

Bodhi, B. (Ed.). (1999). *A comprehensive manual of Abhidhamma: The philosophical psychology of Buddhism*. Seattle, WA: BPS Pariyatti Editions.

Bonadonna, R. (2003). Meditation's impact on chronic illness. *Holistic Nursing Practice, 17*, 309–319.

Boseley, S. (2010, January 5). Meditation on prescription: charity urges alternative remedy for depressed patients. *The Guardian*, p. 4.

Brazier, C. (2003). *Buddhist psychology: Liberate you mind, embrace life*. London: Constable & Robinson.

Brazier, D. (1995). *Zen therapy*. London: Robinson.

Brown, D., Forte, M., & Dysart, M. (1984a). Visual sensitivity and mindfulness meditation. *Perceptual and Motor Skills, 58*, 775–784.

Brown, D., Forte, M., & Dysart, M. (1984b). Differences in visual sensitivity among mindfulness meditators and non-meditators. *Perceptual and Motor Skills, 58*, 727–733.

Brown, R. P., & Gerbarg, P. L. (2005a). Sudarshan kriya yogic breathing in the treatment of stress, anxiety and depression: Part I—neurophysiologic model. *Journal of Alternative and Complementary Medicine, 11*, 189–201.

Brown, R. P., & Gerbarg, P. L. (2005b). Sudarshan kriya yogic breathing in the treatment of stress, anxiety and depression: Part II—clinical applications and guidelines. *Journal of Alternative and Complementary Medicine, 11*, 711–717.

Brown, R. P., & Gerbarg, P. L. (2009). Yoga breathing, meditation and longevity. *Annals of the New York Academy of Sciences, 1172*, 54–62.

Bushell, W. C. (2009). Longevity: Potential life span and health span enhancement through practice of the basic yoga meditation regimen. *Annals of the New York Academy of Sciences, 1172*, 20–27.

Cahn, B. R., & Polich, J. (2006). Meditation states and traits: EEG, ERP, and neuroimaging studies. *Psychological Bulletin, 132*, 180–211.

Caraman, P. (1990). *Ignatius Loyola: A biography of the founder of the Jesuits*. San Francisco: Harper & Row.

Castillo, R. J. (2003). Trance, functional psychosis and culture. *Psychiatry, 66*, 9–21.

Cleary, T. (2000). *Taoist meditation: Methods for cultivating a healthy mind and body*. Boston: Shambala.

Cohen, J. M. (Trans.). (1957). *The life of Saint Theresa of Ávila by herself*. London: Penguin.

Corliss, R. (2001). The power of yoga. *Time, 157*, 54–64.

Cunningham, L. S. (1999). *Thomas Merton: The monastic vision*. Grand Rapids, MI: Wm. B. Eerdmans.

Dalai, A. S. (1991). *Psychology, mental health and yoga*. Twin Lakes, WI: Lotus Press.

Dandelion, P. (2007). *An introduction to Quakerism*. Cambridge, England: Cambridge University Press.

D'Aquili, E., & Newberg, A. (2000). The neuropsychology of aesthetic, spiritual, and mystical states. *Zygon, 35*, 39–51.

Das, L. S. (1997). *Awakening to the Buddha within: Tibetan wisdom for the western world*. London: Bantam.

Davis, A. (Ed.). (2000). *Meditation from the heart of Judaism*. Woodstock, VT: Jewish Lights Publishing/LongHill Partners.

De Nicolás, A. T. (1996). *St. John of the Cress: Alchemist of the soul*. York Beach, ME: Samuel Weiser.

De Silva, P. (2005). *An introduction to Buddhist psychology* (4th ed.). London: Palgrave Macmillan.

Deikman, A. J. (1977). Sufism and psychiatry. *Journal of Nervous and Mental Diseases, 165*, 318–329.

Deshmukh, V. D. (2006). Neuroscience of meditation. *Scientific World Journal, 6*, 2239–2253.

DiGiuseppe, R. (1999). End piece: Reflections on the treatment of anger. *Journal of Clinical Psychology, 55*, 365–379.

Draper, R. (2009). Called to the holy mountain. *National Geographic, 216*, 134–149.

Drubach, D. A., & Claassen, D. O. (2008). Perception and the awareness of God: The importance of neuronal habituation in the context of the Jewish and Christian faiths. *Journal of Religion and Health, 47*, 541–548.

Emmanuel, R. (2001). A-void- an exploration of defences against sensing nothingness. *International Journal of Psychoanalysis, 82*, 1069–1084.

Epstein, M. (2007). *Psychotherapy without the self: A Buddhist perspective*. New Haven, CT and London: Yale University Press.

Ernst, C. W. (1998). The psychophysiology of ecstasy in Sufism and yoga. *North Carolina Medical Journal, 59*, 182–184.

Feuerstein, G. (1992). *Yoga-sūtra of Patañjali: A new translation and commentary*. Rochester, VT: Inner Traditions International.

Flood, G. (1996). *An introduction to Hinduism*. Cambridge, England: Cambridge University Press.

Frager, R., & Fadiman, J. (Eds.). (1997). *Essential Sufism*. San Francisco: Harper San Francisco

Fromm, E., Suzuki, D., & Demartino, R. (1960). *Zen Buddhism and psychoanalysis*. New York: Harper & Row.

Garland, E., & Gaylord, S. (2009). Envisioning a future contemplative science of mindfulness: Fruitful methods and new content for the next wave of research. *Complementary Health Practice Review, 14*, 3–9.

Germer, C. K., Siegel, R. D., & Fulton, P. R. (Eds.). (2005). *Mindfulness and psychotherapy*. New York: The Guilford Press.

Gethin, R. (1998). *The foundations of Buddhism*. Oxford, England: Oxford University Press.

Greeson, J. M. (2009). Mindfulness research update: 2008. *Complementary Health Practice Review, 14*, 10–18.

Hamilton, E. (1982). *Life of Saint Teresa of Avila*. Westminster, MD: Christian Classics.

Hanson, R. (2009). *Buddha's brain: The practical neuroscience of happiness, love and wisdom*. Oakland, CA: New Harbinger Publications.

Harinath, K., Malhotra, A. S., Pal, K., Prasad, R., Kumar, R., Kain, T. C., ... Sawhney, R. C. (2004). Effects of Hatha yoga and Omkar meditation on cardiorespiratory performance, psychologic profile and melatonin secretion. *Journal of Alternative and Complementary Medicine*, *10*, 261–268.

Harris, P. (Ed.). (2001). *John Main: A biography in text and photos*. Oro Valley, AZ: Medio Media.

Harvey, P. (1990). *An introduction to Buddhism: Teachings, history and practices*. Cambridge, England: Cambridge University Press.

Hayes, S. C. (2002). Buddhism and acceptance and commitment therapy. *Cognitive and Behavioural Practice*, *9*, 58–66.

Janakiramaiah, N., Gangadhar, B. N., Murthy, P. J., Harish, M. G., Subbakrishna, D. K., & Vedamurthachar, A. (2000). Antidepressant efficacy of Sudarshan Kriya (SKY) in melancholia: A randomised comparison with electroconvulsive therapy (ECT) and imipramine. *Journal of Affective Disorders*, *57*, 255–259.

Johansson, M., & Hassmén, P. (2008). Acute psychological responses to Qigong exercise of varying durations. *American Journal of Chinese Medicine*, *36*, 449–458.

Karamustafa, A. T. (2007). *Sufism: The formative period*. Edinburgh, Scotland: Edinburgh University Press.

Kavanagh, K. (2000). *John of the Cross: Doctor of light and love*. New York: Crossroad Publishing Company.

Kelly, B. D. (2008). Buddhist psychology, psychotherapy and the brain: A critical introduction. *Transcultural Psychiatry*, *45*, 5–30.

Kelly, B. D., & Feeney, L. (2007). Coping with stressors: Racism and migration. In D. Bhugra, & K. Bhui (Eds.), *Textbook of cultural psychiatry* (pp. 550–560). Cambridge, England: Cambridge University Press.

Kenney, J. P. (2005). *The mysticism of Saint Augustine: Rereading the Confessions*. New York: Routledge.

Khumar, S. S., Kaur, P., & Kaur, S. (1993). Effectiveness of Shavasana on depression among university students. *Indian Journal of Clinical Psychology*, *20*, 82–87.

Krisanaprakornkit, T., Krisanaprakornkit, W., Piyavhatkul, N., & Laopaiboon, M. (2006). Meditation therapy for anxiety disorders. *The Cochrane Database of Systematic Reviews*, *1*, CD004998.

Kulkarni, D. D., & Bera, T. K. (2009). Yogic exercises and health—a psycho-neuro-immunological approach. *Indian Journal of Physiology and Pharmacology*, *53*, 3–15.

Kumar, S. M. (2002). An introduction to Buddhism for the cognitive-behavioural therapist. *Cognitive and Behavioural Practice*, *9*, 40–43.

Leavy, S. A. (2009). Psychoanalysis and religious mysticism. *Journal of the American Psychoanalytic Association*, *57*, 477–489.

Leifer, R. (1999). Buddhist conceptualization and treatment of anger. *Journal of Clinical Psychology*, *55*, 339–351.

Leung, Y., & Singhal, A. (2004). An examination of the relationship between Qigong meditation and personality. *Social Behaviour and Personality: An International Journal*, *32*, 313–320.

Lockhart, R. B. (1999). *Halfway to heaven: The hidden life of the Carthusians*. London: Cistercian Publications.

Logsdon-Conradsen, S. (2002). Using mindfulness meditation to promote holistic health in individuals with HIV/AIDS. *Cognitive and Behavioural Practice*, *9*, 67–72.

Lopez, D. S., Jr. (2008). *Buddhism and science: A guide for the perplexed*. Chicago and London: The University of Chicago Press.

Lundberg, P. C., & Trichorb, K. (2001). Thai Buddhist patients with cancer undergoing radiation therapy: Feelings, coping, and satisfaction with nurse-provided education and support. *Cancer Nursing*, *24*, 469–475.

Lutz, A., Greischar, L. L., Rawlings, N. B., Ricard, M., & Davidson, R. J. (2004). Long-term meditators self-induce high-amplitude gamma synchrony during mental practice. *Proceedings of the National Academy of Sciences USA*, *101*, 16369–16373.

MacCulloch, D. (2009). *A history of Christianity: The first three thousand years*. London: Allen Lane.

Mace, C. (2008). *Mindfulness and mental health: Therapy, theory and science*. Hove, England: Routledge.

Main, J. (2006). *Word into silence: A manual for Christian meditation*. Norwich, England: Canterbury Press.

Maritain, J. (2008). *The angelic doctor: The life and thought of Saint Thomas Aquinas*. Whitefish, MT: Kessinger Publishing.

Marlatt, G. A. (2002). Buddhist philosophy and the treatment of addictive behaviour. *Cognitive and Behavioural Practice*, *9*, 44–49.

Mascaro, J. (2005) *The Upanishads*. London: Penguin.

Massaro, T., & Shannon, T. A. (Eds.). (2002). *American Catholic social teaching*. Collegeville, MN: The Liturgical Press.

Matt, D. C. (1996). *The essential Kabbalah: The heart of Jewish mysticism*. New York: HarperCollins

McDaniel, J. (2007). Hinduism. In J. Corrigan (Ed.), *The Oxford handbook of religion and emotion* (pp. 52–53). Oxford, England: Oxford University Press.

McElroy-Cox, C. (2009). Alternative approaches to epilepsy treatment. *Current Neurology and Neuroscience Reports*, *9*, 313–318.

McGrath, P. (1998). A spiritual response to the challenge of routinization: A dialogue of discourses in a Buddhist-initiated hospice. *Qualitative Health Research*, *8*, 801–812.

Merton, T. (1968). *Zen and the birds of appetite*. New York: New Directions.

Newberg, A., Alavi, A., Baime, M., Pourdeehnad, M., Santanna, J., & d'Aquili, E. (2001). The measurement of regional cerebral blood flow during the complex cognitive task of meditation: A preliminary SPECT study. *Psychiatry Research*, *106*, 113–122.

Newberg, A., Pourdehnad, M., Alavi, A., & d'Aquili, E. G. (2003). Cerebral blood flow during meditative prayer: Preliminary findings and methodological issues. *Perceptual and Motor Skills*, *97*, 625–630.

Newberg, A. B., & Iversen, J. (2003). The neural basis of the complex mental task of meditation: Neurotransmitter and neurochemical considerations. *Medical Hypotheses*, *61*, 282–291.

Nurbakhsh, D. (1978a). Sufism and psychoanalysis. Part one: What is Sufism? *International Journal of Psychiatry*, *24*, 204–212.

Nurbakhsh, D. (1978b). Sufism and psychoanalysis. Part two: A comparison between Sufism and psychoanalysis. *International Journal of Psychiatry*, *24*, 213–219.

Oldstone-Moore, J. (2003). *Understanding Taoism*. London: Duncan Baird Publishers.

Olson, T. (2003). Buddhism, behavior change, and OCD. *Journal of Holistic Nursing*, *21*, 149–162.

Palmer, R. L. (2002). Dialectical behaviour therapy for borderline personality disorder. *Advances in Psychiatric Treatment*, *8*, 10–16.

Pearsall, J., & Trumble, B. (Eds.). (1996). *Oxford English reference dictionary* (2nd ed.). Oxford, England: Oxford University Press.

Pretorius, E. (2009). The role of alternative and complementary treatments of asthma. *Acupuncture and Electro-therapeutics Research, 34*, 15–26.

Robins, C. J. (2002). Zen principles and mindfulness practice in dialectical behaviour therapy. *Cognitive and Behavioural Practice, 9*, 50–57.

Robinson, G. (2000). *Essential Judaism: A complete guide to beliefs, customs and rituals.* New York: Pocket Books/Simon & Schuster.

Saper, R. B., Eisenberg, D. M., Davis, R. B., Culpepper, L., & Phillips, R. S. (2004). Prevalence and patterns of adult yoga use in the United States: Results of a national survey. *Alternative Therapies in Health and Medicine, 10*, 44–49.

Segal, Z. V., Williams, M. G., & Teasdale, J. D. (2001). *Mindfulness-based cognitive therapy for depression: A new approach to preventing relapse.* New York: The Guilford Press.

Shapiro, D., Cook, I. A., Davydov, D. M., Ottaviani, C., Leuchter, A. F., & Abrams, M. (2007). Yoga as a complementary treatment of depression: Effects of traits and moods on treatment outcome. *Evidence-Based Complementary and Alternative Medicine, 4*, 493–502.

Shapiro, R. M. (2000). The teaching and practice of Reb Yerachmiel ben Yisrael. In A. Davis (Ed.), *Meditation from the heart of Judaism* (pp. 17–34). Woodstock, VT: Jewish Lights Publishing/LongHill Partners.

Shelov, D. V., Suchday, S., & Friedberg, J. P. (2009). A pilot study measuring the impact of yoga on the trait of mindfulness. *Behavioural and Cognitive Psychotherapy, 37*, 595–598.

Simpkins, C. A., & Simpkins, A. M. (2009). *Meditation for therapists and their clients.* New York and London: W. W. Norton.

Squire, L. R., Berg, D., Bloom, F., Du Lac, S., & Ghosh, A. (2008). *Fundamental neuroscience* (3rd ed.). Burlington, MA: Academic Press/Elsevier.

Storey, W. G. (2004). *A prayer book of Catholic devotions.* Chicago: Loyola Press.

Talbot, J. M. (2002). *Come to the quiet: The principles of Christian meditation.* New York: Tarcher/Putnam.

Tapanya, S., Nicki, R., & Jarusawad, O. (1997). Worry and intrinsic/extrinsic religious orientation among Buddhist (Thai) and Christian (Canadian) elderly persons. *International Journal of Aging and Human Development, 44*, 73–83.

Tobin, S. (1996). *The Cistercians: Monks and monasteries of Europe.* New York: The Overlook Press.

Tzu, L., & Mitchell, S. (1999). *Tao Te Ching: An illustrated journey.* London: Frances Lincoln.

Wachholtz, A. B., & Pargament, K. L. (2005). Is spirituality a critical ingredient of meditation? Comparing the effects of spiritual meditation, secular meditation, and relaxation on spiritual, psychological, cardiac, and pain outcomes. *Journal of Behavioural Medicine, 28*, 369–384.

Wallace, B. A. (2007). *Contemplative science: Where Buddhism and neuroscience converge.* New York: Columbia University Press.

Williams, M., Teasdale, J., Segal, Z., & Kabat-Zinn, J. (2007). *The mindful way through depression: Freeing yourself from chronic unhappiness.* New York and London: The Guilford Press.

Translation of Eastern Meditative Disciplines Into Western Psychotherapy

Randye J. Semple *and* Sean P. Hatt

Abstract

This chapter describes the history and influence of Buddhist meditative disciplines on Western psychotherapy. Beginning with an overview of Buddhist traditions, a brief discussion of some of the foundational tenets of Buddhist psychology is offered. An overview of the dialog between Buddhism and psychotherapy from the early 1900s to the present is traced. The shift from meditation as a spiritual discipline to mindfulness as a secular practice is explored. Four of the most widely studied and practiced mindfulness-oriented psychotherapies are described: mindfulness-based stress reduction (MBSR), dialectical behavioral therapy (DBT), acceptance and commitment therapy (ACT), and mindfulness-based cognitive therapy (MBCT). The chapter ends with an invitation to consider the reciprocal influence of meditation as a spiritual discipline and as a secular practice. What benefits might be realized by reevaluating the therapeutic secularization of these ancient and profound spiritual practices? We consider the desirability, form, and likelihood of a possible reintegration.

Key Words: Buddhism, meditation, mindfulness, psychology, psychotherapy, spirituality, transpersonal

Introduction

I have discovered a nectarlike truth,
Deep, calm, and simple, lucidly awake and unformed.
Whomever I explain it to, no one will understand;
So I will remain silent in the jungle.
—Buddha Shakyamuni (in Schmidt & Tweed, 2003, p. 17)

Although meditative practices of most Eastern spiritual traditions are present in the rapidly expanding Western psychological and psychotherapeutic discourse, we do not have sufficient space here to discuss the subtle and complex relationships of all of them. Thus, we have chosen to discuss what we know best: Buddhism and Buddhist contemplative practices. From the jungle temples of Southeast Asia, Himalayan meditation caves, and incense-shrouded monasteries of Japan and China,

Buddhist meditative practices have migrated into the laboratories and consulting rooms of Western research scientists and clinicians. Therapies that include meditative components show promise in being effective interventions to treat mental and behavioral health problems (Baer, 2003; Grossman, Niemann, Schmidt, & Walach, 2004). Meditation has become an accepted part of contemporary psychotherapy, psychiatry, behavioral health, and psychosomatic medicine. Exploring the history of the relationship between Buddhist meditative disciplines and psychotherapy will help us understand how and why contemplative practices entered the armamentarium of Western psychotherapists.

This chapter is organized in three sections. First, is an overview of Buddhism and Buddhist meditation practices, tracing the path of how this esoteric Eastern spiritual practice came to dialog with and influence Western psychotherapeutic thinking. Second, is a review of the evolution of contemporary meditation research and practice. The current state of meditation in psychotherapy, recent research, and clinical applications of four mindfulness-oriented therapies are described. Third, we consider possible futures for spiritually informed psychotherapies and, in particular, how Buddhist contemplative disciplines may influence research and clinical practice. We close by exploring several philosophical questions concerning the broader relationship between these curious bedfellows.

Buddhism: A Uniquely Adaptable Tradition

Buddhism has migrated around the world from its original home in Northern India. As it did so, it adopted many cultural nuances and rituals from indigenous religions. These migrations have produced two major Buddhist schools and hundreds of smaller sects and teaching lineages. The first major school is *Theravāda* Buddhism, sometimes called the Path of the Elders. Practiced primarily in Sri Lanka, Myanmar (Burma), Laos, Vietnam, and Thailand, this tradition emphasizes *vipassana*,[1] or insight meditation. Vipassana practices are believed to cultivate mindfulness and insight into the nature of reality. The Theravāda school represents itself as being closest to the original teachings and practices of the historical Buddha (Thanissaro Bhikkhu, 1996). The second school, *Mahayana* Buddhism, is based on *bodhicitta*, which is the wish to achieve enlightenment not purely for one's own sake, but for the sake of all sentient beings. Mahayana has further divided to become *Zen* Buddhism and *Vajrayāna* Buddhism. Zen Buddhism originated in China and then migrated to Vietnam, Korea, and Japan. It is the tradition that may be most familiar to many Westerners. Zen emphasizes gaining wisdom through experience rather than knowledge based on theoretical or intellectual understandings. Zen students practice *zazen* ("just sitting"), a concentrative breath meditation, and *shikantaza* ("whole-hearted sitting"), a form of mindfulness meditation. Zen practices also include *koans,* which are short teaching stories or sentences that

initially seem paradoxical. Koans are intended to radically alter perceptions of reality by thwarting the student's attempts to comprehend that which cannot logically be comprehended (Suzuki, 1970). *Vajrayāna* Buddhism developed in Tibet and is practiced in Nepal, Bhutan, northern India, and parts of China. Most consider Vajrayāna to be a branch of Mahayana Buddhism, but some view it as a separate school (Kitagawa, 2002). Tibetan practices encompass a number of complex, multifaceted contemplative techniques that range from simple breathing exercises to elaborate, tantric visualization rituals (sGam.Po.Pa, 1986). Some are devotional practices not typically applied in secular contexts (e.g., *guru yoga*).

Is Buddhism a Religion or a Method?

Buddhism may be unique among major spiritual traditions, as it generally eschews monotheism or other deific beliefs. Literally translated, the word "buddha" simply means "one who is awake." Siddhārtha Gautama (who later became Shakyamuni Buddha) is considered the founder of Buddhism. Gautama was born in Lumbini around 400 BCE (Cousins, 1996) near the Himalayas in modern-day Nepal (Schmidt & Tweed, 2003). The Buddha's boundless compassion for all beings would not allow him to teach anything less than what he saw as the ultimate truth about reality (Thurman, 1995). Thus, he refused to offer a religious solution to the human condition, including a deific belief in himself, or any god, dogma, or ritual.

Batchelor (1997) suggested that the Buddha was not a mystic and his awakening was not meant to be interpreted as some privileged or esoteric insight into the nature of the universe. Batchelor maintains that the increasingly ritualized, religious practices of Buddhism have been responsible for imputing such claims to Shakyamuni Buddha's insights, while the only claim Shakyamuni made about himself was that he had "freed his heart and mind from the compulsions of craving." The Buddha called this "the taste of the *dharma*" (Batchelor, 1997, p. xi). *Dharma* (or *dhamma* in Pali) usually refers to the Buddhist teachings, but it may also mean those aspects of reality and experience with which those teachings are concerned. A similar position is held by His Holiness the 17th Gyalwa Karmapa, Trinlay Thaye Dorje (as cited in Thurman, 1995). As spiritual leader of the Kagyu lineage of Tibetan Buddhism, the Karmapa maintains that Buddhism should be viewed simply as a method, rather than as a religion or philosophy. He commented that

Buddhism as a method was designed to simply and directly connect us to our true essence so that we might see through confusion and see with clarity the existence of *samsara* (Pellarin, Talley, Lehnert, & Webb, 2003).

On Suffering and the End of Suffering

Before we continue, understanding what Trinlay Thaye Dorje meant by *samsara* may help explain the affinity between psychotherapy and the meditative disciplines. *Samsara* is defined as being the "cyclic existence" of birth, death, and rebirth that is espoused in Buddhism (Schmidt, 1999, p. 180). Samsara is synonymous with the state of ordinary human existence, characterized by *dukkha*, which is generally translated to mean suffering but includes all forms of dissatisfaction, including discomfort, dis-ease, and unpleasant emotions. Dukkha arises from the desire to cling to objects or experiences that are unattainable or impermanent, and the desire to push away unwanted experiences.

The Affinity Between Buddhism and Psychotherapy

Interest in suffering and the ending of suffering provides one point of intersection between Buddhism and psychotherapy. Although Western psychologists maintain boundaries between psychotherapy and spiritual practice, the desire shared by spiritual teachers and psychotherapists to relieve suffering may partly explain the interest in exploring their synergies. Alan Watts (1961) suggested a reframing of Buddhism by observing, "If we look deeply into such ways of life as Buddhism...we do not find either philosophy or religion...we find something more nearly resembling psychotherapy (p. 3). He identified their similarities, noting that "the main resemblance between Eastern ways of life and Western psychotherapy is in the concern of both with bringing about changes of consciousness, changes in our ways of feeling our own existence and our relation to human society and the natural world" (pp. 3–4). Some of the practices associated with the Theravāda, Zen, and Vajrayāna traditions are now being explored by Western scientists and psychotherapists.

Despite their many dissimilarities, all Buddhist schools were founded on an anthology of scriptures known as the *Tripitika* (literally meaning three baskets). The first "basket" is the *Vinaya*, which is the disciplinary code of conduct for monks. Second is the *Pali Canon*, which contains the collected discourses (*suttas* in Pali; *sutras* in Sanskrit) of the

Buddha. The third, and most relevant to this discussion, is the *Abhidhamma*, which contains more abstruse scriptures that deal with philosophy, metaphysics, and psychology (Bhikkhu Bodhi, 1993). The *Abhidhamma* might be considered the world's first psychology textbook. It is a scholarly text that thoroughly describes attributes of consciousness and relationships between mental states. The *Abhidhamma* discusses how to attain and stabilize those mind states that are helpful, while dispelling those that are destructive or harmful. Goleman (1972a) suggested that the *Abhidhamma* is perhaps the broadest and most encyclopedic treatment of higher states of consciousness in existence. The *Abhidhamma* is the principal source of Buddhism's psychology of mind and is referenced often in contemporary meditation research literature. This wealth of scholarly psychological insights makes the Buddhist paradigm particularly suited to engage with Western scientists.

Tension Between the Secular and the Religious

For millions of people around the world, Buddhism is more than a practical method to achieve happiness; it is an ancient and venerated spiritual path. With its long oral and written traditions, Buddhism is contemplative and rich in mysticism and prophesies. While the focus of this chapter is primarily secular, two predictions attributed to Padmasambhava (a revered 8th-century Tibetan sage) frame an interesting tension for modern practitioners who seek to explore the intersection of body, mind, and spirit using Buddhist spiritual practices in clinical settings.

A Prophet and His Prophesies

A rich oral tradition can trace the teachings of Padmasambhava in a direct lineage of teacher to teacher up to the present day. Padmasambhava made these predictions: "When the iron bird flies, and horses run on wheels, the Tibetan people will be scattered like ants across the World, and the Dharma will come to the land of the red-faced people" (Das, 1997, p. 23). In writing about the dharma's ability to transcend temporal and cultural constraints, Goldstein (2002) suggested that Padmasambhava was foretelling both the invasion of Tibet by China and the emergence of Buddhism in the West. Goldstein holds that Buddhism has retained the integrity of its core principles while expanding far beyond its cultural origins. These principles include meditative techniques, the expression of compassion, and the perfection of wisdom that identifies both the causes of suffering and the means to end it.

In another prophesy that is directly relevant to our current model of teaching mindfulness in psychotherapy, Padmasambhava was said to have cautioned against the teaching of these profound practices for the liberation of suffering by those who have not received proper permission from the lineage holders of that tradition. He specifically warned against the use of meditation as a means of helping others by those who were not themselves accomplished practitioners.

> In the future, when the dark age of degeneration arrives, some people who claim to be practitioners will desire to teach others without having received permission. Without having practiced themselves, they will instruct others in meditation. Without being liberated themselves, they will pretend to give instructions for liberation. Without being devoid of self-interest, they will instruct others to cast away their fetters of attachment and be generous (*Schmidt*, 1999, p. 150).

Holding this cautionary statement in mind, let us look back to when the Buddha's teachings began to influence Western psychology.

Tracing a Lineage of Increasing Influence
Buddhism and Psychotherapy: 1900–1950

William James was an early proponent of Buddhism as a psychology. When the Buddhist monk Dharmapāla attended one of James's lectures at Harvard, James is quoted as saying to him, "Take my chair. You are better equipped to lecture on psychology than I." Following one of Dharmapāla's own lectures, James declared, "This is the psychology everybody will be studying twenty-five years from now" (as cited in Scott, 2000, p. 335). Although feeling that Buddhism was generally a pessimistic psychology, in *Varieties of Religious Experience* (1902) James strongly endorsed the functional value of meditation.

In the early 1900s, the Freudian psychoanalytic tradition began an ongoing dialog with Buddhism. Although Freud himself quickly dismissed belief in all religions as a form of psychosis (Freud, 1927/1964), some of his followers disagreed. Sun (1924) compared Buddhist teachings with tenets of psychoanalysis and found some philosophical confluence. In particular, he noted the similarity between consciousness as an "endopsychic organ" and the Buddhist quality of *mano*, which is loosely considered to be the consciousness that is aware of

the self. Sun also found similarities in the psychoanalytic view of unconscious neurotic suffering and the Buddhist conception of *dukkha*. Both could only be mastered by substituting conscious insight for unconscious phantasy (p. 41). He felt that Buddhism and psychoanalysis were similarly dedicated to the arising of wisdom to replace the "evils of illusion" (p. 40). Sun noted that Freudian and Buddhist teachings on the subject of determinism were similar, citing the first line of the *Dhammapada*,[2] which says, "All that we are, is the result of what we have thought; it is founded on our thoughts, it is made up of our thoughts" (p. 40) and comparing this with Freud's comment, "We are what we are because we have been what we have been. And what is needed to solve the problem of human life is not moral estimates, but more knowledge" (p. 40).

Psychoanalyst Franz Alexander (1931) was rather less charitable in his analysis of Buddhism, calling its theoretical framework and practices "nihilistic" (p. 132). He believed that Buddhist meditation practices would trigger a reversal of normal psychological development to an infantile, narcissistic state. According to Alexander, meditative training was purely an egocentric and regressive exercise. He wrote, "... it is clear that Buddhist self-absorption is a libidinal, narcissistic turning of the urge for knowing inward, a sort of artificial schizophrenia with complete withdrawal of libidinal interest from the outside world" (p. 130). Alexander also surmised that meditative practices resulted in a psychological state of "emotionlessness." He first erroneously conflated emotionlessness with *nirvana*, and then defined nirvana as being similar to the condition of a fetus in the womb—an "oceanic feeling" akin to an artificial catatonia. In stark contrast to Alexander's interpretation, Buddhist thinking considers nirvana to be a state of awareness that is beyond discursive thought and free from all desires or suffering. Although later moderating his extreme position, Alexander further suggested that the major difference between Buddhism and psychoanalysis was that Buddhism denies reality, while analysis seeks to help one try to adjust to it.

Carl Jung acted as a psychological interpreter of Buddhism. He expanded the dialog with Buddhism beyond Freudian psychoanalysis when he published the foreword to D. T. Suzuki's *Introduction to Zen Buddhism* (Jung, 1939/1968, pp. 540–541), where he expressed his awareness of the significance of Buddhist practices but criticized early efforts to invoke Western psychology to gain understandings of spiritual enlightenment (*satori*). While Jung understood the fascination of Western audiences for esoteric Zen practices, he also maintained that the Western mind was utterly incapable of grasping such ineffable mysteries as enlightenment. In a seemingly contradictory statement, Jung then noted that the very fact of Buddhism's existence for 25 centuries, during which "many brilliant minds have worked...is sufficient reason for at least venturing a serious attempt to bring such processes within the realm of scientific understanding" (p. 544), and concluded that psychotherapy was the only Western discipline that could gain some understanding of the quest for *satori* (p. 553).

Jung (1943/1968) continued to explore the differences between East and West, astutely noting that Europeans had produced a "medical psychology dealing specifically with the *kleshas*" (p. 572) or the core defilements of the mind[3] that Buddhism proposes to overcome. The difference, Jung felt, between the tortured psyche of Western therapy patients and the psyche of Buddhist practitioners was that psychoanalysis was entangled in the problem of the shadow and its influence on consciousness, while Buddhist practitioners were comfortably acquainted with the shadow in the form of the kleshas. "The spirit of India grows out of nature; with us, spirit is opposed to nature" (p. 572). Psychotherapists spend more time attending to psychopathology than they do cultivating the natural spirit of humanity in their patients, and limited vision may constrain our goals. Freud (1895/2000) believed that maximum therapeutic effectiveness was achieved "...if we succeed in transforming [*our client's*] neurotic misery into common unhappiness" (p. 305). A Buddhist psychotherapist would settle for no less than the complete end to all suffering for all sentient beings.

Buddhism and Psychotherapy: 1950–1960

The psychoanalytic dialog during the 1950s continued to explore primarily Zen theory and practices. Stunkard (1951) identified the way in which Zen masters interacted with their students as having a particular connection with psychoanalysis. He saw similarities in the need to maintain a careful balance between "encouragement necessary to maintain the subject's participation, and the frustration required for his continued self examination" (p. 424). Stunkard, however, advocated for a child-like reliance upon a parent-like teacher, and by analog, the psychoanalyst, which seems more attuned to the devotional practices of Vajrayāna than to Zen.

Rather than calling on the West to adopt Eastern ways of being, Sato (1957) called upon Western science to help Zen Buddhism to free itself from rigidity, emphasizing psychotherapy as a key contributor to this change. Sato found that Zen and psychoanalysis shared a recognition of the importance of attention to intrapsychic experiences occurring in the present moment. He also found parallels in his understanding of the Buddhist concept of "no-mind" and analytic free association. Sato's ideas are consistent with modern thinking in one important area. He identified a clear difference between Zen, which emphasizes the importance of intuition and attending to discrete experiences, and Western psychology, which has a propensity to label, categorize, and judge phenomena.

Not limiting itself to theoretical psychological discourse, Zen began to inform specific psychotherapy interventions. For example, *Morita therapy* is a Japanese protocol developed by Japanese psychiatrist Shoma Morita (Rhyner, 1988). Originally, Zen did not directly influence Morita; however, his thinking later "converged to the Zen mode of thought" (Kora & Sato, 1957, p. 219). The initial therapy was subsequently refined by some of Morita's students, one of whom was a former Zen monk. Developed to help patients suffering from neurasthenia,[4] one aim of Morita therapy was to help the patient stop struggling against or fleeing from reality. Similar to contemporary mindfulness-based approaches, the patient was encouraged to "accept the sufferings and worries just as they are," becoming "open-minded," and avoiding any kind of "repulsive tendency" toward the self or one's experiences (p. 221).

Kondo (1958) explored Zen *shikantaza* meditation as a therapeutic intervention. He noted that initially, his patients found the practice almost unbearable—at times feeling that it was intensifying their suffering. Kondo explained this as the experience of having normal patterns of "scattering their energy" blocked, leaving the patient nowhere to go but inward. The inward movement resulted in a juggling of ideas and fantasies, again to avoid directly facing the causes of suffering. Nonetheless, Kondo encouraged his patients to continue "just sitting." Eventually, they described experiences of increased energy and vitality. One patient was reported to say, "When I sit, I feel I am rooted and full of sap, where before I felt helplessly buffeted by every emotional wind or storm" (p. 63). Kondo defined these experiences as knowing the "real self" and believed that experiential understanding was equally important in psychoanalysis and Zen meditation.

The concept of a "real self" was central to the theories of neo-Freudian feminist psychoanalyst

Karen Horney. She too expressed an affinity for Zen, although she only began to develop the interest near the end of her life. Horney was particularly interested in the work of D. T. Suzuki, citing him in her writings as early as 1945, but not meeting him until the early 1950s (Morvay, 1999). She also approached Kondo to explore incorporating the Zen practice of "just sitting" into psychotherapy as a way of cultivating the "real self." Horney delighted in the fact that Zen could provide her with something she had been unable to find, namely a means to verify the existence of the "real self" (Morvay, 1999, p. 28). Traveling to Japan to study with Suzuki and Kondo deepened Horney's understanding of Zen. She came to understand that good therapy required a certain quality of presence of mind in the therapist that Horney defined as being "wholehearted." To Horney, wholeheartedness had begun to seem much like the results of Zen meditation practice. She eventually concluded that wholeheartedness required the therapist to become "fully present in the moment through a kind of forgetting of the self," thereby freeing herself to "be there with an unlimited receptivity to impressions, feelings, etc." (Morvay, 1999, p. 29).

The humanistic psychoanalyst Erich Fromm was also interested in the work of Zen master D. T. Suzuki. Fromm began exploring the relationship between Buddhism and psychoanalysis with an acknowledgment of the gulf that lies between them. He admitted that his interest in Zen arose in response to the sense of spiritual crisis he felt in many of his patients. He framed the spiritual pain in decidedly existential terms as a "deadening of life" and the "alienation [of man] from himself, from his fellow man and from nature" (Fromm, Suzuki, & De Martino, 1960, pp. 78–79). In 1957, Fromm invited Suzuki and Richard De Martino to collaborate in a series of talks in Cuernavaca, Mexico, which resulted in the seminal book, *Zen Buddhism and Psychoanalysis* (Fromm et al., 1960). In the book's foreword, Fromm noted that a couple of decades earlier, it would have been inconceivable to find that high level of interest among his colleagues in such an esoteric tradition as Zen, adding that Dr. Suzuki had "stimulated, inspired, and refreshed" all those in attendance. Fromm attributed this positive reception to the development of psychoanalytic theory, changes in the intellectual and spiritual climate of the West, and the popularity and accessibility of Suzuki's writing to Western therapists. Suzuki was careful to state that Zen did not stand in opposition to science, but he did suggest that Zen might

inform Western scientists, noting that the Western approach to reality may not be the only one worthy of consideration. Fromm held that Buddhism was superior to Western religions in its use of rationality and realism. In Zen practices, Fromm saw promise for a resolution of the existential suffering that the psychoanalyst alone could not resolve for his patients.

Buddhism and Psychotherapy: 1960–1980

Increasing interest in Zen among psychoanalysts invited sharp criticisms from philosopher Ernest Becker (1960). He cautioned that uncritically accepting Stunkard's (1951) relating the Zen master's relationship to his student to the relationship between the analyst and analysand would open up Western psychotherapy to coercion rather than healing. Becker (1961a) felt that Zen teachers (and by analogy, like-minded psychoanalysts) were essentially engaged in a surreptitious process of converting students to their own perspectives. On the whole, he experienced Zen as an irreconcilable dichotomous paradox, with "poignant esthetic musings about man and nature" struggling against a "blatant denial of life" (1961b, p. 13).

Despite Becker's harsh critique, the East-West dialog continued. In Japan, Kishimoto (1962) wrote about an integrative *self-awakening therapy* that blended Eastern philosophical traditions with Fromm's humanistic psychoanalysis, Horney's self-realization theory, and Frankl's existential psychology. According to Kishimoto, the well-being of the body and soul must be improved using Zen meditation and koan practice as a method of catechesis, by which the mind's conflicts might be "scraped off" (p. 431). For Kishimoto, Zen was less about treating neurosis than it was about finding well-being by forging a sense of unity with the world. Self-awakening therapy was a stepwise process. At the outset, the client would engage in a free-association-like talk therapy in an attempt to establish the desired sense of unity with the world. If unsuccessful, then the client was directed to meditate three to five times daily, combining deep breathing and koan practices. Once the desired sense of unity with the world was attained, then the client would join a like-minded group, share his or her suffering, and encourage other suffering people to support one another until all were freed from neurotic suffering (Kishimoto, 1962).

Maupin (1962) noted the important connection between meditative practice and the therapeutic benefits of relaxation by drawing similarities between *zazen*, autogenic training (Schultz & Luthe, 1959), and progressive muscle relaxation (Jacobson, 1938). Like Kishimoto (1962), Maupin sought to understand how Zen helped patients cultivate a new relationship with the world. He saw the Zen concept of *satori* as being a way of experiencing oneself and the world as a unified whole, and he felt this was a point of interest for psychotherapy. He contrasted satori to the experience of a separate, neurotic, and conceptual self. Whereas the latter is held to be something stable, objective, and in need of defense, the satori experience sees through this illusion to "the real self, the true author of one's behavior, which at the same time is a part of the whole flux of the universe" (Maupin, 1962, pp. 363–364).

Sutherland (1966) similarly speculated about the conjunction of Eastern spirituality and Western psychotherapy in a nondualistic paradigm. He wrote about the Eastern way of experiencing the world, not as a collection of separate objects and separate subjects but rather as "a great organic action," with all apparent divisions being the consequence of artificial constructions that served "ease in communication and not inherently the nature of reality itself" (p. 10). Sutherland tied his ideas directly to Western psychotherapy by promoting an emphasis on here-and-now experiences and a radical acceptance of suffering and joy alike, with "faith in an order beyond technology and world politics, beyond anything the mind can grasp" (p. 12). This radical opening to the present moment was to be cultivated through meditation and the asking of unanswerable questions that might "lead to new ways of knowing" (p. 12). Practiced in this way, proposed Sutherland, psychotherapy might perceive the psychopathology in the individual person as being important, but it would also see and value "the eternal," thus allowing meaning to stretch beyond the limits of the bounded, individual self in order to touch the realm of spirit, soul, and God. In some ways, Sutherland seemed to make little differentiation between spiritual practices and psychotherapy.

Koji Sato (1968) took a more pragmatic approach that mirrors more closely the secular clinical versions of mindfulness practiced today. He chose sitting meditation as being a "psychophysiological adjustment" (p. 8) that was equated to other Eastern practices observed over centuries to have positive impacts upon physical and emotional health. He reported these beneficial effects as ranging from raising vital, sexual energy, to curing chronic psychosomatic illnesses, kidney and heart disease, gynecological problems, and high blood pressure. According to

Sato, psychophysiological adjustment was but one of the 10 virtues that Zen practitioners could expect to cultivate, the 10 virtues covering every aspect of human existence in mind, body, and spirit.

Sato's integration of mind, body, and spirit in Zen as a therapeutic intervention coincided with the birth of a new paradigm in psychology sometimes known as the "fourth force." Transpersonal psychology initially developed out of the human potential movement. In a talk given at the Esalen Institute in 1967, Abraham Maslow (1969) eloquently defined this emergent discipline as a psychology that might study "that which motivates, gratifies and activates the fortunate, developed self-actualizing person" (pp. 3–4). Lajoie and Shapiro (1992) later recognized the evolution of this new paradigm and the shift away from its human potential movement roots, by expanding their definition of transpersonal psychology to include "humanity's highest potential, with the recognition, understanding, and realization of unitive, spiritual, and transcendent experiences" (p. 91).

Ram Dass, a former Harvard University professor turned spiritual teacher, provides one example that exemplifies the paradigm shift that began in the 1960s. During this period, meditation research briefly moved away from strictly academic scholarship and toward experiential scholarship that was integrated with personal spiritual practices. As a Western scholar and a meditation practitioner, Dass embarked on a lifelong trajectory aimed at unifying body, mind, and spirit into a singular psychology, but not purely for the sake of science. His intent was to do this while advancing his own spiritual path. He preferred not to pursue these aims in a Himalayan cave but rather "in New York City in the United States with television and loving people around and great cooks and advertising and total support for all of the attachments" (Dass, 1970, p. 92). This, Dass said, was his own personal *sadhana*, or spiritual journey.

Other academic psychologists (for example, Jack Kornfield, Daniel P. Brown, Richard J. Davidson, John D. Teasdale, and Alan C. Marlatt) and psychiatrists (for example, Deane H. Shapiro, Jr. and Roger N. Walsh) adopted a similar path that, in the world of transpersonal psychology, changed what it meant to be a scholar-practitioner. The philosopher Alan Watts (1961) was another voice that encouraged East and West to influence one another, discussing the complementary aims of meditative practices and psychotherapy, in terms of both "being a transformation of consciousness, of the inner feeling of one's own existence; and…the release of the individual from forms of conditioning imposed upon him…" (p. 18).

Beginning in the 1970s, another scholar-practitioner, Daniel Goleman, wrote extensively about meditation and meditation research (see Goleman, 1972a, 1972b, 1979, 1981, 1984, 1988). Goleman's (1971) concept of meditation as a "metatherapy" may best describe the harmony between spirituality and psychotherapy that was sought by transpersonal therapists. Goleman defined metatherapy as "…a procedure that accomplishes the major goals of conventional therapy and yet has as its end-state a change far beyond the scope of therapies…an altered state of consciousness" (p. 4). Goleman then gradually moved away from meditation research as he extended his work on emotional intelligence to a more general audience (Goleman, 1995).

In 1977, the American Psychiatric Association released a position statement that called for a critical examination of the clinical effectiveness of meditation practices:

> The association strongly recommends that research be undertaken in the form of well-controlled studies to evaluate the possible specific usefulness, indications, contraindications, and dangers of meditative techniques.
>
> (p. 720)

The APA taskforce suggested that meditative practices may reduce the need for psychotropic medications and facilitate psychotherapy. With the endorsement of this respectable and conservative mental health organization, the stage was set for a new wave of scientific study and the further secularization of these profound practices into Western research laboratories and clinical settings.

Many of the meditation studies conducted during this period measured physiological responses such as heart rate and oxygen consumption (Benson, 1975; Benson, Beary, & Carol, 1974), blood pressure (Seer & Raeburn, 1980), and electroencephalogram (EEG) alpha rhythms (Davidson, Schwartz, & Rothman, 1976). Findings from many systematic investigations made it clear that meditation practices affect a variety of hypometabolic responses and lower cortical arousal (Woolfolk, 1975). West (1980) suggested that the practice of meditation reduces arousal and increases relaxation for four reasons: (a) the repetition of a single stimulus produces habituation of the orienting reaction, (b) the eyes are closed so that external visual stimuli are blocked, (c) the setting itself is quiet, and (d) the meditator has expectations of deep relaxation and states of peace. Benson (1975) named this hypometabolic response the *Relaxation Response*, thereby framing meditation as a self-regulation strategy rather than as a consciousness discipline. Walsh (1996) later observed that heart rate and respiration are comparatively gross and objective measures relative to the subtle and subjective shifts in awareness, values, and emotions that have constituted the traditional goals of meditation. Several well-controlled studies found that the hypometabolic effect was not unique to meditation but is shared with other relaxation techniques such as yoga, progressive muscle relaxation, biofeedback, autogenic training, and self-hypnosis (see review by Walsh, 1996). Comparison studies found that meditation practices resulted in cognitive and affective changes beyond the hypometabolic "relaxation response" that was produced by other self-relaxation methods (Lazar et al., 2000; Lehrer, Woolfolk, Rooney, McCann, & Carrington, 1983; Semple, 1999; Weinstein & Smith, 1992). Research focus began to shift from simply examining the psychophysiology of meditation toward cultivating a deeper understanding of cognitive and affective correlates of meditative practices.

The Modern Zeitgeist: From Meditation to Mindfulness

Concurrent with research that placed meditation in a theoretical framework of cognitive and affective processes, a subtle shift in terminology happened that seemed to move meditation in the context of psychotherapy even further from the sacred and plant it more firmly in the secular world. Academic journal articles began to appear that used the phrase "mindfulness meditation" in relationship to clinical interventions (Brown & Engler, 1980; Brown, Forte, & Dysart, 1984a, 1984b; Forte, Brown, & Dysart, 1988; Kabat-Zinn, 1984; Kabat-Zinn, Lipworth, & Burney, 1985; Kutz, 1985). Then, Jon Kabat-Zinn published *Full Catastrophe Living* (1990), which described a structured group program of mindfulness meditation that had been developed and researched at the University of Massachusetts Medical Center during the previous decade. Fueled by the emergence of the Mindfulness-Based Stress Reduction program, the term "meditation" began to be used less frequently, gradually transforming into "mindfulness." After defining "mindfulness" as it is used in contemporary psychotherapy, we will briefly describe what may be called the four foundations of therapeutic mindfulness—the four principal therapies that incorporate mindfulness-based approaches.

Mindfulness

In Buddhism, the word "mindfulness" derives from the Pali word *sati*, which comes from a root word that means "to remember." Sati is a subtle concept loosely related to conscious awareness, attention, remembering (to be fully present in this moment), and maintaining a constant presence of mind (Bhikkhu Bodhi, 1993). As a mental factor, *sati*

> ...signifies presence of mind, attentiveness to the present rather than the faculty of memory regarding the past. It has the characteristic of not wobbling, i.e., not floating away from the object.[5] Its function is absence of confusion or non-forgetfulness.
>
> (p. 86)

"Not wobbling" refers to a stability of attention on the percept of interest, while "absence of confusion" refers to the aim of cultivating discerning wisdom that arises from seeing reality clearly (i.e., seeing what *is*, with no preconceived expectations or judgments).

In Western psychology, mindfulness is generally described as being a special kind of attention. Mindfulness practices are frequently referred to as exercises in training attention. One often quoted definition is "the awareness that emerges through paying attention on purpose, in the present moment, and nonjudgmentally to the unfolding of experience moment by moment" (Kabat-Zinn, 2003, p. 145). The term "mindfulness" is often used interchangeably with *mindful awareness* or *mindful attention*. Bishop and his colleagues (2004) proposed a two-component operational definition, suggesting that mindfulness is "...a process of regulating attention in order to bring a quality of nonelaborative awareness to current experience and a quality of relating to one's experience within an orientation of curiosity, experiential openness, and acceptance" (p. 234).

Mindfulness is considered to be both the dynamic activity of refocusing attention to present-moment events and the state of mind that results from practicing mindfulness. The process of mindfulness is simply the practice of bringing nonjudgmental attention to internal and external events as they arise, moment by moment, then returning the "wobbly" attention whenever awareness arises that the attention has drifted away. Internal events include thoughts, emotions, perceptions, and body sensations. External events include interpersonal, situational, and environmental experiences. Practicing mindfulness is simply the returning of attention, to what Kabat-Zinn (2005) described as the *nowscape*, by which he meant the multifaceted and rich inner and outer world of perceptions and felt experiences. Mindful awareness is open and receptive to immediate experience. Mindfulness is characterized by an attitude of curiosity and non-judgmental acceptance—regardless of whether a given event is interpreted as being pleasant or unpleasant. Qualities of mindful awareness include increased attention to the experience itself; greater awareness of thoughts *about* the experience; and fewer attempts to rationalize, extend, avoid, criticize, or change the experience.

In its psychological context, mindfulness is defined without reference to its spiritual context. Essentially, mindfulness is the application of attention in a specific manner, while maintaining an explicit relationship to the object of attention, and with recognition and awareness that internal cognitive and affective factors can influence one's perceptions. It is generally believed that mindfulness can be cultivated and that it enhances self-management of attention (Baer, 2003; Bishop et al., 2004; Boals, 1978; Kabat-Zinn, 1994; Kumar, 2002; Segal, Williams, & Teasdale, 2002; Semple, Lee, Rosa, & Miller, 2009).

Mindfulness and Psychotherapy: 1980–2000

Along with a movement toward more sophisticated psychotherapy research methods, mindfulness changed its primary allegiance—migrating from the psychodynamic camp to become firmly aligned with the cognitive sciences. During this time, cognitive and information-processing theories became (and still are) the dominant paradigm in clinical psychology and psychotherapy research. Cognitive-behavioral therapies (CBT) had accumulated a great deal of research evidence that supported their effectiveness in the treatment of mood, anxiety, and other mental disorders. CBT helps patients to identify their cognitive biases, appreciate the associations between thoughts, emotions, and behavior, distance themselves from their own idiosyncratic perspectives, and develop more realistic self-statements (Overholser, 1995). Some have argued that consistent meditation practice encourages precisely the same changes (Teasdale, 1999). Cognitive and mindfulness-based therapists are united by the desire to understand the workings of the mind and apply that understanding to reduce human suffering. These therapy models share the insight that thoughts are not always accurate reflections of reality. In other ways, however, they are based on opposite and incompatible worldviews, and reconciling the dialectic can sometimes be a challenge for Western psychotherapists.

MINDFULNESS-BASED STRESS REDUCTION

During the 1970s and most of the 1980s, meditation research had been quietly marginalized. The Mindfulness-Based Stress Reduction (MBSR) program (Kabat-Zinn, 1990, 1994) provided impetus for a renewed surge of interest by academic psychologists. With colleagues at the University of Massachusetts Medical Center, Jon Kabat-Zinn developed MBSR to help patients cope with intractible pain and better manage stress associated with chronic illnesses (Kabat-Zinn, 1984; Kabat-Zinn & Chapman-Waldrop, 1988; Kabat-Zinn et al., 1985). The Stress Reduction Clinic opened at the university medical center in 1979. Since then, more than 18,000 people have completed the 8-week MBSR program at what is now called the Center for Mindfulness in Medicine, Health Care, and Society. MBSR groups are conducted in more than 200 medical centers in the United States and are frequently used to help individuals manage the pain and stressors associated with major medical illnesses.

MBSR provides an intensive, 8-week group training in meditations similar to Vipassana practices. MBSR participants learn to engage more skillfully with their lives by enhancing present-focused awareness. Guided instructions in three specific mindfulness practices are taught: (1) mindfulness of the breath, (2) mindfulness of the body (body scan), and (3) mindful movement practice (simple yoga postures). Simple, sensory-focused exercises (such as eating one raisin with mindfulness) provide further practice in being fully present in the moment. Group discussions and guided inquiries follow each exercise. Participation in an MBSR course demands a significant personal commitment; up to 45 minutes of daily home practice, 6 days each week. The efforts required to develop a consistent daily meditation practice provide much practical experience in mindful awareness. Instructor training programs are also available for those interested in teaching MBSR. Somewhat more aligned with spiritual practices than some therapies developed later, a personal, experiential understanding of mindfulness is believed to be essential. MBSR instructors are therefore expected to have cultivated and maintain their own personal mindfulness practices.

Research has shown that MBSR increases stress management skills for patients coping with chronic pain, general hospital patients (Kabat-Zinn et al., 1985; Miller, Fletcher, & Kabat-Zinn, 1995), and individuals with more serious conditions such as cancer (Carlson, Ursuliak, Goodey, Angen, & Speca, 2001; Kwekkeboom, 2001; Shapiro, Bootzin,

Figueredo, Lopez, & Schwartz, 2003), traumatic brain injuries (Bédard et al., 2003), and HIV (Creswell, Myers, Cole, & Irwin, 2009; Sibinga et al., 2008). Teachers (Anderson, Levinson, Barker, & Kiewra, 1999), medical school students (Shapiro, Schwartz, & Bonner, 1998), inner-city residents (Roth & Robbins, 2004), prison inmates (Bowen et al., 2006), and others in chronically stressful situations have also found MBSR practices beneficial.

A scientist-practitioner model of training encouraged clinicians to utilize evidence-based practices to treat their patients. Nearly a mantra in the 1990s, the phrase "what works for whom" was heard often. Matching a specific therapy to the particular mental health problems of the patient became prevalent; however, MBSR was not intended to be a psychotherapy. Although many MBSR teachers are clinicians, they are referred to as instructors, not therapists. Nonetheless, variants of MBSR have now been evaluated as a treatment for mood and anxiety disorders (Ramel, Goldin, Carmona, & McQuaid, 2004), social anxiety disorder (Koszycki, Benger, Shlik, & Bradwejn, 2007), posttraumatic stress disorder (Simpson et al., 2007), substance use (Bowen et al., 2006; Witkiewitz, Marlatt, & Walker, 2005), and as an adjunct to other psychotherapies (Weiss, Nordlie, & Siegel, 2005). Other therapies began to emerge that were focused on treating specific disorders. Some included mindfulness-informed approaches; one of which was dialectical behavior therapy.

DIALECTICAL BEHAVIORAL THERAPY

Dialectical behavioral therapy (DBT) was developed to treat patients diagnosed with borderline personality disorder (Linehan, 1993a, 1993b), but it was later expanded to include other disorders associated with dysregulated emotions (Lynch, Chapman, Rosenthal, Kuo, & Linehan, 2006). Some core principals of DBT derive from Zen Buddhism (Robins, 2002), but they are incorporated into a structured set of cognitive interventions (e.g., cognitive reframing) and behavioral techniques (e.g., applied functional analysis, social skills training, and exposure).

The principal dialectic in DBT refers to a core struggle within the patient between unconditional acceptance of themselves exactly as they are, thwarted by an accurate recognition of the need to make behavioral changes. Not unlike a Westernized koan practice, DBT aims to resolve the dialectic by finding a way to integrate these opposing positions. DBT teaches skills to cultivate acceptance (mindfulness, distress tolerance) and skills to implement behavioral changes (interpersonal effectiveness, emotional regulation). Mindfulness supports the resolution of the dialectic tension between acceptance and change. Two subsets of mindfulness skills are directly taught. Some focus on *what* mindfulness is (e.g., observing, describing, and participating), and others focus on *how* mindfulness is practiced (e.g., nonjudgment, one-mindfulness, and acting with effectiveness). Mindfulness exercises include noting and counting breaths, and mindful walking, listening to music, eating, or writing. Although patients in DBT do not learn traditional meditation practices, DBT seems to have successfully integrated an acceptance-based mindfulness paradigm with a change-based cognitive-behavioral model (Lau & McMain, 2005).

Research and Clinical Practice in the Nowscape: 2000 to the Present

The success of MBSR and DBT encouraged additional therapy models. One of them, acceptance and commitment therapy, is grounded in the philosophy of functional contextualism, in which events and actions are believed to have meaning only in relationship to the contexts in which they develop. Acceptance and commitment therapy (ACT) is a nonspecific approach to treating a variety of psychopathologies. Another, mindfulness-based cognitive therapy (MBCT), was adapted from MBSR, but it was intended to be a prophylactic treatment for the prevention of depressive relapse.

ACCEPTANCE AND COMMITMENT THERAPY

Acceptance and commitment therapy (ACT) combines elements of mindfulness and acceptance with behavioral therapies (Hayes & Strosahl, 2004). ACT is based on relational frame theory, which is a constructivist theory of language and cognition. The model of pathology underlying ACT is based on concepts of cognitive fusion and experiential avoidance. Cognitive fusion is the belief that thoughts and other intrapsychic events are accurate reflections of reality, which then influence our behavioral responses. Experiential avoidance results from attempts to avoid, manage, or control thoughts, emotions, and sensations, even when the avoidant behaviors are unhelpful (Fletcher & Hayes, 2005). Cognitive fusion and experiential avoidance are believed to lead to psychological inflexibility and suffering. ACT helps patients develop psychological flexibility, formulate personal values, and make commitments to change. Core concepts include identification of acceptance, values, cognitive defusion, contact with the present moment, observing

the self, and committed action (Hayes, Strosahl, & Wilson, 1999). This therapy makes extensive use of metaphors and paradox to increase understanding of how cognitive fusion and experiential avoidance influence behaviors. Experiential exercises include brief meditation-like practices (e.g., mindfulness of thoughts, emotions, the breath, or other physical sensations). Similar to DBT, ACT is informed by a mindfulness paradigm; however, neither model includes specific teachings or practices traditionally associated with Eastern contemplative disciplines. Research support for ACT is still limited, but it has shown preliminary indications of effectiveness for a variety of problems, including anxiety and depression, addictions, smoking cessation, chronic pain, psychosis, workplace stress, and management of diabetes (Hayes, Luoma, Bond, Masuda, & Lillis, 2006).

MINDFULNESS-BASED COGNITIVE THERAPY

Mindfulness-based cognitive therapy (MBCT; Segal et al., 2002) is similar to the MBSR program in that MBCT is also an 8-week group protocol that teaches traditional breath and body meditation techniques. MBCT synthesizes the theories and techniques of MBSR with strategies borrowed from cognitive therapy. Unlike MBSR, MBCT was developed as a psychotherapy for clinical populations. The aims of MBCT are to help patients (1) become more aware of thoughts, body sensations, and feelings; (2) develop a new way of relating to their own thoughts, body sensations, and feelings, specifically by learning mindful observation, acknowledgment, and acceptance of unwanted thoughts and feelings; (3) redefine ruminative cognitions as being events in the mind rather than immutable truths; (4) recognize the onset of negative moods using mindful awareness as kind of "early warning" system; and (5) learn to disengage or "decenter" from the negative moods or thoughts before they escalate into a full depressive relapse. Initial clinical trials of MBCT suggest that, for patients with three or more major depressive episodes, MBCT significantly reduced relapse rates (Ma & Teasdale, 2004; Teasdale et al., 2000). MBCT has since been evaluated as an acute phase treatment for depression (Barnhofer et al., 2009; Kenny & Williams, 2007; Smith, Graham, & Senthinathan, 2007), bipolar disorder (Williams et al., 2008), anxiety disorders (Craigie, Rees, Marsh, & Nathan, 2008; Evans et al., 2008; Kim et al., 2009), and been adapted for use with children (Lee, Semple, Rosa, & Miller, 2008; Semple, et al., 2009).

Beyond the Nowscape: Envisioning a Mindful Future

As we retraced the historical influence of Eastern meditative disciplines on psychotherapy, we found an interesting progression. The early scholarly dialogs that thoughtfully explored similarities and differences between Zen Buddhism and psychoanalysis became the motivation for some scholar-practitioners to find a way to synthesize the two. This effort evolved into a scientific engagement that searched for underlying commonalities between these distinctly different traditions and produced a "fourth force" in psychology: the transpersonal movement. Transpersonal psychology directly borrowed from contemplative techniques, pulling them from the context of their spiritual home, and subjected them to systematic inquiry using assumptions grounded in a very different worldview. Although transpersonal researchers collected much valuable information, their efforts never quite achieved the status of mainstream academic respectability. Psychology then responded to the American Psychiatric Association's 1977 call to scientifically study the efficacy of meditation as a treatment for psychopathology. What resulted was a bifurcation—a splitting between clinical and transpersonal psychology. The transpersonal world returned to scholarly theoretical dialogs, while clinical psychology further secularized meditation, examining the process, mechanisms, and outcomes of meditation, both clinically and using state-of-the-art biomedical technologies. The results of these recent scientific endeavors have provided much support for the effectiveness of Westernized contemplative practices in treating a host of psychological and physical health problems.

The National Institutes of Health (NIH) direct the overall path of biomedical research in America. At the NIH, meditation studies are no longer being funded only by the National Center for Complementary and Alternative Medicine (NCCAM) but also through a diversity of other institutes such as the National Institute of Mental Health (NIMH), National Cancer Institute (NCI), National Institute on Drug Abuse (NIDA), National Institute of Diabetes and Digestive and Kidney Diseases (NIDDK), National Heart, Lung, and Blood Institute (NHLBI), National Institute on Aging (NIA), and others. To date, the NIH has funded nearly 700 research studies involving mindfulness meditation. The cognitive psychologists appear to have achieved what the transpersonal psychologists could not. Mindfulness is no longer considered an "alternative" intervention; it has landed firmly in the mainstream of biomedical research.

We now know much more about how meditation practices ameliorate the debilitating effects of chronic stress associated with severe medical conditions such as cancer (Massion, Teas, Hebert, Wertheimer, & Kabat-Zinn, 1995; Speca, Carlson, Goodey, & Angen, 2000), heart disease (Tacon, McComb, Caldera, & Randolph, 2003), and HIV (Creswell et al., 2009; Sibinga et al., 2008) and how secular programs of mindfulness training can help in the treatment of these and other medical conditions. We understand more about the neuropsychology of attention processes and affect regulation in meditation, and how these interact with psychiatric symptomatology (Rubia, 2009). Evidence suggests that mindfulness practices activate neural structures involved in attention and emotion self-regulation (Davidson, Kabat-Zinn, & Schumacher, 2003; Davidson et al., 2002; Jha, Krompinger, & Baime, 2007; Tang et al., 2007, 2009), and that these may be the underlying mechanisms by which mindfulness exerts its therapeutic effects.

We have begun to understand a bit more about how mindfulness practices enhance well-being. Psychiatrist Daniel Siegel is known for his work in *interpersonal neurobiology*, which is an interdisciplinary science that aims to understand subjective and interpersonal experiences. Siegel studies neurological and interpersonal components of healthy human functioning by synthesizing research in neuroplasticity (Schore, 2003a, 2003b), the relational functions of a specialized neural circuitry known as mirror neurons (Iacoboni et al., 1999), and attachment theory (Ainsworth & Bowlby, 1991; Bowlby, 1978). He developed a model of well-being that includes three components: the physical brain, the mind (defined as a system for organizing energy and information), and attuned relationships (Siegel, 2007), suggesting that it was the relationship between these components that was essential to psychological health and well-being. Siegel believes that this integration is mediated by the prefrontal cortex, an area of the brain that has shown structural and functional changes in meditation practitioners (Lazar et al., 2005).

Concluding Thoughts

Notwithstanding the remarkable advances that have been made in the integration of meditative disciplines with psychotherapy, transpersonal psychologists still speculate on what might be lost as we continue to secularize these profound practices. Roger Walsh (1993) observed that in bringing mindfulness into clinics and laboratories "more attention has been given to heart rate than heart opening" (p. 66), and he encouraged more focus on transpersonal goals such as ethical behaviors, love, compassion, generosity, wisdom, and service. Mindfulness-based stress reduction includes the practice of *metta*, which is the prayerful generating and radiating of loving kindness and compassion for the benefit of all beings. Its secular cousin, mindfulness-based cognitive therapy, does not ordinarily include this practice, although some therapists have incorporated *metta* practices in their MBCT groups. Would augmenting MBCT with *metta* practices enhance its effectiveness as a treatment for mood and anxiety disorders? Could opening the heart in this way provide for stronger or more sustained therapeutic effects to the individual or provide other benefits to those people around the meditator?

Walsh's lament brings us to introduce two rhetorical questions for your consideration. First, how do we harness the power of these practices to relieve psychopathological suffering while remaining true to their original spiritual intentions? Second, if these practices in their secular, clinical manifestations do effectively relieve suffering, need we concern ourselves with anything more profound than that? We would like to close by questioning the possibility or desirability of integrating spirituality and psychotherapy. Is there any way to completely integrate them, and might we even want to do so? The Buddha taught that all experiences in life, including mental and psychological events, are marked by three characteristics: suffering (*dukkha*), impermanance (*anicca*), and egolessness (*anatta*). A thorough understanding of what are known as the "three marks of existence" is believed to be one path that leads to the end of suffering (Ross, 1980). Ken McLeod, a contemporary meditation teacher, once translated the three marks into "life is tough...it will put you through some changes...but don't take it personally." Meditative disciplines and psychotherapy share a desire to end human suffering. Yet life is indeed "tough." A complete integration of Eastern spirituality with psychotherapy might require Western psychotherapy to stop reifying mental illnesses as being "me" or "mine." Psychiatric disorders could no longer be solely brain or genetic dysfunctions. Can we let go of the notion that human unhappiness is the result of chemical imbalances in the brain? More radically, we would need to stop reifying the notion of a bounded and permanent self, let go of the a priori belief that changes are required before happiness can arise, and radically expand our thinking about ways to attain a permanent solution to the human condition. Then we wonder...could any psychotherapy that seeks to cultivate unconditioned awareness of the ultimate nature of ourselves and our world ever be anything other than a spiritual practice?

Notes

1. Theravāda terms are mostly noted in Buddhism's original language of Pali. Mahayana terms are mostly noted in their more common Sanskrit translations. For example, *Dhamma* is the Pali word for teachings of the Buddha, while *Dharma* is the equivalent word in Sanskrit. Zen-specific terms are generally Japanese.

2. The *Dhammapada* is a collection of 423 Buddhist scriptures that are attributed directly to the historical Buddha.

3. In the *Abhidhamma*, 10 defilements or unwholesome mind states are identified. The first three, sometimes known as the "three poisons" (greed, hatred, and delusion), are considered to be the roots of suffering.

4. Neurasthenia is a disorder characterized by depressed mood, fatigue, anxiety, irritability, headaches, dizziness, and central or peripheral neuralgia (World Health Organization, 2007).

5. Objects can be internal (e.g., thoughts, emotions, and body sensations) or external, tangible objects.

References

Ainsworth, M. D., & Bowlby, J. (1991). An ethological approach to personality development. *American Psychologist*, *46*, 333–341.

Alexander, F. (1931). Buddhistic training as an artificial catatonia. *Psychoanalytic Review*, *18*, 129–145.

American Psychiatric Association. (1977). Position statement on meditation. *American Journal of Psychiatry*, *134*, 720.

Anderson, V. L., Levinson, E. M., Barker, W., & Kiewra, K. R. (1999). The effects of meditation on teacher perceived occupational stress, state and trait anxiety, and burnout. *School Psychology Quarterly*, *14*, 3–25.

Baer, R. A. (2003). Mindfulness training as a clinical intervention: A conceptual and empirical review. *Clinical Psychology: Science and Practice*, *10*, 125–143.

Barnhofer, T., Crane, C., Hargus, E., Amarasinghe, M., Winder, R., & Williams, J. M. G. (2009). Mindfulness-based cognitive therapy as a treatment for chronic depression: A preliminary study. *Behaviour Research and Therapy*, *47*, 366–373.

Batchelor, S. (1997). *Buddhism without beliefs: A contemporary guide to awakening*. New York: Riverhead Books.

Becker, E. (1960). Psychotherapeutic observations on the Zen discipline: One point of view. *Psychologia*, *3*, 100–112.

Becker, E. (1961a). The psychotherapeutic meeting of East and West. *American Imago*, *18*, 3–20.

Becker, E. (1961b). *Zen: A rational critique*. New York: W. W. Norton.

Bédard, M., Felteau, M., Mazmanian, D., Fedyk, K., Klein, R., Richardson, J.,...Minthorn-Biggs, M. B. (2003). Pilot evaluation of a mindfulness-based intervention to improve quality of life among individuals who sustained traumatic brain injuries. *Disability and Rehabilitation*, *25*, 722–731.

Benson, H. (1975). *The relaxation response*. New York: William Morrow.

Benson, H., Beary, J. F., & Carol, M. P. (1974). The relaxation response. *Psychiatry, 37*, 37–46.

Bhikkhu, Bodhi. (Ed.). (1993). *A comprehensive manual of Abhidhamma*. Kandy, Sri Lanka: Buddhist Publication Society.

Bishop, S. R., Lau, M., Shapiro, S., Carlson, L., Anderson, N. D., Carmody, J.,…Devins, G. (2004). Mindfulness: A proposed operational definition. *Clinical Psychology: Science and Practice, 11*, 230–241.

Boals, G. F. (1978). Toward a cognitive reconceptualization of meditation. *Journal of Transpersonal Psychology, 10*, 143–182.

Bowen, S., Witkiewitz, K., Dillworth, T. M., Chawla, N., Simpson, T. L., Ostafin, B. D.,…Marlatt, G. A. (2006). Mindfulness meditation and substance use in an incarcerated population. *Psychology of Addictive Behaviors, 20*, 343–347.

Bowlby, J. (1978). Attachment theory and its therapeutic implications. *Adolescent Psychiatry, 6*, 5–33.

Brown, D., & Engler, J. (1980). The stages of mindfulness meditation: A validation study. *Journal of Transpersonal Psychology, 12*, 143–192.

Brown, D., Forte, M., & Dysart, M. (1984a). Differences in visual sensitivity among mindfulness meditators and non-meditators. *Perceptual and Motor Skills, 58*, 727–733.

Brown, D., Forte, M., & Dysart, M. (1984b). Visual sensitivity and mindfulness meditation. *Perceptual and Motor Skills, 58*, 775–784.

Carlson, L. E., Ursuliak, Z., Goodey, E., Angen, M., & Speca, M. (2001). The effects of a mindfulness meditation-based stress reduction program on mood and symptoms of stress in cancer outpatients: Six month follow-up. *Supportive Care in Cancer, 9*, 112–123.

Cousins, L. S. (1996). The dating of the historical Buddha: A review article. *Journal of the Royal Asiatic Society, 3*, 57–63.

Craigie, M. A., Rees, C. S., Marsh, A., & Nathan, P. (2008). Mindfulness-based cognitive therapy for generalized anxiety disorder: A preliminary evaluation. *Behavioural and Cognitive Psychotherapy, 36*, 553–568.

Creswell, J. D., Myers, H. F., Cole, S. W., & Irwin, M. R. (2009). Mindfulness meditation training effects on CD4+ T lymphocytes in HIV-1 infected adults: A small randomized controlled trial. *Brain, Behavior, and Immunity, 23*, 184–188.

Das, L. S. (1997). *Awakening the Buddha within*. New York: Broadway Books.

Dass, R. (1970). Baba Ram Dass lecture at the Menninger Foundation. *Journal of Transpersonal Psychology, 2*, 91–139.

Davidson, R. J., Kabat-Zinn, J., & Schumacher, M. (2003). Alterations in brain and immune function produced by mindfulness meditation. *Psychosomatic Medicine, 65*, 564–570.

Davidson, R. J., Lewis, D. A., Alloy, L. B., Amaral, D. G., Bush, G., Cohen, J. D.,…Peterson, B. S. (2002). Neural and behavioral substrates of mood and mood regulation. *Biological Psychiatry, 52*, 478–502.

Davidson, R. J., Schwartz, G. E., & Rothman, L. P. (1976). Attentional style and the self-regulation of mode-specific attention: An electroencephalographic study. *Journal of Abnormal Psychology, 85*, 611–621.

Evans, S., Ferrando, S., Findler, M., Stowell, C., Smart, C., & Haglin, D. (2008). Mindfulness-based cognitive therapy for generalized anxiety disorder. *Journal of Anxiety Disorders, 22*, 716–721.

Fletcher, L., & Hayes, S. C. (2005). Relational frame theory, acceptance and commitment therapy, and a functional analytic definition of mindfulness. *Journal of Rational-Emotive and Cognitive Behavior Therapy, 23*, 315–336.

Forte, M., Brown, D. P., & Dysart, M. (1988). Differences in experience among mindfulness meditators. *Imagination, Cognition and Personality, 7*, 47–60.

Freud, S. (1964). *The future of an illusion* (W. D. Robson-Scott, Trans.). Garden City, NY: Doubleday. (Original work published 1927).

Freud, S. (2000). The psychotherapy of hysteria (J. Strachey, Trans.). In J. Breuer & S. Freud (Eds.), *Studies on hysteria* (pp. 253–305). New York: Basic Books. (Original work published 1895).

Fromm, E., Suzuki, D. T., & De Martino, R. (1960). *Zen Buddhism and psychoanalysis*. New York: Harper & Brothers.

Goldstein, J. (2002). *One Dharma: The emerging Western Buddhism*. New York: HarperCollins.

Goleman, D. (1971). Meditation as meta-therapy: Hypotheses toward a proposed fifth state of consciousness. *Journal of Transpersonal Psychology, 3*, 1–25.

Goleman, D. (1972a). The Buddha on meditation and states of consciousness: Part I: The teachings. *Journal of Transpersonal Psychology, 4*, 1–44.

Goleman, D. (1972b). The Buddha on meditation and states of consciousness: Part II: A typology of meditation techniques. *Journal of Transpersonal Psychology, 4*, 151–210.

Goleman, D. (1979). A taxonomy of meditation-specific altered states. *Journal of Altered States of Consciousness, 4*, 203–213.

Goleman, D. (1981). Buddhist and Western psychology: Some commonalities and differences. *Journal of Transpersonal Psychology, 13*, 125–136.

Goleman, D. (1984). The Buddha on meditation and states of consciousness. In D. H. Shapiro, Jr. & R. N. Walsh (Eds.), *Meditation: Classical and contemporary perspectives* (pp. 317–360). Hawthorne, NY: Aldine.

Goleman, D. (1988). The meditative mind: The varieties of meditative experience. Los Angeles: Jeremy P. Tarcher.

Goleman, D. (1995). *Emotional intelligence*. New York: Bantam Books, Inc.

Grossman, P., Niemann, L., Schmidt, S., & Walach, H. (2004). Mindfulness-based stress reduction and health benefits: A meta-analysis. *Journal of Psychosomatic Research, 57*, 35–43.

Hayes, S. C., Luoma, J. B., Bond, F. W., Masuda, A., & Lillis, J. (2006). Acceptance and commitment therapy: Model, processes and outcomes. *Behaviour Research and Therapy, 44*, 1–25.

Hayes, S. C., & Strosahl, K. D. (Eds.). (2004). *A practical guide to acceptance and commitment therapy*. New York: Springer.

Hayes, S. C., Strosahl, K. D., & Wilson, K. G. (1999). *Acceptance and commitment therapy: An experiential approach to behavior change*. New York: The Guilford Press.

Iacoboni, M., Woods, R. P., Brass, M., Bekkering, H., Mazziotta, J. C., & Rizzolatti, G. (1999). Cortical mechanisms of human imitation. *Science, 286*, 2526–2528.

Jacobson, E. (1938). *Progressive relaxation* (2nd ed.). Chicago: University of Chicago Press.

James, W. (1990). *The varieties of religious experience: A study in human nature*. New York: Random House (Original work published 1902).

Jha, A. P., Krompinger, J., & Baime, M. J. (2007). Mindfulness training modifies subsystems of attention. *Cognitive, Affective and Behavioral Neuroscience, 7*, 109–119.

Jung, C. G. (1968). Foreword to Suzuki's "Introduction to Zen Buddhism." In H. Read, M. Fordham, G. Adler, & W. McGuire (Eds.), *The collected works of C.G. Jung* (2nd ed.,

Vol. 11, pp. 538–557). Princeton, NJ: Princeton University Press. (Original work published 1939).

Jung, C. G. (1968). The psychology of Eastern meditation. In H. Read, M. Fordham, G. Adler, & W. McGuire (Eds.), *The collected works of C.G. Jung* (2nd ed., Vol. 11, pp. 558–575). Princeton, NJ: Princeton University Press. (Original work published 1943).

Kabat-Zinn, J. (1984). An outpatient program in behavioral medicine for chronic pain patients based on the practice of mindfulness meditation: Theoretical considerations and preliminary results. *Revision, 7,* 71–72.

Kabat-Zinn, J. (1990). *Full catastrophe living.* New York: Bantam Doubleday Dell.

Kabat-Zinn, J. (1994). *Wherever you go there you are: Mindfulness meditation for everyday life.* New York: Hyperion.

Kabat-Zinn, J. (2003). Mindfulness-based interventions in context: Past, present, and future. *Clinical Psychology: Science and Practice, 10,* 144–156.

Kabat-Zinn, J. (2005). Coming to our senses: Healing ourselves and the world through mindfulness. New York: Hyperion.

Kabat-Zinn, J., & Chapman-Waldrop, A. (1988). Compliance with an outpatient stress reduction program: rates and predictors of program completion. *Journal of Behavioral Medicine, 11,* 333–352.

Kabat-Zinn, J., Lipworth, L., & Burney, R. (1985). The clinical use of mindfulness meditation for the self-regulation of chronic pain. *Journal of Behavioral Medicine, 8,* 163–190.

Kenny, M. A., & Williams, J. M. G. (2007). Treatment-resistant depressed patients show a good response to mindfulness-based cognitive therapy. *Behaviour Research and Therapy, 45,* 617–625.

Kim, Y. W., Lee, S-H., Choi, T. K., Suh, S. Y., Kim, B., Kim, C. M.,... Yook, K. H. (2009). Effectiveness of mindfulness-based cognitive therapy as an adjuvant to pharmacotherapy in patients with panic disorder or generalized anxiety disorder. *Depression and Anxiety, 26,* 601–606.

Kishimoto, K. (1962). A preliminary theory about psychotherapy based on Oriental thought. *Acta Psychotherapeutica et Psychosomatica, 10,* 428–438.

Kitagawa, J. M. (Ed.). (2002). The religious traditions of Asia: Religion, history, and culture (2nd ed.). New York: Routledge.

Kondo, A. (1958). Zen in psychotherapy: The virtue of sitting. *Chicago Review, 12,* 57–64.

Kora, T., & Sato, K. (1957). Morita therapy: A psychotherapy in the way of Zen. *Psychologia, 1,* 219–225.

Koszycki, D., Benger, M., Shlik, J., & Bradwejn, J. (2007). Randomized trial of a meditation-based stress reduction program and cognitive behavior therapy in generalized social anxiety disorder. *Behaviour Research and Therapy, 45,* 2518–2526.

Kumar, S. M. (2002). An introduction to Buddhism for the cognitive-behavioral therapist. *Cognitive and Behavioral Practice, 9,* 40–43.

Kutz, I. (1985). Meditation as an adjunct to psychotherapy: An outcome study. *Psychotherapy and Psychosomatics, 43,* 209–218.

Kwekkeboom, K. L. (2001). Pain management strategies used by patients with breast and gynecologic cancer with postoperative pain. *Cancer Nursing, 24,* 378–386.

Lajoie, D. H., & Shapiro, S. I. (1992). Definitions of transpersonal psychology: The first twenty-three years. *Journal of Transpersonal Psychology, 24,* 79–98.

Lau, M. A., & McMain, S. F. (2005). Integrating mindfulness meditation with cognitive and behavioural therapies: The challenge of combining acceptance- and change-based strategies. *Canadian Journal of Psychiatry - Revue Canadienne de Psychiatrie, 50,* 863–869.

Lazar, S. W., Bush, G., Gollub, R. L., Fricchione, G. L., Khalsa, G., & Benson, H. (2000). Functional brain mapping of the relaxation response and meditation. *Neuroreport: An International Journal for the Rapid Communication of Research in Neuroscience, 11,* 1581–1585.

Lazar, S. W., Kerr, C. E., Wasserman, R. H., Gray, J. R., Greve, D. N., Treadway, M. T.,... Fischl, B. (2005). Meditation experience is associated with increased cortical thickness. *Neuroreport, 16,* 1893–1897.

Lee, J., Semple, R. J., Rosa, D., & Miller, L. (2008). Mindfulness-based cognitive therapy for children: Results of a pilot study. *Journal of Cognitive Psychotherapy, 22,* 15–28.

Lehrer, P. M., Woolfolk, R. L., Rooney, A. J., McCann, B., & Carrington, P. (1983). Progressive relaxation and meditation: A study of psychophysiological and therapeutic differences between two techniques. *Behaviour Research and Therapy, 21,* 651–662.

Linehan, M. M. (1993a). *Cognitive-behavioral treatment of borderline personality disorder.* New York: The Guilford Press.

Linehan, M. M. (1993b). *Skills training manual for treating borderline personality disorder.* New York: The Guilford Press.

Lynch, T. R., Chapman, A. L., Rosenthal, M. Z., Kuo, J. R., & Linehan, M. M. (2006). Mechanisms of change in dialectical behavior therapy: Theoretical and empirical observations. *Journal of Clinical Psychology, 62,* 459–480.

Ma, H. S., & Teasdale, J. D. (2004). Mindfulness-based cognitive therapy for depression: Replication and exploration of differential relapse prevention effects. *Journal of Consulting and Clinical Psychology, 72,* 31–40.

Maslow, A. (1969). The farther reaches of human nature. *Journal of Transpersonal Psychology, 1*(1), 1–9.

Massion, A. O., Teas, J., Hebert, J. R., Wertheimer, M. D., & Kabat-Zinn, J. (1995). Meditation, melatonin and breast/prostate cancer: hypothesis and preliminary data. *Medical Hypotheses, 44,* 39–46.

Maupin, E. W. (1962). Zen Buddhism: A psychological review. *Journal of Consulting Psychology, 26,* 362–378.

Miller, J. J., Fletcher, K., & Kabat-Zinn, J. (1995). Three-year follow-up and clinical implications of a mindfulness meditation-based stress reduction intervention in the treatment of anxiety disorders. *General Hospital Psychiatry, 17,* 192–200.

Morvay, Z. (1999). Horney, Zen, and the real self: Theoretical and historical connections. *American Journal of Psychoanalysis, 59,* 25–35.

Overholser, J. C. (1995). Cognitive-behavioral treatment of depression: III. Reducing cognitive biases. *Journal of Contemporary Psychotherapy, 25,* 311–329.

Pellarin, G., Talley, A., Lehnert, T., & Webb, B. (2003). Interview with H. H. The 17th Gyalwa Karmapa Trinlay Thaye Dorje. *Buddhism Today, 13.*

Ramel, W., Goldin, P. R., Carmona, P. E., & McQuaid, J. R. (2004). The effects of mindfulness meditation on cognitive processes and affect in patients with past depression. *Cognitive Therapy and Research, 28,* 433–455.

Rhyner, B. (1988). Morita psychotherapy and Zen Buddhism: A comparison of theoretical concepts. *Psychologia: An International Journal of Psychology in the Orient, 31,* 7–14.

Robins, C. J. (2002). Zen principles and mindfulness practice in dialectical behavior therapy. *Cognitive and Behavioral Practice, 9*, 50–57.

Ross, N. W. (1980). *Buddhism: A way of life and thought.* New York: Random House.

Roth, B., & Robbins, D. (2004). Mindfulness-based stress reduction and health-related quality of life: Findings from a bilingual inner-city patient population. *Psychosomatic Medicine, 66*, 113–123.

Rubia, K. (2009). The neurobiology of meditation and its clinical effectiveness in psychiatric disorders. *Biological Psychology, 82*, 1–11.

Sato, K. (1957). Psychotherapeutic implications of Zen. *Psychologia, 1*, 213–218.

Sato, K. (1968). Zen from a personological viewpoint. *Psychologia: An International Journal of Psychology in the Orient, 11*, 3–24.

Schmidt, M. B. (Ed.). (1999). *Dakini teachings: Padmasambhava's oral instructions to Lady Tsogyal. From the revelations of Nyang Ral Nyima Ozer, Sangye Lingpa and Dorje Lingpa. Translated from the Tibetan according to the teachings of Kyabje Tulku Urgyen Rinpoche by Erik Pema Kunsang (Erik Hein Schmidt).* Kathmandu, Nepal: Rangjung Yeshe Publications.

Schmidt, M. B., & Tweed, M. (Eds.). (2003). *A Tibetan Buddhist companion.* Boston: Shambhala.

Schore, A. N. (2003a). *Affect dysregulation and disorders of the self.* New York: W.W. Norton.

Schore, A. N. (2003b). *Affect regulation and the repair of the self.* New York: W.W. Norton.

Schultz, J. H., & Luthe, W. (1959). *Autogenic training: A psychophysiologic approach in psychotherapy.* New York: Grune & Stratton.

Scott, D. (2000). William James and Buddhism: American pragmatism and the orient. *Religion, 30*, 333–352

Seer, P., & Raeburn, J. M. (1980). Meditation training and essential hypertension: A methodological study. *Journal of Behavioral Medicine, 3*, 59–71.

Segal, Z. V., Williams, J. M. G., & Teasdale, J. D. (2002). *Mindfulness-based cognitive therapy for depression: A new approach to preventing relapse.* New York: The Guilford Press.

Semple, R. J. (1999). *Enhancing the quality of attention: A comparative assessment of concentrative meditation and progressive relaxation.* Unpublished Master's thesis, University of Auckland, New Zealand.

Semple, R. J., Lee, J., Rosa, D., & Miller, L. F. (2009). A randomized trial of mindfulness-based cognitive therapy for children: Promoting mindful attention to enhance social-emotional resiliency in children. *Journal of Child and Family Studies.*

sGam.Po.Pa. (1986). *The jewel ornament of liberation* (H. V. Guenther, Trans.). Boston: Shambhala.

Shapiro, S. L., Bootzin, R. R., Figueredo, A. J., Lopez, A. M., & Schwartz, G. E. (2003). The efficacy of mindfulness-based stress reduction in the treatment of sleep disturbance in women with breast cancer: An exploratory study. *Journal of Psychosomatic Research, 54*, 85–91.

Shapiro, S. L., Schwartz, G. E., & Bonner, G. (1998). Effects of mindfulness-based stress reduction on medical and premedical students. *Journal of Behavioral Medicine 21*, 581–599.

Sibinga, E. M. S., Stewart, M., Magyari, T., Welsh, C. K., Hutton, N., & Ellen, J. M. (2008). Mindfulness-based stress reduction for HIV-infected youth: A pilot study. *Explore: The Journal of Science and Healing, 4*, 36–37.

Siegel, D. J. (2007). *The mindful brain: Reflection and attunement in the cultivation of well-being.* New York: W. W. Norton.

Simpson, T. L., Kaysen, D., Bowen, S., MacPherson, L. M., Chawla, N., Blume, A.,…Larimer, M. (2007). PTSD symptoms, substance use, and Vipassana meditation among incarcerated individuals. *Journal of Traumatic Stress, 20*, 239–249.

Smith, A., Graham, L., & Senthinathan, S. (2007). Mindfulness-based cognitive therapy for recurring depression in older people: A qualitative study. *Aging and Mental Health, 11*, 346–357.

Speca, M., Carlson, L. E., Goodey, E., & Angen, M. (2000). A randomized, wait-list controlled clinical trial: The effect of a mindfulness meditation-based stress reduction program on mood and symptoms of stress in cancer outpatients. *Psychosomatic Medicine, 62*, 613–622.

Stunkard, A. (1951). Some interpersonal aspects of an Oriental religion. *Psychiatry: Journal for the Study of Interpersonal Processes, 14*, 419–431.

Sun, J. T. (1924). Psychology in primitive Buddhism. *Psychoanalytic Review, 11*, 39–47.

Sutherland, R. S. (1966). East, West, and psychotherapy. *Main Currents in Modern Thought, 23*, 10–13.

Suzuki, S. (1970). *Zen mind, beginner's mind.* New York: Weatherhill.

Tacon, A. M., McComb, J., Caldera, Y., & Randolph, P. (2003). Mindfulness meditation, anxiety reduction, and heart disease: A pilot study. *Family and Community Health, 26*, 25–33.

Tang, Y-Y., Ma, Y., Fan, Y., Feng, H., Wang, J., Feng, S.,…Fan, M. (2009). Central and autonomic nervous system interaction is altered by short-term meditation. *Proceedings of the National Academy of Sciences USA, 106*, 8865–8870.

Tang, Y-Y., Ma, Y., Wang, J., Fan, Y., Feng, S., Lu, Q., .. Posner, M. I. (2007). Short-term meditation training improves attention and self-regulation. *Proceedings of the National Academy of Sciences USA, 104*, 17152–17156.

Teasdale, J. D. (1999). Metacognition, mindfulness and the modification of mood disorders. *Clinical Psychology and Psychotherapy, 6*, 146–155.

Teasdale, J. D., Segal, Z. V., Williams, J. M. G., Ridgeway, V. A., Soulsby, J. M., & Lau, M. A. (2000). Prevention of relapse/recurrence in major depression by mindfulness-based cognitive therapy. *Journal of Consulting and Clinical Psychology, 68*, 615–623.

Thanissaro Bhikkhu. (1996). *The wings to awakening: An anthology from the Pali Canon* (G. DeGraff, Trans.). Barre, MA: Dhamma Dana Publications.

Thurman, R. A. F. (1995). *Essential Tibetan Buddhism.* Edison, NJ: Castle Books.

Walsh, R. N. (1993). Meditation research: The state of the art. In R. N. Walsh & F. Vaughan (Eds.), *Paths beyond ego: The transpersonal vision* (pp. 60–66). Los Angeles: Tarcher/Perigree.

Walsh, R. N. (1996). Meditation research: The state of the art. In B. W. Scotton & A. B. Chinen (Eds.), *Textbook of transpersonal psychiatry and psychology* (pp. 167–175). New York: Basic Books.

Watts, A. (1961). *Psychotherapy east and west.* New York: Random House.

Weinstein, M., & Smith, J. C. (1992). Isometric squeeze relaxation (progressive relaxation) vs. meditation: Absorption and focusing as predictors of state effects. *Perceptual and Motor Skills, 75,* 1263–1271.

Weiss, M., Nordlie, J. W., & Siegel, E. P. (2005). Mindfulness-based stress reduction as an adjunct to outpatient psychotherapy. *Psychotherapy and Psychosomatics, 74,* 108–112.

West, M. A. (1980). The psychosomatics of meditation. *Journal of Psychosomatic Research, 24,* 265–273.

Williams, J. M. G., Alatiq, Y., Crane, C., Barnhofer, T., Fennell, M. J. V., Duggan, D. S., Goodwin, G. M. (2008). Mindfulness-based cognitive therapy (MBCT) in bipolar disorder: Preliminary evaluation of immediate effects on between-episode functioning. *Journal of Affective Disorders, 107,* 275–279.

Witkiewitz, K., Marlatt, G. A., & Walker, D. (2005). Mindfulness-based relapse prevention for alcohol and substance use disorders. *Journal of Cognitive Psychotherapy, 19,* 211–228.

Woolfolk, R. L. (1975). Psychophysiological correlates of meditation. *Archives of General Psychiatry, 32,* 1326–1333.

World Health Organization. (2007). *International classification of diseases and related health problems, 10th revision.* Geneva, Switzerland: Author.

Eastern Traditions, Consciousness, and Spirituality

Kartikeya C. Patel

Abstract

This chapter discusses the constructs of consciousness and spirituality in the Eastern tradition of early Buddhism. The descriptive explanations of the following basic and yet complex questions are offered: What are the contents of consciousness? Are there content-less states of consciousness? What is spiritual inquiry? If states of consciousness are multileveled and multifaceted, how one can understand the process of transformation and attainment of these states? Although a comprehensive presentation of various Eastern traditions is not possible in a brief book chapter, it is hoped that a detailed look at early Buddhism will give the reader a taste of the issues that Eastern theories and practices attempt to address.

Key Words: awareness, spirituality, Eastern perspectives on consciousness, spiritual inquiry, enlightenment, nirvana

Introduction

Eastern traditions hold an important place in world spirituality and consciousness studies. There is a growing interest in the field of modern psychology to compare and integrate the teachings of Eastern wisdom traditions (Dimidjian, & Linehan, 2003; Miculas, 2007; Mijares, 2003; Nauriyal, Drummond, & Lal, 2006). In discussing Eastern traditions, however, one should first clarify the scope of inquiry and state what one intends to cover under the umbrella term "Eastern traditions." As Nakamura (1964) stated, there is no unambiguous way of referring to some traditions or ways of thinking as belonging to what may be conveniently referred to as the "East." The diversity of traditions originating in the Eastern regions of our planet precludes the possibility of offering generalized theories applicable to all traditions "Eastern." Hence, the scope of this book chapter is limited to one particular

tradition: early Buddhism. Early Buddhism, originating in India, has shaped and influenced other traditions of the East, including, but not limited to, those originating in China, Japan, Nepal, Myanmar, Sri Lanka, Thailand, and Indonesia (Forman, 1999; Motoyama, 2008; Nakamura, 1964; Rao, 2002). Although early Buddhism may not provide us with theories and concepts that are applicable to all Eastern traditions, it provides us with the foundational material from which many other Eastern traditions derive their conceptual framework and the practices that lead to their stated soteriological goals.

Definitions

We are unable clearly to circumscribe the concepts we use not because we don't know their real definition, but because there is no real "definition" to them. To suppose that there must be would be like supposing that whenever children play with a ball they play a game according to strict rules.

—Ludwig Wittgenstein

The problem of precise definition is not limited to the term "Eastern traditions," however. The other terms under consideration—"early Buddhism," "consciousness," "spirituality," and "spiritual inquiry"—also lack precise definitions and are highly contested terms. But if one were to forego the pursuit of a precise definition of a term or concept and agree with Wittgenstein (1953/1986) that we could make up the rules and alter them as we go along, then we can offer workable but imprecise definitions of the terms under consideration. Furthermore, we may be able to refine our understanding of the terms or concepts as we go along.

Early Buddhism

Early Buddhism is understood throughout this chapter to mean "the Buddhism of the five *Nikayas*." The *Nikayas*—the *Khuddaka Nikaya*, the *Majjhima Nikaya*, the *Samyutta Nikaya*, the *Digha Nikaya*, and the *Anguttara Nikaya*—composed in Pali, may be described as the collection of the Buddha's teachings. The discourses of the Buddha were orally preserved by the monks and later formalized and put in a canonical body of literature by the four Buddhist councils that convened over the course of centuries (c. 480 BCE–20 BCE). The five *Nikayas* form the *Sutta Pitaka* (the casket containing the *suttas*) of the *Pali* canon. The *Vinaya Pitaka* (the casket containing the rules of conduct) and the *Abhidhamma Pitaka* (the casket containing the "higher truths") are the other two caskets besides the *Sutta Pitaka* that form the *Pali* canon. The *Nikayas*, that is, the *Sutta Pitakas*, are thought to have been composed earlier than the other two *Pitakas* and contain much of the important information about the Buddha's teachings, the sociocultural situation of his time, and the Buddha's dialog with other contemporary teachers and laypeople.

Early Buddhism is distinguished from other Buddhist traditions such as *Theravada Buddhism*, "the school whose particular ideas are found mostly in the *Abdhidhamma* and *Pali* commentaries and in certain late *sutta* materials" (Harvey, 1994, p. 100), or *Mahayana Buddhism* whose particular ideas, concepts, and theories are found in such works as the *Mula-madhyamaka Karika* of Nagarjuna. These two traditions, and sixteen others for that matter, could be construed as selective interpretations and applications of the early Buddhist teachings contained in the five *Nikayas*. These later traditions depend on early Buddhism, but they do not form it.

Consciousness

Vimal (2009) recently identified 33 definitions of consciousness that have found footing in contemporary consciousness dialog. An impressive array of contemporary consciousness studies scholars (e.g., Seager, 2007; Velmans, 2009; Wilkes, 1984) have acknowledged that it is challenging to offer a single and universally applicable definition of "consciousness." For our purpose, "consciousness" could be defined as multifaceted and multileveled awareness and the ground of our experience that is more of a process rather than substance, is usually dependent on the senses but could be independent of it, is intentional in nature, could be with content or content-less, and has reflexive quality to it.

Spirituality and Spiritual Inquiry

Spirituality is often confused with religion. How these two terms should be distinguished from each other is a subject that has provoked an intense debate and generated as many questions as it has tried to answer. For our purpose, "spirituality" is defined as a study area and an experimental lab that attempts to understand the existential search of a human being to seek the meaning and purpose of human life and to accomplish that purpose of human life *free of* (a) the dictates of organized entities such as the religious orders and social hierarchies; (b) authority in form of the *ultimate* creator, scripture, or teacher; and (c) the rules and rituals that control human behavior and endeavor. Spirituality deals with the existential journey of a human being and the states of consciousness of a human being who is on such a journey. Spirituality is concerned with consciousness and awareness.

"Spiritual inquiry" is defined here as an existential search of a human being to seek and find the meaning and purpose of life. Such spiritual inquiry has no predetermined and charted path, no predetermined and given method, and its goal may or may not be defined. The *process* of spiritual inquiry is as important as the attainment of the end goal, if any. To engage in spiritual inquiry is to grow, to choose, and to define one's existential choices.

To better understand the aforementioned terms and concepts from an early Buddhist perspective, let us begin with a look at the life and teachings of the Buddha.

Siddhartha's Spiritual Inquiry

The Buddha (the enlightened one), known to his relatives as Siddhartha, to the masses as Sakyamuni, and to his contemporaries as Gotama, was a historical figure who lived and taught during a specific time of our human history. There are many traditional and modern accounts of the Buddha's life story, but the one that held personal meaning for me and that influenced my own interpretation of the Buddha's life is the one that appears in Paul Carus's *The Gospel of the Buddha* (Carus, 1894/1981).

The Buddha (the enlightened one) was born as Siddhartha, in a Hindu royal family to Suddhodhana and Mayavati in 563 BCE in northeast India. When the Buddha was born, it was predicted that he would either become the king of kings or the monk of monks. Suddhodhana, the father, was alarmed by this prediction. To prevent or minimize the possibility of Siddhartha becoming the monk of monks, Suddhodhana decided to ensnare Siddhartha in a life of pleasure. To this end, many seasonal palaces were built for Siddhartha and all entertainment was provided to keep him happy. The painful events of life were hidden from Siddhartha's sight and every attempt was made to prevent him from experiencing the cyclical nature of life. This stratagem of Suddhodhana was successful, and Siddhartha appeared to be happy and content with his lifestyle.

When Siddhartha was of the proper age, he was married to his cousin Yashodhara. Siddhartha fathered a son, Rahula, with Yashodhara. Because of Siddhartha's marriage and fatherhood, to Suddhodhana it appeared that the chances of his son becoming a monk had diminished to a great extent, and consequently he loosened his grip on Siddhartha's life and started to give more liberty to Siddhartha. One day, Siddhartha desired to visit the world beyond the confines of his seasonal palaces and on his outing, he encountered the painful events of human existence, namely, old age, disease, and death, caused by the cyclical nature of human life. He, however, also encountered a monk who appeared to be very peaceful amid all these changes and unperturbed by the events that bothered Siddhartha. These experiences profoundly impacted his perception of life and opened his mind to the larger questions concerning human life. Upon returning to his palace, Siddhartha became a contemplative and started to spend his time reflecting on the nature of human existence.

During one of such contemplative quests under his favorite tree, a divine figure (*samana*) came in his vision and told him that renunciation of life was the most suitable way to inquire about and discover the answers to the existential questions that concerned him (Carus, 1894/1981). The divine figure told Siddhartha that the life of the householder was painful and compared it with the life of a monk, which was peaceful. This prompted Siddhartha to think about renunciation, but he felt that renouncing the world at such an early age as his was against the religious and social injunctions of his time. However, the divine figure confided that all ages were appropriate for renunciation and his age should not prevent him from becoming a wandering monk. Siddhartha found assurance in the words of the divine figure and decided to renounce the world. In the *Ariyapariyesana Sutta* of the *Majjhima Nikaya*, the Buddha recalls his experience of renunciation of his house-holder life: "Then I, monks, after a time, being young, my hair coal-black, possessed of radiant youth, in the prime of my life—although my unwilling parents wept and wailed—having cut off my hair and beard, having put on yellow robes, went forth from home into homelessness" (Horner, 1954/1967, p. 207).

After renouncing his life of comfort, Siddhartha wandered around in various parts of northern India. He went to many different teachers and engaged in lively discussion with many spiritual leaders of his time. Siddhartha was an experimenter of truth. He wanted to evaluate a variety of possible means of spiritual development and maturity. Siddhartha desired to understand the path that leads one to the end goal as well as examine the end goal(s) of the movements of his time (Patel, 1998). Among the many spiritual teachers that he met, he was most enthusiastic and impressed by the teachings of Alara Kalama and Uddaka Ramaputta (Horner, 1954/1967). Both of these leaders belonged to the Upanishadic tradition and sincerely practiced what they preached. The Buddha refers to these teachers as the beings who know and see.

The Buddha refers to the teachings of these teachers and provides a general outline of their views. Alara Kalama believed in a state of *nothingness*. He propounded that this state can be achieved by following a spiritual discipline consisting of faith, energy, mindfulness, concentration, and intuitive insight. In other words, to attain *nothingness*, one would need to cultivate faith, have spiritual energy, be mindful of the psychophysical events and the contexts in which they occur, practice concentration, and develop intuitive insight. This spiritual discipline would lead one to the state where no psychophysical events happened or any visible and definable substance could be found. Furthermore, according to Alara Kalama, the knowledge of the *nothingness* would lead to self-realization for the individual of the sort that "As I am, so are you; as you are, so am I." In other words, the realization of *nothingness* would lead to the ultimate unity of all beings or the realization of one indivisible self without duality. The *Mundaka Upanishad* (Radhakrishnan & Moore, 1957/1989) explains this state of realization of *nothingness* with reference to the salt water. Just as the dissolved salt is in no particular part of the water but is in all of the water, the state of *nothingness* is the state of all pervasive reality.

The Buddha outlines the teachings of Uddaka Ramaputta in a similar fashion. The spiritual discipline recommended by Uddaka Ramaputta was the same as the one prescribed by Alara Kalama. But their goals differed. Whereas for Alara Kalama, the spiritual discipline led one to the state of *nothingness*, for Uddaka Ramaputta, it led the individual to the state of *neither perception nor nonperception*. This state was a state in which the working of perception, and the absence thereof, ceased. Siddhartha soon realized the truth about the states of *nothingness* and *neither perception nor nonperception*; however, upon realizing these truths, he felt that they did not lead to dispassion, awakening, or to *nibbana*. After evaluating the efficacy of the goals of *nothingness* and *neither perception nor nonperception* teachings as taught by Alara Kalama and Uddaka Ramaputta, Siddhartha felt that these could not be the ultimate goals of his path. The Buddha thought that the experience of the states of *nothingness* and *neither perception nor nonperception* failed to cultivate dispassion, tranquility, getting rid of the unwholesome states of consciousness, super knowledge, awakening, or *nibbana*. For him, dispassion, awakening, and *nibbana* were far more important goals. Therefore, he left these two spiritual teachers and embarked on the next phase of his spiritual journey.

After leaving Alara Kalama and Uddaka Ramaputta, the Buddha joined a group of ascetics who practiced extreme self-mortification as means to liberation. He almost died because of practicing extreme self-mortification. Siddhartha was revived by a kind young woman who gave him a bowl of rice pudding. The Buddha soon realized that the denial of the senses does not lead one to enlightenment. After leaving the practice of self-mortification, the Buddha traveled on his own path in an effort to obtain that state of dispassion, tranquility, super knowledge, and *nibbana*.

After a final resolve and complete concentration, the Buddha achieved enlightenment, a state in which he experienced the unborn, undecaying, boundless, undying *nibbana*. Knowledge and vision arose in him and he realized that he had attained *nibbana*. The Buddha, the enlightened one, understood that this state was deep, difficult to see, difficult to understand, tranquil, excellent, beyond the dialectic of language, and subtle. It was difficult to see and understand for those who delighted and rejoiced in sensual pleasure, and who had a strong attachment to the senses. But for those learned who calmed their senses, renounced all attachments, cultivated dispassion, and destroyed craving, this reality was not difficult to see (Horner, 1954/1967, p. 212).

Soon after his enlightenment, the Buddha felt that it was time for him to pass on because even if he were to transmit his message of *nibbana* to people, they would not be able to understand his message. It would only bring useless fatigue and weariness. Lord Brahma (a divine figure in Hindu spirituality), however, persuaded the Buddha to teach about the *dhamma*. After consenting to Lord Brahma's request, the Buddha traveled throughout northeastern India and taught the spiritual means that led him to *nibbana* (Horner, 1954/1967, p. 212).

The Buddha's Spiritual Method

Before we offer our summary of the Buddha's spiritual method, it needs to be pointed out that the Buddha's spiritual method is a postexperiential construction of his spiritual inquiry that led him to enlightenment. The spiritual method evolved as the Buddha engaged in the process of spiritual inquiry and as he made existential choices on the path. The path got carved out, in bits and pieces, from Siddhartha's evolving experience. To assume that the Buddha knew his path prior to embarking on his journey would be to suppose that the Buddha had a priori knowledge of all his existential choices and when he was to make those choices. To borrow Hilary Putnam's words, for Siddhartha "to have made all possible existential choices is precisely to have stopped growing, to have become utterly rigid as human being" (Putnam, 1989, pp. 22–23). Although the Buddha taught for nearly 50 years after his enlightenment, one of his last messages was "Be your own light."

Four Noble Truths

The Buddha taught that an individual who is on a spiritual path first needs to recognize and comprehend the truth(s) about suffering. He or she must know that there is suffering (*dukkha*) in the world. Second, he or she must realize that there is a cause for the arising of the suffering (*dukkhasamudaya*).

Third, this suffering can be prevented (*dukkhanirodha*). Fourth, there is a way that leads to the prevention of this suffering. The Buddha called the recognition and acceptance of suffering as the four noble truths (*ariya-sacca*). The first noble truth concerns what is or can be characterized as suffering. In his first discourse, *Dhammacakkappavattana Sutta*, the Buddha spelled out the notion of suffering as follows:

> Birth is suffering; old age is suffering; sickness is suffering; death is suffering. Sorrow, lamentation, and dejection are suffering. To receive what one does not like (i.e., what is not pleasant), and to not receive what one likes (i.e., what is pleasant) is suffering. Being in contact with what is unpleasant and to be separated from what one intensely likes is suffering. In short, clinging to the five aggregates of the personality—body, feeling, perception, disposition, and consciousness—is suffering. (Rhys Davids & Woodward, 1917–1930, p. 421)

According to the Buddha, the human suffering arises because of the three main factors: (a) the cyclical existence of life; (b) clinging to the five aggregates of which the human personality is made of and thinking of these aggregates as oneself; and (c) having likes and dislikes about the world. Furthermore, the Buddha explained theses causes of suffering (as well as the causes of liberation as explained in the next section) as a causal link that his followers termed as codependent arising (*paticcasamuppada*). This codependent arising consists of the following 12 factors: (1) ignorance, (2) dispositions, (3) consciousness, (4) psychophysical personality, (5) six senses, (6) contact, (7) feeling, (8) craving, (9) grasping, (10) becoming, (11) birth, and (12) old age, death.

The second truth about suffering concerns the fact that the aforementioned factors of causation are the causes of suffering. For instance, in the conceptual realm, attachment to views, and the grasping of systems, doctrines, concepts, and theories of any kind can lead to disputes, verbal warfare of the sort "my doctrine or view alone is true, everything else is false," and consequently cause suffering. In the psychological realm, attachment to desires, feelings, craving, and clinging to some dearly believed doctrines, rules, and rituals lead to suffering. In the physical realm, attachment to the bodily sensations, feelings, and so on lead to suffering. The Buddha taught that there is a way that leads one to the cessation of the cyclical existence and hence to the cessation of suffering.

Eightfold Path

He characterized this way as an eightfold path. The eight steps of this path are as follows: (1) balanced view infused with equanimity (*samma ditthi*); (2) balanced resolution infused with equanimity (*samma sankappa*); (3) balanced speech infused with equanimity (*samma vaca*); (4) balanced action infused with equanimity (*samma kamma*); (5) balanced livelihood infused with equanimity (*samma jiva*); (6) balanced effort infused with equanimity (*samma vayama*); (7) balanced mindfulness infused with equanimity (*samma sati*); and (8) balanced concentration infused with equanimity (*samma samadhi*). It is important to note that most scholars of Buddhism interpret the word *samma* as "right," but if that is the case the Buddha would have used the word "*sacca*" (right or true) to convey the correct and clear meaning. The word "*samma*" has the same meaning as the Sanskrit word "*samyak*," which means a balanced approach infused with equanimity. Furthermore, the Buddha was against both the right and wrong views and had considered them to be equally problematic. From his own spiritual journey, the Buddha had learned that one could get attached both to the right views and wrong views, codes of conduct, rites, and rituals. In the *Sutta Nipata* (Saddhatissa, 1994), it is stated that the monks who had happily renounced the views and theories that bound them to the life of householder now found themselves attached to the "highest" views, purity, and rules:

> When a man in the world, abiding in views, esteems something especially (as) "the highest," then he says that all others are inferior; in this way he is not beyond disputes.
> Those who hold rules to be the highest thing, thinking purity comes from (practice of) self-restraint, take up rites and observe them (dutifully), (thinking) "if we learn this, then we'll have purity." When someone is deficient in rule and ritual, having failed to perform some act, he trembles, he yearns and longs for purity here, like one who has left home   (but) lost the caravan. (p. 105)

To avoid the pitfalls of attachment and craving, one needs to transcend the material realm and the conceptual realm.

States of Consciousness

According to the texts (Horner, 1954/1967, pp. 106–107), the process of transcendence of the material and conceptual realm involves experiencing the higher states of consciousness. The higher states of consciousness help one break the causal chain that binds one to suffering. Just as there is a causal chain that binds one to suffering, the *Samyutta Nikaya* (Rhys Davids & Woodward, 1982, p. 25–27) states that there is a causal chain that leads one to liberation from suffering. Figure 22.1 depicts both the causal chain that leads one to suffering and also the causal chain that leads one to liberation. Both these chains are linked and one could say that this in fact is one chain with two parts.

The components of the causal chain that leads one to liberation (e.g., concentration, joy, rapture, happiness, serenity) are the components that constitute the higher states of consciousness in early Buddhism. In what follows, four different states of consciousness—with content and without content—are explored: (1) states of consciousness with content (*Rupa jhanas*); (2) states of contentless consciousness (*Arupa jhanas*); (3) enlightenment with content (*Saupadisesha Nibbana*); and (4) enlightenment without content (*Anupadisesha Nibbana*). To this end, let us begin with a discussion of the *jhanas*.

The *jhanas* may be seen as successive states of consciousness in which "unification" or "concentration" (*ekaggata*) is attained by gradually giving up the lower states of consciousness for the higher states. There are numerous passages in the *Nikayas* that describe the *jhanas* in detail. These passages offer some description of the various *jhanas* and the conditions preceding and succeeding each *jhana*. Let us begin by considering some key descriptions. In the *Sallekha Sutta*, we read:

> The situation occurs, Cunda, when a monk here, aloof from pleasures of the senses, aloof from unskilled states of mind, may enter on and abide in the first *jhana* which is accompanied by initial thought and discursive thought, is born of aloofness, and is rapturous and joyful.
>
> When some monk here, by allaying initial thought and discursive thought, with the mind subjectively tranquillized and fixed on one point, may enter on and abide in the second *jhana* which is devoid of initial and discursive thought, is born of concentration, and is rapturous and joyful.

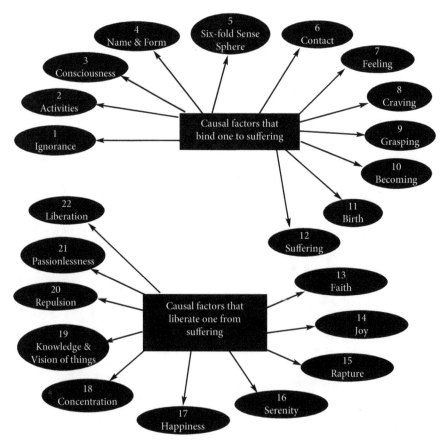

Figure 22.1. The causal factors of suffering and liberation in early Buddhism. Adapted from the *Samyutta Nikaya* (Rhys Davids & Woodward, 1982, pp. 25–26).

When some monk here, by the fading out of rapture, may abide with equanimity, attentive, and clearly conscious, and may experience in his person that joy of which the *ariyans* say: "Joyful lives he who has equanimity and is mindful," and may enter on and abide in the third *jhana*.

When some monk here, by getting rid of joy, by getting rid of anguish, by the going down of his former pleasures and sorrows, may enter on and abide in the fourth *jhana* which has neither anguish nor joy, and that is entirely purified by equanimity and mindfulness.

When some monk here, by wholly transcending perceptions of material shapes, by the going down of perceptions due to sensory impressions, by not reflecting on the perceptions of multiformity, aware that "Ether is unending," may enter on and abide in the plane of infinite ether.

When some monk here, by wholly transcending the plane of infinite ether, aware that "Consciousness is unending," may enter on and abide in the plane of infinite consciousness.

When some monk here, by wholly transcending the plane of infinite consciousness, aware that "There is no-thing," may enter on and abide in the plane of no-thing. When some monk here, by wholly transcending the plane of no-thing, may enter on and abide in the plane of neither-perception-nor-non-perception. (*Horner*, 1954/1967, pp. 52–53.

Let us look at another *sutta* from the *Nikayas* to get a better sense of the *jhanas*. In the *Mahamoggallana Sutta*, Maha Moggallana, a direct disciple of the Buddha recounts his *jhanic* experience as follows:

Now what is the first *jhana*? Herein when a brother, aloof from sensuality, aloof from unwholesome states, attains the first *jhana* which is accompanied by thought directed and sustained, which is born of solitude, full of zest and ease, and abides therein, this is called "the first *jhana*." Now, friends, aloof from sensuality, aloof from evil states, I entered on the first *jhana* and abode therein. But, friends, when I had remained in this condition, perception and work of mind connected with sensuality still continued. Thereupon, friends, the Exalted One [the Buddha] by accomplishment [*iddhi*] came to me and said: Moggallana, Moggallana, do not indulge in the first *jhana*...make steadfast thy mind in the first *jhana*. In the first *jhana* make the mind one-pointed. In the first *jhana* compose the mind. So after that, I entered upon...and abode in the first *jhana*.

Now what is the second *jhana*? Herein when a brother, by the absence of thought directed and sustained (*avitakka*), attains the inward calm, that one-pointedness of will, apart from thought directed and sustained, born of concentration, zestful and full of ease, which is the second *jhana*, and abides in the second *jhana*, and abides therein, this is called "the second *jhana*."

Now what is the third *jhana*? Herein a brother, by fading out of zest, abides balanced and remains mindful and composed, and experiences with the body that ease of which the *Ariyans* aver: "The balanced, thoughtful man dwells happily." Thus he enters on and abides in the third *jhana*. This is called "the third *jhana*."

Now what is the fourth *jhana*? Herein a brother, rejecting pleasure, rejecting pain, by the coming to an end of the joy and sorrow which he had before, enters on and abides in the fourth *jhana*, which is freed from pleasure, freed from pain, but is a state of perfect purity of balance and equanimity. This is called "the fourth *jhana*."

Now what is the realm of infinite space? Herein a brother, passing utterly beyond the perception of objects, by the coming to an end of the perception of resistance, by not attending to perception of diversity, with the idea of "infinite is space," enters on and abides in the realm of infinite space. This is called "the realm of infinite space."

Now what is that realm of infinite consciousness? Herein a brother, passing utterly beyond the realm of infinite space, with the idea: "Endless is consciousness," enters on and abides in the realm of infinite consciousness. This is called "the realm of infinite consciousness."

Now what is that realm of nothingness? Herein a brother, passing utterly beyond the realm of infinite consciousness, with the idea of "there is nothing at all," enters on and abides in the realm of nothingness. This is called "the realm of nothingness."

Now what is that realm of neither-perception-nor-non-perception? Herein a brother, passing utterly beyond the realm of nothingness, enters on the realm where he neither perceives nor perceives not. This is called "the realm of neither-perception-nor-non-perception."

Now what is that unconditioned consciousness [*animitta ceto-samadhi*]? Herein a brother, paying no attention to any or all distinguishing marks, enters on and abides in that rapture...which is without conditions. This is called "the unconditioned." (*Woodward*, 1927/1980, pp. 179–185)

These two *suttas* give us a good understanding of the progression of consciousness and the distinguishing factors of each *jhana*. In Table 22.1, each *jhanic* state of consciousness is depicted, where the factors designated as absent have made the experience of the state of consciousness of that *jhana* possible. The present factors are the ones that are present in this state of consciousness, but they will need to be transcended if the individual wanted to move forward. The *Sallekha Sutta* is designated as

Table 22.1 Absent and Present Phenomena in the Higher States of Consciousness in the *Sallekha Sutta* of the *Majjhima Nikaya* (S1) and the *Mahamoggallana Sutta* of the *Samyutta Nikaya* (S2)

Jhanas	S1	S2	Present Factors	Absent Factors	Causing Factors
Jhana 1	X	X	Discursive thought	Sense desires	Aloofness from desires
	X	X	Discursive reasoning	Unwholesome states	Giving up of sense desires
	X	X	Zest		and other unskilled states
		X			One-pointed concentration
Jhana 2	X	X	Rapture, joy	Discursive thought	One-pointed concentration
	X	X		Discursive reasoning	Giving up of discursive
					reasoning and thought
	X	X			Tranquilization of the senses
Jhana 3	X	X	Mindfulness, joy	Rapture	Concentration of mind
	X	X	Indifference		
Jhana 4	X	X	Indifference	Joy, anguish,	Rejection of pleasure and
	X	X	Mindfulness	pleasure, sorrow	pain
		X			One-pointed concentration
Jhana 5	X	X	Endless space	Perception of	End of perception of
	X	X		multiplicity	resistance; Non attention to
					perception of multiplicity
		X			One-pointed concentration
Jhana 6	X	X	Endless consciousness	Endless space	Transcendence of space
		X			One-pointed concentration
Jhana 7	X	X	Nothingness	Endless	Transcendence of infinite
				consciousness	consciousness
		X			One-pointed concentration
Jhana 8	X	X	Neither perception	Nothingness	Transcendence of
			nor nonperception		nothingness
		X			One-pointed concentration
Animitta		X	Unconditioned	Consciousness with	Nonattention to
Ceto			Consciousness	duality	distinguishing marks
Samadhi		X			One-pointed concentration

S1, and the *Mahamoggallana Sutta* is designated as *S2*. The presence of present factors, absent factors, and causing factors in each *jhanic* state in each *sutta* is marked by an "X."

These two *suttas* give us enough information about the *jhanic* states, except that neither of the *suttas* directly mentions the state of cessation of perception and feeling (*sanna-vedayita-nirodha*) that is mentioned in the *Madhupindika Sutta* (Horner, 1954/1967) as that state of consciousness which precedes the state of unconditioned consciousness. Besides these two *suttas*, there are numerous other *suttas* in the *Nikayas* that discuss these *jhanic* states of consciousness (Horner 1954/1967, pp. 27–29, 155–156, 259–263). We will take their aid in illuminating our discussion as the need arises.

States of Consciousness With Content (Rupa Jhanas)

Simply stated, the first *jhana* is the beginning of the gradual removal and transcendence of the ordinary consciousness associated with the world of senses and sense objects. The main characteristics of this state of consciousness are the separation (*vivicceva*) of sense desires (*kamehi*) and unwholesome mental states (*akusalehi dhammehi*) and the attainment of liking (*piti*) and happiness (*sukha*) born of such separation. The activities of wholesome discursive thought and reasoning are said to continue in this state of consciousness since the state is described as "with discursive reasoning and thought (*savitakkam savicharam*)."

In the second *jhana*, the one-pointedness of mind, inner tranquility along with liking, and pleasure are present, but the factors of discursive reasoning and thought along with other mental defilements are absent. The inner tranquility (*ajjhattam sampasadanam*) is said to arise because of the giving up or transcending of discursive reasoning and thought (*vitakkavicaranam vupasama*). Also, happiness is attained after giving up these factors. Whereas in the first *jhana*, the liking was born of discrimination (*viveka-ja*) based on discursive reasoning and thought, in this *jhana* the liking is said to arise because of concentration (*samadhi-ja*). The one-pointedness is said to be without discursive reasoning and thought (*ekodibhavam avitakkam avicaram*).

In the third *jhana*, indifference (*upekkha*), awareness, and knowledge based on equanimity (*satisampajanna*) are present. This state of consciousness is attained by transcending the liking associated with the first and second *jhanic* states as

well as by developing one-pointed concentration. Furthermore, whereas in the first *jhana*, happiness and liking were associated with discrimination, and in the second *jhana* with concentration, in this third *jhana* it is associated with the body. What one experiences in this state is the bodily sensation without its mental associations. Here the activities of the mind and speech are presumably subsiding while those of the body are continuing.

The fourth *jhana* is concerned with relinquishing the joy (*somanassa*) and sorrow (*domanassa*), pain (*dukkha*), and pleasure (*sukha*). This relinquishment leads one to purity of mindfulness (*sati*) and indifference (*upekkha*). What is meant here is that the state of indifference is the result of one's renunciation of the experience of pleasure and pain, and sorrow and joy.

From the earlier description, it is evident that common to all four *jhanas* is the initial presence of psychophysical elements associated with thinking, feeling, and connation, and the gradual transcendence of these states to be replaced by a pure, refined, concentrated state of consciousness. Thus, wholesome or unwholesome thinking; pleasant, neutral, or unpleasant feelings; and actions based on wholesome and unwholesome desires gradually give way to one-pointed state of consciousness accompanied by knowledge based on equanimity and indifference. In essence, what one experiences in these states of consciousness is the gradual elimination or absence of rationality-based actions and events (*avitakkam avicaram*) and the incremental emergence of wisdom based on successive and more refined states of consciousness. Also, the one-pointedness of mind is fundamental to all four states.

Another point that needs to be observed is that whereas the typical experience associated with unwholesome mental states, discursive reasoning, and discursive thought was that of pain and suffering, the typical experience related to these states of consciousness is that of happiness and joy: "He drenches, steeps, saturates, and suffuses his body with this rapture and happiness born of seclusion, so that there is no part of his entire body which is not suffused by this rapture and happiness" (Bhikkhu Bodhi, 1989, pp. 41–42).

States of Content-less Consciousness (Arupa Jhanas)

The *arupa jhanas* can be characterized as gradually deepening states of consciousness in which the ordinary experiences of the world, as defined and understood by the sixfold senses, and the sense spheres of the senses along with the objects and our notions of space and time, are all displaced by a refined, unitive, unsupported, and unconditioned (*animitta*) consciousness. Crucial to the content-less *jhanas* are the absence of discursive reasoning and thought, and the cessation of the activities of mind, speech, and feeling. There is also a joyful and gradual immersion into reality that is void (*sunno*) in the sense that only awareness per se is present without the sense-objects or the senses.

The fifth *jhana* adds to the process of transcendence of the *rupa jhanas*, the realm of perception with regard to the material perceptions. It divides perceptions into material perceptions (*rupa-sanna*), impact perceptions (*patigha-sanna*), and the variety perceptions or perceptions related to multiforms (*nanatta-sanna*).

The material perceptions can be characterized as those perceptions in which the object is perceived as having specific physical characteristics such as color, shape, the material it is made of, and so on. The impact perceptions can be characterized as those perceptions in which the impact of materiality on the senses when the object is cognized as having such and such color, shape, form, and so on is the focus of one's awareness of the perceptions. The variety perceptions are perceptions concerned with all diverse sense objects and the sense spheres.

The cessation of these three aforementioned perceptions is the transcendence of the perceptual realm. Once the perceptual realm is transcended, one enters into and moves about in the realm of endless space—space that is not bound by one's perception of space with form (*rupa*). In other words, in this realm, all limitations imposed by the concept of "space" are given up. Secondly, the perception of space does not impact one's senses with the idea that the space is limited or bound. Thirdly, the variety perceptions concerned with space are given up, paving the way for the realization that space is not bound, or to put it positively, the space is without end or infinite (*ananto akaso*).

In the sixth *jhana*, the realm of endless consciousness (*vinnanacayatana*), is attained by transcending the realm of "space." According to the *Potthapada Sutta*, the consciousness of space, that there is space, is transcended in this realm (Max Muller, 1899/1977, p. 250). This would seem to suggest that with the transcendence of the consciousness of space, one's consciousness regarding materiality is completely transcended.

The seventh *jhana* is the realm of nothingness (*akincannayatana*) that the meditation practitioner attains because of the transcendence of the realm of consciousness. It could be taken to mean that consciousness without the object is not about something, or in other words, it is about nothing. The realm of nothingness indicates that the consciousness is without object or the conception of or the image of an object. Such a state of consciousness is characterized as content-less (*sunna*).

The eighth *jhana* is called the realm of neither perception nor nonperception (*n'eva sanna nasannayatana*). It is rather perplexing to determine what is meant by the phrase "neither perception nor nonperception." The three types of perceptions are supposed to have been transcended in the fifth realm, so it seems rather odd to realize in this eight *jhana* that perceptions in their entirety were not transcended. Maybe what is suggested here is that only the material perceptions were transcended in the earlier realm, but the perception regarding the mental contents, however empty, still continued. In other words, the awareness regarding content-less perception may have continued. Such awareness of content-less perception is given up here.

The next two states of consciousness, the cessation or prevention of perception and feeling, and the state of unconditioned consciousness occupy an important place in early Buddhism. The state of neither perception nor nonperception is reported by the complete prevention or cessation of perception and feeling (*sannavedayitanirodha*), or simply, the accomplishment of prevention (*nirodhasamapatti*) (Horner, 1954/1967, p. 261). The word *nirodha* is often translated as cessation or stopping, but its literal meaning conveys the sense of prevention, that is, temporary cessation rather than final cessation. The sense of prevention implies that there is a temporary cessation of the activities, but that the "prevented" activities could be renewed, if one so wanted. Thus, the term *nirodha* can be used in two senses: (a) temporary cessation and (b) complete cessation. We will interpret and employ the term in either of these two senses given the context in which it occurs. The state of cessation or prevention of perception and feeling lacks perception and feeling. From this it becomes clear that the state of neither perception nor nonperception, which we discussed earlier, can signify the continuation of perception of "empty" mental events. Such continuation is prevented in the state of cessation of perception and feeling.

The state of unconditioned consciousness (*animittacetosamadhi*) is a state in which the support of consciousness, meaning the senses and the sense objects, is absent. The unconditioned consciousness is literally the consciousness without any marks (Woodward, 1927/1980, pp. 184–185). The state of unconditioned consciousness is regarded the same as the "accomplishment of cessation." In both these states, consciousness regarding the material and mental spheres is totally stopped. The importance of this "unsupported consciousness" is expressed in the *Udana*: "For the supported there is instability, for the unsupported there is no instability; when there is no instability there is serenity; when there is serenity there is no subservience; when there is no subservience there is no coming-and-going; when there is no coming-and-going there is no decease-and-uprising; when there is no decease-and-uprising there is neither 'here' nor 'beyond' nor 'in between the two.' Just this is the end of suffering" (Ireland, 1990, p. 110).

Lastly, the *arupa jhanas*, like the *rupa jhanas*, are accompanied by one-pointed concentration and happiness (*sukha*). The difference between the one-pointed concentration in the *arupa jhanas* as opposed to that in the *rupa jhanas* is that, concentration in these states either has a highly refined object or no object at all. The one-pointed concentration in these realms does not have any object and is not disturbed by the constant onslaught of sense objects and sense impressions.

This one-pointed concentration is explained by the Buddha in the *Mahaparinibbana Sutta* via a story about his own experience:

Once, Pukkusa, when I was staying at Atuma, at the threshing-floor, the rain-god streamed and splashed, lightening flashed and thunder crashed, and two farmers, brothers, and four oxen were killed. And a lot of people went out of Atuma to where the two brothers and the four oxen were killed. And, Pukkusa, I had at that time gone out of the door of the threshing-floor and was walking up and down outside. And a man from the crowd came to me, saluted me and stood to one side. And I said to him: Friend, why are all these people gathered here? (He replied:) Lord, there has been a great storm and two farmers, brothers, and four oxen have been killed. But, you, Lord, where have you been? (I said:) I have been right here, friend. (The inquirer:) But what did you see, Lord? (I said:) I saw nothing, friend. (The inquirer:) Or what did you hear, Lord. (I said:) I heard nothing, friend. (The inquirer:) Were you sleeping, Lord. I was not sleeping, friend. (The inquirer:) Then, Lord, were you conscious? Yes, friend. (He asked:) So, Lord, being conscious and awake you neither saw nor heard the great rainfall

and floods and the thunder and lightening? (I said:) That is so, friend.
(*Walshe,* 1987, p. 259)

The one-pointed concentration described here is a concentration without any support since it does not have any object as such. This concentration is the consciousness of the consciousness per se ("*atthi ceto*" *vati*). One of the passages explains this endless consciousness in the following way:

Consciousness which is non-manifestive, endless, lustrous on all sides,
    Here it is that earth and water, fire and wind, no footing find.
    Here again are long and short, subtle and gross, pleasant and unpleasant Name and form, all cut off without exceptions.

(*Rhys Davids & Rhys Davids,* 1899–1921)

The *arupa jhanas* are also accompanied by happiness. The happiness experienced in the *rupa jhanas* was described as the happiness pertaining to the feeling, thinking, and conation aspects. On the other hand, the happiness experienced during the highest stage of the *arupa jhanas* is not happiness that arises from the sense sphere or sense objects; rather, it is happiness per se that does not depend on the feeling, thinking, or conation. The Buddha explains this happiness:

Here, Ananda, a monk, by wholly transcending the plane of neither-perception-nor-non-perception, enters and abides in the stopping of perceiving and feeling. This, Ananda, is the other happiness that is more excellent and exquisite than that happiness. But the situation occurs, Ananda, when wanderers belonging to other sects may speak thus: "The recluse Gotama speaks of the stopping of perceiving and feeling, and lays down that this belongs to happiness. Now what is this, now how is this?" Ananda, wanderers belonging to other sects who speak thus should be spoken to thus: "Your reverences, the Lord does not lay down that it is only pleasant feeling that belongs to happiness; for, your, reverences, the Tathagata lays down that whenever, wherever, whatever happiness is found that belongs to happiness."
(*Horner,* 1957/1975, p. 69)

Earlier in the *sutta*, it is claimed that each *arupa jhana* is accompanied by happiness associated with the experience of consciousness related to that realm. For example, in the realm of infinite consciousness, one experiences the happiness related to the moving about (*viharati*) in the realm of consciousness.

Lastly, the cessation of perception and feeling and the attainment of the unconditioned consciousness are shown as either directly culminating in wisdom (*panna*) or in liberation (*nibbana*), or they are thought of themselves as liberation (*nibbana*). Thus, it is said, "...attaining the cessation of perception and feeling, he dwells therein, and having seen by wisdom, the cankers (*asavas*) are completely destroyed. Thus far, sir, without qualification has *nibbana* in this visible world been spoken by the Lord" (Woodward & Hare, 1932–1936, p. 454). The meditator (*jhayin*) who attains the state of cessation of perception and feeling is variously described as the *arahant*, the *Tathagata*, or the Buddha.

The *suttas* describe this higher reality as infinite space, infinite consciousness, a place where there is a complete cessation of perception and feeling. This state of cessation of perception and feeling, however, is not a final state. This state is succeeded by the state of consciousness in which one experiences the normal reality with the knowledge that one is liberated. This state of consciousness is called the cessation of the cyclical existence with residue (*saupadisesa nibbana*). The Buddha taught that in the final state of consciousness, one achieves the cessation of the cyclical existence without residue (*anupadisesa nibbana*).

Enlightenment With Residue (Saupadisesha Nibbana)

The *nibbana* in which the purified senses continue to operate is called the enlightenment with remainder (*saupadisesha nibbana*). Such liberation is described in the *Itivuttaka* (38):

Here, monks, a monk is meritorious, one who has destroyed the cankers, who has lived the life, done what was to be done, laid down the burden, won the goal, worn out the fetter of becoming, one released by perfect knowledge. In him the five sense faculties still remain, through which, as they have not yet departed, he experiences sensations both pleasant and unpleasant, experiences pleasures and painfulness. In him the end of lust, hatred, and delusion, monks, is called the condition of *nibbana* with the basis still remaining.
(*Windisch,* 1889, p. 38)

The hallmark of the enlightenment with remainder is that the enlightened individual continues to normally function in this world. He or she, for instance, returns to the world of senses and experiences pleasure and pain as a normal person does. The Buddha clarifies the enlightenment with

remainder in response to a query by Ananda, his direct disciple:

Ananda: May it be said, Venerable Sir, that a monk's achievement of concentration may be of such a sort that, though he does not attend to the eye or visible shapes, ... to the body or touchables, ... to solidity, ... to the sphere of infinite space, ... infinite consciousness; though, whatever is seen, heard, sensed, discerned, attained, sought after, through round by mind—to all that he does not attend, and yet he *does* attend?

The Buddha answers: Herein, Ananda, a monk attends thus—This is the real, this is the excellent; ... the renunciation of all substrate, the destruction of craving, detachment, stopping, *nibbana*. (*Woodward & Hare,* 1932–1936, pp. 321–323)

From this passage it appears that even though the sense sphere continues to be operative, due to detachment born of enlightenment, one is able to experience the sense sphere, such as pleasure and pain. Yet the sense sphere, the substrate, is said to be given up because of the destruction of craving and detachment. In another *sutta* (Woodward, 1927/1980, pp. 202–203), a monk, Kamabhu, explains the attainment of cessation of perception and feeling by claiming that the activities of speech, discursive reasoning, and thought are abandoned first, followed by those of mind and body, such as breathing, perception, and feeling. Next, he tells that the attainment of cessation of perception and feeling is not accomplished by thinking, such as: I shall attain, I am attaining the ceasing of perception and feeling; rather, the state is attained by practice of mind that leads him to the state of being such (*tathattaya upaneti*). Then, on being asked, "How does one who has attained cessation of perception and feeling differ from a dead person?" Kamabhu replies that the person who has attained cessation of perception and feeling retains vitality (*pana*) and heat (*tejo*) and his faculties become clarified. A person who has attained the cessation of perception and feeling, first knows the world as void (*sunnato*), signless (*animitto*), and aimless (*appanihito*), and secondly, as a result of the attainment of cessation and perception, he develops detachment.

Second, the presence of sense faculties does not entail the continuation of their activity. Indeed, this is precisely what is emphasized in the *sutta*:

Now, your reverence, are these properties of vitality states that are to be felt, or are the properties of vitality one thing, states are to be felt another?

Your reverence, these properties of vitality are not themselves states to be felt. If, your reverence, these properties of vitality were themselves states to be felt, no emergence could be shown for a monk who has had won to the stopping of perception and feeling. But because, your reverence, the properties of vitality are one thing and states to be felt another, therefore the emergence of a monk who has won to the stopping of perception and feeling can be shown. (*Woodward*, 1927/1980, pp. 202–203)

Thus, one can say that in enlightenment with remainder, the enlightened individual gradually recedes back to the world of senses and experiences the normal world but now his senses are more purified and he experiences the sense sphere with detachment.

Enlightenment Without Residue (*Anupadisesha Nibbana*)

The total cessation of perception and feeling may be characterized as that content-less state of consciousness in which liberation is achieved without remainder. The following is the description of an Arahat who has achieved liberation without remainder: "Herein, monks, a monk is an Arahat with cankers destroyed, who has lived the life, laid down the burden, attained his own goal, the fetter becoming utterly destroyed, released by perfect gnosis" (Harvey, 1995, p. 180). In the *Aggivacchagotta Sutta*, we read,

Even so, Vaccha, that material shape by which one recognizing the *Tathagata* might recognize him—that material shape,…feeling,…perception,…habitual tendencies,…consciousness,…has been got rid of by the *Tathagata*, cut off at the root, made like a palm-tree stump that can come to no further existence and is not liable to arise again in the future. Freed from denotation by material shape, perception,…feeling,…habitual tendencies,…consciousness,…is the *Tathagata*, Vaccha, he is deep, immeasurable, unfathomable as is the great ocean. (*Horner*, 1954/1967, p. 166)

One can interpret this passage to mean that the enlightenment without remainder is the enlightenment in which the individual has given up the senses, sense sphere, and has passed on. It would seem that the total cessation of the senses has been indicated and likened to the analogy of a cut palm tree. Just as a palm tree whose roots have been cut is said to have ceased to exist, likewise, in the enlightenment without remainder, all activities have ceased.

This enlightenment without remainder could be explained as the final enlightenment in which the material body, along with its psychological accompaniments (*nama-rupa*), is given up.

This final state of consciousness, the enlightenment without remainder, is described as follows:

Monks, there is a not-born, not-become, not-made, not-dispositionally conditioned. Monks, if that not-born, not-become, not-made, not-dispositionally conditioned were not, no escape from the born, become, made, dispositionally conditioned would be known here. But, monks, since there is a not-born, not-become, not-made, not-dispositionally-conditioned, therefore an escape from the born, become, made, dispositionally-conditioned is known. (*Woodward*, 1931, pp. 80–81)

Conclusion

This last quote from the *Nikayas* brings us to a full circle. We began with Siddhartha's attempt to face and understand the cyclical events of human life. The old age, disease, death, and the human pain prompted Siddhartha to embark on his spiritual journey to seek and find answers to the questions that bothered him. Siddhartha's spiritual inquiry led him to many teachers and many teachings of his time. As discussed in the previous sections, although Siddhartha experimented with many teachings of his time, they did not answer his questions or point a way out of the causal chain of dependent co-origination that bound one to suffering and the cyclical existence of human life. As part of his existential search, the Buddha developed his own method and charted his own path. The knowledge of the higher states of consciousness and the transcendence practice developed by the Buddha help us understand that just as there is a causal chain that binds one to suffering, that there is a causal chain that liberates one from suffering. Both these causal chains are linked, although their contents are very different. As it is said in the *Sutta Nipata*, "Even as the white lotus sprung up in the water with its thorny stalk is not sullied by water and mud, even so the sage who professes peace and is free from avarice is not sullied by the sense desires and by the world" (Saddhatissa, 1994, p. 99). The Buddha's spiritual inquiry into the nature of reality and his spiritual method help us understand both the arising and passing of the ordinary states of consciousness as well as the arising of the higher states of consciousness.

Future Directions

Since the advent of logical positivism and empiricism, cross-cultural scholarship has placed heavy emphasis on applying the Buddhist teachings to our experiences originating in our day-to-day world and limited to our ordinary senses. A great many scholars and practitioners of psychotherapy and medicine have emphasized the usefulness of Buddhist meditation practices to reduce stress, treat obsessive-compulsive disorders, or to improve emotional intelligence. These empirical and positivist approaches utilize some aspects of the Buddha's teachings. The following future directions might help us better benefit from the Buddha's teachings from a broader and comprehensive perspective. The following recommendations are made to augment the current synthesis and expand it in new directions: ·

1. The relevance and usefulness of the Buddha's teachings for the emerging trends in psychology, such as positive psychology, cultural psychology, parapsychology, and transpersonal psychology, need to be studied in more detail. For instance, how could the early Buddhist teachings on consciousness help us better understand the nature of near-death experience? How could the early Buddhist teachings of the cultivation of wholesome state, such as compassion or love, help us advance the field of positive psychology?

2. Within Buddhist scholarship, a greater emphasis needs to be placed on the study of nonordinary states of consciousness. To this end, the distinction between the *Dhammika* monks and the *Jhayin* monks as described in the *Nikayas* needs to be explored in more detail. The field will also benefit from exhibiting the flexibility and openness that the life and teachings of the Buddha attest to.

3. The field of religion and spirituality could benefit from the Buddha's teachings by reevaluating the role and experience of the individual in religious and spiritual quest.

4. The early Buddhist sources on the nature of higher states of consciousness should be utilized more broadly to inform the contemporary debate on what is termed as *the problem of pure consciousness.*

5. Lastly, the psychological implications of our infatuation and attachment to views and theories need to be studied. We have become, what may be popularly termed, an *argument culture*. Early Buddhist teachings on the nature and efficacy of arguments, theories, and views might help us better understand the psychological implications of an *argument culture.*

References

Bhikkhu Bodhi. (Trans.). (1989). *The discourse on the fruits of recluseship*. Kandy, Sri Lanka: Buddhist Publication Society.

Carus, P. (1981). *The gospel of the Buddha*. New Delhi, India: National Book Trust of India. (Original work published 1894).

Dimidjian, S., & Linehan, M. (2003). Defining an agenda for future research on the clinical applications of mindfulness practice. *Clinical Psychology: Science and Practice, 10*(2), 166–171.

Forman, R. K. C. (1999). *Mysticism, mind, consciousness*. Albany, NY: SUNY Press.

Harvey, P. (1994). Consciousness mysticism in the discourses of the Buddha. In K. Werner (Ed.), *The yogi and the mystic: Studies in Indian and comparative mysticism* (pp. 82–102). Richmond, England: Curzon Press.

Harvey, P. (1995). *The selfless mind: Personality, consciousness and Nirvana in early Buddhism*. Richmond, England: Curzon Press.

Horner, I. (Trans.). (1967). *The collection of the middle-length sayings (Majjhima-Nikaya)* (Vol. 1). London: Luzac & Company. (Original work published 1954).

Horner, I. (Trans.). (1975). *The collection of the middle-length sayings (Majjhima-Nikaya)* (Vol. 2). London: Luzac & Company. (Original work published 1957).

Ireland, J. (Trans.). (1990). *The Udana: Inspired utterances of the Buddha*. Kandy, Sri Lanka: Buddhist Publication Society.

Max Muller, F. (Ed.). (1977) *Sacred book of the Buddhists* (Vol. 2). London: Pali Text Society. (Original work published 1899).

Miculas, W. (2007). Buddhism and Western psychology: Fundamentals of integration. *Journal of Consciousness Studies, 14*(1), 4–49.

Mijares, S. (Ed.). (2003). *Modern psychology and ancient wisdom: Psychological healing practices from the world's religious traditions*. New York: Haworth Press.

Motoyama, H. (2008). Consciousness evolution of the Buddha until he attained *Satori*. In K. R. Rao, A. Paranjpe, & A. Dalal (Eds.), *Handbook of Indian psychology* (pp. 539–554). New Delhi, India: Cambridge University Press India Pvt Ltd.

Nakamura, H. (1964). *Ways of thinking of Eastern peoples: India, China, Tibet, Japan*. Honolulu: University Press of Hawaii.

Nauriyal, D., Drummond, M., & Lal, Y. (2006). *Buddhist thought and applied psychological research: Transcending the boundaries*. New York: Routledge.

Patel, K. (1998). *Rationality and mysticism in early Buddhism*. Unpublished Ph.D. dissertation, California Institute of Integral Studies, San Francisco.

Putnam, H. (1989). Rationality in decision theory and ethics. In S. Biederman & B. Scharfstein (Eds.), *Rationality in question: On Eastern and Western views of rationality* (pp. 19–28). Leiden, The Netherlands: E. J. Brill.

Radhakrishnan, S., & Moore, C. (Eds.). (1989). *A sourcebook in Indian Philosophy*. Princeton, NJ: Princeton University Press. (Original work published 1957).

Rao, R. K. (2002). *Consciousness studies: Cross-cultural perspectives*. Jefferson, NC: McFarland.

Rhys Davids, C. A. F., & Woodward, L. (Trans.). (1917–1930). *The book of kindred sayings (Samyutta Nikaya)* (Vol. 5). London: Pali Text Society.

Rhys Davids, C. A. F., & Woodward, F. (Trans.). (1982). *The book of kindred sayings (Samyutta Nikaya)* (Vol. 2). London: Pali Text Society.

Rhys Davids, C. A. F., & Rhys Davids, T. W. (Trans.). (1899–1921). *Dialogues of the Buddha* (Vol. 1). London: Pali Text Society.

Saddhatissa, H. (Trans.). (1994). *The Sutta-nipata*. Richmond, England: Curzon Press.

Seager, W. (2007). A brief history of the philosophical problem of consciousness. In P. Zelado, M. Moscovitch, & E. Thompson (Eds.), *The Cambridge handbook of consciousness* (pp. 9–35). New York: Cambridge University Press.

Velmans, M. (2009). How to define consciousness: And how not to define consciousness. *Journal of Consciousness Studies, 16*(5), 139–156.

Vimal, R. L. P. (2009). Meanings attributed to the term "consciousness": An overview. *Journal of Consciousness Studies, 16*(5), 9–27.

Walshe, M. (Trans.). (1987). *Thus have I heard*. London: Wisdom Publications.

Wilkes, K. (1984). Is consciousness important? *British Journal for the Philosophy of Science, 35*(3), 223–243.

Windisch, E. (Ed.). (1889). *Itivuttaka*. London: Pali Text Society.

Wittgenstein, L. (1986). *Philosophical investigations* (G.E.M. Anscombe, Trans.). Oxford, England: Basil Blackwell Ltd. (Original work published 1953).

Woodward, F. (Trans.). (1931). *Minor anthologies* (Vol. 2). London: Pali Text Society.

Woodward, F. (Trans.). (1980). *The book of the kindred sayings (Samyutta Nikaya)* (Vol. 4). London: Pali Text Society. (Original work published 1927).

Woodward, F., & Hare, E. (Trans.). (1932–1936). *The book of the gradual sayings (Anguttara Nikaya)* (Vol. 4). London: Pali Text Society.

Select Glossary

The terms in the following list are identified by a letter indicating their language as follows: P, Pali; S, Sanskrit. Some terms explained in the main body of the text are not repeated here.

Abhidhamma <P>: The higher *dhamma* or advanced teaching. One of the three caskets of the *Pali* canon. The *Theravada* school of Buddhism relies heavily on the teachings of *Abhidhamma*.

Acintiya <P>: Inconceivable.

Akala <P>: Timeless.

Amata <P>: Deathless.

Anatta <P>: No-self.

Anicca <P>: Impermanent.

Animitta-ceto-samadhi <P>: Signless concentration of consciousness.

Anupadisesha <P>: Without remainder.

Appamana <P>: Immeasurable, the opposite of *pamana*.

Arahat <P, S arahant>: Enlightened person who has the Buddha as his/her teacher. The *Pali canon* identifies some direct disciples of the Buddha as *arahat*.

Ariya-sacca <P>: The four noble truths.

Arupavacara <P>: The formless sphere (of consciousness).

Ayatana <P>: Sense sphere.

Bhagava <P, S bhagvan>: The Blessed One.

Domanassa <P>: Sorrow.

Ekagatta <P, S ekagrata>: One-pointed concentration.

Iddhi <P, S siddhi>: Paranormal accomplishment such as flying through the air or appearing from nowhere.

Kilesa <P, S klesha>: Defilement of the mind leading to a conflict.

Kusala/Akusala <P>: Wholesome/unwholesome states of mind.

Magga <P, S marga>: Path. In early Buddhism and Theravada Buddhism, it refers to the eightfold path.

Paccakha <P, S pratyaksha>: Perception.

Pamana <P, S pramana>: Proof of evidence based on measurement.

Panna <P>: Wisdom.

Paramattha <P, S paramartha>: Ultimate. This is in contrast to conventional (*vohara*).

Paticcasamuppada <P, S pratiyasamutpada>: Codependent origination.

Phalasamapatti <P>: Attainment of fruit.

Saddha <P, S sraddha>: Faith.

Sankappa <P, S sankalpa>: Resolve.

Sankhara <P, S sanskara>: Sense-impression.

Sanna <P>: Perception.

Sati <P>: Awareness based on the arising and passing of the phenomena.

Sunna <P>: Void or empty.

Sutta <P, S sutra>: A concise and unambiguous explanatory description of a concept or a theory.

Tanha <P>: Craving.

Tipitaka <P, S tripitaka>: Three caskets of the Pali canon.

Upadana <P>: Clinging to an arising.

Vedana <P, S>: Feeling (generally identified as a painful feeling).

Vimokkha <P, S vimoksha>: Special liberation.

Yathabhutam <P, S>: The reality as is.

PART 6

Physical Health and Spirituality

23 Spirituality, Science, and the Human Body

Wayne B. Jonas, Matt Fritts, Gail Christopher, Maeba Jonas, Susan Jonas

Abstract

Cultures throughout the world and over millennia have described the intimate relationship between spirit and body. Presently, we have an unprecedented opportunity to bring sophisticated scientific methods to the study of this relationship. In this chapter, we present a unified model of the whole person (spirit, mind, and body) and describe examples of practices from Eastern and Western traditions that are grounded in the assumption of body-mind-spirit unity. In addition, we give an overview of modern physical measurement options, such as neuroimaging and genomics, which allow for more detailed study of the spiritual interactions with the body. A fuller understanding of this relationship can lead to deep healing.

Key Words: spirituality, stress, allostatic load, neuroimaging, molecular biology

Introduction

In this chapter we describe opportunities for the scientific exploration of the connection between the body and the spirit and its relevance to the healing process. We will clarify what we mean by "spiritual" as opposed to "psychological" and explore how the new tools of science for assessing the health of the body such as neuroimaging, genetics, and metabolomics have created these opportunities. We will also provide some examples of spiritual practices (both ancient and modern) meant to influence the body and soul. Finally, we will close by making some recommendations on how to better understand the relationship of the body to spirituality in the light of modern science.

New Technologies in Biology and Medicine

The focus on the physical body by modern science has provided great advances in the cure and management of many physical and some psychological diseases, but it has also come with a cost. That cost is in the depersonalized, non-patient-centered approach of our modern medical treatment system. In the rush to identify and eliminate the physical causes of disease, medical care has often left the well-being of both the practitioners and the patients on the sidelines. Finally, by failing to attend to the more subjective signs of spiritual, physical, and psychological imbalance, medicine has been required to adopt ever-more sophisticated and expensive technologies for the management of disease in late stages. These approaches are unsatisfactory for many involved in delivering care and have resulted in a health care system that neither creates health nor facilitates care. It is because of this expensive, impersonal, and dehumanizing system that we have a compelling need to reexamine the relationship between medical care and the more subtle, deeply human spiritual aspects of life. Using the tools of modern science, we can understand the ways in which spirituality influences the body's health and empowers healing at its deepest levels.

A Model of the Whole Person

To better conceptualize both the distinction and blending of the relationship of mind-body-spirit, and to better define what we mean by "spiritual," we use the conceptual model of the "whole person" illustrated in Figure 23.1. In this figure we view the whole person as being like a wedge in space and time. On the outermost plane of the wedge is the physical aspect of the person, manifested as the body. On this level, time and space are clear and distinct and follow fixed physical laws. Person 1 and Person 2, for example, are closer to each other than to Person 3. Communication and interaction between Person 1 and Person 2 is faster than with Person 3. Just below this physical plane is the psychological level, which is the traditional realm of imagination and the mind. Here the distance between Person 1, 2, and 3 matters somewhat less than on the physical level. On this level interaction in memory, visualization, and emotion can occur rapidly. In the center of the figure, Persons 1, 2, and 3 link completely. This is the "spiritual" realm in which the distance in either time or space between persons merges and is indistinguishable. Time, space, and causality do not operate on this level in the way that they do on the physical level. The whole person involves all of these levels and so allows for a distinct ego and body subject to normal casual laws, and it "simultaneously" allows for all distinct persons to also participate in a "universal" link where all things exist in eternity and no physical distinction exists.

While we have drawn lines to distinguish these different "levels" of a person, there is no reason to think they are actually distinct or separate. In reality these "realms" merge and interact continuously, making it somewhat arbitrary to delineate between the physical, psychological, and spiritual. Still, certain characteristics emerge clearly in each level and so they can be defined, examined, and their interaction studied. In this chapter we explore the direct interaction between the outside, physical level and the innermost "spiritual" level, realizing that these levels have differing characteristics and even, possibly, scientific rules. With this model in mind, let us go on to define what we mean by "spiritual."

Defining Spirituality

It is important to describe what we mean by "spiritual" in order to more thoroughly consider the relationship between spirituality and the body. What do we mean by "spiritual"? The definition of "spiritual" and related terms has been problematic in health and academic circles for years. Often the word "spiritual" is used as shorthand to indicate innate human capacities in general, or behavior related to one's religious beliefs. The *Oxford English Dictionary* gives the following definition, "1. Pertaining to or affecting the spirit or soul especially from a religious aspect" (Brown, 1993). This meaning has been relatively stable since the Middle Ages. "Spirit," in addition, means, "1. The animating principle in humans and animals; 2. The immaterial part of corporal being" (Brown, 1993). For our purposes, "spirituality" means the individual's relationship to the characteristics of the divine nature of human experience that go beyond the corporeal nature of the body and the psychological constructs of the "ego." It involves assumptions about forces that extend outside of time and space and involve intelligent entities apparently not located in the physical body or the brain. By the "body" we mean the physical aspects of a human being that can be seen, touched, and examined through various instruments starting with conception and birth and going through to physical death.

The term "psychospiritual" can refer to a larger realm where spirituality intersects with psychology. For example, "belief," "meaning," and "purpose" are words often associated with spirituality, but they also have a nonspiritual meaning. In the latter case, a technique such as mindfulness-based meditation can be used for mitigating the effects of stress in a secular way, although it originated from Buddhist philosophy. We believe that there are several demarcating factors that are useful in distinguishing psychological from spiritual phenomena. These factors include phenomena that go beyond normal conceptions of time and space; they are nonlocal and they deal with beliefs, practices, and virtues, such as universal love or unconditional love, that can best be understood outside of conventional psychological, physical, and social frameworks. Another fruitful area in which to explore the relationship of the body and spirituality is the realm of spiritual healing—especially when its effects can be distinguished from psychological and placebo effects. Extensive research has shown that perception and consciousness can go beyond the bounds of normal time and space, interacting with and perhaps even influencing biology and physical phenomena in the past, the future, and at a distance. Much of this research was critically summarized by Jonas and Crawford (2003b). Throughout this chapter we

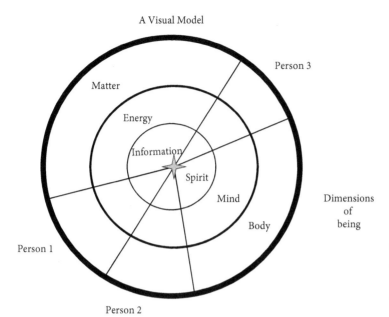

A Visual Model

Matter

Energy

Information

Spirit

Mind

Body

Person 1

Person 2

Person 3

Dimensions of being

Figure 23.1 Model of the whole person. (Adapted with permission from: Jonas, W. B., & Crawford, C.C. (2004). The healing presence: Can it be reliably measured? *Journal of Alternative and Complementary Medicine 10*(5), 751–756.)

will illustrate how some of this research dovetails with spiritual concepts.

The majority of the major religions describe characteristics of the divine as going beyond time and space. Examples of such characteristics are omnipresence, omnipotence, eternality, nonmaterial nature, omniscience, causality, and beneficence. Various religious and spiritual traditions describe these in different ways; yet they all share some core cross-cutting characteristic related to nonlocality. A distinguishing feature here is that not only do these experiences and behaviors transcend the ego, that is, go beyond one's own individual perception, they actually transcend space and time with practices demonstrating impact in the past and future or at distances beyond which normal physical and psychological mechanisms can explain. Thus, when time- and space-independent phenomena occur, one could more precisely define these as spiritual events. When those events are correlated with or have an impact on bodily functions or biological functions, we would then more precisely define these as measuring the biology of spirituality. Likewise, when spiritual experiences become mystical and transcend the normal socialization behaviors that would occur in psychosocial realms, such as when death becomes meaningless or love becomes unconditional, this too would circumscribe a circumstance in which the spirituality of biology could be explored.

The concept of the spirit, consciousness, or soul leaving and returning to the physical body has

been captured in the modern Western scientific documentation of patients' descriptions of near-death experiences. There have been several systematic studies of these experiences. For example, Dutch cardiologist Pim van Lommel conducted a prospective study of 344 heart attack survivors. He interviewed them within a week of resuscitation. The survivors' medical records confirmed that they were clinically dead, despite their reports of perceptions, experiences, and recollections during these time periods of clinical death. Sixty two, or 18%, of van Lommel's study participants reported these types of experiences while clinically dead. Many reported being out of their physical bodies but hearing and seeing activities around their physical bodies. Various spiritual traditions, such as Shamanism and Tibetan Buddhism, describe specific disciplines, rituals, and related practices that enable intentional, out-of-body experiences to be undertaken in the service of the person in need (Beauregard & O'Leary, 2008). We would submit that experiences that transcend space and time are areas for fruitful investigation of the intersection between the body and spirituality.

Spirituality and the Body: A Brief History

The history of humanity has described, up until recently, an intimate relationship between spirituality and the body throughout cultures. In this section, we will give a brief sampling of some of those concepts to demonstrate the global perspective. It is not the purpose of this section to provide an in-depth analysis of how spiritual traditions have dealt with the body nor to construct a philosophical argument for survival of consciousness; rather, its purpose is to highlight the areas that have been addressed in other chapters of this volume in order to frame our focus on measurement of spiritual events in the body.

Eastern Traditions

From the Western (Aristotelian, Cartesian, and Newtonian) perspective, the "I" is permanent and independent, there is a fixed duality of observer and object, and the ego/individual self is to be strengthened. In contrast, many Eastern traditions posit that the "I" is impermanent and interdependent and the self (or ego) is an illusion and source of suffering that is dissipated as the meditator realizes the interconnectedness and impermanence of experiences, objects, and mental phenomena. While we will later describe several Eastern traditions in which spirituality is united with the body, it is important to note that the early history of Eastern religions also includes "disembodied" views, such as the Hindu distinction between *purusha* (pure, unmanifested existence) and *prakruti* (the seed of physical form and nature; Lad, 2000); Jain and other ascetic practices that focus on the body as repulsive and a source of suffering; the Raja Yoga ideal of transcending the *annamayakosha* (gross physical body) to achieve higher *kayas* (levels of awareness); and Vedanta's concept that liberation (*videhamukti*) is possible only upon death (Ferrer, 2008).

Ayurveda and Yoga

An example of how the body and spiritual principles have been intertwined is in the traditional use of consciousness in Hatha Yoga and the medical discipline of Ayurveda, a system of traditional Indian medicine that is often considered the world's oldest healing system. The components of the word "Ayurveda" are "Ayur" (meaning life) and "Veda" (meaning science or knowledge). The formative and organizing principle underlying Ayurvedic medicine is the application of therapeutic techniques to change one's perception and consciousness. But the perception that Ayurvedic medicine seeks to change is not simply a psychological concept; it has spiritual characteristics.

Counseling for the process of changing perception is a primary component of Ayurvedic practices; much of the Ayurvedic physician's focus is on causing in the patient a change in *mahad* (cosmic consciousness). When one enters traditional Ayurvedic treatment, one begins with an astrological assessment to determine the particular cosmic ailment, its progress, and its connection to the universe. *Pachamakarma*—a treatment that involves cathartics, the application of oil to the body and forehead, and other purification practices—is designed to cleanse not just the body but also the mind in order to allow a more accurate perception of divine will. Even Ayurvedic herbal products and formulations are used to change one's perception of the nature of reality. From an Ayurvedic point of view, analysis of active chemical ingredients within those herbal products is, while interesting, off base and largely irrelevant to their use. Sometimes major differences in combinations are used for patients with the same diagnoses, depending upon the effect on perception and experiences that are produced (Lad, 1999).

Ayurveda codeveloped out of yogic philosophy and Hindu spirituality as part of a unified system to heal body, mind, and spirit. Rather than just a technique to restore physical health, yoga is described in ancient texts as an "inner science" and comprehensive way of life. The ultimate purposes of yoga are reunion of the individual self with a Higher Self (the word "yoke" shares its etymology with the Sanskrit root for yoga, "yug") and stilling the mind to allow clearer perception of reality and universal spiritual principles (Satchidananda, 1990). Assumptions and principles underlying both yoga and Ayurveda include nonduality of self and universe; the individual body-mind as microcosm for the universe; parallel rhythms of the body, day, season, and year (Lad, 1984); and that what leads to physical change in the body is immersion into "cosmic consciousness," an ordering principle that increases balance and accelerates spontaneous healing. Change in the body results from change in the spirit.

Qi

The concept and use of *qi* in Chinese medicine offers another example of how a tradition has intertwined spiritual and physical concepts. *Qi* is closest in conception and use to the "vital force" in the vitalism traditions of the West and is often translated as "energy" in the West and "prana" in Sanskrit. Indeed, *qi* does have a number of characteristics similar to energy in the West, such as the ability to be accumulated and projected; however, it also has a number of characteristics that differ from physical energy and phenomena and behave more like a spiritual force. For example, *qi* has a nonlocal characteristic in that it can be directed by attention and thoughts and delivered over great distances, beyond the domain of where the Western concept of energy operates. Yet fundamental physical changes are attributed to the manipulation, projection, and balance of *qi*. While acupuncture is a local manipulation of *qi* in therapeutic settings, *qigong* has local and nonlocal applications in therapeutic settings (Lee & Lei, 1999).

Buddhism

Like other religious and spiritual systems, the aims of Buddhist practice are happiness, genuine love, and inner peace. In contrast to other approaches, however, this aim is achieved in Buddhism not by looking to an outside god or savior, but by turning inward to connect to a deeper aspect of our minds, which when pacified, creates a backdrop from which our innate serenity, insight, and concern for others can emerge. The purpose of many Buddhist practices is to look for, and eventually fail to find, an individual and independent self who is fundamentally separate from others and the Divine. It is to do a deep dive into the center of the person depicted in Figure 23.1.

As both a psychological and spiritual system, Buddhist teachings can be categorized into three general groups: (1) Theravada (a.k.a. Hinayana) Buddhism, focused on stabilizing the mind with monastic asceticism and discipline; (2) Mahayana Buddhism, focused on dissolving the rigid boundary of an independent self and awakening genuine compassion and realization of the interdependence of humanity; and (3) Vajrayana (a.k.a. Tantric) Buddhism, focused on attaining enlightenment as quickly as possible in order to be of maximum benefit to humanity.

Theravada philosophy focuses largely on individual liberation (mocha) from an endless cycle of worldly suffering through behavioral restraint, ethical discipline, the eventual extinction of desires (nirvana), and final enlightenment (parinirvana) after bodily death. While very effective at stabilizing and pacifying the mind (Astin, 1997), Theravada practices such as Vipassana and Mahayana schools such as Zen are primarily focused on the mental sphere and may view the body as a hindrance to spiritual realization. As a result, they may exclude innate sources of knowledge in the emotional and physical spheres. By contrast, and in common with Ayurvedic philosophy described earlier, Vajrayana teachings (in particular, the completion stages of the Highest Yoga Tantra systems) (Gray, 2007) include yogic practices designed to purify blockages to wisdom and elicit spiritual transformation quickly,

while in this body and this world. The Vajrayana teachings share another feature of Ayurvedic philosophy: In scientific manner and with great detail, The Kalachakra ("cycles of time") Tantra describes the parallel relationship among external cycles of time, through which the universe passes; internal cycles, through which energy and the body pass; and cycles of spiritual progression (Dalai Lama, 1999).

While Tibetan yogas differ greatly from Hindu-based Hatha Yoga practices described earlier, they share the same goal; the Tibetan word for yoga (*Nel-jor*) is often translated as "primordial wisdom." The esoteric yogas described in Vajrayana texts were originally transmitted only privately from teacher to selected students and with great secrecy, due to their potential not only for powerful transformation but also for individual ruin. These practices are based on the manipulation of vital energy (Skt "prana," Tib "lung") and are intended to develop a "heightened awareness of one's actual (as opposed to conceptualized) experience of the body...[as] open, ever changing, and basically intangible (empty). Within this emptiness, there is a continual play of energy (prana), as consciousness (bindu) moves along certain pathways (nadi)" (Ray, 2002).

An example of these esoteric practices, which have until only recently been shrouded in secrecy, is the Six Yogis of Naropa (Mullin, 2006), which include practices such as Trul Khor (yogic exercises to open the energy channels; Chaoul, 2003) and Tummo (inner fire that has demonstrable physical effects). These practices defy conventional scientific explanation and blur the Cartesian line between mind and body. For example, it has been documented in medical journals that practitioners of Tummo can generate intense internal heat for spiritual purposes, increase temperature of extremities by as much as 8°C (Benson et al., 1982), and endure immersion in ice for over an hour, wearing only shorts and without significant lowering of core body temperature (Diaz & Chenetz, 2010).

Western Traditions
Vitalism

The concept of "vitalism" runs through a number of nonmainstream practices throughout the West. The idea is that the body has a fundamental energetic organizing principle that is responsible for biological and bodily changes in health. When magnetism and electromagnetism were discovered in the 17th century, many scientists and practitioners at the time believed they had discovered the underlying spiritual principle of vitalism that explained how these ethereal processes influence the body. They thought that this spiritual principle could therefore do away with religious and spiritual explanations. The long history of vitalism in medicine includes Hippocrates's idea that it is nature (*physis*) in the organism that heals the patient. In his history of vitalism, Matthew Wood (2000) weaves together kindred concepts of shamanism, various healing doctrines, religious beliefs, and rational philosophies that evolved over the centuries into diverse systems of healing. Ethereal and spiritual concepts were eventually reconceptualized in terms of magnetic and electromagnetic energy and in terms of an organizing nonmaterial entity. The vital force (*vis*) became the foundation for a number of Western practices such as naturopathy, chiropractic, homeopathy, and osteopathy.

As practiced today, many alternative or non-mainstream systems of health care offer individuals a connection or reconnection with benign, coherent, potent, and meaningful powers (Kaptchuk, 1996). Many manual medicine systems, such as osteopathy, chiropractic, and naturopathy, claim to treat the body, mind, and spirit as a whole unit. These integrated systems demonstrate the interrelated, reciprocal nature of structure and function, while helping the person to recognize and mobilize the body's innate self-healing, self-regulating, and self-regenerating capabilities. Homeopathy speaks of a spiritual "vital essence," and botanical or herbal practitioners draw from knowledge of the traditional uses of herbs by healers from indigenous populations such as Native American shamans. Shamanic ceremonies, rituals, and healing sessions draw upon the spirit of the herbal medicines, honoring the vital power and strength imbued by nature.

Judeo-Christian Approaches to the Body

This chapter is not meant to be a full discussion of the major religious traditions and their teachings on the physical body and its relationship to the spirit. There are numerous examples of sacred writings on this subject; later, we delineate a few that serve to illustrate this discussion.

In the Hebrew Scriptures, we find that Yahweh created humans in his own image: "male and female he created them" (Genesis 1:27). In the gospel of John in the New Testament, "the word was made flesh" (John 1:14), in that the Word existed before its embodiment and became flesh in the body of Jesus of Nazareth. In various religions, the physical body has been interpreted as the container of the spirit, created by divine providence, and thus to

be cared for and cherished. The physical body has also been seen as an impediment to transcendence and a vehicle for sin and earthly pleasure. To further explore the body and its connection to the spiritual, we must acknowledge this dichotomy and embrace a "both-and" rather than an "either-or" view of the nature of the body. The physical is not either sacred or material; rather, it is both sacred and a manifestation of the material world in all of its complexity. As our model illustrates, the person is both separate and unified with the Divine.

Transpersonal Psychology and "Embodied Spirituality"

After the formal development of psychology, established by Freud and his followers, a number of thinkers and writers have moved outside standard intrapersonal psychological components to describe more spiritual-like phenomena in these areas. While this chapter is focused primarily on spiritual concepts and the body, we should at least mention the field of depth psychology and the concept of "embodied spirituality" that's described in related fields. Extensive writing in depth psychology, such as that by Michael Washburn (1994, 2003), and in transpersonal psychology by Jorge Ferrer (2001) and others has used the term "embodied spirituality." Jan van den Berg has written about pastoral anthropology, which also uses this term (2008). Other writers also relate the concept of embodied spirituality to depth and transpersonal psychology, notably the Feldenkrais method (2010) and other therapeutic body work methods such as somatic spiritual psychology, Adorata, and embodied teshuvah (Schreiburg, 2010).

In addition, many traditional and modern Judeo-Christian traditions include concepts that relate to spirituality and the body, such as Pope John Paul's *The Theology of the Body* (John Paul II, 1997), the Roman Catholic Eucharist (in which the body of Christ becomes present in the Eucharistic bread), and Jewish movement facilitators such as those in the Institute for Embodied Spirituality. There are several extensive overviews of these fields and how they touch on the topic of the relationship of spiritual characteristics to physical measurement. Readers are referred to overviews of this extensive area such as Michael Murphy's *The Future of the Body* (1992) and the Kelly and Kelly's *Irreducible Mind: Toward a Psychology for the 21st Century* (2007). We've chosen *not* to use the term "embodied spirituality," in order to distinguish this chapter's focus on new techniques of physical measurement of spiritual characteristics and on spiritual phenomena from physical or bodily interactions.

Feminine Concepts of Spirituality and the Body

The relationship of the female body and feminine spirit to spirituality is another area of exploration that should be mentioned. In recent years, feminist scholarship has produced new knowledge about women's spirituality, the female body, and the feminine face of the divine (Ferguson, 1994). Theologians and anthropologists are uncovering and discovering ancient goddess cultures that reflect an early identification of the female body with the creative force of the divine. These cultures were later replaced with patriarchal, divine warrior-centered cultures that devalued the female body and its ability to procreate. Women's experiences of birthing and raising children, caring for the elderly, and mundane work associated with the earthly and material world have been interpreted as separating them from the masculine spiritual and intellectual life of the mind (Fischer, 1995). As a result of this disconnection, women experience self-hatred, shame, and disengagement in relationship to their bodies, and in many cultures, they are taught to sacrifice their selves and the care of their own bodies so that they may better serve others. Feminist scholars have called for the acknowledgment, reconnection, and reintegration of the female body and spirit.

The Virtues

Living in an intentional way through practice of human virtues impacts the body. In *Why Good Things Happen to Good People* (Post & Neimark, 2007), Stephen Post describes 10 ways of giving of oneself to others and the effect that this has on happiness and longevity: generosity, forgiveness, courage, humor, respect, compassion, loyalty, listening, and creativity. Post describes the research that has been conducted on these virtues and the effect that they have on health. For example, the research on forgiveness is extensive and tends to show that emotional forgiveness, where a person replaces negative emotions with positive forgiving emotions, induces psycho-physiological changes and has direct effects on health and well-being (Worthington Jr., Witvliet, Pietrini, & Miller, 2007). Forgiveness of self and an altruistic motive to forgive others seems to have the most benefit on physical and mental health (Worthington Jr., van Oyen, Lerner, & Scherer, 2005). Forgiveness therapy and interventions may be beneficial to the treatment and management of chronic diseases such as obesity, addictions, and cirrhosis that often have social and interpersonal dynamics (Elliott, 2010). We know that the human condition is such that saintly, well-meaning, and altruistic people also suffer tragedies and untimely illnesses and death (Dossey, 1993), but we also know that people who live loving, generous lives tend to be happier and healthier.

Ultimately whether we are describing spirituality or religion, we are referencing beliefs about truth, the perceived divine, and trust in it and life's guiding forces. These religious and spiritual beliefs can (and often do) become the basis of a person's worldview. For spirituality, these beliefs usually motivate behaviors and relationships of the individual, while religious beliefs motivate an individual's behaviors and relationships within a larger context of organized communities that adhere to doctrines and tenets based on collective beliefs. Both spiritual and religious belief systems espouse virtues or factors associated with good, excellence, and/or right actions. Despite the diversity of religious and spiritual traditions historically and in the modern world, many share common virtues.

Unconditional love emerges as the overarching virtue from which many other aspects of human behavior and aspirations flow. Hope, or the ability to believe in the possibility of fulfillment, is another overarching virtue. And finally there is charity or generosity. These qualities generate many other ideals such as kindness, forgiveness, humility, gratitude, and fidelity. Most spiritual disciplines and religious systems promote practices designed to develop these virtues. Prayer, meditation, service, confession, deep listening, storytelling, as well as lifestyle and dietary modifications, and community rituals such as song and dance are among the practices that help to develop virtues and virtuous states. Examples from research on "the virtues" also illustrate biological impact. Common religious practices in some traditions can be described as confession or exploration of deep, meaningful experiences. Every spiritual tradition imbeds storytelling as a way of reinforcing the experience of that tradition. Deep storytelling can have profound biological effects, especially when it gets at the root of transego and transtemporal phenomena. For example, Pennebaker and others have described extensive research showing that the process of "opening up" as done in confession and storytelling can have an impact on immune function, symptomatology, and even health care utilization (Pennebaker, 1990). Smyth and colleagues, in an article published in the *Journal of the American*

Medical Association, demonstrated that a single episode of deep therapeutic storytelling can have significant impact on objective measures of lung function in asthmatics and subjective measures of pain in patients with rheumatoid arthritis (1999). Love and altruism are other virtues with a growing area of research support on their physical effects.

Spiritual Healing

Spiritual healing is another area in which the relationship between spirituality and the body can be explored. In a study that examined the common characteristics that cut across spiritual and nonmaterial healing traditions, the authors identified a number of core characteristics of those events (Jonas & Crawford, 2003a). Table 23.1 illustrates the healers who were brought together to describe their core characteristics. These healers were then asked to a Delphi process to identify the two characteristics that they thought were part of divine healing. Table 23.2 lists the characteristics that they said these disciplines described. The two characteristics that emerged across all disciplines were divine love and intentionality. Divine love was described as the power that impacted physical events, and intention was the characteristic that directed it toward the desired goal of healing. Thus, when these two characteristics exist in a spiritual healing session, they claimed this provides a fruitful realm for the examination of the intersection of the body and biology and spirituality. Research has established strong links between spirituality and physical, psychological, and medical health (Ai, Dunkle, Peterson, & Bolling, 1998; Helm, Hays, Flint, Koenig, & Blazer, 2000; Koenig, McCullough, & Larson, 2001; Koenig, Pargament, & Nielsen, 1998; Williams, Larson, Buckler, Heckmann, & Pyle, 1991). The following benefits are documented in Koenig, McCullough,

Table 23.1. Healing Traditions Sampled

Ayurvedic	Christian Evangelical
TCM	African Shamanism
Greek Orthodox	Psychotherapy
Kabalistic	Christian Science
Sufi	Spiritual Healing
Native American Medicine	Brazilian Psychic Surgery

Jonas, W. B., & Crawford, C.C. (2004). The healing presence: Can it be reliably measured? *Journal of Alternative and Complementary Medicine 10*(5), 751–756.

Table 23.2. Common Components of a Healing Presence (number of traditions identifying the component)

Love (11)	Good intention (11)
Spiritual Grace (6)	Belief (5)
Focused Awareness (5)	Direction of Energy
Openness to Healing (4)	Listening (3)
Creativity (3)	Reconciliation (3)
Imagination (2)	Connectedness (3), Relationship (3)

Jonas, W. B., & Crawford, C.C. (2004). The healing presence: Can it be reliably measured? *Journal of Alternative and Complementary Medicine 10*(5), 751–756.

and Larson's 2001 *Handbook of Religion and Health* (which incorporates spiritual and religious factors and analyzed 1,200 studies): hope and optimism, less depression, fewer suicides, less anxiety, less alcohol and drug abuse, greater marital stability, less risky behavior, and lower mortality from various causes (Koenig et al., 2001).

Examples of Spiritual-Body Practices

In this section, we describe several examples of how spiritual activities result in physical changes or how physical activities result in spiritual experiences. This is not a comprehensive description, and there are many more, but it is in these realms we believe that further research would shed light and further understanding on the relationship between the body and spirituality as we have described it here.

Shalom

As example of a practical approach to the type of divine healing mentioned earlier, we look to an interview with a healer appropriately called "Love Is an Intention" (Hession, 2003). In it, Jerry Jud, the founder of the Shalom Process, describes the development of the "Principles and Skills of Loving." These tenets are the foundation of an integrative approach to healing through exploration of the energetic blocks created in our bodies by traumas that prevent us from being fully alive and experiencing the fullness of divine love. Drawing on work being done at other retreat centers like Esalen, Kirkridge, DaySpring, and the like, this healing process incorporates psychological techniques of core and bioenergetics, Neo Reichian theories, guided meditation, and some of the primal therapy techniques developed by Dr. Arthur Janov. It posits that the body "re-members" (i.e., incorporates energetically in a specific place in the body) all past experiences of trauma in the form of fear, anger, grief, or shame. By intentionally allowing these energies to arise and cathartically move through the body and complete the natural cycle of energetic release, the person in process can access the flipside to these emotions, which are excitement, passion, joy, and fully being seen. Unlike most therapeutic techniques, the Shalom Process is done in an intentionally created community, through a group process that gives deliberate attention to community building and is rooted in intentional and unconditional loving, which is the foundation of this transformational process. The community furthers the Shalom Process work such that the living body of the people present may energetically hold the intention of divine love for the person engaged in the process. This process claims that by being seen in our darkest shadows by others in loving witness, we are also, in an energetic sense, being witnessed by divine love itself. By practicing love as an intention in this way, healing has the opportunity to emerge quickly and profoundly (http://www.shalommountain.com/).

Transcendental Meditation

We summarize work on meditative practices later in this chapter but will describe one example here. In a National Institutes of Health (NIH)–funded randomized clinical trials, stress-reducing meditation (Transcendental Meditation)was two and half times more effective in reducing systolic and diastolic blood pressure than conventional relaxation. Effects were comparable to standard pharmacological treatment, but without negative side effects (Schneider et al., 1995). Results of another research study, published in *Archives of Internal Medicine* in June 2006, demonstrated the effects of transcendental meditation (a meditative practice derived from the Ancient Vedic traditions) on coronary heart disease and related health challenges (Paul-Labrador et al., 2006).

The study participants (103, in total) had coronary heart disease. Fifty-two were instructed in transcendental meditation and 51 control patients received health education. Eighty-four patients completed the study. At the end of the trial, patients in the transcendental meditation group had significantly lower blood pressure; improved fasting blood glucose and insulin levels, with slightly reduced

insulin resistance; and more stable functioning of the autonomic nervous system. The authors concluded that transcendental meditation may modulate the body's response to stress rather than alter the stress itself, similar to the physiological impact of exercise on conditioning (Paul-Labrador et al., 2006).

Spiritual practices such as meditation, prayer, mindfulness, and yoga alter brain neurochemistry and reduce the biochemical markers of stress (see later for details). Spiritual practices such as meditation and prayer can have beneficial effects on breathing rates, metabolism, blood flow, and heart rates. These effects can be measured and a summary of those changes from recent research is described in a later section of this chapter. As Andrew Newberg and Mark Robert Waldman delineate in their book *How God Changes Your Brain*, "the more we engage in spiritual practices, the more control we gain over body, mind and fate" (2009, p. 63).

Heart Rate Coherence Training

One example of application of the use of heart rate variability (HRV) in psychospiritual training has been done by the HeartMath Corporation (http://www.heartmath.com/). In this process, individuals are trained to regulate heart rate coherence (described later)—usually by cultivating a sense of appreciation and loving kindness. Most of the research has demonstrated improved psychological functioning, decreased stress and depression, and reduced hypertension as example changes in the body (McCraty, 2002). Preliminary research has shown that when individuals are practicing heart rate coherence they also can have impact on the physiological changes of others near them and even at a distance (McCraty, Atkinson, Tomasino, & Bradley, 2006). The latter, the impact of heart rate coherence of others at a distance, would be an area for exploration of the connection between the biological phenomena (heart rate) and the spiritual characteristic of omnipresence.

Prayer and Laying On of Hands

The last example comes from the growing body of literature examining the physical and psychological effects of religious and spiritual practices around the area of prayer and the laying on of hands. These studies have been extensively reviewed in books by Jonas and Crawford (2003b), Dossey (1993), and Benor (2001) and others examining how prayer, love, psychological intention, and laying on of hands can influence biological processes. Many spiritual healing traditions use laying on of hands, or touch, as a therapeutic medium. A growing body of research indicates that the psychological and biological effects observed from these practices may not all be due to the placebo effect. A recent review of these so-called energy practices by Jain and Mills (2009) illustrates the current quality and quantity of research in these areas. This is a fruitful domain for exploring the relationship of spirituality and the body.

Relaxation Response

The final example we will present is the relaxation response (RR) (Benson, 1975). RR is a coordinated physiological response, first described by Herbert Benson, MD, in 1974 and which occurs in association with a state of "well-being." Relaxation training can be used to manage the demands of stress and to maintain optimal levels of energy and capacity for work (Benson, Beary, & Carol, 1974; Wallace, Benson, & Wilson, 1971). The RR is hypothesized to oppose the physiological changes caused by stress and the "fight-or-flight" response (Cannon, 1914). Elicitation of the RR is characterized by a set of measurable, predictable, and reproducible physiologic changes (Beary & Benson, 1974; Benson, 1994; Benson et al., 1974; Benson, Dryer, & Hartley, 1978; Benson, Frankel, et al., 1978; Benson & Goodale, 1981; Benson, Greenwood, & Klemchuk, 1975; Benson, Steinert, Greenwood, Klemchuk, & Peterson, 1975; Greenwood & Benson, 1977; Peters, Benson, & Peters, 1977; Wallace et al., 1971). The RR has been widely utilized to counteract the dysphoric, undesired physiologic and psychological responses to stress (Jevning, Anand, Biedebach, & Fernando, 1996). The consciously motivated behaviors that elicit the RR may counteract adverse physiologic and hormonal responses to stress, and regular practice of the RR may result in sustained physiological changes that can reduce subsequent development of undesired stress responses (Benson, 1984). While scientific investigations of the physiological and structural characteristics of the RR have been undertaken only in the last few decades, RR elicitation has been an important component of many religious and spiritual traditions throughout the world for thousands of years.

Science, Technology, and the Body

The relationship of spirituality to the body requires reexamination in light of recent biological and chemical scientific advances in medicine. Science has moved almost completely in the materialistic direction, resulting in an ever-widening gap

between the spirit and body in both professional and popular culture, as illustrated by phrases such as "it's all in your head." In the premodern scientific era, the material or physical arose from the spiritual or at least had equal footing to it. In the modern era, the spiritual is largely a phenomenon of the material that is explained through physics and chemistry (Lakoff & Johnson, 1999). The tools for dissecting and measuring these physical phenomena have now become so sophisticated that new opportunities exist for exploring the core physical explanations of life and health and their relationship with spiritual concepts and experiences.

Over the last 100 years, there have been tremendous strides in the ability to understand and measure biological and physical events. In the last 20 years especially, technologies have been developed that allow real-time imaging of functional measures within the body and the brain. This includes physiological measurement of the heart, brain imaging, and imagery of metabolism and increasingly sophisticated assessments of cellular function through genomics, proteomics, and metabalomics (van der Greef et al., 2007). Sophisticated computer analysis and mapping of these functions now allow us to put these measures back together in a way that approximates the whole organism. Increasingly, these measures are being applied to the more subtle areas of psychological and social interaction. In this section of the chapter, we look at a few of those measures and how they might be used to assess spiritual phenomena.

Modulation of the Stress Response

The concept of stress, developed by Hans Selye in the early part of the last century (1950), has taken on increased prominence in recent times as further refinements of how the body responds to perceived threats and safety occur. Selye's original concepts of "fight or flight" manifest physiologically through autonomic reactions of the sympathetic and the parasympathetic nervous systems. These concepts have now been extended to ever-finer biological dimensions, including the assessment of organ-specific and cellular-specific reactions to perceived threat and safety. At its core, the concept of stress is a person's response to a real or perceived threat to safety. This response can be offset by perceptions of love, safety, and protection, which then mitigate stress. Spiritual ideals from many traditions—such as, benevolence, universal love, and safety—can help the faithful mitigate the fear of death and modify perceived threat. Faith, belief, and spiritual practices—such as prayer, meditation, or mindfulness—can be stress modulators and buffers to the biological and psychological response to threat, and they can change how practitioners experience, interpret, and relate to stressful situations (Stanley, 2007). With ever-more refined ways of measuring body functions, we can now explore how spiritual practices influence those behaviors.

Subjective Measures of Spirituality

In addition to high-tech approaches that are described later, it is important to note several "lower tech" measures. Many scientists who are well trained in Aristotelian empiricism have concluded that these phenomena simply cannot be understood or measured at all (Batchelor, 1998; Ekman, Davidson, Ricard, & Wallace, 2010; Wallace, 2003, 2007). From the perspective of many of the world's contemplative traditions, it *is* possible to understand these phenomena "from the inside out," such as through rigorous first-person methodologies An example of rigorous neurophenomological approaches, which combine quantitative measures with first-person data and involve active collaborations with the subject under study, is Lutz et al.'s study of naive and experienced meditators whose neuroelectric activity was recorded while describing their experience and performing a visual protocol (Lutz, Lachaux, Martinerie, & Varela, 2002).

Scales for assessment of spirituality are by their nature subjective, and most have been validated in either seriously ill patients or the elderly. Despite these limitations, current evidence provides a growing basis of support for the effect of spirituality and spiritual practices on the body and its physiological processes. These benefits have been recently summarized in an analysis of over 1,000 studies (Koenig et al., 2001). This research shows that the buffering and/or reversing of the stress response by secular mind-body practices—such as mindfulness-based stress reduction (MBSR; Kabat-Zinn et al., 1992) and RR training (Benson, 1975) can be amplified by linking those practices with spirituality and belief. These practices can help to create meaning around stressful and traumatic experiences. Evidence shows that cultivating purpose and meaning, which includes the ability to find religious significance (Pargament, Koenig, & Perez, 2000; Pargament, Smith, Koenig, & Perez, 1998), improves coping ability (The army chaplaincy, *Professional bulletin of the Unit Ministry Team.Summer-Fall 2010*). Construing positive meaning is also associated with greater acceptance of difficult situations and opportunities for posttraumatic growth leading to

spiritual resilience (Litz et al., 2009), better psychological adjustment (Owens, Steger, Whitesell, & Herrera, 2009; Schok, 2009), less remorse, and fewer self-condemning thoughts (Litz et al., 2009). Furthermore, these mind-body practices enable salutogenic cognitive reframing of stressful events, increased situational and self-awareness, and a pause between stressors and habitual, unconscious, and emotional reactions. Introducing this "choice point" thereby enables decisions that are more supportive of personal and spiritual goals.

Physiological Markers of Spirituality

Bidirectional communication between the brain and the body (including the heart) occurs via the autonomic nervous system, the endocrine system, and the immune system. Since the cognitive functions described earlier (such as reframing and construing meaning) have been shown to be assisted by spiritual practices, these three systems become important sources of possible physiologic correlates of spirituality. Next, we present one example from each of these systems (autonomic nervous, endocrine, and immune) as possible physiologic measures of spirituality.

An example of a physiological measure within the autonomic nervous system is HRV, which refers to the change in rate of heart contractility between beats. The time/distance between contractility will change depending upon the environment, emotions, and breathing and how those are translated through the brain to the autonomic regulation of the heart rate. Numerous studies have shown that the more inflexible the HRV, or the more chaotic, the less functional an individual is and the higher risk he or she has for a number of conditions, including hypertension, diabetes, cardiovascular disease, and depression (McCraty, Atkinson, & Tomasino, 2003). Practicing a spiritual discipline such as meditation and prayer, using stress and emotional management, and feeling appreciation can bring HRV into a more coherent (a regular, sinusoidal, variability) pattern, in contrast to the chaotic pattern that occurs during anxiety and perceived threat (McCraty, 2002). HRV is a useful psycho-physiological tool for assessing spiritual phenomena that go beyond the psychological. For example, recent research has shown that heart rate coherence can not only influence the brain of the individual in which the coherence occurs but also in individuals nearby (McCraty et al., 2006). Apparently, electromagnetic waves are detected by the other person's heart and brain, which respond accordingly. This provides a possible physical mechanism for the experience of "deep peace" that one feels in the presence of some spiritual masters. Individuals with coherent HRV may be providing a physically calming influence that occurs even in the absence of any overt behavior. Heart rate coherence has also been shown to be correlated with a number of the more classical hormonal markers of stress, including cortisol, DHEA, and oxytocin (McCraty, Barrios-Choplin, Rozman, Atkinson, & Watkins, 1998).

An example of a possible physiological marker of spirituality from the endocrine system is the finding that transcendental meditation leads to a decrease in cortisol levels and normalization of hormone levels (Mohan, Sharma, & Bijlani, 2011); additional examples are provided later. Finally, a possible marker from the immune system is found in several studies (Rosenkranz et al., 2003) that have found that individuals with high left prefrontal activation (which can be amplified by mind-body practices and predisposes to positive mood) have higher antibody titers in response to an immunological insult (e.g., influenza vaccine).

Correlates of Spirituality in the Central Nervous System

Neuroelectric techniques, such as electroencephalography (EEG), offer another potential marker for religious and spiritual experiences. Spectral analysis and EEG mapping of the RR demonstrate that "by changing mental activity we can demonstrate measurable changes in central nervous system activity" (Jacobs, 2001, p. S83). Over 100 studies and several reviews (Davidson et al., 2003; Lutz, Brefczynski-Lewis, Johnstone, & Davidson, 2008) have described EEG changes from a restful to meditative state, changes in oscillatory rhythms (e.g., alpha and theta), or the effect of meditation on response to external stimuli. Examples of these many studies are greater alpha coherence over frontal electrodes during transcendental meditation practice (Morse, Martin, Furst, & Dubin, 1977), increased alpha or theta activity during calm-abiding (focused awareness) meditation (Davidson et al., 2003), self-induced sustained EEG high-amplitude gamma-band oscillations and phase synchrony in long-term Tibetan Buddhist meditators (Lutz, Greischar, Rawlings, Ricard, & Davidson, 2004).

There is evidence that mental training can alter and enhance specific aspects of awareness and attention. Several random controlled trials have indicated that mindfulness and body-mind training can improve attention and self-regulation (Tang et al., 2007). Example findings include meditation-induced, long-term increases in the efficiency of the executive attentional network (Chan & Woollacott, 2007), enhanced attentional stability and reduced mean reaction time following 3 months of intensive training in focused-attention meditation (Lutz et al., 2009), protection against functional impairments in working memory capacity (used in managing cognitive demands and emotion regulation; Jha, Stanley, Kiyonaga, Wong, & Gelfand, 2010), improved ability to orient attention after MBSR training, and improved alerting skills following concentrative meditation (Jha, Krompinger, & Baime, 2007).

Measurement of Spirituality With Neuroimaging

A number of other tools that may be useful for measuring spiritual characteristics have also rapidly evolved in the last few years. These include functional magnetic resonance imaging (fMRI), positron emission topography (PET), superconducting quantum interference devices (SQUIDS), magnetoencephalography (MEG), and fast computer topography (CT). These techniques have become so dynamic and sophisticated that it is now possible to image certain changes in the brain that occur with both short-term thoughts and emotions (such as thinking about pain versus experiencing pain versus perceiving another experiencing pain) and longer term changes that occur with learning and other cognitive practices (such as meditation). Examples of research in this area are a PET study of blood flow changes during Yoga Nidra practice (Lou et al., 1999), single-photon emission computed tomography studies of Tibetan Buddhist meditators engaging in focused/active meditation (Newberg et al., 2001), an fMRI study of Kundalini yoga adepts and functional imaging to study brain activity during loving kindness/compassion meditation (Lutz et al., 2009). These studies of different types of meditation have demonstrated increased activity in different parts of the brain. Key findings are that even short-term (30 min) training in emotion regulation can reliably alter brain function (Urry et al., 2006), and MBSR can alter prefrontal brain activity in ways that have been shown to accompany positive affect (Davidson, 2003). Spectral analysis and topographic EEG mapping of the RR elicited by many mind-body practices demonstrate that by changing mental activity we can demonstrate measurable changes in central nervous system activity (Jacobs, 2001).

But do mind-body practices produce long-term effects? This question is still open, but research on neuroplasticity (the ability of the brain to physically change as a result of experiences) has expanded over the last decade. Studies on neuroplasticity and meditative practice have found larger hippocampi in taxi drivers than matched controls (Maguire et al., 2000) and increased cortical thickness in regions associated with attention, introspection, and sensory processing in meditators compared to controls (Lazar et al., 2005).

Care must be taken in setting up neuroimaging of spirituality. First, brain changes and complex imaging patterns are often hard to interpret and individual and variations can be considerable from one scan to the next, especially when looking for subtle changes. One person may use differing brain areas and processes than another for similar functions. A recent systematic review of neuroimaging studies of meditation showed a number of changes, but of such variety that generalizable comparison and a meta-analysis were not feasible (Clausen, Crawford, & Ives, 2011). Even more care is needed when attempting to use neuroimaging (or other biological measures) for the measurement of nonlocal phenomena—a core area for assessment of the central (in our model) spiritual domains' interaction with the body. A series of studies have examined neurological correlates of bonded individuals when isolated or at a distance and shown correlated responses (Schmidt, Schneider, Utts, & Walach, 2004; Standish, Kozak, Johnson, & Richards, 2004; Wackermann, Seiter, Keibel, & Walach, 2003). However, if no nonlocal events occur, then the neuroimaging cannot be used to examine that domain. For example, Moultan and Kosslyn did a series of fMRI scans on subjects engaged in a psi experiment and reported no changes. However, since no psi events occurred, the fact that there were not consistent neurocorrelates with that is meaningless (Moulton & Kosslyn, 2008).

Genetic and Cellular Measures of Spirituality

What produces and mediates stress and its health consequences has come under increased study in the last several decades. Some factors are not under major control of an individual; they may be socially or spiritually influenced. Other factors can more easily be modulated by individuals in the community. Recently, an understanding of common cellular and physiological links between stress, coping mechanisms, and stress mediators has emerged. The term "allostasis" or "allostatic load" describes how interactions between the external (social and physical) and internal (psychological and genetic) environments of the person are validated parameters of stress, aging, and a chronic illness (McEwen, 2003). These parameters are arranged in a hierarchical set. Primary mediators (chemical messengers with widespread influence throughout the body, such as cortisol, noradrenalin, epinephrine, and DHEA) influence secondary mediators (markers of abnormal metabolism and physiology such as blood pressure, glycosylated hemoglobin, cholesterol, HDL ratio, and heart rate variability), which in turn lead to tertiary outcomes (diseases consequences such as depression, cardiovascular disease, obesity, diabetes, and decreased mental and physical capacity). Increasingly, the genomic, proteomic, and metabolic consequences of stress can be traced and tracked. This provides an opportunity to assess effects at the cellular and subcellular levels that are influenced by spiritual parameters.

For example, inflammatory mediators have been found to be increasingly connected to stress modulation. Inflammatory mediators such as those influenced by NFK-B in turn influence a cascade of other cytokines and mediators (including interleukin-2 and interleukin-10), which then impact cellular function and disease. Stress also seems to modulate a shift between M1 and M2 immune functioning, which represent the defense versus the repair modes of the body. An imbalance between defense versus repair can aggravate chronic inflammation, resulting in a whole host of cellular and tissue dysfunctions (Seeman, Singer, Ryff, & Levy-Storms, 2002). The area of psychoneuroimmunology has rapidly grown with an increased understanding and ability to measure these mediators. For example, Kiecolt-Glaser has demonstrated that a single conflictual encounter between spouses can result in alteration in cytokine and inflammatory markers in the tissues, resulting in a full-day delay of wound healing as compared to a loving and peaceful interaction between those same spouses (Kiecolt-Glaser et al., 1993). Recently, other markers such as oxytocin have been shown to play a key role in the mitigation or acceleration of stress components, including posttraumatic stress disorder (Olff, Langeland, Witteveen, & Denys, 2010). To the extent that these psychological constructs can be influenced by spiritual practices and events, we enter the realm of measuring the effects of spirituality of the body. One of the most comprehensive and innovative thinkers in this area has been Ernest Rossi. For the last several decades, Rossi has explored the research demonstrating a link between both psychological and spiritual phenomena to a dynamic fluctuation in genetic and cellular changes in the body (Rossi, 2002).

As indicated by the aforementioned examples, the fields of neuroscience, neuroimaging, genomics, and metabolomics are rapidly evolving with the application of these tools to psychological phenomena. We posit that these same tools can be useful for understanding a neuroscience of spirituality (Jonas, 2011).

Spirituality, Science, and Suffering

Ultimately, the importance of directly studying the interaction of spirituality and the body is the understanding it provides to relieve suffering at the deepest and most profound level. One area where the relevance of this can be seen is in the experience, science, and treatment of pain. A recent article by Giordano and Kohls describes the interaction between the subjective, psychospiritual and objective, physical aspects of pain (2008).

The experience of pain, particularly severe chronic pain, is inextricably bound up with one's sense of identity—the ego or "soul"—as well as one's role in the community. The suffering of pain is purely subjective and unique to each individual's personal beliefs and life circumstances, as well as the culture of the surrounding community. Pain can also create a feeling of "ego or soul loss," which may lead people to define themselves narrowly in terms of their pain, losing the identity they project to the rest of the world. In describing his own experience of severe cancer pain, Freud wrote, "My world is a small island floating on a sea of indifference" (http://historyannex.com/20th-century-Europe/Nineteenth-century/psychoanalytic-freud.html). The personal crises of pain and suffering, however, are often associated with, and may in fact prompt, spiritual experiences. Such experiences may be religious or secular—such as meditation or contemplation. As described in this chapter, there is accumulating evidence that spiritual experiences may, in turn, have health-promoting (salutogenic) effects. Regular spiritual practices of any kind could be considered coping mechanisms for distress caused by ego or soul loss. The communal spiritual practices previously described may have persisted in part because of their public health benefits, promoting hardiness and resistance to disease, possibly through improved functions of the endocrine and immune systems.

Not only may spiritual practices reduce the emotional distress associated with pain, they may also contribute to mitigating the pain itself. The biochemical relationships between pain and spiritual experiences may lead to cellular changes in the brain, which in turn may benefit organs and smooth muscle. Thus, physical changes in the brain associated with spiritual practices may include the production of neurotransmitters that promote positive emotions (such as euphoria) as well as analgesic (pain-reducing) molecules.

Thus, spiritual experiences and practices are important and potentially relevant to clinical medicine, particularly with respect to pain management. Medicine should be more than applied science; it must also have a humanitarian dimension that acknowledges patients as spiritual beings and respects their personal preferences and spiritual choices. Pain management should therefore be multidisciplinary, including clergy and other spiritual counseling to address patients' religious needs. Optimal healing environments—including meditative or contemplative spaces—would provide patients with the opportunity for more secular spiritual experiences and enrichment (Chez & Jonas, 2005).

Conclusions and Future Directions

In this chapter, we have explored the relationship between biology, the body, and selected characteristics of spirituality; provided some examples from medical and spiritual practices; and summarized the biological assessment opportunities provided by recent scientific technologies. The implications of this exploration are numerous, but we put forth the following as appropriate implications. First, despite the extensive advances in science, biology, and psychology, there are still fundamental characteristics of the spiritual nature of humanity that are not yet explained or even sufficiently described by this science. Thus, a field for the scientific exploration of spirituality is warranted as a distinct entity. Second, the recent advances in measurement technology in biology provide tremendous opportunities to better understand the nature of spirituality. We should explore and understand the characteristics of spirituality in relationship to the body using these technologies. This will bring us to a new level of refined knowledge and may open up a variety of new modalities and uses for both areas. Finally, there remains a profound power within the area of spirituality for healing. This is a universal human behavior, which has not been sufficiently brought into health care delivery. If we apply our most sophisticated scientific tools to the direct study of spiritual and divine characteristics in healing, we will likely open up new realms of knowledge with broad application across the domains of health, healing, and human flourishing. In the health care of the future, the chaplain, the minister, the spiritual master, and the mother may no longer be called in simply for comfort and palliation during treatment or at the end of life but may be an integral part of the therapeutic team. Spiritual practices would be both evidence based and broadly applicable across the continuum of health and disease.

Both the desire for spirituality and religion and the desire for healing grow out of common human needs to end suffering and to transcend pain and perceived isolation or separation. Modern science now affords the conceptual framework and related tools to better explore the physical value of spirituality to address fundamental human needs. As we gain a deeper, more nuanced understanding of how the human system adapts to perceived threat and to perceived bliss, the stress response is emerging as a unifying concept for health and healing. As a result, the importance of spirituality, spiritual practices, religious beliefs, and secular virtues will gain a more prominent place in medicine and health care.

Acknowledgments

We would like to thank Jarrad Davis and Cindy Crawford for their input and assistance in preparation of this manuscript. This work was partially funded by the Rockefeller Program on Brain, Mind and Healing.

References

Ai, A. L., Dunkle, R. E., Peterson, C., & Bolling, S. F. (1998). The role of private prayer in psychological recovery among midlife and aged patients following cardiac surgery. *Gerontologist, 38*(5), 591–601.

The army chaplaincy, *Professional bulletin of the Unit Ministry Team.Summer-Fall 2010* PB 16–09-2 Head Quarters Department of the Army. Retrieved January 25, 2012 from http://www.chapnet.army.mil/Documents/Summer-Fall_2010.pdf

Astin, J. (1997). Stress reduction through mindfulness meditation: Effects on psychological symptomatology, sense of control, and spiritual experiences. *Psychother Psychosom, 66*(2), 97–106.

Batchelor, S. (1998). *Buddhism without beliefs: A contemporary guide to awakening.* New York: Riverhead Trade.

Beary, J. F., & Benson, H. (1974). A simple psychophysiologic technique which elicits the hypometabolic changes of the relaxation response. *Psychosomatic Medicine, 36*(2), 115–120.

Beauregard, M., & O'Leary, D. (2008). *The spiritual brain: A neuroscientist's case for the existence of the soul.* New York: Harper One.

Benor, D. (2001). *Spiritual healing: Scientific validation of a healing revolution.* Southfield, MI: Vision Publications.

Benson, H. (1975). *The relaxation response.* New York: William Morrow.

Benson, H. (1984). *Beyond the relaxation response.* New York: Times Books.

Benson, H. (1994). Increases in positive psychological characteristics with a new relaxation-response curriculum in high school students. *Journal of Research and Development in Education, 27,* 226–231.

Benson, H., Beary, J. F., & Carol, M. P. (1974). The relaxation response. *Psychiatry, 37*(1), 37–46.

Benson, H., Dryer, T., & Hartley, L. H. (1978). Decreased VO2 consumption during exercise with elicitation of the relaxation response. *Journal of Human Stress, 4*(2), 38–42.

Benson, H., Frankel, F. H., Apfel, R., Daniels, M. D., Schniewind, H. E., Nemiah, J. C.,…Rosner, B. (1978). Treatment of anxiety: A comparison of the usefulness of self-hypnosis and a meditational relaxation technique. An overview. *Psychother Psychosom, 30*(3–4), 229–242.

Benson, H., & Goodale, I. L. (1981). The relaxation response: Your inborn capacity to counteract the harmful effects of stress. *Journal of the Florida Medical Association, 68*(4), 265–267.

Benson, H., Greenwood, M. M., & Klemchuk, H. (1975). The relaxation response: Psychophysiologic aspects and clinical applications. *International Journal of Psychiatry in Medicine, 6*(1–2), 87–98.

Benson, H., Lehmann, J., Malhotra, M., Goldman, R., Hopkins, J., & Epstein, M. (1982). Body temperature changes during the practice of g Tum-mo yoga. *Nature, 295*(5846), 234–236.

Benson, H., Steinert, R. F., Greenwood, M. M., Klemchuk, H. M., & Peterson, N. H. (1975). Continuous measurement of O_2 consumption and CO_2 elimination during a wakeful hypometabolic state. *Journal of Human Stress, 1*(1), 37–44.

Brown, L. (1993). *The new shorter Oxford English dictionary on historical principles.* Oxford, England: Clarendon Press.

Cannon, W. (1914). Emergency function of the adrenal medulla in pain and the major emotions. *American Journal of Physiology, 33,* 356.

Chan, D., & Woollacott, M. (2007). Effects of level of meditation experience on attentional focus: is the efficiency of executive or orientation networks improved? *Journal of Alternative and Complementary Medicine, 13*(6), 651–657.

Chaoul, M. (2003, May). Yogic practices (rtsarlung 'phr ul' khor) in the Bon tradition and possible applications as a CIM (complementary and integrative medicine) therapy. *Proceedings of the Tenth Seminar of the IATS, 2003. Volume 9: The Mongolia-Tibet Interface Oxford,* UK.

Chez, R. A., & Jonas, W. B. (2005). Challenges and opportunities in achieving healing. *Journal of Alternative and Complementary Medicine, 11*(Suppl 1), S3–6.

Clausen, S., Crawford, C., & Ives, J. (2011). Does neuroimaging provide evidence of meditation-mediated neuroplasticity? In S. Schmidt (Ed.), *Neuroscience, consciousness and spirituality.* Berlin: Springer.

Dalai Lama, H. (1999). *Kalachakra Tantra: Rite of initiation* (3rd ed.): Wisdom Publication.

Davidson, R. J. (2003). Affective neuroscience and psychophysiology: Toward a synthesis. *Psychophysiology, 40*(5), 655–665.

Davidson, R. J., Kabat-Zinn, J., Schumacher, J., Rosenkranz, M., Muller, D., Santorelli, S. F.,…Sheridan, J. F. (2003). Alterations in brain and immune function produced by mindfulness meditation. *Psychosomatic Medicine, 65*(4), 564–570.

Diaz, J., & Chenetz, R. (2010). Utter endurance: 'Iceman' and 'Ultramarathon Man': Science at a loss to explain feats of staggering endurance in world's most hostile climates. Retrieved from http://abcnews.go.com/2020/iceman-marathon-man-feats-human-endurance/story?id=10731229&page=1

Dossey, L. (1993). *Healing words: The power of prayer and the practice of medicine.* New York: Harper Collins.

Ekman, P., Davidson, R., Ricard, M., & Wallace, B. (2010). Buddhist and psychological perspectives on emotions and well-being. *Current Direction in Psychological Science, 19*(4), 59–64.

Elliott, V. (2010). Forgiveness therapy: A clinical intervention for chronic disease. *Journal of Religion and Health, 50,* 240–247.

Feldenkrais, M. (2010). *Embodied wisdom: The collected papers of Moshe Felenkrais.* Berkley, CA: North Atlantic Books.

Ferguson, M. (1994). *Women and religion.* New York: Prentice Hall.

Ferrer, J. (2001). *Revisioning transpersonal theory.* Albany, NY: SUNY Press.

Ferrer, J. N. (2008). What does it mean to live a fully embodied spiritual life? *International Journal of Transpersonal Studies, 27,* 1–11.

Fischer, K. (1995). Spiritual direction with women. In R. Wicks (Ed.), *Handbook of spirituality for ministries* (pp. 96–114). New York: Paulist Press.

Giordano, J., & Kohls, N. (2008). Self, suffering and spirituality: The neuroscience of being, pain and spiritual experiences and practices. *Mind and Matter, 6*(3), 179–192.

Gray, D. (2007). *The Cakrasamvara tantra: A study and annotated translation.* : American Institute of Buddhist Studies (p. 472). New York: Columbia University Press. http://cuplive.ifactory.com/book/978-0-9753734-6-0/the-cakrasamvara-tantra

Greenwood, M. M., & Benson, H. (1977). The efficacy of progressive relaxation in systematic desensitization and a proposal for an alternative competitive response—the relaxation response. *Behavioral Research Therapy, 15*(4), 337–343.

Helm, H. M., Hays, J. C., Flint, E. P., Koenig, H. G., & Blazer, D. G. (2000). Does private religious activity prolong survival? A six-year follow-up study of 3,851 older adults. *Journal of Gerontology A: Biological Sciences and Medical Sciences, 55*(7), M400–405.

Hession, J. (2003). *Love is an intention: An interview with Jerry Jud about the principles and skills of Loving.* Ecoprint. http://ebookbrowse.com/love-is-an-intention-by-jim-hession-pdf-pdf-d51029783

Jacobs, G. D. (2001). The physiology of mind-body interactions: the stress response and the relaxation response. *Journal of Alternative and Complementary Medicine, 7*(Suppl 1), S83–92.

Jain, S., & Mills, P. (2009). Biofield therapies: Helpful or full of hype? A best evidence synthesis. *International Journal of Behavioral Medicine, 12*(1), 1–16.

Jevning, R., Anand, R., Biedebach, M., & Fernando, G. (1996). Effects on regional cerebral blood flow of transcendental meditation. *Physiology and Behavior, 59*(3), 399–402.

Jha, A. P., Krompinger, J., & Baime, M. J. (2007). Mindfulness training modifies subsystems of attention. *Cognitive, Affective, and Behavioral Neuroscience, 7*(2), 109–119.

Jha, A. P., Stanley, E. A., Kiyonaga, A., Wong, L., & Gelfand, L. (2010). Examining the protective effects of mindfulness training on working memory capacity and affective experience. *Emotion, 10*(1), 54–64.

John Paul II. (1997). *The theology of the body: Human love in the divine plan.* Boston: Pauline Books.

Jonas, W. (2011). Toward a neuroscience of spirituality. In H Walach, S. Schmidt, W Jonas (Eds.), *Neuroscience, consciousness and spirituality* (Vol. viii, 298, p. 16)Berlin: Springer.

Jonas, W., & Crawford, C. (2003a). Healing presence: Can it be scientifically investigated? *Journal of Alternative and Complementary Medicine, 10*(5),751–6.

Jonas, W., & Crawford, C. (2003b). *Healing, intention, and energy medicine.* New York: Churchill Livingstone.

Kabat-Zinn, J., Massion, A. O., Kristeller, J., Peterson, L. G., Fletcher, K. E., Pbert, L.,…Santorell, S. F. (1992). Effectiveness of a meditation-based stress reduction program in the treatment of anxiety disorders. *American Journal of Psychiatry, 149*(7), 936–943.

Kaptchuk, T. (1996). History of vitalism. In M. Micozzi (Ed.), *Fundamentals of complementary and integrative medicine* (pp. 54–66). Saint Louis, MO: Elsevier.

Kelly, E., & Kelly, E. (2007). *Irreducible mind: Toward a psychology.* Lanham, MD: Rowman & Littlefield.

Kiecolt-Glaser, J., Malarkey, W. B., Chee, M., Newton, T., Cacioppo, J. T., Mao, H-Y., & Glaser, R. (1993). Negative behavior during marital conflict associated with immunological down regulation. *Psychosomatic Medicine, 55*(5), 395–409.

Koenig, H., McCullough, M., & Larson, D. (2001). *Handbook of religion and health.* New York: Oxford University Press.

Koenig, H. G., Pargament, K. I., & Nielsen, J. (1998). Religious coping and health status in medically ill hospitalized older adults. *Journal of Nervous and Mental Disorders, 186*(9), 513–521.

Lad, D. (1999). Ayurvedic medicine. In W. Jonas & J. Levin (Eds.), *Essentials of complementary and alternative medicine* (pp. 200). Baltimore: Lippincott Williams & Wilkins.

Lad, V. (1984). *Ayurveda: The science of self-healing.* Twin Lakes, WI: Lotus Press.

Lad, V. (1984). *Ayurveda: Natural health practices for your body type from the world's oldest healing tradition.* Twin Lakes, WI: Lotus Press.

Lakoff, G., & Johnson, M. (1999). *Philosophy in the flesh: The embodied mind and its challenge to western thought.* New York: Basic Books.

Lazar, S. W., Kerr, C. E., Wasserman, R. H., Gray, J. R., Greve, D. N., Treadway, M. T.,…Fischl, B. (2005). Meditation experience is associated with increased cortical thickness. *Neuroreport, 16*(17), 1893–1897.

Lee, C., & Lei, T. (1999). Qigong. In W. Jonas & J. Levin (Eds.), *Essentials of complementary and alternative medicine* (pp. 392). Baltimore: Lippincott Williams & Wilkins.

Litz, B. T., Stein, N., Delaney, E., Lebowitz, L., Nash, W. P., Silva, C., & Maquen, S. (2009). Moral injury and moral repair in war veterans: a preliminary model and intervention strategy. *Clinical Psychology Review, 29*(8), 695–706.

Lou, H. C., Kjaer, T W., Friberg, L., Wildschiodtz, G., Holm, S., & Nowak, M. (1999). A 15O-H2O PET study of meditation and the resting state of normal consciousness. *Human Brain Mapping, 7*(2), 98–105.

Lutz, A., Brefczynski-Lewis, J., Johnstone, T., & Davidson, R. J. (2008). Regulation of the neural circuitry of emotion by compassion meditation: effects of meditative expertise. *PLoS One, 3*(3), e1897.

Lutz, A., Greischar, L. L., Rawlings, N. B., Ricard, M., & Davidson, R. J. (2004). Long-term meditators self-induce high-amplitude gamma synchrony during mental practice. *Proceedings of the National Academy of Sciences USA, 101*(46), 16369–16373.

Lutz, A., Lachaux, J. P., Martinerie, J., & Varela, F. J. (2002). Guiding the study of brain dynamics by using first-person data: Synchrony patterns correlate with ongoing conscious states during a simple visual task. *Proceedings of the National Academy of Sciences USA, 99*(3), 1586–1591.

Lutz, A., Slagter, H. A., Rawlings, N. B., Francis, A. D., Greischar, L. L., & Davidson, R. J. (2009). Mental training enhances attentional stability: Neural and behavioral evidence. *Journal of Neuroscience, 29*(42), 13418–13427.

Maguire, E. A., Gadian, D. G., Johnsrude, I. S., Good, C. D., Ashburner, J., Frackowiak, R. S., Frith, C. D. (2000). Navigation-related structural change in the hippocampi of taxi drivers. *Proceedings of the National Academy of Sciences USA, 97*(8), 4398–4403.

McCraty, R. (2002). Heart rhythm coherence: An emerging area of biofeedback. *Biofeedback, 20*(1), 23–25.

McCraty, R., Atkinson, M., & Tomasino, D. (2003). Impact of a workplace stress reduction program on blood pressure and emotional health in hypertensive employees. *Journal of Alternative and Complementary Medicine, 9*(3), 355–369.

McCraty, R., Atkinson, M., Tomasino, D., & Bradley, R. (2006). *The coherent heart: Heart-brain interaction, psychophysiological coherence, and the emergence of system-wide order.* Boulder Creek, CA: HeartMath Research Center, Institute of HeartMath.

McCraty, R., Barrios-Choplin, B., Rozman, D., Atkinson, M., & Watkins, A. D. (1998). The impact of a new emotional self-management program on stress, emotions, heart rate variability, DHEA and cortisol. *Integrative Physiological and Behavioral Science, 33*(2), 151–170.

McEwen, B. (2003). Interacting mediator of allostasis and allostatic load: Towards an understanding of resilience in aging. *Metabolism, 52*(10), 10–16.

Mohan, A., Sharma, R., & Bijlani R. L. (2011). Effect of meditation on stress-induced changes in cognitive functions. *Journal of Alternative and Complementary Medicine, 17*(3), 207–12.

Morse, D. R., Martin, J. S., Furst, M. L., & Dubin, L. L. (1977). A physiological and subjective evaluation of meditation, hypnosis, and relaxation. *Psychosomatic Medicine, 39*(5), 304–324.

Moulton, S., & Kosslyn, S. (2008). Using neuroimaging to resolve the psi debate. *Journal of Cognitive Neuroscience, 20*(1), 182–192.

Mullin, G. (2006). *The practice of the six yogas of Naropa* (2nd ed.). Ithaca, NY: Snow Lion Publications.

Murphy, M. (1992). *The future of the body: Explorations into the further evolution of human nature.* New York: Tarcher/Putnam.

Newberg, A., Alavi, A., Baime, M., Pourdehnad, M., Santanna, J., & d'Aquili, E. (2001). The measurement of regional cerebral blood flow during the complex cognitive task of meditation: A preliminary SPECT study. *Psychiatry Research, 106*(2), 113–122.

Newberg, A., & Waldman, M. R. (2009). *How God changes your brain.* New York: Ballubine Books Trade Paperbacks.

Olff, M., Langeland, W., Witteveen, A., & Denys, D. (2010) A psychobiological rationale for oxytocin in he treatment of post-traumatic stress disorder. *CNS Spectrum, 15*(8), 436–444.

Owens, G. P., Steger, M. F., Whitesell, A. A., & Herrera, C. J. (2009). Posttraumatic stress disorder, guilt, depression, and meaning in life among military veterans. *Journal of Trauma and Stress, 22*(6), 654–657.

Pargament, K., Koenig, H., & Perez, L. (2000). The many methods of religious coping: Development and initial validation of the RCOPE. *Journal of Clinical Psychology, 56,* 519–543.

Pargament, K., Smith, B., Koenig, H., & Perez, L. (1998). Patterns of positive and negative religious coping with major life stressors. *Journal for the Scientific Study of Religion, 37,* 710–724.

Paul-Labrador, M., Polk, D., Dwyer, J. H., Velasquez, I., Nidich, S., Rainforth, M.,...Merz, C. N. (2006). Effects of randomized controlled trial of transcendental meditation on components of metabolic syndrome in subjects with coronary heart disease. *Archives of Internal Medicine, 166,* 1218–1224.

Pennebaker, J. (1990). *Opening up: The healing power of confiding in others.* New York: William Morrow.

Peters, R. K., Benson, H., & Peters, J. M. (1977). Daily relaxation response breaks in a working population: II. Effects on blood pressure. *American Journal of Public Health, 67*(10), 954–959.

Post, S., & Neimark, J. (2007). *Why good things happen to good people.* New York: Broadway Books.

Ray, R. What is Tibetan Buddhism? Retrieved January 30, 2012 from http://www.thopaga.org/TibetanBuddhism.pdf

Rosenkranz, M. A., Jackson, D. C., Dalton, K. M., Dolski, I., Ryff, C. D., Singer, B. H.,...Davidson, R. J. (2003). Affective style and in vivo immune response: Neurobehavioral mechanisms. *Proceedings of the National Academy of Sciences USA, 100*(119), 11148–11152.

Rossi, E. (2002). *The psychobiology of gene expression.* New York: Norton.

Satchidananda, S. (1990). *The yoga sutras of Patanjali: Commentary on the raja yoga sutras* Buckingham, VA: Integral Yoga Publications.

Schmidt, S., Schneider, R., Utts, J., & Walach, H. (2004). Distant intentionality and the feeling of being stared at: Two meta-analyses. *British Journal of Psychology, 95*(Pt 2), 235–247.

Schneider, R., Staggers, F., Alxander, C. N., Sheppard, W., Rainforth, M.,...King, C. G. (1995). A randomized control trial of stress reduction for hypertension in older african americans. *Hypertension, 26,* 820–827.

Schok, M. (2009). *Meaning as a mission: Making sense of war and peacekeeping.* Uitgeverij, Belgium: Eburon.

Schreiburg, J. (2010). *Embodied Jewish spirituality.* Retrieved January 25, 2012, from http://www.discover-yourself.com/Spirituality.htm

Seeman, T., Singer, B., Ryff, C., & Levy-Storms, L. (2002). Psychological factors and the development of allostatic load. *Psychosomatic Medicine, 64,* 395–406.

Selye, H. (1950). Stress and the general adaptation syndrome. *British Medical Journal, 1*(4667), 1383–1392.

Smyth, J., Stone, A. A., Hurewitz, A., & Kaell, A. (1999). Effects of writing about stressful experiences on symptom reduction in patients with asthma or rheumatoid arthritis. *Journal of the American Medical Association, 281,* 1304–1309.

Standish, L. J., Kozak, L., Johnson, L. C., & Richards, T. (2004). Electroencephalographic evidence of correlated event-related signals between the brains of spatially and sensory isolated human subjects. *Journal of Alternative and Complementary Medicine, 10*(2), 307–314.

Stanley, E. (2007, October). *Mindfulness and military effectiveness in counterinsurgency operations.* Paper presented at the Conference of the Inter-University Seminar of Armed Forces and Society, Chicago, IL.

Tang, Y. Y., Ma, Y., Wang, J., Fan, Y., Feng, S., & Lu, Q. (2007). Short-term meditation training improves attention and self-regulation. *Proceedings of the National Academy of Sciences USA, 104*(43), 17152–17156.

Urry, H. L., van Reekum, C. M., Johnstone, T., Kalin, N. H., Thurow, M. E., Schaefer, H. S.,...Davidson, R. J. (2006). Amygdala and ventromedial prefrontal cortex are inversely coupled during regulation of negative affect and predict the diurnal pattern of cortisol secretion among older adults. *J Neurosci, 26*(16), 4415–4425.

Van den Berg, J. (2008). An embodied spirituality: Perspectives for a bodily pastoral anthropology. *Acta Theologica, 28*(2), 118–132.

van der Greef, J., Martin, S., Juhasz, P., Adourian, A., Plasterer, T., Verheij, E. R., & McBurney, R. N. (2007). The art and practice of systems biology in medicine: Mapping patterns of relationships. *Journal of Proteome Research, 6*(4), 1540–1559.

Wackermann, J., Seiter, C., Keibel, H., & Walach, H. (2003). Correlations between brain electrical activities of two spatially separated human subjects. *Neuroscience Letters, 336*(1), 60–64.

Wallace, B. (2003). *Buddhism and science: Breaking new ground.* New York: Columbia University Press.

Wallace, B. (2007). *Contemplative science: Where Buddhism and neuroscience converge.* New York: Columbia University Press.

Wallace, R. K., Benson, H., & Wilson, A. F. (1971). A wakeful hypometabolic physiologic state. *American Journal of Physiology, 221*(3), 795–799.

Washburn, M. (1994). *Transpersonal psychology in psychanalytic perspective.* New York: SUNY Press.

Washburn, M. (2003). *Embodied spirituality in a sacred world.* New York: SUNY Press.

Williams, D. R., Larson, D. B., Buckler, R. E., Heckmann, R. C., & Pyle, C. M. (1991). Religion and psychological distress in a community sample. *Social Science and Medicine, 32*(11), 1257–1262.

Wood, M. (2000). *Vitalism: The history of herbalism, homeopathy, and flower essences.* Berkley, CA: North Atlantic Books.

Worthington, E., Jr., van Oyen, W., Lerner, A., & Scherer, M. (2005). Forgiveness in health research and medical practice. *Explore, 1*(3), 169–176.

Worthington, E., Jr., Witvliet, C., Pietrini, P., & Miller, A. (2007). Forgiveness, health, and well-being: A review of evidence for the emotional versus decisional forgiveness, dispositional forgiveness and reduced unforgiveness. *Journal of Behavioral Medicine, 30*(4), 291–302.

Spirituality, Emotions, and Physical Health

Crystal L. Park *and* Jeanne M. Slattery

Abstract

This chapter focuses on relations between religion/spirituality (R/S) and physical health, focusing on the role of emotions as mediating these links. First, we review the literature regarding the effects of R/S on physical health and the effects of physical health on R/S. We then present a model of the reciprocal influences of R/S and health and the pathways of positive and negative emotions as important mediators of the R/S–health relationships. We review and summarize theory and research findings regarding these links and conclude the chapter by suggesting questions that may guide future research.

Key Words: religion, spirituality, positive emotions, negative emotions, physical health

Introduction

It is well established in the scientific literature that religiousness and spirituality (R/S) and physical health and well-being are related (see, for example, McCullough, Hoyt, Larson, Koenig, & Thoresen, 2000; Powell, Shahabi, & Thoresen, 2003). However, these relationships are complex, and the mechanisms underlying them are poorly understood. The directionality of these influences appears to go both ways: R/S can affect physical health, and physical health can affect R/S. Furthermore, many pathways have been proposed to explain these linkages, but little evidence exists regarding many of these proposed pathways. Among those pathways that have been demonstrated to mediate both the influence of R/S on health status and the influence of health status on R/S is that of emotion. The present chapter focuses explicitly on the role of emotions as mediating the link between R/S and health. First, we review the literature demonstrating that (1) R/S affects health and (2) health affects R/S. We then present a model of the reciprocal influences of R/S and health and propose that emotion

is an important mediator of the R/S-health links. We examine the literature regarding these links and summarize current knowledge. We conclude the chapter with questions that should be addressed with further research.

Relationships Between Religiousness/Spirituality and Health

Religiousness/Spirituality Affects Health

In recent years, researchers have become increasingly interested in the influence of religion and spirituality on physical health (for reviews, see George, Ellison, & Larson, 2002; Hill & Pargament, 2003; Lee & Newberg, 2005, 2010; Powell et al., 2003). Epidemiological studies have long demonstrated that higher levels of religiousness, as assessed by membership and service attendance, are related to lower mortality rates (e.g., Koenig & Hays, 1999; Koenig & Vaillant, 2009; McCullough et al., 2000; Powell et al., 2003). These relationships between R/S and health appear to be stronger for women than for men (Koenig & Vaillant, 2009). Although these superior health outcomes appear to be related to a variety of factors, including that people attending religious services are more likely to receive social support and to engage in positive health-related behaviors like exercise and less likely to engage in health-averse behaviors (cf. Hill & Pargament, 2003; Lee & Newberg, 2010; Strawbridge, Shema, Cohen, & Kaplan, 2001), the positive health consequences of religiousness hold up even when potential covariates such as baseline health, social support, and health behaviors are taken into account (Oman, Kurata, Strawbridge, & Cohen, 2002).

Religiousness and spirituality have also been reported to have negative consequences on health. For example, as summarized by Lee and Newberg (2005), some religions oppose certain health interventions (e.g., transfusions, contraception, abortions) and may stigmatize certain illnesses, thus preventing adherents from receiving medical help early; members of religious groups who expect divine intervention with their illnesses delay medical care relative to people with other beliefs; prejudice against members of religious or spiritual groups may cause stress that, in turn, causes problems in mental or physical health; and perceived spiritual and religious transgressions can cause spiritual pain and decrements in physical health. Some religions promote a more fatalistic approach to life, which can interfere with health-promoting behaviors (Hess & McKinney, 2007). These problems can be further increased by religious leaders or church members who predict dire outcomes, including hell, for those who violate religious beliefs and precepts.

Recognizing the multidimensional nature of religiousness and spirituality, researchers have more recently broadened their focus from group membership and religious service attendance to additional aspects of religion and spirituality, such as private religious behaviors, commitment, spiritual transcendence, and religious coping (Hill & Pargament, 2003). Research has yielded generally positive, although somewhat mixed findings regarding relationships between religiousness/spirituality and health (Powell et al., 2003). For example, aspects of religiousness predict lower rates of disability and of a range of illnesses, including alcoholism, cardiovascular disease, hypertension, and myocardial infarction (see Miller & Thoresen, 2003). Specific religious activities like prayer, meditation, and yoga are associated with positive physical and mental health outcomes (Lee & Newberg, 2005, 2010). In addition, to the extent that individuals regard their bodies as sanctified (e.g., as a temple of God), they are more likely to engage in higher levels of health behaviors (Mahoney et al., 2005).

One difficulty in understanding this literature is that religiousness and spirituality are related to other factors, which may themselves cause changes in health. These factors include smoking, substance use, social support, and education (Koenig & Vaillant, 2009). There is, however, some evidence that R/S itself, rather than its covariates, influences subsequent health (cf. Hill & Pargament, 2003; Lee & Newberg, 2010; Oman et al., 2002). For example, in a sample of people recently diagnosed as HIV+, those who increased their self-ratings of religiousness and spirituality had greater preservation of CD4 cells over a 4-year period and better control of viral load, results that held after controlling for a host of covariates (Ironson, Stuetzle, & Fletcher, 2006).

In addition, R/S may facilitate adherence to treatment regimens (Park, 2007), which can substantially improve physical health (DiMatteo & Haskard, 2006), but little research has tested this proposition. One recent study of congestive heart failure (CHF) patients found differential effects for different dimensions of religion and spirituality on different aspects of adherence (Park, Moehl, Fenster, Suresh, & Bliss, 2008). In particular, religious commitment predicted adherence to CHF-specific behaviors (e.g., fluid/weight monitoring) and advice regarding alcohol and tobacco use. Religious social support also predicted self-reported adherence to advice regarding substance use. No religious or spiritual variables were related to adherence to diet, and neither positive nor negative religious coping was related to adherence to treatment.

On the other hand, some aspects of R/S are related to worse health outcomes. For example, an extrinsic religious orientation (i.e., one in which religion is considered a means to other ends) has, in several studies of older adults, been found to relate to exaggerated cardiac reactivity (Masters, Hill, Kircher, Benson, & Fallon, 2004; Masters, Lensegrav-Benson, Kircher, & Hill, 2005), which is related to poorer cardiovascular health.

Health Affects Religiousness/Spirituality

Health crises have been documented to lead to both positive and negative shifts in religious and spiritual dimensions. For example, in a study of medical rehabilitation patients, 37% reported that they became significantly more spiritual during their rehabilitation (Kim, Heinemann, Bode, Sliwa, & King, 2000).

A large body of literature has documented reports of posttraumatic growth in those with physical health problems (Park et al., 2008), ranging from heart disease (Sheikh, 2004) to tinnitus (Davis & Morgan, 2008) and Meniere's disease (Dibb, 2009). Increased spirituality and a closer relationship with God are among the most commonly reported positive changes (e.g., Cole, Hopkins, Tisak, Steel, & Carr, 2008). The majority of the research on posttraumatic growth has been conducted with cancer survivors (Park, 2008); it should be noted that while self-reports of increased spirituality are common, cancer survivors typically do not appear to differ in their spirituality on objective measures from control participants when appropriate covariates are included in analyses (e.g., Andrykowski et al., 2005; Costanzo, Ryff, & Singer, 2009; cf. Helgeson & Tomich, 2005).

On the other hand, not everyone reports an increased sense of meaning or closeness to God when experiencing a health crisis (Cole et al., 2008). In times of sickness, people may withdraw from God and their religious and spiritual beliefs (Kremer, Ironson, & Kaplan, 2009). For example, in the aforementioned study of medical rehabilitation patients, 32% reported that they became significantly *less* spiritual (Kim et al., 2000). Finally, some people may withdraw from their religious and spiritual activities because their poor health interferes with their ability to engage in them (Idler & Kasl, 1997; Lee & Newberg, 2005).

The opposite may be true for those in good health, in that those who are feeling healthy and able-bodied may become more engaged in the everyday details of life and their focus may drift away from existential concerns. On the other hand, as Koenig and Vaillant (2009) speculated, being able-bodied

and healthy may allow people to attend services and other religious or spiritual programming such as congregational life and volunteer work. However, we were unable to locate research examining how healthiness or lack of disability directly related to aspects of R/S other than service attendance (Idler & Kasl, 1997).

A Model of Religiousness/Spirituality–Health Relationships

To better understand the complex relationships between physical health and dimensions of R/S, we developed a model, shown in Figure 24.1, which highlights the reciprocal nature of these influences and specifically focuses on the mediational role of emotions in the R/S-health links.

Although R/S and health are clearly associated, the direction of this influence is less clear. Research has mostly been conducted using cross-sectional designs, and even longitudinal studies have rarely adequately tested alternative directions of influence. Our model is based on the presumption that both directions of influence are not only plausible but likely (e.g., Park, Edmondson, & Mills, 2010). That is, aspects of R/S influence physical health and well-being, and physical health and well-being influence aspects of R/S. Moreover, given that these influences likely recur over a lifetime, a recursive or circular model seems to best represent these influences, as we illustrate in Figure 24.1.

In addition, our model examines a mediational pathway that likely operates in both directions. Many theories have been advanced to explain *how* religion and spirituality may exert salutary influences on well-being (cf. Lee & Newberg, 2005, 2010; Levin & Vanderpool, 1989; Oman & Thoresen, 2005; Park, 2007). For example, people attending

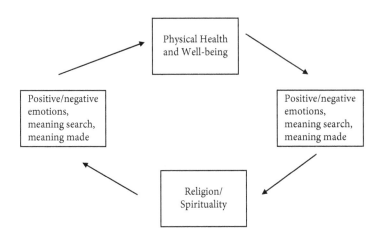

Figure 24.1 Reciprocal model of hypothesized relationships among religiousness/spirituality, health, and emotion.

religious services were more likely to receive social support and to engage in positive health-related behaviors like exercise and less likely to engage in health-averse behaviors like smoking, alcohol abuse, and risky sexual behavior (Strawbridge et al., 2001). The stories told by religious traditions and the modeling of R/S leaders may also influence health behaviors in either positive or negative ways (Oman & Thoresen, 2005, 2007; Thoresen, Oman, & Harris, 2005).

Among the many pathways linking R/S and health is emotion (Park, 2007), which appears to mediate both directions of the reciprocal model (i.e., R/S to health and health to R/S). Copious research has demonstrated that emotions and affect are related to health, in part by influencing the immune (Bower, Moskowitz, & Epel, 2009; Pressman & Cohen, 2005; Seeman, Dubin, & Seeman, 2003), cardiovascular (Masters, in press; Seeman et al., 2003), and endocrine systems (Denson, Spanovic, & Miller, 2009; Seeman et al., 2003) but also by influencing coping and health behaviors (Aldwin, 2007). A large but fairly separate body of literature has linked R/S and emotions (e.g., Koenig & Vaillant, 2009; Oman & Thoresen, 2005). In this chapter, we focus on emotions as mediators of the reciprocal R/S–health relationships. It is important to note that our model is not intended to minimize the influence of mediators other than emotion on R/S–health relationships but rather focuses, for purposes of explication, on this particular piece of the puzzle.

Emotion as the Mediator of the Influences of Religiousness/Spirituality on Health

Clearly, different dimensions of R/S can have different influences on emotions, which would be expected to have a variety of effects on health. For example, R/S may promote positive emotions through religious practices such as prayer and meditation; through religious beliefs, many of which provide comfort and salutary interpretations that help to buffer potentially stressful life events; and through particular spiritual-related states such as gratitude, forgiveness, or compassion, which have been shown to be related to better physical health. In addition, there are ways by which R/S can also lead to negative emotions, which can have deleterious effects on health. These positive and negative influences are detailed next.

Religious beliefs can be comforting in the face of major illnesses and can also provide avenues for coping that may lead to better physical as well as emotional outcomes (Pargament, 1997). Most religions provide ways to understand, reinterpret, and even redeem suffering as well as ways to find the work of a loving or purposeful God within it (Park, 2005), and individuals commonly turn to religion in their coping efforts (e.g., Koenig, George, & Siegler, 1998; Thuné-Boyle, Stygall, Keshtgar, & Newman, 2006). Research has documented that positive religious coping has positive effects on psychological as well as physical health, plausibly mediated through decreased positive emotions (e.g., Pargament, Koenig, & Perez, 2000; Yanez et al., 2009). For example, in a study of survivors of a variety of cancers, daily spiritual experiences, mediated through a type of positive emotion, self-assurance, was related to better health behavior and adherence (Park, Edmondson, Hale-Smith, & Blank, 2009). Religious and spiritual coping predicted mental health status, but not physical health status, for a sample of patients who had had a stroke (Johnstone, Franklin, Yoon, Burris, & Shigaki, 2008). However, in longitudinal research, Yanez and her colleagues (2009) reported that early breast cancer survivors who had found higher levels of meaning and peace, but had lower levels of faith, experienced relatively greater declines in depression and increases in self-reported vitality.

Furthermore, many religious traditions promote forgiveness (McCullough & Worthington, 1999) and gratitude (McCullough, Kilpatrick, Emmons, & Larson, 2001), states that are related to better health (Park, 2007). Regarding forgiveness, a national probability sample found it to be related to better self-reported mental and physical health, especially for middle-aged and older adults (Toussaint, Williams, Musick, & Everson, 2001). In a college student sample, participants who had greater trait levels of forgiveness had lower blood pressure levels and recovered from stress more rapidly (Lawler et al., 2003). Furthermore, participants who had forgiven a person who had "deeply hurt" them had lower blood pressure levels, heart rates, and rate pressure product.

The effects of gratitude on physical health are less clear, although suggestive of a positive relationship between gratitude and positive health. A study focused explicitly on a sense of gratitude toward God in a national sample of older adults found that feeling more grateful to God buffered the chronic stresses of aging, effects that were stronger for women than for men (Krause, 2006). Another study induced gratitude in both a college student sample and a sample of individuals with neuromuscular diseases; it found increased positive affect and subjective well-being but mixed physical effects, including increased exercise among college students, and improved sleep and sleep quality for the group with neuromuscular diseases (Emmons & McCullough, 2003). Emmons and McCullough's research was limited, though, in that it was a relatively brief intervention—2 or 3 weeks depending on the study—and unlikely, as a result, to shift health symptoms and complaints, which are probably more stable qualities.

In addition to forgiveness and gratitude, religions often promote other positive states such as compassion, optimism, and hope (Krause, 2002; Steffen & Masters, 2005). While researchers have proposed that these qualities may lead to positive affect and thus to higher levels of positive physical as well as psychological well-being, to date little evidence exists tracing the physical health effects of religion or spirituality to or through these positive psychological qualities and concomitant positive emotions (Park, 2007).

Some aspects of religion and spirituality have detrimental influences on health and well-being, much of which involves negative emotions associated with spiritual strain or religious struggle, including anger, guilt, or doubts about the existence of God (Exline, 2002). For example, in a random sample of nearly 2,000 Americans, having doubts about one's religious faith was related to poorer mental health, including depression, anxiety, hostility, and somatization (Galek, Krause, Ellison, Kudler, & Flannelly, 2007). One widely cited prospective study found that, for a sample of inpatients with a variety of problems, the use of negative religious coping in the hospital (in particular, interpersonal religious discontent and appraisals of the illness as a punishment from God) was associated with subsequent declines in health and increased mortality rates of 19%–28% at the 2-year follow-up, even controlling for relevant demographic and baseline characteristics (Pargament, Koenig, Tarakeshwar, & Hahn, 2001). Similarly, among a sample of lung transplant candidates, people perceiving their illness as a punishment from God were more depressed and anxious, and had higher levels of disability (Burker, Evon, Sedway, & Egan, 2005). Religious coping uniquely predicted measures of distress and disability over and above nonreligious measures of coping. Among a sample of general rehabilitation patients, negative religious coping and anger at God were risk factors for recovery and significantly related to lower levels of activities of daily living when assessed 1 month later (Fitchett, Rybarczyk, DeMarco, & Nicholas,

1999). Similarly, negative spiritual experiences (as well as positive ones) were associated with general health perception in another sample of rehabilitation patients (Johnstone & Yoon, 2009). In the aforementioned study of survivors of a variety of cancers, spiritual struggle, mediated through guilt, was related to poorer health behaviors and adherence (Park et al., 2009). Another study of men (55 or older) who were rehabilitating from elective heart surgery found that those who reported experiencing comfort from their religion were much more likely to survive 6 months following surgery than those reporting no comfort (Oxman, Freeman, & Manheimer, 1995).

Emotion Mediates the Impact of Health on Religiousness/Spirituality

The bulk of the literature on the role of emotions mediating the impact of physical health on subsequent R/S regards negative health states and physical disability. As noted earlier, studies of medical patients dealing with various health issues have shown that a significant number become less religious and spiritual following their diagnosis, although a significant number also become more religious and spiritual during the same period (Chen & Koenig, 2006; Kim et al., 2000). It is plausible that these changes depend on changes in emotion, but to date the literature is merely suggestive. Extensive research has demonstrated that reports of posttraumatic growth (including a spiritual component) following serious illness, cited earlier, are common (Park, 2008). This growth is often associated with higher levels of positive affect and lower levels of negative affect (Bower et al., 2009). For example, in a study of cancer survivors that specifically focused on changes in spirituality, perceptions of spiritual growth were related to higher levels of positive affect while perceptions of spiritual decline were related to higher levels of negative affect (Cole et al., 2008). However, the direction of any causal influences has not been clearly demonstrated in the research.

As noted earlier, there is little research documenting that positive health states and able-bodiedness influence R/S. There is even less literature regarding the potential for emotion to mediate this influence. It is plausible that individuals who are healthy feel gratitude and happiness, which may lead them to a deeper level of spirituality; such links await scholarly examination, but it may be a fruitful direction based on recent work in positive emotions. For example, in an experimental analog study in which participants were shown films, Saroglou, Buxant, and Tilquin (2008) demonstrated that inducing intense positive emotions, such as wonder and awe, led to increased religious beliefs. Positive emotions following from one's own heightened sense of vigor and health might function similarly.

Conclusions

Although connections between religiousness and spirituality and physical health are well established, the direction of these relationships and the pathways of influence remain only partly understood. It appears that R/S and physical health influence one another in multiple and reciprocal ways. We propose a model in which positive and negative emotions are mediators of both directions of effect. In reviewing the literature regarding this model, evidence regarding some of these links is fairly strong (e.g., between spiritual struggle and subsequent health decrements), while for others, the links remain merely speculative (e.g., between healthfulness and subsequent R/S). However, the model we have developed in this chapter is quite promising as a framework for future theory and research to develop a solid understanding of these relationships.

Future Directions

Given that much remains to be learned about links between R/S and physical health, and the potential roles of emotions in these linkages, we propose several particularly promising directions for future research.

Recursive Relationships

Our model supposes that R/S and health influence each other, such that R/S can lead to changes in health status, and health status can lead to changes in R/S. We view this recursive relationship as taking place across time, such that, in the course of a lifetime, many such transactions may take place. Descriptive studies of retrospective recollections of these influences could be quite useful for generating hypotheses; even more useful, albeit much more difficult, would be longitudinal research to track these interchanges between health status and R/S across time. As most research on R/S and health is correlational in nature, longitudinal research could help establish causality and the nature of the causal relationship (Lee & Newberg, 2010).

The Influences of Positive Health on Religiousness and Spirituality

Our search of the literature found much to suggest that R/S can be a resource for promoting positive health, and that negative health states can spur changes in R/S. However, we found no literature examining the question of how positive physical health states (e.g., vitality, strength, healthfulness) related to subsequent R/S dimensions. Given the prominence of positive psychology in recent years (Snyder & Lopez, 2002), the question of how positive health states might influence an individual (including his or her religious or spiritual life) seems an obvious one to ask. Research remains to be conducted.

Emotions as Mediators of Religiousness/ Spirituality-Health Linkages

Many potential mediators of the relations between R/S and physical health have been proposed (Park, 2007). Our model homes in on only one of these: emotion. Emotional states have been related to health outcomes in a variety of illnesses (e.g., Danner, Snowdon, & Friesen, 2001; Folkman & Moskowitz, 2000; Moskowitz, Epel, & Acree, 2008), as well as to mortality (Xu & Roberts, 2010). Furthermore, positive and negative emotions have been shown to be two distinct constructs, each uniquely related to health outcomes (Folkman & Moskowitz, 2000; Xu & Roberts, 2010). We propose that positive and negative emotions may prove to be a key mediator of the mutual influences of R/S and health. However, our review suggests that these linkages are still largely conjectural. That is, the positive health outcomes of forgiveness, for example, may be primarily due to cognitive or behavioral changes, rather than the associated affective changes per se. Future research could profitably address how positive and negative health states may lead to R/S changes though various positive and negative emotions, and how R/S influences the experiencing of positive and negative emotions, which may lead to changes in physical well-being.

Given that positive and negative emotions have been shown to be two distinct constructs (Folkman & Moskowitz, 2000), researchers must be careful to assess a variety of both positive and negative states in examining emotion's ability to mediate between R/S and health outcomes. Furthermore, researchers must determine whether religiousness and spirituality provide a unique contribution to predicting health outcomes, over and above their ability to elicit positive or negative affect.

Individual Differences

Findings regarding the relationships between R/S and health are intriguing, yet readers must keep in mind that these findings comprise averages of groups of individuals, and that within these groups, large individual differences exist. For example, in Kremer et al.'s (2009) study of HIV+ participants, many identified their HIV diagnosis as a positive turning point leading to increased spirituality; however, others found their diagnosis to have led to decreased spirituality. Some Arab women living in Israel reported religious and cultural values encouraging breast and cervical cancer screenings (e.g., body sanctification), while others described beliefs interfering with those screenings (e.g., fatalism and believing that one's life and death are in God's hands) (Azaiza & Cohen, 2008). Similar differences have been noted by other researchers (e.g., Cole et al., 2008). Ultimately, research needs to understand more about the roles of religiousness and spirituality, especially what causes some people to perceive negative health states as positive turning points, leading to greater religiousness and spirituality, while others perceive these changes more negatively, becoming more alienated from their faith.

Difficulties in Measuring Religiousness and Spirituality

Finally, most research on the relationship between religiousness and spirituality and health has been conducted using self-report measures. There are a variety of problems with these sorts of measures, including participants who make inaccurate observations and reports of religious behaviors (e.g., Marler & Hadaway, 1999; Nisbett & Wilson, 1977), respond according to social desirability biases (Marler & Hadaway, 1999), cannot read materials (Hill & Pargament, 2003), or are not engaged by the research and assessment process (Hill & Pargament, 2003). Alternative assessments of beliefs, attitudes, and behavior (e.g., children's drawings of God, narrative responses about coping with illness, observations of religious behavior) may further elucidate the relationships between R/S and health (Hill & Pargament, 2003; Lee & Newberg, 2010).

References

Aldwin, C. M. (2007). *Stress, coping, and development: An integrative approach* (2nd ed.). New York: The Guilford Press.

Andrykowski, M. A., Bishop, M. M., Hahn, E. A., Cella, D. F., Beaumont, J. L., Brady, M. J.,... Wingard, J. R. (2005). Long-term health-related quality of life, growth, and spiritual well-being after hematopoietic stem-cell transplantation. *Journal of Clinical Oncology, 23,* 599–608.

Azaiza, F., & Cohen, M. (2008). Between traditional and modern perceptions of breast and cervical cancer screenings: A qualitative study of Arab women in Israel. *Psycho-Oncology, 17,* 34–41.

Bower, J. E., Moskowitz, J. T., & Epel, E. (2009). Is benefit finding good for your health? Pathways linking positive life changes after stress and physical health outcomes. *Current Directions in Psychological Science, 18,* 337–341.

Burker, E. J., Evon, D. M., Sedway, J. A., & Egan, T. (2005). Religious and non-religious coping in lung transplant candidates: Does adding God to the picture tell us more? *Journal of Behavioral Medicine, 28,* 513–526.

Chen, Y. Y., & Koenig, H. G. (2006). Do people turn to religion in times of stress?: An examination of change in religiousness among elderly, medically ill patients. *Journal of Nervous and Mental Disease, 194,* 114–120.

Cole, B. S., Hopkins, C. M., Tisak, J., Steel, J. L., & Carr, B. I. (2008). Assessing spiritual growth and spiritual decline following a diagnosis of cancer: Reliability and validity of the spiritual transformation scale. *Psycho-Oncology, 17,* 112–121.

Costanzo, E. S., Ryff, C. D., & Singer, B. H. (2009). Psychosocial adjustment among cancer survivors: Findings from a national survey of health and well-being. *Health Psychology, 28,* 147–156.

Danner, D. D., Snowdon, D. A., & Friesen, W. V. (2001). Positive emotions in early life and longevity: Findings from the nun study. *Journal of Personality and Social Psychology, 80,* 804–813.

Davis, C. G., & Morgan, M. S. (2008). Finding meaning, perceiving growth, and acceptance of tinnitus. *Rehabilitation Psychology, 53,* 128–138.

Denson, T. F., Spanovic, M., & Miller, N. (2009). Cognitive appraisals and emotions predict cortisol and immune responses: A meta-analysis of acute laboratory social stressors and emotion inductions. *Psychological Bulletin, 135,* 823–853.

Dibb, B. (2009). Positive change with Ménière's disease. *British Journal of Health Psychology, 14,* 613–624.

DiMatteo, M. R., & Haskard, K. (2006). Further challenges in adherence research: Measurements, methodologies, and mental health care. *Medical Care, 44,* 297–299.

Emmons, R. A., & McCullough, M. E. (2003). Counting blessings versus burdens: An experimental investigation of gratitude and subjective well-being in daily life. *Journal of Personality and Social Psychology, 84,* 377–389.

Exline, J. J. (2002). Stumbling blocks on the religious road: Fractured relationships, nagging vices, and the inner struggle to believe. *Psychological Inquiry, 13,* 182–189.

Fitchett, G., Rybarczyk, B. D., DeMarco, G. A., & Nicholas, J. J. (1999). The role of religion in medical rehabilitation outcomes: A longitudinal study. *Rehabilitation Psychology, 44,* 333–353.

Folkman, S., & Moskowitz, J. T. (2000). Positive affect and the other side of coping. *American Psychologist, 55,* 647–654.

Galek, K., Krause, N., Ellison, C. G., Kudler, T., & Flannelly, K. J. (2007). Religious doubt and mental health across the lifespan. *Journal of Adult Development, 14,* 16–25.

George, L. K., Ellison, C. G., & Larson, D. B. (2002). Explaining the relationships between religious involvement and health. *Psychological Inquiry, 13,* 190–200.

Helgeson, V. S., & Tomich, P. L. (2005). Surviving cancer: A comparison of 5-year disease-free breast cancer survivors with healthy women. *Psycho-Oncology, 14,* 307–317.

Hess, R. F., & McKinney, D. (2007). Fatalism and HIV/AIDS beliefs in rural Mali, West Africa. *Journal of Nursing Scholarship, 39,* 113–118.

Hill, P. C., & Pargament, K. I. (2003). Advances in the conceptualization and measurement of religion and spirituality: Implications for physical and mental health research. *American Psychologist, 58,* 64–74.

Idler, E. I., & Kasl, S. V. (1997). Religion among disabled and nondisabled persons I: Cross-sectional patterns in health practices, social activities, and well-being. *The Journals of Gerontology Series B: Psychological Sciences and Social Sciences, 52B,* S294–S305.

Ironson, G., Stuetzle, R., & Fletcher, M. A. (2006). An increase in religiousness/spirituality occurs after HIV diagnosis and predicts slower disease progression over 4 years in people with HIV. *Journal of General Internal Medicine, 21*(Suppl 5), S62–S68.

Johnstone, B., Franklin, K. L., Yoon, D. P., Burris, J., & Shigaki, C. (2008). Relationships among religiousness, spirituality, and health for individuals with stroke. *Journal of Clinical Psychology in Medical Settings, 15,* 308–331.

Johnstone, B., & Yoon, D. P. (2009). Relationships between the Brief Multidimensional Measure of Religiousness/Spirituality and health outcomes for a heterogeneous rehabilitation population. *Rehabilitation Psychology, 54,* 422–431.

Kim, J., Heinemann, A. W., Bode, R. K., Sliwa, J., & King, R. B. (2000). Spirituality, quality of life, and functional recovery after medical rehabilitation. *Rehabilitation Psychology, 45,* 365–385.

Koenig, H. G., George, L. K., & Siegler, I. C. (1998). The use of religion and other emotion-regulating coping strategies among older adults. *The Gerontologist, 28,* 303–310.

Koenig, H. G., & Hays, J. C. (1999). Does religious attendance prolong survival? A six-year follow-up study of 3,968 older adults. *Journals of Gerontology Series A: Biological Sciences and Medical Sciences, 54A,* M370–M376.

Koenig, L. B., & Vaillant, G. E. (2009). A prospective study of church attendance and health over the lifespan. *Health Psychology, 28,* 117–124.

Krause, N. (2002). Church-based social support and health in old age: Exploring variations by race. *Journals of Gerontology Series B: Psychological Sciences and Social Sciences;57B,* S332–S347.

Krause, N. (2006). Gratitude toward God, stress, and health in late life. *Research on Aging, 28,* 163–183.

Kremer, H., Ironson, G., & Kaplan, L. (2009). The fork in the road: HIV as a potential positive turning point and the role of spirituality. *AIDS Care, 21,* 368–377.

Lawler, K. A., Younger, J. W., Piferi, R. L., Billington, E., Jobe, R., Edmondson, K., & Jones, W. H. (2003). A change of heart: Cardiovascular correlates of forgiveness in response to interpersonal conflict. *Journal of Behavioral Medicine, 26,* 373–393.

Lee, B. Y., & Newberg, A. B. (2005). Religion and health: A review and critical analysis. *Zygon, 40,* 443–468.

Lee, B. Y., & Newberg, A. B. (2010). The interaction of religion and health. In D. A. Monti & B. D. Beitman (Eds.), *Integrative psychiatry* (pp. 408–444). New York: Oxford University Press.

Levin, J. S., & Vanderpool, H. Y. (1989). Is religion therapeutically significant for hypertension? *Social Science and Medicine, 29,* 69–78.

Mahoney, A., Carels, R. A., Pargament, K. I., Wachholtz, A., Leeper, L. E., Kaplar, M., & Frutchey, R. (2005). The sanctification of the body and behavioral health patterns of college students. *International Journal for the Psychology of Religion, 15,* 221–238.

Marler, P. L., & Hadaway, C. K. (1999). Testing the attendance gap in a conservative church. *Sociology of Religion, 6,* 175–186.

Masters, K. S. (in press). Religion, spirituality and cardiovascular disease. In S. Waldstein, W. Kop, & L. Katzel, & (Eds.), *Cardiovascular behavioral medicine.* New York: Springer.

Masters, K. S., Hill, R. D., Kircher, J. C., Benson, T. L. L., & Fallon, J. A. (2004). Religious orientation, aging, and blood pressure reactivity to interpersonal and cognitive stressors. *Annals of Behavioral Medicine, 28,* 171–178.

Masters, K. S., Lensegrav-Benson, T. L., Kircher, J. C., & Hill, R. D. (2005). Effects of religious orientation and gender on cardiovascular reactivity among older adults. *Research on Aging, 27,* 221–240.

McCullough, M. E., Hoyt, W. T., Larson, D. B., Koenig, H. G., & Thoresen, C. (2000). Religious involvement and mortality: A meta-analytic review. *Health Psychology, 19,* 211–222.

McCullough, M. E., Kilpatrick, S., Emmons, R. A., & Larson, D. (2001). Is gratitude a moral affect? *Psychological Bulletin, 127,* 249–266.

McCullough, M. E., & Worthington, E. L. (1999). Religion and the forgiving personality. *Journal of Personality, 679,* 1141–1164.

Miller, W. R., & Thoresen, C. E. (2003). Spirituality, religion, and health: An emerging research field. *American Psychologist, 58,* 24–35.

Moskowitz, J. T., Epel, E. S., & Acree, M. (2008). Positive affect uniquely predicts lower risk of mortality in people with diabetes. *Health Psychology, 27,* S73–S82.

Nisbett, R. E., & Wilson, T. D. (1977). Telling more than we can know: Verbal reports on mental processes. *Psychological Review, 84,* 231–259.

Oman, D., Kurata, J. H., Strawbridge, W. J., & Cohen, R. D. (2002). Religious attendance and cause of death over 31 years. *International Journal for Psychiatry in Medicine, 32,* 69–89.

Oman, D., & Thoresen, C. E. (2005). Do religion and spirituality influence health? In R. F. Paloutzian & C. L. Park (Eds.), *Handbook of the psychology of religion and spirituality* (pp. 435–459). New York: The Guilford Press.

Oman, D., & Thoresen, C. E. (2007). How does one learn to be spiritual? The neglected role of spiritual modeling in health. In T. G. Plante & C. E. Thoresen (Eds.), *Spirit, science, and health: How the spiritual mind fuels physical wellness* (pp. 39–54). Westport, CT: Praeger.

Oxman, T. E., Freeman, D. H., Jr., & Manheimer, E. D. (1995). Lack of social participation or religious strength and comfort as risk factors for death after cardiac surgery in the elderly. *Psychosomatic Medicine, 57,* 5–15.

Pargament, K. I. (1997). *The psychology of religion and coping.* New York: The Guilford Press.

Pargament, K. I., Koenig, H. G., & Perez, L. M. (2000). The many methods of religious coping: Development and initial validation of the RCOPE. *Journal of Clinical Psychology, 56,* 519–543.

Pargament, K. I., Koenig, H. G., Tarakeshwar, N., & Hahn, J. (2001). Religious struggle as a predictor of mortality among medically ill elderly patients: A 2-year longitudinal study. *Archives of Internal Medicine, 161,* 1881–1885.

Park, C. L. (2005). Religion and meaning. In R. F. Paloutzian & C. L. Park (Eds.), *Handbook of the psychology of religion and spirituality* (pp. 295–314). New York: The Guilford Press.

Park, C. L. (2007). Religiousness/spirituality and health: A meaning systems perspective. *Journal of Behavioral Medicine, 30*, 319–328.

Park, C. L. (2008). Overview of theoretical perspectives. In C. L. Park, S. Lechner, M. H. Antoni, & A. Stanton (Eds.), *Positive life change in the context of medical illness: Can the experience of serious illness lead to transformation?* (pp. 11–30). Washington, DC: American Psychological Association.

Park, C. L., Edmondson, D., Hale-Smith, A., & Blank, T. O. (2009). Religiousness/spirituality and health behaviors in younger adult cancer survivors: Does faith promote a healthier lifestyle? *Journal of Behavioral Medicine, 32*, 582–591.

Park, C. L., Edmondson, D., & Mills, M. A. (2010). Reciprocal influences of religiousness and global meaning in the stress process. In T. Miller (Ed.). *Coping with life transitions* (pp. 485–501). New York: Springer.

Park, C. L., Moehl, B., Fenster, J. R., Suresh, D. P., & Bliss, D. (2008). Religiousness and treatment adherence in congestive heart failure patients. *Journal of Religion, Spirituality and Aging, 20*, 249–266.

Powell, L. H., Shahabi, L., & Thoresen, C. E. (2003). Religion and spirituality: Linkages to physical health. *American Psychologist, 58*, 36–52.

Pressman, S. D., & Cohen, S. (2005). Does positive affect influence health? *Psychological Bulletin, 131*, 925–971.

Saroglou, V., Buxant, C., & Tilquin, J. (2008). Positive emotions as leading to religion and spirituality. *Journal of Positive Psychology, 3*, 165–173.

Seeman, T. E., Dubin, L. F., & Seeman, M. (2003). Religiosity/spirituality and health: A critical review of the evidence for biological pathways. *American Psychologist, 58*, 53–63.

Sheikh, A. I. (2004). Posttraumatic growth in the context of heart disease. *Journal of Clinical Psychology in Medical Settings, 11*, 265–273.

Snyder, C. R., & Lopez, S. (Eds.). (2002). *Handbook of positive psychology*. New York: Oxford University Press.

Steffen, P. R., & Masters, K. S. (2005). Does compassion mediate the intrinsic religion-health relationship? *Annals of Behavioral Medicine, 30*, 217–224.

Strawbridge, W. J., Shema, S. J., Cohen, R. D., & Kaplan, G. A. (2001). Religious attendance increases survival by improving and maintaining good health practices, mental health, and stable marriages. *Annals of Behavioral Medicine, 23*, 68–74.

Thoresen, C. E., Oman, D., & Harris, A. H. S. (2005). The effects of religious practices: A focus on health. In. W. R. Miller & H. D. Delaney (Eds.). *Judeo-Christian perspectives on psychology: Human nature, motivation, and change* (pp. 205–226). Washington, DC: American Psychological Association.

Thuné-Boyle, I. C., Stygall, J. A., Keshtgar, M. R., & Newman, S. P. (2006). Do religious/spiritual coping strategies affect illness adjustment in patients with cancer? A systematic review of the literature. *Social Science and Medicine, 63*, 151–164.

Toussaint, L. L., Williams, D. R., Musick, M. A., & Everson, S. A. (2001). Forgiveness and health: Age differences in a U.S. probability sample. *Journal of Adult Development, 8*, 249–257.

Xu, J., & Roberts, R. E. (2010). The power of positive emotions: It's a matter of life or death—Subjective well-being and longevity over 27 years in a general population. *Health Psychology, 29*, 9–19.

Yanez, B., Edmondson, D., Stanton, A. L., Park, C. L., Kwan, L., Ganz, P. A., & Blank, T. O. (2009). Facets of spirituality as predictors of adjustment to cancer: Relative contributions of having faith and finding meaning. *Journal of Consulting and Clinical Psychology, 77*, 730–741.

Spirituality, Religion, and Psychological Counseling

Thomas G. Plante *and* Carl E. Thoresen

Abstract

A substantial majority of people believe in God in some form and consider themselves to be spiritual, religious, or both. However, most psychologists and other mental health professionals perceive themselves as not religious and have little if any training in spirituality and religious diversity. Psychologists can use spiritual principles and practices to better serve clients, even if they do not share the same or any religious or spiritual perspective. We review and illustrate the emerging relationship between psychology, spirituality, and religion and its current status. Benefits of religious/ spiritual engagement for physical, social, and mental health are outlined. We also comment on religious hazards to health. Spiritual tools commonly found in major religious traditions are discussed and suggested for use by counseling psychologists and others under certain conditions. A brief spiritual inquiry method is presented. Results of a spiritually focused intervention using spiritual practices serve as an example. Ethical and research issues are also discussed, along with important questions to consider.

Key Words: spirituality, religion, faith, health, counseling, psychotherapy, professional issues

Introduction

> We are not human beings trying to be spiritual.
> Rather we are spiritual beings trying to be human.
> —Jacquelyn Small

> Where is the wisdom we have lost in knowledge?
> Where is the knowledge we have lost in information?
> —T. S. Eliot

What accounts for the growing interest in health-related disciplines and professions, such as psychology and medicine, in religion and spirituality, especially its relationship to health, disease, and well-being? In this decade, many professional books have appeared (e.g., Koenig, McCullough & Larson, 2001; Paloutzian & Park, 2005; Plante & Thoresen, 2007). Literally hundreds of mostly empirical articles have appeared (e.g., McCullough, Hoyt, Larson, Koenig, & Thoresen, 2000; Miller

& Thoresen, 2003) and scores of conferences and workshops have been conducted for health care professionals. The topic has been featured since 2000 in almost all popular news magazine and television news programs (e.g., third appearance as cover of *Time*, February 2009). In part, the growing interest has come from a public fascinated with spirituality and its connection with health (e.g., Oprah introduced "Spirituality 101" in 2008 as a regular feature of her popular television program).

The popular interest also comes from a society seeking a greater sense of meaning, purpose, and significance in life, especially recently in the wake of the economic recession that started in 2008. What really matters in life? What is sacred? Help with these questions is not readily found in today's time-pressured society where there is less involvement in social and community groups and organizations, less involvement in developing and maintaining close personal and intimate relationships, and diminishing participation in religious organizations that provide a majority of society's social and moral capital (Putnam, 2000).

Current intrigue with spirituality and religion is found not only among the general population and some health care professionals but also among the psychological and counseling community. Although indifferent and antagonistic toward religion and spirituality for decades, psychology, among other disciplines, seems to be rediscovering its religious and spiritual roots with renewed interest (Oman & Thoresen, 2002). This renaissance seems most apparent in the professional services side of psychology (Miller & Thoresen, 2003).

In this chapter we discuss the growing relationship between psychology and religion and spirituality, especially as it pertains to psychological practice, such as counseling. We discuss empirical research of the mental and physical health benefits of spiritual and religious involvement. We also note some of its hazards to health. Also mentioned are spiritual and religious principles and tools that counselors can use ethically with sensitivity in their professional work, regardless of their personal beliefs or religious affiliation. We also mention ethical mandates and issues as well as some empirical problems deserving consideration.

In the spirit of full disclosure, we as authors perceive ourselves as spiritually and religiously active persons. We are committed to fostering a greater overall understanding of the role of spirituality and religion in psychology as a scientific discipline and as a health-related helping profession. As empirical scholars and health professionals, we use a variety of quantitative and qualitative research methods in addition to our teaching, supervising, and consulting roles.

Definitions, Ethics, and Diversity Issues

Before continuing, we need to address three important issues. They concern defining key terms, ethical precautions, and diversity issues.

Defining Religion, Spirituality, and the Sacred

People are often confused about the definition of the words "religion" and "spirituality." Such confusion is understandable since these terms are multidimensional (e.g., social, emotional, cognitive) and multilevel concepts (e.g., processes within the person, within local organizations, within regions, within nation-states, and within the world at large). For example, the term "religion" can be used on a societal level as a social institution with organizational structures. It can also be defined on a group level as a faith community or on an individual level as involved with the search for significance in life in ways related to what is perceived as sacred (Pargament, 2007). Emmons and Paloutzian (2003), in reviewing theory and research over the past 25 years, observed that the past decade in particular has seen major changes in how religion and spirituality are conceptualized. Mention is made of changing religious landscapes in the broader culture, especially with a "new breed of spirituality that is often distinct from traditional conceptions of religion" (p. 381). Zinnbauer and Pargament (2005) offer the many pros and cons of viewing spirituality as a part of religion or viewing religion as a part of spirituality.

One of the biggest changes has been the broadening perspective of how spirituality is conceived. Essentially the term is no longer exclusively tied directly or indirectly to religious institutions and traditions. Now it is also applied to situations and experiences that are independent of any formal ties with religion. One of the most significant recent developments concerning spirituality has been the emerging relationship of spirituality with positive emotions viewed from an evolutionary perspective (e.g., Vaillant, 2008). We discuss this development later in the chapter.

We view *religion* broadly as a social institution with organizational and community structures that offer ways for people to understand and honor the wisdom traditions, generally through scriptures or religious writings and through rituals viewed as sacred. Religious institutions generally offer an articulated doctrine or belief structure describing the specific values and beliefs of a traditional faith community. Stated somewhat differently, religion commonly provides answers to what have been called perennial questions about life and death (e.g., What really matters? Why do people suffer? What happens after I die?). Religion especially highlights one or more revered religious leaders or spiritual models to emulate, such as Jesus, Buddha, or Mohammed. For a comprehensive discussion of the seminal role of spiritual modeling and how spirituality is primarily "caught not taught," see Oman and Thoresen (2003), Bandura, (2003), and Oman and Thoresen (2005).

The world's major religious faith traditions include Christianity, Judaism, Buddhism, Hinduism, Islam,

Taoism, and Confucianism. Each tradition includes various branches, some highly similar and some quite differing from others in specific beliefs, values, and practices. For example, Christianity includes Roman Catholics, many Protestant denominations, such as Methodists and Baptists, and countless nondenominational churches not affiliated with an organized religion but based on their interpretation of the Bible and the teachings of Jesus. Within the Jewish tradition variations exists as well, such as Orthodox or Reform versions of Judaism. As noted earlier, a key role of a religion as an organized faith community is to help members and others better understand and relate to what is sacred through community and through rituals, traditions, beliefs, and practices. While some religions are quite centralized and highly structured (e.g., the Roman Catholic Church), others are much decentralized with little organizational structure (e.g., Buddhism).

We view *spirituality* primarily at the level of the individual's experiences in seeking what is perceived as sacred in life and associated in some way with the transcendent belief that a higher power or spirit exists that is greater than oneself. This connection might be to God however defined or understood, to religious models, such as Jesus or Buddha, or to the natural world in general. The word "spirituality" comes from the Latin word, *spiritus*, meaning that which is absolutely vital to life, such as the breath or life force (Hage, 2006). William James (1902/1936) defined spirituality in relational terms as "the feelings, acts and experiences of individual men in their solitude, as far as they apprehend themselves to stand in relation to whatever they may consider the divine" (p. 32). In many ways spirituality can be perceived as a blend of positive emotions mixed with prosocial behaviors, such as the joy of feeling connected to something greater than oneself or with "heartfelt" gratitude associated with feeling loved or loving another person (see Fredrickson, 2009, for an excellent overview of positive emotions).

Sacred we view as what is perceived as holy, divine, eternal, or meaningful. Pargament (2007) defines the sacred as "...concepts of God, the divine, and transcendent reality, as well as other aspects of life that take on divine character and significance by virtue of their association with or representation of divinity...at the heart of the sacred lies God, divine beings, or a transcendent reality" (pp. 32–33). In effect, a person can perceive many different things and experiences as sacred. Clarifying what a person deems as sacred can help

one better understand a major basis of motivation and focus in that person's life.

The phrase "spiritual but not religious" has recently become a popular way to describe some people's religious/spiritual identity. Estimates of those identifying themselves in the United States as spiritual but not religious range from 20% to 35% (Fuller, 2001; Hood, 2005). For example, in a recent study of 1,010 college students in four American universities (in the West, East, and South), 30% described themselves as "spiritual but not religious" while 41% saw themselves as "spiritual and religious" (Oman et al., 2009). Interestingly such data compare favorably to other major studies of spirituality and religion in young adults (Astin et al., 2005).

Keep in mind that the "spiritual but not religious" designation represents a fairly heterogeneous group. Some have rejected religious organizations for many reasons, such as their perceived rigid dogma, decrees, demands to be submissive, and requirements to accept unquestionably specific religious beliefs and traditions. For some, the connotation of being spiritual is currently perceived as quite positive while being religious is viewed as fairly negative. Fewer see spirituality as a "New Age" phenomenon that is unnecessary if not antireligious and thus very negative, with religion seen as quite positive (in 10%–15% range).

Pargament (2007) reports that psychologists and other contemporary mental health professionals often view spirituality among their clients as a good thing while religiousness is typically a bad thing. The extremely negative press associated with various religious scandals as well as religiously inspired terrorism and violence has contributed to the notion that organized religion is destructive, hypocritical, and outdated (e.g., Hitchens, 2007). Perhaps it is a typical American penchant to be very individualistic, such that they seek and select some elements of spirituality and religion that work for them and simply reject the rest (Fuller, 2001). Yet while some have rejected organized religion altogether, others have held fast onto their faith traditions and communities, even following remarkable religious scandals and embarrassments.

It is interesting to note the results of the first major national study of spirituality and religion of the so-called millennium generation, those born in the mid to late 1980s and now attending college (Astin et al., 2005). In this study of 112,232 college youth attending 236 American colleges and universities, a clear majority viewed themselves as both spiritual and religious. Of these students, four out of five believe in God, have attended at least one religious service in the past year, and frequently have discussed religion with friends and family. Almost one out of two believe that it is "essential" or "very important" to seek ways to grow spiritually, 69% pray regularly, and over 75% reported that they are searching for greater meaning and purpose in life. These students expressed a great deal of interest in spiritually related questions, such as "What am I going to do with my life?" "What kind of person do I want to be?" "How do I know I am doing the right thing?" Almost two out of three indicated that most people can grow spiritually without being religious.

Importantly, a great deal of diversity emerged among students in different faith traditions and from attending colleges in different regions of the United States. For example, students in Southeastern colleges and universities were less likely to be interested in spirituality (cf. religion) than students from other regions. Those who identified with more conservative denominations were less likely to be interested in social issues, such as gender and sexual orientation, and they were less interested in worldwide humanitarian issues (e.g., world hunger, poverty, discrimination). Clearly the topic of spirituality and religion holds substantial interest among current young adults.

Ethical and Diversity Issues

Several ethical concerns deserve comment. First, when it comes to matters of spirituality and religion, counselors need to work within their area of competence and must not overstep professional bounds. We as psychologists and other professionals are obligated to perform our duties consistent with our training and experience. That means following ethical guidelines of competence as well as legal requirements that license to practice demands. Second, professionals must carefully avoid potential dual relationships, especially when their clients are members of their own faith tradition and perhaps part of the same church community. Unforeseen dual relationships and conflicts can easily emerge. One must be very sensitive to potential exploitive dual relationships as well as the unforeseen consequences that can unfold when working with fellow congregants. Finally, professionals must be careful to avoid potential bias by not promoting one particular religious belief system over another, especially their own.

Professionals, as well as the general population, often may have certain positive or negative perceptions about particular religious or spiritual communities. As noted earlier, we need to be very attentive to the rich diversity of beliefs and practices, even within each particular religious or spiritual tradition. We must steer clear of religious stereotyping of others, a problem that is highly prevalent in many cultures. This is especially true for those psychologists who have had little or no contact with members of a particular religious group in either their professional or personal lives.

Literally all religious and spiritual communities, along with their beliefs, rituals, and practices, exist as a part of a particular culture or subculture. Spiritual and religious customs are commonly steeped in ethnic diversity. For example, Roman Catholics from Eastern Europe may engage in different religious traditions and practices relative to Catholics from Latin America. Jews from Israel may experience their faith and cultural tradition quite differently than those from parts of Eastern Europe or North America. Subtle and not-so-subtle cultural, ethnic, geographic, and political differences may be part of religious experience, customs, and traditions. In fact, many religious and spiritual beliefs and practices originated within a particular ethnic and cultural community before being adopted more broadly by a particular religious tradition. Two very simple examples: Christmas trees and Easter bunnies. The point here is that specific cultural influences are often intimately woven into religious and spiritual experience and expression (American Psychological Association, 2003).

Benefits of Religious and Spiritual Engagement

Mills (2002) reported that almost 1,700 empirical studies of religion and health had been published in professional and research-oriented journals by the year 2000. During the same time about 700 had been published on spirituality and health. We suspect that since the year 2000 well over 3,000 articles and reports have appeared, given the exponential rate of annual publications documented by Mills (2002).

The term "health" itself has been expanding to include not only "conditions of the body" but, more important, "states of mind" (Ryff & Singer, 1998; Thoresen & Eagleston, 1985). While most people still associate health with medicine, biology, and disease, many are expanding its meaning to include a person's overall life experiences. Examples include the hospice care movement, global environmental factors, and positive emotions. Some have suggested that while in the 20th century, psychology first lost its soul and then its mind, it is now beginning to recall them both in the 21st century. In doing so, psychology may be becoming more focused on human nature and the whole person in context, rather than only focused on a person's behaviors, cognitions, or personality (Miller & Delaney, 2005).

The vast majority of high-quality research supports a positive relationship between religious involvement and beneficial health outcomes (Koenig et al., 2001; Pargament, 1997; Plante & Sherman, 2001; Plante & Thoresen, 2007; Richards & Bergin, 2005). People engaged in participating regularly in a religious and spiritual tradition tend to be healthier, happier, maintain better habits, and experience more social support compared to those less active or not at all involved.

Mental Health Benefits of Spirituality and Religion

An extensive review of research involving literally hundreds of studies of mental health benefits of spirituality and religious involvement suggests that it is related to less anxiety, depression, chronic stress, and greater perceived well-being and self-esteem (Koenig et al., 2001; Plante & Sharma, 2001; Thoresen, 2007). They often tend to cope better with major and minor life stress. They are, for example, less likely to have alcohol and other substance abuse problems, eating disorders, be divorced, and less likely to attempt suicide, homicide, or engage in criminal behavior. Generally, they live a healthier overall lifestyle, with better social support, usually avoiding health-damaging behavior patterns. In general they have better mental health functioning, including mood and general affect control, than those not regularly involved religiously or spiritually.

Despite hundreds of studies, the evidence does not demonstrate or prove that religion or spirituality by itself *directly* causes better mental or physical health. Instead the evidence clearly implicates spiritual or religious practices over time in processes involved with better physical and mental health compared with non–religiously active people. Specific causes of this beneficial relationship, however, remain unclear (Thoresen, 2007). We strongly suspect that religion and spirituality serve as a positive factor in good health and well-being but not as the only factor. Rather, spiritual and religious factors appear to serve as one of many other *indirect* but significant factors in promoting good health and well-being (see Thoresen & Harris, 2002).

Physical Health and Longevity

To date, the physical health benefits associated with spirituality and religious involvement have been impressive (Powell, Shahabi, & Thoresen, 2003). Spiritual and religiously active people tend to live longer, are less likely to develop serious medical illnesses, and recover faster from illnesses than others. In fact, meta-analytic research based on long-term prospective studies involving tens of thousands of adults shows that religiously oriented people, in general, live on average 7 years longer than non–religiously minded people. This is the case even when statistically controlling for age; gender; socioeconomic status; family history of disease; health behaviors, such as smoking, drinking alcohol, and diet; and other known risk factors for risk of mortality, such as social support (McCullough et al., 2000; Oman & Thoresen, 2005; Powell et al., 2003). For example, Hummer, Rogers, Nam, and Ellison (1999) investigated over 21,000 adults in a national sample examining disease and mortality. They controlled for 15 likely factors that influence health outcome, such as those mentioned previously plus others. Compared to the highest religious attendance group (attending some kind of religious service more than once per week), the non–religious attendance group suffered 50% more deaths, the occasional religious attendance group (defined as once per month) had 24% more deaths, and the group attending religious services once per week had 15% more deaths. Examining results in years of life, the highest religious attendance group lived 7.6 more years than nonattendees. These results provide the kind of evidence that mandates the need to clarify what factors best explain these results. Unstudied, however, in most studies were indicators of quality of life and several other mental health indicators, particularly positive indicators that could shed even more light on these extraordinary findings.

When 29 independent studies of religious involvement were reviewed using meta-analysis totaling 125,826 adults and 15 potentially influencing factors were controlled, weekly or more religious attendance yielded 29% fewer deaths than nonattendance. This figure dropped to 23% when social support was included in the analysis. The longevity benefit for frequent church attendance was 7 additional years of life (McCullough et al., 2000). Using a more qualitative review process focused on the quality of the research designs, statistical analyses used, and precision of other measures, Powell, Shahabi, and Thoresen (2003) found that in nine highly rated studies, higher religious service attendance mortality rates were 25% lower than nonattendees in general population samples of reasonably healthy adults.

In recent years, for the first time, the National Institutes of Health convened an expert panel (see Miller & Thoresen, 2003; Powell et al., 2003) to conduct a critical evaluation using rigorous scientific criteria. The panel concluded that "persuasive" evidence exists that active religious and spiritual involvement is significantly correlated over time in controlled prospective studies with lower all-cause mortality. The overall results indicated a 25% to 30% reduction in mortality. On average, people who are active in religious or spiritual activities can expect to live about 7 years longer than nonreligious or less religiously active people. In one major study African Americans males lived almost 14 years longer than nonactive African males (see Powell et al., 2003). Clearly, active religious and spiritual engagement for many consistently appears to enhance their health broadly viewed over time.

Tragically, many mental and physical health problems are self-inflicted and thus could be prevented. Roughly 50% of all deaths in Americans and in the developed world are due to lifestyle habits and behaviors, such as smoking cigarettes, excessive eating and drinking, and lack of regular physical exercise (Centers for Disease Control and Prevention, 2004). As already discussed, those who are actively engaged in religious and spiritual practices live a healthier lifestyle than those less active or not at all active. In doing so, they minimize many risks associated with the major chronic diseases, such as various cardiac diseases (e.g., Koenig et al., 2001; Oman & Thoresen, 2005; Powell et al., 2003).

In response to these and other findings, the Association of American Medical Colleges has expressed the value of spirituality and religion in quality health care, stating:

> Spirituality is recognized as a factor that contributes to health in many persons. The concept of spirituality is found in all cultures and societies. It is expressed in an individual's search for ultimate meaning through participation in religion and/or belief in God . . . (and) . . . can influence how patients and health care professionals perceive health and illness and how they interact with one another.
>
> (*Association of American Medical Colleges*, 1999, pp. 25–26)

Community Benefits

Many community benefits exist for active spiritual and religious involvement. Since those who tend to be religious and spiritual also tend to stay married and are less likely to engage in behaviors that could harm others, such as unsafe sexual practices, drunk driving, and criminal activity, spirituality and religiousness appears to foster a more livable and healthy community. Spiritually and religiously oriented people tend to take better care of their local as well as the global community, supporting charitable causes, and especially participating in volunteerism. In fact, an added benefit of helping others in need through volunteerism is less disease and longer life (Oman & Thoresen, 2005).

To illustrate, in one major study, Oman, Thoresen, and McMahon (1999) followed almost 2,000 older persons in Northern California for over two decades in terms of how many regularly volunteered to help others in the community (i.e., they received no material compensation). Roughly one-third of the sample volunteered regularly on a scheduled basis for 4 to 6 hours a month. Volunteers had 40% fewer deaths than those who did not regularly volunteer. That difference increased to over 60% fewer deaths if the person who volunteered also was religiously active. These dramatic differences were found even after statistically controlling for over 12 known mortality risk factors. In a large nationally stratified sample, Harris and Thoresen (2005) found about 15% volunteered regularly. They experienced significantly fewer deaths, but when the other factors known to predict higher deaths were added to the analysis, only those who volunteered *and* who were regularly religiously active had significantly fewer deaths (30% fewer deaths).

Those engaged in spiritual and religious activities tend to be good citizens of the world who make the community a better place for others. In doing so, they also seem to benefit themselves by gaining a greater sense of meaning and significance in life as well as enjoying better health and longevity along with heightened quality of life.

How Could Religious Involvement Benefit Health?

Several theories have been suggested. First, religious involvement is often conducted within a particular social structure termed a congregation. This social structure provides for many ready-made groups (including smaller groups) with similar interests and values often providing invaluable social and emotional support. Supportive congregational activities may help prevent mental health problems from developing or may help reduce these problems by offering better ways to cope with serious challenges and troubles. Second, spiritual and religious practices often involve activities similar to secular relaxation or mind-calming strategies. Mental health professionals often suggest various kinds of relaxation strategies to help clients cope with anxiety, depression, substance abuse, and other mental health problems. Many spiritual and religious practices, such as meditation, prayer, and attending various kinds of services, can be considered as forms of mental and physical relaxation strategies. However, such practices also offer, compared to secular relaxation practices, the added value of bolstering a diminished sense of meaning or significance in life, along with strengthening perceptions of self-efficacy about coping better with life's challenges (Oman & Thoresen, 2005). This strengthened perceived self-efficacy to cope with mental health challenges may depend on the person's perception that a relationship exists for him or her with a higher power or source, such as God.

McAdams (2006), for example, offers a fascinating perspective based on the study of personal narratives ("life stories") focused on Erikson's stage of generativity (the person's concern and commitment to promoting the well-being of others, such as future generations). Some who are actively involved in religion and spirituality seem to benefit greatly in having been able to reframe their suffering and pain as actually beneficial to them (sometimes called "benefit finding"). For such persons the pain and suffering is often viewed as having redemptive consequences.

We also note that the field of positive psychology with its focus on human virtues (e.g., courage, humanity, and transcendence) and specific character strengths (e.g., hope, forgiveness, and gratitude) are significantly related to better mental health functioning (Seligman, Steen, Park, & Peterson, 2005; Snyder & Lopez, 2007). Spiritual and religious people are much more likely, for instance, to forgive others, express compassion, display gratitude, and engage in volunteerism (helping others in need without material compensation). Not surprisingly, positive psychology endorses the need for more positive emotions in daily life that may result in better mental health functioning. It is possible that the relationship between spirituality and religious involvement and positive mental health benefits and outcomes could most likely be indirectly related through a variety of causal mechanisms or pathways.

Recently, positive emotions and positive social behaviors, mentioned earlier, have been described in evolutionary terms when it comes to spirituality. For example, Keltner (2009) in *Born To Be Good*, makes a compelling case that humans survived over thousands of years not only because of their individual fitness but because of their collaborative kindness, and their spiritual and social capacities as well. That is, survival of the human species over 200 million years was not due to their physical genetics as much as due to their social and spiritual capacities, especially those selected for positive and prosocial emotions toward others. These included, for example, faith, hope, love, joy, compassion, and gratitude. One could argue that it was more of a survival of the kindest than just a survival of the fittest, especially fitness viewed only as physical and intellectual abilities. This spiritual evolutionary perspective finds support in several recent studies, primarily in psychology, neuroscience, ethology/animal studies, and cultural anthropology (see, for example, Balter, 2005; Dalai Lama & Ekman, 2008; Damasio, 1994; Panksepp, 1998).

In an excellent overview, Vaillant (2008) makes a strong case that spirituality as positive emotional experiences within social contexts, such as hope and compassion, have evolved over the past 200 million years. Some of the major points he makes include the following:

• Three kinds of evolution exist—genetic, cultural, and individual—having evolved and having continually influenced each other. For example, evolving cultural changes have altered the size and functions within the brain, leading to more likely selection for those living in more supportive, affiliative, and cooperative cultures characterized as fostering positive social emotions and strong social attachments.

• The human brain shares with all mammals and primates, a part of the brain called the limbic system (or paleomammalian brain), the neurophysiological home of positive emotions, empathy, and communal bonding and cooperation. This limbic system processes information from other organs of the body, coordinates emotions with past memories, and sends and receives information from the neocortex (the left prefrontal cortex), leading to more subtle and nuanced thoughts and motivation.

• The supremacy of words, texts, logic, and language in Western science (the primary domain of the left prefrontal cortex) has construed human experience and consciousness much too narrowly, leaving out the vital role of emotional thinking and intuitive wisdom in understanding human experiences, perceptions, decisions, and judgments.

• Spirituality is clearly not the same as religion. Spirituality is individual oriented, more emotional, universal in humans, more experiential, and more tolerant; religion is institutional and interpersonal oriented, more cognitive, more culture bound, more dogmatic, and less tolerant. Note, however, that religion is the greatest depository of spiritual resources, such as religious texts, rituals, music, and prayers/meditations.

This evolutionary perspective in highlighting the primary role of positive emotions in spirituality can help dispel the oversimplified dichotomy about cognitions and emotions, science and spirituality, and causes and effects.

Oman and Thoresen (2002) proposed a combination of four major causal pathways that could in combination explain mental and physical health benefits of spiritual and religious factors: (1) strong social and emotional support; (2) health-enhancing behaviors (e.g., no or moderate drinking, not smoking); (3) positive psychological states (e.g., faith, hope, inner peace, positive emotions); and (4) subtle processes not yet understood scientifically (e.g., nonlocal processes such that cognitions can be transmitted over long distances). While contemporary science cannot at present assess some of these unidentified factors, this does not necessarily mean that they do not exit. The history of science is a story of phenomena that at one time were thought to be inconceivable yet alone measurable, such as the proposition that Earth revolves around the Sun or that emotions are linked to certain areas of the brain or to the body's immune system.

If religious and spiritually minded people tend to live a healthier lifestyle, live more ethically, act more compassionately, and are more forgiving toward others and toward themselves, then they are more likely to have better psychological functioning that, in turn, could influence several physiological processes. Thus, the processes involved mutually enhance each other and other related processes. For example, engaging in daily spiritual meditation can lead to more social support and less depression, which, in turn, can foster more spiritual fellowship as well as more optimistic thoughts and expectations. All of these may impact several major organ systems of the body (e.g., immune competence, cardiovascular functioning, and metabolism) and may also, for example, impact left prefrontal cortical processes, related to more positive self-perceptions, wiser decisions and judgments, and a richer consciousness.

Methodological Concerns

Conducting well-controlled studies, such as randomized experiments or prospective longitudinal studies, to examine important research and clinical questions has always been challenging. This is especially true in examining the influence of religion and spirituality on mental, social, and physical health. Researchers, for example, obviously cannot randomly assign people to different religious and nonreligious groups and then examine health outcomes. Researchers are of course not permitted to coerce people to engage in randomly assigned religious activities, prayer, meditation, or to attend religious services. Therefore, most research in this area to date has been mostly limited to correlational designs, including nonexperimental or quasi-experimental designs that do not randomize participants to different groups.

However, many important problems related to human health and well-being have been successfully studied without having to randomize some participants to the hypothesized disease condition. For example, decades of successful research on the effects of tobacco on health did not require randomizing participants to become smokers for several years nor has successful research on the causes and processes of morbid obesity required randomizing normal weight participants to become clinical obese over time. Science clarifies causality by gathering and critically examining patterns of evidence from a variety of sources and settings over time. There is no one best scientific method used in understanding complex human experience, such as the health effects of spiritual or religious practices that can unequivocally establish causality. Instead, there are a variety of research designs using a variety of data and analytic techniques, depending on the specific topic, that can shed light on the role of spiritual and religious factors in health. Clearly the almost exclusive use of self-report questionnaires or inventories is inadequate for many topics in spirituality and religion (Hill & Pargament, 2003; Oman & Thoresen, 2002). Studies need to also include behavioral observation data, for example, along with assessments of physiological markers indicative of the issue or question being studied.

To illustrate, Ironson et al. (2002) demonstrated that a comprehensive spiritual and religious self-report measure failed to directly predict mortality in HIV/AIDS patients. Instead, the relationship was mediated by reduced cortisol, which in turn predicted less mortality. In the same way, the behavior of helping others significantly mediated the relationship between overall spirituality and mortality. Such studies highlight an important point cited earlier: The spirituality and religion connection with all-cause mortality exists because of several health-related factors that mediate the relationship rather than having an independent, direct influence (Oman & Thoresen, 2002).

Most studies to date have focused on questions as to whether religious people or those actively engaged in spiritual and religious practices tend to benefit overall from better mental and physical health when compared to those not engaging in spiritual and religious behaviors. This kind of correlational research is clearly worthwhile, especially longitudinal studies that assess participants more than once over time (often called prospective designs). However, correlational evidence has important limitations in trying to pin down possible causes of observed change, such as improved health. Well-designed prospective studies, sometimes with relatively small prospective samples ($n = 25$ to 50), can nevertheless shed valuable light on identifying possible causes. For example, the fascinating finding of a small study of participants' daily ratings for one month of the effectiveness of their spiritual coping in reducing chronic pain that day turned out to be the most powerful predictor of actual pain experienced the very next day (Keefe et al., 2001). Such evidence encourages consideration of why that happened and how spiritual coping could be linked to reduced pain. One possibility is that reduced pain from a spiritual coping practice, such as using a short mantra (viz., short sacred word or phrase often repeated during the day), could alter the person's perception of his or her perceived competence (self-efficacy) to manage pain.

The Down Side of Religion and Health Outcomes

Are there mental and physical health hazards to health and well-being associated with religion and spirituality? The answer is yes (Pargament, 2007). For some the policies and practices of organized religion, including the actions of religious professionals (e.g., pastors, priests, sisters, rabbis), have at times been harmful, if not devastating, to a person's or a group's health and well-being. Historically, over hundreds of years, grave abuses were authorized and sometimes implemented by religious authorities based upon a variety of reasons and doctrines. Some have noted that even today abuses associated with religion continue to happen (e.g., Hitchens, 2007; Plante, 2004).

One area of religious hazards to health lies in those experiencing religious struggles, that is, when a person perceives that he or she is being punished or abandoned by God in the face of a major trauma or by a perceived threat to one's existence. While some religious beliefs and worldviews offer a greater sense of meaning and purpose as well as direction in life along with sources of comfort and support, for others certain beliefs and worldviews can create very serious problems and threats that endanger health. When a person struggles chronically with his or her faith, doing so can lead to serious health problems, sometimes with fatal consequences.

For example, Edmondson, Park, Chaudoir, and Wortmann (2008) studied the negative impact of religious struggles in terminally ill heart failure patients suffering from their fear of death. Those struggling in terms of their religious beliefs were much more likely to suffer more serious depressive symptoms that were linked to their elevated fears of death. Such concerns were found to fully mediate the positive relationship of religious struggles and depression, which is a serious mortality risk for those suffering from advanced cardiac diseases.

Religious involvement can be destructive to self, to others, and to the community. Tragically, religious beliefs have been used to wage war, oppress women, murder others who do not share the same religious beliefs and practices, and to instill guilt, depression, and anxiety among many. Religiousness can also be associated with harmful if not fatal health practices, such as the rejection on religious grounds to seek needed medical and psychiatric care. Religious beliefs and practices can and unfortunately continue to be used in certain areas of the world to enflame group conflicts as well. Curiously, religious conflicts about moral transgressions can be significant predictors of panic disorder (Trenholm, Trent, & Compton, 1998). Patients with HIV/AIDS can suffer poorer health if they hold a more rigid view of a punishing and judgmental God, compared to a compassionate and forgiving view of God or an impersonal view of God or higher power (Kremer & Ironson, 2007).

Clearly, empirical evidence exits that religion can be mentally and physically hazardous to health under certain circumstances. These negative effects unfortunately remain understudied and deserve more study using well-controlled research designs. Such designs need to be especially sensitive to assessing ongoing cognitive, social, and emotional experiences as well as specific contexts (e.g., time, place, others present, cultural factors, internal narratives in the setting). Methods are available to capture much of this but seldom have been used. Tennen, Affleck, Armeli, and Carney (2000) offer, for example, useful research designs to study daily processes, such as very specific experiences. These could include specific ways to cope with distress, such as perceived spiritual support and daily spiritual self-efficacy perceptions. As mentioned, Keefe et al. (2001) offer an excellent example of this kind of much needed research.

Keep in mind that almost all of the world's major religions have urged people, for example, to avoid smoking, excessive drinking (or no use of alcohol), unsafe sexual practices, and to engage regularly in physical exercise and eat healthy foods. While these health behaviors are vital to better health and to preventing disease, religious traditions also have long been focused on helping people cope or manage a broad variety of major and minor life stressors and distress associated with enhanced psychological functioning. These coping approaches have included optimism, positive emotions, compassion for self and others, forgiveness of others, and they have resulted in less anxiety, depression, and perceived stress (Plante & Thoresen, 2007).

Overall, research clearly supports the many mental, physical, and community health benefits for those who engage in spiritual and religious activities. It is likely that many spiritual and religious people generally lead lifestyles that are more health promoting and less health damaging than those who are not actively religious or spiritual. They also have generally provided a variety of ways that offer social support through involvement in their religious communities that help people to cope with life's challenges and troubles. Finally, the focus on love, compassion, and serving others in need, along with emphasis on ethical conduct, linked to specific religious and spiritual beliefs and traditions, can have an effect of making the world a better place to live. This is especially true for the vast majority of people who often live impoverished and marginalized lives. However, as discussed, there is evidence that involvement in some religious communities contributes to personal and social problems, such as anxiety, panic, obsessive-compulsive symptoms, terrorism, and various forms of abuse, oppression, violence, and hatred. Typically, for most normal expressions of spiritual and religious beliefs and practices, positive mental and physical health benefits can be expected. We believe it is therefore reasonable for professionals to expect that spiritual and religious engagement could be useful and to at least

consider the role of spiritual and religious factors in an overall counseling treatment plan.

Above all, given the fact that the clear majority of Americans are religious or spiritually active, we believe that the counseling psychologist, as well as other psychologists, should at least broach the topic of religious and spiritual involvement initially with a client. But how would one do that in a way that would not be perceived as offensive or insensitive?

Barriers to Spirituality and Health Benefits in Counseling
Public Is Religious, Psychologists Are Not

The vast majority of people in the United States and across the globe describe themselves as being spiritual, religious, or both. Most belong to a traditional faith community and are affiliated and identified with a major religious tradition. Others view themselves as spiritual but not being interested in organized religion. Most participate in regular formalized religious services, celebrate religious holidays, and pray often or daily. In fact, over 95% of Americans report that they believe in God and 40% attend religious services once a week or more (Gallup & Lindsay, 1999). According to Gallup polls, most Americans are Christian with 85% affiliated with either a Protestant (59%) or Catholic (26%) denomination. About 2% are Jewish while Hindu, Muslim, and Buddhists together account for 3% of the population. Only 6% of Americans are not affiliated with any religious group (Gallup & Lindsay, 1999). More than 80% of Americans report that they wish to grow spiritually (Myers, 2000). Thus, religion and spirituality is clearly an important component to life for most people.

By contrast, most psychologists are not spiritual or religious. Only 33% are affiliated with a religious tradition, only 72% report belief in God or a higher power, and 51% report that religion is *not* important to them (Shafranske, 2000). Miller and Delaney (2005) poignantly observed that in the 20th century, of all the scientific, professional, or academic disciplines, psychology became by far the one least interested in religion and spirituality in the United States. Despite the work of some early major psychologists (e.g., William James, Gordon Allport, and Carl Jung) in the 20th century on spirituality and religion, Miller and Delaney (2005) observed that at best, "The modal response of psychologists to religion in research, practice, and training, however, became one of silence and neglect" (p. 4).

Recently, 68% of current training directors of clinical psychology internship programs state that they "*never* foresee religious/spiritual training being offered in their program" (Russell & Yarhouse, 2006, p. 434). Perhaps people who pursue a career as a psychologist are more secular and less religious or spiritual than the average person. Perhaps psychologists develop a "trained incapacity" in college or graduate school such that they view religion as inherently antiscientific or spirituality as involving supernatural hocus-pocus. Shafranske (2000) suggested that most psychologists who bring this topic into their research or clinical practice do so because of a unique training experience, compared to anything systematic in their training program, or to their own personal faith commitment. Whatever the reason, the fact is that while most people are religious, spiritual, or both, most psychologists studying or serving people are neither religious nor spiritual.

As noted, some of our famous and influential psychology forefathers, such as William James, Carl Jung, and Gordon Allport, wrote extensively about the relationship between psychology and religion (e.g., Allport, 1950; James, 1890, 1902/1936; Jung, 1938). Nevertheless, the topic of religious and spiritual beliefs, attitudes, and behavior has been largely ignored by psychological writers (Collins, 1977). Glancing through the subject index of any basic psychology text, for example, one seldom finds mention of religion or spirituality. Psychologists in the 20th century undoubtedly have been influenced by the perspectives of important leaders in the field, such as Sigmund Freud, B. F. Skinner, John Watson, and Albert Ellis. These leaders seldom had anything positive to say about religion or spirituality (e.g., Ellis, 1971; Freud, 1927/1961; Watson, 1924/1983). For example, in *Future of an Illusion*, Freud referred to religion as an "obsessional neurosis" (Freud, 1927/1961, p. 43). Watson referred to religion as a "bulwark of medievalism" (Watson, 1924/1983, p. 1). These and other leaders clearly implied that religious interest or concerns typically served as signs of pathology, not good health.

Psychology has long prided itself in working hard to be viewed as a rigorous, empirical, "hard science" discipline. Many psychologists appear to hold a dualistic if not stereotyped perception about religious and spiritual constructs; that is, if a construct is perceived as religious or spiritual, then it is viewed by definition as nonscientific or antiscientific. This dualistic attitude about anything religious or spiritual as antiscientific has been especially evident in the applied professional areas of psychology. For example, the recent efforts to focus on empirically

supported and manualized treatments (Task Force on Promotion and Dissemination of Psychological Procedures, 1995) as well as more rigorous scientific approaches to psychological services is evidence for the continuing emphasis on science, which may have little if any interest in spiritual or religious issues.

A related issue concerns the secularization of traditional religious or spiritual practices used in interventions (e.g., procedures to manage distress, calm the body, or quiet the mind). This may have been done, in part, to make them more acceptable to the professional community. For example, the field of positive psychology has categorized some topics as major *virtues* (e.g., humanity, wisdom, transcendence) and related subtopics as *specific character strengths* (e.g., love, gratitude, forgiveness). These topics have been secularized for the most part, that is, presented outside of any religious tradition or practice (see Seligman et al., 2005). The widely used mindfulness-based stress reduction (Kabat-Zinn, 1990; Shapiro & Walsh, 2007) also offers an example of secularizing of spiritual and religious practices (e.g., Buddhist meditation). Perhaps a secular approach was perceived as less controversial or more subject to empirical study than using a spiritual or religious approach.

A question worthy of attention, given that most clients or patients are religiously active and seeking greater spirituality in their lives, is to ask whether spiritual practices when secularized have the same effectiveness as those used within a spiritual or religious tradition. We know of few such studies. One, however, is worthy of some detailed comment because it is based on a well-controlled randomized clinical trial design in an area lacking any such studies (Wachholtz & Pargament, 2008).

The study examined a spiritually focused meditation practice to reduce the frequency of long-term chronic migraine headache sufferers compared with two highly similar meditations and a relaxation control procedure without any spiritual focus. Two questions were asked in the investigation: Is spiritual meditation more effective in enhancing pain tolerance and in reducing the frequency of migraine headaches over a 30-day period? Does spiritual meditation create better mental, physical, and spiritual health outcomes compared to secular meditation and relaxation techniques? Eighty-three headache sufferers were randomized to one of four conditions. One included the spiritual meditation group in which each person selected among a list of spiritually focused meditations such as "God is love" or "God is peace." Participants in two other secular experimental groups (internal or external meditations) selected meditation statements, such as "I am joy" or "I am good" in the internal group or "Sand is soft" or "Grass is green" in the external group. Progressive muscle relaxation was used in the fourth comparison group.

After 30 consecutive days of 20-minute daily meditations, outcome results were impressive. Those in the spiritually focused experimental condition experienced significant reductions in headaches compared to modest reductions in the other three secular conditions. Reductions in pain tolerance (using the cold pressor task where participants place their hand in circulating freezing water until pain is too great to tolerate) were significant and dramatic as well. The baseline pain tolerance for all four groups was 45 seconds. The spiritual meditation group's pain tolerance rose to almost 2 minutes, while the other three groups showed either no change or modest gains up to only 20 seconds. Gains in spiritual measures such as existential well-being and spiritual experiences also favored the spiritual meditation group as well as reductions in trait anxiety and negative emotions.

The Wachholtz and Pargament (2008) intervention study suggests that the inclusion of a spiritual focus might enhance, if used in a sensitive, appropriate, and respectful manner, the effectiveness of psychological practices and interventions. Hopefully, other researchers will pursue this promising topic using appropriate research designs and assessments exemplified by Wachholtz and Pargament (2008).

Perhaps more problematic, if not destructive, is the fact that often secular and nonreligious psychologists working with religiously oriented or spiritually minded clients may unwittingly preconceive or interpret their client's interest in spirituality and religion as a sign or symptom of pathology, delusion, or weakness. Or a psychologist may be oblivious of how clients could draw upon their religious or spiritual beliefs or practices in trying to overcome problems. Are the interests of a client best served if a psychologist ignores completely anything in the spiritual and religious realm or would a client be better served if a psychologist at least inquires about the client's interests and perceptions about spirituality and religion? We discuss this and other related questions later in this chapter.

Despite the long history of "silence and neglect" in modern psychology of spirituality and religion, in recent years, change has come. A greater recognition of the value of religious and spiritual concerns in psychology is under way, and in other social and behavioral sciences. This recognition seems greatest in health and disease, where professional and public support is expanding (Hartz, 2005; Koenig et al., 2001). Many secular professional organizations, such as the Society of Behavioral Medicine, now offer special interest groups that focus on spirituality and health research and practice. Major foundations such as Templeton, Lilly, and Fetzer, as well as government granting agencies such as the National Institute of Health, have also funded large research projects in this area.

The American Psychological Association has also embraced these changes. For example, the 1999 National Multicultural Conference and Summit sponsored by the American Psychological Association stated: "spirituality is a necessary condition for a psychology of human existence" and that "people are cultural and spiritual beings" (Sue, Bingham, Porche-Burke, &Vasquez, 1999, p. 1065). The ethics code for psychologists states: "Psychologists are aware of and respect cultural, individual, and role differences, including those based on age, gender, gender identity, race, ethnicity, culture, national origin, religion, sexual orientation, disability, language, and socioeconomic status and consider these factors when working with members of such groups" (American Psychological Association, 2002, p. 1064). Thus, being "aware of and respect(ful)" of religious issues is now demanded by the ethics code. Finally, the American Psychological Association has itself published a dozen books on psychology, spirituality, and religion during the past 10 years when previously they offered almost none.

Psychology Can Learn From Religion and Spirituality

Psychology as a scientific discipline has been around for a little more than 100 years, while religion and spirituality has been around for thousands of years. Perhaps psychology could learn something from its older cousin. After all, the goal of counseling and psychological services is, in part, about developing more healthy strategies for living and better ways of coping with many stressful life events. Counseling seeks to help people manage their lives in a more thoughtful, significant, and healthy way. Since spiritual and religious traditions have long offered wise council on these issues for thousands of years, perhaps the counseling community could learn a few things from the collective wisdom of these faith traditions. We believe that at least one needs to consider carefully and respectfully ways to incorporate some spiritual concepts and practices into one's scientific and professional work in psychology.

What concepts or practices might be considered? Some possibilities include the following: focusing on forgiveness (self, situations, others), promoting greater acceptance of others as well as self-acceptance, using significant rituals, providing group and community support (i.e., physically, socially, emotionally, and materially), emphasizing selfless love, encouraging kindness, and volunteering regularly to serve others in need. At a broader level, the concept of learning to perceive oneself as a part of something much larger than just oneself (i.e., less egoistic) seems significant as does the concept of enhancing a greater sense of meaning and purpose in life. Note that these and others topics have been thoughtfully considered in many ways in all of the major religious and spiritual wisdom traditions over thousands of years (Armstrong, 2006; Smith, 1991).

The field of psychology has indeed matured as an independent and international discipline, offering rigorous scientific inquiry with state-of-the-art methodologies and statistics to study many human issues, some quite challenging. The many complexities of human perception and judgment, for example, continue to be better understood by using more sophisticated concepts and methods. The study of personality is another complex, multidimensional, if not multilevel topic. The field of psychology deals with complex and challenging concepts and it is capable with sustained commitment of dealing with the complexities of spiritual and religious concepts as they relate to health and well-being (Miller & Delaney, 2005).

While relatively few psychologists, with the exception of those in Division 36 (Psychology of Religion), have studied religion or spirituality, noticeably more are now starting to do so, thus helping to expand the scope and depth of inquiry. Psychology as a discipline can and will benefit from the challenge of trying to better understand, especially empirically, the number of religious and spiritual constructs and practices involved. Psychology as a behavioral and social science discipline is known for its primary focus on the individual and the many differences within and among individuals. Spirituality is eminently personal and individual as well as experiential. It works within each person at various levels of conscious personal experiences, seasoned by a range of beliefs, emotions, and behaviors across time (past, present moment, future). Religions were created by people in part to help individuals within

a perceived community deal with issues of making life more meaningful, gaining a greater sense of purpose and direction, such as how to live a "good life." Building and sustaining communities of faith that provide support for living a values-centered life is what religions seek to do. How successful they are in doing so is another issue.

As psychologists we need to be more attentive to the broad range of diversity issues that individuals represent, such as religious and spiritual beliefs and practices. Since the American Psychological Association ethics code (2002) mandates that psychologists be respectful and mindful of cultural diversity that includes religious traditions and beliefs, psychologists should not ignore or automatically pathologize religious and spiritual issues among their clients and students.

Implementing Spiritually Oriented Interventions
What the Religious and Spiritual Traditions Offer the Counselor

Given the fact that religion and spirituality may offer many mental and physical health benefits, how might professional counselors use the research findings to enhance their clinical activities with clients? First, let us briefly introduce two important steps in ways to think about what the religious and spiritual traditions offer the professional counselor.

In the now classic book, *The World's Religions* (1991), Huston Smith well articulates an ancient view that the world's great religions are much more similar than different. He refers to the Hindu notion that the "various religions are but different languages through which God speaks to the human heart" (p. 73). Quoting Ris-Veda (4000 bce), the often quoted Hindu sage, states, "Truth is one; sages call it by different names" (p. 73).

Smith provides an illustration of how to understand the world's religions that we believe can be helpful to use. He states: "It is possible to climb life's mountain from any side, when the top is reached the trails converge. At base, in the foothills of theology, ritual, and organizational structure, the religions are distinct. Differences in culture, history, geography, and collective temperament all make for diverse starting points" (p. 73). He then describes that as we move higher toward the top of the mountain, the world's religious traditions become one path seeking truth stating, "But beyond these differences, the same goal beckons" (p. 73). He quotes Sri Ramakrishna, a 19th-century Hindu teacher, stating: "God has made different religions to suit different aspirations, times, and countries. All doctrines are only so many paths; but a path is by no means God Himself. Indeed, one can reach God if one follows any of the paths with whole-hearted devotion. One may eat a cake with icing either straight or sideways. It all taste[s] sweet either way" (p. 74). At their best and most thoughtful, the religious traditions converge and ultimately saying much of the same thing but with different languages, customs, and traditions.

Concepts from all of the major contemporary religious traditions as well as Greek philosophical rationalism can be traced to the 9th-century bce during the Axial age in four different regions of the then civilized world (Armstrong, 2006). They all struggled with similar questions and came to similar conclusions about religious, ethical, and social views. This includes "the spirit of compassion . . . lies at the core of all our traditions" (Armstrong, 2006, p. 476). However, all of the religious traditions have "fallen prey to exclusivity, cruelty, superstition, and even atrocity. But at their core, the Axial faiths share an ideal of sympathy, respect, and universal concern" (Armstrong, 2006, p. 466). The Golden Rule, or treating others as you would like to be treated, is the main point and is well articulated in the sacred texts of all of the religious traditions (Armstrong, 2006; Pargament, 2007; Peterson, 1986). In fact, Armstrong states that the Axial sages concluded that "religion *was* the Golden Rule" (Armstrong, 2006, p. 468).

Some Spiritual Principles and Tools for the Counselor

What do religious traditions at their best offer the psychological community? At the top of the metaphorical mountain where the traditions converge, there are a number of highly desirable and useful principles and values that are beneficial. These include a focus on the sacredness of life and of the world, ethical behavior toward others, prayer and meditation, community and service involvement, and love and respect for all. Many also conveyed the notion that God, while existing in many forms and settings, could be found within every person, regardless of status and gender, as well as in other life and inanimate forms. The task of the person, however, was to use spiritual practices to access this divine presence within. The religious traditions emerging from the Axial age all emphasized compassion toward oneself and toward all others. These values and principles can be helpful to many, regardless of their particular religious traditions or affiliations, including those with no interest in any religious traditions or beliefs.

The variety of empirically supported treatment programs and protocols now available can integrate spiritual and religious tools and perspectives in services offered by psychologists and other mental health professionals. Alcoholics Anonymous (AA) is perhaps the oldest and most well-known self-help and peer-led program that integrates spiritual and religious perspectives (Alcoholics Anonymous World Services, 1977). Of course, AA is not an empirically supported treatment program administered by mental health professionals. However, the program well illustrates the popular integration of spirituality into self-help services for alcohol and other addictions. In recent years, professionally developed empirically supported treatments have been developed and tested that integrate spiritual and religious principles in professionally administered treatment services. This includes interventions for substance abuse, eating disorders, and marital discord, to name a few; they have used bibliotherapy, meditation, forgiveness training, and other spiritual and religiously based interventions with roots in all of the major religious traditions. In addition to mental health and relationship problems, interventions have also been developed to help those coping with a number of medical disorders as well such as HIV/AIDS and coronary heart disease. A list of empirically supported treatment interventions that integrate spiritual and religious principles and tools, along with an appropriate reference for further information, is provided in Table 25.1.

Caregiving of Health Professionals: A Spiritual Practices Example

How might a practicing psychologist or other health professional use spiritual practices in a work setting? We use the example of a large Denver hospital that was seeking help to reduce perceived stress of staff and foster better care of patients and their families (Oman, Hedberg, & Thoresen, 2006). A physician connected with the hospital suggested that a comprehensive, spiritually based, nonsectarian program called the Eight-Point Program (EPP) be used (Easwaran, 1991/1978; Flinders, Oman, & Flinders, 2007). Box 25.1 provides a brief description of each spiritual practice drawn from the wisdom traditions spanning all major religions. See also an introductory primer that provides case material and narratives focusing on using the mantra, slowing down, and one-pointed attention to reduce

Table 25.1 Examples of Empirically Supported Spiritual/Religious Interventions for Counseling

Name of Intervention Program	Reference
Opening Your Heart (coronary heart disease and prevention)	Ornish, 1990
Christian Marriage Counseling	Worthington, 1990
Becoming a More Forgiving Christian	Worthington, 2004
Coping With Divorce	Rye & Pargament, 2003
Solace for the Soul	Murray-Swank & Pargament, 2005
Lighting the Way (group treatment for women with HIV/AIDS)	Pargament et al., 2004
Spiritual Renewal (eating disorders)	Richards, Hardman, & Berrett, 2000
Re-Creating Your Life (group treatment for serious mental illness)	Cole & Pargament, 1998
From Vice to Virtue	Ano, 2005
Eight-Point Spiritual Skills Program	Easwaran, 1978/1991
Mindfulness Meditation	Kabat-Zinn, 2003
Mantra Training	Bormann et al., 2006
REACH Model for Forgiveness	Worthington, 2004

worries, foster inner peace, and encourage kindness (Easwaran, 2005).

Working with a psychologist and other health professionals, this physician, with others assisting, conducted eight weekly, 2-hour sessions on the EPP for 29 professionals with another 30 randomized to a wait group condition. A variety of assessments were conducted just before the weekly group started, at the end, and at 8-week and 19-week follow-ups, spanning almost 6 months. Over 90% remained active in the study, and attendance at weekly sessions was above 85%.

Briefly, participants were mostly female (86%), had at least 5 years of full-time work experience, identified themselves as "spiritual but not religious" (50%) or "spiritual and religious" (45%), or neither (5%). Of all, 77% stated that they were very or moderately spiritual. Very few stated they were "very religious." Each session focused on one or more of the eight points with initial attention on what is termed "passage meditation," use of the mantra, slowing down, and being more one-pointed in attention.

Results were encouraging. First, the reductions in perceived stress were impressive and were maintained through the last follow-up (roughly 6 months). Effect sizes were significant at post treatment and at follow-ups: -0.63, -1.00, -0.84, respectively. Translated into levels (%) for this measure in

national populations samples, baseline scores for these health professionals were in the high stress range (above 80%), while the immediate posttreatment score dropped to 50% or average stress level. The two follow-up levels stayed below 50%.

In addition, the Caregiving Self-Efficacy Scale (32 items tapping the perceived confidence level to do something successfully, such as "Control my temper with patients," "Help families of patients to deal with the death of patients," and "Sense the needs of other co-workers (so I can help them without being asked)" was used. Encouraging effect sizes were found in the moderately strong range (0.48, 0.59, 0.47). Improvements in other mental health indicators were less significant but all in the desired direction. Importantly, no evidence emerged that practicing the specific eight points from a spiritual perspective was associated with any kind of negative effect on health and well-being (see Oman, Richards, Hedberg, & Thoresen, 2008, for detailed information on a qualitative, structured interview narrative study that offers some confirmation of the results cited earlier).

Conducting a Spiritual Inquiry in the Initial Interview

Recently, a team of psychologists with others developed a simple, short, yet sensitive and respectful

1. Passage Meditation: Silent repetition in the mind of memorized inspirational passages from the world's great religions, such as the 23rd Psalm, the Prayer of Saint Francis, or the Discourse on Good Will of the Buddha's *Sutta Nipata*. Practiced for one-half hour each morning.
2. Repetition of a Holy Word or Mantra: Silent repetition in the mind at times other than meditation of a single chosen Holy Name, hallowed phrase, or mantra from a major religious tradition.
3. Slowing Down: Setting priorities and reducing the stress and friction caused by hurry.
4. Focused/One-Pointed Attention: Giving full concentration to the matter at hand.
5. Training the Senses: Overcoming conditioned habits and learning to enjoy what is beneficial.
6. Putting Others First: Gaining freedom from selfishness and separateness; finding joy in helping others.
7. Spiritual Association: Spending time regularly with others following the Eight-Point Program for mutual inspiration and support.
8. Inspirational Reading: Drawing inspiration from writings by and about the world's great spiritual figures and from the scriptures of all religions.

way to do conduct a spiritual inquiry. Jean Kristeller and others, including physicians, learned from survey data that a majority of physicians believed that a patient's spirituality could be important in understanding the patient's health status, but that in fact physicians seldom (less than 10%) brought the topic up with patients. When asked why, physicians often mentioned that they were unsure how to do so and did not want to be seen as imposing upon the patient's privacy. Kristeller and others developed a standardized brief protocol called the Patient-Centered Spirituality protocol that could be routinely used by physicians (Kristeller, Rhodes, Cripe, & Sheets, 2005). They conducted a controlled study with 118 oncology patients to assess the effect of using this protocol with oncology patients. Patients were alternately assigned to intake with a brief spiritual inquiry group included or the usual intake interview group. Most patients were Caucasian, 55% were women with mixed diagnoses, and 81% identified themselves as being Christian in background.

Assessments of mental health factors plus patient and physician ratings of the interview were conducted just before the initial interview and 3 weeks later. Physicians rated themselves comfortable with inquiry with 85% of patients and 76% of patients rating inquiry as somewhat or very useful. At 3 weeks follow-up patients in the spiritual inquiry group showed significant improvements compared to the comparison group (at least $p < .05$) in quality of life, spiritual well-being, and perceived sense of interpersonal caring by their physician. The major

steps in this protocol with some of the suggested words in quotes used by the health professional are as follows:

1. Introduce the issue in neutral inquiring manner.

"When dealing with this problem, many people draw on religious or spiritual beliefs to help cope with it. It would be helpful to me to know how you feel about this."

2. Inquire further, adjusting inquiry to client's initial response. If it is a:
   a. Positive-Active Faith Response: "What have you found most helpful about your beliefs since this problem came up?"
   b. Neutral-Receptive Response: "How might you draw on your faith or spiritual beliefs to help you?"
   c. Spiritually Distressed Response (e.g., anger or guilt): "Many people feel that way...what might help you come to terms with this?"
   d. Defensive-Rejecting Response: "It sounds like you're uncomfortable I brought this up. What I'm really interested in is how you are coping...can you tell me about that?"

3. Continue to explore further as indicated:
   "I see. Can you tell me more (about...)?"
4. Inquire about ways of finding meaning and a sense of peace:
   "Is there some way in which you are able to find a sense of meaning or peace in the midst of this?"
5. Inquire about resources.

"Whom do you have to talk to about this/these concerns?"

6. Offer assistance as appropriate and available.

"Perhaps we can arrange for you to talk to someone...there's a support group."

7. Bring inquiry to a close.

"I appreciate you discussing these issues with me. May I ask about it again?"

Obviously, the wording would need to be modified to fit the specific mental or physical health problem (e.g., posttraumatic stress disorder, marital conflict, leadership management issues). But the general format can provide a structure that could be taught in graduate training programs and also used by practicing psychologists with some brief training. Doing so could help the client and also could help psychologists fill the mandate of honoring the spiritual and religious diversity of their clients.

Plante (2009) outlined 13 spiritual and religious tools useful for counselors to have in their therapeutic toolbox, regardless of their interest in specific religious faith traditions. These include (1) meditation; (2) prayer; (3) seeking a sense of vocation, meaning, purpose, and calling in life; (4) bibliotherapy, including sacred scripture reading; (5) attending community services, ceremonies, and rituals; (6) volunteering and charitable works and service; (7) ethical values and behavior with others; (8) approaching others with forgiveness, gratitude, love, kindness, and compassion; (9) engaging in social justice issues; (10) learning from spiritual models; (11) accepting oneself and others (even with faults); (12) being part of something larger than yourself; and (13) understanding the sacredness of life. Some are likely to be appropriate and helpful with particular clients and counselors, while others are not. We believe these tools can add value to the effectiveness of professional services and research offered by counseling and other psychologists involved in health.

Some Conclusions and Future Directions

The religious and spiritual wisdom traditions have evolved over thousands of years. A careful reading of the history and development of these traditions indicates that all have grappled with much of the same theological and philosophical issues. Wisdom traditions also offer guidance in how to live a more satisfying, happy, and meaningful life, one based on a foundation of knowing and understanding perennial human virtues and character strengths (Armstrong, 2006). These traditions offer advice about learning how to discover the sacred in life and make specific suggestions about building and maintaining intimate relationships with others, including a transcendent relationship with a power or spirit greater than oneself, sometimes called God. Ways to manage major and minor stressful life events have also been recommended in dealing with common problems in the contexts of marriage, family, work, and community.

Although religious traditions use different languages, customs, beliefs, and rituals about life's perennial questions, they have reached very similar conclusions over thousands of years. "When religions [traditions] are sifted for their best qualities," wrote Houston Smith (1991), the eminent scholar of the world's major religions, "they begin to look like data banks that house the winnowed wisdom of the human race" (p. 5). Undoubtedly as human institutions, organized religions have also been a source of hatred, fear, violence, deprivation, and hypocrisy. At times certain religious policies and practices have contradicted the essence of spirituality and the sacred, such as love, hope, and compassion. We need, however, to look beyond specific cultural differences and the dogma that goes along with very questionable practices and acknowledge and seek what religions offer at their best.

Every major religion, for example, offers life stories, in effect spiritual models, that convey admirable human qualities and character strengths (e.g., Jesus, Buddha, Gandhi, Moses, Mother Teresa). These traditions and historical spiritual exemplars also have been used to illustrate how persons faced with great challenges were able to deal with them by using spiritual practices and perspectives. We can learn from spiritual exemplars, regardless of the status of our own spiritual and religious affiliation, beliefs, and practices ("Spirituality is caught more than taught").

Empirical evidence clearly supports the view that people actively engaged in spiritual or religious activities on average are physically, socially, and mentally far better off than those seldom or not engaged. This robust empirical relationship between active involvement and health, as noted earlier, does not demonstrate that a direct and specific cause-and-effect relationship exists, such as religion directly causes better health. Rather, what has been demonstrated is that a consistent relationship exists between active spiritual and religious involvement and health benefits for most people. Studies also suggest that clients prefer to have their religious and spiritual issues and traditions at least acknowledged and possibly integrated into their professional health care services.

As noted, the great wisdom traditions provide a variety of useful tools and practices used over more than three millennia. These can be employed by the competent and interested psychologists. Importantly, many of these practices can be used in a secular manner, depending of course on particular circumstances. For example, mindfulness-based stress reduction has been often used in secular settings, yet it has roots in a particular religious tradition (Tibetan Buddhism). While clients are not required to be religious or spiritually active to benefit from the tools derived from religious traditions, it remains unclear if use of a completely secularized practice is more or less effective than when used in a more spiritually or religiously framed manner.

Religious and spiritual beliefs and practices clearly can be harmful and hazardous to overall health. Frankly, this topic has been seldom examined rigorously, and with the needed sensitivity. Candid and comprehensive examinations of possible negative effects merit using rigorous empirical methods, and the collaboration of professional colleagues are needed in such areas such as specific religious beliefs and spiritual practices (Thoresen, Oman, & Harris, 2005).

Most people report that they are religious, spiritual, or both. Some such as Vaillant (2008) discussed earlier believe that all humans are by nature spiritual but not religious due to cultural factors. Overall, a clear majority of people in the United States are affiliated with a religious tradition, believe in God (however defined), and pray regularly. Roughly 40% of Americans attend spiritual or religious ceremonies, services, or rituals weekly or more often. By contrast, in Northern European cultures only a clear minority are actively religious. Interestingly, a clear majority of mental health professionals in the United States and in European cultures are not active religiously or spiritually nor identified with a particular religious tradition. Furthermore, while there has been considerable focus on cultural diversity in recent years, the vast majority of graduate training programs in the mental health professions continue to ignore religious and spiritual issues, offering no instruction or training on religious diversity. The American Psychological Association ethics guidelines (and other codes) in the mental health disciplines now require attention, training, and respect for religious diversity. Since a majority of clients studied and served by psychologists and other health professionals are religiously engaged and spiritually focused, we believe that it makes good professional and clinical

sense for counseling psychologists and other health professionals to at least understand the role of spiritual and religious factors.

The field of counseling psychology has a long history within the discipline of psychology as a specialty devoted to understanding and serving those dealing with life's inevitable "normal" problems, compared to those with severe mental, physical, or social health problems. How can the field of counseling psychology capitalize on the collective wisdoms of the world's major religions discussed earlier? Much of this wisdom relates to fundamental issues of character, conduct, and consciousness. Recently, the terms "virtues" and "character strengths" have been essentially reintroduced in psychology by the positive psychology movement (e.g., Seligman, Steen, Park, & Peterson, 2005; Snyder & Lopez, 2007). As noted earlier, these virtues (e.g., humanity, temperance, and transcendence) each involve several character strengths (e.g., humanity includes love, kindness, and leadership; temperance includes forgiveness, humility, and self-regulation; and transcendence includes gratitude, hope, and humor). Most would view these character strengths as important if not essential personal and social qualities.

How do people learn to be virtuous and to honor a character in their daily lives that displays such strengths as forgiveness, humility, and gratitude in their thoughts and actions? We believe that an important future direction for counseling psychology lies in focusing more on virtues and character strengths, given that many can benefit from acquiring these virtues and strengths: the person, the family, the community, and in effect all on Earth. Recent work in spiritual modeling, drawing on social cognitive theory and the distilled wisdom of all major religious traditions, offers an empirical-based strategy to help people learn spiritual skills and practices that can enhance health in its broadest sense (Bandura, 2003; Oman & Thoresen, 2003, 2007).

Four important future directions for work in this area of spirituality and religion clarify some major current issues:

1. Exploring the growing trend in American as well as other cultures of those who perceive themselves as "spiritual but not religious"

2. Studying relationships between social, mental, and physical factors among those who are more spiritually or religiously active compared to those less or not active

3. Identifying and understanding possible mediating factors that may help explain how a

spiritual or religious factor may play a causal role in one's overall health status. Possible mediators include various forms of meditation, volunteering to serve others, attending religious or spiritual services weekly or more often, and experiencing positive social emotions.

4. Consider further the evolutionary evidence that spirituality is inherently linked to positive emotions, suggesting that humans are by nature spiritual but may need certain cultural experiences to express their spirituality in positive, prosocial ways

We currently know little about the segment of the population that identify themselves as only spiritual. As indicated earlier, studies have found sizable numbers (from 15% to 30%) identified as spiritual but not religious. In what ways is this group a mix of several subgroups as to such factors as age, gender, socioeconomic status, educational level, ethnic identity, and geographical region? Are there significant differences among spiritual but not religious compared to other subgroups (e.g., religious only or spiritual and religious) when it comes to health? What does it mean in terms of attitudes, beliefs, and actions for one who describes oneself as spiritual but not religious? What difference exists, if any, in the kind of problems persons present for counseling services if identified as spiritual only or religious only or both or neither?

Few studies, if any, have documented the relationships of those who are very active spiritually and those less or not active in terms of physical, mental, and social health problems. Typically, studies have seldom used a variety of assessments other than survey questions, especially not different modes of assessment (interviews, structured diaries, daily behavior ratings, ambulatory electronically based devices). Issues of assessing one's spiritual beliefs and practices have been usually based on one short questionnaire. Seldom has one's experiences of what is sacred in life been assessed. Little has been done in gathering a person's "narrative identity" with a focus on spiritual experiences, as discussed by McAdams (2006). Interviews can provide data that speak more deeply to a person's spiritually related experiences, especially if gathered on more than one occasion. Rather than using only interviews or only surveys, using both can provide confirming evidence that survey questions could never reveal. See the Oman, Richards, Hedberg, and Thoresen (2008) study for an example of using repeated interviews to complement a variety of survey measures used on four

occasions in a hospital-based spiritual intervention with health professionals.

How might a spiritual practice, such as frequent attendance at religious or spiritual services, play a causal role in less stress or less mortality? Recall that this attendance and mortality relationship offers to date the strongest empirical evidence in the United States that spirituality and religion may enhance health in most people (Miller & Thoresen, 2003). This question reveals the impressive complexity of factors at play in seeking answers. For example, what is there about attending services that "gets under the skin" in ways that alters at some points in time physiological processes that in turn leads eventually to death? Such a question speaks to the search for mediators, factors that help explain what can be called indirect causes of an outcome, such as the connection between attendance and mortality. To date, several possible answers have been suggested involving lifestyle issues, such as health behaviors (e.g., less smoking, high-risk behaviors), beliefs, perceptions and emotions (e.g., believe in something greater than oneself, sense of meaning and significance), community/social and spiritual support (e.g., emotional support from congregation), and possible processes not assessable by current scientific methods. Counseling psychologists and other health professionals can help clients understand that a number of factors are at work that will help mediate the solutions to their problems. Spiritual practices and perspectives can be good candidates to serve as mediators in helping clients work out solutions to their problems of living.

As long as counseling psychologists and other health professionals are open minded, well trained, have access to appropriate consultation, and closely monitor ethical issues with competence, respect, integrity, and responsibility in mind, they can learn a great deal from spiritual and religious wisdom traditions. In doing so, their clients can benefit greatly as well.

Further Reading

Fredrickson, B. (2009). *Positivity*. New York: Random House.

Miller, W. R. (Ed.) (1999). *Integrating spirituality into treatment: Resources for practitioners*. Washington, DC: American Psychological Association.

Pargament, K. I. (2007). *Spiritually integrated psychotherapy: Understanding and addressing the sacred*. New York: The Guilford Press.

Plante, T. G. (2009). *Spiritual practices in psychotherapy: Thirteen tools for enhancing psychological health*. Washington, DC: American Psychological Association.

Plante, T. G., & Thoresen, C. E. (Eds.). (2007). *Spirit, science and health: How the spiritual mind fuels physical wellness*. Westport, CT: Praeger/Greenwood.

Richards, P. S., & Bergin, A. E. (Eds.). (2003). *Casebook for a spiritual strategy in counseling and psychotherapy*. Washington, DC: American Psychological Association.

Richards, P. S., & Bergin, A. E. (2005). *A spiritual strategy for counseling and psychotherapy, Second edition*. Washington, DC: American Psychological Association.

Vaillant, G. E. (2008). *Spiritual evolution: A scientific defense of faith*. New York: Broadway.

References

Alcoholics Anonymous World Services (1977). Alcoholics Anonymous: The twelve steps and twelve traditions, third edition. New York: Author.

Allport, G. W. (1950). *The individual and his religion: A psychological interpretation*. New York: Macmillan.

American Psychological Association. (2002). Ethical principles of psychologists and code of conduct. *American Psychologist*, *57*, 1060–1073.

American Psychological Association. (2003). Guidelines on multicultural education, training, research, practice, and organizational change for psychologists. *American Psychologist*, *58*, 377–402.

Ano, G. A. (2005). *Spiritual struggles between vice and virtue: A brief psychospiritual intervention*. Unpublished Ph.D. dissertation, Bowling Green State University, Bowling Green, OH.

Armstrong, K. (2006). *The great transformation: The beginning of our religious traditions*. New York: Anchor Books.

Association of American Medical Colleges. (1999). *Report III: Contemporary issues in medicine: Communication in medicine, medical school objectives project*. Washington, DC: Association of American Medical Colleges.

Astin, A. W., Astin, H. S., Lindholm, J. A., Bryant, A. N., Calderone, S., & Szelenyi, K. (2005). *The spiritual life of college students: A national study of college students' search for meaning and purpose*. Los Angeles: Higher Education Research Institute, University of California.

Balter, M. (2005). Are human brains still evolving? Brain genes show signs of selection. *Science*, *309*, 1662–1663.

Bandura, A. (2003). On the psychosocial impact and mechanisms of spiritual modeling. *The International Journal for the Psychology of Religion*, *13*, 167–174.

Bormann, J. E., Gifford, A. L., Shively, M., Smith, T. L., Redwine, L., Kelly, A., . . . Belding, W. (2006). Effects of spiritual mantra repetition on HIV outcomes: A randomized controlled trial. *Journal of Behavioral Medicine*, *29*, 359–376.

Centers for Disease Control and Prevention. (2004). *National vital statistics report*. Washington, DC: Author.

Cole, B. S., & Pargament, K. I. (1998). Re-creating your life: A spiritual/psychotherapeutic intervention for people diagnosed with cancer. *Psycho-Oncology*, *8*, 395–407.

Collins, G. R. (1977). *The rebuilding of psychology: An integration of psychology and Christianity*. Wheaton, IL: Tyndale House.

Dali Lama, & Ekman, P. (2008). *Emotional awareness: Overcoming the obstacles to psychological balance and compassion*. New York: Times Books.

Damasio, A. (1994). *Descartes' error*. New York: Penguin.

Easwaran, E. (1991). *Meditation: A simple eight-point program for translating spiritual ideals into daily life*. Tomales, CA: Nilgiri Press. (Original work published 1978).

Easwaran, E. (2005). *Strength in the storm: Creating calm in difficult times*. Tomales, CA: Nilgiri Press.

Edmondson, D., Park, C. L., Chaudoir, S. R., & Wortmann, J. H. (2008). Death without God: Religious struggle, death concerns, and depression in the terminally ill. *Psychological Science*, *19*, 754–758

Ellis, A. (1971). *The case against religion: A psychotherapist's view*. New York: Institute for Rational Living.

Emmons, R. A., & Paloutzian, R. F. (2003) The psychology of religion. *Annual Review of Psychology*, *54*, 377–402.

Flinders, T., Oman, D., & Flinders, C. L. (2007). The eight-point program of passage meditation: Health effects of a comprehensive program. In T. G. Plante & C. E. Thoresen (Eds.), *Spirit, science, and health: How the spiritual mind fuels physical wellness* (pp. 72–93). Westport, CT: Praeger/Greenwood.

Fredrickson, B. (2009). *Positivity*. New York: Random House

Freud, S. (1961). *The future of an illusion* (J. Strachey, Ed. and Trans.). New York: W. W. Norton. (Original work published 1927).

Fuller, R. C. (2001). *Spiritual but not religious*. New York: Oxford University Press.

Gallup, G., Jr., & Lindsay, D. M. (1999). *Surveying the religious landscape: Trends in U.S. beliefs*. Harrisburg, PA: Morehouse.

Hage, S. M. (2006). A closer look at the role of spirituality in psychology training. *Professional Psychology: Research and Practice*, *37*, 303–310.

Harris, A. H. S., & Thoresen, C. E. (2005). Volunteering is associated with delayed mortality in older people: Analysis of the longitudinal study of aging. *Journal of Health Psychology*, *10*, 739–752.

Hartz, G. W. (2005). *Spirituality and mental health: Clinical applications*. Binghamton, NY: Haworth Pastoral Press.

Hill, P., & Pargament, K. I. (2003). Advances in the conceptualization and measurement of religion and spirituality. *American Psychologist*, *58*, 64–74.

Hitchens, C. (2007). *God is not great: How religion poisons everything*. New York: Twelve Books.

Hood, R.W., Jr. (2005). Mystical, spiritual, and religious experiences. In R. F. Paloutzian & C. L. Park (Eds.), *Handbook of the psychology of religion and spirituality* (pp. 348–364). New York: The Guilford Press.

Hummer, R. A., Rogers, R. G., Nam, C. B., & Ellison, C. G. (1999). Religious involvement and U.S. adult mortality. *Demography*, *36*, 272–285.

Ironson, G., Solomon, G. F., Balbin, E. G., O'Cleirigh, C., George, A., & Kumar, M., . . . Woods, T. E. (2002). The Ironson-Woods Spirituality/Religiousness Index is associated with long survival, health behaviors, less distress, and low cortisol in people with HIV/AIDS. *Annals of Behavioral Medicine*, *24*, 34–48.

James, W. (1890). *Principles of psychology*. New York: Holt.

James, W. (1936). *The varieties of religious experience: A study in human nature*. New York: Modern Library. (Original work published 1902).

Jung, C. G. (1938). *Psychology and religion*. New Haven, CT: Yale University Press.

Kabat-Zinn, J. (1990). *Full catastrophe living*. New York: Delacorte Press.

Kabat-Zinn, J. (2003). Mindfulness-based interventions in context: Past, present, and future. *Clinical Psychology: Research and Practice*, *10*, 144–156.

Keefe, F. J., Affleck, G., Lefebvre, J., Underwood, L., Caldwell, D. S., & Drew, J. (2001). Living with rheumatoid arthritis: The role of daily spirituality and daily religious and spiritual coping. *Journal of Pain*, *2*, 101–110.

Keltner, D. (2009). *Born to be good: The science of a meaningful life*. New York: W. W. Norton.

Koenig, H. G., McCullough, M. E., & Larson, D. B. (2001). *Handbook of religion and health*. New York: Oxford University Press.

Kremer, H., & Ironson, G. (2007). Spirituality and HIV/AIDS. In T. G. Plante & C. E. Thoresen (Eds.), *Spirit, science, and health: How the spiritual mind fuels physical wellness* (pp. 176–190). Westport, CT: Praeger/Greenwood.

Kristeller, J. L., Rhodes, M., Cripe, L. D., & Sheets, V. (2005). Oncologist assisted spiritual intervention study (OASIS): Patient acceptability and initial evidence of effects. *International Journal of Psychiatry in Medicine, 35*, 329–347.

McAdams, D. P. (2006). *The redemptive self: Stories Americans live by*. New York: Oxford University Press.

McCullough, M. E., Hoyt, W. T., Larson, D. B., Koenig, H. G., & Thoresen, C. E. (2000). Religious involvement and mortality: A meta-analytic review. *Health Psychology 19*, 211–221.

Miller, W. R., & Delaney, H. D. (Eds.). (2005). *Judeo-Christian perspectives on psychology*. Washington, DC: American Psychological Association.

Miller, W. R., & Thoresen, C. E. (2003). Spirituality, religion and health: An emerging research field. *American Psychologist, 58*, 24–35.

Mills, P. J. (2002). Spirituality, religiousness, and health: From research to clinical practice. *Annals of Behavioral Medicine, 24*, 1–2.

Murray-Swank, N. A., & Pargament, K. I. (2005). God, where are you? Evaluating a spiritually-integrated intervention for sexual abuse. *Mental Health, Religion and Culture, 8*, 191–203.

Myers, D. (2000). *The American paradox: Spiritual hunger in a land of plenty*. New Haven, CT: Yale University Press.

Oman, D., Hedberg, J., & Thoresen, C. E. (2006). Passage meditation reduces stress in health professionals: A randomized controlled trial. *Journal of Consulting and Clinical Psychology, 74*, 714–719.

Oman, D., Richards, T. A., Hedberg, J., & Thoresen, C. E. (2008). Passage meditation improves caregiving self-efficacy among health professionals: A randomized clinical trial. *Journal of Health Psychology, 13*, 922–1007.

Oman, D., & Thoresen, C. E. (2002). Does religion cause health? Differing interpretations and diverse meanings. *Journal of Health Psychology, 7*, 365–380.

Oman, D., & Thoresen, C. E. (2003). Spiritual modeling: A key to spiritual and religious growth? *The International Journal for the Psychology of Religion, 13*, 149–165.

Oman, D., & Thoresen, C. E. (2005). Do religion and spirituality influence health? In R. F. Paloutzian & C. L. Park (Eds.), *Handbook of the psychology of religion and spirituality* (pp. 435–459). New York: The Guilford Press.

Oman, D. & Thoresen, C. E. (2007). How does one learn to be spiritual? The neglected role of spiritual modeling in health. In T. G. Plante & C. E. Thoresen (Eds.), *Spirit, science and health: How the spiritual mind fuels physical wellness* (pp. 39–56). Westport, CT: Praeger/Greenwood.

Oman, D., Thoresen, C. E., & McMahon, K. (1999). Volunteerism and mortality among the community-dwelling elderly. *Journal of Health Psychology, 4*, 301–316.

Oman, D., Thoresen, C. E., Park, C. L., Shaver, P. R., Hood, R. W., & Plante, T. G. (2009). How does one become spiritual? The spiritual modeling inventory of life environments. *Mental Health, Religion and Culture, 12*, 427–456.

Ornish, D. (1990). *Dr. Dean Onrush's program for reversing heart disease: The only system scientifically proven to reverse disease without drugs or surgery*. New York: Galantine Books.

Paloutzian, R. F., & Park, C. L. (Eds.). (2005). *Handbook of the psychology of religion and spirituality*. New York: The Guilford Press.

Panksepp, J. (1998) *Affective neuroscience: The foundation of human and animal emotion*. New York: Oxford University Press.

Pargament, K. I. (1997). *The psychology of religious coping: Theory, research, practice*. New York: The Guilford Press.

Pargament, K. I. (2007). *Spiritually integrated psychotherapy: Understanding and addressing the sacred*. New York: The Guilford Press.

Pargament, K. I., McCarthy, S., Shah, P., Anon, G., Tarakeshwar, N., Wachholtz, A. B.,...Duggan, J. (2004). Religion and HIV: A review of the literature and clinical implications. *Southern Medical Journal, 97*, 1201–1209.

Peterson, R. (1986). *Everyone is right: A new look at comparative religion and its relation to science*. Marina del Ray, CA: DeVorss.

Plante, T. G. (Ed.). (2004). *Sin against the innocents: Sexual abuse by priests and the role of the Catholic Church*. Westport, CT: Praeger/Greenwood.

Plante, T. G. (2009). *Spiritual practices in psychotherapy: Thirteen tools for enhancing psychological health*. Washington, DC: American Psychological Association.

Plante, T. G., & Sharma, N. (2001). Religious faith and mental health outcomes. In T. G. Plante & A. C. Sherman (Eds.), *Faith and health: Psychological perspectives* (pp. 240–261). New York: The Guilford Press.

Plante, T. G., & Sherman, A. S. (Eds.). (2001). *Faith and health: Psychological perspectives*. New York: The Guilford Press.

Plante, T. G., & Thoresen, C. E. (Eds.). (2007). *Spirit, science and health: How the spiritual mind fuels physical wellness*. Westport, CT: Praeger/Greenwood.

Powell, L., Shahabi, L., & Thoresen, C. E. (2003). Religion and spirituality: Linkages to physical health. *American Psychologist, 58*, 36–52.

Putnam, R. D. (2000). *Bowling alone: The collapse and revival of the American community*. New York: Simon & Schuster.

Richards, P. S., & Bergin, A. E. (2005). *A spiritual strategy for counseling and psychotherapy* (2nd ed.). Washington, DC: American Psychological Association.

Richards, P. S., Hardman, R. K., & Berrett, M. E. (2000). *Spiritual renewal: A journal of faith and healing*. Orem, UT: Center for Change.

Russell, S. R., & Yarhouse, M. A. (2006). Religion/Spirituality within APA-accredited psychology predoctoral internships. *Professional Psychology: Research and Practice, 37*, 430–436.

Rye, M., & Pargament, K. I. (2003). *Coping with divorce: A journey toward forgiveness*. Unpublished manual, University of Dayton, OH.

Ryff, C. D., & Singer, B. (1998). The contours of positive human health. *Psychological Inquiry, 9*, 1–28.

Seligman, M. E. P., Steen, T. A., Park, N., & Peterson, C. (2005). Positive psychology progress: Empirical validation of interventions. *American Psychologist, 60*, 410–421.

Shafranske, E. P. (2000). Religious involvement and professional practices of psychiatrists and other mental health professionals. *Psychiatric Annals, 30*, 525–532.

Shapiro, S. L., & Walsh, R. (2007). Meditation: Exploring the farther reaches. In T. G. Plante & C. E. Thoresen (Eds.), *Spirit, science, and health: How the spiritual mind fuels physical wellness* (pp. 57–71). Westport, CT: Praeger/Greenwood.

Smith, H. (1991). *The world's religions: Our great wisdom traditions*. San Francisco: Harper San Francisco.

Snyder, C. R., & Lopez, S. J. (2007). *Positive psychology: The scientific and practical explorations of human strengths*. Thousand Oaks, CA: Sage.

Sue, D. W., Bingham, R. P., Porche-Burke, L., &Vasquez, M. (1999). The diversification of psychology: A multicultural revolution. *American Psychologist, 54*, 1061–1069.

Task Force on Promotion and Dissemination of Psychological Procedures. (1995). Training in and dissemination of empirically validated psychological treatments: Report and recommendations. *Clinical Psychologist, 48*, 3–23.

Tennen, H., Affleck, G., Armeli, S., & Carney, M. A. (2000). A daily process approach to coping: Linking theory, research, and practice. *American Psychologist, 55*, 626–636.

Thoresen, C. E. (2007). Spirituality, religion and health: What's the deal? In T. G. Plante & C. E. Thoresen (Eds.), *Spirit, science, and health: How the spiritual mind fuels physical wellness* (pp. 3–10). Westport, CT: Praeger/Greenwood.

Thoresen, C. E., & Eagleston, J. R. (1985). Counseling for health. *The Counseling Psychologist, 13*, 15–87

Thoresen, C. E., & Harris, A. H. S. (2002). Spirituality and health: What's the evidence and what's needed? *Annals of Behavioral Medicine, 24*, 3–13.

Thoresen, C. E., Oman, D., & Harris, A. H. S. (2005). The effects of religious practices: A focus on health. In W. R. Miller & H. D. Delaney (Eds.), *Judeo-Christian perspectives on psychology* (pp. 205–226). Washington, DC: American Psychological Association.

Trenholm, P., Trent, J., & Compton, W. C. (1998). Negative religious conflict as a predictor of panic disorder. *Journal of Clinical Psychology, 54*, 59–65.

Vaillant, G. E. (2008). *Spiritual evolution: A scientific defense of faith*. New York: Broadway.

Wachholtz, A. B., & Pargament, K. I. (2008). Migraines and meditation: Does spirituality matter? *Journal of Behavioral Medicine, 31*, 351–366.

Watson, J. B. (1983). *Psychology from the standpoint of a behaviorist*. Dover, NH: Frances Pinter. (Original work published 1924).

Worthington, E. L., Jr. (1990). Marriage counseling: A Christian approach to counseling couples. *Counseling and Values, 35*, 3–15.

Worthington, E. L., Jr. (2004). *Experiencing forgiveness: Six practical sessions for becoming a more forgiving Christian*. Unpublished manuscript, Virginia Commonwealth University, Richmond, VA.

Zinnbauer, B. J., & Pargament, K. I. (2005). Religiousness and spirituality. In R. F. Paloutzian & C. L. Park (Eds.), *Handbook of the psychology of religion and spirituality* (pp. 21–42). New York: The Guilford Press.

Spirituality and Recovery From Serious Mental Problems

David Lukoff

Abstract

This chapter summarizes theory, research, and treatment regarding spirituality and recovery from serious mental problems (SMPs). The incorporation of spirituality into the recovery model was initiated by consumers starting in the 1970s and has become widely accepted in the United States and around the world. Support for this comes from research showing the generally beneficial effects of spirituality on health, including mental health problems; surveys documenting the role that spiritual beliefs and practices play in many who are recovering from SMPs; and the importance of religious coping for people facing serious health problems, including SMPs. Some successful therapeutic approaches for integrating spirituality into recovery are discussed.

Key Words: recovery, religion, spirituality, schizophrenia, bipolar disorder, coping

Introduction

While the significance of spirituality in substance abuse treatment has been acknowledged for many years due to widespread recognition of the therapeutic value of 12-step programs, this is a new development in the treatment of serious mental problems (SMPs) such as bipolar disorder and schizophrenia. The incorporation of spirituality into treatment is part of the recovery model that has become widely accepted in the United States and around the world. In 1999, the Surgeon General in a landmark report on mental health urged that *all* mental health systems adopt the recovery model (US Surgeon General, 1999).

What distinguishes the recovery model from prior approaches in the mental health field is the perspective that people can fully recover from even the most severe forms of mental disorders. Thus, services and research should be reoriented toward recovery from severe or long-term mental illnesses (Anthony, 1993) because recovery creates an orientation of hope rather than the "kiss of death" that diagnoses like schizophrenia once held. One hundred years ago, Emil Kraepelin identified the disorder now known as schizophrenia as dementia praecox, a chronic, unremitting, gradually deteriorating condition, which has a progressive downhill course that ends in dementia and incompetence (Kraepelin, 1904). However, researchers in the past two decades in Japan, Germany, Switzerland, Scotland, France, and the United States have established that people diagnosed with schizophrenia and other serious mental disorders are capable of regaining significant roles in society and of running their own lives. There is strong evidence that most persons, even with long-term and disabling forms of schizophrenia, do "recover," that is, enjoy lengthy periods of time free of psychotic symptoms and partake of community life as independent citizens (Lukoff, Wallace, Liberman, & Burke, 1986). Daniel Fisher, a former patient, now a psychiatrist and internationally recognized advocate for the recovery model, maintains that,

Believing you can recover is vital to recovery from mental illness. Recovery involves self-assessment and personal growth from a prior baseline, regardless of where that baseline was. Growth may take the overt form of skill development and resocialization, but it is essentially a spiritual revaluing of oneself, a gradually developed respect for one's own worth as a human being. Often when people are healing from an episode of mental disorder, their hopeful beliefs about the future are intertwined with their spiritual lives, including praying, reading sacred texts, attending devotional services, and following a spiritual practice.

(Fisher, 2006)

Recovery Versus Medical Model

The medical model tends to define recovery in negative terms (e.g., symptoms and complaints that need to be eliminated, disorders that need to be cured or removed). Mark Ragins (2006) observed that focusing on recovery does not discount the seriousness of the conditions:

For severe mental illness it may seem almost dishonest to talk about recovery. After all, the conditions are likely to persist, in at least some form, indefinitely... The way out of this dilemma is by realizing that, whereas the illness is the object of curative treatment efforts, it is the persons themselves who are the objects of recovery efforts.

Drawing on the 12-step approach to recovery from addictions, Ragins (2006) outlined an alternative to the medical model approach that he helped to develop for individuals at Village Integrated Services Agency in Long Beach, California:

1. Accepting having a chronic, incurable disorder, that is a permanent part of them, without guilt or shame, without fault or blame
2. Avoiding complications of the condition (e.g., by staying sober)
3. Participating in an ongoing support system both as a recipient and a provider
4. Changing many aspects of their lives, including emotions, interpersonal relationships, and spirituality, both to accommodate their disorder and grow through overcoming it

In the recovery model, health care professionals act as coaches helping to design a rehabilitation plan that supports the patient's efforts to achieve a series of functional goals. The focus is on motivating the patient's own efforts to help himself or herself. Respecting and supporting a patient's spiritual

journey, as described later in this chapter, is often an important component of his or her recovery. Ridgeway provides this definition: "Recovery is an on-going journey of healing and transformation. It involves reclaiming hope and a positive sense of self despite the experience of psychiatric disability, self-managing one's life and mental health to reduce psychiatric symptoms and achieve higher levels of wellness, and reclaiming a life and roles beyond being a consumer in the mental health system" (Onken, Dumont, Ridgway, Dornan, & Ralph, 2002, p. 2). McAdams et al. (2001) conducted studies of people recovering from a range of adversities and based on his findings and the extant literature concluded that successful recovery often depends on developing a positive sense of self:

The take home message from the empirical literature on benefit-finding is that people who perceive benefits in adversity tend to show better recovery from and adjustment to the negative events that brought them into adversity in the first place... survivors of illness and trauma often report increased self-reliance and broader self-understanding, enhanced self-disclosure and emotional expressiveness in relationships and a changed philosophy of life.

(p. 485)

Davidson and Strauss (1992) interviewed 66 people who were recovering from SMPs. Twenty-five were diagnosed with schizophrenia; 17 with schizoaffective disorder; and 24 with mood disorders. They found the following themes in the recovery of self:

Discovering a more active self
Taking stock of the self
Putting the self into action
Appealing to the self

These findings suggest that the process of recovery can occur even while the person continues to experience symptoms.

Importance of Spirituality in the Consumer Movement

The increasing adoption of the recovery model has evolved from the growing movement throughout the United States and the world of people calling themselves consumers, survivors, or ex-patients. Having been diagnosed with mental disorders, they began working together with health professionals to make changes in the mental health system and in society. The recognition of spirituality as an important component of recovery has been driven by these consumer and family grassroots movements. In the late 1950s, with the advent of the civil rights movement, people began organizing to fight against inequality and social injustice. By 1970, the women's movement, gay rights movement, and disabilities rights movement had emerged. In this context, in 1975, former patients in several cities across the country began what was first known as the antipsychiatry movement with groups such as the Network Against Psychiatric Assault. The consumer movement grew out of the idea that individuals who have experienced similar problems, life situations, or crises can effectively provide support to one another. Ex-mental patients organized drop-in centers, artistic endeavors, and businesses.

Sally Clay, a pioneer of this movement and founder of the Portland Coalition for the Psychiatrically Labeled, wrote a seminal article in 1987 on spirituality and recovery that illustrated consumer concerns about the neglect of spirituality in their treatment. She has written about the important role that spiritual experiences played in her recovery following 2 years of hospitalization when she was diagnosed with schizophrenia at the Yale-affiliated Hartford Institute of Living (IOL). While hospitalized, she had a powerful spiritual experience that led her to attend religious services.

> My recovery had nothing to do with the talk therapy, the drugs, or the electroshock treatments I had received; more likely, it happened in spite of these things. My recovery did have something to do with the devotional services I had been attending. At the IOL I attended both Protestant and Catholic services, and if Jewish or Buddhist services had been available, I would have gone to them, too. I was cured instantly—healed if you will—as a direct result of a spiritual experience. (*Clay, 1987*, p. 91)

Many years later Clay went back to the IOL to review her case records and found herself described as having "decompensated with grandiose delusions with spiritual preoccupations" (Clay, 1987, p. 90). She complains that "Not a single aspect of my spiritual experience at the IOL was recognized as legitimate; neither the spiritual difficulties nor the healing that occurred at the end" (p. 92). Clay is not denying that she had an SMP at the time, but she makes the case that, in addition to the disabling effects she experienced as part of her SMP, there was also a profound spiritual component that was ignored. She describes how the lack of sensitivity to the spiritual dimensions of her experience on the part of both mental health and religious professionals was detrimental to her recovery. Nevertheless, she has persevered in her belief that,

> For me, becoming "mentally ill" was always a spiritual crisis, and finding a spiritual model of recovery was a question of life or death. Finally I could admit openly that my experiences were, and always had been, a spiritual journey—not sick, shameful, or evil. (Clay, 1994)

The consumer movement has maintained since its early days that recovery from an SMP is experienced by many as part of their spiritual journey. This was eloquently expressed by Jay Mahler, consumer advocate and program director of the Mental Health Division of Contra Costa County. During a conversation with Dan Weisburd, then editor of the CAMI, Jay mentioned that he viewed his disorder as a spiritual journey. When Dan questioned how a devastating mental disorder could be a spiritual journey, Jay responded:

> Regardless of what anyone else chooses to call it, that's what it's been for me. The whole medical vocabulary puts us in the role of a "labeled" diagnosed victim. . . . But as they go through trial and error to control your symptoms, it doesn't take a genius to realize they haven't got the answers. No clue about cures! And oh boy, those side effects! I don't say medications can't help, or that treatments won't have value. But, what I do say is that my being aware that I'm on a spiritual journey empowers me to deal with the big, human "spiritual" questions, like: "Why is this happening to me? Will I ever be the same again? Is there a place for me in this world? Can my experience of life be made livable? If I can't be cured can I be recovering . . . even somewhat? Has my God abandoned me?" Bottom line is . . . we who have it have to wonder whether what remains constitutes a life worth living. That's my spiritual journey, that wondering. That's my search. (*Weisburd*, 1997, p. 2)

Jay Mahler and Frank Leonard started organizing spirituality groups in the San Francisco Bay Area in the 1970s. But it was in later conferences that consumers, mental health professionals, and religious professionals started holding dialogs and began networking to deal with the issue of addressing spirituality in recovery more effectively. Among the many events funded by National Institute of Mental Health was the 1993 Alternatives Conference, "A Celebration of Our Spirit." Held in

Columbus, Ohio, it was organized by the National Empowerment Center (http://www.power2u.org). (For a comprehensive review of the mental health rights movement, see http://www.theopalproject.org) The anitpsychiatry activities of the 1970s have transformed into a movement of consumers who are taking an active role in shaping the recovery model that is being widely adopted throughout the mental health system.

A grassroots network of family members of consumers also organized and founded The National Alliance for the Mentally Ill (now called "NAMI"). Their FaithNet network (http://www.nami.org/namifaithnet) was founded by California physician Guannar Christiansen, MD, and has published a newsletter on outreach and engagement of faith communities with mental health since 1998. NAMI's national conventions have featured many programs on spirituality, such as the 2006 NAMI Conference presentation on "Mental Illness as Spiritual Journey" by Rev. Susan Gregg-Schroeder. Jay Mahler and David Lukoff have also presented on spirituality at NAMI conferences (Lukoff, Mahler, & Mancuso, 2009).

Pat Deegan, who is both a consumer and a psychologist, also makes the point that an episode of SMP can be a genuine route to spirituality:

> Distress, even the distress associated with psychosis, can be hallowed ground upon which one can meet God and receive spiritual teaching. When we set aside neurobiological reductionism, then it is conceivable that during the passage that is madness, during that passage of tomb becoming womb, those of us who are diagnosed can have authentic encounters with God. These spiritual teachings can help to guide and encourage the healing process that is recovery.
> (*Deegan*, 2004)

Studies have shown that religious content occurs in 22% to 39% of psychotic symptoms (Cothran & Harvey, 1986; Siddle, Haddock, Tarrier, & Faragher, 2002). One study of hospitalized bipolar patients found that religious delusions were present in 25% and over half of the hallucinations were brief, grandiose, and usually religious (Goodwin & Jamison, 1990). They suggest that there "have been many mystics who may well have suffered from manic-depressive illness—for example, St. Theresa, St. Francis, St. John" (p. 362). Conversely, Podvoll pointed out that genuine mystical experiences occur in manic states often:

> There is a general agreement among those who have experienced it, that religious truths are realized, the

religious truths, the ones of the desert fathers and the great mystics.
> (*Podvoll*, 1990, p. 118)

Psychotic and spiritual experiences have been associated since the earliest recorded history. Hallucinatory and visionary experiences of biblical prophets and saints have played an essential role in religion for thousands of years. The Old Testament uses the same term to refer to madness sent by God as a punishment for the disobedient, and to describe the behavior of prophets (Rosen, 1968). Socrates, who had a personal Daemonic voice that guided him, declared, "Our greatest blessings come to us by way of madness, provided the madness is given us by divine gift" (Dodds, 1951, p. 61).

Based on a cross-cultural survey, anthropologist Prince (1992) concluded that:

> Highly similar mental and behavioral states may be designated psychiatric disorders in some cultural settings and religious experiences in others…Within cultures that invest these unusual states with meaning and provide the individual experiencing them with institutional support, at least a proportion of them may be contained and channeled into socially valuable roles.
> (*Prince*, 1992, p. 289)

Thus, psychotic experiences that have religious/spiritual content can be explored to find sources of strength, hope, and belief that can provide spiritual support.

Research on Spirituality and Recovery From Serious Mental Problems

Studies have found that people with SMPs value religion as highly as the general population and they turn even more to religion during crises (Fitchett, Burton, & Sivan, 1997). In one study, 94% of people with SMPs indicated a belief in God or higher power and 70% reported they were "moderately," "considerably," or "very" religious (Kroll & Sheehan, 1989). In a study of the religious needs and resources of people hospitalized for SMPs, Fitchett et al. found that 88% of the patients reported three or more current religious needs. Their overall spiritual well-being scores were lower and they were less likely to have talked with their clergy. Only 5% of Fitchett et al.'s patient group said that religion was not a source of strength and comfort for them. Fitchett and colleagues concluded that religion is important for the psychiatric patients, but they may need assistance to find resources to address their religious needs. Neeleman and Lewis (1994) refer to the religious beliefs strongly endorsed by many in their study as "comfort beliefs" because they reflect religion's capacity to reassure and offer solace. Lindgren and Coursey (1995) interviewed people in psychosocial rehabilitation programs and found that 80% said that spirituality/religion had been helpful to them. In a UK study, 61% of the interviewees reported that they had used religion for coping with their SMPs (Kirov, Kemp, Kirov, & David, 1998) among their sample of 74 patients with acute psychotic symptoms.

A number of studies show that spirituality plays an important role in the recovery process for many and that the intensity of religious beliefs is not associated with psychopathology (Pfeifer & Waelty, 1995). In fact, religious practices such as worship and prayer appear to protect against severity of psychiatric symptoms and hospitalization, and enhance life satisfaction and speed recovery from SMPs (Koenig, McCullough, & Larson, 2001). Fallot (1998, 2001) analyzed the key religious and spiritual themes in recovery narratives drawn from spiritual discussion groups, trauma recovery groups, and other clinical groups at Community Connections, a mental health facility for people diagnosed with SMPs. He found that although organized religion had been experienced as stigmatizing and rejecting on some occasions, on the whole a personal, spiritual experience of a relationship with God was helpful in building hope, a sense of divine support and love, the courage to change, and to accept what cannot be changed. Participation in church and other faith communities provided them with supporting practices such as prayer, meditation, religious ritual, religious reading, and listening to religious music. Fallot and colleagues found three main themes. First, spirituality played a positive role in coping with stressful situations, using prayer and religious role models, as well as avoiding drug use and negative activities. Second, church attendance and a belief in a higher power provided social and emotional support. Third, spirituality enhanced the sense of being whole. Sullivan (1993) conducted a qualitative study involving 40 participants that sought to uncover factors associated with the successful adjustment of former and current consumers of mental health services. Spiritual beliefs and practices were identified as essential by 48% of the consumers.

Jacobson (2001) applied the technique of thematic dimensional analysis to 30 recovery narratives. She identified "spiritual or philosophical" as an important theme in most of the narratives:

In this model the "what happened" is a spiritual or philosophical crisis during which the self is destroyed and then recreated in the light of a newly realized truth. The crisis is an altered state of being… The greatest help comes when individuals are able to connect with some source of enlightenment; a community of practicing Buddhists, the Bible, treatises of philosophy or physics. Recovery is about enduring and coming out the other side… Coming back to life, in a recreated and enlightened self, the individual discovers new "wisdom and compassion." Those who have recovered, then, are obligated to demonstrate this wisdom and to practice compassion by reaching out to others who are in the midst of their own crises.

Many patients make use of use of religious and spiritual practices during their recovery. Among a sample of 157 patients, of whom 86% were on psychotropic medications, 50% reported using religious/spiritual reading, 31% meditation, and 20% yoga (Russinova, Wewiorski, & Cash, 2002). Another study of 74 patients with acute psychotic symptoms followed up every 6 months for 2 years found that 30.2% of these patients reported an increase in religious faith after the onset of the illness, and 61.2% reported they used religion to cope with their illness and to get better (Kirov et al., 1998). Eighty-three percent of psychiatric patients in a different study felt that spiritual beliefs had a positive impact on their illness through the comfort it provided and the feelings it engendered of not being alone (Lindgren & Coursey, 1995).

Randal, Simpson, and Laidlaw (2003) conducted a study to assess whether a recovery-focused multimodal therapy can improve the symptoms and functioning of treatment-resistant psychotic patients Their treatment included medication, supportive therapy, focus on recovery, spirituality, and cognitive-behavioral therapy, as well as psychoeducation and affective regulation. The researchers explored issues of religious and spiritual beliefs. Although the sample size was small (nine patients), they found improvement in both positive and negative symptoms. One example they cite is of a participant who "spoke of her relationship with God deepening significantly, she attributed her increased sense of well-being and confidence to God's faithfulness, which she saw as enabling her to move into supported accommodation, and she started part-time work" (p. 722).

Contemporary research on religious coping has generally supported the value of spirituality for persons with SMPs (Phillips, Lukoff, & Stone, 2009). Most of the studies have employed qualitative methods or simple questionnaires using closed-ended items, while a few studies have used validated scales of religion and spirituality. Sullivan (1993) interviewed 40 individuals with SMPs who were considered to be in recovery (living on their own, working or going to school, having avoided psychiatric hospitalization for at least 2 years). Using an ethnographic research method, he found that 19 out of 40 individuals spontaneously reported that their religious beliefs and behaviors helped them recover. Eighty percent of a group of 406 individuals with SMPs in Los Angeles reported that their religious beliefs or behaviors helped them cope with their symptoms (Tepper, Rogers, Coleman, & Malony, 2001). Thirty percent of this group agreed to the statement that religious beliefs and practices "were the most important thing that kept [them] going" (Tepper et al., 2001, p. 662). Some benefits from religion include feelings of optimism and comfort from giving up some sense of control over the difficulties surrounding SMPs, instead placing that control in the belief of a divine force (Sullivan, 1993). Sullivan (1993), as well as others, noted that for persons with SMPs, spirituality provides a sense of connection and support through contacts with like-minded individuals (Bussema & Bussema, 2000; Fallot, 1998) and a higher power (Fitchett et al., 1997). Hope and security can also be derived from religious figures and texts that provide a model for persevering in the face of adversity, and attributing difficult life circumstances to part of a divine plan in which the individual has a purpose (Fallot, 1998). Many people with SMPs experience fear, confusion, and helplessness that disrupt the internal order of their personality. According to Fallot (2001), "Religious faith develops in an unconscious, involuntary way. The faith creates an internal source of security; it offers the individual peace, inner strength and hope...faith in these circumstances can be regarded as the strongest defense mechanisms" (p. 115).

However, some patients have been found to hold dysfunctional spiritual beliefs. One study of 52 psychiatric inpatients found that 23% believed that sin-related factors, such as sinful thoughts or acts, were related to the development of their illness (Sheehan & Kroll, 1990). This is clearly a guilt-inducing belief for which there is no evidence, and one that the vast majority of religious professionals would challenge. When I was a psychologist at Camarillo State Hospital, I collaborated with a rabbi in leading groups for patients, and this was one of the beliefs we regularly encountered. He made a point of disputing such assertions when they were voiced, using both Old and New Testament citations.

Pieper (2004) used the Religious Problem Solving Scale (Pargament, Koenig, & Perez, 2000) to explore issues of control and spirituality in psychiatric inpatients in the Netherlands. The inpatients reported rarely using two religious problem-solving methods that have been associated with poorer outcomes in other samples: (a) deferring religious coping in which individuals place their concerns in the hands of a higher power and believe they should submit control to a divine plan; and (b) self-directing religious coping in which individuals rely on themselves and believe that the divine has the capacity to help them deal with stress. Inpatients were more likely to use a third form of religious problem solving to deal with stress—collaborative religious coping in which individuals work with the divine by doing what they can and expecting help from a divine force regarding obstacles out of their control. The inpatients used this method of coping, which has been found to be associated with better adjustment to stress, at rates similar to the general population (Pargament et al., 2000). In addition, spirituality may play a role in reducing substance abuse among people with SMPs, a well-documented problem that interferes with recovery (Huguelet, Borras, Gillieron, Brandt, & Mohr, 2009).

Phillips and Stein (2007) used a longitudinal design to examine religious attributions and their relationship with adjustment to SMPs. They administered subscales of the RCOPE (Pargament et al., 2000), a well-validated measure of religious coping, and measures of psychological adjustment to young adults living with bipolar disorder and schizophrenia in 2000 (Time 1) and again 1 year later (Time 2). These participants, compared to nonpsychiatric samples from previous studies, were just as likely to use benevolent religious reappraisals (viewing one's challenges such as SMPs as part of a divine plan and an opportunity to grow spiritually). This form of spiritual coping has traditionally been associated with positive outcomes from a stressful life event (Pargament, Koenig, Tarakeshwar, & Hahn, 2004) and use of such appraisals was related to better outcomes in this study as well. Examining correlations between measures given at the same time (e.g., contrasting Time 1 benevolent religious reappraisal scores with Time 1 well-being), benevolent religious reappraisals were correlated with greater psychological well-being and personal growth from having dealt with SMPs. However, participants' benevolent religious reappraisal scores at Time 1 (2000) did not significantly predict the measures of adjustment 1 year later. In terms of other religious attributions, this sample of individuals with SMPs was more likely to believe that their mental problem was a punishment from God than nonpsychiatric samples in previous studies (Pargament et al., 2000). When examining measures at the same point in time, "punishing God reappraisals" were linked to higher levels of distress and greater feelings of loss of a normal life from having an SMP. Furthermore, participants' Time 1 punishing God reappraisal score was associated with higher distress 1 year later (Phillips & Stein, 2007). Similarly, while Tepper and colleagues (2001) found a positive relationship between general religious coping methods and outcomes—the more time spent utilizing religion to cope with mental problems, the fewer symptoms patients reported—some specific religious coping activities were associated with poorer outcomes. For instance, those who prayed the most had lower GAF (global assessment of functioning) scores, and those who met with their spiritual leaders more frequently were more likely to report distress. These studies suggest that research in the field of religious coping is documenting the importance of spirituality in persons with SMPs.

It is possible to integrate mainstream psychological theory of religious coping and transpersonal psychological concepts. Pargament, Smith, Koenig, and Perez (1998) have described transformational religious coping, which involves aspects of religion and spirituality that call for a radical change in living, a change in the major objectives in life ("ends") and ways to obtain these end states ("means"). Certain psychotic states, such as those described by Perry (1998), Grof and Grof (1989), and Lukoff (2007), could fits these criteria. The psychotic break in this situation is a spiritual crisis and involves the restructuring of one's worldview. Pargament (2007) spoke mostly of traditional conversion experiences and rituals of purification and forgiveness as examples of transformational religious coping. Spiritual emergencies may be another form of religious coping that can lead to transformation. With further refinement, mainstream psychological theory may be able to integrate transpersonal insights with regard to the spiritual dimensions of some psychotic episodes.

Treatment of Serious Mental Problems

To illustrate the role spirituality can play in therapy, I will describe how spirituality was important in my own recovery from an SMP (see Lukoff, 1991

for a fuller account). Joseph Campbell once said if there was a sign in a hallway that said: "Lecture on God turn right. Meet God turn left," most people would go to the lecture. I was one of those who not only turned left to meet God but became God—or at least Buddha and Christ. This happened in 1971 when, at the age of 23, I spent 2 months firmly convinced that I was a reincarnation of both Buddha and Christ. I spent many sleepless nights holding conversations with the "spirits" of eminent thinkers in the social sciences and humanities, including talks with R. D. Laing, Margaret Mead, Freud, and Jung. I also conversed with Bob Dylan and Cat Stevens to learn about how to make my book popular with millions of people. Based on these exchanges, I compiled what I learned into a "Holy Book" that would unite all the peoples of the world. I began this sacred endeavor by making photocopies of the book and giving them to my family and friends, and passing them out in the streets of Berkeley, California.

For those 2 months, my episode met the diagnostic criteria for Acute Schizophrenic Reaction in the *Diagnostic and Statistical Manual II* (which was in use at the time). In the current *DSM-IV-TR*, that experience could be diagnosed as a Hallucinogen Induced Delusional Disorder or a Brief Psychotic Disorder. As has happened to others (Lukoff & Everest, 1985), I could have been diagnosed with a psychotic disorder if I hadn't been supported by friends who took me in for weeks at a time while I was going through that episode. They provided sanctuary for me and helped me to get grounded again in the everyday social world and consensual reality. Without their help, I might have been confined in a psychiatric hospital, diagnosed with a lifelong psychotic disorder, and "treated" with medication. Being taken care of by friends is one of the many experiences in my life for which I am deeply grateful.

The support of my friends during this time emulated the Diabysis program that was developed by in 1974 in San Francisco by Jungian analyst John Perry for people undergoing a first psychotic break. Diabysis created a homelike atmosphere where diagnostic labels were not used. Staff members were selected for their ability to be comfortable with the intensive inner processes of persons in psychotic states. In this environment, patients in such vulnerable states were able to follow their inner journeys while being protected from harm. Perry (1998) has published some data on the program, which closed down after a few years due to budget cutbacks in the mental health system. The average length of stay was

48 days. He reported that severely psychotic clients became coherent within 2–6 days *without* medication. The outcomes appeared better for those who had had fewer than three previous psychotic episodes. Unfortunately, other quantitative data were not collected for this sample.

Soteria is a similar program that was operated in San Jose, California, from 1969 to 1971. Its founder, Loren Mosher (1999), described the core of Soteria as "the 24 hour a day application of interpersonal phenomenologic interventions by a nonprofessional staff, usually without neuroleptic drug treatment, in the context of a small, homelike, quiet, supportive, protective, and tolerant social environment" (p. 142). Soteria or Soteria-based houses are currently operating in Sweden, Germany, Switzerland, Hungary, and some other countries. Several studies found that most patients recovered in 6–8 weeks without medication (Mosher et al., 2004). A recent meta-analysis of data from two carefully controlled studies of Soteria programs found better 2-year outcomes for Soteria patients in the domains of psychopathology, work, and social functioning compared to similar clients treated in a psychiatric hospital (Bola & Mosher, 2003).

However, after my delusional episode was over in 2 months, I was intensely embarrassed about having believed myself to be such grandiose figures and distributing a "Holy Book" to family and friends. For years I talked with absolutely no one about my experience—not my wife, my parents, nor even my therapist.

Six years after this episode, I entered Jungian analysis and had a dream in which a large red book appeared. My analyst asked for my associations to the book. Memories of my "Holy Book" leaped into my consciousness. I had not discussed my episode with anyone in 7 years, and my heart raced at the prospect of having to share my story with someone in my own profession. But recognizing therapy as a sacred place where one can safely tell secrets, I blurted out the details—about believing myself to be a reincarnation of Buddha and Christ, and having a mission to save the world by writing the new "Bible." To show that I was now a sane member of the psychology profession, I described these as "grandiose delusions" and "visual hallucinations." At the end of my description, she said, "Well, I don't think that's craziness. Sounds like something important was happening to you on a deep level." She invited me to bring the book to the next session, and so I got to tell my story for the first time.

James Hillman (1983) pointed out, "Recovery means recovering the divine from within the disorder, seeing that its contents are authentically religious" (p. 10). After that therapy session, I began my own process of "recovering the divine." During the past 30 years in my clinical practice as a psychologist at UCLA-NPI, Camarillo State Hospital, the San Francisco VA Medical Center, and private practice, I have often found myself face to face with individuals who have had delusions similar to mine. I believe that my ability to work effectively with those individuals has been aided by being given a rare opportunity to journey through the complete cycle and phenomenology of a naturally resolving psychotic episode. Thus, beyond serving as a spiritual awakening, my journey held within it the archetypal gift of the Wounded Healer, providing me with the ability to connect more deeply with persons recovering from episodes of mental disorders.

Psychotherapy can help patients shape their SMP into a coherent narrative, to see the "message" contained in their experiences, and to create a life-affirming personal myth (belief system) that integrates their experience. As I have illustrated in published case studies (Lukoff, 1988, 1993; Lukoff & Everest, 1985) and found in my clinical practice, psychotherapy can help some individuals probe the personal meaning of their symptoms and also see the universal dimensions of their experiences. Based on what I learned from my own SMP, and through my work with other individuals who had similar episodes, psychotherapy focused on integrating such experiences involves three phases:

Phase 1: Telling One's Story
Phase 2: Tracing Its Symbolic/Spiritual Heritage
Phase 3: Creating a New Personal Mythology

Phase 1: Telling One's Story

People with SMPs are usually not asked to recount or reflect on their experiences. Yet telling one's story is an important first step in recovery. Some clinicians have expressed the concern that having patients discuss their delusional experiences could exacerbate their symptoms by reinforcing them. I developed and led a 12-week holistic health program conducted at a state psychiatric hospital in which participants were encouraged to actively explore their psychotic symptoms. They participated in groups such as "Schizophrenia and Growth," which encouraged them to compare their experiences to mystical experiences, Native American vision quests, and shamanic initiatory crises. Patients were assessed biweekly for psychopathology, and the data showed that telling their stories did not result in exacerbation of symptoms (Lukoff et al., 1986).

Phase 2: Tracing Its Symbolic/Spiritual Heritage

Jungian analyst John Beebe (1982) has noted that,

> Minimally, the experience of psychotic illness is a call to the Symbolic Quest. Psychotic illness introduces the individual to themes, conflicts, and resolutions that may be pursued through the entire religious, spiritual, philosophical and artistic history of humanity. This is perhaps enough for an event to achieve.
>
> (p. 252)

But also like others I have worked with who developed grandiose delusions such as that they were god or the messiah, these stereotypical delusions of power and possibly inappropriate behavior were embarrassing to me later. Father Jerome Stack (1997), a Catholic chaplain for 25 years at Metropolitan State Hospital in Norwalk, California, has observed that people with SMPs often do have genuine religious experiences: "Many patients over the years have spoken to me of their religious experience and I have found their stories to be quite genuine, quite believable. Their experience of the divine, the spiritual, is healthy and life giving... It is important not to presume that certain kinds of religious experience or behavior are simply "part of the illness'" (p. 23).

This search for genuine spiritual dimensions in SMPs by exploring parallels in traditional myths and religious texts has played a role recovery of many people. My personal search began after discovering the works of Joseph Campbell a few months after my episode. He identified three stages in the Hero's Journey that he saw as similar to the inward journey of schizophrenia (Campbell, 1972). Campbell posits that whereas myths are metaphors for journeys into the psyche, psychosis is an actual journey into the psyche.

When I did begin to reflect on my experiences in therapy, I really had very little knowledge of Christ or Buddha at the time I assumed their identity. These experiences led me to explore Christianity, Buddhism, and other forms of spirituality for the first time in my life. Perry (1998) noted that after a psychotic episode, "What remains... is an ideal model and a sense of direction which one can use to complete the transformation through his own

purposeful methods" (p. 34–35). I now view my own experience of having "been" Buddha and Christ as revealing ideal models for my spiritual life.

Phase 3: Creating a New Personal Mythology

Personal mythology is an individual's belief system of complementary and contradictory themes that shape a person's view of the world, shape expectations, and guide decisions (Feinstein & Krippner, 2008). Personal myths address life's most important concerns and questions, including the following:

1. Identity (Who am I? Why am I here?)
2. Direction (Where am I going? How do I get there?)
3. Purpose (What am I doing here? Why am I going there? What does it all mean?)

Weaving the experience of an SMP into a life-affirming personal mythology is essential for recovery. Unfortunately, many beliefs that people develop around an episode of an SMP are dysfunctional myths that emphasize pathological qualities. Since these are not attuned to the person's actual needs, capacities, or circumstances, such myths do not serves as constructive guides during recovery.

Experiences of nonconsensual reality, such as dreams and parapsychological events, as well as the altered state of consciousness (ASC) experiences from an SMP can play a significant role in shaping positive personal mythologies. All of these involve transcendence of ordinary life concerns and an experience with a "higher" or "deeper" reality. Such spiritual experiences can become the foundation for a new personal mythology that is growth-enhancing and spiritually supportive.

My personal journey has involved publishing an account of my own and others SMPs and presentations targeted to increasing the awareness of mental health professionals about the important role of spirituality in recovery and in mental health in general. This work contributed to the addition of a new category to the *DSM-IV* entitled Religious or Spiritual Problem (V62.89), which I coauthored.

Consumer Movements Focused on Spirituality

In November 2004, the passage of Proposition 63—the Mental Health Services Act—by voters in California provided the California Department of Mental Health with increased funding to support county mental health programs. Longtime consumer advocate Jay Mahler saw this as an opportunity to develop a systematic approach to remediating the neglect of spirituality in the public mental health system. In August 2006 Mahler invited a diverse group of 20 consumers, family members, and service providers, including this author, to form a "spirituality workgroup." This group convened monthly in its first year to share knowledge about diverse spiritual practices, religious traditions, and ethnic and cultural experiences in recovery. This dialog led to the development of a concept paper for a state-wide project to find effective, collaborative means to lead the public mental health system in California to inquire about, embrace, and support the spiritual lives of the people it serves. The recently formed California Mental Health & Spirituality Initiative was funded by 53 of the state's 58 counties. Specific activities of the initiative have included conferences on mental health and spirituality, a Web site, community dialogs, teleconferences, development of online and face-to-face curricula, as well as surveys of mental health service recipients (individuals and families), provider agencies, and county mental health directors. These resources are available at http://www.mhspirit.org.

One of the objectives of this initiative involves the recognition of the spiritual dimension of ASC experiences that frequently occur in SMPs. This is an excerpt from the Values Statement of the California Mental Health & Spirituality Initiative available from the Web site (caps in the original):

SPIRITUAL EXPERIENCES CAN OCCUR DURING ALTERED STATES
Some people experience altered states with a spiritual component that can support the journey toward wellness and recovery. For some, this can be a life-changing event. Too often, this spiritual component has been ignored, labeled, or confused with delusions or other symptoms. Providers should respond respectfully and appropriately when clients ask for assistance with these experiences.

The surveys (Lukoff & Blum, 2010) conducted by the Initiative found that more than 90% of the County Behavioral Health Directors said "strongly agree" or "agree" in response to the following three statements.

Q1. "Spirituality is an important recovery resource in mental health treatment." (92%)
Q2. "Spirituality is an important wellness resource in mental health prevention." (94%)
Q3. "Spirituality is an important element of multicultural competency for mental health providers." (98%)

This was even higher than the percentage of consumers who agreed that "Spirituality is important to my mental health"—75%. These findings provide support for county and other public mental health programs to include spirituality as a component of recovery and also to incorporate wellness approaches (many of which are drawn from spiritual practices).

For two days in November 2009, The National Alliance for the Mentally Ill STAR (Support, Technical Assistance, and Resource) Center, with funding from the Substance Abuse & Mental Health Services Administration, convened a working conference to develop a written guide for mental health consumers, and recommendations for consumer supporters, regarding, "What is most important in helping people with intense spiritual experiences?"

The final report included 20 Principles for Honoring Intense Spiritual Experiences with the first one being:

1. Authentic spiritual experiences can occur during altered states.
and the last one being:
2. Spirituality can be part of a holistic approach to mental health. While being careful not to impose any aspect of spirituality or religious beliefs, programs should strive to promote balance of body, mind, and spirit among service recipients, staff, and the community.

These two consumer-initiated and led initiatives illustrate how important the spiritual dimension has become to people recovering from SMPs.

Conclusion

The mental health professions have a long history of ignoring and pathologizing religion. For instance, Freud reduced the "oceanic experience" of mystics to "infantile helplessness" and a "regression to primary narcissism" and described religion as an obsessional neurosis (Freud, 1989/1927). Albert Ellis asserted, "The less religious [patients] are, the more emotionally healthy they will tend to be" (Ellis, 1980, p. 637). But the data reviewed earlier show otherwise: Religion is overwhelmingly associated with positive mental health. For many people, both with and without an SMP, having a relationship with a higher power is the foundation of their psychological well-being. Providing spiritual support involves supporting a person's sense of connection to a higher power (i.e., God or other transcendent force) that is actively supporting, protecting, guiding, teaching, helping, and healing. Some researchers have suggested that the subjective experience of spiritual support may form the core of the spirituality-health connection (Mackenzie, Rajagopal, Meibohm, & Lavizzo-Mourey, 2000).

In most cases, psychologists can provide spiritual support to people coping with SMPs by devoting some time to exploring spiritual issues and asking questions to discover a client's perspective on the deeper meanings in his or her life. They can initiate support of a patient's spirituality through a spiritual assessment such as the FICA interview (Puchalski & Romer, 2000), now taught at over two-thirds of medical schools, which includes four questions that can be administered in 3–5 minutes about a client's: (1) faith, (2) interest in spirituality, (3) connection to a spiritual community, and (4) how the interviewer can address any client concerns about spirituality. In American Psychological Association (APA)-accredited clinical psychology programs, currently about 50% of institutions cover religion and spirituality to some degree (Brawer, Handal, Fabricatore, & Wajda-Johnston, 2002).

Other ways psychologists can provide spiritual support that are both evidence based and appropriate include the following:

Educating the client about recovery as a spiritual journey with a potentially positive outcome

Encouraging the client's involvement with a spiritual path or religious community that is consistent with the client's experiences and values

Encouraging the client to seek support and guidance from credible and appropriate religious or spiritual leaders

Encouraging the client to engage in religious and spiritual practices consistent with his or her beliefs (e.g., prayer, meditation, reading spiritual books, acts of worship, ritual, forgiveness, and service). At times, this might include engaging in a practice together with the patient such as meditation, silence, or prayer.

Modeling one's own spirituality (when appropriate), including a sense of purpose and meaning, along with hope and faith in something transcendent

People recovering from SMPs have rich opportunities for spiritual growth, along with challenges to its expression and development. They will find much needed support when they are clinically guided to explore their spiritual lives.

References

Anthony, W. (1993). Recovery from mental illness: The guiding vision of the mental health service system in the 1990s. *Psychosocial Rehabilitation Journal, 2*(3), 17–25.

Beebe, D. (1982). Notes on psychosis. *Spring, 9*, 233–252.

Bola, J. R., & Mosher, L. R. (2003). Treatment of acute psychosis without neuroleptics: Two year outcomes from the Soteria Project. *The Journal of Nervous and Mental Disease, 191*(4), 219–229.

Brawer, P., Handal, P., Fabricatore, A. R., & Wajda-Johnston, V. (2002). Training and education in religion/spirituality within APA-accredited clinical psychology programs. *Professional Psychology: Research and Practice, 33*, 203–206.

Bussema, K., & Bussema, E. (2000). Is there a balm in Gilead? The implications of faith in coping with a psychiatric disability. *Psychosocial Rehabilitation, 24*(2), 117–124.

Campbell, J. (1972). *Myths to live by.* New York: Viking Press.

Clay, S. (1987). Stigma and spirituality. *Journal of Contemplative Psychotherapy, 4*, 87–94.

Clay, S. (1994). *The wounded prophet.* Retrieved November 2006, from http://www.sallyclay.net/Z.text/Prophet.html

Cothran, M. M., & Harvey, P. D. (1986). Delusional thinking in psychotics: Correlates of religious content. *Psychological Reports, 58*, 191–199.

Davidson, L., & Strauss, J. S. (1992). Making sense of self in recovery from severe mental illness. *British Journal of Medical Psychology, 65*, 131–145.

Deegan, P. (2004). *Spiritual lessons in recovery.* Retrieved November 2006, from http://www.patdeegan.com/blog/archives/000011.php

Dodds, E. (1951). *The Greeks and the irrational.* Berkeley: University of California Press.

Ellis, A. (1980). Psychotherapy and atheistic values: A response to A, E. Bergin's "Psychotherapy and religious issues." *Journal of Consulting and Clinical Psychology, 48*, 635–639.

Fallot, R. (1998). Spiritual and religious dimensions of mental illness recovery narratives. In R. Fallot (Ed.), *Spirituality and religion in recovery from mental illness.* Washington, DC: New Directions for Mental Health Services.

Fallot, R. (2001). Spirituality and religion in psychiatric rehabilitation and recovery from mental illness. *International Review of Psychiatry, 13*(2), 110–116.

Feinstein, D., & Krippner, S. (2008). *Personal mythology: Using ritual, dreams, and imagination to discover your inner story.* Fulton, CA: Energy Psychology Press.

Fisher, D. (2006). *Believing you can recover is vital to recovery from mental illness.* Retrieved November 2006, from http://www.power2u.org/articles/recovery/believing.html

Fitchett, G., Burton, L. A., & Sivan, A. B. (1997). The religious needs and resources of psychiatric patients. *Journal of Nervous and Mental Disorder, 185*, 320–326.

Freud, S. (1989). *The future of an illusion.* New York: W. W. Norton. (Original work published 1927).

Goodwin, F., & Jamison, K. (1990). *Manic-depressive illness.* New York: Oxford University Press.

Grof, S., & Grof, C. (Eds.). (1989). *Spiritual emergency: When personal transformation becomes a crisis.* Los Angeles: Tarcher.

Hillman, J. (1983). *Healing fiction.* New York: Station Hill Press.

Huguelet, P., Borras, L., Gillieron, C., Brandt, P., & Mohr, S. (2009). Influence of spirituality and religiousness on substance misuse in patients with schizophrenia or schizo-affective disorder. *Substance Use and Misuse, 44*, 502–513.

Jacobson, N. (2001). Experiencing recovery: A dimensional analysis of recovery narratives. *Psychiatric Rehabilitation Journal, 24*, 248–256.

Kirov, G., Kemp, R., Kirov, K., & David, A. S. (1998). Religious faith after psychotic illness. *Psychopathology*, *31*(5), 234–245.

Koenig, H., McCullough, M., & Larson, D. (Eds.). (2001). *Handbook of religion and health*. New York: Oxford University Press.

Kraepelin, E. (1904). *Lectures in clinical psychiatry* (T. Johnstone, Trans.). New York: Hafner Publishing.

Kroll, J., & Sheehan, W. (1989). Religious beliefs and practices among 52 psychiatric inpatients in Minnesota. *American Journal of Psychiatry*, *146*, 67–72.

Lindgren, K. N., & Coursey, R. D. (1995). Spirituality and serious mental illness: A two-part study. *Psychosocial Rehabilitation Journal*, *18*(3), 93–111.

Lukoff, D. (1988). Transpersonal therapy with a manic-depressive artist. *Journal of Transpersonal Psychology*, *20*(1), 10–20.

Lukoff, D. (1991). Divine madness: Shamanistic initiatory crisis and psychosis. *Shaman's Drum*, *22*, 24–29.

Lukoff, D. (1993). Case study of the emergence of a contemporary shaman. In R. I. Heinze (Ed.), *Proceedings of the Ninth International Conference on Shamanism and Alternate Healing* (pp. 122–131). Berkeley, CA: Asian Scholars Press.

Lukoff, D. (2007). Visionary spiritual experiences. *Southern Medical Journal*, *100*(6), 635–641.

Lukoff, D., & Blum, P. (2010, August). *Survey on mental health, spirituality, and recovery*. Presentation at the 118th Annual American Psychological Association Meeting, San Diego, CA.

Lukoff, D., & Everest, H. C. (1985). The myths in mental illness. *Journal of Transpersonal Psychology*, *17*(2), 123–153.

Lukoff, D., Mahler, J., & Mancuso, L. (2009). Mental health and spirituality initiative. *California Psychologist*, *42*, 14–18.

Lukoff, D., Wallace, C. J., Liberman, R. P., & Burke, K. (1986). A holistic health program for chronic schizophrenic patients. *Schizophrenia Bulletin*, *12*(2), 274–282.

Mackenzie, E. R., Rajagopal, D. E., Meibohm, M., & Lavizzo-Mourey, R. (2000). Spiritual support and psychological well-being: Older adults' perceptions of the religion and health con. *Alternative Therapies in Health and Medicine*, *6*(6), 37–45.

McAdams, D. P., Reynolds, J., Lewis, M., Patten, A., H., & Bowman, P. J. (2001). When bad things turn good and good things turn bad: Sequences of redemption and contamination in life narratives and their relation to psychosocial adaptation in midlife adults and students. *Personality and Social Psychology Bulletin*, *27*, 474–485.

Mosher, L. (1999). Soteria and other alternatives to acute psychiatric hospitalization: A personal and professional review. *Journal of Nervous and Mental Diseases*, *187*(3), 142–149.

Mosher, L., Hendrix, V., & Fort, D. (2004). *Soteria: Through madness to deliverance*. Philadelphia: Xlibris Corporation.

Neeleman, J., & Lewis, G. (1994). Religious identity and comfort beliefs in three groups of psychiatric patients and a group of medical controls. *International Journal of Social Psychology*, *40*, 2124–2134.

Onken, S., Dumont, J., Ridgway, P., Dornan, D., & Ralph, R. (2002). *Mental health recovery: What helps and what hinders?* Washington, DC: National Technical Assistance Center for State Mental Health Planning.

Pargament, K. (2007). *The psychology of religion and coping: Theory, research, and practice*. New York: The Guilford Press.

Pargament, K., Koenig, H., & Perez, L. (2000). The many methods of religious coping: Development and initial validation of the RCOP. *Journal of Clinical Psychology*, *56*(4), 519–543.

Pargament, K., Koenig, H. G., Tarakeshwar, N., & Hahn, J. (2004). Religious coping methods as predictors of psychological, physical and spiritual outcomes among medically ill elderly patients: A two-year longitudinal study. *Journal of Health Psychology*, *9*(6), 713–730.

Pargament, K. I., Smith, B. W., Koenig, H. G., & Perez, L. (1998). Patterns of positive and negative religious coping with major life stressors. *Journal for the Scientific Study of Religion*, *37*(4), 710–724.

Perry, J. (1998). *Trials of the visionary mind: Spiritual emergency and the renewal process*. Albany, NY: SUNY Press.

Pfeifer, S., & Waelty, U. (1995). Psychopathology and religious commitment—a controlled study. *Psychopathology*, *28*(2), 70–77.

Phillips, R., Lukoff, D., & Stone, M. (2009). Integrating the spirit within psychosis: Alternative conceptualizations of psychotic disorders. *Journal of Transpersonal Psychology*, *41*, 61–79.

Phillips, R., & Stein, C. (2007). God's will, God's punishment, or God's limitations: Religious coping strategies reported by young adults living with serious mental illness. *Journal of Clinical Psychology*, *63*(6), 529–540.

Pieper, J. (2004). Religious coping in highly religious psychiatric inpatients. *Mental Health, Religion, and Culture*, *7*(4), 349–363.

Podvoll, E. (1990). *The seduction of madness: Revolutionary insights into the world of psychosis and a compassionate approach to recovery at home*. New York: Harper Collins.

Prince, R. H. (1992). Religious experience and psychopathology: Cross-cultural perspectives. In J. F. Schumacher (Ed.), *Religion and mental health* (pp. 281–290). New York: Oxford University Press.

Puchalski, C., & Romer, A. (2000). Taking a spiritual history allows clinicians to understand patients more fully. *Journal of Palliative Medicine*, *3*, 129–137.

Ragins, M. (2006). *Recovery with severe mental illness: Changing from a medical model to a psychosocial rehabilitation model*. Retrieved March 2012, from http://www.village-isa.org/Ragin's%20Papers/recov.%20with%20severe%20MI.htm

Randal, P., Simpson, A., & Laidlaw, T. (2003). Can recovery-focused multimodal psychotherapy facilitate symptom and function improvement in people with treatment-resistant psychotic illness? A comparison study. *Australian and New Zealand Journal of Psychiatry*, *37*(6), 720–727.

Rosen, G. (1968). *Madness in society*. New York: Harper & Row.

Russinova, Z., Wewiorski, N., & Cash, D. (2002). The integration of psychiatric rehabilitation services in behavioral health care structures: A state example. *Journal of Behavioral Health Services Research*, *29*(4), 381–393.

Sheehan, W., & Kroll, J. (1990). Psychiatric patients' belief in general health factors and sin as causes of illness. *American Journal of Psychiatry*, *147*(1), 112–113.

Siddle, R., Haddock, G., Tarrier, N., & Faragher, E. (2002). Religious delusions in patients admitted to hospital with schizophrenia. *Social Psychiatry and Psychiatric Epidemiology*, *37*(3), 130–138.

Stack, J. (1997). Organized religion is but one of the many paths toward spiritual growth. *The Journal*, *8*(4), 23–26.

Sullivan, W. (1993). "It helps me to be a whole person": The role of spirituality among the mentally challenged. *Psychosocial Rehabilitation Journal*, *16*(3), 125–134.

Tepper, L., Rogers, S. A., Coleman, E. M., & Malony, H. N. (2001). The prevalence of religious coping among persons with persistent mental illness. *Psychiatric Services, 52*(5), 660–665.

U.S. Surgeon General. (1999). *Mental health: A report of the surgeon general.* Bethesda, MD: U.S. Department of Health and Human Services.

Weisburd, D. (1997). Publisher's note. *The Journal of the California Alliance for the Mentally Ill, 8,* 1–2.

Weiser, M., Kutz, I., Jacobson, S., & Weiser, D. (1995). Psychotherapeutic aspects of the martial arts. *American Journal of Psychotherapy, 49*(1), 118–127.

PART 7

Positive Psychology and Spirituality

Positive Psychology and Spirituality: A Virtue-Informed Approach to Well-Being

Joseph W. Ciarrocchi[1]

Abstract

This chapter brings together a number of observations from scholars in disparate fields critiquing the character strengths and virtue model of positive psychology in light of classical and contemporary virtue ethics. The legitimacy of these criticisms is acknowledged and some suggestions are made for broadening the character strengths and virtue approach to incorporate practical strategies based on these criticisms as well as offering conceptual adjustments for creating a virtue-informed positive psychology. Data were reviewed indicating that contemporary culture fosters psychological myopia, thus making character-building strategies highly relevant. Finally, on both conceptual and empirical grounds the utility of religion and spirituality for countering psychological myopia and self-regulation failure was highlighted with an emphasis on the role spirituality plays in building positive emotions.

Key Words: positive psychology, spirituality, virtues, well-being

Introduction

Positive psychology, the science of human flourishing, is itself flourishing. The doubling of issues annually for the *Journal of Positive Psychology* attests to the increment in quality research. From the beginning, religion and spirituality played a central role as distinctive character strengths contributing to flourishing by activating the virtue of transcendence (Peterson & Seligman, 2004, pp. 599–624). Positive emotions and positive institutions are two other legs of the three-legged stool comprising positive psychology.

Anyone familiar with the history of the psychology of religion in mainstream American psychology (Gillespie, 2001) would view this as a bold stroke given that the role of religion and spirituality as a valid construct in psychological research has not gone unquestioned (Funder, 2002). At the same time the centrality of religion and spirituality in the lives of the majority of the global population warrants such a universal feature of human nature as

worthy of scientific investigation (Micklethwait & Wooldridge, 2009).

The leaders in the classification of positive psychology's character strengths and virtues intentionally move psychology into a research program beyond the parameters of simply understanding what makes people feel good. Their agenda was strikingly ambitious. taking on no less than the ancient philosophical question of "How should one live?" That is, what constitutes the good life in the sense of complete human flourishing? Posed this way, the question assured entering the territory of what it means to have, develop, and express a good character with certain moral dispositions.

For its part the classification system respected and built on many traditions—philosophical, religious, and cultural—that reflect on this age-old question. For its purposes the leaders chose the virtue ethics tradition as a sensible starting point for framing the qualities that could capture agreement on what constitutes moral character. Their intention was rewarded when research revealed that the standard virtues appear as praiseworthy human qualities central to geographically and culturally diverse philosophical, religious, and spiritual wisdom traditions. Their conclusion in making the argument for a science of character strengths and virtues illustrates how deeply they drew on the virtue ethics tradition for their system.

> In sum, we can describe our classification as the social science equivalent of virtue ethics, using the scientific method to inform philosophical pronouncements about the traits of a good person. (*Peterson & Seligman*, 2004, p. 89)

Response

The success of positive psychology as an intellectual movement is impressive. Philosophers, theologians, economists, and other specialists in fields for whom virtue ethics are relevant responded quickly and in depth (Haybron, 2008; Martin, 2007; Nussbaum, 2008; Offer, 2007; Tiberius, 2008; Titus, 2006). Philosophers especially are out front in this dialog with the formation of a subspecialty, "the now-vibrant field of empirically-oriented ethics" (Haybron, 2008, p. xi).

Now that philosophy and other specialties have responded, is it not appropriate for a reciprocal subspecialty such as philosophically informed positive psychology? Or perhaps Blaine Fowers's phrasing is more apt even though broader, "a virtue-informed psychology" (Fowers, 2005, p. 205). The classification leaders in positive psychology made their debt to the virtue ethics tradition evident from the outset, and this chapter is an attempt to analyze and respond to a limited range of virtue ethics' reflections on positive psychology. The goal is to take stock of the conversation to date in order to discover what fine tuning is necessary to help orient positive psychology's research agenda in light of these critiques.

Return to the Sources

In any discussion of the contribution of virtue ethics to positive psychology, religion and spirituality have an important place at the table. Fowers's (2005) wonderful volume attempts to situate positive and other branches of psychology within the framework of classical virtue ethics, maintaining an outlook neither in favor of nor opposed to religious virtue ethics traditions. This chapter goes further by incorporating insights from religious and spiritual traditions to better understand research in the psychology of religion.

While paying due respect to the virtue ethics tradition in ancient Greek philosophy, Peterson and Seligman mistakenly describe the waning of virtue ethics in the Christian religious tradition by its emphasis on following divine law. In fact, virtue ethics played a vigorous and majority role in the Middle Ages. The preservation of Aristotle's works in Muslim countries led to a resurgence of interest in ancient Greek ethics by Muslim scholars who shared their work with Jewish and Christian theologians and philosophers. The leading Catholic theologian in that era, Thomas Aquinas, whose influence today remains central in that tradition, centered his ethical teaching on his synthesis of Augustine and ancient Greek ethics (Pope, 2002; Porter, 1990).

The shift in emphasis from virtue ethics to moral law in the Christian tradition came about due to Protestant Reformation theology in the 16th century, which viewed virtue ethics suspiciously as suggesting that people could somehow develop their own moral characters without the help of God. Thus, when Catholic philosophers in the 20th century renewed philosophy's interest in virtue ethics, this represented a return to the sources for virtue ethics that had dominated Christian spirituality in its first fifteen centuries (Anscombe, 1997; Foot, 1997; MacIntyre, 1984).

Virtue-Informed Positive Psychology

To understand the role religion and spirituality can play in positive psychology means addressing a series of questions that philosophy raises about the degree to which scientific virtue ethics is an adequate paradigm. Many of these questions challenge whether positive psychology has properly understood the virtue ethics tradition in its structure and assumptions. In this chapter, I shall discuss a number of these potential objections with the hope that the critiques can enlighten positive psychology in its next steps.

Facts and Values

An immediate contrast between virtue ethics and the positivist empirical tradition is the assumption in modern science and philosophy of the complete separation between facts and values. Introduced by David Hume (1711–1776), and adhered to by many subsequent philosophers and scientists, the distinction rests on the observation that no logical connection exists between factual observations and perceived values. Something that "is" a certain way in no way justifies an "ought" in terms of specific moral behavior. To make that leap is referred to in logic as the naturalistic fallacy. The realms are entirely different.

Psychology as well as most social sciences attempt to maintain value neutrality in terms of their findings. That is, they do not derive normative moral conduct on the basis of their research outcomes. Virtue ethics and most religious theologies hold a different view. From that viewpoint if human nature is genuinely of a certain kind, moral values can be derived in the sense that they fulfill one's nature. The fact-value distinction falls away and moral values actually build on the facts of human nature (Pojman, 2006). In virtue ethics disputes over human nature can still be resolved at least in general outline, again eliminating any need for a hard and fast dichotomy between facts and values.

A second contrast is the subtle influence of Enlightenment science on psychological worldviews regarding the values it does cultivate (Fowers, 2005). Science has elevated personal freedom in its highest pantheon. What enhances freedom is good; what constrains it is bad. Classical virtue ethics prefers to ask how freedom is used. It enters into the moral realm with regard to the content of the choices exercised with one's freedom, not with its unbridled expression. To further illustrate the contrast, virtue ethics often enjoins behavior based on our human nature. In this sense virtue ethics says we can use freedom to fulfill who we are; but who we are is a given, not something created out of nothing.

How Virtues Hang Together

Among the many questions virtue ethics raises for positive psychology are the assumptions and organizational structure behind character strengths and virtues. A perceptive discussion (Schwartz & Sharpe, 2006) focuses on the role practical wisdom plays in virtue ethics and how attention to it would improve the character strengths and virtue model. In their view practical wisdom is not just one of the six major virtues that positive psychology describes; rather it functions as the executive judgment that guides the person in choosing which specific action is good for the person in this specific situation. A corollary of this is that virtues need to be integrated and in some sense are hierarchical. That is, some virtues such as practical wisdom count more. Positive psychology, on the other hand, views virtues as independent. Although disagreements exist as to how the virtues are integrated, the concept of unity among the virtues is an ancient one (Annas, 1993, pp. 66–84). From this perspective practical wisdom guides a person's decision, taking into account what

is correct in terms of her life as a whole (Annas, 1993, pp. 78–79). Positive psychology, on the contrary, focuses on people developing signature strengths without attending to practices cultivating all the major virtues. In accord with ancient virtue ethics, Schwartz and Sharpe see this as an analogous to a physical fitness buff overdeveloping one set of muscles disproportionately to his body as a whole (2006, p. 380).

Positive psychology and virtue ethics view the end development of virtues differently. Positive psychology works on a linear model, where more of a virtue is better. An example of this might be optimism; intuition suggests a person should have an optimal balance between too little and too much optimism. Interestingly, the empirical evidence concludes that more optimism is generally better (Carver & Scheier, 1999). Virtue ethics, in contrast, maintains virtue is a mean between extremes. Courage, for example, stands between cowardliness and rashness. From the standpoint of ethical theory, positive psychology's methodology resembles utilitarian models that rest on seeking out the greatest good for the greatest number (Hursthouse, 2003).

How might positive psychology respond to these observations and what contribution, if any, could religion and spirituality make? From a methodological standpoint, positive psychology can determine the linear or curvilinear aspects of a measured virtue, thereby testing whether a measurable virtue is indeed a mean between extremes. Most work on character strengths continues to support the linear hypothesis that more is better. Perhaps more research looking for moderation effects of character strengths will bring to life the nuances virtue ethics suggest. Peterson and Seligman intentionally selected personality traits for their measurement template of character strengths. Traits operate at a broad level of human dispositions, whereas practical wisdom in the virtue ethics scheme is situation specific. Hence, this creates an argument for identifying the situation-specific features of character strengths and whether differing levels of situations or other character strengths influence outcomes.

Positive Psychology Clinical Responses

The philosophical criticisms of significant strengths' approach to virtue development are conceptually coherent within a virtue ethics framework. These criticisms, however, fail to understand how clinical applications can work in practice.

One approach would be to use systematic behavioral practices to develop essential virtues within a person. I elaborated such a model for problem gambling (Ciarrocchi, 2002). Worksheets included in the clinical manual targeted core character strengths and virtues for countering a pathological gambling lifestyle such as temperance (delay of gratification), humility (coming to grips with the notion that one's personal control does not extend to random events), honesty (truthfulness), responsible conscience (becoming more attuned to ethical judgments about right and wrong), and so forth. This approach absorbs the virtue-informed suggestions by focusing on an individual's life as a whole and invites a person to engage in practices that build up character strengths inimical to a gambling disposition for each specific individual.

A second approach, more in keeping with Peterson and Seligman's original signature strength model, would be to conduct an individualized signature strength assessment through a tool such as the Values in Action Inventory, an online 240-item questionnaire free to the public at the time of this writing (http://www.viacharacter.org/). In keeping with analog research, a client or counselor would work with a finite number of character strengths (Seligman, Park, & Peterson, 2005), for example, one's top five, to address a specific psychological concern. It would be necessary for a counselor or person interested in self-directed change to use the signature strengths as assets to build in gradually targeted virtues, rather than to leap immediately into building up a deficient virtue directly.

Using drinking problems as a clinical example, research tells us that on average a person with a drinking problem will score low in the character strength of conscientiousness (Piedmont & Ciarrocchi, 1999). Conscientiousness is a personality trait that indicates a disposition to delay gratification and act in a plan-full matter to fulfill one's duties and obligations. In short, conscientiousness is a good measure of the aggregate qualities encompassing personal responsibility. Assuming that a person with low conscientiousness will not score high on this character strength on the Values in Action Inventory, the practical clinical issue is how to build up the strength when the Inventory tells us that the client is strong in, say, the character strength of humanity. How does that strength help shape the person toward the ones that are essential for reducing alcohol use? The clinical approach here is to use the signature strength as a motivational tool for engaging in practices that *can* develop the essential virtue of temperance. This is an alternative to the direct approach suggested in the gambling example.

In that case the counselor or person directly assessed and worked on building up deficient character strengths. In the second approach the counselor or person is using signature strengths to move incrementally toward practices that enact the deficient character strength more fully.

Humanity (compassion and caring for others) now becomes the energy source for behavioral and emotional focusing on how love and concern for others can translate into self-regulatory strategies. In other words, which loving practices could the person engage in that are linked to temperance? The belief in the unity of virtues that many virtue ethics' approaches propose should be of help here. Humanity ought to be connected to temperance in some way even if this is not immediately evident. Coaching children in a sports league would be a simple example of a humanity practice that could take the person away from sitting in front of the television on Saturday afternoon drinking beer. In this way, signature strengths become a path to the core virtue with the additional merit of building on qualities that are intrinsically important to the person.

A similar approach is already used with considerable effectiveness in the evidence-based treatment for addiction known as motivational interviewing (Miller & Rollnick, 2002). In that intervention clients assess themselves on their top values through a card-sort method. These values then form the basis of a dialog with the counselor in terms of how the value could be used in a way to assist the client in reaching her abstinence goal. The strengths-based approach utilized in positive psychology, therefore, is not contrary to a virtue ethics model that considers developing all the virtues as essential. It is not a contradiction to use a specific strength as a foundation to build a more comprehensive character. Finally, given the pervasiveness of spirituality as a meaning-making system, the potential for the character strengths approach as a building block for character development is an enormous untapped resource. Indeed, spirituality has been a cornerstone of the mutual support Alcoholics Anonymous group for generations (Kurtz, 1999).

Religion and Spirituality as Meaning Making

From the standpoint of religion and spirituality, this is an appropriate place to point out another misreading within the character strength and virtue model. Religion and spirituality are only one type of character strength comprising the virtue of transcendence—a virtue that forges "connections to the larger universe and provide[s] meaning" (Peterson & Seligman, 2004, p. 30). Other character strengths in this cluster are purpose, appreciation of beauty and excellence, gratitude, hope, optimism, and humor or playfulness. Bundling humor with spirituality as an aspect of transcendence is at least one problem in the characterization of this virtue. Most people would probably see the connections that meaning gives to a life as a central organizing principle for a life well lived. Meaning and spirituality in their ultimate contexts are not one asset among many but integral to the remaining virtues.

Positive psychology may have trouble balancing its positivist empirical heritage from utilitarian ethics with the character strengths and virtue interests that are more congenial with ancient and contemporary virtue ethics (Fowers, 2005). Philosopher Julia Annas frames the difference between other contemporary moral theories and virtue ethics:

> In our society we have to turn to popular self-help manuals to find extensive discussion of questions of the best life, self-fulfillment, the proper role of the emotions, personal friendships and commitments, topics which in the ancient world were always treated in a more intellectual way as part of ethics. (1995, p. 10)

The basis for this evolution has to do with how modern ethical theories tend to think of the good life compared with the ancients. Contemporary moral theories look at happiness as "the production of good states of affairs" (Annas, p. 8). Virtue ethics instead aims for "living in a certain way" (Annas, p. 38) so that the idea of maximizing a virtue such as temperance is meaningless. In virtue ethics temperance is called for in specific situations so that when I am behaving with temperance I am sufficiently good. It is not as if some temperance allows me to eat only half the lemon meringue pie, while more temperance allows me to eat none of it. I don't need more temperance; I simply need enough of it. Temperance is about eating *the right amount* of lemon meringue pie and ultimately takes into consideration what kind of a person one would like to be. This notion of reflecting on one's life as a whole is crucial for living the right kind of life, which Hellenistic Jewish and Christian spiritualities later adopted from ancient virtue ethics (Hadot, 1995).

Positive psychology's heritage from positivism and utilitarian ethics of flourishing as a good state of affairs also contrasts methodologically. Flourishing according to virtue ethics, as Schwartz and Sharpe

point out, are about judgments and prudence. Linear models do not work well here. Positive psychology is based on signature strengths; virtue ethics judges what is the right thing to do in this situation. A signature strength of self-regulation (under the virtue of temperance in the character strengths and virtue system) points to the degree of self-regulation rather that its context.

Leo Tolstoy's short story "Father Sergius" (Tolstoy, 1912/2009) tells of a 19th-century Russian hermit monk living in his small cell in the wilderness, who is tempted by an attractive woman who bets her friends she can spend the night with the monk. The monk goes through multiple religious prayers and suppression practices until he finally gains control of his impulses by grabbing the ax used for cutting firewood and chops off his finger.

Such spiritual practices to manage temptations are not unknown in the history of spirituality, yet the consensus is this is not true virtue. By way of contrast, consider the story of the highly abstemious medieval saint, Francis of Assisi, whose religious brothers came to him concerned about a friar who was starving himself to death through fasting and whose cries of pain rang out in the night. Francis assembled the entire community, including the fasting friar, and had all available food set before them. The normally ascetic Francis began to eat, and he fed the starving friar himself while admonishing the community that the Lord gives food and drink to care for our bodies. The narrative fully accords with the abstract theological virtue ethics system that Thomas Aquinas wrote in this same 13th century (Aquinas, 1984). Virtue is about judging what is correct. The fasting friar's signature strength of self-regulation was several standard deviations above the mean—even in that ascetic community. But no one considered his behavior virtuous anymore than people today would consider Father Sergius virtuous.

A related contribution for religion and spirituality to the character strengths and virtue discussion is that spirituality is a form of meaning making that describes *the whole point* of the good life, rather than a single virtue among others that constitutes the good life. As philosopher Mike Martin (2007) suggests, it is more comprehensible to place transcendence "as an axis that cuts across all the virtues when they are linked to spirituality (and of course not everyone will have an interest in that linkage)" (p. 97). Absent from the positive psychology classification is the key understanding of religion captured in the statement of the eminent sociologist of religion, Peter Berger, that "Religion is the audacious attempt to conceive of the entire universe as being humanly significant" (1967, p. 28). Large sets of empirical literature in the psychology of religion can now take a meaningful place in positive psychology (Hood, Hill, & Spilka, 2009). Research on intrinsic/extrinsic religiosity, the degree to which a person views religion and spirituality as an end (intrinsic) or as a means to an end (extrinsic), tackles the thorny problem of religious motivation. In general, using religion to further one's personal status in the community fails to deliver in terms of positive outcomes, whereas seeing religion as important in itself correlates with mostly positive outcomes. Concerned about intentions in the character strengths and virtue schema is usually absent, although intentions are central to virtue ethics.

Fowers (2005) critiqued psychology's emphasis on instrumentalism, the idea that external goods in the environment are sources of personal fulfillment. It is tempting for positive psychology and the psychology of religion to fall into this same trap, that is, to see religion and spirituality in a purely functional way. Certainly aspects of religion and spirituality have functional qualities. Indeed, entire systems of understanding religion in this way are quite enlightening (Geyer & Baumeister, 2005). Research on intrinsic and extrinsic religiosity, however, indicate that more is gained from viewing religion noninstrumentally, just as psychology is coming to realize that intrinsic motivations are stronger in maintaining crucial outcomes such as learning than are extrinsic ones (Fowers, 2005). An emphasis on acts that are worthy for building character in and of themselves and not as a means to an end also opposes the mainstream psychological research tradition, yet it is the foundation for virtue ethics.

Happiness

Just as the physical universe is captured under the umbrella of meaning, so too is the totality of human behavior, differentiating virtue and vice. Diverse religious and spiritual systems can recognize a variety of human goods to pursue, but each system maintains that the final end it points to privileges the aim of all other goods. It so happens that having a single final end—happiness—is the starting point for reflecting on what is a good life in virtue ethics. This makes virtue ethics quite compatible with religion and spirituality despite the many definitions of happiness these systems generate.

The centrality of happiness as the single final end of human beings provides yet another link between virtue ethics, religion and spirituality, and positive psychology when interpreted through this lens. In virtue ethics the need to understand how to live, a search to identify what one's ultimate goal is, and the discovering of the concrete forms of happiness for an individual combine to create much overlap with positive psychology's agenda despite Seligman's stated goal of remaining descriptive rather than prescriptive. Positive psychology might claim no interest in the "ought" of virtue ethics or other moral theories, yet its foundation in virtue ethics' traits immerses it in multiple foundational questions. These are the very questions contemporary philosophers have taken aim at for purposes of both clarification and criticism.

The critical schema in the form of questions for reflecting on my life looks something like this (Annas, p. 34):

- Overall, where is my energy going?
- In pursuit of which specific goals do I direct this energy?
- Although I have many goals, how do they hang together?
- What is their common theme?
- Pursuing these goals indicates I see my life *as a whole* going in what direction?
- Upon reflection am I satisfied with where my life is going?

Nussbaum (2008) criticizes positive psychology for not emphasizing what role reflection and deliberation have in a flourishing life. The source of her discontent is obvious from the aforementioned analysis. The ancients realized that only self-examination could reveal the answer to these questions, and so they had many statements similar to the well-known one, "The unexamined life is not worth living." Classical virtue ethics and its heirs such as Christianity and forms of Islamic and Judaic spirituality adopted and refined the reflective practices to promote an examined life. Philippe Hadot (1995) describes these practices in considerable detail illustrating the similarities between classical virtue-ethic practices with traditional religious and spiritual practices.

Nonetheless, contemporary philosophers recognize that ancient virtue ethics as well as later religious and spiritual traditions had a certain naïveté regarding the struggles for self-knowledge. British philosopher John Cottingham (1998) points out the historical failures to achieve self-understanding in practical philosophy and demonstrates the contribution that clinical psychology and psychiatry brought to bear on this process. Freud preeminently unlocked the store of many out-of-awareness motivations. Although Cottingham stops with psychoanalysis, the story continues with empirical work on the "new unconscious," which refines in greater detail the neuroscience mechanisms that render motivations hidden (Hassin, Uleman, & Bargh, 2007).

A further philosophical criticism of positive psychology classification comes from points of view attacking positive psychology traits as equally oriented toward flourishing. Virtue ethics views flourishing as what we ultimately desire and differs in kind from each character strength and virtue. Flourishing is not an aggregate of a select number or even all the character strengths and virtues. The virtues needed for my flourishing depend on how I view the goal of my life as a whole. I might desire to be a highly skilled clinical psychologist in order to relieve pain but if empathy (the virtue of humanity in the positive psychology scheme) is not a "signature strength," it is unlikely that developing my signature strength of temperance will result in achieving my goal. For my stated goal I have no choice but to try to cultivate empathy. Eventually feedback may cause a shift in goals, but for now the path is clear.

This train of reasoning raises some serious dilemmas in positive psychology's embrace of virtue ethics. If living an active life of virtue is the final form happiness takes, the positivist methodology positive psychology utilizes misses the mark. Positive psychology measures character strengths and virtues dimensionally, that is, determining how much of a given signature strength a person reports. Virtue ethics does not view happiness as a quantitative accumulation, but as an activity wherein a person exemplifies the right disposition at the right time to the right degree. The notion of more does not capture this; in fact, it may better define a vice. Too much altruism directed toward a child might prevent a son or daughter from learning skills to act independently.

Religion and spirituality provide solutions when the final end is a specific viewpoint about how to coordinate virtues for one's life as a whole. Qualitative or narrative research may fit better in evaluating behavior that stands at the "mean" or in other ways that suggest engagement at the right time and to the right degree. These narratives can incorporate the goal of viewing one's activities under such standards as love of God and neighbor. They do so by coordinating the activity of the virtues in terms of the right amount of which virtues, rather than a greater amount of whatever the person happens to be strong in.

Religion and spirituality have also found, in some systems, concrete approaches to unifying the virtues toward the goal of happiness. First, many religions pull together the virtues through their emphasis on charity, love of God and others, or negating the self. Rather than having virtue stand alone, there is an integral connection with the more practical social virtues known from tradition as the cardinal virtues. These virtues named from the Latin *cardo* meaning "hinge" form a unity under the virtue of love. Practical wisdom determines the situations requiring love in the right amount, at the right time, and with the correct feelings. Wisdom considers what is the loving thing in terms of what is just. Finally, wisdom disposes a person to love with the proper emotions of courage and temperance, and their component parts such as resilience and the proper appreciation of creation's pleasurable gifts. The organizing virtues inherent in diverse religious and spiritual systems may prove to be a useful marker for understanding belief systems and practices both for mutual dialog in pluralistic societies as well as clinical applications for individuals seeking to grow psychologically in ways consistent with their religion and spirituality.

Which Is the Master Virtue?

A debate has ensued over the concept of a master virtue. Baumeister and colleagues have reviewed the central role self-regulation plays with regard to individual and societal well-being (Baumeister & Exline, 1999; Baumeister, Zell, & Tice, 2005), and from this basis developed a functional view of religion as contributing to society's well-being through the promotion of self-regulation (Geyer & Baumeister, 2005). A critique from the standpoint of Christian psychology is the self is "*inadequate* to win the struggle for virtue on its own" (Worthington & Berry, 2005, p. 157, emphasis in original). The authors quote a well-known (for Christians) passage in the New Testament from St. Paul acknowledging that he is unable on his own to do the good he wants (Romans 7:15). Baumeister, however, does not claim an ability to measure the Christian concept of grace that underlies the critique. A later comment also seems off track: "Imagine, however, that Baumeister had spent 10 years studying love instead of evil" (p. 158). In fact, Baumeister had done considerable empirical and conceptual work on love (Baumeister & Leary, 1995; Baumeister, Wotman, & Stillwell, 1993).

A critique from within the framework of virtue ethics where Baumeister begins (Baumeister & Exline,

1999) might more accurately maintain that self-control technically is not a virtue at all. Certainly it is a human strength but needs to be properly understood within the unity-of-virtues framework. The highly developed framework from the medieval scholastic period onward maintains that practical wisdom or prudence is the master virtue.

> The argument that no proper moral virtue can exist without prudence makes more sense if one recalls that a virtue cannot be put to bad use. The ability to face danger, in its own right, would go just as well to make a daring bank robber as an admirable war hero. A person needs prudence to judge correctly which dangers would be *good* to face.
>
> (*Kent*, 2002, p. 123, emphasis in original)

Practical wisdom, similarly, judges what the right amount of self-control is for the person in the situation. The virtue ethics traditions all formulate a spiritual or philosophical virtue to inform practical wisdom. Aquinas, as noted earlier, considers charity as having primacy. Other philosophers and theologians mention other qualities.

Even these viewpoints, however, do not necessarily make Baumeister's position incompatible with traditional virtue ethics. If one examines the entire body of research and variables constituting self-regulation, evidence exists for seeing self-regulation as a mean between extremes, and not just as a dimensional strength. For example, self-regulation theory speaks to the issue of persistence and the importance of knowing when it is appropriate to give up on a task. Persisting beyond any hope of accomplishment may be as detrimental as lacking perseverance. Here as in most self-regulatory events common sense or practical wisdom determines what is reasonable. Baumeister's work emphasized this point on persistence from the very beginning (Baumeister, Heatherton, & Tice, 1994).

Now More Than Ever

If the cliché that timing is everything is correct, our culture may have reached a "tipping point" for the utility of positive psychology's emphasis on character strengths and virtues. Next we touch on only some of the issues indicating that the modern world for all its technological progress in health, economic development, and simple creature comforts is struggling with serious barriers to quality of life. These barriers have surfaced even in the wealthiest nations and puzzle social scientists who try to understand growing psychological unrest despite seeming plenty. In a brief period three books appeared by reputable social scientists with the word "paradox" in the title to capture this phenomena. The subtitles may be even more revealing: *The American Paradox: Spiritual Hunger in an Age of Plenty* (Myers, 2000a); *The Paradox of Choice: Why More Is Less* (Schwartz 2004); and *The Progress Paradox: How Life Gets Better While People Feel Worse* (Easterbrook, 2003). The messages are similar; we have a good deal and we are not enjoying it.

If the empirical research is valid, then positive psychology's moment may be here to assist people living today to see that happiness resides more in the kind of people we are than in our possessions. Religious and spiritual people of good will are no doubt eager to support this worldview. For such countercultural views to prevail, however, requires changes in outlook supported by enormously powerful social and cultural forces. Those forces do not seem to be at work currently, and it is essential to review those forces if virtuous standards are to have a renewed impact. What follows is a discussion of salient barriers that a range of thinkers, including psychologists, philosophers, and economists, have described.

Economics and the Psychology of Myopia

Israeli economist Avner Offer (2007) developed these themes from the viewpoint of economics while using the psychology of myopia for an explanatory lens. His primary thesis as he surveyed the impact of affluence in both developed and developing countries was, "Affluence breeds impatience, and impatience undermines well-being" (p. 1). Myopia is the label for how impatience breeds; people respond to novelty with great impatience for even more novel products, entertainments, and even relationships. The image of myopia as near-sightedness is nearly identical with the notion of transcendence failure as a primary mechanism in self-regulatory failure (Baumeister et al., 1994). Transcendence failure, like myopia, means people make short-term decisions that are detrimental to their long-term well-being. The image here is one of time: failing to transcend time for immediate gratification. Myopia uses an image of space or sight, wherein one fails to see beyond the present object. Offer's contribution is to relate myopia directly to affluence. More technically what mediates loss of well-being is the disinhibition of self-control that affluence promotes. Without prudence both individuals and cultures as a whole are ill equipped to manage the demands of our rapidly changing affluent society.

A personally useful if less-than-serious way to make sense of the contemporary political scene is to compare two reputable newspapers on either end of the liberal-conservative spectrum to see which issues they agree on editorially. My choices are the *Washington Post* (liberal) and the *Wall Street Journal* (conservative). An issue both agree on is psychological myopia when applied to governments. Each paper has castigated regional governments for passing pension and benefit packages for public sector employees so generous that future generations cannot possibly fund them without monumental tax increases. One jurisdiction, the state of California, passed pension benefit laws in 1999 based on the assumption that the stock market would earn, in perpetuity, more than 8% interest annually.

One way that affluence undermines well-being is through the well-known hedonic treadmill effect. This effect is based on adaptation-level theory, which is also reminiscent of habituation in physiology. Organisms adapt or get used to novel stimuli whether positive or negative and return to their prior level of responding. Both lottery winners and paraplegics over time resemble the general population in terms of levels of happiness. Obtaining that cherished salary raise provides a brief boost to happiness, but eventually the amount of positive emotions resembles the person's baseline level. Hence, the image is one of a person running on a treadmill with regard to happiness and making no progress.

The perverse nature of this effect is evident when people reach minimal levels of material goods. Beyond a certain minimum level of material goods happiness does not increase beyond a brief burst of excitement. Wealth in the United States doubled between 1957 and 1995 in terms of average per capita income from $8,000 to $20,000 annually, yet the percentage of people describing themselves as "very happy" declined from 35% to 33% (Myers, 2000b). During that same period, "the divorce rate doubled. Teen suicide tripled…violent crime nearly quadrupled" (p. 61). As Offer and others have noted, a marginal amount of wealth influences our happiness, and sizable monetary increments have negligible impact.

Perhaps the most direct and startling connection between the necessity of prudence for happiness is Offer's observation that "freedom of choice is not a secure foundation for social well-being" (2007, p. 41). Affluence, rather, points to the need for self-restraint amidst an abundance of short-term rewards against the costs of long-term losses. A number of lines of evidence demonstrate how giving in to short-term rewards lowers subjective well-being. Research on the trait of conscientiousness illustrates a moderate positive correlation between conscientiousness and subjective well-being (Ciarrocchi, Dy-Liacco, & Deneke, 2008; DeNeve & Cooper, 1998). Longitudinal experimental studies demonstrate that preschool children's delay of gratification predicts social maturity and higher scholastic performance in adolescence (Mischel, Shoda, & Peake, 1988).

Offer illustrates how affluence influences "commitment technologies"—what behaviorists would term "stimulus control strategies" for altering the environment to resist short-term temptations. His examples include increasing percentages of early-onset sexual activity, decreased household savings, a rise in obesity, increased divorce rates, increases in mental illness and suicide, extraordinary high levels of television viewing, and overworking. Paradoxically, as personal wealth increases, household savings decrease—especially at lower ends of the economic scale; "about half the population have none at all [financial assets]" (2007, p. 67). Similarly paradoxical is that people derive considerable satisfaction from work but, like income, up to a certain level more work results in satisfaction decline. Working very hard ceases to be enjoyable and almost no amount of salary increase compensates for this decreased satisfaction.

Health and weight control exemplifies some of the more curious examples of self-control. The annual costs of adult weight dyscontrol in developed countries run in the billions of dollars. Nine percent of US health care dollars are due to overweight—a rate comparable to the health effects of tobacco (Offer, 2007, p. 165). Affluence itself in country after country drives these numbers. An economic analysis of factors related to increased body mass index in the United States since the 1980s found the density of fast-food restaurants was the single largest factor. The United States spends 14% of its gross national product on health care, far more than any affluent country, yet it ranks 15th among nations in reaching minimally important health care goals.

The inability of people to resist short-term temptations in cultures that promote an ever-increasing variety of compelling attractions whether directly injurious to health and well-being (high-fat, high-caloric diets with low nutritional value), or indirectly through sedentary technological entertainment, points to the necessity of prudence and other virtues as an offset to the psychology of myopia.

At the same time neglecting the virtue of justice would be erroneous. Nations that witness the largest happiness "gap" are those where inequality is the greatest. Groups that are highly unequal to the majority culture exhibit even larger self-control dis-inhibition. They intuitively have less household savings but also have greater weight control problems, have higher rates of alcohol and drug abuse, watch more television, and lead more sedentary lives—all of which contribute to greater health problems. In the language of economic theory, more education is related to making use of and having greater access to commitment technologies that support prudential long-term decisions over harmful short-term ones. Nutritious foods are more expensive in general; inexpensive fast-food restaurants serve high-fat meals to larger numbers of the poor. Memberships in exercise gyms and other weight-loss facilities are costly.

In summary, affluence creates a greater abundance of less-expensive, short-term rewards. Myopic choice theory holds that it requires time, effort, and trial-and-error feedback to develop efficient commitment technologies that enact prudential self-regulation strategies to counter with long-term benefits. In the short run, myopic choices will overrun a culture to its detriment until rational decision making supersedes. How cultures evolve prudential self-regulation is not well understood. One argument this chapter makes is that exploring classical virtue ethics where prudence is the master virtue encouraging delay of gratification is a reasonable starting point. Positive psychology will need to decide whether it wants to play a role in extending its study of character strengths and virtues to the moral dimension of what it means to live a quality life amid the gifts and burdens of affluence. Delayed gratification is a value choice in a culture that spends 2%–3% of its gross national product advertising the message, "We can have it all now." Or, as the commercial for the luxury car would have it, those who say money can't buy happiness just don't know how to spend it. In a culture wherein the average person views 30,000 television commercials annually, prudence is not an optional virtue. Whatever positive psychology chooses to do with its findings, the fields of moral and religious education will want to consider what it offers to teaching prudence.

Religion, Spirituality, and Positive Emotions

Although positive emotions are not the entire focus of positive psychology, they represent one major component. Extensive empirical work now exists on the relationship between religion and spirituality with positive emotions as well as many other

positive outcomes. To summarize, positive religion and spirituality relate to improved health, psychological well-being, and fewer impulsive behaviors such as substance abuse, domestic violence, criminal behavior, and divorce (Ciarrocchi & Brelsford, 2009; Hood et al., 2009; Pargament, 1997; Pargament, Ano, & Wachholtz, 2005). Religious struggles such as believing God is punishing or abandoning the person are related to decreased health and psychological well-being, and higher mortality (Ciarrocchi & Brelsford, 2009; Ciarrocchi et al., 2008; Pargament, Koenig, Tarakeshwar, & Hahn, 2001). Fredrickson (2002) suggested the effects for positive emotions are due to religion and spirituality's relationship to positive affect, which mediates the outcomes for resilience. Direct tests of that hypothesis so far have failed to provide support (Ciarrocchi et al., 2008). Religion and spirituality are only partially mediated by positive emotion or personality.

An intriguing finding in an early study by personality psychologists Anna Lee Clark and David Watson found a relationship between religiosity and positive effect but not with negative effect (Clark & Watson, 1999; Watson & Clark, 1993). This finding contradicts a wide range of studies illustrating that religion and spirituality relate to both positive and negative emotions (e.g., Pargament, 1997). Piedmont (Chapter 7, this volume) argues on both conceptual and empirical grounds that religion and spirituality should control for personality as a covariate for greater confidence in their effects. Studies that control for personality have replicated Clark and Watson's findings that religion and spirituality are indeed related to positive but not negative affect. The robustness of these findings is attested to in the large variation of populations studied and the multiple measures used for the variables of interest. To date, research has confirmed this differential pattern in the general population (Ciarrocchi & Deneke, 2004), Protestant clergy (Golden, Piedmont, Ciarrocchi, & Rodgerson, 2004), Maltese college students (Galea, Ciarrocchi, Piedmont, & Wicks, 2007), nuns and seminarians in India (Mendonca, Oakes, Ciarrocchi, Sneck, & Gillespie, 2007), sex offenders (Geary, Ciarrocchi, & Scheers, 2006), and pathological gamblers (Walsh, Ciarrocchi, Piedmont, & Haskins, 2007).

These findings, taken together, point to religion and spirituality's function in the positive psychology system as related to increased positive emotion rather than decreased negative emotion. In that sense religion and spirituality are specifically related to flourishing. Spiritual struggles can reduce flourishing both by increasing negative emotions and decreasing positive emotions. Nevertheless, positive forms of religion and spirituality relate directly to one of the major legs of positive psychology, namely positive emotions. This confirms Peterson and Seligman's original insight in naming religion and spirituality as an important character strength within positive psychology. Ultimately, as these findings continue to be replicated, the functional psychological contribution of religion and spirituality will be to increase joy. Although religions have never lost sight of happiness as a consequence of faith, it is not a misleading generalization to say that religion is more frequently viewed as something to access in times of pain and suffering. The proverb that there are no atheists in foxholes, however, may be misleading according to this research. Perhaps there are fewer atheists where people are having positive emotional experiences such as weddings and graduations.

Note

1. Joseph Ciarrocchi died in October, 2010. This work represents his last contribution to the field. Joe had a creative, wide ranging intellect that was philosophically trained and psychologically focused. His published works reflected a thoughtful, analytical approach that could always find new connections and insights. His synthetic skills are evidenced in this chapter as he weaves together the underlying concepts of Positive Psychology with classical philosophy and virtue ethics. He is able to show convergence among ideas that are seen as disparate. And so it was with the man himself, able to bring harmony, joy, and happiness to the many different personalities around him. Joe was a priceless colleague who is dearly missed.

References

Annas, J. (1993). *The morality of happiness.* New York: Oxford University Press.

Anscombe, G. E. M. (1997). Modern moral philosophy. In R. Crisp & M. Slote (Eds.), *Virtue ethics* (pp. 26–44). Oxford, England: Oxford University Press.

Aquinas, T. (1984). *Treatise on the virtues* (J. A. Oesterle, Trans.). Notre Dame, IN: University of Notre Dame Press.

Baumeister, R. F., & Exline, J. J. (1999). Virtue, personality, and social relations: Self-control as the moral muscle. *Journal of Personality, 67,* 1165–1194.

Baumeister, R. F., Heatherton, T. F., & Tice, D. M. (1994). *Losing control: How and why people fail at self-regulation.* San Diego, CA: Academic Press.

Baumeister, R. F., & Leary, M. R. (1995). The need to belong: Desire for interpersonal attachments as a fundamental human motivation. *Psychological Bulletin, 117,* 497–529.

Baumeister, R. F., Wotman, S. R., & Stillwell, A. M. (1993). Unrequited love: On heartbreak, anger, guilt, scriptlessness, and humiliation. *Journal of Personality and Social Psychology, 64,* 339–363.

Baumeister, R. F., Zell, A. L., & Tice, D. M. (2007). How emotions facilitate and impair self-regulation. In J. J. Gross (Ed.), *Handbook of emotion regulation* (pp. 408–428). New York: The Guilford Press.

Berger, P. (1967). *The sacred canopy: Elements of a sociological theory of religion.* Garden City, NY: Doubleday Anchor.

Carver, C. S., & Scheier, M. F. (1999). Optimism. In C. R. Snyder (Ed.), *Coping: The psychology of what works* (pp. 182–204). New York: Oxford University Press.

Ciarrocchi, J. W. (2002). *Counseling problem gamblers: A self-regulation manual for individual and family therapy.* San Diego, CA: Academic Press.

Ciarrocchi, J. W., & Brelsford, G. M. (2009). Spirituality, religion, and substance coping as regulators of emotions and meaning-making: Different effects on pain and joy. *Journal of Addictions and Offender Rehabilitation, 30,* 24–36.

Ciarrocchi, J. W., & Deneke, E. (2004). Happiness and the varieties of religious experience: Religious support, practices, and spirituality as predictors of well-being. *Research in the Social Scientific Study of Religion, 15,* 209–233.

Ciarrocchi, J. W., Dy-Liacco, G., & Deneke, E. (2008). Gods or rituals? Relational faith, spiritual discontent, and religious practices as predictors of hope and optimism. *Journal of Positive Psychology, 3*(2), 120–136.

Clark, L. A., & Watson, D. (1999). Temperament: A new paradigm for trait psychology. In L. A. Pervin & O. P. John (Eds.), *Handbook of personality: Theory and research* (2nd ed., pp. 399–423). New York: The Guilford Press.

Cottingham, J. (1998). *Philosophy and the good life: Religion and the passions in Greek, Cartesian and psychoanalytic ethics.* Cambridge, England: Cambridge University Press.

DeNeve, K. M., & Cooper, H. (1998). The happy personality: A meta-analysis of 137 personality traits and subjective well-being. *Psychological Bulletin, 124,* 197–229.

Easterbrook, G. (2003). *The progress paradox.* New York: Random House.

Foot, P. (1997). Virtues and vices. In R. Crisp & M. Slote (Eds.), *Virtue ethics* (pp. 163–177). Oxford, England: Oxford University Press.

Fowers, B. J. (2005). *Virtue and psychology: Pursuing excellence in ordinary practices.* Washington, DC: American Psychological Association.

Fredrickson, B. (2002). How does religion benefit health and well-being? Are positive emotions active ingredients? *Psychological Inquiry, 13,* 209–212.

Funder, D. (2002). Why study religion? *Psychological Inquiry, 13,* 213–214.

Galea, M., Ciarrocchi, J. W., Piedmont, R. L., & Wicks, R. J. (2007). Child abuse, personality, and spirituality as predictors of happiness in Maltese college students. *Research in the Social Scientific Study of Religion, 18,* 141–154.

Geary, B., Ciarrocchi, J. W., & Scheers, N. J. (2006). Sex offenders, spirituality, and recovery. *Counselling and Spirituality, 25,* 47–71.

Geyer, A. L., & Baumeister, R. F. (2005). Religion, morality, and self-control: Values, virtues, and vices. In R. F. Paloutzian & C. L. Park (Eds.), *Handbook of the psychology of religion and spirituality* (pp. 412–434). New York: The Guilford Press.

Gillespie, C. K. (2001). *Psychology and American Catholicism: From confession to therapy.* New York: Crossroad.

Golden, J., Piedmont, R. L., Ciarrocchi, J. W., & Rodgerson, T. (2004). Spirituality and burnout: An incremental validity study. *Journal of Psychology and Theology, 32,* 115–125.

Hadot, P. (1995). *Philosophy as a way of life: Spiritual exercises from Socrates to Foucault.* Malden, MA: Blackwell.

Hassin, R. R., Uleman, J. s., & Bargh, J. A. (Eds.). (2007). *The new unconscious.* Oxford, England: Oxford University Press.

Haybron, D. M. (2008). *The pursuit of unhappiness: The elusive psychology of well-being.* Oxford, England: Oxford University Press.

Hood, R. W., Hill, P. C., & Spilka, B. (2009). *The psychology or religion* (4th ed.). New York: The Guilford Press.

Hursthouse, R. (2003). Normative virtue ethics. In R. Crisp (Ed.), *How should one live? Essays on the virtues* (pp. 19–36). Oxford, England: Oxford University Press.

Kent, B. (2002). Habits and virtues. In S. J. Pope (Ed.), *The ethics of Aquinas* (pp. 116–130). Washington, DC: Georgetown University Press.

MacIntyre, A. (1984). *After virtue: A study in moral theory* (2nd ed.). Notre Dame, IN: University of Notre Dame Press.

Martin, M. W. (2007). Happiness and virtue in positive psychology. *Journal for the Theory of Social Behavior, 37,* 89–103.

Mendonca, D., Oakes, K. E., Ciarrocchi, J. W., Sneck, W. J., & Gillespie, C. K. (2007). Spirituality and God-attachment as predictors of subjective well-being for seminarians and nuns in India. *Research in the Social Scientific Study of Religion, 18,* 121–140.

Micklethwait, J., & Wooldridge, A. (2009). *God is back: How the global revival of faith is changing the world.* New York: Penguin Press.

Mischel, W., Shoda, Y., & Peake, P. K. (1988). The nature of adolescent competencies predicted by preschool delay of gratification. *Journal of Personality and Social Psychology, 54,* 687–696.

Myers, D. (2000a). *The American paradox: Spiritual hunger in an age of plenty.* New Haven, CT: Yale University Press.

Myers, D. (2000b). The funds, friends, and faith of happy people. *American Psychologist, 55,* 56–67.

Nussbaum, M. C. (2008). Who is the happy warrior? Philosophy poses questions to psychology. *Journal of Legal Studies, 37,* S81–S113.

Offer, A. (2007). *The challenge of affluence: Self-control and well-being in the United States and Britain since 1950.* Oxford, England: Oxford University Press.

Pargament, K. I. (1997). *The psychology of religion and coping.* New York: The Guilford Press.

Pargament, K. I., Ano, G. G., & Wachholtz, A. B. (2005). The religious dimension of coping: Advances in theory, research, and practice. In R. F. Paloutzian & C. L. Park (Eds.), *Handbook of the psychology of religion and spirituality* (pp. 479–495). New York: The Guilford Press.

Pargament, K. I., Koenig, H. G., Tarakeshwar, N., & Hahn, J. (2001). Religious struggle as a predictor of mortality among medically ill elderly patients: A two-year longitudinal study. *Archives of Internal Medicine, 161,* 1881–1885.

Peterson, C., & Seligman, M. E. P. (Eds.). (2004). *Character strengths and virtues: A handbook and classification.* Oxford, England: American Psychological Association & Oxford University Press.

Piedmont, R. L., & Ciarrocchi, J. W. (1999). The utility of the revised NEO Personality Inventory in an outpatient, drug rehabilitation context. *Psychology of Addictive Behaviors, 13,* 213–236.

Pojman, L. P. (2006). *Who are we? Theories of human nature.* Oxford, England: Oxford University Press.

Pope, S. J. (Ed.). (2002). *The ethics of Aquinas.* Washington, DC: Georgetown University Press.

Porter, J. (1990). *The recovery of virtue: The relevance of Aquinas for Christian ethics.* Louisville, KY: Westminster/John Knox Press.

Schwartz, B. (2004). *The paradox of choice: Why more is less.* New York: Harper Collins.

Schwartz, B., & Sharpe, K. E. (2006). Practical wisdom: Aristotle meets positive psychology. *Journal of Happiness Studies, 7,* 377–395.

Seligman, M. E. P., Park, N., & Peterson, C. (2005). Positive psychology progress: Empirical validation of interventions. *American Psychologist, 60,* 410–421.

Tiberius, V. (2008). *The reflective life: Living wisely with our limits.* Oxford, England: Oxford University Press.

Titus, C. S. (2006). *Resilience and the virtue of fortitude: Aquinas in dialogue with the psychosocial sciences.* Washington, DC: Catholic University of America Press.

Tolstoy, L. (2009). *Father Sergius and other stories.* Retrieved from http://www.amazon.com/Father-Sergius-Other-Stories-ebook/dp/B0028AEFOW/ref=sr_1_9?s=books&ie=UTF8&qid=1330368871&sr=1–9 (Original published in 1912).

Walsh, J. M., Ciarrocchi, J. W., Piedmont, R. L., & Haskins, D. (2007). Spiritual transcendence and religious practices in recovery from pathological gambling: Reducing pain or enhancing quality of life? *Research in the Social Scientific Study of Religion, 18,* 155–175.

Watson, D., & Clark, L. A. (1993). Behavioral disinhibition versus constraint: A dispositional perspective. In D. M. Wegner & J. W. Pennebaker (Eds.), *Handbook of mental control* (pp. 506–527). Upper Saddle River, NJ: Prentice Hall.

Worthington, E. L., & Berry, J. W. (2005). Virtues, vices, and character education. In W. R. Miller & H. D. Delaney (Eds.), *Judeo-Christian perspectives on psychology: Human nature, motivation, and change* (pp. 145–164). Washington, DC: American Psychological Press.

Spirituality, Resilience, and Positive Emotions

Bruce W. Smith, J. Alexis Ortiz, Kathryn T. Wiggins, Jennifer F. Bernard, *and* Jeanne Dalen

Abstract

This chapter examines the relationships between spirituality, resilience, and positive emotions. We begin by defining all three constructs, important related constructs, and theoretical models that may help us frame our understanding of the relationship between spirituality, resilience, and positive emotions. Next, we review the research and thinking about the relationship between (1) spirituality and positive emotion, (2) spirituality and resilience, and (3) positive emotions and resilience. These reviews suggest that healthy spirituality may be related to increases in both resilience and positive emotions and that resilience and positive emotions may have a reciprocal influence on each other. Finally, we present a preliminary model of the relationship between spirituality, resilience, and positive emotions and make suggestions for research that may increase our understanding of the relationship between them.

Key Words: spirituality, resilience, positive emotions, personal meaning, purpose in life, posttraumatic growth

Introduction

Positive psychology is a recent branch of psychology that focuses on what enables people to live and function at their best. Positive emotions and resilience are major foci of the emerging studies in positive psychology, and both may be related in several important ways to spirituality. The purpose of this chapter is to examine the relationships among spirituality, positive emotions, and resilience. We will begin by defining all three and some important related constructs and presenting some theoretical models that may help frame our thinking about their relationship. Next, we review the research and thinking about the relationship between (1) spirituality and positive emotion, (2) spirituality and resilience, and (3) positive emotions and resilience. Finally, we will present a preliminary model of how the three may be related, how they all may affect overall

health and well-being, and what may be important directions for future research.

Definitions and Relevant Models
What Is Spirituality?

While there are no universally agreed-upon definitions of "spirituality" or "religion" in the psychological literature, many researchers use similar definitions (Dyson, Cobb, & Forman, 1997; Selway & Ashman, 1998; Weaver, Flannelly, Flannelly, Koenig, & Larson, 1998). Spirituality is generally understood as the thoughts, feelings, and behaviors that an individual engages in search of a relationship with the sacred or the transcendent. It can be understood as a search for that relationship or a process through which a person seeks to discover, hold on to, and even transform whatever it is that he or she holds sacred (Hill & Pargament, 2008). It is the personal quest for understanding the answers to ultimate questions about life which may (or may not) lead to or arise from the development of religious rituals and the formation of community (Zinnbauer & Pargament, 2005).

The meanings associated with "spirituality" are often contrasted with those associated with "religion." Religion has been conceptually defined as a collective concept that relates to common behaviors and beliefs while spirituality has been conceived to be a phenomenon that is unique to different individuals but also focuses on relationships and connections with other people (Dyson et al., 1997; Selway & Ashman, 1998; Weaver et al., 1998). The fundamental difference is that spirituality is generally understood as the thoughts, feelings, and behaviors involved in search of a relationship with the sacred, and religiousness is generally defined as those spiritual thoughts, feelings, and behaviors that are specifically related to a formally organized and identifiable religion (Zinnbauer & Pargament, 2005).

What Are Positive Emotions?

The study of positive emotions has traditionally not been given the same attention in research as negative emotions (Fredrickson, 2001). The term "positive affect" is often used synonymously with positive emotions. Positive affect generally is defined as the extent to which an individual feels alert, enthusiastic, and active (Watson, Clark, & Tellegen, 1988). A state of high positive affect has been characterized as involving high levels of energy, concentration, and pleasurable engagement in activities (Watson et al., 1988). Trait positive affect refers to consistently highly levels of positive affect and broadly corresponds to the personality characteristic of extraversion (Tellegen, 1985; Watson & Clark, 1984). Positive affect is beneficial because it facilitates approach behavior to the environment (Cacioppo, Gardner, & Berntson, 1999; Davidson, 1993; Watson, Wiese, Vaidya, & Tellegen, 1999) and continued action within the environment (Carver & Scheier, 1990; Clore, 1994).

Low positive affect has been implicated as a distinguishing characteristic of depression (Tellegen, 1985). Meanwhile, frequent positive affect, along with infrequent negative affect, has been characterized as both a necessary and sufficient condition to produce a state of happiness or affective well-being (Diener, Sandvik, & Pavot, 1991). High positive affect has been shown to indicate as well as promote optimal well-being or flourishing (Fredrickson, 2001). The Positive and Negative Affect Schedule

(PANAS; Watson et al., 1988) is probably the most widely used measure of positive and negative affect. It has demonstrated high internal consistency and good convergent and discriminant validity (Watson et al., 1988). The scales also possess adequate test-retest reliability over periods of a few weeks to a couple months (Watson et al., 1988).

What Is Resilience?

During the past decade, resilience has increasingly become a focus of research in the behavioral and medical sciences (Charney, 2004; Masten, 2001). Resilience has been defined in a variety of ways, including the ability to adapt to stressful circumstances, to not become ill despite significant adversity, and to function above the norm in spite of significant stress or adversity (Carver, 1998; Tusaie & Dyer, 2004). However, resilience in its original and most basic meaning is defined as the ability to bounce back or recover from stress (Agnes, 2005). The origin for the English word "resilience" is the word "resile," which means "to bounce or spring back" (from re- "back" + salire- "to jump, leap"; Agnes, 2005). Carver (1998) provides a clear distinction between "resilience" as returning to the previous level of functioning (e.g., bouncing back or recovery) and "thriving" as moving to a superior level of functioning following a stressful event.

Additionally, there are those who highlight the reestablishment of equilibrium following adversity (Wagnild & Young, 1990) or the protective factors that serve as a buffer against the negative effects of adversity (Rutter, 1990), as being most indicative of resilience. Ego resiliency (Block & Block, 1980; Block & Kremen, 1996) has been defined as a relatively stable personality trait that is reflective of one's adaptability to changing environments, including identifying opportunities, adjusting to environmental constraints, and recovering from adversity. Those with low resilience have a difficult time coping with negative experiences and are unable to recover from them (Klohnen, 1996; Rutter, 1987). In contrast, those with high resilience are able to "ride out the storm," handle anxiety, and tolerate frustration even when faced with stressful events (Carver, 1998; Saarni, 1999).

What Constructs Are Closely Related to Spirituality, Positive Emotions, and Resilience?

There are three additional constructs related to spirituality, positive emotions, and resilience that are often studied or referred to in the psychological literature.

These constructs may help us to better understand the relationship between spirituality, positive emotions, and resilience. We will refer to these constructs as "personal meaning," "purpose in life," and "posttraumatic growth." All three of these constructs can be understood in more general terms as forms or sources of positive meaning in a person's life.

Personal meaning has been defined as the cognizance of order, a sense of coherence, the pursuit and attainment of worthwhile goals, and an accompanying sense of fulfillment (Antonovsky, 1979; Reker, 2000). A person with a high degree of personal meaning has a clear sense of purpose in life, a sense of directedness, strives for goals consistent with his or her life purpose, feels satisfied with past achievements, and is determined to make the future meaningful. Thus, personal meaning and a sense of purpose in life are closely related in that personal meaning involves a sense of purpose in life. In addition, personal meaning is rooted within an individual's culture and, although influenced by life experiences, is often reasonably stable by the end of early adulthood (Antonovsky, 1979; Battista & Almond, 1973; Frankl, 1963).

While personal meaning and purpose in life refer more generally to the whole of one's life, posttraumatic growth is used more specifically to refer to what occurs in the context or aftermath of traumatic or stressful events. Posttraumatic growth is also sometimes referred to as "stress-related growth" (Park, Cohen, & Murch, 1996) or "benefit finding" (Affleck & Tennen, 1996). Posttraumatic growth involves positive changes such as improved relationships, changes in the value ascribed to one's life, changes in priorities, viewing oneself as a stronger or better person, and even spiritual growth (Siegel & Schrimshaw, 2000; Tedeschi & Calhoun, 2004). Although posttraumatic growth may not only be about positive meaning, it always involves finding or attributing something positive or meaningful to having experienced stressful or traumatic events.

How are personal meaning, purpose in life, and posttraumatic growth related to spirituality, positive emotions, and resilience? Although we will address this question more at the end of the chapter, it may be helpful to make some initial comments here. First, spirituality often facilitates a sense of personal meaning and purpose in life and may encourage and facilitate posttraumatic growth. Second, because personal meaning, purpose in life, and posttraumatic growth generally provide positive meaning to a person's life, the positive attributions about one's life experience may also result in positive emotions.

Third, a sense of purpose in life has often been thought to be a key aspect or source of resilience, and resilience may have a reciprocal and interacting relationship with finding positive meaning, especially in response to stressful events (Connor & Davidson, 2003; Smith & Zautra, 2004).

What Are Some Useful Models for Understanding Spirituality, Positive Emotions, and Resilience?

One of the greatest theoretical limitations of stress and coping models has been their focus on reducing vulnerability to the negative effects of immediate stressors rather than improving well-being and building resources for increasing resilience (Zautra, Johnson, & Davis, 2005). There is a strong need to incorporate recent research and theory regarding the value of positive personal characteristics and emotions into the literature on coping with stressful events. Not surprisingly, the positive psychology movement has provided an impetus and fertile ground for incorporating positive characteristics, relationships, and emotions into theoretical models. This may also be one of the greatest contributions of the positive psychology movement to understanding the relationship between spirituality, positive emotions, and resilience.

Zautra and colleagues have developed a "two-factor model" that provides a framework for understanding the differential effects of positive and negative personal characteristics on emotions and social relationships (Smith & Zautra, 2008; Zautra, 2003). This model is based on studies showing that there may be separate positive and negative domains of emotion, personal characteristics, and social interactions (Bradburn, 1969; Davidson, 1992; Watson et al., 1999). In the two-factor model, personal characteristics may uniquely influence social and emotional domains of the same valence. For example, positive personal characteristics may increase the likelihood of experiencing both positive social interactions and positive emotion but have little effect on negative social interactions and negative emotions. Similarly, negative personal characteristics may increase the likelihood of negative social interactions and negative emotion but have little effect on positive social interactions and positive emotion.

In addition, investigators also have begun to propose models suggesting that positive emotions are important psychological resources that a person may gather over time and use to aid in coping efforts during times of stress (Fredrickson & Joiner, 2002;

Hobfoll, 1989). In Fredrickson's "broaden-and-build" theory (Fredrickson, 2001), positive emotions are thought to enhance well-being by broadening and building personal resources. Specifically, positive emotions are thought to "broaden people's momentary thought-action repertoires, which in turn serve to build their enduring personal resources, ranging from physical and intellectual resources to social and psychological resources" (Fredrickson, 2001, p. 218). Similarly, Hobfoll (1989) has developed a theory suggesting that positive personal, social, and economic resources add up over time and that these resources enable a person to cope with stressful events.

Finally, the "dynamic model of affect" proposed by Zautra and colleagues (2001) is based on the premise that positive emotions may play an important role in the context of stress. This model proposes that a deficit in positive emotions increases vulnerability to negative emotions during stress and that the presence of positive emotions may be critical to the preservation of well-being during these times. Zautra and colleagues have conducted studies showing that positive affect and psychological well-being can be resources for resilience in coping with stressful events (Davis, Zautra, & Smith, 2004; Zautra, Smith, Affleck, & Tennen, 2001). While both the broaden-and-build theory and the dynamic model of affect place value on positive emotions in times of stress, the dynamic model of affect focuses on the value of state-positive emotion while the broaden-and-build theory focuses more on trait-positive emotion.

How are the two-factor model, broaden-and-build theory, and dynamic model of affect relevant for understanding the relationship between spirituality, positive emotions, and resilience? While the study of positive emotion has been neglected until recently, each of these three models proposes a unique role for positive emotions in health and functioning. The two-factor model suggests that positive characteristics, including spirituality and resilience, may have their strongest effects on positive emotions. The broaden-and-build theory suggests that a consistently high level of positive emotions may improve functioning and increase resilience in times of stress. The dynamic model of affect suggests that even high state levels of affect may improve resilience, functioning, and health. Taken together, these theories suggest that spirituality, in as far as it is a positive personal resource, may have a unique influence on positive emotions and that positive emotions may enhance resilience.

Spirituality and Resilience

How is spirituality related to resilience? The study of resilience in psychology is increasing as researchers begin to identify "protective factors" as strengths against developing mental disorders and adapting to chronic and acute stressors. Protective factors are conditions that buffer, interrupt, or prevent problems from occurring. Research has frequently identified spirituality and religion as being related various measures of resilience (Connor & Davidson, 2003; Pargament, 1997). Thus, spirituality and religion may be important protective factors or "resilience resources" that may contribute to or promote a person's resilience to adversity.

How may religion and spirituality serve as resources for resilience? Spirituality, religious faith, the belief in something larger than oneself, and the ability to find meaning following stress events are often discussed as playing an important role in development of resilience. Seaward (2005) suggests that the foundations of all forms of spirituality include four cornerstones: relationships, values, meaning in life, and connectedness. These have all been related directly to better coping with life stressors. Thus, spirituality may increase resilience by its influence on relationships, life values, personal meaning, and coping.

Spirituality Increasing Resilience by Affecting Relationships

In all the major world religions and most forms of spirituality, there is an emphasis on ethical conduct in relationships with other people. At its most basic level, religion promotes human kindness through civil conduct, dedication to community, and in communal worship. This is exemplified in the occurrence of a version of the Golden Rule across cultures and religions (Smith, 1991). This often takes the form of formal scripture or sage advice to treat others as one would like to be treated and build relationships on values such as love, acceptance, and mutual respect. Often, whether it is implicit or explicit, spirituality and religion support dedication to community. Through spirituality or religion, many people come to see a need to build and maintain a sense of community by developing quality and lasting relationships.

Additionally, religion and spirituality often support healthy relationships and social support through encouraging communal worship and fellowship. Social support is a key factor in resilience and coping with stress (Cohen & Wills, 1985) and its relationship with better health has been well documented (Uchino, Cacioppo, & Kiecolt-Glaser, 1996). Cook (2000) suggests that some individuals have characteristics that lead them to become involved in religion and that they derive important benefits from this involvement. This may be encouraged by social influences, such as the participation of other family members in the religious or spiritual communities. In a study of resilience in remarriages, parents were asked what they thought helped their family through stressful times, and they reported that spirituality and religion were the primary coping resources outside of the family (Greeff & Du Toit, 2009).

Spirituality Increasing Resilience by Affecting Life Values

In every form of religion and spirituality, there are rules or ethical guidelines placed on ways of living. These may be viewed as either external mandates or as functioning to cultivate internal values. Many of these take the shape of formal rules and structured guidelines that may prevent or reduce stress (e.g., prayer, meditation, reading sacred scriptures, dietary guidelines). Others serve as virtues of the kind of person that one should strive for, such as humility, charity, and veracity (Smith, 1991). Saint Thomas Aquinas distinguished theological virtues from those of intellect and morality. The theological virtues (faith, hope, and charity) were considered distinct and supernatural in comparison with intellectual or moral virtues and known through one's relationship with God, rather than through reason alone (Browning & Cooper, 2004).

Additionally, religion often explicitly fosters forgiveness and reconciliation as virtues. In fact, some form of forgiveness is espoused in the religious doctrines of Judaism, Christianity, Islam, Buddhism, and Hinduism. It is important to distinguish the inner process of forgiveness from the relational process of reconciliation. The former involves more of an internal process of making peace while recognizing pain (Van Dyke & Elias, 2007), and the latter involves the restoration of a relationship. The former involves a level of emotional and cognitive processing that may support meaning making and acceptance, and the latter has implications for improving relationships and increasing social support. Worthington and Scherer (2004) describe forgiveness as an emotion-focused coping strategy that promotes resilience by reducing stressful reactions to a perceived transgression.

Spirituality Increasing Resilience by Increasing Personal Meaning

Religiousness and spirituality are strongly related to a personal quest for understanding of questions about life, meaning, and what is perceived as sacred. Spirituality and religious beliefs offer meaning to human existence, and religious tenets provide guides for living (Geertz, 1975). During his experiences in the Nazi concentration camps, Viktor Frankl (1963) witnessed, in himself and in others, how strong beliefs and a desire to find meaning amid the suffering could improve resilience in the context of devastation and loss of life. A study by Greene, Galambos, and Lee (2003) involved interviewing people in health-related professions associated with trauma to gain a clearer understanding of what they believed helped buffer life stress and contribute to resilience. Over half of the participants (55%) stated that spirituality/religion was of central importance to them as they experienced adverse events.

Families use spirituality to frame crisis situations in terms of shared beliefs and goals as a way to achieve harmony and work together in coping with them (McCubbin, Thompson, & McCubbin, 1996). In a study of Black families in South Africa, researchers asked open-ended questions about factors or strengths that had recently helped their families (Greeff & Loubser, 2008). They found that people identified spirituality as an important coping resource. Additionally, six themes emerged related to successful adaptation: gifts from God, guidance, God's works, God's plan, prayer, and faith. McGrath (2006) posited that the distinctive strength of Christian spirituality may be that it makes it possible to view suffering and adversity as potentially valuable and that it is a means of thriving in the midst of stressful experiences.

Religion and spirituality may also help people cope with stressors by guiding or reorganizing behavior during times of uncertainty and providing a larger structure under which they can find meaning in their experience. Lazarus and DeLongis (1983) have theorized that personal meaning can positively influence stress management and coping. Specifically, if one feels a strong sense of commitment to a value, goal, or person, and this commitment is challenged by stress, then a threat is perceived that can drive the individual toward trying to eliminate the stressor. From a cognitive perspective, spirituality may enhance resilience to trauma by building narratives that involve overcoming or learning from stressful experiences. This may facilitate the integration of fragmented memories from a trauma into a new cognitive synthesis, thus working to decrease posttraumatic symptoms (Peres, Moreira-Almeida, Nasello, & Koenig, 2007).

Spirituality Increasing Resilience by Improving Coping

Pargament and colleagues have done seminal work examining the use of spirituality and religion in coping with stress (Pargament, 1997). "Religious coping" is the term that is most often used to describe the coping behaviors associated with spirituality or religion. Ways of using religion or spirituality to cope include things like seeking God's love and care, looking for a stronger connection with God, and trying to put one's plans and actions together with God (Pargament, Smith, Koenig, & Perez, 1998). Recent data suggest that religious behaviors and beliefs can reduce the impact of adverse life events on physical and mental health. A study examining religious coping by church members following a large flood found that religious dispositions, attributions, and coping activities were related to better psychological and religious outcomes (Smith, Pargament, Brant, & Oliver, 2000). The results showed that religious attribution and coping activities prospectively predicted better psychological and religious outcomes after controlling for flood exposure and demographics.

Similarly, another study found that religiosity affects ways of thinking about a stressful situation through religious attribution and that religious attribution was related to more positive affect but was not related to distress. Ways of thinking about the stressful situation included the belief that God was enabling them to bear their troubles (religious/spiritual support), that it was all for the best, and that everything is ultimately controlled by God (Loewenthal, Macleod, Goldblatt, Lubitsh, & Valentine, 2000). This study examined people of both Protestant and Jewish faith and did not find any significant differences in religiosity. Religiosity was related to greater positive affect independent of negative affect. Additionally, this study used structural equation modeling to test the causal pathways through which religiosity interacted with cognitions and affect. Overall, religiosity was found to have the strongest relationship with the thoughts that everything would work out for the best and that God

provided religious/spiritual support. Thinking that God provided spiritual/religious support through adverse events was the only direct cognitive pathway to positive affect.

A study of inner-city "at-risk" youths, Cook (2000) found that "church alignment" was related to resilience. Two groups were interviewed and administered questionnaires: a church-aligned group and a non-churchgoing group. Church alignment was measured by church attendance of more than once per week and at least one of the following: a mentor in the church, the church had helped to solve a personal dilemma, or another family member attended church regularly. The results found that the church-aligned group had greater stability in their lives and were less likely to show externalizing problems than the non-churchgoing group of youths. These results were interpreted as a measure of resilience defined as successful adaptation despite challenging and threatening circumstances. Another study with a vulnerable population of youth conducted focus groups with homeless "street youth" aged 18–24 and found that spirituality was one of the strengths that helped them to cope with street life (Bender, Thompson, McManus, Lantry, & Flynn, 2007).

Additionally, religious and spiritual coping appears to vary between ethnic groups and major religions and is influenced by group cultures and practices. A recent study by Bhui, King, Dein, and Connor (2008) confirmed earlier findings that Muslim and Black Caribbean Christians most often use religious coping strategies compared with other religious groups. In contrast, the British and Irish people in this study did not tend to use religious coping. Younes (2007) discussed the importance of religion in increasing resilience in Israeli families in the context of political strife and violence since 1948. She highlighted a culturally shared sense of suffering and religious faith as contributors to resilience. These studies provide greater understanding for how the effects of spirituality and religion on resilience may vary with different cultural and historical contexts.

Limitations of Past Research

There are important limitations to consider in evaluating the association between religion and spirituality with resilience. One common problem with the research on religion and spirituality is the way that they are defined and measured. Studies investigating spirituality and religion often do not precisely measure or differentiate between different facets of spirituality and religion. This can make it difficult to get a clear picture of the complex ways that religious and spirituality may be related to resilience (Bergin, Stinchfield, Gaskin, Masters, & Sullivan, 1988). Thus, it is important for future researchers to assess multiple aspects of spirituality and religion and use research design and analyses approaches that can do justice to their potentially subtle and complex relationships with resilience.

Similarly, the evidence supporting the effects of religion or spirituality and resilience may be overgeneralized. Many people appear to have oversimplified views of the role that spirituality or religion may play in people's lives, such as viewing it as being all bad or all good (Pargament, 1997; Silberman, 2003). Just as spirituality is not always a bad thing, it is also not always related to better health and adjustment. Pargament et al. (1998) have identified forms of both "positive" and "negative" religious coping that are usually related to better and worse health outcomes, respectively. Their measure of negative religious coping they developed includes items like "wondered whether God had abandoned me," "felt punished by my God for lack of devotion," "questioned God's love for me," and "questioned God's power."

Summary and Future Directions

In summarizing the research and thinking regarding spirituality and resilience, it is likely they both may often be important resources for resilience. Spirituality may increase resilience by affecting relationships, life values, personal meaning, and the ways that people cope with stress. At the same time, the relationship between spirituality and resilience may be complex or subtle and it may be tempting to oversimplify their relationship. One important reason for this complexity is that spirituality and religion can be either helpful or harmful influences on health and functioning depending on what specific aspects of spirituality and religion are assessed. In addition, as we saw earlier, resilience can also be defined and measured in several different ways, and it is likely that the relationship of spirituality or religion with resilience will vary according. Finally, because of all of the potential pathways (e.g., relationship, values, meaning, coping) by which spirituality may influence resilience, it may be misleading to focus too much on a direct relationship between them. Future research should be careful to be clear about defining and assessing different aspects of spirituality and resilience, attempt to measure a full range of potential mediators, and examine how their relationship may unfold over time using prospective designs.

Spirituality and Positive Emotions

How is spirituality related to positive emotions? The study of both spirituality and positive emotions has grown tremendously in that past 20 years, although researchers have only begun to examine the relationship between the two. While the earlier models of spirituality and health focused on the relationship between spirituality and negative emotions, researchers are just beginning to study the potential role of spirituality in relation to positive emotions. While it is undeniable that there have been harmful manifestations of spirituality and religion, psychology is becoming more open to the possibility that there may also be more helpful aspects of spirituality and religion. While the two-factor model would suggest that these negative aspects would primarily influence and increase negative emotion and its correlates, this model would also suggest that the positive aspects of spirituality and religion would primarily affect positive emotion.

How might spirituality affect our emotional experience? Emotions are dynamic aspects of personal experience involving facial expressions, subjective feelings, cognitive appraisals, and physiological changes. While all of these components may be a part of the experience of an emotion, appraisal theories of emotion (Lazarus, 1991) emphasize the idea that how we think about an event may influence the emotions that we experience in response to the event. For example, if a person construes a stressful event as an opportunity for growth rather than a cause of harm, he or she is more likely to experience positive emotions such as interest or excitement than negative emotions such as anxiety or fear. Because spirituality may inform how a person thinks about what happens in his or her life, it may influence what emotions the person experiences in relation to these events (Fredrickson, 2002). For example, a person may experience more positive emotions such as gratitude if his or her spiritual or religious beliefs encourage the interpretation of positive experiences as blessings from God.

Spirituality and religion often provide people with opportunities and encouragement to cultivate positive emotions as well as to find positive meaning in everyday events and in major life stressors. Many forms of spirituality place a high value on and foster basic positive emotions such as love, joy, and contentment. The idea of loving a deity or loving one's neighbor is at the heart of many world religions (Smith, 1991). While love can be thought of as including attitudinal and behavioral components, it is also often defined and experienced as an emotion that is fostered by specific spiritual and religious beliefs and practices. Joy is another emotion that is strongly encouraged in religious contexts, even in the midst of pain and suffering. Contentment is a positive emotion that is actively addressed and developed as a goal of achieving serenity and inner peace in many spiritual practices (Emmons & Paloutzian, 2003; Watts, 1996). Many different forms of meditation, prayer, and worship have been developed that may either directly or indirectly evoke these emotions (Seaward, 2005; Smith, 1991).

What has research shown about the relationship between spirituality and positive emotions? There are a growing number of studies examining the relationship between general and specific measures of spirituality and religion and spirituality and measures of positive emotions and well-being. The majority of studies have only involved cross-sectional data, but a growing number are beginning to examine prospective relationships and the effects of spiritually oriented interventions on positive emotion. We will present representative studies examining the relationship between positive emotions and a variety of measures, including general measures of spirituality, daily spiritual experiences, religious or spiritual coping, and religious involvement measures. We will also present the results of studies of spiritually oriented interventions on positive emotion or measures of psychological well-being.

Spirituality Measures

In a cross-sectional study of 120 undergraduates at a religious affiliated college, Fabricatore, Handal, and Fenzel (2000) examined the relationship between personal spirituality and life satisfaction. Personal spirituality was assessed by the Spiritual Involvement Scale (Fenzel, 2002) and the results showed that this measure was positively correlated with life satisfaction. Kim and colleagues (Kim, Seidlitz, Ro, Evinger, & Duberstein, 2004) examined spirituality and positive affect in a population of 287 employees of a South Korean hospital. They assessed spirituality with the Spiritual Transcendence Index (STI; Seidlitz et al., 2002). For participants who reported religious affiliation, they found that spirituality was related to positive affect.

In another cross-sectional study, Ekas, Whitman, and Shivers (2009) examined religiosity, spirituality, and several aspects of socioemotional functioning in mothers of children with autism spectrum disorder. They found that religious belief and spirituality were related to higher levels of positive affect and other positive outcomes (child-related enjoyment,

life satisfaction, psychological well-being) and lower levels of negative outcomes (depression, negative affect, negative life events). Religiosity and spirituality were measured using the Multidimensional Measure of Religiousness/Spirituality developed by the Fetzer Institute (1999).

Daily Spiritual Experiences Measures

The Daily Spiritual Experiences Scale (DSES; Underwood & Teresi, 2002) has been used in several large studies that have also examined happiness or positive emotions. The DSES has the advantage over general questions about spirituality (e.g., "How much do you see yourself as a spiritual person?") of asking participants to report about specific daily events and occurrences. The measure asks participants about how much during the day they experience things such as "I feel God's presence," "I find strength or comfort in my religion," and "I am spirituality touched by the beauty of creation" (Fetzer Institute, 1999, p. 85).

The 1998 National Opinion Research Center's General Social Survey (GSS) used a short form of the DSES to survey 1,445 individuals about their religiosity/spirituality. Using this data, Maselko and Kubzansky (2006) found that daily spiritual experiences were related to greater happiness in both men and women. They also found that religious participation was related to greater happiness in men but not women. Using data from the 2004 GSS, which included the full DSES measure, Ellison and Fan (2008) again found that daily spiritual experiences were associated with greater happiness for both men and women. They also found that daily spiritual experiences were more consistently associated with positive aspects of mental health, such as excitement with life, as opposed to negative aspects, such as psychological distress.

In a recent study by Greenfield, Vaillant, and Marks (2009), a modified version of the DSES was included again on a large national survey, the National Survey of Midlife in the United States (MIDUS). Greenfield and colleagues modified the DSES by eliminating several of the original items' references to "God," "religion," "creation," and "blessings," in an effort to conceptualize spiritual experiences in a manner that did not require involvement in organized religion. To differentiate their modified construct, they referred to spiritual experiences as "spiritual perceptions." These researchers found that more frequent spiritual perceptions were positively related to positive affect. In post-hoc meditational analyses, they found that when formal religious participation was entered into models that did not include the measure of spiritual perceptions, formal religious participation was also associated with higher levels of positive affect. This suggests that spiritual perceptions mediate the association between formal religious participation and positive affect.

The DSES is particularly well suited to daily diary and experience sampling studies because it asks about discrete events that can occur multiple times during the day. Keefe et al. (2001) used the DSES to examine the relationship between daily spiritual experiences and positive mood, negative mood, and social support in 35 people with rheumatoid arthritis. First, they found that participants reported daily spiritual experiences on a relatively frequent basis. Second, they found that daily spiritual experiences were related to higher daily positive mood and lower daily negative mood. Third, daily spiritual experiences were also related to greater social support, an important resource for resilience and coping with stress.

Religious or Spiritual Coping Measures

Several researchers have also examined the relationship between religious or spiritual coping and positive emotion or related aspects of psychological well-being. As with the measure of daily spiritual experiences, measures of religious coping are more tied to specific thoughts and behaviors than are general measures of spirituality or religiosity. Bush et al. (1999) found that positive religious coping was associated with positive affect in a sample of 61 people with chronic pain. Religious coping was assessed using the Religious Appraisal and Coping Survey (Pargament, Ensing, Falgout, & Olsen, 1990).

In a study examining religious coping in a large sample of 1,260 Presbyterian clergy, 823 lay leaders/elders, and 735 church members, religiosity seemed to have differential effects on positive and negative affect depending on how closely their lives were tied to religion (Pargament, Tarakeshwar, Ellison, & Wulff, 2001). The researchers found that while all three groups used religious coping, the clergy used religious coping most often and for that group, positive religious coping had a larger effect in reducing negative affect than in the other two groups. In addition, negative religious coping was associated with lower positive affect. The researchers speculated that for the clergy and to a lesser degree for the lay leaders, their role as spiritual leaders and their religious training led them to use more religious coping.

Religious Involvement Measures

Other studies have examined the relationship between religious involvement and participation in religious activities and positive affect. In a cross-sectional study of recently bereaved widows, McGloshen and O'Bryant (1998) found that religious involvement was associated with higher levels of positive affect. In a longitudinal study examining 305 bereaved AIDS caregivers, Folkman (1997) found that religious/spiritual beliefs and activities were consistently related to more positive affect.

Spiritually Oriented Interventions

Finally, researchers have begun to study the effects of spiritually oriented interventions on positive emotions and psychological well-being. Fredrickson has suggested that mindfulness exercises may be used to increase feelings of contentment (Fredrickson, 2000, 2002). Mindfulness is thought to cultivate nonstriving, a nonjudgmental attitude, and moment-to-moment awareness (Kabat-Zinn, 1990). Contentment involves behavioral passivity, much like nonstriving, and the full awareness of and openness to momentary experiences. While the practice of mindfulness does not necessarily need to be viewed as a religious practice, it has been a component of organized religion and is commonly practiced in the pursuit of a sense of transcendence and the sacred.

Goldstein (2007) described an intervention designed to increase well-being (including positive affect) by cultivating "sacred moments." In a randomized controlled trial, he found that the intervention was just as effective in increasing feelings of well-being as a therapeutic writing intervention. The sacred moment intervention consisted of spending at least 5 minutes a day for 5 days a week practicing mindfulness techniques and then shifting attention to a personally chosen object that held special, precious, or sacred meaning for the individual. Examples of these "sacred objects" included wedding rings or family heirlooms, but they could also include a mantra or insubstantial objects, such as clouds, as long as the chosen object of attention held sacred meaning for the participant. During the time spent in reflection on the object, participants were asked to be open to whatever was sacred in the moment. The control group spent a similar amount of time in a daily writing exercise in which they wrote about their daily activities. There were no significant group differences between the intervention and control groups, but both did show increases in positive affect.

Wachholtz and Pargament (2005) compared the effects of spiritual meditation, secular meditation, and relaxation in predicting spiritual, psychological (including positive and negative affect), and physiological outcomes (heart rate, pain ratings). While this was a prospective study, positive affect was only measured during a posttest. At the posttest, there were significant between-group differences in positive affect. The spiritual meditation group reported significantly more positive affect than the secular meditation or the relaxation groups. The researchers performed several post-hoc analyses and found that spirituality and existential well-being were related to less negative mood, and daily spiritual experiences were related to more positive mood.

Summary and Future Directions

In summarizing the findings regarding spirituality and positive emotions, researchers have found that measures of spirituality, daily spiritual experiences, positive forms of religious coping, and religious participation have consistently been related to measures of positive emotion and related measures of psychological well-being. In accord with the two-factor model, these spirituality measures have been most frequently and more strongly related to more positive emotion than to less negative emotion. Thus, to be able to fully understand the relationship between spirituality and health, it may be critical to assess positive emotions and other aspects of psychological well-being. The main limitations of the research on the relationship between spirituality and positive emotions is the small number of prospective and intervention studies. These kinds of studies are necessary for better understanding the causal nature of the relationship between spirituality and positive emotions.

Another potentially important future direction is to do studies that differentiate between low and high arousal positive emotion because their relationship with spirituality may vary. In fact, there is evidence that high arousal positive emotion (e.g., excitement, enthusiasm) is valued more in Western cultures and traditions and that low arousal positive emotion (e.g., calm, contentment) is valued more in Eastern cultures and traditions (Tsai, Knutson, & Fung, 2006). If this is the case, then it may be particularly interesting to compare Western and Eastern spiritual and religious beliefs and practices to determine whether they result in more high arousal and low arousal positive emotion, respectively.

Resilience and Positive Emotions

The role of both resilience and positive emotions in health has been receiving an increasing

amount of attention in the psychological literature. The study of resilience in children and adolescence precedes the emergence of the positive psychology movement. However, much of the research on positive emotions has evolved in parallel with the study of positive psychology. While researchers refer to "positive emotions," "positive affect," or "positive mood," the questionnaires that assess them are often made up of the same or very similar items. In contrast, resilience has been assessed using a variety of approaches and a variety of different instruments. Although there is debate about how much resilience may be a stable personal characteristic versus a more context-dependent phenomenon (Bonanno, 2005), it has been most commonly studied using measures assuming it is a stable characteristic.

The following is a brief presentation of several measures of resilience as a stable personal characteristic. These measures include the Resilience Scale (Wagnild & Young, 1993), the Connor-Davidson Resilience Scale (CD-RISC; Connor & Davidson, 2003), the Ego Resilience scale (Block & Kremen, 1996), and the Brief Resilience Scale (Smith et al., 2008). We already discussed the most frequently used measure of positive affect, the Positive and Negative Affect Schedule (PANAS; Watson et al., 1988), in the section "Definitions and Relevant Models." After reviewing the resilience measures, we will provide an overview of representative studies on the relationship between resilience and positive emotions.

Resilience Measures

The Resilience Scale (Wagnild, 2009; Wagnild & Young, 1993) was the first widely used instrument to measure resilience and is still used today, especially with adolescents (Ahern, Kiehl, Lou Sole, & Byers, 2006). It is intended to measure several factors that support resilience, including equanimity, perseverance, self-reliance, existential aloneness, and meaningfulness. The CD-RISC (Connor & Davidson, 2003) is one of the most highly validated resilience assessment tools, especially with adult psychiatric and normal populations (Campbell-Sills, Cohan, & Stein, 2006). It is intended to measure several protective factors, including self-efficacy, sense of humor, faith, patience, and optimism. The Ego Resiliency Scale (Block & Kremen, 1996) assesses resilience as a dynamic capacity to adapt to the changing demands of the environment. The Brief Resilience Scale (Smith et al., 2008) is the most recently developed resilience measure. It specifically attempts to assess resilience itself rather than the general protective factors that are thought to promote resilience (Smith et al., 2008). The Brief Resilience Scale assesses resilience as the ability to bounce back or recover from stressful events.

The Effects of Resilience on Positive Emotions

Despite adversity, individuals are often still able to experience positive affect and effectively manage stress and their responsibilities and challenges (Bonanno & Mancini, 2008; Bonanno, Moskowitz, Papa, & Folkman, 2005; Tugade & Fredrickson, 2004). Ego resiliency, which reflects one's ability to adapt to changing environments (Block & Kremen, 1996), has been associated with a number of significant life outcomes (Cohn, Fredrickson, Brown, Mikels, & Conway, 2009). These include fewer early childhood behavioral problems (Conway & McDonough, 2006), enhanced social adjustment over time (Klohnen, 1996), and faster cardiovascular recovery following laboratory stressors (Tugade & Fredrickson, 2004).

The benefits of resilience on positive affect have been studied with a number of different types of adversity. Individuals categorized as resilient were found to demonstrate greater levels of positive affect during bereavement following an interpersonal loss (e.g., the death of a spouse, a child, or a partner) (Bonanno et al., 2005). Resilience has also been associated with higher positive affect as well as lower internalizing in children of alcoholics (Carle & Chassin, 2004). Engdahl, Harkness, Eberly, Page, and Bielinski (1993) studied prisoners of war (POWs) 20 to 40 years after their release. They found that resilience (as indexed by age and education at capture) and captivity trauma were the strongest predictors of the POW's response to trauma (including both positive and negative affect). Resilience was related to the Time 1 measures of trauma response, and both resilience and trauma captivity were related to Time 2 trauma response. In addition, the effects of resilience and Time 1 trauma response had approximately the same effect on Time 2 trauma response.

Fredrickson, Tugade, Waugh, and Larkin (2003) examined resilience and positive emotions prospectively in response to the September 11th terrorist attacks. They assessed resilience using the Ego Resiliency Scale (Block & Kremen, 1996). They found that those who possessed high levels of resilience reported higher levels of postcrisis positive emotions (gratitude, interest, and love) in the midst of the negative emotions (anger, sadness, and fear) that they experienced following the attacks on September 11th.

Contrary to previous thought, recent research indicates that many individuals who are confronted with highly aversive events experience relatively minor and temporary interruptions in normal functioning (Bonanno et al., 2005; Shalev, 2002). When confronted with stressors, individuals high in resilience report experiencing higher levels of positive emotions when compared to their less resilient peers despite experiencing similar levels of negative emotions (Cohn et al., 2009). The difference in the levels of positive emotions may account for the greater resilience, including an enhanced ability to bounce back from stress and adversity, avoid depression, and continue to grow over time (Fredrickson et al., 2003; Ong, Bergeman, Bisconti, & Wallace, 2006; Tugade & Fredrickson, 2004). Fredrickson and Joiner (2002) contend that resilience produces positive emotions, which lead to an upward spiral in that the resilience and positive emotions sustain each other and build over time.

An example of a study that further illuminates the effects of resilience on positive emotions involved volunteering behavior in older adults (Greenfield & Marks, 2004). Volunteering was found to be a protective factor (contributor to increased resilience) for older adults who were at risk for poor psychological well-being. Greater risk was associated with a larger number of role-identity absences in primary life domains (partner, employment, parental). Participants who had a greater number of role-identity absences experienced increased negative affect and decreased positive affect and less purpose in life. However, volunteering was related to higher positive affect and appeared to reduce the adverse effects of a greater number of primary role-identity absences on participants' purpose in life.

Ong et al. (2006) examined the role that resilience and positive emotions may play for older adults in relation to naturally occurring daily stressors. They discovered that positive emotions aided participants in adjustment to daily stress. They found that differences in levels of resilience among the participants accounted for significant variation in their daily emotional responses to stress. They also found that daily positive emotion both moderated stress reactivity and mediated recovery from stress.

Positive affect and resilience have also been examined together in studies of chronic pain patients. Strand et al. (2006) found that positive affect was most influential in diminishing negative affect during weeks of increased pain for participants with rheumatoid arthritis. They concluded that positive affect may be a source of resilience that helps people with chronic pain experience less distress during periods of increased pain.

The Effects of Positive Emotions on Resilience

Just as being resilient may lead to positive emotions, the experience of positive emotions may also cause a person to be more resilient (Fredrickson, 2001). For example, resilience has been found to predict positive affect before and after a time-sensitive speech task (Fredrickson, 2001). In another study, individuals who experienced greater levels of positive emotions were found to be more resilient to adversity and to demonstrate increased coping skills (Fredrickson & Joiner, 2002). These increased coping skills included broad-minded coping, which involves increasing the scope of one's attention and cognition and allows for creative and flexible thinking (Aspinwall, 1998, 2004; Isen, 1990).

Additional research on the relationship between positive affect and resilience has indicated that positive emotions are predictive of increases in resilience as well as life satisfaction. Cohn et al. (2009) examined these associations in a study that was designed as a test of the broaden-and-build theory of positive emotions (Fredrickson, 2001). In this study, the researchers utilized a sample of students and assessed their emotions daily over the period of a month. They found that positive emotions were related to increases in both resilience and life satisfaction. Conversely, negative emotions demonstrated either weak or null effects on these measures and did not interfere with the benefits of positive emotions. Moreover, positive emotions, but not life satisfaction, were found to mediate the relationship between resilience from baseline to the final measurement (Cohn et al., 2009).

Zautra and colleagues' dynamic model of affect (Davis et al., 2004; Reich, Zautra, & Davis, 2003; Zautra, 2003) suggests that when resilient individuals are confronted with loss, they will experience more varied and complex affect. Coifman, Bonanno, and Rafaeli (2007) examined the dynamic model of affect in a sample of bereaved individuals and defined affective complexity as higher levels of independence between positive and negative affect. The results of the study supported the prediction of the dynamic model of affect in that the resilient bereaved participants demonstrated weaker (or less negative) correlations between negative and positive affect when compared to symptomatic bereaved participants. This

relationship remained even after controlling for self-reported distress. These findings indicate that people who are resilient may have the capacity for more complex experiences of affect and that this capacity may be beneficial following aversive life events.

The relationship between resilience and positive affect has also been examined in other populations. Maguen et al. (2008) examined the effects of resilience and risk factors on medical personnel in the military who were preparing for deployment to Iraq. They found that predeployment positive affect was strongly associated with resilience factors, including trait resilience, as assessed by the CD-RISC (Connor & Davidson, 2003), and positive military experiences. Studies have also been conducted on the relationship between resilience and positive affect in younger age groups. Steinhardt and Dolbier (2008) conducted a resilience intervention with college students experiencing academic stress. The participants in the intervention group reported higher levels of positive affect, resilience, problem-focused coping, and lower levels of avoidant coping than did the wait-list control group.

Summary and Future Directions

In summarizing the results regarding resilience and positive emotions, it is clear that they may be closely linked and also that they may lead to increases in each other over time. Positive emotions are beneficial in the process of coping with stress in that individuals who are more resilient tend to utilize coping strategies that elicit positive emotions, including benefit finding and positive reappraisal (Affleck & Tennen, 1996; Folkman & Moskowitz, 2000), humor and meaning making (Folkman, Moskowitz, Ozer, & Park, 1997; Ong, Bergeman, & Bisconti, 2004), and problem-focused coping (Billings, Folkman, Acree, & Moskowitz, 2000). Positive emotions may serve as protective factors that are helpful in promoting both short-term coping and in promoting long-term health (Folkman & Moskowitz, 2000; Tugade, Fredrickson, & Barrett, 2004).

Additionally, resilient persons may possess a more complex understanding of the positive emotions that they experience and utilize this knowledge in order to adapt to stress in a more resourceful and flexible manner (Tugade et al., 2004). While earlier studies have examined the effects of resilience on positive emotions, more recent studies have shown that positive emotion may increase resilience (Fredrickson & Joiner, 2002; Zautra et al., 2005). Trait-positive emotion may broaden and build resources for resilience (Fredrickson,

2001), whereas state-positive emotion may increase resilience in the context of immediate stressors and negative events (Zautra et al., 2001). Ultimately, people who are high in resilience may not only cultivate positive emotions in themselves but also be adept at eliciting positive emotions in others with whom they have close relationships. This generates a supportive social network, which may assist the person in the coping process (Demos, 1989; Kumpfer, 1999; Werner & Smith, 1992).

The main limitation for research examining the relationship between resilience and positive emotions is that resilience has been defined and measured in so many different ways. It is important for researchers to distinguish between resilience resources such as are assessed in the Resilience Scale (Wagnild & Young, 1993) and the CD-RISC (Connor & Davidson, 2003), resilience as the ability to adapt and maintain equilibrium in the face of change as with the Ego Resiliency Scale (Block & Kremen, 1996), and resilience as the ability to bounce back as with the Brief Resilience Scale (Smith et al., 2008). It is also important for researchers to continue to study resilience as the actual recovery or maintainence of health in the face of stressful events (Bonanno et al., 2005; Zautra et al., 2005). Most important, the self-report measures of trait resilience need to be examined across multiple contexts to determine their stability and their relationship with actual recovery or maintenance of health and adjustment despite stress. Being clear and precise in the definition and measurement of resilience and using prospective designs will make it possible to develop a more sophisticated understanding of how the relationship between resilience and positive emotions unfolds over time.

Toward a Model of Spirituality, Positive Emotions, and Resilience

The final goal of this chapter is to present an initial model for understanding the relationship between spirituality, positive emotions, and resilience. Ideally, this would be based on an integration of the most useful and well-developed theories and a long line of programmatic research building upon and refining these theories. In reality, as with the positive psychology movement and much research focusing on positive characteristics and aspects of health and well-being, the relevant theory and research are in their relative infancy. In our minds, there are three great unmet challenges to developing the most useful model for understanding the relationship between spirituality, positive emotions, and resilience. First, there are few previous models that have attempted to include or directly addressed spirituality, positive emotions, or resilience. Second, the definition and measure of spirituality and resilence have often been too varied, broad, and imprecise. Third, the great majority of the research that has been conducted examining the relationship between any two of these three variables has been cross-sectional, making it impossible to understanding how they may influence each another over time.

While keeping these challenges in mind, we would like to present a preliminary model for understanding the most important ways that these three variables may interact. This model is displayed in Figure 28.1. First, we think that it is safe to assume that spirituality, positive emotions, and resilience are generally positively related to each other and that they all generally may have a beneficial effect on health and well-being. There are undoubtedly notable exceptions with regard to spirituality such as with negative religious coping as identified by Pargament and colleagues (Pargament et al., 1998). There are also times positive emotions may be problemmatic such as when humor may not convey empathy during a tragedy or when high arousal positive emotions may be a risk factor for poorer health (Pressman & Cohen, 2005). Despite these caveats and exceptions, we presented research suggesting

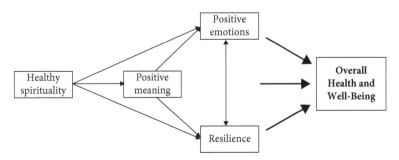

Figure 28.1 Model of the effects of spirituality, positive emotions, and resilience on health and well-being.

that all spirituality, resilience, and positive emotions are probably positive related in most contexts.

Second, while we presented evidence that resilience and positive emotions have often been related and that they may have a reciprocal influence on each other, we suspect that spirituality is most often the cause rather than the result of resilience and positive emotions. We cited research suggesting that resilience and positive emotion may influence each other over time in a way that may lead to an upward spiral or snowball effect (Cohn et al., 2009; Fredrickson & Joiner, 2002). In contrast, although there is little research examining the prospective relationship between spirituality, positive emotions, and resilience, we think that there are more plausible ways that spirituality may influence resilience and positive emotions than the reverse. Along these lines, we argued that spirituality may increase resilience in at least four ways, including through relationships, life values, personal meaning, and coping. We also discussed how we thought that spirituality and religion may increase positive emotions such as love, joy, and contentment through ethical guidelines and various religious and spiritual beliefs and practices.

Third, we identified personal meaning, purpose in life, and posttraumatic growth as three additional contructs that all involve attributing positive meaning to one's life and that may be important for understanding the relationship between spirituality, resilience, and positive emotions. Specifically, we think that the ability to attribute a positive meaning to one's life and experiences may be a key mediator of the effects of spirituality on both positive emotions and resilience. Spirituality and religion often specifically address ways of finding meaning and purpose in life and ways of making sense of and growing through times of stress and suffering (Zinnbauer & Pargament, 2005). In addition, appraisal theories of emotion (Lazarus, 1991) strongly suggest that positive attributions about one's life and experience increase the frequency of positive emotions. Finally, the work of Frankl (1963) and others (Smith & Zautra, 2004) strongly suggests that meaning and purpose enhance the ability to be resilient or cope with even some of life's greatest stressors.

We think that this preliminary model points to the importance of examining the pathways by which spirituality may be related to both positive emotions and resilience. While we suggested some possible means by which spirituality may increase both, we think that the most important directions for future research involve testing these and other

possible theoretically important mediators in prospective designs. In addition, we suspect it will be important to assess negative characteristics such as neuroticism, negative affect, and potential negative aspects of spirituality or spiritual experience, such as negative religious coping, to control for them and develop a full model and understanding of the relationship between spirituality, positive emotions, and resilience. We think that including these negative aspects of experience will reduce the chance of committing the same error that positive psychologists have often indicted past research for: neglecting one-half of human experience.

Most important, we would suggest prospective studies that examine individuals facing ongoing stressors or those who are at risk for facing traumatic or major one-time stressors. Multiple aspects and components of spirituality should be assessed at baseline and follow-ups and would ideally include general measures of spirituality, daily spiritual experiences, positive and negative aspects of religious coping, and measures of specific religious and spiritual beliefs and practices. Similarly, multiple measures of resilience could be used and a resilient group could be identified by how they well they adapt to or how quickly they recover from stressful events. In addition, both high and low arousal positive emotions, including measures of specific positive emotions such as love, contentment, and joy, could be assessed. Another fruitful research direction may be to do more intervention studies where different spiritual or religious practices that may affect both positive emotions and resilience could be compared to nonspiritual or nonreligious interventions. For example, the effects of a loving-kindness meditation or a centering prayer exercise could be compared with a more neutral condition, and the effects on positive emotions and resilience to stress could be examined over time.

Conclusion

In conclusion, resilience and positive emotions may be two of the most important mediators of spirituality on human health and well-being. The initial research on the relationship between spirituality, resilience, and positive emotions suggests that healthy spirituality may be related to higher levels of both resilience and positive emotions. In addition, at least part of the influence of spirituality on resilience and positive emotions may be through the way that it may increase positive meaning, including what have been calling personal meaning, purpose in life, and posttraumatic growth. Finally, while there is little current evidence or theory predicting that resilience and positive emotions may influence spirituality, there is growing evidence that resilience and positive emotions may have a mutual influence on each other that may build over time. Future research should continue to explore the potentially complex relationships among spirituality, resilience, and positive emotion using well-developed and specific measures of all three in both prospective and intervention studies.

Questions for Future Research

1. Which aspects of spirituality and religion (e.g., general spirituality/religiosity, daily spiritual experiences, religious coping) have the strongest effects on resilience and positive emotion?

2. How do specific spiritual or religious practices (e.g., meditation, prayer, worship, sacred reading) affect resilience and positive emotions?

3. Do Western spiritual practices have a stronger effect on high arousal positive emotions and Eastern spiritual practices have a stronger effect on lower arousal positive emotions?

4. How much are the effects of spirituality on resilience and positive emotions mediated by increases in positive meaning (e.g., personal meaning, purpose in life, posttraumatic growth)?

5. What are the other important mediators of the effects of spirituality and religion on resilience and positive emotions (e.g., social relationships, ethical values, coping processes)?

6. How much might resilience or positive emotions affect spirituality and religious beliefs and practices over time?

7. What are the best ways to distinguish between healthy and unhealthy spirituality and religious beliefs and practices?

8. Does healthy spirituality have stronger effects on positive affect, and unhealthy spirituality have stronger effects on negative affect, as the two-factor model would predict?

References

Affleck, G., & Tennen, H. (1996). Construing benefits from adversity: Adaptational significance and dispositional underpinnings. *Journal of Personality, 64*, 899–922.

Agnes, M. (Ed.). (2005). *Webster's new college dictionary.* Cleveland, OH: Wiley.

Ahern, N., Kiehl, E., Lou Sole, M., & Byers, J. (2006). A review of instruments measuring resilience. *Issues in Comprehensive Pediatric Nursing, 29*, 103–125.

Antonovsky, A. (1979). *Health, stress, and coping.* San Francisco: Jossey-Bass.

Aspinwall, L. (1998). Rethinking the role of positive affect in self-regulation. *Motivation and Emotion, 22*, 1–32.

Aspinwall, L. (2004). Dealing with adversity: Self-regulation, coping, adaptation, and health. In M. Brewer & M. Hewstone (Eds.), *Applied social psychology* (pp. 3–27). Malden, MA: Blackwell.

Battista, J., & Almond, R. (1973). The development of meaning in life. *Psychiatry, 36*, 409–427.

Bender, K., Thompson, S. J., McManus, H., Lantry, J., & Flynn, P. M. (2007). Capacity for survival: Exploring strengths of homeless street youth. *Child and Youth Care Forum, 36*, 25–42.

Bergin, A., Stinchfield, R., Gaskin, T., Masters, K. & Sullivan, C. (1988). Religious life-styles and mental health: An exploratory study. *Journal of Counseling Psychology, 35*, 91–98.

Bhui, K., King, M., Dein, S., & O'Connor, W. (2008). Ethnicity and religious coping with mental distress. *Journal of Mental Health. 17*, 141–151.

Billings, D., Folkman, S., Acree, M., & Moskowitz, J. (2000). Coping and physical health during caregiving: The roles of positive and negative affect. *Journal of Personality and Social Psychology, 79*, 131–142.

Block, J. H., & Block, J. (1980). *The role of ego-control and ego-resiliency in the organization of behavior.* Hillsdale, NJ: Erlbaum.

Block, J., & Kremen, A. M. (1996). IQ and ego-resiliency: Conceptual and empirical connections and separateness. *Journal of Personality and Social Psychology, 70*, 349–361.

Bonanno, G. A. (2005). Resilience in the face of potential trauma. *Current Directions in Psychological Science, 14*, 135–138.

Bonanno, G. A., & Mancini, A. D. (2008). The human capacity to thrive in the face of potential trauma. *Pediatrics, 121*, 369–375.

Bonanno, G. A., Moskowitz, J. T., Papa, A., & Folkman, S. (2005). Resilience to loss in bereaved spouses, bereaved parents, and bereaved gay men. *Journal of Personality and Social Psychology, 88*, 827–843.

Bradburn, N. M. (1969). *The structure of psychological well-being.* Oxford, England: Aldine de Gruyter.

Browning, D., & Cooper, T. (2004). *Religious thought and the modern psychologies* (2nd ed.). New York: Fortress Press.

Bush, E. G., Rye, M. S., Brant, C. R., Emery, E., Pargament, K. I., & Riessinger, C. A. (1999). Religious coping with chronic pain. *Applied Psychophysiology and Biofeedback, 24*, 249–260.

Cacioppo, J., Gardner, W., & Berntson, G. (1999). The affect system has parallel and integrative processing components: Form follows function. *Journal of Personality and Social Psychology, 76*, 839–855.

Campbell-Sills, L., Cohan, S., & Stein, M. (2006). Relationship of resilience to personality, coping, and psychiatric symptoms in young adults. *Behaviour Research and Therapy, 44*, 585–599.

Carle, A. C., & Chassin, L. (2004). Resilience in a community sample of children of alcoholics: Its prevalence and relation to internalizing symptomatology and positive affect. *Journal of Applied Developmental Psychology, 25*, 577–595.

Carver, C. (1998). Resilience and thriving: Issues, models, and linkages. *Journal of Social Issues, 54*, 245–266.

Carver, C., & Scheier, M. (1990). Origins and functions of positive and negative affect: A control-process view. *Psychological Review, 97*, 19–35.

Charney, D. S. (2004). Psychobiological mechanisms of resilience and vulnerability: Implications for successful adaptation to extreme stress. *American Journal of Psychiatry, 161*, 195–216.

Clore, G. C. (1994). Why emotions are felt. In P. Ekman & R. J. Davidson (Eds.), The nature of emotion: Fundamental questions (pp. 103–111). New York: Oxford University Press.

Cohen, S., & Wills, T. A. (1985). Stress, social support, and the buffering hypothesis. *Psychological Bulletin*, 98, 310–357, 1985.

Cohn, M., Fredrickson, B., Brown, S., Mikels, J., & Conway, A. (2009). Happiness unpacked: Positive emotions increase life satisfaction by building resilience. *Emotion*, 9, 361–368.

Coifman, K. G., Bonanno, G. A., & Rafaeli, E. (2007). Affect dynamics, bereavement and resilience to loss. *Journal of Happiness Studies*, 8, 371–392.

Connor, K. M., & Davidson, J. R. T. (2003). Development of a new resilience scale: The Connor-Davidson Resilience Scale (CD-RISC). *Depression and Anxiety*, 18, 76–82.

Conway, A., & McDonough, S. (2006). Emotional resilience in early childhood. *Resilience in Children*, 1094, 272–277.

Cook, K. (2000). "You have to have somebody watching your back and if that's God then it's mighty big": The Church's role in the resilience of inner-city youth. *Adolescence*, 35, 717–730.

Davidson, R. J. (1992). Emotion and affective style: Hemispheric substrates. *Psychological Science*, 3, 39–43.

Davidson, R. J. (1993). The neuropsychology of emotion and affective style. In M. Lewis & J. Haviland (Eds.), *Handbook of emotions* (pp. 143–154). New York: The Guilford Press.

Davis, M., Zautra, A., & Smith, B. (2004). Chronic pain, stress, and the dynamics of affective differentiation. *Journal of Personality*, 72, 1133–1160.

Demos, E. V. (1989). Resiliency in infancy. In T. F. Dugan & R. Coles (Eds.), *The child in our times: Studies in the development of resilient* (pp. 3–22). New York: Brunner/Mazel.

Diener, E., Sandvik, E., & Pavot, W. (1991). Happiness is the frequency, not the intensity, of positive versus negative affect. *Subjective Well-Being: An Interdisciplinary Perspective*, 21, 119–139.

Dyson, J., Cobb, M., & Forman, D. (1997). The meaning of spirituality: A literature review. *Journal of Advanced Nursing*, 26, 1183–1188.

Ekas, N. V., Whitman, T. L., & Shivers, C. (2009). Religiosity, spirituality, and socioemotional functioning in mothers of children with autism spectrum disorder. *Journal of Autism and Developmental Disorders*, 39, 706–719.

Ellison, C. G., & Fan, D. (2008). Daily spiritual experiences and psychological well-being among US adults. *Social Indicators Research*, 88(2), 247–271.

Emmons, R. A., & Paloutzian, R. F. (2003). The psychology of religion. *Annual Review of Psychology*, 54, 377–402.

Engdahl, B., Harkness, A., Eberly, R., Page, W., & Bielinski, J. (1993). Structural models of captivity trauma, resilience, and trauma response among former prisoners of war 20 to 40 years after release. *Social Psychiatry and Psychiatric Epidemiology*, 28, 109–115.

Fabricatore, A. N., Handal, P. J., & Fenzel, L. M. (2000). Personal spirituality as a moderator of the relationship between stressors and subjective well-being. *Journal of Psychology and Theology*, 28, 221–228.

Fenzel, L. M. (2002, April). *The development of the Spiritual Involvement Scale: Examining the spiritual lives of late adolescents*. Poster presented at the Biennial Conference of the Society for Research on Adolescence, New Orleans, LA.

Fetzer Institute. (1999). *Multidimensional measurement of religiousness/spirituality for use in health research: A report of the Fetzer Institute/National Institute on Aging*. Kalamazoo, MI: Author.

Folkman, S. (1997). Positive psychological states and coping with severe stress. *Social Science and Medicine*, 45, 1207–1221.

Folkman, S., & Moskowitz, J. T. (2000). Stress, positive emotion, and coping. *Current Directions in Psychological Science*, 9, 115–118.

Folkman, S., Moskowitz, J. T., Ozer, E. M., & Park, C. L. (1997). Positive meaningful events and coping in the context of HIV/AIDS. In B. H. Gottlieb (Ed.), *Coping with chronic stress* (pp. 293–314). New York: Plenum.

Frankl, V. E. (1963). *Man's search for meaning*. New York: Pocket Books.

Fredrickson, B. (2001). The role of positive emotions in positive psychology: The broaden-and-build theory of positive emotions. *American Psychologist*, 56, 218–226.

Fredrickson, B. L. (2000). Cultivating positive emotions to optimize health and well-being. *Prevention and Treatment*, 3(1), doi: 10.1037/1522–3736.3.1.31a.

Fredrickson, B. L. (2002). How does religion benefit health and well-being? Are positive emotions active ingredients? *Psychological Inquiry*, 13, 209–213.

Fredrickson, B. L., & Joiner, T. (2002). Positive emotions trigger upward spirals toward emotional well-being. *Psychological Science*, 13, 172–175.

Fredrickson, B. L., Tugade, M. M., Waugh, C. E., & Larkin, G. R. (2003). What good are positive emotions in crisis? A prospective study of resilience and emotions following the terrorist attacks on the United States on September 11th, 2001. *Journal of Personality and Social Psychology*, 84, 365–376.

Geertz, C. (1975). *The interpretation of cultures*. London: Hutchinson.

Goldstein, E. D. (2007). Sacred moments: Implications on well-being and stress. *Journal of Clinical Psychology*, 63, 1001–1019.

Greeff, A., & Du Toit, C. (2009). Resilience in remarried families. *American Journal of Family Therapy*, 37, 114–126.

Greeff, A., & Loubser, K. (2008). Spirituality as a resiliency quality in Xhosa-speaking families in South Africa. *Journal of Religion and Health*, 47, 288–301.

Greene, R., Galambos, C., & Lee, Y. (2003). Resilience theory: Theoretical and professional conceptualizations. *Journal of Human Behavior in the Social Environment*, 8, 75–91.

Greenfield, E., & Marks, N. (2004). Formal volunteering as a protective factor for older adults' psychological well-being. *Journals of Gerontology Series B: Psychological Sciences and Social Sciences*, 59, S258.

Greenfield, E. A., Vaillant, G. E., & Marks, N. E. (2009). Do formal religious participation and spiritual perceptions have independent linkages with diverse dimensions of psychological well-being? *Journal of Health and Social Behavior*, 50, 196–212.

Hill, P. C., & Pargament, K. I. (2008). Advances in the conceptualization and measurement of religion and spirituality: Implications for physical and mental health research. *Psychology of Religion and Spirituality*, 58, 3–17.

Hobfoll, S. E. (1989). Conservation of resources. A new attempt at conceptualizing stress. *American Psychologist*, 44, 513–524.

Isen, A. M. (1990). The influence of positive and negative affect on cognitive organization: Some implications for development. In N. Stein, B. Leventhal, & J. Trabasso (Eds.), *Psychological and biological approaches to emotion* (pp. 75–94). Hillsdale, NJ: Erlbaum.

Kabat-Zinn, J. (1990). *Full catastrophe living*. New York: Delta.

Keefe, F. J., Affleck, G., Lefebvre, J., Underwood, L., Caldwell, D. S., Drew, J.,...Pargament, K. I. (2001). Living with rheumatoid arthritis: The role of daily spirituality and religious and spiritual coping. *The Journal of Pain, 2*, 101–110.

Kim, Y., Seidlitz, L., Ro, Y., Evinger, J. S., & Duberstein, P. R. (2004). Spirituality and affect: A function of changes in religious affiliation. *Personality and Individual Differences, 37*, 861–870.

Klohnen, E. (1996). Conceptual analysis and measurement of the construct of ego-resiliency. *Journal of Personality and Social Psychology, 70*, 1067–1079.

Kumpfer, K. (1999). Factors and processes contributing to resilience: The resilience framework. In M. Glantz & J. Johnson (Eds.), *Resilience and development: Positive life adaptations* (pp. 179–224). New York: Kluwer.

Lazarus, R. S. (1991). *Emotion and adaptation*. New York: Oxford University Press.

Lazarus, R. S., & DeLongis, A. (1983). Psychological stress and coping in aging. *American Psychologist, 38*, 245–254.

Loewenthal, K. M., Macleod, A., Goldblatt, V., Lubitsh, G., & Valentine, J. D. (2000). Comfort and joy? Religion, cognition, and mood in Protestants and Jews under stress. *Cognition and Emotion, 14*, 355–374.

Maguen, S., Turcotte, D. M., Peterson, A. L., Dremsa, T. L., Garb, H. N., McNally, R. J., & Litz, B. T. (2008). Description of risk and resilience factors among military medical personnel before deployment to Iraq. *Military Medicine, 173*, 1–9.

Maselko, J., & Kubzansky, L. D. (2006). Gender differences in religious practices, spiritual experiences and health: Results from the US General Social Survey. *Social Science and Medicine, 62*, 2848–2860.

Masten, A. S. (2001). Ordinary magic: Resilience processes in development. *American Psychologist, 56*, 227–238.

McCubbin, H., Thompson, A., & McCubbin, M. (1996). *Family assessment: Resiliency, coping and adaptation—inventories for research and practice*. Madison: University of Wisconsin Publishers.

McGloshen, T. H., & O'Bryant, S. L. (1988). The psychological well-being of older, recent widows. *Psychology of Women Quarterly, 12*, 99–116.

McGrath, J. (2006). Post-traumatic growth and the origins of early Christianity. *Mental Health, Religion and Culture, 9*, 291–306

Ong, A., Bergeman, C., & Bisconti, T. (2004). The role of daily positive emotions during conjugal bereavement. *Journals of Gerontology Series B: Psychological Sciences and Social Sciences, 59*, P168.

Ong, A. D., Bergeman, C. S., Bisconti, T. L., & Wallace, K. A. (2006). Psychological resilience, positive emotions, and successful adaptation to stress in later life. *Journal of Personality and Social Psychology, 91*, 730–749.

Pargament, K. (1997). *The psychology of religion and coping*. New York: The Guilford Press.

Pargament, K. I., Ensing, D. S., Falgout, K., & Olsen, H. (1990). God help me: I. Religious coping efforts as predictors of the outcomes to significant negative life events. *American Journal of Community Psychology, 18*, 793–824.

Pargament, K. I., Smith, B. W., Koenig, H. G., & Perez, L. (1998). Patterns of positive and negative religious coping with major life stressors. *Journal for the Scientific Study of Religion, 37*, 710–724.

Pargament, K. I., Tarakeshwar, N., Ellison, C. G., & Wulff, K. M. (2001). Religious coping among the religious: The relationships between religious coping and well-being in a national sample of Presbyterian clergy, elders, and members. *Journal for the Scientific Study of Religion, 40*, 497–513.

Park, C. L., Cohen, L. H., & Murch, R. L. (1996). Assessment and prediction of stress-related growth. *Journal of Personality, 64*, 71–105.

Peres, J., Moreira-Almeida, A., Nasello, A., & Koenig, H. (2007). Spirituality and resilience in trauma victims. *Journal of Religion and Health. 46*, 343–350

Pressman, S., & Cohen, S. (2005). Does positive affect influence health? *Psychological Bulletin, 131*, 925–971.

Reich, J., Zautra, A., & Davis, M. (2003). Dimensions of affect relationships: Models and their integrative implications. *Review of General Psychology, 7*, 66–83.

Reker, G. T. (2000). Theoretical perspective, dimensions, and measurement of existential meaning. In G. T. Reker & K. Chamberlain (Eds.), *Exploring existential meaning: Optimizing human development across the life span* (pp. 39–55). Thousand Oaks, CA: Sage.

Rutter, M. (1987). Psychosocial resilience and protective mechanisms. *American Journal of Orthopsychiatry, 57*, 316–331.

Rutter, M. (1990). Psychosocial resilience and protective mechanisms. *Risk and Protective Factors in the Development of Psychopathology, 3*, 49–74.

Saarni, C. (1999). *The development of emotional competence*. New York: The Guilford Press.

Seaward, B. L. (2005). *Managing stress* (5th ed.). Boston, MA: Jones & Bartlett.

Seidlitz, L., Abernethy, A. D., Duberstein, P. R., Evinger, J. S., Chang, T. H., & Lewis, B. L. (2002). Development of the Spiritual Transcendence Index. *Journal for the Scientific Study of Religion, 41*, 439–453.

Selway, D., & Ashman, A. F. (1998). Disability, religion and health: A literature review in search of the spiritual dimensions of disability. *Disability and Society, 13*, 429–439.

Shalev, A. Y. (2002). Acute stress reactions in adults. *Biological Psychiatry, 51*, 532–543.

Siegel, K., & Schrimshaw, E. W. (2000). Perceiving benefits in adversity: Stress-related growth in women living with HIV/AIDS. *Social Science and Medicine, 51*, 1543–1554.

Silberman, I. (2003). Religion as a meaning system: Implications for the new millennium *Journal of Social Issues, 61*, 641–663.

Smith, B. W., Dalen, J., Wiggins, K., Tooley, E., Christopher, P., & Bernard, J. (2008). The brief resilience scale: Assessing the ability to bounce back. *International Journal of Behavioral Medicine, 15*, 194–200.

Smith, B. W., Pargament, K. I., Brant, C., & Oliver, J. M. (2000). Noah revisited: Religious coping and the impact of a flood. *Journal of Community Psychology, 28*, 169–186.

Smith, B. W., & Zautra, A. J. (2004). The role of purpose in life in recovery from knee surgery. *International Journal of Behavioral Medicine, 11*, 197–202.

Smith, B. W., & Zautra, A. J. (2008). Vulnerability and resilience in women with arthritis: Test of a two-factor model. *Journal of Consulting and Clinical Psychology, 76*, 799–810.

Smith, H. (1991). *The world's religions: Our great wisdom traditions*. New York: Harper Collins.

Steinhardt, M., & Dolbier, C. (2008). Evaluation of a resilience intervention to enhance coping strategies and protective factors and decrease symptomatology. *Journal of American College Health, 56*, 445–453.

Strand, E. B., Zautra, A. J., Thoresen, M., Ødegård, S., Uhlig, T., & Finset, A. (2006). Positive affect as a factor of resilience in the pain—negative affect relationship in patients with rheumatoid arthritis. *Journal of Psychosomatic Research, 60,* 477–484.

Tedeschi, R., & Calhoun, L. (2004). Posttraumatic growth: Conceptual foundations and empirical evidence. *Psychological Inquiry, 15,* 1–18.

Tellegen, A. (1985). Structure of mood and personality and their relevance to assessing anxiety, with an emphasis on self-report. In A. H. Tuma & J. D. Maser (Eds.), *Anxiety and the anxiety disorders* (pp. 681–706). Hillsdale, NJ: Erlbaum.

Tsai, J. L., Knutson, B., & Fung, H. H. (2006). Cultural variation in valuation of affect. *Journal of Personality and Social Psychology, 90,* 288–307.

Tugade, M., Fredrickson, B., & Barrett, L. (2004). Psychological resilience and positive emotional granularity: Examining the benefits of positive emotions on coping and health. *Journal of Personality, 72,* 1161.

Tugade, M. M., & Fredrickson, B. L. (2004). Resilient individuals use positive emotions to bounce back from negative emotional experiences. *Journal of Personality and Social Psychology, 86,* 320–333.

Tusaie, K., & Dyer, J. (2004). Resilience: A historical review of the construct. *Holistic Nursing Practice, 18,* 3–10.

Uchino, B. N., Cacioppo, J. T., & Kiecolt-Glaser, J. K. (1996). The relationship between social support and physiological processes: A review with emphasis on underlying mechanisms and implications for health. *Psychological Bulletin, 119,* 488–531.

Underwood, L. G., & Teresi, J. A. (2002). The Daily Spiritual Experience Scale: Development, theoretical description, reliability, exploratory factor analysis, and preliminary construct validity using health-related data. *Annals of Behavioral Medicine, 24,* 22–33.

Van Dyke, C., & Elias, M. (2007). How forgiveness, purpose, and religiosity are related to the mental health and well-being of youth: A review of the literature. *Mental Health, Religion and Culture, 10,* 395–415.

Wachholtz, A. B., & Pargament, K. I. (2005). Is spirituality a critical ingredient of meditation? Comparing the effects of spiritual meditation, secular meditation, and relaxation on spiritual, psychological, cardiac, and pain outcomes. *Journal of Behavioral Medicine, 28,* 369–384.

Wagnild, G. (2009). A review of the resilience scale. *Journal of Nursing Measurement, 17,* 105–113.

Wagnild, G., & Young, H. (1990). Resilience among older women. *Journal of Nursing Scholarship, 22,* 252–255.

Wagnild, G., & Young, H. (1993). Development and psychometric evaluation of the resilience scale. *Journal of Nursing Measurement, 1,* 165–178.

Watson, D., & Clark, L. (1984). Negative affectivity: The disposition to experience aversive emotional states. *Psychological bulletin, 96,* 465–490.

Watson, D., Clark, L. A., & Tellegen, A. (1988). Development and validation of brief measures of positive and negative affect: The panas scales. *Journal of Personality and Social Psychology, 54,* 1063–1070.

Watson, D., Wiese, D., Vaidya, J., & Tellegen, A. (1999). The two general activation systems of affect: Structural findings, evolutionary considerations, and psychobiological evidence. *Journal of Personality and Social Psychology, 76,* 820–838.

Watts, F. N. (1996). Psychological and religious perspectives on emotion. *International Journal for the Psychology of Religion, 6*(2), 71–87.

Weaver, A. J., Flannelly, L. T., Flannelly, K. J., Koenig, H. G., & Larson, D. B. (1998). An analysis of research on religious and spiritual variables in three major mental health nursing journal, 1991–1995. *Issues in Mental Health Nursing, 19,* 263–276.

Werner, E., & Smith, R. (1992). *Overcoming the odds: High risk children from birth to adulthood.* New York: Cornell University Press.

Worthington, E., & Scherer, M. (2004). Forgiveness is an emotion-focused coping strategy that can reduce health risks and promote health resilience: Theory, review, and hypotheses. *Psychology and Health, 19,* 385–405

Younes, M. (2007). The resilience of families in Israel: Understanding their struggles and appreciating their strengths. *Marriage and Family Review, 41,* 101–117.

Zautra, A. (2003). *Emotions, stress, and health.* New York: Oxford University Press.

Zautra, A. J., Johnson, L. M., & Davis, M. C. (2005). Positive affect as a source of resilience for women in chronic pain. *Journal of Consulting and Clinical Psychology, 73,* 212–220.

Zautra, A. J., Smith, B. W., Affleck, G., & Tennen, H. (2001). Examination of chronic pain and affect relationships from two contrasting approaches: Stress and coping and a dynamic model of affect. *Journal of Consulting and Clinical Psychology, 69,* 786–795.

Zinnbauer, B. J., & Pargament, K. I. (2005). Religiousness and spirituality. In R. F. Paloutzian & C. L. Park (Eds.), *Handbook of the psychology of religion and spirituality* (pp. 21–42). New York: The Guilford Press.

Constructing the Connection Between Spirituality, Work, and Family

Lee Joyce Richmond

Abstract

The chapter is a discussion of the connection between spirituality, work, and family. First, an explanation is offered of how social change has necessitated a renaissance of interest in meaning and purpose. This is followed by an historical perspective of work from the standpoint of religion, culture, and psychology. Next, there is a brief introduction to the postmodern theories and definitions that make possible serious study of spirituality as it is perceived by individuals at home and at work. Practical issues that people face and their implications for therapy are illustrated. Finally, the importance to psychologists and psychotherapists of understanding the connection that exists between spirituality, work, and family is illustrated.

Key Words: work, career, vocation, meaning, purpose, family, social construction, postmodern

Introduction

The socioeconomic climate in which people find employment has changed. The long-term work situations that were characteristic in the past are no longer the norm. Today, people can expect to engage in a series of occupational transitions, many of which lead to jobs that offer families little security. Family structures have also changed. Blended families, sometimes multiply blended, are common. Single-parent families are also common, and same-sex couples with children are becoming less rare.

Technology has replaced people in many occupations that in the past had been labor intensive, and new jobs requiring a more educated but smaller workforce have emerged as a result. Economics driven by technology affects demographics in that people generally live where they can find work, and the work people do influences how they live, their social culture, and their worldview. The present is a period of transition. The major meaning systems that prevailed from the 17th century to the latter quarter of the 20th century have weakened, and so

has the promise of logical positivism (Richmond, 1995). The postrenaissance empiricism that ushered in the era of modern science is eroding and different ways of knowing have evolved (Eppig, 2008).

When worldview changes, new perceptions and understandings are added to what was believed before, and new ways of looking at things alter perceptions of what was deemed valuable in the past. Some psychologists think that the linear "either/ or" reasoning upon which vocational psychology was originally based is insufficient for now. Major change often ushers in a period of confusion that, in turn, causes people to search for meaning. The current quest for meaning has led to a renaissance of interest in spirituality, especially as it affects work and family life. Postmodern epistemological theory allows for research and practice models that include the use of subjective perspectives and story in the understanding of human behavior. Models based on these theories have made it possible to study the connection between spirituality, work, and family in new ways.

Although the upsurge of public interest in spirituality in work and family is new, the connection between work, family, and religion dates back to antiquity, and the connection has not always been positive. When the ancient Greeks spoke of work, they used the word *ponos*, a word that means sorrow as well as work (Hill, 1992, 1996). In those days most Athenians experienced *ponos*, because the manual labor of many supported an elite few who spent their lives engaging a search for truth and beauty. Highly valued leisure, the study of philosophy, music, and mathematics, was allotted only to the privileged group.

Not philosophers, the ancient Hebrews explained the drudgery of manual labor in a different way. In their creation story, the hardships of manual labor occurred as a result of human disregard for instructions given to them by their Creator. Because man and woman ate from the Tree of Knowledge, a tree from which they were told not to eat, the ground was cursed. The Bible describes the scene as follows: *By toil shall you eat of it all the days of your life: Thorns and thistles shall it sprout for you. But your food shall be the grasses of the field: by the sweat of your brow shall you get food to eat* (Genesis 3:17). Nevertheless, the Hebrew people did not denigrate the idea of physical labor. In fact, they acknowledged the positive value of work because they realized that it sustains the human family. Moreover, according to their thinking, work is a divinely ordained activity. Even the Eternal One, before resting on the seventh day, "worked" making an entire world that included a garden for man and woman, the highest of creation. Because of this, 6 days of labor coupled with 1 day per week for rest was regarded as a good way to live (Ottaway, 2003).

Christian theology, concerned with the meaning of work, has viewed work in various ways: as necessity, as a good in itself, as vocation, and as cocreation (Huntley, 1997). However, understanding God's will in relation to the work of human beings is the province of theology, and therefore not the subject of this chapter. Understanding human behavior as it relates to choosing, finding, and maintaining self in an occupation is the task of vocational and counseling psychologists and a topic of consideration here. Unfortunately, until very recently, modern psychology did not include spirituality in its purview. It was as if psychology abandoned meaning and mattering to psychotherapy, and psychotherapy was concerned only when peoples' choices threatened their emotional well-being.

Well-known therapists declared that meaning in life, frequently found in one's occupation, was an absolute necessary for emotional well-being. Carl Jung (1933) wrote the following: "About a third of my cases are suffering from no clinically definable neurosis, but from the senselessness and emptiness of their lives. It is difficult to treat patients of this particular kind by rational methods because they are in the main socially well adapted individuals of considerable ability...the ordinary expression for this situation is: "I am stuck'" (p. 56). It seems as though finding meaningful work was seen as a way to become unstuck. And Jung was not the only therapist to address the importance of meaning and its connection to work. A Holocaust survivor, Viktor Frankl (1963) believed that meaninglessness was the existential issue of his time. Psychological problems were the result of failure to find meaning and purpose in one's activity and being. According to Frankl, meaning, or will to meaning, could be found in attitude toward suffering, aesthetic values, and, most basically, engagement in work that one considers important. Out of his personal suffering Frankl came to believe that living a meaningful life counteracts mass neurotic symptoms and that "a man who becomes conscious of the responsibility he bears toward a human being who affectionately waits for him, or to an unfinished work, will never be able to throw away his life" (p. 122).

Abraham Maslow (1969) viewed meaning and work from a different angle and came to the same conclusion. His research pointed to the fact that self-actualizing people have a sense of purpose. In his studies of metamotivation, Maslow found that "self-actualizing people are devoted to some task, call, vocation, beloved work outside themselves" (p. 155). Ultimately Maslow claimed that "the value life (spiritual, religious, philosophical, axiological etc.) is an aspect of human biology" (pp. 179–180), and that spirituality is the highest part of our biological life. Concurrently, Sidney Jourard (1971) stated: "There is increasing scientific evidence that man's physical and psychological health are profoundly affected by the degree to which he has found meaning, direction and purpose in his existence" (p. ix).

It would seem as though these value statements by well-known therapists would influence the field of career development at its origins, but that was not to be. The beginnings of the scientific study of career come from a different source, and they followed a different trajectory. Frank Parsons (1909), frequently called the Father of Career Counseling in the United States, is often credited with the trait and factor theory of career choice. His goal was to help people find work by using logic and by applying the scientific method as a framework for career decision making. He postulated three basic premises. First, one must understand self, which involves the understanding of one's aptitudes, abilities, interests, resources, and limitations. Second, one must have a clear understanding of the advantages and disadvantages of work situations, and of the human requirements demanded by job tasks. Third, an individual should use true reasoning in order to ascertain the relationship between the two.[1] However, the connection between sprit and work was not included in Parson's theory nor was it in the career theories that followed his. Although personality theories and developmental theories gradually entered the field, spirituality did not find a home in vocational psychology or in the workplace throughout most of the 20th century. This is true also of counseling psychology, which did not become a separate discipline until after World War II. The connection between spirituality, career, and the workplace became a professional issue very slowly, burgeoning only in the late 1980s and 1990s.

Prior to the 1970s, *vocation*, *occupation*, *job*, and *work* were words widely used by professionals, but *career* was not. The word *career* entered the psychology lexicon gradually as did its definition(s). In the 1980s Carl McDaniels (1984) defined career, not solely as work, that which one was paid to do, but also as leisure, that which one enjoyed doing when not working for pay. His equation, career = work + leisure caught on as a definition. Other psychologists also began talking about career ladders and lattices that described upward mobility and/or deviant paths. Super (1980) widened the definition when he posited that career consists of the many roles one plays in life. Citizen, leisurite, child, student, and homemaker along with worker were roles comprising Super's Life Career Rainbow, clearly indicating that career is a life-span, life-space concept.

Anna-Miller Tiedeman broadened the definition even more. She made *career* almost synonymous with *life*, combined the words *life* and *career*, and trademarked the word LIFECAREER. She championed the idea that career is an internal process, and she referred to it as quantum careering, a "living life as process" (Miller- Tiedeman,1999, p. 19). Miller-Tiedeman suggests that rather than "breaking oneself against life," one should realize that life "generally unfolds intelligently" (Miller-Tiedeman,1999, p. 14); each individual can identify what is needed in order to mature his or her career philosophy. According to Miller-Tiedeman, one's career identity, more than one's job, is a process

of becoming that occurs in accordance with one's intentions. Rather than using what she called an outdated model of career counselor as parent/therapist, Miller-Tiedeman suggested that a more suitable role for the therapist is that of one who walks beside the client, offering support for the client during the client's quest. In summary, Miller-Tiedeman suggests that "the new careering "(Miller- Tiedeman,1999, p. 15) leads people on a personal journey back to their own knowing. Her theory is empowering for the client, and although subjective to each individual, it can be universally applied.

The Origins of a Postmodern Connection Between Work and Spirit

The postmodern view of career had its infant but dynamic start in the early 1960s when David V. Tiedeman, then professor of education at the Harvard University Graduate School, challenged the basic theoretical understandings of his time. Dissatisfied with what he thought was a hodgepodge of data that marked the vocational psychology of the 1950s, Tiedeman claimed that although statistics is a logical and useful tool for understanding the validity of many concepts, no statistic can explain how a particular person decides on an occupation or enables him or her to understand what work means personally (Tiedeman, 1952, as reported in Savickas, 2008). Different from his academic peers, Tiedeman defined career as "the imposition of meaning on work."[2]

Finding meaning and taking purposeful action are life-enhancing activities, and as such are spiritual activities. Savickas, (1997) wrote, "Career counseling that envisions work a quest for self and place to nourish one's spirit, helps clients learn to use work as a context for self-development" (p. 3). He added: "Career counseling that cares for the spirit attends to both career and the person who constructs the career. By dealing with both the personal preoccupation and the public occupation, counselors help clients to manifest their spirit and character through work" (p. 14). These words challenge career therapists and counselors to consider the connection between spirit and work in their professional role with clients.

Career therapy has been confronted by additional professionals, some of whom were women, who linked career and mental health with family well-being. In her noted book, *Meaning Making; Therapeutic Processes in Adult Development*, clinical psychologist Mary Baird Carlsen (1988)reported that she informs her career-seeking clients that she will work with them as "whole persons" rather just people seeking jobs (p.191). Her goal is to help all clients exercise their full creative potential. In brief, Carlsen did not separate job issues from mental health issues and from wellness objectives. Neither did career theorist and feminist L. Sunny Hansen. Her lifelong work with women's equity culminated in the publication of a landmark book titled *Integrative Life Planning: Critical Tasks for Career Development and Changing Life Patterns*. Hansen (1997) states that integrative life planning consists of the following six critical tasks: (1) finding work that needs doing in changing global contexts, (2) weaving life into a meaningful whole, (3) connecting work and family, (4) valuing pluralism and inclusivity, (5) exploring spirituality and life purpose, and (6) managing personal transitions and organizational change. Hansen offers information and suggestions about how to meet the challenges of these tasks, and in so doing she emphasizes that spirituality is central to both work and family life. She defines spirituality as something that exists at the core of a person and gives meaning to life: a yearning for higher power and a need to contribute to community and give back to society.

Bloch and Richmond (1998) viewed the connection between spirit and work as nonlinear, nonlocalized, and nonlogical. They noted that career paths include uncertainty, complementarity, and synchronicity. Based on these premises they designed a model that can be used to better understand the unfolding of career. The model contains seven themes: change, balance, energy, calling, harmony, community, and unity. There are spiritual underpinnings to each of them. In brief, it suggests that one should expect change to happen, and that seemingly small events can have huge effects. Balance is essential, but it is a process, not a place. To achieve balance, it is necessary to recognize the existing and the emerging in all of life's roles. Life should be viewed in terms of waves of energy to be recognized, drawn from, and used in community life. Community encompasses awareness of oneness with others. Calling suggests discovering mission in life, which requires listening to an inner voice signaled by values, interests, abilities, and gifts of spirit. Harmony is sought while examining calling in the light of that which needs doing in the world. Unity is to sense the oneness of all that is. Unity is wholeness, the beginning and the end, the first and the last, the One in which all being exists. Unity can be experienced by loving others as self, and by participating in one's life work with joy.

Perhaps no modern writer goes further in connecting spirituality to work than Mathew Fox (1994). Fox holds that people face more of a work crisis than a job crisis. He states: "Life and livelihood ought not to be separated but to flow from the same source, which is Spirit, for both life and livelihood are about Spirit" (p. 1). Fox claims that work is the way that human beings collaborate with God in the ongoing task of cocreating the universe. His work challenges psychology to discover ways to explore the self in relationship with that which is seen as greater than self.

A deep sense of connectedness appears to be the unspoken therapeutic need of many people. One need only search Google, Amazon, or the shelves of a bookstore to discover the current demand for books that relate to spirituality. More than a few are about finding work that can feed the soul as well as the family. Pick up almost any popular magazine and there will be an article or two on the subject. According to Blustein (2006), large corporations are becoming unbounded, and organizations are becoming ungrounded, forcing more and more employees to become contingent, temporary, and/or freelance workers. As corporations restructure for economic survival, they frequently grow larger in size, smarter with technology, and smaller in staff. They are said to become right sized and right fitted. It is little wonder that employees are insecure and mobile with hopes of finding the wherewithal to self-provide health insurance and retirement income. Synchronicity between one's personal self-doubts and circumstances of the external work world link hope for the future, and fear of it, to an inward turning: to interest in purpose, self-dependence, connectedness, and meaning. Psychotherapists need to be aware of work-related issues and the concomitant search for the spiritual, and they need to be ready to work with clients who are not sick by clinical definition but nevertheless need help to bring to light resources that may exist darkly within the self.

There is now an urgency to connect spirituality and career. As William James, a century ago, sought to find methods with which to study and "legitimize" religious experience, including mystical experience and even saintliness, and as Wilhelm Wundt found methods with which to study human consciousness, contemporary psychologists and psychotherapists are currently seeking and finding new methods with which to understand the human quest for spirituality in work and family.[3] However, a problem lay in agreeing upon exactly what spirituality is. Some psychologists hold that it is synonymous with religion. Others claim that it is not. Because of the lack of a unified approach, arguments occur over whether one can study spirituality independently of religion. Transcendence is part of each, but religion is associated with ritual and spirituality is not; hence, the two are not synonymous. Nevertheless, some researchers abandon the attempt to separately define spirituality precisely because it has been so closely associated with religion, and an academic debate about whether one can be spiritual but not religious evokes strong opinions on both sides. Necessity, however, demands that spirituality be understood separately from organized religion because understanding spirituality independent of organized religion makes it possible to discuss spirituality in work and family without getting mired in practice differences between religions, religious denominations, and sects.

The argument that human spirituality as it pertains to work and family cannot be operationally defined, cannot be measured, and therefore cannot be a legitimate avenue for study should no longer hold. Peoples' perceptions of what spirituality is and its purpose in their lives are worth knowing. Sink and Richmond (2004, p. 291) define spirituality as "an overarching notion that reflects a person's attempts to make sense of his or her world," and Bloch and Richmond (1998, p. vii) call it "the experience of connection to something that transcends our ordinary lives" These and other definitions connote purpose, meaning, connection, and a yearning for direction that seems to be felt deeply within the self. Defined as such, spirituality can be discussed in schools and in the workplace.

Family Spirituality and Its Connection to Career

Spirituality as a career concern does not usually begin in adulthood. It develops early in life, and it becomes a part of the personality of children and adolescents. Exactly how spirituality develops within the family has been a topic of interest to developmental and child psychologists. Fowler (1981) described the early stages of faith development and suggested that imagination is the operative agent between age 3 to 7 years. It is probably also the operative agent in spiritual development. From 7 years of age until puberty, the child takes on the beliefs and symbols that he or she sees around him: beliefs and symbols that are either deepened or dropped between puberty and adulthood. The family, therefore, is the first place where most children have the opportunity to develop the sense of

meaning that is later carried into adult life. This sense of meaning includes a value system that can reach beyond ego and self-interest, to be later carried into the work world by adults. However, adolescents who exist in unstable environments where they are assaulted by drugs, sex, gang brutality, cult practices, and marriage breakups frequently have difficulty developing the inner fortitude that is necessary in order to defend against these and other assaults (Bruce & Cockreham, 2004).

There is hardly an adolescent in the United States who does not have vivid images of airplanes crashing into buildings and people jumping from windows to their certain death. Additionally, as a result of constant television news the devastation caused by Hurricane Katrina, by earthquakes, and by wartime violence is etched in the visual memory of children. Studies of traumatic happenings, and of their effect on children, point to a positive correlation between psychopathology and the experience of traumatic events (Breslau, 2002; Pine, 2003; Steinberg & Avenevoli, 2000). Such findings make spiritual guidance in schools a must. However, within public schools in the United States, spiritual support must not involve religion. Spirituality, defined as that which gives meaning and purpose, evokes a sense of compassion, and encourages hope, has been introduced to the personal social track of many comprehensive counseling programs where it is integrated into a program that also includes academic and career guidance (Allen & Coy, 2004; Sink, 2004). School guidance programs that are focused on helping students find meaning, moral purpose, and a compassionate understanding of others have been found to be very useful, especially for those students who have had scant spiritual exposure in the home (Richmond & Margulies, 2008).

To determine whether spiritual beliefs help children and young adults work through difficult and traumatic situations, Rayburn and Richmond (2004) developed the *Traumatic Experiences and Adolescents' and Children's Health* (TEACH), a 41-item questionnaire containing items designed to tap children's' reactions and feelings after very bad experiences happen, and whether spiritual beliefs mediate their feelings. Using the TEACH, followed by personal interviews, it was found that adolescents feel sad, bad, angry, scared, and puzzled when bad things happen. They do not understand why they happen, and if religious, the role of God in allowing the bad things. However, findings indicate that, religious or not, young people who approach life from a spiritual base manage their reactions and feelings better than those who claimed no spiritual influence (Coleman & Ganong, 2004; Richmond, 2005).

The subject of the effect of religion on family has been frequently researched (Ammons & Edgell, 2007; Heston & Goodman, 1985; Thomas & Cornwall, 1990; Thomas & Henry, 1985). General findings indicate that a sense of gratitude and hope, belonging, being loved, and good self-esteem are characteristic of families where religion is practiced. These qualities may also be found in families that are spiritual but do not practice any religion. However, this has not been documented in family therapy texts. In recent years there has been an increase in the quality and quantity of research related to religiosity in families (Dolihite, Marks, & Goodman, 2004) and the effect of religiosity on children of intermarriage, divorce, and remarriage. Little is known about their effect on children from families that may be spiritual but not religious, though there is recognition that more needs to be known. By separating spirituality from religion in family studies, more could be learned about what happens in atheistic or agnostic families where members may hold spiritual values.

Perhaps the reason that there is scant study of family spirituality outside of religion is that many researchers think of spirituality, not as defined in this chapter, but as ephemeral. Like metaphor and mystery, spirituality points to that which often exists beyond itself, and, as such, outside of the realm of a psychology solely based on logical positivism. However, spirituality is not outside the realm of language, which is studied, and, like poetry, spirituality can illuminate the choices people make. One can study family spirituality by contrasting it to that which it is not. Career theorist Hansen (1997) tackles the issue of spirituality within the family by juxtaposing it against negative cultural forces. She differentiates spiritual values from the values of separatism and materialism (pp. 313–314) and treats spirituality as a family value that includes a sense of community and connectedness. The family that carries a sense of gratitude and hope, meaning and purpose is more likely to better deal with life's events than the separatist, materialistic family that does not, and where parents in these families "practice what they preach" adolescents are frequently able to handle the difficult situations that challenge them.

Miller (2008) brings spirituality into her practice of family psychotherapy. In her model of spiritual awareness psychotherapy (SAP) with children and families, the child, introduced as *truth seeker and exemplar of compassion*, becomes a spiritual teacher or guide to parents in conflict. Parents serve as spiritual advisors for their children in that parents are called upon to *support their children on their own sacred paths*. Miller states that this call is *absolute* (p. 227). She carefully explains the important role of the child in healing the family and the sacredness of the spiritual bond between parent and child. She holds that the child offers parents the opportunity to heal and grow because, according to Miller, *the child lives in the presence of the Creator* (p. 235).

In the work of both Miller and Hansen, the family is the vehicle for presenting and preserving foundational spiritual values. These values are builders of strength. Transcendental, they pertain to all religious faiths, but they are not limited to a specific religion. Values related to meaning and purpose, sense of mission, sense of the sacred, awareness of beauty, and awareness of suffering, and courage to be are the contents of spirituality, and anything that has contents can be studied. Content should determine method, not the other way around. Postmodern psychology has considered language as a basis for new methods by which numinous phenomena can be researched. Narrative, constructivist, and social construction theory, have taken recent root, and, along with complexity theory, allow for the development of new ways by which to examine the subjective experiences of people. Studies of this kind will link spirituality to work and to family. The new theories and the subjective methods that they spawn are already in use.

Career Development: New Theoretical and Practical Perspectives

Influenced by the physics of Bohm (1980),[4] David Tiedeman and Anna Miller-Tiedeman believed that people creatively adapt to changing environments. Rather than concentrate on characteristics of personality as the determinant of career, they focused on the quantum physics model of the self-organization of parts, an adaptation that can be considered by the social sciences as emergence in the ongoing quest for best fit between self and environment. Both Tiedeman and Miller-Tiedeman believed that the self arranges and rearranges into ever more complex patterns, attaining higher levels of consciousness as it seeks new fitness peaks. Career, therefore, is what one was, is, and will become instead of something one does. In the process of being and becoming each individual constructs career in the most effective manner possible, based on perception of self and circumstances. The process is universal, but the content is subjective.

Therefore, understanding the actions of individuals, like understanding the actions of subatomic particles, depends upon the perspective of the viewer. In physics, that which is being measured may have both mass and energy, but an observer cannot see both at the same time. The Heisenberg uncertainty principle indicates one cannot possibly determine simultaneously and with any accuracy both the velocity and position of subatomic particles. That is, if an observer seeks to measure mass, mass is what is seen, but if the observer wants to measure energy, mass is not seen.[5] Niels Bohr[6] thought that particle and wave are not opposites but complements of the same reality. Extrapolated to career theory, the understanding of human behavior depends on one's perspective, on the direction from where one is looking, and what one is looking for.

The "new careering" of Anna Miller-Tiedeman (1999) suggests that the therapist help the client listen to the guidance that comes from inner wisdom rather than focus on setting goals. The theory of Savickas (2005) suggests that that careers are constructed, not discovered. Therefore, counselors concerned with the spirit should help clients focus on self-conceiving, more than on self-concept, and acknowledge the self-organizing life force. Accordingly, the materials used by counselors should do the same. Career interest inventories are tools that give people a schema with which to think about self in relation to work, and a vocabulary with which to talk about self in relation to the way the work world is organized. They should be used for discussion, not prediction (Savickas, 2007).

Theories held by Miller-Tiedeman and Savickas encourage and empower people by placing knowledge gained from personal experience at least on par with conventional wisdom if not above it. In essence, one lives in a social milieu and inherently knows and moves toward what he or she believes to be the best choice at any given time. Recognition of that which inheres in self occurs when one opens to the fullness of personal experience and uses intelligence and intuition to learn from it.[7] Thus, the role of a career counselor, or career therapist, is to help a client recognize and activate what is already deeply there, and encourage him or her to exercise inherent potential to conceive of, and become, all that he or she feels called to be. These are spiritual ideas, and they have found their way into business and industry. Two illustrative examples are the leadership development program of the maintenance division of the US Postal Service and a program of staff development program designed to assist with the merger of American Lutheran Church and the Lutheran Church in America.[8] The commonality shared by the two very different programs is "new careering" philosophy. Their convergence occurred as follows.

In 1983 David and Anna Miller-Tiedeman convened a National Assembly to Advance Career held at the University of Southern California. Attendees roomed in dorms, and, unbeknownst to me when I enrolled, I was chosen by lottery to become Anna's roommate. Everything that happened during the 3 days of the Assembly was new and very exciting to me. I had, of course, heard of David, but I knew little of Anna and, at the time, even less about a connection between quantum theory and the psychology of careers. Though I didn't know much, I knew that Anna and David were on to something that had the potential of transforming the career counseling field. My employer at that time was The Johns Hopkins University, where I taught and coordinated graduate programs in counseling. I begged Anna and David to come to Hopkins to teach a special graduate seminar for people interested in career counseling, and I was very pleased that they agreed to do it. People who enrolled were largely corporate personnel who came from everywhere and held previously acquired advanced degrees. Memorable among the students were Linda Kemp, and Harvey Huntley, Jr. Dr. Huntley had the unique task of helping employees of the two separate church bodies adjust to the merger process during which everyone's job was up for grabs: no easy fete in a corporate culture where employees believed that they held their positions by the will of God. Linda Kemp was the director of career development for the US Postal Service, and she had a different agenda. A quasi-governmental corporation, the postal service, at the time, employed 900,000 people who bought into the company philosophy that moving up in the organization was the only way to success. In reality only 10% of the workforce would ever be promoted to management. With postal reorganization and downsizing, Linda's job was to change the corporate culture without destroying motivation. Moving up was not the only way to find work satisfaction with the corporation about to downsize.

Both Harvey and Linda came to the seminar to get ideas, and both designed and implemented career development programs. Both were national in scope, both were based on the same philosophy, and both were spiritual. The similarity ended there. The program in the church used religious metaphor and imagery. Employees, like the Apostle Paul, traveled through turbulent seas, got shipwrecked on the shoals of discontent, and used their career compass, their intelligence, experience, and their intuition to chart the course to calm shores. Participants searched their souls and prayed (self-organization) to become conscious of the gifts that might carry them to a higher place (fitness peak) where they could best answer their call. The program in the US Postal Service was also spiritual but quite different. It used no religious imagery or biblical metaphor. Its spirituality was based on helping people find their passion and meaning in life while looking for purpose not only in their work role but also in learning, leisure, and family roles.

As for me, I was left wondering about the synchronicity of it all. I could not have choreographed that script had I tried. Was it chance or the hand of God that I went to the 1983 Assembly to Advance Career and met the Tiedemans? After almost deciding not to go, I became Anna's roommate by the drawing of straws. Was it only chance that the Tiedemans came to Hopkins, that Harvey and Linda attended the seminar, and that their two separate programs have served hundreds of people since? Chaos theory, sometimes called complexity theory, also new to career development, might hold that strange attractors were operant.[9] Religion might call it hand of God. Either way, the two programs by now have served hundreds of people, but they are like a drop of water in the large sea of career programs that exist in corporate America today, many of which are undergirded by a theory that includes a spiritual and ethical foundation.

In a national study, Mitroff and Denton (1999) described the workplace as "one of the most important settings in which people come together daily to accomplish what they cannot do on their own, that is to realize their full potential as human beings" (p.7). They believe strongly that organizations should not erect walls that separate spiritual development from the workplace. Spirituality is for them the ultimate source of meaning: universal and timeless, transcendent of separatist religious practice. Though they admit to problems in definition, Mitroff and Denton describe spirituality as intensely personal, consisting of the basic belief that everyone has a purpose, that all things are interconnected, and that most people strive to do good. Spirituality is connected to caring, hope, love, and optimism. All of these things, the researchers hold, are good for business as well as individuals. In *A Spiritual Audit of Corporate America*, they discuss several organizations that are innovative and effective precisely because they hold a spiritual philosophy. They state that at present there is a split in corporate America between companies that acknowledge the soul and those that do not. However, their research shows that it is becoming ever more evident that attention to the spirit is health promoting, cuts down on worker absenteeism, and as such adds to the economic health of organizations and to the creativity of employees. Mitroff and Denton claim that corporations that do not attempt to deal directly with the spiritual concerns of workers will not be effective in meeting the challenges of the 21st century.

Special Work and Family Concerns of Women and of Minority Populations

Developing a spiritual approach to life takes time, but time taken to nurture spiritual growth can lead to a better balance and a healthy approach to work, leisure, and community and family relations. The pressure of not having enough time weighs heavy on women as well as men. In 2009, for the first time in history, women became the majority of the American workforce. Today, approximately 70% of all women work, and most working women are married with children. Whereas working men focus primarily on career issues, working women give equal priority to family (Stoltz-Loike, 1997). This frequently results in role conflict. In addition to the strain of bearing responsibility for most of the household chores, women bear the primary burden of child-related variables. The idea of Superwoman, the woman who could do it all, spread widely during the late 1960s and early 1970s, but before the turn of the century amid a rising divorce rate, being Superwoman proved unrealistic and far less than ideal. Many, if not most working mothers experience exhaustion from trying to balance work, housework, and healthy family living. Professor Nicole B. Porter (2006), of the University of Toledo School of Law, described the "maternal wall" as a barrier that stops aspiring women dead, long before they reach a glass ceiling.[10] She writes of the difficulties facing women working in high-powered law firms, possibly pregnant, and with other young children in the home, who need doctor and dental appointments, and rides to and from school and afterschool activities. Even though women may love their work and be very good at doing what they do, female lawyers may not have the time to provide as many billable hours as do their male counterparts and therefore may not earn as much nor advance at the same rate. Porter further claims that not only female lawyers but all working mothers may face the same maternal wall that barricades them from promotion.

Obligations to their children may make it impossible for many women to accept corporate jobs that require travel, yielding advantage to men who can and will travel. Because of the limitations of double duty that many working women endure, some firms attach a stigma to being a working mother. A brilliant female professor related to me that when she was an assistant professor with outstanding promise, the president of her university told her that should she wish to move quickly up the ranks and attain the position in academe commensurate with her capability, she should not become pregnant. She never did! And she regretted it.

Though many women try, few have all that it takes to be a successful and happy wife, mother, and professional woman. Though not superwomen, most women are good enough mothers, workers, and wives. Nevertheless, working mothers frequently suffer guilt for not doing enough for their children and for the companies in which they work. The name of the game for working mothers is to seek the best balance possible at any particular stage of life and be gentle with themselves when falling short of a self-set mark. For the female perfectionist client who cannot achieve her objectives, the therapist might, along with some cognitive restructuring, offer her the spiritual gift of support, as well as encouragement to be gentle with herself. But psychologists and psychotherapists can also help mothers, and the corporations that employ them, by advocating for the special needs of working women with children for whom flex scheduling, backup child care, and sick child care may well be a crying need.

Working mothers are not the only people who need child care help. According to Garey and Arendell (2004), 60% of American children will spend some of their lifetime in single-parent households (p. 297). Thirteen percent of single-parent households are currently headed by fathers whose need for flex time, child care, and abbreviated travel responsibilities may be equal or greater than those of working mothers. Furthermore, many single fathers have parent-to-child communication issues. Few studies prior to the 1970s have dealt with male household duties. More recent studies of family life show a significant trend toward the sharing of child care and more active household involvement (Coltrane, 2004). Communication is an important issue in raising children if they are to acquire a sense of meaning and purpose in life, and psychology has an important role in teaching parents, particularly

fathers, how to effectively communicate with their offspring.

Various religious groups have special work/family issues. For example, observant Orthodox Jews will not work on the Sabbath, which, for them, begins at sundown on Friday evening and does not end until sundown on Saturday. In the Northern Hemisphere sundown can occur quite early in the winter. At its start time, the observant Orthodox Jew must not only have left his job for home but also be bathed and ready for evening prayer and dinner. This limits him or her from accepting jobs that demand employees put in a full day on Friday and/or work on Saturday. It is difficult for most employers to offer the kind of flexible of hours that some observant Orthodox Jews require, and it is sometimes difficult for these potential employees to understand the position of employers. As a result, some Jewish men take jobs with limited salary and benefits in order to accommodate their religious practice. This in turn puts added burden on women who frequently have large families, huge household responsibility, and also must work outside of their household duties for pay. Subject to the same Sabbath restrictions as men, the type of work that they can acquire is limited and, more often than not, low paying.

Dietary laws also restrict some people from attending working lunches held in restaurants where kosher food is not served. This includes Seventh Day Adventists, who also observe a Saturday Sabbath and have dietary restrictions as well. Observant Muslims may limit lunch and other corporate meals during Ramadan when fasting is required. Psychotherapists and counselors who work with members of diverse religious groups must understand the culture of the people with whom they work, empathize with their special needs, and teach their clients how to advocate for their religious needs when applying for jobs.

Needless to say, the groups mentioned earlier are not the groups with special employment needs. The physically and mentally challenged certainly have special needs and the workplace is not always friendly, accommodating only that which is demanded by law. Nor is it always friendly to employees from openly gay or lesbian families. Many new immigrants do not understand why professional degrees and certifications earned in their country of origin are not accepted for licensed professional practice in the United States; and non-English-speaking immigrants are often able to acquire only manual labor or day work, making it difficult for them to get health insurance for their families and/or scholarship aid for their college age children. Furthermore, many new immigrants will need to obtain English-speaking skills to find work. Spiritually sensitive therapists and counselors advocate for justice for all social groups and for equity and excellence for workers and workplace alike. Census surveys indicate that diversity will increase in the United States and diverse populations bring their spiritual practices with them. It is beyond the scope of this chapter to discuss in any detail the various ways that gender, religious practice, ethnicity, socioeconomic factors, physical and mental ability, or lack thereof influence workers, the work they do, and where they do it, though all of this certainly bears further discussion.

The Big Philosophical Difference

There is a huge philosophical difference between conventional career and family therapy, and therapy that involves spirituality. Most counseling issues relate to transitions, and counseling that includes spiritual issues considers not only the transition to be made but also its value in the overarching meaning of the client's life. Career transitions begin in the family but extend to school, college, and the work world. All transitions require decision making, and values, which to a large extent determine outcome, are involved in whatever decision is made.

Dr. Nancy Schlossberg (1989) defines transition as an event or nonevent that results in change, and she recommends that therapists who counsel people in transition have their clients clearly take stock of the situation and examine whether it is internally or externally caused, and whether it is an event or nonevent (something that one expected to happen but did not). She suggests that clients look at resources that exist within self and community in order to discover support. Finally, counselors help clients develop strategies with which to best manage the situation. Schlossberg's model seems to work with most clients. Whether it involves spirituality depends on what clients bring to the therapy sessions and what counselors are comfortable with.

A more spiritual way of looking at transitions is that they are gifts, opportunities for deep self-examination. Donald Winnecott (1989) [11] described transitional space as the space between the inner and the outer worlds in which all intimate relationships and creativity occur. Cultural experience exists in that space, and so does psychotherapy. In therapy, the boundary between inner and outer world becomes porous. Thus, transitional space is sacred space

where the therapist becomes a transitional object that a client can "hold" as the client moves more deeply into his or her true self. Therefore, the transition gap is not something to be rapidly bridged, but rather deeply explored. The empty space that the transition provides is a place of mystery where the client's imagination can play with who he or she is. It is also the place for what exists in potential, signaling what the client can become.

Spirit-centered therapy as applied to work and family looks at seeming opposites and contradictions as potential compliments. Neils Bohr is frequently quoted as follows: "There are two types of truth, the trivial truth and the great truth; while the opposite of a trivial truth is plainly false the opposite of a great truth is also true." There are many therapy stories that illustrate how opposing experiences can both be true when seen in the light of a larger truth. One example is that of two young brothers who were fighting over a toy. The 7-year-old grabbed it from the 10-year-old and ran away with it. The 10-year-old angrily exclaimed: "I hate you and I wish you were dead." The younger brother cried and replied, "I wish you were dead, too!" When their mother heard this, she became both angry and sad. In family therapy, she related the incident to the therapist in front of the children. "Will they ever forgive one another?" she asked the therapist. At this point both boys, almost simultaneously, exclaimed, "Of course. He's my brother," indicating the greater truth of their love and attachment to each other. Psychotherapist Estelle Frankle (2003) discusses this concept in detail. When dealing with wholeness and healing, she presents the Kabalistic concept of opposites actually being complements when seen in the light of a larger whole. The Kabalistic concept is much like the complementarity principle in that it reconciles opposites by means of a greater truth, and taking a middle path to balance many of life's contradictions.

Many people have difficulty living with contradictions. For example, at the most mundane level, if career is thought of as a job and job is identified with who a person is, the loss of a job is tragic. However, if job is seen as only one of many important roles that one plays, its loss, though inconvenient, is not tragic. Contradiction at the ultimate level, as between life and death, can be looked at in the same manner. When one thinks that whether one lives or dies one continues to exist in the Eternal, the contradiction disappears: lost, as it were, in a larger meaning. To learn to see small truths as a part of a larger truth and to contain difficult or opposing polarities within self as parts of a whole is important in achieving balance, gaining energy, enriching community, and finding harmony between one's inner and outer world.

Conclusion: The End and the Beginning—Moving Forward

A goal of this chapter has been to demonstrate that spirituality is important to family and to career, and that a spiritual approach to career and family therapy can make a huge difference. That counselors and therapists include spirituality in family and career issues is more than a call to a cosmetic change in contemporary psychology. If academic psychology and clinical psychotherapy are to find a way to unite modern to postmodern thought, spirituality may prove to be key to professional career unity. Currently we have the theoretical background and the methodology to incorporate spiritual content into every aspect of our research, our teaching, and our practice. David Blustein (2006) stated that more than ever before "we are in a much better position to create a fully engaged psychology that supports working as a fundamental human right that is the birthright of each person" (p. 316). He further claimed that it is the birthright of people to "*find* meaningful and dignified work, support their families, and connect to the social world." A spiritual psychology of work and family is a humane science that engages the art of reconciliation. It allows for disparate things to come together, substituting narrow either/or thinking for broader, more inclusive thinking. It is not only possible but beneficial to combine predictive empirical assessment with subjective personal narrative. Causes of family and career events that are hard for people to understand may occur as a result of many factors, but whether happenstance and/or hand of God, what is important to the spiritually centered therapist is to understand how people perceive events, interpret their meaning, and make use of them. Theories from postmodern physics, coupled with those of modernity and the philosophy of premodern mystical theology, may all be of use to the therapist.

Regardless of whether acknowledged, spirituality occurs everywhere because it inheres in everyone. Poets and mystics have compared spirit to a spark. A spark may be so small it can barely be seen, or so large that it can become a flame. Career counselors regularly help people identify their aptitudes and abilities. This is familiar language, but whether one calls them aptitudes and abilities, or sparks, they are spiritual gifts when used to enable people to exercise meaning and purpose in life. Both the workplace and the family are venues where people nourish their sparks and unite them with the sparks of others. When sparks become evident, gifts are recognized, compassion expands, and interconnectedness increases.

Elkins (1998) claims that the majority of psychologists find spirituality important in their personal lives even when they are not involved in organized religion. He joins with Hillman (1996) and others who talk about psychotherapy as "nurturing and healing the soul." If it is true, as has been said, that life is understood by the stories one tells, then the story told by psychology about itself will determine its future. By deconstructing the narrative of a career and a family psychotherapy almost devoid of spirituality, and reconstructing it as one that is replete with work and family spirituality, psychology may be nurturing its own soul. This is done not by forsaking the past but by adding to it.

Notes

1. Parsons makes this quite clear on page 5 of *Finding a Vocation*, which is available in print and in PDF format on the Internet.

2. In 2008 the National Career Development Association's journal, *The Career Development Quarterly*, devoted a special section as a tribute to David Valentine Tiedeman (1919–2004). Articles describing his major contributions, and the section that references Tiedeman's complete works, are included in the section.

3. James taught experimental psychology at Harvard and later became a pragmatist whose thoughts and lectures on the topic of religion were published in *The Varieties of Religious Experience*.

4. Physicist David Bohm wrote *Wholeness and the Implicate Order*. He believed that humans are a microcosm of the universe and that meaning exists between consciousness and matter.

5. Heisenberg's uncertainty principle was developed at the Neils Bohr Institute. It is commonly associated with observer effect: how a thing is observed affects the measurement of it. It is important to remember that both Bohr and Heisenberg were working within a logical positivist framework.

6. Neils Bohr is credited with the principle of complementarity.

7. Miller-Tiedeman calls experience, intelligence, and intuition a "career compass."

8. The two branches merged into what is now called the Evangelical Lutheran Church in America.

9. For a discussion of strange attractors, see "Applying Chaos Theory to Careers: Attraction and Attractors," *Journal of Vocational Behavior*, *71*(3), December 2007.

10. Both the abstract and the article are available on the Internet. The abstract has a direct link to the paper.

11. The original publication was 1973, and it was culled from material presented at a series of lectures given earlier.

References

Allen, J. M., & Coy, D. R. (2004). Linking spirituality and violence prevention in school counseling. *Professional School Counseling*, *75*, 351–355.

Ammons, S. K., & Edgell, P. (2007). Religious influences on work-family trade-offs. *Journal of family issues, 28*, 794–826.

Bloch, D. P., & Richmond, L. J. (1998). *Soulwork: Finding the work you love, loving the work you have*. Palo Alto, CA: Davies Black.

Blustein, D. L. (2006). *The psychology of working*. Mahwah, NJ: Erlbaum.

Bohm, D. (1980). *Wholeness and the implicate order*. Boston: Routledge.

Breslau, N. (2002) Psychiatric morbidity in adult survivors of childhood trauma. *Seminars in Clinical Neuropsychiatry, 2*, 80–88.

Bruce, M. A., & Cockreham, D. (2004). Enhancing the spiritual development of adolescent girls. *Professional School Counseling, 75*, 334–342.

Carlsen, M. B. (1988). *Meaning making: Therapeutic processes in adult development*. New York: W. W. Norton.

Coleman, M., & Ganong. L. H. (2004). *Handbook of contemporary families*. Thousand Oaks, CA: Sage.

Coltrane, S. (2004). Fathering: Contradictions and dilemmas. In M. Coleman & L. H. Ganong (Eds.), *Handbook of contemporary families* (pp. 224–243). Thousand Oaks, CA: Sage.

Dolihite, D. C., Marks, L. D., & Goodman, M. A. (2004). Families and religious beliefs, practices, and communities: Linkages in a diverse and dynamic cultural context. In M. Colman & L. H. Ganong (Eds.), *Handbook of contemporary families* (pp. 409–411). Thousand Oaks, CA: Sage.

Elkins, D. N. (1998). *Beyond religion*. Wheaton, IL: Quest Books.

Eppig, E. (2008). Worldviews and women's spirituality. In C. A. Rayburn & L. Comas-Diaz (Eds.), *WomanSoul: The inner life of women's spirituality* (pp. 4–17). Westport, CT: Praeger.

Fox, M. (1994). *The reinvention of work*. San Francisco: Harper.

Fowler. J. W. (1981), *Stages of faith: The psychology of human development and the quest for meaning*. San Francisco: Harper & Row.

Frankl, V. E. (1963). *Man's search for meaning: An introduction to logotherapy* (I. Lasch, Trans.) New York: Washington Square Press. (Original work published 1946 as Ein Psycholog erlebt das Konzentrationslager).

Frankle, E. (2003). *Sacred therapy: Jewish spiritual teaching on emotional healing and inner wellness*. Boston: Shambhala.

Garey, A. I., & Arendell, T. (2004). Children, work and family: Some thoughts on "mother-blame." In R.A. Hertz & N. L. Marshall (Eds.), *Working families* (pp. 293–303). Berkeley: University of California Press.

Hansen, S. L. (1997). *Integrative life planning*. San Francisco: Jossey Bass.

Heston, T. B., & Goodman, K. L. (1985). Religion and family formation. *Review of Religious Research. 26*, 343–359.

Hill, R. B. (1992, 1996) *History of work ethic*. Retrieved December 2011, from http://www.coe.uga.edu/~rhill/workethic/hist.htm

Hillman, J. (1996). *The soul's code: In search of character and calling*. New York: Warner Books. (Original work published 1966).

Huntley, H. L. (1997). How does God-talk speak to the workplace? In D. P. Bloch & L. J. Richmond (Eds.), *Connections between spirit and work in career development: New approaches and practical perspectives* (pp.115–136). Palo Alto, CA: Davies-Black.

James, W. (1958). *The varieties of religious experience*. New York: Mentor Books. Jourard, S. M. (1971). *The transparent self*. New York: Van Nostrand.

Jung, C. G. (1933). *Modern man in search of a soul* (W. S. Dell & C. F. Baynes, Trans.). New Haven, CT: Yale University Press.

Jung, C. G. (1938). *Modern man in search of a soul* (W. S. Dell & C. F. Baynes, Trans.). Orlando, FL: Harcourt Brace. (Original work published 1931).

Maslow, A. H. (1969). A theory of motivation: the biological rooting of value life. In A. J. Sutich & M. A. Vich (Eds.), *Readings in humanistic psychology*. New York: Free Press.

McDaniels, C. (1984). The role of leisure in career development. *Journal of Career Development. 11*, 64–70.

Miller, L. (2008). Spiritual awareness in life and psychotherapy. In C. A. Rayburn & L. Comas-Diaz (Eds.), *WomanSoul: The inner life of women's spirituality* (pp. 221–236). Westport, CT: Praeger.

Miller-Tiedeman, A. (*new careering*. Ann Arbor, MI: 1999). *Learning, practicing and living the* Accelerated Development Press. Taylor and Francis

Mitroff, I., & Denton, E. (1999). *A spiritual audit of corporate America*. San Francisco: Jossey Bass.

Ottaway, R. N. (2003). Defining spirituality at work. *International Journal of Value Based Management, 16*, 23–35.

Parsons, F. (1909). Choosing a vocation. Boston: Riverside Press.

Pine, D. (2003). The effects of trauma on children: Working to define roles for mental health professionals. *International Psychiatry, 2*, 3–5.

Porter, N. B. (2006). Re-defining superwoman: An essay on overcoming the "maternal wall" in the legal workplace. *Duke Journal of Gender Law and Policy, 13*, 55.

Rayburn, C. A., & Richmond, L. J. (2004). *Traumatic Experiences and Adolescents' and Children's Health (TEACH)*. Washington, DC: US Copyright Office.

Richmond, L. J. (1995) Values/work/education: Definitions and context. In S. M. Natalie & M. Rothchild (Eds.), *Work values: Education organization and religious concerns*. Amsterdam, The Netherlands: Rodopi.

Richmond, L. J. (2005). *Religion and spirituality: Helping children cope with hard times*. Paper presented at the American Psychological Association Annual Convention Symposium on Perceived Meaningfulness of Religion and Spirituality, August. Washington, DC.

Richmond, L. J., & Margulies, D. R. (2008). Spirituality and school counseling. In J. M. Allen (Ed.), *Empowering the 21st century professional school counselor* (pp. 299–304). Anne Arbor, MI: Counseling Outfitters.

Savickas, M. L. (1997). The spirit in career counseling: Fostering self-completion through work. In D. P. Bloch & L. J. Richmond (Eds.), *Connections between spirit and work in career development: New approaches and practical perspectives* (pp. 3–28). Palo Alto, CA: Davies-Black.

Savickas, M. L. (2005). The theory and practice of career construction. In S. D. Brown & R. W. Lent (Eds.), *Career development and counseling: Putting theory and research to work* (pp. 42–70). Hoboken, NJ: Wiley.

Savickas, M. L. (2007, August 17–20). *Reviewing scientific models of career as social constructions*. Paper presented at the American Psychological Association Annual Convention, San Francisco, CA.

Savickas, M. L. (2008). David V. Tiedeman: Engineer of career construction. *The Career Development Quarterly, 56*, 217–224.

Schlossberg, N. (1989). *Overwhelmed: Coping with life's ups and downs*. Boston: Lexington Books.

Sink, C. A. (2004). Collaborating with student's spirituality. *Professional School Counseling, 75*, 293–299.

Sink, C. A., & Richmond, L. J. (2004). Introducing spirituality to professional school counseling. *Professional School Counseling, 75,* 291–292.

Steinberg, L., & Avenevoli, S. (2000).The role of context in the development of psychopathology: A conceptual framework. *Child Development, 71,* 66–74.

Stoltz-Loike, M. (1997). Creating personal and spiritual balance: Another dimension in career development. In D. P. Bloch & L. J. Richmond (Eds.), *Connections between spirit and work in career development: New approaches and practical perspectives* (pp. 139–163). Palo Alto, CA: Davies-Black.

Super, D. E. (1980). Life career rainbow. *Journal of Vocational Behavior, 16,* 281–298.

Tiedeman, D. V. (1952). Occupational choice: An Approach to a General Theory. *Harvard Educational Review, 22,* 184–190.

Thomas, D. L., & Cornwall, M. (1990). Religion and family in the 80's: Discovery and development. *Journal of Marriage and the family, 52,* 983–992.

Thomas, D. L., & Henry, G. C. (1985). The religion and family connection: Increasing dialogue in the social sciences. *Journal of Marriage and the Family, 47,* 369–379.

Winnecott, D. E. (1989). *Playing and reality.* New York: Routledge. (Original work published 1971).

Glossary

Empirical: experimental.

Logical positivism: definiteness; a philosophy of science that holds that observable empirical evidence is indispensible in knowing a thing.

Postmodern: after modernist philosophy; skeptical of logical positivism.

Social construction: a theory based on the premise that things such as careers develop in a social context. (Social construction is similar to constructivism, which is a philosophy that states that we construct our own evidence and understanding of the world.)

Spirituality and Positive Youth Development

Peter L. Benson, Eugene C. Roehlkepartain, *and* Peter C. Scales

Abstract

This chapter discusses the integration of theories of youth spiritual development with theories of positive youth development, a relatively recent phenomenon in developmental psychology. It reviews the literature showing the intersection of positive youth development with both institutional and personal expressions of spirituality, and it specifically notes the mediating role played by youth experience of developmental assets in the empirically observed linkage of religious and spiritual engagement and positive developmental outcomes among youth. It presents initial research advancing a new theory of youth spiritual development as a universal domain of development, describing spiritual development as a constant, ongoing, and dynamic interplay between one's inward journey and one's outward journey. Several central animating dynamics are presented: awareness, connecting, and integrating these into a purposeful way of living. Research is discussed from a religiously diverse global sample of more than 7,000 youth ages 12–25 years from eight countries in North America, Europe, Asia, and Africa, showing that higher scores on those elements of spiritual development predict positive outcomes across nations and affiliations, including volunteerism, self-rated overall health, environmentalism, and risk behaviors. Moreover, as predicted, high scores occur with and without active engagement with religious traditions. Finally, integration of the spiritual development domains—having high scores in each area—increases with age, as would be expected in a valid developmental process. Although the model does not work equally well with all countries and religions, it marks a significant advance beyond the traditional spiritual development models that have been based on Western and Christian samples and measures and represented the great majority of the literature.

Key Words: positive youth development, developmental assets, spirituality, spiritual development, religious engagement

Introduction

Two lines of scientific inquiry and practice in adolescent psychology have blossomed in the last two decades. They are positive youth development and spiritual development. These two approaches commonly share certain ideas, including strength-based approaches to development, the dynamic interplay between person and context, and the active role of youth in the developmental process.

In this chapter, we will first define these two approaches and then explore the role of spiritual development and spirituality in youth development.

Positive Youth Development

Positive youth development is an umbrella term that covers many streams of work. It is variously a field of interdisciplinary research, a policy approach, a philosophy, an academic major, a program description, and a professional identity (e.g., youth development worker). The "idea" of positive youth development reaches into a number of fields, including child and adolescent developmental psychology, public health, health promotion, prevention, sociology, social work, medicine, and education. One recent review of positive youth development (Benson & Pittman, 2001) suggests four distinguishing features of this field. First, it is comprehensive in its scope, linking a variety of (a) ecological contexts (e.g., relationships, programs, families, schools, neighborhoods, congregations, communities) to (b) the production of experiences, supports, and opportunities known to (c) enhance positive developmental outcomes. Second, its primary organizing principle is (d) promotion of youth access to positive experiences, resources, and opportunities and of developmental outcomes useful to both self and society. Third, it is, as the term implies, developmental, with emphasis on growth and an increasing recognition that youth can (and should) be deliberate actors in the production of positive development. Indeed, some scholars (see Lerner, 2002) argue that positive youth development is only possible when youth and context are essentially "fused" in a bidirectional spiral of growth, with each mutually enhancing the other. And fourth, it is symbiotic, drawing into its orbit ideas, strategies, and practices from many lines of inquiry (e.g., resiliency, prevention, public health, community organizing, developmental psychology).

Damon (2004; Damon & Gregory, 2003) argues that positive youth development represents a sea change in psychological theory and research, with observable consequences for a variety of fields, including education and social policy. Three central themes are noted here. In Damon's view, positive youth development takes a strength-based approach to defining and understanding the developmental process. More precisely, it "emphasizes the manifest potentialities rather than the supposed incapacities of young people..." (2004, p. 15). There is more to this statement than initially meets the eye. In actuality, it connotes a significant critique of mainstream psychological inquiry that is quite ubiquitous in the positive youth development literature. This critique is that understandings of child and adolescent development have been so dominated by the exploration and remediation of pathology and deficit that we have an incomplete—if not distorted—view of how organisms develop. Indeed, the relatively recent emergence of the field of positive psychology as a force reshaping contemporary psychological thought is grounded in precisely this critique (Seligman & Csikszentmihalyi, 2000).

Secondly, Damon, like many other positive youth development proponents, holds up the centrality of community as both an incubator of positive development as well as a multifaceted setting in which young people can exercise agency and inform the settings, places, people, and policies that in turn impact their development. Finally, Damon notes that positive youth development, in its efforts to identify the positive attitudes and competencies that energize healthy developmental trajectories, is not afraid to identify values, moral perspectives, and religious worldviews as constructive developmental resources even though this "flies in the face of our predominantly secular social-science traditions" (2004, p. 21).

A number of scholars argue that the definition of developmental success most deeply entrenched in public policy and practice conceives of health as the absence of disease or pathology. In recent decades, the dominant framework driving interventions with youth has been that of risk behaviors, including alcohol use, tobacco use, other drug use, nonmarital pregnancy, suicide, antisocial behavior, violence, and school dropout (Benson, 1997; Hein, 2003; National Research Council & Institute of Medicine, 2002; Takanishi, 1993). While positive youth development advocates readily accept that reductions in these health-compromising behaviors are important markers of developmental success (see Scales, 1999), there is simultaneously a growing interest in defining "the other side of the coin"—that is, the attributes, skills, competencies, and potentials needed to succeed in the spheres of work, family, and civic life. This dichotomy is well captured in the youth development mantra "problem free is not fully prepared" (Pittman & Fleming, 1991). Accordingly, an important aspect of current positive youth development science is the conceptualization and measurement of dimensions of positive developmental success. Among these areas of work are efforts to define indicators of child well-being (Moore, 1997; Moore, Lippman, & Brown, 2004), thriving (Benson, 2003; Benson & Scales, 2009; Lerner, 2004; Scales & Benson, 2005; Theokas et al., 2005), and flourishing (Keyes, 2003). Within this inquiry on positive markers of success, an emerging issue has to do with expanding the conceptualization of developmental success to include not only what promotes individual well-being but also what promotes the social good (Benson & Leffert, 2001; Benson, Mannes, Pittman, & Ferber, 2004; Damon, 1997; Lerner, 2004).

In their theory of positive youth development (shown in Fig. 30.1), Benson, Scales, Hamilton, and Sesma, Jr. (2006) suggest that the core constructs include (A) developmental contexts, that is, places, settings, ecologies relationships with the potential to generate supports, opportunities, and resources); (B) the nature of the child, which accents an inherent capacity to grow and thrive (and actively engage with supportive contexts); (C) developmental strengths (attributes of the person, including skills, competencies, values, and dispositions important for successful engagement in the world); and two complementary conceptualizations of developmental success: (D) the reduction of high-risk behavior and (E) the promotion of thriving. The bidirectional arrows intend to convey the dynamic nature of person–ecology interactions prominent in recent expositions of positive youth development (Lerner, 2003, 2004).

The authors suggest that there is no definition that encompasses all of this conceptual territory, but the fullness of these constructs is evident when integrating a representative sample of published definitions. Hamilton, Hamilton, & Pittman, (2004) noted that the term has been used in three ways. Their first definition reflects an articulation of the nature of the child (B in Fig. 30.1): "youth development has traditionally been and is still most widely used to mean a natural process: the growing capacity of a young person to understand and act on the environment" (2004, p. 3). Their second definition

picks up the role of contexts (A in Fig. 30.1) in the development of strengths (C): "in the 1990s the term youth development came to be applied to a set of principles, a philosophy or approach emphasizing active support for the growing capacity of young people by individuals, organizations and institutions, especially at the community level" (2004, p. 4). Finally, youth development also refers to a "planned set of practices, or activities, that foster the developmental process in young people" (2004, p. 4). These practices occur within the context portion (A) of Figure 30.1 and can be delivered via programs, organizations, or community initiatives.

Catalano, Berglund, Ryan, Lonczak, and Hawkins (1999, 2004) conducted a major review of the positive youth development field with support from the National Institute of Child Health and Human Development (NICHD). Among its purposes were to "research and establish both theoretical and empirical definitions of positive youth development" (1999, p. ii). Arguing that no comprehensive definition of the term could be found, they created a definition that named the objectives of positive youth development approaches. Hence, positive youth development seeks to promote one or more of the following: bonding, resilience, social competence, emotional competence, cognitive competence, behavioral competence, moral competence, self-determination, spirituality, self-efficacy, positive identity, belief in the future, recognition for positive behavior, opportunities for prosocial involvement,

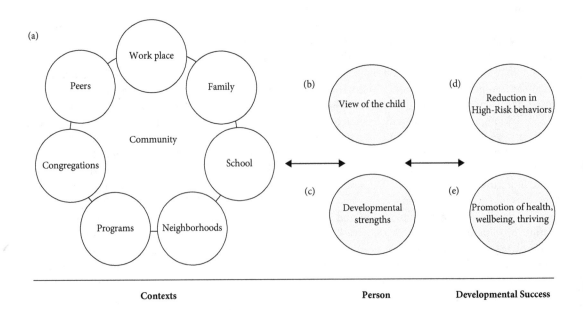

Figure 30.1 Core positive youth development constructs.

and prosocial norms. This definition, then, focuses on describing the territories of (C) developmental strengths and (E) well-being in Figure 30.1.

In 2002, the National Research Council and Institute of Medicine released the influential report *Community Programs to Promote Youth Development.* Though this report did not offer a clear definition of the term, its focus was on defining (and advocating for) two of the constructs in Figure 30.1: "the personal and social assets" young people need "to function well during adolescence and adulthood" (p. 3) and the features of positive developmental settings. These two represent constructs C and A in Figure 30.1.

Larson (2000) contrasts positive youth development with developmental psychopathology and suggests the former is about "how things go right," while the latter focuses on "how things go wrong." Hence, his focus is on positive youth development as a line of inquiry regarding "the pathways whereby children and adolescents become motivated, directed, socially competent, compassionate and psychologically vigorous adults" (p. 170). The pathways organically link contexts (A), developmental strengths (C), and developmental success (D and E). In a similar vein, Lerner's definition (Lerner, Fisher, & Weinberg, 2000) contrasts pathology-reducing and asset-building approaches. "Preventing the actualization of youth risk behaviors is not the same thing as taking actions to promote positive youth development (e.g., the inculcation of attributes such as caring/compassion, competence, character, connection, and confidence). Similarly, programs and policies that prevent youth problems do not necessarily prepare youth to contribute to civil society" (p. 12). Benson and Scales (2005) framed the essential problem with the deficit-reduction approach thusly: "What if *no* young people abused drugs, dropped out of school, committed antisocial behaviors, or became involved in an adolescent pregnancy? Would they then be prepared to be healthy and happy persons, loving and responsible parents, hardworking and productively engaged in a rewarding line of work, caring and involved citizens? To ask those questions is to answer them" (p. 341, emphasis in original).

Some recent definitions place additional accent on the processes and dynamics of designing and mobilizing developmental contexts (A in Figure 30.1) to enhance C, D, E, and their intersection. Benson and Saito (2001), for example, suggested that "youth development mobilizes programs, organizations, systems and communities to build developmental strengths in order to promote health and wellbeing" (p. 144). Finally, Small and Memmo (2004) identify a variant on positive youth development that places an important accent on mobilizing youth to shape their contexts and communities. Called *Community Youth Development* (Hughes & Curnan, 2000; Perkins, Borden, & Villarruel, 2001; Perkins, Crim, Silberman, & Brown, 2004), this approach takes seriously the bidirectional arrow in Figure 30.1 connecting A with B and C.

While there are many models that describe development strengths (C) in positive youth development theory and research, "one of the most widespread and influential positive youth development frameworks" (Small & Memmo, 2004, p. 7) is called *developmental assets* (Benson, 2006; Benson, Scales, & Syvertsen, 2011; Scales & Leffert, 2004). These are an integrated set of supports, experiences, and opportunities known to prevent risk behavior and promote thriving. Because a number of studies of spirituality and religion use this framework of developmental assets, it is presented here in Table 30.1. We will return to it when reviewing the literature on spirituality.

Spirituality and Spiritual Development

Interest in adolescent religious and spiritual development has gained momentum in the last decade. This trend is likely due to a combination of scientific, political, and societal factors. The interdisciplinary field of positive youth development (Benson & Pittman, 2001) has recently given more pronounced attention to religious engagement as a developmental resource that lessens risk behavior and/or enhances positive outcomes, a consistent research finding over at least the last 20 years (Bridges & Moore, 2002; National Research Council, 2002; Scales & Leffert, 2004). This, in turn, has led to renewed interest in the study of spirituality and religion in the fields of public health, social work, education, developmental psychology, and prevention. At the same time, new global conflicts have heightened interest in the role of religious ideology in creating and/or exacerbating intertribal and international animosity.

The vast majority of researchers agree that spirituality has multiple domains. For example, Scott (as cited in Zinnbauer, Pargament, & Scott, 1999) analyzed the content of scientific definitions of religiousness and spirituality published in the last half of the 20th century. Although she found no consensus or even dominant approaches, Scott identified nine content categories in definitions of spirituality:

Table 30.1 The Framework of Developmental Assets

Category	External Assets	Definition
Support	1. Family support	Family life provides high levels of love and support.
	2. Positive family communication	Young person and her or his parent(s) communicate positively, and young person is willing to seek advice and counsel from parents.
	3. Other adult relationships	Young person receives support from three or more nonparent adults.
	4. Caring neighborhood	Young person experiences caring neighbors.
	5. Caring school climate	School provides a caring, encouraging environment.
	6. Parent involvement in schooling	Parent(s) are actively involved in helping young person succeed in school.
Empowerment	7. Community values youth	Young person perceives that adults in the community value youth.
	8. Youth as resources	Young people are given useful roles in the community.
	9. Service to others	Young person serves in the community 1 hour or more per week.
	10. Safety	Young person feels safe at home, school, and in the neighborhood.
Boundaries and Expectations	11. Family boundaries	Family has clear rules and consequences and monitors the young person's whereabouts.
	12. School boundaries	School provides clear rules and consequences.
	13. Neighborhood boundaries	Neighbors take responsibility for monitoring young people's behavior.
	14. Adult role models	Parent(s) and other adults model positive, responsible behavior.
	15. Positive peer influence	Young person's best friends model responsible behavior.
	16. High expectations	Both parent(s) and teachers encourage the young person to do well.
Constructive Use of Time	17. Creative activities	Young person spends 3 or more hours per week in lessons or practice in music, theater, or other arts.
	18. Youth programs	Young person spends three or more hours per week in sports, clubs, or organizations at school and/or in community organizations.
	19. Religious community	A young person spends one hour or more per week in activities in a religious institution.
	20. Time at home	Young person is out with friends "with nothing special to do" two or fewer nights per week.

(continued)

Commitment to Learning	21. Achievement motivation	Young person is motivated to do well in school.
	22. School engagement	Young person is actively engaged in learning.
	23. Homework	Young person reports doing at least 1 hour of homework every school day.
	24. Bonding to school	Young person cares about her or his school.
	25. Reading for pleasure	Young person reads for pleasure 3 or more hours per week.
Positive Values	26. Caring	Young person places high value on helping other people.
	27. Equality and social justice	Young person places high value on promoting equality and reducing hunger and poverty.
	28. Integrity	Young person acts on convictions and stands up for her or his beliefs.
	29. Honesty	Young person "tells the truth even when it is not easy."
	30. Responsibility	Young person accepts and takes personal responsibility.
	31. Restraint	Young person believes it is important not to be sexually active or to use alcohol or other drugs.
Social Competencies	32. Planning and decision making	Young person knows how to plan ahead and make choices.
	33. Interpersonal competence	Young person has empathy, sensitivity, and friendship skills.
	34. Cultural competence	Young person has knowledge of and comfort with people of different cultural/racial/ethnic backgrounds.
	35. Resistance skills	Young person can resist negative peer pressure and dangerous situations.
	36. Peaceful conflict resolution	Young person seeks to resolve conflict nonviolently.
Positive Identity	37. Personal power	Young person feels he or she has control over "things that happen to me."
	38. Self-esteem	Young person reports having high self-esteem.
	39. Sense of purpose	Young person reports that "my life has a purpose."
	40. Positive view of personal future	Young person is optimistic about her or his personal future.

Source: From Benson, P. (2006). *All kids are our kids: What communities must do to raise caring and responsible children and adolescents.* San Francisco: Jossey-Bass.

experiences of connectedness or relationship; processes leading to greater connectedness; behavioral responses to something (either sacred or secular); systems of thought or beliefs; traditional institutional structures; pleasurable states of being; beliefs in the sacred, transcendent, and so forth; and existential questions. In another study, MacDonald (2000) analyzed 20 measures of spirituality, identifying five "robust dimensions of spirituality"

(p. 185): cognitive orientation, an experiential/phenomenological dimension, existential well-being, paranormal beliefs, and religiousness.

Because of its multidimensionality, spirituality does not fit neatly inside any particular domain of social science. Hill et al. (2000) noted that religion and spirituality inherently involve developmental, social-psychological phenomena, cognitive phenomena, affective and emotional phenomena, and personality. They note that "few phenomena may be as integral across life span development as religious or spiritual concerns" (p. 53). Furthermore, Piedmont (1999) presents evidence that spirituality may be an independent dimension of personality. Thus, a multidisciplinary approach is essential to develop a comprehensive understanding of the domain.

A persistent and important definitional, measurement, and philosophical challenge is distinguishing spirituality from religiosity and distinguishing spiritual development from religious development. Is spirituality the experiential dimension of religion? Are spirituality and religiousness unique, polarized domains? Is one embedded within the other? How are they related and distinct? The answers to those questions depend, of course, on how one defines both religion and spirituality.

Furthermore, in the same way that spirituality is itself complex and multidimensional, so is religion (Hood, Spilka, Hunsberger, & Gorsuch, 1996). Pargament (1997) defined religion broadly as "a search for significance in ways related to the sacred" (p. 34). Koenig, McCullough, and Larson (2001) defined religion more specifically as "an organized system of beliefs, practices, rituals, and symbols designed (a) to facilitate closeness to the sacred or transcendent (God, higher power, or ultimate truth/reality) and (b) to foster an understanding of one's relationship and responsibility to others in living together in community" (p. 18). In examining the relationship between religion and spirituality, Reich (1996) identified four possibilities: religion and spirituality as synonymous or fused; one as a subdomain of the other; religion and spirituality as separate domains; and religion and spirituality as distinct but overlapping domains.

There is considerable evidence (largely from studies of adults in the United States) that people experience religion and spirituality as overlapping but not synonymous domains. For example, a nationally representative sample of 1,422 US adults who responded to a special ballot on religion and spirituality as part of the 1998 General Social Survey found high correlation (0.63) between self-perceptions of religiosity and spirituality (Shahabi et al., 2002). Similarly, Marler and Hadaway (2002) examined data from several national US studies (again, of adults) that examined this question and concluded that:

the relationship between "being religious" and "being spiritual" is not a zero-sum. In fact, these data demonstrate that "being religious" and "being spiritual" are most often seen as distinct but interdependent concepts.... Indeed, the most significant finding about the relationship between "being religious" and "being spiritual" is that most Americans see themselves as both. (p. 297)

Spirituality and Youth Development: Major Research Themes

Even though the definitional debates continue, a significant body of literature is emerging about the intersection of positive youth development with both institutional and personal expressions of spirituality. Reviews of this intersection are also becoming more common (see, for example, Benson & Roehlkepartain, 2008; King & Roeser,2009; Lerner, Roeser, & Phelps, 2008; Roehlkepartain, Benson, & Scales, 2011). Although adolescent spiritual development as a research subject has been almost wholly absent from mainstream developmental psychology (Benson, Roehlkepartain, & Rude, 2003), it is notable that almost all the major positive psychology and positive youth development frameworks and theories of the last 20 years include some explicit reference to religious community or spirituality in their core concepts, such as Search Institute's developmental assets framework (Benson, Leffert, Scales, & Blyth, 1998), the National Research Council's personal and social assets (National Research Council, 2002), the protective factors approach of Hawkins, Catalano, and colleagues (Catalano et al., 2004), the values in action approach of Seligman and colleagues (Seligman, Steen, Park, & Peterson, 2005), and the work on adolescent thriving promulgated by Benson and Scales (2009) and Lerner and colleagues (Lerner, Alberts, Anderson, & Dowling, 2006).

In capturing the major themes connecting spirituality to youth development theory, it is useful to revisit Figure 30.1 and the interplay of ecology (A), person (B and C), and outcome (D and E). Using this framework, the literature can be organized around four themes: spirituality as human capacity (B); the role of religious community in promoting developmental strengths (A to C); the role of spiritual/religious variables in risk behavior (C to D); and the link of these same variables to adolescent thriving (C to E).

Human Capacity

Work is emerging on several fronts that expands our understanding of child and adolescent capacities and enhances the view of how persons actively connect with and engage the world. Hart (2006) refers to these as spiritual capacities. They include awe, wonder, "intuitive knowing," and openness to experiences of connectedness, transcendence, and the sacred. Some authors have suggested that children may have spiritual abilities and capacities that are underappreciated and that become attenuated in part due to their lack of explicit nurture. Gordon Allport (1955), one of the pioneers in the psychology of religion, suggested that "the religion of childhood may be of a very special order" (p. 101). Nelson and Hart (2003) report that nearly 80% of young adults experience wonder and awe about the natural world, with a high percentage recalling such experiences earlier than age 18. These kinds of capacities may be catalytic for spiritual development, but these relationships have heretofore been poorly explored.

Benson, Roehlkepartain, and Rude (2003) argue that spirituality may be one of the most dynamic and impactful of human capacities, serving as a wellspring for the best of human life (e.g., generosity, sacrifice, altruism) as well as for our darkest side (e.g., slavery, genocide, terrorism). Though research is on the upswing, the baseline has been extraordinarily low. Between 1990 and 2002, for example, less than 1% of articles in six leading child and adolescent development journals addressed issues of spirituality, spiritual development, or religion.

The relatively new focus on human virtues within the positive psychology movement helps to position spirituality as a human strength. Synthesizing volumes of inventories of human virtue, both historical and contemporary, Peterson and Seligman (2004) place transcendence as one of the six major categories of human strength. In turn, these are as follows: the strengths of wisdom and knowledge, courage, humanity, justice, temperance, and transcendence. The latter includes awe, wonder, gratitude, hope, faith, and purpose. Benson and Scales (2009) also posited that spiritual development (defined as affirming the importance of a sacred or transcendent force and the role of their spirituality or faith in shaping everyday thoughts and actions) was one of the key markers of adolescent thriving, and they confirmed that factor in a sample of more than 2,000 middle and high school students. Many of these terms and concepts now serve as bridges between the study of spirit and the study of youth development.

Religious and Spiritual Community and Developmental Strengths

Though emerging theory emphasizes the interaction of many contexts with spiritual development (Roehlkepartain, Benson, & Scales, 2011), the extant research focuses heavily on the place of religious or spiritual communities in religious and spiritual development. One of the most robust findings in the scientific study of spirituality and religion is the link with health and well-being. In a recent review of this literature, Benson and King (2005) noted the consistent negative association between religious participation and alcohol and other drug use, crime, violence and delinquency, depression, risk taking, and early sexual behavior. On the other side of the coin, religious involvement is consistently related to volunteerism and service, school success, physical health, positive identity formation, and life satisfaction.

What accounts for this consistent and generalizable relationship between involvement in religious/spiritual community—whether mosque, synagogue, parish, church, or temple—with both the suppression of risk behavior and the enhancement of thriving? A fairly recent line of inquiry supports the hypothesis that developmental assets (in particular, religious contexts that function as asset-building resources) mediate the influence of religion. See Figure 30.1 for this ecology-to-developmental strengths dynamic in the theory of positive youth development.

A recent analysis provides strong evidence that religious engagement does enhance the developmental asset landscape (Wagener, Furrow, King, Leffert, & Benson, 2003). The authors argue that religious engagement, then, wields its influence via building developmental strengths. A related study, using a national sample of 614 adolescents (ages 12 to 17), provides strong evidence that frequency of attendance enhances positive engagement with adults outside of one's family (Scales et al., 2003). Such networks of adult relationships can be powerful influences on both risk behaviors and thriving (Scales & Leffert, 2004). A line of publications over the last 15 years reflects and builds on this research and suggests strategies for enhancing the developmental impact of religious communities within many faith traditions (e.g., Roehlkepartain, 1998, 2003a, 2003b; Roehlkepartain & Patel, 2006; Roehlkepartain & Scales, 1995).

Consistent with this reasoning, Kerestes, Youniss, and Metz (2004) suggest that religious engagement promotes social integration (into adult relationships and prosocial values). Tracking four religious development trajectories during the high school years, they found that stable or upward trajectories were associated with greater civic participation and less alcohol and other drug use in comparison to low or downward trajectories.

Regnerus and Elder (2003) offer an important extension to this line of thinking. They find that more public forms of religious expression, such as church attendance, are associated with educational progress, particularly in economically stressed neighborhoods. With considerable caution and creativity these authors propose a theoretical frame for understanding these findings. It suggests that church attendance functions as a protective mechanism in high-risk neighborhoods, generating relationships, values, and sanctions that build "a transferable skill set of commitments and routines" (p. 646) useful for promoting success.

Roehlkepartain (1998) created specific hypotheses for the asset-building capacity of religious/spiritual communities, using the developmental asset taxonomy displayed in Table 30.1. In particular, he named this set of assets as viable candidates for developmental growth: family support (asset 1), positive family communication (2), intergenerational community (3), community value for youth (7), youth as resources (8), service to others (9), adult role models (14), positive peer influence (15), high expectations (16), engagement in structured time use (17–20), the nurture of positive values (26–31), and social competencies (32–36).

Scales (2007a) analyzed a data set of 148,189 middle and high school students who had taken, in 2003, Search Institute's *Profiles of Student Life: Attitudes and Behaviors*. This survey measures each of the 40 developmental assets and a wide range of risk and thriving behaviors. It also includes items about the frequency of religious engagement and the importance of "being religious or spiritual." The asset scores for students active in religious engagement were appreciably higher than for less active youth. The largest differences were in the asset categories of support and empowerment.

On many assets, increases of 50% or more were found comparing active and less active youth. Among these were positive family communication (asset 2), parental involvement in schooling (6), community values youth (7), youth as resources (8), service to others (9), engagement in creative activities (12), engagement in youth programs (18), and the value of restraint (31).

The developmental asset profiles that favor active youth are consistent with work that connects religious/spiritual engagement to higher levels of social capital (King & Furrow, 2004; Putnam, 2000). As King and Roeser (2009) put it: Faith communities

have particular capacity "to build trustworthy cross-generational relationships and link youth to sources of helpful information, resources and opportunities" (p. 459).

Often left out of discussions of the impact of religion and spirituality is the specific role of faith-based youth programs. Larson, Hansen, and Moneta (2006) provide a rare and important exception. They looked at a representative sample of 2,280 11th graders to profile their developmental experiences in extracurricular and community-based organized activities. Comparisons were made among six categories of organized activity: sports, arts, academic, community, service, and faith based. Students in faith-based youth groups reported significantly higher rates than youth in other activities on each of the six developmental experiences measured. These were identity work, initiative, emotional regulation, teamwork and social skills, positive relationships and adult networks, and social capital.

The Link to Risk Behavior

There have been many reviews establishing the link between spiritual and/or religious variables and risk behaviors (Benson, Donahue, & Erickson, 1989; Benson, Masters, & Larson, 1997; Benson, Roehlkepartain, & Rude, 2003; King & Benson, 2006; King & Roeser, 2009). Several mechanisms for explaining this relationship have been reviewed previously in this chapter, including the way that religious ecologies (A in Figure 30.1) lead to the building of developmental strengths (C in the model), which in turn are instrumental in risk behavior reduction (D in the model). Other research has documented the highly significant role of developmental assets on behavior. Many studies have replicated the finding that increases in developmental assets promote significant decrease in 10 risk behavior patterns, including alcohol use, tobacco use, illicit drug use, onset of sexual activity, depression and attempted suicide, antisocial behavior, violence, school problems, driving and alcohol use, and gambling (Benson, 2006). Employing a risk behavior index comprised of these 10 behaviors, Leffert et al. (1998) found that demographic background explained 9% of the variance in risk behavior. Developmental assets explained an additional 57%. This point illuminates the importance of developmental ecologies in the theory of positive youth development (see Fig. 30.1). Furthermore, it illuminates the potential of multiple ecologies (e.g., congregation, family, schools, community) working in concert to enrich young people's developmental asset landscape. Scales (2007b) reported that religious engagement and/or spiritual importance explained about 5% of the variance in risk behavior apart from other ecological influences. That is not insignificant, of course. It does suggest, however, that the influence of religious and spiritual community is less about a straight-line suppression of risk behavior and is more about its potential to catalyze community partnerships to collaborate in enhancing developmental assets.

Two other constructs are commonly used to study the spirituality-behavior link. Both of these are variants on the theme of developmental strengths. One construct is the concept of protective factors, which has a rich and long research tradition in the fields of medicine and public health (Hawkins, Catalano, & Miller, 1992; Resnick, 2000). In this line of inquiry, religious and spiritual identity serve as one of a series of protective mechanisms against multiple health risk behaviors, with an impact on a par with self-esteem, grades in school, and family connectedness (Blum & Rinehart, 1992; Blum, Beuhring, & Rinehart, 2000).

Resilience is a second and overlapping construct commonly used to describe the role of religious and spiritual identity in development. Resilience refers to the process of positive adaptation to adverse life events, including poverty, abuse, and violence. Several researchers (Crawford, Wright, & Masten, 2006; Masten, 2004; Werner & Smith, 1982, 1992) have documented the significant relationship of spirituality in the process of "rebounding," positioning resilience as a key developmental strength.

While the evidence on spirituality has been on its constructive influence in development, there are important exceptions to this rule. As suggested by the inclusion of Religious and Spiritual Problem in the *Diagnostic and Statistical Manual of Mental Disorders* (*DSM-IV-TR*) (American Psychiatric Association, 2000), certain forms of spiritual beliefs, practices, and experiences can distort reality or cause harm to self or others. These harmful effects can include narcissism, conflict-ridden or authoritarian spiritual practices, denial of reality, spiritual delusions, or terrorism (Hill et al., 2000; MacDonald, 2000; Wagener & Malony, 2006). The dark side of religious and spiritual development—including their capacity to nurture racism, exclusion, violence, and terrorism—has received considerable press attention and far too little quality research.

The Link to Thriving

Youth development has a long tradition in research and advocacy for positioning positive indicators of development as central for both a richer understanding of development and a more comprehensive social policy (Benson, Scales, Hamilton, & Sesma, Jr., 2006). Thriving has emerged both as a term encompassing a range of positive behaviors (e.g., compassion, volunteering, leadership) and as an approach to understanding processes and dynamics of optional human development (i.e., construct E in Fig. 30.1).

A number of studies show significant relationships between religion-spirituality and indicators of thriving (Benson, Scales, Sesma, & Roehlkepartain, 2005). As with risk behaviors, the correlations with thriving indicators are generally significant and modest. Additionally, analogous to the argument presented in the previous section, a primary mechanism by which religion-spirituality promotes the indicators of thriving is via building developmental strengths/assets. Furrow, King, and White (2004) supported this idea with a study of urban high school students. Results suggested that religious identity led to enhanced meaning and fulfillment (developmental assets), which in turn led to higher prosocial concerns (an element of thriving).

In the literature, spirituality and religion are too rarely distinguished. An exception is the work of Dowling and colleagues (Dowling et al., 2004). They distinctly operationalized two phenomena, with religion defined as institutional affiliation and participation with a religious tradition and spirituality defined as experiencing transcendence and defining the self in relationship to others. Benson, Williams, and Johnson (1987) noted in a secondary analysis of Search Institute's *Young Adolescents and Their Parents* data set (N = 8,165 youth and 10,467 parents), both religion and spirituality had direct effects on thriving indicators. In addition, religion mediated the effects of spirituality on thriving. These findings suggest that both religion and spirituality may play a role in the development of thriving.

New efforts are under way to understand the process of thriving (Benson & Scales, 2011). Lerner and his colleagues (Lerner et al., 2008) characterize thriving as the bidirectional process of regulating the healthy interplay between individual strengths and the opportunities for positive growth within one's social ecology. Benson and Scales (2009) define thriving "as the dynamic and bi-directional interplay of a young person intrinsically animated and energized by discovering his/her specialness, and the developmental contexts (people, places) that know, affirm, celebrate, encourage and guide its expression" (p. 85). In both theories, spiritual development is prominent. For Lerner, spirit connects with the idea of transcendence, defined as a commitment to ideas or institutions that transcend the self. This concept fuels the capacity of persons to dynamically forge self and context into a prosocial life orientation. The Benson and Scales theory (2009) positions spirituality as either an external or internal resource that animates persons to identify their "spark" and to seek or create relationships and opportunities to nourish it.

A Theory of Spiritual Development

The literature on spirituality and positive youth development continues, by and large, to treat spirituality and religion as synonyms and/or as siblings, with one more experiential and the other more institutional and doctrinal. Very little attention has been focused on defining spiritual development. One key question is what part of us develops when we talk about spiritual development. What are the developmental "tasks" addressed by this potential dimension of development?

A definition of spiritual development posed by Benson, Roehlkepartain, and Rude (2003) was created as a precursor for establishing the parameters for a theoretical approach. Embedded in it are assumptions about three dynamics of human development, each of which need to be explicated in any theory of human development: (1) the core developmental processes at play that are deemed intrinsic to the nature of human life; (2) the goals or purposes of development; and (3) the contexts that inform how developmental processes play themselves out. First, here is the "working" definition they pose:

> Spiritual development is the process of growing the intrinsic human capacity for self-transcendence, in which the self is embedded in something greater than the self, including the sacred. It is the developmental "engine" that propels the search for connectedness, meaning, purpose and contribution. It is shaped both within and outside of religious traditions, beliefs and practices.
> (pp. 205–206)

The clauses in this definition can be arrayed as follows, per the three issues posed earlier:

• The core developmental processes at play: "Spiritual development is the process of growing

the intrinsic capacity for self-transcendence, in which the self is embedded in something larger than the self, including the sacred."

• The goals or purposes of development: "connectedness, meaning, purpose and contribution."

• The contexts that inform how such development plays itself out: "It is shaped both within and outside of religious traditions, beliefs and practices."

Furthermore, the definition provides two linkages to the arena of religion and "spirit." The first is in the definition of self-transcendence and the referent to embedding the self in the sacred. Note, however, that this form of self-transcendence (e.g., placing oneself in the context of God, gods, a chosen people, a divine plan) is assumed to be only one possible variant on the theme of "something greater than the self." Conceivably, other options include embedding the self in non-sacred traditions of thought, ideology, community or vocation. The second referent is to the role of religious traditions, beliefs, and practices as among the cultural and social contexts that can, but do not necessarily, inform how development proceeds.

Hence, this "working" definition stands solidly on the idea that spiritual development is a universal domain of development that can be dramatically informed by ideas and practices that are theological and/or religious. Explicit in the definition is the possibility that spiritual development also occurs independently of religion and/or conceptions of sacred, ultimate, or alternative forms of reality.

In 2006, Search Institute received a major grant from the John Templeton Foundation to deepen the definitional and theoretical work on spiritual development and doing so in an international context to expand understanding of the possibility of universal dynamics and the reality of cultural and social dynamics in development. As one strategy, we engaged an international network of 120 scientific, theological, and practice advisors in a Web-based consensus-building process around the processes of spiritual development. Through this structured process, advisors critiqued and recommended criteria, ranked various dimensions of spiritual development, and offered other guidance as we sought to create a framework for understanding child and adolescent spiritual development as an integral part of human development. As we began our work with the international advisors, we asked them to identify, then rank, various criteria for defining spiritual development. Table 30.2 shows all the criteria that were rated as essential by a majority of advisors within each tradition, discipline, and culture that are represented among the advisors.

What has emerged from the literature review, focus groups, interviews, and the advisor consensus-building process is the idea that "spirit" is an intrinsic capacity that propels young people to link their discovery of self and the world in pursuit of a flourishing life. As Johnson (2008) puts it, spiritual development is "a distinct human capacity to become aware of what is truly vital in life.... [It] is about orienting life toward what most vitally matters. It is about fostering richer, deeper, fuller life by carefully attending to its spirit" (p. 26).

From this perspective, *spiritual development is a constant, ongoing, and dynamic interplay between one's inward journey and one's outward journey*. This process presses persons to look outward to connect or embed their lives with all of life, including being in relationship with family, community, the world, and, for many, the sacred, divine, or some form of universal reality. It also compels us to look inward to accept or discover one's potential to grow, learn, contribute, and matter (Benson & Roehlkepartain, 2008). The central animating dynamics, we have posited, include awareness and awakening, connecting, and integrating these into a proactive and purposeful way of living.

To test this model and to test its generalizability across cultures and tradition, we embedded measures of these constructs in a recent international field study. Awareness was split into two constructs (self and world). This yielded four measures, defined as follows:

A. *Awareness or Awakening—Self:* Developing an awareness of one's inherent strength. In some traditions, this process has to do with "awakening" to one's true essence or spirit. A variant on this theme is Search Institute's new work on "sparks"—the apprehension of what about oneself is "good, beautiful, and useful." Other metaphors are commonplace throughout the world for this phenomenon.

B. *Awareness or Awakening—World:* Developing an awareness of the beauty, majesty, and wonder of the universe. The experience of awe is formative here. Though other perceptions of the world are possible, the lens of a hospitable and benevolent world is instrumental for animating a life toward strength.

C. *Interconnecting and Belonging:* Developing the perspective that life is interconnected and interdependent. This idea has deep roots in most of the metaphysical traditions of the world. It is not lost on us how central the idea has also become in the biological and physical sciences.

Table 30.2 Criteria Deemed "Essential" by International Advisors in Seeking to Define Spiritual Development

1. Articulate that spiritual development—though a unique stream of human development—cannot be separated from other aspects of one's being.

2. Avoid suggesting that the definition is final or comprehensive, thus inviting continued dialog and exploration.

3. Be relevant (though not uniform) across gender, age, socioeconomic, and cultural and ethnic differences.

4. Recognize that spiritual development involves both an inward journey (inner experiences and/or connections to the infinite or unseen) and an outward journey (being expressed in daily activities, relationships, and actions).

5. Add conceptual value to how human development is currently understood by articulating what is unique about spiritual development and how it is connected to other areas of development.

6. Recognize that spiritual development is a dynamic, nonlinear process that varies by individual and cultural differences.

7. Highlight broad domains of spiritual development while recognizing that these are approached and manifested in many different ways among individuals, cultures, and traditions.

8. Conceptually distinguish spiritual development from religious development or formation while also recognizing that they are integrally linked in the lived experiences of some people, traditions, and cultures.

9. Recognize that spiritual development has the potential to contribute to the health and well-being of self and/or others or to harm self and/or others.

10. Be understandable and accessible to people from many walks of life, including the general public.

D. *Living a Life of Strength*: Developing a life orientation grounded in hope, purpose, and gratitude. These are common and widespread human aspirations that are simultaneously grounded in the great philosophical, spiritual, cultural, and religious traditions of the world.

It is also important that the model articulates the relationship among religion, spiritual practice, and the processes named earlier. Though there are a variety of approaches to defining religion, we approach it as a particularistic set of beliefs, practices, narratives, symbols, dogmas, and communities that shape one's worldview in relation to an ultimate power or reality. It encompasses ancestral or cultural narratives, myths, and traditions, as well as personal faith and religious experiences.

We propose that many people utilize or access religion as a guiding narrative and normative community for shaping their spiritual development. When this occurs, one's spiritual development can be closely aligned with one's religious beliefs, identity, and worldview. However, one can develop spiritually without religious institutions, beliefs, or practices. Furthermore, the broader ecology of community, relationships, and social norms also influences and shapes the spiritual development of those persons who are devoutly religious (Roehlkepartain, Benson, & Scales, 2011). Thus, these two phenomena are related and overlapping for many persons. But they are different.

This is a critical point, and one of our key hypotheses. That is, the development of the core processes of awareness, connecting, and creating a life of strength can occur without direct engagement with the narratives, symbols, and practices of religious and spiritual traditions. On the other hand, these traditions, we would argue, have been created—wholly or in part—to nourish the processes we have identified. One of the most important issues we are exploring is the way young people access, appropriate, influence, and utilize these traditions in their development. This line of work has major implications for informing why young people opt in or out of religious engagement, an issue we propose merits in-depth exploration.

Putting these elements together leads to this definition: Spiritual development is the dynamic and active process by which persons (1) go about the "work" of awareness/connecting/creating a life of strength, and (2) interact with religious and spiritual ideals, symbols, practices, and traditions in "negotiating" these developmental processes.

This model was tested in our recently completed international study of 7,600 12–25-year-olds. One interest was how well this model and the hypotheses undergirding it would hold up across nations (Australia, Cameroon, Canada, India, Thailand, Ukraine, United Kingdom, United States) and five self-reported religious affiliations: Buddhist, Christian, Hindu, Muslim, and agnostic/atheist/none. (Jewish participants were sought, but fewer than 50 took part, precluding analysis.)

The findings of this international field test are promising. Each of several hypotheses receives support (Benson, 2009). For example:

1. Scores on the four constructs (A, B, C, D) predict behaviors as hypothesized. These patterns generalize across nations and affiliations.

2. As predicted, youth who most highly integrate the four processes exhibit relative strength on a number of "outcomes," including volunteerism, environmental stewardship, self-rated overall health, and risk behaviors.

3. As predicted, integration of the four processes (A, B, C, D) can occur without active engagement with religious and spiritual traditions. This happens with about 20% of the integrated subsample in the larger sample of 7,600. However, most youth who score high on each of the four processes do engage and connect with religious/spiritual community at rates higher than their less integrated counterparts.

4. Development, we would argue, moves in the direction of integration. In this case, this means weaving A, B, C, and D together into whole cloth. One proximal test of this is to look at whether the percent of youth who demonstrate this integration (i.e., having high scores in each of A, B, C, and D) increases with age. This hypothesis is supported when comparing youth 12–14, 15–17, 18–21, and 22–25. Integration becomes stronger with each advance in age.

5. In multivariate analyses, we confirm that the four processes, after controlling for gender, age, and religious/spiritual engagement, significantly explain variance on *each* of the seven indicators of thriving, health, and risk behaviors included in the study.

These results, though preliminary, suggest that the model has viability across many social locations. Subsequent modeling analyses using confirmatory factor analysis suggested a more mixed picture, with the model described here better supported for all the countries except India and Cameroon, and for

Buddhists, Christians, and the none/atheist/other group, but not for Hindus and Muslims. This may suggest that we have much of the elements of the model correctly identified (the constructs and many of the items), but either (a) not all the necessary elements have been named yet, or (b) we do not yet have the right hypothesis about *how* they are connected into a model, or both. Nevertheless, the collective results of our analyses so far suggest that much of this theoretical approach to spiritual development can be reasonably applied beyond the religious, particularly Christian, and Western frames of reference that have historically predominated in spiritual development research. The next phase of the research will, of course, provide deeper tests and refinements of the model, with a set of methods to also explore the dynamic interplay between the four processes and mediators such as age and gender, as well as young people's active engagement with both their religious/spiritual contexts and the ecologies of family, peers, school, and community.

Spirituality and Positive Youth Development: Next Steps

A new era is being launched in the scientific study of human development. For decades in adolescent research, religion was seen primarily as a control or prevention mechanism that reduced the odds of high-risk behavior. With the emergence of positive youth development on the one hand, and the framing of spirituality on the other, it has become more commonplace to also look to the place of spirituality and religion as a generator of strength. Hence, we see new literatures emerging on spirituality and well-being, thriving, and flourishing.

Moving forward, there are some significant challenges that must be addressed. While there is a rapidly expanding literature seeking to define religious and spiritual development and their interrelationship (see, for example, Hill & Hood, 1999), this period of intellectual and definitional "storming" yields as much fog as light when trying to define terms. If this emerging field of religious and spiritual development is to make its way into mainstream social science, some consensus-based resolution of terms and meanings is essential.

Closely aligned with this issue is the equally daunting task of measurement. Two themes dominate the measurement literature: First is the overwhelming tendency to measure religious salience (i.e., importance) and the quantity of engagement, such as frequency of attendance (Benson et al., 2005). Second is the proliferation of scales to measure various types of religious beliefs and sentiments, most of which do not generalize well across many ways adolescents experience the spiritual and religious domains. One hopes for the time when work focuses on new measures that are theoretically grounded and purposefully intended to measure the most salient dimensions within the religious and spiritual domains.

A related issue is that current research strongly emphasizes religious development and religious contexts. This emphasis builds on a rich tradition in the field of psychology of religion (Donelson, 1999; Hood et al., 1996), and it is important to continue this line of inquiry. At the same time, as spirituality emerges as a theme and focus, it is important also to launch focused research that examines the dimensions of the spiritual life both within and outside of religious traditions. This parallel emphasis will strengthen the field and contribute to the conceptual clarity that is needed to gain widespread acceptance in the social sciences.

Much of the extant research has utilized samples of Christians in fairly conventional (i.e., institutional) settings. Much less is known scientifically about spiritual or religious development in other cultures and traditions (see Boyatzis, 2003; Bridges & Moore, 2002), though there are significant efforts globally to broaden the knowledge base (see, for example, de Souza, Francis, O'Higgins-Norman, & Scott, 2010; Roehlkepartain, King, Wagener, & Benson, 2006). Accordingly, many of the efforts to measure deeper themes and dimensions utilize items and scales tailored to these samples. If there is any trend that describes the spiritual/religious landscape, it is the growth and spread of new religious beliefs, practices, forms, and movements (Eck, 2001; King, 2001). Hence, a critical measurement issue has to do with how to capture this rich diversity of spiritual and religious energy.

In addition, little is known about religious and spiritual development in cultures within the United States other than the European American culture. For example, Mattis and Jagers (2001) noted that the vast majority of conceptualization and research in the area of spirituality has emphasized the individual "quest" rather than the social and relational context of spiritual development. This individual emphasis has "failed to situate African American religiosity and spirituality in an explicitly relational context" (Mattis & Jagers, 2001, p. 523), which they find to be integral to the African American experience of spiritual and religious development.

Another remaining challenge is to contextualize the relatively unique patterns of religion and spirituality in the United States with religious and spiritual development globally. Little scientific attention is paid to the dynamics of spiritual or religious development in other parts of the world (Stifoss-Hanssen, 1999). Given emerging data suggesting that religious and spiritual vitality and salience may be most prominent in the developing world (Gallup International Association, 1999; Lippman & Keith, 2006), we can greatly enrich theory and practice by learning from nonindustrialized and developing contexts.

The global research described in the previous section in this chapter points in a promising direction. It seeks to identify core (and perhaps) universal developmental processes that can be informed by experiences with more formalized religious and/or spiritual practice. Much more theoretical and empirical work is needed to determine the fruitfulness of this approach.

It is reasonable, however, to suggest that the realm of spirituality represents, or responds to, a hidden and unclaimed core dimension of human development. As Benson (2003) has argued, among the most interesting and impactful human capacities are the lifelong pursuits of meaning, purpose, connectedness, and self-transcendence. These "higher" pursuits are universal and are addressed with or without institutional engagement and with or without an embrace of a higher power or entity. This dynamic, lifelong "work" is as psychologically and socially compelling as any other dimension of human development. The fact that these pursuits can present themselves in the form of creed, doctrine, membership, or idolatry ought not blind the scientific community to the developmental processes out of which they spring, nor to the more unseen and unacknowledged experiences of the same pursuit (e.g., altruism, forgiveness, civic engagement, temperance, the pursuit of social justice, generosity, seeking to make a difference, and pursuing noble purpose).

It is time—indeed, way past time—for psychology to claim and honor spiritual development as a core developmental process that deserves equal standing in the pantheon of universal developmental processes. So doing will not only greatly expand and enrich understanding of human development, but it will also strengthen society's capacity to nurture healthy development. We will know this recognition has been achieved when references to spiritual development in developmental psychology textbooks are as voluminous as they are for emotional, physical, social, and cognitive development.

In Memoriam

While this chapter was in production, the first author, Peter L. Benson, passed away after a battle with cancer. In itself, the chapter highlights the breadth and depth of his contributions to the understanding of youth development and spiritual development, including his pioneering work on the developmental assets, which has impacted theory, research, policy, and practice around the world; his theoretical exploration of thriving in adolescence; and his leadership in pushing the field of adolescent development to integrate spiritual development as an integral dimension of human development. When he was 43, Benson received the American Psychological Association's William James Award for career achievement in the scientific study of religion. More than 20 years later, he continued to embody the spirit of that award, remaining a visionary, energetic, creative, and compassionate scholar and leader until his premature passing at age 65.

Acknowledgments

The authors gratefully acknowledge support from the John Templeton Foundation in the preparation of this manuscript.

References

Allport, G. (1955). *The individual and his religion*. New York: Macmillan.

American Psychiatric Association. (2000). *Diagnostic and statistical manual of mental disorders* (4th ed., Text rev.). Arlington, VA: Author.

Benson, P. L. (1997). *All kids are our kids: What communities must do to raise caring and responsible children and adolescents*. San Francisco: Jossey-Bass.

Benson, P. L. (2003). Developmental assets and asset building communities: Conceptual and empirical foundations. In R. M. Lerner & P. L. Benson (Eds.), *Developmental assets and asset-building communities: Implications for research, policy, and practice* (pp. 19–43). Norwell, MA: Kluwer Academic.

Benson, P. L. (2006). *All kids are our kids: What communities must do to raise caring and responsible children and adolescents* (2nd ed.). San Francisco: Jossey-Bass.

Benson, P. L. (2009, April 2–4). *Adolescent spiritual development: Initial findings from an international field test survey*. Presentation at the Society for Research in Child Development Biennial Meeting, Denver, CO.

Benson, P. L., Donahue, M. J., & Erickson, J. A. (1989). Adolescence and religion: A review of the literature from 1970 to 1986. *Research in the Social Scientific Study of Religion, 1*, 153–181.

Benson, P. L., & King, P. E. (2005). Adolescence. In H. R. Ebaugh (Ed.), *Handbook of religion and social institutions* (pp. 121–138). New York: Springer.

Benson, P. L., & Leffert, N. (2001). Childhood and adolescence: Developmental assets. In N. J. Smelser & P. G. Baltes (Eds.), *International encyclopedia of the social and behavioral sciences* (pp. 1690–1697). Oxford, England: Pergamon.

Benson, P. L., Leffert, N., Scales, P. C., & Blyth, D. A. (1998). Beyond the "village" rhetoric: Creating healthy communities for children and adolescents. *Applied Developmental Science*, 2(3), 138–159.

Benson, P. L., Mannes, M., Pittman, K., & Ferber, T. (2004). Youth development, developmental assets and public policy. In R. M. Lerner & L. Steinberg (Eds.), *Handbook of adolescent psychology* (2nd ed., pp. 781–814). New York: John Wiley.

Benson, P. L., Masters, K. S., & Larson, D. B. (1997). Religious influences on child and adolescent development. In J. D. Noshpitz (Ed.), *Handbook of child and adolescent psychiatry: Varieties of development* (Vol. 4, pp. 206–219). New York: John Wiley.

Benson, P. L., & Pittman, K. J. (2001). *Trends in youth development: Visions, realities and challenges*. Boston: Kluwer Academic.

Benson, P. L., & Roehlkepartain, E. C. (2008). Spiritual development: A missing priority in youth development. *New Directions for Youth Development* [Special issue: Spiritual Development], 118, 13–28.

Benson, P. L., Roehlkepartain, E. C., & Rude, S. P. (2003). Spiritual development in childhood and adolescence: Toward a field of inquiry. *Applied Developmental Science*, 7(3), 205–213.

Benson, P. L., & Saito, R. N. (2001). The scientific foundations of youth development. In P. L. Benson & K. J. Pittman (Eds.), *Trends in youth development: Visions, realities, and challenges* (pp. 135–154). Norwell, MA: Kluwer Academic.

Benson, P. L., & Scales, P. C. (2005). Developmental assets. In R. Lerner & C. Fisher (Eds.), *Applied developmental science encyclopedia* (pp. 340–343). Thousand Oaks, CA: Sage.

Benson, P. L., & Scales, P. C. (2009). The definition and preliminary measurement of thriving in adolescence. *Journal of Positive Psychology*, 4(1), 85–104.

Benson, P. L., & Scales, P. C. (2011). Thriving and sparks. In R. J. R. Levesque (Ed.), *Encyclopedia of adolescence* (pp. 2963–2976). New York: Springer.

Benson, P. L., Scales, P. C., Hamilton, S. F., & Sesma, A. (2006). Positive youth development: Theory, research, and applications. In W. Damon & R. M. Lerner (Eds.), *Handbook of child psychology* (6th ed., pp. 894–941). New York: John Wiley.

Benson, P. L., Scales, P. C., Sesma, A., Jr., & Roehlkepartain, E. C. (2005). Adolescent spirituality. In K. A. Moore & L. Lippman (Eds.), *What do children need to flourish? Conceptualizing and measuring indicators of positive development* (pp. 25–40). New York: Springer.

Benson, P. L., Scales, P. C., & Syvertsen, A. K. (2011). The contribution of the developmental assets framework to positive youth development theory and practice. In R. M. Lerner, J. V. Lerner, & J. B. Benson (Eds.). *Advances in Child Development and Behavior, Vol. 41* (pp. 197–230). Burlington: Academic Press.

Benson, P. L., Williams, D., & Johnson, A. (1987). *The quicksilver years: The hopes and fears of early adolescence*. San Francisco: Harper and Row.

Blum, R. W., Beuhring, T., & Rinehart, P. M. (2000). *Protecting teens: Beyond race, income and family structure*. Minneapolis, MN: Center for Adolescent Health, University of Minnesota.

Blum, R. W., & Rinehart, P. M. (1992). *Reducing the risk: Connections that make a difference in the lives of youth*. Minneapolis, MN: Division of General Pediatrics and Adolescent Health, University of Minnesota.

Boyatzis, C. J. (2003). Religious and spiritual development: An introduction. *Review of Religious Research*, 44, 213–219.

Bridges, L., & Moore, K. A. (2002). *Religion and spirituality in childhood and adolescence*. Washington, DC: Child Trends.

Catalano, R. F., Berglund, M. L., Ryan, J. A. M., Lonczak, H. S., & Hawkins, J. D. (1999). *Positive youth development in the United States: Research findings on evaluations of positive youth development programs*. Washington, DC: National Institute of Child Health and Human Development.

Catalano, R. F., Berglund, M. L., Ryan, J. A. M., Lonczak, H. S., & Hawkins, J. D. (2004). Positive youth development in the United States: Research findings on evaluations of positive youth development programs. *Annals of the American Academy of Political and Social Science*, 591, 98–124.

Crawford, E., Wright, M. O., & Masten, A. S. (2006). Resilience and spirituality in youth. In E. C. Roehlkepartain, P. E. King, L. Wagener, & P. L. Benson (Eds.), *Handbook of spiritual development in childhood and adolescence* (pp. 355–370). Thousand Oaks, CA: Sage.

Damon, W. (1997). *The youth charter: How communities can work together to raise standards for all our children*. New York: Free Press.

Damon, W. (2004). What is positive youth development? *Annals of the American Academy of Political and Social Science*, 591(1), 13–24.

Damon, W., & Gregory, A. (2003). Bringing in a new era in the field of youth development. In R. M. Lerner & P. L. Benson (Eds.), *Developmental assets and asset-building communities: Implications for research, policy, and practice* (pp.47–64). New York: Kluwer Academic/Plenum Press.

de Souza, M., Francis, L. J., O'Higgins-Norman, J., & Scott, D. (Eds.). (2010). *International handbook of education for spirituality, care and wellbeing*. New York: Springer+Business Media.

Donelson, E. (1999). Psychology of religion and adolescents in the United States: Past to present. *Journal of Adolescence*, 22, 187–204.

Dowling, E. M., Gestsdottir, S., Anderson, P. M., von Eye, A., Almerigi, J., & Lerner, R. M. (2004). Structural relations among spirituality, religiosity, and thriving in adolescence. *Applied Developmental Science*, 8(1), 7–16.

Eck, D. L. (2001). *A new religious America: How a "Christian country" has become the world's most religiously diverse nation*. New York: Harper.

Furrow, J. L. & King, P. E., & White, K. (2004). Religion and positive youth development: Identity, meaning, and prosocial concerns. *Applied Developmental Science*, 8(1), 17–26.

Gallup International Association. (1999). *Gallup international millennium survey*. Zurich, Switzerland: WIN/Gallup International Association.

Hamilton, S. F., Hamilton, M. A., & Pittman, K. (2004). Principles for youth development. In S. F. &. H. M. A. Hamilton (Eds.), *The youth development handbook: Coming of age in American communities* (pp. 3–22). Thousand Oaks, CA: Sage.

Hart, T. (2006). Spiritual experiences and capacities of children and youth. In E. C. Roehlkepartain, P. E. King, L. Wagener, & P. L. Benson (Eds.). *The handbook of spiritual development in childhood and adolescence* (pp.163–177). Thousand Oaks, CA: Sage.

Hawkins, J. D., Catalano, R. F., & Miller, J. Y. (1992). Risk and protective factors for alcohol and other drug problems in adolescence and early adulthood: Implications for substance abuse prevention. *Psychology Bulletin*, 112, 64–105.

Hein, K. (2003). Enhancing the assets for positive youth development: The vision, values, and action agenda of the W. T. Grant Foundation. In R. M. Lerner & P. L. Benson (Eds.), *Developmental assets and asset-building communities: Implications for research, policy, and practice* (pp. 97–117). New York: Kluwer Academic/Plenum.

Hill, P. C., & Hood, R. W. (1999). *Measures of religiosity*. Birmingham, AL: Religious Education Press.

Hill, P. C., Pargament, K. I., Hood, R. W., McCullough, M. E., Swyers, J. P., Larson, D. B., & Zinnbauer, B. J. (2000). Conceptualizing religion and spirituality: Points of commonality, points of departure. *Journal for the Theory of Social Behavior, 30*(1), 52–77.

Hood, R. W., Jr., Spilka, B., Hunsberger, B., & Gorsuch, R. (1996). *The psychology of religion: An empirical approach*. (2nd ed). New York: The Guilford Press.

Hughes, D., & Curnan, S. P. (2000). Community youth development: A framework for action. *CYD Journal, 1*(1), 7–13.

Johnson, B. (2008). A tale of two religious effects: Evidence for the protective and prosocial impact of organic religion. In K. K. Kline (Ed.), *Authoritative communities: The scientific case for nurturing the whole child* (pp. 341–351). New York: Springer.

Kerestes, M., Youniss, J., & Metz, E. (2004). Longitudinal patterns of religious perspective and civic engagement. *Applied Developmental Science, 8*(1), 39–46.

Keyes, C. L. M. (2003). Complete mental health: An agenda for the 21st century. In C. L. M. Keyes & J. Haidt (Eds.), *Flourishing: Positive psychology and the life well-lived* (pp. 293–312). Washington, DC: American Psychological Association.

King, P. E., & Benson, P. L. (2006). Spiritual development and adolescent well-being and thriving. In E. C. Roehlkepartain, P. E. King, L. Wagener, & P. L. Benson (Eds.), *Handbook of spiritual development in childhood and adolescence* (pp. 384–398). Thousand Oaks, CA: Sage.

King, P. E., & Furrow, J. L. (2004). Religion as a resource for positive youth development: Religion, social capital, and moral outcomes. *Developmental Psychology, 40*(5), 703–713.

King, P. E., & Roeser, R. W. (2009). Religion and spirituality in adolescent development. In R. M. Lerner & L. Steinberg (Eds.) *Handbook of adolescent psychology: Vol. 1. Development, relationships and research methods* (3rd ed., pp. 435–478). Hoboken, NJ: Wiley.

King, U. (Ed.). (2001). *Spirituality and society in the new millennium*. Brighton, England: Sussex Academic Press.

Koenig, H. G., McCullough, M. E. , & Larson, D. B.(2001). *Handbook of religion and health*. New York: Oxford University Press.

Larson, R. M. (2000). Towards a psychology of positive youth development. *American Psychologist, 55*, 170–183.

Larson, R. M., Hansen, D., & Moneta, G. (2006). Differing profiles of developmental experiences across types of organized youth activities. *Developmental Psychology, 42(5)*, 849–863.

Leffert, N., Benson, P. L., Scales, P. C., Sharma, A. R., Drake, D. R., & Blyth, D. A. (1998). Developmental assets: Measurement and prediction of risk behaviors among adolescents. *Applied Developmental Science, 2*(4), 209–230.

Lerner, R. M. (2002). *Concepts and theories of human development* (3rd ed.). Mahwah, NJ: Erlbaum.

Lerner, R. M. (2003). Developmental assets and asset-building communities: A view of the issues. In R. M. Lerner & P. L. Benson (Eds.), *Developmental assets and asset-building communities: Implications for research, policy, and practice* (pp. 3–18). New York: Kluwer Academic/Plenum Press.

Lerner, R. M. (2004). *Liberty: Thriving and civic engagement among America's youth*. Thousand Oaks, CA: Sage.

Lerner, R. M., Alberts, A. E., Anderson, P. M., & Dowling, E. M. (2006). On making humans human: Spirituality and the promotion of positive youth development. In E. C. Roehlkepartain, P. E. King, L. Wagener, & P. L. Benson (Eds.), *Handbook of spiritual development in childhood and adolescence* (pp. 60–72). Thousand Oaks, CA: Sage.

Lerner, R. M., Fisher, C. B., & Weinberg, R. A. (2000). Toward a science for and of the people: Promoting civil society through the application of developmental science. *Child Development, 71*, 11–20.

Lerner, R. M., Roeser, R. W., & Phelps, E. (2008). Positive development, spirituality, and generosity in youth: An introduction to the issues. In R. M. Lerner, R. W. Roeser, & E. Phelps (Eds.), *Positive youth development and spirituality* (pp. 3–24). West Conshohocken, PA: Templeton Foundation Press.

Lippman, L. H., & Keith, J. D. (2006). The demographics of spirituality among youth: International perspectives. In E. C. Roehlkepartain, P. E. King, L. Wagener, & P. L. Benson (Eds.), *Handbook of spiritual development in childhood and adolescence* (pp. 109–123). Thousand Oaks, CA: Sage Publications.

MacDonald, D. A. (2000). Spirituality: Description, measurement, and relation to the five factor model of personality. *Journal of Personality, 68*(1), 157–197.

Marler, P. L., & Hadaway, C. K. (2002). "Being religious" or "being spiritual" in America: A zero-sum proposition? *Journal for the Scientific Study of Religion, 41*, 289–300

Masten, A. S. (2004). Regulatory processes, risk and resilience in adolescent development. In R. E. Dahl & E. L. P. Spear (Eds.), *Annals of the New York Academy of Sciences: Vol. 1021. Adolescent brain development: Vulnerabilities and opportunities* (pp. 310–319). New York: New York Academy of Sciences.

Mattis, J. S., & Jagers, R. J. (2001). A relational framework for the study of religiosity and spirituality in the lives of African Americans. *Journal of Community Psychology, 29*, 519–539.

Moore, K. A. (1997). Criteria for indicators of child well-being. In R. M. Hauser, B. V. Brown, & W. R. Prosser (Eds.), *Indicators of children's well-being* (pp. 36–44). New York: Russell Sage Foundation.

Moore, K. A., Lippman, L., & Brown, B. (2004). Indicators of child well-being: The promise for positive youth development. *The Annals of the American Academy of Political and Social Science, 591*, 125–147.

National Research Council and Institute of Medicine. (2002). *Community programs to promote youth development*. Washington, DC: National Academy Press.

Nelson, P. L., & Hart, T. (2003). *A survey of recalled childhood spiritual and non-ordinary experiences: Age, rate and psychological factors associated with their occurrence*. Retrieved January 2012, from http://childspirit.org/wp-content/uploads/2011/09/Child-Spirit-Carrollton-Survey-childhood-exp.pdf

Pargament, K. (1997). *The psychology of religious coping*. New York: The Guilford Press.

Perkins, D. D., Crim, B., Silberman, P., & Brown, B. B. (2004). Community development as a response to community-level adversity: Ecological theory and research and strengths-based policy. In K. I. Maton, C. J. Schellenbach, B. J. Leadbeater, & A. L. Solarz (Eds.), *Investing in children, youth, families, and communities: Strengths-based research and policy* (pp. 321–340). Washington, DC: American Psychological Association.

Perkins, D. F., Borden, L. M., & Villarruel, F. A. (2001). Community youth development: A partnership for change. *School Community Journal, 11*, 39–56.

Peterson, C., & Seligman, M. E. P. (2004). *Character strengths and virtues: A handbook and classification.* Washington, DC: APA Press and Oxford University Press.

Piedmont, R. L. (1999). Does spirituality represent the sixth factor of personality? Spiritual transcendence and the five-factor model. *Journal of Personality, 67*(6), 985–1013.

Pittman, K. J., & Fleming, W. E. (1991, September). *A new vision: Promoting youth development.* Written transcript of live testimony by Karen J. Pittman given before The House Select Committee on Children, Youth and Families. Washington, DC: Center for Youth Development and Policy Research.

Putnam, R. D. (2000). *Bowling alone: The collapse and revival of American community.* New York: Simon & Schuster.

Regnerus, M. D., & Elder, G. H., Jr. (2003). Staying on track in school: Religious influences in high and low-risk settings. *Journal for the Scientific Study of Religion, 42*, 633–649.

Reich, K. H. (1996). A logic-based typology of science and theology. *Journal of Interdisciplinary Studies, 8*(1–2), 149–167.

Resnick, M. D. (2000). Protective factors, resiliency, and healthy youth development. *Adolescent Medicine: State of the Art Reviews, 11*(1), 157–164.

Roehlkepartain, E. C. (1998). *Building assets in congregations: A practical guide for helping youth grow up healthy.* Minneapolis, MN: Search Institute.

Roehlkepartain, E. C. (2003a). Making room at the table for everyone: Interfaith engagement in positive child and adolescent development. In D. Wertlieb, F. Jacobs, & R. M. Lerner (Eds.), *Handbook of applied developmental science: Promoting positive child, adolescent, and family development through research, policies, and programs: Vol. 3. Promoting positive youth and family development: Community systems, citizenship, and civil society* (pp. 535–563). Thousand Oaks, CA: Sage.

Roehlkepartain, E. C. (2003b). Building strengths, deepening faith: Understanding and enhancing youth development in Protestant congregations. In R. M. Lerner, F. Jacobs, & D. Wertlieb (Eds.), *Handbook of applied developmental science: Promoting positive child, adolescent, and family development through research, policies, and programs: Vol. 3. Promoting positive youth and family development: Community systems, citizenship, and civil society* (pp. 515–534). Thousand Oaks, CA: Sage.

Roehlkepartain, E. C., Benson, P. L., Scales, P. C. (2011). Spiritual identity: Contextual perspectives. In Schwartz, S. J., Luyckx, K., & Vignoles, V. L. (Eds.). *The handbook of identity theory and research: Vol. 2—Domains and categories* (pp. 545–562). New York: Springer.

Roehlkepartain, E. C., King, P. E., Wagener, L., & Benson, P. L. (2006). *The handbook of spiritual development in childhood and adolescence.* Thousand Oaks, CA: Sage.

Roehlkepartain, E. C., & Patel, E. (2006). Congregations: Unexamined crucibles of spiritual development. In E. C. Roehlkepartain, P. E. King, L. M. Wagener, and P. L. Benson (Eds.). *The handbook of spiritual development in childhood and adolescence* (pp. 324–336). Thousand Oaks, CA: Sage.

Roehlkepartain, E. C., & Scales, P. C. (1995). *Youth development in congregations: An exploration of the potential and barriers.* Minneapolis, MN: Search Institute.

Scales, P. C. (1999). Reducing risks and building developmental assets: Essential actions for promoting adolescent health. *Journal of School Health, 69*(3), 113–119.

Scales, P. C. (2007a). Early spirituality and religious participation linked to later adolescent well-being. Retrieved January 2012, from http://www.search-institute.org/csd/articles/fast-facts/early-spirituality

Scales, P. C. (2007b). Spirituality and adolescent well-being: Selected new statistics. Retrieved January 2012, from http://www.search-institute.org/csd/articles/fast-facts/selected-statistics

Scales, P. C., & Benson, P. L. (2005). Adolescence and thriving. In R. Lerner & C. Fisher, (Eds.), *Applied developmental science encyclopedia* (pp. 15–19). Thousand Oaks, CA: Sage.

Scales, P.C., Benson, P. L., Mannes, M., Hintz, N. R., Roehlkepartain, E. C., & Sullivan, T. K. (2003). *Other people's kids: Social expectations and American adults' involvement with children and adolescents.* New York: Kluwer Academic/Plenum.

Scales, P. C., & Leffert, N. (2004). *Developmental assets: A synthesis of the scientific research on adolescent development* (2nd ed.). Minneapolis, MN: Search Institute.

Seligman, M. E. P., & Csikszentmihalyi, M. (2000). Positive psychology: An introduction. *American Psychologist, 55*(1), 5–14.

Seligman, M. E. P., Steen, T., Park, N., & Peterson, C. (2005). Positive psychology progress: Empirical validation of interventions. *American Psychologist, 60*(5), 410–421.

Shahabi, L., Powell, L. H., Musick, M., Pargament, K. I., Thoresen, C. E., Williams, D.,…Ory, M. A. (2002). Correlates of self-perceptions of spirituality in American adults. *Annals of Behavioral Medicine, 24*(1), 59–68.

Small, S., & Memmo, M. (2004). Contemporary models of youth development and problem prevention: Toward an integration of terms, concepts, and models. *Family Relations, 53*, 3–11.

Stifoss-Hanssen, H. (1999). Religion and spirituality: What a European ear hears. *International Journal for the Psychology of Religion, 9*, 25–33.

Takanishi, R. (1993). An agenda for the integration of research and policy during early adolescence. In R. M. Lerner (Ed.), *Early adolescence: Perspectives on research, policy, and intervention* (pp. 457–470). Hillsdale, NJ: Erlbaum.

Theokas, C., Almerigi, J., Lerner, R. M., Dowling, E., Benson, P. L., Scales, P. C., & von Eye, A. (2005). Conceptualizing and modeling individual and ecological asset components of thriving in early adolescence. *Journal of Early Adolescence, 25*(1), 113–143.

Wagener, L. M., Furrow, J. L., King, P. E., Leffert, N., & Benson, P. L.(2003). Religion and developmental resources. *Review of Religious Research, 44*, 271–284.

Wagener, L. M., & Malony, H. N. (2006). Spiritual and religious pathology in childhood and adolescence. In E. C. Roehlkepartain, P. E. King, L. Wagener, & P. L. Benson (Eds.), *Handbook of spiritual development in childhood and adolescence* (pp. 137–149). Thousand Oaks, CA: Sage.

Werner, E. E., & Smith, R. S. (1982). *Vulnerable but invincible: A study of resilient children.* New York: McGraw-Hill.

Werner, E. E., & Smith, R. S. (1992). *Overcoming the odds: High risk children from birth to adulthood.* Ithaca, NY: Cornell University Press.

Zinnbauer, B. J., Pargament, K. I., & Scott, A. B. (1999). The emerging meanings of religiousness and spirituality: Problems and prospects. *Journal of Personality, 67*(6), 889–919.

PART 8

The Brain and Spiritual Experience

Transformation of Brain Structure and Spiritual Experience

Andrew B. Newberg

Abstract

This chapter will review the transformations of brain structure and function associated with spiritual experiences by considering the current state of neurophysiological investigations of spiritual experiences in terms of brain imaging, neurotransmitter studies, hormone function, and immune function. There are currently a number of techniques for studying the brain and its related functions. Such techniques include single photon emission computed tomography (SPECT), positron emission tomography (PET), and functional magnetic resonance imaging (fMRI). As will be discussed in this chapter, these imaging techniques can observe the very broad function of different structures of the brain as well as detailed neurotransmitter systems with regard to spiritual experience. Additional studies of various hormone levels, autonomic activity, and immune function can also be integrated into a comprehensive model that can be utilized to help better understand the biological correlates of spiritual experiences.

Key Words: brain, spirituality, religion, experience, fMRI, PET, SPECT, neurotransmitter

Introduction

The study of spiritual experience is ultimately the study of a complex mental process. However, the study of spiritual experience is also potentially one of the most important areas of research that may be pursued by science in the next decade. This may not be an understatement since spiritual experience offers a fascinating window into human consciousness, psychology, and experience; the relationship between mental states and body physiology; emotional and cognitive processing; and the biological correlates of religious and spiritual experiences. In the past 30 years, scientists have explored the biology of various components of spiritual experiences and practices in some detail. Many studies have focused on specific practices such as prayer or meditation rather than the specific moment of transformation that might be associated with such practices. However, since these practices can lead to spiritual experiences, there certainly is value in understanding them. Thus, initial studies of such spiritual practices have measured changes in autonomic activity such as heart rate and blood pressure as well as electroencephalographic changes. More recent studies have explored changes in hormonal and immunological function associated with meditation. While many of these studies have utilized peripheral measurements of different substances, they are consistent with a number of central neurochemical changes. Studies have also explored the clinical effects of such practices in both physical and psychological disorders. Functional neuroimaging has opened a new window into the investigation of states associated with spiritual practices by exploring the neurobiological correlates of these experiences.

Neuroimaging techniques include positron emission tomography (PET; Herzog et al., 1990–1991; Lou et al., 1999), single photon emission computed tomography (SPECT; Newberg et al., 2001), and functional magnetic resonance imaging (fMRI; Lazar et al., 2000). Each of these techniques provides different advantages and disadvantages in the study of meditation. Functional MRI, while having improved resolution over SPECT and the ability of immediate anatomic correlation, can be very difficult to utilize for the study of a variety of spiritual practices because the noise from the machine and the requirement of having the subject lie down, often is not conducive to spiritual practices. With regard to spiritual experiences, brain imaging studies are also somewhat problematic since the actual moment of a spiritual experience is almost impossible to predict, and if it were interrupted in order to obtain a scan or assess the exact mental state, then the spiritual experience might be severely altered. On the other hand, individuals performing spiritual practices, especially those with great proficiency, can often engage in their practice despite the distractions. One other possibility would be to image individuals before and then after a spiritual experience has occurred, to determine longer term, or "trait" related, changes in the brain's function. Thus, functional brain imaging offers potentially important techniques for studying spiritual experiences and their associated practices, although the best approach may depend on a number of factors.

By reviewing the existing data on neurophysiology and physiology with regard to spiritual experiences and the practices that may bring on such experiences, we can attempt to integrate the existing data into a comprehensive neurophysiological model. However, there are many possible neurophysiological changes that may occur during spiritual practices or experiences, even though they may not occur in every type of practice or experience, or in each individual. This model might be based upon practices such as deep meditation or prayer, which have been the initial target of research. We can also consider a variety of experiential elements of spiritual experiences to determine how each element may be related to specific brain processes. As will be described next, a neurobiological model of the effects of such practices on spiritual experiences (Fig. 31.1) may provide a framework of the neurological and physiological correlates of spiritual experiences and create a springboard for future research.

Activation of the Prefrontal and Cingulate Cortex

Since some approaches to spiritual experience involve practices in which the person on his or her own volition attempts to enter into such a state, we can begin with the structures of the brain that might be associated with the human will. Brain imaging studies suggest that willful acts and tasks that require sustained attention are initiated via activity in the prefrontal cortex (PFC), particularly in the right hemisphere (Frith, Friston, Liddle, & Frackowiak, 1991; Ingvar, 1994; Pardo, Fox, & Raichle, 1991; Posner & Petersen, 1990). The cingulate gyrus has also been shown to be involved in focusing attention, probably in conjunction with the PFC (Vogt, Finch, & Olson, 1992). Since spiritual practices such as meditation or prayer require intense focus of attention, it seems that there should be activation of the PFC as well as the cingulate gyrus. This notion is supported by the increased activity observed in these regions on several brain imaging studies of volitional types of meditation (Destexhe, Contreras, & Steriade, 1998; Kjaer et al., 2002; Streeter et al., 2007). For example, a study of Tibetan Buddhist meditators, who meditated for approximately 1 hour were found to have increased activity in the PFC bilaterally (greater on the right) and the cingulate gyrus during the practice of meditation.

Therefore, meditation appears to start by activating the prefrontal and cingulate cortex associated with the will or intent to clear the mind of thoughts or to focus on an object. Of course, meditation does not necessarily lead to spiritual experiences, so frontal lobe activity alone does not seem to provide a complete understanding of these experiences. In fact, some spiritual experiences are associated with feelings in which the self feels "overtaken" by the experience itself. The self feels as if it becomes absorbed or lost into the experience. If the frontal lobe is involved in willful activity, then a spiritual experience associated with a feeling of losing the self or of the original self being overcome by something spiritual, might be associated with a lack of activity in the frontal lobes. This has also been evaluated with a recent study of the practice of speaking in tongues, which is the Pentecostal practice associated with having the self surrender to the spirit of God. During such a practice, the vocalizations that occur sound like language, although they do not correlate with any particular language (Newberg, Wintering, Morgan, & Waldman, 2006). For the individual, the practice is experienced as the spirit of God "moving through them." During brain scan studies of speaking in tongues, the frontal lobes, particularly the areas involved in the willful generation of language, had reduced activity compared to the normal production of language. Thus, if the frontal lobe

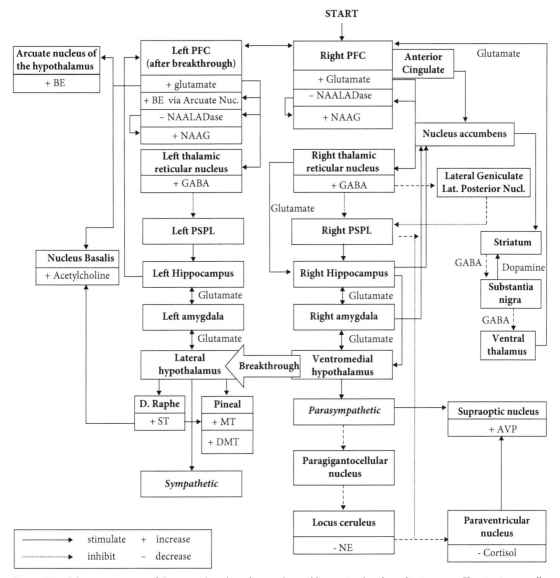

START

				Glutamate

Arcuate nucleus of the hypothalamus
+ BE

Left PFC (after breakthrough)
+ glutamate
+ BE via Arcuate Nuc.
– NAALADase
+ NAAG

Right PFC
+ Glutamate
– NAALADase
+ NAAG

Anterior Cingulate

Left thalamic reticular nucleus
+ GABA

Right thalamic reticular nucleus
+ GABA

Nucleus accumbens

Lateral Geniculate Lat. Posterior Nucl.

Left PSPL

Glutamate

Right PSPL

Striatum

Nucleus Basalis
+ Acetylcholine

Left Hippocampus

Right Hippocampus

GABA   Dopamine

Substantia nigra

Glutamate

Glutamate

Left amygdala

Right amygdala

GABA

Glutamate

Glutamate

Ventral thalamus

Lateral hypothalamus

Breakthrough

Ventromedial hypothalamus

D. Raphe
+ ST

Pineal
+ MT
+ DMT

Parasympathetic

Supraoptic nucleus
+ AVP

Sympathetic

Paragigantocellular nucleus

Locus ceruleus
– NE

Paraventricular nucleus
– Cortisol

⟶ stimulate   + increase
⋯⋯▸ inhibit   – decrease

Figure 31.1 Schematic overview of the neurophysiological network possibly associated with meditative states. The circuits generally apply to both hemispheres; however, much of the initial activity is on the right. AVP, vasoconstrictor arginine vasopressin; BE, beta-endorphin; GABA, gamma aminobutyric acid; NAAG, N-acetylaspartylglutamate; NE, norepinephrine; PFC, prefrontal cortex; PSPL, posterior superior parietal lobule.

activity increases, the spiritual experience might be perceived as having intense focus while if the frontal lobe decreases, the spiritual experience might be perceived as losing the sense of willful focus.

Thalamic Activation

Several animal studies have shown that the PFC, when activated, innervates the reticular nucleus of the thalamus (Cornwall & Phillipson, 1988), particularly as part of a more global attentional network (Portas et al., 1998). Such activation may be accomplished by the PFC's production and distribution of

the excitatory neurotransmitter, glutamate, which the PFC neurons use to communicate among themselves and to innervate other brain structures (Cheramy, Romo, & Glowinski, 1987). The thalamus itself governs the flow of sensory information to cortical processing areas via its interactions with two structures called the lateral geniculate and lateral posterior nucleus and also likely uses the glutamate system in order to activate neurons in other structures (Armony & LeDoux, 2000). The lateral geniculate nucleus receives raw visual data from the optic nerve and routes it to the visual cortex for processing (Andrews, Halpern, & Purves, 1997). The lateral posterior nucleus of the thalamus provides the posterior superior parietal lobule (PSPL) with the sensory information it needs to help determine the body's spatial orientation (Bucci, Conley, & Gallagher, 1999).

When excited, the reticular nucleus elaborates the inhibitory neurotransmitter, gamma aminobutyric acid (GABA), onto the lateral geniculate and lateral posterior nucleus, cutting off input to the PSPL and visual centers in proportion to the reticular nucleus activation (Destexhe et al., 1998). During practices such as meditation or prayer, because of the increased activity in the PFC, particularly on the right, there should be a concomitant increase in the activity in the reticular nucleus of the thalamus. While brain imaging studies of meditation have not had the resolution to distinguish the reticular nucleus, several recent SPECT studies have demonstrated a general increase in thalamic activity that was proportional to the activity levels in the PFC. This is consistent with, but does not confirm the specific interaction between the PFC and reticular nuclei. If the activation of the right PFC causes increased activity in the reticular nucleus during meditation, the result may be decreased sensory input entering into the PSPL, also called "deafferentation." Several studies have demonstrated an increase in GABA during meditation, possibly reflecting increased central GABA activity (Elias, Guich, & Wilson, 2000; Streeter et al., 2007). This functional deafferentation related to increased GABA would mean that fewer distracting outside stimuli would arrive at the visual cortex and PSPL enhancing the sense of focus. During spiritual experiences, similar mechanisms might be in place, although the interaction between the frontal lobe and the thalamus might be more complex such that some states may be associated with mutual increases, some with mutual decreases, and some with one turned on and the other off. The mechanism of the later is less clear at this time.

It should also be noted that the dopaminergic system, via the basal ganglia, is believed to participate in regulating the glutamatergic system and the interactions between the prefrontal cortex and subcortical structures. A PET study utilizing 11C-Raclopride to measure the dopaminergic tone during Yoga Nidra meditation demonstrated a significant increase in dopamine levels during the meditation practice (Kjaer et al., 2002). They hypothesized that this increase may be associated with the gating of cortical–subcortical interactions that leads to an overall decrease in readiness for action that is associated with this particular type of meditation. Similarly, there might eventually be a reciprocal decrease in prefrontal cortex activity associated with the inhibitory function of the thalamus. This decrease may effectively take the frontal lobes "off-line" and result in the sense of losing control. It is also well known that the dopaminergic system is involved in euphoric states and thus may be associated with spiritual experiences of high emotional states. Future studies will be necessary to elaborate on the role of dopamine in spiritual experience as well as the interactions between dopamine and other neurotransmitter systems.

Posterior Superior Parietal Lobule Deafferentation

The PSPL is involved in the analysis and integration of higher order visual, auditory, and somaesthetic information (Adair, Gilmore, Fennell, Gold, & Heilman, 1995). It is also involved in a complex attentional network that includes the PFC and thalamus (Fernandez-Duque & Posner, 2001). Through the reception of auditory and visual input from the thalamus, the PSPL is able to help generate a three-dimensional image of the body in space, provide a sense of spatial coordinates in which the body is oriented, help distinguish between objects, and exert influences in regard to objects that may be directly grasped and manipulated (Lynch, 1980). These functions of the PSPL might be critical for distinguishing between the self and the external world. It should be noted that another study has suggested that the superior temporal lobe may play a more important role in body spatial representation (Karnath, Ferber, & Himmelbach, 2001). While it remains to be seen what is the actual relationship between the parietal and temporal lobes in terms of spatial representation, these structures likely play a mutual role in the spatial effects associated with spiritual experiences.

In particular, deafferentation of these orienting areas of the brain may be an important aspect in the physiology of spiritual practices and experiences. If, for example, there is deafferentation of the PSPL by the reticular nucleus's GABAergic effects, the person may begin to lose his or her usual ability to spatially define the self and help to orient the self. This is an experience frequently associated with meditative and prayer practices as well as more generally with spiritual experiences. Deafferentation of the PSPL has also been supported by imaging studies demonstrating decreased activity in this region during intense meditation (Destexhe et al., 1998; Streeter et al., 2007). Furthermore, brain imaging studies have also shown a correlation between increasing activity in the thalamus and decreasing activity in the PSPL.

Hippocampus and Amygdala Activation

In addition to the complex cortical-thalamic activity, spiritual practices and experiences might also be associated with altered activity in the limbic system, particularly since stimulation of limbic structures is associated with profound emotional responses (Fish, Gloor, Quesney, & Oliver, 1993; Saver & Rabin, 1997). The hippocampus acts to moderate cortical arousal and responsiveness, via rich and extensive interconnections with the prefrontal cortex, other neocortical areas, the amygdala, and the hypothalamus (Joseph, 1996). Hippocampus stimulation has been shown to diminish cortical responsiveness and arousal; however, if cortical arousal is initially at a low level, then hippocampal stimulation tends to augment cortical activity (Redding, 1967). The ability of the hippocampus to stimulate or inhibit neuronal activity in other structures likely relies upon the glutamate and GABA systems, respectively (Newman & Grace, 1999).

It has been suggested that the blocking of sensory information (i.e., deafferentation) of the PSPL might be associated with the loss of the sense of self and/or the orientation of that self to other objects in the world (d' Aquili & Newberg, 1993). Since this loss of orientation of the self is often described in spiritual experiences, the deafferentation of the PSPL might be an important mechanism underlying such experiences. If partial deafferentation of the right PSPL occurs during a spiritual experience, the result may be stimulation of the right hippocampus because of the inverse relationship between hippocampus and cortical activity. If, in addition, there is simultaneous direct stimulation of the right hippocampus via the thalamus (as part of the known attentional network) and mediated by glutamate, then a powerful recruitment of stimulation of the right hippocampus might occur. Right hippocampal activity may ultimately enhance the stimulatory function of the PFC on the thalamus via a structure called the nucleus accumbens, which gates the neural input from the PFC to the thalamus via the neuromodulatory effects of dopamine (Chow & Cummings, 1999; Newman & Grace, 1999).

The hippocampus greatly influences the amygdala, such that they complement and interact in the generation of attention, emotion, and certain types of imagery (Sudsuang, Chentanez, & Veluvan, 1991). It seems that much of the prefrontal modulation of emotion is via the hippocampus and its connections with the amygdala (Poletti & Sujatanond, 1980). Because of this reciprocal interaction between the amygdala and hippocampus, the activation of the right hippocampus likely stimulates the right amygdala as well. The results of several imaging studies support the notion of increased activity in the regions of the amygdala and hippocampus during practices such as meditation (Kjaer et al., 2002). However, whether such functional changes are associated with spiritual experience more broadly remains to be seen.

Hypothalamic and Autonomic Nervous System Changes

The hypothalamus is extensively interconnected with the limbic system. Stimulation of the right amygdala has been shown to result in stimulation of the hypothalamus with a subsequent stimulation of the peripheral parasympathetic system (Davis, 1992). Increased parasympathetic activity should be associated with the subjective sensation first of relaxation, and eventually, of a more profound quiescence. Activation of the parasympathetic system would also cause a reduction in heart rate and respiratory rate. All of these physiological responses have been observed during meditation (Jevning, Wallace, & Beidebach, 1992). Spiritual experiences can have a number of strong emotional responses ranging from bliss to ecstasy. Blissful elements of such experiences may be mediated in part by activity in the parasympathetic system.

Typically, when breathing and heart rate slow down, the paragigantocellular nucleus of the medulla in the brain stem ceases to innervate a structure called the locus ceruleus (LC), also in the brain stem. The LC produces and distributes the stress molecule, norepinephrine (NE, Foote, 1987), a neuromodulator that increases the susceptibility of brain regions to sensory input by amplifying strong stimuli, while simultaneously gating out weaker activations and cellular "noise" that fall below the activation threshold (Waterhouse, Moises, & Woodward, 1998). Decreased stimulation of the LC should result in a decrease in the level of NE (Van Bockstaele & Aston-Jones, 1995). The breakdown products of catecholamines such as NE and epinephrine have generally been found to be reduced in the urine and plasma during meditation practices (Infante et al., 2001; Walton, Pugh, Gelderloos, & Macrae, 1995), which may simply reflect the systemic change in autonomic balance. However, it is not inconsistent with a cerebral decrease in NE levels as well. During a spiritual practice, the reduced firing of the paragigantocellular nucleus may cut back its innervation of the locus ceruleus, which densely and specifically supplies the PSPL and the lateral posterior nucleus with NE (Janal, Colt, Clark, & Glusman, 1984). Thus, a reduction in NE would decrease the impact of sensory input on the PSPL, contributing to its deafferentation described earlier, and helping to enhance the experience of the loss of the sense of self and space. Thus, spiritual experiences could be facilitated by such neuronal interactions.

If the aforementioned processes occur during spiritual practices, it might be expected that the locus ceruleus would also deliver less NE to the hypothalamic paraventricular nucleus. The paraventricular nucleus of the hypothalamus typically secretes corticotropin-releasing hormone (CRH) in response to innervation by NE from the locus ceruleus (Ziegler, Cass, & Herman, 1999). This CRH stimulates the anterior pituitary gland to release adrenocorticotropic hormone (ACTH) (Livesey, Evans, Mulligan, & Donald, 2000). ACTH, in turn, stimulates the adrenal cortex to produce cortisol, one of the body's primary stress hormones (Davies, Keyon, & Fraser, 1985). Decreasing NE from the locus ceruleus during meditation or prayer would likely decrease the production of CRH by the paraventricular nucleus and ultimately decrease cortisol levels (Albin & Greenamyre, 1992; Jevning, Wilson, & Davidson, 1978; Sudsuang et al., 1991), reflecting a reduced stress state.

A drop in blood pressure associated with increased parasympathetic activity would be expected to relax the arterial baroreceptors that monitor blood pressure and lead to the caudal ventral medulla in the brain stem to decrease its GABAergic inhibition of the supraoptic nucleus of the hypothalamus. This lack of inhibition can provoke the supraoptic nucleus to release the vasoconstrictor arginine vasopressin (AVP), thereby tightening the arteries and returning blood pressure to normal (Renaud, 1996). But AVP has also been shown to contribute to the general maintenance of positive mood (Pietrowsky, Braun, Fehm, Pauschinger, & Born, 1991), decrease self-perceived fatigue and arousal, and significantly improve the consolidation of new memories and learning (Weingartner et al., 1991). During spiritual practices, plasma AVP has been shown to increase dramatically, although it is not known whether there will be a similar increase associated with more spiritual experiences (O'Halloran et al., 1985). AVP could help to enhance the memory of a particular experience, perhaps explaining the subjective phenomenon that meditative experiences are remembered and described in very vivid terms.

Prefrontal Cortex Effects on Other Neurochemical Systems

As PFC activity increases, it produces increasing levels of glutamate in the brain. Increased glutamate can stimulate the arcuate nucleus of the hypothalamus to release beta-endorphin (Kiss, Kocsis, Csaki, Gorcs, & Halasz, 1997). Beta-endorphin (BE) is an endogenous opioid produced, and it is distributed to the brain's subcortical areas (Yadid, Zangen, Herzberg, Nakash, & Sagen, 2000). BE is known to depress respiration, reduce fear, reduce pain, and produce sensations of joy and euphoria (Janal et al., 1984). That such effects have been described during spiritual practices and experiences may implicate some degree of BE release related to the increased PFC activity. Furthermore, the joy and euphoric feelings associated with spiritual experience might similarly implicate the endogenous opioid system. Meditation has been found to disrupt diurnal rhythms of BE and ACTH, while not affecting diurnal cortisol rhythms (Infante et al., 1998). Thus, the relationship between opioid receptors and various spiritual experiences is not clear, especially in light of one very limited study demonstrating that blocking the opiate receptors with naloxone did not affect the experience or EEG associated with meditation (Sim & Tsoi, 1992).

Glutamate itself activates N-methyl d-Aspartate (NMDA) receptors, but excess glutamate can kill the neurons expressing the NMDA receptors through excitotoxic processes (Albin & Greenamyre, 1992). If glutamate levels approach excitotoxic concentrations during intense spiritual experiences, the brain might limit its production of N-acetylated-alpha-linked-acidic dipeptidase, which converts the endogenous NMDA antagonist N-acetylaspartylglutamate (NAAG) into glutamate (Thomas, Vornov, Olkowski, Merion, & Slusher, 2000). The resultant increase in NAAG would protect cells from excitotoxic damage. However, there is an important side effect since the NMDA receptor inhibitor, NAAG, is functionally analogous to the disassociative hallucinogens ketamine, phencyclidine, and nitrous oxide (Jevtovic-Todorovic, Wozniak, Benshoff, & Olney, 2001). These NMDA receptor antagonists produce a variety of states that may be characterized as either schizophrenomimetic or mystical, such as out-of-body and near-death experiences (Vollenweider et al., 1997). Whether such substances are elaborated within the brain during the short interval associated with a spiritual experience is not yet clear.

Autonomic-Cortical Activity

In the early 1970s, Gellhorn and Kiely developed a model of the physiological processes involved in meditation based almost exclusively on autonomic nervous system (ANS) activity, which while somewhat limited, indicated the importance of the ANS during such experiences (Gellhorn & Keily, 1972). These authors suggested that intense stimulation of either the sympathetic or parasympathetic system, if continued, could ultimately result in simultaneous discharge of both systems (what might be considered a "breakthrough" of the other system). If such a breakthrough was associated with the most intense, and potentially most spiritual types of spiritual experiences (d'Aquili & Newberg, 1993), it might help explain some of the conflicting subjective descriptions of these experiences—namely that they involve feelings of both high energy and intense bliss. Several studies have demonstrated predominant parasympathetic activity during meditation practices associated with decreased heart rate and blood pressure, decreased respiratory rate, and decreased oxygen metabolism (d'Aquili & Newberg, 1993; Travis, 2001; Yadid et al., 2000). However, recent studies of different meditative techniques suggested a mutual activation of parasympathetic and sympathetic systems by demonstrating an increase in the variability of heart rate during these practices (Peng et al., 1999). The increased variation in heart rate was hypothesized to reflect activation of both the parasympathetic and sympathetic arms of the autonomic nervous system. This notion also fits the characteristic description of meditative states in which there is a sense of overwhelming calmness as well as significant alertness. Also, the notion of mutual activation of both arms of the ANS is consistent with recent developments in the study of autonomic interactions (Hugdahl, 1996).

Serotonergic Activity

Activation of the autonomic nervous system can result in intense stimulation of structures in the lateral hypothalamus and median forebrain bundle that are known to produce both ecstatic and blissful feelings when directly stimulated (Olds & Forbes, 1981). Stimulation of the lateral hypothalamus can also result in changes in serotonergic activity. In fact, several studies have shown that after meditation, the breakdown products of ST in urine are significantly increased, suggesting an overall elevation in ST levels during meditation (Albin & Greenamyre, 1992). Serotonin is a neuromodulator that densely supplies the visual centers of the temporal lobe, where it strongly influences the flow of visual associations generated by this area (Janal et al., 1984). The cells of the dorsal raphe near the brain stem produce and distribute ST when innervated by the lateral hypothalamus (Aghajanian, Sprouse, & Rasmussen, 1987) and also when activated by the prefrontal cortex (Juckel, Mendlin, & Jacobs, 1999). Moderately increased levels of ST appear to correlate with positive affect, while low ST often signifies depression (Van Praag & De Haan, 1980). This relationship has clearly been demonstrated with regard to the effects of the selective serotonin reuptake inhibitor medications, which are widely used for the treatment of depression. When cortical ST receptors (especially in the temporal lobes) are activated, however, the stimulation can result in a hallucinogenic effect. Tryptamine-based psychedelic drugs such as psylocybin and LSD seem to take advantage of this mechanism to produce their extraordinary visual associations (Aghajanian & Marek, 1999). The mechanism by which this appears to occur is that ST inhibits the lateral geniculate nucleus, greatly reducing the amount of visual information that can pass through (Funke & Eysel, 1995; Yoshida, Sasa, & Takaori, 1984). If combined with reticular nucleus inhibition of the lateral geniculate, ST may increase the fluidity of temporal visual associations in the absence of sensory input, possibly resulting in the internally generated imagery that has been described during certain spiritual states.

Increased ST levels can affect several other neurochemical systems. An increase in serotonin has a modulatory effect on dopamine, suggesting a link between the serotonergic and dopaminergic system that may enhance feelings of euphoria (Vollenweider, Vontobel, Hell, & Leenders, 1999), frequently described during spiritual states. Serotonin, in conjunction with the increased glutamate, has been shown to stimulate another structure called the nucleus basalis to release acetylcholine, which has important modulatory influences throughout the cortex (Manfridi, Brambilla, & Mancia, 1999; Zhelyazkova-Savova, Giovannini, & Pepeu, 1997). Increased acetylcholine in the frontal lobes has been shown to augment the attentional system and in the parietal lobes to enhance orienting without altering sensory input (Walton et al., 1995). Increased serotonin combined with lateral hypothalamic innervation of the pineal gland may lead the latter to increase production of the neu-rohormone melatonin (MT) from the conversion of ST (Moller, 1992). Melatonin has been shown to depress the central nervous system and reduce pain sensitivity (Shaji & Kulkarni, 1998). During meditation, blood plasma MT has been found to increase sharply (Tooley, Armstrong, Norman, & Sali, 2000), which may contribute to the feelings of calmness and decreased awareness of pain (Dollins et al., 1993). Under circumstances of heightened activation, pineal enzymes can also endogenously synthesize the powerful hallucinogen 5-methoxy-dimethyltryptamine (DMT) (Monti & Christian, 1981). Several studies have linked DMT to a vari-ety of mystical states, including out-of-body experi-ences, distortion of time and space, and interaction with supernatural entities (Strassan & Clifford, 1994; Strassman, Clifford, Qualls, & Berg, 1996). Hyperstimulation of the pineal at this step, then, could also lead to DMT production that can be associated with the wide variety of mystical-type experiences associated with that hallucinogen.

Conclusion

Much work still needs to be done to better elu-cidate the intricate neurobiological processes asso-ciated with spiritual experiences. Most available studies have explored specific spiritual practices such as meditation or prayer upon which much of the hypothetical model presented in this chapter is based. However, the lack of data on the larger topic of spiritual experiences places much of these theo-ries on speculative grounds. Regardless, the neuro-physiological effects that have been observed during spiritual practices and experiences seem to outline a consistent pattern of changes involving certain key brain structures in conjunction with autonomic nervous system and hormonal changes. These changes are also reflected in neurochemical changes involving the endogenous opioid, GABA, norepi-nephrine, serotonergic, and dopaminergic receptor systems. The model presented here, based on cur-rent literature about the interaction of these systems as well as brain imaging studies of spiritual practices, is an integrated hypothesis that may help elucidate the mechanism underlying the physical and psycho-logical effects of such practices and experiences. It should also be mentioned in closing that whatever neurophysiological basis of spiritual experience is eventually discovered, it does not necessarily reduce such experience to mere biology. The subjective state and the phenomenology of such experiences cannot be ignored or dismissed, especially considering that

such experiences carry with them not only spiritual properties but a very strong sense they represent a more fundamental sense of reality compared to that observed by science. Furthermore, the physiological means of entering into a spiritual state may simply reflect the brain's response to that experience rather than establish a true causal relationship. Regardless of the ultimate basis of such experiences, elucidat-ing their physiological and psychological basis can only help in our overall understanding of how spir-itual experience comes about.

Future Directions

1. More studies are required in order to expand the database regarding the relationship between an extensive variety of spiritual practices and experiences to neurobiological correlates.

2. More studies are required to address the relationship between neurotransmitter systems and spiritual experiences.

3. More studies are required to try to capture specific moments that spiritual experiences occur.

4. More studies are required to evaluate how specific interventions that stimulate spiritual experiences relate to neurobiology.

5. More studies are required to correlate the subjective components of spiritual experiences to neurobiological correlates.

6. More studies should be conducted to evaluate other aspects of religious and spiritual phenomena, such as theological concepts, forgiveness, and altruism.

7. More scholarship is required to assess the causal relationship between neurobiology and spirituality.

References

Adair, K. C., Gilmore, R. L., Fennell, E. B., Gold, M., & Heilman, K. M. (1995). Anosognosia during intracarotid barbiturate anaesthesia: Unawareness or amnesia for weak-ness. *Neurology, 45,* 241–243.

Aghajanian, G. K., & Marek, G. J. (1999). Serotonin and hal-lucinogens. *Neuropsychopharmacology, 21,* 16S–23S.

Aghajanian, G., Sprouse, J., & Rasmussen, K. (1987). In H. Meltzer (Ed.), *Psychopharmacology, the third generation of progress* (pp. 141–149). New York: Raven Press.

Albin, R., & Greenamyre, J. (1992). Alternative excitotoxic hypotheses. *Neurology, 42,* 733–738.

Andrews, T. J., Halpern, S. D., & Purves, D. (1997). Correlated size variations in human visual cortex, lateral genicu-late nucleus, and optic tract. *Journal of Neuroscience, 17,* 2859–2868.

Armony, J. L., & LeDoux, J. E. (2000). How danger is encoded: Toward a systems, cellular, and computational understand-ing of cognitive–emotional interactions in fear. In M. S.

Gazzaniga (Ed.), The new cognitive neurosciences (pp. 1073–1074). Cambridge, MA: MIT Press.

Bucci, D. J., Conley, M., & Gallagher, M. (1999). Thalamic and basal forebrain cholinergic connections of the rat posterior parietal cortex. *Neuroreport, 10*, 941–945.

Cheramy, A., Romo, R., & Glowinski, J. (1987). Role of corticostriatal glutamatergic neurons in the presynaptic control of dopamine release. In M. Sandler, C. Feuerstein, & B. Scatton (Eds.), *Neurotransmitter interactions in the basal ganglia* (pp. 131–133). New York: Raven Press.

Chow, T. W., & Cummings, J. L. (1999). In B. L. Miller & J. L. Cummings (Eds.), *The human frontal lobes* (pp. 3–26). New York: The Guilford Press.

Cornwall, J., & Phillipson, O. T. (1988). Mediodorsal and reticular thalamic nuclei receive collateral axons from prefrontal cortex and laterodorsal tegmental nucleus in the rat. *Neuroscience Letters, 88*, 121–126.

d'Aquili, E. G., & Newberg, A. B. (1993). Religious and mystical states: A neuropsychological model. *Zygon, 28*, 177–199.

Davies, E., Keyon, C. J., & Fraser, R. (1985). The role of calcium ions in the mechanism of ACTH stimulation of cortisol synthesis. *Steroids, 45*, 557.

Davis, M. (1992). The role of the amygdala in fear and anxiety. *Annual Review of Neuroscience, 15*, 353–375.

Destexhe, A., Contreras, D., & Steriade, M. (1998). Mechanisms underlying the synchronizing action of corticothalamic feedback through inhibition of thalamic relay cells. *Journal of Neurophysiology, 79*, 999–1016.

Dollins, A. B., Lynch, H. J., Wurtman, R. J., Deng, M. H., Kischka, K. U., Gleason, R. E., & Lieberman, H. R. (1993). Effect of pharmacological daytime doses of melatonin on human mood and performance. *Psychopharmacology, 112*, 490–496.

Elias, A. N., Guich, S., & Wilson, A. F. (2000). Ketosis with enhanced GABAergic tone promotes physiological changes in transcendental meditation. *Medical Hypotheses, 54*, 660–662.

Fernandez-Duque, D,, & Posner, M. I. (2001). Brain imaging of attentional networks in normal and pathological states. *Journal of Clinical and Experimental Neuropsychology, 23*, 74–93.

Fish, D. R., Gloor, P., Quesney, F. L., & Oliver, A. (1993). Clinical responses to electrical brain stimulation of the temporal and frontal lobes in patients with epilepsy. *Brain, 116*, 397–414.

Foote, S. (1987). Extrathalamic modulation of cortical function. *Annual Review of Neuroscience, 10*, 67–95.

Frith, C. D., Friston, K., Liddle, P. F., & Frackowiak, R. S. (1991). Willed action and the prefrontal cortex in man. A study with PET. *Proceedings of the Royal Society of London B: Biological Sciences, 244*, 241–246.

Funke, K., & Eysel, U. T. (1995). Possible enhancement of GABAergic inputs to cat dorsal lateral geniculate relay cells by serotonin. *Neuroreport, 6*, 474–476.

Gellhorn, E., & Kiely, W. F. (1972). Mystical states of consciousness: Neurophysiological and clinical aspects. *Journal of Nervous and Mental Disorders, 154*, 399–405.

Herzog, H., Lele, V. R., Kuwert, T., Langen, K. J., Rota Kops, E., & Feinendegen, L. E. (1990–1991). Changed pattern of regional glucose metabolism during Yoga meditative relaxation. *Neuropsychobiol, 23*, 182–187.

Hugdahl, K. (1996). Cognitive influences on human autonomic nervous system function. *Current Opinion in Neurobiology, 6*, 252–258.

Infante, J. R., Peran, F., Martinez, M., Roldan, A., Poyatos, R., Ruiz, C., ... Garrido, F. (1998). ACTH and beta-endorphin in transcendental meditation. *Physiology and Behavior, 64*, 311–315.

Infante, J. R., Torres-Avisbal, M., Pinel, P., Vallejo, J. A., Peran, F., Gonzalez, F., ... Latre, J. M. (2001). Catecholamine levels in practitioners of the transcendental meditation technique. *Physiology and Behavior, 72*, 141–146.

Ingvar, D. H. (1994). The will of the brain: Cerebral correlates of willful acts. *Journal of Theoretical Biology, 171*, 7–12.

Janal, M., Colt, E., Clark, W., & Glusman, M. (1984). Pain sensitivity, mood and plasma endocrine levels in man following long-distance running: Effects of naxalone. *Pain, 19*, 13–25.

Jevning, R., Wallace, R. K., & Beidebach, M. (1992). The physiology of meditation: A review. A wakeful hypometabolic integrated response. *Neuroscience and Biobehavioral Review, 16*, 415–424.

Jevning, R., Wilson, A. F., & Davidson, J. M. (1978). Adrenocortical activity during meditation. *Hormones and Behavior, 10*, 54–60.

Jevtovic-Todorovic, V., Wozniak, D. F., Benshoff, N. D., & Olney, J. W. (2001). A comparative evaluation of the neurotoxic properties of ketamine and nitrous oxide. *Brain Research, 895*, 264–267.

Joseph, R. (1996). *Neuropsychology, neuropsychiatry, and behavioral neurology*. New York: Williams & Wilkins.

Juckel, G. J., Mendlin, A., & Jacobs, B. L. (1999). Electrical stimulation of rat medial prefrontal cortex enhances forebrain serotonin output: Implications for electroconvulsive therapy and transcranial magnetic stimulation in depression. *Neuropsychopharmacology, 21*, 391–398.

Karnath, H. O., Ferber, S., & Himmelbach, M. (2001). Spatial awareness is a function of the temporal not the posterior parietal lobe. *Nature, 411*, 950–953.

Kiss, J., Kocsis, K., Csaki, A., Gorcs, T. J., & Halasz, B. (1997). Metabotropic glutamate receptor in GHRH and beta-endorphin neurons of the hypothalamic arcuate nucleus. *Neuroreport, 8*, 3703–3707.

Kjaer, T. W., Bertelsen, C., Piccini, P., Brooks, D., Alving, J., & Lou, H. C. (2002). Increased dopamine tone during meditation-induced change of consciousness. *Brain Research Cognitive Brain Research, 13*(2), 255–259.

Lazar, S. W., Bush, G., Gollub, R. L., Fricchione, G. L., Khalsa, G., & Benson, H. (2000). Functional brain mapping of the relaxation response and meditation. *Neuroreport, 11*, 1581–1585.

Livesey, J. H., Evans, M. J., Mulligan, R., & Donald, R. A. (2000). Interactions of CRH, AVP and cortisol in the secretion of ACTH from perifused equine anterior pituitary cells: "Permissive" roles for cortisol and CRH. *Endocrinology Research, 26*, 445–463.

Lou, H. C., Kjaer, T. W., Friberg, L., Wildschiodtz, G., Holm, S., & Nowak, M. (1999). A 15O-H2O PET study of meditation and the resting state of normal consciousness. *Human Brain Mapping, 7*, 98–105.

Lynch, J. C. (1980). The functional organization of posterior parietal association cortex. *Behavioral and Brain Sciences, 3*, 485–499.

Manfridi, A., Brambilla, D., & Mancia, M. (1999). Stimulation of NMDA and AMPA receptors in the rat nucleus basalis of Meynert affects sleep. *American Journal of Physiology, 277*, R1488–1492.

Moller, M. (1992). Fine structure of pinealopetal innervation of the mammalian pineal gland. *Microscopy Research and Technique, 21*, 188–204.

Monti, J. A., & Christian, S. T. (1981). N-N-dimethyltryptamine: An endogenous hallucinogen. *International Review of Neurobiology, 22*, 83–110.

Newberg, A. B., Alavi, A., Baime, M., Pourdehnad, M., Santanna, J., d'Aquili, E. (2001). The measurement of regional cerebral blood flow during the complex cognitive task of meditation: A preliminary SPECT study. *Psychiatry Research: Neuroimaging, 106*, 113–122.

Newberg, A., Wintering, N. A., Morgan, D., & Waldman, M. R. (2006). The measurement of regional cerebral blood flow during glossolalia: A preliminary SPECT study. *Psychiatry Research: Neuroimaging, 148*(1), 67–71.

Newman, J., & Grace, A. A. (1999). Binding across time: The selective gating of frontal and hippocampal systems modulating working memory and attentional states. *Consciousness and Cognition, 8*, 196–212.

O'Halloran, J. P., Jevning, R., Wilson, A. F., Skowsky, R., Walsh, R. N., & Alexander, C. (1985). Hormonal control in a state of decreased activation: potentiation of arginine vasopressin secretion. *Physiology and Behavior, 35*, 591–595.

Olds, M. E., & Forbes, J. L. (1981). The central basis of motivation, intracranial self-stimulation studies. *Annual Review of Psychology, 32*, 523–574.

Pardo, J. V., Fox, P. T., & Raichle, M. E. (1991). Localization of a human system for sustained attention by positron emission tomography. *Nature, 349*, 61–64.

Peng, C. K., Mietus, J. E., Liu, Y., Khalsa, G., Douglas, P. S., Benson, H., & Goldberger, A. L. (1999). Exaggerated heart rate oscillations during two meditation techniques. *International Journal of Cardiology, 70*, 101–107.

Pietrowsky, R., Braun, D., Fehm, H. L., Pauschinger, P., & Born, J. (1991). Vasopressin and oxytocin do not influence early sensory processing but affect mood and activation in man. *Peptides, 12*, 1385–1391.

Poletti, C. E., & Sujatanond, M. (1980). Evidence for a second hippocampal efferent pathway to hypothalamus and basal forebrain comparable to fornix system: A unit study in the monkey. *Journal of Neurophysiology, 44*, 514–531.

Portas, C. M., Rees, G., Howseman, A. M., Josephs, O., Turner, R., & Frith, C. D. (1998). A specific role for the thalamus in mediating the interaction attention and arousal in humans. *Journal of Neuroscience, 18*, 8979–8989.

Posner, M. I., & Petersen, S. E. (1990). The attention system of the human brain. *Annual Review of Neuroscience, 13*, 25–42.

Redding, F. K. (1967). Modification of sensory cortical evoked potentials by hippocampal stimulation. *Electroencephalography Clinical Neurophysiology, 22*, 74–83.

Renaud, L. P. (1996). CNS pathways mediating cardiovascular regulation of vasopressin. *Clinical and Experimental Pharmacology and Physiology, 23*, 157–160.

Saver, J. L., & Rabin, J. (1997). The neural substrates of religious experience. *Journal of Neuropsychiatry and Clinical Neuroscience, 9*, 498–510.

Streeter, C. C., Jensen, J. E., Perlmutter, R. M., Cabral, H. J., Tian, H., Terhune, D. B.,...Renshaw, P. F. (2007). Yoga Asana sessions increase brain GABA levels: A pilot study. *Journal of Alternative and Complementary Medicine, 13*(4), 419–426.

Sudsuang, R., Chentanez, V., & Veluvan, K. (1991). Effects of Buddhist meditation on serum cortisol and total protein

levels, blood pressure, pulse rate, lung volume and reaction time. *Physiology and Behavior, 50*, 543–548.

Shaji, A. V., & Kulkarni, S. K. (1998). Central nervous system depressant activities of melatonin in rats and mice. *Indian Journal of Experimental Biology, 36*, 257–263.

Sim, M. K., & Tsoi, W. F. (1992). The effects of centrally acting drugs on the EEG correlates of meditation. *Biofeedback and Self Regulation 17*, 215–220.

Strassan, R. J., & Clifford, R. (1994). Dose-response study of N,N-dimethyltrypamine in humans. I: Neuroendocrine, autonomic, and cardiovascular effects. *Archives of General Psychiatry, 51*, 85–97.

Strassman, R. J., Clifford, R., Qualls, R., & Berg, L. (1996). Differential tolerance to biological and subjective effects of four closely spaced doses of N,N-dimethyltrypamine in humans. *Biological Psychiatry, 39*, 784–795.

Thomas, A. G., Vornov, J. J., Olkowski, J. L., Merion, A. T., & Slusher, B. S. (2000). N-Acetylated alpha-linked acidic dipeptidase converts N-acetylaspartylglutamate from a neuroprotectant to a neurotoxin. *Journal of Pharmacology and Experimental Therapeutics, 295*, 16–22.

Tooley, G. A., Armstrong, S. M., Norman, T. R., & Sali, A. (2000). Acute increases in night-time plasma melatonin levels following a period of meditation. *Biological Psychology, 53*, 69–78.

Travis, F. (2001). Autonomic and EEG patterns distinguish transcending from other experiences during transcendental meditation practice. *International Journal of Psychophysiology, 42*, 1 9.

Van Bockstaele, E. J., & Aston-Jones, G. (1995). Integration in the ventral medulla and coordination of sympathetic, pain and arousal functions. *Clinical and Experimental Hypertension, 17*, 153–165.

Van Praag, H., & De Haan, S. (1980). Depression vulnerability and 5-Hydroxytryptophan prophylaxis. *Psychiatry Research, 3*, 75–83.

Vogt, B. A., Finch, D. M., & Olson, C. R. (1992). Functional heterogeneity in cingulate cortex: the anterior executive and posterior evaluative regions. *Cerebral Cortex, 2*, 435–443.

Vollenweider, F. X., Leenders, K. L., Scharfetter, C., Antonini, A., Maguire, P., Missimer J., & Angst, J. (1997). Metabolic hyperfrontality and psychopathology in the ketamine model of psychosis using positron emission tomography (PET) and [18F]fluorodeoxyglucose (FDG). *European Neuropsychopharmacology, 7*, 9–24.

Vollenweider, F. X., Vontobel, P., Hell, D., & Leenders, K. L. (1999). 5-HT modulation of dopamine release in basal ganglia in psilocybin-induced psychosis in man—a PET study with [11C]raclopride. *Neuropsychopharmacology,20*, 424–433.

Walton, K. G., Pugh, N. D., Gelderloos, P., & Macrae, P. (1995). Stress reduction and preventing hypertension: preliminary support for a psychoneuroendocrine mechanism. *Journal of Alternative and Complementary Medicine, 1*, 263–283.

Waterhouse, B. D., Moises, H. C., & Woodward, D. J. (1998). Phasic activation of the locus coeruleus enhances responses of primary sensory cortical neurons to peripheral receptive field stimulation. *Brain Research, 790*, 33–44.

Weingartner, H., Gold, P., Ballenger, J. C., Smallberg, S. A., Summers, R., Rubinow, D. R.,...Goodwin, F. K. (1981). Effects of vasopressin on human memory functions. *Science, 211*, 601–603.

Yadid, G., Zangen, A., Herzberg, U., Nakash, R., & Sagen, J. (2000). Alterations in endogenous brain beta-endorphin release by adrenal medullary transplants in the spinal cord. *Neuropsychopharmacology, 23*, 709–716.

Yoshida, M., Sasa, M., & Takaori, S. (1984). Serotonin-mediated inhibition from dorsal raphe neurons nucleus of neurons in dorsal lateral geniculate and thalamic reticular nuclei. *Brain Research, 290*, 95–105.

Zhelyazkova-Savova, M., Giovannini, M. G., & Pepeu, G. (1997). Increase of cortical acetylcholine release after systemic administration of chlorophenylpiperazine in the rat: An in vivo microdialysis study. *Neuroscience Letters, 236*, 151–154.

Ziegler, D. R., Cass, W. A., & Herman, J. P. (1999). Excitatory influence of the locus coeruleus in hypothalamic-pituitary-adrenocortical axis responses to stress. *Journal of Neuroendocrinology, 11*, 361–369.

Neuroimaging and Spiritual Practice

Mario Beauregard

Abstract

In this chapter, we first define religious, spiritual, and mystical experiences (RSMEs). We then review clinical data suggesting a role for the temporal lobe in RSMEs. The possibility of experimentally inducing such experiences by stimulating the temporal lobe with weak electromagnetic currents is examined. The limbic-marker hypothesis is also presented. In the following section, we examine the findings of neuroimaging studies of RSMEs conducted to date. Since meditation is often associated with spiritual practice, we review in the fourth section neuroimaging studies of diverse meditative states. In the next section, we discuss neuroimaging data and phenomenology of RSMEs with respect to the mind-brain problem. In the last section, we provide a few concluding remarks and propose new opportunities for expanding the neuroscience of spirituality.

Key Words: neuroimaging, brain, temporal lobe, religious, spiritual, and mystical experiences (RSMEs), meditation, mind-brain problem

Introduction

The past decade has seen the emergence of the neuroscience of spirituality. The central objective of this domain of research is to use neuroscience methods (e.g., brain imaging, stimulation, psychopharmacological, electrophysiological recordings) to explore the neural mechanisms mediating religious, spiritual, and mystical experiences (RSMEs). These experiences relate to a fundamental dimension of human existence and are frequently reported across all cultures (Hardy, 1975; Hay, 1990). One of the basic assumptions of this emergent field is that RSMEs are brain mediated; that is, they have neurophysiological correlates, as are all other aspects of human experience. Regarding this issue, it is important to fully appreciate that elucidating the neural substrates of RSMEs does not diminish or depreciate their meaning and value.

Religious experiences arise from following a religious tradition and involve a contact with the divine or a religious figure. Spiritual experiences are subjective experiences that do not arise from following a religious tradition. These experiences, however, can also bring the experiencer into contact with the divine or a transcendent reality. Mysticism refers to the pursuit of an altered state of consciousness that enables the mystic to commune with, or identify with, a divinity or ultimate reality through an immediate, direct, intuitive knowledge and experience. James (1902) proposed that ineffability, noetic quality, transiency, and passivity are the most important features of mystical experiences. Other characteristics attributed to mystical experiences include feelings of unity, peace and bliss, numinosity, sense of incommunicability of the experience, loss of ego, an altered perception of space and time, and profound transformative changes (i.e., changes in one's worldview, belief system, relationships, and sense of self) (Stace, 1960; Waldron, 1998).

In the second section of this chapter, we review data suggesting a role for the temporal lobe and the limbic system in RSMEs. In the following section, we examine the findings of brain imaging studies of RSMEs conducted to date. Since meditation is often associated with spiritual practice, we review in the fourth section neuroimaging studies of diverse meditative states. In the next section, we discuss neuroimaging data and phenomenology of RSMEs with respect to the mind-brain problem. Finally, in the last section, we provide a few concluding remarks and propose new opportunities for expanding the neuroscience of spirituality.

Role of the Temporal Lobe and the Limbic System in Religious, Spiritual, and Mystical Experiences

Temporal Lobe Epilepsy

Clinical observations suggest an association between temporal lobe epilepsy (TLE) and RSMEs during (ictal), after (postictal), and in between (interictal) seizures (Devinsky & Lai, 2008). Howden (1872–1873) first observed a man who had a religious conversion after a generalized seizure in which he experienced being transported to "heaven." Afterward, Mabille (1899) described a patient who, following a seizure, reported that God had given him a mission to bring law to the world. A few years later, Spratling (1904) reported a religious aura or a premonitory period of hours or several days associated with religiosity in 52 of 1,325 patients with epilepsy (4%). Furthermore, Boven (1919) reported the case of a 14-year-old boy who, after a seizure, saw God and the angels, and heard celestial music.

More recently, Dewhurst and Beard (1970) reported six patients with TLE who underwent sudden and often lasting religious conversions in the postictal period. Some of these patients had prior or active psychiatric disorders. There was an obvious temporal relationship between conversion and first seizure or increased seizure frequency in five patients.

Studies have shown that between 0.4% and 3.1% of TLE patients had ictal RSMEs, while postictal RSMEs occurred in 2.2% of patients with TLE. Ictal RSMEs occur most often in patients with right TLE, whereas there is a predominance of postictal and interictal RSMEs in TLE patients with bilateral seizure foci. Of note, many of the epilepsy-related religious conversion experiences occur postictally (Devinsky & Lai, 2008).

From an experiential perspective, ictal religious experiences during seizures can be accompanied by intense emotions of God's presence, the sense of being connected to the infinite (Alajouanine, 1963), hallucinations of God's voice (Hansen & Brodtkorb, 2003), the visual hallucination of a religious figure (Karagulla & Robertson, 1955), or repetition of a religious phrase (Ozkara et al., 2004). It has been suggested that some of the greatest religious figures in history (e.g., Saint Paul, Muhammad, Joan of Arc, Joseph Smith) were probably suffering from TLE (Saver & Rabin, 1997).

Naito and Matsui (1988) described an elderly woman whose seizures were characterized by joyful visions of God. Interictal electroencephalography (EEG) revealed spike discharges in the left anterior and middle temporal areas during sleep. Morgan (1990) described a patient whose seizures were associated with feelings of ineffable contentment and fulfillment; visualizing a bright light recognized as the source of knowledge; and sometimes visualizing a bearded young man resembling Jesus Christ. A computed axial tomography (CAT) scan displayed a right anterior temporal astrocytoma. Following anterior temporal lobectomy, ecstatic seizures vanished. Along the same lines, Picard and Craig (2009) described the case of a 64-year-old right-handed woman who has had epileptic seizures with an ecstatic aura. During her ecstatic epileptic seizures, she reported experiencing immense joy above physical sensations as well as unimaginable harmony with life, the world and the "All." Cerebral MRI showed a meningioma in the left temporal pole region. An interictal EEG revealed left anterior temporofrontal epileptiform activity.

Ogata and Miyakawa (1998) examined 234 Japanese epileptic patients for ictus-related religious experiences. Three (1.3%) patients were found to have had such experiences. All three cases had TLE with postictal psychosis, and interictal experiences with hyperreligiosity. Patients who had ictus-related or interictal religious experiences did not believe only in Buddhism (a traditional religion in Japan), but rather in a combination of Buddhism and Shintoism, new Christian sects, contemporary Japanese religions, and/or other folk beliefs. This suggests that these experiences were related not only to the personality characteristic of TLE but also to the social circumstances and conditions under which such experiences occur in contemporary Japan. These findings indicate that manifestations of religious experience in postictal psychosis were influenced by some psychosocial factors.

Interictal Personality Syndrome of Temporal Lobe Epilepsy

Waxman and Geschwind (1975) suggested that hyperreligiosity is a core feature of a distinctive interictal personality syndrome of TLE (also called the Geschwind syndrome). A heightened state of religious conviction, an increased sense of personal destiny, intense philosophical and cosmological concerns, and strong moral beliefs usually characterize interictal religiosity. The putative temporal-lobe personality type is also characterized by hypermoralism, deepened affects, humorlessness, aggressive irritability, and hypergraphia.

Support for this hypothetical syndrome was provided by Bear and Fedio (1977) who found that religiosity trait scores were significantly higher in TLE patients than in healthy control participants. In keeping with this, Roberts and Guberman (1989) found that 60% of 57 consecutive patients with epilepsy had excessive interests in religion. Subsequent studies using religion questionnaires, however, failed to find any differences regarding interictal religiosity between patients with TLE versus idiopathic generalized epilepsy, or between patients with epilepsy and normal control participants (Tucker, Novelly, & Walker, 1987; Willmore, Heilman, Fennel, & Pinnas, 1980). It has been proposed that differences in religiosity measures and in control group selection account for some of the discrepancy among studies (Saver & Rabin, 1997).

Interestingly, Wuerfel et al. (2004) used magnetic resonance imaging (MRI) to investigate mesial temporal structures in 33 patients with refractory partial epilepsy, comparing 22 patients without and 11 patients with hyperreligiosity. High ratings on the religiosity scale were correlated with a significantly smaller hippocampus in the right hemisphere. The hippocampal atrophy may reflect the duration and severity of hyperreligiosity. This does not mean that the right hippocampus is the critical cerebral structure for religious experience (Devinsky & Lai, 2008).

The Limbic-Marker Hypothesis

Saver and Rabin (1997) have theorized that temporolimbic discharges underlie each of the core features of RSMEs (e.g., the noetic and the ineffable; the sense of having touched the ultimate ground of reality; the sense of incommunicability of the experience; the experience of unity, timelessness, and spacelessness; feelings of positive affect, peace, and joy). The limbic system integrates external stimuli with internal drives and is part of a distributed neural circuit that marks the valence (positive or negative) of stimuli and experiences (Damasio, Tranel, & Damasio, 1991). Saver and Rabin (1997) posited that temporolimbic discharges may mark experiences as (1) depersonalized or derealized; (2) crucially important and self-referent; (3) harmonious, indicative of a connection or unity between disparate elements; and (4) ecstatic, profoundly joyous.

According to the limbic-marker hypothesis, the perceptual and cognitive contents of an RSME are comparable to those of ordinary experience, except that they are tagged by the limbic system as of deep importance, as united into a whole, and/or as joyous. Therefore, descriptions of the contents of the RSME resemble descriptions of the contents of ordinary experience, and the feelings associated with them cannot be captured fully in words. As in the case of strong emotions, these limbic markers can be named but cannot be communicated in their full visceral intensity, resulting in a report of ineffability.

The temporal lobe and the limbic system may not be the only cerebral structures involved in RSMEs. About this question, Devinsky and Lai (2008) hypothesized that alterations in frontal functions in the right hemisphere may contribute to increased religious interests and beliefs as a personality trait. This hypothesis is based on the finding that dramatic changes in self, defined as a change in political, social, or religious views can be seen in patients with a dysfunction affecting selectively the right frontal lobe (Miller et al., 2001).

Stimulation of the Temporal Lobe

Persinger (1983) speculated that RSMEs are evoked by transient, electrical microseizures within deep structures of the temporal lobe, and that it is possible to experimentally induce RSMEs by stimulating the temporal lobe with weak electromagnetic currents. Persinger and Healey (2002) tested this hypothesis by exposing 48 university students to weak (100 nanoTesla to 1 microTesla) complex, pulsed electromagnetic fields. These fields were applied in one of three ways: over the right temporoparietal region, over the left temporoparietal region, or equally across the temporoparietal region of both hemispheres of the brain (one treatment per group). Fields were applied for 20 minutes while participants were wearing opaque goggles in a very quiet room. A fourth group was exposed to a sham-field condition; that is, participants were not exposed to an electromagnetic field, although all participants were told that they might be. Beforehand, the Hypnosis Induction Profile (Spiegel, Aronson, Fleiss, & Haber, 1976) was administered to participants (psychology students), to test for suggestibility.

Two-thirds of the participants reported a sensed presence under the influence of the electromagnetic fields. But 33% of the control (sham-field) group reported a sensed presence, too. In other words, Persinger and Healey (2002) found that twice as many participants reported a sensed presence under the influence of the electromagnetic field as those who reported one without an electromagnetic field. About half of these participants stated that they felt "someone else" in the chamber. Another approximate half of the group described a sentient being who moved when they tried to "focus attention" upon the presence. About one-third of participants attributed the presence to a deceased member of the family or to some cultural equivalent of a "spirit guide." In the study, those who had received stimulation over the right hemisphere or both hemispheres reported more unusual phenomena than those who had received stimulation over the left hemisphere.

Persinger and Healey (2002) concluded two things: that the experience of a sensed presence can be manipulated by experiment, and that such an experience may be the source for phenomena attributed to visitations by spiritual entities.

A research team at Uppsala University in Sweden, headed by Granqvist (Granqvist et al., 2005), mirrored Persinger's experiment by testing 89 undergraduate students, some of whom were exposed to the electromagnetic fields and some of whom were not. Using Persinger's equipment, the Swedish researchers could not reproduce his key results. They attributed their findings to the fact that they ensured that neither the participants nor the experimenters interacting with them had any idea who was being exposed to the electromagnetic fields.

Granqvist and colleagues made sure that their experiment was double blind by using two experimenters for each trial. The first experimenter, who was not told about the purpose of the study, interacted with the participants. The second experimenter switched electromagnetic fields off or on without advising either the first experimenter or the subject. So if the subject had not already been advised that an RSME was likely at Granqvist's laboratory, the study experimenters were not in a position to provide that clue.

Study participants included undergraduate theology students as well as psychology students.

Neither group was asked for prior information on spiritual or paranormal experiences, nor was any participant told that there was a sham-field (control) condition. Rather, participants were told only that the study investigated the influence of weak electromagnetic fields on experiences and feeling states. Personality characteristics that might predispose a person to report an unusual experience were used as predictors for which participants would report one. These characteristics included absorption (the ability to become completely absorbed in an experience), signs of abnormal temporal-lobe activity, and a "New Age" lifestyle orientation.

No evidence was found for a "sensed presence" effect of weak electromagnetic fields. The characteristic that significantly predicted the outcomes was personality. Of the three participants who reported strong spiritual experiences, two were members of the control group. Of the twenty-two who reported "subtle" experiences, eleven were members of the control group. Those participants who were rated as highly suggestible on the basis of a questionnaire filled out after they completed the study reported paranormal experiences whether the electromagnetic field was on or off while they were wearing the stimulation helmet. Granqvist and colleagues also noted that they had found it difficult to evaluate the reliability of Persinger's findings, because no information on experimental randomization or blindness was provided, which left his results open to the possibility that psychological suggestion was the best explanation.

Taken together, the clinical studies of epileptic patients suggest that the temporal lobe and the limbic system can be involved in the experiential aspect of RSMEs. However, the relationship between these brain regions and RSMEs is still poorly understood since (1) most people who have these experiences are not epileptics; and (2) very few epileptics report RSMEs during seizures. In addition, the experimental induction of such experiences by stimulating the temporal lobes with weak electromagnetic currents does not appear easily achievable when psychological suggestibility is controlled using a randomized, double-blind, placebo approach.

Brain Imaging Studies of Religious, Spiritual, and Mystical Experiences

The first brain imaging study of a religious experience was conducted by Azari et al. (2001). These researchers studied a group of six self-identified religious participants, who attributed their religious experience to biblical Psalm 23. These participants, who were members of a "Free Evangelical Fundamentalist Community" in Germany, all reported having had a conversion experience (related to the first verse of biblical Psalm 23, which states "The LORD is my shepherd; I shall not be in want"), and interpreted biblical text literally as the word of God. Religious participants were compared to six nonreligious individuals. The texts used for the different tasks were "religious" (first verse of biblical Psalm 23), "happy" (a well-known German children's nursery rhyme), and "neutral" (instructions on using a phone card from the Düsseldorf telephone book).

Participants were scanned with positron emission tomography (PET) during various conditions: reading silently or reciting biblical Psalm 23; reading silently or reciting the children's nursery rhyme; reading silently the set of instructions; and while lying quietly. The PET images revealed a significant activation of the right dorsolateral prefrontal cortex in the religious participants during the religious state (relative to other readings) as compared with nonreligious participants. During the religious state, the religious participants showed additional loci of activation, including the dorsomedial frontal cortex and the right precuneus. Limbic areas did not show regional cerebral blood flow (rCBF) changes.

According to Azari and colleagues (2001), these results strongly support the view that religious experience is a cognitive attributional phenomenon, mediated by a preestablished neural circuit, involving dorsolateral prefrontal, dorsomedial frontal, and medial parietal cortex. Religious attributions are based on religious schemata, which consist of organized knowledge about religion and religious issues, and include reinforced structures for inferring religiously related causality of experienced events (Spilka & McIntosh, 1995). Azari and coworkers (2001) proposed that the dorsolateral prefrontal and medial parietal cortices were probably involved in the subject's own religious schemata, whereas the dorsomedial frontal cortex was implicated in the felt immediacy of religious experience.

The central limitation in this study is that, phenomenologically, there was no measure of a religious state. Therefore, it is conceivable that the regional brain activations were not related to a genuine religious experience.

Newberg et al. (2003) used single-photon emission computed tomography (SPECT) to scan three Franciscan nuns while they performed a "centering prayer" to open themselves to the presence of God. This prayer involved the internal repetition of a particular phrase. Compared to baseline, the prayer condition scan showed increased rCBF in the prefrontal cortex, inferior parietal lobes, and inferior frontal lobes. There was a strong inverse correlation between the rCBF changes in the prefrontal cortex and in the ipsilateral superior parietal lobule. Newberg et al. (2003) hypothesized that increased frontal rCBF reflected focused concentration, whereas changed rCBF in the superior parietal lobule was related to an altered sense of space experienced by the nuns during prayer. In this pilot study, there was no attempt to analyze and quantify in a rigorous and systematic manner the nuns' subjective experiences during their "centering prayer." In other words, Newberg and colleagues could not determine whether focusing attention on a phrase from a prayer over a period of time really led the nuns to feel the presence of God.

Newberg et al. (2006) also used SPECT to investigate changes in cerebral activity during glossolalia ("speaking in tongues"). This unusual mental state is associated with specific religious traditions. Glossolalia is one of the "gifts of the Spirit" according to Saint Paul and, hence, some fundamentalist religious traditions see it as a sign of being visited by the Spirit. This is due to the Pentecost experience, where, according to the Acts of the Apostles, the Apostles "spoke in the tongues" of all those present, that is, made themselves understood to everybody, whereby later on just babbling something became synonymous with glossolalia. In this state, the individual seems to be speaking in an incomprehensible language over which he or she claims to have no voluntary control. Yet the individual perceives glossolalia to have great personal and religious meaning. In their study, Newberg and colleagues examined five practitioners (women) of glossolalia. Participants described themselves as Christians in a Charismatic or Pentecostal tradition who had practiced glossolalia for more than 5 years. Structured clinical interviews excluded current psychiatric conditions. Glossolalia was compared to a religious singing state since the latter is similar except that it involves actual language (English). Earphones were used to play music to sing and to perform glossolalia (the same music was used for both conditions). Several significant rCBF differences were noted between the glossolalia and singing state. During glossolalia (compared to the religious singing state), significant decreases were found in the prefrontal cortices, left caudate, and left temporal pole. Decreased activity in the prefrontal lobe is consistent with the participants' description of a lack of volitional control over the performance of glossolalia. Newberg et al.

(2006) proposed that the decrease in the left caudate may relate to the altered emotional activity during glossolalia.

Recently, we sought to identify the neural correlates of a mystical experience (as understood in the Christian sense) in a group of contemplative nuns using functional magnetic resonance imaging (fMRI) (Beauregard & Paquette, 2006). Fifteen Carmelite nuns took part in the study. Blood oxygen–level dependent (BOLD) signal changes were measured during a mystical condition, a control condition, and a baseline condition. In the mystical condition, participants were asked to remember and relive the most intense mystical experience ever felt in their lives as a member of the Carmelite Order. This strategy was adopted given that the nuns told us before the onset of the study that "God can't be summoned at will." In the Control condition, participants were instructed to remember and relive the most intense state of union with another human ever felt in their lives while being affiliated with the Carmelite Order. The week preceding the experiment, participants were requested to practice these two tasks. The baseline condition was a normal restful state. Immediately at the end of the scan, the intensity of the subjective experience during the control and mystical conditions was measured using numerical rating scales ranging from 0 (no experience of union) to 5 (most intense experience of union ever felt); self-report data referred solely to the experiences lived during these two conditions, not to the original experiences recalled to self-induce the control and mystical states. The phenomenology of the mystical experience during the mystical condition was assessed with 15 items of the Mysticism Scale (Hood, 1975). This scale, which comprises 32 items, aims at measuring reported mystical experience (for each participant, scores of 15 or above were considered significant for a given item). In addition, qualitative interviews were conducted after the experiment to obtain additional information regarding the nature of the subjective experiences during the control and mystical conditions.

As regards the phenomenology of the subjective experience during the mystical condition, summed scores of 15 or above were noted for three items of the Mysticism Scale: (1) "I have had an experience in which something greater than my self seemed to absorb me" (average score: 15); (2) "I have experienced profound joy" (average score: 22); and (3) "I have had an experience which I knew to be sacred" (average score: 20). During the qualitative interviews conducted at the end of the experiment, several participants mentioned that, during the mystical condition, they felt the presence of God, His unconditional and infinite love, as well as plenitude and peace. All participants reported that from a first-person perspective, the experiences lived during the mystical condition were different than those used to self-induce a mystical state. Participants also reported the presence of visual and motor imagery during both the mystical and control conditions. In addition, the participants experienced a feeling of unconditional love during the control condition.

The mystical versus baseline contrast produced significant loci of BOLD activation in the right medial orbitofrontal cortex (Brodmann area [BA] 11), right middle temporal cortex (BA 21), right inferior parietal lobule (BA 40) and superior parietal lobule (BA7), right caudate, left medial prefrontal cortex (BA 10), left dorsal anterior cingulate cortex (BA 32), left inferior parietal lobule (BA 7), left insula (BA 13), left caudate, and left brainstem. A few loci of activation were also seen in the extrastriate visual cortex.

Based on the studies indicating a relationship between RSMEs and the temporal lobe, we posited that the right middle temporal activation noted during the mystical condition was related with the subjective impression of contacting a spiritual reality. We also proposed that the caudate activations reflected feelings of joy and unconditional love since the caudate nucleus has been systematically activated in previous functional brain imaging studies implicating positive emotions such as happiness (Damasio et al., 2000), romantic love (Bartels & Zeki, 2000), and maternal love (Bartels & Zeki, 2004). Concerning the brainstem, there is some empirical support for the view that certain brainstem nuclei map the organism's internal state during emotion (Damasio, 1999). Given this, it is conceivable that the activation in the left brainstem was linked to the somatovisceral changes associated with the feelings of joy and unconditional love. As for the insula, this cerebral structure is richly interconnected with regions involved in autonomic regulation (Cechetto, 1994). It contains a topographical representation of inputs from visceral, olfactory, gustatory, visual, auditory, and somatosensory areas and is proposed to integrate representations of external sensory experience and internal somatic state (Augustine, 1996). The insula has been seen activated in several studies of emotional processing and appears to support a representation of somatic and visceral responses accessible to consciousness

(Critchley, Wien, Rotshtein, Ohman, & Dolan, 2004; Damasio, 1999). It is plausible that the left insular activation (BA 13) noted in our study was related to the representation of the somatovisceral reactions associated with the feelings of joy and unconditional love.

In addition, we suggested that the left medial prefrontal cortical activation (BA 10) was linked with conscious awareness of those feelings. Indeed, the results of functional neuroimaging studies indicate that the medial prefrontal cortex is involved in the metacognitive representation of one's own emotional state (Lane & Nadel, 2000). This prefrontal area receives sensory information from the body and the external environment via the orbitofrontal cortex and is heavily interconnected with limbic structures, such as the amygdala, ventral striatum, hypothalamus, midbrain periaqueductal gray region, and brainstem nuclei (Barbas, 1993; Carmichael & Price, 1995). In other respects, brain imaging findings (Lane, Fink, Chau, & Dolan, 1997; Lane et al., 1998) support the view that the activation of the left dorsal anterior cingulate cortex (BA 32) reflected that aspect of emotional awareness associated with the interoceptive detection of emotional signals during the mystical condition. This cortical region projects strongly to the visceral regulation areas in the hypothalamus and midbrain periaqueductal gray (Ongur, Ferry, & Price, 2003). Regarding the medial orbitofrontal cortex, there is mounting evidence that this prefrontal cortical region codes for subjective pleasantness (Kringelbach, ODoherty, Rolls, & Andrews, 2003). The medial orbitofrontal cortex has been found activated with regard to the pleasantness of the taste or smell of stimuli (de Araujo, Rolls, Kringelbach, McGlone, & Phillips, 2003; Rolls, Kringelbach, & de Araujo, 2003) or music (Blood & Zatorre, 2001). It has reciprocal connections with the cingulate and insular cortices (Carmichael & Price, 1995; Cavada, Company, Tejedor, Cruz-Rizzolo, & Reinoso-Suarez, 2000). The right medial orbitofrontal cortical activation (BA 11) noted in the mystical condition was perhaps related to the fact that the experiences lived during the mystical state were considered emotionally pleasant by the participants.

Given that the right superior parietal lobule is involved in the spatial perception of self (Neggers, Van der Lubbe, Ramsey, & Postma, 2006), it is conceivable that the activation of this parietal region (BA 7) reflected a modification of the body schema associated with the impression that something greater than the participants seemed to absorb them.

Moreover, there is evidence that the left inferior parietal lobule is part of a neural system implicated in the processing of visuospatial representation of bodies (Felician, Ceccaldi, Didic, Thinus-Blanc, & Poncet, 2003). Therefore, the left inferior parietal lobule activation in the mystical condition was perhaps related to an alteration of the body schema. In keeping with this, there is some evidence indicating that the right inferior parietal lobule is crucial in bodily consciousness and the process of self/other distinction (Ruby & Decety, 2003). However, the inferior parietal lobule plays an important role in motor imagery (Decety, 1996). It is thus plausible that the activations in the right (BA 40) and left (BA 7) inferior parietal lobules were related to the motor imagery experienced during the mystical condition. Last, regarding the loci of activation found in the extrastriate visual cortex during this condition, it has been previously shown (Ganis, Thompson, & Kosslyn, 2004) that this region of the brain is implicated in visual mental imagery. It is likely that the BOLD activation in visual cortical areas was related to the visual mental imagery reported by the nuns.

The main limitation of this study is that the participants were asked to remember and relive a mystical experience rather than actually try to achieve one. Such a strategy was used because the participants told us a priori that they were not capable of reaching a mystical state at will. In our view, this does not represent a major problem since the phenomenological data indicate that the participants actually experienced genuine mystical experiences during the mystical condition. These mystical experiences felt subjectively different than those used to self-induce a mystical state.

Brain Imaging Studies of Meditative States

The word *meditation* refers to practices that self-regulate the body and mind, thereby affecting mental processes by engaging a specific attentional set. Since the control of attention is the common denominator across the various methods of meditation (Davidson & Goleman, 1977), meditative techniques are generally classified into two types—mindfulness and concentrative—depending on how the attentional processes are regulated (Andresen, 2000; Shapiro & Walsh, 1984; Wallace, 1999). Mindfulness practices involve allowing any sensations, thoughts, or feelings to arise while maintaining awareness of the phenomenal field as an attentive and nonattached observer without judgment or analysis. Examples include Zen and Vipassana. Concentrative meditational techniques involve focusing on selective sensory or mental activity: specific body sensations such as the breath, a repeated sound, or an imagined image. Examples include forms of yogic meditation and the Buddhist Samatha meditation focus on the sensation of breath. These two types of meditative techniques elicit a deep sense of calm peacefulness, a slowing of the mind's internal dialog, and a meta-cognitive shift toward expanded experience of self not centered on the individual's body representations and mental contents (Wallace, 1999).

Positron Emission Tomography and Single-Photon Emission Computed Tomography Studies

Using positron emission tomography (PET), Herzog et al. (1990) measured the regional cerebral metabolic rate of glucose (rCMRGlc) in eight members of a yoga meditation group during a meditation state and a normal control state (participants were instructed to think of daily affairs). The ratios of frontal versus occipital rCMRGlc were significantly elevated during the meditation condition. These altered ratios were caused by a small increase of frontal rCMRGlc and a more pronounced decrease in primary and secondary visual areas. Herzog and colleagues (1990) suggested that the decrease in the occipital cortical areas might reflect an inhibition of visual processing during yogic meditation, whereas the increase in the frontal cortex could reflect the sustained attention requested for meditation.

Another PET study was performed in nine highly experienced yoga teachers during Yoga Nidra meditation (which is characterized by a diminished level of desire for action) and during the resting state of normal consciousness (Lou et al., 1999). Regional cerebral blood flow (rCBF) was measured with the [^{15}O] H$_2$O technique. The meditation condition consisted of diverse exercises focusing on body sensation, abstract joy, visual imagery, and symbolic representation of self. Each of the guided meditation phases was correlated with different regional activations relative to the control condition: body sensation was accompanied by increased parietal and superior frontal activation; abstract joy was associated with left parietal and superior temporal activation; visual imagery induced robust occipital lobe activation (excluding V1); and symbolic representation of self was correlated with bilateral activation of parietal lobes. In the resting state of normal consciousness (compared with meditation as a baseline), differential activity was found in dorsolateral and orbital frontal cortex, anterior cingulate gyri, left temporal gyri, left inferior parietal lobule,

striatal and thalamic regions, pons and cerebellar vermis and hemispheres. Interestingly, the control condition was characterized by increased activity for executive–attentional systems and the cerebellum.

The same research team used ^{11}C-raclopride PET to investigate dopaminergic changes during Yoga Nidra meditation (^{11}C-raclopride selectively and competitively binds to D2 receptors, such that the amount of binding inversely correlates with endogenous dopamine levels) (Kjaer et al., 2002). Eight healthy meditation teachers underwent two ^{11}C-raclopride PET scans, one while attending to speech with eyes closed, and one during active meditation. Results revealed a 7.9% decrease in ^{11}C-raclopride binding in the ventral striatum during meditation. This reduction corresponds to an approximate 65% increase in dopamine release. In addition, increased striatal dopamine release was associated with the experience of reduced readiness for action. Since in the striatum, dopamine modulates excitatory glutamatergic synapses of the projections from the frontal cortex to striatal neurons, which in turn project back to the frontal cortex via the pallidum and ventral thalamus, these results suggest that being in the Yoga Nidra meditative state produces a suppression of cortico-striatal glutamatergic transmission.

A SPECT study was conducted on eight experienced Tibetan Buddhist meditators (Newberg et al., 2001a) and nine control individuals. Participants were injected at baseline with HMPAO and scanned 20 min later for 45 min. The Buddhist meditators then meditated for 1 hr at which time they were injected again with HMPAO and scanned 20 min later for 30 min. Experientially, the meditators reported "becoming one with" the visualized image during the meditative state. The baseline activation patterns revealed a difference in the thalamic laterality index in which meditators displayed a greater rightward dominance of thalamic rCBF compared to controls. Increased rCBF was measured in the cingulate gyrus, inferior and orbital frontal cortex, dorsolateral prefrontal cortex, midbrain, and thalamus during meditation relative to baseline. Newberg and colleagues (2001a) suggested that the increased frontal rCBF may reflect focused concentration while thalamic increases may be correlated with increased cortical activity during meditation. These researchers also proposed that midbrain activation may be related to alterations in autonomic activity during meditation. Decreased rCBF activity in the left posterior superior parietal lobe was negatively correlated with the activity increase noted in left dorsolateral prefrontal cortex. Newberg et al. (2001a) postulated that this negative correlation may reflect an altered sense of space experienced during meditation.

Functional Magnetic Resonance Imaging

Lazar et al. (2000) used fMRI to identify the brain regions that are active during a form of Kundalini yoga consisting of a mantra combined with heightened breath awareness. The control task was the mental construction of animal names. The five participants had practiced Kundalini yoga for at least 4 years. Significant BOLD signal increases were detected in the dorsolateral prefrontal and parietal cortices, hippocampus/parahippocampus, temporal lobe, pregenual anterior cingulate cortex, striatum, and pre- and postcentral gyri during meditation (compared with the control condition). The results suggest that the practice of meditation activates brain regions implicated in attention (frontal and parietal cortex) and arousal/control of the autonomic nervous system (pregenual anterior cingulate, amygdala, midbrain, and hypothalamus). Additionally, marked activity increases in these areas and a greater number of activation foci and larger signal changes were found during the late meditation states. These findings indicate that neural activity during meditation is slowly evolving throughout the duration of meditation practice.

Individuals with considerable training in this form of Kundalini yoga (mantra-based) or Vipassana (mindfulness-based) meditation were compared with fMRI during meditation and control tasks (e.g., resting state, production of a random list of numbers, paced breathing) (Lazar et al., 2003). Nonoverlapping frontal and parietal cortices as well as subcortical structures were activated in the two meditator groups during the meditation condition. The main locus of common activation was the dorsal anterior cingulate cortex. Lazar and her colleagues (2003) concluded that distinct forms of meditation seem to engage different cerebral structures.

A group of 11 experienced Zen meditation practitioners were scanned with fMRI using an on-off design of 45 sec blocks in which meditators focused on counting their breath as in normal daily practice (experimental condition) and engaged in random thoughts (control condition). Comparing meditation with the control condition revealed increased activity in the right medial prefrontal cortex and basal ganglia, bilaterally. Decreased activity was noted in the superior occipital gyrus and

anterior cingulate cortex (Ritskes, Ritskes-Hoitinga, Stodkilde-Jorgensen, Baerentsen, & Hartman, 2003). Activity decrease in this prefrontal cortical area was attributed to a reduced experience of will in the meditative state.

Recently, Shimomura et al. (2008) utilized fMRI to identify the brain regions activated during praying of the Namo Amida Butsu (Nembutsu) and the reciting of Buddhist scriptures (Sutra) in eight highly trained Japanese monks. Relative to a resting condition, the task of repeating the Nenbutsu activated the medial frontal gyrus, whereas the task of reciting the Sutra activated the left lateral middle frontal gyrus and right parietal cortices (angular gyrus, supramarginal gyrus).

Neuroscience; Religious, Spiritual, and Mystical Experiences; and the Mind-Brain Problem

Physicalism is the mainstream metaphysical view of modern neuroscience with respect to the mind-body problem, that is, the explanation of the relationship that exists between mental processes and bodily processes. According to this view, consciousness and mental events (e.g., thoughts, emotions, desires) can be reduced to their neural correlates, that is, the brain electrical and chemical processes whose presence necessarily and regularly correlates with these mental events. Physicalist philosophers and neuroscientists believe that mental events are equivalent to brain processes. About this issue, it is important to bear in mind that neural correlates do not yield a causal explanation of mental events; that is, they cannot explain how neural processes become mental events. Indeed, correlation does not entail causation. And the external reality of "God" or ultimate reality can neither be confirmed nor disconfirmed by neural correlates.

Newberg and colleagues (Newberg, d'Aquili, & Rause, 2001b) submitted that the most important criterion for judging what is real is the subjective vivid sense of reality. They argued that individuals usually refer to dreams as less real than waking (baseline) reality when they are recalled within baseline reality. In contrast, RSMEs (e.g., "cosmic consciousness" states, religious visions, near-death experiences) appear more real to the experiencers than waking (baseline) reality when they are recalled from baseline reality.

A major problem with this criterion is its subjectivity. This problem is well illustrated by the fact that individuals suffering from psychosis are unable to distinguish personal subjective experience from the reality of the external world. They experience hallucinations and/or delusions as being very real. From a neuroscientific perspective, a more satisfactory approach to evaluate the "objective" ontological reality of RSMEs is to determine whether it is possible for a human being to have a spiritual experience during a state of clinical death, that is, when her or his brain is not functioning. In this state, vital signs have ceased: the heart is in ventricular fibrillation, there is a total lack of electrical activity on the cortex of the brain (flat EEG), and brainstem activity is abolished (loss of the corneal reflex, fixed and dilated pupils, and loss of the gag reflex).

The thought-provoking case of a patient who apparently underwent a profound spiritual experience while her brain was not functioning has been reported by cardiologist Michael Sabom (1998). In 1991, 35-year-old Atlanta-based singer and songwriter Pam Reynolds began to suffer dizziness, loss of speech, and difficulty moving. A CAT scan revealed that she had a giant basilar artery aneurysm (a grossly swollen blood vessel in the brain stem). If it burst, it would kill her. But attempting to drain and repair it might kill her too. Her doctor offered no chance of survival using conventional procedures. Reynolds heard about neurosurgeon Robert Spetzler, at the Barrow Neurological Institute in Phoenix, Arizona. He was a specialist and pioneer in a rare and dangerous technique called hypothermic cardiac arrest, or "Operation Standstill." He would take her body down to a temperature so low that she was clinically dead but then bring her back to a normal temperature before irreversible damage set in. At a low temperature, the swollen vessels that burst at the high temperatures needed to sustain human life become soft. Then they can be operated upon with less risk. Also, the cooled brain can survive longer without oxygen, though it obviously cannot function in that state. So for all practical purposes, Reynolds would actually be clinically dead during the surgery. But if she didn't agree to it, she would soon be dead anyway with no hope of return. So she consented.

As the surgery began, her heart and breathing ceased, the blood was completely drained from her head, and her EEG brain waves flattened into total silence (indicating no cerebral activity; during a cardiac arrest, the brain's electrical activity disappears after about 10 seconds—Clute & Levy, 1990). Her brainstem became unresponsive (her eyes had been taped shut and her ears had been blocked by molded ear speakers), and her temperature fell to 15°C. When all of Reynolds's vital signs were

stopped, the surgeon began to cut through her skull with a surgical saw. She reported later that at that point, she felt herself "pop" outside her body and hover above the operating table. From her out-of-body position, she could see the doctors working on her lifeless body. She described, with considerable accuracy for a person who knew nothing of surgical practice, the Midas Rex bone saw used to open skulls. Reynolds also heard and reported later what was happening during the operation and what the nurses in the operating room had said. At a certain point, she became conscious of floating out of the operating room and traveling down a tunnel with a light. Deceased relatives and friends were waiting at the end of this tunnel, including her long-dead grandmother. She entered the presence of a brilliant, wonderfully warm and loving Light and sensed that her soul was part of God and that everything in existence was created from the Light (the breathing of God) (Sabom, 1998).

The anecdotal case of Pam Reynolds strongly challenges the physicalist doctrine in regard to the mind-brain problem. This case suggests that mental processes and events (consciousness, perception, cognition, emotion) can be experienced at the moment that the brain seemingly no longer functions (as evidenced by a flat EEG) during a period of clinical death. This case also suggests that RSMEs can occur when the brain is not functioning; that is, these experiences are not necessarily delusions created by a defective brain. In other words, it would be possible for humans to experience a transcendent reality during an altered state of consciousness in which perception, cognition, identity, and emotion function independently from the brain. This raises the possibility that when a spiritual experience happens while the brain is fully functional, the neural correlates of this experience indicate that the brain is de facto connecting with a transcendent level of reality.

It should be noted that since Pam Reynolds did not die, there were likely residual brain processes not detectable by EEG that persisted during the clinical death period at sufficient levels so as to permit return to normal brain functioning after the standstill operation. Yet it is difficult to see how the brain could generate higher mental functions in absence of cortical and brainstem activity. Scientific research is clearly needed to investigate the possibility that a functioning brain may not be essential to higher mental functions and spiritual experiences. It is noteworthy that near-death experiences are reported by 10%–18% of cardiac arrest survivors

(Greyson, 2003; Parnia, Waller, Yeates, & Fenwick, 2001; van Lommel, van Wees, Meyers, & Elfferich, 2001).

The case of Pam Reynolds and many cases of near-death experiences during cardiac arrest (Greyson, 2003; Parnia et al., 2001; van Lommel et al., 2001) stand against the physicalist credo as regards RSMEs and the mind-brain problem. Collectively, these cases point out the possibility that RSMEs can happen when the brain is seemingly not functioning (i.e., there is no cerebral activity detectable by EEG). In this context, it is conceivable that the neural correlates of RSMEs reflect the actual connection of the brain with a spiritual level of reality. Solid scientific research is required to tackle this fascinating issue. One way to address this question is to conduct an experiment aiming to test the veridicity of out-of-body perceptions with randomly changing pictures presented (on a video screen) in the operating room during hypothermic cardiac arrest.

More than a century ago, William James (1898/1960) proposed that the brain may serve a permissive/transmissive/expressive function rather than a productive one, in terms of the mental events and experiences it allows (just as a prism—which is not the source of the light—changes incoming white light to form the colored spectrum). Following James, Henri Bergson (1914) and Aldous Huxley (1954) posited that the brain acts as a filter or reducing valve by blocking out much of, and allowing registration and expression of only a narrow band of, perceivable reality. Bergson and Huxley believed that over the course of evolution, the brain has been trained to eliminate most of those perceptions that do not directly aid our everyday survival. This outlook implies that the brain normally limits the human capacity to have an RSME. A significant alteration of the electrochemical activity of the brain would be necessary for the occurrence of an RSME (Beauregard & O'Leary, 2007).

Conclusion and Future Directions

Contrary to the assertion that neural discharges in the temporal lobe and limbic system underlie each of the main features of RSMEs (Saver & Rabin, 1997), brain imaging studies conducted during the last decade indicate that several brain regions and networks mediate the diverse aspects of these experiences (perception, cognition, emotion, etc.). This conclusion should not come as a surprise given that these experiences are complex and multidimensional; that is, they implicate changes in perception, self-awareness, cognition, and emotion. Along the same lines, the results of the neuroimaging studies of meditation suggest that different patterns of brain activation and deactivation support the different types of meditative states.

One of the principal limitations of the studies reviewed in this chapter being the relatively small sample size, future neuroimaging investigations of RSMEs and meditation should involve larger numbers of participants.

Correlating subjective (first-person, phenomenological) data and objective (third-person, neurophysiological) data represents a crucial issue in the neuroscience of spirituality (Newberg & Lee, 2005). The employment of "first-person methods," which are disciplined practices individuals can use to increase their sensitivity to their own mental experiences at various time-scales and produce more refined descriptive reports, intensify self-awareness (Lutz & Thompson, 2003). Given this, the collection of first-person data from phenomenologically trained individuals of different religious/spiritual traditions should be used to interpret the neurophysiological processes pertaining to various types of RSMEs and meditative states.

While the segregation principle states that some functional processes specifically engage well-localized and specialized brain regions, it is now widely believed that higher mental functions emerge through integration of information flows across distributed cerebral structures (Frackowiak et al., 2004; Varela, Lachaux, Rodriguez, & Martinerie, 2001). In this view, it is not only a collection of brain areas that is hypothesized to process functional tasks, but rather large-scale networks, that is, sets of brain regions dynamically interacting with one another. Accordingly, future neuroimaging studies of RSMEs and meditation should entail the measurement of functional connectivity within dynamic, large-scale brain networks. Such measurement may significantly improve our knowledge and understanding of the brain mechanisms underlying spiritual experiences.

Electroencephalography (EEG) and fMRI provide complementary advantages with regard to spatial and temporal resolution in studying brain activity. Indeed, EEG has a weak spatial resolution but a very high temporal resolution, whereas fMRI has an excellent spatial resolution but a relatively poor temporal resolution. As a consequence, these two techniques could be combined to shed more light on the neural correlates of RSMEs and meditative states.

References

Alajouanine, T. (1963). Dostoiewski's epilepsy. *Brain, 86,* 209–218.

Andresen, J. (2000). Meditation meets behavioural medicine: The story of experimental research on meditation. *Journal of Consciousness Studies, 7,* 17–73.

Augustine, J. R. (1996). Circuitry and functional aspects of the insular lobe in primates including humans. *Brain Research Reviews, 22,* 229–244.

Azari, N. P., Nickel, J., Wunderlich, G., Niedeggen, M., Hefter, H., Tellmann, L., … Seitz, R. J. (2001). Neural correlates of religious experience. *European Journal of Neuroscience, 13,* 1649–1652.

Barbas, H. (1993). Organization of cortical afferent input to the orbitofrontal area in the rhesus monkey. *Neuroscience, 56,* 841–864.

Bartels, A., & Zeki, S. (2000). The neural basis of romantic love. *NeuroReport, 11,* 3829–3834.

Bartels, A., & Zeki, S. (2004). The neural correlates of maternal and romantic love. *Neuroimage, 21,* 1155–1166.

Bear, D., & Fedio, P. (1977). Quantitative analysis of interictal behavior in temporal lobe epilepsy. *Archives of Neurology, 34,* 454–467.

Beauregard, M., & O'Leary, D. (2007). *The spiritual brain.* New York: Harper Collins.

Beauregard, M., & Paquette, V. (2006). Neural correlates of a mystical experience in Carmelite nuns. *Neuroscience Letters, 405,* 186–190.

Bergson, H. (1914). Presidential address. *Proceedings of the Society for Psychical Research, 27,* 157–175.

Blood, A., & Zatorre, R. (2001). Intensely pleasurable responses to music correlate with activity in brain regions implicated in reward and emotion. *Proceedings of the National Academy of Sciences USA, 98,* 11818–11823.

Boven, W. (1919). Religiosité et épilepsie. *Schweiz Archives of Neurological Psychiatry, 4,* 153–169.

Carmichael, S. T., & Price, J. L. (1995). Limbic connections of the orbital and medial prefrontal cortex in macaque monkeys. *Journal of Comparative Neurology, 363,* 615–641.

Cavada, C., Company, T., Tejedor, J., Cruz-Rizzolo, R. J., & Reinoso-Suarez, F. (2000). The anatomical connections of the macaque monkey orbitofrontal cortex, a review. *Cerebral Cortex, 10,* 220–242.

Cechetto, D. F. (1994). Identification of a cortical site for stress-induced cardiovascular dysfunction. *Integrative Physiological and Behavioral Science, 29,* 362–373.

Clute, H. L., & Levy, W. J. (1990). Electroencephalographic changes during brief cardiac arrest in humans. *Anesthesiology, 73,* 821–825.

Critchley, H. D., Wien, S., Rotshtein, P., Ohman, A., & Dolan, R. J. (2004). Neural systems supporting interoceptive awareness. *Nature Neuroscience, 7,* 189–195.

Damasio, A. R. (1999). *The feeling of what happens: Body and emotion in the making of consciousness.* New York: Harcourt Brace.

Damasio, A. R., Grabowski, T. J., Bechara, A., Damasio, H., Ponto, L. L., Parvizi, J., & Hichwa, R. D. (2000). Subcortical and cortical brain activity during the feeling of self-generated emotions. *Nature Neuroscience, 3,* 1049–1056.

Damasio, A. R., Tranel, D., & Damasio, H. (1991). Somatic markers and the guidance of behaviour. In H. Levin, H. Eisenberg, & A. Benton (Eds.), *Frontal lobe function and dysfunction* (pp. 217–228). New York: Oxford University Press.

Davidson, R. J., & Goleman, D. J. (1977). The role of attention in meditation and hypnosis: A psychobiological perspective on transformations of consciousness. *International Journal of Clinical and Experimental Hypnosis, 25,* 291–308.

de Araujo, I. E., Rolls, E. T., Kringelbach, M. L., McGlone, F., & Phillips, N. (2003). Taste-olfactory convergence, and the representation of the pleasantness of flavour, in the human brain. *European Journal of Neuroscience, 18,* 2059–2068.

Decety, J. (1996). Do imagined and executed actions share the same neural substrate? *Cognitive Brain Research, 3,* 87–93.

Devinsky, O., & Lai, G. (2008). Spirituality and religion in epilepsy. *Epilepsy and Behavior, 12,* 636–643.

Dewhurst, K., & Beard, A. W. (1970). Sudden religious conversions in temporal lobe epilepsy. *British Journal of Psychiatry, 117,* 497–507.

Felician, O., Ceccaldi, M., Didic, M., Thinus-Blanc, C., & Poncet, M. (2003). Pointing to body parts: A double dissociation study, *Neuropsychologia, 41,* 1307–1316.

Frackowiak, R. S. J., Friston, K. J., Frith, C. D., Dolan, R. J., Price, C. J., Zeki, S.,… Penny, W. (Eds.). (2004). *Human brain function* (2nd ed.). San Diego, CA: Academic Press.

Ganis, G., Thompson, W. L., & Kosslyn, S. M. (2004). Brain areas underlying visual mental imagery and visual perception: An fMRI study. *Cognitive Brain Research, 20,* 226–241.

Granqvist, P., Fredrikson, M., Unge, P., Hagenfeldt, A., Valind, S., Larhammar, D., & Larsson, M. (2005). Sensed presence and mystical experiences are predicted by suggestibility, not by the application of transcranial weak complex magnetic fields. *Neuroscience Letters, 379,* 1–6.

Greyson, B. (2003). Incidence and correlates of near-death experiences in a cardiac care unit. *General Hospital Psychiatry, 25,* 269–276.

Hansen, B. A., & Brodtkorb, E. (2003). Partial epilepsy with "ecstatic" seizures. *Epilepsy and Behavior, 4,* 667–673.

Hardy, A. (1975). *The biology of god.* New York: Taplinger.

Hay, D. (1990). *Religious experience today: Studying the facts.* London: Mowbray.

Herzog, H., Lele, V. R., Kuwert, T., Langen, K. J., Kops, E. R., & Feinendegen, L. E. (1990). Changed pattern of regional glucose metabolism during yoga meditative relaxation. *Neuropsychobiology, 23,* 182–187.

Hood, R.W., Jr. (1975). The construction and preliminary validation of a measure of reported mystical experience. *Journal for the Scientific Study of Religion, 14,* 21–41.

Howden, J. C. (1872–1873). The religious sentiments in epileptics. *Journal of Mental Science, 18,* 491–497.

Huxley, A. (1954). *The doors of perception.* New York: Harper & Row.

James, W. (1902). *The varieties of religious experience: A study in human nature.* New York: Longmans, Green.

James, W. (1898/1960). Human immortality: Two supposed objections to the doctrine. In G. Murphy & R. O. Ballou (Eds.), *William James on psychical research* (pp. 279–308). New York: Viking.

Karagulla, S., & Robertson, E. E. (1955). Psychical phenomena in temporal lobe epilepsy and the psychoses. *British Medical Journal, 1,* 748–752.

Kjaer, T. W., Bertelsen, C., Piccini, P., Brooks, D., Alving, J., & Lou, H. C. (2002). Increased dopamine tone during meditation-induced change of consciousness. *Cognitive Brain Research, 13,* 255–259.

Kringelbach, M. L., O'Doherty, J., Rolls, E. T., & Andrews, C. (2003). Activation of the human orbitofrontal cortex to a

liquid food stimulus is correlated with its subjective pleasantness. *Cerebral Cortex*, 13, 1064–1071.

Lane, R. D., Fink, G. R., Chau, P. M. L., & Dolan, R. J. (1997).
Neural activation during selective attention to subjective
emotional responses. *NeuroReport*, 8, 3969–3972.

Lane, R. D., & Nadel, L. (2000). *Cognitive neuroscience of emotion*. New York: Oxford University Press.

Lane, R. D., Reiman, E. M., Axelrod, B., Yun, L. S., Holmes, A.,
& Schwartz, G. E. (1998). Neural correlates of levels of emotional awareness. Evidence of an interaction between emotion and attention in the anterior cingulate cortex. *Journal of
Cognitive Neuroscience*, 10, 525–535.

Lazar, S. W., Bush, G., Gollub, R. L., Fricchione, G. L., Khalsa, G.,
& Benson, H. (2000). Functional brain mapping of the relaxation response and meditation. *NeuroReport*, 11, 1581–1585.

Lazar, S. W., Rosman, I. S., Vangel, M., Rao, V., Dusek, H.,
Benson, H., Gollub, R. L. (2003, November). Paper pre-
sented at the meeting of the Society for Neuroscience, New
Orleans, LA.

Lou, H. C., Kjaer, T. W., Friberg, L., Wildschiodtz, G., Holm,
S., & Nowak, M. (1999). A 15O-H2O PET study of medi-
tation and the resting state of normal consciousness. *Human
Brain Mapping*, 7, 98–105.

Lutz, A., & Thompson, E. (2003). Neurophenomenology.
Journal of Consciousness Studies, 10, 31–52.

Mabille, H. (1899). Hallucinations religieuses dans l'épilepsie.
Annales Médicopsychologiques, 9–10, 76–81.

Miller, B. L., Seeley, W. W., Mychack, P., Rosen, H. J., Mena,
I., & Boone, K. (2001). Neuroanatomy of the self: Evidence
from patients with frontotemporal dementia. *Neurology*, 57,
817–821.

Morgan, H. (1990). Dostoevsky's epilepsy: A case report and
comparison. *Surgical Neurology*, 33, 413–416.

Naito, H., & Matsui, N. (1988). Temporal lobe epilepsy with
ictal ecstatic state and interictal behavior of hypergraphia.
Journal of Nervous and Mental Diseases, 176, 123–124.

Neggers, S. F., Van der Lubbe, R. H., Ramsey, N. F., & Postma,
A. (2006). Interactions between ego- and allocentric neuronal representations of space. *Neuroimage*, 31, 320–331.

Newberg, A., Alavi, A., Baime, M., Pourdehnad, M., Santanna,
J., & d'Aquili, E. (2001a). The measurement of regional
cerebral blood flow during the complex cognitive task of
meditation: A preliminary SPECT study. *Psychiatry Research*,
106, 113–122.

Newberg, A., d'Aquili, E., & Rause, V. (2001b). *Why God won't
go away*. New York: Ballantine Books.

Newberg, A., & Lee, B. Y. (2005). The neuroscientific study of
religious and spiritual pheneomena: Or why God doesn't use
biostatistics. *Zygon*, 40, 469–489.

Newberg, A., Pourdehnad, M., Alavi, A., & d'Aquili, E. G.
(2003). Cerebral blood flow during meditative prayer:
Preliminary findings and methodological issues. *Perceptual
and Motor Skills*, 97, 625–630.

Newberg, A. B., Wintering, N. A., Morgan, D., & Waldman, M.
R. (2006). The measurement of regional cerebral blood flow
during glossolalia: A preliminary SPECT study. *Psychiatry
Research*, 148, 67–71.

Ogata, A., & Miyakawa, T. (1998). Religious experiences in
epileptic patients with a focus on ictus-related episodes.
Psychiatry and Clinical Neuroscience, 52, 321–325.

Ongur, D., Ferry, A. T., & Price, J. L. (2003). Architectonic sub-
division of the human orbital and medial prefrontal cortex.
Journal of Comparative Neurology, 460, 425–449.

Ozkara, C., Sary, H., Hanoglu, L., Yeni, N., Aydogdu, I., &
Ozyurt, E. (2004). Ictal kissing and religious speech in a
patient with right temporal lobe epilepsy. *Epileptic Disorders*,
6, 241–245.

Parnia, S., Waller, D. G., Yeates, R., & Fenwick, P. (2001). A
qualitative and quantitative study of the incidence, features
and aetiology of near death experiences in cardiac arrest survivors. *Resuscitation*, 48, 149–156.

Persinger, M. A. (1983). Religious and mystical experiences as
artifacts of temporal lobe function: a general hypothesis.
Perceptual and Motor Skills, 57, 1255–1262.

Persinger, M. A., & Healey, F. (2002). Experimental facilitation
of the sensed presence: Possible intercalation between the
hemispheres induced by complex magnetic fields. *Journal of
Nervous and Mental Diseases*, 190, 533–541.

Picard, F., & Craig, A. D. (2009). Ecstatic epileptic seizures: A
potential window on the neural basis for human self-awareness. *Epilepsy and Behavior*, 16, 539–546.

Ritskes, R., Ritskes-Hoitinga, M., Stodkilde-Jorgensen, H.,
Baerentsen, K., & Hartman, T. (2003). MRI scanning
during Zen meditation: The picture of enlightenment?
Constructivism in the Human Sciences, 8, 85–90.

Roberts, J. K., & Guberman, A. (1989). Religion and epilepsy.
Psychiatry Journal University of Ottawa, 14, 282–286.

Rolls, E. T., Kringelbach, M. L., & de Araujo, I. E. (2003).
Different representations of pleasant and unpleasant odours
in the human brain. *European Journal of Neuroscience*, 18,
695–703.

Ruby, P., & Decety, J. (2003). What you believe versus what
you think they believe: A neuroimaging study of conceptual perspective-taking. *European Journal of Neuroscience*, 17,
2475–2480.

Sabom, M. (1998). *Light and death: One doctor's fascinating account of near-death experiences*. Grand Rapids, MI:
Zondervan.

Saver, J. L., & Rabin, J. (1997). The neural substrates of religious experience. *Journal of Neuropsychiatry and Clinical
Neuroscience*, 9, 498–510.

Shapiro, D. H., & Walsh, R. N. (1984). *Meditation: Classical
and contemporary perspectives*. New York: Aldine de Gruyter.

Shimomura, T., Fujiki, M., Akiyoshi, J., Yoshida, T., Tabata, M.,
Kabasawa, H., & Kobayashi, H. (2008). Functional brain
mapping during recitation of Buddhist scriptures and repetition of the Namu Amida Butsu: A study in experienced
Japanese monks. *Turkish Neurosurgery*, 18, 134–141.

Spiegel, H., Aronson, M., Fleiss, J. L., & Haber, J. (1976).
Psychometric analysis of the Hypnotic Induction Profile.
International Journal of Clinical and Experimental Hypnosis,
24, 300–315.

Spilka, B., & McIntosh, D. N. (1995). Attribution theory and
religious experience. In R. W. Hood (Ed.), *Handbook of religious experience* (pp. 421–445). Birmingham, AL: Religious
Education Press.

Spratling, W. P. (1904). *Epilepsy and its treatment*. Philadelphia:
W. B. Saunders.

Stace, W. T. (1960). *Mysticism and philosophy*. New York:
Macmillan.

Tucker, D. M., Novelly, R. A., & Walker, P. J. (1987).
Hyperreligiosity in temporal lobe epilepsy: Redefining the
relationship. *Journal of Nervous and Mental Diseases*, 175,
181–184.

van Lommel, P., van Wees, R., Meyers, V., & Elfferich, I.
(2001). Near-death experience in survivors of cardiac

arrest: A prospective study in the Netherlands. *Lancet, 358,* 2039–2045.

Varela, F. J., Lachaux, J-P., Rodriguez, E., & Martinerie, J. (2001). The brainweb: Phase synchronization and large-scale integration. *Nature Reviews Neuroscience, 2,* 229–239.

Waldron, J. L. (1998). The life impact of transcendent experiences with a pronounced quality of noesis. *Journal of Transpersonal Psychology, 30,* 103–134.

Wallace, B. A. (1999). The Buddhist tradition of Samatha: Methods for refining and examining consciousness. *Journal of Consciousness Studies, 6,* 175–187.

Waxman, S. G., & Geschwind, N. (1975). The interictal behavior syndrome of temporal lobe epilepsy. *Archives of General Psychiatry, 32,* 1580–1586

Willmore, L. J., Heilman, K. M., Fennell, E., & Pinnas, R. M. (1980). Effect of chronic seizures on religiosity. *Transactions of the American Neurological Association, 105,* 85–87.

Wuerfel, J., Krishnamoorthy, E. S., Brown, R. J., Lemieux, L., Koepp, M., Tebartz van Elst, L., & Trimble, M. (2004). Religiosity is associated with hippocampal but not amygdala volumes in patients with refractory epilepsy. *Journal of Neurology Neurosurgery and Psychiatry, 75,* 640–642.

The Psychology of Near-Death Experiences and Spirituality

Bruce Greyson

Abstract

Near-death experiences (NDEs) occur in 10%–20% of people who come close to death, and they are similar to mystical experiences occurring in other settings. Their incidence and features are not influenced by prior religious beliefs, although cultural background may affect the interpretation of some of those features. However, NDEs profoundly influence one's subsequent sense of spirituality, leading to increased compassion, altruism, and sense of purpose in life, and to decreased fear of death, competitiveness, and materialistic interests. They do not necessarily lead to an increased involvement in organized religion but rather tend to foster an internal sense of connection to the divine and to something greater than the self. The mechanism by which NDEs bring about these changes is unclear, but it may be related to their inescapable challenge to the materialistic model of mind-brain identity and the implication that there is a spiritual component to humans that appears, under extreme circumstances, to function independent of the physical body.

Key Words: near-death experience, spirituality, mystical experience, consciousness, mind-body problem

Introduction

Some individuals when they come close to death report having unusual experiences that they interpret as spiritual or religious. These profound experiences, which have come to be called near-death experiences (NDEs), often include a sense of separation from the physical body, cosmic unity, divine revelation, ineffability, a sense that the experience transcends personal ego, and encounters with religious figures and a mystical or divine presence. Moody, who coined the term *near-death experience* in 1975, defined them as "profound spiritual events that happen, uninvited, to some individuals at the point of death" (Moody & Perry, 1988, p. 11).

This phenomenon was first described as a discrete syndrome by Heim in 1892 (translated into English by Noyes & Kletti, 1972), and recent research has suggested that it occurs in 10%–20% of people who are clinically dead (Greyson, 1998). Although the

term *near-death experience* and its acronym *NDE* were not coined until 1975, accounts of similar events can be found in the folklore and writings of European, Middle Eastern, African, Indian, East Asian, Pacific, and Native American cultures.

NDEs are reported by individuals who were pronounced clinically dead but then resuscitated; by individuals who actually died but were able to describe their experiences in their final moments (often called *deathbed visions*); and by individuals who, in the course of accidents or illnesses, simply feared that they were near death. Although all elements of the NDE can be reported by individuals who merely perceive themselves to be near death, certain features, such as enhanced cognitive function, an encounter with a brilliant light, and positive emotions are more common among individuals whose closeness to death is documented by medical records (Owens, Cook, & Stevenson, 1990).

Closeness to death may be an even more significant factor among children: In one study, although NDEs were recounted by up to half of those children who survived critical illnesses, they were not recounted by children who suffered serious illnesses that were not potentially fatal (Morse et al., 1986).

Phenomenology of Near-Death Experiences

In coining the term *near-death experience*, Moody (1975) identified 15 elements that seemed to recur in NDE reports: ineffability, hearing oneself pronounced dead, feelings of peace, hearing unusual noises, seeing a dark tunnel, being out of the body, meeting spiritual beings, encountering a bright light or "being of light," panoramic life review, a realm where all knowledge exists, cities of light, a realm of bewildered spirits, supernatural rescue, border or limit, and coming back into the body. He later (Moody, 1977) added four recurrent aftereffects: frustration upon relating the experience to others, broadened or deepened appreciation of life, elimination of fear of death, and corroboration of out-of-body visions.

Moody noted that no two NDE accounts were precisely the same, that no experience in his collection included more than 12 of these original 15 elements, that no one element appeared in every narrative, and that the order in which elements appeared varied from one experience to another (1975); and he warned that his list was intended as a rough theoretical model rather than a fixed definition (Moody, 1977). Children's NDEs are similar to those of adults, except that they tend not to include a life review or meetings with deceased friends and relatives, two differences that might be expected, in light of children's brief experience with life (Bush, 1983; Morse et al., 1986).

The most common features of NDEs can be grouped into four components. Most NDEs include features from all four components, although many experiences are dominated by one or more component (Greyson, 1985). The first component, *cognitive features* reflecting changes in thought processes, includes distortions in the sense of time, acceleration of thought processes, a life review or panoramic memory, and a sense of revelation or sudden understanding. The second component, *affective features* reflecting changes in emotional state, includes a sense of peace and well-being, feelings of joy, a sense of cosmic unity, and an encounter with a brilliant light that seems to radiate unconditional love. The third component, *paranormal features* reflecting apparent psychic phenomena, includes extraordinarily vivid physical sensations, apparent extrasensory perception, precognitive visions, and a sense of being out of the physical body. The final component, *transcendental features* reflecting apparent otherworldly phenomena, includes apparent travel to a mystical or unearthly realm or dimension, an encounter with a mystical being or presence, visible spirits of deceased or religious figures, and a border beyond which one cannot return to earthly life.

Explanatory Models for Near-Death Experiences

How can these phenomena best be understood? No variables that have yet been studied, such as age, gender, race, or history of mental illness, predict either the occurrence or type of NDE. There has been ample speculation about the cause of NDEs but very few data bearing on the question.

A plausible physiological model has attributed NDEs to decreased oxygen (hypoxia) or to complete lack of oxygen (anoxia), since that appears to be the final common pathway to death (Whinnery, 1997). However, hypoxia or anoxia generally produces idiosyncratic, frightening hallucinations and leads to agitation and belligerence, quite unlike the peaceful NDE with consistent, universal features. Furthermore, studies of people near death have shown that those who have NDEs do not have lower oxygen levels than those who do not have NDEs (Sabom, 1982; van Lommel et al., 2001).

A recent report suggested that increased carbon dioxide (hypercapnia) was associated with NDEs in cardiac arrest survivors (Klemenc-Ketis, Kersnik, & Grmec, 2010), although other studies reported decreased (Sabom, 1982) or normal levels of carbon dioxide (Parnia, Waller, Yeates, & Fenwick, 2001) in the same population. However, this unconfirmed correlation may simply reflect the known association between hypercapnia and increased cardiac output, which would lead to less amnesia following cardiac arrest. That is, this correlation may reflect simply that patients who are able to recall more of their cardiac arrest also report more NDEs (Greyson, 2010a). The meaning of a correlation of NDEs with blood levels of carbon dioxide is further complicated by the fact that levels of carbon dioxide in the blood do not necessarily reflect levels in the brain (Gliksman & Kellehear, 1990).

Another frequently cited physiological model has attributed NDEs to medications given to dying persons. However, although some drugs may on occasion induce experiences that bear superficial similarities to NDE, comparative studies have shown that patients who receive medications in fact report *fewer* NDEs than do patients who receive no medication (Greyson, 1982; Osis & Haraldsson, 1977; Sabom, 1982).

NDEs have also been speculatively linked to a number of neurotransmitters in the brain, most frequently endorphins (Carr, 1982), although other models have implicated serotonin, adrenaline, vasopressin, and glutamate (Jansen, 1997; Morse, Venecia, & Milstein, 1989; Saavedra-Aguilar & Gómez-Jeria, 1989). NDEs have also been speculatively linked to a number of anatomic locations in the brain, most often the right temporal lobe (Blanke, Ortigue, Landis, & Seeck, 2002) or the left temporal lobe (Britton & Bootzin, 2004), although other neuroscientists have argued for involvement of the frontal lobe attention area, the parietal lobe orientation area, the thalamus, the hypothalamus, the amygdala, and the hippocampus (Azari et al., 2001; Fenwick, 2001; Newberg & d'Aquili, 1994). These putative neurological mechanisms, for which there is little empirical evidence, may suggest brain pathways through which NDEs are expressed or interpreted, but they do not necessarily imply causal mechanisms.

Recently, an association has been suggested between NDEs and "REM intrusion," the intrusion into waking consciousness of thought processes typical of rapid eye movement sleep (Nelson, Mattingly, Lee, & Schmitt, 2006). NDEs and REM intrusion share common elements of extraordinary light and a sense of being immobilized yet alert to the surroundings, and a sense of being dead; and it has been suggested that other aspects of NDEs, including autoscopy, light, visual experience, pleasant feelings, and transcendent qualities, can also occur in other conditions associated with REM intrusion.

However, the survey on which this correlation with REM intrusion was based drew its NDE sample from people who shared their experiences on the Internet, suggesting an unusual willingness to acknowledge anomalous experiences, albeit anonymously; whereas the comparison sample was "recruited from medical center personnel or their contacts" and queried in face-to-face interviews, possibly inhibiting their endorsement of symptoms they would likely identify as pathological. In fact, only 7% of the comparison group acknowledged hypnagogic hallucinations, about one-fourth of that in the general population (Ohayon, Priest, Zully, Smirne, & Paiva, 2002).

Data arguing against the contribution of REM intrusion to NDEs include features, such as fear, typical in sleep paralysis but rare in NDEs, and the occurrence of typical NDEs under general anesthesia and other drugs that inhibit REM (Cronin, Keifer, Davies, King, & Bixler, 2001). Finally, a correlation between REM intrusion, if it were to be corroborated by additional research, might suggest either that REM intrusion contributes to NDE phenomenology or that NDEs enhance subsequent REM intrusion. The latter interpretation is supported by the increased REM intrusion in posttraumatic stress disorder (Husain, Miller, & Carwile, 2001) and the increased posttraumatic stress symptoms following NDEs (Greyson, 2001).

Psychological models have also been proposed, attributing NDEs to psychological defense mechanisms, depersonalization, wishful thinking, retroactive confabulation, and expectation (Greyson, 1983b). While plausible, none of these psychological models are supported by empirical evidence. Expectations likely influence an experiencer's interpretation of certain features of the NDE, but they do not appear to influence the experience itself: Children who are too young to have internalized expectations of death or of an afterlife describe the same NDE features as do adults (Bush, 1983; Herzog & Herrin, 1985; Morse et al., 1986); cross-cultural studies show few differences in NDE content from differing societies (Holck, 1978–1979; McClenon, 1994); and NDE descriptions are not affected by the experiencer's prior knowledge of NDEs or expectations of the dying process or of an afterlife (Athappilly, Greyson, & Stevenson, 2006; Greyson, 1991; Greyson & Stevenson, 1980).

Similarity of Near-Death and Mystical Experiences

Four years before Moody coined the term "near-death experience," Noyes (1971, 1972) noted that altered states of consciousness in people as they approached death often have mystical, transcendental, cosmic, or religious features. He included in those features ineffability, transcendence of time and space, sense of truth, loss of control, intensified emotion, and disordered perception.

Many of the experiential features of mystical experiences in general are similar to those of NDEs. The feelings of peace and joy, the ineffability of the experience, the sense of being in the presence of something greater than oneself, and the experience of a bright light or "being of light" are all features common to both NDEs and mystical experiences. Cressy (1994) compared typical NDE phenomenology and aftereffects to the ongoing mystical experiences of medieval Catholic mystics St. Theresa of Avila and St. John of the Cross, and concluded that they shared ecstatic out-of-body travel, visions of God, clairvoyance, loss of fear of death, and healing transformations. She noted that nearness to death has always played a role in the spiritual path, and that for Sts. Theresa and John, mysticism was a preparation for death. She pointed out, however, that unlike mystics, those who have NDEs are thrust suddenly into spiritual consciousness without any preparation and then returned to a community in which such experiences are not valued.

Just as with NDEs, the onset of a mystical experience is often signaled by overwhelming feelings of joy, happiness, and peace (James, 1902). People sometimes describe a feeling of sudden release in a mystical experience, and although they may sometimes use the term "release" metaphorically, some reports definitively describe literal out-of-body experiences. Many people also report enhanced mental functioning or heightened perception in mystical experiences, just as in NDEs. A sensory phenomenon that is particularly common to both NDEs and mystical experiences is the sense of seeing a bright light of unusual quality. As with "release," some people seem to use the phrase "seeing the light" in a figurative sense, but others are clearly referring to what seemed to them to be a real and vivid sensory phenomenon.

Pahnke and Richards (1966) delineated nine aspects of mystical experience, based on the previous work of James (1902) and Stace (1960): a sense of cosmic unity or oneness, transcendence of time and space, deeply felt positive mood, sense of sacredness, noetic quality or intuitive illumination, paradoxicality, ineffability, transiency, and persistent positive aftereffects. All nine of these features are commonly reported as part of the NDE (Pennachio, 1986). However, whereas all of these features can be seen in NDEs, typical NDEs differ from classical mystical experiences in three respects: the persistence of individual identity, such as in the life review and encounters with deceased relatives; the clarity of perceived events; and the lower frequency of union with the divine, which is a defining characteristic of mystical experience (Wulff, 2000).

Perhaps the most important feature common to both mystical experiences and NDEs, however, is the transformative impact of the experience. NDEs generally have a profound and lasting impact on many people who experience them. They often precipitate a significant change in values, attitude toward death, and a new sense of purpose or meaning in life. Similarly, mystical experiences have been recognized for more than a century as leading to sudden and lasting changes in character and values (James, 1902), including changes in the person's relationship with God, perception and appreciation of nature, attitude toward self, and, perhaps most significantly, attitude toward other people (Starbuck, 1906).

This transformative aspect of NDEs has not been reported in connection with the various fragmentary experiences that are sometimes equated with NDEs, such as the "dreamlets" induced by hypoxia or other abnormalities of blood-gas concentrations (Whinnery, 1997) or experiences reported by patients receiving temporal lobe stimulation (Blanke et al., 2002). Moreover, the transformative features associated with NDEs differ from those associated with coming closing to death but not having an NDE (Greyson, 1983a; Ring, 1984; van Lommel, van Wees, Meyers, & Elfferich, 2001).

Near-Death Experiences and Prior Religiosity or Spirituality

Since religion addresses fundamental human concerns such as death and dying, it is plausible that religious orientation might influence NDEs (McLaughlin & Maloney, 1984). One skeptical view of the NDE is that it represents essentially a religiously inspired illusion: The crisis of impending death triggers a series of hallucinations in keeping with an individual's religious belief system and expectations concerning an afterlife.

Several studies have searched for associations between religion or religiosity and subsequent NDEs. In a cross-cultural study in the United States and India, Osis and Haraldsson (1977) did not find any straightforward relationship between religiousness and deathbed visions, although they did find that an individual's belief system influenced the *interpretation* of the experience. Sabom and Kreutziger (1978), in a study of 107 survivors of cardiac arrest, also found no relationship between NDEs and extent of prior religious involvement. In a study of people who had come close to death from a suicide attempt, I found that NDEs were associated neither with religious preference or religiosity, nor with prior expectations of death, dying, or postmortem survival (Greyson, 1991).

Ring (1980a) interviewed 102 survivors of near-death crises, asking a number of questions that collectively provided an overall index of religiousness, including degree of religiosity, strength of belief in God, conviction about life after death, and belief in heaven and hell. He too concluded that "neither the likelihood nor the depth of a near-death experience was systematically related to individual religiousness [or] religious affiliation" (1980a, p. 4). However, Ring found, as did Osis and Haraldsson (1977), "that the *interpretation* that was placed on the experience by the individual was markedly influenced by his religious belief system.... Also, one's *emotional reaction* to the experience may be affected by one's prior belief system, as one would expect" (Ring, 1980a, p. 4).

McLaughlin and Maloney (1984) speculated that intrinsically oriented religious persons, who tend to have more positive views of death and hope in an afterlife of reward, might be more likely to have deeper NDEs; and that people who have a vital relationship with God might be more receptive to an NDE. They interviewed 40 people who had NDEs, including Protestants, Roman Catholics, Jews, followers of the Baha'i faith, and people with no religious affiliation. They administered to their participants a standardized measure of religious orientation that included three basic religious attitudes: compliance to religion for personal gain (extrinsic religious orientation), identification with religion for support (consensual religious orientation), and internalization of religion for its own intrinsic value (intrinsic religious orientation). They found no significant relationship between depth of NDE and various measures of religious orientation or other religious measures.

Near-Death Experiences and Subsequent Religiosity or Spirituality

If NDEs are not influenced by prior religious belief or religiosity, do the experiences themselves affect *subsequent* religious preference, religiosity, or spirituality? Several studies have documented that NDEs can permanently and dramatically alter the individual experiencer's attitudes, beliefs, and values, often leading to profound and lasting personal transformations. Those who have NDEs tend to see themselves as integral parts of a benevolent and purposeful universe in which personal gain, particularly at others' expense, is no longer relevant. Aftereffects most often reported include increases in spirituality, concern for others, and appreciation of life; a heightened sense of purpose; and decreases in fear of death, in materialistic attitudes, and in competitiveness (Bauer, 1985; Flynn, 1982, 1986; Grey, 1985; Greyson, 1983a, 1992; McLaughlin & Maloney, 1984; Noyes, 1980; Ring, 1980b, 1984; Ring & Valarino, 1998; Sabom, 1982, 1998). These

changes that follow NDEs meet the definition of spiritual transformation as "a dramatic change in religious belief, attitude, and behavior that occurs over a relatively short period of time" (Schwartz, 2000, p. 4).

In studies comparing the attitudes of those who have had NDEs before and after their experiences, Noyes (1980) found that they reported a reduced fear of death, a sense of relative invulnerability, a feeling of special importance or destiny, and a strengthened belief in postmortem existence. Ring (1980b, 1984) found that those who have had NDEs reported a greater appreciation for life, a renewed sense of purpose, greater confidence and flexibility in coping with life's vicissitudes, increased value of love and service, greater compassion for others, a heightened sense of spiritual purpose, decreased concern with personal status and material possessions, and a greatly reduced fear of death.

Ring (1980a) collected information on religious aftereffects among 102 survivors of near-death crises. He found that those who had had NDEs did describe themselves as more religious than they were before, whereas those near-death survivors who reported no NDE did not report any change in their religiousness. However, although those who had had NDEs said they felt more religious, they did not attend church more often than they had prior to their experiences, nor did they participate in other modes of formal religious worship:

> Rather, there is a heightened *inward* religious feeling that is often indicated which does not seem to require a conventional religious format for it to be manifested. Instead, near-death survivors will describe themselves as feeling closer to God, as more inwardly prayerful, or as having a greater awareness of God's presence. This personal sense of God is sometime so strong that conventional religious observances seem irrelevant or unnecessary.
> (*Ring*, 1980a, p. 4)

Furthermore, even though those who had had NDEs expressed indifference toward organized religion, they also described "an overall tolerance for all ways of religious worship. From this point of view, there is no one religion or religious denomination which is superior or 'true'; rather, all religions are expression of a single truth" (Ring, 1980a, p. 4). In summarizing these changes, Ring concluded that those who had had NDEs emphasized the importance of love, caring, and compassion for others: "if there was a single value which seemed to epitomize the comments of near-death survivors... it was their increased emphasis on the need for *unconditional love* or *acceptance* for others" (Ring, 1980a, p. 4).

Ring focused his second book on NDEs (1984) on the radical reorientation in spiritual values and life directions that often follow NDEs. Unlike many authors who based their conclusions on subjective testimonies of experiencers, Ring included a number of objective measures of psychospiritual changes to bolster his arguments. In his most recent book on NDEs, Ring (Ring & Valarino, 1998) focused on the spiritual meaning and "soul-making" significance of NDEs.

Flynn (1982) found that those who had had NDEs reported a greatly increased concern for others, increased belief in an afterlife, increased religious interest and feeling, decreased fear of death, and lessened desire for material success and approval of others. Subsequently, Flynn (1986) described the life-transforming nature of NDEs, changing experiencers' values, decreasing their fear of death, and giving their lives new meaning. He argued that NDEs produce the same aftereffects as religious conversion experiences: Those who faced death return with a love of the divine light that transformed their own lives and a mission to bring that love to others. He concluded that NDEs lead to (a) a shift from ego-centered to other-centered consciousness, (b) disposition to love unconditionally, (c) heightened empathy, (d) decreased interest in status symbols and material possessions, (e) reduced fear of death, and (f) deepened spiritual consciousness.

McLaughlin and Maloney (1984) measured religious orientation and religious change as a result of the NDE in 40 experiencers who were interviewed in depth and completed a series of questionnaires. They found strong associations between depth of NDE and various measures of religious change *after* the experience. Those who had had NDEs placed greater importance on religion after the NDE and became more active in their religion; and the strength of those changes was positively associated with the depth of their NDE. For many experiencers, the NDE was an experiential reaffirmation of the reality of the spiritual realm they had believed in previously, and it served to intensity their relationship with God. This increase in religious activity contradicted Ring's finding that NDEs led to inward spiritual change but no change in religious activity. McLaughlin and Maloney concluded that NDEs represent a spiritual intervention in the lives of people, regardless of their religious orientations or beliefs beforehand. They found that the NDE reaffirmed religious faith for some experiencers, had no effect on beliefs of others, and led still others to abandon their prior belief systems.

Lorimer (1990) reported that NDEs, and particularly the moral assessment in the life review, provided an experiential basis for moral order based on "empathic resonance" with other people, meaning the direct perception of an intrinsic interconnectedness and interdependence of all living beings. He argued that in the life review one experiences firsthand, with compassionate and empathic understanding, how one's thoughts, feelings, and actions affect others. This experience, he reported, leads to a new appreciation of the Golden Rule—"whatsoever you wish that men would do unto you, do so to them" (Matthew 7:12) —as not just a prescription for moral conduct but also an accurate description of the interconnectedness of the universe. Lorimer concluded that the ego-shattering effect of NDEs reveals the illusion of separate individual egos by inducing direct experience of cosmic unity.

Sutherland (1990) interviewed 50 people who had had NDEs and specifically asked them to differentiate changes in their spirituality from changes in their religiosity. Her subjects largely rejected describing themselves as "religious," often vehemently, but did describe themselves as "spiritual." They reported "dramatic change in religious affiliation, especially from organized religion, of whatever denomination, to no religion" (1990, p. 24). Following their NDEs, 76% of her interviewees described themselves as "spiritual," an increase from 16% prior to their NDEs; whereas 6% described themselves as "religious," a decrease from 24% prior to their NDEs. None of her subjects described the NDE as a religious experience, but 70% described it as a spiritual experience. Asked an open-ended question about the most significant change resulting from the NDE, the single most common response (31% of respondents) was "spirituality" or "spiritual growth."

In studies comparing the attitudes of those who had had NDEs with those of other groups, including persons who had come close to death but not had NDEs, I found that experiencers placed significantly lower value on social status, professional and material success, and fame (Greyson, 1983a), and found death less threatening (Greyson, 1992). Although decreased fear of death may be associated with increased suicidal risk (Shneidman, 1971), those who have had NDEs paradoxically express stronger objections to suicide than do comparison samples, primarily on the basis of increased transpersonal or transcendental beliefs (Greyson,

1992–1993). These profound changes in attitudes and in behavior have been corroborated in long-term studies of those who have had NDEs and in interviews with their significant others (Ring, 1984). More specifically (and seemingly paradoxically, given the positive nature of most experiences and the reluctance of many experiencers to return to the body), those who experience an NDE as the result of a suicide attempt rarely attempt suicide again, in contrast to most other suicide attempters. This effect may be the result of an increased sense of purpose and appreciation for life (Greyson, 1981, 1992–1993).

Musgrave (1997) surveyed 51 people who had had NDEs about changes in their attitudes, beliefs, and behavior. She found that the majority of her respondents claimed that since the NDE they were more helpful toward others (82%), more compassionate or understanding (82%), more open minded in general (82%), more spiritually or religiously open (80%), more intuitive (78%), more aware of guidance by a higher power (75%), more appreciative of life (73%), emotionally stronger (69%), more purposeful (65%), and less fearful of life (51%). Absolute belief in God increased from 24% before the NDE to 82% after the experience; definite belief in an afterlife increased from 22% to 92%; 89% reported a decreased fear of death; and 88% reported a positive change in spirituality. In general, a sense of spirituality or inner connection to God gained in the NDE took precedence over subscribing to religious doctrine. Those believing that there was more than one path to God increased from 28% before the NDE to 65% after the experience; 77% claimed that their lives had changed dramatically as a result of the NDE; and 73% reported that the NDE led them to discover their life purpose.

Sabom (1998), after completing a study of 116 NDEs and then observing NDEs and their aftereffects in his own patients over 20 years as a cardiologist, found that NDEs produced a stronger faith and a higher level of commitment to traditional religious practice. Although he had originally approached the study of NDEs as a skeptical medical scientist, expecting to find that these experiences were misfirings of a dying brain, he eventually concluded that they were instead powerful spiritual experiences, whose underlying message was consistent with divine revelation from more traditional sources.

Bauer (1985), using an instrument based on Frankl's (1969) logotherapy, found that NDEs led to significant positive changes in the purpose and meaning of life and in death acceptance. A large study of survivors of cardiac arrest showed that, after both a 2-year and an 8-year follow-up interval, people who had NDEs had a significant decrease in their fear of death and a significant increase in their belief in survival after death, whereas those who had not had an NDE tended not to believe in survival (van Lommel et al., 2001).

Theological Implications of Near-Death Experiences

Mainstream theologians have tended to greet NDEs with what Fox (2003) called "deafening silence." Perhaps some theologians regard NDEs as so expected at the point of death that they do not merit discussion, whereas others ignore the phenomenon out of general academic distrust of any paranormal phenomena. Zaleski (1987) suggested that many theologians felt more comfortable regarding NDEs as metaphors or literary motifs rather than as actual encounters with the divine, and Couliano (1991) placed NDEs within the cross-cultural tradition of fantastic accounts of otherworld journeys. Indeed, the Buddhist perspective on visions of the dying, as described in *The Tibetan Book of the Dead* (Evans-Wentz, 1957), is that they occur in the mind of the experiencer; and Küng's response to NDEs was that they are psychological experiences of dying that have no bearing on what happens after death (Küng, 1984).

Whatever the reason for the disinterest in NDEs among theologians, the result is that most of what has been written about the theological implications of NDEs has come from psychologists. Ring, for example, wrote:

> When an individual knows with a sense of
> unshakable certitude that he can exist outside of his
> own body, he intuitively understands that physical
> death is not an end.... Such a view does not logically
> require a *religious* interpretation of the afterlife, but,
> in practice, it is usually put that way.
> (*Ring,* 1980b, p. 110)

He further noted that those people who see visions of deceased loved ones in their NDEs become convinced that life beyond death is more than "a vague emotional yearning" (Ring, 1980b, p. 110). Fox has opined that

> many of the claims that near-death experiencers
> (NDErs) have made in the last quarter-century
> are such that they may well be said to *demand* a

response which goes to the very heart of the West's understanding of what it is to be human, and what it is for human beings to die.

(*Fox*, 2003, p. 5)

Adherents to various religions have claimed NDEs as empirical support of their particular doctrines. It has been argued that NDEs provide striking parallels to the teachings of the Hindu *Upanishads* and to early Babylonian, Egyptian, and Zoroastrian texts (Holck, 1978–1979), to shamanism (Green, 2001), to Taoism (Hermann, 1990), to Sino-Japanese Pure Land Buddhism (Becker, 1981), to Tibetan Buddhism (Becker, 1985; Holck, 1978–1979), to Gnostic Christianity of the 2nd through 4th centuries (Bain, 1999), to medieval Christian religious treatises (Zaleski, 1987), to Mormon doctrine (Lundahl, 1983), to Christian Universalism (Vincent, 2003), to Spong's New Christianity (Gibbs, 2005), and to New Age spirituality (Lee, 2003). Regarding these "religious wars" over NDEs, Ring has expressed regret that "the body of the NDE, like some sort of sacred relic or corrupted corpse, is fought over by warring parties either for rights of possession or unceremonious burial" (Ring, 2000, p. 240). As Fox concluded, "NDEs cannot unambiguously be used as apologetic tools for the propagation of any one particular religious or spiritual tradition or be somehow fitted into any one tradition to the exclusion of all others" (2003, p. 339).

Ring (1980b) found beliefs common among those who have had NDEs that seemed consistent with a Judaeo-Christian worldview. More than half of his sample of those who have had NDEs reached a point where a decision was made either by or for them as to whether they would return to physical life, and 40% of those described an encounter with a presence (not always seen) that included an auditory or telepathic conversation. Sometimes the presence would describe specific consequences of the decision whether to return, including information about what would occur if the experiencer chose to return to life. This was often accompanied by a life review and sometimes a preview of events to come, in which the experiencer evaluated his or her life. Most experiencers interpreted this sequence of events as a direct encounter with God and with His unconditional love.

Ring himself interpreted this sequence of events not as an encounter with an external deity, but rather with the experiencer's "higher self," of which the individual personality is only a fragment. This higher self seems to have divine aspects and is clearly omniscient with respect to the personality; Ring speculated that experiences of this encounter may give rise to the Christian concept of the "guardian angel" (1980b).

Ring later documented further changes in attitude and belief in those who have had NDEs consistent with the dominant Western Judaeo-Christian heritage (Ring & Valarino, 1998). He argued that NDEs lead directly to the Golden Rule and to Jesus's admonition that "as you did it to one of the least of these my brethren, you did it unto me" (Matthew 25:40). In fact, Ring argued, in concert with Lorimer (1990), that for those who have had NDEs, the Golden Rule is no longer just a commandment one is taught to obey, but rather an indisputable law of nature, as inevitable as gravity. They know it is the way the universe works because they have experienced it firsthand in suffering directly the effects of their actions upon others. Though they do not feel punished or judged for their misdeeds, they do receive back as part of their life review everything they have ever given out, measure for measure.

Some Christian theologians have corroborated this view of NDEs as consistent with their teachings. Hampe conducted a study of dying people's experiences before Moody coined the term "near-death experience." Working independently of Moody, he reported a similar phenomenon, concluding that the expansion of consciousness at death implied separation of the soul from the body and that the continued fellowship with God reported by many people who have had NDEs reinforced New Testament teachings (Hampe, 1979). That conclusion was shared by other theological scholars: "What appears to happen is that the soul leaves the body and begins to move on to another mode of existence" (Badham & Badham, 1982, p. 89).

However, whereas some religious scholars view NDEs as proof of spiritual capacities in humans and of divine grace, others see them as Satanic deceptions that contradict Christian teachings. The conflicting and often negative views of psychic phenomena held by many religious people extend to their interpretations of NDEs (McLaughlin & Maloney, 1984).

Fox (2003) pointed out ways that NDEs appear to contradict traditional Christian beliefs in the afterlife. First, NDEs suggest a separation of a disembodied soul from the physical body at the point of death, which seems to contradict the Christian belief in resurrection of an embodied soul. Second, NDEs imply that survival of death is a universal human birthright, rather than a gift of grace. Third, a judgment at the time of death appears to contradict the belief in a far-off judgment day when Christ returns. (However, Fox did note that there is a belief going back at least to the 3rd century in two judgments: first a "friendly warning" at death and later the earth-shattering finality of the judgment day.) Fourth, the divine being of light is often encountered by non-Christians, who do not identify it as Christ. Finally, people of varying religious backgrounds who have had NDEs seem equally likely to describe a blissful or "heavenly" experience, regardless of whether they were saved, born again, or baptized.

Fox reconciled these discrepancies by invoking the traditional Christian belief that death ushers in a type of sleep that lasts until the judgment day, but that that sleep is accompanied by a dream, which we have come to call an NDE. Others suggested that apparent insights from NDEs cannot challenge traditional concepts of death because

> near-death experiences may be too brief an experience of the dying process to reveal much knowledge about the ultimate nature of death. The person may not have entered deeply enough into the dying process to experience the ultimate nature of death.
> (*McLaughlin & Maloney*, 1984, p. 157)

Some Christians have claimed that NDEs not only contradict biblical religion but furthermore foster an anti-Christian "New Age" moral code. Although the interpretation of NDEs as deceptions perpetrated by "fallen spirits" has been espoused by at least one Eastern Orthodox theologian (Rose, 1980), this perspective has been put forward primarily by Fundamentalist Protestant authors. They have argued that NDEs must have a Satanic rather than divine source, because they present death as a benign event in which the Grim Reaper is replaced by a nonjudgmental Being of Light who extends unconditional love to all souls, regardless of whether they are born-again Christians:

> Paul warns us that Satan's emissaries regularly disguise themselves, and that Satan himself appears as an "angel of light" (II Corinthians 11:14).... [Death] was the result of sinful disobedience. Death is preeminently the sign of that fall, and the symbol of God's rejection of sin... *not* regarded biblically as a normal and benign complement to the process of life, but as something alien and abnormal....
>
> For those who accept the values of [near-death experiencers]...the atoning death...of Jesus Christ

is not only unnecessary, it is meaningless and altogether irrelevant.
(*Albrecht & Alexander*, 1977, pp. 10–11)

Fox (2003) argued that this view implies that Satan's deception is more powerful than God's grace. He asked, if the loving being of light in NDEs is actually Satan pulling an appalling deception, then where is the Christian God of grace and truth, the real light? Vincent likewise argued, "Satan may be a neon sign, but God is the Light of the Universe" (Vincent, 2003, p. 64). Ring countered the argument that the being of light that seems to love everyone unconditionally must be Satanic by appealing to Jesus's dictum that "you will know them by their fruits" (Matthew 7:20). By that criterion, Ring argued, NDEs should be judged by their fruits of increased compassion, humility, honesty, and altruism (Ring & Valarino, 1998).

Regarding the question of whether unconditional love renders the atoning death of Christ irrelevant, Vincent (2003) argued that NDEs are compatible theologically with Christian Universalism, the Doctrine of Universal Salvation, a classical Christian position that was declared heretical at one point but has been espoused by a large number of theologians from Origen in the 3rd century to Barth in the 20th. This belief postulates that God, despite his wrathfulness and judgment, wills the eventual redemption of all people rather than condemnation to eternal hell, which would be inconsistent with the nature of God as loving. Vincent noted that virtually all the major religions include some kind of belief in universal salvation, but that Christian Universalism allows for a temporary hellish state to "shape up" if necessary before the ultimate reward. He argued that there is more biblical support for the doctrine of universal salvation than for the belief in salvation *for only those born again*, and he cited biblical passages favoring the doctrines that Jesus saves everyone, that humanity can be saved by good works, and that hell is not permanent.

Other religious writers have decried NDEs for holding out the false promise of "cheap grace," which they define as the unconditional forgiveness of sins without any required contrition (Tracy, 1993; Zaleski, 1987). The promise of "cheap grace" so defined may well be part of the popular image of NDEs, but it does not seem to play a role in the actual experience.

In fact, Ring argued, the unconditional love that those who have experienced NDEs report does not gloss over their sins or excuse their future behavior

(Ring & Valarino, 1998). Quite to the contrary, those who have had NDEs experience firsthand in their NDEs the painful consequences of their sinful behavior, and they return to earthly life as confirmed disciples, who understand from their own experience that their behavior does indeed matter far more than they could have imagined. Those who have had NDEs do not come back with a sense that they are perfect beings as they are now, but rather they return committed to work toward perfection and to carry out the work of a higher power, often at great emotional as well as material sacrifice. Far from encouraging indiscriminate behavior, the unconditional love they experienced confers on them the self-esteem, courage, and self-knowledge to bring about the kind of life changes demanded of disciples. Values and beliefs are changed, but those who have had NDEs still struggle to change their behaviors.

Cressy (1994) pointed out that NDEs differ from many other mystical experiences in that they do not occur in the context of a conscious search for meaning or resolution of spiritual crisis; a single encounter with mystical consciousness may start one on a spiritual path, but the NDE by itself does not confer sainthood: "One mystical experience does not make a mystic" (1994, p. 64). The empirical data support her view that all NDEs do not lead to immediate transformation; but whereas *all* NDEs do not lead to radical changes, those NDEs that *do* transform do so through a process that is characteristic of other spiritual encounters, sometimes evolving over a period of many years (van Lommel et al., 2001). Expanding on this theme of the NDE as a mere taste of mystical consciousness, Ring (1984) described NDEs as "spiritual catalysts" fostering spiritual awakening and development. He argued that this spiritual catalysis is linked particularly to the later stages of NDEs in which one transcends space and time, communes with a divine light, and is overcome with peace and joy.

Conclusion

Near-death experiences are common events, occurring in 10%–20% of people who come close to death, and bear many similarities to mystical experiences occurring in other settings. Their incidence and phenomenological features are not influenced by the experiencer's prior religious beliefs, although cultural background may affect the experiencer's interpretation of some of those features. However, NDEs profoundly influence the experiencer's subsequent sense of spirituality, leading to increased compassion, altruism, and sense of purpose in life, and to decreased fear of death, competitiveness, and materialistic interests. They do not necessarily lead to an increased involvement in organized religion, but rather they tend to foster an internal sense of connection to the divine and to something greater than the self. Furthermore, NDEs may have significant moral impact on people who do not experience them but only encounter them indirectly. Flynn (1986) described a project in which his college students practiced unconditional love, after having studied the message of NDEs, and were themselves transformed by the exercise. Like Flynn, Ring reported that his students, having studied NDEs, also became more empathic and spiritually oriented through applying the lessons of NDEs: that death is not fearsome, that life continues beyond, that love is more important than material possessions, and that everything happens for a reason (Ring & Valarino, 1998).

There are also suggestions that NDEs may have more widespread spiritual implications. Twentieth-century intellectuals as diverse as Toynbee, Jung, and Schweitzer have written that "nothing short of a worldwide spiritual revolution will suffice" to save human civilization (Lorimer, 1990, p. 259). Ring suggested "that the NDE can be viewed as an *evolutionary device* to bring about this transformation" (1984, p. 7) and that NDEs and similar mystical experiences may point the way toward unlocking humankind's dormant spiritual potential.

Ring (1984) speculated that, with increasing resuscitation technology enabling more and more individuals to return from the brink of death, the cumulative impact of their uplifting testimonies may foster the spiritual evolution of the collective consciousness of humanity. The title of his book on NDE aftereffects, *Heading Toward Omega*, comes from Teilhard de Chardin's notion of the "Omega point," a hypothetical end point in human history representing an evolutionary culmination in the highest strivings of human culture. Likewise, Badham (1997) argued that NDEs revitalize society's belief in God and hope for an afterlife.

Future Directions

Despite the extensive research into the religious and spiritual aftereffects of NDEs, there have been few studies of this topic among non-Christian populations (Kellehear, 2009). The differential impact of NDEs on people from different faith backgrounds remains to be elaborated.

Likewise, there remain questions about the trajectory of spiritual growth following NDEs. Most studies of NDE effects have been cross-sectional, leaving open the question of longitudinal changes in degree and quality of religiosity and spirituality over the course of a lifetime, and how NDE effects may interact with other influences on religious or spiritual development.

There is ample evidence *that* NDEs foster spiritual growth; what is not clear is *how* they do so. For example, it remains to be explored whether religious or spiritual growth is more closely associated with particular features of NDEs than with others, such as a sense of leaving the body, an apparent encounter with the divine, or an experience of unconditional love. It is plausible that NDEs alter experiencers' beliefs about their relationship to the divine and about their place in the universe by raising questions about basic assumptions about the relationship between the spiritual and the physical in general, and about the relationship between mind and brain in particular. How the mind–brain relationship may be altered at the approach of death may be the most fruitful direction for future investigation of the psychology of NDEs and spirituality.

Until the early 20th century, classical mechanics was the foundation for all sciences, on the assumption that observations of all sciences might someday be reduced to the laws of mechanics. At the heart of the classical worldview was materialist reductionism, the idea that any complex phenomenon could be understood by reducing it to its individual components, and eventually down to elementary material particles. This materialist worldview permeated psychology as it did other sciences, even though this reductionism required psychologists to focus exclusively on phenomena that could be described objectively by independent observers and ignore consciousness. Materialist psychology was epitomized by Watson, who asserted: "Psychology, as the behaviorist views it, is a purely objective, experimental branch of natural science which needs consciousness as little as do the sciences of chemistry and physics" (1914, p. 27). It is ironic that while Watson was aligning behaviorist psychology with classical mechanics, physicists were already moving beyond that model with a quantum physics that could not be formulated without reference to consciousness.

Classical physics, anchored in materialist reductionism, offered adequate descriptions of everyday mechanics but ultimately proved insufficient for describing the mechanics of extremely high speeds or small sizes, and was supplemented nearly a century ago by quantum physics, which by necessity includes consciousness in its formulation. Materialist psychology, modeled on the reductionism of classical physics, likewise offered adequate descriptions of everyday mental functioning but ultimately proved insufficient for describing cognition under extreme conditions. The exploration of mental function in such extraordinary circumstances reveals the limitations of the current model of mind-brain identity and the need for a more comprehensive explanatory model. For example, there have been more than 80 documented cases of the unexpected return of mental clarity and memory shortly before death in patients suffering from irreversible brain deterioration as in Alzheimer's disease (Nahm & Greyson, 2009), as well as rigorous studies of individuals with normal to high cognitive function despite having both cerebral hemispheres reduced by severe hydrocephalus to as little as 5% of the normal volume (Lorber, 1983).

NDEs include phenomena that challenge materialist reductionism (Greyson, 2003; Parnia et al., 2001; Schwartz, Stapp, & Beauregard, 2005; van Lommel et al., 2001), such as enhanced cognition and memory during cerebral impairment, accurate perceptions from a perspective outside the body, and reported visions of deceased persons, including surprising visions of those not previously known to be deceased (Greyson, 2010b). Complex consciousness, including cognition, perception, and memory, under conditions such as cardiac arrest and general anesthesia, when it cannot be associated with normal brain function, require a revised psychology anchored not in 19th-century classical physics but rather in 21st-century quantum physics that includes consciousness in its conceptual formulation.

For example, in five published studies alone, more than 100 NDEs have been reported occurring under conditions of cardiac arrest (Greyson, 2003; Parnia et al., 2001; Sabom, 1982; Schwaninger, Eisenberg, Schechtman, & Weiss, 2002; van Lommel et al., 2001). In cardiac arrest, blood flow and oxygen uptake in the brain plunge swiftly, with electroencephalographic (EEG) signs of cerebral ischemia detectable within 6 to 10 seconds, progressing to flat-line EEGs within 10 to 20 seconds (Parnia & Fenwick, 2002; van Lommel et al., 2001). There have been recent reports of brief increases in brain electrical activity at the point of death (Chawla, Akst, Junker, Jacobs, & Seneff, 2009) or even after cardiac death, during organ donation (Auyong et al., 2010). However, these reports were not based on standard EEGs but rather the bispectral index, a derivative measure of brain electrical activity that is notoriously vulnerable to artifact pollution from a wide variety of physiological and environmental sources, leading to spurious signals that can be misinterpreted as brain activity (Dahaba, 2005; Myles & Cairo, 2004).

In sum, the primary challenge in the study of NDEs and spirituality lies in asking how complex cognition, sensory perception, and memory can occur under conditions such as cardiac arrest in which current physiological models of mind deem it impossible. This conflict between a materialist model of brain-mind identity and the occurrence of NDEs under conditions of general anesthesia and/or cardiac arrest is profound and inescapable. Expanding our model of the mind–brain relationship to accommodate extraordinary experiences such as NDEs may lead to a greater understanding of consciousness and its relation to brain, and of the relationship of spirituality to its physical correlates.

References

Albrecht, M., & Alexander, B. (1977). Thanatology: Death and dying. *Journal of the Spiritual Counterfeits Project, 1*(1), 5–11.

Athappilly, G. K., Greyson, B., & Stevenson, I. (2006). Do prevailing societal models influence reports of near-death experiences? Comparison of accounts reported before and after 1975. *Journal of Nervous and Mental Disease, 194*, 218–222.

Auyong, D. B., Klein, S. M., Gan, T. J., Roche, A. M., Olson, D., & Habib, A. S. (2010). Processed electrocardiogram during donation after cardiac arrest. *Anesthesia and Analgesia, 110*, 1428–1432.

Azari, N. P., Nickel, J., Wunderlich, G., Niedeggen, M., Hefter, H., Tellmann, L., . . . Seitz, R. J. (2001). Neural correlates of religious experience. *European Journal of Neuroscience, 13*, 1649–1652.

Badham, P. (1997). *Religious and near-death experience in relation to belief in a future life.* Second Series Occasional Paper 13. Oxford, England: Religious Experience Research Centre.

Badham, P., & Badham, L. (1982). *Immortality or extinction?* (2nd ed.). London: SPCK.

Bain, B. A. (1999). Near-death experiences and Gnostic Christianity: Parallels in antiquity. *Journal of Near-Death Studies, 17*, 205–209.

Bauer, M. (1985). Near-death experiences and attitude change. *Anabiosis: Journal of Near-Death Studies, 5*(1), 39–47.

Becker, C. B. (1981). The centrality of near-death experiences in Chinese Pure Land Buddhism. *Anabiosis: Journal of Near-Death Studies, 1*, 154–171.

Becker, C. B. (1985). Views from Tibet: Near-death experiences and *The book of the dead. Anabiosis: Journal of Near-Death Studies, 5*(1), 3–19.

Blanke, O., Ortigue, S., Landis, T., & Seeck, M. (2002). Stimulating illusory own-body perceptions. *Nature, 419*, 269–270.

Britton, W. B., & Bootzin, R. R. (2004). Near-death experiences and the temporal lobe. *Psychological Science, 15*, 254–258.

Bush, N. E. (1983). The near-death experience in children: Shades of the prison-house reopening. *Anabiosis: Journal of Near-Death Studies, 3*, 177–193.

Carr, D. (1982). Pathophysiology of stress-induced limbic lobe dysfunction: A hypothesis for NDEs. *Anabiosis: Journal of Near-Death Studies, 2*, 75–89.

Chawla, L. S., Akst, S., Junker, C., Jacobs, B., & Seneff, M. G. (2009). Surges of electroencephalographic activity at the time of death: A case series. *Journal of Palliative Medicine, 12*, 1095–1100.

Couliano, I. (1991). *Out of this world: Otherworld journeys from Gilgamesh to Albert Einstein.* Boston: Shambhala.

Cressy, J. (1994). *The near-death experience: Mysticism or madness?* Boston: Christopher.

Cronin, A. J., Keifer, J. C., Davies, M. F., King, T. S., & Bixler, E. O. (2001). Postoperative sleep disturbance: Influences of opioids and pain in humans. *Sleep, 24*, 39–44.

Dahaba, A. A. (2005). Different conditions that could result in the bispectral index indicating an incorrect hypnotic state. *Anesthesia and Analgesia, 101*, 765–773.

Evans-Wentz, W. Y. (Ed.). (1957). *The Tibetan book of the dead.* London: Oxford University Press.

Fenwick, P. (2001). The neurophysiology of religious experience. In I. Clarke (Ed.), *Psychosis and spirituality: Exploring the new frontier* (pp. 15–26). London: Whurr.

Flynn, C. P. (1982). Meanings and implications of NDEr transformations: Some preliminary findings and implications. *Anabiosis: Journal of Near-Death Studies, 2*, 3–13.

Flynn, C. P. (1986). *After the beyond: Human transformation and the near-death experience.* Englewood Cliffs, NJ: Prentice-Hall.

Fox, M. (2003). *Religion, spirituality and the near-death experience.* London: Routledge.

Frankl, V. (1969). *The will to meaning: Foundations and applications of logotherapy.* New York: World.

Gibbs, J. C. (2005). What do near-death experiencers and Jesus have in common? The near-death experience and Spong's New Christianity. *Journal of Near-Death Studies, 24*, 61–95.

Gliksman, M. D., & Kellehear, A. (1990). Near-death experiences and the measurement of blood gases. *Journal of Near-Death Studies, 9*, 41–43.

Green, J. T. (2001). The near-death experience as a shamanic initiation: A case study. *Journal of Near-Death Studies, 19*, 209–225.

Grey, M. (1985). *Return from death: An exploration of the near-death experience.* London: Arkana.

Greyson, B. (1981). Near-death experiences and attempted suicide. *Suicide and Life-Threatening Behavior, 11*, 10–16.

Greyson, B. (1982, May). *Organic brain dysfunction and near-death experiences.* Paper presented at the American Psychiatric Association 135th Annual Meeting, Toronto, Canada.

Greyson, B. (1983a). Near-death experiences and personal values. *American Journal of Psychiatry, 140*, 618–620.

Greyson, B. (1983b). The psychodynamics of near-death experiences. *Journal of Nervous and Mental Disease, 171*, 376–381.

Greyson, B. (1985). A typology of near-death experiences. *American Journal of Psychiatry, 142*, 967–969.

Greyson, B. (1991). Near-death experiences precipitated by suicide attempt: Lack of influence of psychopathology, religion, and expectations. *Journal of Near-Death Studies, 9*, 183–188.

Greyson, B. (1992). Reduced death threat in near-death experiencers. *Death Studies, 16,* 533–546.

Greyson, B. (1992–1993). Near-death experiences and antisuicidal attitudes. *Omega, 26,* 81–89.

Greyson, B. (1998). The incidence of near-death experiences. *Medicine and Psychiatry, 1,* 92–99.

Greyson, B. (2001). Posttraumatic stress symptoms following near-death experiences. *American Journal of Orthopsychiatry, 71,* 358–373.

Greyson, B. (2003). Incidence and correlates of near-death experiences in a cardiac care unit. *General Hospital Psychiatry, 25,* 269–276.

Greyson, B. (2010a). Hypercapnia and hypokalemia in near-death experiences. *Critical Care, 14,* 420.

Greyson, B. (2010b). Seeing dead people not known to have died: "Peak in Darien" experiences. *Anthropology and Humanism, 35,* 159–171.

Greyson, B., & Stevenson, I. (1980). The phenomenology of near-death experiences. *American Journal of Psychiatry, 137,* 1193–1196.

Hampe, J. C. (1979). *To die is gain: The experience of one's own death.* Atlanta, GA: John Knox.

Heim, A. von St. G. (1892). Notizen über den tod durch absturz [Remarks on fatal falls]. *Jahrbuch der Schweizerischen Alpclub, 27,* 327–337.

Hermann, E. J. (1990). The near-death experience and the Taoism of Chuang Tzu. *Journal of Near-Death Studies, 8,* 175–190.

Herzog, D. B., & Herrin, J. T. (1985). Near-death experiences in the very young. *Critical Care Medicine, 13,* 1074–1075.

Holck, F. H. (1978–1979). Life revisited: Parallels in death experiences. *Omega, 9,* 1–11.

Husain, A. M., Miller, P. P., & Carwile, S. T. (2001). REM sleep behavior disorder: Potential relationships to post-traumatic stress disorder. *Journal of Clinical Neurophysiology, 18,* 148–157.

James, W. (1902). *The varieties of religious experience: A study in human nature.* New York: Longman, Green.

Jansen, K. L. R. (1997). The ketamine model of the near-death experience: A central role for the N-methyl-D-aspartate receptor. *Journal of Near-Death Studies, 16,* 5–26.

Kellehear, A. (2009). Census of non-Western near-death experiences to 2005: Observations and critical reflections. In J. M. Holden, B. Greyson, & D. James (Eds.), *The handbook of near-death experiences: Thirty years of investigation* (pp. 135–158). Santa Barbara, CA: Praeger/ABC-CLIO.

Klemenc-Ketis, Z., Kersnik, J., & Grmec, S. (2010). The effect of carbon dioxide on near-death experiences in out-of-hospital cardiac arrest survivors: A prospective observational study. *Critical Care, 14,* R56.

Küng, H. (1984). *Eternal life? Life after death as a medical, philosophical, and theological problem.* Garden City, NY: Doubleday.

Lee, R. L. M. (2003). The reenchantment of death: Near-death, death awareness, and the New Age. *Journal of Near-Death Studies, 22,* 117–131.

Lorber, J. (1983). Is your brain really necessary? In D. Voth (Ed.), *Hydrocephalus im frühen kindesalter: Fortschritte der grundlagenforschung, diagnostik und therapie* (pp. 2–14). Stuttgart, Germany: Enke Verlag.

Lorimer, D. (1990). *Whole in one: The near-death experience and the ethic of interconnectedness.* London: Arkana.

Lundahl, C. R. (1983). The Mormon explanation of near-death experiences. *Anabiosis: Journal of Near-Death Studies, 3,* 97–106.

McClenon, J. (1994). *Wondrous events: Foundations of religious belief.* Philadelphia: University of Pennsylvania Press.

McLaughlin, S. A., & Maloney, H. N. (1984). Near-death experiences and religion: A further investigation. *Journal of Religion and Health, 23,* 149–159.

Moody, R. A. (1975). *Life after life.* Covington, GA: Mockingbird Books.

Moody, R. A. (1977). *Reflections on life after life.* St. Simon's Island, GA: Mockingbird Books.

Moody, R. A., & Perry, P. (1988). *The light beyond.* New York: Bantam.

Morse, M. L., Castillo, P., Venecia, D., Milstein, J., & Tyler, D. C. (1986). Childhood near-death experiences. *American Journal of Diseases of Children, 140,* 1110–1114.

Morse, M. L., Venecia, D., & Milstein, J. (1989). Near-death experiences: A neurophysiologic explanatory model. *Journal of Near-Death Studies, 8,* 45–53.

Musgrave, C. (1997). The near-death experience: A study of spiritual transformation. *Journal of Near-Death Studies, 15,* 187–201.

Myles, P. S., & Cairo, S. (2004). Artifact in the bispectral index in a patient with severe ischemic brain injury. *Anesthesia and Analgesia, 98,* 706–707.

Nahm, M., & Greyson, B. (2009). Terminal lucidity in patients with chronic schizophrenia and dementia: A survey of the literature. *Journal of Nervous and Mental Disease, 197,* 942–944.

Nelson, K. R., Mattingly, M., Lee, S. A., & Schmitt, F. A. (2006). Does the arousal system contribute to near death experience? *Neurology, 66,* 1003–1009.

Newberg, A. B., & d'Aquili, E. G. (1994). The near-death experience as archetype: A model for "prepared" neurocognitive processes. *Anthropology of Consciousness, 5*(4), 1–15.

Noyes, R. (1971). Dying and mystical consciousness. *Journal of Thanatology, 1,* 25–41.

Noyes, R. (1972). The experience of dying. *Psychiatry, 35,* 174–184.

Noyes, R. (1980). Attitude change following near-death experiences. *Psychiatry, 43,* 234–242.

Noyes, R., & Kletti, R. (1972). The experience of dying from falls. *Omega, 3,* 45–52.

Ohayon, M. M., Priest, R. G., Zully, J., Smirne, S., & Paiva, T. (2002). Prevalence of narcolepsy symptomatology and diagnosis in the European general population. *Neurology, 58,* 1826–1833.

Osis, K., & Haraldsson, E. (1977). *At the hour of death.* New York: Avon.

Owens, J. E., Cook, E. W., & Stevenson, I. (1990). Features of "near-death experience" in relation to whether or not patients were near death. *Lancet, 336,* 1175–1177.

Pahnke, W. N., & Richards, W. A. (1966). Implications of LSD and experimental mysticism. *Journal of Religion and Health, 5,* 175–208.

Parnia, S., & Fenwick, P. (2002). Near-death experiences in cardiac arrest: Visions of a dying brain or visions of a new science of consciousness. *Resuscitation, 52,* 5–11.

Parnia, S., Waller, D. G., Yeates, R., & Fenwick, P. (2001). A qualitative and quantitative study of the incidence, features and aetiology of near death experiences in cardiac arrest survivors. *Resuscitation, 48,* 149–156.

Pennachio, J. (1986). Near-death experience as mystical experience. *Journal of Religion and Health, 25,* 64–72.

Ring, K. (1980a). Religiousness and near-death experiences: An empirical study. *Theta, 8*(3), 3–5.

Ring, K. (1980b). *Life at death: A scientific investigation of the near-death experience.* New York: Coward, McCann & Geoghegan.

Ring, K. (1984). *Heading toward omega: In search of the meaning of the near-death experience.* New York: Morrow.

Ring, K. (2000). Religious wars in the NDE movement: Some personal reflections on Michael Sabom's *Light and death. Journal of Near-Death Studies, 18,* 215–244.

Ring, K., & Valarino, E. E. (1998). *Lessons from the light: What we can learn from the near-death experience.* New York: Plenum/Insight.

Rose, S. (1980). *The soul after death: Contemporary "after-death" experiences in the light of the Orthodox teaching of the afterlife.* Platina, CA: St. Herman Press.

Saavedra-Aguilar, J. C., & Gómez-Jeria, J. S. (1989). A neurobiological model for near-death experiences. *Journal of Near-Death Studies, 7,* 205–222.

Sabom, M. B. (1982). *Recollections of death: A medical investigation.* New York: Harper & Row.

Sabom, M. B. (1998). *Light and death: One doctor's fascinating account of near-death experiences.* Grand Rapids, MI: Zondervan.

Sabom, M. B., & Kreutziger, S. A. (1978). Physicians evaluate the near-death experience. *Theta, 6*(4), 1–6.

Schwaninger, J., Eisenberg, P. R., Schechtman, K. B., & Weiss, A. N. (2002). A prospective analysis of near-death experiences in cardiac arrest patients. *Journal of Near-Death Studies, 20,* 215–232.

Schwartz, A. (2000). *The nature of spiritual transformation.* Radnor, PA: John Templeton Foundation.

Schwartz, J. M., Stapp, H. P., & Beauregard, M. (2005). Quantum physics in neuroscience and psychology. *Philosophical Transactions of the Royal Society B, 360,* 1309–1327.

Shneidman, E. S. (1971). On the deromanticization of death. *American Journal of Psychotherapy, 25,* 4–17.

Stace, W. T. (1960). *Mysticism and philosophy.* Philadelphia: Lippincott.

Starbuck, E. D. (1906). *The psychology of religion: An empirical study of the growth of religious consciousness.* New York: Walter Scott.

Sutherland, C. (1990). Changes in religious beliefs, attitudes, and practices following near-death experiences: An Australian study. *Journal of Near-Death Studies, 9,* 21–31.

Tracy, D. (1993). God of history, God of psychology. *Concilium, 1993*(5), 101–111.

van Lommel, P., van Wees, R., Meyers, V., & Elfferich, I. (2001). Near-death experiences in survivors of cardiac arrest: A prospective study in the Netherlands. *Lancet, 358,* 2039–2045.

Vincent, K. R. (2003). The near-death experience and Christian Universalism. *Journal of Near-Death Studies, 22,* 57–71.

Watson, J. B. (1914). *Behavior.* New York: Holt.

Whinnery, J. E. (1997). Psychophysiologic correlates of unconsciousness and near-death experiences. *Journal of Near-Death Studies, 15,* 231–258.

Wulff, D. M. (2000). Mystical experience. In E. Cardeña, S. J. Lynn, & S. Krippner (Eds.), *Varieties of anomalous experience: Examining the scientific evidence* (pp. 397–440). Washington, DC: American Psychological Association.

Zaleski, C. G. (1987). *Otherworld journeys: Accounts of near-death experience in medieval and modern times.* New York: Oxford University Press.

PART 9

Sacred Consciousness and Healing: Postmaterial Spiritual Science

Nonlocality, Intention, and Observer Effects in Healing Studies: Laying a Foundation for the Future

Stephan Schwartz *and* Larry Dossey

Abstract

All research domains are based upon epistemological assumptions. Periodic reassessment of these assumptions is crucial because they influence how we interpret experimental outcomes. Perhaps nowhere is this reassessment needed more than in the study of prayer and intention experiments: If positive results from this field of research are sustained, the reality of nonlocal consciousness must be confronted. This chapter explores the current status of healing and intention research, citing a number of major studies and using the "Study of the Therapeutic Effects of Intercessory Prayer (STEP) in Cardiac Bypass Surgery Patients: A Multicenter Randomized Trial of Uncertainty and Certainty of Receiving Intercessory Prayer" as a case study of this line of research. The chapter argues that the dose-dependent model typical of drug trials, and adopted for use in the STEP and other studies, is not the optimal model for intention-healing research, and critiques this approach in detail, citing apposite research from which we draw our recommendations and conclusions. The chapter suggests that the usual assumptions concerning blindness and randomization that prevail in studies using the pharmacological model must be reappraised. Experimental data suggest that a nonlocal relationship exists among the various individuals participating in a study, one which needs to be understood and taken seriously. We argue that it is important to account for and understand the role of both local and nonlocal observer effects, since both can significantly affect outcome. Research is presented from an array of disciplines to support why we feel these issues of linkage, belief, and intention are so important to a successful, accurate, and meaningful study outcome. Finally, we offer suggestions for new lines of research and new protocol designs that address these observer-effect issues, particularly the nonlocal aspects. The chapter finally suggests that if these effects occur in intention studies, they must necessarily exist in all studies, although in pharmacological studies they are often overshadowed by the power of chemical and biological agents.

Key Words: intention, prayer, healing, observer effect, consciousness, placebo, nonlocal consciousness

Introduction

Periodic reassessment of what constitutes good research is crucial because this process gives us the ability to distinguish justified belief from opinion. Perhaps nowhere is this distinction of greater significance than in the study of prayer and intention experiments: If the positive results from this field of research are sustained, the reality of nonlocal consciousness must be taken seriously. This chapter explores the current status of healing and intention research, cites a number of major studies, and uses the "Study of the Therapeutic Effects of Intercessory Prayer (STEP) in Cardiac Bypass Surgery Patients: A Multicenter Randomized Trial of Uncertainty and Certainty of Receiving Intercessory Prayer" conducted by Herbert Benson et al. (2006) as a case study of this line of research. In April 2006, researchers from Harvard Medical School published this long-awaited study in the *American Heart Journal* (Benson et al., 2006). The $2.4 million study was funded in large part by the John Templeton Foundation, which promotes the study of the intersection of religion and science. Its publication grabbed headlines across America for two main reasons: It originated from Harvard Medical School, and it had an unexpected result—patients who were prayed for, and knew they would be prayed for, fared the worst of the three intervention groups.

Because of its venue, its level of funding, and the media attention the study has engendered, we have selected this study as a case demonstrating issues common to much of this research field, and we use it to explore those issues. In the process, we also examine attitudes that prevail in the arguments of both proponents and skeptics of prayer and intention research. What we seek is a discussion on the basic assumptions implicit, but usually unacknowledged, in these studies, and a reappraisal of the design parameters upon which prayer and intention studies have been grounded. In our view, STEP is a noble failure; noble because it was done with integrity, on the basis of imperfect understanding, and because its failure has much to teach us.

STEP Background

The STEP experiment involved 1,802 patients undergoing coronary artery bypass surgery at six US hospitals (Benson et al., 2006). These 1,802 patients were then assigned to one of three sub-populations. Therapeutic intention in the form of prayer was provided by one Protestant and two Catholic groups, whose members were told to pray for a quick recovery with no complications. They were provided only with the first name and the initial of the last name of the prayer participants—for example, "John D." Prayers were initiated on the eve or the day of surgery and continued for 2 weeks thereafter.

The three groups consisted of the following (the group names are our designation):

• Group A: 604 patients who were told they might or might not be prayed for, and were; of this group, 52% had postsurgical complications
• Group B: 597 patients who were told they might or might not be prayed for, and were not; among this group, 51% had postsurgical complications
• Group C: 601 patients who were told they would be prayed for, and were; among this group, 59% had postsurgical complications

To many skeptics in both media and science, it was this last result that was the headline of the study, suggesting that prayers for the sick might actually be harmful.

How can these results be understood? To begin with, the differences between the two blind groups, those who were told they might or might not be recipients, one of which eventually was prayed for, whereas the other was not, are nonsignificant. *The only significant outcome in the study is between those who were blind and those who were not* ($p = .003$; $z = 2.8$). Yet an attempt to analyze this result is almost wholly absent in both the published report and much of the commentary about it (Casatelli, 2006; Freed, 2006; Giberson, 2006; Kalb, 2006).

We are disturbed by the fact that not only skeptics but the researchers themselves turned a blind eye to this challenging result, and we are not alone. Duke University Medical Center cardiologist Mitchell W. Krucoff, and his research partners, Suzanne W. Crater and Kerry L. Lee, explain this carefully in their article accompanying the publication of the STEP study in the *American Heart Journal* (2006). They say:

> [T]he most striking element of the STEP report is in the interpretation of the study results showing significantly worsened outcomes in one of the experimental arms.... [T]he investigators take an almost casual approach toward any explanation, stating only that it "may have been a chance finding." It is rather unusual to attribute a statistically significant result in the primary end point of a prospective, multicenter randomized trial to "chance."
>
> In fact, such attribution is antithetical to the very definition of what error and statistical certainty imply: that the worse outcomes are almost certainly related to the therapy and not the play of chance. If the results had shown benefit rather than harm, would we have read the investigators' conclusion that this effect "may have been a chance finding," with absolutely no other comments, insight, or even speculation?" (p. 763)

Observer-Expectancy Effects, Both Local and Nonlocal

The randomized, double-blind clinical trial is widely considered the gold standard of judging the efficacy of any therapy. If a study is adequately randomized and blinded, it is assumed that the effects of belief, intention, and conviction of subjects and researchers are bypassed. Applying this logic to prayer experiments, it is assumed that what an experimenter privately thinks about the intercession is irrelevant. Yet experimental results suggest it is not that simple.

Rather, data suggest that intention, belief, attitude, and expectancy, on the part of everyone involved with a study, expressed both locally and nonlocally, can be determining variables. Chemist Douglas Dean and parapsychologist Karlis Osis showed that different experimenters carrying out the same experiment got different results (Osis & Dean, 1964). Psychologists Gertrude Schmeidler and Michaeleen Maher made videos of well-known researchers conducting experiments and then played them for students with the volume turned so low as to be inaudible (Schmeidler & Maher, 1981). The students were asked to describe the researchers, assigning them words like "friendly" or "cold." Estimates were then made as to how experiments conducted by these researchers would turn out. Those with "cold" type responses were estimated to have respondents who produced lower scores; the converse was true for researchers described as "friendly." The actual results of the experiments were then compiled. Those with "cold" type adjectives did in fact have informants who scored lower (Schmeidler & Maher, 1981).

Perhaps the starkest example, however, showing the observer latency effect of belief is an experiment series done by psychologist Richard Wiseman, a leading denier of nonlocal consciousness, and anthropologist Marilyn Schlitz, a researcher long associated with successful studies exploring whether an individual knows through some kind of linkage that he or she is being stared at, even by a person at a distance looking at his or her image on a closed-circuit television (Wiseman & Schlitz, 1997). The measurement for this effect was galvanic skin response. Schlitz had earlier worked with psychologist William Braud and carried out a series of studies demonstrating this effect (Braud & Schlitz, 1989).

Wiseman sought to replicate these studies and made three attempts, all unsuccessful. Schiltz then proposed that she and Wiseman do a new series, a kind of hyperreplication *using his same laboratory, the same protocol, and the same participant pool*. Once again with Schlitz as the principal investigator, the study was successful. Once again, the participants being stared at showed significant physiological response that was absent when they were not being focused on (Wiseman & Schlitz, 1997). Wiseman then ran the same study again, without success, confirming his passionate negative expectation.

Hazelrigg et al. (1991) examined "personality moderators of experimenter expectancy effects" and focused on five, looking at them from the perspective of both researcher and participant. They reported, "Experimenters with stronger interpersonal control orientations, more positively evaluated interpersonal interaction styles, and greater ability to encode nonverbal messages are believed to be more likely to produce expectancy bias" (Hazelrigg, Cooper, & Strathman, 1991). They also looked at subjects with greater need for social approval and greater nonverbal decoding ability, and hypothesized that such individuals would be more susceptible to bias.

They reported two "moderators" mattered: "the experimenter control orientation and subject need for social approval hypotheses. There was also evidence for a boomerang effect— subjects low in need for social approval gave ratings opposite to the experimenter's outcome expectancy. Finally, effects appeared stronger when positive expectancies were communicated than when expectancies were negative" (Cooper & Hazelrigg, 1988, p. 569; Hazelrigg et al., 1991, p. 576).

None of these factors are discussed in the STEP report. They are absent in most other similar studies as well, and they will continue to be a confounding problem until they are addressed and understood. No intention study, whether it involves intercessory prayer or some other variety of therapeutic intent, should be conducted without careful consideration of observer effects as part of the protocol, and we believe it should be extended to all research exploring nonlocal consciousness with any protocol.

It would be helpful if the STEP study answered questions, such as "Did the experimenters believe that intercessory prayer would work in the world, or were they expecting neutral outcomes?" "Could the negative beliefs of critics who knew about the STEP study during the several years it was in progress, and who may have wished to see it fail, have affected the outcome?" "What about the impact of the attitudes of religious individuals who believe in prayer but don't want to see prayer studies done because of doctrinal objections?"

Questions such as these are awkward and make people uncomfortable. In our culture, probing such concerns is considered indelicate and intrusive. But this does not mean they are irrelevant. We suggest that an intention study cannot be properly designed if it does not take the intentions and beliefs of everyone involved with the study into consideration.

It strikes us as odd that observer effects were not considered in the STEP study, when Benson himself addressed observer effects in his previous work and has apparently long believed in their importance. In 1979, Benson and David McCallie coauthored a paper on a range of treatments for angina pectoris, including placebo. In this study, they refer to "Three recognized components of the placebo effect—the beliefs and expectations of the physician, the beliefs and expectations of the patient, and the physician-patient relationship" (Benson & McCallie, 1979, p. 1424). Why would the beliefs and expectations of physicians and researchers not apply in the STEP study?

This Benson paper reports that treatments which enjoyed efficacy rates as high as 90% when a treatment was new and enthusiasm in the medical community was high fell back to the typical 30% to 40% effectiveness when studies critical of the treatment began to emerge in the literature (Benson & McCallie, 1979). The attitude of the clinician, locally mediated through subliminal body clues, tone of voice, or choice of words, was judged by Benson and McCallie (1979) to be important factors in this huge spectrum of response and to be clinically important. (We would add that a physician's intentions can act nonlocally as well, bypassing the senses, to shape therapeutic responses.) In their paper, as an historical grace, note they cite 19th-century French physician, Armand Trousseau, who observed sarcastically, "You should treat as many patients as possible with the new drugs while they still have the power to heal" (Benson & McCallie, 1979, p. 1425).

Because the evidence favoring belief and intention in affecting clinical outcomes is so strong, why aren't belief and intention—"expectation," as Benson and McCallie would have it—more carefully considered in intention studies? Psychologist William Braud (2003) has explored the influence of intention. He notes, "I think the reason that the intentions of other persons are not taken into consideration in most prayer studies is that the investigators are not aware of the possible influence and alternative processes that might be involved, but instead, consider prayer outcomes only in terms of entreaties to, and actions of, the Divine" (W. Braud, personal communication, August 2006). This seems to us a very limited view. We see the "Observer Effect," in its most generous interpretation, as one of the fundamental questions to be addressed in future work.

Without sacrificing any rigor in the process of randomization and blinding, what other factors need to be controlled for an intention or prayer study? Which factors operate locally, mediated via the senses? Which operate locally sourced sensory mediation? How do both local and/or nonlocal influences affect experimental outcomes? Do they operate concurrently or independently?

The classic "sheep/goat effect" is an example of the kind of variable we have in mind. First reported by physicist Robert McConnell and psychologist Gertrude Schmeidler (who coined the terms), this belief effect is now recognized as one of the most consistently determinative variables in the intention research literature (Schmeidler & McConnel, 1958). Sheep—those who accept that nonlocal phenomena exist in the context of the experiment *in which they are taking part*—generally achieve higher scores in controlled studies than goats, who are skeptics. But is the effect local or nonlocal, or both? The STEP study doesn't address this kind of question, and neither do most other intention studies. They should.

The Question of Time

Nonlocality also opens another consideration important to understanding intention/prayer studies: the issue of time. Consider the retroactive intercessory prayer study carried out by Israeli immunologist Leonard Leibovici (2001). Highly skeptical of the claims of intention/prayer studies, Leibovici designed an experiment that only some kind of nonlocal linkage could explain. The very idea of such an effect challenges many assumptions. Yet retrocausality has become an area of intense research. The American Association for the Advancement of Science, in conjunction with the American Institute of Physics, held a conference on this topic, and a reader interested in pursuing retrocausality in the context within which it is discussed in this paper should read the published conference papers (Radin, 2006; Sheehan, 2006). They suggest that from a physics perspective, Leibovici's research is conceptually plausible.

Leibovici's protocol was a hospital-sited, "double blind, parallel group, randomized controlled trial of *a retroactive intervention* [emphasis added]" (Leibovici, 2001, p. 1450). It was a study with a large enough *N* to have gravitas. In July 2000, Leibovici identified 3,393 adult patients each of whom had suffered from a bloodstream infection that was detected while they were in the Rabin Medical Center, in Israel, between 1990 and 1996—that is to say, *4–10 years earlier*. All of these individuals were long out of the hospital. These 3,393 *former hospital patients* were randomized into two populations;

1,691 were assigned to the intervention treatment group and 1,702 to the control group. The treatment group was the focus of therapeutic intention in the form of prayer, which "was said for the well-being and full recovery of the intervention group" (Leibovici, 2001, p. 1450).

The study discovered that "length of stay in hospital and duration of fever were significantly shorter in the intervention group than in the control group (p = .01 and p = .04, respectively)." Leibovici concluded, "Remote, retroactive intercessory prayer said for a group is associated with a shorter stay in hospital and shorter duration of fever in patients with a bloodstream infection and should be considered for use in clinical practice" (Leibovici, 2001, p.1451).

For this study to have worked, it seems that therapeutic intention from the "future" must have affected the "past" *when it was the present* to produce a biased outcome—not to have changed the past, but to have produced the original effect in the first instance. No local explanation can subsume what happened. (A possible alternative nonlocal explanation is based on decision augmentation theory [DAT], which we shall examine shortly.) Leibovici's study is an extreme example of an intention study because of its retrocausal essence, but all intention studies must consider that intention is not blocked by time. To understand intention/prayer studies, we must expand our horizons.

Dosage

The STEP study required prayer for only 14 days. Is a 2-week intervention an adequate test of prayer? What about the duration of each prayer session? One positive prayer study required an hour of prayer (Sicher, Targ, Moore, & Smith, 1998); one failed study required 5 minutes (Matthews, Conti, & Sireci, 2001). Is duration the determinant factor here? Many studies do not even consider this issue. What is the requisite dosage of therapeutic intention? Does this question even make sense given the nonlocal nature of the effect? We are aware of only one study by Schwartz (coauthor of this paper) et al. (1990) that examined the relationship of time and effect, a study measuring changes across 5, 10, and 15 minutes, and no significant differences were observed.

One might reasonably expect that long repetitive experience would lead to insincerity and boredom, and that freshness and sincerity are more likely to be found in those new to an endeavor. And yet this is another area where our actual knowledge is slight. In the chemical drug model, dosage and composition are crucial. This leads to a fundamental question: What do dosage and composition mean in an intention/prayer study? Do these concepts apply?

Experimental evidence suggests that reiterated acts of intention—which could be seen as a kind of dosage—produce a cumulative nonlocal field effect. Biologists Graham and Anita Watkins carried out a series of experiments in which they anesthetized mice from the same line, which were then put in one of two cradles, one designated "treated," the other "control" (1971). The task of the influencer/healer was to awaken the treated mouse through mental intention alone. There was no physical contact. The revival times of the "treated" mice were compared with those randomly assigned as controls. The results were statistically significant (Watkins & Watkins, 1971). Without planning initially for this effect, but having been consistent in their assignment pattern, they then wondered what would happen if no healer was involved. In subsequent sessions, those mice assigned to the "treated" cradle continued to awaken more quickly than the controls (Beloussov & Popp, 1995).

Another attempt to model this cumulative effect can be found in the concept of a field, which has some of the properties of a wave and some of a particle, which was independently developed in the 1920s by Russian biologist Alexander Gurwitsch, who also discovered ultraweak photon emission from living systems (Watkins & Watkins, 1971), and Austrian biologist Paul Weiss. They called them morphogenetic fields, or biological fields. In the interests of historical accuracy, perhaps it would be best to say they called them biological fields.

Most recently, this line of research has been taken up and expanded by English biologist Rupert Sheldrake (1981). This work suggests that not only do individual acts of observation—observer awareness, one might call it—cause an observer effect, but that the effect becomes stronger as more iterations of awareness occur. Perhaps the best illustration of this can be seen in two contemporaneous studies, one designed by psychologist Gary Schwartz, then of Yale, the other by psychologist Alan Pickering of Hatfield Polytechnic in England (Sheldrake, 1995). Their protocols were different but essentially the same. In Schwartz's case the study involved different reactions non-Hebrew speakers and readers had to real words as compared to Hebrew letters randomly assembled to create nonsense words. In Pickering's study, the words and nonsense letter combinations used were in Farsi. Both studies were highly significant, and alternative explanations were systematically eliminated (Sheldrake, 1995). The oldest words, the ones that had been the subject of the most acts of intentioned awareness, produced stronger effects than did the new words, and they more than the nonsense words.

A third facet of this cumulative effect has shown up in nonlocal perception studies, particularly in experimental studies using a protocol known as remote viewing, in which individuals, under rigorously controlled conditions during an experimental session, are typically asked to describe persons, places, or objects that are not designated as targets until after the sensory and descriptive data have been recorded. Literally millions of these remote viewing sessions have been carried out, and they show that targets which have been the focus of reiterated acts of intentioned awareness, particularly in a state of heightened emotion (whether positive or negative does not seem to matter), say, for instance, a religious shrine, are easier than other targets, perhaps a rice paddy, which may be visually more arresting but harder to perceive in nonlocal awareness. Why? Because, we suggest, targets such as shrines have become numinous (Otto, 1958). The term *numinous*, coined in 1917 by the German Protestant philosopher and theologian Rudolf Otto (1869–1937), is based on the Latin word *numen* (Beloussov & Popp, 1995). The word, *numen*, which dates to early 17th-century Latin, represents a prescientific attempt to explain the sense of nonlocal awareness associated with totemic things and places by imputing this numinous empirical experience to a divine power or spirit over that thing or place. The particular quality that seems apposite to intention research was described by Carl Jung: "We should not be in the least surprised if the empirical manifestations of unconscious contents bear all the marks of something illimitable, something not determined by space time. This quality is numinous…numina are psychic entia…" (1974, p. 256).

Research also suggests this numinous quality is not something inherent to the target, but instead, accumulated within the nonlocal information architecture linked to a physical target. Obviously then different viewers respond to the same target differently. An Irish lyre has a special meaning for an Irishman that it does not have for a Czech. Different individual viewers perceive the same target differently because it holds a different numinosity for each. Different groups and cultures similarly invest images with differing numinous significance. In terms of intention studies, consider the now-classic study done by cardiologist Randolph Byrd (1988).

His study was conducted with Christian healers because of Byrd's personal beliefs. This leads one to ask, in intention/prayer studies, what is the intention observer effect created by a researcher with strong religious beliefs? Also, what is the effect if the study protocol conflicts in some way with those beliefs?

The "field" concept, of course, is admittedly a hand-waving term whose meaning is imprecise. Even so, field effects appear to be lawful in the scientific sense, particularly in studies such as those reported by Watkins and Watkins (1971). We believe this dimly understood cumulative intention effect is a significant variable that must be better understood if intention/prayer research is to advance.

Blindness and Randomization

For over 30 years, research has suggested that both randomization and blindness do not perform the same functions in experiments involving nonlocal perception or perturbation, of which intention/prayer studies are a subcategory, as they are assumed to do in drug trials. The literature supporting this conclusion is now so large that we will simply mention three studies: two involving perception—remote viewing and Ganzfeld protocol studies—and perturbation—direct mental interactions with living systems (DMILS) studies.

As in Leibovici's (2001) study, a time factor is often involved, because accurate impressions are frequently obtained before a target is even selected, making these experiments truly triple blind.

In 1995, the US Congress commissioned the American Institutes for Research, a Washington, DC–based, not-for-profit think tank with close government ties, and a long history of work in human performance, to assess the validity of remote viewing research that the US government had previously funded. That body of research was just a fraction of similar research that had been conducted up to that point. To make the assessment, American Institutes for Research selected statistician Jessica Utts of the University of California, Davis, and psychologist Ray Hyman of the University of Oregon, a fellow of the Committee for the Scientific Investigation of Claims of the Paranormal. Hyman was selected for his avowed skepticism, Utts because of her reputation as an academic statistician. Both had previously published in the field of nonlocal awareness and were notably sophisticated in the issues involved. Utts had previously addressed the question the US Congress was asking in a 1991 paper published in the journal *Statistical Science* (Utts, 1991). In their joint report, Utts concluded:

> Using the standards applied to any other area of science…(this) functioning (Remote Viewing) has been well established. The statistical results of the studies examined are far beyond what is expected by chance. Arguments that these results could be due to methodological flaws in the experiments are soundly refuted. Effects of similar magnitude have been replicated at a number of laboratories across the world. Such consistency cannot be readily explained by claims of flaws or fraud. The magnitude of…functioning exhibited appears to be in the range between what social scientists call a small and medium effect. That means that it is reliable enough to be replicated in properly conducted experiments, with sufficient trials to achieve the long-run statistical results needed for replicability.
>
> (*Utts,* 1995, p. 3-2)

And Hyman, responding to Utts's statement, wrote:

> I want to state that we agree on many…points. We both agree that the experiments (being assessed) were free of the methodological weaknesses that plagued the early…research. We also agree that the…experiments appear to be free of the more obvious and better known flaws that can invalidate the results of parapsychological investigations. We agree that the effect sizes reported…are too large and consistent to be dismissed as statistical flukes.
>
> (*Hyman,* 1995)

A similar meta-analysis used a related but quite different Ganzfeld protocol, also used by laboratories and universities around the world. In a Ganzfeld experiment, the person providing the impressions is in a state of sensory deprivation and is exposed to white noise. The Ganzfeld meta-analysis was carried out by psychologist Daryl Bem, of Cornell University, and Charles Honorton, then at the University of Edinburgh (Bem & Honorton, 1994). It reached conclusions similar to those of Utts in the Utts and Hyman meta-analysis.

A third protocol, DMILS, designed by psychologist William Braud and anthropologist Marilyn Schlitz, explored whether people could detect when they were the focus of another person's intentioned awareness (Braud & Schlitz, 1991). This was achieved by placing one person in a room and measuring his or her electrodermal activity, which correlates with sympathetic autonomic activity, while a closed-circuit video feed of this individual was sent to another person in a room some distance away, beyond the reach of sensory communication. In the distant room, the second person either viewed the televised image of the individual or listened to white noise. The image was shown randomly for a few seconds. The results showed that when the target person's picture was being viewed on the monitor, his or her physiology reacted with a deviation in electrodermal activity (Schwartz, De Mattei, Brame, & Spottiswoode, 1990). These findings have been replicated numerous times; the only notable failure being the Wiseman and Schlitz study (1997) when a self-defined skeptic served as one of the researchers. The DMILS protocol is of particular relevance to intention research because it is a very close approximation of the healing intention protocol. It raises the question, could one be aware when one was being prayed for? No one seems to have asked this important question.

These three protocols suggest that randomization and blindness, although they prevent conventional biases, are not the absolute barriers they are presumed to be. As far as intention/prayer studies are concerned, we propose that the prevailing perception of blindness be reexamined, and that the intentions of *all* the participants in the study be evaluated. The STEP study makes no such consideration, nor do most other intention/prayer experiments.

Agent of Action

One of the most pressing questions future intention research must consider is who is the agent of action? Is there only one? What would the effect be if all the participants were somehow linked—or there are no such linkages at all? Positive prior studies suggest that something nonlocal is happening, but exactly what? Are the results achieved because of a person's therapeutic intention? Or is the outcome determined by the beliefs of the person who is the overt focus of the intention? Or, even more fundamentally, does the person who selects the participating subjects produce a successful or unsuccessful outcome? Or do all these factors operate simultaneously? Our ignorance runs deep; we do not even know if the healing effect results from the healer's intention producing a perturbation in the recipient's body, or whether the healer nonlocally provides information to the recipient, who then uses that information to stimulate his or her own psychophysical self-regulation.

One compelling line of research known as decision augmentation theory (DAT) specifically addresses some of these questions. DAT proposes that researcher intention, not healer intention, can be the determining factor in any experiment's outcome. This hypothesis, initially called intuitive data sorting, was first developed by an interdisciplinary team headed by physicist Ed May, experimental psychologist Dean Radin, and statistician Jessica Utts (May, Radin, Hubbard, Humphrey, & Utts, 1985). Subsequently, DAT has been explored by other researchers, and its essential tenets have been confirmed (May, Paulinyi, & Vassy, 2005; May, Utts, & Spottiswoode, 1995). The theory proposes that the outcome of an experiment can be determined by the decisions made by the experimenters, *and that nonlocal perception on the part of the researcher—not nonlocal perturbation in the form of intercessory prayer or any other variety of therapeutic intent—is responsible for the outcome.* That is, if investigators could optimize (via nonlocal perception) their decisions while designing and carrying out an experiment, and take advantage of natural fluctuations in disease outcomes or differences in patients' inherent ability to heal, then by such favorable selections, placing these individuals in the intention group, a successful experimental result would be achieved. But it would not be due to healing intervention; rather, it would be due to the experimenters' "augmented" decisions. This hypothesis requires nonlocal perception on the part of the experimenters, and as such is as controversial as nonlocal perturbation, but it is plausible and more important, it provides a dramatically different interpretation of successful healing studies, so we feel researchers should take DAT into consideration when planning their experiments.

One possible approach would be to conduct healing studies with two groups. Group A might contain two patients, and group B, 15 patients. Each group would have one healer assigned to them. Neither recipients nor healers would know how many others were within each of the two groups. There would also be two similar-sized groups, C and D, to provide a (blindly) matched nonintention control condition. Assume that on average the hypothesized intentional healing effect operates with the same effectiveness on each patient, say e. Then, the overall statistical outcome for the healing measurement of interest in group A would be approximately $e \times \sqrt{(2)}$, whereas in group B it would be $e \times \sqrt{(15)}$. That is, group B would achieve a greater level of statistical significance than group A. This is a simple consequence of the greater statistical power provided by group B. If such a study produced a statistically significant outcome (beyond the results of the control groups C and D), it would provide evidence in favor

of healing as a nonlocal perturbation, not as a result of "augmented" selection.

However, if the statistical outcomes of groups A and B were about the same (not the effect size e, but rather the resulting P values), then the assumption that intentional healing operates about the same on each patient would not be supported, and the observed effects would be more likely due to the investigators' augmented decisions. This is because under DAT, no healing is assumed to occur in these tests, and so the only way to obtain results that favor the experimental hypothesis is by taking advantage of natural "noisy" fluctuations and selecting individuals with a strong capacity for spontaneous healing, thus producing the positive outcome intended by the hypothesis. There are fewer opportunities to select strongly favorable fluctuations out of larger groups of 15 patients than from smaller groups of two patients.

There are two studies known to us that address the DAT issue, although this was not the authors' intention in either case. One of the largest therapeutic intention studies, the 2005 MANTRA II research conducted by Mitchell Krucoff at Duke, and researchers at eight other medical centers, involved a total of 748 patients (Krucoff et al., 2005).

Each of these individuals had been diagnosed with coronary artery disease and was scheduled to undergo percutaneous coronary intervention, or elective cardiac catheterization with possible percutaneous coronary intervention. All were enrolled between May 1999 and December 2002. They were randomized equally to each of the two noetic therapies or standard care, creating four treatment groups. "One group (189 patients) received both off-site intercessory prayer and music, imagery, and touch (MIT) therapy; a second group (182 patients) received off-site intercessory prayer only; a third group (185 patients) received MIT therapy only, while the fourth group (192 patients) received neither the intercessory prayer nor the MIT therapy" The interventional heart procedures were all conducted according to each institution's standard practice, and the study called for a 6-month period of follow-up.

Initially, this was a standard single-tier research project—one group of healers prays for one group of recipients. However, MANTRA II underwent a major protocol redesign part way through the study. Following the terror attacks of September 11, 2001, enrollment rates in the study fell sharply for approximately 3 months. During that time, the research team adopted a two-tiered prayer strategy. Twelve additional "second-tier" prayer groups were formed and added. "These groups were given a list of the primary tier prayer groups, and asked on notification *to pray for the prayers of the prayer groups*"

Patients treated with two-tiered prayer had absolute 6-month death and rehospitalization rates that were about 30% lower than control patients. This was statistically characterized as "a suggestive trend," and these results suggest that it is therapeutic intention and not DAT that at least sometimes is operative, and that researcher selection would not explain these results.

The MANTRA II researchers explicitly created this two-tier protocol to emulate an earlier study by Cha and Wirth (2001) in which a three-tier design had been employed to explore the effect of therapeutic intention/prayer on the success of in vitro fertilization. This in vitro study, became notorious after publication, because of a criminal conviction of the second author for behavior in another area of his life, having nothing to do with the study. As a result the insights afforded by this well-designed research often are overlooked. It may be the clearest guidance we have concerning the DAT hypothesis.

The study was a prospective, double-blind, randomized clinical trial in which patients and providers were not informed about the intervention. Statisticians and investigators were masked until all the data had been collected and clinical outcomes were known.

> The setting was an IVF-ET program at Cha Hospital, Seoul, Korea. IP was carried out by prayer groups in the United States, Canada and Australia. The investigators were at a tertiary medical center in the United States. The patients were 219 women aged 26 to 46 years who were consecutively treated with IVF-ET over a four-month period. Randomization was performed after stratification of variables in two groups: distant IP versus no IP. The clinical pregnancy rates in the two groups were the main outcome measure.
>
> After clinical pregnancies were known, the data were unmasked to assess the effects of IP after assessment of multiple comparisons in a log-linear model. The IP group had a higher pregnancy rate as compared to the no-IP rate (50% vs. 26%, $P = 0.0013$). The IP group showed a higher implantation rate (16.3% vs. 8%, $P = 0.0005$). Observed effects were independent of clinical or laboratory providers and clinical variables. (*Cha & Wirth*, 2001, p. 781)

The statistical effect size of the study is what everyone focused on. But, in terms of the issues raised by DAT, the most important finding is this one: "The people praying…were separated into three groups. One group received pictures of the women and prayed for an increase in their pregnancy rate. Another group prayed to improve the effectiveness of the first group. A third group prayed for the two other groups" (Cha & Wirth, 2001, p. 783).Once again it would seem that DAT is not the explanation, and that therapeutic intention is. The DAT issue may be far from settled, but one thing seems very clear to us. In the future, therapeutic intention/prayer studies must accommodate themselves to DAT and design protocols accordingly.

Can Prayer Harm?

Biologist Carroll Nash of St. Joseph's College, Philadelphia, carried out a therapeutic intention study involving bacterial colonies, cultured in common, and then split into three independent subpopulations (Nash, 1982). His purpose was to replicate earlier studies by nun and biochemist Sister Justa Smith (1973) and nursing pioneer Dolores Krieger (1974), who along with Dora Kunz would later develop the nonsectarian approach to therapeutic intent known as therapeutic touch. Smith's studies had shown significant differences between treated and controls measuring changes in hemoglobin and enzyme activity, which were the focus of the expressed intention. But Nash had a second question. He asked, "Could intention alone not merely affect the cell colonies, but could it do so both positively *and* negatively, when compared to controls?" (Nash, 1982, p. 63). The results showed that it could, although positive intention produced a more significant result than negative intention. Nash's experiments provide a clue that intention can do harm, and that it can be value weighted.

In their critique of the STEP study, Krucoff et al. (2006) agree saying, "Leading researchers such as the STEP team should be underlining the imperative that…even well intentioned intercessory prayer…must be scrutinized for safety issues at an equal or even higher level than efficacy measures if medically important and useful knowledge in this arena is to truly step forward" (p. 764).

If one considers the STEP study, for example in this "can prayer harm" context, the relevance of the issue to good protocol design becomes clear. Let's imagine what the results of the STEP experiment might have been under three conditions:

(1) if prayer is effective, (2) if prayer is ineffective, or (3) if prayer is harmful:

1. *If prayer is effective*, groups A and C should have benefited equally from it, with C having the added benefit of the placebo response owing to the certainty of receiving prayer. Group C, then, should have had the best clinical outcome of the three groups. This was not the case; C had the worst outcome. So "effective prayer" is unable to explain the outcome of the STEP study.

2. *If prayer is ineffective*, it should not have exerted any effect on any of the three groups, but group C should have done better because of the certainty of receiving prayer, thus benefiting from the placebo effect. But group C did the worst of all the groups. So "ineffective prayer" is unable to explain the outcome of the experiment.

3. *If prayer harms*, both A and C should have demonstrated worse outcomes than B, which was spared prayer, in which case B would have done better than the other two groups. But B responded equally with A. Therefore, harmful or negative prayer cannot explain the results of the STEP study.

The STEP researchers essentially ignored the possibility that prayer might be harmful in their report, simply saying that the worst outcome in group C "may have been a chance finding." They were taken to task for this in Krucoff et al. (2006) in the *American Heart Journal*. The criticism is appropriate in view of the anthropological evidence that negative beliefs and intentions can be lethal (curses, hexes, spells), as well as the controlled laboratory studies showing that negative intentions can retard or harm living, nonhuman systems (Dossey, 1997).

What other possible explanations are there for STEP's outcome?

Extraneous Prayer

Randomized, controlled studies in prayer in humans acknowledge that patients in both treatment and control groups may pray for themselves and that their loved ones may pray for them as well, but it is assumed that the effects of this extraneous prayer is equally distributed between the intervention and control groups and does not create statistical differences between the two. This assumption may or may not be true, and in any case does not eliminate the problems posed by extraneous prayer in controlled studies. The positive effects of extraneous prayer, if they exist, may diminish the effect size between the two groups, therefore limiting one's ability to detect the effects of assigned prayer in the intervention group. As one of the coauthors of the STEP study said in a news release from Harvard Medical School, "One caveat [of STEP] is that with so many individuals receiving prayer from friends and family, as well as personal prayer, it may be impossible to disentangle the effects of study prayer from background prayer" (Harvard Medical School Office of Public Affairs, 2006).

An analogy would be a pharmaceutical study in which the intervention group is treated with 10 mg of the drug being tested, and the control group with 9 mg. Even if the medication were effective, could the effect be detected?

No one knows how extraneous prayer could be eliminated in human prayer-and-healing studies. It may be impossible to do so, especially in American culture, where the great majority of individuals pray routinely when they are *well*. Trying to eliminate prayer in a control group may be unethical as well, for who has the right to extinguish personal prayer and prayer by loved ones during sickness? In contrast, extraneous prayer can be handily eliminated in nonhuman studies involving animals, plants, or microbes. They presumably do not pray for themselves, and neither do their fellow beings pray for them. In these studies, one often sees profoundly positive effects of healing intentions (Dossey, 1993).

Randomization Differences

In May 2008, Ariel et al. examined the demographic differences between the three groups in the Harvard study and found that group C, which had the highest rate of postoperative complications, may have been predisposed to do worse. This group had a higher incidence of chronic obstructive pulmonary disease (emphysema and chronic bronchitis), a higher incidence of smoking history, a higher rate of three-vessel coronary bypass surgery, and a lower rate of beta-blocker use prior to surgery, which many experts consider to be cardio-protective during coronary bypass surgery, when compared with the other two groups. For a fair trial of prayer, the study should have established a level playing field between all three groups through proper randomization, such that no group was worse off than any other going into the study.

Psychological Factors

The overall design of the study may have created psychological dynamics in groups A and B that could have led to the results that were observed.

Patients in A and B were told they might or might not be prayed for by the intercessors. Think for a moment what this means. Surveys show that around 80% or 90% of Americans pray regularly when they are well, and it can be assumed that even more pray when they are sick. Faced with the prospect of being denied prayer in the study, the subjects in A and B may therefore have aggressively solicited prayer from their loved ones to make up for the possible withholding of prayer in the experiment, and they may have redoubled their personal prayers for themselves. Thus, a paradox may have resulted in which A and B received more prayer—not less—than C, even though this was not the intent of the study. If prayer is effective, this additional unforeseen, extraneous prayer may have lifted A and B above C in terms of clinical outcomes, accounting for the study's results.

Another possibility is that patients in group C, who knew that many outsiders were praying for them, felt stressed and pressured to do well. Moreover, "It might have made them uncertain, wondering, 'Am I so sick they had to call in their prayer team?'" said cardiologist Charles Bethea, MD, a member of the STEP research team (Cromie, 2006, p. 2). "We found increased amounts of adrenalin, a sign of stress, in the blood of patients who knew strangers were praying for them," said STEP researcher Jeffrey A. Dusek, PhD, associate research director of Harvard's Mind/Body Medical Institute at Massachusetts General Hospital. "It's possible that we inadvertently raised the stress levels of these people" (Cromie, 2006, p. 2).

For many believers—including believing researchers—the idea that prayer might harm is a horrifying consideration. Yet, as we have noted, it is completely consistent with both ethnohistorical traditions—negative prayer outcome is an iconic part of voodoo, and it can be found in the Tibetan *Bön* faith—as well as the major scriptural texts of several religions, including Christianity.

The Bible is full of events in which people and things were harmed or killed when people invoked prayer for destructive ends. In the New Testament, Jesus cursed and killed a fig tree (Matthew 21:9; Mark 11:13–14, 20–22). The apostle Paul cursed a sorcerer and made him blind (Acts 12:11). In the Old Testament, the prophet Elisha cursed 42 children and caused them to be devoured by bears because they made fun of his baldness (II Kings 2:23–24).

Although not often acknowledged as such, veiled negative prayer is very much a part of our culture.

To cite an obvious example: When you pray for victory in the current second Iraq War, are you explicitly praying for the defeat, destruction, and the killing of those who oppose us? Do you think others might be doing this, and if so, how prevalent do you think this is? A 1994 Gallup poll found that 5% of Americans explicitly admitted to praying that harm will come to others—and that's only the 1 in 20 who will own up to it (Gallup, 1994). Television and history tell us daily that death and destruction are the handmaidens of victory in war. Can there be any doubt that some prayers for victory hold an implicit negative intention toward the opponent? The truth is, although we do not want to admit it explicitly, we consider prayer as capable of harm as good.

The placebo literature also shows this. As long ago as 1955, physician Henry Beecher admonished researchers to pay attention to the negative aspects of intention expressed as a "nocebo" effect, saying, "Not only do placebos produce beneficial results, but like other therapeutic agents they have associated toxic effects. In a consideration of 35 different toxic effects of placebos that we had observed in one or more of our studies, there is a sizable incidence of (such) effects attributable to the placebo" (p. 1605). What is not known is what aspect of intention is local and what is nonlocal.

Experimental data, placebo evidence, and ethnohistorical and religious traditions all point in one direction. Intention can be expressed in both positive and negative ways. It is increasingly clear that this reality needs to be better understood and incorporated into study design. We also need to study the differences between positive and negative intention and how they manifest. The STEP study was silent on all this, as are all too many other research efforts.

Healers, Rituals, and Prayers

We know very little about what qualifies a person to successfully express therapeutic intention as a healer. Most investigators believe that the sincerity and genuineness of prayer must surely make a difference, but in most prayer experiments these factors are merely assumed without being rigorously assessed. In contrast, the skills of the cardiac surgeons in the STEP study were not assumed; the surgeons had met stringent objective requirements that qualified them for their role. Intention/prayer must incorporate these kinds of considerations into experiment design. One place to begin might be employing empathy rating scales like those used to rate the empathic capacity of therapists who work as caregivers and counselors (La Monica, 1981). Or, if children and parents are involved in an intention study, perhaps the Parent-Child Relationship Inventory (Coffman, Guerin, & Gottfried, 2006). And there are sure to be other considerations that may affect outcome. The point here is that a number of useful measures have already been established and may be of use in intention/prayer research. Research teams should incorporate specialists in these areas.

Ethnohistory and anthropological research suggest that the role of form and ritual is important to understand. Yet few intention studies consider this. Left to themselves, people generally pray according to the dictates of their heart. In the STEP experiment, although intercessors were free to pray as they saw fit, an 11-word prescribed prayer was required of all of them. In other studies, the expression of therapeutic intention is more free form. What role does form of expression play in these studies?

There is also the issue of God. Some intercessors follow a nondirected or "Thy will be done" approach in prayer, whereas others are more comfortable with a more traditional, formally religious, directed form in which they pray for a specific outcome according to their religious belief. Some presume no involvement of a deity at all, as in therapeutic touch. What is the role of religious belief?

Experience and the role of intention-focusing disciplines, religious or secular, are also factors that have received inadequate study. In a study looking at changes in the molecular structure of water exposed to healing intention, Schwartz (2007) compared the performance of two subpopulations: one consisting of individuals who defined themselves as healing practitioners, and had some established approach to expressing their intention, and a second group who had never done such work or even considered it. Each sample was independently significant, but the experienced practitioners were much more effective (experienced, $p = .001$; naive, $p = .04$; Schwartz et al, 1990). The comparison showed, "Those who trained in some kind of therapeutic technique, and characteristically involved themselves in such activities, produced more significant results than those who had not undergone such training or who did not characteristically involve themselves in such activities, although even with no training, or regular practice, it is possible…if the intent is strong" (Schwartz, 1990). This study looked at changes in the structure of water, but clinical studies support the same conclusion. Some of the most effective

healing studies employed dedicated healers with decades of experience. To us this suggests expressing effective healing intention may be a skill set attained like any other. That is, one's innate talent can be more effectively expressed by mastering a technique to enhance it, and then practicing it.

One place to begin research into techniques is by examining the meditation literature—both ancient and modern. One ancient source of particular interest is the Patanjali Yoga sutras, which date at least to the 2nd century BCE (Patañjali, 1998). The Sutras speak at length about moving into nonlocal awareness through meditation.

Braud, who has made a particular study of this, notes: "The sixth, seventh, and eight 'limbs' of ashtanga Yoga are *dharana* (concentration), *dhyana* (meditation), and *samadhi* (profound absorption), respectively" (Braud, 2008, p. 228).

The Patanjali source refines this further: "The repeated continuation, or uninterrupted stream of that one point of focus is called absorption in meditation (*dhyana*), and is the seventh of the eight steps (*tatra pratyaya ekatanata dhyanam*)" (Yoga sutras of Patanjali, 3.2. n.d.). Braud continues:

> When these three are practiced together, the composite process is called *samyama*. *Samyama* might be translated as *constraint; thorough, complete, or perfect restraint;* or *full control*; it might also be translated as *communion* or *mind poise*. *Samyama* conveys a sense of knowing through being or awareness through becoming what is to be known. Through mastery of *samyama* comes insight (*prajna*), and through its progressive application, in stages, come knowledge of the Self and of the various principles of reality (*tattvas*). With increasing yogic practice come a variety of mystical, unitive experiences, states, conditions, or fulfillments—the various *samadhis*—along with the attainments or powers (*siddhis*).
>
> (*W. Braud, private communication,* October 2008)

Although couched in Eastern terms, the Sutras describe the same insights and processes concerning nonlocal functioning that have been elucidated by a modern peer-reviewed meditation literature too large to cite—including papers and a best-selling book, *The Relaxation Response*, by Benson and Klipper (2000).

Meditation is also potentially important because it produces placebo-like effects, as Benson et al. (1990) reported. In a small study, Buddhist meditators using several different meditative practices were able to raise their resting metabolism (VO2; up by

61%) or lower it (down by 64%; Cromie, 2006). The reduction from rest was the largest ever reported when the paper was published in 1990. On the electroencephalogram measure, there was marked asymmetry in alpha and beta activity between the hemispheres, and increased beta activity (Cromie, 2006).

Honorton (1981) carried out a study explicitly to explore this linkage of Patanjali and modern research involving nonlocal phenomena. Radin, for several years now, has been conducting an online experiment involving nonlocal awareness expressed through several protocols. It is a study that now has a baseline of data numbering into the millions of trials. He reports that the strongest predictor of success with his protocols is whether the person participating is a meditator (Radin, n.d.). Therapeutic intent, expressed through intercessory prayer, is another manifestation of nonlocal consciousness and, not surprisingly, prayer and some kind of discipline to develop focused awareness is a part of almost every spiritual tradition.

It seems obvious to us that understanding the role of mind-altering disciplines such as meditation may have much to say to intention/prayer research. Like placebo research, meditation research tells us about the power of intention to produce psychophysical effects. Understanding this will help us comprehend how healing occurs. Is it something the intercessor does, or is it something stimulated by the healer but activated by the recipient, much like a placebo response?

The STEP study paid little heed to any of this and, once again, is representative of intention research as a whole. It drew no attention, for instance, to the fact that the study did not generate the expected placebo response among the participants who knew for certain they were the focus of prayer intention. This is an odd lacuna, given that Benson is one of the pioneers of both placebo and meditation research and, as long ago as 1975, entitled one of his papers, "The Placebo Effect—a Neglected Asset in the Care of Patients" (Benson & Epstein, 1975).

Evidence Ignored

To place the STEP study in context, one would expect that critics and analysts would cite and compare it with earlier prayer studies that reported positive outcomes. This has not happened. Study of the Therapeutic Effects of Intercessory Prayer has become such a marked feature of the healing intention debate that it often goes unchallenged and is assumed to be the final word. This seems an undeniable bias—a position counter to accepting science's fundamental commitment to go where sound data lead. Why is this area of inquiry so threatening, particularly positive studies of intention/prayer? We think it is because it requires extending our concept of consciousness to include the nonlocal; it gives us a model that is not exclusively physiological. How can this bias be seen as any different than the creationist's dismissal of all evolutionary science in the service of his bias? Why is this not a form of scientific superstition? In response to the critics' eagerness to declare the further study of intention expressed through intercessory prayer moribund, we say, look at the data. And look across the spectrum of science. Consider, for instance, the "Quantum Cooperation of Insects," reported by Austrian scientist Johann Summhammer (2005), which suggests nonlocal linkage between insects, a provocative new area for further study. And the last several years have seen many papers involving quantum physics, largely in the context of Bell's theorem (Bell, 2004) and string theory (Josephson, 2003), in which observer effects are fundamental.

Even within just the medical literature, the research is compelling to the objective observer. Wayne B. Jonas, former director of the National Institute of Health's National Center for Complementary and Alternative Medicine, and his colleague Cindy C. Crawford, recently surveyed the literature for studies involving prayer and directed intentions (Jonas & Crawford, 2003). They discovered 80 randomized controlled trials in humans and 122 controlled laboratory studies involving cells, tissues, animals, plants, microbes, and inanimate devices such as random number generators. Using accepted Consolidated Standards of Reporting Trials criteria specifically designed to allow readers to understand and compare protocol design, procedure, analysis, and the interpretations advanced, to evaluate the quality of medical research, they found that the laboratory intention studies merited an "*A*" or "good" grade, and the human trials a "*B*" or "fair grade."

In addition to the Jonas and Crawford review (2003), many systematic and meta-analyses have been published, nearly all of which are positive (Dossey & Hufford, 2005). Most of the prayer-and-healing studies are abstracted, reviewed, and analyzed by psychiatrist Daniel Benor in his book *Healing Research* (2002).

How to Do a Prayer Study

Four months before the Harvard study was published, mind-body researcher Jeanne Achterberg, a veteran explorer of indigenous healing methods and the role of imagery and visualization in health care, published an experiment incorporating many of the propositions we raise here (Achterberg et al., 2005). The work of Achterberg and her team was ignored by the nation's media, which, we believe, was a shame, because it is the kind of next-generation study needed if we are to more fully understand the effects of intention. That the study of Achterberg et al. (2005) with its positive findings was overlooked, whereas the ambiguous STEP study received international attention, we suggest, is not a coincidence but another expression of the bias we have discussed. Achterberg's work began with an attempt to understand the culture of the people with whom she would be working and to find a way to incorporate their worldview into a rigorous, meticulously designed, modern scientific protocol without compromising either, which is exactly the sort of approach we think will lead us to real understanding concerning intention/prayer. This led her to the island of Hawaii, where she spent 2 years observing the culture and healing methods of indigenous healers, many of whom took her into their confidence and shared their healing methods with her.

Achterberg was interested in exploring whether healers can exert a positive influence on a distant individual with whom they have no sensory contact, as healers universally claim. She and her colleagues at North Hawaii Community Hospital in Waimea recruited 11 indigenous healers to participate in a healing experiment (Achterberg et al., 2005). The healers were not casually interested in healing; they had pursued their healing tradition for an average of 23 years. Each of them was asked to select a person they knew, with whom they had previously worked professionally, and with whom they felt an empathic, compassionate, bonded connection, to serve as the recipient of their healing intentions. Although the researchers summarily referred to the various healing endeavors as distant intention, the healers themselves described what they did in specific ways—prayer, sending energy, good intentions, or wishing for the highest good.

Not only was Achterberg cordial to the idea of remote healing as a result of her prior ethnological work, but she appreciated and respected both how the healers understood what they were being asked to do and why the sociocultural context of the experiment favored its success. The Big Island of Hawaii is often called "the healing island." There, prayer is "in the air"; its effectiveness is assumed. In essence, Achterberg had explicitly designed her study to deal with Benson's beliefs and expectations of the "physician" healer, the beliefs and expectations of the "patient," and the relationship of healer and recipient. We particularly single out the Achterberg study because although she was sensitive to the cultural aspects of this experiment, she made no concessions concerning rigor in her protocol. Each recipient in Achterberg's study was isolated from all forms of sensory contact with the healer and placed in a functional magnetic resonance imaging (fMRI) scanner. The healers then sent their various forms of distant intention to their participants at random, 2-minute intervals that could not have been anticipated by the recipient. When the fMRI brain scans of the participants were analyzed, significant differences in brain function were found between the experimental (send) and control (no-send) conditions. There was approximately 1 chance in 10,000 that these differences could be explained by chance ($p = .0001$). The brain areas that were activated during the healing, or send periods, were the anterior and middle cingulate, precuneus, and frontal regions (Achterberg et al., 2005). When the experiment was repeated, using participants with whom the healers felt no empathic bonding, no significant fMRI changes were found in the recipients during either the send or no-send conditions (Achterberg et al., 2005).

This study suggests that compassionate, empathic healing intentions and prayer can exert measurable effects on a distant recipient, and Achterberg's study does not stand alone. Several earlier experiments demonstrated correlations in brain function between empathic individuals who are widely separated and who have no sensory contact with each other (Duane & Behrendt, 1965; Radin, 2004; Standish, Kozak, Johnson, Johnson, & Richards, 2004; Wadkerman, Seiter, Keibel, & Walach, 2003).

If there was one thing we could have wished included in Achterberg's study, it would be monitoring to ascertain whether, and in what time frame, therapeutic intention altered the course of an illness. Several other studies suggest that this will be a fruitful area for future study.

Future Directions

Therapeutic intention expressed through prayer is now and always has been a universal human activity. We wear different clothes. Speak different languages. Eat different foods, spiced by different condiments, consumed using different implements. We worship different Gods, with different rituals. But the overwhelming majority of us not only believe but operationalize some way of opening ourselves to a greater whole to express therapeutic intention. We pray. Individuals or minority cohorts may dissent, but it is hard to look across the millennia, seeing therapeutic intention expressed in any one of a thousand ways, and conclude that intention effects, such as those claimed for prayer, are only delusion. Yet, for the skeptics, none of this—neither carefully controlled research nor universal practice—seems to evoke the slightest curiosity. To us it seems long past time to ask skeptics to justify their positions by providing not polemics but careful methodological criticism to justify their assertions.

The positive outcomes of prayer research require a new view of consciousness. The conventional local view of the nature of human consciousness, in which the actions of consciousness are confined to the individual brain and body, must eventually yield to a more comprehensive, nonlocal view in which consciousness also acts beyond the brain in ways that transcend direct sensory contact between humans (Dossey, 1989, 1999).

Just asking questions about prayer distresses many religious individuals, who fear that the sacred act of prayer may be swamped and profaned by being examined by what they see as a Godless science, which they consider practically demonic. This is a groundless fear. Therapeutic intent research may tell us how the process works, but in no way does it either prove or disprove the existence of God. This remains as always an illumination of faith and gnosis.

Researcher William Harris and his colleagues, in their 1999 study of prayer in heart patients, suggest that God cannot be either affirmed or denied by prayer research. They say, "We have not proven that God answers prayers or even that God exists.... All we have observed is that when individuals outside the hospital speak (or think) the first names of hospitalized patients with an attitude of prayer, the latter appear to have a 'better' CCU experience" (Harris et al., 1999, p. 2277).

The inability to specify divine action in a prayer study is fortunate, because this discourages any specific religion from using prayer experiments to claim superiority over other faiths. Another way of inhibiting claims of superiority by specific religions is to openly study this issue by using intercessors from various religions in prayer experiments, thus replacing speculation and assertion with data. This is the custom followed in the high-profile MANTRA studies at Duke University Medical Center. In the pilot study, prayer groups around the world prayed for people undergoing urgent cardiac catheterization and angioplasty (Harris et al., 1999). The prayed-for group had 50% to 100% fewer complications (bleeding, arrhythmias, death, etc.) than the group not assigned prayer (Krucoff et al., 2001). In other experiments, healers have been both secular and nonsecular (Achterber et al., 2005). Thus far, there is no compelling evidence from prayer studies that any particular faith enjoys an advantage over any other. Rather, prayer experiments seem to democratize and universalize prayer. They affirm religious tolerance, and that, we believe, may be one of their most valuable contributions.

One area of remote healing research that is particularly productive currently is hypothesis development. Although there is no consensus about how these nonlocal, consciousness-related phenomena occur, hypotheses abound and have been offered by a variety of scholars, including Nobelists, in physics, mathematics, and neurobiology.

Those who prefer theological explanations for prayer's workings need not worry. Physically based theories of how prayer may work are not incompatible with transcendental explanations, just as Darwinian explanations do not rule out operations of the Divine through evolutionary processes.

Is the STEP study an obituary for prayer research, as many claim? Following the premature publication of his obituary in the *New York Journal* on June 2, 1897, Mark Twain wrote, "The reports of my death are greatly exaggerated." So, too, with reports of the death of prayer research. In fact, in our view, we are just beginning to understand the right questions to ask.

Acknowledgments

The authors thank William Braud, PhD, Dean Radin, PhD, and Vernon Neppe, MD, PhD, for their critical review, comments, and suggestions concerning our chapter.

References

Achterberg, J., Cooke, K., Richards, T., Standish, L. J., Kozak, L., & Lake, J. (2005). Evidence for correlations between distant intention and brain function in recipients: A functional magnetic resonance imaging analysis. *Journal of Alternative and Complementary Medicine, 11*, 965–971.

Ariel, H., Dvorkin, L., Steinman, Y., Berman, A., Brenner, F., & Silverman, D. (2008). Intercessory prayer: A delicate celestial orchestration between spiritual and physical worlds [letter to the editor]. *Journal of Altern Complement Medicine, 14*, 351–352.

Beecher, H. (1995). The powerful placebo. *Journal of the American Medical Association, 159*, 1602–1606.

Beloussov, L. V., & Popp, F. A. (Eds.). (1995). *Biophotonics*. Moscow, Russia: BioInform Services.

Bell, J. S. (2004). Speakable and unspeakable in quantum mechanics (2nd ed). Cambridge, England: Cambridge University Press.

Bem, D. J., & Honorton, C. (1994). Does psi exist? (Replicable evidence for an anomalous process of information transfer). *Psychological Bulletin, 115*, 4–8.

Benor, D. J. (2002). Healing research (Vol. 1). Southfield, MI: Vision.

Benson, H., Dusek, J. A., Sherwood, J. B., Lam, P., Bethea, C. F., Carpenter, W.,...Hibberd, P. L. (2006). Study of the Therapeutic Effects of Intercessory Prayer (STEP) in cardiac bypass patients: a multicenter randomized trial of uncertainty and certainty of receiving intercessory prayer. *American Heart Journal, 151*, 934–942.

Benson, H., & Epstein, M. D. (1975). The placebo effect–a neglected asset in the care of patients. *Journal of the American Medical Association, 232*, 1225–1227.

Benson, H., & Klipper, M. (2000). *Relaxation response.* New York: Avon Books.

Benson, H., Malhotra, M. S., Goldman, R. F., Jacobs, G. D., & Hopkins, P. J. (1990). Three case reports of the metabolic and electroencephalographic changes during advanced Buddhist meditation techniques. *Behavioral Medicine, 16*(2), 90–95.

Benson, H., & McCallie, D. (1979). Angina pectoris and the placebo effect. *New England Journal of Medicine, 300*, 1424–1429.

Braud, W. (2003). *Distant mental influence: Its contributions to science, healing, and human interactions.* Charlottesville, VA: Hampton Roads.

Braud, W. (2008). Patanjali Yoga and siddhis: Their relevance to parapsychological theory and research. In K. R. Rao, A. C. Paranjpe, & A. K. Dalal (Eds.), *Handbook of Indian psychology* (pp. 217–243). New Delhi, India: Cambridge University Press (India)/Foundation Books.

Braud, W., & Schlitz, M. (1989). A methodology for the objective study of transpersonal imagery. *Journal of Scientific Exploration, 3*, 43–63.

Braud, W., & Schlitz, M. (1991). Consciousness interactions with remote biological systems: anomalous intentionality effects. *Subtle Energies, 2*(1), 1–46.

Byrd, R. (1988). Positive therapeutic effects of intercessory prayer in a coronary care unit population. *Southern Medical Journal, 81*, 826–829.

Casatelli, C. (2006, May). Study casts doubt on medicinal use of prayer. *Science and Theology News*, pp. 10–11.

Cha, K. Y., & Wirth, D. P. (2001). Does prayer influence the success of in vitro fertilization-embryo transfer? (Report of a masked, randomized trial). *Journal of Reproductive Medicine, 46*, 781–787.

Coffman, J. K., Guerin, D. W., & Gottfried, A. W. (2006). Reliability and validity of the Parent-Child Relationship Inventory (PCRI): Evidence from a longitudinal cross-informant investigation. *Psychological Assessment, 18*, 209–214.

Cooper, H., & Hazelrigg, P. (1988). Personality moderators of interpersonal expectancy effects: An integrative research review. *Journal of Personal and Social Psychology, 55*, 937–949.

Cromie, W. J. (2006, April 6). Prayers don't help surgery patients. *Harvard University Gazette.* Retrieved January 2012, from http://news.harvard.edu/gazette/2006/04.06/05-prayer.html

Dossey, L. (1989). *Recovering the soul.* San Francisco: Harper San Francisco.

Dossey, L. (1993). Healing words: The power of prayer and the practice of medicine. San Francisco: Harper San Francisco.

Dossey, L. (1997). *Be careful what you pray for...you might just get it.* San Francisco: Harper San Francisco.

Dossey, L. (1999). *Reinventing medicine.* San Francisco: Harper San Francisco.

Dossey, L., & Hufford, D. B. (2005). Are prayer experiments legitimate? (Twenty criticisms). *Explore (NY), 1*, 109–117.

Duane, T. D., & Behrendt, T. (1965). Extrasensory electroencephalographic induction between identical twins. *Science, 150*, 367.

Freed, P. T. (2006, April 5). Prayer could hurt hearts. *The Harvard Crimson.* Retrieved January 2012, from http://www.thecrimson.com/article.aspx?ref=512467

Gallup. (1994, March). *The power of prayer: How Americans talk to God. Life*, p. 54–65.

Giberson, K. (2006, May). The great value of nothing. *Science and Theology News*, p. 6.Kalb, C. (2006, April 10). Don't pray for me! Please! *Newsweek*, p. 15.

Harris, W., Gowda, M., Kolb, J. W., Strychacz, C. P., Vacek, J. L., Jones, P. G.,...McAllister, B. D. (1999). A randomized, controlled trial of the effects of remote, intercessory prayer on outcomes in patients admitted to the coronary care unit. *Archives of Internal Medicine, 159*, 2273–2278.

Harvard Medical School Office of Public Affairs. (2006). *Largest study of third-party prayer suggests such prayer not effective in reducing complications following heart surgery.* Retrieved June 2008, from http://web.med.harvard.edu/sites/RELEASES/html/3_31STEP.html

Hazelrigg, P., Cooper, H., & Strathman, A. (1991). Personality moderators of the experimenter expectancy effect: A reexamination of five hypotheses. *Personality and Social Psychology Bulletin, 17*, 569–579.

Honorton, C. (1981). Psi, internal attention states and the Yoga sutras of Patanjali. In B. Shapin & L. Coly (Eds.), *Concepts and theories of parapsychology* (pp. 55–68). New York: Parapsychology Foundation.

Hyman, R. (1995). In M. D. Mumford, A. M. Rose, & D. A. Goslin (Eds.), *An evaluation of remote viewing: Research and applications* (sect 3–2). Washington DC: The American Institutes for Research.

Jonas, W. B., & Crawford, C. (2003). *Healing, intention and energy medicine.* New York: Churchill.

Josephson, B. (2003). *String theory, universal mind, and the paranormal* (arXiv:physics/0312012v3). Retrieved December 2008, from http://arxiv.org/abs/physics/0312012

Jung, C. G. (1974). *Dreams II* (R. F. C. Hull, Trans.). Princeton, NJ: Princeton University Press.

Kreiger, D. (1974). Healing by the laying on of hands as a facilitator of bio-energetic change: The response of in vivo human hemoglobin. *Psychoenergetic Systems, 1*, 121–129.

Krucoff, M. W., Crater, S. W., Gallup, D., Blankenship, J. C., Cuffe, M., Guarneri, M.,...Lee, K. L. (2005). Music, imagery, touch, and prayer as adjuncts to interventional cardiac care: The Monitoring and Actualisation of Noetic Trainings (MANTRA) II randomised study. *Lancet, 366*(9481), 211–217.

Krucoff, M. W., Crater, S. W., Green, C. L., Maas, A. C., Seskevich, J. E., Lane, J. D.,...Koenig, H. G. (2001). Integrative noetic therapies as adjuncts to percutaneous intervention during unstable coronary syndromes: Monitoring and Actualization of Noetic Training (MANTRA) feasibility pilot. *American Heart Journal, 142*, 760–767.

Krucoff, M. W., Crater, S. W., & Lee, K. L. (2006). From efficacy to safety concerns: A STEP forward or a step back for clinical research and intercessory prayer? The Study of Therapeutic Effects of Intercessory Prayer (STEP). *American Heart Journal, 151,* 762–764.

La Monica, E. (1981). Construct validity of an empathy instrument. *Research in Nursing and Health, 4,* 389–400.

Leibovici, L. (2001). Effects of remote, retroactive intercessory prayer on outcomes in patients with bloodstream infection: Randomised controlled trial. *BMJ, 323,* 1450–1451.

Matthews, W. J., Conti, J. M., & Sireci, S. G. (2001). The effects of intercessory prayer, positive visualization, and expectancy on the well-being of kidney dialysis patients. *Alternative Therapies in Health and Medicine, 7,* 42–52.

May, E. C., Paulinyi, T., & Vassy, Z. (2005). Anomalous anticipatory skin conductance response to acoustic stimuli: Experimental results and speculation about a mechanism. *Journal of Alternative and Complementary Medicine, 11,* 695–702.

May, E. C., Radin, D. I., Hubbard, G. S., Humphrey, B. S., & Utts, J. M. (1985). Psi experiments with random number generators: an informational model. In D. H. Weiner & D. I. Radin (Ed.), *Research in parapsychology* (pp. 119–120). Metuchen, NJ: Scarecrow Press.

May, E. C., Utts, J. M., & Spottiswoode, S. J. P. (1995). Decision augmentation theory: applications to the random number generator database. *Journal of Scientific Exploration, 9,* 453–488.

Nash, C. B. (1982). Psychokinetic control of bacterial growth. In W. G. Roll, R. L. Morris, & R. A. White (Eds.), *Research in parapsychology* (pp. 61–64). Metuchen, NJ: Scarecrow Press.

Osis, K., & Dean, D. (1964). The effect of experimenter differences and subject's belief level upon ESP scores. *Journal of the American Society for Psychical Research, 58,* 158–185.

Otto, R. (1958). *The idea of the holy* (J. W. Harvey, Trans.) Oxford, England: Oxford University Press.

Patañjali, V. (1998). *The yoga-system of Patañjali; Or, the ancient Hindu doctrine of concentration of mind: embracing the mnemonic rules, called Yoga-sūtras, of Patañjali and the comment, called Yoga-bhāshya, attributed to Veda-Vyāsa and the explanation, called Tattva-vāicāradī, of Vāchaspati-Miçra* (J. H. Woods, Trans.). Delhi, India: Motilal Banarsidass.

Radin, D. (2004). Event-related electroencephalographic correlations between isolated human subjects. *Journal of Alternative and Complementary Medicine, 10,* 315–323.

Radin, D. I. (2006). Psychophysiological evidence of possible retrocausal effects in humans. In D. P. Sheehan (Ed.), *Frontiers of time: Retrocausation-experiment and theory* (pp. 193–213). San Diego, CA: American Institute of Physics.

Radin, D. (n.d.). *Psi games.* Retrieved Month YYYY, from http://noetic.org/research/project/psi-arcade/

Schmeidler, G. R., & Maher, M. (1981). Judges' responses to the nonverbal behavior of psi-conducive and psi-inhibitory experimenters. *Journal of the American Society for Psychical Research, 75,* 241–257.

Schmeidler, G., & McConnell, R. (1958). *ESP and personality patterns.* New Haven, CT: Yale University Press.

Schwartz, S. (2007). *Opening to the infinite.* Buda, TX: Nemoseen.

Schwartz, S., De Mattei, R., Brame, E., & Spottiswoode, S. (1990). Infrared spectra alteration in water proximate to the palms of therapeutic practitioners. *Subtle Energies, 1,* 43–73.

Sheehan, D. P. (Ed.). (2006). *Frontiers of time: Retrocausation–experiment and theory.* San Diego, CA: American Institute of Physics.

Sheldrake, R. (1981). *A new science of life: The hypothesis of formative causation.* London, England: Blond & Briggs.

Sheldrake, R. (1995). *The presence of the past* (pp. 191–193). Rochester, VT: Park Street Press.

Sicher, F., Targ, E., Moore, D., & Smith, H. S. (1998). A randomized double-blind study of the effect of distant healing in a population with advanced AIDS–report of a small-scale study. *Western Journal of Medicine, 169,* 356–363.

Smith, M. J. (1973). Paranormal effects on enzyme activity. *Human Dimensions, 1,* 12–15.

Standish, L., Kozak, L., Johnson, L., Johnson, L. C., & Richards, T. (2004). Electroencephalographic evidence of correlated event-related signals between the brains of spatially and sensory isolated human subjects. *Journal of Alternative and Complementary Medicine, 10,* 307–314.

Summhammer, J. (2005). *Quantum cooperation of insects* (arXiv:quant-ph/0503136v1). Retrieved May 2010, from http://arxiv4.library.cornell.edu/abs/quant-ph/0503136v1

Utts, J. (1991). Replication and meta-analysis in parapsychology [with discussion]. *Statistical Science, 6,* 363–403.

Utts, J. (1995). In M. D. Mumford, A. M. Rose, & D. A. Goslin (Eds.), *An evaluation of remote viewing: Research and applications* (sect 3–2). Washington DC: The American Institutes for Research.

Wadkerman, J., Seiter, C., Keibel, H., & Walach, H. (2003). Correlations between brain electrical activities of two spatially separated human subjects. *Neuroscience Letters, 336,* 60–64.

Watkins, G., & Watkins, A. (1971). Possible PK influence on the resuscitation of anesthetized mice. *Journal of Parapsychology, 35,* 257–272.

Wiseman, R., & Schlitz, M. (1997). Experimenter effects and the remote detection of staring. *Journal of Parapsychology, 61,* 197–208.

Yoga sutras of Patanjali, 3.2. (n.d.). *HRIH.* Retrieved May 2010, from http://hrih.net/patanjali/download/

Spirituality, Connection, and Healing With Intent: Reflections on Cancer Experiments on Laboratory Mice

William F. Bengston

Abstract

Data from 10 experiments that tested the effect of healing with intent on cancerous laboratory mice are selectively summarized to address the question of whether there is a connection between spirituality and healing. Volunteer healers with no previous experience or belief in healing with intent were successful in producing full life-span cures in cancer models that are normally fatal. Successful healing has been produced by volunteers who have experienced a wide range of subjective sense of connection to their experimental mice. While it may initially seem reasonable to conclude that connection may not be necessary to affect healing, methodological complications resulting from an apparent resonant bonding between experimental and control groups render interpretation problematical. These resonant bonds are interpreted as fluid, with the potential of being both strengthened and weakened by consciousness and shared experience. Some implications of these experiments for the study of the connection between healing and spirituality, and for the mechanistic tradition within science, are discussed.

Key Words: healing with intent, cancer, spirituality and healing, resonant bonds, placebo effects

Introduction

In 10 experiments testing the efficacy of "healing with intent" or "hands-on healing" on laboratory mice infected with fatal cancers, nonbelieving volunteer healers were able to produce an unprecedented high percentage of full cures in the animals (Bengston & Krinsley, 2000; Bengston & Moga, 2007). Participant healers in these experiments have included the author, as well as faculty and student volunteers who had no prior belief or experience in hands-on healing. These experiments were carried out in five different traditional biological laboratories by conventionally trained scientists with extensive experience with these mice, whose cancer normally results in 100% fatality. Additional anomalous results include an apparent "resonant entanglement" between the experimental and control mice, so that a significant percentage of nontreated control mice are also cured under some conditions.

The list of questions and challenges to conventional wisdom generated by these experiments is extensive. The purpose of this paper is to reflect on some of these implications for the study of spirituality and health, and what has been called postmaterialist conceptions of reality. Because the volunteer faculty and student healers in these experiments were prescreened so as to be completely inexperienced as well as nonbelievers in the efficacy of healing with intent, and the mice as healees presumably were the same, the importance of belief in the enhancement of health conditions may be somewhat called into question. In addition, interviews and logs by the volunteer healers themselves indicate a wide variation in their sense of "spiritual connection" to either the mice or to the specific hands-on techniques used in these experiments (Bengston, 2007, 2010). Because all volunteers have had some success in curing their cancerous mice, perhaps the relationship of spiritual connection to healing so prevalent in the literature has also been stated too simply. Finally, the question of whether these healing data bring a significant challenge to materialist science will be discussed, with special attention being given to the methodological implications of the apparent non-local resonant entanglement among the treated and untreated mice.

The Study of Spirituality

One of the classic definitions of r*eligion* comes from William James, who regarded religion as the "feelings, acts, experiences of individual men in their solitude...in relation to whatever they may consider divine" (James, 1961, p. 42). This individualistic view is counterposed by the more communal definition of *religion* as a social and institutional phenomenon (Durkheim, 1965; Weber, 1963).

The conceptual relationship of religion to spirituality is unclear, though religion is usually envisioned as bounded by socially recognizable institutions, and spirituality or transcendence is normally seen more as a personal, subjective experience. About the latter, it must be acknowledged at the outset that there are many definitions of *spirituality* in the literature, perhaps having so much variety as to have no real empirical utility. As just one example, Holmes writes that "Hazarding a definition of spirituality, one can treat it (very inadequately) as the human search for meaning, particularly relationally, and that for many today this incorporates a supernatural/corporeal dimension that suggests many of us have discovered we are more than our physical biology" (Holmes, 2007, p. 24). Indeed, the very vagueness of the use of *spirituality* has probably resulted in a widespread leap of faith among researchers; although it is hard to define, most agree that we can recognize it when it occurs. Similarly, like respondent self-reporting of internal subjective states such as happiness, measures of self-reported spirituality assume that all agree on operational decisions about its extent at any given time. Measures rarely question whether someone who self-classifies as, for example, "somewhat spiritual" has variations in that amount over the course of even short durations of time, or whether the criteria for operational self-diagnosis varies among disparate groups (e.g., Hill, 1999; Hill & Hood, 1999).

Many researchers believe that we cannot study spirituality directly because it is so intangible (Holmes, 2007), though those who study the physiological correlates of spiritual experience would typically adopt at least an implicit reductionist approach to the personal reports of spiritual experience (Glock, 1973). In this case the former would arguably retort that the study of spirituality had been reduced to its outcomes and symptoms, while a more holistic approach of necessity would include the element of mystery and connection to something larger than self (Holmes, 2007).

And so while the argument has been made that we cannot or should not study spirituality scientifically, these often stem from a priori assumptions that if the larger experience cannot be adequately studied, then the effort is for naught. Yet at the same time there is not only a large body of psychology and sociology on the subject, but entire journals have been devoted to its study for decades (e.g., *The Journal for the Scientific Study of Religion*). The argument that spirituality is not amenable to scientific investigation often stems from a materialist perspective. That is, science, by virtue of its method, cannot study spirituality because spiritual tenets are themselves neither observable nor effable (Thomson, 1996). In opposition to this are all the working scientists who routinely study nonobservable phenomena in many disciplines. In reality, of course, the social and behavioral sciences routinely deal with subjective states of consciousness, even including such apparently ineffable personal and profound experiences as mystical union with all of creation (Greeley, 1975).

In recent years the experience of spirituality has been linked to both physical and psychological health (Koenig, 1998; Koenig, Larson, & McCullough, 2000; Miller & Thoresen, 2003). Indeed, a wide variety of academic journals have by now devoted entire issues to the personal and social effects of spirituality. And while authors may differ on specific operational measures of spirituality or transcendence, it is generally the case that these experiences are interpreted as having beneficial effects (Cecero, Bedrosian, Fuentes, & Bornstein, 2006; Greeley, 1975; Miller & Thoresen, 2003).

Spirituality and Healing

The alternative and complementary community has enthusiastically embraced spirituality as a positive corollary to healing. The transcendent experience of wonder is often taken as a sign that a larger force can work through both the healer and healee to produce medically verifiable improvements that would not otherwise occur. Similarly, it is widely assumed that the state of mind can have direct and powerful implications for healing (Benor, 2002;

Cunningham, Stephen, Phillips, & Watson, 2000; Dossey, 1999; Fitzpatrick, Berger, Calabrese, Kim & Polissar, 2007; Lipton, 2008; Soothill et al., 2002).

There are by now long-standing professional societies that regularly have meetings to reinforce such beliefs. For example, the International Society for the Study of Energy and Energy Medicine (ISSEEM) and the Association for Comprehensive Energy Psychology (ACEP) both endorse and celebrate the liberating effects of energy medicine for physical and mental health, although it should be acknowledged that no conventional "energy" has been isolated or shown to have the properties necessary to produce the effects that are purported to occur (Oschman, 2000; Tiller, Dibble, & Kohane, 2001). The lack of traditional scientific acceptance about the existence of these subtle energies demonstrates to the adherents only that traditional science has not kept up with alternative and superior interpretations about the way the world really works. Conventional scientists, by and large, are not aware of this alternative energy medicine world, just as the energy medicine adherents are not necessarily trained in traditional scientific methods of analysis. The energy medicine adherents, however, often seek the mantle of scientific respectability; they hold conferences with such titles as "The Science of the Miraculous" and invite luminaries to address their membership.

There are now numerous peer-reviewed academic journals devoted entirely to the study of alternative and complementary approaches to healing. *The Journal of Alternative and Complementary Medicine* and *Alternative Therapies in Health and Medicine* are probably the oldest, with relative newcomers such as *Explore: The Journal of Science and Healing* following suit. There are numerous online electronic journals that also regularly publish articles on healing, as well as peer-reviewed journals devoted to the scientific study of anomalous phenomena, such as the *Journal of Scientific Exploration*, that also devote some space to healing studies.

The link between healing and spirituality in much of the literature is nicely exemplified by a widely cited reference book in the field, entitled *Spiritual Healing* (Benor, 2002). Though the title contains the word *spiritual* in it, the contents are devoted to an analysis of the quality of the published work on healing. Both in vitro and in vivo studies are examined, and it is instructive that empirically based analyses on the effect of conscious intent on cell cultures is contained within a book entitled *Spiritual Healing*. It is therefore not clear where the boundaries between "spiritual" and "nonspiritual" healing might be located, unless it is simply assumed that all healing is spiritual.

The Cancer Healing Experiments

The data from five of the ten cancer healing experiments referred to in this chapter have been published elsewhere (Bengston &ˑ Krinsley, 2000; Bengston & Moga, 2007), as have the descriptions of the healing techniques used (Bengston, 2007, 2010). And so it is not my intent to summarize all of the technical details here, but rather to generally describe the patterns of healing data with particular emphasis on the role of belief, the subjective sense of connection while healing, and the apparent anomalous resonant entanglement that occurred between the treated experimental mice and the untreated control mice. The subjective sense of resonance will be complemented with objective measurements of brain entanglement that seems to occur during the healing process (Hendricks, Bengston, & Gunkelman, 2010).

In 8 of the 10 experiments (total N = 200), mice with mammary adenocarcinoma (code: H2712; host strain: C3H/HeJ; Strain of Origin C3H/HeHu), which had a predicted 100% fatality between 14 and 27 days subsequent to injection, were treated using various "dosages" of what could be considered "healing with intent." The normal progression of the disease involves nonmetastatic tumor growth until the mouse dies from some combination of malnutrition or the crushing of the internal organs.

When given healing with intent by the volunteers in these experiments, the treated mice developed a blackened area on their tumors, which then ulcerated. Some of these stages can be seen in Figures 35.1 through 35.4.

On days subsequent to these photos, the tumor ulcerations continued to implode without any discharge or infection to full life-span cure.

In two of the experiments, mice with methylcholanthrene-induced sarcomas (strain Balb/C; Background H-2d) were used. The host survival for these mice is unknown, but probably around 45–50 days subsequent to injection, thus making this model also fatal but slightly less aggressive than the mammary model.

When given healing in these experiments, the mice tumors sometimes imploded (see Fig. 35.5), but at other times the tumors simply remitted by shrinking to full cure. At all stages up to the full

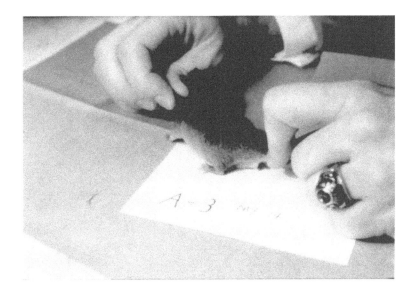

Figure 35.1 A mouse 14 days after being injected with mammary adenocarcinoma.

disappearance of the tumor, histology indicated viable cancer cells present.

This process of cancer cure has been produced both with the volunteer healers in the same room as the treated mice, and by a combination of proximal and distant administrations of healing for various lengths of time and frequency. Among 10 experiments, treatment length varied from 30 minutes to 60 minutes per day until cured. Treatment frequency varied from one treatment per week to daily. The number of mice treated simultaneously in a healing session varied from 1 to 10. The proximity of healer to infected mice varied from hands placed around a cage of mice to healing intention delivered from approximately 600 miles away from the cages.

None of these changes in the parameters of healing seemed to matter in regard to the percentage of mice cured, which generally was in excess of 90%. The only external variable that made any difference was the absolute number of mice in a given experiment. The greater the number of mice, the faster the remission process. This will be discussed in some detail in a later section, and it will involve some speculative ideas about resonant entanglement among experimental mice, as well as the conditions under which resonant bonds are created and destroyed.

Healing, Belief, and Spiritual Connection

Volunteer healers were asked to keep logs of their subjective experiences when practicing the

Figure 35.2 A blackened area begins to develop on the tumor.

Figure 35.3 Tumor ulceration begins 28 days subsequent to injection.

healing techniques and when actually treating the mice. Student volunteers tended to comply with this request; faculty volunteers less so. In regard to the latter, though, extensive informal conversations were conducted in lieu of written logs.

It is uniformly the case that none of the volunteer healers, including myself, could be characterized as a "believer" in the efficacy of the healing techniques. Student and faculty volunteers were prescreened to exclude anyone who had any previous experience with healing or who in any way indicated a priori acceptance of the reality of the phenomenon. The volunteers were trained collectively in weekly meetings for approximately 6 weeks before the arrival of the experimental mice.

Extensive drilling of the techniques was done, and volunteers were asked to practice during the week.

By self-report, the amount that the volunteer healers practiced before and during the experiment varied widely, ranging from not at all to regularly with concerted effort and attention.

All volunteers were encouraged to try to articulate any subjective sensations that they had either while practicing the techniques or during the healing sessions themselves. Here, too, there was a wide range of responses. Some healers felt nothing at all either in the practice sessions or in their healing interactions with the mice. Some felt quite emotional when their mice began to develop tumors, and this experience was only exacerbated during the

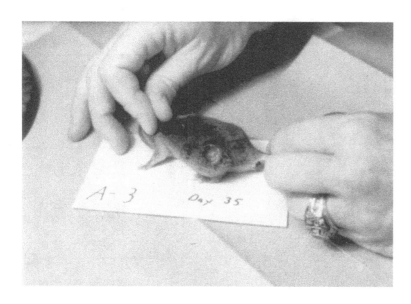

Figure 35.4 Tumor in full ulceration 35 days subsequent to injection.

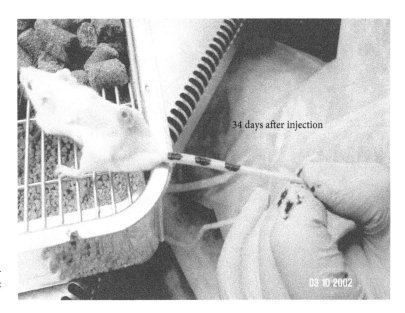

Figure **35.5** Methylcholanthrene-induced sarcoma 34 days subsequent to injection.

34 days after injection

03 10 2002

stages of ulceration. Some reported an intermittent sense of personal connection with their mice that was both surprising and pleasant. In these latter cases, though the word *spiritual* was never explicitly used in a diary or conversation, it would be fair to say that it was implied at least through a sense of an extraordinary "connection" to the mice, though that was usually accompanied by some embarrassment.

The rate and speed of remissions were not related to the presence or absence of either healing technique practice or the subjective sense of spiritual connection to the mice. Upon first inspection this would seem to at the very least minimize the importance of anything approaching a sense of spiritual connection for healing. But a closer examination of the overall patterns of remission presents a serious methodological complication that may have widespread implications.

The Control Group Problem

The traditional model of experimental design randomly separates subjects into experimental and control groups, with only the former receiving any kind of planned stimulus. The postexperimental difference between the two groups is presumed to be due to that active agent. It is universally assumed that the control group represents "what otherwise would have been" had not an active agent been applied, just as it is universally assumed that the experimental and control groups are independent of one another.

Among the more perplexing findings of these experiments has been the pattern of control group cures. In all experiments, there were control mice that went through the same stages of remission as the experimental treated mice.

Since there are innumerable published studies on these mouse models, and since all the experimental biologists were very experienced with these models, it is very much known "what otherwise would have been." All the mice should have died. Furthermore, in some of the experiments, the mice were given twice the known lethal dosage, and at times doubly injected with twice the lethal dosage. There was virtually no chance that any of the mice should have survived without some sort of unprecedented extraordinary intervention.

And yet many of the seemingly untreated control mice also went through the remission stages to full cure, and the patterns of their remissions raise many serious questions. In brief, the control mice would die as predicted unless or until someone who was practicing the healing techniques saw them. Although no conscious healing treatment was ever given to any control mice, the simple occurrence of being seen by a volunteer healer was apparently sufficient to begin the stages of anomalous healing patterns in these mice.

In several experiments, the control mice were dying on schedule, well within the predicted time frame. When either a student or faculty volunteer healer secretly broke protocol and out of curiosity briefly looked at them, the remaining control mice would begin the healing stages of blackened area, ulceration, and tumor implosion despite not being consciously or deliberately treated using the healing techniques. In two experiments we used a second control group sent to another city so that they could not be discovered by any volunteer healers, and these mice all died within the predicted time frame.

In two experiments, a second control group of mice was located inside the same building with the experimental mice and first control group. The healers knew of the existence of the first control group, but not the second. Yet in these experiments the second control group also was cured.

Overall, the percentage of control mice remissions was approximately equal to the percentage of experimental mice remissions subsequent to their being found by a volunteer healer. With one exception, the control mice that were not seen by a volunteer healer died within the predicted time frame, as did the control mice that were sent out of the building and to another city.

Resonant Bonding

These patterns of cure make no sense if the traditional assumption of experimental and control group independence is accurate. The only way that any descriptive pattern emerges is if under some conditions, the experimental and control mice, however spatially separate, are not in fact independent of one another (Bengston, 2004; Bengston & Moga, 2007) but instead are somehow bonded. If that is the case, a healing treatment given to any experimental mouse would in effect result in a treatment being given to all mice in the experiment. Even while the actual mechanism of the healing action remains a mystery, conceptually envisioning the mice as bonded together accounts for the patterns of cure. And it is likely that these resonant bonds are themselves fluid, so that under some conditions they are reinforced and under other conditions they are weakened or broken. The discovery of the conditions of bonding and unbonding might go far in explaining not only the results of these cancer healing experiments but also on other mysterious phenomena such as placebo effects. These same conditions might shed light on potential misinterpretations of experimental data, particularly those that might involve type II errors (Bengston & Moga, 2007).

Consider some facts:

• As already mentioned, upon being observed, the control mice begin the remission process; otherwise they die.

• Traditional dose–response tests show no difference in variability of treatment time. That is,

multiple treatments per week have the same effect as single treatments per week. However,

• The larger the number of mice in the experimental group, the faster all mice go through the remission process. This may be an indirect indication of a dose effect to healing. That is, the larger the number of mice, the greater the number of treatments necessary to administer healing treatments to them. If the mice are in fact bonded together, then the absolute number of "pooled" treatments given will be greater, thus indirectly suggesting a dose response.

If the mice are seen to be members of a bonded group, then these facts make some sense. However, there are more anomalies to consider:

• All experimental mice failures have been associated with biology student volunteers.

• The biology student volunteers who could not cure their lab mice were in fact able to cure mice at home.

• In the experiment where the biology student volunteers failed to cure their lab mice, they were the only ones to stumble upon the control mice. Those control mice began the process of remission even while their laboratory experimentally treated mice died.

• Adjacent to the biology students' mice cages were the other cages being treated by nonbiology student volunteers, who were successful in curing their own mice. All of the cages were regularly and repeatedly seen by all healer volunteers. Yet the biology students' mice died, even as the biology students were the only ones to see the control mice, which were cured.

If the problem is the condition of bonding and unbonding of individuals to a group, and the non-biologists were able to cure their mice, why wasn't there a bonding with the mice of the biologists who were not able to heal their mice? And if the nonbiologists could not heal their mice, why did the control mice remit when only seen by the biologists?

Speculatively, the answer may lie in the bonding/unbonding power of the state of mind and with consciousness itself. The biology students were, by the accounts in their own logs, nervous about being seen in a biology lab, with white coats on, putting their hands around cages of mice. Simply put, they had their professional status on the line in a way that the nonbiologist student volunteers did not. Could this anxious state of mind break the bond of their mice to the group? If so, the successful healing effect produced by the nonbiologists on the adjacent mice cages could not affect their mice, as they had been broken off from the collective.

In one experiment there was a second control group unknown to the volunteer healer that was cured. How to explain this? Obviously, conscious awareness on the part of the healer is unnecessary for healing to occur, but could the consciousness of the other experimenters who knew about the previous control remissions have bonded the mice together? If that is the case, then a treatment given to any mouse would still be a treatment to all. Or, alternatively, could it have been the consciousness or collective experience of the mice themselves, which were raised and shipped together, that somehow bonded them together? These are testable questions that deserve further study.

One final anomaly: Two of the experiments were carried out in a medical school that had many active labs investigating a single mouse model. In these experiments, the experimental mice were always at least 100 meters from the control mice, and there were at least a dozen labs doing more conventional work on the same cancer model between the experimental and control cages. In these experiments, both the experimental and control mice were cured, and there were no reported anomalous healings in any of the labs doing conventional work. A second control cage of mice unknown to the volunteer healer was also cured.

If these healings were done in a way analogous to a morphogenetic field effect (Sheldrake, 1995, 2009), then it follows that the labs which were between the experimental and control cages in the healing experiments would likely have had some anomalous effects. Yet there were no anomalous results reported by any of these labs. Rather, the bonding was selective, increasing the likelihood that bonds are made not necessarily by nondiscriminating field effects, but rather through some specific targeting by consciousness itself. The challenge is to elucidate the laws and patterns of consciousness in binding and unbinding groups together.

Implications for Spirituality and Mechanistic Science

The methodological complications that flow out of the resonant bonding of groups are formidable. Two obvious examples come to mind. The first are the well-known but only relatively recently studied placebo effects (Benedetti, 2009; Guess, Kleinman, Kusek, & Engel, 2002; Kaptchuk, 2001; Zajicek, 1995). Could placebos not simply be the consequence of suggestion, but instead possibly be the effects of resonant bonding between experimental and control subjects? When an experimenter administers an active agent to one group, are the consequences of that administration also felt by the bonded control group? Is the strength of the placebo effect directly proportional to the strength of the bond between subjects? What is the difference between those subjects who have a strong placebo response and those who don't? Instead of simply looking at psychological effects, perhaps there are some underlying physical mechanisms of bonding at work.

And if a placebo group has a strong effect, and there is a bond between the groups, then there will be a diminished chance that data analysis will indicate a difference between experimental and control/placebo groups. In statistical terms, that is known as a type II error, concluding that nothing has occurred when in fact it has. An alternative possibility in the context of resonant bonding is that an effect has occurred to all bonded participants, even those not directly administered a stimulus. Concluding that nothing has occurred might miss elucidating the conditions of bonding and unbonding. In the context of resonant bonding, it would be interesting to examine the data from previous experiments in a wide variety of fields.

The methodological complications extend to the question of whether healing and spirituality are connected. Some of the volunteer healers in the cancer experiments experienced nothing approaching what could be considered spiritual; others from time to time felt a sense of connection to their mice. The methodological conundrum of course is in the context of resonant bonding: Did the actual healing come from only those who felt some sort of connection? Was each volunteer healer actually responsible for healing his or her own mice? Is healing a correlate to the sense of spirituality?

Over the course of the last several decades, there have been attempts to correlate subjective states of connection with more objective physiological and physical measurements. Jahn and Dunne (2005) have widely reported that operators can significantly alter the output of random number generators when there is a feeling of a "resonant bonding" to their machine. Researchers have measured correlations between the brains of spatially separated people to determine whether the subjective sense of connection is associated with measurable alterations in brain activity, and they have found it to be so (Duane & Behrendt, 1965). Is this the same as a spiritual connection?

Of course, the fact of anomalous connection at a distance does not demonstrate that healing actually occurs during these times of connection, nor that this is the same as the subjective experience of spirituality. In a recent study, a volunteer healer and healee were physically separated yet were found to have intermittent brain entrainment that would last between 4 and 14 seconds per interval (Hendricks et al., 2010). While this may be taken as a potential example of a nonlocal physical connection, it does not demonstrate that the moments of brain entrainment correlated with moments of healing.

A further complication is that in the Hendricks study, neither volunteer healer nor healee reported any conscious sense of spiritual connection. It is possible, for example, that although spirituality is by definition subjectively experienced, that actual nonlocal healing is independent of conscious awareness. It is also possible that any conscious experience of healing is experienced as simply the delayed effect of a more autonomic process of healing. Until the moments of healing can be measured, this will be difficult to untangle.

Finally, what are the implications of these experiments for a mechanistic view of reality? Science traditionally assumes that phenomena can be reduced to its material correlates alone, and that there is a world out there that is objective in its existence and independent of the observer. The observer's consciousness, in turn, is really nothing more than an outgrowth of complex nerve firings in the brain.

There have been strongly made arguments (Jahn, 2001a; Tart, 2009) and empirical challenges (Greyson, 2010; Jahn & Dunne, 2005) against such a mechanistic approach to scientific inquiry from many disparate fields, too numerous to survey here. Do the patterns of cancer cures in these mice experiments reinforce these challenges and call into question this mechanistic view?

In the cancer healing experiments reported here, it is consistently the case that the consciousness of the observer affected the disease process, profoundly altering "what otherwise would have been" in both the experimental and control groups of mice. These effects were not dependent on belief, nor necessarily on deliberate intent, and it remains an open question whether those volunteer healers who sensed a "connection" with their mice produced a greater effect than those who did not feel such a connection.

The simple insertion of consciousness, even devoid of intent, clearly altered the outcome of the experimental data reported here, and this is perhaps the greatest challenge to mechanistic science (Jahn, 2001b). In addition, these effects were at times brought about from a distance that defies conventional understanding, and the apparent nonlocal bonding of groups further adds to the conceptual and theoretical challenges.

How are group bonds created and destroyed? How are they strengthened and weakened? How do they challenge the methodological underpinnings of the way we investigate and the way we interpret empirical data? These cancer experiments clearly raise more questions than answers. The good news is that most of the questions will yield testable hypotheses.

References

Benedetti, F. (2009). *Placebo effects: Understanding the mechanisms in health and disease.* New York: Oxford University Press.

Bengston, W. F. (2004). Methodological difficulties involving control groups in healing research. *The Journal of Alternative and Complementary Medicine, 10*(2), 227–230.

Bengston, W. F. (2007). A method used to train skeptical volunteers to heal in an experimental setting. *Journal of Alternative and Complementary Medicine, 13*(3), 329–332.

Bengston, W. F. (Speaker). (2010). *Hands-on healing: A training course in the energy cure.* [Audio CD] Louisville, CO: Sounds True Publishers.

Bengston, W. F., & Krinsley, D. (2000). The effect of the laying-on of hands on transplanted breast cancer in mice. *Journal of Scientific Exploration, 14*(3), 353–364.

Bengston, W. F., & Moga, M. (2007). Resonance, placebo effects, and type II errors: Some implications from healing research for experimental methods. *Journal of Alternative and Complementary Medicine, 13*, 317–327.

Benor, D. (2002). *Spiritual healing: Professional supplement.* Southfield, MI: Vision.

Cecero, J., Bedrosian, D., Fuentes, A., & Bornstein, R. (2006). Religiosity and health dependency as predictors of spiritual well-being. *International Journal for the Psychology of Religion, 16*(3), 225–238.

Cunningham, A. J., Stephen, J. E., Phillips, C., & Watson, K. D. (2000). Psychospiritual therapy. In J. Barraclough (Ed.), *Integrated cancer care: Holistic, complementary and creative approaches* (pp. 173–186). Oxford, England: Oxford University Press.

Dossey, L. (1999). *Reinventing medicine: Beyond mind-body to a new era of healing.* New York: Harper Collins.

Duane, T. D., & Behrendt, T. (1965). Extrasensory electroencephalographic induction between identical twins. *Science, 150*, 367.

Durkheim, E. (1965). *The elementary forms of the religious life.* New York: Free Press.

Fitzpatrick, A. L., Berger, J., Calabrese, C., Kim, J., & Polissar, N. (2007). Survival in HIV-1-positve adults practicing psychological or spiritual activities for one year. *Alternative Therapy Health Medicine, 13*(5), 18–23. Glock, C. (1973). *Religion in sociological perspective: Essays in the empirical study of religion.* Belmont, CA: Wadsorth.

Greeley, A. (1975). *The sociology of the paranormal.* Thousand Oaks, CA: Sage.

Greyson, B. (2010). Implications of near-death experiences for a postmaterialist psychology. *Psychology of Religion and Spirituality, 2*(1), 37–45.

Guess, H., Kleinman, A., Kusek, J., & Engel, L. (2002). *The science of the placebo: Towards an interdisciplinary research agenda*. London: BMJ Books.

Hendricks, L., Bengston, W. F., & Gunkelman, J. (2010). The healing connection: EEG harmonics, entrainment, and Shumann's resonances. *Journal of Scientific Exploration, 24*(3), 419–430.

Hill, P. (1999) *Measures of religiosity*. Birmingham, AL: Religious Education Press.

Hill, P., & Hood, R. (1999). *Measures of religious behavior*. Birmingham, AL: Religious Education Press.

Holmes, P. (2007). Spirituality: Some disciplinary perspectives. In K. Flanagan & P. Jupp (Eds.), *A sociology of spirituality* (pp. 23–42). Burlington, VT: Ashgate.

Jahn, R. (2001a). 20th and 21st century science: Reflections and projections. *Journal of Scientific Exploration, 15*(1), 21–31.

Jahn, R. (2001b). The challenge of consciousness. *Journal of Scientific Exploration, 15*(4), 443–457.

Jahn, R. G., & Dunne, B. (2005). The PEAR proposition. *Journal of Scientific Exploration, 19*(2), 195–245.

James, W. (1961). *The varieties of religious experience*. Cambridge, MA: Harvard University Press.

Kaptchuk, T. J. (2001). The double-blind randomized controlled trial: gold standard or golden calf? *Journal of Clinical Epidemiology. 54*, 541–49.

Koenig, H. G. (1998). *Handbook of religion and mental health*. San Diego, CA: Academic Press.

Koenig, H. G., Larson, D. B., & McCullough, M. E. (2000). *Handbook of religion and health*. New York: Oxford University Press.

Lipton, B. (2008). *The biology of belief: Unleashing the power of consciousness, matter, and miracles*. Carlsbad, CA: Hay House.

Miller, W., & Thoresen, C. (2003). Spirituality, religion, and health: An emerging research field. *American Psychologist, 58*(1), 24–35.

Oschman, J. (2000). *Energy medicine: The scientific basis*. New York: Churchill Livingstone.

Sheldrake, R. (1995). *A new science of life*. Rochester, VT: Park Street Press.

Sheldrake, R. (2009). *Morphic resonance: The nature of formative causation*. Rochester, VT: Park Street Press.

Soothill, K., Francis, B., Harman, J. C., McIllmurray, M. B., Morris, S. M., & Thomas C. (2002). Cancer and faith. Having faith—Does it make a difference among patients and their informal careers? *Scandinavian Journal of Caring Science, 16*(3), 256–263.

Tart, C. (2009). *The end of materialism: How evidence of the paranormal is bringing science and spirit together*. Oakland, CA: Noetic Books.

Thomson, K. S. (1996). The revival of experiments in prayer. *American Scientist, 84*, 532–534.

Tiller, W., Dibble, W., & Kohane, M. (2001). *Conscious acts of creation: The emergence of a new physics*. Walnut Creek, PA: Pavior.

Weber, M. (1963). *The sociology of religion*. Boston: Beacon Press.

Zajicek, G. (1995). The placebo effect is the healing force of nature. *Cancer Journal, 8*(2).

Knowledge, Intention, and Matter

William A. Tiller

Abstract

In human experience, there appear to be at least two uniquely different pathways to accessing knowledge, Logos (physical science) and Mythos (psychoenergetic science). Here, we show that a simple electrical device can serve as an effective host for a specific intention. Such a device can be utilized to (1) raise the electromagnetic gauge symmetry state of an experimental space from the *uncoupled state* to the *coupled state* of physical reality and (2) to tune that space to materialize the property changes implicit in the specific intention. Three uniquely different materials via four different experiments have been robustly successful, one of which has been replicated by others. This work shows that a functioning nature exists beyond our conventional level of electrically charged atom/ molecule world. This impacts domains of reality of serious interest to religions and human spiritual reality. It strongly suggests that higher dimensional domains of reality are held within the overarching potential field of the Divine.

Key Words: Logos, Mythos, physical science, psychoenergetic science, the uncoupled state, the coupled state, intentions, materials, dark matter, dark energy

Introduction

A long, long time ago in human history, there were two accepted and compatible pathways to the acquisition of knowledge. This applies not only to the historically well-known cultures but also to the not-so-well-documented indigenous cultures of the world. These two pathways were called *Mythos* and *Logos* (Armstrong, 2000), with the former designating the human *inner path of revelation* and the latter designating the human *outer path of logic* applied to external observations of Nature. For the many separate indigenous cultures, an intimate inner connection appeared to develop between the humans and the Earth prior to any massive cultural transformations that took place. However, in those early days, these two paths might have been looked at as two loosely intertwining and meandering rivers of thought.

During the subsequent human evolution and culture formation processes, as a consequence of the emergence in the far-flung human family of a number of avatars such as Krishna, Melchizedek, Moses, Lao Tzu, Confucius, Buddha, Jesus, Mohammed, and so on, a wide variety of religions came into being. Some of these became very powerful, political, and dogmatic. In the large cultures, both Mythos and Logos were submerged and exploited for centuries to millennia in this very powerful pathway of human behavior called religion. In these cultures, it dominated human experience, human thought, and the human worldview. Here, the priests took a lead role as privileged dispensers of knowledge to the human populace. For most of the smaller indigenous cultures, this did not happen.

For the major cultures, the first Copernican revolution, of 1600 AD, initiated a serious emergence of Logos from the pathway of religion to contest the long-held centrist view of the priests that both our sun and the other planets revolved around the

Earth. The subsequent experimental and quantitative theoretical findings by Kepler, Galileo, and Newton, and so on, underscored the substantial truth of the Copernican observations and thought. This led to the Industrial Revolution with all its human benefits and horrors. The classical mechanics (CM) paradigm was born and the pathway of Logos morphed into the pathway of science, in serious opposition to the pathway of religion.

Humankind has always been concerned with scientific inquiry because we really want to understand the milieu in which we find ourselves. Our mindset is that we also want to engineer and modulate as much of our environment as possible to sustain, feed, enrich, and propagate our lives. Following this path, the goal of science has been to gain a reliable description of natural phenomena that eventually allows accurate quantitative prediction, within certain error-bar limits of Nature's behavior as a function of an ever-changing environment. As such, past and present science is incapable of providing us with absolute truth. Rather, it seeks to provide us with *relative knowledge*, but internally self-consistent knowledge, about the relationships between different phenomena and between different things (see Fig. 36.1; Lederman & Teresti, 1993) relative to the prevailing paradigm.

The goal of engineering, on the other hand, is to build on this fundamental understanding in order to generate new materials, devices, attitudes, moralities, philosophies, and so on, for producing tangible societal order, for harnessing the various potentials in Nature's many phenomena, and for expanding human capabilities in an ever-changing environment.

In the foregoing, since the time of Descartes (1604) an unstated assumption of establishment science has been that "No human qualities of consciousness, intention, emotion, mind, or spirit can significantly influence a well-designed target experiment in physical reality." Thus, this morphing of Logos into today's science carries with it the complete denial of human consciousness aspects as

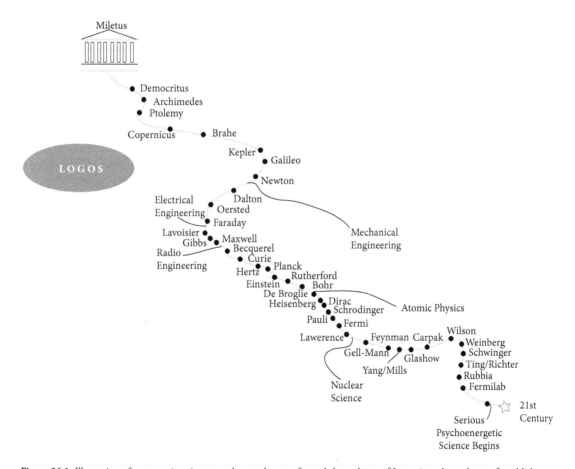

Figure 36.1 Illustration of many major pioneer explorers who transformed the pathway of Logos into the pathway of establishment science (Lederman & Teresti, 1993).

significant and meaningful experimental variables in the study of physics. Furthermore, for internal self-consistency, physics must deny the relevance of Mythos as a viable pathway to "knowing."

In contrast to the previous paragraph, relevant experimental data from the area of psychophysiology should be considered. A relevant beginning is with Gustav Fechner, who, in ~1860 (1966), wrote a book entitled *Elements of Psychophysics* wherein he wrote, "Not only does the world influence the mind but the mind influences the world." By around 1910, Johannes Schultz, via combining various ideas from (a) his medical research, (b) hypnosis, and (c) concepts from yogic methods, developed an inner self-management procedure that he labeled "autogenic training" (Schultz & Luthe, 1959), a self-generated or self-motivated training for attaining a variety of stable emotional/mental states. By the ~1960s, Elmer and Alyce Green (1999) had deeply studied voluntary control of *internal* human states, both psychological and physiological, and strongly promoted the "psychophysiological principle" wherein:

> by an appropriate change in the mental-emotional state, conscious or unconscious, and conversely every change in the human mental-emotional state, conscious or unconscious, is accompanied by an appropriate change in the physiological state. (p. 17–134)

The Greens went on to show that the instrumental monitoring and display, continuous in time, of a particular human physiological parameter can allow an attentive human to voluntarily modify the magnitude of this parameter and thereby alter one's own physiological activity, behavior, or process of consciousness. This work led to the use of biofeedback as an important medical therapeutic procedure. It also generated serious suspicion in some concerning the validity of the long-held, unstated assumption of establishment science: *No human qualities of consciousness, intention, emotion, mind or spirit can significantly influence a well-designed target experiment in physical reality.* Since the experimental work of this chapter has seriously tested the veracity of this critical assumption of establishment science, it is useful to provide three meaningful biofeedback examples as a backdrop for the next major section of this chapter. The first two examples are from the unconscious responses of humans to unique life stimuli, while the third deals with physiological measurement responses, consciously observed, in a typical biofeedback mode.

1. One of the most striking unconscious biofeedback experiments was that carried out in the mid-1930s by Slater (Rock, 1967) involving the use of his "upside-down" glasses. Subjects were asked to continually wear these glasses that distorted perception so that the wearer saw everything in an upside-down configuration. It was very destabilizing for these subjects, but they did so, and after 2–3 weeks depending on the particular subject, there was a "flip" and, with the glasses on, they suddenly saw everything "right side up" and thereafter continued to do so. Then, when the subjects removed these glasses, the world suddenly appeared upside down again for another ~2–3 weeks, depending on the individual, before normal vision was suddenly restored. From this, one might presume that the apparent disparity between the conventional worldview that people walk erect and the special glasses' inverted view caused a force on the brain's dendrites to first construct some type of hard-wired internal *inversion mirror* so that one's expectations are fulfilled and then later dissolved this brain structural element when it was no longer needed. At the very least, it indicates a level of malleability of our brains relative to our expectations.

2. Stewart Wolf did a double-blind study (Norris, 1997) with a group of pregnant women suffering from nausea and vomiting. He did it in two steps. First, he gave an antiemetic to one portion of the group and a placebo to the other. He was surprised to find how many of the women in the placebo subgroup had a cessation of nausea and vomiting. In the second step, he took the placebo subgroup and gave them what he said was a new and strong antiemetic. He observed that all the women overcame their nausea and vomiting. What he didn't tell them was that he actually gave them Ipecac, a very strong emetic that is regularly used to induce vomiting. This is a remarkable psychophysiological result wherein the strength of the women's intention field created a thermodynamic force in their bodies that significantly exceeded the opposite sign force, the strong chemical force known to be present from Ipecac.

3. In the mid-1990s, I worked with colleagues at the Institute of HeartMath in California studying effects of focusing intentional appreciation for someone or something (poem, painting, nature scene, etc.) through the heart on the electrophysiological state of humans (Tiller, 1997). The core biofeedback measurement

instrument was the electrocardiogram (EKG) with subsidiary measurements of respiration (R), pulse transit time (PTT), and electroencephalograph (EEG). The EKG data were automatically converted to heart rate variability (HRV) and displayed for the viewer in real time. Its power spectrum was also obtained. The time trigger for invoking the focused appreciation was labeled "freeze-frame." Figure 36.2 illustrates the real-time changes in HRV, PTT, and R plus the HRV power spectrum both before and after the freeze-frame intention. Figure 36.3 provides power spectra data for all measurement systems before and after freeze-frame onset. What we learn from this data is that the onset of a sincere appreciation focus through the heart brings (a) a state of internal coherence in the real-time HRV, (b) the collapse of both the parasympathetic (high-frequency) and sympathetic (low-frequency) power spectrum HRV information to the baroreflex frequency of ~0.14 Hertz, where the heart interacts strongly with the brain and (c) strong entrainment of all four electrophysiological measurements to the baroreflex frequency. When one regularly practices this freeze-frame/sincere appreciation technique, one also notes a significant change in chemical factory output for the body, that is, DHEA production increases while cortisol

production decreases. Thus, internal stress signatures are decreasing while beneficial hormones are increasing. All of the foregoing signifies an appreciably healthier human via this particular act of directed consciousness.

The useful background for the "meat" of this chapter has now been completed and we can now return to our experimental testing of establishment science's unstated assumption. This next section will prove that unstated assumption to be very, very wrong and that Equations 2b and 2c are fully justified. The final sections of the chapter deal with theoretical exploration of psychoenergetic science.

The Logos Pathway to Scientific Understanding
Pathways to Scientific Understanding

The time-honored method of scientific inquiry for a new phenomenon is to treat it as a "black box" whose internal characteristics are unknown but are amenable to probing and analysis (see the upper section of Fig. 36.4). One applies some appropriately selected input stimulus (IS) to the box and determines its output response (OR) to the specific stimulus. By varying IS and correlating the OR with the IS, one deduces information about the most

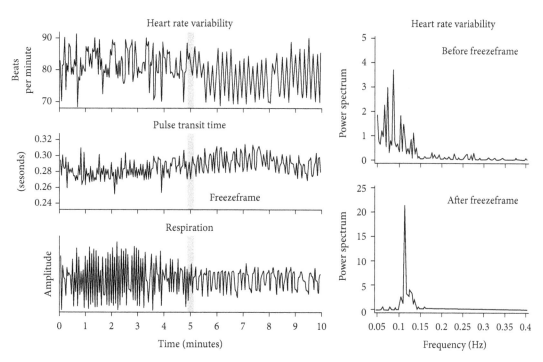

Figure 36.2 Real-time changes in heart rate variability (HRV), pulse transit time (PTT), and respiration (R) plus the HRV power spectrum both before and after the freeze-frame (FF) intention. EEG, electroencephalograph.

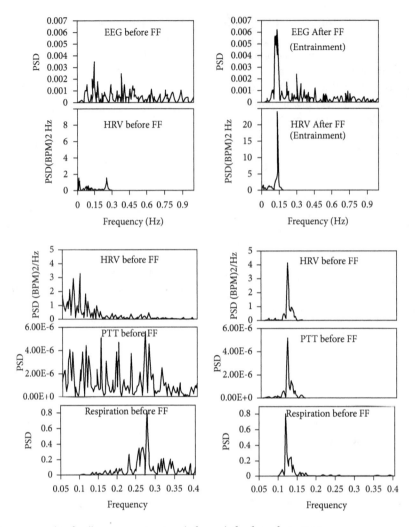

Figure 36.3 Power spectra data for all measurement systems before and after freeze-frame onset.

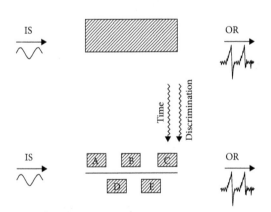

Figure 36.4 Schematic illustration of the "black box" metaphor (*top*) as a time-honored procedure for gaining sufficient understanding of a new phenomenon to recognize it as an interacting system of discriminated pieces of basic physics and chemistry (*bottom*). IS, input stimulus; OR, output response.

probable behavior of the box for this magnitude of stimulus. One then speculates on models of nature that would first qualitatively and ultimately quantitatively reproduce such a spectrum of responses. Then, one proceeds to design critical tests for discriminating between the initially acceptable models (Tiller, 2007).

Since the *full* and lawful nature of the box would have a much more complex and rich expression than we could explain by this limited probing, the exact and complete response function, OR/IS, for the box may be characterized by the following *general* form

$$\frac{OR}{IS} = f\left(V_n, P_m\right) \tag{1a}$$

Here, f represents the *exact and complete* hypothesized functional relationship between all possible experimental variables, V, and material parameters, P, of the system, each having an unlimited range of magnitude. The subscripts n and m refer to the *number* of different variables and parameters involved.

Because at any point in time for our evolving society, one has (1) limited cognitive awareness concerning all of these variables and parameters, (2) a limited array of experimental equipment of the probe stimuli type available with significant accuracy, and (3) limited patience and financial resources available for endless data gathering, to be practical one settles for the following functional expression as the *operational* response function for the box

$$\frac{OR}{IS} \approx f'\left(v_N, \ p_M\right). \qquad (1b)$$

Here, f' has a much less rich functional form than f; N is much smaller than n, M is much smaller than m, any particular v has a much smaller experimental range than V, and p has a much smaller experimental range than P. It is the Equation 1b-type of response function that one tries to match with a theoretical model for this type of black box behavior. Thus, one must always realize that what we call *a successful model* simulates only idealized rather than actual nature.

This is a practical procedure that has been very fruitful for an evolving humanity, and it provides meaningful but relative truth concerning this aspect of nature. With this information, one then begins to speculate on possible models of nature that might *qualitatively* reproduce such a spectrum of experimental results. At this level of analysis, one usually finds that *dozens* of competing models can qualitatively simulate such an OR/IS spectrum. Next, one proceeds to *quantitative* models, which greatly reduces the number of viable candidates. Then, one proceeds to design critical test experiments for sensitively discriminating between the surviving quantitative candidates. Over time, people tend to become attached to the theoretical model that has been fashioned to fit idealized nature (Equation 1b) and *tend to forget* that they are not dealing with actual nature (Equation 1a). This attachment can become so strong that a rather rigid mindset can develop in the scientific community concerning it and it becomes the scientific worldview or paradigm for an overly extended period of time. However, periodically in time, the prevailing paradigm is unable to accommodate some new sets of experimental observations, so pressure begins to develop to change the accepted form of Equation 1b and this would constitute a paradigm shift.

Paradigm shifts in physics do not occur easily because the old mindset of the establishment has great inertia to change for a variety of reasons. Such a shift began a century ago with the then new concepts of discrete quantum packets of change plus the relativistic coupling of the separate coordinates, distance and time, into an indivisible space-time. These new concepts violated certain basic assumptions inherent in the prevailing perspective of classical mechanics, and they were strongly resisted. Today, these concepts of quantum mechanics are well accepted, but it has taken a century of productive and fruitful work to make it so.

Now, a century later, the prevailing physics model is unable to incorporate the robust experimental observations concerning psychoenergetics (e.g., ESP, remote viewing, distant healing, homeopathy, qigong, mind and emotions) into its internally self-consistent picture. Thus, physicists must either deny the existence of such observations as being valid observations or they must expand their model of nature sufficiently to incorporate them. Unfortunately and perhaps predictably, at the moment, most of the scientific establishment has preferred to "sweep all these observations under the rug" rather than accept the limited nature of their present perspective and thus proceed forward to define and explore the larger truth.

Because humankind continues to grow steadily in consciousness while continuing to refine and expand its experimental tools for probing nature, a wise society would periodically assess whether their current formulation of Equation 1b is still a valid approximation to the truth of *all* the experimental observations gathered by their community. One must really expect that, with the passage of time, our old relative truth must be periodically replaced with a new relative truth as a course correction for our trajectory toward enlightenment (Equation 1a).

For the disciplines of physics and chemistry, N and M in Equation 1b are generally small (N + M ~ 4) so f' can be determined with a good degree of accuracy. With the passage of time, our sensing capacity increases, so N + M tends to increase and the experimental ranges for v and p tend to increase. There are time and funds to allow the gathering of ~10 data points along each v and p, so that a good level of theoretical modeling can be reliably tested. Thus, for physics and chemistry, only ~10,000 experimental data points need to be gathered for serious testing of a mathematical form for f' in Equation 1b. If one's apparatus allows the gathering of 10 data points per day, then this becomes a 3 human-year experiment (a typical PhD thesis period).

As a simple illustration, consider the simplest case of M = 1 and N = 1 with a range of 10 data points along each coordinate direction so that the total number of OR/IS data points is 10x10 intersections, as illustrated in Figure 36.5.

Here, our two-dimensional topographic map is represented by the surface plotted above the 100 base-plane intersection points. As M and N increase in magnitude and, if one seeks 10 data points along each coordinate direction (physics level reliability of modeling), then 10 to the power M + N experimental data points must be gathered, 10^{M+N}, to do this. Thus, both the time and cost expenditures to achieve this goal rise strongly with the magnitude of M + N.

To put this in perspective, Table 36.1 provides an approximate value of M + N for a variety of research disciplines. Thus, for the same level of theoretical modeling capability as physics, in engineering ~10 to 1,000 theses (even using dimensionless groups of parameters and variables) would be required. Moving down the first column of Table 36.11 to materials science, one can see that it is impossible in any practical sense to use this simple black box approach, with 10 data points along each coordinate direction in order to gain meaningful theoretical modeling capability because it requires ~1 trillion theses. However, if one shrinks the average number of data points along each coordinate direction to ~2 or 3, practical and useful research can be

Table 36.1 Relative Correlation of Number of Material Parameters Plus Variables, M + N, With Specific Research Disciplines

Discipline	M + N
Physics, chemistry	~ 3–4
Engineering—without dimensionless groups	~ 8–10
Engineering—with dimensionless groups	~ 5–6
Materials science and engineering	~ 20–30
Geology	~ 20–40
Biology	~ 50
Medicine	~ 50–100
Psychology	~ 100–200
Sociology	~ 500–1,000

done but with very low theoretical modeling capabilities. This approach leads to an *art-based technology* containing a number of very useful *recipes* for obtaining some practical utility as an output from the research. This same declaration can be made for all of the lower candidates in Column 1 of Table 36.1. Since M + N is so large for these areas of research activity, it takes an incredibly large number of human-years of research effort to gather sufficient experimental data for one to meaningfully map the OR/IS profile. Thus, just as with materials science, specific *recipes* are developed and an art-based technology exists.

As a sidebar to this discussion, it is important for the reader to recognize that physicists, as a group, are not really more intelligent than workers in the research fields with positions lower down in column 1 of Table 36.1. General respect for physics in our society relates very much to the fact that physicists choose to work on problems where M + N is small. Then, with good tools, they can quickly gather sufficient experimental data so that their data map is rich enough for meaningful theoretical modeling of nature. Thus, in their field of activity, they can dig deeper and deeper into the more microscopic and macroscopic levels of nature. Then, they ultimately become limited by the sophistication and costs of the tools and human teams needed to continue pursuing their investigations. Of course, because they have been able to search more quickly and more

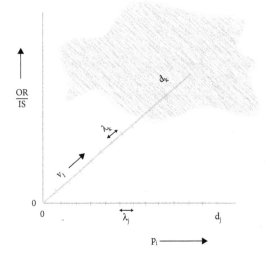

Figure 36.5 Plot of output response (OR)/ input stimulus (IS) for the simplest case, where M = N = 1. Here, λ is the average grid spacing for measurement along any particular coordinate axis and d is the total experimental range along that coordinate direction.

deeply than other disciplines, they have harvested and taught succeeding generations of physicists more necessary new concepts and techniques than other disciplines.

Returning now to our central theme for this section, the "simple black box" research approach is continued in any new area of activity until sufficient information has been uncovered to allow researchers to *discriminate* details of internal structure in this particular box. One then comes to see that it can be effectively described as a *system* of Q subboxes wherein each of these subboxes is a single element of physics. Now, the original, simple black box with large M + N is partitioned with Q subsystems with each having an average number of parameters plus variables equal to (M + N)/Q. Provided each of these is the size of a typical physics problem, and one pays close attention to the interactions between the various subsystems, research progress can now proceed very rapidly in terms of human-years of effort. Now we are not dealing with $10^{(M + N)}$ data points but, defining (M + N)/Q = z, we now require only z 10^z data points. For example, if M + N ≈ 100 and Q = 10 so z = 10, we only need approximately 10^{11} data points instead of 10^{100}. This is a tremendous cost and manpower saving. This more advanced approach ultimately leads to *science-based technologies*.

Finally, in addition to the foregoing research evolution path, it is important to note that some scientists who learn to handle the craft of large M + N disciplines also make good managers, businessmen, and good politicians because these are also large M + N disciplines requiring the acquiring of a good *intuition* for discriminating and predicting the really important regions of parameter/variable space for detailed study (~10 data points along each coordinate in such regions) and for casual study (~2 data points along each coordinate for all other regions). Here we see the beginnings of psychoenergetic science entering the research protocols. From an educational perspective, and ultimately practical perspective for a society, it is probably beneficial for students to take their primary education in physics, mathematics, and chemistry and then follow this with an information synthesis field with appreciably larger M + N-value (like materials science, biology, psychology, etc.).

The Mythos Pathway to Psychoenergetic Science Understanding

From on overly simplistic viewpoint, one could say that, for the past ~400 years or so, establishment science has dealt with multiple aspects of the metaphorical reaction equation

$$MASS \Leftrightarrow ENERGY \qquad (2a)$$

with each term being convertible to the other via Einstein's, $E = mc^2$ equation (E = energy, m = mass, and c = the velocity of electromagnetic [EM] light traveling through the physical vacuum; Tiller, 2007). In Equation 2a, *consciousness* is not allowed as a significant variable, so Equation 2a is an *idealized approximation* to the behavior of nature. Unfortunately, over time, physicists have forgotten that this was just a useful assumption. And it *was* a very useful assumption because we learned how to develop a reliable methodology and set of procedures for the conduct of scientific experiments in the simplest of cases—where the biofields of the experimenters were relatively weak and thus they only negligibly perturb the experimental outcomes. One of the downsides of almost total acceptance of this assumption by scientists is that their philosophical worldview has generally become reductionistic and materialistic. One of the upsides of this assumption was the discovery of many natural laws that were *linear* relationships between various potential differences applied to a material and responses from the material (e.g., Ohm's law, Hooke's law, Fick's law, etc.). This produced great engineering utility for such materials. In addition, in more recent times we have discovered that, when these potential differences become quite large, the response function of the material expands to include second-order and third-order terms and becomes meaningfully *nonlinear*. This latter aspect becomes important in what is to follow.

Returning to Equation 2a, our research of the past decade shows that human biofield effects are no longer of insignificant magnitude and that psychoenergetic effects require an expansion of Equation 2a to the form

$$MASS \Leftrightarrow ENERGY \Leftrightarrow CONSCIOUSNESS. \quad (2b)$$

The term "consciousness" here is used to mean a unique quality of nature that is ultimately convertible to energy (and thus mass), although it also conforms to the typical dictionary usage of being awake, aware, and so on.

Perhaps, instead of asking what consciousness *means*, we should ask what consciousness *does*. When we do this, we almost immediately see that consciousness manipulates *information* in the form of numbers, alphabet letters, jigsaw puzzle pieces, and, most generally, symbols. Thus, Equation 2b becomes more revealing when we phrase it in the following format:

$$\text{MASS} \Leftrightarrow \text{ENERGY} \Leftrightarrow \text{INFORMATION} \Leftrightarrow \text{CONSCIOUSNESS.} \qquad (2c)$$

For the past 50 years or so, establishment science has recognized the existence of a quantitative relationship between information in units of bits and the thermodynamic quality, *entropy*, in units of calories per unit temperature (Brillouin, 1962; Shannon, 1948). For the past ~150 years or so, entropy has been recognized as a very important contribution to the *thermodynamic free energy* functions of Helmholtz (Mayer & Mayer, 1940) and Gibbs (1957). Thus, information in Equation 2c is intimately connected to energy and also to consciousness and is a very important bridge between the two. Because one cannot define either information or consciousness as *spatially* varying qualities or forces, one sees that *space-time* is not an appropriate reference frame (RF) for their utilization. Thus, one also sees that a new RF involving an expansion beyond just space-time will be needed for describing the manifold expressions of nature that involve consciousness as a significant variable.

If information, I, increases in a natural process, then entropy, S, decreases as a consequence of that process. S in the Gibb's thermodynamic free energy function, G, is connected to E via

$$G = PV + E - TS \qquad (3)$$

where P = pressure, V = volume, E = energy, and T = temperature. It is changes in G, ΔG, that drive all processes in nature, and the TS term in Equation 3 is comparable in magnitude to the E term in Equation 3. Most progress in nature (heat transfer, mass transfer, etc.) generates a positive increase in S, which leads to a decrease in G, that is, a decrease in the ability to do work. Only those processes that increase the magnitude of information, I, in the system, decrease the magnitude of S and thus increase G and restore potential to our universe.

As we humans do "inner" work on ourselves, we create infrastructure in the various layers of self, and this new infrastructure is really an information content increase of self and thus constitutes an increase in G (see Equation 3 with $S = S_0 + \Delta I_s$). More will be said about this later.

Inner work, usually involving the practice of meditation, altered states of consciousness, and other inner self-management techniques, leads to other ways of "knowing" than our standard education and Logos paths. Building such infrastructure into the larger self usually requires decades to lifetimes of patient practice. Scientists who would follow both the Logos and the Mythos paths will find that a significant activation barrier exists between practicing the former to practicing the latter. Those who just practice the former have a strong tendency and hubris to think that simple extensions of the Logos path of the prevailing paradigm can answer and explain any phenomenon observed in our space-time world. To illustrate that this is not so, consider statements by Paul Werbos, PhD, a world-class quantum mechanics practitioner and director of the engineering sector for the US National Science Foundation:

(1) All forms of quantum mechanics, Copenhagen, Bohmian, Schwinger, and Werbos types, yield the same type of predictions and none of them can explain "remote viewing."

(2) The world has spent billions of dollars to use quantum electrodynamics in the military to see things far away (remote viewing) and has absolutely failed to do so. An entirely different science approach will be needed if we wish to do so. (Werbos, 2001 p. 81).

Perhaps a more personal example will be illuminating for the reader. My wife, Jean, and I were introduced to the works of Edgar Cayce in the mid to late 1950s and began daily meditations together, via the Cayce method, in 1964. This was followed by weekly Cayce study-group activities in our home in Menlo Park, California, from 1965 to 1969. At these meetings, a very heterogeneous group of 11–13 people meaningfully discussed two books that Cayce had written in the early 1930s, *Search for God*, books I and II, and we meditated together. This meditation procedure involved a 10-minute segment of sharply focused attention on particular affirmations followed by a 10-minute segment of relaxed attunement to that affirmation where the mind was allowed freedom to explore the content. With continued practice, Jean and I expanded our meditation period to 1 hour per day, and I learned how to rapidly switch back and forth from the sharply focused state to the softly attuned state. I found this to be greatly beneficial in (1) my 1965 and onward role as chairman of Stanford's Department of Materials Science and (2) my industrial consulting practice.

At the end of the 1960s, I received a Guggenheim Fellowship for a year's sabbatical leave to Oxford University and, just before we left for England, I purchased a copy of the book *Psychic Discoveries Behind the Iron Curtain* (Ostrander & Schroeder, 1970) for casual reading. I knew a considerable amount about psychics and psychic phenomena by that time, but I was very impressed with both the breadth and scope of the Russian work and, while flying to England, my mind kept returning again and again to the question "how might the universe be constructed so that this 'crazy-seeming' kind of stuff could naturally coexist with the traditional science I was conducting every day with my Stanford graduate students?"

Although in Oxford I started to write the book in my traditional materials science area that I had planned to write, the foregoing question kept coming back into my mind. After about a month of this distracting influence, I decided to switch projects and seriously attempt to answer the question via the use of my meditative process. Once again my wife meditated with me for an hour each morning. Within about 10 minutes a state of comfortable coherence usually developed between us and the room. Then, I would mentally hold "this question" in my mind, like a supplicant seeking and expecting some type of revelatory enlightenment regarding the question. After we came out of meditation, Jean and I would discuss our internal experiences and any insights received. Then, I would go upstairs to my home office and work all day on the kernels or fragments of insight received that day to see if they violated any important experimental data present in the world literature of physics. During this process, new questions arose in my mind and these became "the questions" for our next day's meditation session. This became a daily procedure that was iterated for 6 months, at which time, I had finally arrived at a starting model of a structural and multidimensional nature for our universe that would allow both my orthodox science considerations and my unorthodox considerations to naturally coexist.

To fulfill my goal, I had to postulate the following:

(1) That nature consists of many classes of substance *beyond* the electric atom/molecule substance with which we are quite familiar and that different varieties interact with each other via other than the four fundamental forces of gravity, electromagnetism, the weak nuclear force, and the strong nuclear force.

(2) That these other *classes* of substance all travel at velocities greater than $v = c$, the velocity of electromagnetic light in physical vacuum, and thus cannot be detected via our conventional instrumentation.

(3) A multidimensional RF is needed for discriminating, tracking and understanding the new energy fields and forces involved with these new kinds of substance.

My first visualization of such an RF is that illustrated in Figure 36.6 with the densest substance on the left and the finest substance on the right.

During these meditation sessions, Jean and I both felt an inner communion with what might be called "unseen intelligence" that was somehow assisting my quest for greater insight into these subtle domains of nature. The sessions were definitely Mythos-types of experiences. In analogy with Figure 36.1, Figure 36.7 represents some of the key individuals who have attempted to morph Mythos into a science that meaningfully utilizes human consciousness as a key experimental variable in the study of nature. I have labeled this path as "Psychoenergetic Science."

The Four Key Intention Experiments

Webster's dictionary defines "intention" as the determination to do a specific thing or act in a specified manner; having something in mind as a plan, design, purpose, or goal. My early intention experiments began with gas discharge devices in the mid to late 1970s as an avocational pursuit. They clearly showed that subtle energy (biofield) emissions from humans could influence both micro-avalanche population and magnitude in gas discharges (Tiller, 1990, 1997). They also showed that the specific intention of the human could both enhance or eliminate such micro-avalanche discharges. However, this category of psychoenergetic science began in earnest in the period 1997–2000 and led to the publication of many papers and the seminal book *Conscious Acts of Creation: The Emergence of a New Physics* (Tiller, Dibble, & Kohane, 2001).

The primary goal of this work was to seriously test the long-held unstated assumption of science that "No human qualities of consciousness, intention, emotion, mind, or spirit can significantly influence a well-designed target experiment in physical reality." This was done by designing, constructing and running four carefully designed experiments, just as one does in orthodox science. A specific intention was introduced into each experiment via a novel procedure. Instead of directly utilizing the biofield

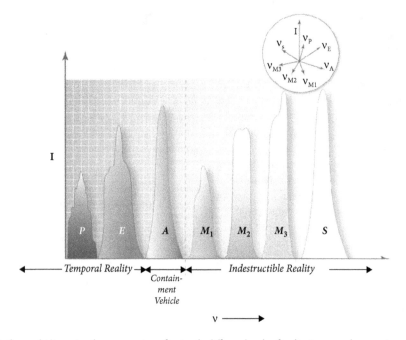

Figure 36.6 My first multidimensional representation of uniquely different bands of reality in spectral terms. A, astral; E, etheric; I, intensity; v= frequency; M_1, instinctive mind; M_2, intellectual mind; M_3, spiritual mind; P, physical; S, spirit.

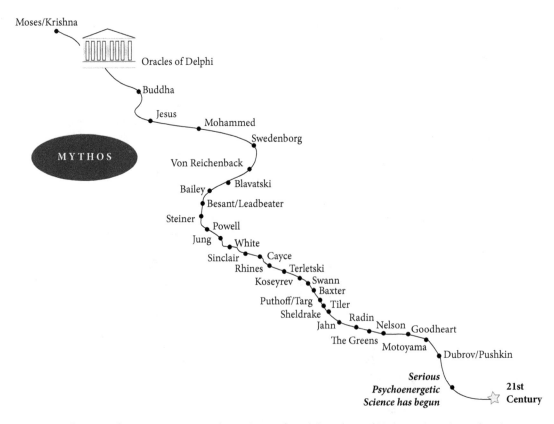

Figure 36.7 Illustration of many major pioneer explorers who transformed the pathway of Mythos to the pathway of psychoenergetic science.

of a human to insert a specific intention into the specific experiment, we first imbedded the intention into a simple electronic device from a deep meditative state (Tiller, 2007; Tiller, Dibble, & Fandel, 2005; Tiller et al., 2001); we next shipped this imprinted device to the laboratory location where the four experiments were being run to gather background data; the specific intention-host device for each experiment was then placed next to its appropriate experimental apparatus, plugged into an electric power outlet, and switched on so as to run in that location for several months while the running experiment was continuously monitored. It should be noted that the total electric power output of an intention-host device was less than 1 microwatt.

An overview perspective on the general experimental results is schematically illustrated in Figure 36.8, where one sees that, for any physical measurement, Q, the qualitative magnitude of property change, Q_M, is plotted versus the degree of locale space conditioning produced by continued intention-host device use. Here, one sees that nothing much happens to Q_M, during exposure of the experimental space to the particular intention-host device for time, t, until a threshold time t_1 ~ 1 month has been passed. Then, Q_M begins to change from Q_{M0}, the background value, always in the direction of the specific intention before it begins to level off and plateau at time t_2 ~ 3 months when $Q_{M1} - Q_{M0} = \Delta Q$ ~ the magnitude of the specific intention originally embedded into the intention-host device from the deep meditative state.

For the first target experiment, the intention was to *increase* the pH of a vessel of water in equilibrium with air at room temperature by +1.0 pH units with

no chemical additions. Our measurement accuracy was ± 0.02 pH units. This experiment was robustly successful in yielding the intended result (Tiller et al., 2001), which was 50 times larger than the noise level. It was visually noted that plots of pH as a function of time were remarkably more *coherent* in an intention-host device conditioned space than in a normal reality unconditioned space.

The second target experiment was with the same type of water in equilibrium with air at room temperature, but, here, the intention was to *decrease* the pH by 1.0 pH units, again with *no* chemical additions. Once again, this experiment was robustly successful. Similar successful results were obtained for alkaline, neutral, and acidic water as the starting substance (Tiller et al., 2001).

For the third target experiment, the material medium was an in vitro biological molecule, alkaline phosphatase (ALP), a liver enzyme. The intention was to *increase* the chemical activity of ALP by a significant amount via just exposing the ALP for a period of 30 minutes to its intention-host device "conditioned" space that had been brought to *the coupled state* of physical reality. Once again, the experimental results (Tiller et al., 2001) were remarkably successful compared to the built-in controls. About a 25%–30% increase in ALP chemical activity was achieved at $p < .001$.

In the fourth target experiment, the material medium was an in vivo living system, fruit fly larvae. Here, the intention was to significantly *increase* the ratio of the cell's energy storage molecule, ATP, to its chemical precursor, ADP, so as to make the larvae more physically fit and thus have a greatly reduced larval development time, τ, to the adult fly stage.

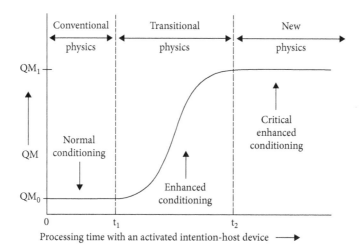

Figure 36.8 For any typical physical measurement, Q, the qualitative magnitude change, Q_M, is plotted versus the degree of locale conditioning produced by continued intention-host device use.

Again, with built-in controls, this living system was exposed to its intention-host device-"conditioned" space for the entire period, $\tau \sim 28$ days. We found that the ratio [ATP/ADP] increased by ~15%–20% with $p < .001$ and τ decreased by ~20%–25% at $p < .001$ (Tiller et al., 2001).

One might ask, "How is it possible for something like this to occur in the physical reality with which we are all so familiar?" The answer is that, from our experimental work of the past 10 years, we have discovered that there are actually *two* levels of physical reality and not just the *one* with which we are all familiar. It is this new level of physical reality that can be significantly influenced by human intention—not our familiar electric atom/molecule level.

The two basic kinds of unique substances inhabiting these two levels of physical reality appear to interpenetrate each other, but, normally, they do not interact with each other. We label this state as *the uncoupled state* of physical reality. In the uncoupled state, with one's five physical senses, we can detect the normal physical environment all around us. This new level of substance, because it appears to function in the physical vacuum (the empty space between the fundamental electric particles that make up our normal electric atoms and molecules), is currently invisible to us and to our traditional measurement instruments. It also appears to be of a magnetic information-wave nature.

It is the use of these intention-host devices that affects the experimental space in such a way that meaningful coupling begins to occur between these two very different kinds of substance. Then, the vacuum level of physical reality becomes partially visible to our traditional measurement instruments. We have labeled this condition *the coupled state* of physical reality. Figure 36.9 metaphorically illustrates a key difference between a material in these two states

of physical reality. In Figure 36.9, the black balls represent the electric substance and the much, much smaller white balls represent the magnetic substance. The black lines joining the black balls to each other represents that they are interacting with each other and, in (a), since no lines connect the white balls with the black balls, this represents that they are *not* interacting with each other—the uncoupled state. In Figure 36.9 (b), the dashed lines connecting the white balls with the black balls represents that use of an intention-host device has caused them to significantly interact with each other and produce the coupled state of physical reality.

The implication of all of this for our world is enormous! However, before proceeding to discuss some major implications of large-scale use of such intention-host devices in scientific laboratories and industrial sites around the world, let us look at a few of our key experimental results upon which I have based the foregoing remarks.

Returning, momentarily to the Figure 36.8 message, this general result can be quantitatively put in a simple equation form as

$$Q_M(t) \approx Q_e + \alpha_{eff}(t)Q_m, \qquad (4)$$

where Q_e is our normal electric atom/molecule value, Q_{M0}, of the uncoupled state, Q_m is the vacuum level value, and α_{eff} is the time-dependent *coupling* coefficient between the two types of substances due to use of the intention-host device as the space transitions from the uncoupled state to the coupled state of physical reality. The magnitude of $\alpha_{eff}Q_m$ $(t > t_2)$ is $\Delta Q_m = Q_{M1}-Q_{M0}$. When $\alpha_{eff} \sim 0$, then Equation 4 replicates data from our normal uncoupled state physical reality. However, when $0.05 < \alpha_{eff} < 1.0$, Equation 4 produces results for coupled state physical reality (Tiller et al., 2001).

One of the key experimental observations concerning an intention-host conditioned space is the significant change in the DC magnetic field polarity effect associated with the transition from the uncoupled state to the coupled state of physical reality (Tiller et al., 2001). The main elements of the experimental setup are illustrated in Figure 36.10. Here, the disk-magnet is first placed with either the N-pole or the S-pole pointing upward for 3–4 days while continuously monitoring the pH. For an *uncoupled state* space, one observes that *no change* in pH occurs regardless of which pole is pointing upward. This is exactly what one should expect because our normal state (uncoupled) of physical reality contains only magnetic dipoles and no single N- or S-pole

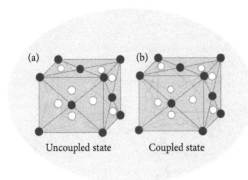

Figure 36.9 The physical reality metaphor; (a) the uncoupled state and (b) the coupled state.

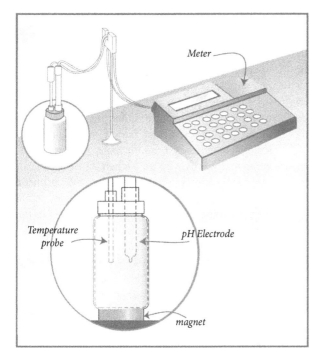

Figure 36.10 Experimental setup for testing changes due to a DC magnet placed under the water vessel with either the N pole or S pole axially and vertically aligned and pointing into the water.

magnetic charges. For such a dipole, the magnetic force and magnetic energy is proportional to H^2 and is independent of dipole orientation. However, for a coupled state space, one observes a result like that shown in Figure 36.11, where a very significant change in pH occurs; the S-pole pointing upward leads to the water becoming more alkaline and the N-pole pointing upward leads to the water becoming more acidic. This result cannot possibly occur if only magnetic dipoles are present in the water. Only the accessing of magnetic monopoles via an Equation 4 kind of process would lead to this kind of behavior. This strongly suggests than an intention-host conditioned space is functioning at an electromagnetic

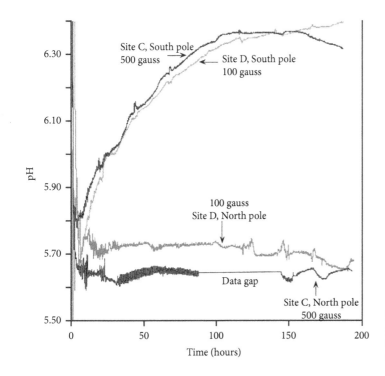

Figure 36.11 pH changes with time for pure water for both N pole up and S pole up axially aligned DC magnetic fields at 100 and 500 gauss.

gauge symmetry level where both electric monopole charges and magnetic monopole charges naturally coexist (the SU(2) EM gauge symmetry state ≡ the coupled state of physical reality).

The second phase of our experimental research began with the performance of a replication study for Experiment 1 because of its simplicity. The study was conducted at 10 sites in the United States and Europe (Tiller, 2007; Tiller et al., 2005).

Three of the intention-host sites, in Arizona, Missouri, and Kansas, had control sites 2 to 20 miles distant. These control sites had exactly the same type of equipment and water but *never* an intention-host device. Excellent experimental replication occurred at all three intention-host device sites with the pH(t) rising exponentially with time in the following fashion:

$$pH(t) = pH_{th} + \Delta pH(1 - e^{-\beta t}) \qquad (5)$$

Here, pH_{th} is the theoretically predicted value for an uncoupled state space at room temperature, ΔpH is the total magnitude of pH change, and is usually quite close to the intended value, while β determines how rapidly the exponential function, e, decays. Both ΔpH and β are site specific. Surprisingly, at the nearby control sites, very similar pH(t)-behavior was observed. This behavior strongly suggested that room temperature, information entanglement was occurring between the intention-host device sites and their control sites 2 to 20 miles away.

To test this hypothesis, we utilized the Baltimore and Bethesda sites as control sites for the Arizona, Missouri, and Kansas intention-host device-sites. We found that within 1 to 2 months the pH(t) was increasing exponentially by ~0.8 pH units. Thus, the room temperature information entanglement was both found to exist and now had been extended to ~1,500 miles (Tiller, 2007; Tiller et al., 2005).

Next, we decided to use the London site, and ~3 months later the Milan site as control sites for the (AZ, MO, and KS) intention-host device sites. Within 3 weeks the ΔpH had increased by ~1 pH unit at the London site and, 3 months later the Milan site went online and within 1 week the ΔpH at that site had increased exponentially to ~1 pH unit. Thus, this information entanglement phenomenon had now been proved to extend *at least 6,000* miles.

The last important result to note regarding the coupled state versus the uncoupled state was discovered by utilizing the services of a world-class kinesiologist (Tiller, Dibble, & Krebs, 2004) to determine whether the human body already has an organ or body system that is at the coupled state of physical reality. The probe utilized was a DC magnet rod of small diameter and tested the strength of various muscle groups under two conditions by bringing the south pole or the north pole of the magnet to within ~1 cm of a particular muscle group. We found that the particular muscle was significantly strengthened for the south pole addressing the group and greatly weakened when the north pole of the magnet addressed the group. This DC magnetic field effect indicates that the human acupuncture meridian system, which is subtly connected to the propriocepters in muscles, is *already* at the *coupled state* of physical reality. Thus, human intentions can significantly influence Qi-flow in the human acupuncture meridians and thus the induced electrical energy flows in the normal tissues and organs of the uncoupled state human body. By sustained and focused, specific intentions, humans can, in principle, develop themselves into adepts, masters, and avatars. Of course, this procedure can be readily utilized for preventive medicine in our society.

Switching gears now, during this replication experiment, we invented a new and novel procedure for quantitatively measuring, for the aqueous H^+-ion, the excess thermodynamic free energy change, $\delta G_H{}^{+*}$, of the coupled state relative to the uncoupled state for an experimental space. Values of $\delta G_H{}^{+*}$ were measured for all 10 sites involved in the replication experiment. Figure 36.12 illustrates experimental data for two intention-host device sites, P_1 and P_7, in the Arizona laboratory and two control sites, the United Kingdom and Italy. The fact that all of the control sites exhibited non-zero values for $\delta G^*_H{}+$ demonstrates very clearly that the control sites are informationally connected to the intention-host device sites even over such huge distances. In energetic terms, the magnitude of the $\delta G^*_H{}+$ -values can be quite large, equivalent thermal energy changes for an uncoupled-state space of ~150 °C to ~500 °C, even though there was no significant change in the measured temperature at these sites (indicative of an entropic change rather than an enthalpic change).

What Is Matter and Where Does It Come From?
Introductory Theoretical Background

As we reflect upon our world and upon the humans that populate its surface, one soon perceives that there are several categories of phenomena and information wherein we need to gain reliable understanding in order to understand our life's journey. These might be classified as (1) things of the

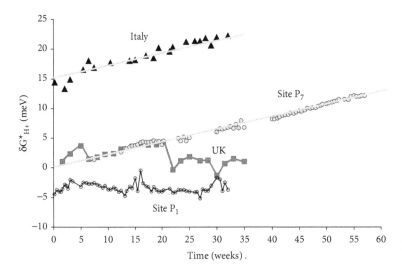

Figure 36.12 $\delta G^{\star}_{H+}$ vs. time at four diverse sites.

physical, (2) things of the psyche, (3) things of emotion, (4) things of the mind, and (5) things of the spirit. In addition, we need a meaningful perspective or RF from which to view these different categories of phenomena and information. Ultimately, our understanding of all these phenomena must be internally self-consistent. Since we are an evolving species, growing in understanding via a bootstrap process, a useful metaphor for what we need is a "ladder of understanding" that guides us from the simple to the more complex—in the sense of various levels of integration of different categories of infrastructure. Thus, Figure 36.13 represents our metaphorical "ladder of understanding" that we must carefully build by our efforts and then climb upon, rung by rung, as we evolve to higher states of being.

The prevailing orthodox science paradigm of our world is (1) quantum mechanics (QM), (2) relativity theory (RT), and (3) the big bang hypothesis. Each of them has serious limitations that need correcting in order to fulfill the goals of this chapter.

Our present form of QM is fine with Equation 2a, where the four fundamental forces are spatially varying and one can use space-time as a suitable RF. However, in Equation 2c and in any psychoenergetic process, information and consciousness are thermodynamic variables that appear to be independent of distance. Thus, both QM and our present RF must be expanded to allow our science to adequately deal with the experimental data described in the previous section.

On this path of necessary change, the experimental data of the previous section reveal the following key insights: (1) two unique levels of physical reality, the electric atom/molecule level and the magnetic information wave level of the physical vacuum appear to exist; (2) two distinct states of interaction, the uncoupled state and the coupled state, for these two unique kinds of substance appear to exist and are both experimentally accessible when an appropriate form of consciousness is brought into play; and (3) when $\alpha_{eff} \sim 0$ in Equation 4, only the uncoupled state is accessible but when an intention-host device is added to the mix, $\alpha_{eff}(t)$ grows in magnitude with time and the coupled state of physical reality becomes instrumentally accessible. All of these factors are keys to the proper design of our new RF. However, there is one more factor that needs to be brought into play.

The two key cornerstones of QM were (1) Max Planck's experimental and theoretical observations that EM radiation emission and absorption by physical matter was in discrete-sized bits (quanta) rather than

Figure 36.13 A metaphorical description of the "ladder of understanding."

continuously variable sized bits and (2) de Broglie's particle/pilot wave concept illustrated in Figure 36.14 where the group wave envelope encloses the particle and guides it via the $v_w > c$ pilot wave components. Harrison (2000) has shown that all the rest of the QM formalism can be generated provided one assumes the simultaneous existence of physical matter as both a particle and wave. One problem for us is that human cognition does not perceive a continuous looking wave like that shown in Figure 36.14. The waves that humans cognitively discriminate are all *modulations of particle densities or modulations of particle fluxes*. It is the bunching of particles to create density variations in space and time that make the waves that we sensorily detect as light, sound, and so on.

Figure 36.14 applies to both matter, the solid seeming kind of stuff we experience around us in our daily lives, and photons, which are particles that have no mass but are the communication vehicles that act between the mass-type of particles. We call these communication vehicles "light." In the electric atom/molecule aspect of our world, there are four uniquely different kinds of forces acting between these mass-type of particles (gravitation, electromagnetism, the weak nuclear force, and the strong nuclear force), each with its own type of communication vehicle. This constitutes the "stuff" of the lowest rung of the "ladder of understanding" depicted in Figure 36.13.

My working hypothesis is that in the metaphors of Figures 36.6 and 36.13, each uniquely different energy band of Figure 36.6 contains a uniquely different kind of substance with new communication vehicles acting between different moieties of

this unique substance, and the ultimately complete package of our scientifically gathered understanding of this "particular stuff" constitutes another single rung on the "ladder of understanding" of Figure 36.13. Now, let us go forward and focus on Figure 36.14 and see how its details illuminate a link between the first two left-side bands of Figure 36.6 and the bottom two rungs of Figure 36.13.

It is important to consider Figure 36.14 and reveal several important consequences that come from applying simple QM and simple RT mathematics to this space-time de Broglie concept (Eisberg, 1961). When this is done, Eisberg (1961) was the first to show that both

$$v_p = v_g \quad \text{and} \quad v_p v_w = c^2 \qquad (6a)$$

Here, v_p = the mass particle velocity, v_g is the wave group velocity, and v_w is the velocity of the pilot wave components that enter and leave the wave group as the group moves along at velocity v_p. Since from RT, one knows that $v_p < c$, always, $v_w > c$, always. Combining the two de Broglie postulates, $\lambda = h/p$ and $\upsilon = E/h$ (where λ = wavelength, p = particle momentum, E = energy and h = Planck's constant) with the total relativistic energy, E, of the particle, one obtains the equation

$$v_w = \upsilon\lambda = \frac{E}{h}\frac{h}{p} = \frac{E}{p} = \frac{\sqrt{c^2 p^2 + (m_0 c^2)^2}}{p}$$
$$= c\sqrt{1 + (m_0 c / p)^2} \qquad (6b)$$

which clearly shows that $v_w > c$. Thus, an actual set of waves, that move faster than the speed of electromagnetic light, c, is *directing* a wave group moving at a speed slower than c, which is, in turn, directing a positive mass particle moving at velocity v_p. Since the de Broglie particle/pilot wave process has been confirmed experimentally, and truth is always in the experimental data, what must be operating in nature to allow such waves to interact across the light barrier at v = c *without* violating relativity theory? These directing waves cannot be seen by today's electromagnetic (EM) instrumentation because they are superluminal and EM signals are subluminal.

This author has chosen to resolve this and other theoretical dilemmas by proposing three postulates:

(1) That there exists in the domain of emotion, a moiety called *deltron* that can be consciousness activated to serve as a coupler substance between the $v_p < c$ electric atom/molecule substances and the

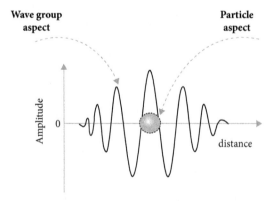

Wave group aspect

Particle aspect

Amplitude

0

distance

Figure 36.14 The de Broglie particle/pilot wave concept of the 1920s, for which he won a Nobel Prize, proposed that every particle had a group wave envelope enclosing it and moving at the particle's velocity. Faster than EM-light, c, unseen pilot waves of the physical vacuum move through the group from left to right at velocity $v_w > c$.

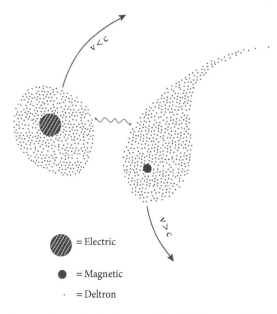

= Electric

= Magnetic

· = Deltron

Figure 36.15 A higher dimensional level of substance, labeled deltrons, falling outside the constraints of relativity theory and able to move at velocities greater than and less than c, acts as a coupling agent between the electric monopole types of substance and the magnetic monopole types of substance to produce both electromagnetic (EM) and magnetoelectric (ME) types of mediator fields exhibiting a special type of "mirror" principle relationship between them.

$v_w > c$ magnetic information wave substances (see Fig. 36.15)

(2) That a duplex RF for viewing physical reality, consisting of two, four-dimensional, reciprocal subspaces, one of which is space-time, is needed to replace our present space-time only RF (see Fig. 36.16)

(3)   That this particular duplex RF is imbedded in a larger reality RF consisting of the higher dimensional domains of emotion (9D to 11D), mind (12D to 14D), and spirit (15D and up) (see Fig. 36.17)

Figure 36.17 provides both a structural representation (a) and an energy band representation (b) of these two nested RFs. Since the duplex physical RF are reciprocals, the conjugate physical is a frequency domain; and, if all the higher domains are also frequency domains, then sympathetic resonance between the higher domain substances and the magnetic information wave substance of the conjugate physical domain can occur so the deltron coupler (α_{eff} in Equation 4) can transfer the information to the electric atom/molecule level of physical reality. Figures 36.15 and 36.16 illustrate how the deltrons could produce interaction between the electric stuff and the magnetic stuff plus between the particle and pilot wave in the two coordinate systems of the duplex RF, respectively.

Figure 36.18 illustrates qualitatively how a particular intention from the domain of spirit can create a correlated information imprint on the domain of mind. This, in turn, both (1) radiates a correlated information map to the magnetic information wave domain and (2) activates more deltrons so that this new information map becomes α_{eff}-coupled to the measuring instruments of our electric atom/molecule world. This, we believe, is how one can account for

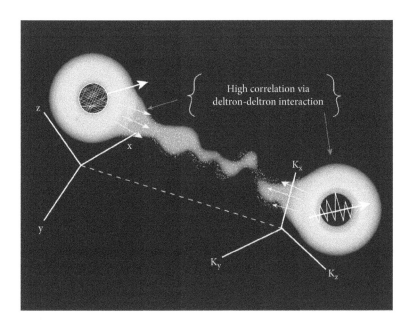

Figure 36.16 Illustration of how deltron-deltron coupling (α_{eff}) allows the two unique levels of physical reality to interact with each other.

(a)
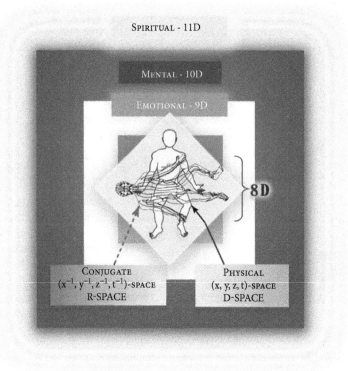

(b)
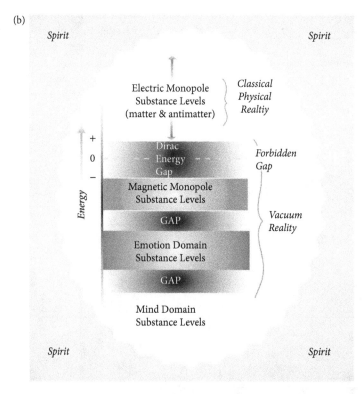

Figure 36.17 (a) A structural representation of our reference frame (RF) with the duplex space in the center. If one counts the duplex space as a unique member of the general 8-dimensional space, then our RF is 11 dimensional. (b) An energy-level diagram embracing both classical physical substances and "unseen" vacuum substances.

the four target experiment results and the long-range information entanglement results of the previous section.

Expanding the Dirac Matter Creation Concept to Replace the Big Bang Hypothesis

Dirac, in 1931, was the first to answer the question "Where do all the elementary electric particles physicists have discovered come from?" (Aitchison & Hey, 1982). At that time, it was well known that the total relativistic energy, E, of a particle is given via the Equation

$$E^2 = c^2p^2 + (m_0c^2)^2 \qquad (7)$$

which seemed to allow both positive and negative energy solutions for E. A schematic model, consistent with Equation 7 and created by Dirac (Aitchison & Hey, 1982), is given in Figure 36.19.

Here, we see a plenum of negative energy states separated from a plenum of positive energy states by a band gap of disallowed energy states with the zero energy origin located in the middle of this band gap. Dirac's key assumption was that the physical vacuum consisted of a plenum of negative energy states; that is, the physical vacuum is not empty but is filled with unknown "stuff."

Despite the fact that physicists generally hate the concept of a negative energy, because they do not know what that could possibly mean (however, energy states bound in a potential well are always

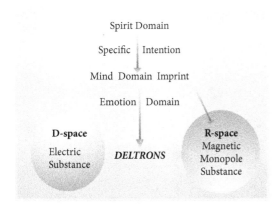

Figure 36.18 Human consciousness, and specifically human intention, can activate this deltron population, and thereby modulate this electric/magnetic monopole substance coupling, so as to alter the specifics of the electromagnetic state of the space wherein an object rests and thus the experimentally measurable properties of that object.

negative relative to the dissociation energy, which can be taken as the zero energy state; thus, I would postulate that all the negative energy states represented in Figure 36.17b have that mathematical sign of energy because they all function within a massive potential well created by the Divine Source of All), Dirac was a truly superior mathematician and pursued his matter creation concept anyway. He proposed that, by stimulating the negative energy plenum via a cosmic ray (an EM photon) of sufficient energy, a particle (electron, say) may be photo-ejected across a band gap into the positive energy states plenum and become physically real; that is, detectable via our present-day instrumentation. The hole left behind in the negative energy plenum was shown to have a positive electric charge and a positive energy and was called the positron. This was the first bit of antimatter to be theoretically discovered and detected experimentally several years later. At this point in time, antimatter particles have been experimentally observed for all the particles known to today's physics.

With respect to the initial Dirac equation for the electron, it gave the initial spectrum for the hydrogen atom at the time and a calculated energy for the electron that was 99.9% of that found experimentally. This error arose because he neglected the electron/photon interaction (which everyone did at that time). Eventually the orthodox physics community rejected Dirac's concept because they couldn't live with the concept of negative energy states even though it led to the discovery of antimatter (see Eisberg, 1961, for an expanded discussion). It is a little strange that no orthodox physicist to date seems to have reflected deeply on the fact that when two electric particles (electron and proton, say) come close together to form a hydrogen atom, they form a potential well wherein the possible bound states all have a negative energy *relative* to the unbound state at large particle separation in space-time. If we hypothesize (speculate) that space-time itself is situated in a larger thermodynamic potential well of a non-space-time force field, then negative energy solutions should not be a problem.

Turning to the orthodox big bang concept, it postulates that, in the beginning, there was nothing, not even space, and for some unknown reason, suddenly there was a gigantic explosion leading to a fireball of tremendous proportions, which, on cooling, led to our observable cosmos. This author prefers an alternate but richer, multidimensional model more along the lines provided by Figure 36.17 wherein a prephysical structure already existed in the physical vacuum. This prephysical structure is proposed to consist of the emotion, mind, and spirit domains of Figure 36.17 acting a womb for the creation of the duplex substances (1) magnetic information wave domain stuff and (2) electric atom/molecule domain stuff via what one might call Divine intention from the hierarchy of the "unseen" intelligences inhabiting these higher dimensional domains. This concept is beyond the scope of this chapter and has been more fully described elsewhere (Tiller, 2007).

An important point of this new hypothesis is that, via the use of Figure 36.17b with radiations passing upward from unseen finer levels of substance to coarser levels of substance, one can provide a possible explanation for the following five physically observable phenomena:

1. Why the matter/antimatter ratio in physical reality is different than unity
2. The origin of dark matter in nature
3. The origin of dark energy in nature
4. Why the outer envelope of our physical universe is accelerating rather than decelerating
5. Why levitation of objects and humans might be possible

Explanations

1. Physicists have experimentally observed that the matter/antimatter ratio for various fundamental particles in nature is greater than unity. However, the Dirac concept for their original creation based on Figure 36.19 is 1:1. Utilizing just the Figure 36.19 picture, it is difficult to provide an explanation for such a result. Taking into account the intrinsic silicon model of Figure 36.17b, there is a remote possibility that limited "hole" reconstruction could produce an additional set of unique configurational states in addition to unreconstructed "hole" states in the vacuum plenum. However, a more realistic possibility comes from consideration wherein activation of some moiety from the lower emotion domain band (and less likely from the mind domain band) to jump upward and fill some of these antimatter sites (hole sites) originally created via the Dirac-proposed process. This would definitely annihilate some but not all of these antimatter sites and produce a matter/antimatter ratio of greater than unity. Such a proposed process would, in principle, allow deltrons to react with information wave substance, converting it perhaps to a magnetic charge-like character that can still interact across the $v = c$ light barrier with electric substance.

2. Both relativity theory and experiment have taught us that spatial energy density variations locally alter the curvature of space and that this gives rise to gravitational forces. With their telescopes, astronomers have for centuries visually observed the effects of standard gravitational forces on the movements of celestial bodies. However, in the past half-century, astronomers have also begun to observe celestial body movements associated with "unseen" attractors. They have observed gravitational-type force effects that cannot be correlated with the presence of an observed celestial body so, to quantitatively account for their observations, they have postulated the presence, first of dark matter and later also of dark energy, with both of these having produced spatial curvature effects without any correlated electromagnetic instrument detection. Ultimately, these experimental observations indicated that the majority of the mass and radiant energy present in our universe was of the dark matter and dark energy type and not of our EM mass and EM energy type. Today's orthodox physics community seems somewhat confused as to the origins of such effects; however, Figure 36.19 alone should "shout out" an obvious candidate.

Traditional gravitational forces involve positive mass–positive mass interactions of the $m_1 m_2 / r$-type plus EM radiation acting as the communication vehicle between positive masses. This is due to the $E > 0$ region ($E^2 > 0$) of substance in Figure 36. 19. This region of substance with $v_p < c$, is instrumentally observable via today's EM technology.

Nontraditional gravitational forces involve negative mass–negative mass interactions of the negative mass x negative mass type plus a different type of radiation acting as the communication vehicle between this negative mass substance that

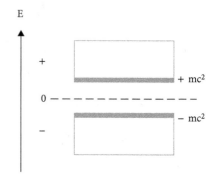

Figure 36.19 Schematic energy spectrum associated with the Dirac equation.

this author has labeled magnetoelectric (ME) energy (moving magnetic charges inducing electric fields in the physical vacuum). This is due to the $E < 0$ region ($E^2 > 0$) of substance in Figure 36.19. This region of substance, with $v_w > c$, is not instrumentally observable with today's EM technology.

3. If one now adds some level of activated deltrons to the cosmic mix of positive mass substance and negative mass substance, the $v_w > c$ substance can interact with the $v_p < c$ substance to produce repulsive gravitational forces rather than just attractive gravitational forces. If one also accepts the small amount of experimental data suggesting that $v_w > c$ substance and energy of the physical vacuum speed up rather than slow down on entering dense matter, whereas the opposite is true for the EM counterpart, then dark matter and dark energy in the cosmos should tend to partition to those regions of space that are densest in EM substance. Thus, such accumulation regions of dark matter and dark energy should not be at the outermost regions of the cosmos but, rather, somewhere well within the outermost envelope. Also, the dark matter mass and energy to normal matter mass and energy ratio is significantly greater than unity so that the gravitational force at the outermost envelope of observable planets and stars will be repulsive rather than attractive. This should lead to acceleration rather than deceleration of the observable planets and stars at the outer envelope of the cosmos. Of course, the population distribution of activated deltrons in the cosmos will change the calculated numerics of the aforementioned concepts.

4. In the human body, just as in inanimate bodies, Figure 36.19 and Figure 36.17b should hold and experimentally human intention has been shown to interact with this $v_w > c$ vacuum information wave substance. Thus, one should expect that sufficiently inner-self-managed humans should, in principle, be capable of intentionally drawing into their body, from the outside environment, a sufficient amount of the $v_w > c$ substance so that the net gravitational force interaction between their body and the Earth shifts from a strongly attractive force to a neutral force and ultimately to a repulsive force. Then, the human will be observed to be levitating relative to the Earth.

One might also speculate that, when these new concepts are ultimately accepted by orthodox physics and understood in a quantitative way, technology will be developed to make the levitation of inanimate objects a practical industry.

Closing Comments

In this chapter I have shown both experimentally, and via a new theoretical model, that human intention and thus human consciousness can (1) significantly alter both the properties of materials and physical reality in a straightforward scientific manner, (2) provide a richer explanation for the formation of our physical universe than the current big bang theory, (3) provide an internally self-consistent explanation for the presence of dark energy and dark matter in our physical universe, (4) provide a viable pathway for the beneficial enhancement of all present-day industries plus create new ones, and (5) provide a model via which humans can consciously expand their spiritual capacities and their capabilities by building new infrastructure (information) into themselves. Thus, it provides a new pathway via which science can expand its capabilities toward the understanding of nature, via which religions can gain greater perspective of their ultimate goal and via which Logos and Mythos can once again be compatible pathways to the acquisition of knowledge.

References

Aitchison, I. J. R., & Hey, A. J. G. (1982). *Gauge theories in particle physics*. Bristol, England: Adam Hilger.

Armstrong, K. (2000). *The battle for God*. New York: Ballantine.

Brillouin, L. (1962). *Science and information theory* (2nd ed.). New York: Academic Press.

Eisberg, R. M. (1961). *Fundamentals of modern physics*. New York: Wiley.

Fechner, G. (1860/1966). *Elements of psychophysics* (Vol. 1, H. Adler, Trans.). New York: Holt, Rinehart & Winston.

Gibbs, J. W. (1957). *The collected works of J. Willard Gibbs* (Vols. 1–2). New Haven, CT: Yale University Press.

Green, E., & Green, A. (1999). Biofeedback and self-regulation. *Subtle Energies and Energy Medicine, 10*, 17–134.

Harrison, W. A. (2000). *Applied quantum mechanics*. Singapore: World Scientific.

Lederman, L., & Teresti, D. (1993). *The God particle*. New York: Dell Publishing.

Mayer, J. E., & Mayer, M. G. (1940). *Statistical mechanics*. New York: Wiley.

Norris, P. (1997). Current conceptual trends in biofeedback and self-regulation. *Subtle Energies and Energy Medicine, 10*, 61.

Norretranders, T. (1999). *The user illusion*. New York: Penguin Books.

Ostrander, S., & Schroeder, L. (1970). *Psychic discoveries behind the Iron Curtain*. Englewood Cliffs, NJ: Prentice Hall.

Rock, I. (1967). *The nature of perceptual adaptation*. New York: Basic Books.

Schultz, J. H., & Luthe, W. (1959). *Autogenic training: A physiological approach in psychotherapy*. New York; Grune & Stratton.

Shannon, C. E. (1948). A mathematical theory of communication. *The Bell Systems Technical Journal, 27*, 379–423, 623–656.

Tiller, W. A. (1990). A gas discharge device for investigating focused human attention. *Journal of Scientific Exploration, 2*, 255.

Tiller, W. A. (1997). *Science and human transformation: Subtle energies, intentionality and consci*ousness. Walnut Creek, CA: Pavior.

Tiller, W. A. (2007). *Psychoenergetic science: A second Copernican-scale revolution*. Walnut Creek, CA: Pavior.

Tiller, W. A., Dibble, W. E., Jr., & Fandel, J. G. (2005). *Some science adventures with real magic*. Walnut Creek, CA: Pavior.

Tiller, W. A., Dibble, W. E., Jr., & Kohane, M. J. (2001). *Conscious acts of creation: The emergence of a new physics*. Walnut Creek, CA: Pavior.

Tiller, W. A., Dibble, W. E., Jr., & Krebs, C. T. (2004). Instrumental response to advanced kinesiology treatments in a conditioned space. *Subtle Energies and Energy Medicine, 13*(2), 91–108.

Werbos, P. (2001). What do neural nets and quantum theory tell us about mind and reality? In K. Yasue, M. Jiba, & T. D. Senta (Eds.), *No matter, never mind* (pp. 81). Philadelphia: John Benjamins.

Appendix: Some Questions and Answers

Q_1. *Need there be a sort of dualism by positing two distinct realms of reality—relying on consciousness as coming from a separate realm into the electric realm to achieve the coupled state?*

Since the substance of one of these levels of physical reality travels at v < c and the substance of the second level of physical reality, needed to form the coupled state, travels at v > c (see Equation 6b) and both are constrained by relativity theory (RT) to not reach the light barrier, v = c, in order to interact with each other, a coupling substance *from beyond the reach of space-time RT* is required (see Fig. 36.15). Thus, there is a need for a type of dualism. This is more fully dealt with via the author's "Whole Person Metaphor" described Tiller (2007), pp. 147–149.

Q_2. *Might it be possible that consciousness constantly exists throughout, and informs the electric realm, but that consciousness itself tends to be scattered, that is, not focused in most cases (for instance, prior to introducing the imprinted machine)? Left willy-nilly, consciousness may exist in many short bursts (not big "t") and points in many directions; therefore, it cancels itself out in its impact on the electrical state. Might consciousness exert influence constantly but not in a focused single direction?*

In my model, consciousness does exist throughout the smallest particle/pilot wave complex (see Fig. 36.14) in physical reality. This requires some amount of coupler substance to be present locally in order to bind these two moieties together and move at $v_p = v_g$ (see Equation 6a). Since the coupled substance also embodies the property of consciousness, then consciousness is essentially present *everywhere* in space-time; however, it is filling an essential role in nature and not easily diverted from that role by applied human consciousness (possible but not very probable).

Q_3. *Two realms versus one continuous realm?*

The substance of these different realms interpenetrate each other in the same general space and thus, it appears to be a continuous realm from one perspective but, without the presence of a sufficient amount of coupler substance, they cannot come into an intimate and lawful relationship. When they do, a material phase transformation has occurred on an incredibly microscopic scale, that of a single atom. Then, not only do electrons orbit a single nucleus but also magnetic monopole/deltron complexes are orbiting that same nucleus in some kind of electromagnetic dance together.

Q_4. *Coupling depends on the notion that consciousness arrives anew into the electric realm. Two distinct realms. Is it possible that E can move fluidly across c such that there is not a "wall" or separate divide between v < c and v > c? Is c more than a marker of speed? Why is c a barrier (pardon me if I do not understand something about c as a barrier)? If c is a barrier, then might you clarify that for a more naïve reader.*

In space-time, c is very definitely a barrier because current relativity theory shows that any particle with positive mass must be given an *infinite* amount of energy to increase its speed to v = c. For particles with negative mass, to decelerate them to v = c, they must be given an infinite amount of negative energy. Thus, the barrier is an energy barrier—not a physical barrier.

Q_5. *Why do we need a deltron to convey information? Might you clarify in a paragraph the need for the concept of the deltron? Why can there not be continuous movement of energy through the "two" different realms—from electric to magnetic and back. If the deltron resolves a question, please might you highlight what is resolved by the deltron.*

Once again, I ask the reader to look at Figure 36.15 and my response to Question 4. Without the proposed deltron coupler, Figure 36.14 could not exist in physical reality and atoms, molecules, and macroscopic substances of any kind could not exist in this world. Thus, life of any form could not exist because bare interactions between electric charge-based particles of positive mass (v < c) cannot directly interact with magnetic charged-base moieties of negative mass (v > c) because of the infinite energy constraint at v = ±c. However, with a coupler substance from a higher dimensional domain having the property of both v < c and v > c, such an interaction can occur *indirectly* as illustrated in Figure 36.15 via coupler–coupler interaction.

Q_6. *Does it take energy to transpose E from the form of thought wave into matter? Is there something about formation into matter, per se, that requires energy?*

First, I would expect a thought wave to be associated with a photon-like entity from the mind domain identified in Figure 36.17b. Each of these discrete bands of energy is associated with a unique category of substance. You might call them finer forms of matter than we know in our electric charge-based matter, indicated in the top energy band of Figure 36.17b. Since we don't yet know anything about the domain of mind, its specific substances, their force/energy interactions and their mediators (photons), we can only speculate (and not well). However, we can use the electric charge-based matter plus its electromagnetic (EM) photons and today's television technology to provide an analogy-type answer.

Here, we take actors (matter) in a studio, bounce EM photons in the form of visible light off of them continuously over time, and gather these scattered EM photons collectively via video cameras. These are then digitized, amplified, and processed by special electronic equipment before being broadcast through the air to remote locations. There, individual receiver sets absorb the EM waves containing the digitized information concerning the events that occurred in the distant studio. Your television set is designed to replicate the scene from that distant studio event and display it for you on your own television screen.

Does it take energy to cause all of this to happen? Yes, of course it does. Can we take EM energy and convert it into electric charged-based matter? Yes, of course we can via a procedure Dirac first taught us about (see Fig. 36.19). Can we go in the other direction; that is, take electric charge-based matter and convert it into EM energy? Yes, of course we can. The atomic bomb is an example of just such a process ($E = mc^2$).

Q_7. *Might you speak to the lived experience on nonlocality of thought wave? Does the nonlocality of thought wave account for the simultaneous awareness of an event (such as the death of someone) in different material locations? Does the nonlocality of thought wave account for the simultaneous awakening of ideas in human history across the globe?*

Once one accepts the reality of Equation 4 and the author's duplex space model (direct space plus reciprocal space), long-range information entanglement such as seen in Figure 36.12 is a natural consequence (Payson to Italy). How this is thought to happen has been described in Tiller (2007), p. 138.

Reciprocal space is a frequency domain, so that when a specific space-time event is deltron-manifested in reciprocal space, the pattern is now everywhere and everywhen so the information is now available to any space-time location. This is how certain individuals can heal other humans across the Earth via a simple telephone linkage.

Q_8. *The E moves from the highest realm of spirit to matter, and back, suggesting to me that all expressions of E and all of creation are sacred. This is a unifying model that I read as referring back to your opening statement about early human's Mythos and relationship with the Earth. If this read is correct, what do you view as the implications of a unified model of E? Might you consider highlighting the point that your model suggests that the same E is everywhere, and contrasts to the belief that the sacred is not in this world of matter/Earth.*

I tend to see this world of matter/Earth primarily as a classroom for human soul development with the soul connected to this classroom via its present-day personality self (see Tiller, 2007, pp. 147–149). Thus, for me, it is all sacred—the sacredness just varies in degree as one moves from the *visible* Earth-type matter to the presently invisible, spirit of the Earth-type substance (a much finer form of matter).

To me, we are all spirits having a physical experience as we "ride the river of physical life" together. Our spiritual parents dressed us in these biobodysuits and put us in this playpen that we call a universe—in order to grow in coherence; in order to develop our gifts of intentionality; and in order to become what we were intended to eventually become. which is co-creators with our spiritual parents.

Q_9. *In your final conclusion, point 5 on enhancing the possibility of the human journey: Might you expand upon the possibility for humanity associated with expanding our consciousness. Do we have access to all knowledge? Is all knowledge in the universe, given the nonlocality demonstrated with the imprinted machines in Arizona, Missouri, and around the globe? What type of information might be accessible to us or benefit humanity? How might we be avatars? What is our possibility told through images or examples?*

We have experimentally shown that the human acupuncture meridian system is already at the coupled state level of physical reality (see Fig. 36.9) so that, in principle, all humans have the possibility, via their disciplined and sustained intentions, to build large amounts of infrastructure into the various unseen levels of themselves. This appears to allow more spirit substance to enter our bodies and attach to this new infrastructure. Since one of my working hypotheses is that "consciousness" is a biproduct of spirit entering dense matter, this would speed us along the path from normal to adept to master and ultimately to avatar.

In addition, it appears that, even at just the five physical senses level, the information handling capabilities of the human unconscious is about a million times that of the electric charge-based human brain. Thus, it is the *human unconscious* that gathers all the information being radiated by both local and nonlocal nature. This information gets catalogued, processed, and edited before small kernels are prepared and sent to the conscious brain so that the conscious brain can experience the dynamics of life. However, it appears that these kernels of information are only of the type that the conscious brain have heretofore given meaning (Norretranders, 1999). It appears that the rest of the information is "dumped." Thus, for one to grow in consciousness, one should give more things meaning in his or her life (Norretranders, 1999).

Q_{10}. *When you mention the potential practical applications of this model, I started thinking about valuative questions. As a leader among scientists, might you comment about the ethical applications of this model? Where does ethics come into our engagement with the realm of information? Is the universe essentially valuative? In other words, are there axioms of consciousness that sustain or laws that suggest certain uses of consciousness? Is the universe sacred? Is there good/life source, and is there evil or destruction in the higher realms?*

Ethical considerations enter at all stages of personal development: (a) To thine own self be true, (b) treat your neighbor as you would treat yourself, (c) never take away the free will of choice by a neighbor, (d) put your ego and talents in service to the larger whole, (e) love and nourish those around you, (f) this Earth domain is a classroom, have compassion but let others grow by their own choices, (g) we are indestructible at the soul level, so it is only the biobodysuit of the personality self that can be destroyed, and so on. The realm of information is linked thermodynamically to the realm of energy, which, in turn is linked to the realm of matter ($E = mc^2$). It is just another kind of stuff to deal with. Purity of intent is the guiding principle for all of one's actions in the space-time classroom.

Ultimately, everything is quantitative and thus valuative, but the very large number of factors that enter the quantitative evaluation is beyond our present evolutionary ability to discriminate. Here, one must trust one's intuition, guided by a balanced heart and brain.

Our universe is a sacred device, a vehicle for us to learn and grow and become. It is for us to become the ultimate sensor of all that is, built into ourselves with no need for any instrumentation to use as training wheels or a crutch. Only then can we graduate to the level of worthy co-creators.

I know that there is good/life source, and I have experienced evil acting in this realm. Being an optimist, I think that it has a purpose: "If you wish to create, if the medium offers you no resistance you can make no durable impression!"

Q_{11}. *You share early in the Chapter that our instruments can probe only certain sides of existence. What might be in reality that we have not explored through science (might you give an example or two)? Do you have a sense or direct experience of qualities of reality that are not considered by a scientific model of dimensions?*

All of the natural phenomena of what we presently call parapsychology have quantitative expressions that lie completely outside of the internal self-consistency requirements of today's orthodox science based upon a distance-time-only RF. Remote viewing is the most extensively studied member of the parapsychology class of phenomena. Governments of the world have, collectively, spent billions of dollars via use of all types of quantum mechanics trying to "see" things at a far distance and have failed completely (Werbos, 2001). Orthodox medicine is still disclaiming very loudly that homeopathy is a fraud because the results are not internally self-consistent with orthodox science and medicine's accepted rules and protocols. Many other examples could be given.

Q_{12}. *Are there real-life examples of our tendency to tap into the realm of information in current normative experience? For instance, through relationship do we align or harmonize? A mother knows moments before her baby wakes and cries. People around the world are picking up 9–11 information prior to the events of September 11, 2001. Is this done through the energetic meridian system that you highlight?*

My answer is yes to the last sentence. In our experimental work just as we daily see information entanglement over small and large distances, weekly to monthly we see information entanglement over time. In many cases, this is days ahead of its actual manifestation in space-time (which Einstein showed us is a four-dimensional construct with time treated as a mathematically imaginary distance coordinate—$x_4 = ict$).

Perhaps the best documentation concerning your question is provided by the ~10,000 recorded and preserved trance readings of Edgar Cayce, the Sleeping Prophet. These are available from the archives of the Association for Research and Enlightenment (A.R.E.) located in Virginia Beach, VA. Hundreds of books have been written about this very spiritual and religious man who lived in the first half of the 1900s. The A.R.E. is still very active today.

Consciousness, Spirituality, and Postmaterialist Science: An Empirical and Experiential Approach

Gary E. Schwartz

Abstract

Consciousness and spirituality are inherently experiential processes. The definition of "spirituality" ranges from (I) personal opinions regarding the meaning of life and being part of something greater, through (2) experiences of transcendental states and oneness, to (3) beliefs regarding the existence of spirit, life after death, reincarnation, angels and guides, and some sort of omnipresent infinite intelligence and power. Academic psychology has typically taken a materialistic view toward consciousness and spirituality; both are interpreted as neurobiological processes shaped by genetics and developmental and cultural factors. However, as reviewed in this chapter, contemporary consciousness research provides emerging proof-of-concept evidence suggesting that (I) mind is separate from brain, (2) spirit and soul are comparable to energy and information that persist in the vacuum of space, (3) people can receive intuitive information that is accurate and useful in their individual and collective lives, and (4) physical and psychological health can be fostered by active loving spiritual processes. The evidence points toward the emergence of a postmaterialist paradigm in psychology and science in general.

Key Words: consciousness, spirituality, materialism, postmaterialism, the mind–brain relationship, the Big Five, parapsychology, survival of consciousness, continuity of consciousness, spirit, soul, information, energy, intuition, energy healing, spiritual healing, angels, guides, infinite intelligence, God

When Kepler found his long-cherished belief did not agree with the
most precise observation, he accepted the uncomfortable fact.
He preferred the hard truth to his dearest illusions;
that is the heart of science.
—Carl Sagan

Do not bite my finger; look where I am pointing.
—Warren McCulloch

Introduction

The broad title of this chapter—"Consciousness, Spirituality, and Postmaterialist Science: An Empirical and Experiential Approach"—was suggested by the editors. It provides a unique opportunity for the author and readers to explore the relationship between empirical research and theory in consciousness and spirituality and to integrate them with real-life experiences.

Consciousness is inherently an experiential process (Tart, 2009); it is only witnessed directly by the person having the experiences. The same applies to spirituality (Walsh, 2000). Whether we define "spirituality" as (1) a set of personal opinions about the meaning of life and/or as being part of something greater, (2) experiences of transcendence and/or feeling a sense of oneness with everything, or (3) beliefs about the actual existence of a greater spiritual reality, including spirits, life after death, reincarnation, angels and guides, and/or some sort of omnipresent and omnipotent intelligence, they all involve conscious processes.

The scope of this chapter, as proposed by the title, invites us to examine contemporary consciousness research as it relates to spirituality and postmaterialist science, from both an empirical and experiential point of view. It turns out that research on the cutting edge of consciousness science points strongly to the possibility that (3) some sort of larger spiritual reality actually exists (Schwartz, 2011; Tart, 2009). In light of this possibility, the emerging proof-of-concept research has profound potential implications for the field of psychology as a whole. It also has significant potential implications and applications to virtually all aspects of human life. This chapter integrates state-of-the-art proof-of-concept research and theory on consciousness and postmaterialist science as it relates to the existence of a greater spiritual reality, with examples of real life applications.

The chapter focuses on "proof-of-concept" research primarily because much of the research is in its early stages. Given the nature of the topic—that is, the possible existence of a greater spiritual reality and its relationship to consciousness—the research is inherently controversial, at least as viewed by conventional psychology, neuroscience, and mainstream science in general. However, the collection of proof-of-concept research findings, when considered as a whole, not only demonstrate the feasibility of conducting large-scale systematic research in this area, but it illustrates the promise of this research for increasing our understanding of human nature (and nature in general) as well as evolving our behavior as a species.

The chapter begins with the fundament "mind-brain" problem—is consciousness a by-product of brain function, or is it separate from the brain? It illustrates how mainstream theory in electronics and electrical engineering, combined with state-of-the-art empirical research addressing the survival of consciousness (SOC) after death hypothesis, point to the serious possibility that *consciousness as a process is ultimately separate from the brain*. Included is a discussion of the challenge of determining whether consciousness has intention, and whether evidence of intention is observed in afterlife research. The

theoretical question of the potential existence of "spirit" and "soul" is examined in light of parallels involving energy and information.

The chapter then examines the possibility that people can intuitively receive information from "spirit" that is potentially accurate as well as useful in real-life situations. Research is reviewed on medical intuition, and examples are provided involving the author and his research staff that illustrate how "spirit-assisted" intuition can be practiced in daily life.

The relationship of spirituality to health is examined next from the theoretical possibility of "spirit-assisted" healing. Exemplary proof-of-concept research and observations are reviewed that illustrate how psychology and medicine are being potentially expanded and advanced in this area.

Finally, the chapter looks to the future and considers some of the profound implications for psychology and society that stem from the possibility that this emerging vision of consciousness and spirituality is valid. The implications range from experimental designs, through alternative interpretations of psychological and neuroscience data, to new postmaterialist applications in technology and education. The concept of "self-science" is explored as an emerging paradigm for integrating contemporary consciousness and spirituality research and fostering "evidence-based spirituality" in daily life.

Materialism and the Mind-Brain Problem

Mainstream psychology, neuroscience, and science in general typically adopt a materialistic view of nature and the universe. Materialism is the belief that (1) what is real is physical matter, that (2) only matter exists, and that (3) everything that happens in nature and the universe can be understood and explained in materialistic terms (Tart, 2009). In psychology this belief is expressed in terms of the relationship of mind and brain; consciousness is assumed to be a by-product or "epiphenomenon" of brain function (e.g., an emergent property of neural networks). Note that a materialistic interpretation of the mind–brain relationship precludes the possibility that a greater spiritual/nonmaterial reality could, in principle, exist.

There is no question that adopting a materialistic perspective helped science historically break away from the constraints and biases (including censorship) of various religious institutions. Moreover, scientific methods based upon materialistic philosophy have been highly successful in not only increasing our understanding of nature and the universe but also in obtaining greater control and freedom through advances in technology. It is understandable how materialism became the cardinal assumption in mainstream science.

Not surprisingly, when the assumption of materialism is questioned today, it typically evokes confusion and criticism, if not consternation, by conventional scientists. The history of materialism is comprehensively reviewed, and seriously challenged, in Tart's (2009) visionary and controversial book *The End of Materialism*. A distinguished researcher at the frontiers of consciousness science, Tart reviews what he calls the "Big Five" areas of "anomalous" consciousness research—often labeled as parapsychology—which together question the foundation of a simple materialistic perspective. The five areas are as follows:

(1) Precognition, the ability to predict the future. The information sometimes comes as a vision, a mental flash, or a dream.

(2) Telepathy, often called mind reading or mind-to-mind communication. It literally means "distant feeling."

(3) Clairvoyance, the ability to perceive remote places, objects, or people. In science it is typically referred to as "remote viewing."

(4) Psychokinesis, the ability to move objects with the power of mind only.

(5) Healing, spiritual practices (often equated with energy) that may afford gradual relief from pain or sickness and may sometimes bring about a sudden "miraculous" healing.

Space precludes reviewing the substantial body of replicated research in each of these five areas that together strongly justify Tart's sweeping conclusion. What is important to recognize here is that a large body of methodologically sound research exists in these five separate areas and serves as a compelling challenge to the conclusion that consciousness can be explained solely as a by-product of brain processes.

A sixth area of research—on the possibility of SOC after physical death (Braude, 2003; Fontana, 2005; Schwartz, 2002, 2005, 2011; van Lommel, 2010)—is emerging that potentially provides "proof" that materialism is in error, and that some sort of a postmaterialist paradigm is called for. The word "proof" is used here intentionally because *if* the findings from this emerging research are valid— the word *if* is important here—then an essential core prediction of the materialistic premise will have been effectively disproved.

The logic is as follows: If the brain is solely responsible for the existence of consciousness, then when the brain dies, consciousness should die. There are no ifs, ands, or buts to the logic; this is an essential, even absolute, prediction of materialism. It follows that if empirical SOC research documented that consciousness continued after physical death, the materialistic interpretation would be resoundingly refuted.

Before we review contemporary SOC research, it is helpful to examine how psychology and neuroscience routinely come to the conclusion that consciousness is created by the brain, followed by the compelling logic that clearly explains how this assumed-to-be-true conclusion is actually (and ultimately fatally) flawed.

Does Consciousness Require a Brain?

There are three types of experimental evidence that together seem to point to the conclusion that consciousness is created by the brain. The word "seem" is emphasized here because careful examination of the totality of evidence, when viewed from the perspective of electronics and electrical engineering, reveals how the evidence is actually *as consistent with the explanation that the mind is separate from the brain as it is with the explanation that the mind is created by the brain.* Unfortunately it is not widely appreciated by mainstream scientists that the three experimental approaches used to investigate mind–brain relationships do *not*, by themselves, require a materialistic conclusion—and they are wholly consistent with a nonmaterialistic (postmaterialist) explanation.

The three kinds of evidence are as follows:

1. *Evidence from recordings*—Neuroscientists record brain waves (via electroencephalograms [EEGs]) using sensitive electronic devices. For example, it is well known that occipital alpha waves decrease when people see visual objects or imagine them.

2. *Evidence from stimulation*—Various areas of the brain can be stimulated using electrodes placed inside the head or magnetic coils placed outside the head. For example, stimulation of the occipital cortex is typically associated with people experiencing visual sensations and images.

3. *Evidence from ablation*—Various areas of the brain can be removed with surgical techniques (or areas can be damaged through injury or disease). For example, when areas of the occipital cortex are damaged, people and lower animals lose aspects of vision.

The generally accepted—and seemingly commonsense—neuroscience interpretation of this set of findings is that visual experience is created by the brain.

However, the critical question is whether this *creation of consciousness* explanation is the *only* possible interpretation of this set of findings. The answer is actually no. The three kinds of evidence are *also consistent with* the brain as being a *receiver of external consciousness information* (Schwartz, 2002, 2005, 2011).

The reasoning is straightforward and is illustrated in electronics and electrical engineering. Though it is rare to discuss an electronics example in the context of a psychology monograph (especially one focused on religion and spirituality), it turns out to be prudent and productive to do so here.

Consider the television (be it analog or digital). It is well known—and generally accepted—that televisions work as *receivers* for processing information carried by *external* electromagnetic fields oscillating in specific frequency bands. Television receivers do *not create* the visual information (i.e., they are *not the source* of the information) —they *detect* the information, *amplify* it, *process* it, and *display* it.

Apparently it is not generally appreciated that electrical engineers conduct the same three kinds of experiments as neuroscientists do. The parallel between the brain and the television is essentially perfect.

1. *Evidence from recordings*—Electrical engineers can monitor signals inside the television set using sensitive electronic devices. For example, electrodes can be placed on particular components in circuits that correlate with the visual images seen on the screen.

2. *Evidence from stimulation*—Electrical engineers can stimulate various components of the television using electrodes placed inside the television set or magnetic coils placed outside the set. For example, particular circuits can be stimulated with specific patterns of information, and replicable patterns can be observed on the TV screen.

3. *Evidence from ablation*—Electrical engineers can remove various components from the television (or areas can be damaged or wear out). For example, key components can be removed and the visual images on the screen will disappear.

However, do these three kinds of evidence imply that the *source* or *origin* of the TV signals is *inside* the television—that is, that the television *created* the signals? The answer is obviously no.

It should be clear how this basic logic—as applied to television receivers—can equally be applied to neural network (brain) receivers. The three kinds of evidence (correlation, stimulation, and ablation) only allow us to conclude that television sets—as well as brains—play some sort of *role* in visual experience. The truth is that the three kinds of evidence, by themselves, do *not* tell us whether either television sets or brains:

(1) "self-create" the information internally— the materialist assumption, or

(2) function as complex receivers of external information—which allows for both survival of consciousness after death and a larger spiritual reality.

In other words, the three kinds of evidence, by themselves, do not speak to (and do not enable us to determine) whether the signals—the information fields—are:

(1) coming from *inside* the system (the materialistic interpretation applied to brains),

or

(2) coming from *outside* the system (the interpretation routinely applied to televisions).

It follows that *additional kinds of experiments* are required to distinguish between the "self-creation" versus "receiver" hypotheses.

Experiments on the SOC hypothesis with skilled research mediums provide an important fourth kind of evidence that can neither be predicted nor explained by the self-creation (i.e., materialism) hypothesis, but it can be predicted and explained by the receiver hypothesis (Schwartz, 2002, 2005, 2011).

It should be noted that in physics, external electromagnetic fields are not labeled as being "material" per se. These fields do *not* have mass (e.g., they do not have weight) and are invisible; they are described by a set of equations that characterize an as-yet-unexplained property of the "vacuum" of space (which may be empty of "mass" but is actually full of energy and information).

Contemporary Experiments on Survival of Consciousness

The SOC hypothesis has been investigated for more than 100 years. Gauld's (1984) book, *Mediumship and Survival: A Century of Investigations*, provides a comprehensive review of this research up to the early 1980s.

Though much of this research was conducted in England, influential research was also conducted in the United States, most notably by William James, the father of experimental psychology. James investigated a number of mediums—individuals who purportedly receive information from deceased individuals—especially Mrs. Piper (see Blum, 2007; Gauld, 1984).

Contemporary research has been conducted in the Laboratory for Advances in Consciousness and Health (formally the Human Energy Systems Laboratory) at the University of Arizona (reviewed in Schwartz, 2002, 2005, 2011).

The early experimental designs were mostly single blinded; the medium was blind to the identity of the sitters (e.g., Schwartz & Russek, 2001; Schwartz, Russek, & Barentsen, 2002; Schwartz, Russek, Nelson, & Barentsen, 2001). Some exploratory experiments designs were double blinded; not only was the medium blind to the identity of the sitters, but the sitters were blind to the identity of their personal readings (Schwartz, 2002). This was accomplished by not allowing the sitter to hear the readings when they occurred. The sitters later received transcripts of their personal readings as well as the readings of others, and they blindly score all the information.

Also, some experiments were double-blinded in that the medium was blind to the identity of the sitters and the experimenter was blind to information regarding the sitter's deceased loved ones (Schwartz, 2002;2005).

The most recent experimental designs were triple blinded; for example, the research assistant who received the transcripts, and interacted with the sitters, was blind to which readings were associated with which sitters (e.g., Beischel & Schwartz, 2007.

All of the experiments (single, double, or tripled blinded) eliminated visual cues. Depending upon the study, the medium and sitter were in the same room, separated by a screen, or the medium and sitters were in separate locations, separated by hundreds or thousands of miles of distance, and the readings were conducted by phone (and even e-mail).

Some experiments eliminated auditory cues. Depending upon the study, the medium may have spent the first 10 minutes attempting to receive whatever information she or he could get about the sitter in the room, but the medium was not allowed to ask questions, and the sitter was not allowed to speak (termed the "sitter silent condition"), or the medium conducted the reading in his or her own home and conveyed the information via the

Internet, and the sitter, located in a different state, did not know when the reading had taken place.

All information—including initials, names, historical facts, physical descriptions, and personal descriptions—were typically scored, item by item, using a 7-point scale, from –3 (a complete miss) to +3 (a complete hit). In some experiments the sitters scored more than a thousand items.

A growing group of research-oriented mediums ($n = 15$) who (1) claimed high success rates in their private practice of mediumship, (2) were interested in the science of mediumship and typically donated their time, and (3) recognized the risks involved (for example, they knew that if they were caught cheating, they would be exposed) have participated in as few as one experiment or as many as eight experiments. A larger group of research-oriented sitters (approximate total $n = 50$) who (1) experienced one or more significant deaths of loved ones, (2) were interested in the SOC hypothesis for personal and/or scientific reasons and typically donated their time, and (3) agreed to spend the many hours necessary to score the transcripts, sometimes under sitter-blinded conditions, have participated in as few as one experiment or as many as four experiments.

Space precludes presenting a detailed review of these experiments here (they are reviewed in Schwartz, 2002, 2005, 2011). Briefly, the average accuracy (counting only +3's as hits, a conservative estimate of accuracy per experiment) has ranged from 40% to 80% for actual readings compared to 10% to 40% for control readings. Sitters have varied widely in how readily mediums obtain information about their deceased loved ones; the range for individual sitters' readings is from 0% (very rare, but observed on a few occasions) to 100% (also rare, but observed on a few occasions).

The totality of the experiments effectively rules out potential conventional psychological explanations of (1) fraud, (2) "cold reading" techniques used by fake mediums (psychic entertainers) to coax information from sitters, (3) visual, auditory, and olfactory cues, (4) sitter rater bias, (5) vague, general information, (6) statistical guessing, and (7) experimenter effects.

The totality of the experiments also essentially rules out one potential anomalous (i.e., paranormal) explanation: the possibility of telepathy (or mind reading) by the medium of the sitter's mind. For example, in numerous experiments research mediums obtained information that the sitter did *not* know, which was subsequently confirmed by relatives or friends living hundreds or thousands of miles from the sitter and the medium. And in triple-blinded experiments, the experimenter (the proxy "sitter") was blind to information about the sitter; hence, the mediums could not have been reading the mind of the proxy sitter (experimenter) to obtain the accurate information they received about the sitter's deceased loved ones.

Schwartz has concluded that when the findings are viewed collectively as a whole, the simplest and most parsimonious explanation of the data (Ockham's razor) —including "dazzle shots" of remarkably specific and unique pieces of information that may be unknown to the sitter—is the SOC hypothesis.

Schwartz et al.'s findings have been independently replicated in Scotland (Roy & Robertson, 2001, 2004) as well as by researchers at the University of Virginia (Kelly & Arcangel, 2011)). At the time this chapter was written, a complex quintuple-blind experiment was being carried out by Dr. Beishel and colleagues at the Windbridge Institute.

Is The Emerging Evidence Proof of Survival of Consciousness?

Though this collection of experiments, taken together, point strongly to some sort of nonconventional mechanism of information reception on the part of the mediums, they do not establish the *source* of the information.

Various authors have written about alternative possible paranormal explanations—sometimes called "super-psi" —that might be imagined to possibly explain these observations (e.g., Braude, 2003). The most speculative is the notion that mediums somehow retrieve information about the deceased that was presumably left, and continues to exist, in the "vacuum" of space—in physics this is termed the "quantum hologram" (also the "zero-point field"). The implication here is that although the information continues to exist, it is "dead information." In other words, the speculation presumes that the information is not "conscious" and therefore does not indicate the presence of a living, conscious mind.

Schwartz (2002, 2005, 2008, 2011) has pointed out that in astrophysics it is assumed that photons of light emitted by distant stars continue to travel in the vacuum of space long after a given star has "died." The foundation of astrophysics is based on the assumption that photons in the vacuum of space do not significantly lose their information. The patterns of star light as witnessed in a dark night sky, or as sensitively recorded with contemporary low-light

CCD cameras, are presumed to reflect the *accurate history* of star light traveling for millions or billions of years.

It is well established that the human body as whole, and each of its individual organs and cells, reflect and emit super-complex patterns of photons that also travel out into space and continue to do so. This fact has been documented by super-sensitive spy satellites in space that can not only see humans on Earth but record other frequencies of photon emission that identify individuals, including infrared and ultraviolet frequencies of light. Like the information from star light, the photonic information reflected and emitted by biological systems is presumed to be nonliving and nonconscious.

Interestingly, the information received by research mediums does *not* appear to be "dead." Mediums do not describe the process of receiving the information as if they are watching a movie or reading a book. *They describe the information retrieval process as being dynamic, interactive, often surprising, and even sometimes confrontational. In other words, the information seems like communication with a living person.*

The information appears as if it is "intentional." Various authors have described instances where the information evidences compelling qualities of intentionality (reviewed in Fontana, 2005; Gauld, 1984); however, no laboratory research to date has examined this observation systematically.

Schwartz and colleagues have begun to examine the apparent intentional nature of SOC communications. Schwartz (2011) has reviewed a set of compelling case examples, some observed in the context of double-blinded laboratory experiments that provide significant proof-of-concept observations, which individually and collectively support the intentionality hypothesis. The combined evidence points to the experiential as well as empirical nature of this work.

Integrating Experiential and Empirical Approaches to Survival of Consciousness

In one example, Schwartz (2005) explains how immediately after Susy Smith, a famous lay scientist and author of 30 books in parapsychology and SOC had died (e.g., Smith, 2000), information was received by mediums that continued for months. Schwartz came to know Ms. Smith well before she died. Though the information received could not be explained by conventional psychological mechanisms (e.g., fraud, rater bias, sensory leakage), the information per se did not rule out possible "super-psi" explanations.

A particular research medium participated in a private personal exploratory investigation with Schwartz (reported in Schwartz, 2011). The medium conducted long-distance readings by e-mail 5 days a week for more than 10 weeks; the medium lived more than 1,000 miles from Tucson. The medium was kept blind to Schwartz's activities, including his travel schedule. The medium was requested to contact Ms. Smith in the mornings on Mondays through Fridays and ask her two questions: (1) what had Ms. Smith witnessed Schwartz doing in the previous 24 hours, and (2) what did she see happening within the next 24 hours that might be memorable or meaningful for Schwartz.

The accuracy of the information received (scored by Schwartz using the procedures described previously) averaged around 80%. Though the information appeared to be communication-like in nature, and though this is a necessary condition for inferring intentionality, it is not by itself sufficient to establish intentionality, and Schwartz was well aware of this fact.

Then, something completely unexpected happened that proved to be scientifically propitious as well as productive. Schwartz was on the East Coast, meeting with a woman whose younger sister, a surgeon, had recently died of brain cancer. The older sister asked Schwartz to meet with her parents who were Holocaust survivors and were grieving the death of their younger daughter.

In the car on the way to the parents' home on a Saturday morning, the sister shared how she wished she could have had a compelling reading with a gifted psychic who could convince her that her younger sister was okay and still with them. Schwartz recounted how in the car he thought about how fortunate he had been for having received over 50 evidential (i.e., accurate) readings with a medium via e-mail, and he secretly wished this family could have had a similar experience with a medium.

The next morning, Schwartz received an unexpected and surprising e-mail from the medium. She apologized for e-mailing him on a Sunday, but she explained that something strange had happened. She had been driving on Saturday morning when purportedly Ms. Smith showed up unannounced in the car, accompanied by an unknown deceased woman, and Susy insisted that the medium do a reading on the mystery woman ASAP. The medium claimed that she pulled over to the side of the road and, as allegedly requested, did a reading with the unknown woman. The medium carefully wrote down the information; Ms. Smith then supposedly instructed her to e-mail the information to Schwartz, who presumably would know what to do with the information.

Schwartz wondered whether the unknown woman allegedly read by the medium could be the deceased sister. Mustering his courage, he called the older sister. He explained the strange circumstances of the unexpected and surprising e-mail reading and asked her whether she would be willing to score the information. Schwartz read her the information, item by item, over the phone. The scoring took about an hour. The sister's scoring of the accuracy of the e-mail reading was greater than 80%. Both the sister and Schwartz were moved by the spontaneity, timing, and accuracy of this apparent "spirit-initiated" reading.

What actually convinced Schwartz that this might be a genuine reading was a highly specific and novel piece of information regarding eagles. The medium claimed that the deceased sister wanted her family to know that she loved eagles, and that eagles were important to her life. Sobbing on the phone, the older sister explained the following: (1) her deceased sister had indeed loved eagles; (2) she collected statues of eagles, (3) that instead of her ashes being present at the memorial service, one of her deceased sister's favorite eagle statues was displayed, and (4) the song "Fly Like an Eagle" was selected to be played at the service. To prove this to Schwartz, the older sister later mailed him a VHS video tape of the service verifying these facts.

At this point Schwartz had witnessed hundreds of research readings, and he knew that at no time had a medium ever spontaneously brought up information about an eagle. Moreover, he realized that what he had just witnessed was extraordinary—*the possibility that one deceased person could intentionally bring a second deceased person to a medium.* Moreover, in this instance not only was the medium blind to the identity of the second "mystery" deceased person, but the medium was blind to the possibility that this could happen in the first place. A very unusual and compelling set of circumstances

This unexpected observation inspired the creation of what Schwartz called the "double-deceased" research paradigm. He further realized that double-blinded experiments could be designed using this "spirit-mediated" double-deceased research paradigm. As described in Schwartz (2011), collaborating with a second scientist on the East Coast, they conducted a dual-location, double-blinded, double-deceased proof-of-concept personal exploratory experiment, and obtained promising positive results.

Space precludes discussing additional proof-of-concept observations (1) where the deceased appear to have "minds of their own," as well as (2) various ways in which the spirit intentionality hypothesis can be operationalized and put to experimental test (see Schwartz, 2011). What is important to recognize here is that not only can such research be designed and conducted, but that intentional-like spirit behavior can be observed and appreciated in real-life situations (as well as in the laboratory). In fact, Schwartz illustrates how innovative proof-of-concept experimental paradigms are being suggested by sophisticated deceased individuals who seemingly are participating in current SOC research.

On the Scientific Meanings of the Words "Spirit" and "Soul"

When the author was a graduate student at Harvard University in the late 1960s, words like "consciousness," "thoughts," "feelings," and "mind" were generally considered to be taboo. This was the era of the emerging shift from behaviorism to cognitive psychology. The "C" words ("cognition" and "consciousness") were perceived as being controversial (if not illusory) and often denigrated if not dismissed.

However, by the late 1990s, the zeitgeist had radically changed. Cognitive psychology, cognitive neuroscience, and cognitive-behavioral therapy were well established in universities worldwide. Moreover, a growing set of universities, such as The University of Arizona, were creating Centers for Consciousness Studies; and the topic of consciousness was on the road to becoming mainstream.

Meanwhile, during the same time period "S" words like "spirit" and "soul" were generally considered to be taboo. Even in 2011 (the year this chapter was written), despite increasing research on the psychology of religion and spirituality, words like "spirit" and "soul" are generally frowned upon (and words such as "angels" and "guides" typically evoke even stronger negative reactions).

If (1) materialism is an incomplete description of nature and the universe, and if (2) "nonphysical" concepts like energy (including fields) and information are necessary for a more complete and accurate portrayal of nature and the universe, then (3) it is useful to consider how the spiritual terms "spirit" and "soul" may relate to the scientific concepts of "energy" and "information."

Schwartz (1997) proposed that the concepts of spirit and soul have a curious and potentially fundamental parallel with the concepts of energy and information. In physics, energy refers to the capacity to do work and overcome resistance. Energy reflects power, force, vibration, vitality. Interestingly the term "spirit" is often associated with life, vitality, passion, strength, conviction. Note that by definition, the existence of energy is *inferred* from its effects on matter (for example, the force of gravity is *inferred* from the observation that objects fall to the earth, or that planets are observed to revolve around stars); the existence of spirit is also *inferred* by its effects. Take together, the terms "spirit" and "energy" both share an implicit (i.e., inferred) sense of the capacity to act and have effects on things.

In physics, information refers to patterns, form, nonrandom sequences, structure, and complexity. Interestingly, the word "soul" is often associated with person, identity, the essence that describes something about the person, and memory.

Stimulated by the apparent parallels of (1) spirit with energy, and (2) soul with information, Schwartz (1997) wrote a science-based spiritual poem, which expresses these parallels. The first few stanzas of this science-based spiritual poem introduce the core parallels; the stanzas are included at the end of this chapter to honor the experiential side of consciousness and spirituality.

Though drawing an energy and information distinction between spirit and soul is useful heuristically and potentially theoretically, scientists and laymen alike typically use the spirit and soul synonymously. In keeping with the overarching theme of consciousness and spirituality in this chapter, the term "spirit" is being used broadly here to refer to (1) potentially living minds of deceased beings, as well as (2) purportedly higher level beings (e.g., hypothesized angels, guides, and the Source).

The author understands that some readers may experience the words "spirit" and "soul" negatively, a response not unlike his reaction to raw oysters. Briefly, the author never developed a taste for raw oysters. Quite the contrary, to him oysters appear slimy and gooey, and they make him gag. However, just as the author finds it significantly easier to write about oysters than to actually eat them, he is inviting the reader to merely think about the concepts of spirit and soul—and not necessarily swallow them.

If Spirits Exist, Can They Play a Practical Role in Daily Life?

Let us imagine for the moment that future controlled laboratory research on SOC continues to generate positive evidence consistent with the continuity of consciousness hypothesis. Furthermore, let us imagine that future innovative experimental designs will document the presence of intentionality (including properties of thinking, information processing, memory, decision making, choice, having preferences, the capacity to withhold information, and even giving false information). Finally, let us imagine that the future research justifies the conclusion that consciousness is in some sense similar to the light from distant stars in that the organized energy and information continues to exist long after the brain has died—not only consisting of accurate information but of conscious intentionality as well.

If Spirit exists, and if the claims of well-researched and genuine (not fraudulent) mediums are to be considered, then it will be prudent for scientists to keep an open mind about the possibility that numerous so-called paranormal capabilities—including Tart's (2009) Big Five—may be mediated by spirit assistance to various degrees. This could be called the "spirit partnership" hypothesis (it is sometimes also called the sacred partnership hypothesis; Schwartz, 2011).

One example of purported spirit assistance is the controversial area of medical intuition. Medical intuition is a form of clairvoyance (third on Tart's list) as applied to medical diagnosis. There is a long history of claims of medical intuition, including the beliefs and practices of ancient Greek physicians, shamans throughout the world, healers in India, and Edgar Cayce in America. In more recent times exploratory research has been conducted on medical intuitives, including practitioners of therapeutic touch, Silva Mind Control, and Mind Dynamics in Sweden. However, no double-blinded studies had been conducted to evaluate the purported accuracy of diagnosing illnesses using medical intuition.

To address this gap, Attig and Schwartz (2006) conducted a double-blind experiment using seven practicing medical intuitives. The study involved 20 pairs of congestive heart failure patients (10 males and 10 females) and their respective spouses; the spouses (who did not have congestive heart failure) served as matched controls. As a result of counterbalancing for the sex of the patients, the average age of the patient and control groups was comparable.

A cardiologist collected medical data on the patients with congestive heart failure as well as on their spouses. As anticipated, given the consequences of congestive heart failure, on the average the patients (males and females) were found to have a significantly greater number of other medical conditions (in addition to congestive heart failure) than their respective spouses (females and males).

The medical intuitives (who lived in various states across the country) were asked to provide medical diagnoses for all subjects; hence, the medical diagnoses were made from a distance. The intuitives were given only the subjects' names, dates of birth, gender, and the city and state in which they lived. They were kept blind to the patient selection criteria (i.e., they were not informed that the patients had been selected for congestive heart failure). Complete data were available on 19 pairs for scoring. Undergraduate students were trained to count the number of diagnoses given to each subject by each intuitive. Two cardiologists rated the likelihood of a diagnosis being congestive heart failure for each diagnosis given by the intuitives. Both groups of raters were blind to which subjects were patients versus controls.

The results for the undergraduate raters revealed that on average the intuitives gave significantly more medical diagnoses to the subjects who were originally diagnosed by the cardiologist as having congestive heart failure (the patients) than to the subjects who did not have congestive heart failure (the controls). Moreover, the cardiologists rated the patients as significantly more likely to have the diagnosis of congestive heart failure—based on the symptoms reported by the medical intuitives—compared to the controls.

This proof-of-concept experiment documented that for this relatively small sample ($n = 7$) of skilled medical intuitives, clairvoyant/remote-viewing diagnoses could be made in patients versus controls that were significantly greater than chance. Though the experiment validated the primary claims of the medical intuitives that they could make statistically accurate diagnoses, the study does not address the secondary claims made by a majority of the medical intuitives that they were able to achieve this degree of accuracy because of the active assistance of their "spirit guides."

Medical intuitives typically believe in spirit assistance, and many claim that the spirits provide most if not all of the information. Of the seven intuitives, the one participant who had the greatest accuracy (a high school–educated grandmother) claimed that she received much of her information directly from the deceased Edgar Cayce (whom she affectionately referred to as "Eddie") as well as other alleged spirits and angels.

Their life histories are revealing and potentially meaningful. One intuitive explained that early in her medical intuitive training, she was diagnosed with breast cancer. She went to numerous oncologists who confirmed the diagnosis and recommended a double mastectomy. However, her "guides" insisted that she did not have cancer. She ultimately decided to ignore her guides' persistent advice and chose to undergo the surgery. To her shock and dismay, subsequent laboratory examination of her tissues revealed that her intuitions (allegedly from her guides) were correct; she did not have cancer. Her surgery had indeed been unnecessary. The critical question arises, Was this merely a chance occurrence, a lucky guess, or did it involve spirit assistance as claimed by the intuitive? It is not possible to reach a conclusion based on a single case.

The author has witnessed a number of highly visible medical intuitives practice their art; one of the most visible is Mary Occhino on her popular daily Sirius XM radio show. Ms. Occhino provided medical diagnoses as well as medical predictions that are often uncannily accurate and later verified to be true. Moreover, listeners regularly called into Ms. Occhino's radio show recounting instances where their alleged spirit guides have helped them in everyday situations ranging from selecting the right book to read, to avoiding a life-threatening car accident. Ms. Occhino claims that the reason that she is personally able to be so accurate is because of the skilled and dependable assistance of her spirit guides; her show is aptly called "Angels on Call."

Understandably, mainstream academic psychology has been reluctant to examine such controversial claims closely and put them to experimental test. Speaking metaphorically, the actual process of designing and conducting such research would be for many psychologists like eating oysters would be for the author.

However, *if* (1) medical intuition is a genuine phenomenon (the key word here is "if"), and *if* (2) their explanation for the mechanism of how it works involves an active partnership with spirits (again, "if"), then (3) the implications for the science of consciousness and spirituality, psychology, and science in general, is sufficiently substantial as to warrant serious consideration. We will return to this challenging issue at the end of the chapter.

Potential Applications of Consciousness and Spirit to Healing

One of the most controversial of all claims in religion and spirituality involves reports of spiritual healing and associated "miracles." Throughout recorded history, certain individuals—including shamans and medicine men and women, the most notable healer being Jesus of Nazareth—purportedly

had extraordinary healing powers that they attributed to their ancestors, angels, or the Great Spirit/God/the Sacred (etc.).

In contemporary complementary and alternative medicine, spiritual healing is typically considered in the context of "energy" healing, a less controversial and more physical/materialistic phrasing (and reframing) of the phenomenon. A growing body of research in complementary and alternative medicine, including double-blinded experiments, documents that energy/spiritual healing sometimes has measurable basic as well as clinical effects (reviewed in Schwartz, 2008; Tart, 2009).

Mainstream psychologists and physicians generally assume (incorrectly so) that if significant healing effects are actually observed, that they must be due to expectancy and belief (i.e., placebo effects). There is a large body of research in psychophysiology and mind-body medicine documenting how the mind of the patient can affect his or her physiology and healing (Schlitz, Amorok, & Micozzi, 2004). However, the totality of the research that specifically addresses energy and spiritual healing indicates that expectancy and belief effects, though important, *cannot fully account for the effects observed*.

For example, Baldwin and Schwartz (2006) conducted a controlled animal experiment investigating the effects of a Japanese spiritual energy healing technique (Reiki) on microvascular inflammation and leakage in the capillary beds of the guts of noise-stressed rats. Noise stress has been shown to produce significant increases in (1) the number of leaks and (2) the size (areas) of leaks, measured microscopically in the rat's capillary beds. In these studies the microscopic analyses of the tissues samples were conducted blindly by the technicians (i.e., the samples were not identified in terms of experimental conditions).

The Baldwin and Schwartz (2006) study included four groups of animals:

1. No noise controls
2. Noise alone
3. Noise plus Reiki
4. Noise plus Sham Reiki

The duration of the experiment was 21 days per group. For the Noise plus Reiki group, skilled Reiki practitioners visited the laboratory each day and performed Reiki healing. They did not touch the animals or the cages; the healings were done silently.

For the Noise plus Sham Reiki group, research assistants who had no background in healing and no intention to heal were taught to mimic the hand movements of the Reiki practitioners.

Both groups were videotaped; it was not possible by watching the recordings to discern who the true versus sham practitioners were. Using this experimental design, the question of possible belief and expectancy effects (on the part of the rats) was not relevant and therefore could be ruled out.

Though compared to noise alone, the presence of the sham practitioners was associated with a small decrease in both the number and size of the stress-induced leaks; the decreases were not statistically significant. However, the presence of genuine Reiki treatments was associated with substantial and statistically significant decreases in both the number and size of the stress-induced leaks. The findings comparing true versus sham practitioners were replicated three times.

Again, similar to Attig and Schwartz's (2006) experiment on medical intuition discussed previously, the Baldwin and Schwart (2006) experiment only demonstrates the presence of an effect; it does not address the potential mechanism (s) of the effects. Though the experimental design rules out conventional explanations of the findings (most notably placebo effects), the design does not make it possible to determine whether any portion of the observed effect can be attributed to spirit assistance per se (as apposed to the consciousness and energy of the practitioner per se).

Nonetheless, the practitioners insist that they are being assisted by ancestors, spirit guides, and the "Source" (they use many different terms, from Universal Intelligent Energy to Divine Mind and God). The question becomes, Can their spirit-assistance claim be addressed experimentally?

The answer in principle is yes. For example, Schwartz (2011) described a proof-of-concept experiment that tested the claims of a spiritual energy healer that a deceased physician was present in his healing sessions and provided assistance. The healer claimed that when the spirit physician entered the healing, his hands became warm. The healer further claimed that sometimes the deceased physician showed up earlier in the session, and other times late in the session. This precise claim was tested experimentally.

With the aid of a skilled research medium, Schwartz requested that the medium contact the deceased physician, and together they would decide whether the spirit physician would show up (1) early or (2) late for a given healing session. The healer, who was kept blind to this decision, would then conduct an energy healing session and record whether his hands warmed up (1) early or (2) late in the session. Schwartz was also kept blind to the alleged decisions. After ten sessions—five purportedly when the deceased physician would enter early, and five when he would enter late—the data were unblinded and analyzed. The results revealed that the match between the medium's alleged decisions with the deceased physician regarding early versus late, and the hand warming times recorded by the healer concerning early versus late, was 100%.

Presuming that (1) fraud was not involved in this experiment, and that (2) this was not a spurious or chance finding, explanations other than spirit assistance can still be imagined. For example, one could speculate whether it possible that the healer somehow read the mind of the medium (who was located over a thousand miles from the healer). In principle, the answer could be yes; however, future research could be conducted to test directly whether the healer could actually read the mind of the distant healer.

Note that even if the spirit-*presence* hypothesis were ultimately established, the question would still remain: Did the presence of the spirit actually play a *healing role* in the recovery of the patient? Again, this is a question that can be addressed in future research. What is important to recognize here, at this early proof-of-concept stage of research, is that challenging questions such as these can be raised and carefully addressed in future research.

Proof-of-concept observations can sometimes be made in the laboratory of one's personal life. Schwartz (2011) recounted a personal experience where he was suffering from a severe flu, and on three separate occasions he was unknowingly given distant healing by a person who practiced a divine-focused spiritual healing tradition. He was not told when the healings would be provided; in fact, he did not even request that healings be offered (and he was not aware that they were being provided). There were three significant moments in his recovery: (1) when his fever broke after 5 days, (2) when his persistent coughing broke a few days later, and (3) when his severe coughing reappeared, and then broke. To his surprise, each significant moment in his healing happened to have been preceded, within an hour, by an essentially secret distant spiritual healing session. One such pairing (a secret healing preceding symptom relief) could have been a coincidence; two such pairings might have been a coincidence as well. However, the replicated occurrence of three separate and precise pairings suggests that more than coincidence was taking place.

It is one thing to read about an experiment in a publication (or even to conduct such an experiment); it is another thing to experience the phenomenon in real life. The fact that Schwartz happened to be thoroughly blind to the occurrences and timings of the healings speaks to the possibility that a genuine spiritual healing effect was occurring. This personal scientific account demonstrates how blinded spiritual healing experiments (with appropriate human subjects consenting) can be carried out in the future.

Conclusion

There are special moments in the history of science when major conceptual breakthroughs occur. They are sometimes called paradigm shifts or changes (Kuhn, 1996). Classic examples of paradigm changes include the shift in thinking that (1) the Earth was *flat*, to the Earth being *spherical*, that (2) the Sun revolved around the Earth, to the Earth revolving around the Sun, that (3) matter was *solid and fixed* (how we conventionally experience it), to matter being mostly "*empty space*" and *dynamically probabilistic* (quantum physics), and (4) the vacuum being "*empty*," to space being *filled with invisible energy and information* (the zero-point field).

Major advances linking quantum physics (and other more innovative and visionary physics) with consciousness and spirituality is capturing the imagination of contemporary researchers (Goswami, 2001; Radin, 2006), and some of the core underpinnings of the materialistic worldview are being seriously challenged if not disproved. Visionary scientists (as exemplified in this Handbook) are beginning to explore what science might look like from a postmaterialist perspective.

As Schwartz (2011) illustrates, new advances in technology (including the recording of patterns of cosmic rays as well as individual photons of light) are making it possible to address the presence and effects of a greater spiritual reality. A recent paper documents how a super-sensitive silicon photomultiplier system can be used to monitor the presence of spirit and potentially serve as a communication device (Schwartz, 2010). Though the idea of technology advancing to the point of creating a reliable spirit-communication device—what Schwartz playfully calls the "soul phone" —might sound like science fiction, the history of science reminds us of countless instances where what was once viewed as science fiction became science fact.

If there is a greater spiritual reality, and *if* consciousness is the key to it, then psychology will need to revise and expand its vision of (1) what is mind, (2) how does mind operate, and (3) what are its limitations and potentials. Just as the television set is required to receive and convert the external electromagnetic field signals into viewable information and energy that can be processed by human beings, the brain as a receiver may be needed in a parallel fashion.

Interestingly, the hypothesis that the brain might serve as a receiver (as well as a transmitter) of information and energy for consciousness has an illustrious history. The brain-receiver hypothesis was seriously entertained by William James, the founding father of American psychology; Wilder Penfield, a distinguished Canadian neurosurgeon who mapped consciousness and the brain; and Sir John Eccles, a British neurophysiologist who won the Nobel Prize in Medicine for discoveries involving the neuron. These luminaries may have had the correct thesis (van Lommel, 2010).

Future Directions

If the mind is not limited to the brain per se, but it extends into space and can operate independently of the brain (Kelly et al., 2009; Schwartz, 2011; van Lommel, 2010; Beauregard, 2012), then the nature of the scientific method needs be carefully reexamined. It is possible that the beliefs and expectations of the experimenter may sometimes directly influence what they discover, regardless of their specialty (Radin, 2006). Researchers may be "participant-observers" in what they are investigating, even at a fundamental quantum level (termed the Heisenberg uncertainty principle). Additional experimental control conditions will need to be designed and employed. For example, in postmaterialist science even physics and chemistry experiments may need to manipulate (or at least monitor) the beliefs and expectations of technicians.

Moreover, if minds other than those of the experimenters can directly influence the physical world— that is, the spirit-assistance hypothesis—then we may need to take spirit-assisted mechanisms into account to better explain and predict certain laboratory findings. Many seemingly anomalous phenomena in physics, chemistry, biology, and psychology may be predictable and explainable by taking into account hypothesized spirit-assisted processes.

Also, improving healing and health may require that processes involving spirit and soul be addressed and included as part of diagnosis, treatment, and prevention. This not only includes the possibility of spirit-assisted healing, but the idea that healing may require a broad collaboration between the physical and the spiritual, including so-called past-life information. The emerging frontier research in consciousness and spirituality should serve to encourage scientists to *resist the inclination to simply dismiss or denigrate such ideas* (what Tart calls "scientism"); instead, a more "agnostic" and cautiously open-minded approach is indicated if psychology, and science in general, are to advance with responsibility and integrity. This chapter was written following the framework suggested by Warren McCulloch: "Do not bite my finger; look where I am pointing." The strong version of this open-minded philosophy is expressed in Carl Sagan's quote that introduces the chapter: "This is the heart of science."

Unfortunately, the politics of science promises to make progress difficult. Conventional funding agencies, as well as mainstream scientific journals, are strongly materialistic. They are typically threatened by the serious possibility that their core assumptions will need to be expanded and revised. University politics for promotion and tenure require acceptance by the mainstream.

Meanwhile, the public is increasingly becoming interested in matters of consciousness and spirit. This is evidenced by numerous successful televisions—documentaries, reality shows, and fictional series—spanning parapsychology, mediumship, "ghost hunting," angels, and spiritual healing. Support from the private sector appears to be necessary to foster and promote future research in this area.

In closing, it should be remembered that certain discoveries in consciousness and spirituality, by their very nature, can only be made by individuals directly experiencing them. Adding the scientific method to daily life becomes a prudent and effective practice (Walsh, 2000). When the scientific method is integrated with everyday activities, life becomes a living laboratory of personal exploration and evolution.

Schwartz (2011) illustrates how "self-science" can fruitfully be employed in discovering a wide variety of spiritual phenomena, including developing one's intuitions and charting complex patterns of events (called synchronicities). Self-science can foster the development of evidence-based spirituality as a practical consequence of a postmaterialist paradigm. Let us close with the first four stanzas of Schwartz's (1997) poem "Soul as Information, Spirit as Energy":

What, pray tell, are Spirit and Soul?
Are they one and the same?
Are Soul and Spirit a functional Whole?

Derived from a common Name?
Or is it the case that Soul and Spirit
Reflect two sides of a coin:
Where Soul reflects the Information that fits?
And Spirit, the Energy that joins?
Is Soul the story, the Plan of Life?
The music we play, our score?
Is Spirit the passion, the Fire of Life?
Our motive to learn, to soar?
Soul directs the paths we take,
The guidance that structures our flow.
Spirit feels very alive, awake,
The force that moves us to grow.

References

Attig, S., & Schwartz, G. E. (2006). *Remote diagnosis of medical conditions: A double-blind experiment of medical intuition.* Paper presented at Toward a Science of Consciousness. Tucson, AZ.

Baldwin, A. L., & Schwartz, G. E. (2006). Personal interaction with a Reiki practitioner decreases noise-induced microvascular damage in an animal model. *Journal of Alternative and Complementary Medicine, 12*(1), 15–22.

Beischel, J., & Schwartz, G. E. (2007). Anomalous information reception by research mediums demonstrated using a novel triple blind design. *EXPLORE: The Journal of Science and Healing.* 3(1), 23–27.

Beauregard, M. (2012). *Brain Wars.* New York City, NY: HarperOne.

Blum, D. (2007). *Ghost hunters.* New York: Penguin.

Braude, S. E. (2003). *Immortal remains: The evidence for life after death.* Lanham, MD: Rowman & Littlefield.

Fontana, D. (2005). *Is there an afterlife?* Oakland, CA: O Books.

Gauld, A. (1984). *Mediumship and survival.* Chicago: Academy Chicago Publishers.

Goswami, A. (2001). *Physics of the soul.* Newburyport, MA: Hampton Roads.

Kelly, E. F., Kelly, E. W., Crabtree, A., Gauld, A., Grosso, M., & Greyson, B. (2009). *Irreducible minds.* Lanham, MD: Rowman & Littlefield.

Kelly, E.W., & Arcangel, D. (2011). An investigation of mediums who claim to give information about deceased persons. *Journal of Nervous and Mental Disease, 199*, 11–17.

Kuhn, T. S. (1996). *The structure of scientific revolutions.* Chicago: University of Chicago Press.

Radin, D. (2006). *Entangled minds.* New York: Paraview Pocket Books/Simon & Schuster.

Roy, A. E., & Robertson, T. J. (2001). A double-blind procedure for assessing the relevance of a medium's statements to a recipient. *Journal of the Society for Psychical Research, 65*(3), 161–174.

Roy, A. E., & Robertson, T. J. (2004). Results of the application of the Robertson- Roy protocol to a series of experiments with mediums and participants. *Journal of the Society for Psychical Research, 68*(1), 18–34.

Schlitz, M., Amorok, T., & Micozzi, M. (2004). *Consciousness and healing.* Oakland, CA: New Harbinger.

Schwartz, G. E. (1997). Energy and information: The soul and spirit of mind-body medicine. *Advances: The Journal of Mind-Body Health, 13*(1), 75–77.

Schwartz, G. E. (2002). *The afterlife experiments.* New York: Atria Books/Simon & Schuster.

Schwartz, G. E. (2005). *The truth about medium*. Charlottesville, VA: Hampton Roads.

Schwartz, G. E. (2008). *The energy healing experiments*. New York, NY: Atria/Simon & Schuster.

Schwartz, G. E. (2010). Possible application of silicon photo-multiplier technology to detect the presence of spirit and intention: Three proof-of-concept experiments. *EXPLORE: The Journal of Science and Healing* 7(2), 100–109.

Schwartz, G. E. (2011). *The sacred promise*. Hillsboro, OR: Beyond Words/Atria/Simon & Schuster.

Schwartz, G. E. R., & Russek, L. G. S. (2001). Evidence of anomalous information retrieval between two mediums: telepathy, network memory resonance, and continuance of consciousness. *Journal of the Society for Psychical Research, 65*(4), 257–275.

Schwartz, G. E. R., Russek, L. G. S., & Barentsen, C. (2002). Accuracy and replicability of anomalous information retrieval: replication and extension. *Journal of the Society for Psychical Research, 66*(3), 144–156.

Schwartz, G. E. R., Russek, L. G. S., Nelson, L. A., & Barentsen, C. (2001). Accuracy and replicability of anomalous after-death communication across highly skilled mediums. *Journal of the Society for Psychical Research, 65*(1), 1–25.

Smith, S. (2000). *The afterlife codes*. Charlottesville, VA: Hampton Roads.

Tart, C. T. (2009). *The end of materialism*. Oakland, CA: New Harbinger.

Van Lommel, P. (2010). *Consciousness beyond life*. San Francisco, CA: Harper One.

Walsh, R. N. (2000). *Essential spirituality*. San Francisco: Wiley.

A Postmaterialist Human Science and Its Implications for Spiritual Activism

Amit Goswami

Abstract

Various models of postmaterialist science are introduced with a brief exposition of the quantum physics and primacy-of-consciousness-based model that integrates all the various approaches.

Key Words: quantum physics, primacy of consciousness

Introduction

Materialist science is science based on the meta-physics of scientific materialism—everything is made of matter and material interactions. As such, it is an exclusive science; scientific materialism is a dogma that excludes an important part of the human experience—spirituality—except as a causally inef-ficacious epiphenomenon of matter. If materialist science's contention is true, then spiritual values and transformation toward upholding these values in one's life, which are the basis for all religions and spiritual traditions, can only be regarded as super-fluous. In this way religions and with them spiri-tuality have lost much ground in our societies and cultures worldwide.

Additionally, for justifiable reasons, most coun-tries have adopted the idea of secularism—the separation of state and church. As a consequence, religious ideas and with them spirituality and spir-itual values cannot be taught in public schools. In contrast, scientific materialism and its materialist values find unbridled expression in the education offered in public schools. Hence, spiritual activism, with the ideas of upholding spiritual values and emphasizing the importance of spiritual transfor-mation, is important.

Much of the current movement of spiritual activism has originated in the religions themselves.

In the West, especially in the United States, spiritual activism has been politicized in such attempts as to legalize prayer and meditation in public schools or teach creationism as an alternative to evolutionism.

More recently, spiritual activism has found expression outside of religions in the movement for better ethics in our society; in the movement for replacing the "shallow" ecology of the environmen-tal movement by a "deep" ecology—a caring for not only our physical external environment but also our subtle mental and vital internal environments; in the movement for alternative medicine whose goal is to heal not only the gross aspects of our body (that allopathic conventional materialist medicine treats) but also "subtle" aspects of our bodies; and finally, in the movement for a transpersonal psychology whose goal is not only to address our material ego needs but also to the spiritual needs of the superconscious transpersonal self beyond the ego.

Unfortunately, the approach of these latter activ-ist movements has been one of a continuous apol-ogy. Dazzled by the success of materialist science and technology, spiritual activism under the aegis of these movements has shied away from a direct confrontation with scientific materialism. Instead, they have invoked dubious ideas such as holism or evidence-based science to establish their authentic-ity. Even when a movement is solidly founded on an inclusive worldview, transpersonal psychology, for example, which is based on the philosophy of monistic idealism—consciousness, not matter, is the ground of all being—no attempt is made to bridge the chasm of spirit and matter. Instead, a phenomenological approach is pursued (Wilber, 2006) that retains a spirit-matter dichotomy. In the absence of such integration, it is easy for scientific materialists to ignore these efforts of spiritual activism as "unscientific," however unjustified that may be. Ours is a scientific culture; science works. If ethics and spiritual transformation are not scientifically innate aspects of us, but only philosophical imperatives, why bother? Thus a lot of coordinated effort to discredit the idea of God for which a straw God—the God of popular Christianity—is the usual target (Dawkins, 2006; Hawking & Mlodinow, 2010). A recent advert on London double-deckers puts the materialist position well: God probably does not exist. So relax and enjoy life.

Fortunately, more recently, the research of many scientists has helped expose the fact that materialist science is showing signs of inadequacy in the form of philosophical paradoxes and anomalous data. As a result of their work, a new science is aborning, replacing the metaphysics of the primacy of matter with one based on the primacy of consciousness.

Fundamentally, materialist science treats humans as genetically and environmentally conditioned machines. In contrast, the new science is a human science; it not only includes causal efficacy of the human consciousness, but being based on quantum physics, it enables us to treat all human experiences—both external and internal—on equal footing. In particular, this new science shows unambiguously that spirituality is innate in us. And ethics and spiritual transformation are imperative because of our evolutionary drive.

In this article, I will introduce this postmaterialist human science and discuss its implications for spiritual activism—an activism directed toward reenchanting humanity with its innate spiritual values.

A Brief History of the Chasm Between Science and Spirit

Although materialist science is rooted in the mechanistic theories of Newton and others, its early years were spent embedded in a worldview truce called modernism. Also called Cartesian dualism, modernism gave value to both matter and mind, to both our external and internal experiences. In modernism, matter is causally deterministic, its movements predictable and controllable; but mind is recognized to have free will. Thus, in this truce was created the unprecedented creative opportunity for the exploration of the human potential that gave us the Industrial Revolution, capitalism, democracy, and liberal education. In the West, before modernism, the worldview was exclusive—the religious worldview of Christianity. In that worldview, ordinary people's exploration of meaning was confined to religion that emphasized the afterlife much more than this life. No wonder that given this history, Karl Marx has labeled religion the opium of the people. It was. In contrast, modernism brought a breath of fresh air, nay, a gale of strong wind to blow the barriers away against ordinary people's exercise of free will and creativity.

But the truce did not last. From the beginning, there was a question of great unease: How do matter and mind, dual objects with nothing in common, interact? In the 19th century, science discovered energy and its law of conservation—the energy of the material world alone is always a constant. The unease grew further: It must take energy-carrying signals to mediate the interaction of matter and mind. But if that were so, the energy conservation law had to be violated.

Then came Darwin with his theory that purported to explain the fossil data with the idea that humans evolved from animals that were regarded by both physicalists and mentalists as machines. If humans evolved from animals, how could one not see that humans must also be machines? The final clincher was the discovery of the structure of the DNA molecule that created molecular biology with great promise to explain all facets of life, including its origin.

Thus, it was in the 1950s (when DNA structure was unraveled) that modern science officially became materialist science—everything is matter; everything, including the mind, could be reduced to matter and its interactions. A three-prong project was begun: (1) to manufacture life in the laboratory starting with the base molecules. This was to keep the proponents of vital energy or life force at bay. (2) To produce computing machines with mind—artificial intelligence. This was to keep mentalists on defense. And (3) to discover the elementary particles of matter to prove beyond doubt that reductionism works. It didn't help the cause of the mentalists that in spite of the valiant work of many philosophers, a monism based on the primacy of the mind could not find even philosophical grounding let alone scientific backing.

Let's now remember, that modern science, before the Cartesian truce, grew up in an environment of open hostility between science and religion (in the form of Christianity). As Darwin's theory found increasing footing in empirical data, hostility broke open once again. And in the 1950s, the battle seemed to have been decided in favor of materialist science. But still people did not become atheists overnight. It took s lot of hard scientific success in the form of actually finding the elementary particles of matter, a lot of successful technology in the form of weaponry and computers mainly, and last but not least a lot of philosophical sophistry in the form of postmodern deconstructionism before a substantial number of people declared themselves to be atheists—nonbelievers of religion, even spirituality. A major role in this conversion has been played by the concept of secularism, separation of church and state—originally intended to keep the Christian Church at bay from the affairs of the government.

Unfortunately secularism created a different monster. It was not recognized until recently that a science based on the exclusive philosophy of scientific materialism is also a dogma just like Christianity is. The exclusivity of the spirit has been replaced by the exclusivity of matter. The new exclusivity was bought lock stock and barrel by the media and the governments of most countries, but is reality really exclusive? Doubts lingered.

After all, of the three promises of materialist science at its inauguration, only one has materialized. Reductionism works for matter: elementary particles make atoms, atoms make molecules, molecules make larger conglomerates of macro-matter, including living cells, and cells make biological organs such as the brain. Material forces work through upward causation—cause rises upward from the base-level elementary particles

But, then, are all our internal experiences—feeling, thinking, and intuition—and our consciousness itself brain epiphenomena as materialists contend? Recent research is giving an answer: a resounding no.

Paradoxes and Anomalies of Materialist Science

Unheralded by the media and unrecognized by the government (in the form of research grants), a few scientists continued in their search of reality, not totally convinced that material monism is the final answer to the logically inconsistent Cartesian philosophy of dualism. Soon the efforts of these truth seekers began to reveal unexpected holes in the dogma of matter supremacy:

Item: Quantum physics says objects are waves of possibility and, furthermore, material interactions can never change possibility waves into actual events observed in experiments. If everything is matter, how can one explain the observer effect? In the presence of an observer, possibility waves are always found to have collapsed to actual events in the observer's experience. This is called the quantum measurement paradox (von Neumann, 1955).

Item: The movement of quantum objects exhibits nonlocality (signal-less communication) and discontinuity (quantum leaps). But material interactions are always locality and continuity bound.

Item: Objects and their interactions can only produce other objects, never a subject experiencing objects as we do whenever we are aware. The philosopher David Chalmers (1995) has called this the hard question of neurophysiology.

Item: The philosopher John Searle (1994) and the physicist Roger Penrose (1991) have established that a computer can process mental content and content alone, not mental meaning. A nonphysical mind is needed for processing mental meaning. And if meaning is not computable, then intuitive values (the archetype of love, for example) that belong to a higher category of logic cannot be computable either.

This is not good news for those materialist philosophers, who claim that our capacities for processing meaning and values emerge from Darwinian evolution, from survival necessity. But if matter cannot even process meaning and values, this claim is obviously unjustified.

Item: Cell differentiation that is required for biological form making (morphogenesis) smacks of nonlocality (how does the cell know where it is in the body?). The biologist Rupert Sheldrake (1981) argued that since matter cannot process nonlocality, the fields responsible for morphogenesis (call them morphogenetic fields) must be nonphysical. In other words, a nonphysical world of morphogenetic fields, call it the vital world, is required to explain biological form making.

Item: Where do physical laws come from? If there is only matter and its interactions and the movements these interactions cause, then the laws of movement of matter must originate from material movement itself. But all attempts to derive these laws from the random motion of matter have failed. Hence, Plato's theory that physical laws are examples of the archetype of truth and that archetypes belong to a subtle archetypal world of reality still stands.

These are only a few highlights of the theoretical difficulties with scientific materialism and materialist science. There are many more (Goswami, 2008a). And materialist science does not fare any better in the experimental arena either. Here are some examples of anomalous data:

Item: The physicist Alain Aspect and his collaborators have verified quantum nonlocality between quantum objects and the neurophysiologist Jacobo Grinberg and his collaborators (1994) have demonstrated quantum nonlocality between human brains in the form of transfer of electric potential from one brain to another without electrical connection. These data have been replicated repeatedly (Sabel, Clarke, & Fenwick, 2001; Standish, Kozak, Clark Johnson, & Richards, 2004; Wackerman, Seiter, & Holder, 2003). Once again I emphasize: material interactions cannot cause nonlocal phenomena.

Item: There is now an enormous amount of data demonstrating spontaneous communication between humans and other living beings at a distance (Targ & Catra, 1998). They are all examples of quantum nonlocality (Goswami, 2008a).

Item: It has been experimentally demonstrated that when electrons penetrate an energy barrier in a transistor, they do it by quantum leaping, without going through the intervening space. In the same vein, creativity researchers have demonstrated with many case studies that creative insights come to us via a discontinuous movement of thought (Briggs, 1990). The subjective experience of this quantum leap is surprise, aha! This is why a creative experience is sometimes called "an aha experience."

Item: The fossil gaps in the fossil records of biological evolution similarly demonstrate discontinuous movements of species creativity (Eldredge & Gould, 1972; Goswami, 2008b).

Item: Discontinuous quantum leaps also occur in the phenomenon of spontaneous healing also called quantum healing (Chopra, 1990).

Item: The data on survival after death and reincarnation are now very solid (Goswami, 2001, 2008a). What survives? A personalized nonphysical subtle body (consisting of personalized mental and vital components). In this way these phenomena empirically prove the existence of the subtle, mental and vital, bodies.

Item: How does acupuncture work? Via needed movement of vital energy. How does homeopathy work when not even one physical molecule is administered in the medicine proffered? The answer

once again: via the infusion of healing vital energy (Goswami, 2004).

The conclusion is obvious. Scientific materialism is not a valid metaphysics for science. We have to recognize a nonmaterial source of causation and nonmaterial subtle worlds in addition to our gross material world.

A Brief Summary of the New Science Within Consciousness

For the sake of brevity, I will not present the details of the new science (see Blood, 2001; Goswami, 1993, 2008a; Stapp, 1993). It will suffice to recap the basic elements of the developing science within the primacy of consciousness as we begin to apply it to spiritual activism:

• Consciousness is the ground of all being. Its possibilities follow quantum laws; that is, they are quantum possibilities. Consciousness has causal efficacy (call it downward causation in contrast to material upward causation) consisting of choice from the many-faceted quantum possibilities the one facet that becomes the conscious experience of the actuality of an object.

• Downward causation is nonlocal and is applied in a discontinuous manner.

• Downward causation requires a tangled hierarchical device, that is, a device with circularly acting components. The brain is such a device; the circular components are a hierarchical system of apparatuses that produce perception and another hierarchical system of apparatuses that produce memory. Notice the circularity: Perception requires memory, but memory requires perception. In the transition from the micro-level to the macro-level, the circularity makes the entire hierarchy tangled. As a result of the tangled hierarchy of the brain, consciousness identifies with it and we have self-reference, an abbreviation for its subject-object split (Goswami, 1993; Hofstadter, 1980).

• The quantum possibilities of consciousness are four-fold: material (which we sense); vital energy (which we feel); mental meaning (which we think); and supramental discriminating contexts such as physical laws, contexts of meaning and feeling such as ethics and love and aesthetics (which we intuit). The material is called gross: because at the macro-level of matter, quantum movement is much suppressed producing a Newtonian fixity in the way we experience it. Fixity makes the experience sharable and objective and apparently external. The movement of the nonmaterial objects remains quantum always (there is no micro-macro division in the worlds they inhabit); no two people can ordinarily collapse the same experience giving the impression that their experiences are private and internal. In this way, these internal experiences make up the subtle domain of reality.

• Conscious choice is nonlocal without involving signals; in this way, dualism is avoided. Instead, nonlocal consciousness mediates the interactions between the four worlds of experience.

• Experience makes memory, and previously experienced stimulus is experienced not only as a primary experience but also as a secondary experience upon reflection from the mirror of previous memory. As memories accumulate, the response to a learned stimulus becomes conditioned in favor of previous responses. Eventually, as we grow up, our identity shifts from the "quantum self" of the primary experience to a secondary conditioned ego that is ordinarily capable of experiencing only after the reflection from the memory of previous experiences.

• It is ego conditioning that produces habit patterns, or the "character" consists of nonlocal memory (Goswami, 2001). The nonlocality of these memory patterns enables them to recycle from one incarnation to another. This is the explanation of reincarnation.

• When consciousness chooses from the possibilities the actual event of its experience (with physical, vital, mental, and supramental components), the physical has the opportunity of making representations of the subtle. The physical acts like computer hardware; the subtle is represented in the physical as software.

• Biological organs are software representations of the vital morphogenetic fields. Consciousness uses these fields as blueprints for making biological form (the organs). When consciousness collapses the organ corresponding to a particular biological function, it also collapses the associated morphogenetic field. It is the movement of the correlated morphogenetic fields that we feel at the points around which the important organs of the body are situated. These points of the body are called the chakras.

• Our capacity for making physical representation of the subtle evolves via alternative stages of slow tempo (of Darwinian vintage) and fast tempo (of quantum leaps of biological creativity). First, the capacity for making representations of the vital evolved through the evolution of life via more and more sophisticated organs to represent the living functions such as maintenance, and reproduction, and sensing. Next the capacity of making more and more sophisticated representations of the mental evolved. This is the stage of evolution that we are in right now (Aurobindo, 1996; Goswami, 2008b; Teilhard de Chardin, 1961; Wilber, 1981).

• Our capacity to represent the supramental has not evolved yet. However, there is evolutionary pressure on us in this direction; it is the primary reason some of us are attracted to meaning, values, and spirituality even in these times of "Newton's sleep." Indeed, even today, for some of us, ethics and spirituality become categorical imperatives as Kant envisioned.

• In times of cataclysmic crisis, survival needs bring many more people into creativity looking for solutions. Evolution takes place via the effect of this collective biological creativity.

In this way, the new science gives us a powerful new perspective for spiritual activism. First of all, it gives us back free will and creativity in the form of discontinuous movements of downward causation from a nonlocal state of consciousness. Transformation is no longer a dubious proposition.

Ethics is now solidly based on a metaphysics that fundamentally recognizes the interconnectedness of all humans. Why ethics is no longer the question, but how ethics.

Since the external and the internal are treated on the same footing, clearly shallow ecology must give way to a deep ecology that cares for both. Again, the question shifts from why to how.

Alternative medicine's search for more than material healing is now seen as clearly justified. If the vital is diseased, we must heal it before the physical (the representations) can be healed. Similarly, the disease of the mental will block the movement of the vital energy; therefore, the diseased mind needs to be healed first. Finally, it is clearly recognized that, ultimately, healing involves acquiring spiritual wholeness.

Transpersonal psychology's emphasis on a superconscious state beyond ego is now seen as eminently scientific. It is the state of the self in any event of downward causation that involves full freedom of choice of the nonlocal consciousness. Prime examples are creative experiences, experiences that are called paranormal, experiences of love, and aesthetics.

Next we will delve into each of these fields with further elaborations. However, a most important aspect of the new science is that it allows us to distinguish between spirituality and religion. This distinction opens the door for a new era of postsecularism.

Postsecularism

The new science includes spiritual values as an important domain of possibilities for human experience, which, evolutionarily speaking, is just opening up for human exploration en masse (see later). The new science also restores our free will and creativity and legitimizes our efforts toward spiritual transformation. In other words, under the aegis of the new science, spirituality is scientific: It has both scientific theory and empirical data supporting it. Religions, on the other hand, have a dogmatic side. All religions hold that their scriptures, which are exclusive, are infallible. But such infallibility cannot be subjected to scientific investigation.

Postsecularism is then the idea that we move beyond secularism by distinguishing between spirituality and religion. Where state and religion should still maintain separation, there is no longer a need to keep spirituality out of the functions of the state.

It should be clear, however, that paradigms take a while to change and materialist science is very entrenched right now. For one thing, as the novelist Upton Sinclair said, "It is difficult to make a man understand something when his salary depends upon his not understanding it." So spiritual activism is needed to reenchant our classrooms with spiritual (but not religious) values.

Conventional spiritual activism, however, needs to adapt to the new science when it broaches the subject of spiritual transformation. Quantum physics gives us the concept of downward causation, but downward causation has an entrance requirement. You cannot access it without a quantum leap from your ordinary state of ego consciousness. And quantum leaps require you to engage with the creative process.

Most popular religions maintain that just by being a member of that religion you are "saved," or that members of a religion are "God's chosen people." The new science is clear on this: No one is saved or can claim to be God's chosen without spiritual awakening, and this takes a creative quantum leap and the arduous work that the manifestation stage of the creative process demands (Goswami, 2008a).

We need a redefinition: Spiritual activism is activism geared to revive spiritual values and to emphasize spiritual transformation using the transformative process of quantum creativity.

In an era of postsecularism, the following question is bound to come up: Is there any need for religion once we develop a science of spirituality as we have now? The answer is a resounding yes. This may require some explanation, however. It may seem that since God is objective in our scientific approach, God experience must be the same for all of us. God is nonlocal consciousness; everyone's God is the same nonlocal cosmic quantum consciousness as mystics have declared throughout history. Any private experience of God must be secondary.

But in our regular ego consciousness, we cannot see God outside of ourselves the way we see matter, so God is not public in the same way that the material world is public. It is more subtle than that. We can still verify that God is objective because we can experience the nonlocality of God consciousness with others; the company of God-loving others helps us experience the public side of God consciousness more easily.

The parapsychologist Dean Radin (2006) took random number generators to meditation halls and found that indeed their behavior deviated substantially from randomness. As the philosopher Gregory Bateson said, the opposite of randomness is choice. In the company of others, we become more prone to access the quantum freedom of choice of nonlocal consciousness. This substantiates what Buddha tried to do with his idea of *sangha* (meaning community), what Hindus do with *satsang* (meaning the company of people in search of reality), and what Jesus meant when he said,

When two or more meditate in my name
There I am in the midst of them.

Religions, communities of spiritually motivated people, grow out of the intuition of quantum nonlocality of God consciousness.

Spiritual Activism and Evolution

The psychologist Abraham Maslow said, "If you have a hammer in your hand, you tend to see the world as nails." Creationists (religious activists under the aegis of Christian fundamentalism) have their hammer in the form of the biblical story of Genesis. So they only see the homeostatic parts of the fossil data. Conventional biologists have their hammer in the slow-and-continuous evolution theory of Darwinism; they see only the slow and continuously changing part of the fossil data. The rest they rationalize: We will fill up the gaps of the fossil data later. Only when we have injected quantum physics in biology can we use the idea of quantum creativity and quantum leaps to explain the fossil gaps as epochs of fast tempo in evolution (Eldredge & Gould, 1972; Goswami, 2008b).

Immediately, other things fall into place. Evolution is now seen as the purposive evolution of consciousness, the purpose being to evolve better and better representations of the heavenly archetypes in earthly manifestations. The biological arrow of time, the overall evolution of life from simple to complex, is now explained.

Most important, human evolution is now seen as the evolution of meaning giving capacity of the mind. First comes the physical mind with the capacity of giving meaning to the physical world (the hunter-gatherer era). Second, the vital mind of giving meaning to feelings (the horticultural era of small-scale agriculture). Third comes the rational mind with the capacity for giving meaning to meaning itself that evolved with the coming of large-scale agriculture. The agricultural era has given way to industry and technology, but we are still in the evolutionary era of the rational mind.

Not that we have not discovered intuition; we have. Even inner creativity that we call spirituality has been in vogue for the last 2,600 years at least; with inner creativity we have been exploring archetypes such as love and goodness and truth. But mind of the human species as a whole has not evolved much; mind has not even achieved full rationality, let alone the next stage of its evolution: the intuitive mind.

The problem can be traced to the presence of neurophysiological brain circuits of negative emotions that are instinctual, and the remedy has been identified. It is to collectively evolve brain circuits of positive emotions to balance the negative. Our new science is saying that even if a relatively few of us strive to achieve such brain circuits of spiritual transformations, it is likely that in a few generations, all of humanity will benefit; all human beings will be born with positive emotional instincts (Goswami, 2008b; Sheldrake, 1981). This, then, is the focus of spiritual activism in the form of quantum activism.

Evolutionary Ethics

Why ethics? If we are nonlocally connected via a quantum consciousness, then ethics—being good to others—makes sense. However, when we identify with the ego, the nonlocality is obscure and, therefore, ethics does not make complete sense anymore.

There are two points to consider. First, we always have the capacity for intuiting the supramental archetypal domain. Through intuition, we can glimpse the archetype of goodness at any age. Second, during our early development, most of us make mental representations of the archetype of goodness that are no doubt influenced by our family, our educators, and our society. To the extent we live up to these mental representations, we may develop some brain circuits that correspond to ethical actions. So whenever the question of ethics or moral judgment comes up, these brain circuits may be triggered, arousing our "conscience."

But not all of us follow the dictates of our conscience; in fact, today fewer and fewer of us do. Environmental conditioning has much to do with the efforts we make to follow up our intuitions about goodness. Growing up today under the aegis of scientific materialism with religions undermined as they are does not help to grow a healthy conscience.

In a postsecular era, we can bring back spirituality to our schools; we can bring back creativity and transformation. Thus, ethics can be taught, and spiritual transformation can be emphasized, helping students to grow a good conscience.

Intelligent students will still ask this: If there is no God to punish us, why should we follow ethics blindly? The new science has a clear answer on this: If we don't learn our archetypes, in this case the archetype of goodness, we will reincarnate and again we have to go through suitable comeuppance for violating ethics.

There is a second aspect of the new ethics that emerges when we look at spirituality and ethics not from the old-fashioned mystical view but from a new-fashioned scientific view. There is a social dimension of spirituality. Spirituality is not only satisfying the personal goal of awakening to God consciousness but also to evolving the cream of God consciousness: the supramental archetypes, our spiritual values such as ethics in all humanity.

Whereas reincarnation is a reactive reason to follow ethics, evolution gives us the proactive incentive, the categorical imperative. The ethics that is imperative is *evolutionary ethics*: the idea that I cannot make personal progress in my spiritual path without making some effort to help my fellow humans to evolve, too. In this way, under the new science the old idea of spiritual activism must give way to what I call quantum activism: to transform self and society using the quantum transformative principles of nonlocality, discontinuity, and tangled hierarchy.

Deep Ecology

The root Greek word for "eco" is *eikos*, meaning the place we live, and "logy" comes from Greek *logos*, meaning knowledge. Ordinary ecology is about the knowledge of our physical environment. But as the ecologist Arne Ness knew (Devall & Sessions, 1985), we live not only in a physical world, we also live in the three subtle worlds—vital, mental, and supramental. Deep ecology in this way refers to the knowledge of both our external and internal worlds and it asks us to have ethical responsibility for all of these environments in which we live.

But to materialist scientists, deep ecology is meaningless. If you hold to scientific materialism, you will be asking too much of yourself, you will be asking a machine (you) to have relationships with other machines, less sophisticated at that, and to have relationships based on unjustified rules of ethics.

Only when we become established in an evolutionarily ethical relationship with all our fellow human beings, it is time to ponder our ethical responsibility to all creatures, great and small, including the responsibility to our nonliving environment. Only then it makes sense to ask, What is our responsibility to the planet Earth, to Gaia?

Deep ecology requires not only abiding by a few rules for preserving our ecosystem or passing a few governmental laws preventing environmental pollution but also taking actions in ambiguous situations that demand a creative quantum leap. When you take such a quantum leap, you realize one astounding thing: *I choose, therefore I am, and my world is.* The world is not separate from you. When we do this en masse, we leap into a truly Gaia consciousness (Lovelock, 1982). Naturally, movement toward deep ecology is part and parcel of quantum activism.

Integrative Medicine

In the new science, we have a body in each of our worlds of experience: a physical body of senses, a vital body of feeling, a mental body of meaning, and a supramental body of archetype. These four bodies are embedded in the whole—the ground of all being—consciousness itself. We can call it a fifth body.

All these bodies ideally function in perfect synchrony. Lack of synchrony (ease) will be experienced as disease. Five bodies, five sources of lack of synchrony, five kinds of disease. Hence, to heal we need to go to the source of the disease and, therefore, five kinds of healing.

Conventional allopathy or so-called modern medicine is physical body medicine in this terminology. Traditional Chinese medicine (that includes acupuncture), the Indian ayurveda, and homeopathy correspond to vital body medicine, and mind-body medicine is mental body medicine.

In materialist science, only allopathy, physical body medicine, is valid. But "healing" and "wholeness" come from the same root Greek word. Ultimately, healing requires total harmony in wholeness; this is the same objective as that of spiritual transformation. All the bodies must act in synchrony. Hence, to bring alternative medicine to our culture that heals the subtle bodies has been an important emphasis of spiritual activism. This is good because alternative medicine is literally sacred technology. To experience the causal efficacy of alternative medicine is to experience downward causation.

If you are a nonscientist, you probably do not have any direct knowledge—theoretical or experimental—of electricity. Why do you believe in the science of electricity then? Because when you flip an electric switch, the light comes on! That is convincing. The same with alternative medicine. When you meditate and it slows your mind down, relieving mental stress and reducing your blood pressure, that is equally convincing about the causal efficacy of consciousness.

The new science, treating all the bodies on the same footing, integrates conventional and alternative medicine systems into an integrative medicine (Goswami, 2004). In integrative medicine, the healing dynamics have a two-fold perspective. Whereas the healee is interested primarily in regaining physical health and the relief of physical symptoms, why is the healer engaged? The materialist answer is money, but most healers would disagree. The new science says, in healing a patient with whom the healer has a tangled hierarchical relationship gives the healer an excellent chance to achieve wholeness, positive health. This defines no less than a healing path to spiritual transformation.

And because quantum principles are used in spiritual activism using the healing path of integrative medicine, such activism is quantum activism. To their credit, alternative healing researchers (quantum activists all) have been aware of the importance of quantum principles for healing for quite a while. As early as 1982, the physician Larry Dossey (1982) emphasized the importance of quantum nonlocality in healing. In 1988, the physician Randolph Byrd (1988) did the first controlled experiment on distant healing, and it remains one of the convincing demonstrations of quantum nonlocality. And in 1989, Deepak Chopra (1990) became famous with his idea of quantum healing as the explanation of spontaneous healing without medical intervention.

Transpersonal Psychology

In psychology, materialist psychology in the form of behavioral/cognitive branches of psychology dominates the academia. In this approach our behavior originates from psychosocial conditioning, although the effects of evolutionary conditioning in the form of the genetic makeup are also acknowledged. However, in psychology, the causal efficacy of consciousness was introduced by no other than Sigmund Freud in the form of the psychological drive of the unconscious id. Clinical psychology to this day is dominated by Freudian psychoanalysis. In this way, in the field of psychology the battle of matter versus consciousness (which is primary?) remains undecided.

Transpersonal psychology began with the idea of bringing spirituality to the way healing in mental health is practiced. Instead of emphasizing the behavioral ego, it emphasizes the higher self of spiritual vintage; the higher self is more like the Holy Spirit of Christianity and the superconscious Samadhi state of Hinduism. Instead of analytical therapy for exploring the unconscious, transpersonal psychotherapy depends more on superconscious "peak experiences" for healing the mind.

But although based on nonduality, transpersonal psychology is only marginally more successful than dualism-based spiritual activism in terms of credibility. When transpersonal psychology is formulated within the quantum worldview and science within consciousness and its ideas become experimentally verifiable, the credibility question will undoubtedly improve.

Unfortunately, many exponents of the field, such as Ken Wilber, have taken an antiscience position. Wilber bypasses the question of worldview altogether through the use of phenomenology. Everyone must agree that there are first-person, second-person, and third-person descriptions of conscious experiences. Of these, conventional (materialist) science only deals with the third-person consciousness, says Wilber. The other two, then, must be in the jurisdiction of the transpersonal approach. This seems to legitimize the transpersonal approach. Unfortunately it introduces an outer (scientific) and inner (transpersonal/spiritual) dichotomy that can only be integrated, it is said, from the internal vantage point of mystical realization. Obviously, this is an elitist position. In the new science within

consciousness, the external/internal dichotomy is resolved from the get-go (Goswami, 2000) and is resolvable by anyone by simple reasoning and looking at his or her own experience.

The nondual spiritual philosophy adapted by transpersonal psychology is not, per se, able to distinguish between conscious and the unconscious. This gives rise to unnecessary competition between this "height" psychology of the superconscious and the depth psychology with emphasis on the unconscious. The new science explains the distinction of the unconscious, conscious, and superconscious states. Incorporating transpersonal psychology within the new science thus integrates transpersonal psychology with depth psychology. And all the somewhat quaint arguments between the two postmaterialist forces of psychology are resolved (Goswami, 2008a).

On the practical side, adapting the transpersonal psychology movement within the more general movement of the new science paradigm identifies transpersonal psychology as an important new technology of the new science, the technology of positive mental health.

Spiritual Activism and Social Change

Due to the perceived success of materialist science, our social sciences, economics and political science, for example, are dominated by the behavioral/cognitive approach to ourselves. In the field of economics, this approach has resulted in a surreptitious corruption of Adam Smith's capitalism into a materialist economics (Goswami, 2011). The result on our society has been disastrous; witness the economic meltdown of 2007–2009.

The new science, besides giving us integrative technologies for physical and mental health, is finding a most relevant social application in the form of a spiritual economics. Adam Smith (1776/1994) recognized only our material need. The basic idea of spiritual economics is to recognize Maslow's hierarchy of needs, which posits that besides our material needs we have subtle needs of feeling, meaning, and values in our lives, and then include these subtle needs in our economic demand-supply equation (Goswami, 2011).

Similarly, the new science shows us the way back for politicians. They can dedicate their political power to the advancement of meaning processing in the lives of increasingly large numbers of humans, which is the purpose of democracy.

Finally, the new science gives us the proper ammunition to take our education system back from its current job emphasis to its Jeffersonian liberal arts emphasis (Goswami, 2011). However, much activism, call it spiritual activism or quantum activism, will be needed to bring about all this social change.

My vision is that we are right on track. Via the aforementioned social changes, more and more people will be able to make their livelihood meaningfully and purposively. This is a prerequisite for becoming a quantum activist. Quantum activism with much help from the Internet will produce communities dedicated to collective transformation. The creativity of these communities will get a boost from the crisis conditions brought about by materialist science. Soon a threshold will be reached and the collective transformation of today's efforts of activism will become inheritable instinctual positive emotional brain circuits of tomorrow.

References

Aurobindo, S. (1996). *The life divine*. Pondicherry, India: Sri Aurobindo Ashram/Tarcher/Putnam.

Blood, C. (2001). *Science, sense, and soul*. Los Angeles: Renaissance Books.

Briggs, J. (1990). *Fire in the crucible*. Los Angeles: Tarcher/Penguin.

Byrd, R. C. (1988). Positive therapeutic effects of intercessor prayer in a coronary care unit population. *Southern Medical Journal, 81*, 826–829.

Chalmers, D. (1995). *Toward a theory of consciousness*. Cambridge, MA: MIT Press.

Chopra, D. (1990). *Quantum healing*. New York: Bantam-Doubleday.

Dawkins, R. (2006). *The God delusion*. Boston: Houghton Mifflin.

Devall, W., & Sessions, G. (1985). *Deep ecology*. Salt Lake City, UT: Peregrine Smith.

Dossey, L. (1982). *Space, time and medicine*. New York: Bantam.

Eldredge, N., & Gould, S. J. (1972). Punctuated equilibria: An alternative to phyletic gradualism. In T. J. M. Schopf (Ed.), *Models of paleontology* (pp. 82–115). San Francisco: Freeman.

Goswami, A. (1993). *The self-aware universe: How consciousness creates the material world*. New York: Tarcher/Putnam.

Goswami, A. (2000). *The visionary window: A quantum physicist's guide to enlightenment*. Wheaton, IL: Quest Books.

Goswami, A. (2001). *Physics of the soul*. Charlottsville, VA: Hampton Roads.

Goswami, A. (2004). *The quantum doctor*. Charlottsville, VA: Hampton Roads.

Goswami, A. (2008a). *God is not dead*. Charlottsville, VA: Hampton Roads.

Goswami, A. (2008b). *Creative evolution*. Wheaton, IL: Theosophical Publishing House.

Goswami, A. (2011). *How quantum activism can save civilization*. San Francisco: Hampton Roads.

Grinberg-Zylberbaum, J., Delaflor, M., Attie, L., & Goswami, A. (1994). Einstein Podolsky Rosen paradox in the human brain: The transferred potential. *Physics Essays, 7*, 422–428.

Hawking, S., & Mlodinow, L. (2010). *The grand design*. New York: Bantam.

Hofstadter, D. (1980). *Godel, Escher, Bach: An eternal golden braid*. New York: Basic Books.

Lovelock, J. E. (1982). *Gaia: A New Look at Life on Earth*. Oxford: Oxford University Press.

Sabel, A., Clarke, C., & Fenwick, P. (2001). Intersubject EEG correlations at a distance—the transferred potential. In C. S. Alvarado (Ed.), *Proceedings of the 46th Annual Convention of the Parapsychological Association* (pp. 419–422). New York.

Searle, J. (1994). *The rediscovery of the mind*. Cambridge, MA: MIT Press.

Sheldrake, R. (1981). *A new science of life*. Los Angeles: Tarcher.

Smith, A. (1994). *The wealth of nations*. New York: Modern Library. (Original work published 1776).

Standish, L. J., Kozak, L., Clark Johnson, L., & Richards, T. (2004). Electroencephalographic evidence of correlated event-related signals between the brains of spatially and sensory isolated human subjects. *Journal of Alternative and Complementary Medicine, 10*, 307–314.

Stapp, H. P. (1993). *Mind, matter, and quantum mechanics*. New York: Springer.

Targ, R., & Catra, J. (1998). *Miracles of mind*. Novatao, CA: New World Library.

Teilhard de Chardin, P. (1961). *The phenomenon of man*. New York: Harper & Row.

Von Neumann, J. (1955). *The conceptual foundations of quantum mechanics*. Princeton, NJ: Princeton University Press.

Wackermann, J., Seiter, C., & Holger, K. (2003). Correlation between brain electrical activities of two spatially separated human subjects. *Neuroscience Letters, 336*, 60–64.

Wilber, K. (1981). *Up from Eden*. Garden City, NY: Anchor/Doubleday.

Wilber, K. (2006). *Integral spirituality*. Boston: Integral Books.

PART 10

Conclusion

Conclusion

Lisa J. Miller

Abstract

Spiritual psychology, in science and practice, propels psychology into the 21st-century consciousness-based sciences rather than strictly a 20th-century material science. The current postmaterial spiritual psychology propagates a clarification and broadening of ontology. A consciousness-driven psychology unites the human inner life and surrounding physical events into a singular inquiry addressed by a range of formerly separate disciplines. From this postmaterial view, a human science sees human mind as an extension of the fabric of universal consciousness yet dialectically in dialog through perception, awareness, and choice. Science now can wed the vast majority of human history understood through transcendent cosmology and religion, by exploring an intentional universe.

Key Words: Postmaterial, Spiritual Psychology, Conscious Universe

The constellation of research across spiritual psychology represents a broadened ontology, vastly expanding the explanatory power of psychology. Most people (a Gallup poll suggests over 90%) have had moments of great consequence derived from spiritual experience that simply cannot be explained through a psychology based exclusively on mechanism and materialism. These pivotal and illuminating moments, which forge our lives and create our opportunities, call for understanding through a psychology that spans across a broadened ontology. Over the most recent five thousand years, most humans have held a cosmology, often through religion, that engaged transcendent experiences. A 20th century science that refused room for investigation of intentionality in the fabric of the universe or vitality in the physical world precluded the study of major questions, particularly as concerns significant moments of human consciousness.

Psychology, to unite significant inner and outer realities, now becomes a 21st-century science that includes consciousness as bedrock in the nature of reality. This idea is quite familiar within our peer academic disciplines, such as contemporary physics, as pointed out by Everett Worthingon (Chapter 4) or the life sciences as explained out by C. Edward Richards (Chapter 5). We live in an era of consciousness based physical sciences. Our own spiritual psychology, as a consciousness-based science, reaches across once disparate disciplines to view consciousness as extending through humans and the surrounding physical world. In addition to the paradigm shift fueled by physics, biology, and medicine, psychology also benefits from wisdom contained in thousands of years of human healing practice and ritual, and, as Ralph Hood (Chapter 1) points out through academic science carefully engaging ideas in religion. Our current point in intellectual history, as suggested by Worthington, Richards and Hood points to a current concomitant emergence of postmaterial ideas across disciplines that potentiates the unification of disciplines.

That consciousness exists in states other than matter expands our notion of the human brain and is the linchpin of a postmaterial psychology. Within postmaterial science at some ontological levels, there are no differences between the inner life and the outer world because consciousness is continuous, not exclusively local, through space and time. Consciousness is in us, through us, and around us.

A consciousness-driven science can address non-mechanistic interrelatedness across space and time. Many people have premonitions of negativity or anxiety or see related information before a large-scale event of devastation, or joy concomitant with an event of love and harmony, even when it occurs at a great distance without our having been a priori informed.

A consciousness-driven science evokes curiosity around the recurrent patterns across various scientific levels of analysis. While scientific paradigms were previously lodged within level of analysis, religious and spiritual traditions have comfortably made the lead with insights such as "As above, so below." The question of recurrent patterns from great to small is posed through art; for instance, the work of the accomplished photographer Ansel Adams asks: Why does an aerial view of a canyon resemble the close-up view of the bark of a tree?

The notion of a consciousness-driven science opens up explanatory possibility and the opportunity for new models and eventually paradigms for science. For instance, research using electroencephalography shows that spiritual experience in humans is associated with readings of high-amplitude alpha. The wavelength of alpha from the human brain is the same wavelength of Shumann's constant, a long-standing measurement of the energy in the Earth's crust. From the perspective of the postmaterial science in this volume, the brain detects consciousness, not merely constructs consciousness. Therefore, a quantitative reading of the same level of energy in the spiritually engaged brain and the living Earth invites a fascinating, open ended, and certainly much expanded explanation. Is the brain detecting the same form or dimension of energy that is part of the inherent set point or nature of Earth? Is the brain, in a spiritually engaged moment, in the same form of energy or consciousness as other life thriving on Earth? Awareness of the broader relationship invites study on the sameness or deep relationships between the function of the spiritually engaged brain and living beings beyond humans, such as plants, earth, animals, and water. This may be detected, in light of Tiller's contribution (Chapter 35) as consciousness shared at the level of the atom.

The physicists in this Handbook explore the possibility that as humans we function both as a point and as a wave. In other words, we walk on solid earth from home to work and pour water into reliable cups, thus functioning as a point. Then, we suddenly remember or discover an idea at the same moment as our beloved partner back home, thus functioning as a unified wave. Through his meticulous research on Near Death Experiences, Bruce Greyson (Chapter 33) shows human consciousness to be independent of the material brain and to exist in the arena of greater consciousness. A consciousness-driven human science harmonizes with our fellow scientists, as it explains humans living both as discrete points and as wave functions.

Within the "wave function" consciousness healing is possible within us and among us. The model of health and healing proposed by Wayne Jonas and colleagues (Chapter 23) posits a layered model of medical healing that includes a core source of healing through universal sacred consciousness. The model applies at the level of the individual and extends to collective psychological healing of our global village. As for the method of unification and healing with the scared consciousness, there are multiple chariots. Lee Joyce Richmond (Chapter 29) shows relationships and right livelihood to be vehicles for joining in the unified consciousness. Kartikeya Patel (Chapter 22) shows through some Eastern traditions our deliberate contemplative and meditative consciousness work to unite us into what I am calling the wave function of consciousness. Prayer and sacred meditation invoke direct healing, as highlighted by Thomas Plante (Chapter 25) in physical healing, and P. Scott Richards (Chapter 16), Mark McMinns and colleagues (Chapter 17) and David Lukoff (Chapter 26) in psychological healing across faith traditions as well as outside of traditional religious practice.

What physics encouraged human scientists to acknowledge is the notion of a consciousness-driven science in which intention changes the unfolding of material events. Perhaps the greatest emergent contribution of a consciousness-driven science is room for research to explore intentionality in the fabric of the universe. Science can take seriously that we live in a universe propelled by ultimate intention, the Source as referred to by Schwartz (Chapter 36) and expressed throughout space as in the consciousness of an atom, as explained by Tiller (Chapter 34). Many religions view an overarching intention of love and guidance in the universe, and nearly all faith traditions detect some intention to the workings of the world. Until recently, this profound and pressing question has not been touched by science, perhaps due to its historical packaging. From the view of a consciousness-driven science, all of life, to include humans, is not necessarily a so-called random event but may be formed and sustained through intention. Sensing this possibility, popular contemporary culture has taken a rather solipsistic focus upon manifesting human intention as an anthropocentric command upon reality. This model does not explain how humans receptively detect events nor does it explain how humans encounter unenvisioned opportunity. However, a science that views consciousness throughout the fabric of the universe may show that the force of intention supercedes that of hedonic desires of the individual. Joseph W. Ciarrocchi (Chapter 27) advocated for a spiritual positive psychology based upon pursuit of virtues "in and of themselves" rather than as driven by hedonics or for instrumental gain, as common in the 20th Century psychology. Ciarrocchi empirically showed that a broad range of virtues, expressed through sensitivity to the momentary context, can be cultivated, and connect us with the world. The effect of virtues, considered by other authors as intentions of love, compassion and empathy, may in practice be a dynamic dialog or a joining with the ultimate powerful intention throughout the universe. Perhaps right intentions is where human psyche is part of ultimate consciousness.

From the view of epistemology and methodology, post-Enlightenment scientific gains from within materialism exist comfortably alongside scientific postmaterialism. Scientific awareness of materialism as an explanatory paradigm, taken alongside postmaterialism, is an expanded science that states at each moment the operative ontology surrounding the research question and interpretation of data. Too often 20th-centurty science has assumed materialism, without being clear on the ontological context selected by the investigators. Science in this Handbook is presented within a broadened and sophisticated clarity of ontological context. Elegant examples of explicit statement of ontology are stated throughout the handbook. Spiritual psychological science, that unifies material and postmaterial thought, promises a vast horizon.

This expanded science lights a different set of lived daily assumptions that help us better negotiate the 21st-century world. The spiritual psychology in this Handbook is one of dialog between humans and the universe—a discussion that eventuates in life-creating possibility. Consciousness as Tiller explains exists in and through all beings – to include all nature, trees, birds and water – the universe is alive and guiding. Awareness of the consciousness throughout our world allows us to learn from other life forms; our relationship to the environment greatly gains possibility. From a 21st century postmaterial view, humans learn by listening to the environment, in contrast to the 20th century view of controlling or dominating the environment.

The studies in this handbook suggest there is an awe inspiring expedition ahead on the grandness of this dialectic – psyche attuned yet contributing towards consciousness – our role in between consciousness and matter. How precisely we as humans are co-creators is just starting to be discovered–but we have shifted into a different laboratory built on sacred ground. The insights and scientific revelations of these authors are well timed for a rising generation who will need to listen with great openness and intent to find a new way of relating in the world.

INDEX

family relationships (*Cont.*)
  in Judaism, as structural concept, 168–169
  maintenance of, 169–170
  maintenance of, by married couples, 170–171
  through marriage, 169
  between parent-children, 169–170
  in Protestant Christianity, as structural concept, 168
  relational spirituality and, 166, 178
  religious familism, 165–166, 168, 169
  religiousness as influence on, 171
family spirituality, 459–460
"Father Sergius" (Tolstoy), 429
The Favorite Fairytale of Childhood (Dieckman), 294
Fechner, Gustav, 560
feedback loops
  consciousness and, 71
  in levels of learning, 73
Feigl, Herbert, 23
females. *See* women
feminism
  among African American females, 202–203
  Goddess movement and, 187
  mujerismo, 203
fertility goddesses
  for ancient Hebrews, 188
  women as, 187–188, 193
FFM. *See* Five Factor Model for personality
first-person perspectives, 43
Fisher, Daniel, 410–411
Five Factor Model (FFM) for personality, 86
  agreeableness in, 90–91
  ASPIRES Scale and, 105, 116–117
  STS and, 106
Flournoy, Theodore, 288, 289, 296
fMRI. *See* functional magnetic resonance imaging
folk healers, 203
folk Hinduism, 316
forgiveness, physical health influenced by, 382
Forman, Robert, 39
fossil gaps, as anomalies in evolutionary theory, 601
Fowers, Blaine, 426
Fowler, James, 140
Fox, Matthew, 458
fractured identity, from cultural oppression, 198–199
fragmentation, evil as, 131–132
  in Christianity, 131
  future research study for, 135
Frances of Assisi (Saint), 429
Frankl, Viktor, 456
Frankle, Estelle, 464
Freire, Paulo, 202
Freud, Sigmund, 288, 398
  on Buddhist influences on psychotherapy, 329

dream analysis for, 296
dynamic psychology under, 9–10
James and, 10–11
Jung and, 289, 288–289
linking of religion and psychoanalysis by, 7, 9–10
on psi research, 273–274
on religion, 273
sexual theory, 289
on spirituality, 273
Friedman, Thomas L., 59
Fromm, Erich, 331, 331
Frost, Robert, 157
Full Catastrophe Loving (Kabat-Zinn), 333
functional magnetic resonance imaging (fMRI)
  during meditation, 508
  during RSMEs, 505
fundamentalism. *See* religious fundamentalism
Future of an Illusion (Freud), 398
The Future of the Body (Murphy), 366

G

GABA neurotransmitter. *See* gamma aminobutyric acid neurotransmitter
Gadamer, H-G., 28
Gage, Fred, 72
gamma aminobutyric acid (GABA) neurotransmitter, 492
Gariaev, P. P., 70
Gauld, A., 587
gender
  attachment processes by, religiousness and, 90
  conjunctive faith stage and, 184
  in family relationships, 169
  Godhood and, 187
  human body and, spirituality and, 367
  maternal instinct and, 143
  patriarchal nature of religion and, 182
  physical health and, religiousness as influence on, 379–380
  in psychological models of spiritual development, 216
genetics. *See* behavior genetics
German experimental tradition, in psychology, 9
Gertrude of Helfta, 186
Geschwind syndrome. *See* interictal personality syndrome
GIF study. *See* God-image formation study
girls
  during conjunctive stage, of faith development, 184
  maternal influences on faith, 182–183
GISE study. *See* God-image and self-esteem study
glossolalia, 44
God
  in Christian meditation, 314
  the Self and, 292

Goddess movement, 187
Gödel's theorem, 71
God Hates Us All, 131
Godhood
  gender considerations in, 187
  purification procedures for women and, 187
God-image and self-esteem (GISE) study, 29
  epistemological assumptions in, 30–31
  ethical assumptions in, 29–30
  in hermeneutics, 29
  methodological assumptions in, 31
  ontological assumptions in, 29
God-image formation (GIF) study, 29
  epistemological assumptions in, 30–31
  ethical assumptions in, 29–30
  in hermeneutics, 29
  methodological assumptions in, 31
  ontological assumptions in, 29
Goleman, Daniel, 333
good. *See also* love
  bipolar dimensions in, 126
  bottom-up approach to, 125
  definition of, 124–128
  liberalism and, 127–128
  libertarianism and, 128
  in Moral Foundations Theory, 125
  political conservatism and, 127–128
  in Schwartz Value Survey, 127
  self-transcendence and, 128–129
  thematic constructs, 134
  top-down approach to, 125
Gorusch, Richard, 27
The Gospel of the Buddha (Carus), 345
Goswamit, Amit, 66
gratitude, physical health influenced by, 382–383
gratuitous assumptions, in PRS, 22
gravitational forces, 578–579
Green, Alyce, 560
Green, Elmer, 560
Gregg-Schroeder, Susan, 413
Grinberg, Jacobo, 601
Gröning, Philip, 315
group processes, religion and, 38
Gurwitsch, Alexander, 535
Guth, Alan, 66

H

Hadot, Philippe, 430
Hainline, Ross, 300
Hall, G. Stanley, 8, 289
hands on healing. *See* healing with intent, studies in
Hansen, L. Sunny, 458
happiness, 430–431
Harris, William, 545
Hartle-Hawking theory, 65
Hassidism, 211
hate, evil and, 130
  grandiose self-image and, 133–134
Hawkings, Stephen, 68

Koob, Andrew, 70
Kook, Abraham, 138
Kotchnig, Elined, 300
Kraepelin, Emil, 410
Krevsky, George, 302
Krieger, Dolores, 539
Kristeller, Jean, 403
Kuhn, Thomas, 59
kundalini energy, 217
Kunz, Dora, 539

L

Laing, R. D., 416
Lakatos, Imre, 59
Lao Tzu, 318
Lapdron, Machig, 191
Large Hadron Collider (LHC), 67
Latinos, spirituality among
    animism and, 199
    Candomblé, 198, 203
    communal nature of, 202
    curanderismo, 198, 203
    espiritismo, 203
    liberation through, 202
    magical realism and, 200
    mujerismo among, 203
    Santeria, 198, 203
    through syncretism, 198, 203
Latter Day Saints (LDS), 170
Laughlin, Robert, 68
    on organizational system principles, 68
LaVey, Anton, 129
law of nature, 48–49
The Law of Three Stages, 26
    hermeneutics and, 29
    limitations of, 27
laying on of hands, 369–370. *See also*
    healing with intent, studies in
LCI. *See* Life Choices Inventory
LDS. *See* Latter Day Saints
learning, levels of, 75–76, 73
    feedback loops in, 73
    meta-communication, 73–74
    recursion in, 73
    self-awareness and, 73–74
Leonard, Frank, 412
Leuba, James H., 8, 9
LHC. *See* Large Hadron Collider
liberalism, morality and, 127–128
liberation
    during Black theology movement, 202
    for Latinos, through spirituality, 202
    mujerismo and, among Latinas, 203
    racial, for African Americans, 202
    through spirituality, for people of color, 202–203
    womanism and, among African American females, 202–203
libertarianism, morality and, 128
libido transformation theory, 289
Liebovici, Leonard, 534
Life Choices Inventory (LCI), 190
life span psychology, religion and, 38

limbic-marker hypothesis, 502
Lipton, Bruce, 70
literal stage, of faith development, 183
Logos pathway, for knowledge acquisition.
    See also materialist science
    art-based technology in, 564
    qualitative models in, 563
    science-based technology in, 565
    for scientific understanding, 561–565
Lord Kelvin. *See* Thompson, William
love
    altruistic, 128, 132–133
    definition of, 128–129
    erotic, 128
    as positive emotion, 443–444
    self-transcendence and, 128
    unconditional, during NDEs, 522–523
Lukoff, David, 413
Luther, Martin, 186, 312

M

madonnas, 191, 193
    Black, 201
magical realism, 200
magnetoencephalography (MEG), 56–57
Maha Moggallana, 349
Mahayana Buddhism, 327
Maher, Michaeleen, 533
Mahler, Jay, 412, 413, 418
Main, John, 313, 314
males
    attachment processes for, religiousness and, 90
    in psychological models of spiritual development, 216
Man and His Symbols (Jung), 297
marital relationships
    maintenance of, by married couples, 170–171
    parent-child relationships and, 170–171
    quality of, 170
marriage
    family relationships through, 169
    same-faith, 170
    in traditional families, 170
Martin, Malachi, 131
Martin, Mike, 429
Marx, Karl, 599
Maslow, Abraham, 332, 603
    on meaning of work, 456
mass energy consciousness, 565–566
mass energy information consciousness, 566
master virtues, 431–432
materialism. *See also* spiritual materialism
    definition of, 585
    mind-brain problem and, 585–586
materialistic perspective, in psychotherapy, 224–225, 234–235
materialist science. *See also* scientific method
    anomalies in, 600–601
    development history of, 599–600

as dogmatic, 600
    limitations of, 599
    modernism and, 599
    paradoxes of, 600–601
    religious tradition and, conflicts with, 600
    rise of secularism and, 598
maternal instinct, 143
matter, creation of, 572–579
    with Big Bang theory, 577–578
    Dirac theory of, 577–579
    quantum theories of, 572–577
    RF in, 575
Mattis, Jacquie, 152
Maturana, Humberto, 74
May, Ed, 538
MBCT. *See* Mindfulness-Based Cognitive Therapy
MBSR programs. *See* Mindfulness-Based Stress Reduction programs
McCallie, David, 534
McConnell, Robert, 534
McCulloch, Warren, 596
McDaniel, Carl, 457
McLeod, Ken, 338
Mead, Margaret, 416
meaning of life, 258
medical intuition, 592, 592–593
medical model, for SMPs, 411
medicine, new technologies in, 361
meditation. *See also* Buddhist meditation; Christian meditation; neuroimaging, during meditation
    amygdala activation during, 493–494
    cingulate cortex activation through, 490–491
    clinical applications for, 320–321, 337
    in cross-cultural psychology, 322
    future applications for, 319–322
    in Hinduism, 316–317
    Hisbodedus practices, in Judaism, 318
    Hisbonenus practices, in Judaism, 318
    hypothalamic activation during, 493–494
    in Islam, 315–316
    in Judaism, 317–318
    in *Kabbalah*, 317–318
    neuropsychological applications for, 320
    new concepts in, 321–322
    NIH studies on, 337
    physiological effects of, 333
    prayer through, 542
    prefrontal cortex activation through, 490–491
    psychotherapeutic applications for, 311, 319, 326–327
    in Sufism, 316
    in Taoism, 318–319
    universality of, 307
    in Zen Buddhism, 330
Mediumship and Survival: A Century of Investigations (Gauld), 587

MEG. *See* magnetoencephalography
Memories, Dreams, Reflections (Jung), 287, 289, 290
mental health, religion and, 13–14. *See also* serious mental problems
 coping strategies and, 14
 negative effects of, 396–397
mental health, religiousness and, 392
Mental Health Services Act, 418–419
Merton, Thomas, 313, 314
meta-communication, 73–74
Metal: A Headbanger's Journey, 131
metaphysical assumptions
 in hermeneutics, 29
 in PN, 26–27
 in PRS, 22
meta-therapy, 333
methodological assumptions
 in hermeneutics, 31
 operationalization and, 23, 23–24
 in PN, 23–24
 in PRS, 22
Michelson, Albert, 51
mid-life theory, 291. *See also* destiny motif
millennium generation, 390–391
mindfulness
 in Buddhist meditation, 310, 334
 in cognitive therapies, 319, 320
 definition of, 334
 future research applications for, 320–321
 as practice, 334
 in Western psychology, 334
mindfulness, psychotherapy and, 333–336
 from 1980–2000, 334–336
 ACT, 336
 in CBT, 334
 contemporary applications of, 336
 DBT, 335–336
 future applications for, 337–338
 in MBSR programs, 335
 well-being from, 337
Mindfulness-Based Cognitive Therapy (MBCT), 336
Mindfulness-Based Stress Reduction (MBSR) programs, 335
 therapeutic applications, 335
miracles, 271–272
mirror neurons, 66
 embodied simulation with, 275–276
models, conceptual definition of, 209
modernism, 599
modern physics, 51–53. *See also* quantum physics
 black holes in, 68–69
 consciousness and, as study subject, 54–55
 dark energy, 52
 Higgs boson, 53
 Holographic Principle in, 69
 with LHC, 67
 particle physics, 53
 pedagogy and, 77

physical constants in, 66
psychology and, 77
quantum mechanics in, 52, 54, 55
relativity theory in, 51–52
sense of wonder in, 53–54
Standard Model of Particle Physics, 52–53
string theory, 53
Moral Foundations Theory, 125
moral identity, 95
morality, through religion, 95–96. *See also* evil; good
 in Buddhism, 308
 in experimental studies, 95–96
 liberalism and, 127–128
 libertarianism and, 128
 in Moral Foundations Theory, 125
 political conservatism and, 127, 127–128
 in psychological models of spiritual development, 215–216
 in Schwartz Value Survey, 127
 social desirability hypothesis and, 95
 spirituality and, 96
 in theistic integrative psychotherapy, 241
moral reasoning, 95
 altruism and, 143–144
moral virtue, in Buddhism, 308
Morita, Shoma, 330
Morita therapy, 330
Morley, Edward, 51
Mormonism. *See* Latter Day Saints
Mosher, Loren, 417
mothers
 faith influenced by, 182–183
 during intuitive-projective stage of faith development, 183
 during literal stage of faith development, 183
 during synthetic conventional stage, of faith development, 183
Motherhood of God, 185–187, 193
 in Buddhism, 186
 creativity influenced by, 187
 early believers in, 186
 fertility goddesses and, 187–188
motivational interviewing, 428
motives
 in ASPIRES Scale, 107–108
 in STS, 107–108
Muhammad, Elijah, 202
mujerismo, 203
Murphy, Michael, 366
Murray, Kelly, 162
mysticism
 chemically-facilitated, 15–16
 non-chemically facilitated, 16
 psychedelic drugs and, 16
Mysticism Scale, 16, 40
myths. *See also* personal myth
 of man, 293
 of pure evil, 130–131

Mythos pathway, for knowledge acquisition, 558, 565–567
 mass energy consciousness in, 565–566
 mass energy information consciousness in, 566

N

Nadeau, Robert, 69
NAMI. *See* National Alliance for the Mentally Ill
Nanotechnology, 78
Nash, Carroll, 539
National Alliance for the Mentally Ill (NAMI), 413
National and International Religion Report, 185
National Institute of Child Health and Human Development (NICHD), 470–471
National Institutes of Health (NIH), 337
National Longitudinal Study of Adolescent Health, 157
Native Americans, spirituality among, 197
 as culturally relevant, 199–200
 healing activities in, 203
 universal interconnectedness in, 200
naturalism. *See also* positivistic naturalism
 in PRS, 23
natural theology, 43–44
Nature, 64
Nazianzus, Gregory, 186
near death experiences (NDEs), 363
 as challenge to materialist reductionism, 524
 Christianity and, 521–522
 common components of, 515
 criteria for, 514–515
 definition of, 514
 explanatory models of, 515–516
 future research directions for, 523–525
 historical research on, 514
 hypercapnia as cause of, 515
 hypoxia as cause of, 515
 neurotransmitters as causes of, 516
 paradox of, 601
 pharmacological causes of, 515–516
 phenomenology of, 515
 prior religiosity and, 517–518
 psychological models for, 516
 in religious traditions, 521
 REM intrusion and, 516
 RSMEs and, 509–510, 516–517
 as spiritual catalyst, 523
 subsequent religiosity after, 518–520
 technological influences on, 523
 theological implications of, 520–523
 unconditional love felt during, 522–523
negative energy. *See* dark energy
negative intention, as nocebo effect, 541
negative prayer, 541
 nocebo effect, 541
Ness, Arne, 605

neurobiological models, of spiritual
development, 217
kundalini energy and, 217
neuroimaging, during meditation,
506–508
with fMRI, 508
with PET, 507
with SPECT, 507–508
neuroimaging, during RSMEs, 503–506
development of, as discipline, 500–501
with fMRI, 505
future research applications for, 510
as measuring tool, 372–373
with PET, 504
with SPECT, 504–505
neuroplasticity, in brain function, 72
neuroscience, RSMEs and, 508–510
new age religions. *See* spirituality
Newberg, Andrew, 369
new careering, 461
NICHD. *See* National Institute of Child
Health and Human Development
nightmares, 298
NIH. *See* National Institutes of Health
nihilism, 130
nocebo effect, 541
non-chemically facilitated mysticism, 16
nonlocality, in prayer studies, 532–534
agent of action and, 537–539
blindness as variable in, 536–539
dosage variables, 535–536
observer-expectancy effects for,
532–534
randomization in, 536–539, 540
time variables, 534–535
The Non-local Universe (Nadeau/Kafatos),
69
nontraditional families
adults without children, 176
cohabiting heterosexual unions,
173–175
divorced adults with children, 176
religion in, 171–176
same-sex unions, 172–173
single parenthood, 175–176

O

objective consciousness, 65. *See also*
quantum physics
objective psyche, 290
observer effect, 534
Occhino, Mary, 593
"Ode to a Grecian Urn" (Keats), 302
Offer, Avner, 432
*On the Psychology and Pathology of So-
called Occult Phenomena* (Jung),
288
ontological assumptions
in hermeneutics, 29
in PN, 26–27
in PRS, 22
ontological claims, in psychology of
religion, 13, 16–17

openness, 96–97. *See also* prejudice,
religion and
religiousness and, 96–97
spirituality and, 96
operationalization, 23
limitations of, 23–24
oppression, spirituality among peoples of
color and, 198, 198–200
attachments as result of, 198
contemporary, 199
through cultural imperialism, 198
fractured identity as result of, 198–199
through racial microaggressions, 199
skin color and, 198
soul wounds from, 199
optimism, spirituality and, 58
optimistic "law" of big numbers, 48–51
aging world population as influence
on, 50
analysis of, 49–50
assumed law of nature in, 48–49
corollaries in, 48–49
foundations for, 50–51
religious disappointment as influence
on, 50
scientific progress as influence on, 50–51
technological progress as influence
on, 51
The Order of Cistercians, 313–314
organizational psychology, religion and, 38
organizational systems, principles of, 68
Origen, 186
Orthodox Jews, career limitations for, 463
Osis, Karlis, 533
Otto, Rudolf, 292, 536

P

Padmasambhava, 328–329
Pali Canon, 328
PANAS. *See* Positive and Negative Affect
Schedule
paradigm shifts
in psychotherapy, 223–231, 224
in scientific discovery, 595
in spirituality, tangibility of, 595
parapsychology, 17
spiritualism and, 17
parents. *See also* mothers; single
parenthood
in family relationships, 169–170
parent-child conversations about
religion, 154–155
religious conflicts with children, 160
sanctification, 156
as spiritual ambassadors, 154
in traditional families, parent-child
relationship formation, 170
parental-based socialization of religiosity
(PBRS) model, 88
parent-child conversations, about religion,
154–155
parent-centered, 155
youth-centered, 155

parent-child relationships
within families, 169–170
formation of, 170
marital relationship as influence on,
170–171
Parson, Talcott, 12
Parsons, Frank, 456–457
particle physics, 53
Patanjali, 212
patriarchy
female conflicts with, during
conjunctive faith stage, 184
in religious structure, 182
Pauli, Wolfgang, 67
PBRS model. *See* parental-based
socialization of religiosity model
PEAR studies. *See* Princeton Engineering
Anomalies studies
pedagogy
modern physics and, 77
psychology and, 77
Penrose, Roger, 65, 71, 600
people of color, spirituality among. *See
also* African Americans; Asian
Americans, spirituality among;
healing, through spirituality;
Latinos, spirituality among; Native
Americans, spirituality among;
oppression, spirituality among
peoples of color and
as collective unconsciousness, 198
cultural consciousness in, 200–203
as culturally relevant, 199–200
cultural resilience from, 200–201
with histories of oppression, 198–200
immigration as influence on, 198
liberation through, 202–203
main characteristics of, 204
psychological needs addressed by, 199
as source of healing, 197
transpersonality in, 200
personality, religion and, 38. *See also*
attachment processes, religiousness
and; behavior genetics, religiousness
and; Five Factor Model for
personality; prosociality, religion and
age as influence on, 87
agreeableness and, 90–91, 93–94
conscientiousness, 94–95
CPI for, 192
external religiousness and, 87–88
FFM, 105
internal religiousness and, 87–88
morality, 95–96
prejudice and, 96–97
religious orientation, 86
Schwartz Value Survey, 86
self-control, 94–95
theistic integrative psychotherapy and,
241
trait pathways, 90
traits as influence on, 86
values as influence on, 86

quest religiousness and, 97–98
research trends for, 98–99
RF and, 97
Priestly, Joseph, 30
Princeton Engineering Anomalies (PEAR)
studies, 279
Principles of Psychology (James), 9
The Principles of Psychology (James), 72
probability distribution, in quantum
physics, 64
prophecy. *See* failed prophecy, in cognitive
dissonance theory
Proposition 63. *See* Mental Health
Services Act
prosociality, religion and, 91–94, 144.
See also altruism
aggressive retaliatory behaviors and,
92–93
from childhood religious development,
159
experimental evidence for, 92
limits of, 92–94
observer reports of, 91
priming methods for, 92
projective methods for, 92
spirituality and, 93–94
as tribal, 93
universal, 93
vengefulness and, 92–93
Protestant Christianity, 312
conversion to, 9
family as concept within, 168
psychology of religion influenced by, 8
as Western model of spiritual
development, 212
PRS. *See* psychology of religion and
spirituality
psilocybin, 16
psi phenomena
clairvoyance, 272
Freud on, 273–274
intersubjective space and, 283
PEAR studies, 279
psychoanalysis influenced by, 280–281
psychokinesis, 272, 280
quantum space and, 279–280
research on, 279–280
the Source and, 280
spiritual space and, 279–280
superordinate space and, 279–280
telepathy, 272
the unconsciousness and, 272–273
PSPL deafferentation, 492–493
psychedelic drugs, mysticism and, 16
psilocybin, 16
psychoanalysis
academic identity crisis of, 280–281
attunement in, 281–282
countertransference in, 281
criticism of, 10
cultural influence of, 10
decline in religion influenced by, 10
as dynamic psychology, 9–10

female faith development and, 193
future directions of, 280–283
Hindu Indian spirituality in, 193
influence in, 281
intention in, 281
intersubjective theories of, 274–275,
276–278
non-neutrality in, 281
personality of analyst as influence on,
282
psi influence on, 280–281
psychology of religion and, 9–10
religion and, 7, 9–10
resonance in, 281–282
scientific testing of, 10
Sufi philosophy in, 193
Sufism and, comparative considerations
of, 316
telepathy in, 274, 274
time and, 282–283
two-person, 275, 276
the unconscious in, 273–274
psychoanalytic movement, early, 286–287
psychokinesis, 272, 280
psychological models, of spiritual
development, 215–217
extrinsic religion in, 215
Freudian approach in, 216
as gender-biased, 216
intrinsic religion in, 215
morality in, 215–216
seven universal stages in, 216
transpersonal, 216–217
Psychological Types, theory of, 289–290
psychologists
religiosity of, 397–398
spiritual traditions and, therapeutic
applications for, 400–401
Psychologists Interested in Religious Issues
(PIRI), 7
psychology. *See also* positive psychology;
transpersonal psychology
clinical, 44
cognitive, 38
consciousness and, 71–79
cross-cultural, 322
cultural, 38
diversity awareness in, 391
dualism in, 224–225, 235
dynamic, 9–10
emotion and, 38
ethics in, 391
evolutionary, 38, 44
German experimental tradition, 9
as hard science discipline, 398
holism in, 225
interdisciplinary integration within, 37
James theory for, 72
life span, 38
materialistic perspective in, 224–225,
234–235
mindfulness as concept in, 334
modern physics and, 77

as natural science, 10
organizational, 38
pedagogy and, 77
postmaterialistic perspective in,
224–225, 235–236
reductionism in, 224–225
religion and, as research study, 36–38
shadow culture in, 9
of spirituality, 225–226
transpersonal, 216, 216–217, 337
psychology, spirituality and
academic forefathers and, 398
barriers to, 397–400
in care giving, 401–402
empirical support for, 402
EPP in, 401–402, 403
future research applications, 404–406
institutional support for, 399
interdisciplinary benefits from,
399–400
intervention implementation, 400–404
spiritual inquiry in, 402–404
tools and principles for, 401
virtues in, 405
Psychology of Judaism, 38
psychology of myopia, 432–434
psychology of religion. *See also* data,
for psychology of religion;
taxonomies, in psychology of
religion
for Allport, 398
applications for, 44–45
authoritarianism in, 14
for chemically-facilitated mysticism,
15–16
in clinical psychology, 44
cognitive dissonance as theme in, 15
conversion themes in, 14–15
coping strategies and, 14
for dangerous religious forms, 45
deconversion themes in, 14–15
development of, as academic field of
study, 7, 36
early history for, 8–12
faith selectivity limitations, in data,
38–39
faith-specific therapies and, 17
funding agency support for, 17–18
future research prospects for, 16–18
geographic limitations, in data, 38
German experimental tradition and, 9
glossolalia in, 44
for healthy religious processes, 45
interdisciplinary associations, 12–13
interdisciplinary paradigms for, 12
for James, 9, 398
journals on, 37
for Jung, 398
mental health and, 13–14
nomenclature for, development of, 7–8
for non-chemically facilitated
mysticism, 16
ontological claims in, 13, 16–17

resilience *(Cont.)*
  CD-RISC, 446
  constructs in, 438–439
  coping strategies and, 442
  definition of, 438
  dynamic model of affect for, 440
  Ego Resilience Scale, 446
  future research on, 443, 448–450
  live values and, 441
  personal meaning and, 439, 441–442
  positive emotions and, 447–448,
    446–450
  in positive youth development, 477
  posttraumatic growth and, 439
  purpose of life and, 439
  relationships and, 440–441
  research limitations on, 442–443
  Resilience Scale, 446
  spirituality and, 440–443
  two-factor model for, 439–440
Resilience Scale, 446
resonance, in psychoanalysis, 281–282
resonant bonding, in healing with intent
    studies, 554–555, 555
Revelation of Love (Julian of Norwich),
    185–186
Review of Religious Research, 12
Reynolds, Pam, 509, 509
  NDE of, 509–510
RF. *See* religious fundamentalism
RFT. *See* Relational Frame Theory
Ricoeur, Paul, 28
Ring, K., 523
Rinpoche, Gochen Tulku, 191
Robert of Molesme, 313
Rolland, Romain, 273
Roman Catholicism, 312
  same-faith marriage in, 170
RR. *See* relaxation response
RSMEs. *See* religious-spiritual-mystical
    experiences

S

Sabom, Michael, 509
sacraments, in Christianity, 312
the sacred, 390
Saddhatissa, H., 347
Sagan, Carl, 596
same-faith marriage, 170
same-sex unions, 172–173
  formation of, 172
  maintenance of, 172–173
samsara (cycle of existence), 327–328
sanctification, as concept
  for children and adolescents, 153
  of parents, 156
sangomas, 211
Santeria, 198
  healing through, 203
SAP. *See* spiritual awareness psychotherapy
The Satanic Bible (LaVey), 129
Satanism, 129
Sato, Koji, 332

satori (way of experiencing oneself), 332
schizophrenia, recovery model for, 410
Schlitz, Marilyn, 533
Schlossberg, Nancy, 464
Schmeidler, Gertrude, 533, 534
Schore, Allan, 276
Schrödinger, Erwin, 52
Schultz, Johannes, 560
Schwartz, Gary, 535
Schwartz, J. M., 71
Schwartz Value Survey, 86
  morality values in, 127
science. *See also* biology; materialist
    science; modern physics; particle
    physics; postmaterialist science
  sense of wonder in, 53–54
  spirituality as replacement for religion
    influenced by, 55
science fiction. *See also* optimistic "law"
    of big numbers
  mythology in, 48
  religion and, 48–50
  themes in, 48
scientific epistemological cycle, 22
scientific method
  PN and, 27, 28
  religion and, as primary activity, 37–38
scriptural text, as psychological point of
    view, 44
Searle, John, 600
secularism, rise of, 598
segregation principle, 510
SELF. *See* Self-Expansiveness Level Form
the Self
  destiny motif and, 294–296
  development of, 275
  God and, for Jung, 292
  in individuation process, 291–292
self-awakening therapy, 331
self-awareness, 72–79
  attention and, 74, 76
  attraction-aversion distraction cycle, 76
  ground of awareness in, 74
  insight in, 75
  intention in, 75
  levels of learning and, 73–74
  object in, 74, 76–77
  practice of, 75, 76
  reflection in, 75, 77
  subject in, 74, 76–77
  witness capacity of, 76
self-control, 94–95
  affluence and, 433, 434
  conscientiousness and, 94–95
  spirituality and, 96
self-esteem, religiousness and, 88–89
Self-Expansiveness Level Form (SELF),
    216–217
selflessness, in spirituality, 188–189
self-transcendence
  elevation from, 133
  good and, 128–129
  love and, 128

Seligman, Martin, 228, 228
Selye, Hans, 370
SEM. *See* structural equation modeling
serious mental problems (SMPs)
  coping strategies for, 414–415
  dysfunctional spiritual beliefs and, 415
  medical model for, 411
  personal mythology readjustments
    after, 418
  recovery model for, 410–411
  reflection phase for, 417–418
  religiosity levels in patients, 413–414
  Religious Problem Solving Scale, 415
  as route to spirituality, 413
  Soteria programs for, 417
  spirituality incorporated into, 410
  tracing of heritage for, 418
  treatment strategies for, 416–417
serotonergic activity, 495–496
Sexton, Virginia, 7
Shabbat (day of rest), 317
shadow culture, 9
Shalom Process, 368–369
shamanism, 203
  as indigenous model of spiritual
    development, 210–211
  as path of community service, 211
  sangomas and, 211
sheep/goat effect, 534
Sheldrake, Rupert, 535, 600
Shintoism, 212
  spirituality within, 244
Siddhārtha Gautama
  early years of, 345
  eightfold path for, 308, 347
  enlightenment of, 346
  as founder of Buddhism, 307–308,
    327–328
  four noble truths for, 308, 346–347
  spiritual inquiry of, 344–346
  spiritual method of, 346–347
  spiritual teachers for, 345–346
Siegel, Daniel, 337
Sikhism, 244
single parenthood, 175–176
  career development and, 463
  formation of, 175
  maintenance of, 175–176
single photon emission computed
    tomography (SPECT)
  during meditation, 507–508
  during RSMEs, 504–505
singularity problem, in Big bang theory, 66
Skinner, B.F., 72, 398
Smith, Adam, 606
Smith, Clyde, 302
Smith, Esther, 302
Smith, Huston, 400
Smith, Justa, 539
Smith, Susy, 589
Smith, Wilfred Cantwell, 161
SMPs. *See* serious mental problems
SOC. *See* survival of consciousness

social constructionism, 43
social desirability hypothesis, 95
social-ecology approach, to religious
    development, 153
  among African Americans, 156
  children as spiritual emissaries in, 154
  cultural influences on, 154, 157–158
  family structure as influence in, 154
  macrosystems in, 153
  mesosystems in, 153
  microsystems in, 153
  multiple variables in, 155–156
  parental discipline in, 155–156
  parent-child conversations in, 154–155
  peer influences on, 156–157
  religious prejudice and, 158
  sanctification of parental role in, 156
  sibling influences on, 157
  transactional models in, 153–154
social interactionism, 44
social networking, through religious/
    spiritual affiliations, 258
Society for the Scientific Study of
    Religion, 12
Society of Behavioral Medicine, 399
sociology of religion, 44
Sojourners, 127–128
Sorokin, Pitrim, 12, 17
Soteria programs, 417
soul, scientific meaning of, 591
soul wounds, 199
the Source, 280
space-time causality, 67
speaking in tongues. See glossolalia
SPECT. See single photon emission
    computed tomography
Spetzler, Robert, 509
SP hypothesis. See Spirit Partnership
    hypothesis
spirits, 188
  in daily life, practical role for, 591–593
  NDEs and, 363
  as physical concept, 363
  scientific meaning of, 591
Spirit Partnership (SP) hypothesis, 592
  in medical intuition, 592–593
spiritual activism, 598–599, 603–604
  social change from, 606–607
Spiritual Awareness Psychotherapy,
    193. See also spiritually-sensitive
    psychotherapy
spiritual awareness psychotherapy (SAP),
    460
spiritual but not religious, identification
    as, 390, 406
spiritual development, models of. See also
    adolescence, religious development
    during; childhood, religious
    development during; Eastern
    models, of spiritual development;
    psychological models, of spiritual
    development; Western models, of
    spiritual development

awareness measures in, 479–480
barriers identification in, 217
belief organization within, 210
conceptual definitions in, 207–210
conversion and, 208
cross-cultural viability of, 480
defined end purposes in, 209–210
definition criteria for, 478, 479
five-factor model, 208
future research directions for, 218
horizontal, 207
indigenous, 210–211
integrative-philosophical, 213–215
interdisciplinary approach to, 471–474
as interpersonal, 209
as intrapersonal, 209
multidirectional, 207
neurobiological, 217
philosophical aspects of, 210
psychological, 215–216
spiritually-sensitive psychotherapy and,
    227
suddenness of, 210
testing of, 479–480
theory in, 209
traditional, 210–213
as transpersonal, 209
as unidirectionally progressive, 210
vertical, 207
spiritual failure, 259
  poor health outcomes and, 259
spiritual impressions of the heart,
    249–250
spiritual inquiry, 344
  of Siddhārtha Gautama, 344–346
  in spiritually-influenced psychology,
    402–404
spiritual interventions, 250–251
  by psychotherapists, 261
spirituality. See also diversity in spirituality,
    psychotherapy and; faith
    development; family relationships,
    religion and; healing, through
    spirituality; human body,
    spirituality and; mysticism;
    people of color, spirituality
    among; psychology, spirituality
    and; psychology of religion
    and spirituality; psychology of
    spirituality; universal spirituality,
    psychotherapy and
  as adventurous, 58
  among African Americans, 197
  agreeableness and, 93–94
  among Asian Americans, 197–198
  attachment and, 89–90
  benefits of, 208
  broaden-and-build theory for, 440
  within Buddhism, 244
  cellular measures of, 373–374
  within Christianity, 244
  conceptualization of, 166–167
  within Confucianism, 244

conscientiousness and, 96
constructs in, 438–439
in consumer movements, 411–413,
    418–419
counseling resources with, 258
as cultural issue, in psychotherapy,
    256–261
cultural resilience and, 200–201
definitions of, 57–58, 188, 207–209,
    344, 362–363, 389, 390, 437–438
diversity in, psychotherapy and,
    237–238
dynamic model of affect for, 440
dysfunctional beliefs, 415
engagement capacity for, 474–475
epidemiological studies on, 257–258
family, 459–460
five-factor model of, 208
Freud on, 273
genetic measurements for, 373–374
harmful occurrences with, 208
within Hinduism, 244
human body as concept within,
    363–367
Inventory on Spirituality, 189
within Islam, 244
within Judaism, 244
Jung on, 291, 292
among Latinos, through syncretism,
    198
liberation through, for people of color,
    202–203
life expectancy increases and, 392–393
within major religious traditions, 244
as meaning-making, 428–430
meaning of life through, 258
in meaning of work, 457–459
mental health and, 392
among millennium generation,
    390–391
morality through, 96
among Native Americans, 197
negative dimensions of, 259
neuroimaging and, as measurement
    tool, 372–373
openness and, 96
optimism and, 58
overgeneralization of, in psychotherapy,
    256–257
paradigm shift in study of, 595
parapsychology and, 17
parent-child conversations about,
    154–155
as patriarchal, 182
personal meaning in, 439
physical health and, 379–381
in popular culture, 388–389
positive dimensions of, 257–258
positive emotions and, 443–446
posttraumatic growth and, 439
prosociality and, 93–94
psychological markers of, 371–372
psychologization of, 225–226